GARDNER'S ART THROUGH THE AGES

A CONCISE GLOBAL HISTORY

SECOND EDITION

FRED S. KLEINER

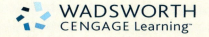

WADSWORTH
CENGAGE Learning™

Australia · Brazil · Japan · Korea · Mexico · Singapore · Spain · United Kingdom · United States

About the Author

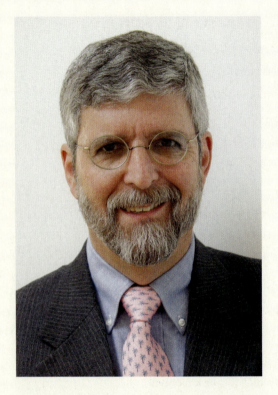

FRED S. KLEINER (Ph.D., Columbia University) is the author of *Gardner's Art through the Ages: A Global History*, 13th edition, and co-author of the 10th, 11th, and 12th editions of *Art through the Ages* as well as more than a hundred publications on Greek and Roman art and architecture, including *A History of Roman Art*, also published by Wadsworth. He has taught the art history survey course for more than three decades, first at the University of Virginia and, since 1978, at Boston University, where he is currently Professor of Art History and Archaeology and Chair of the Art History Department. Long recognized for his inspiring lectures and devotion to students, Professor Kleiner won Boston University's Metcalf Award for Excellence in Teaching as well as the College Prize for Undergraduate Advising in the Humanities in 2002 and is a two-time winner of the Distinguished Teaching Prize in the College of Arts and Sciences Honors Program. He was Editor-in-Chief of the *American Journal of Archaeology* from 1985 to 1998.

Also by Fred Kleiner: *A History of Roman Art* (Wadsworth 2007; ISBN 0534638465), winner of the 2007 Texty Prize as the best new college textbook in the humanities and social sciences. In this authoritative and lavishly illustrated volume, Professor Kleiner traces the development of Roman art and architecture from Romulus' foundation of Rome in the eighth century BCE to the death of Constantine in the fourth century CE, with special chapters devoted to Pompeii and Herculaneum, Ostia, funerary and provincial art and architecture, and the earliest Christian art.

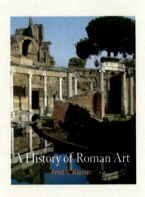

A History of Roman Art
Fred S. Kleiner

About the Cover Art

In a famous 1860 essay entitled "The Painter of Modern Life," the French poet and critic Charles Baudelaire (1821–1867) argued that "modernity is the transitory, the fugitive, the contingent." That definition well describes the paintings of Edgar Degas (1834–1917) and the Impressionists, which stand in forceful opposition to that era's government-sponsored academic art featuring traditional religious, historical, and mythological subjects and highly polished technique. In marked contrast, the Impressionists recorded the contemporary scene. In *The Rehearsal* (1874), Degas abandoned academic subject matter, brushwork, and compositional formulas to capture "the transitory, fugitive, and contingent" on canvas. The frame cuts off the spiral stairs, the windows in the background, and the group of figures in the right foreground. The dancers are not at the center of a classically balanced composition. Instead, a large, off-center, empty space takes up most of the foreground. The figures themselves, blurred as they stretch and pivot, do not even glance at the viewer. Degas's highly personal approach to painting characterizes modern art in general, but it is not typical of many periods of the history of art when artists toiled in anonymity to fulfill the wishes of their patrons, whether Egyptian pharaohs, Roman emperors, medieval monks, or Renaissance princes. *Art through the Ages* surveys the art of all periods from prehistory to the present and examines how artworks of all kinds have always reflected the historical contexts in which they were created.

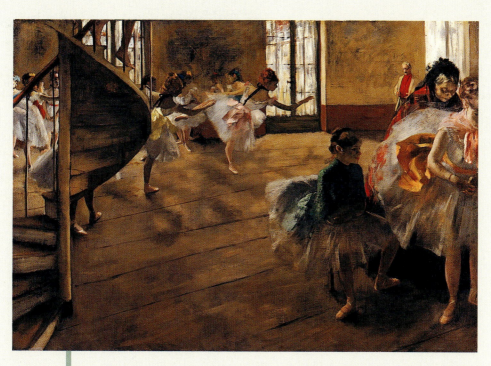

EDGAR DEGAS, *The Rehearsal*, 1874. Oil on canvas, 1′ 11″ × 2′ 9″. Glasgow Art Galleries and Museum, Glasgow (The Burrell Collection).

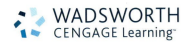
WADSWORTH
CENGAGE Learning™

Gardner's Art through the Ages: A Concise Global History, Second Edition
Fred S. Kleiner

Publisher: Clark Baxter

Senior Development Editor: Sharon Adams Poore

Assistant Editor: Erikka Adams

Editorial Assistant: Nell Pepper

Managing Technology Project Manager: Wendy Constantine

Senior Marketing Manager: Diane Wenckebach

Marketing Assistant: Aimee Lewis

Marketing Communications Manager: Heather Baxley

Senior Content Project Manger, Editorial Production:
    Lianne Ames

Creative Director: Rob Hugel

Senior Art Director: Cate Rickard Barr

Senior Print Buyer: Judy Inouye

Permissions Editor: Bob Kauser

Production Service/Layout: Joan Keyes,
    Dovetail Publishing Services

Text Designer: tani hasegawa

Photo Researcher: Sarah Evertston

Copy Editor: Ida May Norton

Cover Designer: tani hasegawa

Cover Image: Edgar Degas, *The Rehearsal*, 1874. Oil on canvas, 1′ 11″ × 2′ 9″. The Burrell Collection. Culture and Sport Glasgow (Museums). Photo Credit: Edgar Degas, *The Rehearsal*, #35.246. Photo © Culture and Sport Glasgow (Museums).

Compositor: Thompson Type

For product information and technology assistance, contact us at **Cengage Learning Academic Resource Center, 1-800-423-0563**

For permission to use material from this text or product, submit all requests online at **www.cengage.com/permissions**. Further permissions questions can be e-mailed to **permissionrequest@cengage.com**.

Library of Congress Control Number: 2008921019

ISBN-13: 978-0-495-50346-0
ISBN-10: 0-495-50346-0

Wadsworth Cengage Learning
25 Thomson Place
Boston, MA 02210
USA

Cengage Learning products are represented in Canada by Nelson Education, Ltd.

For your course and learning solutions, visit **academic.cengage.com**.
Purchase any of our products at your local college store or at our preferred online store **www.ichapters.com**.

Printed in the United States of America
4 5 6 7 12 11 10

Brief Contents

Contents

Preface

When Helen Gardner published the first edition of *Art through the Ages* in 1926, she could not have imagined that more than 80 years later instructors all over the world would still be using her textbook in their classrooms. Nor could she have foreseen that a new publisher would make her text available in special editions corresponding to a wide variety of introductory art history courses ranging from year-long global surveys to Western- and non-Western-only surveys to the one-semester course for which this concise edition was designed. Indeed, if Professor Gardner were alive today, she would not recognize the book that long ago became—and remains—the most widely read introduction to the history of art and architecture in the English language. During the past half century, successive authors have constantly reinvented Helen Gardner's groundbreaking text, always keeping it fresh and current and setting an ever-higher standard in both content and publication quality with each new edition. I hope both professors and students will agree that this second edition of *Art through the Ages: A Concise Global History* lives up to that venerable tradition.

Certainly, this latest edition offers much that is fresh and new (described later), but some things have not changed, including the fundamental belief that guided Helen Gardner—namely, that the primary goal of an introductory art history textbook should be to foster an appreciation and understanding of historically significant works of art of all kinds from all periods and from all parts of the globe. Because of the longevity and diversity of the history of art, it is tempting to assign responsibility for telling its story to a large team of specialists. The Gardner publishers themselves took this approach for the first edition they produced after Professor Gardner's death, and it has now become the norm for introductory art history surveys. But students overwhelmingly say that the very complexity of the global history of art makes it all the more important for the story to be told with a consistent voice if they are to master so much diverse material. I think Helen Gardner would be pleased to know that this new edition of *Art through the Ages* once again has a single storyteller.

Along with the late Richard Tansey and my more recent collaborator, Christin Mamiya, with whom I had the honor and pleasure of working on several successive editions, I continue to believe that the most effective way to tell the story of art through the ages, especially to someone studying art history for the first time, is to organize the vast array of artistic monuments according to the civilizations that produced them and to consider each work in roughly chronological order. This approach has not merely stood the test of time. It is the most appropriate way to narrate the *history* of art. The principle that underlies my approach to every period of art history is that the enormous variation in the form and meaning of the paintings, sculptures, buildings, and other artworks men and women have produced over the past 30,000 years is largely the result of the constantly changing contexts in which artists and architects worked. A historically based narrative is therefore best suited for a global history of art because it permits the author to situate each work discussed in its historical, social, economic, religious, and cultural context. That is, after all, what distinguishes art history from art appreciation.

In the first (1926) edition of *Art through the Ages*, Helen Gardner discussed Henri Matisse and Pablo Picasso in a chapter entitled "Contemporary Art in Europe and America." Since then many other innovative artists have emerged on the international scene, and the story of art through the ages has grown longer and even more complex. More important, perhaps, the discipline of art history has changed markedly in recent decades, and so too has Helen Gardner's book. This latest edition fully reflects the range of current art historical research emphases yet retains the traditional strengths that have made previous editions of *Art through the Ages* so popular. While maintaining attention to style, chronology, iconography, and technique, I also ensure that issues of patronage, function, and context loom large in every chapter. I treat artworks not as isolated objects in sterile 21st-century museum settings but with a view toward their purpose and meaning in the society that produced them at the time they were produced. I examine not only the role of the artist or architect in the creation of a work of art or a building, but also the role of the individuals or groups who paid the artists and influenced the shape the monuments took. Further, I devote more space than previously to the role of women and women artists in societies worldwide over time. In every chapter, I have tried to choose artworks and buildings that reflect the increasingly wide range of interests among scholars today, while never abandoning the traditional list of "great" works or the very notion of a "canon." I have also expanded the geographical range of the non-Western chapters in this concise edition to include Southeast Asian and Korean art for the first time. In fact, every one of the non-Western chapters includes additional material, as do all the chapters on Western art since the Renaissance. Consequently, although the concise Gardner is an abbreviated survey of the history of art, the selection of works in the second edition encompasses every artistic medium and almost every era and culture, and includes many works that until recently art historians would not have considered to be "art" at all.

The first edition of *Art through the Ages: A Concise Global History* immediately became the number-one choice for one-semester art history survey courses, and for this second edition I have retained all of the features that made its predecessor such a success. Once again, the book boasts roughly 650 photographs, plans, and drawings, virtually all in color and reproduced according to the highest standards of clarity and color fidelity. The second edition, however, also features scores of new or upgraded photos by a host of new photographers as well as redesigned maps and plans and an extraordinary new set of architectural drawings prepared exclusively for *Art through the Ages* by John Burge.

The captions to the illustrations in this edition of *Art through the Ages*, as before, contain a wealth of information, including the name of the artist or architect, if known; the formal title (printed in italics), if assigned, description of the work, or name of the building; the provenance or place of production of the object or location of the building; the date; the material(s) used; the size; and the current location if the work is in a museum or private collection. As in previous editions, scales accompany all plans, but for the first time scales now also appear next to each photograph of a painting, statue, or other artwork. The works illustrated vary enormously in size, from colossal sculptures carved into mountain cliffs and paintings that cover entire walls or ceilings to tiny figurines, coins, and jewelry that can be held in the hand. Although the captions contain the pertinent dimensions, students who have never seen the paintings or statues in person find it daunting to translate those dimensions into an appreciation of the true size of the objects. The new scales provide an effective and direct way to visualize how large or how small a given artwork is and its relative size compared with other objects in the same chapter and throughout the book.

The new concise Gardner also features the Quick-Review Captions that students found so useful in preparing for examinations when I introduced them in 2006 in the first edition. These brief synopses of the most significant aspects of each illustrated artwork or building accompany the captions to all images in the book. In this new edition, however, I have provided two additional tools to aid students in reviewing and mastering the material. Each chapter now ends with a full-page feature called The Big Picture, which sets forth in bullet-point format the most important characteristics of each period or artistic movement discussed in the chapter. Small illustrations of characteristic works discussed accompany the summary of major points. Finally, I have attempted to tie all of the chapters together by providing with each copy of *Art through the Ages* a poster-size Global Timeline. This too features illustrations of key monuments of each age and geographical area as well as a brief enumeration of the most important art historical developments during that period. The timeline has four major horizontal bands corresponding to Europe, the Americas, Asia, and Africa, and 34 vertical columns for the successive chronological periods from 30,000 BCE to the present.

Another popular feature of the first edition that I have retained is the series of boxed essays that appear throughout the book, but in this edition these essays are more closely tied to the main text. Consistent with that greater integration, most boxes now incorporate photographs of important artworks discussed in the text proper that also illustrate the theme treated in the boxed essays. These essays fall under five broad categories, one of which is new to the second edition.

Architectural Basics boxes provide students with a sound foundation for the understanding of architecture. These discussions are concise explanations, with drawings and diagrams, of the major aspects of design and construction. The information included is essential to an understanding of architectural technology and terminology. The boxes address questions of how and why various forms developed, the problems architects confronted, and the solutions they used to resolve them. Topics discussed include how the Egyptians built the pyramids, the orders of classical architecture, Roman concrete construction, and the design and terminology of mosques, stupas, and Gothic cathedrals.

Materials and Techniques essays explain the various media artists employed from prehistoric to modern times. Because materials and techniques often influence the character of artworks, these discussions contain essential information on why many monuments appear as they do. Hollow-cast bronze statues; fresco paintings; Renaissance drawings; engravings, etchings, and lithographs; and daguerreotype, calotype, and wet-plate photographs are among the subjects treated.

Religion and Mythology boxes introduce students to the principal elements of the world's great religions, past and present, and to the representation of religious and mythological themes in painting and sculpture of all periods and places. These discussions of belief systems and iconography give readers a richer understanding of some of the greatest artworks ever created. The topics include the gods and goddesses of Mount Olympus, the life of Jesus in art, Muhammad and Islam, Buddha and Buddhism, Daoism and Confucianism, and Aztec religion.

Art and Society essays treat the historical, social, political, cultural, and religious context of art and architecture.

Topics include Egyptian mummification, Byzantine icons and iconoclasm, pilgrimages and the cult of relics, primitivism and colonialism, public funding of controversial art, the Mesoamerican ball game, and African masquerades.

Artists on Art boxes are a new category in which artists and architects throughout history discuss both their theories and individual works. Examples include Leonardo da Vinci discussing the art of painting, Artemisia Gentileschi talking about the special problems she confronted as a woman artist, Jacques-Louis David on Neoclassicism, Gustave Courbet on Realism, Henri Matisse on color, Diego Rivera on art for the people, and Judy Chicago on her seminal work *The Dinner Party*.

Rounding out the features in the book is a Glossary containing definitions of all terms introduced in the text in italics and a Bibliography of books in English, including both general works and a chapter-by-chapter list of more focused studies. The second edition of *Art through the Ages: A Concise Global History* is not, however, a stand-alone text but one element of a complete package of learning tools. In addition to the Global Timeline, every new copy of the book comes with a password to *ArtStudy Online*, a Web site with access to a host of multimedia resources that students can employ throughout the course, including image flashcards, tutorial quizzes, podcasts, vocabulary, and more. Instructors have access to a host of teaching materials, including the Digital Image Library with zoom capabilities, video, and Google™ Earth coordinates.

A work as extensive as a global history of art could not be undertaken or completed without the counsel of experts in all areas of world art. As with previous editions, the publisher has enlisted more than a hundred art historians to review every chapter of *Art through the Ages* to ensure that the text lived up to the Gardner reputation for accuracy as well as readability. I take great pleasure in acknowledging here the important contributions to the 13th edition of *Art through the Ages* (of which this is an abbreviated version) made by Charles M. Adelman, University of Northern Iowa; Kirk Ambrose, University of Colorado–Boulder; Susan Ashbrook, Art Institute of Boston; Zainab Bahrani, Columbia University; Susan Bakewell, University of Texas–Austin; James J. Bloom, Florida State University; Suzaan Boettger, Bergen Community College; Colleen Bolton, Mohawk Valley Community College; Angi Elsea Bourgeois, Mississippi State University; Kimberly Bowes, Fordham University; Elizabeth Bredrup, St. Christopher's School; Lawrence E. Butler, George Mason University; Alexandra Carpino, Northern Arizona University; Jane Carroll, Dartmouth College; Hipolito Rafael Chacon, The University of Montana; Catherine M. Chastain, North Georgia College & State University; Violaine Chauvet, Johns Hopkins University; Daniel Connolly, Augustana College; Michael A. Coronel, University of Northern Colorado; Nicole Cox, Rochester Institute of Technology; Jodi Cranston, Boston University; Kathy Curnow, Cleveland State University; Giovanna De Appolonia, Boston University; Marion de Koning, Grossmont College; John J. Dobbins, University of Virginia; Erika Doss, University of Colorado–Boulder; B. Underwood DuRette, Thomas Nelson Community College; Daniel Ehnbom, University of Virginia; Lisa Farber, Pace University; James Farmer, Virginia Commonwealth University; Jerome Feldman, Hawaii Pacific University; Sheila ffolliott, George Mason University; Ferdinanda Florence, Solano Community College; William B. Folkestad, Central Washington University; Jeffrey Fontana, Austin College; Mitchell Frank, Carleton University; Sara L. French, Wells College; Norman P. Gambill, South Dakota State University; Elise Goodman, University of Cincinnati; Kim T. Grant, University of Southern Maine; Elizabeth ten Grotenhuis, Silk Road Project; Sandra C. Haynes, Pasadena City College; Valerie Hedquist, The University of Montana; Susan Hellman, Northern Virginia Community College; Marian J. Hollinger, Fairmont State University; Cheryl Hughes, Alta High School; Heidrun Hultgren, Kent State University; Joseph M. Hutchinson, Texas A&M University; Julie M. Johnson, Utah State University; Sandra L. Johnson, Citrus College; Deborah Kahn, Boston University; Fusae Kanda, Harvard University; Catherine Karkov, Miami University; Wendy Katz, University of Nebraska–Lincoln; Nita Kehoe-Gadway, Central Wyoming College; Nancy L. Kelker, Middle Tennessee State University; Cathie Kelly, University of Nevada–Las Vegas; Katie Kempton, Ohio University; John F. Kenfield, Rutgers University; Herbert L. Kessler, Johns Hopkins University; Monica Kjellman-Chapin, Emporia State University; Ellen Konowitz, State University of New York–New Paltz; Kathryn E. Kramer, State University of New York–Cortland; Carol Krinsky, New York University; Lydia Lehr, Atlantic Cape Community College; Krist Lien, Shelton State Community College; Ellen Longsworth, Merrimack College; David A. Ludley, Clayton State University; Henry Luttikhuizen, Calvin College; Christina Maranci, University of Wisconsin–Milwaukee; Dominic Marner, University of Guelph; Jack Brent Maxwell, Blinn College; Anne McClanan, Portland State University; Brian McConnell, Florida Atlantic University; Amy McNair, University of Kansas; Patrick McNaughton, Indiana University; Heather McPherson, University of Alabama–Birmingham; Cynthia Millis, Houston Community College–Southwest; Cynthia Taylor Mills, Brookhaven College; Keith N. Morgan, Boston University; Johanna D. Movassat, San Jose State University; Helen Nagy, University of Puget Sound; Heidi Nickisher, Rochester Institute of Technology; Bonnie Noble, University of North Carolina–Charlotte; Abigail Noonan, Rochester Institute of Technology; Marjorie Och, University of Mary Washington; Karen Michelle O'Day, University of Wisconsin–Eau Claire; Edward J. Olszewski, Case Western Reserve University; Allison Lee Palmer, University of Oklahoma; Martin Patrick, Illinois State University; Glenn Peers, University of Texas–Austin; Jane Peters, University of Kentucky; Julie Anne Plax, University of Arizona; Frances Pohl, Pomona College; Virginia C. Raguin, College of the Holy Cross; Donna Karen Reid, Chemeketa Community College; Albert W. Reischuch, Kent State University; Jonathan Ribner, Boston University; Cynthea Riesenberg, Washington Latin School; James G. Rogers Jr., Florida Southern College;

Carey Rote, Texas A&M University–Corpus Christi; David J. Roxburgh, Harvard University; Conrad Rudolph, University of California–Riverside; Catherine B. Scallen, Case Western Reserve University; Denise Schmandt–Besserat, University of Texas–Austin; Natasha Seaman, Berklee College of Music; Malia E. Serrano, Grossmont College; Laura Sommer, Daemen College; Natasha Staller, Amherst College; Nancy Steele-Hamme, Midwestern State University; Andrew Stewart, University of California–Berkeley; John R. Stocking, University of Calgary; Francesca Tronchin, Ohio State University; Frances Van Keuren, University of Georgia; Kelly Wacker, University of Montevallo; Carolynne Whitefeather, Utica College; Nancy L. Wicker, University of Mississippi; Alastair Wright, Princeton University; John G. Younger, University of Kansas; Margaret Ann Zaho, Central Florida University; Michael Zell, Boston University.

In addition, I wish to thank the following individuals for providing critiques of the first concise edition of *Art through the Ages*, which were invaluable in my preparation of the second edition: Mark S. Deka, Edinboro University of Pennsylvania; Barbara Dodsworth, Mercy College; Kevin Glowacki, Texas A&M University; Michael P. Kemling, University of Georgia; Gamble L. Madsen, Mt. San Antonio College; Rose May, Temple University; Heather Shirey, University of St. Thomas; Jerry E. Smith, Collin County Community College.

I am also happy to have this opportunity to express my gratitude to the extraordinary group of people at Wadsworth involved with the editing, production, and distribution of *Art through the Ages*. Some of them I have now worked with on various projects for more than a decade and feel privileged to count among my friends. The success of the Gardner series in all of its various permutations depends in no small part on the expertise and unflagging commitment of these dedicated professionals: Sean Wakely, president Cengage Arts and Sciences; P. J. Boardman, vice president and editor-in-chief Wadsworth Publishing; Clark Baxter, publisher; Sharon Adams Poore, senior development editor; Lianne Ames, senior content project manager; Wendy Constantine, managing technology project manager; Erikka Adams, assistant editor; Nell Pepper, editorial assistant; Cate Barr, senior art director; Scott Stewart, vice president managing director sales; Diane Wenckebach, senior marketing manager; as well as Heather Baxley, Doug Easton, tani hasegawa, Aimee Alcorn Lewis, and Ellen Pettengell.

I am also deeply grateful to the following for their significant contributions to the second edition of *Art through the Ages: A Concise Global History*: Joan Keyes, Dovetail Publishing Services; Ida May Norton, copy editor; Pat Lewis, proofreader; Sarah Evertson and Stephen Forsling, photo researchers; John Pierce, Thompson Type; Don Larson and Rick Stanley, Digital Media Inc., U.S.A.; Cindy Geiss, Graphic World; and, of course, John Burge, for his superb architectural drawings. I also wish to acknowledge my debt to Edward Tufte for an illuminating afternoon spent discussing publication design and production issues and for his insightful contribution to the creation of the scales that accompany all reproductions of paintings, sculptures, and other artworks in this edition.

Finally, I owe thanks to my colleagues at Boston University and to the thousands of students and the scores of teaching fellows in my art history courses during the past three decades. From them I have learned much that has helped determine the form and content of *Art through the Ages* and made it a much better book than it otherwise might have been.

Fred S. Kleiner

Resources

Many teaching and learning tools are available for instructors and students.

FOR STUDENTS

ArtStudy Online
Gives access to a host of multimedia resources including **flashcards** with a new zoom feature as well as a new compare-and-contrast feature that can display two works side by side with critical-thinking questions. Students also gain access to interactive maps, architectural basics materials, video clips of select architectural monuments, museum guides with links, Google™ Earth coordinates with exercises, student test packets, audio study tools, vocabulary of art history, a guide to researching art history online, tips on becoming a successful student, and art links to beneficial Web sites on art, artists, architecture, and more.

Global Timeline
The fold-out global timeline shows the spectacular panorama of art through the ages at a glance. It is enclosed with each new copy of the second edition.

SlideGuide
This lecture companion enables students to take notes alongside representations of the art images shown in class. New to this edition are Google™ Earth coordinates linking satellite images of key cities, monuments, and buildings to textual references and end-of-chapter exercises.

Drawing upon Art
Students will learn through doing with this workbook geared toward students with no or limited art skills. Assignments address the fundamental, historical questions and problems in visual art. It is designed specifically to bring students into direct contact with landmark artistic achievements. This tool challenges students, with simple and direct exercises, to experience for themselves history's most advanced and creative visual art problems and developments.

Book Companion Web Site
Instructors and students have access to a rich array of teaching and learning resources, including chapter-by-chapter online tutorial quizzes, final exam, chapter review, chapter-by-chapter Web links, glossary flashcards, and more.

FOR INSTRUCTORS

Digital Image Library
Bring digital images into the classroom with this one-stop lecture and class presentation tool that makes it easy to assemble, edit, and present customized lectures for your course using Microsoft® PowerPoint®. The Digital Image Library provides high-resolution images (maps, illustrations, and most of the fine art images from the text) for lecture presentations, either in an easy-to-use PowerPoint presentation format, or in individual file formats compatible with other image-viewing software. The **zoom feature** allows you to magnify selected portions of an image for more detailed display in class or display images side by side for comparing and contrasting in your lecture. You can easily customize your classroom presentation by adding your own images to those from the text. The Digital Image Library also includes **Google™ Earth** coordinates that allow you to zoom in on an entire city, as well as key monuments and buildings within it. Flash video clips of architectural landmarks in New York City discussed in the text are also included, and a navigation bar enables you to move around the building/monument and zoom in/out and right/left.

PowerLecture
This CD-ROM includes a Resource Integration Guide, an electronic Instructor's Manual, and a Test Bank with multiple-choice, matching, short-answer, and essay questions in ExamView® computerized format.

JoinIn™ Student Response System
Turn your lecture into a fully interactive experience for your students with text-specific Microsoft® PowerPoint® slides. Take attendance, poll students, check student comprehension of difficult concepts, and even administer quizzes without collecting papers or grading.

WebTutor® on Blackboard and WebCT
WebTutor offers a flexible format that enables you to assign pre-formatted, text-specific content that is available as soon as you log on. You can also customize the WebTutor environment in any way you choose—from uploading images and other resources to adding Web links to creating your own practice materials.

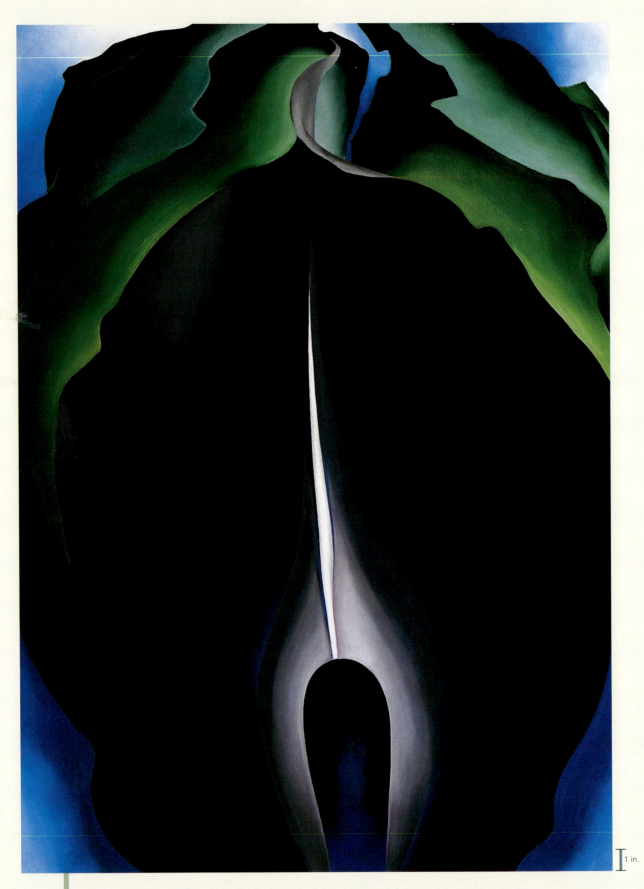

1 in.

I-1 Georgia O'Keeffe, *Jack-in-the-Pulpit No. 4*, 1930. Oil on canvas, 3′ 4″ × 2′ 6″. National Gallery of Art, Washington, D.C. (Alfred Stieglitz Collection, bequest of Georgia O'Keeffe).

Georgia O'Keeffe painted this floral composition without knowing who would purchase it or where it would be displayed, but throughout history most artists created works for specific patrons and settings.

Introduction
What Is Art History?

Except when referring to the modern academic discipline, people do not often juxtapose the words "art" and "history." They tend to think of history as the record and interpretation of past human actions, particularly social and political actions. Most think of art, quite correctly, as part of the present—as something people can see and touch. People cannot, of course, see or touch history's vanished human events. But a visible and tangible artwork is a kind of persisting event. One or more artists made it at a certain time and in a specific place, even if no one now knows who, when, where, or why. Although created in the past, an artwork continues to exist in the present, long surviving its times. The first painters and sculptors died 30,000 years ago, but their works remain, some of them exhibited in glass cases in museums built only a few years ago.

Modern museum visitors can admire these objects from the remote past and the countless others humankind has produced over the millennia without any knowledge of the circumstances that led to the creation of those works. An object's beauty or sheer size can impress people, the artist's virtuosity in the handling of ordinary or costly materials can dazzle them, or the subject depicted can move them. Viewers can react to what they see, interpret the work in the light of their own experience, and judge it a success or a failure. These are all valid responses to a work of art. But the enjoyment and appreciation of artworks in museum settings are relatively recent phenomena, as is the creation of artworks solely for museum-going audiences to view.

Today, it is common for artists to work in private studios and to create paintings, sculptures, and other objects that commercial art galleries will offer for sale, as the American painter GEORGIA O'KEEFFE (1887–1986) did when she created her series of paintings of flowering plants (FIG. I-1). Usually, someone the artist has never met will purchase the artwork and display it in a setting the artist has never seen. But although this is not a new phenomenon in the history of art—an ancient potter decorating a vase for sale at a village market stall probably did not know who would buy the pot or where it would be housed—it is not at all typical. In fact, it is exceptional. Throughout history, most artists created the paintings, sculptures, and other objects exhibited in museums today for specific patrons and settings and to fulfill a specific purpose. Often, no one knows the original contexts of those artworks.

Although people may appreciate the visual and tactile qualities of these objects, they cannot understand why they were made or why they appear as they do without knowing the circumstances of their creation. Art *appreciation* does not require knowledge of the historical context of an artwork (or a building). Art *history* does. Thus, a central aim of art history is to determine the original context of artworks. Art historians seek to achieve a full understanding not only of why these "persisting events" of human history look the way they do but also of why the artistic events happened at all. What unique set of circumstances gave rise to the erection of a particular building or led a specific patron to commission an individual artist to fashion a singular artwork for a certain place? The study of history is therefore vital to art history. And art history is often very important to the study of history. Art objects and buildings are historical documents that can shed light on the peoples who made them and on the times of their creation in a way other historical documents cannot. Furthermore, artists and architects can affect history by reinforcing or challenging cultural values and practices through the objects they create and the structures they build. Thus, the history of art and architecture is inseparable from the study of history, although the two disciplines are not the same. The following pages introduce some of the distinctive subjects art historians address and the kinds of questions they ask, and explain some of the basic terminology art historians use when answering these questions. Armed with this arsenal of questions and terms, readers will be ready to explore the multifaceted world of art through the ages.

ART HISTORY IN THE 21ST CENTURY

Art historians study the visual and tangible objects humans make and the structures they build. From the earliest Greco-Roman art critics on, scholars have studied works that their makers consciously manufactured as "art" and to which the artists assigned formal titles. But today's art historians also study a vast number of objects that their creators and owners almost certainly did not consider to be "works of art." Few ancient Romans, for example, would have regarded a coin bearing their emperor's portrait as anything but money. Today, an art museum may exhibit that coin in a locked case in a climate-controlled room, and scholars may subject it to the same kind of art historical analysis as a portrait by an acclaimed Renaissance or modern sculptor or painter.

The range of objects art historians study is constantly expanding and now includes computer-generated images, for example, whereas in the past almost anything produced using a machine would not have been regarded as art. Most people still consider the performing arts—music, drama, and dance—as outside art history's realm because these arts are fleeting, impermanent media. But recently even this distinction between "fine art" and "performance art" has become blurred. Art historians, however, generally ask the same kinds of questions about what they study, whether they employ a restrictive or an expansive definition of art.

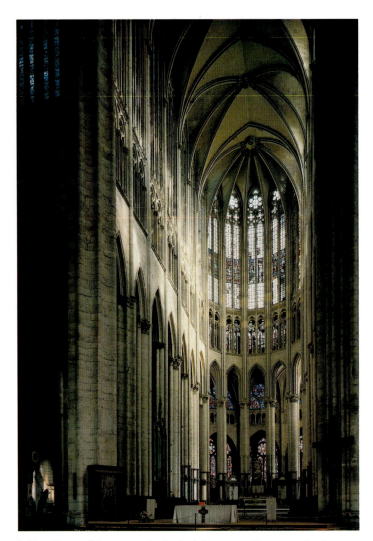

I-2 Choir of Beauvais Cathedral, Beauvais, France, rebuilt after 1284.

The style of an object or building often varies from region to region. This cathedral has towering stone vaults and large stained-glass windows typical of 13th-century French architecture.

The Questions Art Historians Ask

How Old Is It? Before art historians can construct a history of art, they must be sure they know the date of each work they study. Thus, an indispensable subject of art historical inquiry is *chronology*, the dating of art objects and buildings. If researchers cannot determine a monument's age, they cannot place the work in its historical context. Art historians have developed many ways to establish, or at least approximate, the date of an artwork.

Physical evidence often reliably indicates an object's age. The material used for a statue or painting—bronze, plastic, or oil-based pigment, to name only a few—may not have been invented before a certain time, indicating the earliest possible date someone could have fashioned the work. Or artists may have ceased using certain materials—such as specific kinds of inks and papers for drawings—at a known time, providing the latest possible dates for objects made of those materials. Sometimes the material (or the manufacturing technique) of an object or a building can establish a very precise date of production or construction. Studying

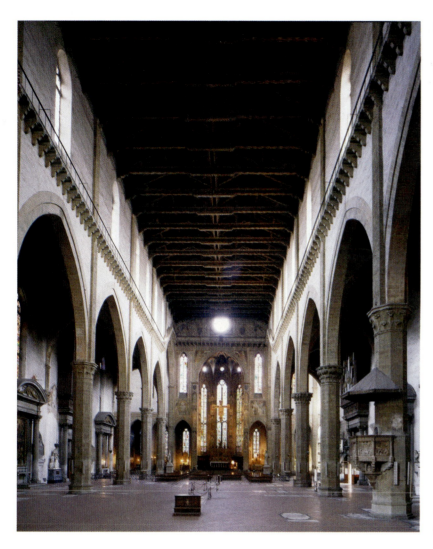

I-3 Interior of Santa Croce, Florence, Italy, begun 1294.

In contrast to Beauvais Cathedral (FIG. I-2), this contemporaneous Florentine church conforms to the quite different regional style of Italy. The building has a low timber roof and small windows.

tree rings, for instance, usually can determine within a narrow range the date of a wood statue or a timber roof beam.

Documentary evidence can help pinpoint the date of an object or building when a dated written document mentions the work. For example, official records may note when a bishop commissioned a new artwork for a church—and how much he paid to which artist.

Internal evidence can play a significant role in dating an artwork. A painter might have depicted an identifiable person or a kind of hairstyle, clothing, or furniture fashionable only at a certain time. If so, the art historian can assign a more accurate date to that painting.

Stylistic evidence is also very important. The analysis of *style*—an artist's distinctive manner of producing an object, the way a work looks—is the art historian's special sphere. Unfortunately, because it is a subjective assessment, stylistic evidence is by far the most unreliable chronological criterion. Still, art historians often find style a very useful tool for establishing chronology.

What Is Its Style? Defining artistic style is one of the key elements of art historical inquiry, although the analysis of artworks solely in terms of style no longer dominates the field the way it once did. Art historians speak of several different kinds of artistic styles.

Period style refers to the characteristic artistic manner of a specific time, usually within a distinct culture, such as "Archaic Greek." But many periods do not display any stylistic unity at all. How would someone define the artistic style of the opening decade of the new millennium in North America? Far too many crosscurrents exist in contemporary art for anyone to describe a period style of the early 21st century—even in a single city such as New York.

Regional style is the term art historians use to describe variations in style tied to geography. Like an object's date, its *provenance*, or place of origin, can significantly determine its character. Very often two artworks from the same place made centuries apart are more similar than contemporaneous works from two different regions. To cite one example, usually only an expert can distinguish between an Egyptian statue carved in 2500 BCE and one made in 500 BCE. But no one would mistake an Egyptian statue of 500 BCE for one of the same date made in Greece or Mexico.

Considerable variations in a given area's style are possible, however, even during a single historical period. In late medieval Europe, French architecture differed significantly from Italian architecture. The interiors of Beauvais Cathedral (FIG. I-2) and the Florentine church of Santa Croce (FIG. I-3) typify the architectural styles of France and Italy, respectively, at the end of the 13th century. The rebuilding of the east end of Beauvais Cathedral began in 1284. Construction commenced on Santa Croce only 10 years later. Both structures employ the *pointed arch* characteristic of this era, yet the two churches differ strikingly. The French church has towering stone ceilings and large expanses of colored windows, whereas the Italian building has a low timber roof and small, widely separated windows. Because the two contemporaneous churches served similar purposes, regional style mainly explains their differing appearance.

Personal style, the distinctive manner of individual artists or architects, often decisively explains stylistic discrepancies among monuments of the same time and place. Georgia O'Keeffe's 1930 painting *Jack-in-the-Pulpit No. 4* (FIG. I-1) is a sharply focused close-up view of petals and leaves. O'Keeffe captured the growing plant's slow, controlled motion while converting the organic form into a powerful abstract composition of lines, shapes, and colors (see the discussion of art historical vocabulary in the next section). Only a year later, another American artist, BEN SHAHN (1898–1969), painted *The Passion of Sacco and Vanzetti* (FIG. I-4), a stinging commentary on social injustice inspired by the trial and execution of two Italian anarchists, Nicola Sacco and Bartolomeo Vanzetti. Many people believed Sacco and Vanzetti had been unjustly convicted of killing two men in a holdup in 1920. Shahn's painting compresses time in a symbolic representation of the trial and its aftermath. The two executed men lie in their coffins. Presiding over them are the three members of the commission (headed by a college president wearing academic cap and gown) that declared the original trial fair and cleared the way for the executions. Behind, on the wall of a stately government building, hangs the framed portrait of the judge who pronounced the initial sentence. Personal style, not period or regional style, sets Shahn's canvas apart from O'Keeffe's. The contrast is extreme here because of the very different subjects the artists chose. But even when two artists depict the same subject, the results can vary widely. The *way* O'Keeffe painted flowers and the *way* Shahn painted faces are distinctive and unlike the styles of their contemporaries. (See the "Who Made It?" discussion.)

The different kinds of artistic styles are not mutually exclusive. For example, an artist's personal style may change dramatically during a long career. Art historians then must distinguish among the different period styles of a particular artist, such as the "Blue Period" and the "Cubist Period" of the prolific 20th-century artist Pablo Picasso.

What Is Its Subject? Another major concern of art historians is, of course, subject matter. Some artworks, such as modern *abstract* paintings, have no subject, not even a setting. But when artists represent people, places, or actions, viewers must identify these aspects to achieve complete understanding of the work. Art historians traditionally separate pictorial subjects into various categories, such as religious, historical, mythological, *genre* (daily life), portraiture, *landscape* (a depiction of a place), *still life* (an arrangement of inanimate objects), and their numerous subdivisions and combinations.

Iconography—literally, the "writing of images"—refers both to the content, or subject of an artwork, and to the study of content in art. By extension, it also includes the study of *symbols*, images that stand for other images or encapsulate ideas. In Christian art, two intersecting lines of unequal length or a simple geometric cross can serve as an emblem of the religion as a whole, symbolizing the cross of Jesus

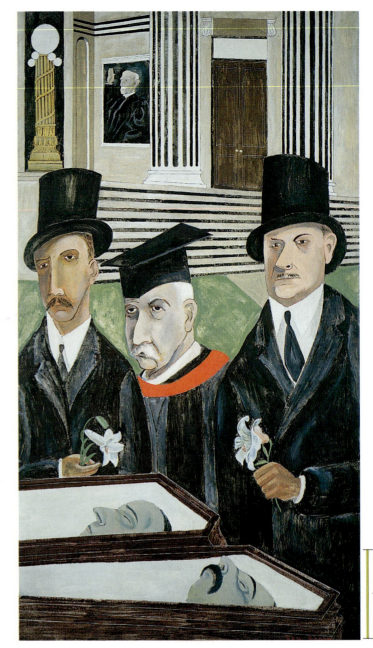

I-4 BEN SHAHN, *The Passion of Sacco and Vanzetti*, 1931–1932. Tempera on canvas, 7'$\frac{1}{2}$" × 4'. Whitney Museum of American Art, New York (gift of Edith and Milton Lowenthal in memory of Juliana Force).

A contemporary of O'Keeffe's (FIG. I-1), Shahn had a markedly different personal style. His paintings are often social commentaries on contemporary events and incorporate readily identifiable human figures.

Christ's crucifixion. A symbol also can be a familiar object the artist imbued with greater meaning. A balance or scale, for example, may symbolize justice or the weighing of souls on Judgment Day.

Artists may depict figures with unique *attributes* identifying them. In Christian art, for example, each of the authors of the New Testament Gospels, the four evangelists, has a distinctive attribute. People can recognize Saint John by the eagle associated with him, Luke by the ox, Mark by the lion, and Matthew by the winged man.

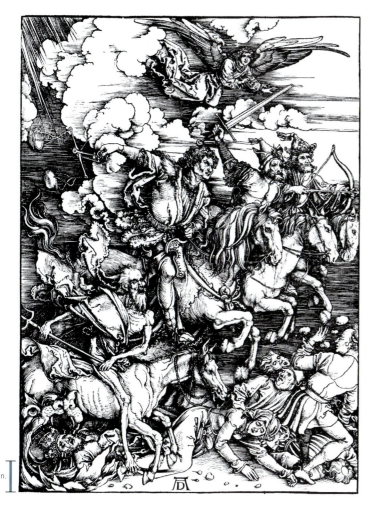

1 in.

I-5 ALBRECHT DÜRER, *The Four Horsemen of the Apocalypse*, ca. 1498. Woodcut, 1′ 3¼″ × 11″. Metropolitan Museum of Art, New York (gift of Junius S. Morgan, 1919).

Personifications are abstract ideas codified in human form. Albrecht Dürer represented Death, Famine, War, and Pestilence as four men on charging horses, each man carrying an identifying attribute.

Throughout the history of art, artists have also used *personifications*—abstract ideas codified in human form. Worldwide, people visualize Liberty as a robed woman with a torch because of the fame of the colossal statue set up in New York City's harbor in the 19th century. *The Four Horsemen of the Apocalypse* (FIG. **I-5**) is a terrifying late-15th-century depiction of the fateful day at the end of time when, according to the Bible's last book, Death, Famine, War, and Pestilence will cut down the human race. The German artist ALBRECHT DÜRER (1471–1528) personified Death as an emaciated old man with a pitchfork. Dürer's Famine swings the scales that will weigh human souls, War wields a sword, and Pestilence draws a bow.

Even without considering style and without knowing a work's maker, informed viewers can determine much about the work's period and provenance by iconographical and subject analysis alone. In *The Passion of Sacco and Vanzetti* (FIG. I-4), for example, the two coffins, the trio headed by an academic, and the robed judge in the background are all pictorial clues revealing the painting's subject. The work's date must be after the trial and execution, probably while the event was still newsworthy. And because the deaths of the two men caused the greatest outrage in the United States, the painter–social critic was probably American.

Who Made It? If Ben Shahn had not signed his painting of Sacco and Vanzetti, an art historian could still assign, or *attribute*, the work to him based on knowledge of the artist's personal style. Although signing (and dating) works is quite common (but by no means universal) today, in the history of art countless works exist whose artists remain unknown. Because personal style can play a large role in determining the character of an artwork, art historians often try to attribute anonymous works to known artists. Sometimes they assemble a group of works all thought to be by the same person, even though none of the objects in the group is the known work of an artist with a recorded name. Art historians thus reconstruct the careers of artists such as "the Achilles Painter," the anonymous ancient Greek vase painter whose masterwork is a depiction of the hero Achilles. Scholars base their attributions on internal evidence, such as the distinctive way an artist draws or carves drapery folds, earlobes, or flowers. It requires a keen, highly trained eye and long experience to become a *connoisseur*, an expert in assigning artworks to "the hand" of one artist rather than another.

Sometimes a group of artists works in the same style at the same time and place. Art historians designate such a group as a *school*. "School" does not mean an educational institution. The term connotes only chronological, stylistic, and geographic similarity. Art historians speak, for example, of the Dutch school of the 17th century and, within it, of subschools such as those of the cities of Haarlem, Utrecht, and Leyden.

Who Paid for It? The interest many art historians show in attribution reflects their conviction that the identity of an artwork's maker is the major reason the object looks the way it does. For them, personal style is of paramount importance. But in many times and places, artists had little to say about what form their work would take. They toiled in obscurity, doing the bidding of their *patrons*, those who paid them to make individual works or employed them on a continuing basis. The role of patrons in dictating the content and shaping the form of artworks is also an important subject of art historical inquiry.

In the art of portraiture, to name only one category of painting and sculpture, the patron has often played a dominant role in deciding how the artist represented the subject, whether the patron or another person, such as a spouse, son, or mother. Many Egyptian pharaohs and some Roman emperors insisted that artists depict them with unlined faces and perfect youthful bodies no matter how old they were when portrayed. In these cases, the state employed the sculptors and painters, and the artists had no choice but to depict their patrons in the officially approved manner.

All modes of artistic production reveal the impact of patronage. Learned monks provided the themes for the sculptural decoration of medieval church portals. Renaissance princes and popes dictated the subject, size, and materials of artworks destined, sometimes, for buildings constructed according to their specifications. An art historian could make a very long list along these lines, and it would indicate that throughout the history of art, patrons have had diverse tastes and needs and demanded different kinds of art. Whenever a patron contracts an artist or architect to paint, sculpt, or build in a prescribed manner, personal style often becomes a very minor factor in the final appearance of the painting, statue, or building. In these cases, the identity of the patron reveals more to art historians than does the identity of the artist or school.

The Words Art Historians Use

Like all specialists, art historians have their own specialized vocabulary. That vocabulary consists of hundreds of words, but certain basic terms are indispensable for describing artworks and buildings of any time and place. They make up the essential vocabulary of *formal analysis*, the visual analysis of artistic form. Definitions of the most important of these art historical terms follow.

Form and Composition *Form* refers to an object's shape and structure, either in two dimensions (for example, a figure painted on a canvas) or in three dimensions (such as a statue carved from a marble block). Two forms may take the same shape but differ in their color, texture, and other qualities. *Composition* refers to how an artist organizes (*composes*) forms in an artwork, either by placing shapes on a flat surface or by arranging forms in space.

Material and Technique To create art forms, artists shape materials (pigment, clay, marble, gold, and many more) with tools (pens, brushes, chisels, and so forth). Each of the materials and tools available has its own potentialities and limitations. Part of all artists' creative activity is to select the *medium* and instrument most suitable to the artists' purpose—or to develop the use of new media and tools, such as bronze and concrete in antiquity and cameras and computers in modern times. The processes artists employ, such as applying paint to canvas with a brush, and the distinctive, personal ways they handle materials constitute their *technique*. Form, material, and technique interrelate and are central to analyzing any work of art.

Line *Line* is one of the most important elements defining an artwork's shape or form. A line can be understood as the path of a point moving in space, an invisible line of sight. But, more commonly, artists and architects make a line concrete by drawing (or chiseling) it on a *plane*, a flat and two-dimensional surface. A line may be very thin, wirelike, and delicate. It may be thick and heavy. Or it may alternate

quickly from broad to narrow, the strokes jagged or the outline broken. When a continuous line defines an object's outer shape, art historians call it a *contour line*. All of these line qualities are present in Dürer's *Four Horsemen of the Apocalypse* (FIG. I-5). Contour lines define the basic shapes of clouds, human and animal limbs, and weapons. Within the forms, series of short broken lines create shadows and textures. An overall pattern of long parallel strokes suggests the dark sky on the frightening day when the world is about to end.

Color Light reveals all colors. Light in the world of the painter and other artists differs from natural light. Natural light, or sunlight, is whole or *additive light*. As the sum of all the wavelengths composing the visible *spectrum*, it may be disassembled or fragmented into the individual colors of the spectral band. The painter's light in art—the light reflected from pigments and objects—is *subtractive light*. Paint pigments produce their individual colors by reflecting a segment of the spectrum while absorbing all the rest. Green pigment, for example, subtracts or absorbs all the light in the spectrum except that seen as green, which it reflects to the eyes.

Red, yellow, and blue are the *primary colors*. The *secondary colors* result from mixing pairs of primaries: orange (red and yellow), purple (red and blue), and green (yellow and blue). *Complementary colors*—orange and blue, purple and yellow, green and red—complete, or "complement," each other, one absorbing colors the other reflects.

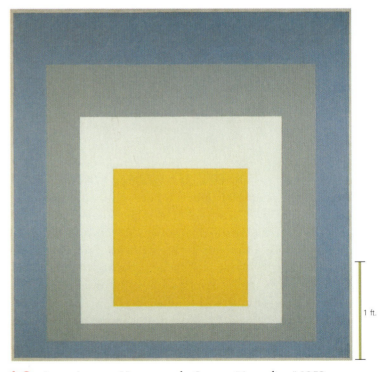

1 ft.

I-6 JOSEF ALBERS, *Homage to the Square: "Ascending,"* 1953. Oil on composition board, 3′ 7½″ × 3′ 7½″. Whitney Museum of American Art, New York.

Josef Albers painted hundreds of canvases with the same composition but employed variations in color saturation and tonality in order to reveal the relativity and instability of color perception.

Artists can manipulate the appearance of colors, however. One artist who made a systematic investigation of the formal aspects of art, especially color, was JOSEF ALBERS (1888–1976), a German-born artist who immigrated to the United States in 1933. In *Homage to the Square: "Ascending"* (FIG. I-6)—one of hundreds of color variations on the same composition of concentric squares—Albers demonstrated "the discrepancy between physical fact and psychic effect."[1] Because the composition remains constant, the *Homage* series succeeds in revealing the relativity and instability of color perception. Albers varied the *saturation* (a color's brightness or dullness) and *tonality* (lightness or darkness) of each square in each painting. As a result, the sizes of the squares from painting to painting appear to vary (although they remain the same), and the sensations emanating from the paintings range from clashing dissonance to delicate serenity. In this way Albers proved "that we see colors almost never unrelated to each other."[2] Artists' comments on their own works are often invaluable to art historians. In *Art through the Ages*, artist commentaries appear frequently in boxed features called "Artists on Art."

Texture *Texture* is the quality of a surface (such as rough or shiny) that light reveals. Art historians distinguish between true texture, or the tactile quality of the surface, and represented texture, as when painters depict an ob-

ject as having a certain texture, even though the pigment is the real texture. Texture is, of course, a key determinant of any sculpture's character. People's first impulse is usually to handle a piece of sculpture—even though museum signs often warn "Do not touch!" Sculptors plan for this natural human response, using surfaces varying in texture from rugged coarseness to polished smoothness. Textures are often intrinsic to a material, influencing the type of stone, wood, plastic, clay, or metal that sculptors select.

Space *Space* is the bounded or boundless "container" of objects. For art historians, space can be the literal three-dimensional space occupied by a statue or a vase or contained within a room or courtyard. Or it can be *illusionistic*, as when painters depict an image (or illusion) of the three-dimensional spatial world on a two-dimensional surface.

Perspective *Perspective* is one of the most important pictorial devices for organizing forms in space. Throughout history, artists have used various types of perspective to create an illusion of depth or space on a two-dimensional surface. The French painter CLAUDE LORRAIN (1600–1682) employed several *perspectival* devices in *Embarkation of the Queen of Sheba* (FIG. I-7), a painting of a biblical episode set in a 17th-century European harbor with a Roman ruin in the left foreground. For example, the figures and boats on the

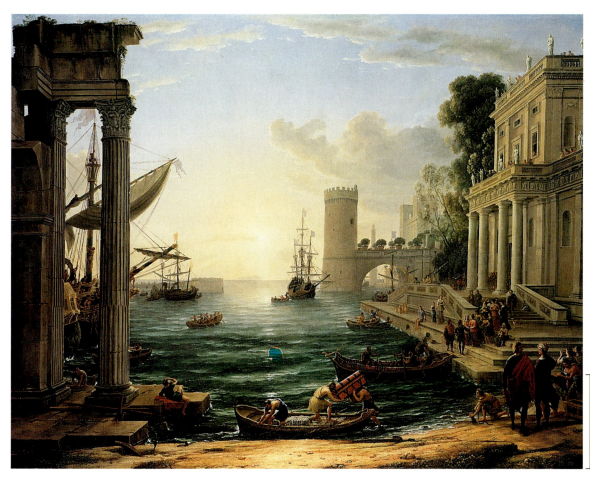

I-7

CLAUDE LORRAIN, *Embarkation of the Queen of Sheba*, 1648. Oil on canvas, 4′ 10″ × 6′ 4″. National Gallery, London.

To create the illusion of a deep landscape, this French painter employed perspective, reducing the size of and blurring the most distant forms. All diagonal lines converge on a single point.

1 ft.

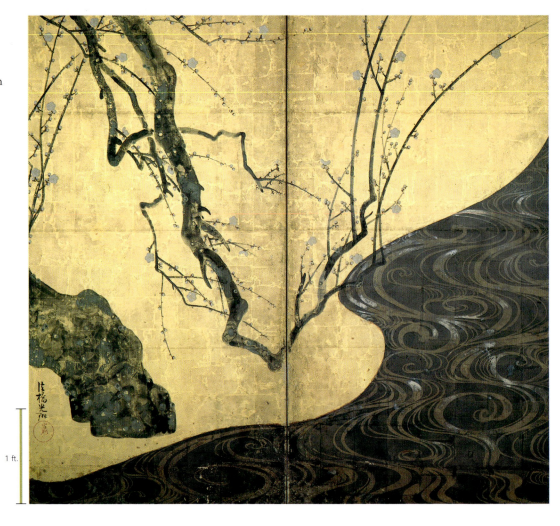

I-8 OGATA KORIN, *White and Red Plum Blossoms*, ca. 1710–1716. Pair of two-fold screens. Ink, color, and gold leaf on paper, each screen 5′ 1⅝″ × 5′ 7⅞″. MOA Art Museum, Shizuoka-ken.

1 ft.

shoreline are much larger than those in the distance. Decreasing an object's size makes it appear farther away from the viewer. Also, the top and bottom of the port building at the painting's right side are not parallel horizontal lines, as they are in a real building. Instead, the lines converge beyond the structure, leading viewers' eyes toward the hazy, indistinct sun on the horizon. These perspectival devices—the reduction of figure size, the convergence of diagonal lines, and the blurring of distant forms—have been familiar features of Western art since the ancient Greeks. But it is important to note at the outset that all kinds of perspective are only pictorial conventions, even when one or more types of perspective may be so common in a given culture that they are accepted as "natural" or as "true" means of representing the natural world.

In *White and Red Plum Blossoms* (FIG. **I-8**), a Japanese landscape painting on two folding screens, OGATA KORIN (1658–1716) used none of these Western perspective conventions. He showed the two plum trees as seen from a position on the ground, while viewers look down on the stream between them from above. Less concerned with locating the trees and stream in space than with composing shapes on a surface, the painter juxtaposed and contrasted the

water's gently swelling curves with the jagged contours of the branches and trunks. Neither the French nor the Japanese painting can be said to project "correctly" what viewers "in fact" see. One painting is not a "better" picture of the world than the other. The European and Asian artists simply approached the problem of picture-making differently.

Foreshortening Artists also represent single figures in space in varying ways. When the Flemish artist PETER PAUL RUBENS (1577–1640) painted *Lion Hunt* (FIG. **I-9**), he used *foreshortening* for all the hunters and animals—that is, he represented their bodies at angles to the picture plane. When in life one views a figure at an angle, the body appears to contract as it extends back in space. Foreshortening is a kind of perspective. It produces the illusion that one part of the body is farther away than another, even though all the forms are on the same surface. Especially noteworthy in *Lion Hunt* are the gray horse at the left, seen from behind with the bottom of its left rear hoof facing viewers and most of its head hidden by its rider's shield, and the fallen hunter at the painting's lower right corner, whose barely visible legs and feet recede into the distance.

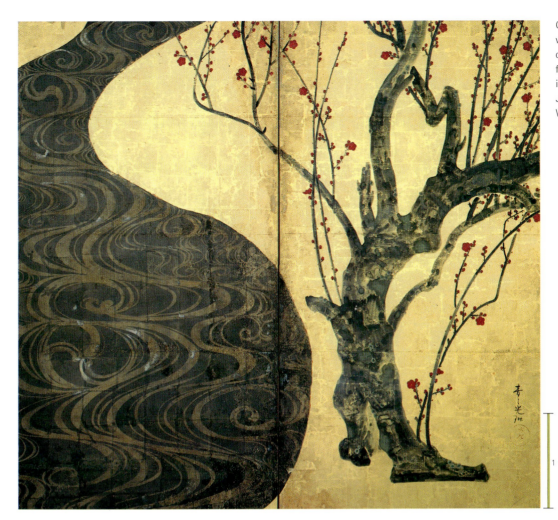

Ogata Korin was more concerned with creating an interesting composition of shapes on a surface than with locating objects in three-dimensional space. Japanese artists rarely employed Western perspective.

1 ft.

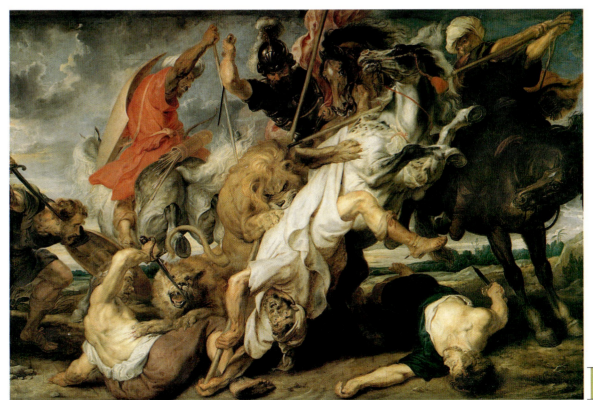

I-9 PETER PAUL RUBENS, *Lion Hunt*, 1617–1618. Oil on canvas, 8′ 2″ × 12′ 5″. Alte Pinakothek, Munich.

Foreshortening—the representation of a figure or object at an angle to the picture plane—is a common device in Western art for creating the illusion of depth. Foreshortening is a kind of perspective.

1 ft.

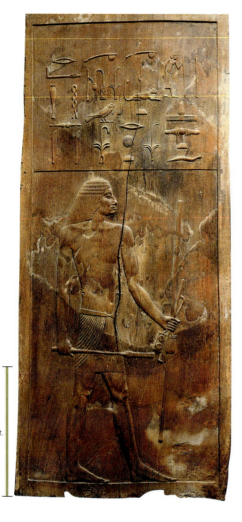

I-10 Hesire, from his tomb at Saqqara, Egypt, Third Dynasty, ca. 2650 BCE. Wood, 3′ 9″ high. Egyptian Museum, Cairo.

Egyptian artists combined frontal and profile views to give a precise picture of the parts of the human body, as opposed to depicting how an individual body appears from a specific viewpoint.

1 ft.

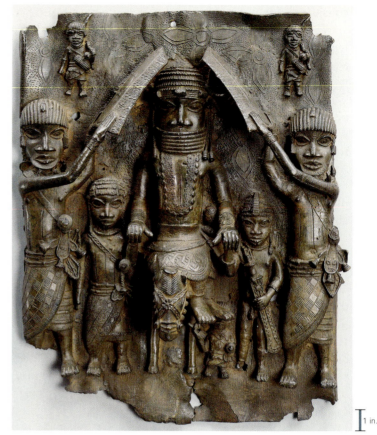

1 in.

I-11 King on horseback with attendants, from Benin, Nigeria, ca. 1550–1680. Bronze, 1′ 7½″ high. Metropolitan Museum of Art, New York (Michael C. Rockefeller Memorial Collection, gift of Nelson A. Rockefeller).

This African artist used hierarchy of scale to distinguish the relative rank of the figures, making the king the largest. The sculptor created the relief by casting (pouring bronze into a mold).

The artist who carved the portrait of the ancient Egyptian official Hesire (FIG. **I-10**) did not employ foreshortening. That artist's purpose was to present the various human body parts as clearly as possible, without overlapping. The lower part of Hesire's body is in profile to give the most complete view of the legs, with both the heels and toes of the feet visible. The frontal torso, however, allows the viewer to see its full shape, including both shoulders, equal in size, as in nature. (Compare the shoulders of the hunter on the gray horse or those of the fallen hunter in *Lion Hunt*'s left foreground.) The result, an "unnatural" 90-degree twist at the waist, provides a precise picture of human body parts. Rubens and the Egyptian sculptor used very different means of depicting forms in space. Once again, neither is the "correct" manner.

Proportion and Scale *Proportion* concerns the relationships (in terms of size) of the parts of persons, buildings, or objects. "Correct proportions" may be judged intuitively ("that statue's head seems the right size for the body"). Or proportion can be a mathematical relationship between the size of one part of an artwork or building and the other parts within the work. Proportion in art implies using a *module*, or basic unit of measure. When an artist or architect uses a formal system of proportions, all parts of a building, body, or other entity will be fractions or multiples of the module. A module might be a *column*'s diameter, the height of a

human head, or any other component whose dimensions can be multiplied or divided to determine the size of the work's other parts.

In certain times and places, artists have formulated *canons*, or systems, of "correct" or "ideal" proportions for representing human figures, constituent parts of buildings, and so forth. In ancient Greece, many sculptors formulated canons of proportions so strict and all-encompassing that they calculated the size of every body part in advance, even the fingers and toes, according to mathematical ratios. Proportional systems can differ sharply from period to period, culture to culture, and artist to artist. Part of the task art history students face is to perceive and adjust to these differences.

In fact, many artists have used disproportion and distortion deliberately for expressive effect. Dürer's Death (FIG. I-5) has hardly any flesh on his bones, and his limbs are distorted and stretched. Disproportion and distortion distinguish him from all the other figures in the work, precisely as the artist intended. In other cases, artists have used disproportion to focus attention on one body part (often the head) or to single out a group member (usually the leader). These intentional "unnatural" discrepancies in proportion constitute what art historians call *hierarchy of scale*, the enlarging of elements considered the most important. On a bronze plaque (FIG. I-11) from Benin, Nigeria, the sculptor enlarged all the heads for emphasis and also varied the size of each figure according to its social status. Central, largest, and therefore most important is the Benin king, mounted on horseback. The horse has been a symbol of power and wealth in many societies from prehistory to the present. That the Benin king is disproportionately larger than his horse, contrary to nature, further aggrandizes him. Two large attendants fan the king. Other figures of smaller size and lower status at the Benin court stand on the king's left and right and in the plaque's upper corners. One tiny figure next to the horse is almost hidden from view beneath the king's feet.

One problem that students of art history—and professional art historians too—confront when studying illustrations in art history books is that although the relative sizes of figures and objects in a painting or sculpture are easy to discern, it is impossible to determine the absolute size of the work reproduced because they all appear at approximately the same size on the page. Readers of *Art through the Ages* can determine the exact size of all artworks from the dimensions given in the captions and, more intuitively, from the scales (in inches or feet) that appear at the lower left or right corner of each illustration.

Carving and Casting Sculptural technique falls into two basic categories, *subtractive* and *additive*. *Carving* is a subtractive technique. The final form is a reduction of the original mass of a block of stone, a piece of wood, or another material. Wooden statues were once tree trunks, and stone statues began as blocks pried from mountains. An unfinished 16th-century marble statue of a bound slave (FIG. I-12) by MICHELANGELO BUONARROTI (1475–1564) clearly reveals the original shape of the stone block. Michelangelo thought of sculpture as a process of "liberating" the statue within the block. All sculptors of stone or wood cut away (subtract) "excess material." When they finish, they "leave behind" the statue—in this example, a twisting nude male form whose head Michelangelo never freed from the stone block.

In additive sculpture, the artist builds up the forms, usually in clay around a framework, or *armature*. Or a sculptor may fashion a *mold*, a hollow form for shaping, or *casting*, a fluid substance such as bronze. That is how the Benin artist made the bronze sculpture of the king and his attendants (FIG. I-11).

Relief Sculpture *Statues* that exist independent of any architectural frame or setting and that the viewer can walk around are *freestanding* sculptures, or *sculptures in the round*. In *relief* sculpture, the subjects project from the background but remain part of it. In *high-relief* sculpture, the images project boldly. In some cases (FIG. I-11), the relief is so high that not only do the forms cast shadows on the background, but some parts are actually in the round. In *low relief*, or *bas-relief* (FIG. I-10), the projection is slight. Relief sculpture, like sculpture in the round, can be produced either by carving (FIG. I-10) or casting (FIG. I-11).

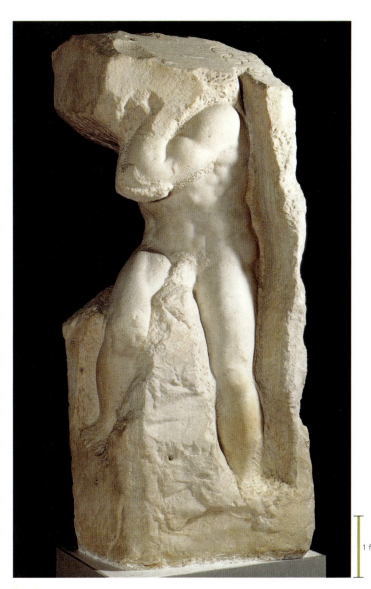

1 ft.

I-12 MICHELANGELO BUONARROTI, unfinished captive, 1527–1528. Marble, 8' 7½" high. Galleria dell'Accademia, Florence.

Freestanding sculpture can also be cast in molds, but artists more frequently carve statues from stone or wood, cutting away excess material to leave behind the shape of a human figure or other subject.

Architectural Drawings Buildings are groupings of enclosed spaces and enclosing masses, such as walls. People experience architecture both visually and by moving through and around it, so they perceive architectural space and mass together. Architects can represent these spaces and masses graphically in several ways, including as plans, sections, elevations, and cutaway drawings.

A *plan*, essentially a map of a floor, shows the placement of a structure's masses and, therefore, the spaces they bound and enclose. A *section*, like a vertical plan, depicts the placement of the masses as if the building were cut through along a plane. Drawings showing a theoretical slice across a structure's width are *lateral sections*. Those cutting through a building's length are *longitudinal sections*. An *elevation* drawing is a head-on view of an external or internal wall. A *cutaway* combines an exterior view with an interior view of part of a building in a single drawing. Illustrated here are the plan

Art History in the 21st Century | 13

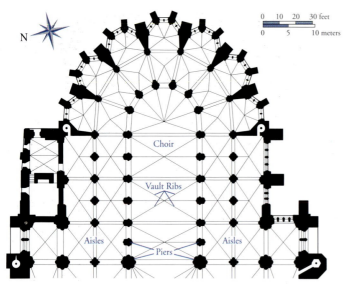

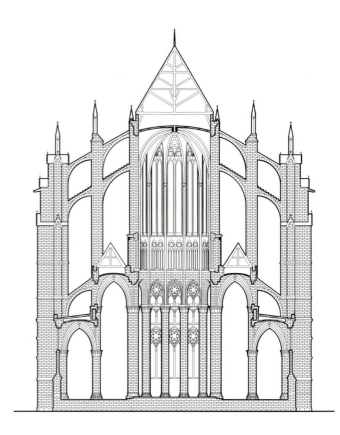

I-13 Plan (*above*) and lateral section (*right*) of Beauvais Cathedral, Beauvais, France, rebuilt after 1284.

Architectural drawings are indispensable aids for the analysis of buildings. Plans are maps of floors, "footprints" of the structure's masses. Sections are vertical "slices," across either the width or length of a building.

and lateral section (FIG. **I-13**) of Beauvais Cathedral, which may be compared to the photograph of the church's *choir* (FIG. I-2). The plan shows not only the choir's shape and the location of the *piers* dividing the *aisles* and supporting the *vaults* above but also the pattern of the crisscrossing vault *ribs*. The lateral section shows not only the interior of the choir with its vaults and *stained-glass* windows, but also the structure of the roof and the form of the exterior *flying buttresses* that hold the vaults in place. Scales accompany all plans in *Art through the Ages* to indicate the size of the building. Many of the architectural photographs include people for the same reason.

This overview of the art historian's vocabulary is not exhaustive, nor have artists used only painting, drawing, sculpture, and architecture as media over the millennia. Ceramics, jewelry, textiles, photography, and computer art are just some of the numerous other arts. All of them involve highly specialized techniques described in distinct vocabularies. As in this introductory chapter, new terms appear in *italics*, accompanied by their definition, whenever they first appear in the text. Definitions of all terms can be found in the comprehensive Glossary at the end of the book.

Art History and Other Disciplines

By its very nature, the work of art historians intersects with that of others in many fields of knowledge, not only in the humanities but also in the social and natural sciences. Today, art historians regularly must go beyond the boundaries of what previous generations considered to be the province of art history. Art historical research in the 21st century is frequently interdisciplinary in nature. To cite one example, in an effort to unlock the secrets of a particular statue, an art

historian might conduct archival research hoping to uncover new documents shedding light on who paid for the work and why, who made it and when, where it originally stood, how contemporaries viewed it, and a host of other questions. Realizing, however, that the authors of the written documents often were not objective recorders of fact but observers with their own biases and agendas, the art historian may also use methodologies developed in fields such as literary criticism, philosophy, sociology, and gender studies to weigh the evidence the documents provide.

At other times, rather than attempting to master many disciplines at once, art historians band together with other specialists in multidisciplinary inquiries. Art historians might call in chemists to date an artwork based on the composition of the materials used or might ask geologists to determine which quarry furnished the stone for a particular statue. X-ray technicians might be enlisted in an attempt to establish whether a painting is a forgery. Of course, art historians often contribute their expertise to the solution of problems in other disciplines. A historian, for example, might ask an art historian to determine—based on style, material, iconography, and other criteria—if any of the portraits of a certain king were made after his death. That would help establish the ruler's continuing prestige during the reigns of his successors.

DIFFERENT WAYS OF SEEING

The history of art can be a history of artists and their works, of styles and stylistic change, of materials and techniques, of images and themes and their meanings, and of contexts and cultures and patrons. The best art historians analyze artworks from many viewpoints. But no art historian (or

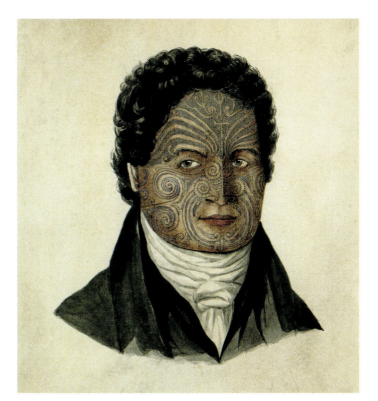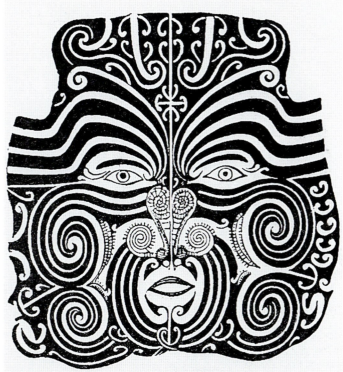

I-14 *Left:* JOHN HENRY SYLVESTER, *Portrait of Te Pehi Kupe*, 1826. Watercolor, $8\frac{1}{4}'' \times 6\frac{1}{4}''$. National Library of Australia, Canberra (Rex Nan Kivell Collection). *Right:* TE PEHI KUPE, *Self-Portrait*, 1826. From Leo Frobenius, *The Childhood of Man* (New York: J. B. Lippincott, 1909).

These strikingly different portraits of the same Maori chief reveal the different ways of seeing of Western and non-Western artists. Understanding the cultural context of artworks is vital to art history.

scholar in any other field), no matter how broad-minded in approach and no matter how experienced, can be truly objective. Like artists, art historians are members of a society, participants in its culture. How can scholars (and museum visitors and travelers to foreign locales) comprehend cultures unlike their own? They can try to reconstruct the original cultural contexts of artworks, but they are limited by their distance from the thought patterns of the cultures they study and by the obstructions to understanding—the assumptions, presuppositions, and prejudices peculiar to their culture—their own thought patterns raise. Art historians may reconstruct a distorted picture of the past because of culture-bound blindness.

A single instance underscores how differently people of diverse cultures view the world and how various ways of seeing can cause sharp differences in how artists depict the world. Illustrated here are two contemporaneous portraits of a 19th-century Maori chieftain (FIG. I-14)—one by an Englishman, JOHN SYLVESTER (active early 19th century), and the other by the New Zealand chieftain himself, TE PEHI KUPE (d. 1829). Both reproduce the chieftain's facial tattooing. The European artist included the head and shoulders and underplayed the tattooing. The tattoo pattern is one aspect of the likeness among many, no more or less important than

the chieftain's dressing like a European. Sylvester also recorded his subject's momentary glance toward the right and the play of light on his hair, fleeting aspects that have nothing to do with the figure's identity.

In contrast, Te Pehi Kupe's self-portrait—made during a trip to Liverpool, England, to obtain European arms to take back to New Zealand—is not a picture of a man situated in space and bathed in light. Rather, it is the chieftain's statement of the supreme importance of the tattoo design that symbolizes his rank among his people. Remarkably, Te Pehi Kupe created the tattoo patterns from memory, without the aid of a mirror. The splendidly composed insignia, presented as a flat design separated from the body and even from the head, is Te Pehi Kupe's image of himself. Only by understanding the cultural context of each portrait can viewers hope to understand why either image appears as it does.

As noted at the outset, the study of the context of artworks and buildings is one of the central concerns of art historians. *Art through the Ages* seeks to present a history of art and architecture that will help readers understand not only the subjects, styles, and techniques of paintings, sculptures, buildings, and other art forms created in all parts of the world for 30 millennia but also their cultural and historical contexts. That story now begins.

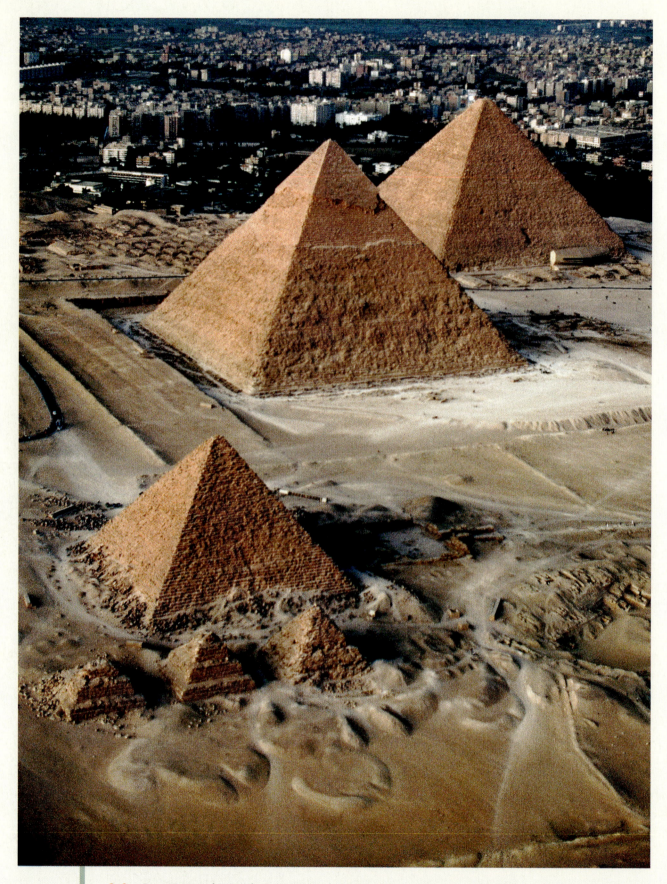

1-1 Great Pyramids, Gizeh, Egypt, Fourth Dynasty. *From left:* Pyramids of Menkaure, ca. 2490–2472 BCE; Khafre, ca. 2520–2494 BCE; and Khufu, ca. 2551–2528 BCE.

The Great Pyramids are the oldest of the Seven Wonders of the world. Their shape echoes the Egyptian sun god's emblem. The sun's rays were the ramp the pharaohs used to ascend to the heavens after death.

Prehistory and the First Civilizations

PREHISTORIC ART

Humankind seems to have originated in Africa in the very remote past. Yet it was not until millions of years later that ancient hunters began to represent (literally, "to present again"—in different and substitute form) the world around them and to fashion the first examples of what people generally call "art." The immensity of this intellectual achievement cannot be exaggerated.

Paleolithic Art

The earliest preserved art objects date to around 30,000 BCE, during the Old Stone Age, or *Paleolithic* period (from the Greek *paleo*, "old," and *lithos*, "stone"). Paleolithic artworks are of an astonishing variety. They range from simple shell necklaces to human and animal forms in ivory, clay, and stone to monumental paintings, engravings, and relief sculptures covering the huge wall surfaces of caves.

Venus of Willendorf One of the oldest sculptures discovered to date, carved using simple stone tools, is the tiny limestone figurine of a woman (FIG. 1-2) nicknamed the *Venus of Willendorf* after its *findspot* in Austria (MAP 1-1). Art historians can only speculate on the function and meaning of this and similar objects because they date to a time before writing, before (or *pre*-) history. Yet the preponderance of female over male figures in the Old Stone Age seems to indicate a preoccupation with women, whose child-bearing capabilities ensured the survival of the species. The anatomical exaggeration of the Willendorf figurine has suggested to many scholars that this and other prehistoric statuettes of women served as fertility images. The breasts of the Willendorf woman are enormous, far larger than the tiny forearms and hands that rest on them. The sculptor also used a stone *burin* to *incise* (scratch) into the stone the outline of the pubic triangle. Sculptors often omitted this detail in other Paleolithic female figurines, however, and many of the women also have far more slender proportions than the Willendorf woman, leading some scholars to question the nature of these figures as fertility images. In any case, the makers' intent seems to have been to represent not a specific woman but womanhood.

Le Tuc d'Audoubert Far more common than Paleolithic representations of humans are sculptures and paintings of animals. An early example of animal sculpture is the pair of clay bison reliefs (FIG. 1-3) in a cave at Le Tuc

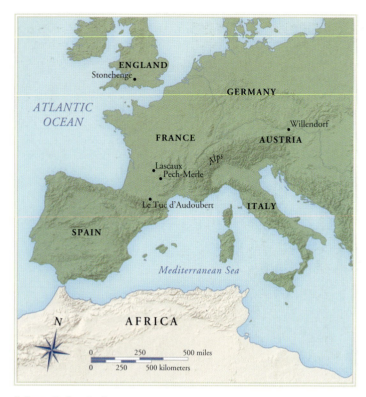

MAP 1-1 Prehistoric Europe.

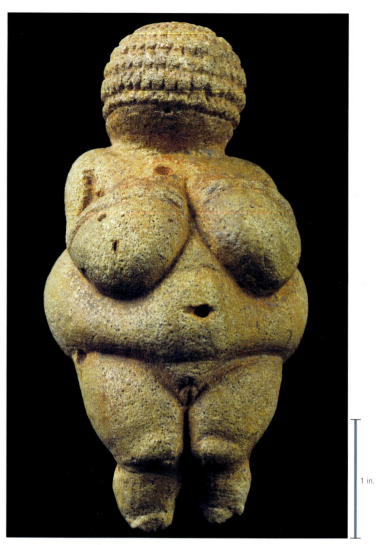

1 in.

1-2 Nude woman (*Venus of Willendorf*), from Willendorf, Austria, ca. 28,000–25,000 BCE. Limestone, $4\frac{1}{4}''$ high. Naturhistorisches Museum, Vienna.

One of the oldest sculptures known, this tiny figurine, with its anatomical exaggeration, typifies Paleolithic representations of women, whose child-bearing capabilities ensured the survival of the species.

d'Audoubert, France. The sculptor modeled the forms by pressing the clay against the surface of a large rock and using both hands to form the overall shape of the animals. Then the artist smoothed the surfaces with a spatula-like tool and used fingers to shape the eyes, nostrils, mouths, and manes. Like nearly every other Paleolithic representation of animals, these bison are in strict profile. The profile is the only view of an animal wherein the head, body, tail, and all four legs can be seen. A frontal view would conceal most of the body, and a three-quarter view would not show either the front or side fully. Because only the profile view is completely informative about the animal's shape, the profile was the almost universal postural choice during the Stone Age. A very long time passed before artists placed any premium on "variety" or "originality," either in subject choice or in representational manner. These are quite modern notions in the history of art. The aim of the earliest sculptors and painters was to create a convincing image of the subject, a kind of pictorial definition of the animal capturing its very essence, and only the profile view met their needs.

Cave Painting The bison of Le Tuc d'Audoubert are among the largest sculptures of the Paleolithic period, but they are dwarfed by the "herds" of painted animals that roam the cave walls of southern France and northern Spain. Examples of Paleolithic painting now have been found at more than 200 European sites. Nonetheless, archaeologists still regard painted caves as rare occurrences, because even though the cave images number in the hundreds, prehistoric artists created them over a period of some 10,000 to 20,000 years. Paleolithic painters drew their subjects using chunks of red

and yellow ocher. For painting, they ground these same ochers into powders they mixed with water before applying. Large flat stones served as *palettes* to hold the pigment. The painters made brushes from reeds, bristles, or twigs and may have used a blowpipe of reeds or hollow bones to spray pigments on out-of-reach surfaces. Some caves have natural ledges on the rock walls upon which the painters could have stood in order to reach the upper surfaces of the naturally formed "rooms" and corridors. To illuminate their work, the painters used stone lamps filled with marrow or fat, perhaps with a wick of moss. Despite the difficulty of making the tools and pigments, modern attempts at replicating the techniques of Paleolithic painting have demonstrated that skilled workers could cover large surfaces with images in less than a day.

Pech-Merle A *mural* (wall) painting (FIG. **1-4**) at Pech-Merle, France, provides insight into why certain subjects were chosen for a specific location. One of the horses (at the

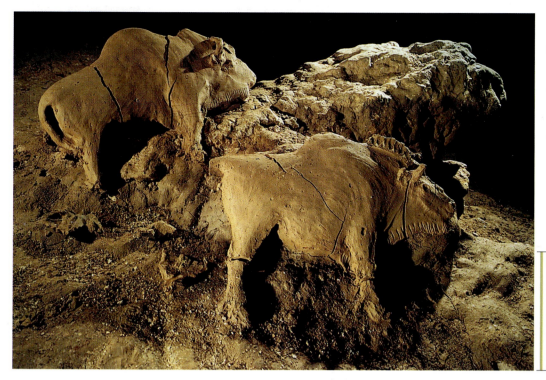

1-3 Two bison, reliefs in the cave at Le Tuc d'Audoubert, France, ca. 15,000–10,000 BCE. Clay, each 2' long.

Animals are far more common than humans in Old Stone Age art. In both relief sculpture and painting, they always appear in profile, the only view completely informative about the animals' shape.

1 ft.

1 ft.

1-4 Spotted horses and negative hand imprints, wall painting in the cave at Pech-Merle, France, ca. 22,000 BCE. 11' 2" long.

Many Paleolithic paintings include abstract signs and handprints. Some scholars think the Pech-Merle painted hands are "signatures" of cult or community members or, less likely, of individual painters.

right in the illustration) may have been inspired by the rock formation in the wall surface resembling a horse's head and neck. Like the clay bison at Le Tuc d'Audoubert, the Pech-Merle horses are in strict profile. Here, however, painted hands accompany them. These and the majority of painted hands at other sites are "negative"—that is, the painter placed one hand against the wall and then brushed or blew or spat pigment around it. Occasionally, the painter dipped a hand in the pigment and then pressed it against the wall, leav-

ing a "positive" imprint. These handprints must have had a purpose. Some scholars have considered them "signatures" of cult or community members or, less likely, of individual painters. Checks, dots, squares, and other abstract signs appear near the painted animals in other Paleolithic caves. Several observers think these signs are a primitive form of writing, but like the hands—and everything else in Paleolithic art—their meaning is unknown (see "Art in the Old Stone Age," page 20).

Prehistoric Art **19**

Art in the Old Stone Age

Since the discovery of the first cave paintings in the late 19th century, scholars have wondered why the hunters of the Old Stone Age decided to cover the walls of dark caverns with animal images (FIGS. 1-3 to 1-6). Various theories have been proposed.

Some scholars have argued that the animals were mere decoration, but this explanation cannot account for the narrow range of subjects or the inaccessibility of many of the representations. In fact, the remoteness and difficulty of access of many of the images, and indications that the caves were in use for centuries, are precisely why other scholars have suggested that the prehistoric hunters attributed magical properties to the images they painted and sculpted.

According to this argument, by confining animals to the surfaces of their cave walls, the Paleolithic hunters believed they were bringing the beasts under their control. Some have even hypothesized that rituals or dances were performed in front of the images and that these rites served to improve the hunters' luck. Still others have stated that the animal representations may have served as teaching tools to instruct new hunters about the character of the various species they would encounter or even to serve as targets for spears.

In contrast, some prehistorians have argued that the magical purpose of the paintings and reliefs was not to facilitate the *destruction* of animal species. Instead, they believe that the first painters and sculptors created animal images to ensure the *survival* of the herds on which Paleolithic peoples depended for their food supply and for their clothing. A central problem for both the hunting-magic and food-creation theories is that the animals that seem to have been diet staples of Old Stone Age peoples are not those most frequently portrayed.

Other researchers have sought to reconstruct an elaborate mythology based on the cave paintings and sculptures, suggesting that Paleolithic humans believed they had animal ancestors. Still others have equated certain species with men and others with women and postulated various meanings for the abstract signs that sometimes accompany the images. Almost all of these theories have been discredited over time, and most prehistorians admit that no one knows the intent of the representations. In fact, a single explanation for all Paleolithic animal images, even ones similar in subject, style, and composition, is unlikely to apply universally. The works remain an enigma—and always will, because before the invention of writing, no contemporaneous explanations could be recorded.

1-5 Hall of the Bulls (left wall), Lascaux, France, ca. 15,000–13,000 BCE. Largest bull 11′ 6″ long.

The purpose and meaning of Paleolithic cave paintings are unknown, but it is clear that painters were concerned solely with representing the animals, not with locating them in a specific place or on a common ground line.

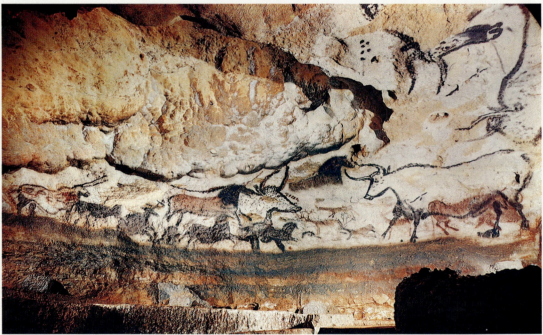

1 ft.

Lascaux Perhaps the best-known Paleolithic cave is that at Lascaux, near Montignac, France, which features a large circular gallery called the Hall of the Bulls (FIG. **1-5**). Not all of the painted animals are bulls, despite the modern nickname, and the several species depicted vary in size. The artists represented many of the animals, such as the great bull at the right in the illustration, using outline alone, but others are colored silhouettes. On the walls of the Lascaux cave, the two basic approaches to drawing and painting in the history of art appear side by side. These differences in style and technique alone suggest that different artists painted the animals at various times. The modern impression of a rapidly moving herd of beasts was probably not the original intent. In any case, the "herd" consists of several kinds of animals of disparate sizes moving in different directions. Although most share a common *ground line* (the horizontal base of the composition), some, like those in the upper right corner of FIG. **1-5**, seem to float above the viewer's head, like clouds in the sky. The painting has no setting, no background, no indication of place. The Paleolithic painter's sole concern was representing the animals, not locating them in a specific place.

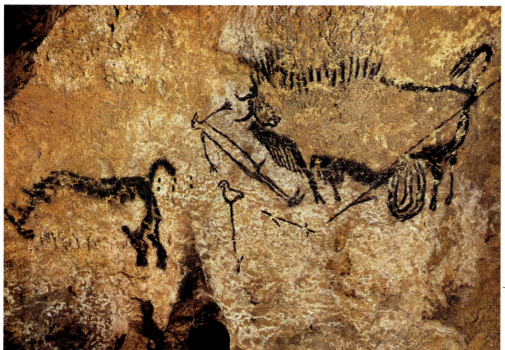

1-6 Rhinoceros, wounded man, and disemboweled bison, painting in the well, Lascaux, France, ca. 15,000–13,000 BCE. Bison, 3′ 8″ long.

If these paintings of two animals and a bird-faced (masked?) man, deep in a well shaft in the Lascaux cave, represent a hunting scene, they constitute the earliest example of narrative art ever discovered.

1 ft.

Another feature of the Lascaux paintings deserves attention. The bulls show a convention of representing horns called *twisted perspective*, because the viewer sees the heads in profile but the horns from the front. Thus, the painter's approach is not strictly or consistently optical (seen from a fixed viewpoint). Rather, the approach is descriptive of the fact that cattle have two horns. Two horns are part of the concept "bull." In strict optical-perspective profile, only one horn would be visible, but to paint the animal in that way would, as it were, amount to an incomplete definition of it.

Probably the most perplexing painting in any Paleolithic cave is the one deep in the well shaft (FIG. **1-6**) at Lascaux, where man (as opposed to woman) makes one of his earliest appearances in prehistoric art. At the left is a rhinoceros, rendered with all the skilled attention to animal detail customarily seen in cave art. Beneath its tail are two rows of three dots of uncertain significance. At the right is a bison, more schematically painted, probably by someone else. The second painter nonetheless successfully suggested the bristling rage of the animal, whose bowels are hanging from it in a heavy coil. Between the two beasts is a bird-faced (masked?) man with outstretched arms and hands with only four fingers. The man is depicted with far less care and detail than either animal, but the painter made the hunter's gender explicit by the prominent penis. The position of the man is ambiguous. Is he wounded or dead or merely tilted back and unharmed? Do the staff (?) with the bird on top and the spear belong to him? Is it he or the rhinoceros who has gravely wounded the bison—or neither? Which animal, if either, has knocked the man down, if indeed he is on the ground? Are these three images related at all? Researchers can be sure of nothing, but if the painter placed the figures beside each other to tell a story, then this is evidence for the creation of narrative compositions involving humans and animals at a much earlier date than anyone had imagined only a few generations ago. Yet it is important to remember that even if a story was intended, very few people would have been able to "read" it. The painting, in a deep shaft, is very difficult to reach and could have been viewed only in flickering lamplight. Like all Paleolithic art, the scene in the Lascaux well shaft remains enigmatic.

Neolithic Art

Around 9000 BCE, the ice that covered much of northern Europe during the Paleolithic period melted as the climate grew warmer. The reindeer migrated north, and the woolly mammoth and rhinoceros disappeared. The Paleolithic gave way to a transitional period, the *Mesolithic*, or Middle Stone Age, when Europe became climatically, geographically, and biologically much as it is today. Then, for several thousand years at different times in different parts of the globe, a great new age, the *Neolithic* (New Stone Age), dawned. Human beings began to settle in fixed abodes and to domesticate plants and animals. Their food supply assured, many groups changed from hunters to herders, to farmers, and finally to townspeople. Wandering hunters settled down to organized community living in villages surrounded by cultivated fields. The new sedentary societies of the Neolithic age originated systematic agriculture, weaving, metalworking, pottery, and counting and recording with tokens.

Çatal Höyük One of the most extensively excavated Neolithic sites is Çatal Höyük on the central Anatolian plateau, a settlement that flourished between 7000 and 5000 BCE in what is now Turkey. Çatal Höyük was one of the world's first experiments in urban living. The regularity of the town's plan suggests that the inhabitants built the

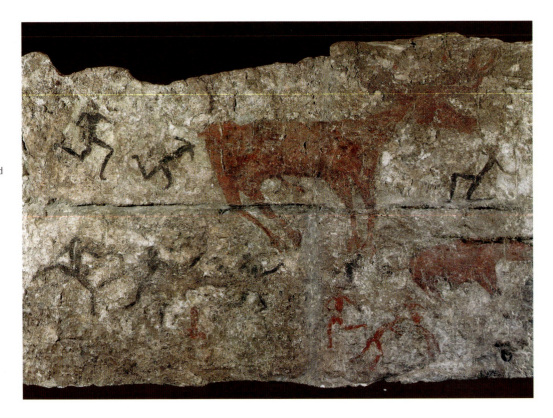

1-7 Deer hunt, detail of a wall painting from level III, Çatal Höyük, Turkey, ca. 5750 BCE. Museum of Anatolian Civilization, Ankara.

This Neolithic painter depicted human figures as a composite of frontal and profile views, the most descriptive picture of the shape of the human body. This format would become the rule for millennia.

settlement to some predetermined scheme. The houses, constructed of mud brick strengthened by sturdy timber frames, varied in size but repeated the same basic plan. The rooms have plastered and painted floors and walls with platforms along the walls that served as sites for sleeping, working, and eating. The living buried the dead beneath the floors.

The excavators have found many rooms decorated with mural paintings and plaster reliefs. These "shrines" had an uncertain function, but their number suggests that the rooms played an important role in the life of the Neolithic settlement. On the wall of one room, archaeologists discovered a painted representation of a deer hunt (FIG. 1-7). The mural is worlds apart from the cave paintings the hunters of the Paleolithic period produced. Perhaps what is most strikingly new about the Çatal Höyük painting and others like it is the regular appearance of the human figure—not only singly but also in large, coherent groups with a wide variety of poses, subjects, and settings. As noted earlier, humans were unusual subjects in Paleolithic painting, and pictorial narratives have almost never been found. Even the "hunting scene" (FIG. 1-6) in the well at Lascaux is doubtful as a narrative. In Neolithic paintings, human themes and concerns and action scenes with humans dominating animals are central.

In the Çatal Höyük hunt, the group of hunters—and no one doubts it is, indeed, an organized hunting party, not a series of individual figures—shows a tense exaggeration of movement and a rhythmic repetition of basic shapes customary for the period. The painter took care to distinguish important descriptive details—for example, bows, arrows, and garments—and the heads have clearly defined noses, mouths, chins, and hair. The Neolithic painter placed all the heads in profile for the same reason Paleolithic painters universally chose the profile view for representations of animals. Only

the side view of the human head shows all its shapes clearly. At Çatal Höyük, however, the torsos are frontal—again, the most informative viewpoint—whereas the painter chose the profile view for the legs and arms. This *composite view* of the human body is quite artificial because the human body cannot make an abrupt 90-degree shift at the hips. But it is very descriptive of what a human body is—as opposed to how it appears from a particular viewpoint. The composite view is another manifestation of the twisted perspective of Paleolithic paintings that combined a frontal view of an animal's two horns with a profile view of the head (FIG. 1-5). The technique of painting also changed dramatically since Paleolithic times. At Çatal Höyük, the artists used brushes to apply the pigments to a white background of dry plaster. The careful preparation of the wall surface is in striking contrast to the direct application of pigment to the rock surfaces of Old Stone Age caves.

Ain Ghazal At Ain Ghazal, near Amman, Jordan, archaeologists have uncovered another important Neolithic settlement. Occupied from the late eighth through the late sixth millennium BCE, Ain Ghazal has produced striking finds, including two caches containing three dozen plaster statuettes (FIG. 1-8) datable to the mid-seventh millennium BCE. The sculptures, which appear to have been ritually buried, are white plaster built up over a core of reeds and twine. The sculptors used black bitumen, a tarlike substance, to delineate the pupils of the eyes, which are inset cowrie shells. Painters added orange and black hair, clothing, and, in some instances, body paint or tattooing. Only rarely did the sculptors indicate the gender of the figures. Whatever their purpose, by their size (a few exceed three feet in height) and sophisticated technique, the Ain Ghazal statuettes differ

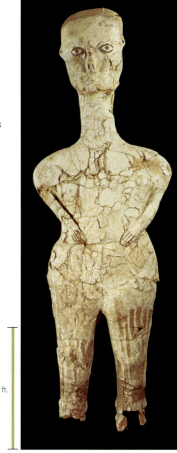

1-8 Human figure, from Ain Ghazal, Jordan, ca. 6750–6250 BCE. Plaster, painted and inlaid with cowrie shell and bitumen, 3′ 5$\frac{3}{8}$″ high. Louvre, Paris.

At Ain Ghazal, archaeologists have uncovered dozens of large white plaster Neolithic statuettes with details added in paint and shell. They mark the beginning of monumental sculpture in the history of art.

1 ft.

found. However, in succeeding millennia, perhaps as early as 4000 BCE, the local Neolithic populations in several areas developed a monumental architecture employing massive rough-cut stones. The very dimensions of the stones, some as tall as 17 feet and weighing as much as 50 tons, have prompted historians to call them *megaliths* (great stones) and to designate the culture that produced them *megalithic*.

Although megalithic monuments are plentiful throughout Europe, the arrangement of huge stones in a circle (called a *henge*), often surrounded by a ditch, is almost entirely limited to Britain. The most imposing of these today is Stonehenge (FIG. **1-9**) on Salisbury Plain in southern England. Stonehenge is a complex of rough-cut sarsen (a form of sandstone) stones and smaller "bluestones" (various volcanic rocks). Outermost is a ring, 97 feet in diameter, of 24-foot-tall *monolithic* sarsen stones supporting *lintels* (stone "beams" used to span an opening). This simple *post-and-lintel system* of construction is still in use today. Next is a ring of bluestones, which in turn encircles a horseshoe (open end facing east) of *trilithons* (three-stone constructions)—five lintel-topped pairs of the largest sarsens, each weighing 45 to 50 tons. Standing apart and to the east (outside the photograph) is the "heel-stone," which, for a person looking outward from the center of the complex, would have marked the point where the sun rose at the summer solstice. Construction of Stonehenge probably occurred in several phases in the centuries before and after 2000 BCE. It seems to have been a kind of astronomical observatory. During the Middle Ages, the Britons believed the mysterious structures were the work of the magician Merlin of the King Arthur legend, who spirited them from Ireland. Most archaeologists now consider Stonehenge a remarkably accurate solar calendar. This achievement is testimony to the rapidly developing intellectual powers of Neolithic humans as well as to their capacity for heroic physical effort.

fundamentally from Paleolithic figurines such as the four-inch-tall Willendorf woman (FIG. **1-2**). They mark the beginning of monumental sculpture in the ancient world.

Stonehenge In western Europe, where Paleolithic paintings and sculptures abound, no comparably developed towns of the time of Çatal Höyük or Ain Ghazal have been

1-9 Aerial view (looking northwest) of Stonehenge, Salisbury Plain, Wiltshire, England, ca. 2550–1600 BCE.

One of the earliest examples of monumental architecture in Neolithic Europe, the circle of 24-foot-tall trilithons at Stonehenge probably functioned as an astronomical observatory and solar calendar.

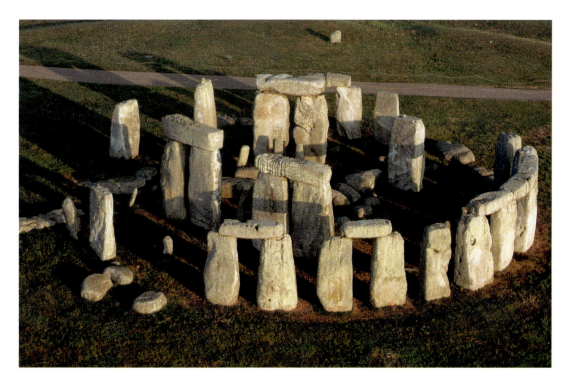

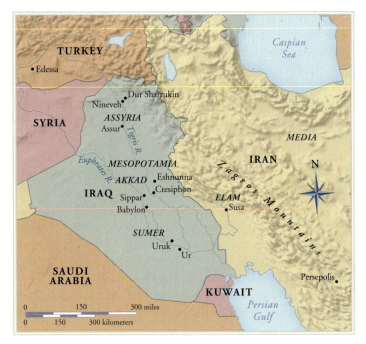

MAP 1-2 The ancient Near East.

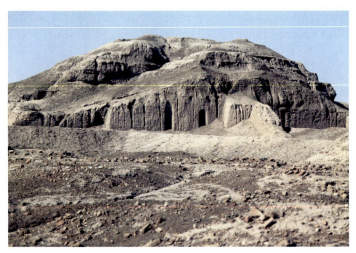

1-10 White Temple and ziggurat, Uruk (modern Warka), Iraq, ca. 3200–3000 BCE.

Using only mud bricks, the Sumerians erected temples on high platforms called ziggurats several centuries before the Egyptians built stone pyramids. The most famous was the biblical Tower of Babel.

ANCIENT NEAR EASTERN ART

The fundamental change in human society from the dangerous and uncertain life of the hunter and gatherer to the more predictable and stable life of the farmer and herder first occurred in Mesopotamia. Mesopotamia—a Greek word that means "the land between the [Tigris and Euphrates] rivers"—is at the core of the region often called the Fertile Crescent, a land mass that forms a huge arc from the mountainous border between Turkey and Syria through Iraq to Iran's Zagros Mountain range (MAP 1-2). There, humans first used the wheel and the plow, learned how to control floods and construct irrigation canals, and established the first great urban communities.

Sumerian Art

The people who transformed the vast, flat, sparsely inhabited lower valley between the Tigris and Euphrates into the giant oasis of the Fertile Crescent were the Sumerians. They also developed the earliest known writing system, using wedge-shaped (*cuneiform*) signs. Ancient Sumer was not a unified nation, however, but about a dozen independent *city-states*. Each was under the protection of a different Mesopotamian deity. The Sumerian rulers were the gods' representatives on earth and the stewards of their earthly treasure. The rulers and priests directed all communal activities, including canal construction, crop collection, and food distribution. The development of agriculture to the point that only a portion of the population had to produce food made it possible for some members of the community to specialize in other activities, including manufacturing, trade, and administration. Labor specialization is a hallmark of the first complex urban societies. In the Sumerian city-states of the fourth millennium BCE, activities that once had been individually initiated became institutionalized for the first time. The community, rather than the family, assumed responsibility for defense against enemies and the caprices of nature. Whether ruled by a single person or a council chosen from among the leading families, these

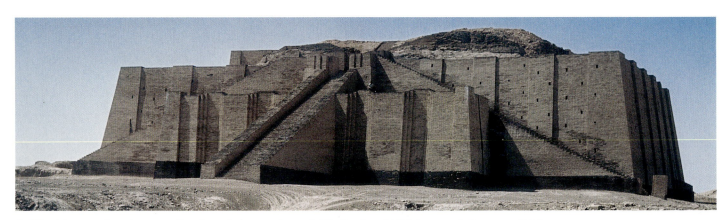

1-11 Ziggurat (northeastern facade with restored stairs), Ur (modern Tell Muqayyar), Iraq, ca. 2100 BCE.

The Ur ziggurat, the best preserved in Mesopotamia, is 50 feet high. It has three ramplike stairways of a hundred steps each that originally ended at a gateway to a brick temple, which does not survive.

communities gained permanent identities as discrete cities. The city-state was one of the great Sumerian inventions.

White Temple, Uruk

The Sumerian city plan reflected the central role of the local god in the daily life of the city-state's occupants. The god's temple formed the monumental nucleus of the city. It was not only the focus of local religious practice but also an administrative and economic center. It was indeed the domain of the god, whom the Sumerians regarded as a great and rich holder of lands and herds, as well as the protector of the city-state. The vast temple complex was a kind of city within a city, where priests and scribes carried on official business. Sumerian temple precincts had both religious and secular functions.

The outstanding preserved example of early Sumerian temple architecture is the 5,000-year-old White Temple (FIG. 1-10) at Uruk, the home of the legendary Gilgamesh. Sumerian builders did not have access to stone quarries and instead formed mud bricks for the superstructures of their temples and other buildings. The fragile nature of the building materials did not, however, prevent the Sumerians from erecting towering works, such as the Uruk temple, several centuries before the Egyptians built their stone pyramids (FIGS. 1-1 and 1-24). This says a great deal about the Sumerians' desire to provide monumental settings for the worship of their deities.

The Uruk temple (whose whitewashed walls lend it its modern nickname) stands on top of a high platform, or *ziggurat*, 40 feet above street level in the city center. A stairway leads to the temple at the top. Like those of other Sumerian temples, the corners of the White Temple point to the cardinal points of the compass. The building, probably dedicated to Anu, the sky god, is of modest proportions (61 by 16 feet) and poorly preserved. By design, it did not accommodate large throngs of worshipers but only a select few, the priests and perhaps the leading community members. The temple had several chambers. The central hall, or *cella*, was set aside for the divinity and housed a stepped altar. The Sumerians referred to their temples as "waiting rooms," a reflection of their belief that the deity would descend from the heavens to appear before the priests in the cella. Whether the Uruk temple had a roof is uncertain.

Ziggurat, Ur

Eroded ziggurats still dominate most of the ruined cities of Sumer. The best preserved is that at Ur (FIG. 1-11), built about a millennium later than the Uruk ziggurat and much grander. The base is a solid mass of mud brick 50 feet high. The builders used baked bricks laid in bitumen for the facing of the entire monument. Three ramplike stairways of a hundred steps each converge on a tower-flanked gateway. From there another flight of steps probably led to the temple proper, which does not survive. The loftiness of the great ziggurats of Mesopotamia made a profound impression on the peoples of the ancient Near East. The tallest ziggurat of all—at Babylon—was about 270 feet high. Known to the Hebrews as the Tower of Babel, it became the centerpiece of a biblical tale about insolent pride. Humankind's desire to build a tower to Heaven angered God. Therefore, the Lord caused the workers to speak different languages, preventing them from communicating with one another and bringing construction of the ziggurat to a halt.

Warka Vase

The Sumerians, pioneers in so many areas, also may have been the first to use pictures to tell complex stories. Sumerian narrative art goes far beyond Stone Age artists' tentative efforts at storytelling. The so-called *Warka Vase* (FIG. 1-12) from Uruk (modern Warka) is the first great work of narrative relief sculpture known. Found within the temple complex dedicated to Inanna, the goddess of love and war, it depicts a religious festival in her honor. The sculptor divided the vase's reliefs into three bands (called *registers* or *friezes*). This new kind of composition marks a significant break with the haphazard figure placement in earlier art. The register format for telling a story was to have a very long future. In fact, artists still employ registers today in modified form in comic books.

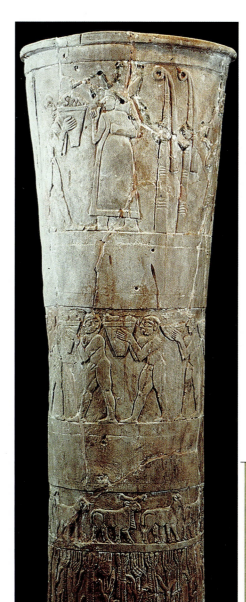

1-12
Presentation of offerings to Inanna (*Warka Vase*), from Uruk (modern Warka), Iraq, ca. 3200–3000 BCE. Alabaster, $3'\frac{1}{4}''$ high. Iraq Museum, Baghdad.

In this oldest known example of Sumerian narrative art, the sculptor divided the tall stone vase's reliefs into registers, a significant break with the haphazard figure placement found in earlier art.

1 ft.

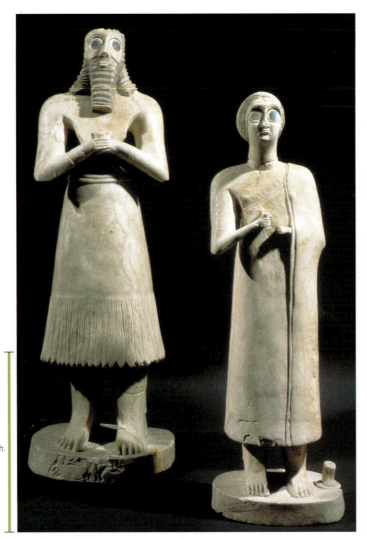

1-13 Statuettes of two worshipers, from the Square Temple at Eshnunna (modern Tell Asmar), Iraq, ca. 2700 BCE. Gypsum inlaid with shell and black limestone, male figure 2′ 6″ high. Iraq Museum, Baghdad.

The oversized eyes probably symbolized the perpetual wakefulness of these substitute worshipers offering prayers to the deity. The figures hold beakers containing libations to pour in honor of the gods.

At the far right is an only partially preserved clothed man usually, if ambiguously, referred to as a "priest-king," that is, both a religious and secular leader. The greater height of the priest-king and Inanna compared with the offering bearers indicates their greater importance, a convention called *hierarchy of scale*. Some scholars interpret the scene as a symbolic marriage between the priest-king and the goddess, ensuring her continued goodwill—and reaffirming the leader's exalted position in society.

Eshnunna Statuettes Further insight into Sumerian religion comes from a cache of soft gypsum statuettes inlaid with shell and black limestone found in a temple at Eshnunna (modern Tell Asmar). The two largest figures (FIG. 1-13), like all the others, represent mortals rather than deities. They hold the small beakers the Sumerians used in religious rites. The men wear belts and fringed skirts. Most have beards and shoulder-length hair. The women wear long robes, with the right shoulder bare. Similar figurines from other sites bear inscriptions with the name of the donor and the god or even specific prayers to the deity on the owner's behalf. With their heads tilted upward, they wait in the Sumerian "waiting room" for the divinity to appear. Most striking is the disproportionate relationship between the inlaid oversized eyes and the tiny hands. Scholars have explained the exaggeration of the eye size in various ways. Because the purpose of these votive figures was to offer constant prayers to the gods on their donors' behalf, the open-eyed stares most likely symbolize the eternal wakefulness necessary to fulfill their duty.

Standard of Ur The spoils of war, as well as success in farming and trade, brought considerable wealth to some of the city-states of ancient Sumer. Nowhere is this clearer than in the so-called Royal Cemetery at Ur, the city that was home to the biblical Abraham. Researchers still debate whether those buried in Ur's cemetery were true kings and queens or simply aristocrats and priests, but their tombs were regal in character. They contained gold helmets and daggers with handles of lapis lazuli (a rich azure-blue stone imported from Afghanistan), golden beakers and bowls, jewelry of gold and lapis, musical instruments, chariots, and other luxurious items.

Although not fashioned from the most costly materials, the most significant artwork found in the "royal" graves is the so-called *Standard of Ur* (FIG. 1-14), a rectangular box of uncertain function. It has sloping sides inlaid with shell, lapis lazuli, and red limestone. The excavator who discovered it thought the Sumerians mounted it on a pole as a kind of military standard, hence its nickname. Art historians usually refer to the two long sides of the box as the "war side" and "peace side," but the two sides may represent the first and second parts of a single narrative. The artist divided each into three horizontal bands. The narrative reads from left to right and bottom to top.

On the war side, four ass-drawn four-wheeled war chariots mow down enemies, whose bodies appear on the

The lowest band on the *Warka Vase* shows ewes and rams—in strict profile, as in the Old Stone Age—above crops and a wavy line representing water. The animals and plants underscore that Inanna has blessed Uruk's inhabitants with good crops and increased herds. Above, naked men carry baskets and jars overflowing with earth's abundance. They will present their bounty to the goddess as a *votive offering* (gift of gratitude to a deity usually made in fulfillment of a vow) and will deposit it in her temple. The spacing of each figure involves no overlapping. The Uruk men, like the Çatal Höyük deer hunters (FIG. 1-7), are a composite of frontal and profile views, with large staring frontal eyes in profile heads. (If the eyes were in profile, they would not "read" as eyes at all, because they would not have their distinctive flat oval shape.)

In the uppermost (and tallest) band is a female figure with a tall horned headdress, probably Inanna but perhaps her priestess. A nude male figure brings a large vessel brimming with offerings to be deposited in the goddess's shrine.

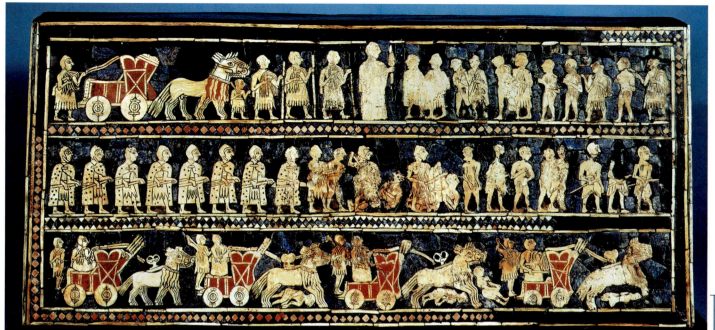

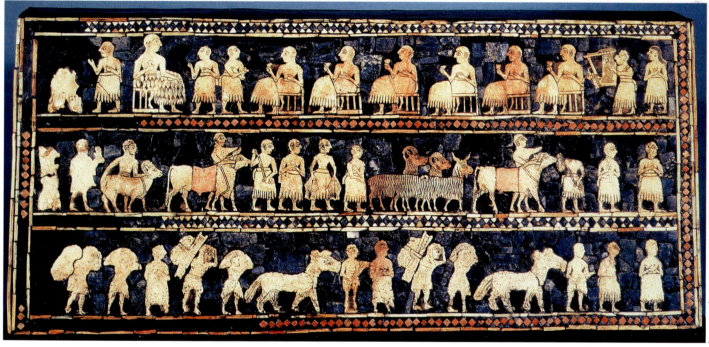

1-14 War side (*top*) and peace side (*bottom*) of the *Standard of Ur,* from tomb 779, Royal Cemetery, Ur (modern Tell Muqayyar), Iraq, ca. 2600 BCE. Wood inlaid with shell, lapis lazuli, and red limestone, 8″ × 1′ 7″. British Museum, London.

Using a mosaic-like technique, this Sumerian artist told the story of battlefield victory and a celebratory feast in three registers. The size of the figures on both sides of the box varies with their relative importance.

ground in front of and beneath the animals. Above, foot soldiers gather up and lead away captured foes. In the uppermost register, soldiers present bound captives (who have been stripped naked to degrade them) to a kinglike figure, who has stepped out of his chariot. His central place in the composition and his greater stature (his head breaks through the border at the top) set him apart from all the other figures.

In the lowest band on the peace side, men carry provisions, possibly war booty, on their backs. Above, attendants bring animals, perhaps also spoils of war, and fish for the great banquet depicted in the uppermost register. There, seated dignitaries and a larger-than-life "king" (third from the left) feast, while a lyre player and singer (at the far right) entertain the group. Scholars have interpreted the scene both as a victory celebration and as a banquet in connection with cult ritual. The two are not necessarily incompatible. The absence of an inscription prevents connecting the scenes with a specific event or person, but the *Standard of Ur* undoubtedly is an early example of historical narrative.

Akkadian Art

In 2334 BCE, the loosely linked group of cities known as Sumer came under the domination of a great ruler, Sargon of Akkad (r. 2332–2279 BCE). Archaeologists have yet to locate the specific site of the city of Akkad, but it was in the vicinity of Babylon. Under Sargon (whose name means "true king") and his followers, the Akkadians introduced a new concept of royal power based on unswerving loyalty to the king rather than to the city-state. During the rule of Sargon's grandson, Naram-Sin (r. 2254– 2218 BCE), governors of cities were mere servants of the king, who called himself "King of the Four Quarters"—in effect, ruler of the earth, akin to a god.

Akkadian Portraiture A magnificent copper head (FIG. **1-15**) representing an Akkadian king embodies this new concept of absolute monarchy. The head is all that survives of a statue knocked over in antiquity, perhaps during the sack of Nineveh in 612 BCE. To make a political statement, the enemy not only toppled the Akkadian royal portrait but gouged out the eyes (once inlaid with precious or semiprecious stones), broke off the lower part of the beard, and slashed the ears. Nonetheless, the king's majestic serenity,

dignity, and authority are evident. So, too, is the masterful way the sculptor balanced *naturalism* and abstract patterning. The artist carefully observed and recorded the distinctive profile of the ruler's nose and his long, curly beard. The sculptor also brilliantly communicated the differing textures of flesh and hair—even the contrasting textures of the mustache, beard, and the braided hair on the top of the head. The coiffure's triangles, lozenges, and overlapping disks of hair and the great arching eyebrows that give such character to the portrait reveal that the artist was also sensitive to formal pattern. No less remarkable is the fact that this is a life-size, hollow-cast metal sculpture (see "Hollow-Casting Life-Size Bronze Statues," Chapter 2, page 66), one of the earliest known. The head demonstrates its maker's sophisticated skill in casting and polishing copper and in engraving the details.

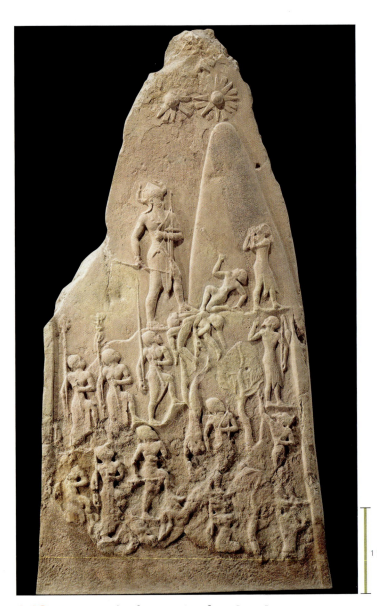

1-15 Head of an Akkadian ruler, from Nineveh (modern Kuyunjik), Iraq, ca. 2250–2200 BCE. Copper, 1' 2⅛" high. Iraq Museum, Baghdad.

The sculptor of this first known life-size hollow-cast head captured the distinctive portrait features of the ruler while also displaying a keen sense of abstract pattern. The head was later vandalized.

1-16 Victory stele of Naram-Sin, from Susa, Iran, ca. 2254–2218 BCE. Pink sandstone, 6' 7" high. Louvre, Paris.

To commemorate his conquest of the Lullubi, Naram-Sin set up this stele showing him leading his army. The sculptor staggered the figures on the mountain, boldly rejecting the traditional register format.

Naram-Sin Stele The godlike sovereignty the kings of Akkad claimed is also evident in the victory stele (FIG. **1-16**) Naram-Sin set up at Sippar. A *stele* is a carved stone slab erected to commemorate a historical event or, in some other cultures, to mark a grave (FIG. **2-45**). Naram-Sin's stele commemorates his defeat of the Lullubi, a people of the Iranian mountains to the east. On the stele, the grandson of Sargon leads his victorious army up the slopes of a wooded mountain. His routed enemies fall, flee, die, or beg for mercy. The king stands alone, far taller than his men, treading on the bodies of two of the fallen Lullubi. He wears a horned helmet—the first time a king appears with the attribute of a god in Mesopotamian art. At least three favorable stars (the stele is damaged at the top and broken at the bottom) shine on his triumph.

By storming the mountain, Naram-Sin seems also to be scaling the ladder to the heavens, the same conceit that lies behind the great ziggurat towers of the ancient Near East. His troops march up the slope behind him in orderly files, suggesting the discipline and organization of the king's forces. The enemy, in contrast, is in disarray, which the artist communicated by depicting the Lullubi in a great variety of postures. (One falls headlong down the mountainside.) The sculptor adhered to older conventions in many details, especially by portraying the king and his soldiers in composite views and by placing a frontal two-horned helmet on Naram-Sin's profile head. But in other respects this work shows daring innovation. Here, the sculptor created one of the first landscapes in the history of art and set the figures on successive tiers within that landscape. This was a bold rejection of the standard compositional formula of telling a story in a series of horizontal registers.

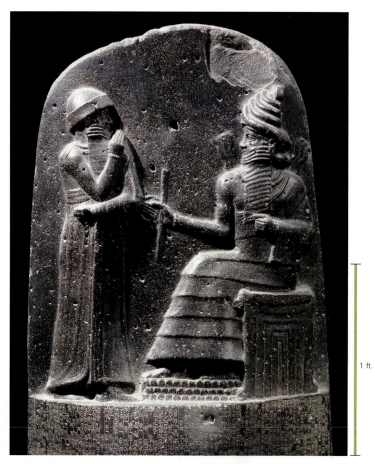

1-17 Hammurabi and Shamash, detail of the stele of Hammurabi, from Susa, Iran, ca. 1780 BCE. Basalt, stele 7′ 4″ high. Louvre, Paris.

The stele that records Hammurabi's remarkably early comprehensive law code also is one of the first examples of an artist employing foreshortening—the representation of a figure or object at an angle.

Babylonian Art

Around 2150 BCE, a mountain people, the Gutians, brought Akkadian power to an end. The cities of Sumer, however, soon united in response to the alien presence, drove the Gutians out of Mesopotamia, and established a Neo-Sumerian state ruled by the kings of Ur. This age, which historians call the Third Dynasty of Ur, saw the construction of the Ur ziggurat (FIG. **1-11**). Sumer's resurgence was short-lived, however. The last king of the Third Dynasty fell at the hands of the Elamites, who ruled the territory east of the Tigris River. The following two centuries witnessed the reemergence of the traditional Mesopotamian political pattern of several independent city-states existing side by side, until one of those cities, Babylon, succeeded in establishing a centralized government that ruled southern Mesopotamia in the 18th and 17th centuries BCE.

Hammurabi Babylon's most powerful king was Hammurabi (r. 1792–1750 BCE). Famous in his own time for his conquests, he is best known today for his law code, which prescribed penalties for everything from adultery and murder to the cutting down of a neighbor's trees. The code is inscribed in 3,500 lines of cuneiform characters on a tall black-basalt stele. At the top (FIG. **1-17**) is a relief depicting Hammurabi in the presence of the flame-shouldered sun god, Shamash. The king raises his hand in respect. The god extends to Hammurabi the rod and ring that symbolize authority. The symbols derive from builders' tools—measuring rods and coiled rope—and connote Hammurabi's capacity to build the social order and to measure people's lives, that is, to render judgments. The sculptor depicted Shamash in the familiar convention of combined front and side views but with two important exceptions. The god's great headdress with its four pairs of horns is in true profile so that only four, not all eight, of the horns are visible. And the artist seems to have tentatively explored the notion of *foreshortening*—a device for suggesting depth by representing a figure or object at an angle, rather than frontally or in profile. Shamash's beard is a series of diagonal rather than horizontal lines, suggesting its recession from the picture plane. Innovations like this and the bold abandonment of the register format in favor of a tiered landscape on the Naram-Sin stele were exceptional in early eras of the history of art. These occasional departures from the normal representational modes testify to the creativity of ancient Near Eastern artists.

Assyrian Art

The Babylonian Empire toppled in the face of an onslaught by the Hittites, an Anatolian people who conquered and sacked Babylon around 1595 BCE. They then retired to their home-land, leaving Babylon in the hands of the Kassites. By around 900 BCE, however, the Assyrians had overtaken Mesopotamia. The new conquerors took their name from Assur, the city of the god Ashur on the Tigris River. At the height of their power, the Assyrians ruled an empire that extended from the Tigris to the Nile and from the Persian Gulf to Asia Minor.

Dur Sharrukin The royal citadel of Sargon II (r. 721–705 BCE) at Dur Sharrukin is the most completely excavated of the many Assyrian palaces. Its ambitious layout reveals the confidence of the Assyrian kings in their all-conquering might, but its strong defensive walls also reflect a society ever fearful of attack during a period of almost constant warfare. The city measured about a square mile in area and

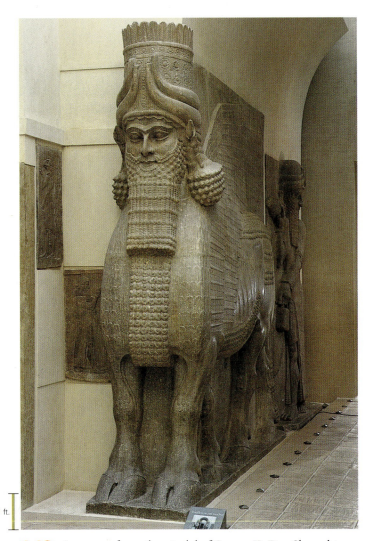

1 ft.

1-18 Lamassu, from the citadel of Sargon II, Dur Sharrukin (modern Khorsabad), Iraq, ca. 720–705 BCE. Limestone, 13′ 10″ high. Louvre, Paris.

Ancient sculptors insisted on showing complete views of animals. This gigantic four-legged Assyrian palace guardian has five legs—two when seen from the front and four in profile view.

included a great ziggurat and six sanctuaries for six different gods. The palace, elevated on a mound 50 feet high, covered some 25 acres and had more than 200 courtyards and timber-roofed rooms. Sargon II regarded his city and palace as an expression of his grandeur. In one inscription, he boasted, "I built a city with [the labors of] the peoples subdued by my hand, whom [the gods] Ashur, Nabu, and Marduk had caused to lay themselves at my feet and bear my yoke." And in another text, he proclaimed, "Sargon, King of the World, has built a city. Dur Sharrukin he has named it. A peerless palace he has built within it."

Guarding the gate to Sargon's palace were colossal lime-stone monsters (FIG. **1-18**), which the Assyrians probably called *lamassu.* These winged, man-headed bulls served to ward off the king's enemies. The task of moving and install-ing these immense stone sculptures was so daunting that sev-eral reliefs in the palace of Sargon's successor celebrate the feat, showing scores of men dragging lamassu figures with the aid of ropes and sledges. The Assyrian lamassu sculp-tures are partly in the round, but the sculptor nonetheless conceived them as high reliefs on adjacent sides of a corner. They combine the front view of the animal at rest with the side view of it in motion. Seeking to present a complete pic-ture of the lamassu from both the front and the side, the sculptor gave the monster five legs (two seen from the front, four seen from the side). The three-quarter view the modern photographer chose would not have been favored in antiq-uity. This sculpture, then, is yet another case of early artists' providing a *conceptual representation* of an animal or per-son and all its important parts, as opposed to a view of the lamassu as it would actually stand in space.

Nineveh For their palace walls the Assyrian kings com-missioned extensive series of narrative reliefs exalting royal power and piety. The sculptures record not only battlefield victories but also the slaying of wild animals. (The Assyrians, like many other societies before and after, regarded prowess in hunting as a manly virtue on a par with success in war-fare.) One of the most extensive cycles of Assyrian narrative reliefs comes from the palace of Ashurbanipal (r. 668–627 BCE) at Nineveh. Throughout the palace, painted gypsum re-liefs sheathed the lower parts of the mud-brick walls below brightly colored plaster. Rich textiles on the floors contrib-uted to the luxurious ambience. The reliefs celebrated the king and bore inscriptions describing his accomplishments.

One of the palace's hunting scenes (FIG. **1-19**) depicts lions charging the king after being released from cages in a large enclosed arena. (The hunt did not take place in the wild but in a controlled environment, ensuring the king's safety and success.) The king is in his chariot with his attendants. He thrusts a spear into a savage lion, which leaps at the king even though it already has two arrows in its body. All around the royal chariot is a pathetic trail of dead and dying animals, pierced by far more arrows than needed to kill them. Blood streams from some of the lions, but they refuse to die. The artist brilliantly depicted the straining muscles, the swelling veins, the muzzles' wrinkled skin, and the flattened ears of

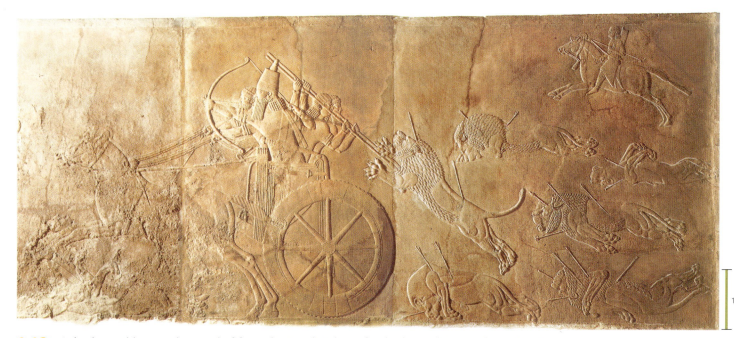

1-19 Ashurbanipal hunting lions, relief from the North Palace of Ashurbanipal, Nineveh (modern Kuyunjik), Iraq, ca. 645–640 BCE. Gypsum, 5′ 4″ high. British Museum, London.

Extensive series of narrative stone reliefs exalting royal power adorned the walls of Assyrian palaces. The hunting and killing of lions were manly virtues on a par with victory in warfare.

the powerful and defiant beasts. Modern sympathies make this scene of carnage a kind of heroic tragedy, with the lions as protagonists. It is unlikely, however, that the king's artists had any intention other than to glorify their ruler by showing the king of men pitting himself against and repeatedly conquering the king of beasts. Portraying Ashurbanipal's beastly foes as possessing courage and nobility as well as strength served to make the king's accomplishments that much grander.

Neo-Babylonian Art

The Assyrian Empire was never very secure, and most of its kings had to fight revolts in large sections of the Near East. During the last years of Ashurbanipal's reign, the empire began to disintegrate. Under his successors, it collapsed from the simultaneous onslaught of the Medes from the east and the resurgent Babylonians from the south. For almost a century beginning in 612 BCE, Neo-Babylonian kings held sway over the former Assyrian Empire.

Ishtar Gate The most renowned Neo-Babylonian king was Nebuchadnezzar II (r. 604–562 BCE), who restored Babylon to its rank as one of the great cities of antiquity. The city's famous hanging gardens were one of the Seven Wonders of the ancient world, and, as noted previously, its enormous ziggurat dedicated to Marduk, the chief god of the Babylonians, was immortalized in the Bible as the Tower of Babel. Nebuchadnezzar's Babylon was a mud-brick city, but dazzling blue glazed bricks faced the most important monuments. Some of the buildings, such as the Ishtar Gate (FIG. **1-20**), with its imposing *arcuated* (arch-shaped) opening flanked by towers, featured glazed bricks with molded reliefs of animals, real and imaginary. The Babylonian artists

molded and glazed each brick separately, then set the bricks in proper sequence on the wall. On Ishtar's Gate, profile figures of Marduk's dragon and Adad's bull alternate. (Ishtar was the Babylonian equivalent of Inanna; Adad was the Babylonian god of storms.) Lining the processional way leading up to the gate were reliefs of Ishtar's sacred lion, glazed in yellow, brown, and red against a blue ground.

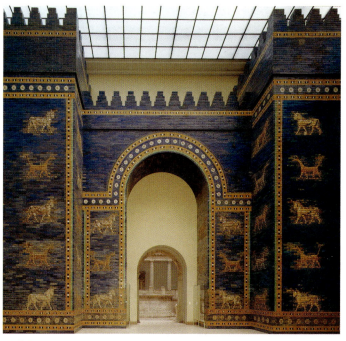

1-20 Ishtar Gate (restored), Babylon, Iraq, ca. 575 BCE. Vorderasiatisches Museum, Staatliche Museen zu Berlin, Berlin.

Babylon under King Nebuchadnezzar II was one of the greatest cities of the ancient world. Glazed bricks depicting Marduk's dragon and Adad's bull decorate the monumental arcuated Ishtar Gate.

Achaemenid Persian Art

Although Nebuchadnezzar, "King of Kings" of the biblical Daniel, had boasted that he "caused a mighty wall to circumscribe Babylon . . . so that the enemy who would do evil would not threaten," Cyrus of Persia (r. 559–529 BCE) captured the city in the sixth century BCE. Cyrus was the founder of the Achaemenid dynasty and traced his ancestry back to a mythical King Achaemenes. Babylon was but one of the Persians' conquests. Egypt fell to them in 525 BCE, and by 480 BCE the Persian Empire was the largest the world had yet known, extending from the Indus River in South Asia to the Danube River in northeastern Europe. Only the successful Greek resistance in the fifth century BCE prevented Persia from embracing southeastern Europe as well (see Chapter 2). The Achaemenid line ended with the death of Darius III in 330 BCE, after his defeat at the hands of Alexander the Great (FIG. 2-50).

Persepolis The most important source of knowledge about Persian art and architecture is the ceremonial and administrative complex on the citadel at Persepolis (FIG. 1-21), which the successors of Cyrus, Darius I (r. 522–486 BCE) and Xerxes (r. 486–465 BCE), built between 521 and 465 BCE. Situated on a high plateau, the heavily fortified complex of royal buildings stood on a wide platform overlooking the plain. Alexander the Great razed the site in a gesture symbolizing the destruction of Persian imperial power. Even in ruins, the Persepolis citadel is impressive. The approach to it led through a monumental gateway called the Gate of All Lands, a reference to the harmony among the peoples of the vast Persian Empire. Assyrian-inspired colossal man-headed winged bulls flanked the great entrance. Broad ceremonial stairways provided access to the platform and the huge royal audience hall, or *apadana*, 60 feet high and 217 feet square, containing 36 colossal *columns*. An audience of thousands could have stood within the hall.

The reliefs decorating the walls of the terrace and staircases leading to the apadana represent processions of royal guards, Persian nobles and dignitaries, and representatives from 23 subject nations bringing the king tribute. Every one of the emissaries wears his national costume and carries a typical regional gift for the conqueror. Traces of color prove that the reliefs were painted, and the original effect must have been very striking. Although the Persepolis sculptures may have been inspired by those in Assyrian palaces, they are different in style. The forms are more rounded, and they project more from the background. Some of the details, notably the treatment of drapery folds, echo forms characteristic of Archaic Greek sculpture (see Chapter 2), and Greek influence seems to be one of the many ingredients of Achaemenid style. Persian art testifies to the active exchange of ideas and artists among Mediterranean and Near Eastern civilizations at this date. A building inscription at Susa, for example, names Ionian Greeks, Medes (who occupied the land north of Persia), Egyptians, and Babylonians among those who built and decorated the palace.

The Sasanians Alexander the Great's conquest of Persia in 330 BCE marked the beginning of a long period of first Greek and then Roman rule of large parts of the ancient Near East. In the third century CE, however, a new power rose up in Persia that challenged the Romans and sought to force them out of Asia. The new rulers called themselves Sasanians. They traced their lineage to a legendary figure named Sasan, said to be a direct descendant of the Achaemenid kings. Their New Persian Empire was founded in 224 CE, when the first Sasanian king, Artaxerxes I (r. 211–241), defeated the Parthians (another of Rome's eastern enemies). The son and successor of Artaxerxes, Shapur I (r. 241–272), succeeded in further extending Sasanian territory. So powerful was the Sasanian army that in 260 CE Shapur I even succeeded in capturing the Roman emperor Valerian near Edessa (in modern Turkey). The New Persian Empire endured more than 400 years, until the Arabs drove the Sasanians out of Mesopotamia in 636 CE, just four years after the death of Muhammad. Thereafter, the greatest artists and architects of Mesopotamia worked in the service of Islam (see Chapter 5).

1-21 Aerial view (looking west) of Persepolis (apadana in the background), Iran, ca. 521–465 BCE.

The imperial Persian capital at Persepolis contained a grandiose royal audience hall with 36 colossal columns. The terraces leading up to it feature reliefs of subject nations bringing tribute to the king.

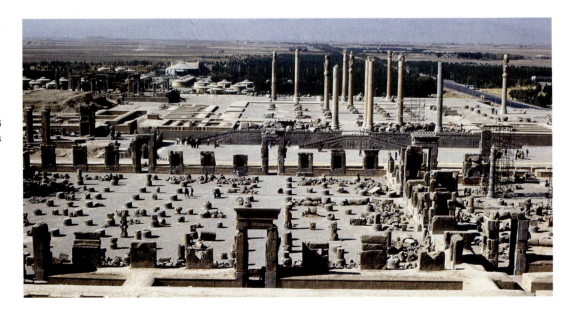

EGYPTIAN ART

Nearly 2,500 years ago, the Greek historian Herodotus wrote, "Concerning Egypt itself I shall extend my remarks to a great length, because there is no country that possesses so many wonders, nor any that has such a number of works that defy description."[1] Even today, many would agree with this assessment. The ancient Egyptians left to the world countless monuments of architecture, sculpture, and painting dating across three millennia. The solemn and ageless art of the Egyptians expresses the unchanging order that, for them, was divinely established.

The backbone of Egypt was, and still is, the Nile River, whose annual floods supported all life in that ancient land (MAP 1-3). Even more than the Tigris and the Euphrates rivers of Mesopotamia, the Nile defined the cultures that developed along its banks. Originating deep in Africa, the world's longest river flows through regions that may not have a single drop of rainfall in a decade. Yet crops thrive from the rich soil that the Nile brings thousands of miles from the African hills. In the time of the *pharaohs*, the ancient Egyptian kings, the land bordering the Nile consisted of marshes dotted with island ridges. Amphibious animals swarmed in the marshes and were hunted through tall forests of *papyrus* and rushes (FIG. 1-28). Egypt's fertility was famous. When Egypt became a province of the Roman Empire after the death of Queen Cleopatra (r. 51–30 BCE), it served as the granary of the Mediterranean world.

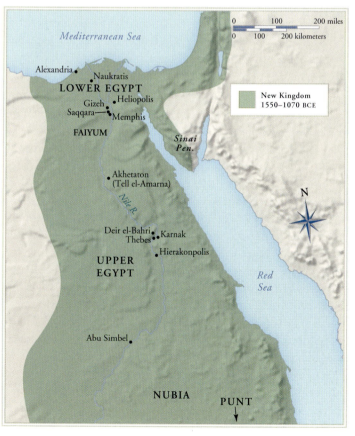

MAP 1-3 Egypt during the New Kingdom.

Predynastic and Early Dynastic Periods

The Predynastic, or prehistoric, beginnings of Egyptian civilization are chronologically vague. But tantalizing remains of tombs, paintings, pottery, and other artifacts from around 3500 BCE attest to the existence of a sophisticated culture on the banks of the Nile. In Predynastic times, Egypt was divided geographically and politically into Upper Egypt (the southern, upstream part of the Nile Valley) and Lower (northern) Egypt. The ancient Egyptians began the history of their kingdom with the unification of the two lands. Until recently, historians thought this event occurred during the rule of the First Dynasty pharaoh Menes.

Palette of King Narmer Many scholars identify Menes with King Narmer, whose image and name appear on both sides of a ceremonial *palette* (stone slab with a circular depression) found at Hierakonpolis. The palette (FIG. 1-22) is an elaborate, formalized version of a utilitarian object commonly used in the Predynastic period to prepare eye makeup. (Egyptians used makeup to protect their eyes against irritation and the glare of the sun.) Narmer's palette is the earliest existing labeled work of historical art. Although historians no longer believe it commemorates the founding of the first of Egypt's 31 dynasties around 2920 BCE (the last ended in 332 BCE),[2] it does record the unification of Upper and Lower Egypt at the very end of the Predynastic period. Scholars now think this unification occurred over several centuries, but the palette reflects the ancient Egyptian belief that the creation of the "Kingdom of the Two Lands" was a single great event.

King Narmer's palette is important not only as a document marking the transition from the prehistorical to the historical period in ancient Egypt but also as a kind of early blueprint of the formula for figure representation that characterized most Egyptian art for 3,000 years. At the top of each side of the palette are two heads of the goddess Hathor, the divine mother of the pharaoh, who nourishes him with her milk and here takes the form of a cow with a woman's face. Between the Hathor heads is a hieroglyph giving Narmer's name within a frame representing the royal palace. Below, the story of the unification of Egypt unfolds in registers.

On the back of the palette, the king, wearing the high, white, bowling-pin-shaped crown of Upper Egypt and accompanied by an official who carries his sandals, slays an enemy. Above and to the right, the falcon with human arms is Horus, the Egyptian god who was the special protector of the pharaohs. The falcon-god takes captive a man-headed hieroglyph with a papyrus plant growing from it that stands for the land of Lower Egypt. Below the king are two fallen enemies. On the front of the palette, the elongated necks of two felines form the circular depression that would have held eye makeup in an ordinary palette not made for display. The intertwined necks of the animals may be another pictorial reference to Egypt's unification. In the uppermost register, Narmer, wearing the red crown of Lower Egypt, reviews

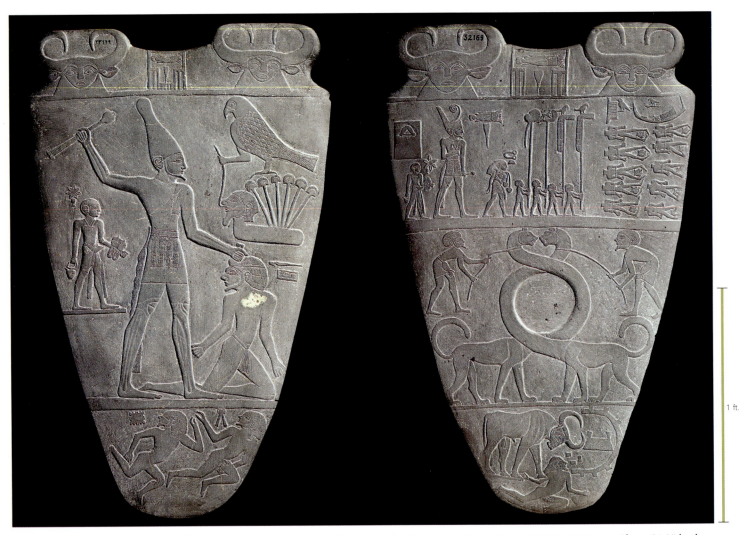

1-22 Palette of King Narmer (*left*, back; *right*, front), from Hierakonpolis, Egypt, Predynastic, ca. 3000–2920 BCE. Slate, 2′ 1″ high. Egyptian Museum, Cairo.

These oldest preserved labeled historical reliefs commemorate the unification of Upper and Lower Egypt. Narmer, the largest figure, effort-lessly defeats a foe on one side, and on the other surveys the beheaded enemy.

the beheaded bodies of the enemy. The artist depicted each body with its severed head neatly placed between its legs. By virtue of his superior rank, the king, on both sides of the palette, performs his ritual task alone and towers over his own men and the enemy. In the lowest band, a great bull knocks down a rebellious city whose fortress walls are seen from above. The bull symbolizes the king's superhuman strength. Specific historical narrative was not the artist's goal in this work. What was important was the characterization of the king as supreme, isolated from and larger than all ordinary men and solely responsible for the triumph over the enemy. Here, at the very beginning of Egyptian history, is evidence of the Egyptian convention of thought, of art, and of state policy that established the pharaoh as a divine ruler.

Tombs and the Afterlife Narmer's palette is exceptional among surviving Egyptian artworks because it is commemorative rather than funerary in nature. In fact, Egyptian tombs provide the principal, if not the exclusive, evidence for the historical reconstruction of Egyptian civilization. The overriding concern in this life was to ensure safety and

happiness in the next life. The majority of monuments the Egyptians left behind reflect this preoccupation (see "Mummification and the Afterlife," page 36).

The standard tomb type in early Egypt was the *mastaba* (FIG. 1-23). The mastaba (Arabic, "bench") was a rectangular brick or stone structure with sloping sides erected over an underground burial chamber. A shaft connected this chamber with the outside, providing the ka with access to the tomb. The form probably developed from earth or stone mounds that marked even earlier tombs. Although mastabas originally housed single burials, as in the illustrated example, during the latter part of the Old Kingdom they accommodated multiple family burials and became increasingly complex. Surrounding the central underground chamber were storage rooms and compartments whose number and size increased with time until the area covered far surpassed that of the tomb chamber. Built into the superstructure, or sometimes attached to the outside, was a chapel housing a statue of the deceased in a small concealed chamber called the *serdab*. Adorning the chapel's interior walls and the ancillary rooms were colored relief carvings and paintings of

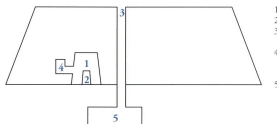

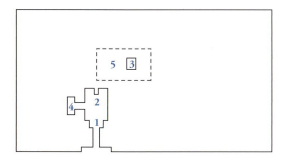

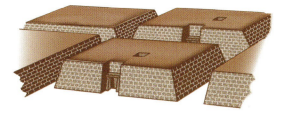

1. Chapel
2. False door
3. Shaft into burial chamber
4. Serdab (chamber for statue of deceased)
5. Burial chamber

1-23 Section (*top*), plan (*middle*), and restored view (*bottom*) of typical Egyptian mastaba tombs.

The standard early form of Egyptian tomb had an underground burial chamber and rooms to house a portrait statue and offerings to the deceased. Scenes of daily life often decorated the interior walls.

scenes from daily life intended magically to provide the deceased with food and entertainment.

Imhotep and Djoser One of the most renowned figures in Egyptian history was IMHOTEP, the royal builder for King Djoser (r. 2630–2611 BCE) of the Third Dynasty. Imhotep was a man of legendary talent who served also as the pharaoh's chancellor and high priest of the sun god Re. After his death, the Egyptians revered Imhotep as a god and in time may have inflated the list of his achievements. Nonetheless, his is the first known name of an artist in recorded history. Imhotep designed the Stepped Pyramid (FIG. **1-24**) of Djoser at Saqqara, near Memphis, Egypt's capital at the time. Djoser's pyramid was the centerpiece of an immense (37-acre) rectangular enclosure surrounded by a monumental wall (34 feet high and 5,400 feet long) of white limestone. The huge precinct also contained a funerary temple, where priests performed daily rituals in celebration of the divine pharaoh. Several structures in the complex were connected with the Jubilee Festival, the event that perpetually reaffirmed the royal existence in the hereafter.

Built before 2600 BCE, Djoser's pyramid is one of the oldest stone structures in Egypt and, in its final form, the first truly grandiose royal tomb. Begun as a large mastaba with each of its faces oriented toward one of the cardinal points of the compass, the tomb was enlarged at least twice before taking on its ultimate shape. About 200 feet high, the Stepped Pyramid seems to be composed of a series of mastabas of diminishing size, stacked one atop another. The tomb's dual function was to protect the mummified king

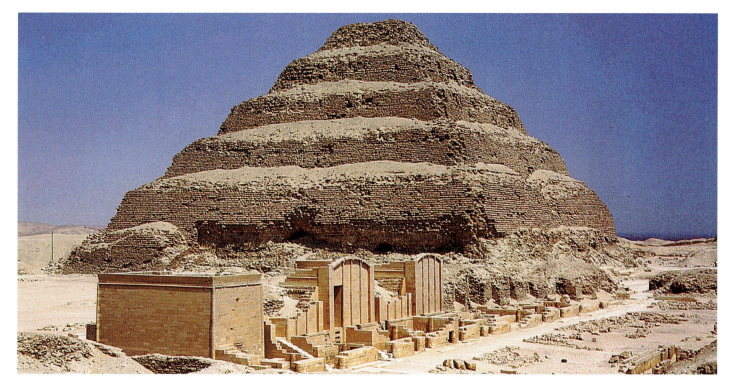

1-24 IMHOTEP, Stepped Pyramid and mortuary precinct of Djoser, Saqqara, Egypt, Third Dynasty, ca. 2630–2611 BCE.

The first pyramid took the form of a series of stacked mastabas. Djoser's Stepped Pyramid was the centerpiece of an immense funerary complex glorifying the god-king and his eternal existence in the hereafter.

Egyptian Art | 35

Mummification and the Afterlife

The Egyptians did not make the sharp distinction between body and soul that is basic to many religions. Rather, they believed that from birth a person had a kind of other self, the *ka* (life force), which, on the death of the body, could inhabit the corpse and live on. For the ka to live securely, however, the body had to remain as nearly intact as possible. To ensure that it did, the Egyptians developed the technique of embalming (*mummification*) to a high art.

Embalming generally lasted 70 days. The first step was the surgical removal of the lungs, liver, stomach, and intestines through an incision in the left flank. The Egyptians thought these organs were most subject to decay. The organs were individually wrapped and placed in four jars for eventual deposit in the burial chamber with the corpse. The brain was extracted through the nostrils and discarded. The Egyptians did not attach any special significance to the brain. But they left in place the heart, necessary for life and regarded as the seat of intelligence.

Next, the body was treated for 40 days with natron, a naturally occurring salt compound that dehydrated the body. Then the Egyptians filled the corpse with resin-soaked linens, and closed and covered the embalming incision with a representation of Horus's eye, a powerful *amulet* (a device to ward off evil and promote rebirth). Finally, they treated the body with lotions and resins and then wrapped it tightly with hundreds of yards of linen bandages to maintain its shape. The Egyptians often placed other amulets within or on the corpse. The mummies of the wealthy had funerary masks (FIG. 1-36) covering their faces.

Preserving the deceased's body by mummification was only the first requirement for immortality. Food and drink also had to be provided, as did clothing, utensils, and furniture. For those who could afford to furnish their tombs, nothing that had been enjoyed on earth was to be lacking in the afterlife. The Egyptians placed statuettes called *ushabtis* (answerers) in their tombs to perform any labor the deceased required in the afterlife, answering whenever his or her name was called. Wealthier families also set up statues of the deceased in shallow recesses. They guaranteed the permanence of the person's identity by providing substitute dwelling places for the ka in case the mummy disintegrated. Wall paintings and reliefs recorded the recurring round of human activities. The Egyptians hoped and expected that the images and inventory of life, collected and set up within the tomb's protective stone walls, would ensure immortality.

---

and his possessions and to symbolize, by its gigantic presence, his absolute and godlike power. Beneath the pyramid was a network of underground galleries resembling a palace. It was to be Djoser's new home in the afterlife.

The Old Kingdom

The Old Kingdom is the first of the three great periods of Egyptian history, called the Old, Middle, and New Kingdoms, respectively. Many Egyptologists now begin the Old Kingdom with the first pharaoh of the Fourth Dynasty, Sneferu (r. 2575–2551 BCE), although the traditional division of kingdoms places Djoser and the Third Dynasty in the Old Kingdom. It ended with the demise of the Eighth Dynasty around 2134 BCE.

Great Pyramids At Gizeh stand the three Great Pyramids (FIG. 1-1), the oldest of the Seven Wonders of the ancient world. The prerequisites for membership in this elite club were colossal size and enormous cost. The Gizeh pyramids testify to the wealth and pretensions of the Fourth Dynasty pharaohs Khufu (r. 2551–2528 BCE), Khafre (r. 2520–2494 BCE), and Menkaure (r. 2490–2472 BCE). The three pyramids, built in the course of about 75 years, represent the culmination of an architectural evolution that began with the mastaba. The pyramid form did not evolve out of necessity. Kings could have indefinitely continued stacking mastabas to make their weighty tombs. The new tomb shape probably reflects the influence of Heliopolis, the seat of the powerful cult of Re, whose emblem was a pyramidal

stone, the *ben-ben*. The Great Pyramids are symbols of the sun. The Pyramid Texts, inscribed on the burial chamber walls of many royal tombs, refer to the sun's rays as the ramp the pharaoh uses to ascend to the heavens. Djoser's Stepped Pyramid (FIG. 1-24) may also have been conceived as a giant stairway. The pyramids were where Egyptian kings were reborn in the afterlife, just as the sun is reborn each day at dawn. As with Djoser's Stepped Pyramid, the four sides of each of the Great Pyramids point to the cardinal points of the compass. But the funerary temples associated with the three Gizeh pyramids are not on the north side, facing the stars of the northern sky, as Djoser's temple did. The temples sit on the east side, facing the rising sun and underscoring their connection with Re.

Of the three Fourth Dynasty pyramids at Gizeh, the tomb of Khufu is the oldest and largest. Except for its internal galleries and burial chamber, it is an almost solid mass of limestone masonry (see "Building the Great Pyramids," page 37)—a stone mountain built on the same principle as the earlier Stepped Pyramid at Saqqara. When its original stone facing was intact, the sunlight it reflected would have been dazzling, underscoring the pyramid's role as a solar symbol. The Gizeh pyramids are immense. At the base, the length of one side of Khufu's tomb is approximately 775 feet, and its area is some 13 acres. Its present height is about 450 feet (originally 480 feet). The structure contains roughly 2.3 million blocks of stone, each weighing an average of 2.5 tons. Napoleon's scholars calculated that the blocks in the three Great Pyramids were sufficient to build a 1-foot-wide and 10-feet-tall wall around France.

Building the Great Pyramids

The three Great Pyramids (FIG. 1-1) of Khufu, Khafre, and Menkaure at Gizeh attest to Egyptian builders' mastery of stone masonry and to their ability to mobilize, direct, house, and feed a huge workforce engaged in one of the most labor-intensive enterprises ever undertaken.

Like all building projects of this type, the process of erecting the pyramids began with the quarrying of stone, in this case primarily the limestone of the Gizeh plateau itself—from which Egyptian sculptors also carved the Great Sphinx (FIG. 1-25). Teams of skilled workers had to cut into the rock and remove large blocks of roughly equal size using stone or copper chisels and wooden mallets and wedges. Often, the Egyptian artisans had to cut deep tunnels to find high-quality stone free of cracks and other flaws. To remove a block, the workers cut channels on all sides and partly underneath. Then they pried the stones free from the bedrock with wooden levers.

After workers liberated the stones, the rough blocks had to be transported to the building site and *dressed* (shaped to the exact dimensions required, with smooth faces for a perfect fit). The Egyptians moved the massive blocks used to construct the Great Pyramids using wooden rollers and sleds. They dressed the blocks by chiseling and pounding the surfaces and, in the last stage, by rubbing and grinding the surfaces with fine polishing stones. The name for this kind of construction, in which carefully cut and regularly shaped blocks of stone are piled in successive rows, or *courses*, is *ashlar masonry*.

To set the ashlar blocks in place, workers erected great rubble ramps against the core of the pyramid. They adjusted their size and slope as work progressed and the tomb grew in height. Scholars still debate whether the Egyptians used simple linear ramps inclined at a right angle to one face of the pyramid or zigzag or spiral ramps akin to staircases. Linear ramps would have had the advantage of simplicity and would have left three sides of the pyramid unobstructed. But zigzag ramps placed against one side of the structure or spiral ramps winding around the pyramid would have greatly reduced the slope of the incline and would have made the dragging of the blocks easier. Some scholars also have suggested a combination of straight and spiral ramps.

The workers used ropes, pulleys, and levers both to lift and to lower the stones, guiding each block into its designated place. Finally, they provided the pyramid with a facing of white limestone cut so precisely that the eye could scarcely detect the joints between the blocks. A few casing stones remain at the apex of the Pyramid of Khafre (FIGS. 1-1, *center*, and 1-25, *left*).

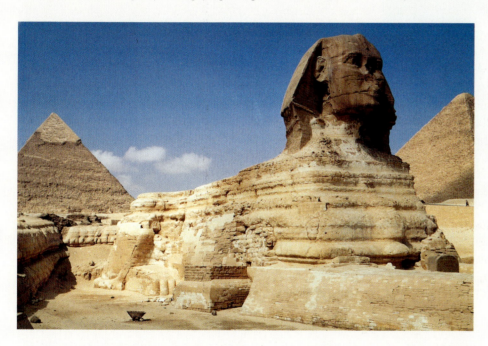

1-25 Great Sphinx (with Pyramid of Khafre in the background at left), Gizeh, Egypt, Fourth Dynasty, ca. 2520–2494 BCE. Sandstone, 65′ high, 240′ long.

Carved from the rock of the Gizeh plateau from which workers quarried the stones for the Great Pyramids, the Great Sphinx is the largest statue in the Near East. The man-headed lion is associated with the sun god.

From the remains surrounding the Pyramid of Khafre, archaeologists have been able to reconstruct an entire funerary complex. The complex included the pyramid itself with the pharaoh's burial chamber; the *mortuary temple* adjoining the pyramid on the east side, where priests made offerings to the dead king; the roofed causeway leading to the mortuary temple; and the *valley temple* at the edge of the floodplain.

According to one theory, the complex served not only as the king's tomb and temple but also as his palace in the afterlife.

Great Sphinx Beside the causeway and dominating the valley temple of Khafre rises the Great Sphinx (FIG. 1-25). Carved from a spur of rock in an ancient quarry, the colossal statue—the largest in the ancient Near East—is probably an image of Khafre, although some scholars believe it portrays Khufu and antedates Khafre's complex. Whoever it portrays, the *sphinx*—a lion with a human head—was associated with the sun god and therefore was an appropriate image for a pharaoh. The composite form suggests that the pharaoh combines human intelligence with the awesome strength and authority of the king of beasts.

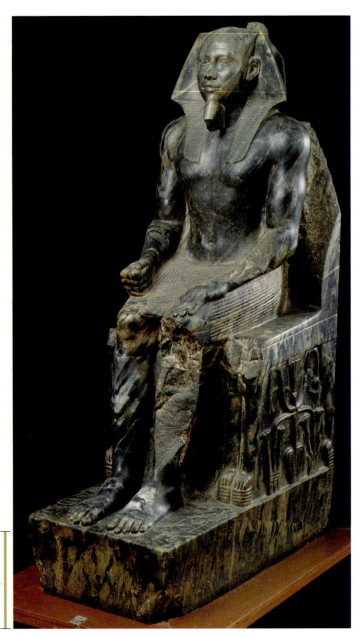

1 ft.

1-26 Khafre enthroned, from Gizeh, Egypt, Fourth Dynasty, ca. 2520–2494 BCE. Diorite, 5′ 6″ high. Egyptian Museum, Cairo.

This portrait from his pyramid complex depicts Khafre as a divine ruler with a perfect body. The rigidity of the pose creates the effect of eternal stillness, appropriate for the timelessness of the afterlife.

Khafre Enthroned Sculptors created images of the deceased to serve as abodes for the ka should the mummies be destroyed. Although the Egyptians used wood, clay, and other materials, mostly for images of those not of the royal or noble classes, the primary material for tomb statuary was stone. The seated statue of Khafre (FIG. **1-26**) is one of a series of similar statues carved for the pharaoh's valley temple near the Great Sphinx. The stone is diorite, an exceptionally hard dark stone brought some 400 miles down the Nile from royal quarries in the south. Khafre wears a simple kilt and sits rigidly upright on a throne formed of two stylized lions' bodies. Between the legs of the throne are intertwined lotus and papyrus plants—symbol of the united Egypt. The falcon-god Horus extends his protective wings to shelter the

pharaoh's head. Khafre has the royal false beard fastened to his chin and wears the royal linen *nemes* headdress with the *uraeus* cobra of kingship on the front. The headdress covers his forehead and falls in pleated folds over his shoulders, as in the Great Sphinx. As befitting a divine ruler, Khafre has a well-developed, flawless body and a perfect face, regardless of his real age and appearance. The Egyptians considered ideal proportions appropriate for representing imposing majesty, and artists used them quite independently of reality. This and all other generalized representations of the pharaohs are not true portraits. Their purpose was not to record individual features or the distinctive shapes of bodies, but rather to proclaim the godlike nature of Egyptian kingship.

The seated king radiates serenity. The sculptor created this effect, common to Egyptian royal statues, in part by giving the figure great compactness and solidity, with few projecting, breakable parts. The form manifests the purpose: to last for eternity. Khafre's body is attached to the unarticulated slab that forms the back of the king's throne. His arms touch the torso and thighs, and his legs are close together and connected to the chair by the stone the artist chose not to remove. The pose is frontal, rigid, and *bilaterally symmetrical* (the same on either side of an axis, in this case the vertical axis). The sculptor suppressed all movement and with it the notion of time, creating an eternal stillness.

To produce the statue, the artist first drew the front, back, and two profile views of the pharaoh on the four vertical faces of the stone block. Next, apprentices used *chisels* to cut away the excess stone on each side, working inward until the planes met at right angles. Finally, the master sculpted the parts of Khafre's body, the falcon, and so forth. The finishing was done by *abrasion* (rubbing or grinding the surface). This subtractive method accounts in large part for the blocklike look of the standard Egyptian statue. Nevertheless, other sculptors, both ancient and modern, with different aims, have transformed stone blocks into dynamic, twisting human forms (for example, FIG. **I-12**).

Menkaure and Khamerernebty The seated statue is one of only a small number of basic formulaic types the Egyptians employed to represent the human figure. Another is the image of a person or deity standing, either alone or in a group, as in the double portrait (FIG. **1-27**) of Menkaure and one of his wives, probably Queen Khamerernebty. The portraits once stood in the valley temple of Menkaure at Gizeh. Here, too, the figures remain wedded to the stone block from which they were carved, and the sculptor used conventional postures to suggest the timeless nature of these eternal substitute homes for the ka. Menkaure's pose, which is duplicated in countless other Egyptian statues, is rigidly frontal with the arms hanging straight down and close to his well-built body. His hands are clenched into fists with the thumbs forward. He advances his left leg slightly, but no shift occurs in the angle of the hips to correspond to the uneven distribution of weight. Khamerernebty stands in a similar position. Her right arm, however, circles around the king's waist, and her left hand gently rests on his left arm.

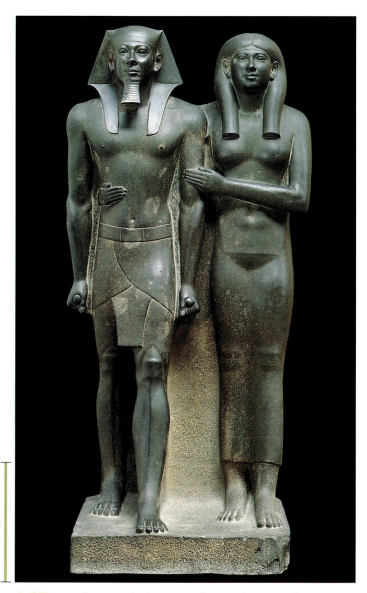

1-27 Menkaure and Khamerernebty(?), from Gizeh, Egypt, Fourth Dynasty, ca. 2490–2472 BCE. Graywacke, 4′ 6½″ high. Museum of Fine Arts, Boston.

This double portrait displays the conventional postures used for Egyptian statues designed as substitute homes for the ka. The frozen gestures signify that the man and woman are husband and wife.

This frozen stereotypical gesture indicates their marital status. The husband and wife show no other sign of affection or emotion and look not at each other but out into space.

Tomb of Ti Egyptian artists also depicted the dead in relief sculpture and in mural painting, sometimes alone—as on the wooden panel of Hesire (FIG. I-10)—and sometimes in a narrative context. The scenes in painted limestone relief (FIG. 1-28) decorating the walls of the mastaba of Ti, a Fifth Dynasty official, typify the subjects Old Kingdom patrons favored for the adornment of their final resting places. Depictions of agriculture and hunting fill his tomb at Saqqara. These activities were associated with the provisioning of the ka in the hereafter, but they also had powerful symbolic overtones. In ancient Egypt, success in the hunt, for example, was a metaphor for triumph over the forces of evil.

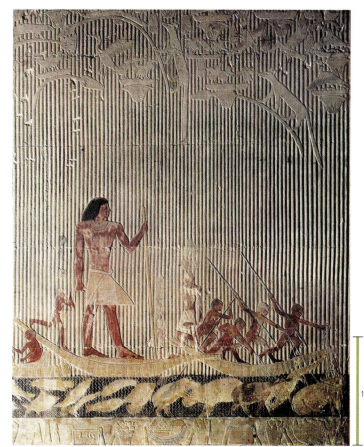

1-28 Ti watching a hippopotamus hunt, relief in the mastaba of Ti, Saqqara, Egypt, Fifth Dynasty, ca. 2450–2350 BCE. Painted limestone, 4′ high.

In Egypt, a successful hunt was a metaphor for triumph over evil. In this painted tomb relief, the deceased stands aloof from the hunters busily trying to spear hippopotami. Ti's size reflects his high rank.

In FIG. 1-28, Ti, his men, and his boats move slowly through the marshes, hunting hippopotami and birds in a dense growth of towering papyrus. The sculptor delineated the reedy stems of the plants with repeated fine grooves that fan out gracefully at the top into a commotion of frightened birds and stalking foxes. Hippopotami and fish occupy the water beneath the boats, which the artist signified by a pattern of wavy lines. Ti's men seem frantically busy with their spears, while Ti, depicted twice their size, stands aloof. The basic conventions of Egyptian figure representation used a half millennium earlier in King Narmer's palette (FIG. 1-22) appear again here. As on the Predynastic palette and the portrait relief of Hesire (FIG. I-10), the artist used the conceptual rather than the optical approach, representing the essence of the subject, instead of a random view of it, and showing its most characteristic parts at right angles to the line of vision. The composite view expressed a feeling for the constant and changeless aspect of things and was well suited for Egyptian funerary art. Ti's outsize proportions bespeak his rank. His conventional pose contrasts with the realistically rendered activities of his tiny servants and with the naturalistically carved and painted birds and animals among the papyrus buds. Ti's immobility suggests that he is not an actor in the hunt. He

Egyptian Art | 39

does not *do* anything. He simply *is*, a figure apart from time and an impassive observer of life, like his ka. Scenes such as this demonstrate that Egyptian artists could be close observers of daily life. The absence of the anecdotal (that is, of the time-bound) from their representations of the deceased both in relief and in the round was a deliberate choice. Their primary purpose was to suggest the deceased's eternal existence in the afterlife, not to portray nature.

The idealized image of Ti is typical of Egyptian relief sculpture. Egyptian artists regularly ignored the endless variations in body types of real human beings. Painters and sculptors did not sketch their subjects from life but applied a strict *canon*, or system of proportions, to the human figure. They first drew a grid on the wall. Then they placed various human body parts at specific points on the network of squares. The height of a figure, for example, was a fixed number of squares, and the head, shoulders, waist, knees, and other parts of the body also had a predetermined size and place within the scheme. This approach to design lasted for thousands of years. Specific proportions might vary from workshop to workshop and change over time, but the principle of the canon persisted.

The New Kingdom

About 2150 BCE, the Egyptians challenged the pharaohs' power, and for more than a century the land was in a state of civil unrest and near anarchy. But in 2040 BCE, the pharaoh of Upper Egypt, Mentuhotep II (r. 2050–1998 BCE), managed to unite Egypt again under the rule of a single king and established the Middle Kingdom (11th to 14th Dynasties), which brought stability to Egypt for four centuries. In the 17th century, it too disintegrated. Power passed to the Hyksos, or shepherd kings, who descended on Egypt from the Syrian and Mesopotamian uplands. They were in turn overthrown by native Egyptian kings of the 17th Dynasty around 1600–1550 BCE. Ahmose I (r. 1550–1525 BCE), final conqueror of the Hyksos and first king of the 18th Dynasty, ushered in the New Kingdom, the most brilliant period in Egypt's long history. At this time, Egypt extended its borders by conquest from the Euphrates River in the east deep into Nubia (the Sudan) to the south (MAP 1-3). A new capital—Thebes, in Upper Egypt—became a great and luxurious metropolis with magnificent palaces, tombs, and temples along both banks of the Nile.

Hatshepsut One of the most intriguing figures in the ancient world was the New Kingdom pharaoh Hatshepsut (r. 1473–1458 BCE). In 1479 BCE, Thutmose II (r. 1492–1479 BCE), the fourth pharaoh of the 18th Dynasty, died. Hatshepsut, his principal wife (and half sister), had not given birth to any sons who survived, so the title of king went to the 12-year-old Thutmose III, son of Thutmose II by a minor wife. Hatshepsut became regent for the boy-king. Within a few years, however, the queen proclaimed herself pharaoh and insisted that her father Thutmose I had chosen her as his successor during his lifetime. Hatshepsut is the first great female monarch whose name has been recorded. For two decades she ruled what was then the most powerful and prosperous empire in the world. As always, Egyptian sculptors produced statues of their pharaoh in great numbers for display throughout the kingdom. Hatshepsut uniformly wears the costume of the male pharaohs, with royal headdress and kilt, and in some cases even a false ceremonial beard. Many inscriptions refer to Hatshepsut as "*His* Majesty."

One of the most impressive of the many grandiose monuments erected by the New Kingdom pharaohs is Hatshepsut's

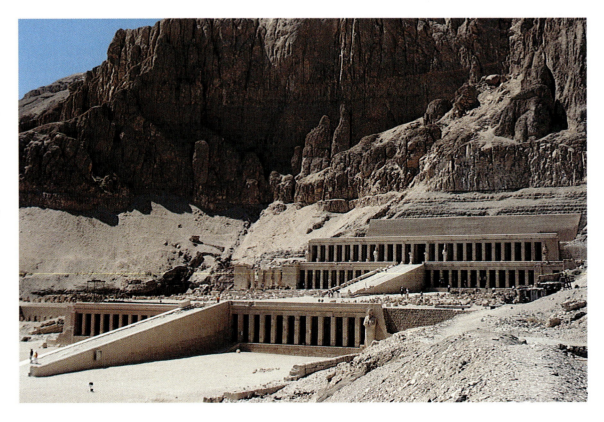

1-29 Mortuary temple of Hatshepsut (looking west), Deir el-Bahri, Egypt, 18th Dynasty, ca. 1473–1458 BCE.

Hatshepsut was the first great female monarch in history. Her immense terraced funerary temple featured an extensive series of painted reliefs recounting her divine birth, coronation, and great deeds.

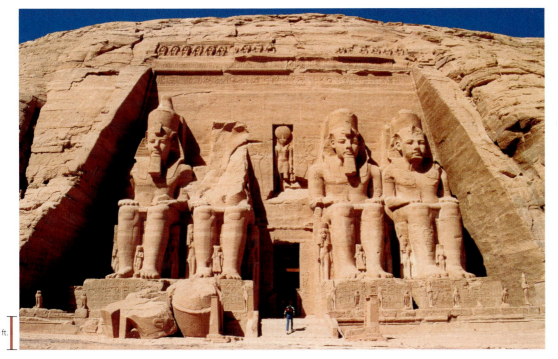

1-30 Facade of the temple of Ramses II, Abu Simbel, Egypt, 19th Dynasty, ca. 1290–1224 BCE. Sandstone, colossi 65' high.

Four rock-cut colossal images of Ramses II seated dominate the facade of his mortuary temple. Inside, more gigantic figures of the long-reigning king depict him as Osiris, god of the dead and giver of eternal life.

10 ft.

Ramses II Perhaps the greatest pharaoh of the New Kingdom was Ramses II (r. 1290–1224 BCE), who ruled Egypt for two-thirds of a century, an extraordinary accomplishment in an era when life expectancy was far shorter than it is today. Four colossal images of Ramses never fail to impress visitors to the pharaoh's mortuary temple (FIG. **1-30**) at Abu Simbel. The portraits, carved directly into the cliff face, are almost a dozen times an ancient Egyptian's height, even though the pharaoh is seated. The grand scale of the *facade* statues extends inside the temple also, where giant (32-foot-tall) figures of the king, carved as one with the *pillars*, face each other across the narrow corridor. Ramses appears in his *atlantids* (statue-columns) in the guise of Osiris, god of the dead and king of the underworld as well as giver of eternal life.

mortuary temple (FIG. **1-29**) on the Nile at Deir el-Bahri. The temple rises in three terraces connected by ramps. It is remarkable how visually well suited the structure is to its natural setting. The long horizontals and verticals of the *colonnades* of the terraces repeat the pattern of the limestone cliffs above. In Hatshepsut's day, the terraces were not the barren places they are now but gardens with frankincense trees and rare plants the pharaoh brought from the faraway "land of Punt" on the Red Sea. Her expedition to Punt figures prominently in the once brightly painted low reliefs that cover many walls of the complex. In addition to representing great deeds, the reliefs also show Hatshepsut's divine birth and coronation. She was said to be the daughter of the sun god, whose sanctuary was on the temple's uppermost level. The reliefs of Hatshepsut's mortuary temple, unfortunately defaced after her death, constitute the first great tribute to a woman's achievements in the history of art.

Temple of Amen-Re, Karnak Colossal scale also characterizes the temples the New Kingdom pharaohs built to honor one or more of the gods. Successive kings often extended the building campaigns for centuries. The temple of Amen-Re (FIG. **1-31**) at Karnak, for example, was largely

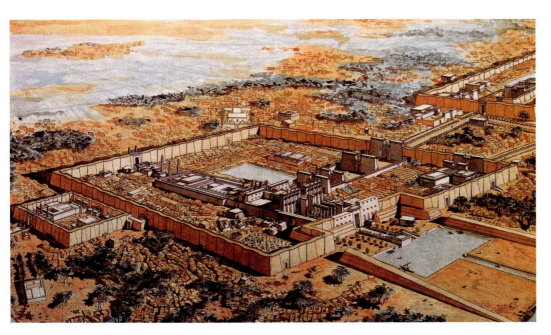

1-31 Restored view of the temple of Amen-Re, Karnak, Egypt, begun 15th century BCE (Jean-Claude Golvin).

The vast Karnak temple complex took centuries to complete. It contained an artificial lake associated with the Egyptian creation myth and a pylon temple whose axial plan conformed to Egyptian religious rituals.

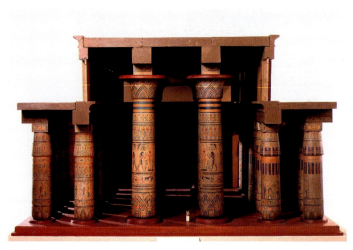

1-32 Model of the hypostyle hall, temple of Amen-Re, Karnak, Egypt, 19th Dynasty, ca. 1290–1224 BCE. Metropolitan Museum of Art, New York.

The two central rows of columns of the hypostyle hall at Karnak are 66 feet high, with capitals 22 feet in diameter. The clerestory beneath the raised roof permitted sunlight to illuminate the hall's interior.

the work of the 18th Dynasty pharaohs, including Hatshepsut, but Ramses II (19th Dynasty) and others also contributed sections. Parts of the complex date as late as the 26th Dynasty.

The Karnak temple has an artificial sacred lake within its precinct, a reference to the primeval waters before creation. The temple rises from the earth as the original sacred mound rose from the waters at the beginning of time. In other respects, however, the temple is a typical, if especially large, New Kingdom *pylon temple*. The name derives from the simple and massive *pylons* (gateways with sloping walls) that are characteristic features of New Kingdom temple design. A typical pylon temple is bilaterally symmetrical along a single axis that runs from an approaching avenue through a colonnaded court and hall into a dimly lit sanctuary. This Egyptian temple plan evolved from ritualistic requirements. Only the pharaohs and the priests could enter the sanctuary. A chosen few were admitted to the great columnar hall. The majority of the people could enter only as far as the open court, and a high wall shut off the site from the outside world. The central feature of the New Kingdom pylon temple plan—a narrow axial passageway through the complex—characterizes much of Egyptian architecture. The approaches to the Old Kingdom pyramids (FIG. 1-1) of Gizeh and to the multilevel mortuary temple of Hatshepsut (FIG. 1-29) at Deir el-Bahri also conform to the Egyptian preference for *axial plans*.

In the Karnak plan, the hall (FIG. **1-32**) between the court and sanctuary has its long axis placed at a right angle to the corridor of the entire building complex. Inside this *hypostyle hall* (one in which columns support the roof) are massive columns that carry the stone slabs of the roof on stone lintels. The lintels rest on cubical blocks that in turn rest on giant *capitals* ("heads"). The central columns are 66 feet high, and the capitals are 22 feet in diameter at the top, large

enough to hold a hundred people. The Egyptians, who used no cement, depended on precise cutting of the joints and the weight of the huge stone blocks to hold the columns in place. Most scholars believe Egyptian columns originated from an early building technique that used firmly bound sheaves of reeds and swamp plants as roof supports in *adobe* structures. Egyptian masons first translated these early and relatively impermanent building methods into stone in Djoser's funerary precinct at Saqqara. The columns' swamp-plant origin is still evident at Karnak, where the columns have bud-cluster or bell-shaped capitals resembling lotus or papyrus (the plants of Upper and Lower Egypt).

In the Amen-Re temple at Karnak and in many other Egyptian hypostyle halls, the builders made the central rows of columns higher than those at the sides. Raising the roof's central section created a *clerestory*. Openings in the clerestory permitted sunlight to filter into the interior, although the stone grilles would have blocked much of the light. This method of construction appeared in primitive form as early as the Old Kingdom in the valley temple of the Pyramid of Khafre. The clerestory seems to be an Egyptian innovation, and its significance hardly can be overstated. Before the invention of the electric light bulb, illuminating a building's interior was always a challenge for architects. The clerestory played a key role, for example, in medieval church design and has remained an important architectural feature up to the present.

Akhenaton The Karnak sanctuary also provides evidence for a period of religious upheaval during the New Kingdom and for a corresponding revolution in Egyptian art. In the mid-14th century BCE, the pharaoh Amenhotep IV, later known as Akhenaton (r. 1353–1335 BCE), abandoned the worship of most of the Egyptian gods in favor of Aton, whom he declared to be the universal and only god, identified with the sun disk. He blotted out the name of Amen from all inscriptions and even from his own name and that of his father, Amenhotep III. He emptied the great temples, enraged the priests, and moved his capital downriver from Thebes to a site he named Akhetaton (after his new god), where he built his own city (now called Tell el-Amarna) and shrines. The pharaoh claimed to be both the son and sole prophet of Aton. Moreover, in stark contrast to earlier practice, artists represented Akhenaton's god neither in animal nor in human form but simply as the sun disk emitting life-giving rays. The pharaohs who followed Akhenaton reestablished the cult and priesthood of Amen and restored the temples and the inscriptions. Akhenaton's religious revolution was soon undone, and his new city largely abandoned.

During the brief heretical episode of Akhenaton, however, profound changes occurred in Egyptian art. A colossal statue (FIG. **1-33**) of Akhenaton from Karnak, toppled and buried after his death, retains the standard frontal pose of pharaonic portraits. But the effeminate body, with its curving contours, and the long face with full lips and heavy-lidded eyes bear no resemblance to the heroically proportioned figures (FIG. 1-27) of Akhenaton's predecessors. Akhenaton's

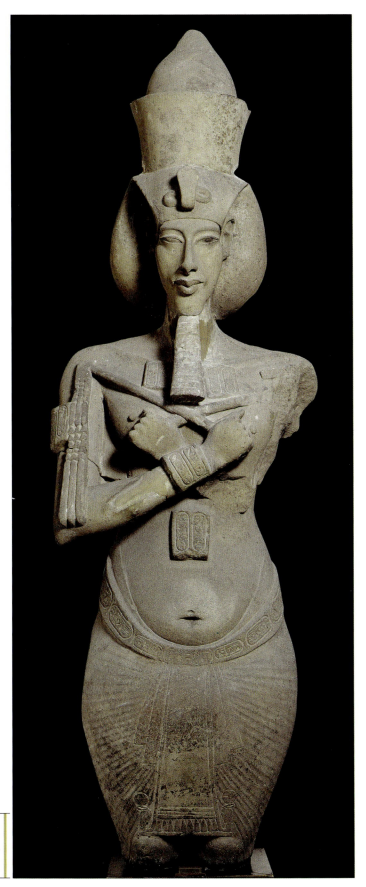

1 ft.

1-33 Akhenaton, from the temple of Aton, Karnak, Egypt, 18th Dynasty, ca. 1353–1335 BCE. Sandstone, 13' high. Egyptian Museum, Cairo.

Akhenaton initiated a religious revolution, and his art is also a deliberate artistic reaction against tradition. This curious androgynous image may be an attempt to portray the pharaoh as Aton, the sexless sun disk.

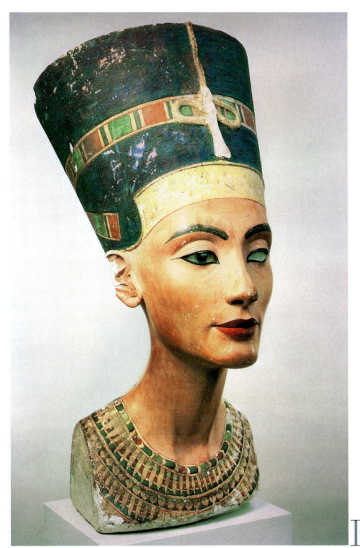

1 in.

1-34 THUTMOSE, Nefertiti, from Tell el-Amarna, Egypt, 18th Dynasty, ca. 1353–1335 BCE. Painted limestone, 1' 8" high. Ägyptisches Museum, Berlin.

Found in the sculptor's workshop, Thutmose's unfinished portrait of Nefertiti, Akhenaton's influential wife, depicts her as an elegant and beautiful musing woman with a long, delicately curved neck.

body is curiously misshapen, with weak arms, a narrow waist, protruding belly, wide hips, and fatty thighs. Modern doctors have tried to explain his physique by attributing a variety of illnesses to the pharaoh. They cannot agree on a diagnosis, and their premise—that the statue is an accurate depiction of a physical deformity—is probably faulty. Some art historians think Akhenaton's portrait was a deliberate artistic reaction against the established style, paralleling the suppression of traditional religion. They argue that Akhenaton's artists tried to formulate a new androgynous image of the pharaoh as the manifestation of Aton, the sexless sun disk. But no consensus exists other than that the style was revolutionary and short-lived.

Nefertiti A painted limestone bust (FIG. **1-34**) of Akhenaton's queen, Nefertiti (her name means "The Beautiful One Has Come"), exhibits a similar expression of entranced musing and an almost mannered sensitivity and

1-35 Innermost coffin of Tutankhamen, from his tomb at Thebes, Egypt, 18th Dynasty, ca. 1323 BCE. Gold with inlay of enamel and semiprecious stones, 6′ 1″ long. Egyptian Museum, Cairo.

Tutankhamen was a boy-king whose fame today is due to the discovery of his unplundered tomb. His mummy was encased in three nested coffins. The innermost one, the costliest, portrays the pharaoh as Osiris.

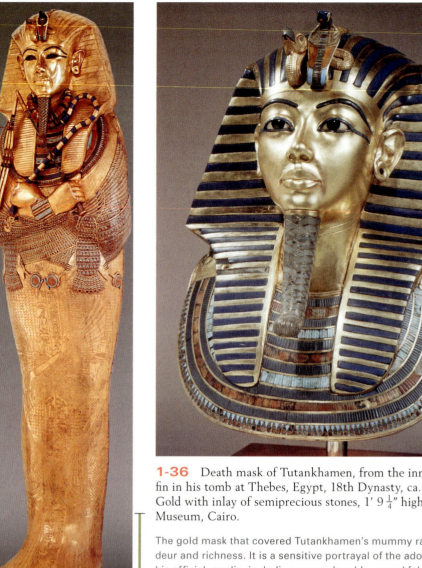

1-36 Death mask of Tutankhamen, from the innermost coffin in his tomb at Thebes, Egypt, 18th Dynasty, ca. 1323 BCE. Gold with inlay of semiprecious stones, 1′ 9¼″ high. Egyptian Museum, Cairo.

The gold mask that covered Tutankhamen's mummy radiates grandeur and richness. It is a sensitive portrayal of the adolescent king in his official regalia, including nemes headdress and false beard.

delicacy of curving contour. Nefertiti was an influential woman during her husband's kingship. She frequently appears in the decoration of the Aton temple at Karnak, portrayed not only as equal in size to her husband but also sometimes wearing pharaonic headgear. Excavators discovered the portrait illustrated here in the workshop of the sculptor THUTMOSE. It is a deliberately unfinished model very likely by the master's own hand. The left eye socket still lacks the inlaid eyeball, making the portrait a kind of before-and-after demonstration piece. With this elegant bust, Thutmose may have been alluding to a heavy flower on its slender stalk by exaggerating the weight of the crowned head and the length of the almost serpentine neck. The Tell el-Amarna sculptor adjusted the true likeness of his subject to match the era's standard of spiritual beauty.

Tutankhamen Probably Akhenaton's son by a minor wife, Tutankhamen (r. 1333–1323 BCE) ruled Egypt for a decade and died at age 18. Although he was a very minor figure in Egyptian history, he is famous today because of the fabulously rich art and artifacts found in his largely unplundered tomb at Thebes, uncovered in 1922. The principal monument in the collection is the enshrined body of the pharaoh himself. The royal mummy reposed in the innermost of three coffins, nested one within the other. The innermost coffin (FIG. **1-35**), the most luxurious of the three, shows Tutankhamen in the guise of Osiris. Made of beaten gold (about a quarter ton of it) and inlaid with such semiprecious stones as lapis lazuli, turquoise, and carnelian, it is a supreme monument to the sculptor's and goldsmith's crafts. The por-

trait mask (FIG. **1-36**), which covered the king's face, is also made of gold with inlaid semiprecious stones. It is a sensitive portrayal of the serene adolescent king dressed in his official regalia, including the nemes headdress and false beard. The general effect of the mask and of the tomb treasures as a whole is of grandeur and richness expressive of Egyptian power, pride, and affluence.

Egypt in Decline During the last millennium BCE, Egypt lost the commanding role it once had played in the ancient Near East. The empire dwindled away, and foreign powers invaded, occupied, and ruled the land, until Alexander the Great of Macedon and his Greek successors and, eventually, the Romans, took control of the land of the Nile. But even after Egypt became a province of the Roman Empire, its prestige remained high. Visitors to Rome today who enter the city from the airport road encounter the tomb of a Roman nobleman who died around 12 BCE. His memorial takes the form of a pyramid, 2,500 years after the Old Kingdom pharaohs erected the Great Pyramids of Gizeh.

Prehistory and the First Civilizations

PREHISTORIC ART

▪ The first sculptures and paintings antedate the invention of writing by tens of thousands of years. No one knows why humans began to paint and carve images or what role those images played in the lives of Paleolithic hunters. Women were far more common subjects than men, but animals, not humans, dominate Paleolithic art (ca. 30,000–9000 BCE). Surviving works range in size from tiny figurines to painted walls and ceilings covered with over-life-size animals, as in the Lascaux cave. Animals always appear in profile in order to show clearly the head, body, tail, and all four legs.

▪ The Neolithic Age (ca. 8000–3500 BCE) revolutionized human life with the beginning of agriculture and the formation of the first settled communities. The earliest known monumental sculptures date to the seventh millennium BCE. In painting, coherent narratives became common, and artists began to represent human figures as composites of frontal and profile views.

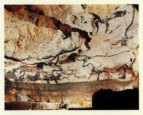

Hall of the Bulls, Lascaux, ca. 15,000–13,000 BCE

ANCIENT NEAR EASTERN ART

▪ The Sumerians (ca. 3500–2332 BCE) founded the world's first city-states and invented writing in the fourth millennium BCE. They were also the first people to build towering temple platforms, called ziggurats, and to place figures in registers to tell coherent stories.

▪ The Akkadians (ca. 2332–2150 BCE) were the first Near Eastern rulers to call themselves kings of the world and to assume divine attributes. Akkadian artists may have been the first to cast hollow life-size bronze sculptures and to place figures at different levels in a landscape setting.

▪ During the Third Dynasty of Ur (ca. 2150–1800 BCE) and under the kings of Babylon (ca. 1800–1600 BCE), the Sumerians constructed one of the largest ziggurats in Mesopotamia at Ur. Babylonian artists were among the first to experiment with foreshortening.

▪ At the height of their power, the Assyrians (ca. 900–612 BCE) ruled an empire that extended from the Persian Gulf to the Nile and Asia Minor. Assyrian palaces were fortified citadels with gates guarded by monstrous lamassu. Painted reliefs glorifying the king decorated the walls.

▪ The Neo-Babylonian kings (612–559 BCE) erected the biblical Tower of Babel and the Ishtar Gate.

▪ The capital of the Achaemenid Empire (559–330 BCE) was Persepolis, where the Persians built a huge palace complex with an audience hall that could accommodate thousands.

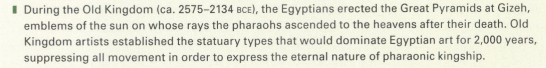

Standard of Ur, ca. 2600 BCE

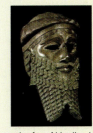

Portrait of an Akkadian king, ca. 2250–2200 BCE

EGYPTIAN ART

▪ The palette of King Narmer, which commemorates the unification of Upper and Lower Egypt around 3000–2920 BCE, established the basic principles of Egyptian representational art for 3,000 years.

▪ Imhotep, architect of the funerary complex of King Djoser (r. 2630–2611 BCE) at Saqqara, is the first known artist in history.

▪ During the Old Kingdom (ca. 2575–2134 BCE), the Egyptians erected the Great Pyramids at Gizeh, emblems of the sun on whose rays the pharaohs ascended to the heavens after their death. Old Kingdom artists established the statuary types that would dominate Egyptian art for 2,000 years, suppressing all movement in order to express the eternal nature of pharaonic kingship.

▪ During the New Kingdom (ca. 1550–1070 BCE), the most significant architectural innovation was the axially planned pylon temple incorporating an immense gateway, columnar courtyards, and a hypostyle hall with clerestory windows. Powerful pharaohs such as Hatshepsut (r. 1473–1458 BCE) and Ramses II (r. 1290–1224 BCE) erected gigantic temples in honor of their patron gods and, after their deaths, for their own worship. Akhenaton (r. 1353–1335 BCE) abandoned the traditional Egyptian religion in favor of Aton, the sun disk, and initiated a short-lived artistic revolution in which undulating curves and anecdotal content replaced the cubic forms and impassive stillness of earlier Egyptian art.

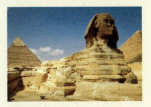

Great Sphinx and Pyramid of Khafre, Gizeh, ca. 2520–2494 BCE

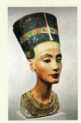

Thutmose, Portrait of Nefertiti, ca. 1353–1335 BCE

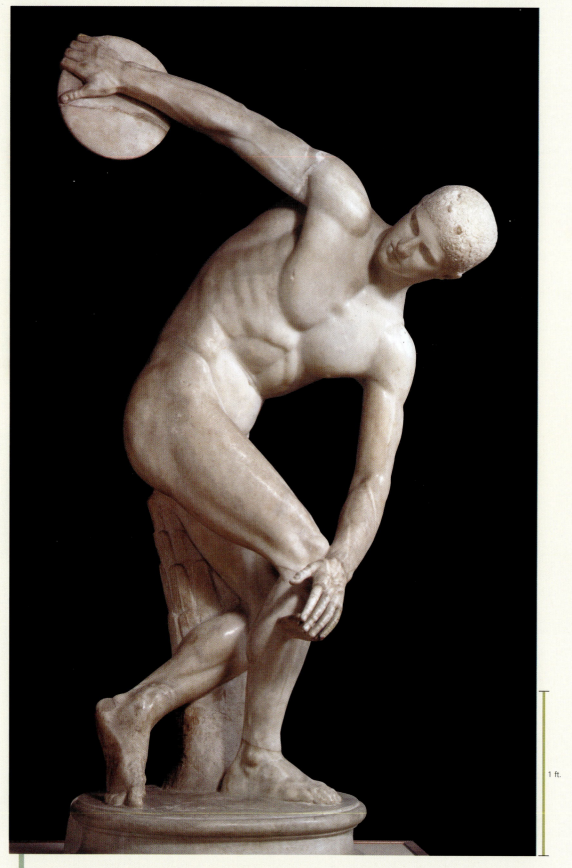

1 ft.

2-1 MYRON, *Diskobolos (Discus Thrower)*. Roman copy after a bronze original of ca. 450 BCE. Marble, 5′ 1″ high. Museo Nazionale Romano—Palazzo Massimo alle Terme, Rome.

In contrast to Near Eastern and Egyptian deities, Greek gods differed from humans only in being immortal. Greek artists depicted both gods and young men such as this discus thrower with perfect nude bodies.

2

Greece

Greek art occupies a special place in the history of art through the ages. Many of the cultural values of the Greeks, especially their honoring of the individual and exaltation of humanity as "the measure of all things," remain fundamental tenets of Western civilization. In fact, these ideas are so completely part of modern Western habits of mind that most people are scarcely aware that the concepts originated in Greece more than 2,500 years ago.

The Greeks, or *Hellenes*, as they called themselves, never formed a single nation but instead established independent city-states on the Greek mainland, on the islands of the Aegean Sea, and on the western coast of Asia Minor (MAP **2-1**). In 776 BCE, the separate Greek states held their first ceremonial games in common at Olympia. From then on, despite their differences and rivalries, the Greeks regarded themselves as sharing a common culture, distinct from the surrounding "barbarians" who did not speak Greek.

Even the gods of the Greeks (see "The Gods and Goddesses of Mount Olympus," page 49) differed in kind from those of neighboring cultures. Unlike the Egyptian and Mesopotamian gods (see Chapter 1), the Greek deities differed from human beings only in that they were immortal. It has been said the Greeks made their gods into humans and their humans into gods. This humanistic worldview led the Greeks to create the concept of democracy (rule by the *demos*, the people) and to make seminal contributions in the fields of art, literature, and science.

The distinctiveness and originality of Greek civilization should not, however, obscure the enormous debt the Greeks owed to the cultures of Egypt and the Near East. Scholars today increasingly recognize this debt, and the Greeks themselves readily acknowledged borrowing ideas, motifs, conventions, and skills from these older civilizations. Nor should a high estimation of Greek art and culture blind historians to the realities of Hellenic life and society. Even "democracy" was a political reality for only one segment of the Greek demos. Slavery was a universal institution among the Greeks, and Greek women were in no way the equals of Greek men. Women normally remained secluded in their homes, emerging usually only for weddings, funerals, and religious festivals. They played little part in public or political life. Nonetheless, the importance of the Greek contribution to the later development of Western civilization and Western art cannot be overstated.

The story of art in Greece does not begin with the Greeks, however, but with their prehistoric predecessors in the Aegean world—the people who would later become the heroes of Greek mythology.

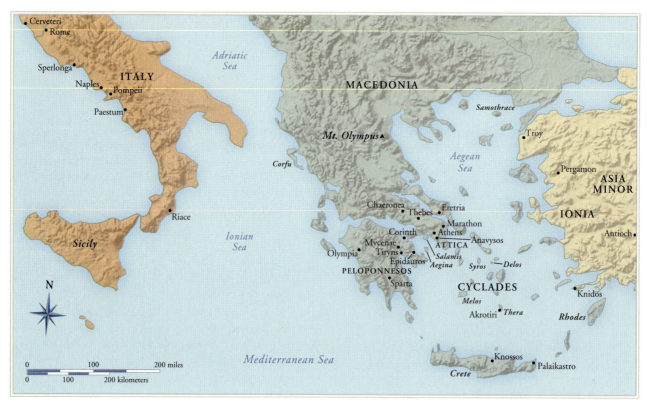

MAP 2-1 The ancient Greek world.

PREHISTORIC AEGEAN ART

Historians, art historians, and archaeologists alike divide the prehistoric Aegean into three geographic areas. Each has a distinctive artistic identity. *Cycladic* art is the art of the Cycladic Islands (so named because they *circle* around Delos) as well as of the adjacent islands in the Aegean, excluding Crete. *Minoan* art, named for the legendary King Minos, encompasses the art of Crete. *Mycenaean* art, which takes its name from the great citadel of Mycenae celebrated in Homer's *Iliad*, the epic tale of the Trojan War, is the art of the Greek mainland.

Cycladic Art

Although the heyday of the prehistoric Aegean was not until the second millennium BCE, humans inhabited Greece as far back as the Paleolithic period. Village life was firmly established in Greece in Neolithic times. However, the earliest distinctive Aegean artworks date to the third millennium BCE and come from the Cyclades.

Cycladic Statuettes Marble was abundant in the Aegean Islands, and many Cycladic marble sculptures survive. Most of these, like their Stone Age predecessors (FIG. 1-2), represent nude women with their arms folded across their abdomens. One example (FIG. **2-2**), about a foot and a half tall, comes from a grave on Syros. It is almost flat, and the sculptor rendered the human body in a highly schematic manner. Large, simple triangles dominate the form—the

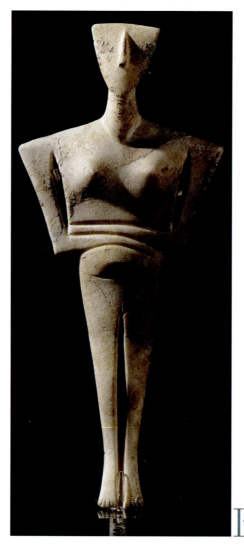

2-2 Figurine of a woman, from Syros (Cyclades), Greece, ca. 2500–2300 BCE. Marble, 1′ 6″ high. National Archaeological Museum, Athens.

Most Cycladic statuettes come from graves and depict nude women, but whether they represent the deceased is uncertain. The sculptor rendered the female body schematically as a series of large triangles.

1 in.

The Gods and Goddesses of Mount Olympus

The Greek deities most often represented in art—not only in antiquity but also in the Middle Ages, the Renaissance, and up to the present—are the 12 gods and goddesses of Mount Olympus. Listed here are the Olympian gods (and their Roman equivalents):

Zeus (*Jupiter*) was king of the gods and ruled the sky. His weapon was the thunderbolt, and with it he led the other gods to victory over the giants, who had challenged the Olympians for control of the world.

Hera (*Juno*), the wife and sister of Zeus, was the goddess of marriage.

Poseidon (*Neptune*), Zeus's brother, was lord of the sea. He controlled waves, storms, and earthquakes with his three-pronged pitchfork *(trident)*.

Hestia (*Vesta*), sister of Zeus, Poseidon, and Hera, was goddess of the hearth.

Demeter (*Ceres*), Zeus's third sister, was the goddess of grain and agriculture.

Ares (*Mars*), the god of war, was the son of Zeus and Hera and the lover of Aphrodite. As father of the twin founders of Rome, Romulus and Remus, Mars looms much larger in Roman mythology and religion than Ares does in Greek.

Athena (*Minerva*) was the goddess of wisdom and warfare. She was a virgin (*parthenos* in Greek), born not from a woman's womb but from the head of her father, Zeus.

Hephaistos (*Vulcan*), the son of Zeus and Hera, was the god of fire and of metalworking. He provided Zeus his scepter and Poseidon his trident, and fashioned the armor Achilles wore in battle against Troy. He was also the "surgeon" who split open Zeus's head when he gave birth to Athena. Hephaistos was lame and, uncharacteristically for a god, ugly. His wife, Aphrodite, was unfaithful to him.

Apollo (*Apollo*) was the god of light and music, and a great archer. He was the son of Zeus with Leto (Latona), daughter of one of the Titans who preceded the Olympians. His epithet *Phoibos* means "radiant," and the Greeks sometimes identified the young, beautiful Apollo with the sun (Helios/Sol).

Artemis (*Diana*), the sister of Apollo, was the goddess of the hunt and of wild animals. Because she was Apollo's twin, the Greeks occasionally regarded Artemis as the moon (Selene/Luna).

Aphrodite (*Venus*), the daughter of Zeus and Dione (one of the *nymphs*—the goddesses of springs, caves, and woods), was the goddess of love and beauty. She was the mother of the Trojan hero Aeneas by Anchises.

Hermes (*Mercury*), the son of Zeus and another nymph, was the fleet-footed messenger of the gods and possessed winged sandals. He was also the guide of travelers and carried the *caduceus*, a magical herald's rod.

Three other gods and goddesses figure prominently in Greek and Roman art:

Hades (*Pluto*), Zeus's other brother, was equal in stature to the Olympian deities, but he never resided on Mount Olympus. Zeus allotted him lordship over the Underworld when he gave the realm of the sea to Poseidon. Hades was the god of the dead.

Dionysos (*Bacchus*) was the god of wine and the son of Zeus and a mortal woman.

Eros (*Amor* or *Cupid*) was the winged child-god of love and the son of Aphrodite and Ares.

---

head, the body itself (which tapers from exceptionally broad shoulders to tiny feet), and the incised triangular pubis. The feet are too fragile to support the figurine. If these sculptures were primarily funerary offerings, as archaeologists believe they were, they must have been placed on their backs in the graves—lying down, as were the deceased themselves. Whether they represent those buried with the statuettes or fertility figures or goddesses is still the subject of debate. As is true of all such images, the artist took pains to emphasize the breasts as well as the pubic area. Traces of paint found on some of the Cycladic figurines indicate that the artists colored at least parts of these sculptures. The now almost featureless faces would have had painted eyes and mouths in addition to the sculpted noses. Red and blue necklaces and bracelets, as well as painted dots on the cheeks, characterize a number of the surviving figurines.

Minoan Art

During the third millennium BCE, both on the Aegean Islands and the Greek mainland, most settlements were small and consisted of simple buildings. Burials containing costly offerings such as the Syros statuette were rare. With the second millennium BCE, in contrast, came the construction of large palaces on Crete. This was the golden age of the prehistoric Aegean, the era when the first great Western civilization emerged. The Cretan palaces were large, comfortable, and handsome, with ample staircases and courtyards for pageants, ceremonies, and games. They also had storerooms, offices, and shrines that permitted these huge complexes to serve as the key administrative, commercial, and religious centers of the island. All of the Cretan palaces have similar layouts. The size and number of the palaces, as well as the

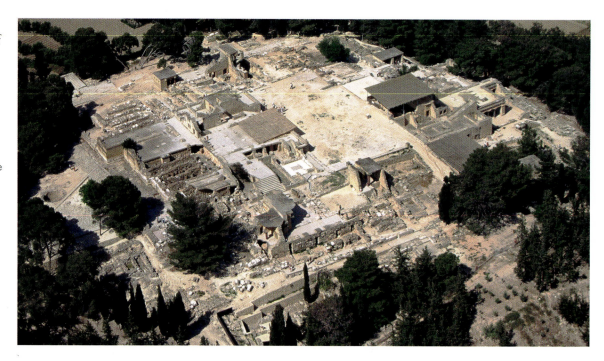

2-3 Aerial view (looking northeast) of the palace at Knossos (Crete), Greece, ca. 1700–1400 BCE.

The largest palace on Crete, this was the legendary home of King Minos. Scores of rooms surround a large rectangular court. The palace's mazelike plan gave rise to the myth of the Minotaur in the labyrinth.

rich finds they have yielded, attest to the power and prosperity of the people archaeologists have dubbed the Minoans, after the legendary King Minos.

Knossos Minos's palace (FIG. **2-3**) at Knossos, the largest on Crete, was the legendary home of the *Minotaur*, a creature half bull and half man. According to the myth, the Minotaur inhabited a vast labyrinth, and when the Athenian king Theseus defeated the monster, he was able to find his way out of the maze only with the aid of Minos's daughter Ariadne. She had given Theseus a spindle of thread to mark his path through the labyrinth and safely find his way out again. The aerial view reveals that the Knossos palace was indeed mazelike in plan. Its central feature was a large rectangular court. The other units—living quarters, ceremonial rooms, and storerooms—were grouped around it. The palace was also complex in elevation. It had as many as three stories around the central court and even more on the south and east sides where the terrain sloped off sharply. Interior staircases (FIG. **2-4**) built around light and air wells provided necessary illumination and ventilation. The Minoans fashioned their columns of wood and usually painted the shafts red. The columns had black, bulbous, cushionlike capitals resembling those of the later Greek Doric order (see "Doric and Ionic Temples," page 59). Minoan column shafts, however, taper from a wide top to a narrower base—the opposite of both Egyptian and later Greek columns.

Mural paintings liberally adorn the Knossos palace, constituting one of its most striking features. The paintings depict many aspects of Minoan life (bull-leaping, processions, and ceremonies) and of nature (birds, animals, flowers, and marine life). Unlike the Egyptians, who painted in *fresco secco (dry fresco)*, the Minoans coated the rough fabric of their rubble walls with a fine white lime plaster and used a *true (wet) fresco* method (see "Fresco Painting," Chapter 7, page 208). The Minoan frescoes required rapid execution and great skill.

The most famous fresco (FIG. **2-5**) from the palace at Knossos depicts the Minoan ceremony of bull-leaping. Only fragments of the full composition survive. (The dark patches are original. The remainder is a modern restoration.) The Minoan artist painted the young women (with fair skin) and the youth (with dark skin) according to a convention for distinguishing male and female also seen in ancient Near Eastern and Egyptian art. The young man is in midair, having,

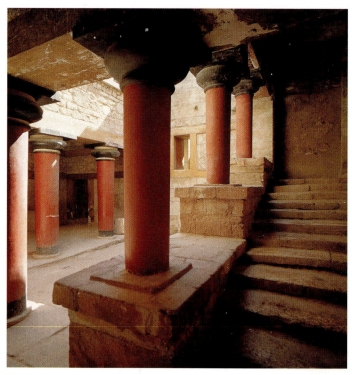

2-4 Stairwell in the residential quarter of the palace at Knossos (Crete), Greece, ca. 1700–1400 BCE.

The Knossos palace was complex in elevation as well as plan. It had several stories on all sides of the central court. Minoan columns taper from top to bottom, unlike Egyptian and Greek columns.

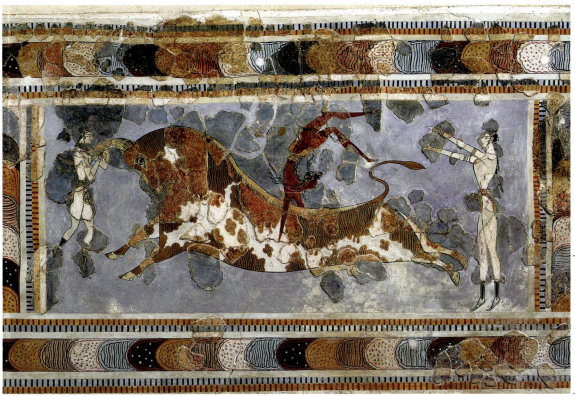

2-5

Bull-leaping, from the palace at Knossos (Crete), Greece, ca. 1450–1400 BCE. Fresco, 2′ 8″ high, including border. Archaeological Museum, Herakleion.

Frescoes decorated the Knossos palace walls. The men and women have stylized bodies with narrow waists. The skin color varies with gender, a common convention in ancient paintings.

1 ft.

it seems, grasped the bull's horns and vaulted over its back in a perilous and extremely difficult acrobatic maneuver. The painter brilliantly suggested the powerful charge of the bull by elongating the animal's shape and using sweeping lines to form a funnel of energy, beginning at the very narrow hindquarters of the bull and culminating in its large, sharp horns and galloping forelegs. The human figures also have stylized shapes, with typically Minoan pinched waists. The elegant, elastic, highly animated Cretan figures, with their long curly hair and proud and self-confident bearing, are easy to distinguish from Mesopotamian and Egyptian figures.

Thera Much better preserved than the Knossos frescoes are those uncovered in the excavations of Akrotiri on the volcanic island of Santorini (ancient Thera), some 60 miles north of Crete. The excellent condition of the Theran paintings is due to an enormous seismic explosion on Santorini that buried Akrotiri in volcanic pumice and ash, probably in 1628 BCE. One almost perfectly preserved Theran mural painting, the *Spring Fresco* (FIG. **2-6**), has nature itself as its sole subject. The artist's aim, however, was not to render the rocky island terrain realistically but rather to capture the landscape's essence and to express joy in the splendid surroundings. The irrationally undulating and vividly colored rocks, the graceful lilies swaying in the cool island breezes, and the darting swallows express the vigor of growth, the delicacy of flowering, and the lightness of birdsong and flight. In the lyrical language of curving line, the artist celebrated the rhythms of spring. This is the first known example of a pure landscape painting, a picture of a place without humans or animals present. *Spring Fresco* represents the polar opposite of the first efforts at mural painting in the caves of Paleolithic Europe, where animals (and occasionally humans) appear as isolated figures without any indication of setting.

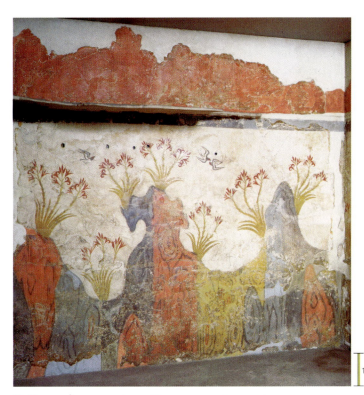

2-6 Landscape with swallows *(Spring Fresco)*, from Room Delta 2, Akrotiri, Thera (Cyclades), Greece, ca. 1650 BCE. Fresco, 7′ 6″ high. National Archaeological Museum, Athens.

Aegean muralists painted in wet fresco, which required rapid execution. In this first known pure landscape, the painter used vivid colors and undulating lines to capture the essence of springtime.

1 ft.

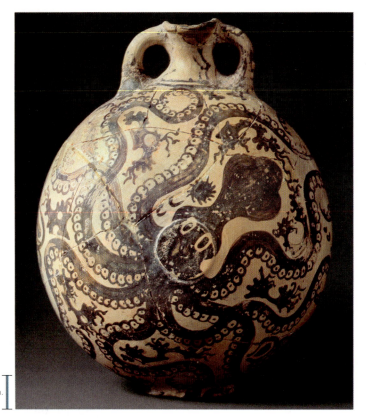

1 in.

2-7 Octopus jar, from Palaikastro (Crete), Greece, ca. 1500 BCE. 11″ high. Archaeological Museum, Herakleion.

The sea figures prominently in Minoan art. This painter perfectly matched the octopus motif to the shape of the vase. The sea creature's tentacles reach out to fill the curving surfaces of the vessel.

Minoan Pottery Minoan painters also decorated small objects, especially ceramic pots, usually employing dark silhouettes against a cream-colored background. On a jar (FIG. **2-7**) found at Palaikastro on Crete, the tentacles of an octopus spread out over the curving surfaces of the vessel, embracing the piece and emphasizing its volume. This is a masterful realization of the relationship between the vessel's decoration and its shape, always a problem for the ceramist.

Snake Goddess In contrast to the Mesopotamians and Egyptians, the Minoans seem to have erected no temples or monumental statues of gods, kings, or monsters, although large wooden images may once have existed. What remains of Minoan sculpture in the round is small in scale, such as the *faience* (low-fired glasslike silicate) statuette known as the *Snake Goddess* (FIG. **2-8**), found in the palace at Knossos. It is one of several similar figurines that some scholars believe may represent mortal attendants rather than deities, although the prominently exposed breasts suggest that these figurines stand in the long line of prehistoric fertility images usually considered divinities. (The Knossos woman holds snakes in her hands and supports a leopardlike feline peacefully on her head. This implied power over the animal world also seems appropriate for a deity.) The frontality of the figure is reminiscent of Egyptian and Near Eastern statuary, but the costume, with its open bodice and flounced skirt, is distinctly Minoan.

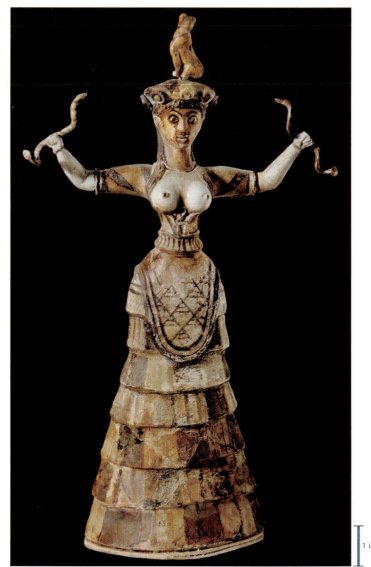

1 in.

2-8 *Snake Goddess*, from the palace at Knossos (Crete), Greece, ca. 1600 BCE. Faience, 1′ 1½″ high. Archaeological Museum, Herakleion.

This Minoan figurine may represent a priestess, but it is more likely a bare-breasted goddess. The snakes in her hands and the leopardlike feline on her head imply that she has power over the animal world.

Minoan Decline Scholars dispute the circumstances surrounding the end of Minoan civilization, although they now widely believe Mycenaeans had already moved onto Crete and established themselves at Knossos in the 15th century BCE. Parts of the palace continued to be occupied until its final destruction around 1200 BCE, but its importance as a cultural center faded soon after 1400 BCE, as the focus of Aegean civilization shifted to the Greek mainland.

Mycenaean Art

Scholars still debate the origins of the Mycenaeans. The only certainty is the presence of these forerunners of the historical Greeks at the beginning of the second millennium BCE. Some researchers believe the mainland was long a Minoan economic dependency, but by 1500 BCE a distinctive Mycenaean culture was flourishing in Greece.

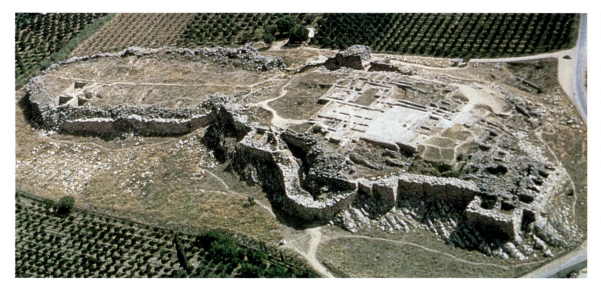

2-9 Aerial view of the citadel at Tiryns, Greece, ca. 1400–1200 BCE.

In the *Iliad,* Homer called the fortified citadel of Tiryns the City of the Great Walls. Its huge, roughly cut stone blocks are examples of Cyclopean masonry, named after the mythical one-eyed giants.

Tiryns The destruction of the Cretan palaces left the mainland culture supreme. Although this civilization has come to be called Mycenaean, Mycenae was but one of several large citadels. The best-preserved and most impressive Mycenaean remains are those of the fortified palaces at Tiryns and Mycenae. Construction of both began about 1400 BCE. Homer, writing in the mid-eighth century BCE, called the citadel of Tiryns (FIG. **2-9**), located about 10 miles from Mycenae, Tiryns of the Great Walls. In the second century CE, when Pausanias, author of an invaluable guidebook to Greece, visited the site, he marveled at the towering fortifications and considered the walls of Tiryns as spectacular as the pyramids of Egypt. Indeed, the Greeks of the historical age believed mere humans could not have erected such edifices and instead attributed the construction of the great Mycenaean citadels to the mythical *Cyclopes,* a race of one-eyed giants. Archaeologists still apply the term *Cyclopean masonry* to the huge, roughly cut stone blocks forming the massive fortification walls of Tiryns and other Mycenaean sites. The walls of Tiryns average about 20 feet in thickness and incorporate blocks often weighing several tons each. The heavily fortified Mycenaean palaces contrast sharply with the open Cretan palaces (FIG. **2-3**) and clearly reveal their defensive character.

Lion Gate, Mycenae The entrance to the citadel at Mycenae was the Lion Gate (FIG. **2-10**), protected on the left by a wall built on a natural rock outcropping and on the right by a projecting bastion of large blocks. Any approaching enemies would have had to enter this 20-foot-wide channel and face Mycenaean defenders above them on both sides. The gate itself consists of two great monoliths capped with a huge lintel. Above the lintel, the masonry courses form a *corbeled arch,* constructed by placing the blocks in horizontal courses and then cantilevering them inward until they meet, leaving an opening that lightens the weight carried by the lintel. The Mycenaean builders filled this *relieving triangle* with a great limestone slab where two lions carved in high relief stand on the sides of a Minoan-type column. The whole design admirably fills its triangular space, harmonizing in dignity, strength, and scale with the massive stones that form the walls and gate. Similar groups appear in miniature on Cretan seals, but the idea of placing monstrous guardian figures at the entrances to palaces, tombs, and sacred places has its origin in the Near East (FIGS. **1-18** and **1-25**). At Mycenae the animals' heads were fashioned separately and are lost. Some scholars have suggested that the "lions" were composite beasts in the Near Eastern tradition, possibly sphinxes.

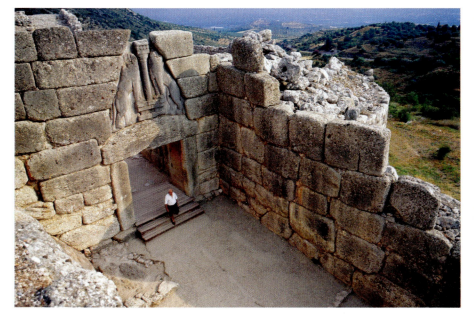

2-10 Lion Gate, Mycenae, Greece, ca. 1300–1250 BCE. Limestone, relief panel 9′ 6″ high.

The largest sculpture in the prehistoric Aegean is the relief panel with confronting lions that fills the relieving triangle of Mycenae's main gate. The gate itself consists of two great monoliths and a huge lintel.

Prehistoric Aegean Art | 53

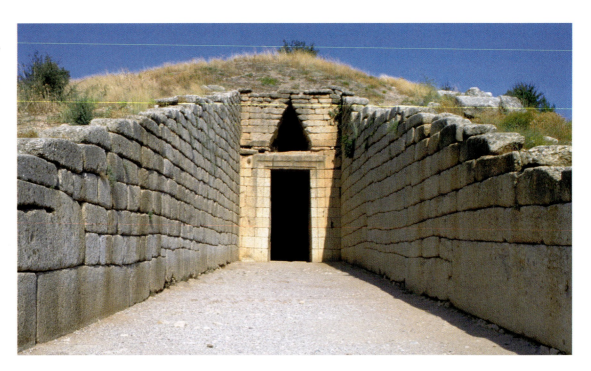

2-11 Treasury of Atreus, Mycenae, Greece, ca. 1300–1250 BCE.

The best-preserved tholos tomb outside the walls of Mycenae is named for Homer's King Atreus. An earthen mound covers the burial chamber, entered through a doorway at the end of a long passageway.

Treasury of Atreus The Mycenaeans erected the Lion Gate and the towering fortification wall circuit of which it formed a part a few generations before the presumed date of the Trojan War. At that time, wealthy Mycenaeans were laid to rest outside the citadel walls in tombs covered by enormous earthen mounds. The best preserved of these is the so-called Treasury of Atreus (FIG. **2-11**), which the later Greeks already mistakenly believed was the repository of the treasure of Atreus, father of King Agamemnon, who waged war against Troy. Approached by a long passageway, a doorway surmounted by a relieving triangle similar to that employed in the roughly contemporaneous Lion Gate led to the beehive-shaped tomb chamber *(tholos)*. Composed of a series of stone corbeled courses laid on a circular base, the tholos (FIG. **2-12**) has a lofty *dome*-shaped *vault*. The builders probably constructed the vault using rough-hewn blocks. After they set the stones in place, the masons had to finish the surfaces with great precision to make them conform to both the horizontal and vertical curves of the wall. The principle involved is no different from a corbeled arch, but the process of constructing a complete dome is much more complicated. About 43 feet high, the tholos of the Treasury of Atreus was the largest vaulted space without interior supports ever built before the Romans.

Gold Masks The Treasury of Atreus had been thoroughly looted long before its modern rediscovery, but excavators have made spectacular finds at graves elsewhere at Mycenae. Just inside the Lion Gate, but predating it by some three centuries, is the burial area archaeologists refer to as Grave Circle A. Here, at a site protected within the circuit of the later walls, six deep shafts served as tombs for kings and their families. The excavation of the royal shaft graves yielded many gold artifacts, including beaten *(repoussé)* gold funerary masks (FIG. **2-13**). (Homer described the Mycenaeans as "rich in gold.") Art historians often compare the Mycenaean mask

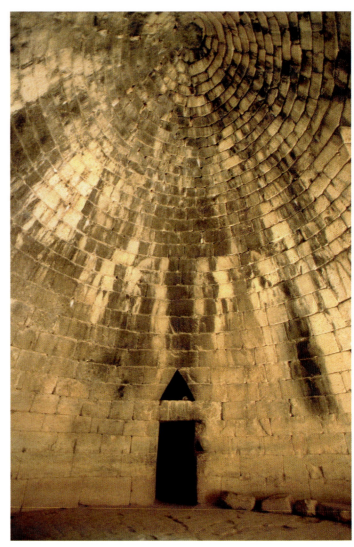

2-12 Interior of the tholos of the Treasury of Atreus, Mycenae, Greece, ca. 1300–1250 BCE.

The beehive-shaped tholos of the Treasury of Atreus is composed of corbeled courses of stone blocks laid on a circular base. The 43-foot-high dome was the largest in the ancient world for almost 1,500 years.

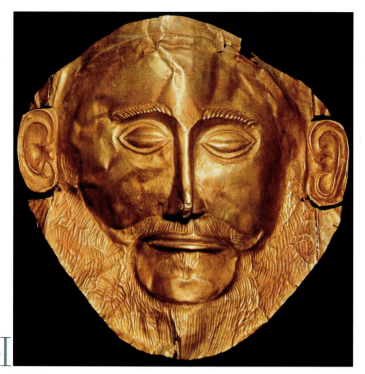

2-13 Funerary mask, from Grave Circle A, Mycenae, Greece, ca. 1600–1500 BCE. Gold, 1' high. National Archaeological Museum, Athens.

Homer described the Mycenaeans as "rich in gold." This repoussé gold mask of a bearded man comes from a royal shaft grave. It is one of the first attempts at life-size sculpture in Greece.

to Tutankhamen's gold mummy mask (FIG. 1-36). The treatment of the human face is, of course, more primitive in the Mycenaean mask. But this was one of the first known attempts in Greece to render the human face at life-size, whereas the Egyptian mask belongs to a long line of monumental sculptures dating back more than a millennium. Whether the Mycenean masks were intended as portraits is unknown, but the goldsmiths recorded different physical types with care. The illustrated mask, with its full beard, must depict a mature man, perhaps a king—although not Agamemnon, as its 19th-century discoverer wished. If Agamemnon was a real king, he lived some 300 years after the manufacture of this mask.

End of Mycenae Despite their mighty walls, the citadels of Mycenae and Tiryns were burned between 1250 and 1200 BCE, when the Mycenaeans seem to have been overrun by northern invaders or to have fallen victim to internal warfare. By Homer's time, the heyday of Aegean civilization was but a distant memory, and the men and women of Crete and Mycenae had assumed the stature of heroes from a lost golden age.

GREEK ART

Disintegration of the Bronze Age social order accompanied the destruction of the Mycenaean palaces. The disappearance of powerful kings and their retinues led to the loss of the knowledge of how to cut masonry, construct citadels and tombs, paint frescoes, and sculpt in stone. Even the arts of reading and writing were forgotten. Depopulation, poverty,

and an almost total loss of contact with the outside world characterized the succeeding centuries, sometimes called the Dark Age of Greece.

Geometric and Archaic Art

Only in the eighth century BCE did economic conditions improve and the population begin to grow again. This era was in its own way a heroic age, a time when the city-states of Greece took shape; when the Greeks broke out of their isolation and once again began to trade with their neighbors both in the east and the west; when Homer's epic poems, formerly memorized and passed down from bard to bard, were recorded in written form; and when the Olympic Games were established. Art historians call the art of this formative period *Geometric*, because Greek vase painting of the time consisted almost exclusively of abstract motifs.

Geometric Krater The eighth century also brought the return of the human figure to Greek art. One of the earliest examples of Geometric figure painting is found on a huge *krater* (FIG. 2-14), a bowl for mixing wine and water,

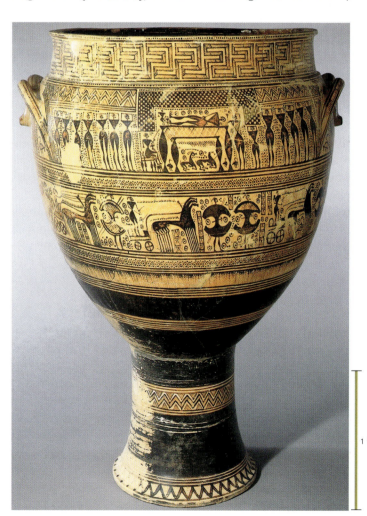

2-14 Geometric krater, from the Dipylon cemetery, Athens, Greece, ca. 740 BCE. 3' 4½" high. Metropolitan Museum of Art, New York.

Figure painting reappeared in Greece in the Geometric period, named for the abstract ornamentation on vessels like this funerary krater featuring a mourning scene and a procession in honor of the deceased.

that marked the grave of an Athenian man buried around 740 BCE. At well over a yard tall, this remarkable vase is a considerable technical achievement. Characteristically for this date, the artist covered much of the krater's surface with precisely painted, abstract angular motifs in horizontal bands. Especially prominent is the *meander* (key) pattern around the rim. But the Geometric painter reserved the widest part of the krater for two bands of human figures and horse-drawn chariots. Befitting the vase's function as a grave marker, the scenes depict the mourning for a man laid out on his bier and the grand chariot procession in his honor. The human figures and the furniture are as two-dimensional as the geometric shapes elsewhere on the vessel. For example, in the upper band, the shroud, raised to reveal the corpse, is an abstract checkerboard-like backdrop. Every empty space has circles and M-shaped ornamentation, further negating any sense that the mourners inhabit a three-dimensional world. The figures are silhouettes constructed of triangular (frontal) torsos with attached profile arms, legs, and heads (with a single large frontal eye in the center), following the age-old convention. To distinguish male from female, the painter added a penis growing out of one of the deceased's thighs. The mourning women, who tear their hair out in grief, have breasts emerging beneath their armpits. In both cases the artist's concern was to specify gender, not anatomical accuracy. Below are warriors, drawn as though they were walking shields, and several chariots. The horses have the correct number of heads and legs but seem to share a common body, countering any sense of depth. Despite the highly stylized and conventional manner of representation, this vessel marks a significant turning point in the history of Greek art. Not only did the human figure reenter the painter's repertoire, but vase painters also revived the art of storytelling.

Lady of Auxerre In the seventh century BCE, the first Greek stone sculptures since the Mycenaean Lion Gate (FIG. 2-10) began to appear. One of the earliest, probably originally from Crete, is a limestone statuette of a goddess or maiden (*kore*; plural, *korai*) popularly known as the *Lady of Auxerre* (FIG. 2-15) after the French town that is her oldest recorded location. Because she does not wear a headdress, as early Greek goddesses frequently do, and the gesture of her right hand probably signifies prayer, the *Lady of Auxerre* is most likely a kore. The style is characteristic of the early *Archaic* period, when Greek artists revived the art of monumental sculpture. The flat-topped head takes the form of a triangle framed by complementary triangles of four long strands of hair each. Also typical are the small belted waist and a fondness for pattern, seen, for example, in the almost Geometric treatment of the long skirt with its incised concentric squares, once brightly painted.

Art historians refer to this early Greek style as *Daedalic*, after the legendary artist Daedalus, whose name means "the skillful one." In addition to his renown as a great sculptor, Daedalus was credited with building the labyrinth of Knossos (FIG. 2-3) and designing a temple at Memphis in Egypt. The historical Greeks attributed to him almost all the great achievements in

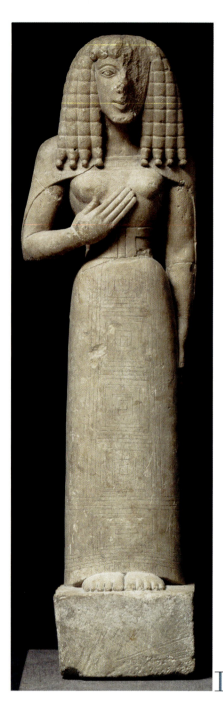

2-15 *Lady of Auxerre*, statue of a goddess or kore, ca. 650–625 BCE. Limestone, 2' 11" high. Louvre, Paris.

One of the earliest Greek stone sculptures, this kore (maiden) typifies the Daedalic style of the seventh century BCE with its triangular face and hair and lingering Geometric fondness for abstract pattern.

early sculpture and architecture. The story that Daedalus worked in Egypt reflects the enormous impact of Egyptian art and architecture on the Greeks.

Kouroi The first life-size Greek statues follow very closely the standard Egyptian format. A marble statue (FIG. 2-16) representing a *kouros* (youth; plural, *kouroi*) is typical in emulating the stance of Egyptian statues (FIG. 1-27). In both cases, the male figure is rigidly frontal with the left foot advanced slightly. The arms are close to the body, and the fists clenched with the thumbs forward. Greek kouros statues differ, however, from their Egyptian models in two important ways. First, the Greek sculptors liberated their figures from the original stone block. The Egyptian obsession with permanence was alien to the Greeks, who were preoccupied with finding ways to represent motion rather than stability in their statues. Second, the kouroi are nude, just as Greek athletes competed nude in the Olympic Games, and, in the absence of attributes, Greek youths as well as maidens are formally indistinguishable from Greek statues of deities.

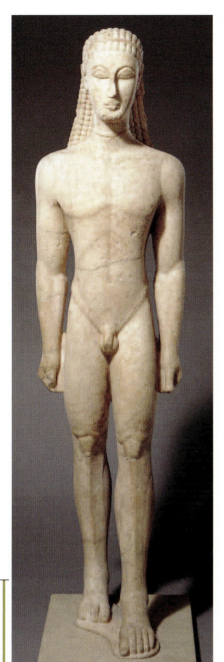

2-16

Kouros, ca. 600 BCE. Marble, 6' ½" high. Metropolitan Museum of Art, New York.

The earliest Greek life-size statues of kouroi (young men) adopt the Egyptian pose for standing figures (FIG. 1-27), but they are nude and free-standing, liberated from the original stone block.

1 ft.

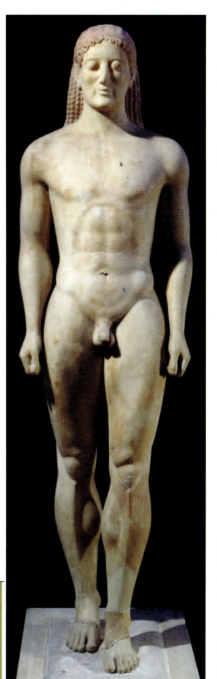

2-17

Kroisos, from Anavysos, Greece, ca. 530 BCE. Marble, 6' 4" high. National Archaeological Museum, Athens.

This later kouros displays increased naturalism in its proportions and more rounded modeling of face, torso, and limbs. Kroisos also smiles—the Archaic Greek sculptor's way of indicating life.

1 ft.

The illustrated kouros shares many traits with the *Lady of Auxerre* (FIG. 2-15), especially the triangular shape of head and hair and the flatness of the face—the hallmarks of the Daedalic style. Eyes, nose, and mouth all sit on the front of the head, and ears on the sides. The long hair forms a flat backdrop behind the head. These traits reflect the working method of the Greek sculptor, who drew the features on four independent sides of the marble block, following the same workshop procedure used in Egypt for millennia. The kouros also has the slim waist of earlier Greek statues and exhibits the same love of pattern. The pointed arch of the rib cage, for example, echoes the V-shaped ridge of the hips, which suggests but does not accurately reproduce the rounded flesh and muscle of the human body.

Kroisos Sometime around 530 BCE, a young man named Kroisos died a hero's death in battle, and his family marked his grave at Anavysos, not far from Athens, with a kouros statue (FIG. 2-17). Although the stance is the same as in the earlier kouros, the sculptor's rendition of human anatomy is more naturalistic. The head is no longer too large for the

body, and the face is more rounded, with swelling cheeks replacing the flat planes of the earlier head. The long hair does not form a stiff backdrop to the face but falls naturally over the back. Rounded hips replace the V-shaped ridges of the earlier statue. Also new is that Kroisos smiles—or seems to. From this time on, Archaic Greek statues always smile—even in the most inappropriate contexts (FIG. 2-29). Art historians have proposed various interpretations of this so-called *Archaic smile*, but the smile should not be taken literally. Rather, it is the Archaic sculptor's way of indicating that the person portrayed is alive. By adopting this convention, the Greek artist signaled a very different intention from Egyptian sculptors' objectives.

Some original paint survives on the Kroisos statue, enhancing the sense of life. Greek artists painted all their stone statues. The modern notion that Greek statuary was pure white is mistaken. The Greeks did not color their statues garishly, however. They left the flesh in the natural color of the stone, which was waxed and polished. They painted the eyes, lips, hair, and drapery in *encaustic*, a technique in which pigment is mixed with hot wax and applied it to the statue.

Greek Art | 57

Unlike men, women are never nude in Archaic art. This smiling statue was a votive offering on the Athenian Acropolis. The woman once held an attribute in her left hand, perhaps identifying her as Athena.

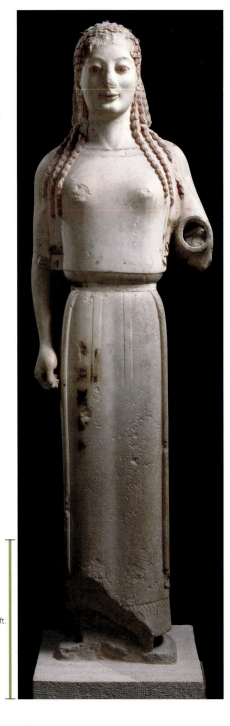

1 ft.

arms, and feet, the sixth-century sculptor rendered the soft female form much more naturally. This softer treatment of the flesh also sharply differentiates later korai from contemporaneous kouroi, which have hard, muscular bodies.

Greek Temples Egypt also had a profound impact on Greek architecture. Shortly after the founding of a Greek trading colony at Naukratis (MAP 1-3) around 650–630 BCE, the Greeks began constructing the first stone buildings since the fall of the Mycenaean kingdoms. Although Greek temples cannot be confused with Egyptian buildings, columnar halls such as that at Karnak (FIG. 1-32) clearly inspired Greek architects.

The basic plan of all Greek temples (see "Doric and Ionic Temples," page 59) reveals an order, compactness, and symmetry that reflect the Greeks' sense of proportion and their effort to achieve ideal forms in terms of regular numerical relationships and geometric rules. The earliest temples tended to be long and narrow, with the proportion of the ends to the sides roughly expressible as a 1:3 ratio. From the sixth century on, temples became slightly longer than twice their width. To the Greek mind, proportion in architecture and sculpture was much the same as harmony in music, reflecting and embodying the cosmic order. The history of Greek temple architecture is the history of Greek architects' unflagging efforts to find the most satisfactory (that is, what they believed were perfect) proportions for each part of the building and for the structure as a whole.

The Greeks gathered outside, not inside, their temples to worship. The altar always lay outside the temple—at the east end, facing the rising sun. The temple proper (FIG. 2-19) housed the *cult statue* of the deity, the grandest of all votive offerings. Both in its early and mature manifestations, the Greek temple was the house of the god or goddess, not of his or her followers.

Figural sculpture played a major role in the exterior program of the Greek temple from early times. Sculptural ornamentation was concentrated in the frieze and pediments. Architectural sculpture, like freestanding statuary, was painted and usually placed only in the building parts that had no structural function. This is true particularly of the Doric order, where decorative sculpture appears only in the metope and pediment "voids." Ionic builders, less severe in this respect as well, were willing to decorate the entire frieze. Occasionally, they replaced their columns with female figures (*caryatids*; FIG. 2-42). The Greeks often painted the capitals, decorative moldings, and other architectural elements. By adding color to parts of the building, the designer could bring out more clearly the relationships of the structural parts and soften the stone's glitter at specific points, as well as provide a background to set off the figures.

Temple of Hera, Paestum The prime example of early Greek efforts at Doric temple design (FIG. 2-20, *left*) is not in Greece but in Italy, at Paestum. The Archaic temple

Peplos Kore A stylistic "sister" to the Anavysos kouros, also with paint preserved, is the smiling *Peplos Kore* (FIG. 2-18), so called because she wears a *peplos,* a simple long, woolen belted garment that gives the female figure a columnar appearance. The kore's missing left arm was extended, a break from the frontal compression of the arms at the sides in Egyptian statues. She once held in her hand an attribute that would identify the figure as a maiden or, as some have suggested, a goddess, perhaps Athena herself, because the statue was a votive offering in that goddess's sanctuary in Athens. Whoever the *Peplos Kore* represents, the contrast with the *Lady of Auxerre* (FIG. 2-15) is striking. Although in both cases the drapery conceals the entire body save for head,

Doric and Ionic Temples

The plan and elevation of Greek temples varied with date, geography, and the requirements of individual projects, but Greek temples have common defining elements that set them apart from both the religious edifices of other civilizations and other types of Greek buildings.

■ **Plan** (FIG. 2-19) The temple core was the *naos,* or *cella,* which housed the cult statue of the deity. In front was a *pronaos,* or porch, often with two columns between the *antae,* or extended walls (columns *in antis,* that is, between the antae). A smaller second room might be placed behind the cella, but more frequently the Greek temple had a porch at the rear *(opisthodomos)* set against the blank back wall of the cella. The purpose was not functional but decorative, intended to satisfy the Greek passion for balance and symmetry. A colonnade could be placed across the front of the temple (*prostyle;* FIG. 2-42), across both front and back (*amphiprostyle;* FIG. 2-43), or, more commonly, all around the cella and its porch(es) to form a *peristyle,* as in FIGS. 2-19, 2-21, and 2-36.

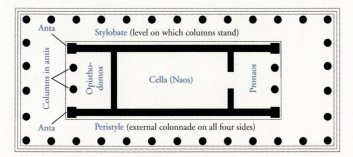

2-19   Plan of a typical Greek peripteral temple.

Greek temples had peripteral colonnades and housed cult statues of the gods in the central room, or cella. Worshipers gathered outside the temples, where priests made offerings at open-air altars.

■ **Elevation** (FIG. 2-20) The elevation of a Greek temple consists of the platform, the colonnade, and the superstructure *(entablature).* In the Archaic period, two basic systems evolved for articulating the three units. These are the so-called *orders* of Greek architecture. The orders differ both in the nature of the details and in the relative proportions of the parts. The names of the orders derive from the Greek regions where they were most commonly employed. The *Doric* (FIG. 2-20, *left*) was formulated on the mainland and remained the preferred manner there and in the western colonies of the Greeks. The *Ionic* (FIG. 2-20, *right*) was the order of choice in the Aegean Islands and on the western coast of Asia Minor. The geographical distinctions are by no means absolute. The Ionic order was, for example, often used in Athens.

In both orders, the columns rest on the *stylobate,* the uppermost course of the platform. The columns have two or three parts, depending on the order: the *shaft,* which is marked with vertical channels *(flutes);* the *capital;* and, in the Ionic order, the *base.* Greek column shafts, in contrast to their Minoan and Mycenaean forebears, taper gradually from bottom to top. The capital has two elements. The lower part (the *echinus*) varies with the order. In the Doric, it is convex and cushionlike, similar to the echinus of Minoan (FIG. 2-4) and Mycenaean (FIG. 2-10) capitals. In the Ionic, it is small and supports a bolster ending in spirals (the *volutes*). The upper element, present in both orders, is a flat block (the *abacus*) that provides the immediate support for the entablature.

The entablature has three parts: the *architrave,* or *epistyle,* the main weight-bearing and weight-distributing element; the *frieze;* and the *cornice,* a molded horizontal projection that together with two sloping *(raking)* cornices forms a triangle that frames the *pediment.* In the Ionic order, the architrave is usually subdivided into three horizontal bands *(fasciae).* In the Doric order, the frieze is subdivided into *triglyphs* (triple vertical projections) and *metopes* (the square plaques between the triglyphs), whereas the Ionic architects left the frieze open to provide a continuous field for relief sculpture.

The Doric order is massive in appearance, its sturdy columns firmly planted on the stylobate. Compared with the weighty and severe Doric, the Ionic order seems light, airy, and much more decorative. Its columns are more slender and rise from molded bases. The most obvious differences between the two orders are, of course, in the capitals—the Doric, severely plain, and the Ionic, highly ornamental.

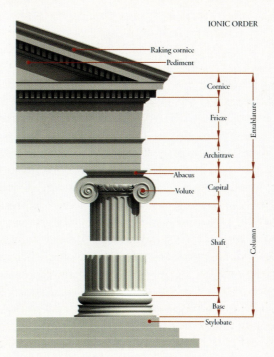

2-20   Elevations of the Doric and Ionic orders.

The major orders of Greek architecture were the Doric and Ionic. They differ primarily in the form of the capitals and the treatment of the frieze. The Doric frieze is divided into triglyphs and metopes.

2-21 Temple of Hera ("Basilica"), Paestum, Italy, ca. 550 BCE.

The peristyle of this huge early Doric temple consists of heavy, closely spaced cigar-shaped columns with bulky, pancakelike capitals, characteristic features of Archaic Greek architecture.

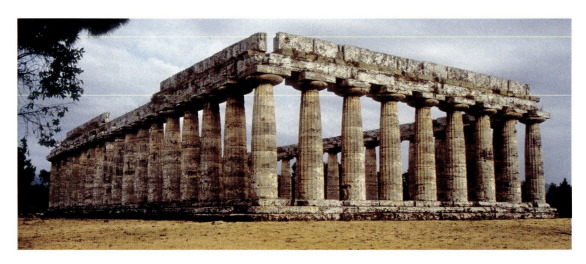

erected there around 550 BCE retains its entire *peripteral* colonnade, but most of the entablature, including the frieze, pediment, and all of the roof, has vanished. Called the Basilica after the Roman columnar hall building type that early investigators felt it resembled, the huge (80 × 170 feet) structure was really a temple of Hera (FIG. **2-21**). The misnomer stems from the building's plan (FIG. **2-22**), which differs from that of most other Greek temples. The unusual feature, found only in early Archaic temples, is the central row of columns that divides the cella into two aisles. Placing columns underneath the *ridgepole* (the timber beam running the length of the building below the peak of the gabled roof) might seem the logical way to provide interior support for the roof structure. But it resulted in several disadvantages. Among these was that this interior arrangement allowed no place for a central statue of the deity to whom the temple was dedicated. Also, the peripteral colonnade, in order to correspond with the interior, had to have an odd number of columns (nine in this case) across the building's facade. At Paestum, the builders also set three columns in antis instead of the standard two, which in turn ruled out a central doorway for viewing the statue. However, the designer achieved a simple 1:2 ratio of facade and flank columns by erecting 18 columns on each side of the temple.

The peristyle consists of heavy, closely spaced columns with a pronounced swelling *(entasis)* at the middle of the shafts, giving the columns a profile akin to that of a cigar. Topping the shafts are large, bulky, pancakelike Doric capitals, which seem compressed by the overbearing weight of the entablature. The columns and capitals thus vividly reveal their weight-bearing function. The heaviness of the design and the narrowness of the spans between the columns probably reflect the Archaic builders' fear that the superstructure would collapse if the columns were thinner and more widely spaced. In later Doric temples, builders placed the columns farther apart, and the shafts became more slender, the entasis subtler, the capitals smaller, and the entablature lighter.

Temple of Artemis, Corfu Even older than the Paestum temple is the Doric temple of Artemis at Corfu, which dates to the early sixth century BCE. The building is unfortu-

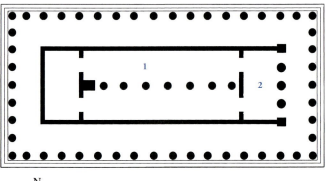

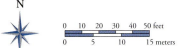

1. Cella with central row of columns
2. Pronaos with three columns in antis

2-22 Plan of the Temple of Hera, Paestum, Italy, ca. 550 BCE.

The plan of the Hera temple also reveals its early date. It has an odd number of columns on the facade and a single row of columns in the cella, allowing no place for a central statue of the goddess.

nately in ruins, but most of the sculpture that embellished its pediments (FIG. **2-23**) survives. Designing figural decoration for a pediment was never an easy task for the Greek sculptor because of the pediment's awkward triangular shape. The central figures had to be of great size (more than nine feet tall at Corfu). As the pediment tapered toward the corners, the available area became increasingly cramped.

At the center of the Corfu pediment is the *gorgon* Medusa, a demon with a woman's body and bird wings. Medusa also had a hideous face and snake hair, and anyone who gazed at her turned to stone. The sculptor depicted her in the conventional Archaic bent-leg, bent-arm, pinwheel-like posture that signifies running or, for a winged creature, flying. To her left and right are two great felines. Together they serve as temple guardians, repulsing all enemies from the sanctuary of the goddess. Between Medusa and the great beasts are two small figures—the human Chrysaor at her left and the winged horse Pegasus at her right (only the rear legs remain). Chrysaor and Pegasus were Medusa's children. They sprang from her head when the Greek hero Perseus severed it with his sword. Their presence here with the living Medusa is therefore a chrono-

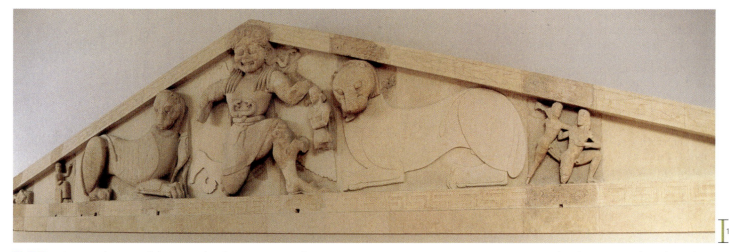

2-23 West pediment of the Temple of Artemis, Corfu, Greece, ca. 600–580 BCE. Limestone, greatest height 9′ 4″ Archaeological Museum, Corfu.

The hideous Medusa and two panthers at the center of this very early pediment serve as temple guardians. To either side, and at much smaller scale, are scenes from the Trojan War and the battle of gods and giants.

logical impossibility. The Archaic artist was not interested in telling a coherent story but in identifying the central figure by depicting her offspring.

In contrast, narration was the purpose of the much smaller groups situated in the pediment corners. To the viewer's right is Zeus, brandishing his thunderbolt and slaying a kneeling giant. In the extreme corner was a dead giant. The *gigantomachy* (battle of gods and giants) was a popular Greek theme that was a metaphor for the triumph of reason and order over chaos. In the pediment's left corner is one of the climactic events of the Trojan War: Achilles' son Neoptolemos kills the enthroned King Priam. The fallen figure to the left of this group may be a dead Trojan.

The master responsible for the Corfu pediments was a pioneer, and the composition shows all the signs of experimentation. The lack of narrative unity in the Corfu pediment and the extraordinary scale diversity of the figures eventually gave way to pedimental designs with figures all acting out a single event and appearing the same size. But the Corfu designer already had shown the way, realizing, for example, that the area beneath the raking cornice could be filled with gods and heroes of similar size if a combination of standing, leaning, kneeling, seated, and prostrate figures were employed in the composition. Also, the Corfu master discovered that animals could be useful space fillers because, unlike humans, they have one end taller than the other.

Black-Figure Painting Greek artists also pioneered a new ceramic painting technique during the Archaic period. Invented in Corinth, *black-figure painting* quickly replaced the simpler silhouette painting favored in the Geometric period. The black-figure painter

did put down black silhouettes on the clay surface, but then used a *graver* (a sharp, pointed instrument) to incise linear details within the forms, usually adding highlights in purplish red or white over the black figures before firing the vessel. The combination of the weighty black silhouettes with the delicate detailing and the bright polychrome overlay proved to be irresistible, and painters in other Greek cities soon copied the technique from the Corinthians.

Exekias The acknowledged master of the black-figure technique was an Athenian named EXEKIAS. An *amphora*, or two-handled storage jar (FIG. **2-24**), found at Vulci, an

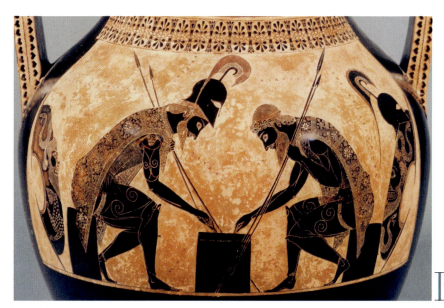

2-24 EXEKIAS, Achilles and Ajax playing a dice game (detail of a black-figure amphora), from Vulci, Italy, ca. 540–530 BCE. Whole vessel 2′ high; detail 8½″ high. Musei Vaticani, Rome.

The dramatic tension, adjustment of the figures' poses to the shape of the vase, and extraordinary intricacy of the engraved details are hallmarks of Exekias, the greatest master of black-figure painting.

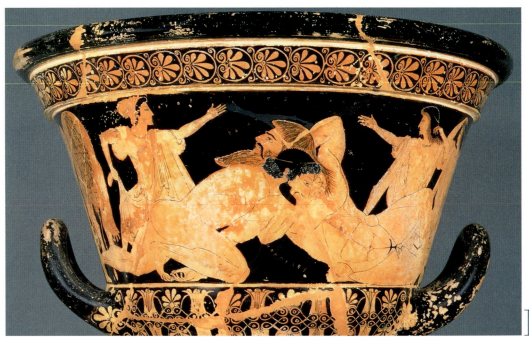

2-25 EUPHRONIOS, Herakles wrestling Antaios (detail of a red-figure calyx krater), from Cerveteri, Italy, ca. 510 BCE. Whole vessel 1′ 7″ high; detail, 7¾″ high. Louvre, Paris.

The early red-figure master Euphronios rejected the age-old composite view for painted figures and instead attempted to reproduce how a person sees the human body from a particular viewpoint.

Etruscan city in Italy, bears his signature as both painter and potter. Such signatures, common on Greek vases, reveal both pride and a sense of self-identity as an "artist." They also served as "brand names" because the ceramic workshops of Athens and Corinth exported their vases widely. Unlike his Geometric predecessors, Exekias used figures of monumental stature and placed them in a single large framed panel. At the left is Achilles, fully armed. He plays a dice game with his comrade Ajax. Ajax has removed his helmet, but both men hold their spears and their shields are nearby. Each man is ready for action at a moment's notice. The gravity and tension that characterize this composition are rare in Archaic art.

Exekias had no equal as a black-figure painter. Note, for example, the extraordinarily intricate engraving of the patterns on the heroes' cloaks (highlighted with delicate touches of white). The composition is also masterful. The arch formed by the backs of the two warriors echoes the shape of the rounded shoulders of the amphora. The shape of the vessel is echoed again in the void between the men's heads and spears. Exekias also used the spears to lead the viewer's eyes toward the thrown dice, where the heroes' eyes are fixed. Of course, those eyes do not really look down at the table but stare out from the profile heads in the old manner. For all his brilliance, Exekias was still wedded to many of the old conventions. Real innovation in figure drawing would have to await the invention of a new ceramic painting technique of greater versatility than black-figure.

Red-Figure Painting The birth of this new technique, called *red-figure painting*, came around 530 BCE. Red-figure is the opposite of black-figure: What was previously black became red, and vice versa. The artist still employed the same black *glaze*. But instead of using the glaze to create the silhouettes of figures, the painter outlined the figures and then colored the background black, reserving the red clay for the figures themselves. For the interior details, the artist

used a soft brush in place of a metal graver. This permitted the painter to vary the glaze thickness, building it up to give relief to hair curls or diluting it to create brown shades, thereby expanding the chromatic range of the Greek vase painter's craft.

Euphronios One of the most admired red-figure painters was EUPHRONIOS, whose krater depicting the struggle between Herakles (Roman Hercules), the greatest Greek hero, and the giant Antaios (FIG. 2-25) reveals the exciting possibilities of the new technique. Antaios was a son of Earth, and he derived his power from contact with the ground. To defeat him, Herakles had to lift him into the air and strangle him while no part of the giant's body touched the earth. Here, the two wrestle on the ground, and Antaios still possesses enormous strength. Nonetheless, Herakles has the upper hand. The giant's face is a mask of pain. His eyes roll and he bares his teeth. His right arm is paralyzed, with the fingers limp.

Euphronios used diluted glaze to show Antaios's un-kempt, golden-brown hair—intentionally contrasted with Herakles' neat coiffure and carefully trimmed beard—and to delineate the muscles of both figures. But rendering human anatomy convincingly was not his only interest. Euphronios also wished to show that his figures occupy space. He deliberately rejected the conventional composite posture for the human figure and attempted to reproduce how a viewer actually sees a particular human body. He presented, for example, not only Antaios's torso but also his right thigh from the front. The lower leg disappears behind the giant, and only part of the right foot is visible. The viewer must mentally make the connection between the upper leg and the foot. Euphronios's panel is a window onto a mythological world with protagonists occupying three-dimensional space—a revolutionary new conception of what a picture is supposed to be.

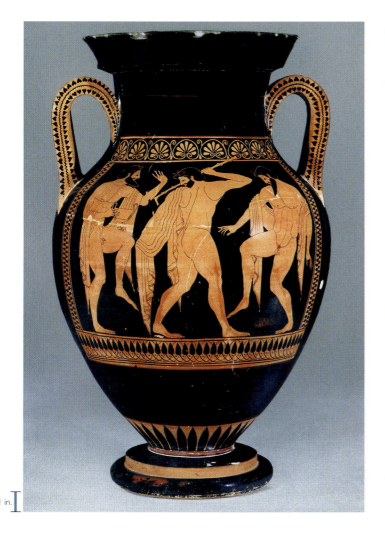

2-26 EUTHYMIDES, Three revelers (red-figure amphora), from Vulci, Italy, ca. 510 BCE. 2′ high. Staatliche Antikensammlungen, Munich.

Euthymides chose this theme in order to represent the human form in unusual positions, including a foreshortened view from the rear. He claimed he surpassed Euphronios as a draftsman.

theme was little more than an excuse for the artist to experiment with representing unusual positions of the human form. It is no coincidence that the bodies do not overlap, for each is an independent figure study. Euthymides cast aside the conventional frontal and profile composite views. Instead, he painted torsos that are not two-dimensional surface patterns but are *foreshortened*, that is, drawn in a three-quarter view. Most noteworthy is the central figure, which Euthymides depicted from the rear with a twisting spinal column and buttocks in three-quarter view. Earlier artists had no interest in attempting such postures because they not only are incomplete but also do not show the "main" side of the human body. For Euthymides, however, the challenge of drawing the figure from such an unusual viewpoint was a reward in itself. With understandable pride he proclaimed his achievement by adding to the formulaic signature "Euthymides painted me" the phrase "as never Euphronios [could do]!"

Temple of Aphaia, Aegina The years just before and after 500 BCE were a time of dynamic transition also in architecture and architectural sculpture. The key monument is the temple (FIG. **2-27**) dedicated to Aphaia, a local goddess, at Aegina. The colonnade is 45 × 95 feet and consists of 6 Doric columns on the facade and 12 on the flanks. This structure is much more compact than the impressive but ungainly Archaic Temple of Hera at Paestum (FIGS. **2-21**

Euthymides A preoccupation with the art of drawing per se is evident in a remarkable amphora (FIG. **2-26**) painted by EUTHYMIDES, one of Euphronios's rivals. The subject is appropriate for a wine storage jar—three tipsy revelers. But the

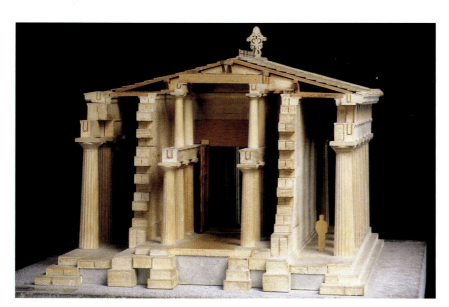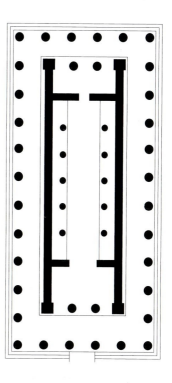

2-27 Model *(left)* and plan *(right)* of the Temple of Aphaia, Aegina, Greece, ca. 500–490 BCE. Model in Glyptothek, Munich.

In this refined Doric design, the columns are more slender and widely spaced, there are only six columns on the facade, and the cella has two colonnades of two stories each framing the cult statue.

Greek Art | 63

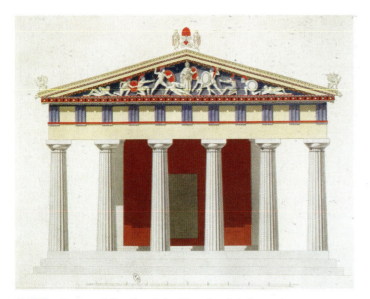

2-28 Restored facade of the Temple of Aphaia, Aegina, Greece, ca. 500–490 BCE (Guillaume-Abel Blouet, 1828).

The Aegina sculptors solved the problem of placing figures in a pediment by using the whole range of postures from upright to leaning, falling, kneeling, and lying. Only Athena is larger than the rest.

and 2-22), even though the ratio of width to length is similar. Doric architects had learned a great deal in the half century that elapsed between construction of the two temples. The columns of the Aegina temple are more widely spaced and more slender. The capitals create a smooth transition from the vertical shafts below to the horizontal architrave above. Gone are the Archaic flattened echinuses and bulging

shafts of the Paestum columns. The Aegina architect also refined the temple plan and internal elevation. In place of a single row of columns down the cella's center is a double colonnade—and each row has two stories. This arrangement allowed the placement of a statue on the central axis and also gave those gathered in front of the building an unobstructed view through the pair of columns in the pronaos.

Painted life-size statuary filled both of the Aegina temple's pediments (FIG. 2-28). The two statuary groups depicted the same subject and had similar compositions. The theme was the battle of Greeks and Trojans, with Athena at the center. She is larger than all the other figures because she is superhuman, but all the mortal heroes are the same size, regardless of their position in the pediment. Unlike the experimental design at Corfu (FIG. 2-23), the Aegina pediments feature a unified theme and consistent scale. The designer achieved the latter by using the whole range of body postures from upright (Athena) to leaning, falling, kneeling, and lying (Greeks and Trojans).

The sculptures of the west pediment were set in place upon completion of the building around 490 BCE. The eastern statues are a decade or two later in date. Comparison of the earlier and later figures is instructive. The sculptor of the west pediment's dying warrior (FIG. 2-29) still conceived the figure in the Archaic mode. The torso is rigidly frontal, and the warrior looks out directly at the spectator—and smiles, in spite of the bronze arrow that punctures his chest. He is like a mannequin in a store window whose arms and legs have been arranged by someone else for effective display. The comparable figure (FIG. 2-30) in the later east pediment is radically different. Not only is his posture more

2-29 Dying warrior, from the west pediment of the Temple of Aphaia, Aegina, Greece, ca. 500–490 BCE. Marble, 5′ 2½″ long. Glyptothek, Munich.

The two sets of Aegina pediment statues were installed 10 to 20 years apart. The earlier statues exhibit Archaic features. This fallen warrior still has a rigidly frontal torso and an Archaic smile.

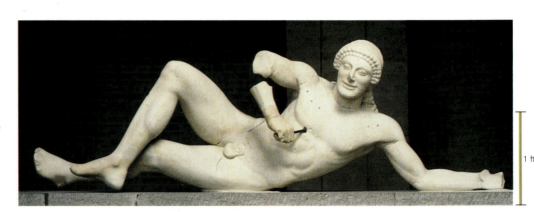

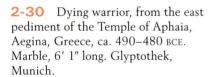

2-30 Dying warrior, from the east pediment of the Temple of Aphaia, Aegina, Greece, ca. 490–480 BCE. Marble, 6′ 1″ long. Glyptothek, Munich.

This later dying warrior already belongs to the Classical era. His posture is more natural, and he exhibits a new self-consciousness. Concerned with his own pain, he does not face the viewer.

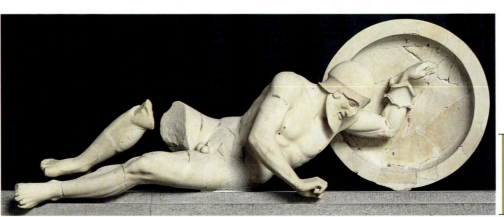

1 ft.

natural and more complex, with the torso placed at an angle to the viewer—he is on a par with the painted figures of Euphronios (FIG. 2-25)—but he also reacts to his wound. He knows death is inevitable, but he still struggles to rise once again, using his shield for support. And he does not look out at the viewer. He is concerned with his pain, nothing else. The two statues belong to different eras. The later warrior is not a creation of the Archaic world, when sculptors imposed anatomical patterns (and smiles) on statues from without. It belongs to the Classical world, where statues move as humans move and possess the self-consciousness of real men and women. This was a radical change in the conception of what a statue should be. In sculpture, as in painting, the Classical revolution had occurred.

Early and High Classical Art

Art historians mark the beginning of the *Classical** age from a historical event—the defeat of the Persian invaders of Greece by the allied Hellenic city-states. Shortly after the sack of Athens in 480 BCE, the Greeks won a decisive naval victory over the Persians at Salamis. It had been a difficult war, and it had seemed at times as though Asia would swallow up Greece, and the Persian king Xerxes (see Chapter 1) would rule over all. The sense of Hellenic identity became so strong after that close escape from domination by Asian "barbarians" that thereafter the civilizations of Europe and Asia took distinctly separate paths. Historians universally consider the decades following the defeat of the Persians as the high point of Greek civilization. This is the era of the dramatists Aeschylus, Sophocles, and Euripides, the historian Herodotus, the statesman Pericles, the philosopher Socrates, and many of the most famous Greek architects, sculptors, and painters.

Kritios Boy The sculptures of the Early Classical period (ca. 480–450 BCE) display a seriousness that contrasts sharply with the smiling figures of the Archaic period. But a more fundamental and significant break from the Archaic style was the rejection of the rigid and unnatural Egyptian-inspired pose of Archaic statuary. The marble statue known as the *Kritios Boy* (FIG. 2-31), so named because scholars once thought it was the work of the sculptor Kritios, is the earliest manifestation of the new style. Never before had a sculptor been concerned with portraying how a human being, as opposed to a stone image, actually stands. Real people do not stand in the stiff-legged pose of the kouroi and korai or their Egyptian predecessors. Humans shift their weight and the position of the main body parts around the vertical, but flexible, axis of the spine. The *Kritios Boy* sculptor was among the first to grasp this fact and to represent it in statuary. The

* In *Art through the Ages*, the adjective "Classical," with uppercase C, refers specifically to the Classical period of ancient Greece, 480–323 BCE. Lowercase "classical" refers to Greco-Roman antiquity in general, that is, the period treated in Chapters 2 and 3.

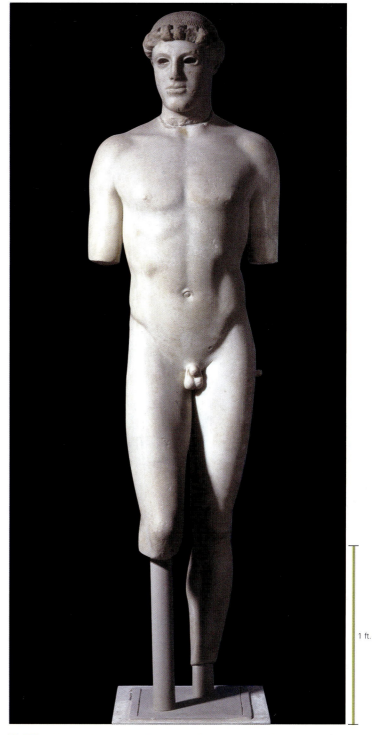

2-31 *Kritios Boy*, from the Acropolis, Athens, Greece, ca. 480 BCE. Marble, 3' 10" high. Acropolis Museum, Athens.

This is the first statue to show how a person really stands. The sculptor represented the figure shifting weight from one leg to the other (contrapposto). The head also turns slightly—and does not smile.

youth has a slight dip to the right hip, indicating the shifting of weight onto his left leg. His right leg is bent, at ease. The head also turns slightly to the right and tilts, breaking the unwritten rule of frontality that dictated the form of virtually all earlier statues. This weight shift, which art historians describe as *contrapposto* (counterbalance), separates Classical from Archaic Greek statuary.

Hollow-Casting Life-Size Bronze Statues

Monumental bronze statues could not be manufactured using a single simple mold, as could small-scale figures. Weight, cost, and the tendency of large masses of bronze to distort when cooling made life-size castings in solid bronze impractical, if not impossible. Instead, sculptors hollow-cast large statues by the *cire perdue* (lost-wax) method. The *lost-wax process* entailed several steps and had to be repeated many times, because bronze workers typically cast monumental statues like the Riace warrior (FIG. 2-32) in parts—head, arms, hands, torso, and so forth.

First, the sculptor fashioned a full-size clay model

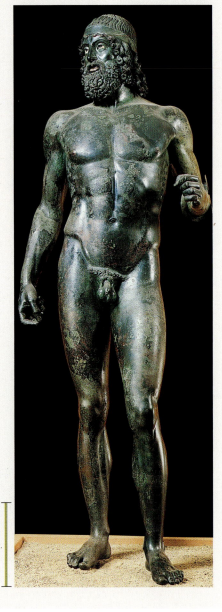

2-32 Warrior, from the sea off Riace, Italy, ca. 460–450 BCE. Bronze, 6′ 6″ high. Museo Archeologico Nazionale, Reggio Calabria.

One of the few surviving Classical bronze statues, the Riace warrior has inlaid eyes, silver teeth and eyelashes, and copper lips and nipples. The sculptor cast the various body parts in individual molds.

1 ft.

of the intended statue. Then a master mold of clay was formed around the model and removed in sections. When dry, the various pieces of the master mold were put back together for each separate body part. Next, a layer of beeswax was applied to the inside of each mold piece. When the wax cooled, the mold was removed, and the sculptor was left with a hollow wax model in the shape of the original clay model. The artist could then correct or refine details—for example, engrave fingernails on the hands, or individual locks of hair on the head.

In the next stage, a final clay mold *(investment)* was applied to the exterior of the wax model, and a liquid clay core was poured inside the hollow wax. The bronze worker then drove metal pins *(chaplets)* through the new mold to connect the investment with the clay core (FIG. 2-33*a*). Next the wax was melted out ("lost") and molten bronze poured into the mold in its place (FIG. 2-33*b*). When the bronze hardened and assumed the shape of the wax model, the sculptor removed the investment and as much of the core as possible. Finally, the artist fit together and soldered the individually cast pieces, smoothed surface imperfections and joins, inlaid eyes, added teeth and eyelashes, provided attributes such as spears and wreaths, and so forth.

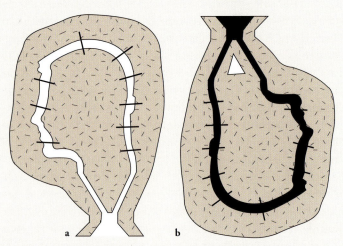

a   b

2-33 Two stages of the lost-wax method of bronze casting (after Sean A. Hemingway).

Drawing *a* shows a clay mold (investment), wax model, and clay core connected by chaplets. Drawing *b* shows the wax melted out and the molten bronze poured into the mold to form the cast-bronze head.

Riace Warrior The innovations of the *Kritios Boy* were carried even further in the bronze statue (FIG. 2-32) of a warrior found in the sea near Riace, Italy. It is one of a pair of almost perfectly preserved statues discovered in a ship that sank in antiquity on its way from Greece probably to Rome. The statue lacks only its shield, spear, and helmet. It is a masterpiece of hollow-casting (see "Hollow-Casting Life-Size Bronze Statues," above), with inlaid eyes, silver teeth and eyelashes, and copper lips and nipples. The weight shift is more pronounced than in the *Kritios Boy*. The warrior's

head turns more forcefully to the right, his shoulders tilt, his hips swing more markedly, and his arms have been freed from the body. Natural motion in space has replaced Archaic frontality and rigidity.

Myron, *Diskobolos* The *Kritios Boy* and the Riace warrior stand at rest, but Early Classical Greek sculptors also explored how to represent figures engaged in vigorous action. The famous *Diskobolos (Discus Thrower)* by MYRON (FIG. 2-1), with its arms boldly extended, body twisted, and left heel raised off the ground, is such a statue. Nothing comparable survives from the Archaic period. The pose suggests the motion of a pendulum clock. The athlete's right arm has reached the apex of its arc but has not yet begun to swing down again. Myron froze the action and arranged the body and limbs to form two intersecting arcs, creating the impression of a tightly stretched bow a moment before the string is released.

The illustrated marble statue, however, is not Myron's, which was bronze. It is a copy made in Roman times. Roman demand for famous Greek statues so far exceeded the supply that it spawned a veritable industry to meet the Roman call for copies to be displayed in both public and private venues. The sculptors usually made the copies in less costly marble, and the change in medium resulted in a different surface appearance. In most cases, the copyist also had to add an intrusive tree trunk to support the great weight of the stone statue and insert struts between arms and body to strengthen weak points. The copies rarely approach the quality of the originals, but they are indispensable today. Without them it would be impossible to reconstruct the history of Greek sculpture after the Archaic period.

Polykleitos, *Doryphoros* One of the most frequently copied Greek statues was the *Doryphoros* (*Spear Bearer*, FIG. 2-34) by POLYKLEITOS, a work that epitomizes the intellectual rigor of High Classical (ca. 450–400 BCE) statuary design. The *Doryphoros* is the culmination of the evolution in Greek statuary from the Archaic kouros to the *Kritios Boy* to the Riace warrior. The contrapposto is more pronounced than ever before in a standing statue, but Polykleitos was not content with simply rendering a figure that stands naturally. His aim was to impose order on human movement, to make it "beautiful," to "perfect" it. He achieved this through a system of cross balance of the figure's various parts. Note, for instance, how the straight-hanging arm echoes the rigid supporting leg, providing the figure's right side with the columnar stability needed to anchor the left side's dynamically flexed limbs. The tensed and relaxed limbs oppose each other diagonally. The right arm and the left leg are relaxed, and the tensed supporting leg opposes the flexed arm, which held a spear. In like manner, the head turns to the right while the hips twist slightly to the left. Although the *Doryphoros* seems to take a step forward, he does not move. This dynamic asymmetrical balance, this motion while at rest, and the resulting harmony of opposites are the essence of the Polykleitan style.

Polykleitos made the *Doryphoros* as a demonstration piece to accompany his treatise on the ideal statue of a nude man. *Spear Bearer* is but a modern descriptive name for the work. The title the artist assigned to the statue was *Canon*. Polykleitos was greatly influenced by the philosopher Pythagoras of Samos, who lived during the latter part of the sixth century BCE. A famous geometric theorem still bears his name. Pythagoras also discovered that harmonic chords in music are produced on the strings of a lyre at regular intervals that may be expressed as ratios of whole numbers—

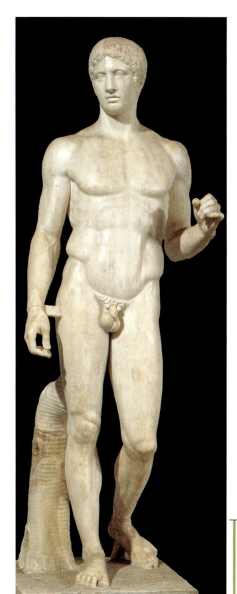

2:1, 3:2, 4:3. He and his followers, the Pythagoreans, believed more generally that underlying harmonic proportions could be found in all of nature, determining the form of the cosmos as well as of things on earth, and that beauty resided in harmonious numerical ratios. By this reasoning, a perfect statue would be one constructed according to an all-encompassing mathematical formula—and that is what Polykleitos achieved in his *Doryphoros*. Galen, a physician who lived during the second century CE, summarized Polykleitos's philosophy as follows:

> [Beauty arises from] the commensurability *[symmetria]* of the parts, such as that of finger to finger, and of all the fingers to the palm and the wrist, and of these to the forearm, and of the forearm to the upper arm, and, in fact, of everything to everything else, just as it is written in the *Canon* of Polykleitos. . . . Polykleitos supported his treatise [by making] a statue according to the tenets of his treatise, and called the statue, like the work, the *Canon*.[1]

This is why Pliny the Elder, writing in the first century CE, maintained that Polykleitos "alone of men is deemed to have rendered art itself [that is, the theoretical basis of art] in a work of art."[2]

Athenian Acropolis While Polykleitos was working out his prescription for the perfect statue, the Athenians, under the leadership of Pericles, were initiating one of history's most ambitious building projects, the reconstruction of the Acropolis (*acropolis* means "high city") after the Persian sack. In 478 BCE, in the aftermath of the Persian defeat, the Greeks formed an alliance for mutual protection against any renewed threat from the east. The new confederacy became known as the Delian League, because its headquarters were on the Cycladic island of Delos. Although at the outset each league member had an equal vote, Athens was "first among equals," providing the allied fleet commander and determining which cities were to furnish ships and which were instead to pay an annual tribute to the treasury at Delos. Continued fighting against the Persians kept the alliance intact, but Athens gradually assumed a dominant role. In 454 BCE, the Athenians transferred the Delian treasury to Athens, ostensibly for security reasons. League members continued to pay tribute, but Pericles did not expend the surplus reserves for the common good of the allied Greek states. Instead, he expropriated the funds to resurrect the Acropolis (FIG. 2-35). Thus, the Periclean building program was not the glorious fruit of Athenian democracy, as commonly thought, but the by-product of tyranny and the abuse of power. Too often art and architectural historians do not ask how a monument was financed. The answer can be very revealing.

The centerpiece of the Periclean Acropolis was the Parthenon (FIG. 2-35, no. 1), the Temple of Athena Parthenos, erected in the remarkably short period between 447 and 438 BCE. (Work on the great temple's ambitious sculptural ornamentation continued until 432 BCE.) Immediately upon completion of the Parthenon, construction commenced on a grand new gateway to the Acropolis, the Propylaia (FIG. 2-35, no. 2). Two later temples, the Erechtheion (FIG. 2-35, no. 3) and the Temple of Athena Nike (FIG. 2-35, no. 4), built after Pericles' death, were probably also part of his original plan.

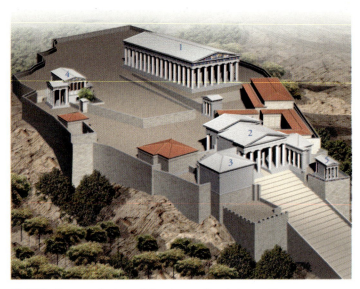

2-35 Restored view of the Acropolis, Athens, Greece (John Burge). (1) Parthenon, (2) Propylaia, (3) Erechtheion, (4) Temple of Athena Nike.

Under Pericles, the Athenians undertook one of history's most ambitious building projects, the reconstruction of the Acropolis after the Persian sack. The funds came from the Delian League treasury.

Parthenon: Architecture Most of the peripteral colonnade of the Parthenon (FIG. 2-36) still stands (or has been reerected), and art historians know a great deal about the building and its sculptural program. The architects were IKTINOS and KALLIKRATES. The statue of Athena was the work of PHIDIAS, who was also the overseer of the temple's sculptural decoration. In fact, Plutarch, who wrote a biography of Pericles in the early second century CE, claims that Phidias was in charge of the entire Periclean building program. Just as the contemporaneous *Doryphoros* is the culmination of nearly two centuries of searching for the ideal proportions of the human body, so, too, the Parthenon may be viewed as

2-36 IKTINOS and KALLIKRATES, Parthenon, the Temple of Athena Parthenos (looking southeast), Acropolis, Athens, Greece, 447–438 BCE.

The architects of the Parthenon believed that perfect beauty could be achieved by using harmonic proportions. The controlling ratio for larger and smaller parts was $x = 2y + 1$ (for example, a plan of 17 by 8 columns).

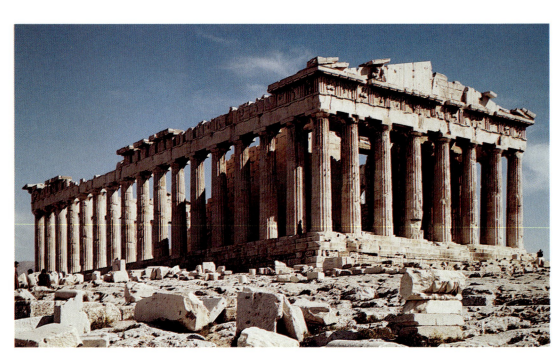

the ideal solution to the Greek architect's quest for perfect proportions in Doric temple design. The Parthenon architects and Polykleitos were kindred spirits in their belief that strict adherence to harmonious numerical ratios produced ideal forms. For the Parthenon, the controlling ratio for the *symmetria* of the parts may be expressed algebraically as $x = 2y + 1$. Thus, for example, the temple's short ends have 8 columns and the long sides have 17, because $17 = (2 \times 8) + 1$. The stylobate's ratio of length to width is 9:4, because $9 = (2 \times 4) + 1$. And so forth throughout the temple.

The Parthenon's harmonious design and the mathematical precision of the sizes of its constituent elements obscure the fact that the architects incorporated in their design pronounced deviations from the strictly horizontal and vertical lines assumed to be the basis of all Greek temples. The stylobate, for example, curves upward at the center on all four sides, forming a kind of shallow dome, and this curvature is carried up into the entablature. Moreover, the peristyle columns lean inward slightly. Those at the corners have a diagonal inclination and are also about two inches thicker than the rest. If their lines continued, they would meet about 1.5 miles above the temple. These deviations from the norm meant that the Athenian masons had to carve virtually every Parthenon block according to the special set of specifications dictated by its unique place in the structure. Vitruvius, a Roman architect of the late first century BCE, explained these adjustments as compensations for optical illusions. According to Vitruvius, if a stylobate is laid out on a level surface, it will appear to sag at the center. He also said that the corner columns of a building should be thicker because they are surrounded by light and would otherwise appear thinner than their neighbors.

One of the ironies of the Parthenon, the world's most famous Doric temple, is that it is "contaminated" by Ionic elements (FIG. **2-37**). Although the cella had a two-story Doric colonnade around Phidias's Athena, the back room—which housed the goddess's treasury and the tribute collected from the Delian League—had four tall and slender Ionic columns as sole supports for the superstructure. And whereas the temple's exterior had a Doric frieze, the inner frieze that ran around the top of the cella wall was Ionic. Perhaps this fusion of Doric and Ionic elements reflected the Athenians' belief that the Ionians of the Cycladic Islands and Asia Minor descended from Athenian settlers and were therefore their kin. Or it may be Pericles' and Iktinos's way of suggesting that Athens was the leader of *all* the Greeks. In any case, a mix of Doric and Ionic features characterizes the fifth-century BCE buildings of the Acropolis as a whole.

Athena Parthenos The Parthenon was more lavishly decorated than any Greek temple before it, Doric or Ionic. Every one of the 92 Doric metopes was decorated with relief sculpture (FIG. **2-37**). So, too, was every inch of the 524-foot-long Ionic frieze. Dozens of larger-than-life-size statues were set in the two pediments. The director of this vast sculptural program was Phidias, though he himself executed only the *Athena Parthenos*, the statue of Athena the Virgin, which stood in the Parthenon's cella. It was a *chryselephantine* statue, that is, fashioned of gold and ivory, and stood 38 feet tall. Athena was fully armed with shield, spear, and helmet, and she held Nike (the winged female personification of victory) in her extended right hand. No one doubts that this Nike referred to the victory of 479 BCE. The memory of the Persian sack of the Acropolis was still vivid, and the Athenians were intensely conscious that by driving back the Persians, they were saving their civilization from the eastern "barbarians" who had committed atrocities against the Greeks of Asia Minor. In fact, the *Athena Parthenos* had multiple allusions to the Persian defeat. On the thick soles of Athena's sandals was a representation of a *centauromachy*, a battle between Greeks and *centaurs* (mythological beasts that were part man, part horse). Emblazoned on the exterior of her shield were high reliefs depicting the battle of Greeks and Amazons *(Amazonomachy)*, in which Theseus drove the Amazons (female warriors) out of Athens. Phidias also painted a gigantomachy on the shield's interior. Each of these mythological contests was a metaphor for the triumph of order over chaos, of civilization over barbarism, and of Athens over Persia.

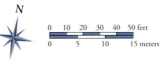

Sack of Troy (32 metopes)

Panathenaic Procession (frieze)

Contest between Athena and Poseidon

Amazonomachy (14 metopes)

Procession (frieze)

Athena Parthenos

Procession (frieze)

Gigantomachy (14 metopes)

Birth of Athena

Panathenaic procession (frieze)

Centauromachy (32 metopes)

N

0 10 20 30 40 50 feet
0   5   10   15 meters

2-37 Plan of the Parthenon, Acropolis, Athens, Greece, with diagram of sculptural program, 447–432 BCE (after A. Stewart).

The Parthenon was lavishly decorated. Statues filled both pediments, and reliefs adorned all 92 Doric metopes as well as the 524-foot Ionic frieze. In the cella was Phidias's colossal gold-and-ivory Athena.

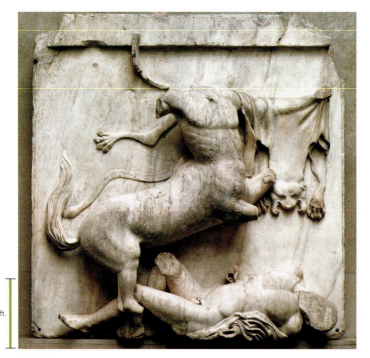

2-38 Lapith versus centaur, metope from the south side of the Parthenon, Acropolis, Athens, Greece, ca. 447–438 BCE. Marble, 4′ 8″ high. British Museum, London.

The Parthenon's centauromachy metopes alluded to the Greek defeat of the Persians. The sculptor of this metope knew how to distinguish the vibrant living centaur from the lifeless Greek corpse.

Parthenon: Metopes These same themes appeared again in the Parthenon's Doric metopes (FIG. 2-37). The south metopes are the best preserved. They depict the battle of Lapiths and centaurs, a combat in which Theseus of Athens played a major role. On one extraordinary slab (FIG. 2-38), a triumphant centaur rises up on its hind legs, exulting over the crumpled body of the Greek it has defeated. The relief is so high that parts are fully in the round. (Some pieces have broken off.) The sculptor knew how to distinguish the vibrant, powerful form of the living beast from the lifeless corpse on the ground. In other metopes the Greeks have the upper hand, but the full set suggests that the battle was a difficult one against a dangerous enemy and that losses as well as victories occurred. The same was true of the war against the Persians.

Parthenon: Pediments The subjects of the two pediments were especially appropriate for a temple that celebrated the Athenians as well as the goddess Athena. The east pediment depicted the birth of Athena. At the west was the contest between Athena and Poseidon to determine which one would become the city's patron deity. Athena won, giving her name to the city and its people. Significantly, in both the story and the pediment, the Athenians are judges of the relative merits of the two gods. This reflects the same arrogance that led to the use of Delian League funds to adorn the Acropolis.

All that remains of the east pediment's statues are the spectators to the left and the right who witnessed Athena's birth on Mount Olympus. At the far left are the head and arms of Helios (the sun) and his chariot horses rising from the pediment floor (FIG. 2-39). Next to them is a powerful male figure usually identified as Dionysos or possibly Herakles, who entered the realm of the gods after he completed 12 impossible labors. At the right are three goddesses (FIG. 2-40), probably Hestia, Dione, and Aphrodite, and then either Selene (the

2-39 Helios and his horses, and Dionysos (Herakles?), from the east pediment of the Parthenon, Acropolis, Athens, Greece, ca. 438–432 BCE. Marble, greatest height 4′ 3″. British Museum, London.

The east pediment of the Parthenon depicts the birth of Athena. At the left, the horses of the sun god emerge from the pediment floor, suggesting the sun rising above the horizon at dawn.

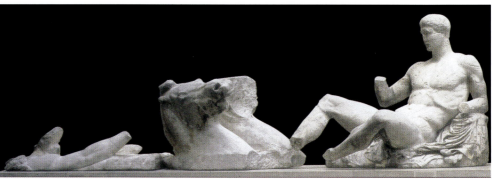

2-40 Three goddesses (Hestia, Dione, and Aphrodite?), from the east pediment of the Parthenon, Acropolis, Athens, Greece, ca. 438–432 BCE. Marble, greatest height 4′ 5″. British Museum, London.

The statues of Hestia, Dione, and Aphrodite conform perfectly to the sloping right side of the Parthenon's east pediment. The thin and heavy folds of the garments alternately reveal and conceal the body forms.

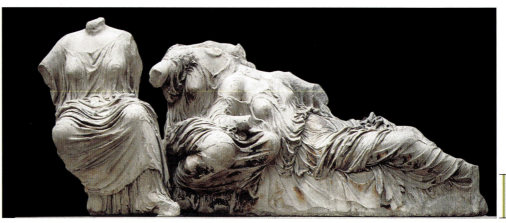

moon) or Nyx (night) and more horses, this time sinking below the pediment floor. Here, Phidias discovered an entirely new way to deal with the awkward triangular frame of the pediment. Its bottom line is the horizon line, and charioteers and their horses move through it effortlessly.

Phidias and his assistants were master sculptors. They fully understood not only the surface appearance of human anatomy, both male and female, but also the mechanics of how muscles and bones make the body move. They mastered the rendition of clothed forms too. In the Dione-Aphrodite group (FIG. 2-40), the thin and heavy folds of the garments alternately reveal and conceal the main and lesser body masses while swirling in a compositional tide that subtly unifies the figures. The articulation and integration of the bodies produce a wonderful variation of surface and play of light and shade. Moreover, all the figures, even the animals, are brilliantly characterized. The horses of the sun, at the beginning of the day, are energetic. Those of the moon or night, having labored until dawn, are weary.

Parthenon: Ionic Frieze   In many ways the most remarkable part of the Parthenon's sculptural program is the inner Ionic frieze (FIG. **2-41**). Scholars still debate the sub-

ject of the frieze, but most agree it is the Panathenaic Festival procession that took place every four years in Athens. The procession began at the Dipylon Gate to the city and ended on the Acropolis, where the Athenians placed a new peplos on an ancient wooden statue of Athena. That statue (probably similar in general appearance to the *Lady of Auxerre*, FIG. **2-15**) stood in the Archaic temple the Persians razed. (The statue survived because the Athenians removed it from the Acropolis on the eve of the Persian attack.) On the Parthenon frieze, the procession begins on the west, that is, at the temple's rear, the side facing the gateway to the Acropolis. It then proceeds in parallel lines down the long north and south sides of the building and ends at the center of the east frieze, over the doorway to the cella housing Phidias's statue. The upper part of the relief is higher than the lower part so that the more distant and more shaded upper zone is as legible from the ground as the lower part of the frieze. This is another instance of the architects' taking optical effects into consideration in the Parthenon's design.

The frieze vividly communicates the procession's acceleration and deceleration. At the outset, on the west side, marshals gather and youths mount their horses. On the north (FIG. **2-41**, *top*) and south, the momentum of the cavalcade

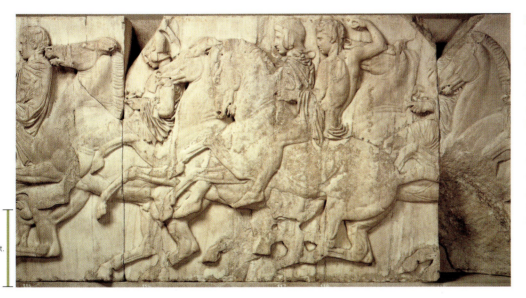

1 ft.

2-41   Two details of the Panathenaic Festival procession frieze, from the Parthenon, Acropolis, Athens, Greece, ca. 447–438 BCE. Marble, 3′ 6″ high. Horsemen of north frieze *(top)*, British Museum, London; elders and maidens of east frieze *(bottom)*, Louvre, Paris.

The Parthenon's Ionic frieze represents the festival procession of citizens on horseback and on foot that took place every four years. The temple celebrated the Athenians as much as the goddess Athena.

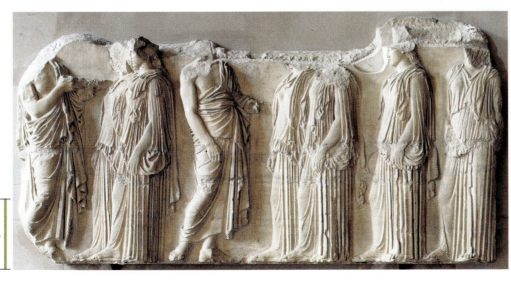

1 ft.

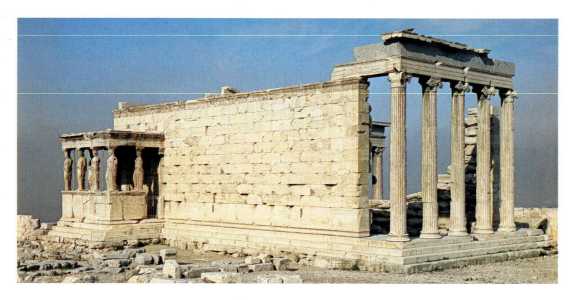

2-42 Erechtheion (looking northwest), Acropolis, Athens, Greece, ca. 421–405 BCE.

The asymmetrical form of the Erechtheion is unique for a Greek temple. It reflects the need to incorporate preexisting shrines into the plan. The decorative details are perhaps the finest in Greek architecture.

picks up. On the east, the procession slows to a halt (FIG. 2-41, *bottom*) in the presence of seated gods and goddesses, the invited guests. The role assigned to the Olympian deities is extraordinary. They do not take part in the festival or determine its outcome but are merely spectators. They watch the Athenian people—by then masters of a new Aegean empire who considered themselves worthy of depiction on a temple. Indeed, the Parthenon celebrated the greatness of Athens and the Athenians as much as it honored Athena.

Erechtheion In 421 BCE work finally began on the temple that was to replace the Archaic Athena temple the Persians had destroyed. The new structure, the Erechtheion (FIG. 2-42), built to the north of the old temple's remains, was to be a multiple shrine. It honored Athena and housed the ancient wooden image of the goddess that was the goal of the Panathenaic Festival procession. But it also incorporated shrines to a host of other gods and demigods who loomed large in the city's legendary past. Among these were Erechtheus, an early king of Athens, during whose reign the ancient wooden idol of Athena was said to have fallen from the heavens, and Kekrops, another king of Athens, who served as judge of the contest between Athena and Poseidon. In fact, the site chosen for the new temple was the very spot where that contest occurred. Poseidon had staked his claim to Athens by striking the Acropolis rock with his trident and producing a salt-water spring. Nearby, Athena had miraculously caused an olive tree to grow.

The asymmetrical plan of the Ionic Erechtheion is unique for a Greek temple and the antithesis of the simple and harmoniously balanced plan of the Doric Parthenon across the way. Its irregular form reflected the need to incorporate the tomb of Kekrops and other preexisting shrines, Poseidon's trident mark, and Athena's olive tree into a single complex. The unknown architect responsible for the building also had to struggle with the problem of uneven terrain. The area could not be made level by terracing because that would disturb the ancient sacred sites. As a result, the Erechtheion has four sides of very different character, and each side rests on a different ground level.

Perhaps to compensate for the awkward character of the building as a whole, the architect took great care with the Erechtheion's decorative details. The frieze, for example, received special treatment. The stone chosen was the dark-blue limestone of Eleusis to contrast with the white Pentelic marble of the walls and columns. Marble relief figures were attached to this dark ground. The temple's most striking and famous feature, however, is its south porch, where caryatids replaced Ionic columns. Although the caryatids exhibit the weight shift that was standard for Phidian-era statues, the vertical flutelike drapery folds concealing their stiff, weight-bearing legs underscore the statues' role as architectural supports. The Classical architect-sculptor successfully balanced the dual and contradictory functions of these female statue-

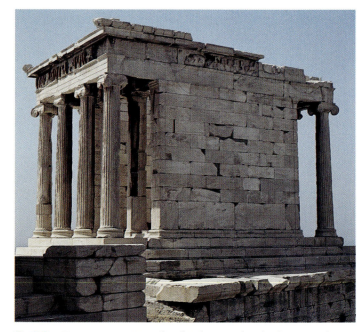

2-43 KALLIKRATES, Temple of Athena Nike (looking southwest), Acropolis, Athens, Greece, ca. 427–424 BCE.

This small temple at the entrance to the Acropolis is a splendid example of Ionic architecture. It celebrated Athena as bringer of victory, and one of its friezes depicts the Persian defeat at Marathon.

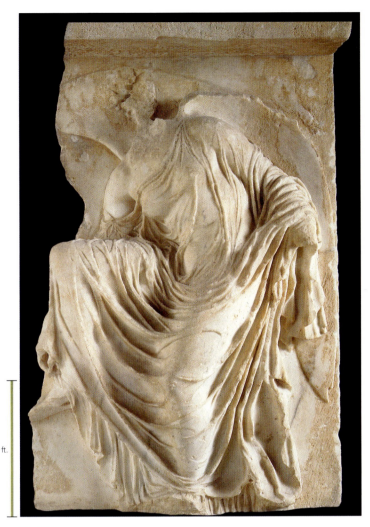

2-44 Nike adjusting her sandal, from the south side of the parapet of the Temple of Athena Nike, Acropolis, Athens, Greece, ca. 410 BCE. Marble, 3′ 6″ high. Acropolis Museum, Athens.

The image of winged Victory appeared dozens of times on the parapet around the Athena Nike temple. Here, the sculptor carved a figure whose garments seem almost transparent.

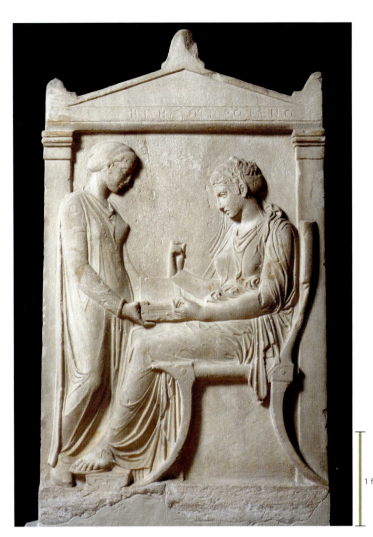

2-45 Grave stele of Hegeso, from the Dipylon cemetery, Athens, Greece, ca. 400 BCE. Marble, 5′ 2″ high. National Archaeological Museum, Athens.

On her tombstone, Hegeso examines jewelry from a box her servant girl holds. Mistress and maid share a serene moment out of daily life. Only the epitaph reveals that Hegeso is the one who has died.

columns. The figures have enough rigidity to suggest the structural column and just the degree of flexibility needed to suggest the living body.

Temple of Athena Nike Another Ionic building on the Athenian Acropolis is the small Temple of Athena Nike (FIG. **2-43**), designed by KALLIKRATES, who worked with Iktinos on the Parthenon. It stands on what used to be a Mycenaean bastion and greets all visitors entering Athena's great sanctuary. As on the Parthenon, here the Athenians also recalled the victory over the Persians—and not just in the temple's name. Part of its frieze represented the decisive battle at Marathon that turned the tide against the Persians—a human event, as in the Parthenon's Panathenaic Festival procession frieze. But now the sculptors chronicled a specific occasion, not a recurring event involving anonymous citizens.

Around the building, at the bastion's edge, was a *parapet* decorated with reliefs. The theme matched that of the temple proper—Nike (victory). Her image appeared dozens of times, always in different attitudes, sometimes erecting trophies bedecked with Persian spoils and sometimes bringing forward sacrificial bulls to Athena. One of the reliefs (FIG. **2-44**) shows Nike adjusting her sandal—an awkward posture rendered elegant and graceful. The sculptor carried the style of the Parthenon pediments (FIG. **2-40**) even further and created a figure whose garments cling so tightly to the body that they seem almost transparent, as if drenched with water. But the drapery folds form intricate linear patterns unrelated to the body's anatomical structure and have a life of their own as abstract designs. Deep carving produced pockets of shade to contrast with the polished marble surface and enhance the ornamental beauty of the design.

Hegeso Stele Decorating temples was not the only job available to sculptors in fifth-century BCE Athens. Around 400 BCE, the family of a young woman named Hegeso, daughter of Proxenos, erected a grave stele (FIG. **2-45**) in the Dipylon cemetery in her memory. Hegeso is the well-dressed woman seated on an elegant chair (with footstool). She examines a piece of jewelry (once rendered in paint, now not visible) she has selected from a box a servant girl brings to her. The maid's simple, unbelted *chiton* contrasts sharply with the more elaborate attire of her mistress. The garments of both women reveal the body forms beneath them, as on the parapet reliefs of the Athena Nike temple. The faces are serene, without a trace of sadness. Indeed, the sculptor depicted both mistress and maid in a characteristic shared moment from daily life. Only the epitaph reveals that Hegeso is the one who has departed.

The simplicity of the scene on the Hegeso stele is deceptive, however. This is not merely a bittersweet scene of tranquil domestic life before an untimely death. The setting itself is significant—the secluded women's quarters of a Greek house, from which Hegeso rarely would have emerged. Contemporaneous grave stelae of men regularly show them in the public domain, as warriors. And the servant girl is not so much the faithful companion of the deceased in life as she is Hegeso's possession, like the jewelry box. The slave girl may look solicitously at her mistress, but Hegeso has eyes only for her ornaments. Both slave and jewelry attest to the wealth of Hegeso's father, unseen but prominently cited in the epitaph. (It is noteworthy that the stele does not give the mother's name.) Indeed, even the jewelry box carries a deeper significance, for it probably represents the dowry Proxenos would have provided to his daughter's husband when she left her father's home to enter that of her husband. In the patriarchal society of ancient Greece, the dominant position of men is manifest even when only women are depicted.

White-Ground Painting All the masterpieces of Classical painting have vanished because they were on wooden panels, but ancient authors describe them as polychrome. The ACHILLES PAINTER was able to emulate the polychromy of monumental panels by using the *white-ground painting* technique for a *lekythos* (flask containing perfumed oil; FIG. **2-46**) he painted about 440 BCE. White-ground painting takes its name from the chalky-white *slip* (liquefied clay) used to provide a background for the figures. Experiments with white-ground painting date to the late sixth century BCE, but the method became popular only toward the middle of the fifth century. White-ground is essentially a variation of the red-figure technique. First the painter covered the pot with a slip of very fine white clay, then applied black glaze to outline the figures, and used diluted brown, purple, red, and white to color them. Other colors—for example, the yellow chosen for the garments of both figures on the illustrated lekythos—also could be employed, but these had to be applied after firing because the Greeks did not know how to make them withstand the intense heat of the kiln. Despite the obvious attractions of the white-ground technique, the impermanence of the expanded range of colors discouraged its use for everyday vessels, such as amphoras and kraters. In fact, ceramists explored the full polychrome possibilities of white-ground painting almost exclusively on

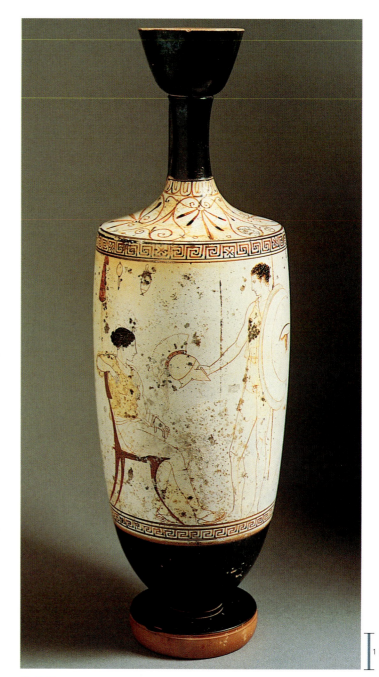

2-46 ACHILLES PAINTER, Warrior taking leave of his wife (white-ground lekythos), from Eretria, Greece, ca. 440 BCE. 1′ 5″ high. National Archaeological Museum, Athens.

White-ground painters applied the colors after firing because most colored glazes could not withstand the kiln's heat. The Achilles Painter here displays his mastery at drawing an eye in profile.

lekythoi, which the Greeks commonly placed in graves as offerings to the deceased. For such vessels designed for short-term use, the fragile nature of the white-ground technique was of little concern.

The subject of the Achilles Painter's lekythos is appropriate for its funerary purpose. A youthful warrior takes leave of his wife. The red scarf, mirror, and jug hanging on the wall behind the woman indicate that the setting is the interior of their home. The motif of the seated woman is strikingly similar to that of Hegeso on her grave stele (FIG. **2-45**), but here the woman is the survivor. It is her husband, preparing to go to war, who will depart, never to return. On his shield is a large painted eye, roughly life-size. Greek shields often bore devices such as the horrific face of Medusa, intended to ward off evil spirits and frighten the enemy. Although recalling this tradition, the eye on this lekythos was little more than an excuse for the Achilles Painter to display superior drawing skills. Since the late sixth century BCE, Greek painters had abandoned the Archaic habit of placing frontal eyes on profile faces and attempted to render the eyes in profile. The Achilles Painter's mastery of this difficult problem in foreshortening is on exhibit here.

Late Classical Art

The Peloponnesian War, which began in 431 BCE, ended in 404 BCE with the complete defeat of a plague-weakened Athens and left Greece drained of its strength. The victor, Sparta, and then Thebes undertook the leadership of Greece, both unsuccessfully. In the middle of the fourth century BCE, an external threat caused the rival Greek states to put aside their animosities and unite for their common defense, as they had earlier against the Persians. But at the battle of Chaeronea in 338 BCE, the Greek cities suffered a devastating loss and had to relinquish their independence to Philip II, king of Macedon. Philip was assassinated in 336, and his son, Alexander III ("the Great"), succeeded him. In the decade before his death in 323 BCE, Alexander led a powerful army on an extraordinary campaign that overthrew the Persian Empire (the ultimate revenge for the Persian invasion of Greece), wrested control of Egypt, and even reached India.

The fourth century BCE was thus a time of political upheaval in Greece, and the chaos had a profound impact on the psyche of the Greeks and on the art they produced. In the fifth century, Greeks had generally believed that rational human beings could impose order on their environment, create "perfect" statues such as Polykleitos's *Canon* (FIG. 2-34), and discover the "correct" mathematical formulas for constructing temples such as the Parthenon (FIG. 2-36). The Parthenon frieze (FIG. 2-41) celebrated the Athenians as a community of citizens with shared values. The Peloponnesian War and the unceasing strife of the fourth century BCE brought an end to the serene idealism of the fifth century. Disillusionment and alienation followed. Greek thought and Greek art began to focus more on the individual and on the real world of appearances rather than on the community and the ideal world of perfect beings and perfect buildings.

Praxiteles The new approach to art is immediately apparent in the work of **PRAXITELES**, one of the great masters of the Late Classical period (ca. 400–323 BCE). Praxiteles did not reject the themes High Classical sculptors favored. His Olympian gods and goddesses retained their superhuman beauty, but in his hands they lost some of their solemn grandeur and took on a worldly sensuousness. Nowhere is this new humanizing spirit more evident than in the statue of Aphrodite (FIG. 2-47) Praxiteles sold to the Knidians after another city had rejected it. The lost marble original is known

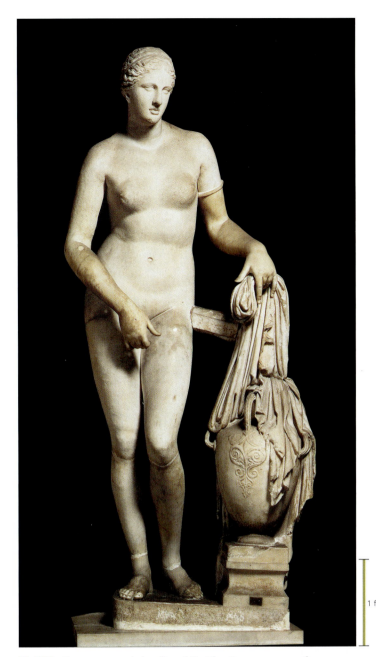

2-47 PRAXITELES, *Aphrodite of Knidos*. Roman copy after an original of ca. 350–340 BCE. Marble, 6′ 8″ high. Musei Vaticani, Rome.

This first nude statue of a goddess caused a sensation. But Praxiteles was also famous for his ability to transform marble into soft and radiant flesh. His Aphrodite had "dewy eyes."

only through copies of Roman date, but Pliny considered it "superior to all the works, not only of Praxiteles, but indeed in the whole world."[3] The statue made Knidos famous, and Pliny reported that many people sailed there just to see it. The *Aphrodite of Knidos* caused such a sensation in its time because Praxiteles took the unprecedented step of representing the goddess of love completely nude. Female nudity was rare in earlier Greek art and confined almost exclusively to paintings on vases designed for household use. The women so depicted also tended to be courtesans or slave girls, not noblewomen or goddesses, and no one had dared fashion a life-size statue of a goddess without her clothes. Moreover,

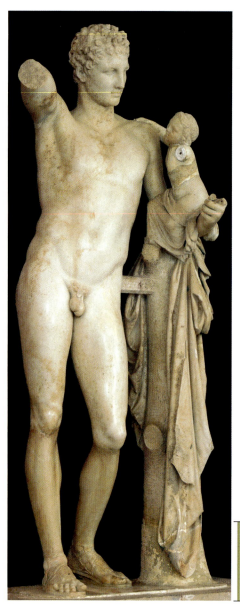

2-48
PRAXITELES, Hermes and the infant Dionysos, from the Temple of Hera, Olympia, Greece. Copy after an original of ca. 340 BCE. Marble, 7' 1" high. Archaeological Museum, Olympia.

Praxiteles' Hermes is as sensuous as his Aphrodite (FIG. 2-47). The god gazes dreamily into space while he dangles a bunch of grapes as temptation for the infant wine god. Praxiteles humanized the Greek deities.

1 ft.

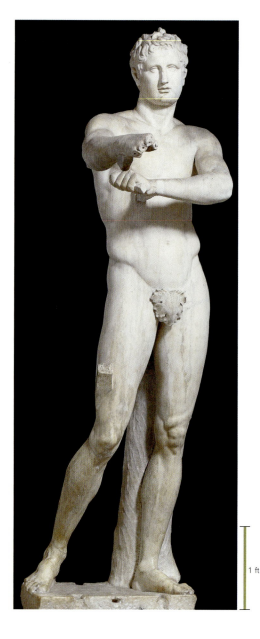

2-49 LYSIPPOS, *Apoxyomenos (Scraper).* Roman marble copy of a bronze original of ca. 330 BCE, 6' 9" high. Musei Vaticani, Rome.

Lysippos introduced a new canon of proportions and a nervous energy to his statues. He also broke down the dominance of the frontal view and encouraged looking at his statues from multiple angles.

1 ft.

Praxiteles' Aphrodite is not a cold and remote image. In fact, the goddess engages in a trivial act out of everyday life. She has removed her garment, draped it over a large *hydria* (water pitcher), and is about to step into the bath. Although shocking in its day, the *Aphrodite of Knidos* is not openly erotic (the goddess modestly shields her pelvis with her right hand), but she is quite sensuous. Lucian, writing in the second century CE, noted that she had a "welcoming look" and a "slight smile" and that Praxiteles became famous for his ability to transform marble into soft and radiant flesh. Lucian mentions, for example, the "dewy quality of Aphrodite's eyes."[4]

Unfortunately, the rather mechanical Roman copies do not capture the quality of Praxiteles' modeling of the stone, but the statue of Hermes and the infant Dionysos (FIG. **2-48**) found in the Temple of Hera at Olympia gives a good idea of the "look" of the *Aphrodite of Knidos*. Once thought to be by the hand of the master himself but now generally considered a copy of the highest quality, the statue depicts Hermes resting in a forest during his journey to deliver Dionysos to the *satyr* (a creature part man, part goat) Papposilenos and

the nymphs, who assumed responsibility for raising the child. Hermes leans on a tree trunk (here an integral part of the composition, not the copyist's addition), and his slender body forms a sinuous, shallow S-curve that is the hallmark of many of Praxiteles' statues. Hermes looks off dreamily into space while he dangles a bunch of grapes (now missing) as a temptation for the infant who is to become the Greek god of the vine. This tender and very human interaction between an adult and a child is common in life, but it had been absent from Greek statuary before the fourth century BCE.

The superb quality of the carving appears to be faithful to the Praxitelean original. The modeling is deliberately smooth and subtle, producing soft shadows that follow the planes as they flow almost imperceptibly one into another. The delicacy of the marble facial features stands in sharp contrast to the metallic precision of Polykleitos's bronze *Doryphoros* (FIG. 2-34), in which even the locks of hair conform to the High Classical sculptor's laws of symmetry and do not violate the skull's perfect curve. A comparison of these two statues reveals the sweeping change in artistic attitude and intent that occurred from the mid-fifth to the mid-fourth century BCE. Sensuous languor and an order of beauty that appeals more to the eye than to the mind replaced majestic strength and mathematical design. In the statues of Praxiteles, the deities of Mount Olympus still possess a beauty mortals can aspire to, although not achieve, but they are no longer remote. Praxiteles' gods have stepped off their High Classical pedestals and entered the Late Classical world of human experience.

Lysippos As renowned in his day as Praxiteles was LYSIPPOS, selected by Alexander the Great to create his official portrait. (Alexander could afford to employ the best. His father, Philip II, hired the leading thinker of his age, Aristotle, as the young Alexander's tutor.) Lysippos introduced a new canon of proportions in which the bodies were more slender than those of Polykleitos—whose own canon continued to exert enormous influence—and the heads roughly one-eighth the height of the body rather than one-seventh, as in the previous century. The new proportions appear in one of Lysippos's most famous works, *Apoxyomenos* (FIG. **2-49**), a bronze statue of an athlete scraping oil from his body after exercising, known, as usual, only from Roman copies in marble. A comparison with Polykleitos's *Doryphoros* (FIG. **2-34**) reveals more than a change in physique. The nervous energy running through the Lysippan

statue is absent in the balanced form of the *Doryphoros*. The *strigil* (scraper) is about to reach the end of the right arm, and at any moment the athlete will switch it to the other hand so that he can scrape his left arm. At the same time, he will shift his weight and reverse the positions of his legs. Lysippos rejected stability and balance as worthy goals for statuary. He also began to break down the dominance of the frontal view in freestanding sculpture and encouraged the observer to look at his statues from multiple angles. Because Lysippos represented the athlete with his right arm boldly thrust forward, the figure breaks out of the shallow rectangular box that defined the boundaries of earlier statues. To comprehend the action, the observer must move to the side and view the work at a three-quarter angle or in full profile.

Battle of Issus The life of Alexander the Great was very much like an epic saga, full of heroic battles, exotic locales, and unceasing drama. Alexander was a man of unique character, an inspired leader with boundless energy and an almost foolhardy courage, who always personally led his army into battle. A Roman *mosaic* not only captures the Macedonian king's unique character but also provides a welcome glimpse of Greek monumental painting during Alexander's time. In the *Alexander Mosaic* (FIG. **2-50**), as it is usually called, the mosaicist employed *tesserae* (tiny stones or pieces of glass cut to the desired size and shape) to "paint"

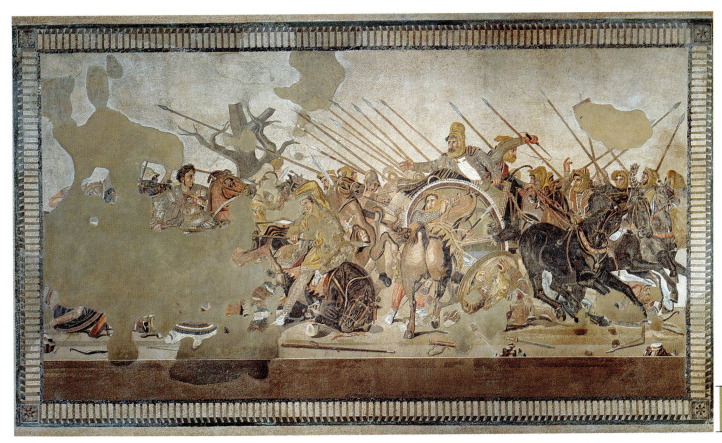

2-50 PHILOXENOS OF ERETRIA, *Battle of Issus*, ca. 310 BCE. Roman copy *(Alexander Mosaic)* from the House of the Faun, Pompeii, Italy, late second or early first century BCE. Tessera mosaic, 8′ 10″ × 16′ 9″. Museo Archeologico Nazionale, Naples.

Philoxenos here reveals his mastery of foreshortening, modeling in color, and depicting reflections and shadows. Most impressive, however, is the psychological intensity of the confrontation between Alexander and Darius.

Greek Art | 77

what art historians believe is a reasonably faithful copy of a famous panel painted around 310 BCE by PHILOXENOS OF ERETRIA. The subject is a great battle between Alexander the Great and the Persian king Darius III, probably the battle of Issus in southeastern Turkey, which Darius fled in humiliating defeat.

Philoxenos's painting is notable for its technical mastery of problems that had long fascinated Greek painters. Even Euthymides (FIG. 2-26) would have marveled at the rearing horse seen in a three-quarter rear view below Darius. And the subtle modulation of the horse's rump through shading in browns and yellows far surpasses anything even a white-ground vase painter (FIG. 2-46) ever attempted. Other details are even more impressive. The Persian to the right of the rearing horse has fallen to the ground and raises, backward, a dropped Macedonian shield to protect himself from being trampled. Philoxenos recorded the reflection of the man's terrified face on the polished surface of the shield. Everywhere in the scene, men, animals, and weapons cast shadows on the ground. Philoxenos and other Classical painters' interest in the reflection of insubstantial light on a shiny surface, and in the absence of light (shadows), stands in marked contrast to earlier painters' preoccupation with the clear presentation of weighty figures seen against a blank background. The Greek painter here truly opened a window into a world filled not only with figures, trees, and sky but also with light.

Most impressive about *Battle of Issus*, however, is the psychological intensity of the drama unfolding before the viewer's eyes. Alexander leads his army into battle without even a helmet to protect him. He drives his spear through one of Darius's bodyguards while the Persian's horse collapses be-neath him. Alexander is only a few yards away from Darius, and he directs his gaze at the king, not at the man impaled on his now-useless spear. Darius has called for retreat. In fact, his charioteer is already whipping the horses and speeding the king to safety. Before he escapes, Darius looks back at Alexander and in a pathetic gesture reaches out toward his brash foe. But the victory has slipped from his hands. Pliny said Philoxenos's painting of the battle between Alexander and Darius was "inferior to none."[5]

Theater of Epidauros

In ancient Greece, plays were not performed repeatedly over months or years as they are today, but only once, during sacred festivals. Greek drama was closely associated with religious rites and was not pure entertainment. At Athens, for example, performers staged the great tragedies of Aeschylus, Sophocles, and Euripides in the fifth century BCE at the Dionysos festival in the theater dedicated to the god on the southern slope of the Acropolis. The finest theater in Greece, however, is at Epidauros (FIG. 2-51). The architect was POLYKLEITOS THE YOUNGER, possibly a nephew of the great fifth-century sculptor.

The precursor of the formal Greek theater was a place where ancient rites, songs, and dances were performed. This circular piece of earth with a hard and level surface later became the *orchestra* (literally "dancing place") of the theater. The actors and the chorus performed there, and at Epidauros an altar to Dionysos stood at the center of the circle. The spectators sat on a slope overlooking the orchestra—the *theatron* ("place for seeing"). When the Greek theater took architectural shape, builders always situated the auditorium (*cavea*, Latin for "hollow place, cavity") on a hillside. The

2-51 POLYKLEITOS THE YOUNGER, aerial view of the theater, Epidauros, Greece, ca. 350 BCE.

Greek theaters were always situated on hillsides, which supported the cavea of stone seats overlooking the circular orchestra. The Epidauros theater is the finest in Greece. It accommodated 12,000 spectators.

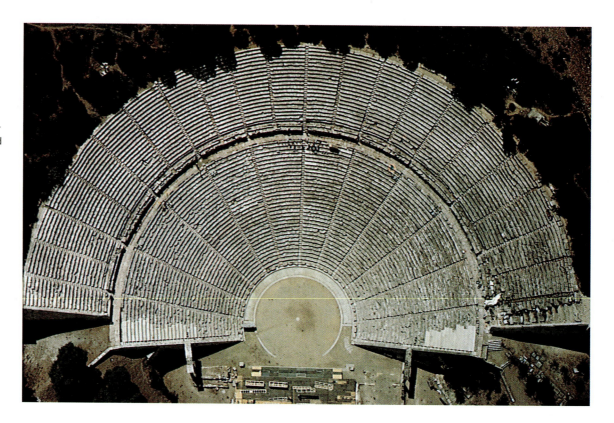

cavea at Epidauros, composed of wedge-shaped sections of stone benches separated by stairs, is somewhat greater than a semicircle in plan. The auditorium is 387 feet in diameter, and its 55 rows of seats accommodated about 12,000 spectators. They entered the theater via a passageway between the seating area and the scene building *(skene)*, which housed dressing rooms for the actors and formed a backdrop for the plays. The design is simple but perfectly suited to its function. Even in antiquity the Epidauros theater was famous for the harmony of its proportions. Although spectators sitting in some of the seats would have had a poor view of the skene, all had unobstructed views of the orchestra. Because of the excellent acoustics of the open-air cavea, everyone in the audience could hear the actors and chorus.

Hellenistic Art

Alexander the Great's conquest of the Near East, Egypt, and India ushered in a new cultural age that historians and art historians alike call *Hellenistic.* The period opened with the death of Alexander in 323 BCE and lasted nearly three centuries, until the double suicide of Queen Cleopatra of Egypt and her Roman consort Mark Antony in 30 BCE after their decisive defeat at the battle of Actium by Antony's rival Augustus. A year later, Augustus made Egypt a province of the Roman Empire.

After Alexander's death, his generals divided his far-flung empire among themselves and established their own regional kingdoms. The cultural centers of the Hellenistic period were the court cities of these Greek kings—Antioch in Syria, Alexandria in Egypt, Pergamon in Asia Minor, and others. An international culture united the Hellenistic world, and its language was Greek. Hellenistic kings became enormously rich on the spoils of the East, priding themselves on their libraries, art collections, and scientific enterprises,

as well as on the learned men they could assemble at their courts. The world of the small, austere, and heroic city-state passed away, as did the power and prestige of its center, Athens. A cosmopolitan (Greek, "citizen of the world") civilization, much like today's, replaced it.

Altar of Zeus, Pergamon The kingdom of Pergamon, founded in the early third century BCE after the breakup of Alexander's empire, embraced almost all of western and southern Asia Minor. The Pergamene kings enjoyed immense wealth and expended much of it on embellishing their capital city, especially its acropolis. The Altar of Zeus, erected about 175 BCE, is the most famous Hellenistic sculptural ensemble. The monument's west front (FIG. 2-52) has been reconstructed in Berlin. The altar proper was on an elevated platform and framed by an Ionic colonnade with projecting wings on either side of a broad central staircase.

All around the altar platform was a sculpted frieze almost 400 feet long, populated by about a hundred larger-than-life-size figures. The subject was the battle of Zeus and the gods against the giants—the most extensive representation Greek artists ever attempted of that epic conflict for control of the world. A similar subject appeared on the shield of Phidias's *Athena Parthenos* and on some of the Parthenon metopes, where the Athenians sought to draw a parallel between the defeat of the giants and the defeat of the Persians. The Pergamene king Attalos I (r. 241–197 BCE) had successfully turned back an invasion by the Gauls in Asia Minor. The gigantomachy of the Altar of Zeus alluded to his victory over those barbarians. The designer of the Pergamene altar also made a deliberate connection with Athens, whose earlier defeat of the Persians was by then legendary, and with the Parthenon, already recognized as a Classical monument—in both senses of the word. The figure

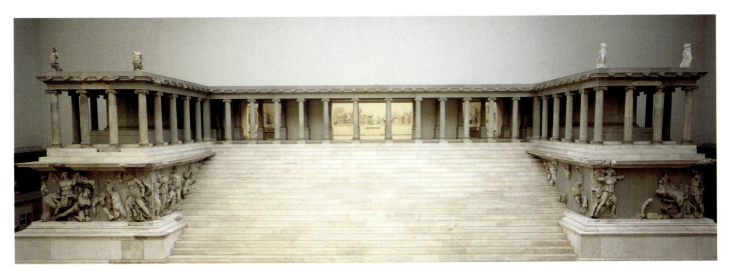

2-52   Reconstructed west front of the Altar of Zeus, from Pergamon, Turkey, ca. 175 BCE. Staatliche Museen, Berlin.

The gigantomachy frieze of Pergamon's monumental altar to Zeus is almost 400 feet long. The battle of gods and giants here alluded to the victory of King Attalos I over the Gauls of Asia Minor.

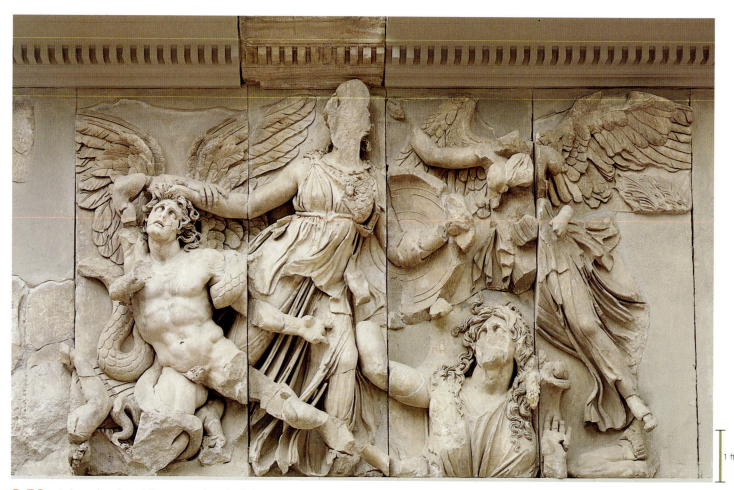

2-53 Athena battling Alkyoneos, detail of the gigantomachy frieze of the Altar of Zeus, Pergamon, Turkey, ca. 175 BCE. Marble, 7' 6" high. Staatliche Museen, Berlin.

The tumultuous gigantomachy of the Pergamon altar has an emotional intensity unparalleled in earlier Greek art. Violent movement, swirling draperies, and vivid depictions of suffering fill the frieze.

2-54 EPIGONOS(?), Dying Gaul. Roman copy after a bronze original from Pergamon, Turkey, ca. 230–220 BCE. Marble, 3' $\frac{1}{2}$" high. Museo Capitolino, Rome.

The defeat of the Gauls was also the subject of Pergamene statuary groups. The barbaric Gauls have bushy hair, mustaches, and neck bands, but the sculptor portrayed them as noble foes.

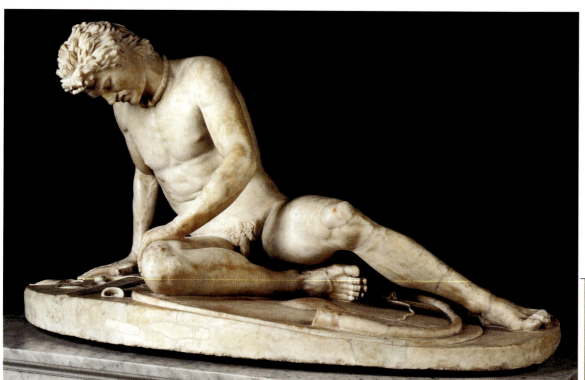

of Athena (FIG. 2-53), for example, who grabs the hair of the giant Alkyoneos as Nike flies in to crown her, is a variation on the Athena from the Parthenon's east pediment. But the Pergamene frieze is not a dry series of borrowed motifs. On the contrary, its tumultuous narrative has an emotional intensity without parallel in earlier monuments. The battle rages everywhere, even up and down the very steps visitors must ascend to reach Zeus's altar (FIG. 2-52). Violent movement, swirling draperies, and vivid depictions of death and suffering are the norm. Wounded figures writhe in pain, and their faces reveal their anguish. Deep carving creates dark shadows. The figures project from the background like bursts of light.

Dying Gaul The Altar of Zeus was not the only monument to celebrate the victory of Attalos I over the Gauls. An earlier Pergamene statuary group had explicitly represented the defeat of the barbarians instead of cloaking it in mythological disguise. The Greek victors, however, were apparently not part of the group. The viewer saw only their Gallic foes and their noble and moving response to defeat. Roman copies of some of these figures survive, including a trumpeter who collapses on his large oval shield as blood pours from the gash in his chest (FIG. 2-54). If this figure is the *tubicen* (trumpeter) Pliny mentioned in his *Natural History*, the sculptor was EPIGONOS. In any case, the sculptor carefully studied and reproduced the distinctive features of the foreign Gauls, most notably their long, bushy hair and mustaches and the *torques* (neck bands) they frequently wore. The artist also closely observed male anatomy. Note the tautness of the fallen Gaul's chest and the bulging veins of his left leg. The trumpeter is reminiscent of the dying warrior (FIG. 2-30) from the east pediment of the Temple of Aphaia at Aegina, but the suffering Gaul's pathos and drama are far more pronounced. Nonetheless, the Pergamene sculptor depicted the fallen Gaul with sympathy. The enemy's powerful body implies that the unseen Greek hero who struck down this noble and savage foe must have been an extraordinary warrior.

Nike of Samothrace Another masterpiece of Hellenistic sculpture is the statue of Nike originally set up in the Sanctuary of the Great Gods on the island of Samothrace. The *Nike of Samothrace* (FIG. 2-55) has just alighted on the prow of a Greek warship. She once raised her right arm to crown the naval victor, just as Nike placed a wreath on Athena on the Altar of Zeus (FIG. 2-53). But the Pergamene relief figure seems calm by comparison. The Samothracian Nike's wings still beat, and the wind sweeps her drapery. Her *himation* (woolen mantle) bunches in thick folds around her right leg, and her linen chiton is pulled tightly across her abdomen and left leg. The statue's original setting amplified its theatrical effect. The war galley was displayed in the upper basin of a two-tiered fountain. In the lower basin were large boulders. The fountain's flowing water created the illusion of rushing waves dashing up against the prow of the ship. The statue's reflection in the shimmering water below accentuated the sense of lightness and move-

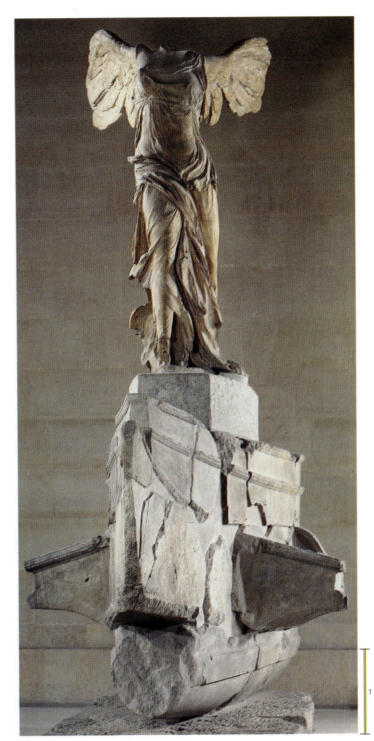

2-55 Nike alighting on a warship *(Nike of Samothrace)*, from Samothrace, Greece, ca. 190 BCE. Marble, figure 8′ 1″ high. Louvre, Paris.

Victory has just landed on a prow to crown a victor at sea. Her wings still beat, and the wind sweeps her drapery. The statue's placement in a fountain of splashing water heightened the dramatic visual effect.

ment. The sound of splashing water added an aural dimension to the visual drama. In the *Nike of Samothrace*, the Hellenistic sculptor combined art and nature and resoundingly rejected the Polykleitan conception of a statue as an ideally proportioned, self-contained entity on a bare pedestal. The Hellenistic statue interacts with its environment and appears as a living, breathing, and intensely emotive presence.

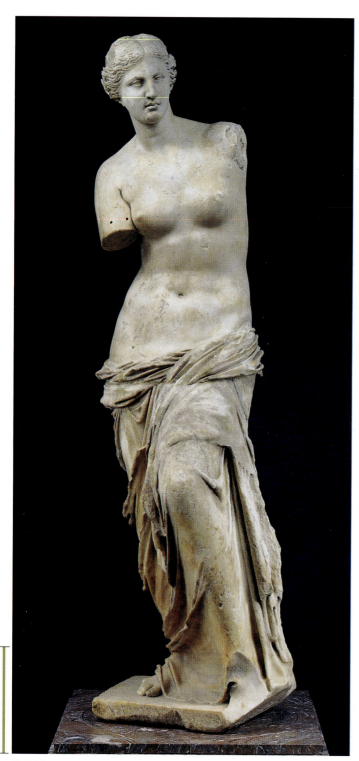

1 ft.

2-56 ALEXANDROS OF ANTIOCH-ON-THE-MEANDER, *Aphrodite (Venus de Milo)*, from Melos, Greece, ca. 150–125 BCE. Marble, 6′ 7″ high. Louvre, Paris.

Displaying the eroticism of many Hellenistic statues, this Aphrodite is more overtly sexual than the Knidian Aphrodite (FIG. 2-47). To tease the spectator, the sculptor gave the goddess a slipping garment.

Venus de Milo In the fourth century BCE, Praxiteles had already taken bold steps in redefining the nature of Greek statuary. His influence on later sculptors was enormous. The undressing of Aphrodite, for example, became the norm, but

Hellenistic sculptors went far beyond Praxiteles to openly explore the eroticism of the nude female form. The *Venus de Milo* (FIG. 2-56) is a larger-than-life-size marble statue of Aphrodite found on Melos together with its inscribed base (now lost) signed by the sculptor, ALEXANDROS OF ANTIOCH-ON-THE-MEANDER. In this statue, the goddess of love is more modestly draped than her Knidos counterpart (FIG. 2-47), but she is more overtly sexual. Her left hand (separately preserved) holds the apple the Trojan hero Paris awarded her when he judged her the most beautiful goddess. Her right hand may have lightly grasped the edge of her drapery near the left hip in a halfhearted attempt to keep it from slipping farther down her body. The sculptor intentionally designed the work to tease the spectator. By so doing he imbued his partially draped Aphrodite with a sexuality lacking in Praxiteles' entirely nude image of the goddess.

Barberini Faun Archaic statues smile at their viewers, and even when Classical statues look away from the viewer they are always awake and alert. Hellenistic sculptors often portrayed sleep. The suspension of consciousness and the entrance into the fantasy world of dreams—the antithesis of the Classical ideals of rationality and discipline—had great appeal for them. This newfound interest can be seen in a statue of a drunken, restlessly sleeping *satyr* (a semihuman follower of Dionysos) known as the *Barberini Faun* (FIG. 2-57) after the Italian cardinal who once owned it. The satyr has consumed too much wine and has thrown down his panther skin on a convenient rock and then fallen into a disturbed, intoxicated sleep. His brows are furrowed, and one can almost hear him snore.

Eroticism also comes to the fore in this statue. Although men had been represented naked in Greek art for hundreds of years, Archaic kouroi and Classical athletes and gods do not exude sexuality. Sensuality surfaced in the works of Praxiteles and his followers in the fourth century BCE. But the dreamy and supremely beautiful Hermes playfully dangling grapes before the infant Dionysos (FIG. 2-48) has nothing of the blatant sexuality of the *Barberini Faun*, whose wantonly spread legs focus attention on his genitals. Homosexuality was common in the man's world of ancient Greece. It is not surprising that when Hellenistic sculptors began to explore the sexuality of the human body, they turned their attention to both men and women.

Old Market Woman Hellenistic sculpture stands in contrast to Classical sculpture in other ways too. Many Hellenistic sculptors had a deep interest in exploring realism—the very opposite of the Classical period's idealism. This realistic mode is evident above all in Hellenistic statues of old men and women from the lowest rungs of the social order. Shepherds, fishermen, and drunken beggars are common—the kinds of people who sometimes appeared on Archaic and Classical vases but were never before thought worthy of monumental statuary. One statue of this type (FIG. 2-58) depicts

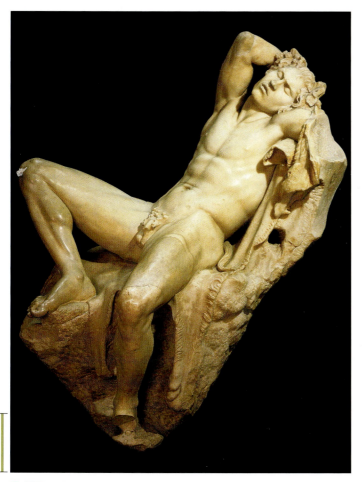

2-57 Sleeping satyr (*Barberini Faun*), from Rome, Italy, ca. 230–200 BCE. Marble, 7′ 1″ high. Glyptothek, Munich.

In this statue of a restlessly sleeping, drunken satyr, a Hellenistic sculptor portrayed a semihuman in a suspended state of consciousness—the antithesis of the Classical ideals of rationality and discipline.

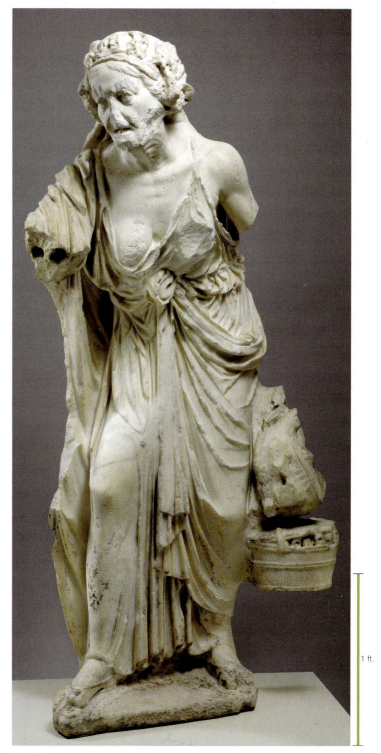

2-58 Old market woman, ca. 150–100 BCE. Marble, 4′ ½″ high. Metropolitan Museum of Art, New York (Rogers Fund, 1909).

Hellenistic art is sometimes brutally realistic. Many statues portray old men and women from the lowest rungs of society—subjects earlier artists considered unsuitable for monumental sculpture.

a haggard old woman bringing chickens and a basket of fruits and vegetables to sell in the market. Her face is wrinkled, her body bent with age, and her spirit broken by a lifetime of poverty. She carries on because she must, not because she derives any pleasure from life. No one knows the purpose of statues like this one, but they attest to an interest in social realism absent in earlier Greek statuary. The Hellenistic world was a cosmopolitan place, and the highborn could not help but encounter the poor and a growing number of foreigners (non-Greek "barbarians") on a daily basis. Hellenistic art reflects this different social climate in the depiction of a much wider variety of physical types, including different ethnic types—for example, Gallic warriors with their shaggy hair, strange mustaches, and golden torques (FIG. 2-54).

Laocoön In the opening years of the second century BCE, the Roman general Flamininus defeated the Macedonian army and declared the old city-states of Classical Greece free once again. They never regained their former glory, however. Greece became a Roman province in 146 BCE. When, 60

years later, Athens sided with King Mithridates VI of Pontus (r. 120–63 BCE) in his war against Rome, the general Sulla crushed the Athenians. Thereafter, Athens retained some of its earlier prestige as a center of culture and learning, but politically it was just another city in the ever-expanding

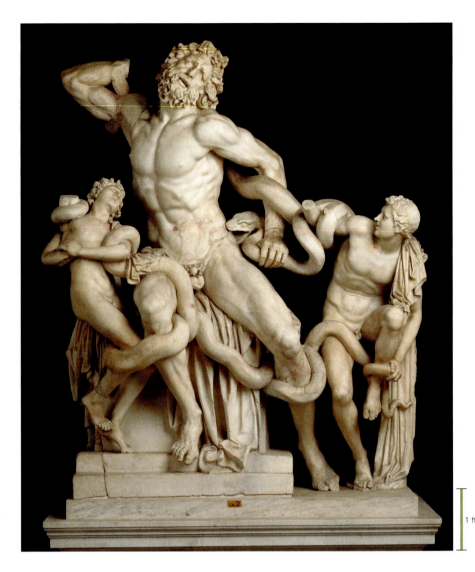

2-59 ATHANADOROS, HAGESANDROS, and POLYDOROS OF RHODES, Laocoön and his sons, from Rome, Italy, early first century CE. Marble, 7' 10½" high. Musei Vaticani, Rome.

Hellenistic style lived on in Rome. Although stylistically akin to Pergamene sculpture (FIG. 2-53), this statue of sea serpents attacking Laocoön and his two sons matches the account given only in the *Aeneid*.

1 ft.

Roman Empire. Nonetheless, Greek artists continued to be in great demand, both to furnish the Romans with an endless stream of copies of Classical and Hellenistic masterpieces and to create new statues *à la grecque* for Roman patrons.

The marble group (FIG. **2-59**) of the Trojan priest Laocoön and his sons is such a work. Long believed to be an original of the second century BCE, it was found in the palace of the emperor Titus (r. 79–81 CE), exactly where Pliny had seen it in the late first century CE. Pliny attributed the statue to three sculptors—ATHANADOROS, HAGESANDROS, and POLYDOROS OF RHODES. Scholars now generally believe these artists worked in the early first century CE. They probably based their group on a Hellenistic masterpiece depicting Laocoön and only one son. Their variation on the original added the son at Laocoön's left (note the greater compositional integration of the two other figures) to conform with the Roman poet Vergil's account in the *Aeneid*. Vergil vividly described the strangling of Laocoön and his *two* sons by sea serpents while sacrificing at an altar. The gods who favored the Greeks in the war against Troy had sent the serpents to punish Laocoön, who had tried to warn his compatriots about the danger of bringing the Greeks' wooden horse within the walls of their city. In Vergil's graphic account, Laocoön suffered in terrible agony. The Rhodian sculptors communicated the torment of the priest and his sons in spectacular fashion in this marble group. The three Trojans writhe in pain as they struggle to free themselves from the death grip of the serpents. One bites into Laocoön's left hip as the priest lets out a ferocious

cry. The serpent-entwined figures recall the suffering giants of the great frieze of the Altar of Zeus at Pergamon, and Laocoön himself is strikingly similar to Alkyoneos (FIG. **2-53**), Athena's opponent. In fact, many scholars believe that a Pergamene statuary group of the second century BCE was the inspiration for the three Rhodian sculptors.

Confirmation that the work seen by Pliny and displayed in the Vatican today was made for Romans rather than Greeks came in 1957 with the discovery of fragments of several Hellenistic-style groups illustrating scenes from Homer's *Odyssey*. Found in a grotto that served as the picturesque summer banquet hall of the seaside villa of the Roman emperor Tiberius (r. 14–37 CE) at Sperlonga, some 60 miles south of Rome, one of the groups bears the signatures of the same three sculptors Pliny cited as the creators of the Laocoön group. At Tiberius's villa and in Titus's palace, Hellenistic sculpture lived on long after Greece ceased to be a political force. When Rome inherited the Pergamene kingdom in 133 BCE, it also became heir to the Greek artistic legacy. What Rome adopted from Greece it passed on to the medieval and modern worlds. If Greece was peculiarly the inventor of the European spirit, Rome was its propagator and amplifier.

Greece

PREHISTORIC AEGEAN

- The major surviving artworks of the third millennium BCE in Greece are Cycladic marble statuettes. Most come from graves and may represent the deceased.

- The golden age of Crete was the Late Minoan period (ca. 1700–1200 BCE). The palace at Knossos was a vast multistory structure so complex in plan that it gave rise to the myth of the Minotaur in the labyrinth of King Minos. Large fresco paintings, usually illustrating palace rituals like bull-leaping, adorned the walls. Minoan sculpture was of small scale.

- The Mycenaeans (ca. 1700–1200 BCE) constructed great citadels at Mycenae, Tiryns, and elsewhere with "Cyclopean" walls of huge, irregularly shaped stone blocks. Masters of corbel vaulting, the Mycenaeans also erected beehive-shaped tholos tombs like the Treasury of Atreus, which had the largest dome in the pre-Roman world. The oldest preserved monumental sculptures in Greece, most notably Mycenae's Lion Gate, date to the end of the Mycenaean period.

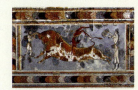

Bull-leaping fresco, Knossos, ca. 1450–1400 BCE

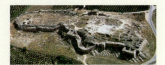

Citadel, Tiryns, ca. 1400–1200 BCE

GEOMETRIC AND ARCHAIC ART

- The human figure returned to Greek art during the Geometric period (ca. 900–700 BCE) in the form of simple silhouettes amid other abstract motifs on vases.

- Around 600 BCE, during the Archaic period (ca. 700–480 BCE), the first life-size stone statues appeared in Greece. The earliest kouroi emulated the frontal poses of Egyptian statues, but artists depicted the young men nude, the way Greek athletes competed in the Olympic Games. During the course of the sixth century BCE, Greek sculptors refined the proportions and added "Archaic smiles" to the faces of their statues to make them seem more lifelike. The Archaic age also saw the erection of the first stone temples with peripteral colonnades and the codification of the Doric and Ionic orders. Vase painters developed in turn the black- and red-figure techniques. Euphronios and Euthymides rejected the age-old composite view for the human figure and experimented with foreshortening.

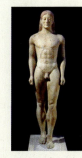

Kroisos, kouros from Anavysos, ca. 530 BCE

CLASSICAL ART

- The fifth century BCE was the golden age of Greece, when Aeschylus, Sophocles, and Euripides wrote their plays, and Herodotus, the "father of history," lived. During the Early Classical period (480–450 BCE), which opened with the Greek victory over the Persians, sculptors revolutionized statuary by introducing contrapposto (weight shift) to their figures.

- In the High Classical period (450–400 BCE), under the patronage of Pericles and the artistic directorship of Phidias, the Athenians rebuilt the Acropolis after 447 BCE. Polykleitos developed a canon of proportions for the perfect statue, and Iktinos and Kallikrates applied mathematical formulas to temple design in the belief that beauty resulted from the use of harmonic numbers.

- In the aftermath of the Peloponnesian War, which ended in 404 BCE, Greek artists began to focus more on the real world of appearances than on the ideal world of perfect beings. During the Late Classical period (400–323 BCE), sculptors humanized the remote deities and athletes of the fifth century. Praxiteles, for example, caused a sensation when he portrayed Aphrodite undressed.

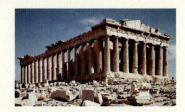

Parthenon, Acropolis, Athens, 447–438 BCE

HELLENISTIC ART

- The Hellenistic age (323–30 BCE) extends from the death of Alexander the Great until the death of Cleopatra, when Egypt became a province of the Roman Empire. The great cultural centers of the era were no longer the city-states of Archaic and Classical Greece but royal capitals such as Pergamon in Asia Minor. Hellenistic sculptors explored new subjects, for example, Gauls with mustaches and necklaces, and impoverished old women, and treated traditional subjects in new ways, as by making goddesses openly erotic. Artists delighted in depicting violent movement and unbridled emotion.

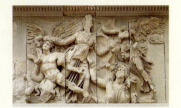

Altar of Zeus, Pergamon, ca. 175 BCE

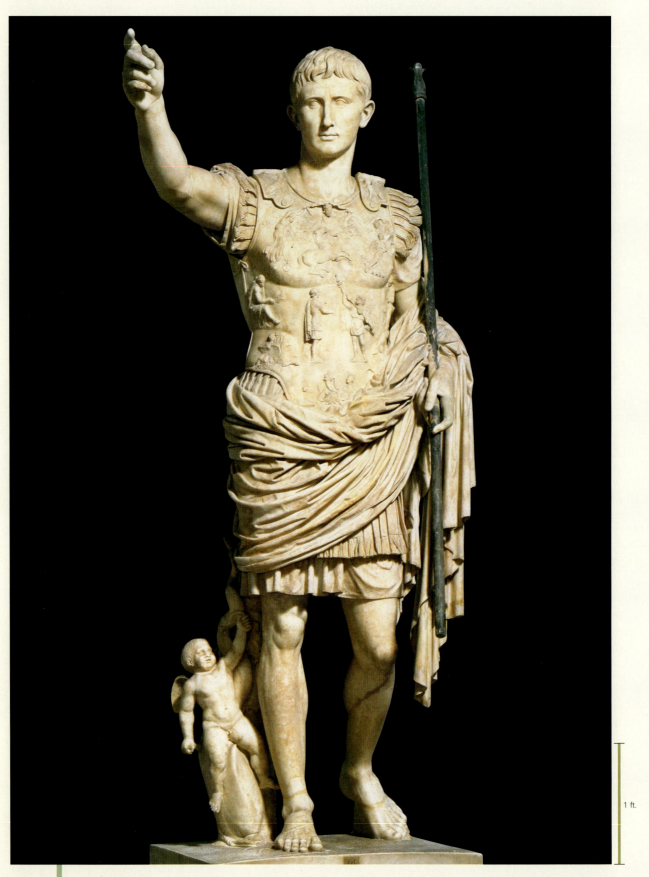

3-1 Portrait of Augustus as general, from Primaporta, Italy, early first century CE copy of a bronze original of ca. 20 BCE. Marble, 6′ 8″ high. Musei Vaticani, Rome.

Portraiture is one of the most important genres of Roman art. Imperial portraits are carefully crafted political images that are not always likenesses. Augustus always appeared as a never-aging son of a god.

1 ft.

The Roman Empire

With the rise and triumph of Rome, a single government ruled, for the first (and last) time in human history, from the Strait of Gibraltar to the Nile, from the Tigris and Euphrates to the Rhine, Danube, Thames and beyond (MAP **3-1**). In Europe, the Middle East, and North Africa today, Roman temples and basilicas have an afterlife as churches. The powerful concrete vaults of ancient Roman buildings form the cores of modern houses, stores, restaurants, factories, and museums. Bullfights, sports events, operas, and rock concerts take place in Roman amphitheaters. Ships dock in what were once Roman ports, and Western Europe's highway system still closely follows the routes of Roman roads.

Ancient Rome also lives on in the Western world in the concepts of law and government, in languages, in the calendar—even in the coins used daily. Roman art speaks in a language almost every Western viewer can readily understand. Its diversity and eclecticism foreshadowed the modern world. The Roman use of art, especially portraits and historical relief sculptures, to manipulate public opinion is similar to the carefully crafted imagery of contemporary political campaigns. And the Roman mastery of concrete construction began an architectural revolution still felt today. But when, according to legend, Romulus founded the future capital of the Western world in 753 BCE, Rome was not the most powerful or the most sophisticated city even in central Italy. In fact, in the sixth century BCE, the rulers of Rome were Etruscan kings.

ETRUSCAN ART

The heartland of the Etruscans was the territory between the Arno and Tiber rivers of central Italy. During the eighth and seventh centuries BCE, the Etruscans, as highly skilled seafarers, enriched themselves through trade abroad. By the sixth century BCE, they controlled most of northern and central Italy from strongholds such as Tarquinia, Cerveteri, Vulci, and Veii. But these cities never united to form a state. They coexisted, flourishing or fading independently. Any semblance of unity among them stemmed primarily from common linguistic ties and religious beliefs and practices. This lack of political cohesion eventually made the Etruscans relatively easy prey for the Romans.

Etruscan Temples In the sixth century BCE, the most innovative artists and architects in the Mediterranean were the Greeks (see Chapter 2). But however eager the Etruscans may have been to emulate Greek works, the vast majority of Archaic Etruscan artworks depart markedly from their Greek prototypes. This is

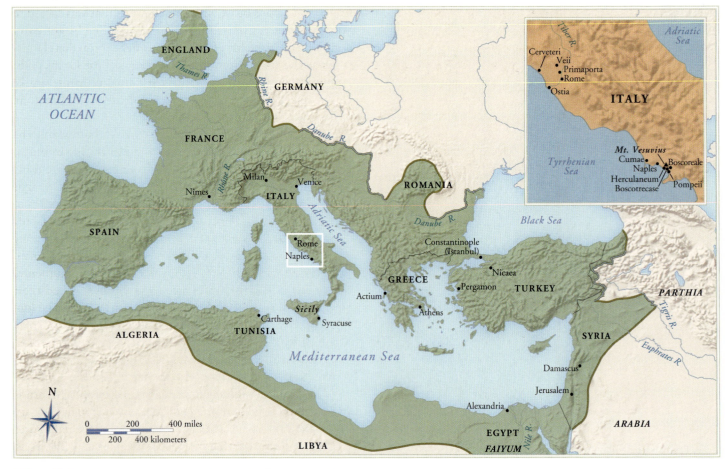

MAP 3-1 The Roman Empire at the death of Trajan in 117 CE.

especially true of religious architecture. Etruscan temple design superficially owes much to Greek architects, but the differences between Greek and Roman temples far outweigh the similarities. Because of the materials Etruscan architects employed, usually only the foundations of Etruscan temples have survived. Supplementing the archaeological record, however, is the Roman architect Vitruvius's treatise on architecture written near the end of the first century BCE. In it, Vitruvius provided an invaluable chapter on Etruscan temples.

The typical Archaic Etruscan temple (FIG. **3-2**) resembled the Greek stone gable-roofed temple (FIGS. **2-27**, *left*, and **2-36**), but it had wooden columns and a wooden roof, and its walls were of sun-dried brick. Entrance was via a narrow staircase at the center of the front of the temple, which sat on a high podium, the only part of the building made of stone. The Etruscans placed columns only on the front of the building, creating a deep porch that occupied roughly half the podium, setting off one side of the structure as the main side. In contrast, the front and rear of a Greek temple were indistinguishable. Steps and columns were on all sides.

Etruscan temples differed in other ways from those of Greece. Etruscan columns (also called *Tuscan columns*) resembled Greek Doric columns (FIG. **2-20**, *left*), but they were wood, unfluted, and had bases. Because of the lightness of the superstructure they had to support, Etruscan columns were, as a rule, much more widely spaced than Greek columns. Unlike their Greek counterparts, Etruscan temples frequently had three cellas—one for each of their chief gods, Tinia (Roman Jupiter/Greek Zeus), Uni (Juno/Hera), and Menrva (Minerva/Athena). Further, pedimental statuary was exceedingly rare in Etruria. The Etruscans normally placed narrative statuary—of hollow-cast *terracotta* instead of carved stone—on the peaks of their temple roofs.

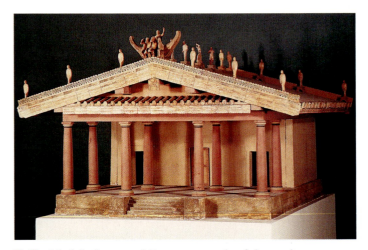

3-2 Model of a typical Etruscan temple of the sixth century BCE, as described by Vitruvius. Istituto di Etruscologia e di Antichità Italiche, Università di Roma, Rome.

Etruscan temples resembled Greek temples but had widely spaced unfluted wooden columns only at the front, walls of sun-dried mud brick, and a narrow staircase at the center of the facade.

Apulu (Apollo), from the roof of the Portonaccio Temple, Veii, Italy, ca. 510–500 BCE. Painted terracotta, 5′ 11″ high. Museo Nazionale di Villa Giulia, Rome.

This Apollo was part of a statuary group depicting a Greek myth. Distinctly Etruscan, however, are the god's vigorous motion and gesticulating arms and the placement of the statue on a temple roof.

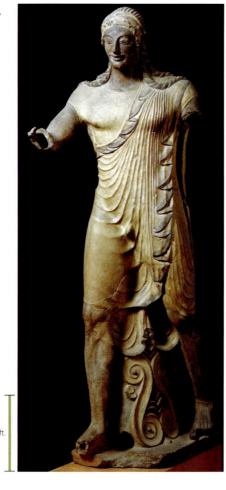

1 ft.

hind, a wondrous beast with golden horns that was sacred to Apulu's sister Artumes (Diana/Artemis). The bright paint and the rippling folds of Apulu's garment immediately distinguish the statue from the nude images of the Greek gods. Apulu's vigorous striding motion, gesticulating arms, fanlike calf muscles, and animated face are also distinctly Etruscan.

Cerveteri Sarcophagus Also made of terracotta, the favored medium for life-size statuary in Etruria, is a *sarcophagus* (FIG. 3-4) in the form of a husband and wife reclining on a banquet couch, from a tomb at Cerveteri. Sarcophagus literally means "flesh-eater," and most ancient sarcophagi contained the bodies of the deceased, but this one contained only ashes. Cremation was the most common means of disposing of the dead in Etruscan Italy. This type of funerary monument had no parallel in Greece, which then had no monumental tombs to house large sarcophagi. The Greeks buried their dead in simple graves marked by a vase (FIG. 2-14), statue (FIG. 2-17), or stele (FIG. 2-45). Moreover, only men dined at Greek banquets. Their wives remained at home, excluded from most aspects of public life. The image of a husband and wife sharing the same banquet couch is unknown in Greece.

The man and woman on the Cerveteri sarcophagus are as animated as the Veii Apulu (FIG. 3-3), even though they are at rest. They are the antithesis of the stiff and formal figures encountered in Egyptian tomb sculptures (FIG. 1-27). Also typically Etruscan, and in striking contrast to contemporaneous Greek statues with their emphasis on proportion and balance, is the manner in which the Etruscan sculptor rendered the upper and lower parts of each body. The legs are only summarily modeled, and the transition to the torso at the waist is unnatural. The artist's interest focused on the upper half of the figures, especially on the vibrant faces and gesticulating arms. The Cerveteri banqueters and the Veii Apulu speak to the viewer in a way that contemporaneous Greek statues never do.

The finest of these rooftop statues to survive today is the life-size image of Apulu (FIG. 3-3)—the Greco-Roman Apollo. It is a brilliant example of the energy and excitement that characterize Archaic Etruscan art in general. Apulu was part of a group of at least four painted terracotta figures that adorned the rooftop of a temple at Veii. The god confronts Hercle (Hercules/Herakles) for possession of the Ceryneian

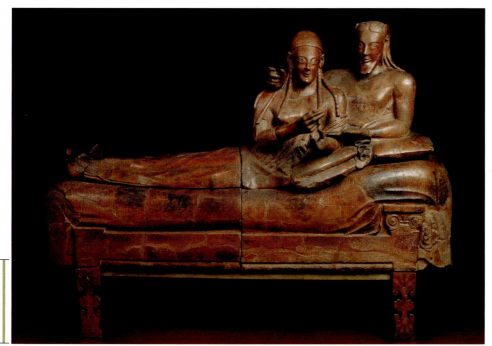

1 ft.

3-4 Sarcophagus with reclining couple, from Cerveteri, Italy, ca. 520 BCE. Painted terracotta, 3′ 9½″ × 6′ 7″. Museo Nazionale di Villa Giulia, Rome.

Sarcophagi in the form of a husband and wife on a dining couch have no parallel in Greece. The artist's focus on the upper half of the figures and the emphatic gestures are also Etruscan hallmarks.

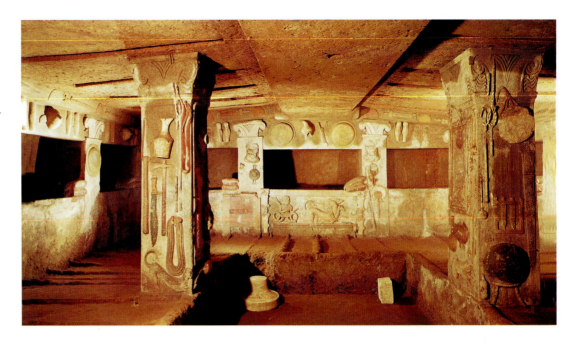

3-5 Interior of the Tomb of the Reliefs, Cerveteri, Italy, third century BCE.

The Cerveteri necropolis had scores of tumuli with underground burial chambers. These Etruscan houses of the dead resembled the houses of the living. This interior has painted stucco reliefs evoking a domestic context.

Banditaccia Necropolis The exact findspot of the Cerveteri sarcophagus is not known, but the kind of tomb that housed Etruscan sarcophagi is well documented. The typical Cerveteri tomb took the form of a mound, or *tumulus*, not unlike the Mycenaean Treasury of Atreus (FIG. **2-11**). But whereas the Mycenaeans constructed their tholos tombs of masonry blocks and then encased them in an earthen mound, each Etruscan tumulus covered one or more subterranean multichambered tombs cut out of the dark local limestone called tufa. These burial mounds sometimes reached colossal size, with diameters in excess of 130 feet. Arranged in an orderly manner along a network of streets, the cemeteries resembled veritable cities of the dead (indeed, Greek *"necropolis"* means "city of the dead"), and were located some distance from cities of the living. The Cerveteri tumuli highlight the very different values of the Etruscans and the Greeks. The Etruscans' temples, constructed of wood and mud brick, no longer stand, but their grand underground tombs are as permanent as the bedrock itself. In contrast, the Greeks employed stone for the shrines of their gods but only rarely built monumental tombs for their dead.

The most elaborately decorated Cerveteri tomb is the so-called Tomb of the Reliefs (FIG. **3-5**), which housed the remains of several generations of a single family. The walls,

3-6 Interior of the Tomb of the Leopards, Tarquinia, Italy, ca. 480–470 BCE.

Mural paintings adorn many Tarquinian tombs. Here, guarded by leopards, banqueting couples, servants, and musicians celebrate the good life. The men have dark skin, the women fair skin.

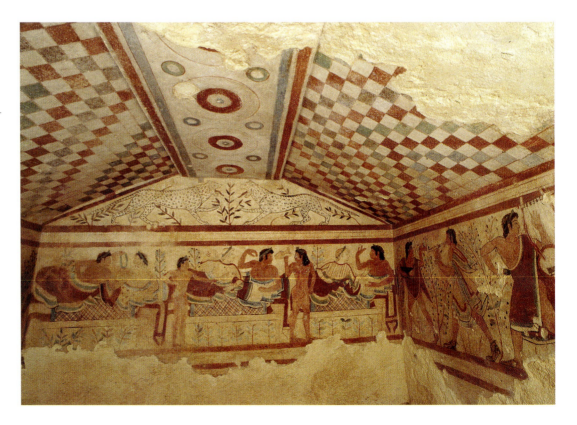

ceiling beams, piers, and funerary couches of this tomb were, as in other Cerveteri tombs, gouged out of the tufa bedrock, but in this instance brightly painted stucco reliefs cover the stone. The stools, mirrors, drinking cups, pitchers, and knives effectively suggest a domestic context, underscoring the visual and conceptual connection between Etruscan houses of the dead and those of the living.

Tomb of the Leopards The Etruscans also decorated their underground burial chambers with mural paintings. Painted tombs are statistically rare, the privilege of only the wealthiest Etruscan families. Most have been found at Tarquinia. A well-preserved example, dating to the early fifth century BCE, is the Tomb of the Leopards (FIG. **3-6**), named for the beasts that guard the tomb from their perch within the rear wall pediment. They recall the panthers on each side of Medusa in the pediment (FIG. **2-23**) of the Archaic Greek Temple of Artemis at Corfu. But mythological figures, whether Greek or Etruscan, are uncommon in Tarquinian murals, and the Tomb of the Leopards has none. Instead, banqueting couples (the men with dark skin, the women with light skin, in conformity with the age-old convention) adorn the walls—painted versions of the terracotta Cerveteri sarcophagus (FIG. **3-4**). Pitcher- and cup-bearers serve them, and musicians entertain them. The banquet takes place in the open air or perhaps in a tent set up for the occasion. In characteristic Etruscan fashion, the banqueters, servants, and entertainers all make exaggerated gestures with unnaturally enlarged hands. The man on the couch at the far right on the rear wall holds up an egg, the symbol of regeneration. The painting is a joyful celebration of life, food, wine, music, and dance, rather than a somber contemplation of death.

Capitoline Wolf The fifth century BCE was a golden age in Greece but not in Etruria. In 509 BCE, the Romans expelled the last of their Etruscan kings, replacing the monarchy with a republican form of government. In 474 BCE, an alliance of Cumaean Greeks and Hieron I of Syracuse defeated the Etruscan fleet off Cumae, effectively ending Etruscan dominance of the seas and with it Etruscan prosperity. These events had important consequences in the world of art and architecture. The number of Etruscan tombs, for example, decreased sharply, and the quality of the furnishings declined markedly. No longer could the Etruscans fill their tombs with golden jewelry and imported Greek vases or mural paintings and terracotta sarcophagi of the first rank. But Etruscan art did not cease.

The best known of these later Etruscan works—one of the most memorable portrayals of an animal in the history of world art—is the *Capitoline Wolf* (FIG. **3-7**). The statue is a somewhat larger than life-size hollow-cast bronze portrayal of the legendary she-wolf that nursed Romulus and Remus after they were abandoned as infants. When the twins grew to adulthood, they quarreled, and Romulus killed his brother. On April 23, 753 BCE, he founded Rome and became the city's first king. The *Capitoline Wolf*, however, is not a work of Roman art, which had not yet developed a distinct identity, but is the product of an Etruscan workshop. (The suckling infants are 16th-century additions.) The vitality accorded the human figure in Etruscan art is here concentrated in the tense, watchful animal body of the she-wolf, with her spare flanks, gaunt ribs, and taut, powerful legs. The lowered neck and head, alert ears, glaring eyes, and ferocious muzzle capture the psychic intensity of the fierce and protective beast as danger approaches.

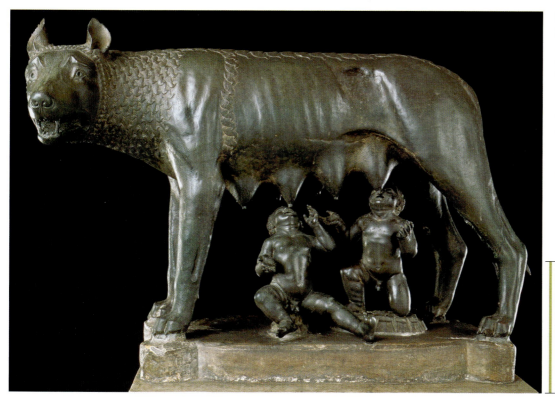

3-7 *Capitoline Wolf*, from Rome, Italy, ca. 500–480 BCE. Bronze, 2' 7½" high. Musei Capitolini, Rome.

An Etruscan sculptor cast this statue of the she-wolf that nursed the infants Romulus and Remus, founders of Rome. The animal has a tense, gaunt body and an unforgettable psychic intensity.

1 ft.

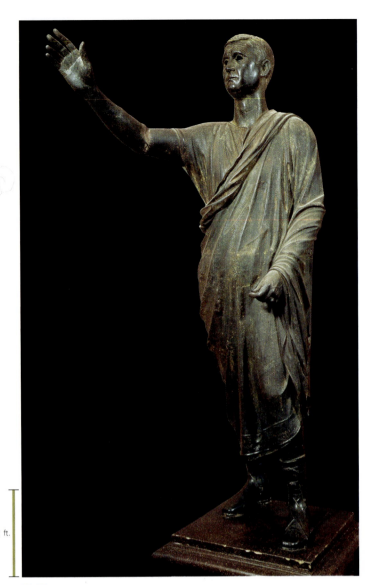

3-8 Aule Metele *(Arringatore)*, from Cortona, near Lake Trasimeno, Italy, early first century BCE. Bronze, 5' 7" high. Museo Archeologico Nazionale, Florence.

Inscribed in Etruscan, this bronze statue of an orator is Etruscan in name only. Aule Metele wears the short toga and high boots of a Roman magistrate, and the style of the portrait is also Roman.

Aule Metele Veii fell to the Romans in 396 BCE, after a terrible 10-year siege. Rome concluded peace with Tarquinia in 351, but by the beginning of the next century, the Romans had annexed Tarquinia too, and they conquered Cerveteri in 273. By the first century BCE, Roman hegemony over the Etruscans became total. A life-size bronze statue (FIG. **3-8**) representing a man named Aule Metele is an eloquent symbol of the Roman absorption of the Etruscans. The man raises his arm to address an assembly—hence the statue's modern nickname, *Arringatore (Orator)*. Although the sculptor inscribed Aule Metele's Etruscan name and the names of both of his Etruscan parents on the statue, the orator wears the short toga and high laced boots of a Roman magistrate. Aule Metele is Etruscan in name only. Scholars still debate the origin of the Etruscan people, but the question of their demise has a ready answer. Aule Metele and his compatriots became Romans, and Etruscan art became Roman art.

ROMAN ART

The Rome of Romulus in the eighth century BCE comprised only small huts of wood, wattle, and daub, clustered together on the Palatine Hill overlooking what was then uninhabited marshland. In the Archaic period, Rome was essentially an Etruscan city, both politically and culturally. Its greatest shrine, the late-sixth-century BCE Temple of Jupiter on the Capitoline Hill, was built by an Etruscan king, designed by an Etruscan architect, made of wood and mud brick in the Etruscan manner, and decorated with an Etruscan sculptor's terracotta statuary. When the Romans expelled the last of Rome's Etruscan kings in 509 BCE, they established a constitutional government, or republic (see "An Outline of Roman History," page 93)—and the she-wolf (FIG. **3-7**) became its emblem.

The Republic

The new Roman Republic vested power mainly in a *senate* (literally, "a council of elders," *senior* citizens) and in two elected *consuls*. Under extraordinary circumstances a *dictator* could be appointed for a specified time and a specific purpose, such as commanding the army during a crisis. Before long, the descendants of Romulus conquered Rome's neighbors one by one: the Etruscans to the north, the Samnites and the Greek colonists to the south. Even the Carthaginians of North Africa, who under Hannibal's dynamic leadership had annihilated some of Rome's legions and almost brought down the Republic, fell before the might of Roman armies.

The year 211 BCE was a turning point for both Rome and Roman art. Breaking with precedent, Marcellus, conqueror of the fabulously wealthy Sicilian Greek city of Syracuse, brought back to Rome not only the usual spoils of war—captured arms and armor, gold and silver coins, and the like—but also the city's artistic patrimony. Thus began, in the words of the historian Livy, "the craze for works of Greek art."[1] Ships filled with plundered Greek statues and paintings became a frequent sight in Rome's harbor at Ostia.

Exposure to Greek sculpture and painting and to the splendid marble temples of the Greek gods increased as the Romans expanded their conquests beyond Italy. Greece became a Roman province in 146 BCE, and in 133 the last king of Pergamon willed his kingdom to Rome (see Chapter 2). Nevertheless, although the Romans developed a virtually insatiable taste for Greek "antiques," their own monuments were not slavish imitations of Greek masterpieces. The Etruscan basis of Roman art and architecture was never forgotten. The statues and buildings of the Roman Republic are highly eclectic, drawing on both Greek and Etruscan traditions.

Temple of Portunus, Rome This Roman eclecticism characterizes the Temple of Portunus (FIGS. **3-9,** no. 1, and **3-10**), the Roman god of harbors, on the east bank of the Tiber. In plan, the temple follows the Etruscan pattern. The high podium can be reached only at the front of the building via a wide flight of steps. Freestanding columns are confined

An Outline of Roman History

Monarchy (753–509 BCE)

Latin and Etruscan kings ruled Rome from the city's founding by Romulus in 753 BCE until the revolt against Rome's last king, Tarquinius Superbus, in 509 BCE (exact dates of rule unreliable).

Republic (509–27 BCE)

The Republic lasted almost 500 years, until the Senate bestowed the title of Augustus on Octavian, the grandnephew of Julius Caesar and victor over Mark Antony in the civil war of 41–31 BCE that ended republican government. Some major figures were

- Marcellus, b. 268(?), d. 208 BCE, consul
- Sulla, b. 138, d. 79 BCE, consul and dictator
- Julius Caesar, b. 100, d. 44 BCE, consul and dictator
- Mark Antony, b. 83, d. 30 BCE, consul

Early Empire (27 BCE–96 CE)

The Early Empire began with the rule of Augustus and his Julio-Claudian successors and continued until the end of the Flavian dynasty. The most important emperors of this period were

- Augustus, r. 27 BCE –14 CE
- Nero, r. 54–68
- Vespasian, r. 69–79
- Titus, r. 79–81
- Domitian, r. 81–96

High Empire (96–192 CE)

The High Empire began with the death of Domitian and the ensuing rule of the Spanish emperors, Trajan and Hadrian, and ended with the last emperor of the Antonine dynasty. The major rulers of this period were

- Trajan, r. 98–117
- Hadrian, r. 117–138
- Marcus Aurelius, r. 161–180

Late Empire (192–337 CE)

The Late Empire began with the Severan dynasty and included the so-called soldier emperors of the third century, the tetrarchs, and Constantine, the first Christian emperor. Some of these emperors were

- Septimius Severus, r. 193–211
- Caracalla, r. 211–217
- Trajan Decius, r. 249–251
- Diocletian, r. 284–305
- Constantine I, r. 306–337

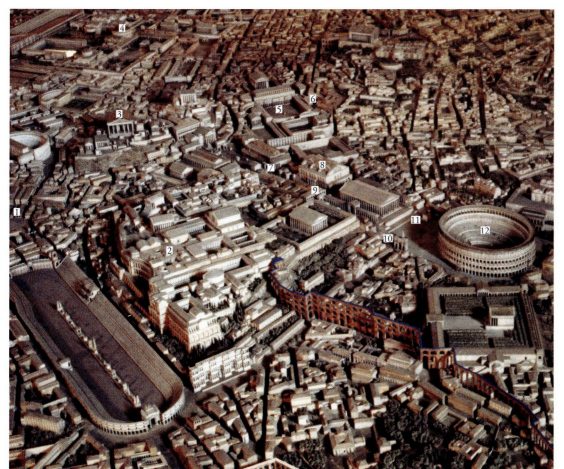

3-9 Model of the city of Rome during the early fourth century CE. Museo della Civiltà Romana, Rome. (1) Temple of Portunus, (2) Palatine Hill, (3) Capitoline Hill, (4) Pantheon, (5) Forum of Trajan, (6) Markets of Trajan, (7) Forum Romanum, (8) Basilica Nova, (9) Arch of Titus, (10) Arch of Constantine, (11) Colossus of Nero, (12) Colosseum.

At the height of its power, Rome was the capital of the greatest empire of the ancient world. The Romans ruled from the Tigris and Euphrates to the Thames and beyond, from the Nile to the Rhine and Danube.

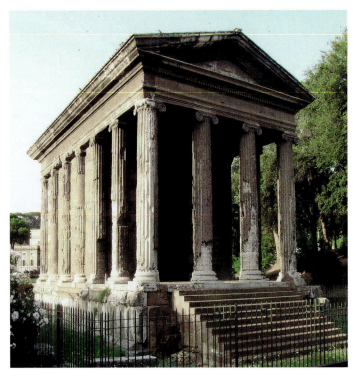

3-10 Temple of Portunus, Rome, Italy, ca. 75 BCE.

Republican temples combine Etruscan plan and Greek elevation. This pseudoperipteral temple employs the Ionic order and is built of stone, but it has a staircase and freestanding columns only at the front.

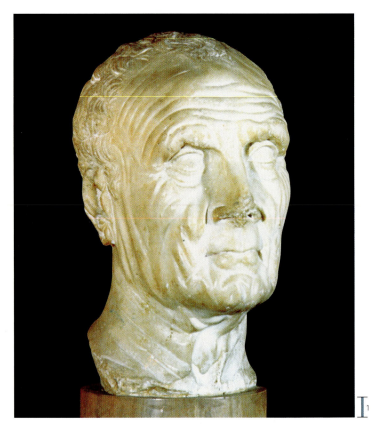

1 in.

3-11 Head of an old man, from Osimo, Italy, mid-first century BCE. Marble, life-size. Palazzo del Municipio, Osimo.

Veristic (superrealistic) portraits of old men from distinguished families were the norm during the Republic. The sculptor of this head painstakingly recorded every detail of the elderly man's face.

to the deep porch. But the builders constructed the temple of stone (local tufa and travertine), overlaid originally with stucco in imitation of the marble temples of the Greeks. The columns are not Tuscan but Ionic, complete with flutes and bases and a matching Ionic frieze. Moreover, in an effort to approximate a peripteral Greek temple yet maintain the basic Etruscan plan, the architect added a series of Ionic *engaged columns* (attached half-columns) around the cella's sides and back. The result was a *pseudoperipteral* temple. Although the design combines Etruscan and Greek elements, it is uniquely Roman.

Verism The patrons of Republican religious and civic buildings were almost exclusively members of the *patrician* class of old and distinguished families, often victorious generals who used the spoils of war to finance public works. These aristocrats were fiercely proud of their lineage. They kept likenesses *(imagines)* of their ancestors in wooden cupboards in their homes and paraded them at the funerals of prominent relatives. The surviving portraits of patricians, which appear to be literal reproductions of individual faces, must be seen in this context. Portraits were one way the patrician class celebrated its elevated position in society. The subjects of these portraits were nearly all men of advanced age, for generally only elders held power in the Republic. These patricians did not ask sculptors to idealize them. Instead, they requested brutally realistic images of distinctive features, in the tradition of the treasured household imagines.

One of the most striking of these so-called *veristic* (superrealistic) portraits is the head of an unidentified elderly man

(FIG. **3-11**) from Osimo. The sculptor painstakingly recorded each rise and fall, each bulge and fold, of the facial surface, like a mapmaker who did not want to miss the slightest detail of surface change. Scholars debate whether such portraits were truly blunt records of real features or exaggerated types designed to make a statement about personality: serious, experienced, determined, loyal to family and state—virtues the patricians greatly admired during the Republic.

Pompeii and the Cities of Vesuvius

On August 24, 79 CE, Mount Vesuvius, a long-dormant volcano, suddenly erupted, burying many prosperous towns around the Bay of Naples, among them Pompeii. This catastrophe for the Romans, however, has been a boon for archaeologists, who have been able to reconstruct the art and life of the Vesuvian towns with a completeness far beyond that possible anywhere else.

The Oscans, one of the many Italic tribes that occupied Italy during the peak of Etruscan power, were the first to settle at Pompeii. Toward the end of the fifth century BCE, the Samnites, another Italic people, took over the town. Under the influence of their Greek neighbors, the Samnites greatly expanded the original settlement and gave monumental shape to the city center. Pompeii fought with other Italian cities on

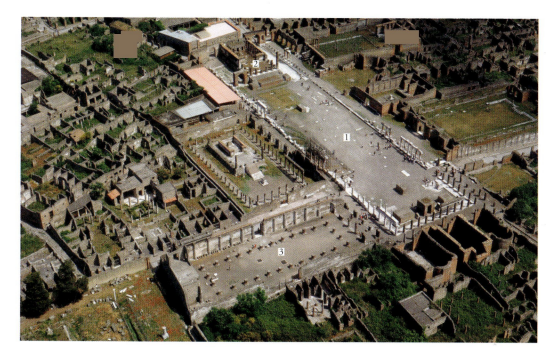

The center of Roman civic life was the forum. At Pompeii, colonnades frame a rectangular plaza with the Capitolium at the northern end. At the southwestern corner is the basilica, Pompeii's law court.

the losing side against Rome in the so-called Social War of the early first century BCE. In 80 BCE, Sulla founded a new Roman colony on the site, with Latin as its official language. The colony's population had grown to between 10,000 and 20,000 when Mount Vesuvius buried Pompeii in volcanic ash.

Forum The center of civic life in any Roman town was its *forum*, or public square. Pompeii's forum (FIG. **3-12,** no. 1) lies in the southwest corner of the expanded Roman city but at the heart of the original town. The forum probably took on monumental form in the second century BCE when the Samnites, inspired by Hellenistic architecture, erected two-story *porticos* (colonnades) on three sides of the long and narrow plaza. At the north end they constructed a temple of Jupiter (FIG. **3-12,** no. 2). When Pompeii became a Roman colony, the Romans converted the temple into a *Capitolium*—a triple shrine to Jupiter, Juno, and Minerva. The temple is of standard Republican type, constructed of tufa covered with fine white stucco and combining an Etruscan plan with Greek columns. It faces into the civic square, dominating the area. This is very different from the siting of Greek temples (FIG. **2-35**), which stood in isolation and could be approached and viewed from all sides, like colossal statues on giant stepped pedestals. The Roman forum, like the Etrusco-Roman temple, has a chief side, a focus of attention.

All around the square, behind the colonnades, were secular and religious structures, including the town's administrative offices. Most noteworthy is the *basilica* at the southwest corner (FIG. **3-12,** no. 3), the earliest well-preserved example of a building type that would have a long history in both Roman and Christian architecture. Constructed during the late second century BCE, the basilica was the town's administrative center and housed the law court. In plan it resembles the forum itself: long and narrow, with two stories of internal columns dividing the space into a central *nave* and flanking *aisles*.

Amphitheater Shortly after the Romans took control of Pompeii, two of the town's wealthiest officials used personal funds to erect a large *amphitheater* (FIG. **3-13**), or "double theater," at the southeastern end of town. Although Roman amphitheaters resemble two Greek theaters put together, the Greeks never built amphitheaters.

Greek theaters were situated on natural hillsides (FIG. **2-51**), but supporting an amphitheater's continuous elliptical *cavea* (seating area) required building an artificial mountain.

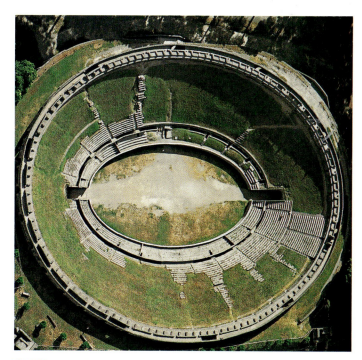

3-13 Aerial view of the amphitheater, Pompeii, Italy, ca. 70 BCE.

Pompeii boasts the earliest known amphitheater. Roman concrete technology made its elliptical cavea possible. The Pompeians staged bloody gladiatorial combats and wild animal hunts in the arena.

Roman Concrete Construction

The history of Roman architecture would be very different if the Romans had been content to use the same building materials as the Greeks, Etruscans, and other ancient peoples. Instead, the Romans developed concrete construction, which revolutionized architectural design. They made *concrete* from a changing recipe of lime mortar, volcanic sand, water, and small stones (*caementa,* from which the English word cement is derived). Builders placed the mixture in wooden frames and left it to dry and to bond with a brick or stone facing. When the concrete dried completely, they removed the wooden molds, leaving behind a solid mass of great strength, though rough in appearance. The Romans often covered the rough concrete with stucco or with marble *revetment* (facing). Despite this lengthy procedure, concrete walls were much less costly to construct than walls of imported Greek marble or even local tufa and travertine.

The advantages of concrete go well beyond cost, however. It is possible to fashion concrete shapes that masonry construction cannot achieve, especially huge vaulted and domed rooms without internal supports. The Romans came to prefer these to the Greek and Etruscan post-and-lintel structures. Concrete enabled Roman builders to think of architecture in revolutionary ways. Roman concrete became a vehicle for shaping architectural space.

The most common types of Roman concrete vaults and domes are

▪ **Barrel Vault** Also called the *tunnel vault,* the *barrel vault* (FIG. 3-14*a*) is an extension of a simple *arch,* creating a semicylindrical ceiling over parallel walls. Pre-Roman builders constructed barrel vaults using traditional ashlar masonry (for example, FIG. 1-20), but those vaults are less stable than concrete barrel vaults. If any of the blocks of a cut-stone vault come loose, the whole may collapse. Also, masonry barrel vaults can be illuminated only by light entering at either end of the tunnel. In contrast, windows can be placed at any point in concrete barrel vaults, because once the concrete hardens, it forms a seamless sheet

of "artificial stone" that builders can puncture almost at will. Whether made of stone or concrete, barrel vaults require *buttressing* (lateral support) of the walls below the vaults to counteract their downward and outward *thrust.*

▪ **Groin Vaults** A *groin,* or *cross, vault* (FIG. 3-14*b*) is formed by the intersection at right angles of two barrel vaults of equal size. Besides appearing lighter than the barrel vault, the groin vault needs less buttressing. The barrel vault's thrust is concentrated along the entire length of the supporting wall. The groin vault's thrust, however, is concentrated along the *groins,* and buttressing is needed only at the points where the groins meet the vault's vertical supports, usually *piers.* The system leaves the covered area open, permitting light to enter. Groin vaults, like barrel vaults, can be built using stone blocks—but with the same structural limitations when compared with concrete vaulting.

When a series of groin vaults covers an interior hall (FIG. 3-14*c*; compare FIGS. 3-36, 3-43, and 3-49,) the open lateral arches of the vaults form the equivalent of a clerestory of a traditional timber-roofed structure (FIGS. 4-4 and 4-5). Such a *fenestrated* (having openings or windows) sequence of groin vaults has a major advantage over wooden clerestories: Concrete vaults are relatively fireproof.

▪ **Hemispherical Domes** If a barrel vault is described as a round arch extended in a line, then a hemispherical *dome* (FIG. 3-14*d*) may be described as a round arch rotated around the full circumference of a circle. Masonry domes (FIG. 2-12), like masonry vaults, cannot accommodate windows without threat to structural stability. Builders can open up concrete domes even at their apex with a circular "eye" *(oculus),* allowing much-needed light to reach the often vast spaces beneath (FIG. 3-39). Hemispherical domes usually rest on concrete cylindrical *drums.*

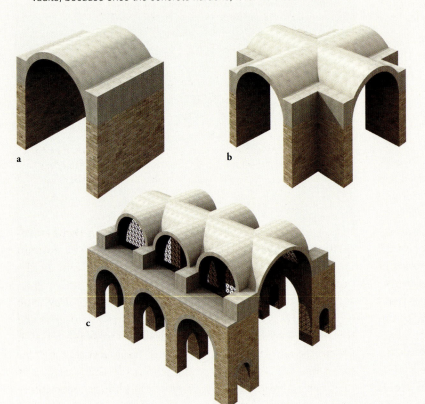

a

b

c

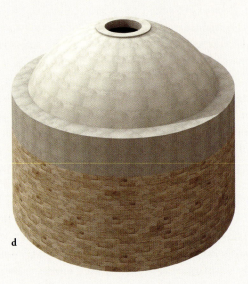

d

3-14 Roman concrete construction. **(a)** barrel vault, **(b)** groin vault, **(c)** fenestrated sequence of groin vaults, **(d)** hemispherical dome with oculus (John Burge).

Concrete domes and vaults of varying designs enabled Roman builders to revolutionize the history of architecture by shaping interior spaces in novel ways.

The Roman House

The entrance to a typical Roman *domus* (private house) was through a narrow foyer *(fauces),* which led to a large central reception area, the *atrium.* The rooms flanking the fauces could open onto the atrium, as in FIG. 3-16, or onto the street, in which case they were rented out as shops. The roof over the atrium was partially open to the sky, not only to admit light but also to channel rainwater into a basin *(impluvium)* below. The water could be stored in cisterns for household use. Opening onto the sides of the atrium were small bedrooms called *cubicula* (cubicles) and *alae* (wings). At the back was the owner's *tablinum,* or "home office." Early Roman houses also had a dining room *(triclinium)* and kitchen at the back or side of the atrium, and sometimes a small garden at the rear of the house. Endless variations of the same basic plan exist, dictated by an owner's personal tastes and means, the size and shape of the lot purchased, and so forth, but all Roman houses of this type were inward-looking in nature. The design shut out street noise and dust, and all internal activity focused on the brightly illuminated atrium at the center of the residence.

During the second century BCE, the Roman house took on Greek airs. Builders added a *peristyle* (colonnaded) garden at the rear, as in FIG. 3-16, providing a second internal illumination source as well as a pleasant setting for meals served in a summer triclinium. The axial symmetry of the plan meant that on entering the fauces of the house, a visitor had a view through the atrium directly into the peristyle garden (as in FIG. 3-15), which often boasted a fountain or pool, marble statuary, mural paintings, and mosaic floors.

3-15 Atrium of the House of the Vettii, Pompeii, Italy, second century BCE, rebuilt 62–79 CE.

Older Roman houses had a small garden behind the atrium, but beginning in the second century BCE, Roman builders added peristyles with Greek columns at the rear, as in the House of the Vettii.

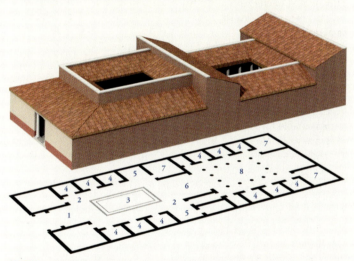

3-16 Restored view and plan of a typical Roman house of the Late Republic and Early Empire (John Burge). (1) fauces, (2) atrium, (3) impluvium, (4) cubiculum, (5) ala, (6) tablinum, (7) triclinium, (8) peristyle.

Roman houses were inward-looking with a central atrium open to the sky and an impluvium to collect rainwater. A visitor standing in the fauces had an axial view through to the peristyle garden.

Only concrete, unknown to the Greeks, could meet that requirement (see "Roman Concrete Construction," page 96). In the Pompeii amphitheater, the earliest known, a series of radially disposed concrete barrel vaults (FIG. 3-14*a*) forms a giant retaining wall that holds up the earthen mound and stone seats. Barrel vaults also form the tunnels leading to the *arena,* the central area where bloody *gladiatorial* combats and wild animal hunts occurred. (Arena is Latin for "sand," which soaked up the blood of the wounded and killed.) The Roman amphitheater stands in sharp contrast, both architecturally and functionally, to the Greek theater, home of refined performances of comedies and tragedies.

House of the Vettii The evidence from Pompeii regarding Roman domestic architecture (see "The Roman House," above) is unparalleled anywhere else. One of the best-preserved houses at Pompeii is the House of the Vettii. A photograph (FIG. 3-15) taken in the *fauces* shows the *impluvium* in the center of the *atrium,* the opening in the roof above, and, in the background, the *peristyle* (FIG. 3-16). Of course, only the wealthy—whether patricians or former slaves like the Vettius brothers, who made their fortune as merchants—could own spacious private houses with internal colonnades. The masses, especially in expensive cities like Rome, lived in multistory apartment houses.

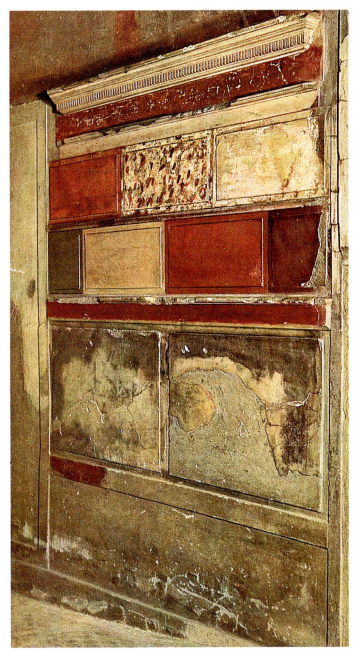

3-17 First Style wall painting in the fauces of the Samnite House, Herculaneum, Italy, late second century BCE.

In First Style murals, the decorator's aim was to imitate costly marble panels using painted stucco relief. The style is Greek in origin and another example of the Hellenization of Republican architecture.

Samnite House The houses and villas around Mount Vesuvius have also yielded the most complete record of the changing fashions in fresco painting anywhere in the ancient world. Art historians divide the various Roman mural types into four so-called Pompeian Styles. In the *First Style*, the decorator's aim was to imitate costly marble panels (for example, those seen in FIG. 3-39) using painted stucco relief. In the fauces (FIG. 3-17) of the Samnite House at Herculaneum, a stunning illusion of walls constructed, or at least faced, with marbles imported from quarries all over the Mediterranean greets visitors to the house. This approach to

wall decoration is comparable to the modern practice of using cheaper manufactured materials to approximate the look and shape of genuine wood paneling. This style is not, however, uniquely Roman. First Style walls are well documented in the Greek world from the late fourth century BCE on. The use of the First Style in Republican houses is yet another example of the Hellenization of Roman architecture.

Villa of the Mysteries The *Second Style*, introduced around 80 BCE, seems to be a Roman innovation and is in most respects the antithesis of the First Style. Second Style painters aimed to dissolve a room's confining walls and replace them with the illusion of an imaginary three-dimensional world. An early example of the new style is the room (FIG. 3-18) that gives its name to the Villa of the Mysteries at Pompeii. Many scholars believe this is the chamber where Pompeian women celebrated, in private, the rites of the Greek god Dionysos (Roman Bacchus). Dionysos was the focus of an unofficial mystery religion popular among Italian women at this time. The precise nature of the Dionysiac rites is unknown, but the figural cycle in the Villa of the Mysteries, illustrating mortals (all female save for one boy) interacting with mythological figures, probably provides some evidence for the cult's initiation rites. In these rites, young women united in marriage with Dionysos. The Second Style painter created the illusion of a shallow ledge on which human and divine actors move around the room. Especially striking is the way some of the figures interact across the corners of the room. For example, a seminude winged woman at the far right of the rear wall lashes out with her whip across the space of the room at a kneeling woman with a bare back (the initiate and bride-to-be of Dionysos) on the left end of the right wall.

Villa at Boscoreale In later Second Style designs, painters created a three-dimensional setting that also extends *beyond* the wall. An example is a cubiculum (FIG. 3-19) from the Villa of Publius Fannius Synistor at Boscoreale, decorated between 50 and 40 BCE. All around the room the painter opened up the walls with vistas of Italian towns, marble temples, and colonnaded courtyards. Painted doors and gates invite the viewer to walk through the wall into the magnificent world the painter created. Knowledge of single-point *linear perspective* (see "Renaissance Perspectival Systems," Chapter 8, page 232) explains in large part the Boscoreale painter's success in suggesting depth. In this kind of perspective, all the receding lines in a composition converge on a single point along the painting's central axis. Ancient writers state that Greek painters of the fifth century BCE first used linear perspective for the design of Athenian stage sets (hence its Greek name, *skenographia*, "scene painting"). In the Boscoreale cubiculum, the painter most successfully used linear perspective in the far corners, where a low gate leads to a peristyle framing a round temple (FIG. 3-19, *right*).

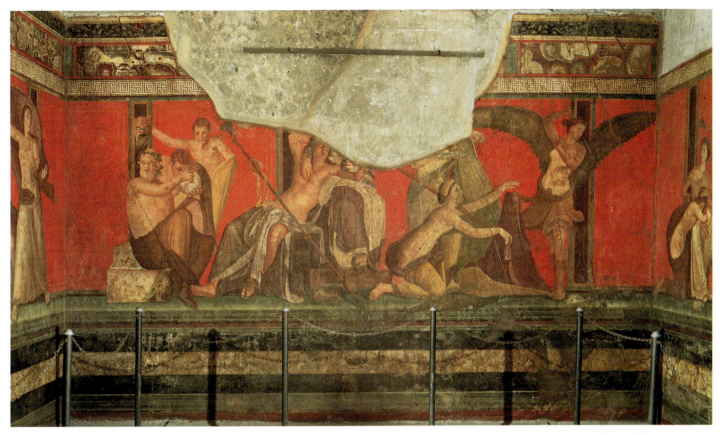

3-18 Dionysiac mystery frieze, Second Style wall paintings in room 5 of the Villa of the Mysteries, Pompeii, Italy, ca. 60–50 BCE. Frieze, 5′ 4″ high.

Second Style painters created the illusion of an imaginary three-dimensional world on the walls of Roman houses. The figures in this room act out the initiation rites of the mystery religion of Dionysos.

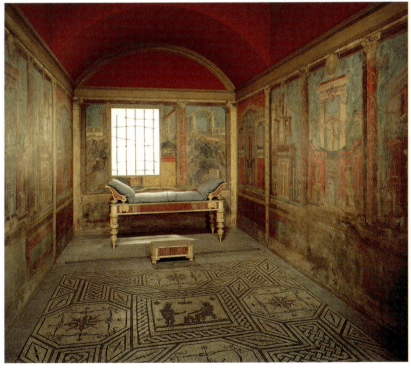
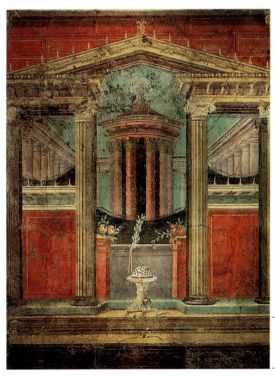

1 ft.

3-19 Second Style wall paintings (general view, *left*, and detail of tholos, *right*) from cubiculum M of the Villa of Publius Fannius Synistor, Boscoreale, Italy, ca. 50–40 BCE. Fresco, 8′ 9″ high. Metropolitan Museum of Art, New York.

In this Second Style bedroom, the painter opened up the walls with vistas of towns, temples, and colonnaded courtyards. The convincing illusionism is due in part to the artist's use of linear perspective.

3-20 Gardenscape, Second Style wall painting, from the Villa of Livia, Primaporta, Italy, ca. 30–20 BCE. Fresco, 6′ 7″ high. Museo Nazionale Romano—Palazzo Massimo alle Terme, Rome.

The ultimate example of a Second Style "picture window" wall is this gardenscape in Livia's villa. To suggest recession, the painter used atmospheric perspective, intentionally blurring the most distant forms.

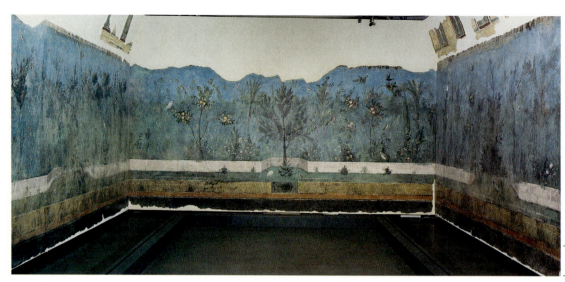

1 ft.

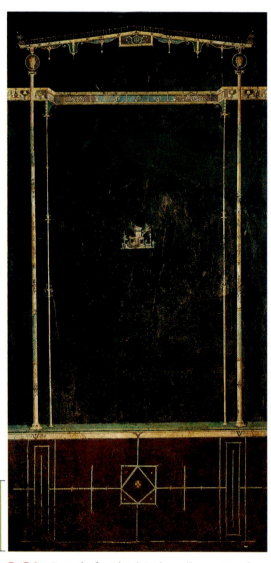

1 ft.

3-21 Detail of a Third Style wall painting, from cubiculum 15 of the Villa of Agrippa Postumus, Boscotrecase, Italy, ca. 10 BCE. Fresco, 7′ 8″ high. Metropolitan Museum of Art, New York.

In the Third Style, Roman painters decorated walls with delicate linear fantasies sketched on predominantly monochromatic backgrounds. A tiny floating landscape is the central motif on the solid black wall.

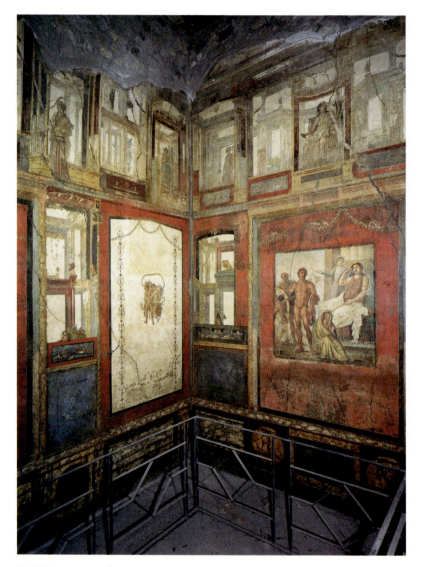

3-22 Fourth Style wall paintings in the Ixion Room (triclinium P) of the House of the Vettii, Pompeii, Italy, ca. 70–79 CE.

Fourth Style murals are often crowded and confused compositions with a mixture of fragmentary architectural vistas, framed panel paintings, and motifs favored in the First and Third Styles.

Villa of Livia The ultimate example of a Second Style "picture window" wall is the gardenscape (FIG. **3-20**) in the Villa of Livia, wife of the emperor Augustus, at Primaporta, just north of Rome. To suggest recession, the painter mastered another kind of perspective, *atmospheric perspective*, indicating depth by the increasingly blurred appearance of objects in the distance. At Livia's villa, the fence, trees, and birds in the foreground are precisely painted, whereas the details of the dense foliage in the background are indistinct.

Villa at Boscotrecase The Primaporta gardenscape is the polar opposite of First Style designs, which reinforce, rather than deny, the heavy presence of confining walls. But tastes changed rapidly in the Roman world, as in society today. Not long after Livia had her villa painted, Roman patrons began to favor mural designs that reasserted the primacy of the wall surface. In the *Third Style* of Pompeian painting, popular from about 15 BCE to 60 CE, artists no longer attempted to replace the walls with three-dimensional worlds of their own creation. Nor did they seek to imitate the appearance of the marble walls of Hellenistic kings. Instead they decorated walls with delicate linear fantasies sketched on predominantly *monochromatic* (one-color) backgrounds. One of the earliest examples of the Third Style is a room (FIG. **3-21**) in the Villa of Agrippa Postumus at Boscotrecase. Nowhere did the artist use illusionistic painting to penetrate the wall. In place of the stately columns of the Second Style are insubstantial and impossibly thin *colonnettes* supporting featherweight canopies barely reminiscent of pediments. In the center of this delicate and elegant architectural frame is a tiny floating landscape painted directly on the jet-black ground. It is hard to imagine a sharper contrast to the panoramic gardenscape at Livia's villa.

Ixion Room In the *Fourth Style*, a taste for illusionism returned once again. This style, fashionable in the two decades before the Vesuvian eruption of 79, is characterized by crowded and confused compositions with a mixture of fragmentary architectural vistas, framed panel paintings, and motifs favored in the First and Third Styles. The Ixion Room (FIG. **3-22**) of the House of the Vettii was probably painted shortly before the eruption. Its Fourth Style design is a résumé of all the previous styles, another instance of the eclecticism noted earlier as characteristic of Roman art in general. The lowest zone, for example, is one of the most successful imitations anywhere of costly multicolored imported marbles. The large white panels in the corners of the room, with their delicate floral frames and floating central motifs, would fit naturally into the most elegant Third Style design. Unmistakably Fourth Style, however, are the fragmentary architectural vistas of the central and upper zones. They are unrelated

to one another, do not constitute a unified cityscape beyond the wall, and incorporate figures that would tumble into the room if they took a single step forward.

The Ixion Room takes its nickname from the mythological painting at the center of the rear wall. Ixion had attempted to seduce Hera, and Zeus punished him by binding him to a perpetually spinning wheel. The paintings on the two side walls (not visible in FIG. **3-22**) also have Greek myths as subjects. The Ixion Room is a small private art gallery with framed paintings decorating the walls, as in many modern homes. Scholars long have believed that the models for these and the many other mythological paintings on Third and Fourth Style walls were lost Greek panels. Although few, if any, of the mythological paintings at Pompeii can be described as true copies of "Old Masters," they attest to the Romans' continuing admiration for Greek art.

Still Life One of the most frequent motifs on Roman painted walls is the *still life*, or painting of inanimate objects, artfully arranged. A still life with peaches and a carafe (FIG. **3-23**), a detail of a painted wall from Herculaneum, demonstrates that Roman painters sought to create illusionistic effects when depicting small objects as well as buildings and landscapes. The artist paid as much attention to shadows and highlights on the fruit, the stem and leaves, and the glass jar as to the objects themselves.

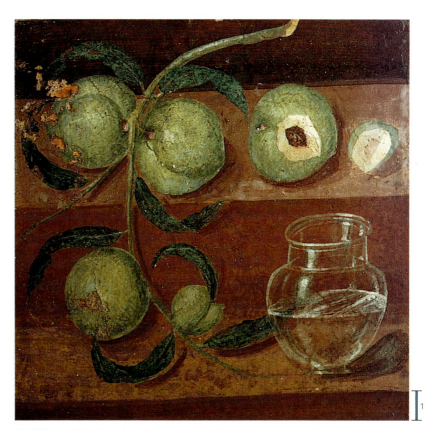

3-23 Still life with peaches, detail of a Fourth Style wall painting, from Herculaneum, Italy, ca. 62–79 CE. Fresco, 1′ 2″ × 1′ 1½″. Museo Archeologico Nazionale, Naples.

The Roman interest in illusionism explains the popularity of still-life paintings. This painter paid scrupulous attention to the play of light and shadow on different shapes and textures.

Early Empire

The murder of Julius Caesar on the Ides of March, 44 BCE, plunged the Roman world into a bloody civil war. The fighting lasted 13 years and ended only when Octavian, Caesar's grandnephew and adopted son, crushed the naval forces of Mark Antony and Queen Cleopatra of Egypt at Actium in northwestern Greece. Antony and Cleopatra committed suicide, and in 30 BCE, Egypt, once the wealthiest and most powerful kingdom of the ancient world, became another province in the ever-expanding Roman Empire.

Augustus Historians mark the passage from the old Roman Republic to the new Roman Empire from the day in 27 BCE when the Senate conferred the majestic title of Augustus (r. 27 BCE–14 CE) on Octavian. The Empire was ostensibly a continuation of the Republic, with the same constitutional offices, but in fact Augustus, as *princeps* (first citizen), occupied all the key positions. He was consul and *imperator* (commander in chief; root of the word "emperor") and even, after 12 BCE, *pontifex maximus* (chief priest of the state religion). These offices gave Augustus control of all aspects of Roman public life.

With powerful armies keeping order on the Empire's frontiers and no opposition at home, Augustus brought peace and prosperity to a war-weary Mediterranean world. Known in his own day as the *Pax Augusta* (Augustan Peace), the peace Augustus established prevailed for two centuries. It came to be called simply the *Pax Romana*. During this time Roman emperors commissioned a huge number of public works throughout their territories, all on an unprecedented scale. The erection of imperial portraits and monuments covered with reliefs recounting the various emperors' great deeds reminded people everywhere of the source of this beneficence. These portraits and reliefs often presented a picture that bore little resemblance to historical fact. Their purpose, however, was not to provide an objective record but to mold public opinion.

When Augustus vanquished Antony and Cleopatra in 31 BCE and became undisputed master of the Mediterranean world, he had not reached his 32nd birthday. The rule by elders that had characterized the Roman Republic for nearly half a millennium came to an abrupt end. Suddenly Roman portraitists were called on to produce images of a *youthful* head of state. But Augustus was not merely young. Caesar had been made a god after his death, and Augustus, while never claiming to be a god himself, widely advertised himself as the son of a god. His portraits were designed to present the image of a godlike leader, a superior being who, miraculously, never aged. The models for Augustus's idealized portraits were Classical Greek artworks. The statue of Augustus (FIG. **3-1**) from Primaporta depicts the emperor as general, standing in the pose of Polykleitos's *Doryphoros* (FIG. **2-34**), addressing his troops with his right arm extended in the manner of the orator Aule Metele (FIG. **3-8**). Although the head is that of an individual and not a nameless athlete, its overall shape, the sharp ridges of the brows, and the tight cap of layered hair

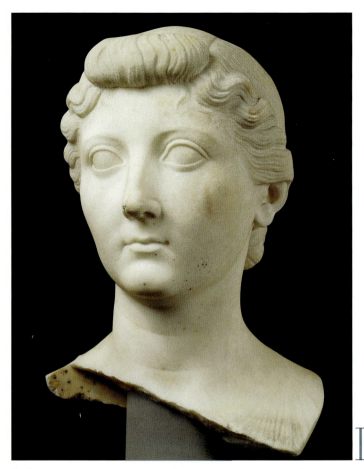

3-24 Portrait bust of Livia, from Arsinoe, Egypt, early first century CE. Marble, 1' 1½" high. Ny Carlsberg Glyptotek, Copenhagen.

Livia sports the latest Roman coiffure, but her youthful appearance and sharply defined features derive from images of Greek goddesses. She lived until 87, but never aged in her portraits.

emulate the Polykleitan style. The reliefs on the emperor's breastplate celebrate a victory over the Parthians. The Cupid at Augustus's feet refers to his divine descent from Venus. Every facet of the portrait carried a political message.

Livia A marble portrait (FIG. **3-24**) of Livia shows that the imperial women of the Augustan age shared the emperor's eternal youthfulness. Although she sports the latest Roman coiffure, with the hair rolled over the forehead and knotted at the nape of the neck, Livia's blemish-free skin and sharply defined features derive from images of Classical Greek goddesses. Livia outlived Augustus by 15 years, dying at age 87. In her portraits, the coiffure changed with the introduction of each new fashion, but her face remained ever young, befitting her exalted position in the Roman state.

Ara Pacis Augustae On Livia's birthday in 9 BCE, Augustus dedicated the Ara Pacis Augustae (Altar of Augustan Peace; FIG. **3-25**), the monument celebrating his most important achievement, the establishment of peace. Acanthus tendrils adorn the altar's marble precinct walls, which have Corinthian *pilasters* at the corners. The *Corinthian capital* was a Greek innovation of the fifth century BCE, but it did not

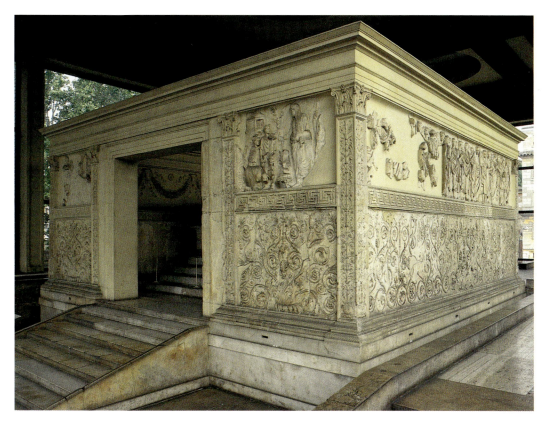

3-25 Ara Pacis Augustae (Altar of Augustan Peace), Rome, Italy, 13–9 BCE.

Augustus sought to present his new order as a Golden Age equaling that of Athens under Pericles. The Ara Pacis celebrates the emperor's most important achievement, the establishment of peace.

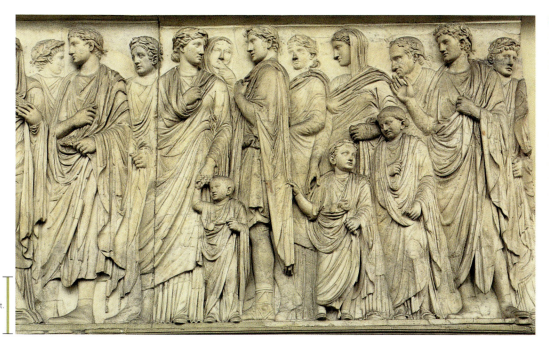

1 ft.

3-26 Procession of the imperial family, detail of the south frieze of the Ara Pacis Augustae, Rome, Italy, 13–9 BCE. Marble, 5′ 3″ high.

Although inspired by the Panathenaic procession frieze of the Parthenon (FIG. 2-41), the Ara Pacis friezes depict recognizable individuals, including children. Augustus promoted marriage and childbearing.

become popular until Hellenistic and especially Roman times. More ornate than either the Doric or Ionic capital, the Corinthian capital consists of a double row of acanthus leaves, from which tendrils and flowers emerge, wrapped around a bell-shaped echinus. The rich floral and vegetal ornament of the altar's exterior alludes to the prosperity that peace brings.

Four panels on the east and west ends of the Ara Pacis depict carefully selected mythological subjects, including (at the right in FIG. 3-25) a relief of Aeneas making a sacrifice. Aeneas was the son of Venus and one of Augustus's forefathers. The connection between the emperor and Aeneas was a key element of Augustus's political ideology for his new

Golden Age. It is no coincidence that Vergil wrote the *Aeneid* during the rule of Augustus. The epic poem glorified the young emperor by celebrating the founder of the Julian line.

Processions of the imperial family (FIG. 3-26) and other important dignitaries appear on the long north and south sides of the Ara Pacis. These parallel friezes were clearly inspired to some degree by the Panathenaic procession frieze of the Parthenon (FIG. 2-41, *bottom*). Augustus sought to present his new order as a Golden Age equaling that of Athens under Pericles. The emulation of Classical models thus made a political as well as an artistic statement. Even so, the Roman procession is very different in character. On the Parthenon,

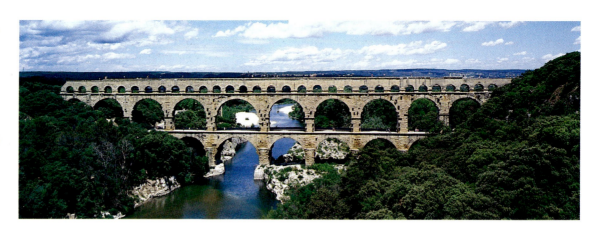

3-27 Pont-du-Gard, Nîmes, France, ca. 16 BCE.

Roman engineers constructed roads, bridges, and aqueducts throughout the Empire. This aqueduct bridge brought water from a distant mountain spring to Nîmes—about 100 gallons a day for each of the city's inhabitants.

anonymous figures act out an Athenian event that recurred every four years. The frieze stands for *all* Panathenaic Festival processions. The Ara Pacis depicts a singular event (probably the inaugural ceremony of 13 BCE) and recognizable contemporary figures. Among those portrayed are children, who restlessly tug on their elders' garments and talk to one another when they should be quiet on a solemn occasion. Augustus was concerned about a decline in the birthrate among the Roman nobility, and he enacted a series of laws designed to promote marriage, marital fidelity, and raising children. The portrayal of men with their families on the Altar of Peace served as a moral exemplar.

Pont-du-Gard During the Pax Romana, Rome sent engineers to construct aqueducts, roads, and bridges throughout its far-flung empire. In southern France, outside Nîmes, still stands the aqueduct-bridge known as the Pont-du-Gard (FIG. 3-27). The aqueduct provided about 100 gallons of water a day for each inhabitant of Nîmes from a mountain spring some 30 miles away. The water flowed over the considerable distance by gravity in channels built with a continuous gradual decline over the entire route from source to city. Roman builders erected the three-story bridge at Nîmes to maintain the height of the water channel where the water crossed the Gard River. Each large arch spans some 82 feet and incorporates blocks weighing up to two tons each. The bridge's uppermost level consists of a row of smaller arches, three above each of the large openings below. They carry the water channel itself. Their quickened rhythm and the harmonious proportional relationship between the larger and smaller arches reveal that the Roman engineer-architect had a keen aesthetic as well as practical sense.

The Flavians For a half century after Augustus's death, Rome's emperors all came from his family, the Julians, or his wife Livia's, the Claudians. But the outrageous behavior of Nero (r. 54–68 CE) produced a powerful backlash. Nero was forced to commit suicide in 68 CE, bringing the Julio-Claudian dynasty to an end and ushering in a year of renewed civil strife. The man who emerged triumphant in this brief but bloody conflict was Vespasian (r. 69–79 CE), a general who had served under Nero. Vespasian, whose family name was Flavius, had two sons, Titus (r. 79–81 CE) and Domitian

(r. 81–96 CE). The Flavian dynasty ruled Rome for more than a quarter century.

Colosseum The Flavian Amphitheater, or Colosseum (FIGS. 3-28 and 3-9, no. 12), was one of Vespasian's first undertakings after becoming emperor. The decision to build the Colosseum was very shrewd politically. The site chosen was on the property Nero had confiscated from the Roman people after a great fire in 64 CE in order to build a private villa for himself. By constructing the new amphitheater there, Vespasian reclaimed the land for the public and provided

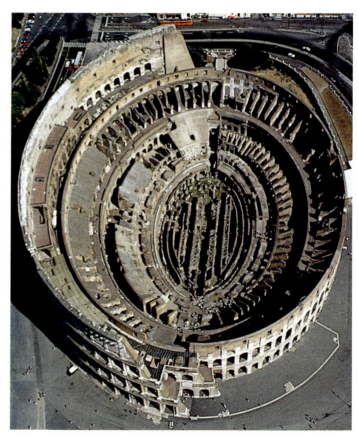

3-28 Aerial view of the Colosseum (Flavian Amphitheater), Rome, Italy, ca. 70–80 CE.

Vespasian built the Colosseum, the world's largest amphitheater, on land that Nero had confiscated from the public. A complex system of concrete barrel vaults once held up the seats for 50,000 spectators.

Romans with the largest arena for gladiatorial combats and other lavish spectacles that had ever been constructed. The Colosseum could hold more than 50,000 spectators, but it takes its name from its location beside the Colossus of Nero (FIG. 3-9, no. 11). The huge statue, which stood at the entrance to his villa, portrayed the emperor as the sun god. To mark the opening of the Colosseum, the Flavians staged games for 100 days. The highlight was the flooding of the arena to stage a complete naval battle with more than 3,000 participants.

The Colosseum, like the much earlier Pompeian amphitheater (FIG. 3-13), could not have been built without concrete. A complex system of barrel-vaulted corridors holds up the enormous oval seating area. This concrete "skeleton" is visible today because the amphitheater's marble seats were hauled away during the Middle Ages and Renaissance. Also exposed are the arena substructures, which housed waiting rooms for the gladiators, animal cages, and machinery for raising and lowering stage sets as well as animals and humans. Ingenious lifting devices brought beasts from their dark dens into the arena's bright light.

The exterior travertine shell (FIG. 3-29) is approximately 160 feet high, the height of a modern 16-story building. The facade is divided into four bands, with large arched openings piercing the lower three. Ornamental Greek orders frame the arches in the standard Roman sequence for multistory buildings: from the ground up, Tuscan Doric, Ionic, and then Corinthian. The use of engaged columns and a lintel to frame the openings in the Colosseum's facade is a common motif on Roman buildings. As in the pseudoperipteral temple (FIG. 3-10), which is an eclectic mix of Greek orders and Etruscan plan, this way of decorating a building's facade combined Greek orders with an architectural form foreign to Greek post-and-lintel architecture, namely the arch. The engaged columns and even the arches had no structural purpose, but they added variety to the surface and unified the multistory facade by casting a net of verticals and horizontals over it.

Flavian Portraiture Flavian portraits survive in large numbers. A marble bust (FIG. 3-30) of a young woman, probably a Flavian princess, is of special interest as an early

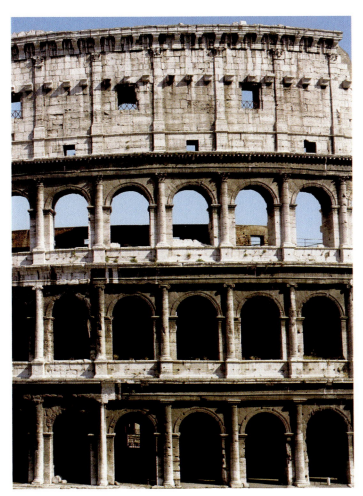

3-29 Detail of the facade of the Colosseum (Flavian Amphitheater), Rome, Italy, ca. 70–80 CE.

Engaged Doric, Ionic, and Corinthian columns frame the arcuated openings of the Colosseum. This eclectic mix of Greek and Roman elements masked the amphitheater's skeleton of concrete vaults.

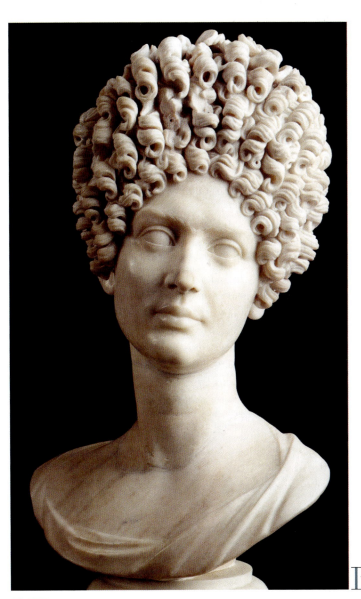

1 in.

3-30 Portrait bust of a Flavian woman, from Rome, Italy, ca. 90 CE. Marble, 2′ 1″ high. Musei Capitolini, Rome.

The Flavian sculptor reproduced the elaborate coiffure of this elegant woman by drilling deep holes for the corkscrew curls, and carved the rest of the hair and the face with hammer and chisel.

3-31 Arch of Titus, Rome, Italy, after 81 CE.

Domitian erected this arch on the road leading into the Roman Forum to honor his brother, the emperor Titus, who became a god after his death. Victories fill the spandrels of the arcuated passageway.

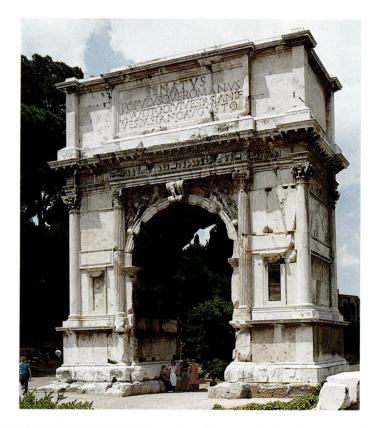

example of the use of the drill in Roman sculpture. The portrait is notable for its elegance and delicacy and for the virtuoso way the sculptor rendered the differing textures of hair and flesh. The artist reproduced the corkscrew curls of the elaborate Flavian coiffure by drilling deep into the stone in addition to carving with the traditional hammer and chisel. The drillwork created a dense mass of light and shadow set off boldly from the softly modeled and highly polished skin of the face and swanlike neck.

Arch of Titus When Titus died in 81 CE, his younger brother, Domitian, who succeeded him as emperor, erected a *triumphal arch* (FIGS. **3-31** and **3-9**, no. 9) in Titus's honor on the road leading into the Roman Forum (FIG. 3-9, no. 7). The Arch of Titus is typical of early triumphal arches in having only one passageway. As on the Colosseum, engaged columns frame the *arcuated* (arch-shaped) opening. Reliefs depict-

3-32 Spoils of Jerusalem, relief panel in passageway of the Arch of Titus, Rome, Italy, after 81 CE. Marble, 7′ 10″ high.

The reliefs inside the bay of the Arch of Titus commemorate the emperor's greatest achievement—the conquest of Judaea. Here, Roman soldiers carry the spoils taken from the Jewish temple in Jerusalem.

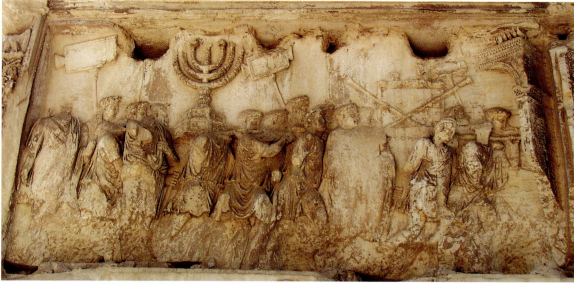

1 ft.

3-33 Triumph of Titus, relief panel in passageway of the Arch of Titus, Rome, Italy, after 81 CE. Marble, 7′ 10″ high.

Victory accompanies Titus in his triumphal chariot. Also present are personifications of Honor and Valor. This is the first known instance of the intermingling of human and divine figures in a Roman historical relief.

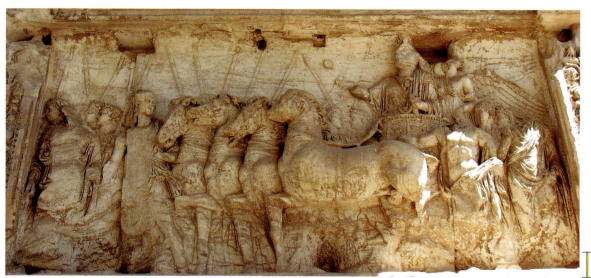

1 ft.

ing personified Victories fill the *spandrels* (the area between the arch's curve and the framing columns and entablature). A dedicatory inscription stating that the Senate erected the arch to honor the god Titus, son of the god Vespasian, dominates the *attic*. (Roman emperors normally were proclaimed gods after they died, as Augustus was, but if they ran afoul of the Senate, they were damned. The statues of those who suffered *damnatio memoriae* were torn down, and their names were erased from public inscriptions. This was Nero's fate.)

Inside the passageway of the Arch of Titus are two great relief panels. They represent the triumphal parade of Titus after his return from the conquest of Judaea at the end of the Jewish Wars in 70 CE. One of the reliefs (FIG. **3-32**) depicts Roman soldiers carrying the spoils from the Temple in Jerusalem. Despite considerable damage to the relief, the illusion of movement is convincing. The parade moves forward from the left background into the center foreground and disappears through the obliquely placed arch in the right background. The energy and swing of the column of soldiers suggest a rapid march. The sculptor rejected the low relief of the Ara Pacis (FIG. 3-26) in favor of extremely deep carving, which produces strong shadows. The heads of the forward figures have broken off because they stood free from the block. Their high relief emphasized their different placement in space from the heads in low relief, which are intact. The play of light and shade across the protruding foreground and receding background figures enhances the sense of movement.

The panel (FIG. **3-33**) on the other side of the passageway shows Titus in his triumphal chariot. Victory rides with the emperor and places a wreath on his head. Below her is a bare-chested youth who is probably a personification of

Honor (Honos). A female personification of Valor (Virtus) leads the horses. These allegorical figures transform the relief from a record of Titus's battlefield success into a celebration of imperial virtues. A similar intermingling of divine and human figures occurs in the Mysteries frieze (FIG. 3-18) at Pompeii, but the Titus panel is the first known instance of divine beings interacting with humans on an official Roman historical relief. (On the Ara Pacis, FIG. 3-25, the gods, heroes, and personifications appear in separate framed panels, carefully segregated from the procession of living Romans.) The Arch of Titus reliefs date after the emperor's death, when Titus was already a god. Soon afterward, however, this kind of interaction between mortals and immortals became a staple of Roman narrative relief sculpture, even on monuments honoring a living emperor.

High Empire

Domitian's extravagant lifestyle and ego resembled Nero's. He so angered the senators that he was assassinated in 96 CE. The first emperor of the second century, chosen with the consent of the Senate, was Trajan (r. 98–117 CE), a capable and popular general. Born in Spain, Trajan was the first non-Italian to rule Rome. During his reign, the Roman Empire reached its greatest extent (MAP 3-1), and the imperial government took on ever greater responsibility for its people's welfare by instituting a number of farsighted social programs.

Forum of Trajan Trajan's major building project in Rome was a huge new forum (FIGS. **3-34** and 3-9, no. 5), which glorified his victories in two wars against the Dacians (who occupied what is now Romania). The architect was

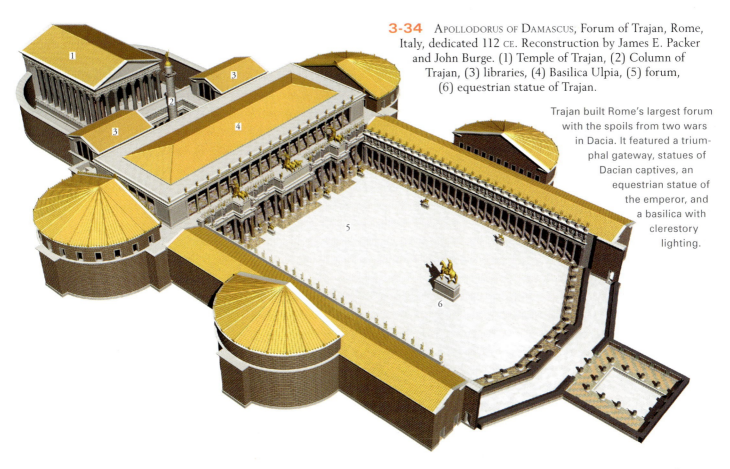

3-34 APOLLODORUS OF DAMASCUS, Forum of Trajan, Rome, Italy, dedicated 112 CE. Reconstruction by James E. Packer and John Burge. (1) Temple of Trajan, (2) Column of Trajan, (3) libraries, (4) Basilica Ulpia, (5) forum, (6) equestrian statue of Trajan.

Trajan built Rome's largest forum with the spoils from two wars in Dacia. It featured a triumphal gateway, statues of Dacian captives, an equestrian statue of the emperor, and a basilica with clerestory lighting.

APOLLODORUS OF DAMASCUS, Trajan's chief military engineer, who had constructed a world-famous bridge across the Danube River. Apollodorus's plan incorporated the main features of most early forums (FIG. 3-12), except that a huge basilica, not a temple, dominated the colonnaded open square. The temple (completed after the emperor's death and dedicated to the newest god in the Roman pantheon, Trajan himself) was set instead behind the basilica. Entry to Trajan's forum was through an impressive gateway resembling a triumphal arch. Inside the forum were other reminders of Trajan's military prowess. A larger-than-life-size gilded-bronze equestrian statue of the emperor stood at the center of the great court in front of the basilica. Statues of captive Dacians stood above the columns of the forum porticos.

The Basilica Ulpia (Trajan's family name was Ulpius) was a much larger and far more ornate version of the basilica in the forum of Pompeii (FIG. 3-12, no. 3). As shown in FIG. 3-34, no. 4, it had *apses* (semicircular recesses) on each short end. Two aisles flanked the nave on each side. The building was vast: about 400 feet long (without the apses) and 200 feet wide. Light entered through *clerestory* windows, made possible by elevating the timber-roofed nave above the colonnaded aisles. In the Republican basilica at Pompeii, light reached the nave only indirectly through aisle windows. The clerestory (used millennia before at Karnak in Egypt; FIG. 1-32) was a much better way to illuminate the interior space.

Column of Trajan

The Column of Trajan (FIG. 3-35), erected between the Basilica Ulpia and the Temple of Trajan, still stands. It is 128 feet high and has a monumental base decorated with captured Dacian arms and armor. A heroically nude statue of the emperor once topped the column. The 625-foot band that winds around the shaft is the first instance of a spiral narrative frieze. The reliefs depict Trajan's two Dacian campaigns. The story unfolds in more than 150 episodes in which some 2,500 figures appear. The relief is very low so as not to distort the contours of the column. Paint enhanced the legibility of the figures, but a viewer still would have had difficulty following

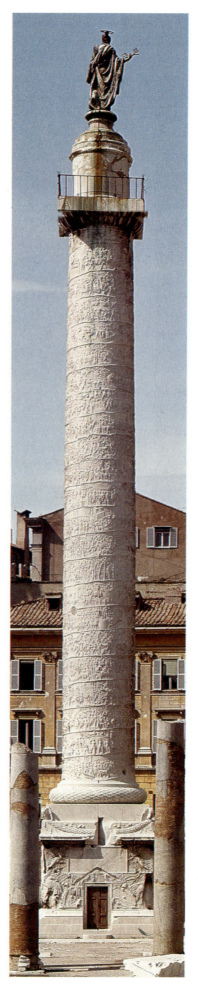

the narrative from beginning to end. That is why much of the frieze consists of easily recognizable compositions: Trajan addressing his troops, sacrificing to the gods, and so on. The narrative is not a reliable chronological account of the Dacian Wars, as was once thought. The sculptors nonetheless accurately recorded the general character of the campaigns. Notably, battle scenes occupy only about a quarter of the frieze. The Romans spent more time constructing forts, transporting men and equipment, and preparing for battle than they did fighting. The focus is always on the emperor, who appears repeatedly in the frieze, but the enemy is not belittled. The Romans won because of their superior organization and more powerful army, not because they were inherently superior beings.

Markets of Trajan

On the Quirinal Hill overlooking the forum, Apollodorus built the Markets of Trajan (FIG. 3-9, no. 6) to house both shops and administrative offices. The transformation of the hill into a multilevel complex was made possible by the use of concrete. The basic unit was the *taberna*, a single-room shop covered by a barrel vault. The shops were on several levels. They opened either onto a hemispherical facade winding around one of the great *exedras* (semicircular recessed areas) of Trajan's forum, onto a paved street farther up the hill, or onto a great indoor market hall (FIG. 3-36) resembling a modern shopping mall. The hall housed two floors of shops, with the upper shops set back on each side and lit by skylights. Light from the same sources reached the ground-floor shops through arches beneath the great umbrella-like groin vaults (FIG. 3-14c) covering the hall.

Pantheon

Upon Trajan's death, Hadrian (r. 117–138 CE), also a Spaniard and a relative of Trajan's, succeeded him as emperor. Almost immediately, he began work on the

3-35 Column of Trajan, Forum of Trajan, Rome, Italy, dedicated 112 CE.

The spiral frieze of Trajan's Column tells the story of the Dacian Wars in 150 episodes. The sculptors represented all aspects of the campaigns, from fierce battles to solemn sacrifices and road and fort construction.

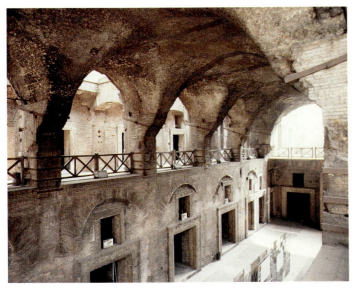

3-36 APOLLODORUS OF DAMASCUS, interior of the great hall, Markets of Trajan, Rome, Italy, ca. 100–112 CE.

The great hall of Trajan's Markets resembled a modern shopping mall. It housed two floors of shops, with the upper shops set back and lit by skylights. Concrete groin vaults covered the central space.

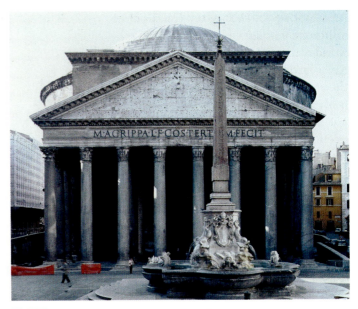

3-37 Pantheon, Rome, Italy, 118–125 CE.

Visitors first saw the facade of Hadrian's "temple of all gods" after entering a columnar courtyard. Like a temple in a Roman forum (FIG. 3-12), the Pantheon stood at one narrow end of the enclosure.

Pantheon (FIGS. **3-37** and **3-9**, no. 4), the temple of all the gods. The Pantheon reveals the full potential of concrete, both as a building material and as a means for shaping architectural space. The approach to the temple was from a columnar courtyard (FIG. **3-38**), and, like temples in Roman forums, the Pantheon stood at one narrow end of the enclo-sure. Its facade of eight Corinthian columns—almost all that could be seen from ground level in antiquity—was a bow to tradition. Everything else about the Pantheon was revolu-tionary. Behind the columnar porch is an immense concrete cylinder covered by a huge hemispherical dome 142 feet in diameter. The dome's top is also 142 feet from the floor

3-38 Restored cutaway view of the Pantheon, Rome, Italy, 118–125 CE (John Burge).

The Pantheon's traditional facade masked its revolutionary cylindrical drum and its huge hemispherical dome. The interior symbolized both the orb of the earth and the vault of the heavens.

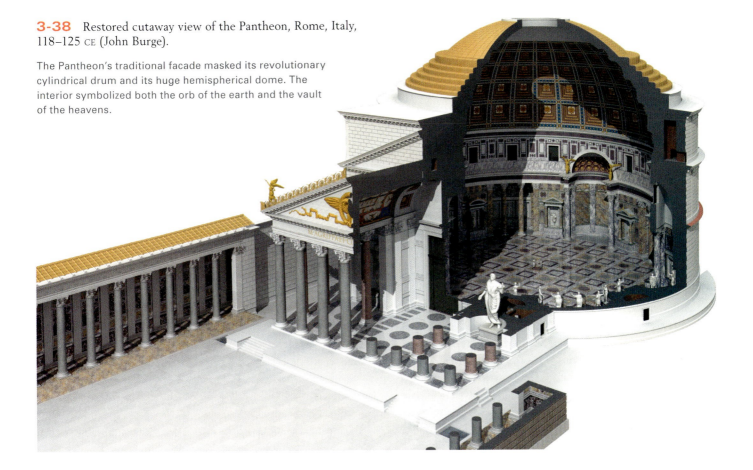

(FIG. **3-39**). The design is thus based on the intersection of two circles (one horizontal, the other vertical) so that the interior space can be imagined as the orb of the earth and the dome as the vault of the heavens.

If the Pantheon's design is simplicity itself, executing that design took all the ingenuity of Hadrian's engineers. They built up the cylindrical drum level by level using concrete of varied composition. Extremely hard and durable basalt went into the mix for the foundations, and the builders gradually modified the "recipe" until, at the top, featherweight pumice replaced stones to lighten the load. The dome's thickness also decreases as it nears the oculus, the circular opening 30 feet in diameter that is the only light source for the interior. The use of *coffers* (sunken decorative panels) reduced the dome's weight, without weakening its structure, and provided a handsome pattern of squares within the vast circle. Renaissance drawings suggest that each coffer once had a glistening gilded-bronze rosette at its center, enhancing the symbolism of the dome as the starry heavens.

Below the dome, much of the original marble veneer of the walls, niches, and floor has survived. In the Pantheon, visitors can get a sense, as almost nowhere else, of how magnificent the interiors of Roman concrete buildings could be. But despite the luxurious skin of the Pantheon's interior, the sense experienced on first entering the structure is not the weight of the enclosing walls but the space they enclose. In pre-Roman architecture, the form of the enclosed space was determined by the placement of the solids, which did not so much shape space as interrupt it. Roman architects were the first to conceive of architecture in terms of units of space that could be shaped by the enclosures. The Pantheon's interior is a single unified, self-sufficient whole, uninterrupted by supporting solids. Through the oculus, the space opens to the drifting clouds, the blue sky, the sun, and the gods. Inside the Pantheon, the architect used light not just to illuminate the darkness but to create drama and underscore the symbolism of the interior shape. On a sunny day, the light that passes through the oculus forms a circular beam, a disk of light that moves across the coffered dome in the course of the day as the sun moves across the sky itself. Escaping from the noise and heat of a Roman summer day into the Pantheon's cool, calm, and

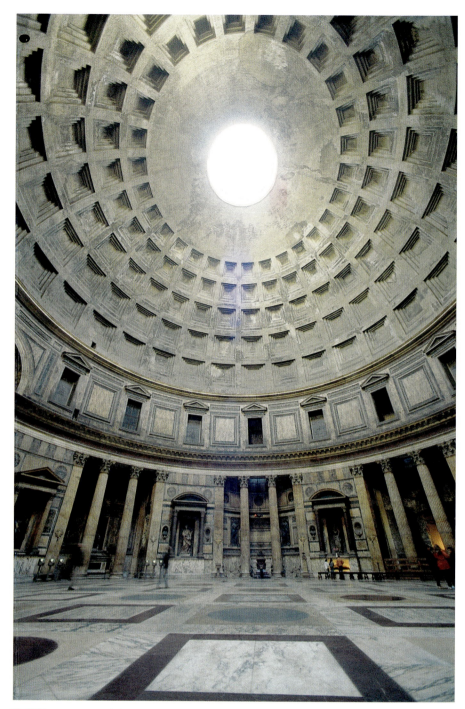

3-39 Interior of the Pantheon, Rome, Italy, 118–125 CE.

The coffered dome of the Pantheon is 142 feet in diameter and 142 feet high. The light entering through its oculus forms a circular beam that moves across the dome as the sun moves across the sky.

mystical immensity is an experience almost impossible to describe and one that should not be missed.

Marcus Aurelius Perhaps the most majestic surviving portrait of a Roman emperor is the larger-than-life-size gilded-bronze equestrian statue (FIG. **3-40**) of Marcus Aurelius (r. 161–180 CE), one of the Antonine emperors who followed Hadrian. Marcus's statue possesses a superhuman grandeur. The sculptor portrayed the emperor as much larger than any normal human would be in relation to his

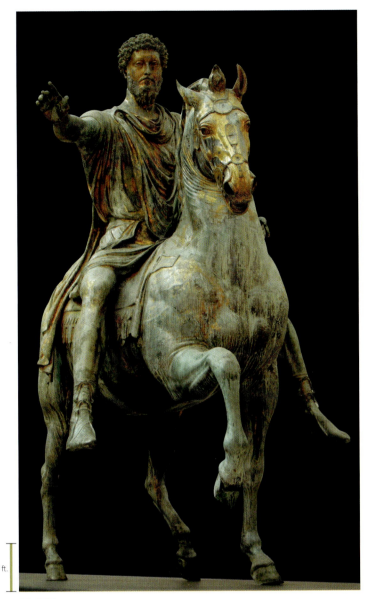

1 ft.

3-40 Equestrian statue of Marcus Aurelius, from Rome, Italy, ca. 175 CE. Bronze, 11′ 6″ high. Musei Capitolini, Rome.

In this portrait on horseback, which conveys the power of the Roman emperor, Marcus Aurelius stretches out his arm in a gesture of clemency. An enemy once cowered beneath the horse's raised foreleg.

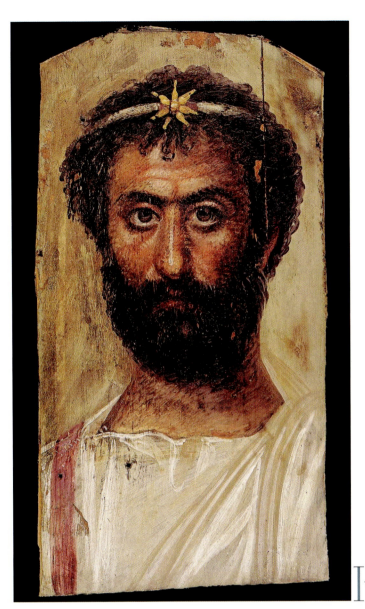

1 in.

3-41 Mummy portrait of a priest of Serapis, from Hawara (Faiyum), Egypt, ca. 140–160 CE. Encaustic on wood, 1′ 4¾″ × 8¾″. British Museum, London.

In Roman times, the Egyptians continued to bury their dead in mummy cases, but painted portraits replaced the traditional masks. This portrait was painted in encaustic, a mixture of colors and hot wax.

horse. He stretches out his right arm in a gesture that is both a greeting and an offer of clemency. Some evidence suggests that beneath the horse's raised right foreleg an enemy once cowered, begging Marcus for mercy. The statue conveys the majestic power of the Roman emperor as ruler of the whole world. This message of supreme confidence, however, is not conveyed by the emperor's head. Marcus has long, curly hair and a full beard, consistent with the latest fashion, but his forehead is lined, and his eyes appear saddened. He seems weary, even worried. For the first time, the strain of constant warfare on the frontiers and the burden of ruling a worldwide empire show in the emperor's face. The Antonine sculptor ventured beyond Republican verism, exposing the ruler's character, his thoughts, and his soul for all to see, as

Marcus revealed them himself in his *Meditations*, a deeply moving philosophical treatise setting forth the emperor's personal worldview. This kind of introspective verism was a profound change from Classical idealism. It marks a major turning point in the history of ancient art.

Mummy Portraits Painted portraits were common in the Roman Empire, but most have perished. In Roman Egypt, however, large numbers have been found because the Egyptians continued to bury their dead in mummy cases (see "Mummification," Chapter 1, page 36), with painted portraits on wood replacing the traditional stylized portrait masks. One example (FIG. 3-41) depicts a priest of the Egyptian god Serapis. The artist probably painted the portrait

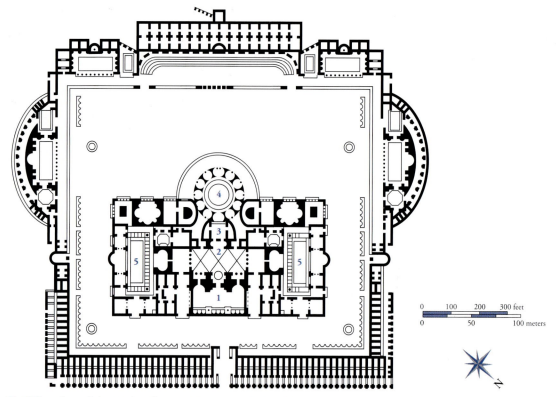

3-42 Plan of the Baths of Caracalla, Rome, Italy, 212–216 CE. (1) natatio, (2) frigidarium, (3) tepidarium, (4) caldarium, (5) palaestra.

Caracalla's baths could accommodate 1,600 bathers. They resembled a modern health spa and included libraries, lecture halls, and exercise courts in addition to bathing rooms and a swimming pool.

while the man was still alive. The technique is *encaustic*, in which the painter mixes colors with hot wax and then applies the mixture with a spatula to a wooden panel. This portrait exhibits the painter's refined use of the brush and spatula, mastery of the depiction of varied textures and of the play of light over the soft and delicately modeled face, and sensitive portrayal of the deceased's calm demeanor. Artists also applied encaustic to stone, and the mummy portraits give some idea of the appearance of Roman marble portraits. According to Pliny, when Praxiteles, perhaps the greatest marble sculptor of the ancient world, was asked which of his statues he preferred, the fourth-century BCE Greek artist replied, "Those that Nikias painted."[2] This anecdote underscores the importance of coloration in ancient statuary.

Late Empire

By the time of Marcus Aurelius, two centuries after Augustus established the Pax Romana, Roman power was beginning to erode. It was increasingly difficult to maintain order on the frontiers, and even within the Empire the authority of Rome was being challenged. Marcus's son Commodus (r. 180–192 CE) was assassinated, bringing the Antonine dynasty to an end. The economy was in decline, and the efficient imperial bureaucracy was disintegrating. Even the official state religion was losing ground to Eastern cults,

Christianity among them, which were beginning to gain large numbers of converts. The Late Empire was a pivotal era in world history during which the pagan civilization of classical antiquity was gradually transformed into the Christian civilization of the Middle Ages.

Baths of Caracalla Civil conflict followed Commodus's death. When it ended, an African-born general named Septimius Severus (r. 193–211 CE) was master of the Roman world. The Severans were active builders in the capital. Septimius's son and successor, Caracalla (r. 211–217 CE), built the greatest in a long line of bathing and recreational complexes erected with imperial funds to win the public's favor. Made of brick-faced concrete and covered by enormous vaults springing from thick walls up to 140 feet high, the Baths of Caracalla (FIG. 3-42) covered an area of almost 50 acres. The design was symmetrical along a central axis, facilitating the Roman custom of taking sequential plunges in warm-, hot-, and cold-water baths in the *tepidarium, caldarium,* and *frigidarium* respectively. There were stuccoed vaults, mosaic floors, marble-faced walls, and colossal statuary throughout the complex, which also featured landscaped gardens, lecture halls, libraries, colonnaded exercise courts (*palaestras*), and a giant swimming pool (*natatio*). Archaeologists estimate that up to 1,600 bathers at a time could enjoy this Roman equivalent of a modern health spa. Both men and women

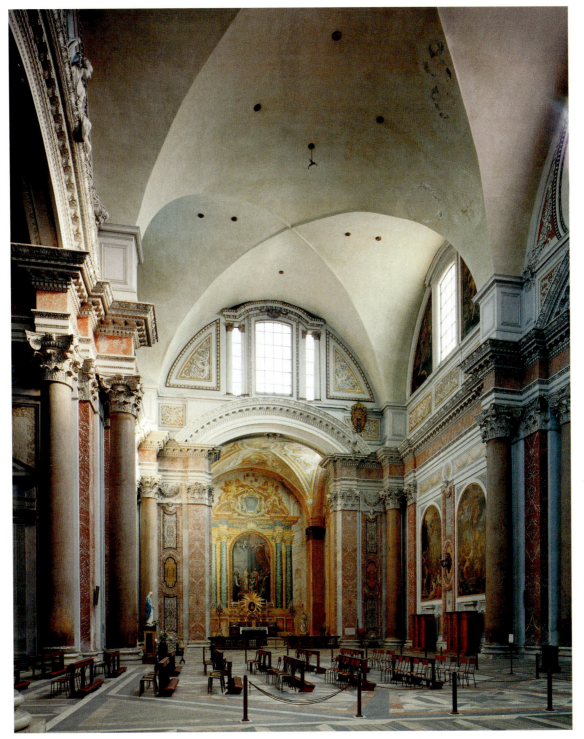

3-43 Frigidarium, Baths of Diocletian, Rome, ca. 298–306 CE (remodeled by Michelangelo as the nave of Santa Maria degli Angeli, 1563).

The groin-vaulted nave of the church of Santa Maria degli Angeli in Rome was once the frigidarium of the Baths of Diocletian. It gives an idea of the lavish adornment of imperial Roman baths.

attended the baths, although at different times of the day. A branch of one of the city's major aqueducts supplied water, and furnaces circulated hot air through hollow floors and walls throughout the complex.

The concrete vaults of the Baths of Caracalla collapsed long ago, but visitors can get an excellent idea of what the central bathing hall once looked like from the nave (FIG. 3-43) of the church of Santa Maria degli Angeli in Rome, which was once the frigidarium of the later Baths of Diocletian. Although the Renaissance interior has many new elements foreign to a Roman bath, its rich wall treatment, colossal columns, immense groin vaults, and clerestory lighting give a better sense of the character of a Roman imperial bathing complex than does any other building in the world.

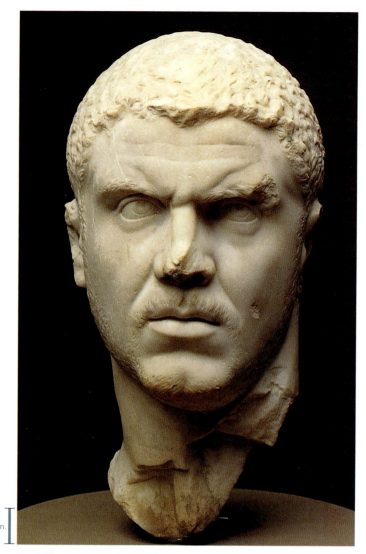

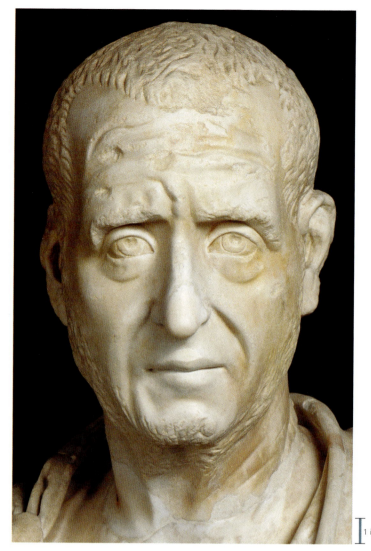

3-44 Portrait of Caracalla, ca. 211–217 CE. Marble, 1′ 2″ high. Metropolitan Museum of Art, New York.

The artist brilliantly captured the emperor's suspicious personality in this portrait. Caracalla's brow is knotted, and he abruptly turns his head over his left shoulder, as if he suspects danger from behind.

3-45 Detail of portrait bust of Trajan Decius, 249–251 CE. Marble, full bust 2′ 7″ high. Musei Capitolini, Rome.

This portrait of a "soldier emperor," who ruled only briefly, depicts an older man with bags under his eyes and a sad expression. The eyes glance away nervously, reflecting the anxiety of an insecure ruler.

Caracalla Caracalla is also remembered for his cruelty. He ruthlessly had his brother (a contender for emperor) murdered, as well as his wife and father-in-law. A marble portrait (FIG. **3-44**) in which the sculptor depicted the short hair and close-cropped beard by etching into the surface brilliantly captures Caracalla's personality. The emperor's brow is knotted, and he abruptly turns his head over his left shoulder, as if he suspects danger from behind. Caracalla had reason to be fearful. An assassin's dagger felled him in the sixth year of his rule.

Trajan Decius The next half century was one of almost continuous civil war. One general after another was declared emperor by his troops, only to be murdered by another general a few years or even a few months later. The unstable times of the so-called soldier emperors nonetheless produced some of the most moving portraits in the history of art. Following the lead of the sculptors of the Marcus Aurelius and Caracalla portraits, artists fashioned likenesses of the soldier emperors

that are as notable for their emotional content as they are for their technical virtuosity. The portraits of Trajan Decius (r. 249–251 CE), for example, the marble head (FIG. **3-45**) illustrated here, depict the emperor (best known for persecuting Christians) as an old man with bags under his eyes and a sad expression. In his eyes, which glance away nervously rather than engage the viewer directly, is the anxiety of a man who knows he can do little to restore order to an out-of-control world. The sculptor modeled the marble as if it were pliant clay, compressing the sides of the head at the level of the eyes, incising the hair and beard into the stone, and chiseling deep lines in the forehead and around the mouth. The portrait reveals the anguished soul of the man—and of the times.

Battle Sarcophagus Beginning under Trajan and Hadrian and especially during the rule of the Antonines, the Romans began to favor burial over cremation. This reversal of funerary practices may reflect the influence of Christian-

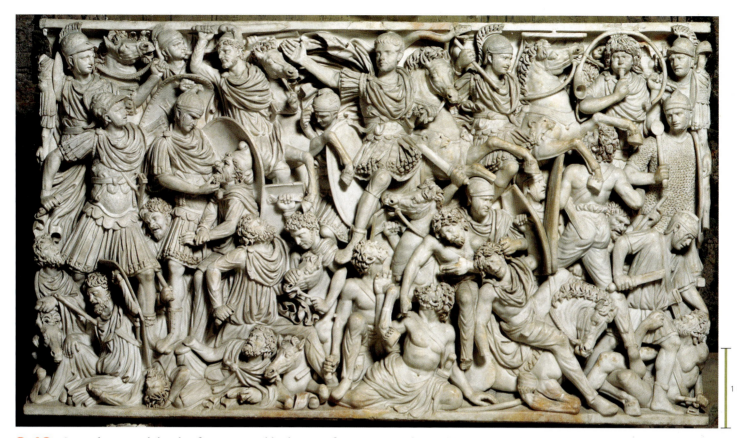

3-46 Sarcophagus with battle of Romans and barbarians, from Rome, Italy, ca. 250–260 CE. Marble, 5′ high. Museo Nazionale Romano—Palazzo Altemps, Rome.

A chaotic scene of battle between Romans and barbarians decorates the front of this unusually large sarcophagus. The sculptor piled up the writhing, emotive figures in an emphatic rejection of perspective.

1 ft.

ity and other Eastern religions, whose adherents believed in an afterlife for the human body. Whatever the explanation, the shift to burial led to a sudden demand for sarcophagi. By the third century CE, burial had become so widespread that even the imperial family adopted burial in place of cremation. An unusually large sarcophagus (FIG. 3-46) of the mid-third century is decorated on the front with a chaotic scene of battle between Romans and one of their northern foes, probably the Goths. The sculptor spread the writhing and highly emotive figures evenly across the entire relief, with no illusion of space behind them. This piling of figures is an emphatic rejection of perspective. Like the contemporaneous "soul portraits" of the soldier emperors, it underscores the increasing dissatisfaction Late Roman artists felt with the Classical style.

Within the dense mass of intertwined bodies, the central horseman stands out vividly. He is bareheaded and thrusts out his open right hand to demonstrate that he holds no weapon. Several scholars have identified him as one of the sons of Trajan Decius. In an age when the Roman army was far from invincible and emperors and would-be emperors constantly murdered imperial rivals, the young general is boasting that he is a fearless commander assured of victory. His self-assurance may stem from his having embraced one of the increasingly popular Eastern mystery religions. On the youth's forehead is the emblem of

Mithras, the Persian god of light, truth, and victory over death. Many shrines to Mithras dating to this period have been found in Rome.

Tetrarchy In 293 CE, in an attempt to restore order to the Roman Empire, Diocletian (r. 284–305 CE), whose troops had proclaimed him emperor a decade earlier, decided to share power with his potential rivals. He established the *tetrarchy* (rule by four) and adopted the title of Augustus of the East. The other three tetrarchs were a corresponding Augustus of the West, and Eastern and Western Caesars (whose allegiance to the two Augusti was cemented by marriage to their daughters). Artists often portrayed the four tetrarchs together and did not try to capture their individual appearances and personalities. They sought instead to represent the nature of the tetrarchy itself—that is, to represent four equal partners in power. In two pairs of porphyry (purple marble) tetrarchic portraits (FIG. 3-47) in Venice, it is impossible to name the rulers. Each of the four emperors has lost his identity as an individual and been subsumed into the larger entity of the tetrarchy. All wear identical breastplates and cloaks, and each grasps a sheathed sword in the left hand. With their right arms they embrace one another in an overt display of concord. The figures have large cubical heads on squat bodies. The drapery is schematic. The faces are emotionless masks, distinguished only

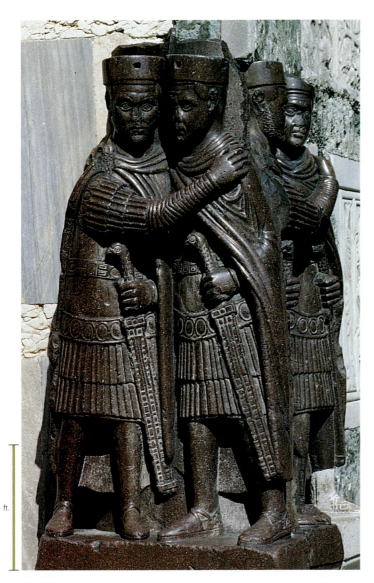

3-47 Portraits of the four tetrarchs, from Constantinople, ca. 305 CE. Porphyry, 4′ 3″ high. Saint Mark's, Venice.

Diocletian established the tetrarchy to bring order to the Roman world. Whenever the four rulers appeared together, artists did not portray them as individuals but as nearly identical partners in power.

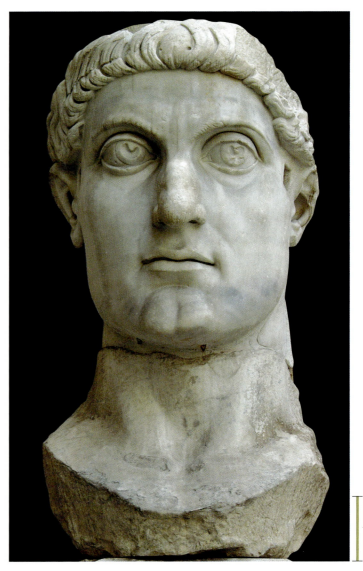

3-48 Portrait of Constantine, from the Basilica Nova, Rome, Italy, ca. 315–330 CE. Marble, 8′ 6″ high. Musei Capitolini, Rome.

Constantine's portraits revive the Augustan image of an eternally youthful ruler. This colossal head is one of several fragments of an enthroned statue of the emperor holding the orb of world power.

by the beard on two of the figures (probably to identify them as the older Augusti, as opposed to the younger Caesars). Nonetheless, each pair is as alike as freehand carving can achieve. In this group portrait, carved eight centuries after Greek sculptors first freed the human form from the formal rigidity of the Egyptian-inspired kouros stance, the sculptor once again conceived the human figure in iconic terms. Idealism, naturalism, individuality, and personality now belonged to the past.

Constantine and Christianity The short-lived concord among the tetrarchs ended with Diocletian's abdication in 305 CE. An all-too-familiar period of conflict among rival Roman armies followed. The eventual victor was Constantine (r. 306–337 CE), son of Constantius Chlorus, Diocletian's Caesar of the West. After the death of his father,

Constantine invaded Italy in 312 and took control of Rome. Constantine attributed his decisive victory at the Milvian Bridge, the gateway to the capital, to the aid of the Christian god. In 313 he and Licinius, Constantine's coemperor in the East, issued the Edict of Milan, ending persecution of Christians. In time, Constantine and Licinius became foes, and in 324 Constantine defeated and executed Licinius near Byzantium (modern Istanbul, Turkey). Constantine was now unchallenged ruler of the entire Roman Empire. Shortly after the death of Licinius, he founded a "New Rome" on the site of Byzantium and named it Constantinople (City of Constantine). A year later, in 325, at the Council of Nicaea, Christianity became the de facto official religion of the Roman Empire. From this point on, paganism declined rapidly. Constantinople was dedicated May 11, 330, "by the commandment of God." Constantine himself was baptized on

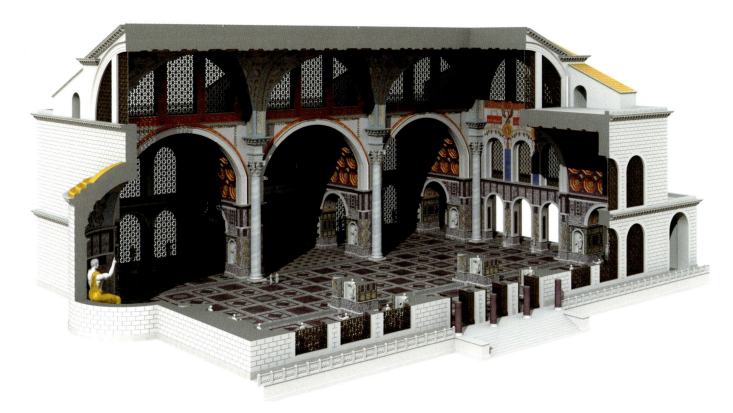

3-49 Restored cutaway view of the Basilica Nova (Basilica of Constantine), Rome, Italy, ca. 306–312 CE (John Burge).

This architect applied the lessons learned in the construction of baths and market halls to the Basilica Nova, where fenestrated concrete groin vaults replaced the clerestory of a traditional stone-and-timber basilica.

his deathbed in 337. For many scholars, the transfer of the seat of power from Rome to Constantinople and the recognition of Christianity mark the beginning of the Middle Ages. Constantinian art is a mirror of this transition from the classical to the medieval world. In Rome, for example, Constantine was a builder in the grand tradition of the emperors of the first, second, and early third centuries, erecting public baths, a basilica near the Roman Forum, and a triumphal arch. But he was also the patron of the city's first churches, including Saint Peter's (FIG. 4-4).

Colossus of Constantine The most impressive by far of Constantine's preserved portraits is an eight-and-one-half-foot-tall head (FIG. 3-48), one of several marble fragments of a colossal enthroned statue of the emperor composed of a brick core, a wooden torso covered with bronze, and a head and limbs of marble. Constantine's artist modeled the seminude seated portrait on Roman images of Jupiter but also resuscitated the Augustan image of an eternally youthful head of state. The emperor held an orb (possibly surmounted by the cross of Christ), the symbol of global power, in his extended left hand. Constantine's personality is lost in this immense image of eternal authority. The colossal size, the likening of the emperor to Jupiter, the eyes directed at no person or thing of this world—all combine to produce a formula of overwhelming power appropriate to Constantine's exalted position as absolute ruler.

Basilica Nova Constantine's gigantic portrait sat in the western apse of the Basilica Nova (FIGS. 3-49 and 3-9, no. 8) he constructed near the Arch of Titus. From its position in the apse, the emperor's image dominated the interior of the "New Basilica" in much the same way enthroned statues of Greco-Roman divinities loomed over awestruck mortals who entered the cellas of pagan temples.

The ruins of the Basilica Nova never fail to impress tourists with their size and mass. The original structure was 300 feet long and 215 feet wide. Brick-faced concrete walls 20 feet thick supported coffered barrel vaults in the aisles. These vaults also buttressed the groin vaults of the nave, which was 115 feet high. The walls and floors were richly marbled and stuccoed and could be readily admired by those who came to the basilica to conduct business, because the groin vaults permitted ample light to enter the nave directly.

The reconstruction in FIG. 3-49 effectively suggests the immensity of the interior, where the great vaults dwarf not only humans but also even the emperor's colossal portrait. The drawing also clearly reveals the *fenestration* of the groin vaults, a lighting system akin to the clerestory of a traditional stone-and-timber basilica (FIG. 3-34, no. 4). In the Basilica Nova, the architect applied to basilica design the lessons learned in the construction of buildings such as Trajan's great market hall (FIG. 3-36) and the Baths of Caracalla and Diocletian (FIG. 3-43).

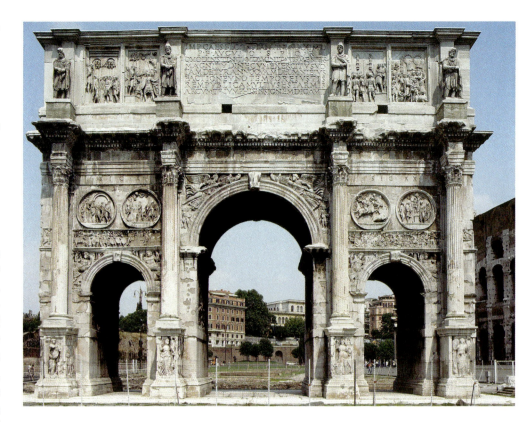

3-50 Arch of Constantine (looking north), Rome, Italy, 312–315 CE.

Constantine's builders took most of the sculptural decoration of his arch from monuments of Trajan, Hadrian, and Marcus Aurelius. Sculptors recut the heads of the earlier emperors with Constantine's features.

Arch of Constantine Also grandiose is Constantine's nearby triple-passageway arch (FIGS. **3-50** and 3-9, no. 10), the largest erected in Rome since the end of the Severan dynasty nearly a century before. Most of the sculptural decoration, however, came from earlier monuments of Trajan, Hadrian, and Marcus Aurelius. Sculptors refashioned the second-century reliefs to honor Constantine by recutting the heads of the earlier emperors with the features of the new ruler. Some scholars have pointed to the Arch of Constantine as evidence of a decline in creativity and technical skill in the waning years of the pagan Roman Empire. Although this judgment is in large part deserved, it ignores the fact that the designer carefully selected older sculptures to associate Constantine with famous emperors of the second century. One of the new Constantinian reliefs above the arch's lateral passageways underscores that message. It shows Constantine on the speaker's platform in the Roman Forum, flanked by statues of Hadrian and Marcus Aurelius.

In another Constantinian relief (FIG. **3-51**), the emperor distributes largesse to grateful citizens who approach him from right and left. Constantine is a frontal and majestic presence, elevated on a throne above the recipients of his munificence. The figures are squat in proportion, like the tetrarchs (FIG. **3-47**). They do not move according to any Classical principle of naturalistic movement but rather with the mechanical and repeated stances and gestures of puppets. The relief is very shallow, the forms not fully modeled, and the details incised. The frieze is less a narrative of action than a picture of actors frozen in time so that the viewer can distinguish instantly the all-important imperial donor (at the center on a throne) from his attendants (to the left and right above) and the recipients of the largesse (below and of smaller stature).

This approach to pictorial narrative was once characterized as a "decline of form," and when judged by the standards of Classical art, it was. But the composition's rigid formality, determined by the rank of those portrayed, was consistent with a new set of values. It soon became the preferred mode, supplanting the Classical notion that a picture is a window

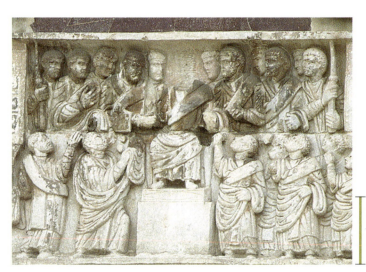

3-51 Distribution of largesse, detail of the north frieze of the Arch of Constantine, Rome, Italy, 312–315 CE. Marble, 3′ 4″ high.

This Constantinian frieze is less a narrative of action than a picture of actors frozen in time. The composition's rigid formality reflects the new values that would come to dominate medieval art.

onto a world of anecdotal action. Comparing this Constantinian relief with a Byzantine icon (FIG. **4-20**) reveals that the new compositional principles are those of the Middle Ages. They were very different from—but not necessarily "better" or "worse" than—those of classical antiquity. The Arch of Constantine is the quintessential monument of its era, exhibiting a respect for the past in its reuse of second-century sculptures while at the same time rejecting the norms of Classical design in its frieze, paving the way for the iconic art of the Middle Ages.

The Roman Empire

ETRUSCAN ART

▪ The Etruscans admired Greek art and architecture but did not copy Greek works. Etruscan temples were made of wood and mud brick instead of stone and had columns and stairs only at the front. Terracotta statuary decorated the roof. Most surviving Etruscan artworks come from underground tomb chambers. At Cerveteri, great earthen mounds (tumuli) covered tombs with interiors sculptured to imitate the houses of the living. At Tarquinia, painters covered the tomb walls with monumental frescoes, usually depicting funerary banquets attended by both men and women.

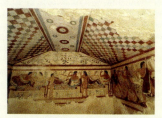

Tomb of the Leopards, Tarquinia, ca. 480–470 BCE

REPUBLICAN ART

▪ In the centuries following the establishment of the Republic (509–27 BCE), Rome conquered its neighbors in Italy and then moved into Greece, bringing exposure to Greek art and architecture. Republican temples combined Etruscan plans with the Greek orders, and houses had peristyles with Greek columns. The Romans, however, pioneered the use of concrete as a building material. The First Style of mural painting derived from Greece, but the illusionism of the Second Style is distinctly Roman. Republican portraits were usually superrealistic likenesses of elderly patricians.

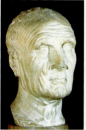

Head of an old man, mid-first century BCE

EARLY IMPERIAL ART

▪ Augustus (r. 27 BCE–14 CE) established the Roman Empire after defeating Antony and Cleopatra. The Early Empire (27 BCE–96 CE) extends from Augustus to the Flavian emperors (r. 68–96 CE).

▪ Augustus revived Classical art. His monuments make frequent references to Periclean Athens, and his portraits always depict him as an idealized youth. Under the Flavians, builders exploited the full potential of concrete in buildings like the Colosseum, Rome's largest amphitheater. The Arch of Titus celebrates the Flavian victory in Judaea. Mount Vesuvius erupted in 79 CE, burying Pompeii and Herculaneum. During the last quarter century of the towns' existence, painters decorated the walls of houses in the Third and Fourth Styles.

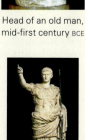

Augustus as general, ca. 20 BCE

HIGH IMPERIAL ART

▪ During the High Empire (96–192 CE), beginning with Trajan (r. 98–117 CE), the Roman Empire reached its greatest extent.

▪ Trajan's new forum and markets transformed the center of Rome. The Column of Trajan commemorated his Dacian campaigns in a spiral frieze filled with thousands of figures. Hadrian (r. 117–138 CE) built the Pantheon, the temple to all the gods, incorporating in its design the forms of the orb of the earth and the dome of the heavens. Under the Antonines (r. 138–192 CE), imperial artists introduced a psychological element in portraiture.

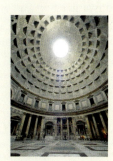

Pantheon, Rome, 118–125 CE

LATE IMPERIAL ART

▪ The Late Empire (193–337 CE) opened with the Severans (r. 193–235 CE) and closed with Constantine (r. 306–337 CE), who ended persecution of the Christians and transferred the imperial capital from Rome to Constantinople in 330.

▪ During the chaotic era of the soldier emperors (r. 235–284 CE), artists revealed the anxiety and insecurity of the emperors in moving portraits. Diocletian (r. 284–305 CE) reestablished order by sharing power. Statues of the tetrarchs portray the four emperors as identical and equal rulers, not as individuals. Constantine restored one-man rule. The abstract formality of Constantinian art paved the way for the iconic art of the Middle Ages.

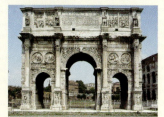

Arch of Constantine, Rome, 312–315 CE

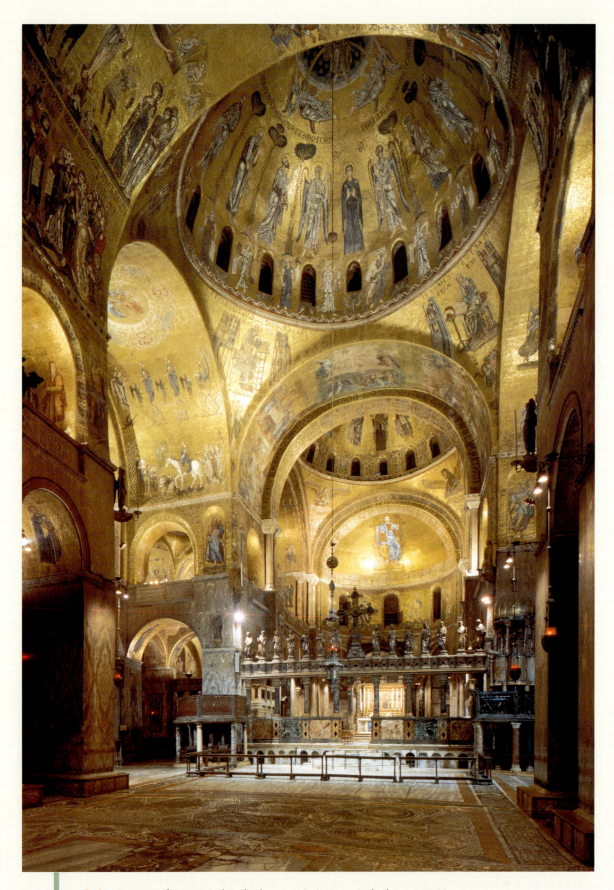

4-1 Interior of Saint Mark's (looking east), Venice, Italy, begun 1063.

In the Middle Ages, Venice was the crucial link between Byzantium and Italy. Saint Mark's has a Greek-cross plan with five domes and features 40,000 square feet of dazzling gold-ground mosaics.

Early Christianity and Byzantium

During the third and fourth centuries,* a rapidly growing number of people throughout the vast Roman Empire had rejected the emperors' polytheism (belief in multiple gods) in favor of monotheism (the worship of a single, all-powerful god). The most prominent of these religions was Christianity. In fact, the emperor Diocletian (r. 284–305; FIG. 3-47) became so concerned by the growing popularity of Christianity in the Roman army ranks that he ordered a fresh round of persecutions in 303 to 305, a half century after the last great persecutions under Trajan Decius (r. 249–251; FIG. 3-45). The Romans hated the Christians because of their alien beliefs—that their god had been incarnated in the body of a man and that the death and resurrection of the god-man Christ made possible the salvation and redemption of all. More important, the Christians refused to pay even token homage to the official gods of the Roman state. As Christianity's appeal grew, so too did the Roman state's fear of weakening imperial authority. Persecution ended only when Constantine (FIG. 3-48) came to believe that the Christian god was the source of his power rather than a threat to it. In 313 he issued the Edict of Milan, which established Christianity as a legal religion with equal or superior standing to the traditional Roman cults.

EARLY CHRISTIAN ART

Very little is known about the art of the first Christians. The phrase "Early Christian art" refers to the earliest preserved artworks having Christian subjects, not the art of Christians at the time of Jesus.

Funerary Art

Most Early Christian art in Rome dates to the third and fourth centuries and is found in the *catacombs*—vast subterranean networks of passageways and chambers designed as cemeteries for burying the Christian dead. The name derives from the Latin *ad catacumbas*, which means "in the hollows." The builders tunneled the catacombs out of the tufa bedrock, much as the Etruscans fashioned the underground tomb chambers (FIG. 3-5) at Cerveteri. The catacombs are less elaborate than the Etruscan tombs but much more extensive. The known underground galleries in Rome run for 60 to 90 miles and housed as many as four million bodies.

* From this point on, all dates are CE unless otherwise indicated.

4-2 The Good Shepherd, the story of Jonah, and orants, painted ceiling of a cubiculum in the Catacomb of Saints Peter and Marcellinus, Rome, Italy, early fourth century.

Early Christian paintings regularly mixed Old and New Testament themes. Jonah was a popular subject because a sea monster swallowed him, but he emerged safely after three days, prefiguring Christ's Resurrection.

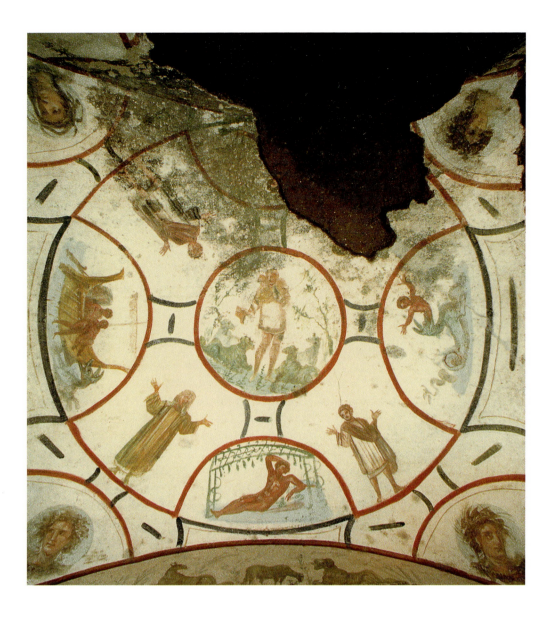

Peter and Marcellinus Often, the Christians carved out small rooms, called *cubicula* (as in Roman houses; FIG. 3-16), to serve as mortuary chapels within the catacombs. The painted ceiling (FIG. 4-2) of a cubiculum in the Catacomb of Saints Peter and Marcellinus in Rome features a large circle with the symbol of the Christian faith, the cross, at its center. The arms of the cross terminate in four *lunettes* (semicircular frames) containing the key episodes from the Old Testament story of Jonah. On the left, the sailors throw him from his ship. He emerges on the right from the "whale" (really a sea dragon) that swallowed him. At the bottom, safe on land, Jonah contemplates the miracle of his salvation and the mercy of God.

From the beginning, the Old Testament played an important role in Christian life and Christian art, in part because Jesus was a Jew and so many of the first Christians were converted Jews, but also because Christians came to view many of the persons and events of the Old Testament as *prefigurations* (prophetic forerunners) of New Testament persons and events. Christ himself established the pattern for this kind of biblical interpretation when he compared

Jonah's spending three days in the belly of the sea monster to the comparable time he would be entombed in the earth before his Resurrection (Matt. 12:40). In the fourth century, Saint Augustine (354–430) confirmed the validity of this approach to the Old Testament when he stated that "the New Testament is hidden in the Old; the Old is clarified by the New."[1]

A man, a woman, and at least one child occupy the compartments between the Jonah lunettes in FIG. 4-2. They are *orants* (praying figures), raising their arms in the ancient attitude of prayer. Together they make up a cross-section of the Christian family seeking a heavenly afterlife. The cross's central medallion shows Christ as the Good Shepherd, whose powers of salvation are underscored by his juxtaposition with Jonah's story. In Early Christian art, Christ often appears as the youthful and loyal protector of the Christian flock, who said to his disciples, "I am the good shepherd; the good shepherd gives his life for the sheep" (John 10:11). Only after Christianity became the Roman Empire's official religion did Christ take on in art imperial attributes, such as the halo, the purple robe, and the throne, which denoted rulership.

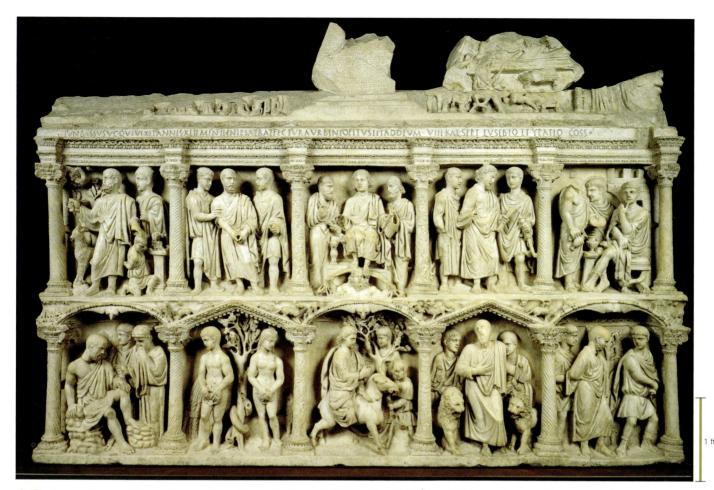

4-3 Sarcophagus of Junius Bassus, from Rome, Italy, ca. 359. Marble, 3′ 10½″ × 8′. Museo Storico del Tesoro della Basilica di San Pietro, Rome.

The wealthiest Christians, like the city prefect Junius Bassus, favored elaborately decorated sarcophagi. Here, biblical episodes from Adam and Eve to Christ before Pilate appear in ten niches in two rows.

Junius Bassus Sarcophagus All Christians rejected cremation, and the wealthiest Christian faithful, like their pagan contemporaries, favored impressive marble sarcophagi. The finest surviving Early Christian sarcophagus (FIG. 4-3) is that of Junius Bassus, city prefect of Rome and a pagan convert to Christianity, who died in 359. His sarcophagus is divided into two registers of five compartments, each framed by columns. Stories from the Old and New Testaments fill the 10 niches. Christ has pride of place and appears in the central compartment of each register: as a teacher enthroned between his chief disciples, or *apostles* (from the Greek for "messenger"), the *saints* Peter and Paul (above), and triumphantly entering Jerusalem on a donkey (below). Appropriately, the sculptor placed the scene of Christ's heavenly triumph above that of his earthly triumph. Both compositions owe a great deal to pagan Roman art. In the upper zone, Christ, like an enthroned Roman emperor, sits above a personification of the sky god holding a billowing mantle over his head, indicating that Christ is ruler of the universe. The scene below derives in part from portrayals of Roman emperors entering cities on horseback, but Christ's steed and the absence of imperial attributes contrast sharply with the imperial models the sculptor used as compositional sources.

The Old Testament scenes chosen for the Junius Bassus sarcophagus were those that had special significance in the early Christian Church. Adam and Eve, for example, are in the second niche from the left on the lower level. Their Original Sin of eating the apple in the Garden of Eden ultimately necessitated Christ's sacrifice for the salvation of humankind. To the right of the entry into Jerusalem is Daniel, unscathed by flanking lions, saved by his faith. At the upper left, Abraham is about to sacrifice Isaac. Christians believe this Old Testament story was a prefiguration of God's sacrifice of his own son, Jesus.

The Crucifixion itself, however, does not appear on the Junius Bassus sarcophagus. Indeed, the subject was very rare in Early Christian art, and unknown prior to the fifth century. Artists emphasized Christ's divinity and exemplary life as teacher and miracle worker, not his suffering and death at the hands of the Romans. This sculptor, however, alluded to the Crucifixion in the scenes in the two compartments at the upper right depicting Jesus being led before Pontius Pilate for judgment. The Romans condemned Jesus to death, but he triumphantly overcame it (see "The Life of Jesus in Art," pages 124–125). Junius Bassus hoped for a similar salvation.

Early Christian Art | 123

The Life of Jesus in Art

Christians believe that Jesus of Nazareth is the son of God, the *Messiah* (Savior, Christ) of the Jews prophesied in the Old Testament. His life—from his miraculous birth from the womb of a virgin mother through his preaching and miracle working to his execution by the Romans and subsequent ascent to Heaven—has been the subject of countless artworks from Roman times through the present day. Although many of the events of Jesus' life were rarely or never depicted during certain periods, it is useful to summarize here the entire cycle with a description of the events as they usually appear in art.

Incarnation and Childhood

The first "cycle" of the life of Jesus consists of the events of his conception, birth, infancy, and childhood.

- **Annunciation to Mary** The archangel Gabriel announces to the Virgin Mary that she will miraculously conceive and give birth to God's son, Jesus. Artists sometimes indicated God's presence at the Incarnation by a dove, the symbol of the Holy Spirit, the third "person" of the Trinity with God the Father and Jesus.

- **Visitation** The pregnant Mary visits Elizabeth, her older cousin, who is pregnant with the future Saint John the Baptist. Elizabeth is the first to recognize that the baby Mary is bearing is the Son of God.

- **Nativity, Annunciation to the Shepherds,** and **Adoration of the Shepherds** Jesus is born at night in Bethlehem and placed in a basket. Mary and her husband, Joseph, marvel at the newborn, while an angel announces the birth of the Savior to shepherds in the field.

- **Adoration of the Magi** A bright star alerts three wise men *(magi)* in the East that the King of the Jews has been born. They travel 12 days to find the Holy Family and present precious gifts to the infant Jesus.

- **Presentation in the Temple** Mary and Joseph bring their son to the temple in Jerusalem, where the aged Simeon, who God said would not die until he had seen the Messiah, recognizes Jesus as the prophesied Savior of humankind.

- **Massacre of the Innocents** and **Flight into Egypt** King Herod, fearful that a rival king has been born, orders the massacre of all infants in Bethlehem, but an angel warns the Holy Family, and they escape to Egypt.

- **Dispute in the Temple** Joseph and Mary travel to Jerusalem for the feast of Passover (the celebration of the release of the Jews from bondage to the pharaohs of Egypt). Jesus, only 12 years old at the time, engages in learned debate with astonished Jewish scholars in the temple, foretelling his ministry.

Public Ministry

The public ministry cycle comprises the teachings of Jesus and the miracles he performed.

- **Baptism** The beginning of Jesus' public ministry is marked by his *baptism* at age 30 by John the Baptist in the Jordan River. God's voice proclaims Jesus as his son.

- **Calling of Matthew** Jesus summons Matthew, a tax collector, to follow him, and Matthew becomes one of his 12 apostles.

- **Miracles** In the course of his teaching and travels, Jesus performs many miracles, revealing his divine nature. In the miracle of loaves and fishes, for example, Jesus transforms a few loaves of bread and a handful of fishes into enough food to feed several thousand people. Other miracles include acts of healing and the raising of the dead, the turning of water into wine, and walking on water.

- **Delivery of the Keys to Peter** The fisherman Peter was one of the first Jesus summoned as a disciple. Jesus chooses Peter (whose name means "rock") as his successor, the rock on which his church will be built, and symbolically delivers to Peter the keys to the Kingdom of Heaven.

- **Transfiguration** Jesus scales a high mountain and, in the presence of Peter and two other disciples, James and John the Evangelist, is transformed into radiant light. God, speaking from a cloud, discloses that Jesus is his son.

- **Cleansing of the Temple** Jesus returns to Jerusalem, where he finds money changers and merchants conducting business in the temple. He rebukes them and drives them out of the sacred precinct.

Passion

The Passion (from Latin *passio,* "suffering") cycle includes the episodes leading to Jesus' death, Resurrection, and ascent to Heaven.

- **Entry into Jerusalem** On the Sunday before his Crucifixion (Palm Sunday), Jesus rides triumphantly into Jerusalem on a donkey, accompanied by disciples.

Architecture and Mosaics

The earliest Christian places of worship were usually remodeled private houses that could accommodate only a small community. Once Christianity achieved imperial sponsorship under Constantine, an urgent need suddenly arose to construct churches. Constantine believed the Christian god had guided him to victory, and in lifelong gratitude he protected and advanced Christianity throughout the Empire, as well as in the obstinately pagan capital city of Rome. As emperor, he was, of course, obliged to safeguard the ancient Roman religion, traditions, and monuments, and, as noted in Chapter 3, he was (for his time) a builder on a grand scale in the heart of the city (FIGS. **3-49** and **3-50**). But eager to provide buildings to house the Christian rituals and venerated burial places, especially the memorials of founding saints, Constantine also was the first major patron of Christian architecture. He constructed elaborate basilicas, memorials, and *mausoleums* not only in Rome but also in Constantinople, his "New Rome" in the East, and at sites sacred to Christianity, most notably Bethlehem, the birthplace of Jesus, and Jerusalem, the site of his Crucifixion. The new buildings had

■ **Last Supper** and **Washing of the Disciples' Feet** In Jerusalem, Jesus celebrates Passover with his disciples. During this Last Supper, Jesus foretells his imminent betrayal, arrest, and death and invites the disciples to remember him when they eat bread (symbol of his body) and drink wine (his blood). This ritual became the celebration of *Mass (Eucharist)* in the Christian Church. At the same meal, Jesus sets an example of humility for his apostles by washing their feet.

■ **Agony in the Garden** Jesus goes to the Mount of Olives in the Garden of Gethsemane, where he struggles to overcome his human fear of death by praying for divine strength. The apostles who accompanied him there fall asleep despite his request that they stay awake with him while he prays.

■ **Betrayal and Arrest** One of the disciples, Judas Iscariot, agrees to betray Jesus to the Jewish authorities in return for 30 pieces of silver. Judas identifies Jesus to the soldiers by kissing him, and Jesus is arrested. Later, a remorseful Judas commits suicide by hanging himself from a tree.

■ **Trials of Jesus** and **Denial of Peter** Jesus is brought before Caiaphas, the Jewish high priest, who interrogates Jesus about his claim to be the Messiah. Meanwhile, the disciple Peter thrice denies knowing Jesus, as Jesus predicted he would. Jesus is then brought before the Roman governor of Judaea, Pontius Pilate, on the charge of treason because he had proclaimed himself as King of the Jews. Pilate asks the crowd to choose between freeing Jesus or Barabbas, a murderer. The people choose Barabbas, and the judge condemns Jesus to death. Pilate washes his hands, symbolically relieving himself of responsibility for the mob's decision.

■ **Flagellation** and **Mocking** The Roman soldiers who hold Jesus captive whip (flagellate) him and mock him by dressing him as King of the Jews and placing a crown of thorns on his head.

■ **Carrying of the Cross, Raising of the Cross,** and **Crucifixion** The Romans force Jesus to carry the cross on which he will be crucified from Jerusalem to Mount Calvary (Golgotha, the "place of the skull," where Adam was buried). He falls three times and is stripped of clothing along the way. Soldiers erect the cross and nail his hands and feet to it. The Virgin Mary, John the Evangelist, and Mary Magdalene mourn at the foot of the cross, while soldiers torment Jesus. One of them (the centurion Longinus) stabs his side with a spear. After suffering great pain, Jesus dies. The Crucifixion occurred on a Friday, and Christians celebrate the day each year as Good Friday.

■ **Deposition, Lamentation,** and **Entombment** Two disciples, Joseph of Arimathea and Nicodemus, remove Jesus' body from the cross (the Deposition) and take him to the tomb Joseph had purchased for himself. Joseph, Nicodemus, the Virgin Mary, Saint John the Evangelist, and Mary Magdalene mourn over the dead Jesus (the Lamentation). (When in art the isolated figure of the Virgin Mary cradles her dead son in her lap, the image is called a *Pietà* [Italian for "pity"]). In representations of the Entombment, his followers lower Jesus into a sarcophagus in the tomb.

■ **Descent into Limbo** During the three days he spends in the tomb, Jesus (after death, Christ) descends into Hell, or Limbo, and triumphantly frees the souls of the righteous, including Adam, Eve, Moses, David, Solomon, and John the Baptist.

■ **Resurrection** and **Three Marys at the Tomb** On the third day (Easter Sunday), Christ rises from the dead and leaves the tomb while the guards outside are sleeping. The Virgin Mary, Mary Magdalene, and Mary, the mother of James, visit the tomb, find it empty, and learn from an angel that Christ has been resurrected.

■ **Noli Me Tangere, Supper at Emmaus,** and **Doubting of Thomas** During the 40 days between Christ's Resurrection and his ascent to Heaven, he appears on several occasions to his followers. Christ warns Mary Magdalene, weeping at his tomb, with the words "Don't touch me" (*Noli me tangere* in Latin), but he tells her to inform the apostles of his return. At Emmaus he eats supper with two of his astonished disciples. Later, Christ invites Thomas, who cannot believe that Jesus has risen, to touch the wound in his side that Longinus inflicted at the Crucifixion.

■ **Ascension** On the 40th day, with his mother and apostles as witnesses, Christ gloriously ascends from the Mount of Olives to Heaven in a cloud.

to meet the requirements of Christian *liturgy* (the ritual of public worship), provide a suitably monumental setting for the celebration of the Christian faith, and accommodate the rapidly growing numbers of worshipers.

Old Saint Peter's The greatest of Constantine's churches in Rome was Old Saint Peter's, probably begun as early as 319. The present-day church (FIGS. 10-2 and 10-3) is a replacement for the fourth-century structure. Old Saint Peter's stood on the spot where Constantine and Pope Sylvester believed that Peter, the first apostle and founder of the Christian community in Rome, had been buried. Excavations in the Roman cemetery beneath the church have in fact revealed a second-century memorial erected in honor of the Christian *martyr* at his reputed grave. The great Constantinian church, capable of housing 3,000 to 4,000 worshipers at one time, therefore fulfilled the words of Christ himself when he said, "Thou art Peter, and upon this rock [in Greek, *petra*] I will build my church" (Matt. 16:18).

The plan and elevation of Old Saint Peter's resemble those of Roman basilicas, such as Trajan's Basilica Ulpia (FIG. 3-34, no. 4), rather than the design of any Greco-Roman temple.

The Christians, understandably, did not want their houses of worship to mimic the form of pagan shrines, but practical considerations also contributed to their shunning the pagan temple type. The Greco-Roman temple housed only the cult statue of the deity, and all rituals took place outside at open-air altars. The classical temple, therefore, could have been adapted only with great difficulty as a building that could accommodate large numbers of people within it. The Roman basilica, in contrast, was ideally suited as a place for congregation, and Early Christian architects eagerly embraced it.

Like Roman basilicas, Old Saint Peter's (FIG. **4-4**) had a wide central *nave* (300 feet long) with flanking *aisles* and an *apse* at the end. Preceding it was an open colonnaded courtyard, very much like the forum proper in the Forum of Trajan (FIG. **3-34**, no. 5) but called an *atrium*, like the central room in a private house (FIG. **3-16**). Worshipers entered the basilica through a *narthex*, or vestibule. When they emerged in the nave, they had an unobstructed view of the altar in the apse. A special feature of the Constantinian church was the *transept*, or transverse aisle, an area perpendicular to the nave between the nave and apse. It housed the relics of Saint Peter that hordes of pilgrims came to see. (*Relics* are the body parts, clothing, or any object associated with a saint or Christ himself; see "Pilgrimages and the Cult of Relics," Chapter 6, page 170.) The transept became a standard element of church design in the West only much later, when it also took on, with the nave and apse, the symbolism of the Christian cross.

Unlike Roman temples, Old Saint Peter's did not have a sculpture-filled pediment to impress those approaching the church. Its exterior consisted of austere brick walls. Inside,

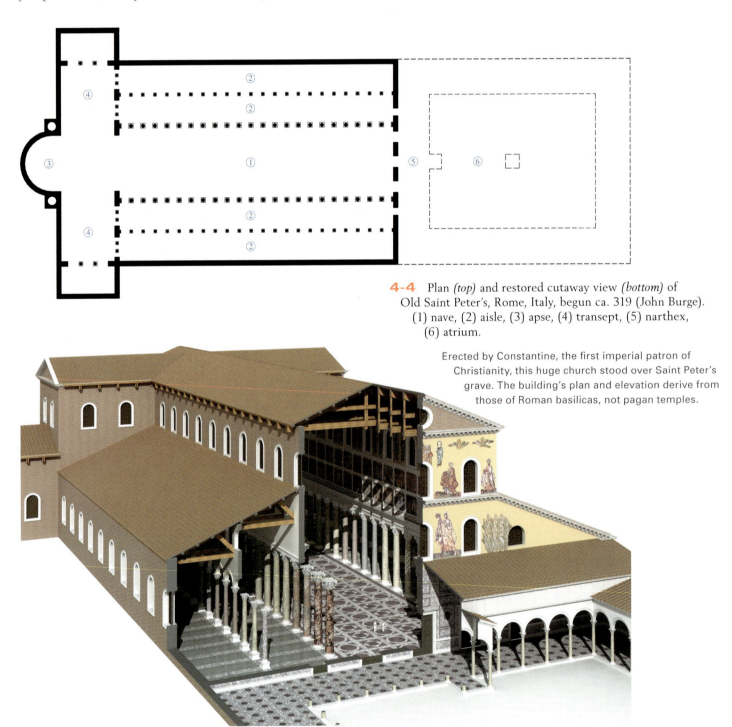

4-4 Plan *(top)* and restored cutaway view *(bottom)* of Old Saint Peter's, Rome, Italy, begun ca. 319 (John Burge). (1) nave, (2) aisle, (3) apse, (4) transept, (5) narthex, (6) atrium.

Erected by Constantine, the first imperial patron of Christianity, this huge church stood over Saint Peter's grave. The building's plan and elevation derive from those of Roman basilicas, not pagan temples.

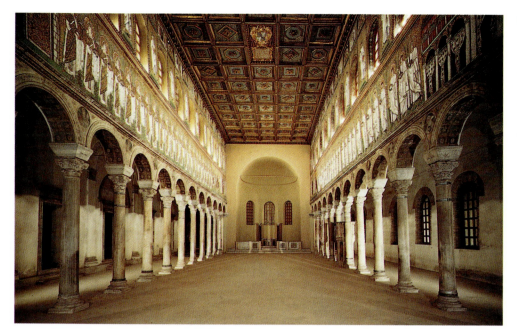

Early Christian basilican churches were timber-roofed and illuminated by clerestory windows. The columns of the nave produced a steady rhythm that focused all attention on the apse, which framed the altar.

however, were frescoes and mosaics, marble columns, grandiose chandeliers, and gold and silver vessels on jeweled altar cloths for use in the Mass. A huge marble *baldacchino* (domical canopy over an altar), supported by four spiral columns, marked the spot of Saint Peter's tomb. Readers can visualize the interior of Old Saint Peter's from the restored view (FIG. **4-4,** *bottom*) and from a photograph (FIG. **4-5**) of the nave of the later Sant'Apollinare Nuovo in Ravenna. In both cases the nave columns produce a steady rhythm that focuses all attention on the apse, which frames the altar. In Ravenna, as in Rome, light drenches the nave from the *clerestory* windows piercing the thin upper wall beneath the timber roof. That light illuminates the mosaics in Sant'Apollinare Nuovo's nave. Mosaics and frescoes commonly adorned the nave and apse of Early Christian churches.

Santa Costanza The rectangular basilican church design featuring a *longitudinal plan* was long the favorite of the Western Christian world. But Early Christian architects also adopted another classical architectural type: the *central-plan* building, a structure in which the parts are of equal or almost equal dimensions around the center. Roman central-plan buildings were usually round or polygonal domed structures. Byzantine architects developed this form to monumental proportions and amplified its theme in numerous ingenious variations (FIGS. **4-1** and **4-13**). In the West, builders generally employed the central plan for structures adjacent to the main basilicas, such as mausoleums, *baptisteries*, and private chapels, rather than for churches, as in the East.

A highly refined example of the central-plan design is Santa Costanza (FIGS. **4-6** and **4-7**) in Rome, built in the

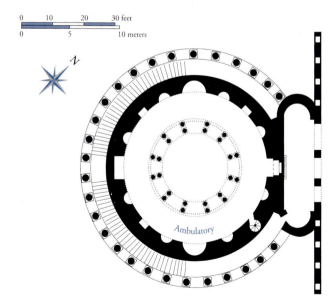

4-6 Interior of Santa Costanza, Rome, Italy, ca. 337–351.

Santa Costanza has antecedents in the domed structures of the Romans, but it is unique in having an ambulatory and 12 pairs of columns. The building once featured rich mosaic ornamentation.

4-7 Plan of Santa Costanza, Rome, Italy, ca. 337–351.

Possibly built as the mausoleum of Constantine's daughter, Santa Costanza later became a church. Its central plan, featuring a domed interior, would become the preferred form for churches in Byzantium.

Early Christian Art | 127

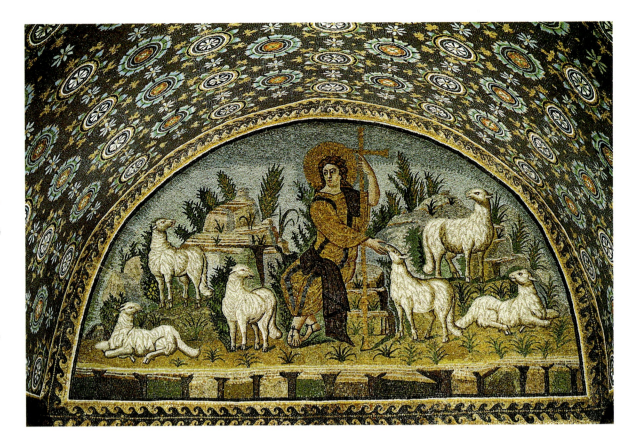

4-8

Christ as the Good Shepherd, mosaic from the entrance wall of the Mausoleum of Galla Placidia, Ravenna, Italy, ca. 425.

Jesus sits among his flock, haloed and robed in gold and purple. The landscape and the figures, with their cast shadows, are the work of a mosaicist still deeply rooted in the naturalistic classical tradition.

mid-fourth century, possibly as the mausoleum for Constantina, the emperor Constantine's daughter. Recent excavations have called the traditional identification into question, but the building housed Constantina's monumental porphyry sarcophagus, even if the structure was not built as her tomb. The mausoleum, later converted into a church, stood next to the basilican Church of Saint Agnes, whose tomb was in a nearby catacomb. Santa Costanza has antecedents in the domed structures of the Romans, such as the Pantheon (FIG. 3-39), but the designer modified the interior to accommodate an *ambulatory*, a ringlike barrel-vaulted corridor separated from the central domed cylinder by 12 pairs of columns. It is as if the builder bent the nave of the Early Christian basilica with its clerestory wall around a circle, the ambulatory corresponding to the basilican aisles. Like Early Christian basilicas, Santa Costanza has a severe brick exterior. Its interior also featured an extensive series of mosaics, although most are lost.

Mausoleum of Galla Placidia Mosaic decoration played an important role in the interiors of Early Christian buildings (see "Mosaics," page 129). When, under Constantine, Christianity suddenly became a public and official religion in Rome, not only were new buildings required to house the faithful, but wholesale decoration programs for the churches also became necessary. To advertise the new faith in all its diverse aspects and to instruct believers, acres of walls in dozens of new churches had to be filled in the style and medium that would carry the message most effectively.

The so-called Mausoleum of Galla Placidia in Ravenna is a rare example of a virtually intact Early Christian mosaic program. Galla Placidia was the half sister of the emperor

Honorius (r. 395–423), who had moved the capital of his crumbling Western Roman Empire from Milan to Ravenna in 404. Galla Placidia's "mausoleum," built shortly after 425, almost a quarter century before her death in 450, is really a chapel to the martyred Saint Lawrence. The building has a characteristically unadorned brick exterior. Inside, however, mosaics cover every square inch above the marble-faced walls.

Christ as Good Shepherd (FIG. 4-8) is the subject of the lunette above the entrance. No earlier version of the Good Shepherd is as regal as this one. Instead of carrying a lamb on his shoulders, Jesus sits among his flock, haloed and robed in gold and purple. To his left and right, the mosaicist distributed the sheep evenly in groups of three. But their arrangement is rather loose and informal, and they occupy a carefully described landscape that extends from foreground to background beneath a blue sky. All the forms have three-dimensional bulk and cast shadows. In short, the panel is full of Greco-Roman illusionistic devices. It is the work of a mosaicist still deeply rooted in the classical tradition.

Sant'Apollinare Nuovo In 476, Ravenna fell to Odoacer, the first Germanic king of Italy, whom Theodoric, king of the Ostrogoths, overthrew in turn. Theodoric established his capital at Ravenna in 493. The mosaics in his palace church, Sant'Apollinare Nuovo (FIG. 4-5), date from different periods, but those the Ostrogoth king installed already reveal a new, much more abstract and formal style. The mosaics above the clerestory windows depict scenes from Christ's life. In the panel showing the miracle of the loaves and fishes (FIG. 4-9), Jesus, beardless, in the imperial dress of gold and purple and now distinguished by the cross-

Mosaics

As an art form, *mosaic* had a rather simple and utilitarian beginning, seemingly invented primarily to provide an inexpensive and durable flooring. Originally, *mosaicists* set small beach pebbles, unaltered from their natural form and color, into a thick coat of cement. They soon discovered, however, that the stones could be arranged in decorative patterns. At first, these *pebble mosaics* were uncomplicated and confined to geometric shapes. Generally, the artists used only black and white stones. The earliest examples of this type date to the eighth century BCE. Eventually, mosaicists arranged the stones to form more complex pictorial designs, and by the fourth century BCE, artists were able to depict elaborate figural scenes using a broad range of colors—yellow, brown, and red in addition to black, white, and gray—and to shade the figures, clothing, and setting to suggest volume.

By the middle of the third century BCE, the Greeks had invented a new kind of mosaic employing *tesserae* (Latin, "cubes" or "dice"). These tiny cut stones gave the artist far greater flexibility because their size and shape could be adjusted at will. Much more gradual gradations of color also became possible, and mosaicists finally could aspire to rival the achievements of panel painters (FIG. 2-50). In Early Christian mosaics (FIGS. 4-8 and 4-9),

the tesserae are usually made of glass, which reflects light and makes the surfaces sparkle. Ancient mosaicists occasionally used glass tesserae, but the Romans preferred opaque marble pieces.

Mosaics quickly became the standard means of decorating walls and vaults in Early Christian buildings, although some churches also contained mural paintings. The mosaics caught the light flooding through the windows in vibrant reflection, producing sharp contrasts and concentrations of color that could focus attention on a composition's central, most relevant features.

Mosaics made in the Early Christian manner were not intended for the subtle tonal changes a naturalistic painter's approach would require. The artists *placed,* not blended, color. Bright, hard, glittering texture, set within a rigorously simplified pattern, became the rule. For mosaics situated high in an apse or ambulatory vault or over the nave colonnade, far above the observer's head, the painstaking use of tiny tesserae seen in Roman floor mosaics became meaningless. Early Christian mosaics, designed to be seen from a distance, employed larger tesserae. The mosaicists also set the pieces unevenly so that their surfaces could catch and reflect the light.

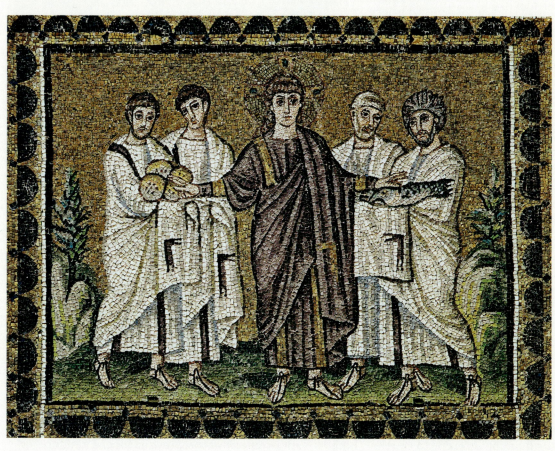

4-9 Miracle of the loaves and fishes, mosaic from the top register of the nave wall (above the clerestory windows) of Sant'Apollinare Nuovo, Ravenna, Italy, ca. 504.

In contrast to FIG. 4-8, Jesus here faces directly toward the viewer. Blue sky has given way to the otherworldly splendor of heavenly gold, the standard background color for medieval mosaics.

inscribed *nimbus* (halo) that signifies his divinity, faces directly toward the viewer. With extended arms he directs his disciples to distribute to the great crowd the miraculously increased supply of bread and fish he has produced. The artist made no attempt to supply details of the event. The emphasis is instead on the holy character of it, the spiritual fact that

Jesus is performing a miracle by the power of his divinity. The fact of the miracle takes it out of the world of time and of incident. The presence of almighty power, not anecdotal narrative, is the important aspect of this scene. The mosaicist told the story with the least number of figures necessary to make its meaning explicit. The artist aligned the figures laterally, moved them close to the foreground, and placed them in a shallow picture box cut off by a golden screen close behind their backs. The landscape setting, which the artist who worked for Galla Placidia so explicitly described, is here merely a few rocks and bushes that enclose the figure group like parentheses. The blue sky of the physical world has given way to the otherworldly splendor of heavenly gold, the standard background color for mosaics from this time forward. Remnants of Roman illusionism appear only in the handling of the individual figures, which still cast shadows and retain some of their former volume. But the shadows of the drapery folds already are only narrow bars.

Manuscript Illumination

The long tradition of placing pictures in manuscripts began in Egypt. Ancient books, however, are very rare. An important invention of the Early Empire period, the *codex*, greatly aided the dissemination of manuscripts as well as their preservation. The codex is much like a modern book, composed of separate leaves *(folios)* enclosed within a cover and bound together at one side. The new format superseded the long manuscript scroll *(rotulus)* used by the Egyptians, Greeks, Etruscans, and Romans. (Christ holds a rotulus in his left hand in FIG. 4-3.) Much more durable *vellum* (calfskin) and *parchment* (lambskin), which provided better surfaces for painting, also replaced the comparatively brittle *papyrus* (an Egyptian plant) used for ancient scrolls. As a result, luxuriousness of ornamentation became increasingly typical. Art historians refer to the painted books produced before the invention of the printing press as *illuminated manuscripts* (from the Latin *illuminare*, meaning "to adorn, ornament, or brighten," and *manu scriptus*, "handwritten").

Vienna Genesis The oldest well-preserved painted manuscript containing biblical scenes is the early sixth-century *Vienna Genesis*, so called because of its present location. The book is sumptuous. The pages are fine calfskin dyed with rich purple, the same dye used to give imperial cloth its distinctive color, and the Greek text is written in silver ink. One lavish page (FIG. 4-10) depicts the story of Rebecca and Eliezer (Gen. 24:15–61). When Isaac, Abraham's son, was 40 years old, his parents sent their servant Eliezer to find a wife for him. Eliezer chose Rebecca because when he stopped at a well, she was the first woman to draw water for him and his camels. The *Vienna Genesis* illustration presents two episodes of the story within a single frame. In the first episode, at the left, Rebecca leaves the city of Nahor to fetch water from the well. In the second episode, she gives water to Eliezer and his 10 camels, while one of them already laps water from the well. The artist painted Nahor as a walled city seen from above, a familiar convention in Roman art. Rebecca walks to the well along the colonnaded avenue of a Roman city. A seminude female personification of a spring is the source of the well water. These are further reminders of the persistence of classical motifs and stylistic modes in Early Christian art even as other artists (FIG. 4-9)

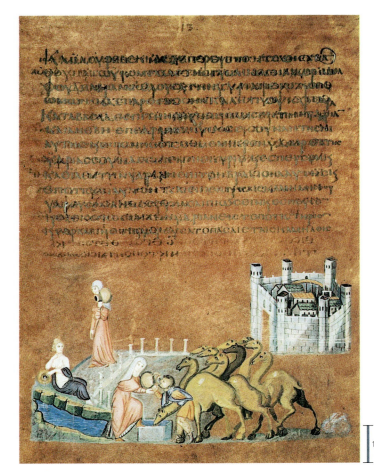

4-10 Rebecca and Eliezer at the well, folio 7 recto of the *Vienna Genesis*, early sixth century. Tempera, gold, and silver on purple vellum, $1'\frac{1}{4}'' \times 9\frac{1}{4}''$. Österreichische Nationalbibliothek, Vienna.

Classical motifs and stylistic modes persist in this sumptuous book— the oldest well-preserved manuscript containing biblical scenes. Two episodes of the story appear in a single setting.

rejected classical norms in favor of a style better suited for a focus on the spiritual instead of the natural world.

BYZANTINE ART

In the decades after the founding in 324 of Constantinople— the New Rome in the East, on the site of the Greek city of Byzantium—the pace of Christianization of the Roman Empire quickened. In 380, Theodosius I (r. 379–395) issued an edict finally establishing Christianity as the state religion. In 391, he enacted a ban against pagan worship. In 394, the emperor abolished the Olympic Games, the enduring symbol of the classical world and its values. Theodosius died in 395, and imperial power passed to his two sons, Arcadius, who became Emperor of the East, and Honorius, Emperor of the West. Though not formally codified, the division of the Roman Empire became permanent. In the western half, the Visigoths, under their king Alaric, sacked Rome in 410. The Western Empire soon collapsed, replaced by warring kingdoms that during the Middle Ages formed the foundations of the modern nations of Europe (see Chapter 6). The eastern half of the Roman Empire, only loosely connected by religion to the west and with only minor territorial holdings

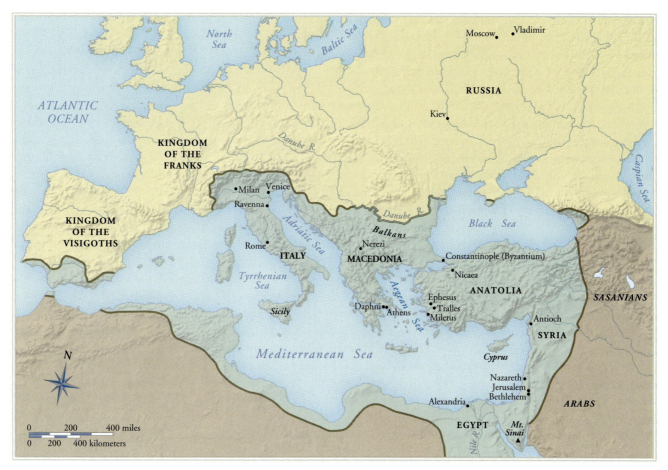

MAP 4-1 The Byzantine Empire at the death of Justinian in 565.

there, had a long and complex history of its own. Centered at New Rome, the Eastern Christian Empire remained a cultural and political entity for a millennium, until the last of a long line of Eastern Roman emperors, ironically named Constantine XI, died at Constantinople in 1453, defending it in vain against the Muslim armies of the Ottoman Turks.

Historians call that Eastern Christian Roman Empire "Byzantium," employing Constantinople's original name, and use the term "Byzantine" to identify whatever pertains to Byzantium—its territory, its history, and its culture. The Byzantine emperors, however, did not use these terms to define themselves. They called their empire Rome and themselves Romans. Though they spoke Greek and not Latin, the Eastern Roman emperors never relinquished their claim as the legitimate successors to the ancient Roman emperors. Nevertheless, Byzantium and Byzantine, though inexact terms, have become in modern times the accepted designations for the Eastern Roman Empire.

The Byzantine emperors considered themselves the earthly vicars of Jesus Christ. Their will was God's will. They exercised the ultimate spiritual as well as temporal authority. As sole executives for church and state, the emperors shared power with neither senate nor church council. They reigned supreme, combining the functions of both pope and caesar, which the Western Christian world kept strictly separate. The Byzantine emperors' exalted position made them quasi-divine. The imperial court was an image of the Kingdom of Heaven.

Art historians divide the history of Byzantine art into three periods. The first, Early Byzantine, extends from the age of the emperor Justinian (r. 527–565; MAP 4-1) to the onset of iconoclasm (the destruction of images used in religious worship) under Leo III in 726. The Middle Byzantine period begins with the renunciation of iconoclasm in 843 and ends with the western Crusaders' occupation of Constantinople in 1204. Late Byzantine corresponds to the period after the Byzantines recaptured Constantinople in 1261 until its final loss in 1453 to the Ottoman Turks.

Early Byzantine Art

The reign of Justinian marks the end of the Late Roman Empire and the beginning of the Byzantine Empire. At this time Byzantine art emerged as a recognizably novel and distinctive style, leaving behind the uncertainties and hesitations of Early Christian artistic experiment. Justinianic art and architecture definitively expressed, with a new independence and power of invention, the unique character of the Eastern Christian culture centered at Constantinople. In the capital alone, Justinian built or restored more than 30 churches, and his activities as builder extended throughout the Byzantine Empire. The historian of his reign, Procopius, declared that the emperor's ambitious building program was an obsession that cost his subjects dearly in taxation. But Justinian's grand monuments defined the Byzantine style in architecture forever after.

Hagia Sophia The most important monument of Early Byzantine art is Hagia Sophia (FIGS. **4-11** to **4-13**), the Church of Holy Wisdom, in Constantinople. ANTHEMIUS OF TRALLES and ISIDORUS OF MILETUS designed and built the church for Justinian between 532 and 537. It is Byzantium's grandest building and one of the supreme accomplishments of world architecture. Its dimensions are formidable: about 270 feet long and 240 feet wide, with a dome 108 feet in diameter whose crown rises some 180 feet above the pavement. In exterior view, the great dome dominates the structure, but the building's external aspects today are much changed from their original appearance. Huge buttresses were added to the Justinianic design, and four towering Turkish *minarets* were constructed after the Ottoman conquest of 1453, when Hagia Sophia became a *mosque* (see Chapter 5).

The characteristic Byzantine plainness and unpretentiousness of the exterior (FIG. **4-11**) scarcely prepare visitors for the building's interior (FIG. **4-13**), which was once richly appointed. Colored stones from all over the known world sheathed the walls and floors. But what distinguishes Hagia Sophia from the equally lavishly revetted and paved interiors of Roman buildings such as the Pantheon (FIG. **3-39**) is the mystical quality of the light that floods the building. The soaring canopy-like dome that dominates the inside as well as the outside of the church rides on a halo of light from 40 windows in the dome's base. The windows create the illusion that the dome is resting on the light that pours through them. Procopius observed that the dome looked as if it were suspended by "a golden chain from Heaven." Said he: "You might say that the space is not illuminated by the sun from the outside, but that the radiance is generated within, so great an abundance of light bathes this shrine all around."[2]

A poet and member of Justinian's court, Paul the Silentiary (official usher), compared the dome to "the firmament which rests on air" and described the vaulting as covered with "gilded tesserae from which a glittering stream of golden rays pours abundantly and strikes men's eyes with irresistible force. It is as if one were gazing at the midday sun in spring."[3] Thus, Hagia Sophia has a vastness of space shot through with light and a central dome that appears to be supported by the light it admits. Light is the mystic element—light that glitters in the mosaics, shines forth from the marbles, and pervades and defines spaces that, in themselves, seem to escape definition. Light seems to dissolve material substance and transform it into an abstract spiritual vision.

Justinian's architects achieved this illusion of a floating "dome of Heaven" by using *pendentives* (see "Pendentives," page 134, and FIG. **4-14**) to transfer the weight from the great dome to the piers beneath rather than to the walls. With pendentives, not only could the space beneath the dome be unobstructed but scores of windows also could puncture the walls themselves (FIGS. **4-12** and **4-13**). This created the impression of a dome suspended above, not held up by, walls. Experts today can explain the technical virtuosity of Anthemius and Isidorus, but it remained a mystery to their contemporaries. Procopius communicated the sense of wonderment experienced by those who entered Justinian's great church: "No matter how much they concentrate . . . they are unable to understand the craftsmanship and always depart from there amazed by the perplexing spectacle."[4]

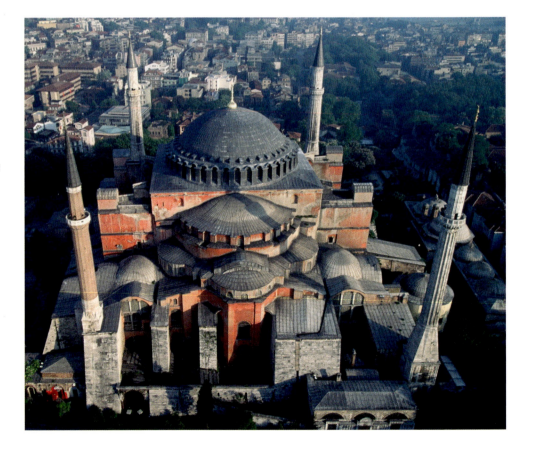

4-11 ANTHEMIUS OF TRALLES and ISIDORUS OF MILETUS, aerial view (looking north) of Hagia Sophia, Constantinople (Istanbul), Turkey, 532–537.

The reign of Justinian marks the beginning of the first golden age of Byzantine art and architecture. Justinian built or restored more than 30 churches in Constantinople alone. Hagia Sophia was the greatest.

By placing a hemispherical dome on a square instead of a circular base, Anthemius and Isidorus succeeded in fusing two previously independent and seemingly mutually exclusive architectural traditions: the vertically oriented central-plan building and the longitudinally oriented basilica. Hagia Sophia is, in essence, a domed basilica (FIG. 4-12)—a uniquely successful conclusion to centuries of experimentation in Christian church architecture. However, the thrusts of the pendentive construction at Hagia Sophia made external buttresses necessary, as well as huge internal northern and southern wall piers and eastern and western half-domes. The semidomes' thrusts descend, in turn, into still smaller half-domes surmounting columned exedrae that give a curving flow to the design.

The diverse vistas and screenlike ornamented surfaces mask the structural lines. The columnar *arcades* of the nave and galleries have no real structural function. Like the walls they pierce, they are only part of a fragile "fill" between the huge piers. Structurally, although Hagia Sophia may seem Roman in its great scale and majesty, it does not have Roman organization of its masses. The very fact that the "walls" in Hagia Sophia are concealed (and barely adequate) piers indicates that the architects sought Roman monumentality as an effect and did not design the building according to Roman principles. Using brick in place of concrete marked a further departure from Roman practice and characterizes Byzantine architecture as a distinctive structural style. Hagia Sophia's eight great supporting piers are ashlar masonry, but the screen walls are brick, as are the vaults of the aisles and galleries and the dome and semicircular half-domes.

The ingenious design of Hagia Sophia provided the illumination and the setting for the solemn liturgy of the Greek Orthodox faith. The large windows along the rim of the great dome poured light down upon the interior's jeweled splendor, where priests staged the sacred spectacle. Sung by clerical choirs, the Orthodox equivalent of the Latin Mass celebrated the sacrament of the Eucharist at the altar in the *apsidal* sanctuary, in spiritual reenactment of Jesus' Crucifixion. Processions of chanting priests, accompanying the *patriarch* (archbishop) of Constantinople, moved slowly to and from the sanctuary and the vast nave. The gorgeous array of their vestments rivaled the interior's polychrome marbles, metals, and mosaics, all glowing in shafts of light from the dome.

The nave of Hagia Sophia was reserved for the clergy, not the congregation. The laity, segregated by gender, watched from the shadows of the aisles and galleries, restrained in

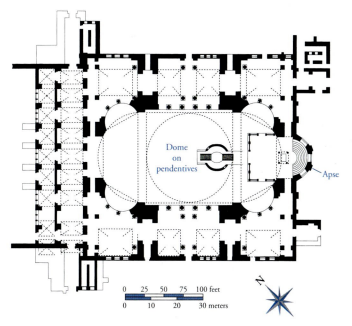

4-12 ANTHEMIUS OF TRALLES and ISIDORUS OF MILETUS, plan (*top*) and restored cutaway view (*bottom*) of Hagia Sophia, Constantinople (Istanbul), Turkey, 532–537 (John Burge).

In Hagia Sophia, Justinian's architects succeeded in fusing two previously independent architectural traditions: the vertically oriented central-plan building and the longitudinally oriented basilica.

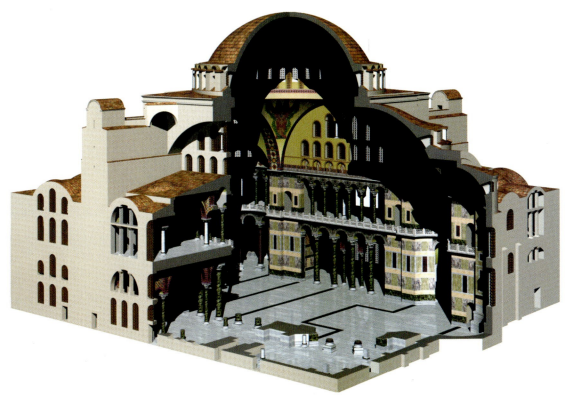

Pendentives

Perhaps the most characteristic feature of Byzantine architecture is the placement of a dome, which is circular at its base, over a square, as at Hagia Sophia (FIGS. 4-12 and 4-13) in Constantinople, Saint Mark's (FIG. 4-1) in Venice, the Church of the Dormition (FIG. 4-21) at Daphni, and countless other churches throughout the Byzantine Empire. The structural device that made this feat possible was the *pendentive* (FIG. 4-14).

In pendentive construction (from the Latin *pendere*, "to hang"), a dome rests on what is, in effect, a second, larger dome. The top portion and four segments around the rim of the larger dome are omitted, creating four curved triangles, or pendentives. The pendentives join to form a ring and four arches whose planes bound a square. The weight of the dome is thus transferred through the pendentives and arches to the four piers from which the arches spring, instead of to the walls. The first use of pendentives on a monumental scale was in Hagia Sophia in the mid-sixth century.

In Roman and Early Christian central-plan buildings, such as the Pantheon (FIGS. 3-38 and 3-39) and Santa Costanza (FIG. 4-6), the dome springs directly from the circular top of a cylinder (FIG. 3-14*d*).

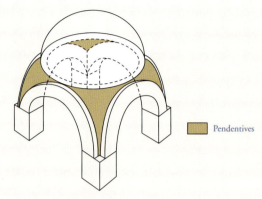

4-14 Dome on pendentives.

Roman domes rested on cylindrical drums (FIG. 3-14*d*). Pendentives (triangular sections of a sphere) made it possible to place a dome on a ring over a square. They became a hallmark of Byzantine architecture.

most places by marble parapets. The complex spatial arrangement allowed only partial views of the brilliant ceremony. The emperor was the only layperson privileged to enter the sanctuary. When he participated with the patriarch in the liturgical drama, standing at the pulpit beneath the great dome, his rule was sanctified and his person exalted. Church and state were symbolically made one, as in fact they were. The church building was then the earthly image of the court of Heaven, its light the image of God and God's holy wisdom. At Hagia Sophia, the ambitious scale of Rome and the mysticism of Eastern Christianity combined to create a monument that is at once a summation of antiquity and a positive assertion of the triumph of Christian faith.

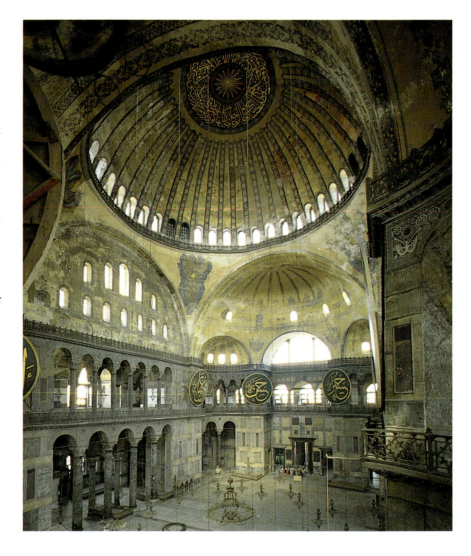

4-13 ANTHEMIUS OF TRALLES and ISIDORUS OF MILETUS, interior (looking southwest) of Hagia Sophia, Constantinople (Istanbul), Turkey, 532–537.

Pendentive construction made possible Hagia Sophia's lofty dome, which seems to ride on a halo of light. A contemporary said the dome seemed to be suspended by "a golden chain from Heaven."

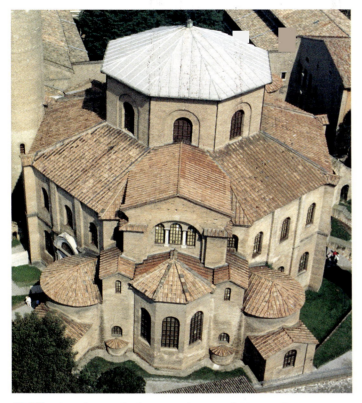

4-15 Aerial view (looking northwest) of San Vitale, Ravenna, Italy, 526–547.

Justinian's general Belisarius captured Ravenna from the Ostrogoths. The city became the seat of Byzantine dominion in Italy. San Vitale honored Saint Vitalis, who suffered martyrdom at Ravenna.

San Vitale In 539, Justinian's general Belisarius captured Ravenna from the Ostrogoths. As the seat of Byzantine dominion in Italy, Ravenna enjoyed unparalleled prosperity, and its culture became an extension of Constantinople's. Its art,

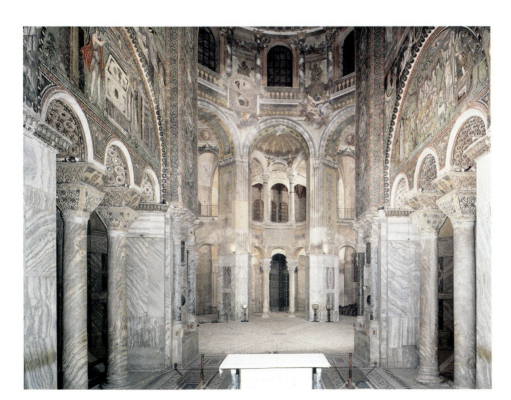

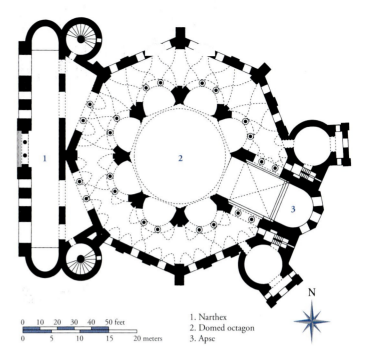

4-16 Plan of San Vitale, Ravenna, Italy, 526–547.

Centrally planned like Justinian's churches in Constantinople, San Vitale is unlike any other church in Italy. The design features two concentric octagons. A dome crowns the taller, inner octagon.

1. Narthex
2. Domed octagon
3. Apse

even more than that of the Byzantine capital (where relatively little outside of architecture has survived), clearly reveals the transition from the Early Christian to the Byzantine style.

San Vitale (FIGS. **4-15** to **4-17**), dedicated by Bishop Maximianus in 547 in honor of Saint Vitalis, who suffered martyrdom at Ravenna in the second century, is the most spectacular building in Ravenna. Construction began under Bishop Ecclesius shortly after Theodoric's death in 526. Julianus Argentarius (Julian the Banker) provided the enormous sum of 26,000 *solidi* (gold coins, weighing in excess of 350 pounds) required to proceed with the work. The church is unlike any of Ravenna's other sixth-century churches (FIG. **4-5**). Indeed, it is unlike any other church in Italy. Although it has a traditional plain exterior and a polygonal apse (FIG. **4-15**), San Vitale is not a basilica. It is centrally planned (FIG. **4-16**), like Justinian's churches in Constantinople.

4-17 Interior (looking from the apse into the choir) of San Vitale, Ravenna, Italy, 526–547.

Light filtered through alabaster-paned windows plays over the glittering mosaics and glowing marbles that cover San Vitale's complex wall and vault shapes, producing a sumptuous effect.

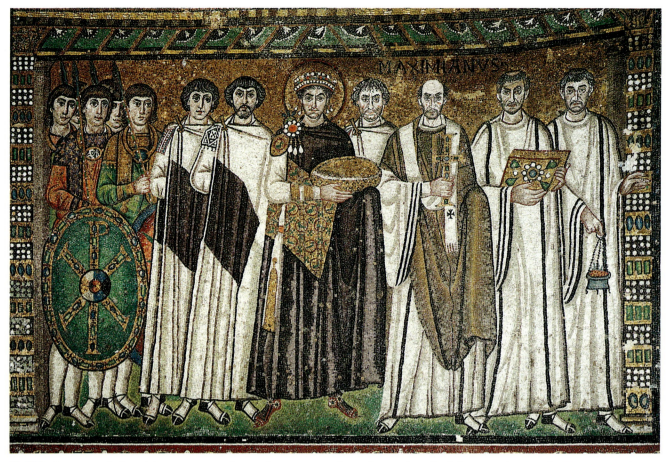

4-18 Justinian, Bishop Maximianus, and attendants, mosaic from the north wall of the apse, San Vitale, Ravenna, Italy, ca. 547.

San Vitale's mosaics reveal the new Byzantine aesthetic. Justinian is foremost among the dematerialized frontal figures who hover before the viewer, weightless and speechless, their positions in space uncertain.

The design features two concentric octagons. The dome-covered inner octagon rises above the surrounding octagon to provide the interior with clerestory lighting. The central space (FIG. 4-17) is defined by eight large piers that alternate with curved, columned exedrae, pushing outward into the surrounding two-story ambulatory and creating, on the plan (FIG. 4-16), an intricate eight-leafed design. The exedrae closely integrate the inner and outer spaces that otherwise would have existed simply side by side as independent units. A cross-vaulted *choir* preceding the apse interrupts the ambulatory and gives the plan some axial stability. The off-axis placement of the narthex, whose odd angle never has been explained fully, weakens this effect, however. (The atrium, which no longer exists, may have paralleled a street that ran in the same direction as the angle of the narthex.)

San Vitale's intricate plan and elevation combine to produce an effect of great complexity. The exterior's octagonal regularity is not readily apparent inside. A rich diversity of ever-changing perspectives greets visitors walking through the building. Arches looping over arches, curving and flattened spaces, and wall and vault shapes seem to change constantly with the viewer's position. Light filtered through alabaster-paned windows plays over the glittering mosaics and glowing marbles that cover the building's complex surfaces, producing a sumptuous effect.

The mosaics that decorate San Vitale's choir and apse, like the building itself, must be regarded as one of the climactic achievements of Byzantine art. Completed less than a decade after the Ostrogoths surrendered Ravenna, the apse and choir decorations form a unified composition, whose theme is the holy ratification of Justinian's right to rule. In the apse vault are Christ, who extends the golden martyr's wreath to Saint Vitalis, the patron saint of the church, and Bishop Ecclesius, who began the construction of San Vitale and offers a model of the new church to Christ. On the choir wall to the left of the apse mosaic appears Justinian (FIG. **4-18**). He stands on the Savior's right side. Uniting the two visually and symbolically are the imperial purple they wear and their halos. A dozen attendants also accompany Justinian, paralleling Christ's 12 apostles. Thus, the mosaic program underscores the dual political and religious roles of the Byzantine emperor.

The positions of the figures are all-important. They express the formulas of precedence and rank. Justinian is at the center, distinguished from the other dignitaries by his purple robe and halo. At his left is Bishop Maximianus, the man responsible for San Vitale's completion. The mosaicist stressed the bishop's importance by labeling his figure with the only identifying inscription in the composition. Some have identified the figure behind and between Justinian and Maximianus as Julius Argentarius, the church's benefactor.

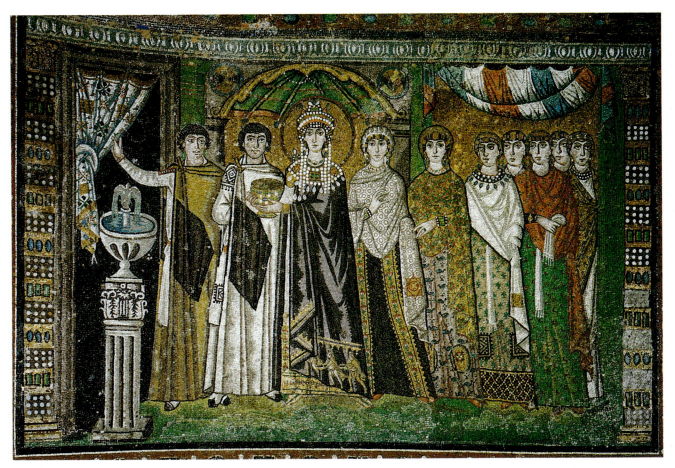

4-19 Theodora and attendants, mosaic from the south wall of the apse, San Vitale, Ravenna, Italy, ca. 547.

Justinian's counterpart on the opposite wall is the empress Theodora, a powerful figure at the Byzantine court. Neither she nor Justinian ever visited Ravenna. San Vitale's mosaics are proxies for the absent sovereigns.

The artist divided the figures into three groups: the emperor and his staff; the clergy; and the imperial guard, one of whom bears a shield with the *Christogram*, the monogram (✠) composed of chi (**X**), rho (**P**), and iota (**I**), the initial letters of Christ's name in Greek. Each group has a leader whose feet precede (by one foot overlapping) the feet of those who follow. The positions of Justinian and Maximianus are curiously ambiguous. Although the emperor appears to be slightly behind the bishop, the golden *paten* (large bowl holding the Eucharist bread) he carries overlaps the bishop's arm. Thus, symbolized by place and gesture, the imperial and ecclesiastical powers are in balance. Justinian's paten, Maximianus's cross, and the attendant clerics' book and censer produce a slow forward movement that strikingly modifies the scene's rigid formality. There is no background. The artist wished the observer to understand the procession as taking place in this very sanctuary. Thus, the emperor appears forever as a participant in the sacred rites and as the proprietor of this royal church and the ruler of the Western Empire.

The procession at San Vitale recalls but contrasts with that of Augustus and his entourage on the Ara Pacis (FIG. 3-26) erected more than a half millennium earlier in Rome. There the fully modeled marble figures have their feet planted firmly on the ground. The Romans talk among themselves, unaware of the viewer's presence. All is anecdote, all very human and of this world, even if the figures themselves conform to a classical ideal of beauty that cannot be achieved in reality. The frontal figures of the Byzantine mosaic, by comparison, hover before the viewer, weightless and speechless, their positions in space uncertain. Tall, spare, angular, and elegant, the figures have lost the rather squat proportions characteristic of much Early Christian work. The garments fall straight, stiff, and thin from the narrow shoulders. The organic body has dematerialized, and, except for the heads, some of which seem to be true portraits, the viewer sees a procession of solemn spirits gliding silently in the presence of the sacrament. Indeed, the theological basis for this approach to representation was the idea that the divine was invisible and that the purpose of religious art was to stimulate spiritual seeing. Theodulf of Orleans summed up this idea around 790 when he wrote "God is beheld not with the eyes of the flesh but only with the eye of the mind."[5] The mosaics of San Vitale reveal the Byzantine world's new aesthetic, one very different from that of the classical world but equally compelling. Blue sky has given way to heavenly gold, and matter and material values are disparaged. Byzantine art is an art without solid bodies or cast shadows, with blank golden spaces, and with the perspective of Paradise, which is nowhere and everywhere.

Justinian's counterpart on the opposite wall of the apse is his empress, Theodora (FIG. **4-19**), who was Justinian's most trusted adviser as well as his spouse. She too is accompanied by her retinue. Both processions move into the apse, Justinian proceeding from left to right and Theodora from right to left, in order to take part in the Eucharist. Justinian carries the paten containing the bread, Theodora the golden cup with the wine. The portraits in the Theodora mosaic exhibit the same stylistic traits as those in the Justinian mosaic, but the mosaicist represented the women within a definite architecture, perhaps the atrium of San Vitale. The empress stands in state beneath an imperial canopy, waiting to follow the emperor's procession. An attendant beckons her to pass through the curtained doorway. The fact that she is outside the sanctuary in a courtyard with a fountain and only about to enter attests that, in the ceremonial protocol, her rank was not quite equal to her consort's. But the very presence of Theodora at San Vitale is significant. Neither she nor Justinian ever visited Ravenna. Their participation in the liturgy at San Vitale is pictorial fiction. The mosaics are proxies for the absent sovereigns. Justinian was represented because he was the head of the Byzantine state, and by his presence he exerted his authority over his territories in the West. But Theodora's portrayal is more surprising and testifies to her unique position in Justinian's court. Theodora's prominent role in the mosaic program of San Vitale is proof of the power she wielded at Constantinople and, by extension, at Ravenna. In fact, the representation of the three magi on the border of her robe suggests that she belongs in the elevated company of the three monarchs who approached the newborn Jesus bearing gifts.

Mount Sinai During Justinian's reign, almost continuous building took place, not only in Constantinople and Ravenna but all over the Byzantine Empire. Between 548 and 565, Justinian rebuilt an important early *monastery* (monks' compound) at Mount Sinai in Egypt where Moses received the Ten Commandments from God. Now called Saint Catherine's, the monastery marked the spot at the foot of the mountain where the Bible says God first spoke to the Hebrew prophet from a burning bush.

The monastic movement began in Egypt in the third century and spread rapidly to Palestine and Syria in the east and as far as Ireland in the west. It began as a migration to the wilderness by those who sought a more spiritual way of life, far from the burdens, distractions, and temptations of town and city. In desert places these refuge seekers lived austerely as hermits, in contemplative isolation, cultivating the soul's perfection. So many thousands fled the cities that the authorities became alarmed—noting the effect on the tax base, military recruitment, and business in general. The origins of organized monasticism are associated with Saints Anthony and Pachomius in Egypt in the fourth century. By the fifth century, regulations governing monastic life began to be codified. Individual monks came together to live according to a rule within a common enclosure, a community under the direction of an *abbot* (see "Medieval Monasteries," Chapter 6, page 165). The monks typically lived in a walled monastery, an architectural complex that included the monks' residence (an alignment of single cells), a *refectory* (dining hall), a kitchen, storage and service quarters, a guest house for pilgrims, and, of course, an *oratory* or monastery church (FIG. 6-9). The monastery at Mount Sinai had been an important pilgrimage destination since the fourth century, and Justinian enclosed it within new walls to protect not only the hermit-monks but also the lay pilgrims during their visits. The Mount Sinai church was dedicated to the Virgin Mary, whom the Council of Ephesus had officially recognized in 431 as the Mother of God (*Theotokos*, "bearer of God" in Greek).

Icons Icons (see "Icons and Iconoclasm," page 139) played an important role in monastic life. Unfortunately, few early icons survive because of the wholesale destruction of images *(iconoclasm)* that occurred in the eighth century. Some of the finest early examples (FIG. 4-20) come from Mount Sinai. The technique is encaustic on wood, continuing a tradition of panel painting in Egypt that, like so much else in the Byzantine world, dates to the Roman Empire (FIG. 3-41). The icon depicts the enthroned Theotokos and Child with Saints Theodore and George. The two guardian saints intercede with the Virgin on the viewer's behalf. Behind them, two angels look upward to a shaft of light where the hand of God appears. The foreground figures are strictly frontal and have a solemn demeanor. Background details are few and suppressed. The forward plane of the picture dominates; space is squeezed out. Traces of Greco-Roman illusionism remain in the Virgin's rather personalized features, in her sideways glance, and in the posing of the angels' heads. But the painter rendered the saints in the new Byzantine manner.

Iconoclasm

The preservation of Early Byzantine icons at the Mount Sinai monastery is fortuitous but ironic, for opposition to icon worship was especially prominent in Syria and Egypt. There, in the seventh century, a series of calamities erupted, indirectly causing the imperial ban on images. The Sasanians, chronically at war with Rome, swept into the eastern provinces early in the seventh century. Between 611 and 617 they captured the great cities of Antioch, Jerusalem, and Alexandria. Hardly had the Byzantine emperor Heraclius (r. 610–641) pressed them back and defeated them in 627 when a new and overwhelming power appeared unexpectedly on the stage of history. The Arabs, under the banner of the new Islamic religion, conquered not only Byzantium's eastern provinces but also Persia itself, replacing the Sasanians in the age-old balance of power with the Christian West (see Chapter 5). In a few years the Arabs launched attacks on Constantinople, and Byzantium was fighting for its life.

These were catastrophic years for the Eastern Roman Empire. They terminated once and for all the long story of imperial Rome, closed the Early Byzantine period, and inaugurated the medieval era of Byzantine history. Almost two-thirds of the Byzantine Empire's territory was lost—many cities and much of its population, wealth, and material resources. The shock of these events persuaded Emperor Leo III (r. 717–741) that God had punished the Christian Roman

Icons and Iconoclasm

Icons (Greek, "images") are small portable paintings depicting Christ, the Virgin, or saints (or a combination of all three, as in FIG. 4-20). Icons survive from as early as the fourth century. From the sixth century on, they became enormously popular in Byzantine worship, both public and private. Eastern Christians considered icons a personal, intimate, and indispensable medium for spiritual transaction with holy figures. Some icons (FIG. 4-25) came to be regarded as wonder-working, and believers ascribed miracles and healing powers to them.

Icons were by no means universally accepted, however. From the beginning, many Christians were deeply suspicious of the practice of making images of the divine, whether on portable panels, on the walls of churches, or especially as statues that reminded them of pagan idols. The opponents of Christian figural art had in mind the Old Testament prohibition of images the Lord dictated to Moses in the Second Commandment: "Thou shalt not make unto thee any graven image or any likeness of anything that is in heaven above, or that is in the earth beneath, or that is in the water under the earth. Thou shalt not bow down thyself to them, nor serve them" (Exod. 20:4, 5).

Opposition to icons became especially strong in the eighth century, when the faithful often burned incense and knelt before them in prayer to seek protection or a cure for illness. Although the purpose of icons was only to evoke the presence of the holy figures addressed in prayer, in the minds of many, icons became identified with the personages represented. Icon worship became confused with idol worship, and this brought about an imperial ban on all sacred images. The term for this destruction of holy pictures is *iconoclasm*.

The consequences of iconoclasm for the history of Byzantine art are difficult to overstate. For more than a century, not only did the portrayal of Christ, the Virgin, and the saints cease, but the *iconoclasts* (breakers of images) also systematically destroyed countless works from the early centuries of Christendom.

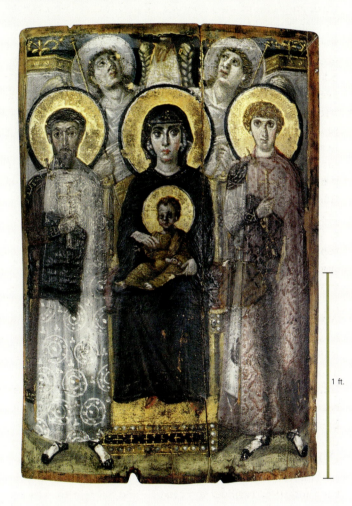

4-20 Virgin (Theotokos) and Child between Saints Theodore and George, icon, sixth or early seventh century. Encaustic on wood, 2′ 3″ × 1′ 7⅜″. Monastery of Saint Catherine, Mount Sinai, Egypt.

Byzantine icons continued the Roman tradition of panel painting in encaustic on wood panels (FIG. 3-41), but their style as well as the Christian subjects broke sharply from classical models.

1 ft.

Empire for its idolatrous worship of icons by setting upon it the merciless armies of the infidel—an enemy that, moreover, shunned the representation in holy places not only of God but of all living things. In 726 he formally prohibited the use of images, and for more than a century Byzantine artists produced little new religious figurative art.

Middle Byzantine Art

In the ninth century, a powerful reaction against iconoclasm set in. New *iconophile* emperors condemned the destruction of images as a heresy, and restoration of the images began in 843. Shortly thereafter, under the Macedonian dynasty, art, literature, and learning sprang to life once again. Basil I (r. 867–886), head of the new line of emperors, thought of himself as the restorer of the Roman Empire. He denounced as usurpers the Frankish Carolingian monarchs of the West (see Chapter 6) who, since 800, had claimed the title "Roman Empire" for their realm. Basil bluntly reminded their emissary that the only true Emperor of Rome reigned in Constantinople. They were not Roman emperors but merely "kings of the Germans."

Daphni Basil I and his immediate successors undertook the laborious and costly task of refurbishing the churches the iconoclasts had defaced and neglected, but they initiated little new church construction. In the 10th century and through the 12th, however, a number of monastic churches arose that are the flowers of Middle Byzantine architecture. They feature a brilliant series of variations on the domed central plan.

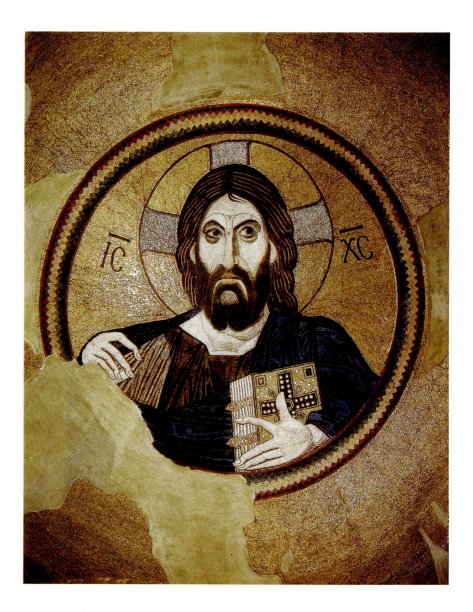

4-21 Christ as Pantokrator, dome mosaic in the Church of the Dormition, Daphni, Greece, ca. 1090–1100.

The fearsome image of Christ as "ruler of all" is like a gigantic icon hovering dramatically in space. The mosaic serves to connect the awestruck worshiper below the dome with Heaven through Christ.

From the exterior, the typical later Byzantine church building is a domed cube, with the dome rising above the square on a kind of cylinder or drum. The churches are small, vertical, and high shouldered, and, unlike earlier Byzantine buildings, their exterior wall surfaces bear vivid decorative patterns, probably reflecting the impact of Islamic architecture.

Mosaics covered the interiors of the new churches. Some of the best-preserved examples are in the monastery Church of the Dormition (from the Latin for "sleep," referring to the ascension of the Virgin Mary to Heaven at the moment of her death), at Daphni, near Athens, Greece. The main elements of the late-11th-century pictorial program are intact, although the mosaics were restored in the 19th century. Gazing down from on high in the central dome (FIG. 4-21) is the fearsome image of Christ as *Pantokrator* (literally "ruler of all" in Greek but usually applied to Christ in his role as Last Judge of humankind). The dome mosaic is the climax of an elaborate hierarchical pictorial program including several New Testament episodes below. The Daphni Pantokrator is like a gigantic icon hovering dramatically in space. The mosaic serves to connect the awestruck worshiper in the church below with Heaven through Christ.

On one of the walls below the Daphni dome, an unknown artist depicted Christ's Crucifixion (FIG. 4-22). Like the Pantokrator mosaic in the dome, the Daphni Crucifixion is a subtle blend of the painterly, Hellenistic style and the later, more abstract and formalistic Byzantine style. The Byzantine artist fully assimilated classicism's simplicity, dignity, and grace into a perfect synthesis with Byzantine piety and pathos. The figures have regained the classical organic structure to a surprising degree, particularly compared with figures from the Justinianic period (compare FIGS. 4-18 and 4-19). The style is a masterful adaptation of classical statuesque qualities to the linear Byzantine manner. In quiet sorrow and resignation, the Virgin and Saint John flank the crucified Christ. A skull at the foot of the cross indicates Golgotha. The artist needed nothing else to set the scene. Symmetry and closed space combine to produce an effect of the motionless and unchanging aspect of the deepest mystery of the Christian religion. The timeless presence is, as it were, beheld in unbroken silence. The picture is not a narrative of the historical event of the Crucifixion, although it contains anecdotal details. Christ has a tilted head and sagging body, and blood spurts from the wound Longinus inflicted on him,

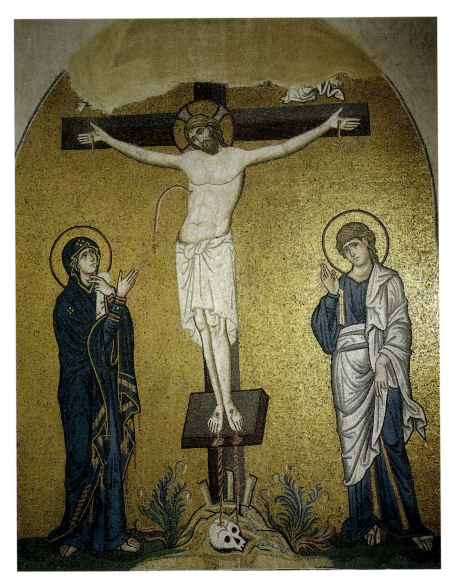

The Daphni Crucifixion is a subtle blend of Hellenistic style and the more abstract Byzantine manner. The Virgin Mary and Saint John point to Christ on the cross as if to a devotional object.

but he is not overtly in pain. The Virgin and John point to the figure on the cross as if to a devotional object. They act as intercessors between the viewer below and Christ, who, in the dome, appears as the Last Judge of all humans.

Saint Mark's, Venice The revival on a grand scale of church building, featuring vast stretches of mosaic-covered walls, extended beyond the Greek-speaking Byzantine East in the 10th to 12th centuries. A resurgence of religious architecture and of the mosaicist's art also occurred in areas of the former Western Roman Empire where ties with Constantinople were the strongest. In the Early Byzantine period, Venice, about 80 miles north of Ravenna on the eastern coast of Italy, was a dependency of that Byzantine stronghold. In 751, Ravenna fell to the Lombards, who wrested control of most of northern Italy from Constantinople. Venice, however, became an independent power. Its *doges* (dukes) enriched themselves and the city through seaborne commerce, serving as the crucial link between Byzantium and the West.

Venice had obtained the relics of Saint Mark from Alexandria in Egypt in 829, and the doges constructed the first Venetian shrine dedicated to the apostle shortly thereafter. In 1063, Doge Domenico Contarini began the construction of the present Saint Mark's. The model for the grandiose new building was the Church of the Holy Apostles at Constantinople, built in Justinian's time. That church no longer exists, but its key elements were a *cruciform* (cross-shaped) plan with a central dome over the crossing and four other domes over the four equal arms of the *Greek cross*, as at Saint Mark's.

The interior (FIG. **4-1**) of Saint Mark's is, like its plan, Byzantine in effect. Light enters through a row of windows at the bases of all five domes, vividly illuminating a rich cycle of mosaics. Both Byzantine and local artists worked on the project over the course of several centuries. Most of the mosaics date to the 12th and 13th centuries. Cleaning and restoration on a grand scale have enabled visitors to experience the full radiance of mosaic (some 40,000 square feet of it) as it covers, like a gold-brocaded and figured fabric, all the walls, arches, vaults, and domes.

In the vast central dome, 80 feet above the floor and 42 feet in diameter, Christ ascends to Heaven in the presence of the Virgin Mary and the 12 apostles. The great arch framing the church crossing bears a narrative of the Crucifixion and Resurrection of Christ and of his descent into Limbo to liberate from death Adam and Eve, Saint John the Baptist, and other biblical figures. The mosaics have explanatory

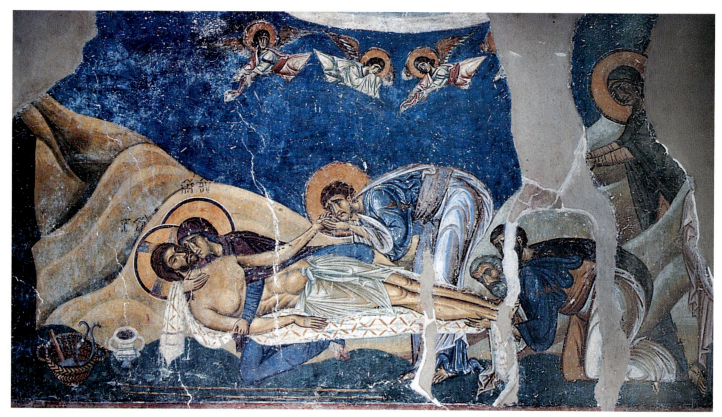

4-23 Lamentation, wall painting, Saint Pantaleimon, Nerezi, Macedonia, 1164.

Working in the Balkans in an alternate Byzantine mode, this painter staged the emotional scene of the Lamentation in a hilly landscape below a blue sky and peopled it with fully modeled figures.

labels in both Latin and Greek, reflecting Venice's position as the key link between Eastern and Western Christendom in the later Middle Ages. The insubstantial figures on the walls, vaults, and domes appear weightless and project from their flat field no more than the elegant Latin and Greek letters above them. Nothing here reflects on the world of matter, of solids, of light and shade, of perspective. Rather, the mosaics reveal the mysteries of the Christian faith.

Nerezi When the emperors lifted the ban against religious images and again encouraged religious painting at Constantinople, the impact was felt far and wide. The style varied from region to region, but a renewed enthusiasm for picturing the key New Testament figures and events was universal. In 1164, at Nerezi in Macedonia, Byzantine painters embellished the Church of Saint Pantaleimon with murals of great emotional power. One of these represents the Lamentation over the dead Christ (FIG. **4-23**). It is an image of passionate grief. The artist captured Christ's followers in attitudes, expressions, and gestures of quite human bereavement. Joseph of Arimathea and the disciple Nicodemus kneel at his feet, while Mary presses her cheek against her dead son's face and Saint John clings to Christ's left hand. In the Gospels, neither Mary nor John was present at the entombment of Christ. Their presence here, as elsewhere in Middle Byzantine art, intensified for the viewer the emotional impact

of Christ's death. Such representations parallel the development of liturgical hymns recounting the Virgin's lamenting her son's death on the Cross.

At Nerezi, the painter set the scene in a hilly landscape below a blue sky—a striking contrast to the abstract golden world of the mosaics favored for church walls elsewhere in the Byzantine Empire. The artist strove to make utterly convincing an emotionally charged realization of the theme by staging the Lamentation in a more natural setting and peopling it with fully modeled actors. This alternate representational mode is no less Byzantine than the more abstract style of Ravenna or the poignant melancholy of Daphni.

Paris Psalter Another example of this classical-revival style is a page from a book of the Psalms of David. The so-called *Paris Psalter* (FIG. **4-24**) reasserts the artistic values of the Greco-Roman past with astonishing authority. Art historians believe the manuscript dates from the mid-10th century—the Macedonian Renaissance, a time of enthusiastic and careful study of the language and literature of ancient Greece, and of humanistic reverence for the classical past. David, the psalmist, surrounded by sheep, goats, and his faithful dog, plays his harp in a rocky landscape with a town in the background. Similar settings appeared frequently in Pompeian murals. Befitting an ancient depiction of Orpheus, the Greek hero who could charm even inani-

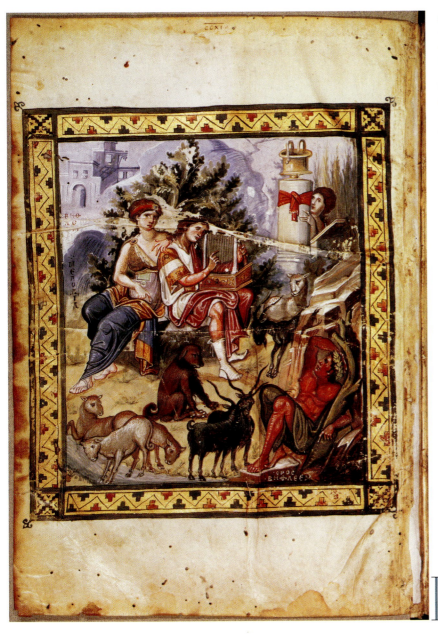

4-24 David composing the Psalms, folio 1 verso of the *Paris Psalter,* ca. 950–970. Tempera on vellum, 1' 2⅛" × 10¼". Bibliothèque Nationale, Paris.

During the so-called Macedonian Renaissance, Byzantine painters revived the classical style. This artist portrayed David as if a Greek hero accompanied by personifications of Melody, Echo, and Bethlehem.

1 in.

mate objects with his music, allegorical figures accompany the Old Testament harpist. Melody looks over his shoulder, while Echo peers from behind a column. A reclining male figure points to a Greek inscription that identifies him as representing the mountain of Bethlehem. These allegorical figures do not appear in the Bible. They are the stock population of Greco-Roman painting. Apparently, the artist had seen a work from the Late Roman Empire or perhaps earlier and partly translated it into a Byzantine pictorial idiom. In works such as this, Byzantine artists kept the classical style alive in the Middle Ages.

Vladimir Virgin Nothing in Middle Byzantine art better demonstrates the rejection of the iconoclastic viewpoint than the return to prominence of painted icons. After the restoration of images, icons multiplied by the thousands to meet public and private demand. In the 11th century, the clergy began to display icons in hierarchical order (Christ,

the Theotokos, John the Baptist, and then other saints) in tiers on the *templon,* the columnar screen separating the sanctuary from the main body of a Byzantine church.

One example is the renowned *Vladimir Virgin* (FIG. **4-25**). Descended from works such as the Mount Sinai icon (FIG. 4-20), the *Vladimir Virgin* clearly reveals the stylized abstraction resulting from centuries of working and reworking the conventional image. Probably painted by a Constantinopolitan artist, the characteristic traits of Byzantine Virgin and Child icons are all present: the Virgin's long, straight nose and small mouth; the golden rays in the infant's drapery; the sweep of the unbroken contour that encloses the two figures; and the flat silhouette against the golden ground. But this is a much more tender and personalized image of the Virgin than that in the Mount Sinai icon. Here Mary is depicted as the Virgin of Compassion, who presses her cheek against her son's in an intimate portrayal of Mother and Child. The image is also infused with a deep pathos as Mary contemplates

4-25 Virgin (Theotokos) and Child, icon (*Vladimir Virgin*), late 11th to early 12th century. Tempera on wood, original panel 2′ 6½″ × 1′ 9″. Tretyakov Gallery, Moscow.

In this Middle Byzantine icon, the painter depicted Mary as the Virgin of Compassion, who presses her cheek against her son's as she contemplates his future. The reverse side shows the instruments of Christ's Passion.

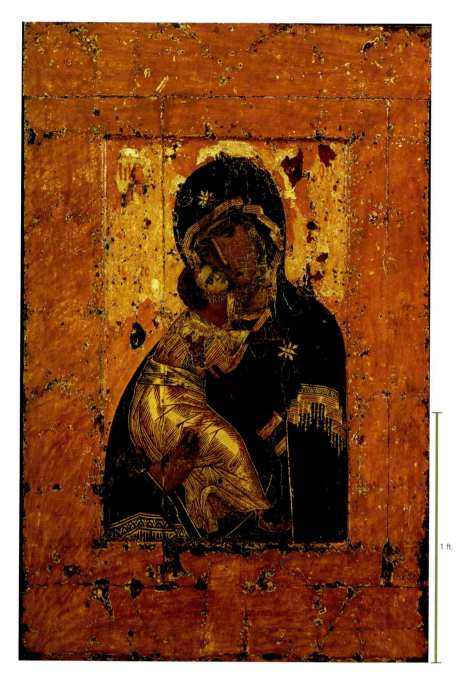

1 ft.

the future sacrifice of her son. (The back of the icon bears images of the instruments of Christ's Passion.)

The icon of Vladimir, like most icons, has seen hard service. Placed before or above altars in churches or private chapels, the icon became blackened by the incense and the smoke from candles that burned before or below it. Frequently repainted, often by inferior artists, only the faces show the original surface. First painted in the late 11th or early 12th century, it was taken to Kiev (Ukraine) in 1131, then to Vladimir (Russia) in 1155 (hence its name), and in 1395, as a wonder-working image, to Moscow to protect that city from the Mongols. The Russians believed the sacred picture saved the city of Kazan from later Tartar invasions and all of Russia from the Poles in the 17th century. The *Vladimir Virgin* is a historical symbol of Byzantium's religious and cultural mission to the Slavic world.

Byzantium after 1204

When rule passed from the Macedonian to the Comnenian dynasty in the later 11th and the 12th centuries, three events of fateful significance changed Byzantium's fortunes for the worse. The Seljuk Turks conquered most of Anatolia. The Byzantine Orthodox Church broke finally with the Church of Rome. And the Crusades brought the Latins (a generic term for the peoples of the West) into Byzantine lands on their way to fight for the Cross against the Saracens (Muslims) in the Holy Land (see "The Crusades," Chapter 6, page 176).

Crusaders had passed through Constantinople many times en route to "smite the infidel" and had marveled at its wealth and magnificence. Envy, greed, religious fanaticism (the Latins called the Greeks "heretics"), and even ethnic enmity motivated the Crusaders when, during the Fourth Crusade in 1203 and 1204, the Venetians persuaded them to divert their expedition against the Muslims in Palestine and to attack Constantinople instead. The Crusaders took the city and sacked it.

The Latins set up kingdoms within Byzantium, notably in Constantinople itself. What remained of Byzantium split into three small states. The Palaeologans ruled one of these, the kingdom of Nicaea. In 1261, Michael VIII Palaeologus (r. 1259–1282) succeeded in recapturing Constantinople. But his empire was no more than a fragment, and even that disintegrated during the next two centuries. Isolated from the Christian West by Muslim conquests in the Balkans and besieged by Muslim Turks to the east, Byzantium sought help from the West. It was not forthcoming. In 1453 the Ottoman Turks, then a formidable power, took Constantinople and brought to an end the long history of Byzantium.

Early Christianity and Byzantium

EARLY CHRISTIAN ART

▌ Very little Christian art or architecture survives from the first centuries of Christianity. "Early Christian art" means the earliest art having Christian subjects, not the art of Christians at the time of Jesus. The major surviving examples are mural and ceiling paintings in the catacombs of Rome and marble sarcophagi depicting Old and New Testament stories.

▌ Constantine's Edict of Milan of 313 granted Christianity legal status equal or superior to the traditional Roman cults. The emperor was the first great patron of Christian art and built the first churches in Rome, including Old Saint Peter's. In 330 he moved the capital of the Roman Empire to Constantinople (Greek Byzantium).

▌ The emperor Theodosius I (r. 379–395) proclaimed Christianity the official religion of the Roman Empire in 380 and banned pagan worship in 391. Honorius (r. 395–423) moved the capital of his Western Roman Empire to Ravenna in 404. Rome fell to Visigoth king Alaric in 410.

▌ Mosaics became a major vehicle for the depiction of Christian themes in the naves and apses of churches, which closely resembled Roman basilicas in both plan and elevation. The first manuscripts with illustrations of the Old and New Testaments date to the early sixth century.

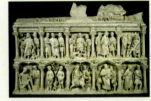

Sarcophagus of Junius Bassus, ca. 359

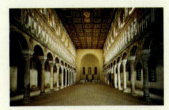

Sant'Apollinare Nuovo, Ravenna, 504

BYZANTINE ART

▌ The reign of Justinian (r. 527–565) opened the first golden age of Byzantine art (527–726). Justinian was a great patron of the arts, and in Constantinople alone he built or restored more than 30 churches. Constructed in only five years, Hagia Sophia, a brilliant fusion of central and longitudinal plans, rivaled the architectural wonders of Rome. Its 180-foot-high dome rests on pendentives.

▌ The seat of Byzantine power in Italy was Ravenna, which enjoyed its greatest prosperity under Justinian. San Vitale is Ravenna's greatest church. Its mosaics, with their weightless, hovering, frontal figures against a gold background, reveal the new Byzantine aesthetic.

▌ Justinian also rebuilt the monastery at Mount Sinai in Egypt, where the finest Early Byzantine icons are preserved. In 726, however, Leo III (r. 717–741) enacted a ban against picturing the divine, initiating the era of iconoclasm (726–843).

▌ Middle Byzantine art (843–1204), which marked the triumph of the iconophiles over the iconoclasts, is stylistically eclectic. Mosaics with mystical golden backgrounds were common, but some paintings, for example those in the *Paris Psalter,* revived the naturalism of classical art.

▌ Middle Byzantine churches have highly decorative exterior walls and feature domes that rest on drums above the center of a Greek cross. The climax of the interior mosaic programs was often an image in the dome of Christ as Pantokrator.

▌ In 1204, Latin Crusaders sacked Constantinople, bringing to an end the second golden age of Byzantine art. In 1261, Michael VIII Palaeologus (r. 1259–1282) succeeded in recapturing the city. Constantinople remained in Byzantine hands until it was taken in 1453 by the Ottoman Turks, marking the end of the Late Byzantine period (1261–1453).

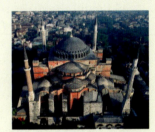

Hagia Sophia, Constantinople, 532–537

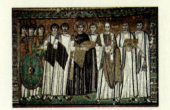

San Vitale, Ravenna, 526–547

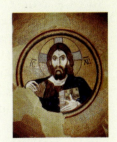

Christ as Pantokrator, Daphni, ca. 1090–1100

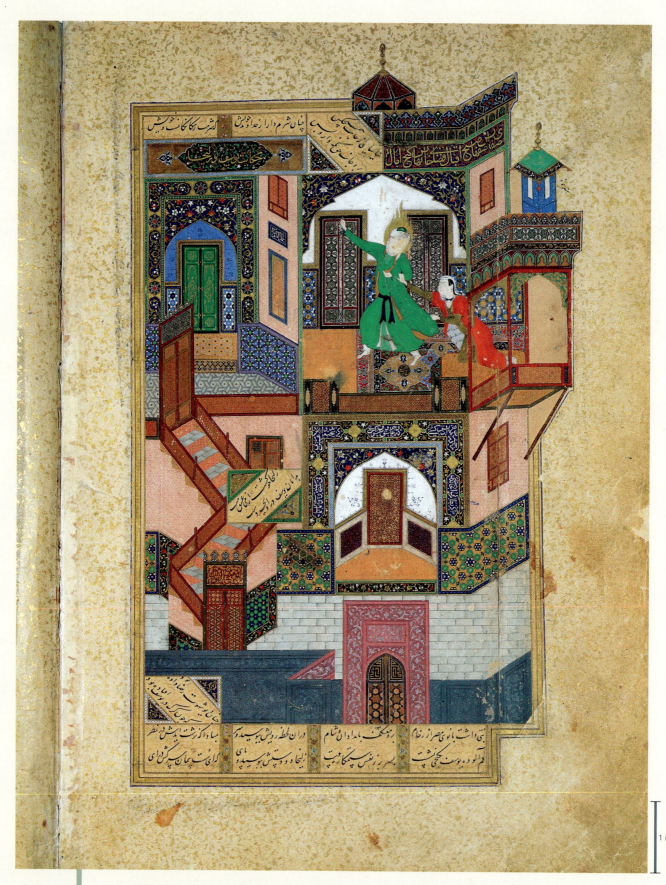

5-1 BIHZAD, *Seduction of Yusuf,* folio 52 verso of the *Bustan* of Sultan Husayn Mayqara, from Herat, Afghanistan, 1488. Ink and color on paper, $11\frac{7}{8}'' \times 8\frac{5}{8}''$. National Library, Cairo.

This manuscript page depicts human figures, which never appear in Islamic religious art. The painting displays vivid color, intricate decorative detailing, and a brilliant balance between pattern and perspective.

The Islamic World

The religion of Islam (an Arabic word meaning "submission to God") arose in the Arabian peninsula early in the seventh century (see "Muhammad and Islam," page 149). At the time, the Arabs were peripheral to the Byzantine and Persian empires. Yet within little more than a century, Muslim armies had subdued the Middle East, and the followers of Muhammad controlled much of the Mediterranean (MAP 5-1). The swiftness of the Islamic advance is among the wonders of world history. By 640, Muslims ruled Syria, Palestine, and Iraq. In 642, the Byzantine army abandoned Alexandria, marking the Muslim conquest of northern Egypt. In 651, the successors of Muhammad brought more than 400 years of Sasanian rule in Iran to an end. By 710, all of North Africa was under Muslim control. A victory in southern Spain in 711 seemed to open the rest of western Europe to the Muslims. By 732, they had advanced north to Poitiers in France. There, however, the Franks turned them back. But in Spain, the Muslim rulers of Córdoba flourished until 1031, and not until 1492 did Islamic influence and power in Iberia end. In the East, the Muslims reached the Indus River in South Asia by 751. In Anatolia, relentless Muslim pressure against the shrinking Byzantine Empire eventually caused its collapse in 1453.

ARCHITECTURE

During the early centuries of Islamic history, the Muslim world's political and cultural center was the Fertile Crescent of ancient Mesopotamia (see Chapter 1). The caliphs of Damascus (capital of modern Syria) and Baghdad (capital of Iraq) appointed provincial governors to rule the vast territories they controlled. These governors eventually gained relative independence by setting up dynasties in various territories and provinces: the Umayyads in Syria and in Spain, the Abbasids in Iraq, and so on. Like other potentates before and after, the Islamic rulers were builders on a grand scale.

Dome of the Rock The first great achievement of Islamic architecture is the Dome of the Rock (FIG. 5-2) in Jerusalem. The Muslims had taken the city from the Byzantines in 638, and the Umayyad caliph Abd al-Malik (r. 685–705) erected the monumental sanctuary between 687 and 692 as an architectural tribute to the triumph of Islam. The Dome of the Rock marked the coming of the new religion to the city that was—and still is—sacred to both Jews and Christians. The Umayyads erected the sanctuary on the site of the Temple of Solomon that the Roman emperor Titus destroyed in 70 (FIG. 3-32). In time, the site took on

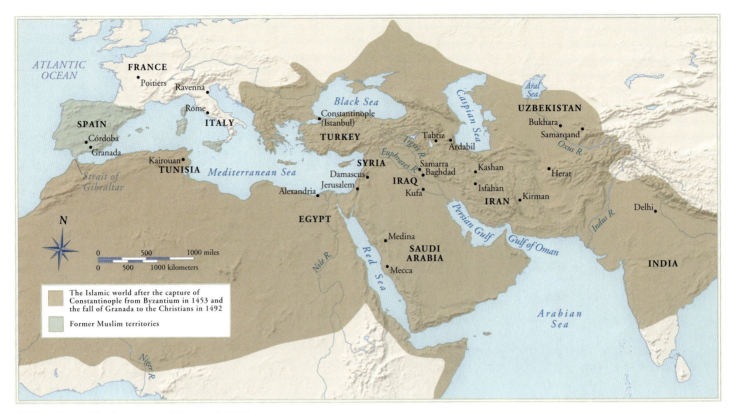

MAP 5-1 The Islamic world around 1500.

additional significance as the reputed place of Adam's burial and the site where Abraham prepared to sacrifice Isaac. It houses the rock (FIG. 5-3) from which Muslims later came to believe Muhammad miraculously journeyed to Heaven and then, in the same night, returned to his home in Mecca.

As Islam took much of its teaching from Judaism and Christianity, so its architects and artists borrowed and transformed design, construction, and ornamentation principles that had been long applied in Byzantium and the Middle East. The Dome of the Rock is a domed octagon resembling San Vitale (FIG. 4-15) in Ravenna in its basic design. In all likelihood, the Dome of the Rock's designers drew inspiration from a Christian monument in Jerusalem, Constantine's Church of the Holy Sepulchre. That fourth-century *rotunda* (a domed round build-

ing) bore a family resemblance to the roughly contemporaneous Santa Costanza (FIG. 4-6) in Rome. The Dome of the Rock is a member of the same extended family. Its double-shelled wooden dome, however, some 60 feet across and 75 feet high, so dominates the elevation as to relegate the

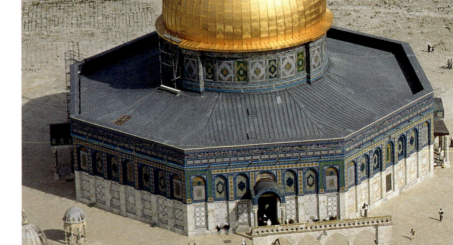

5-2 Aerial view of the Dome of the Rock, Jerusalem, 687–692.

Abd al-Malik erected the Dome of the Rock to commemorate the triumph of Islam in Jerusalem, which the Muslims had captured from the Byzantines. The shrine takes the form of an octagon with a towering dome.

Muhammad and Islam

Muhammad, founder of Islam and revered as its Final Prophet, was a native of Mecca on the west coast of Arabia. Born around 570 into a family of merchants, Muhammad was inspired to prophesy. Critical of the polytheistic religion of his fellow Arabs, he preached a religion of the one and only God ("Allah" in Arabic), whose revelations Muhammad received beginning in 610 and for the rest of his life. Opposition to Muhammad's message among the Arabs was strong enough to prompt the Prophet to flee from Mecca to a desert oasis eventually called Medina ("City of the Prophet"). Islam dates its beginnings from this flight in 622, known as the *Hijra,* or emigration. (Muslims date events beginning with the Hijra in the same way Christians reckon events from Christ's birth.) Barely eight years later, in 630, Muhammad returned to Mecca with 10,000 soldiers. He took control of the city, converted the population to Islam, and destroyed all the idols. But he preserved as the Islamic world's symbolic center the small cubical building that had housed the idols. The Arabs associated the *Kaaba* (from the Arabic for "cube") with the era of Abraham and Ishmael, the common ancestors of Jews and Arabs. Muhammad died in Medina in 632.

The essential meaning of Islam is acceptance of and submission to Allah's will. Believers in Islam are called Muslims ("those who submit"). Islam requires Muslims to live according to the rules laid down in the collected revelations communicated through Muhammad during his lifetime and recorded in the *Koran,* Islam's sacred book. The word "Koran" means "recitations"—a reference to the archangel Gabriel's instructions to Muhammad in 610 to "recite in the name of Allah." The profession of faith in Allah, the one God, is the first of five obligations binding all Muslims.

In addition, the faithful must worship five times daily, facing in Mecca's direction, give alms to the poor, fast during the month of Ramadan, and once in a lifetime—if possible—make a pilgrimage to Mecca. The revelations in the Koran are not the only guide for Muslims. Muhammad's exemplary ways and customs, collected in the *Sunnah,* offer models to the faithful on ethical problems of everyday life. The reward for the Muslim faithful is Paradise.

Islam has much in common with Judaism and Christianity. Its adherents think of it as a continuation, completion, and in some sense a reformation of those other great monotheisms. Islam incorporates many of the Old Testament teachings, with their sober ethical standards and hatred of idol worship, and those of the New Testament Gospels. Muslims acknowledge Adam, Abraham, Moses, and Jesus as the prophetic predecessors of Muhammad. The Final Prophet did not claim to be divine, as did Jesus. Rather, Muhammad was God's messenger, the purifier and perfecter of the common faith of Jews, Christians, and Muslims in one God. Islam also differs from Judaism and Christianity in its simpler organization. Muslims worship God directly, without a hierarchy of rabbis, priests, or saints acting as intermediaries.

In Islam, as Muhammad defined it, religious and secular authority were united even more completely than in Byzantium. Muhammad established a new social order, taking complete charge of his community's temporal as well as spiritual affairs. After Muhammad's death, the *caliphs* (from Arabic "successor") continued this practice of uniting religious and political leadership in one ruler.

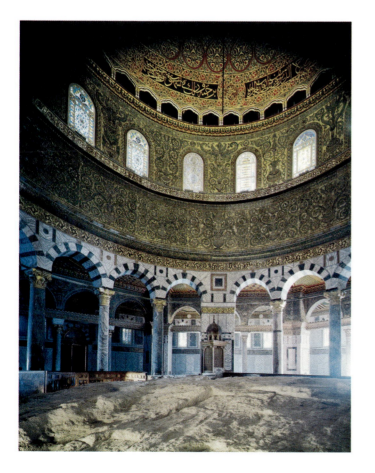

octagon to serving merely as its base. This soaring, majestic unit creates a decidedly more commanding effect than that of Late Roman and Byzantine domical structures (for example, FIG. **4-11**). The silhouettes of those domes are comparatively insignificant when seen from the outside.

The building's exterior has been extensively restored. Tiling from the 16th century and later has replaced the original mosaic. Yet the vivid, colorful patterning that wraps the walls like a textile is typical of Islamic ornamentation. It contrasts markedly with Byzantine brickwork and Greco-Roman sculptured profiling and carved decoration. The interior's mosaic ornamentation (FIG. **5-3**) has been preserved. Consisting of rich floral and vegetal motifs against a field of gold, it conjures the gorgeous places of Paradise awaiting the faithful. The lavish interior mosaics suggest the original appearance of the structure's exterior walls.

5-3 Interior of the Dome of the Rock, Jerusalem, 687–692.

The exterior of the Dome of the Rock has 16th-century tilework, but the interior's original mosaic ornamentation has been preserved. The mosaics conjure the Paradise awaiting the Muslim faithful.

Architecture | **149**

The Mosque

Islamic religious architecture is closely related to Muslim prayer. In Islam, worshiping can be a private act. It requires neither prescribed ceremony nor a special locale. Only the *qibla*—the direction (toward Mecca) Muslims face while praying—is important. But worship also became a communal act when the first Muslim community established a simple ritual for it. To celebrate the Muslim sabbath, which occurs on Friday, the community convened each Friday at noon, probably in the Prophet's house in Medina. The main feature of Muhammad's house was a large, square court with rows of palm trunks supporting thatched roofs along the north and south sides. The southern side was wider and had a double row of trunks. It faced Mecca. During these communal gatherings, the *imam*, or leader of collective worship, stood on a stepped pulpit, or *minbar*, set up in front of the southern (qibla) wall.

These features became standard in the Islamic house of worship, the *mosque* (from Arabic *masjid*, "a place of prostration"), where the faithful gathered for the five daily prayers. The *congregational mosque* (also called the *Friday mosque* or *great mosque*) was ideally large enough to accommodate a community's entire population for the Friday noonday prayer. Both ordinary and congregational mosques usually have a *mihrab*

(FIG. 5-11), a semicircular niche set into the qibla wall. Often a dome over the bay in front of the mihrab marked its position (FIGS. 5-4 and 5-7). The niche may recall the place where the Prophet stood in his house at Medina when he led communal worship.

In some mosques, a *maqsura* precedes the mihrab. The maqsura is the area reserved for the ruler or his representative. Mosques may also have one or more *minarets* (FIGS. 5-4 and 5-5), towers used to call the faithful to worship and to signal the location of a mosque from a distance. Early mosques were generally *hypostyle halls,* communal worship halls with roofs held up by a multitude of columns (FIGS. 5-4 and 5-6). An important later variation is the mosque with four *iwans* (vaulted rectangular recesses), one on each side of a courtyard (FIG. 5-10).

The mosque's origin is still in dispute, although one prototype may well have been the Prophet's house in Medina. Today, mosques continue to be erected throughout the world. Despite many variations in design and detail, and the employment of modern building techniques and materials unknown in Muhammad's day, all mosques, wherever they are built and whatever their plan, are oriented toward Mecca, and the faithful worship facing the qibla wall.

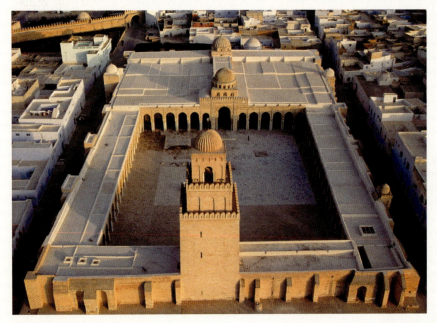

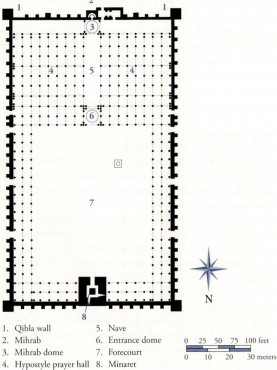

5-4   Aerial view (*above*) and plan (*right*) of the Great Mosque, Kairouan, Tunisia, ca. 836–875.

The hypostyle type of mosque most closely resembles Muhammad's house in Medina. Kairouan's Great Mosque is one of the oldest. An arcaded forecourt resembling a Roman forum leads to the columnar prayer hall.

1. Qibla wall   5. Nave
2. Mihrab   6. Entrance dome
3. Mihrab dome   7. Forecourt
4. Hypostyle prayer hall   8. Minaret

0   25   50   75   100 feet
0   10   20   30 meters

Kairouan   The Dome of the Rock is a unique monument. Throughout the Islamic world, the most important buildings were usually mosques (see "The Mosque," above). Of all the variations, the hypostyle mosque most closely reflects the mosque's supposed origin, Muhammad's house in Medina. One of the oldest, well-preserved hypostyle mosques is the mid-eighth-century Great Mosque (FIG. **5-4**) at Kairouan in Tunisia. Like the Dome of the Rock, the Kairouan mosque owes much to Greco-Roman and Early Christian architecture. The precinct takes the form of a slightly askew parallelogram of huge scale, some 450 by 260 feet. A series of lateral entrances on the east and west lead to an arcaded forecourt bay, the second (no. 3) over the bay that fronts the mihrab (no. 2) set into the qibla wall (no. 1). A raised nave connects the domed spaces and prolongs the north-south axis of the minaret and courtyard. Eight columned aisles flank the nave on either side, providing space for a large congregation. The hypostyle mosque synthesizes elements received from other cultures into a novel architectural unity.

Samarra The three-story minaret of the Kairouan mosque is square in plan and believed to be a near-copy of a Roman lighthouse, but minarets can take a variety of forms. Perhaps the most striking and novel is that of the immense (more than 45,000 square yards) Great Mosque at Samarra, Iraq, the largest mosque in the world. The Abbasid caliph al-Mutawakkil (r. 847–861) erected it between 848 and 852. Known as the Malwiya ("snail shell" in Arabic) minaret (FIG. 5-5) and more than 165 feet tall, it now stands alone, but originally a bridge linked it to the mosque. The distinguishing feature of the brick tower is its stepped spiral ramp, which increases in slope from bottom to top. Too tall to have been used to call Muslims to prayer, the Malwiya minaret, visible from a considerable distance in the flat plain around Samarra, was probably intended to announce the presence of Islam in the Tigris Valley. Unfortunately, in 2005 the minaret suffered some damage during the Iraqi insurgency.

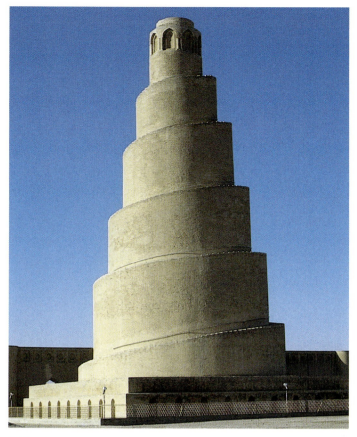

5-5 Malwiya minaret, Great Mosque, Samarra, Iraq, 848–852.

The unique spiral Malwiya (snail shell) minaret of Samarra's Great Mosque is more than 165 feet tall and can be seen from afar. It served to announce the presence of Islam in the Tigris Valley.

(FIG. 5-4, no. 7), reminiscent of Roman forums (FIG. 3-34) and the atriums of Early Christian basilicas (FIG. 4-4). The courtyard is oriented north-south on axis with the mosque's minaret (no. 8) and the two domes (nos. 3 and 6) of the hypostyle prayer hall (no. 4). The first dome (no. 6) is over the entrance

Córdoba At the time the Umayyads built the Kairouan mosque (FIG. 5-4), the Abbasids ruled much of North Africa. In 750, they had overthrown the Umayyad caliphs and moved the capital from Damascus to Baghdad. Abd-al-Rahman I, the only Umayyad notable to escape the Abbasid massacre of his clan in Syria, fled to Spain. There, the Arabs, who had defeated the Christian kingdom of the Visigoths in 711, accepted the fugitive as their overlord, and he founded the Spanish Umayyad dynasty. Their capital was Córdoba, which became the center of a brilliant culture rivaling that of the Abbasids at Baghdad and exerting major influence on the civilization of the Christian West.

The jewel of Córdoba was its Great Mosque, begun in 784 and enlarged several times during the 9th and 10th centuries. The hypostyle prayer hall (FIG. 5-6) has 36 piers and 514 columns topped by a unique system of double-tiered arches that carried a wooden roof (now replaced by vaults). The two-story system was the builders' response to the need to raise the roof to an acceptable height using short columns that had been employed earlier in other structures. The lower arches are

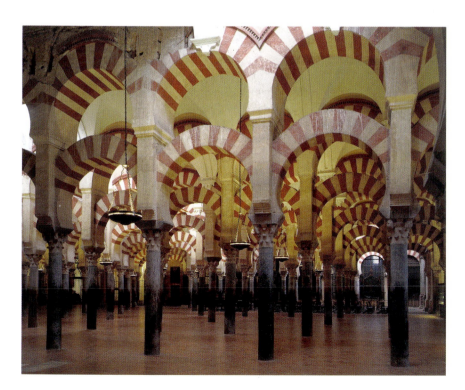

5-6 Prayer hall of the Great Mosque, Córdoba, Spain, 8th to 10th centuries.

Córdoba was the capital of the Umayyad dynasty in Spain. The Great Mosque's prayer hall has 36 piers and 514 columns topped by a unique system of double-tiered, horseshoe-shaped arches.

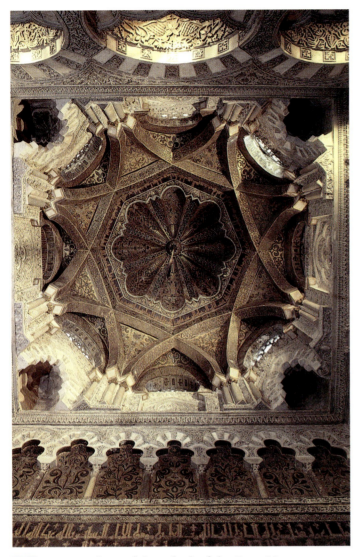

5-7 Dome in front of the mihrab of the Great Mosque, Córdoba, Spain, 961–965.

This dome is a prime example of Islamic experimentation with highly decorative multilobed arches. The rich and varied abstract patterns create a magnificent effect, which mosaics further heighten.

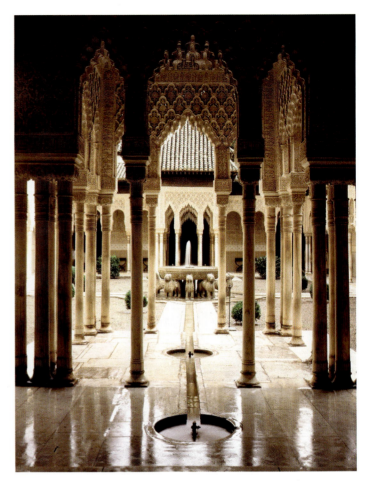

5-8 Court of the Lions, Palace of the Lions, Alhambra, Granada, Spain, 1354–1391.

The Palace of the Lions, named for its unusual statues, is typically Islamic in the use of multilobed pointed arches and the interweaving of Arabic calligraphy and abstract decoration in its stuccoed walls.

horseshoe-shaped, a form perhaps adapted from earlier Near Eastern architecture or of Visigothic origin. In the West, the horseshoe arch quickly became closely associated with Muslim architecture. Visually, these arches seem to billow out like windblown sails, and they contribute greatly to the light and airy effect of the Córdoba mosque's interior.

The 10th-century renovations to the mosque included the addition of a series of domes to emphasize the axis leading to the mihrab. The dome (FIG. **5-7**) that covers the area immediately in front of the mihrab rests on an octagonal base crisscrossed by ribs that form an intricate pattern centered on two squares set at 45-degree angles to each other. It is a prime example of Islamic experimentation with highly decorative, multilobed arches. The builders created rich and varied abstract patterns and further enhanced the magnificent effect of the complex arches by sheathing the surfaces with mosaics. The mosaicists and even the tesserae were brought to Spain from Constantinople.

Alhambra In the early years of the 11th century, the Umayyad caliphs' power in Spain unraveled, and their palaces fell prey to Berber soldiers from North Africa. The Berbers ruled southern Spain for several generations but could not resist the pressure of Christian forces from the north. Córdoba fell to the Christians in 1236. From then until the final Christian triumph in 1492, the Nasrids, an Arab dynasty that had established its capital at Granada in 1230, ruled the remaining Muslim territories in Spain. On a rocky spur at Granada, the Nasrids constructed a huge palace-fortress called the Alhambra ("the Red" in Arabic) because of the rose color of the stone used for its walls and 23 towers. By the end of the 14th century, the complex, a veritable city with a population of 40,000, included at least a half dozen royal residences.

One of those palaces is the Palace of the Lions, named for the courtyard (FIG. **5-8**) that boasts a fountain with marble lions carrying a water basin on their backs. The Alhambra's lion fountain is an unusual instance of freestanding stone sculpture in the Islamic world, unthinkable in a sacred setting. Nonetheless, the design of the courtyard is distinctly Islamic and features many multilobed pointed arches and lavish stuccoed walls in which calligraphy and abstract motifs are interwoven. The builders intended the palace—the

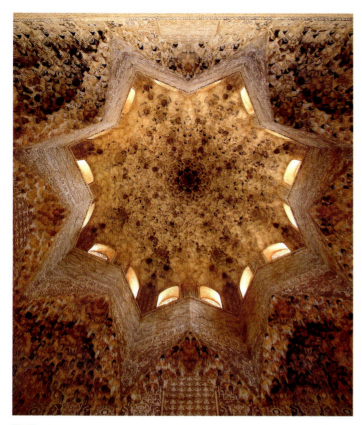

5-9 Muqarnas dome, Hall of the Abencerrajes, Palace of the Lions, Alhambra, Granada, Spain, 1354–1391.

The structure of this dome is difficult to discern because of the intricately carved stucco muqarnas decoration. The prismatic forms catch and reflect sunlight, creating the effect of a starry sky.

rests on an octagonal drum pierced by eight pairs of windows, but its structure is difficult to discern because of the intricate carved stucco decoration. The builders covered the ceiling with some 5,000 *muqarnas*—tier after tier of stalactite-like prismatic forms that seem aimed at denying the structure's solidity. The purpose of the muqarnas ceiling was to catch and reflect sunlight as well as to form beautiful abstract patterns. The lofty vault in this hall and others in the palace symbolized the dome of Heaven. The flickering light and shadows create the effect of a starry sky as the sun's rays move from window to window during the day. To underscore the symbolism, the palace walls were inscribed with verses by the court poet Ibn Zamrak, who compared the Alhambra's lacelike muqarnas ceilings to "the heavenly spheres whose orbits revolve."

Isfahan At the opposite end of the Islamic world, in Iran, successive dynasties erected a series of mosques at Isfahan. The largest is the Great Mosque (FIG. **5-10**), which Muslim architects remodeled several times over nearly a millennium. The earliest mosque on the site, of the hypostyle type, was constructed in the eighth century during the caliphate of the Abbasids. Seljuk *sultans* (rulers) transformed the structure in the 11th century, and later alterations further changed the mosque's appearance. The present mosque, which retains its basic 11th-century plan, consists of a large courtyard bordered by a two-story arcade on each side. Four iwans open onto the courtyard, one at the center of each side (see "The Mosque," page 150). The southwestern iwan leads into a dome-covered room in front of the mihrab. It functioned as a maqsura reserved for the sultan and his attendants. It is uncertain whether the first use of this plan, with four iwans and a dome before the mihrab, was in the Great Mosque at Isfahan, but it became standard in Iranian mosque design. In four-iwan mosques, the qibla iwan is always the largest. Its size (and the dome that often accompanied it) immediately indicated to worshipers the proper direction for prayer.

residence of Muhammad V (r. 1354–1391)—and its courtyards, lush gardens, and luxurious carpets and other furnishings to conjure the image of Paradise.

The Palace of the Lions is noteworthy also for its elaborate stucco ceilings. A spectacular example is the dome (FIG. **5-9**) of the so-called Hall of the Abencerrajes. The dome

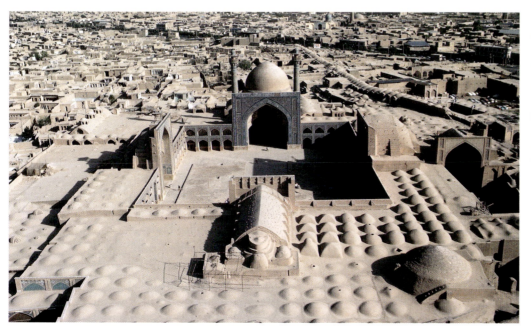

5-10 Aerial view (looking southwest) of the Great Mosque, Isfahan, Iran, 11th to 17th centuries.

Mosques take a variety of forms. In Iran, the standard type of mosque has four iwans opening onto a courtyard. The largest iwan leads into a dome-covered maqsura in front of the mihrab.

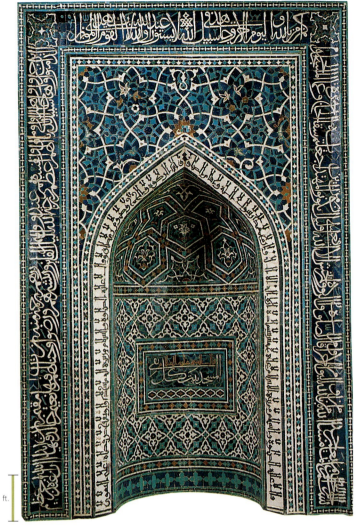

1 ft.

5-11 Mihrab from the Madrasa Imami, Isfahan, Iran, ca. 1354. Glazed mosaic tilework, 11' 3" × 7' 6". Metropolitan Museum of Art, New York.

This mihrab is one of the masterworks of Iranian tilework, but it is also a splendid example of Arabic calligraphy. In the Islamic world, the walls of buildings often displayed the sacred words of the Koran.

Madrasa Imami The iwans of the Isfahan mosque feature soaring pointed arches framing tile-sheathed muqarnas vaults. The muqarnas ceilings probably date to the 14th century. The ceramic-tile revetment on the walls and vaults is the work of the 17th-century Safavid rulers of Iran. The use of glazed tiles has a long history in the Middle East. Even in ancient Mesopotamia, gates and walls sometimes had a colorful facing of baked bricks (FIG. 1-20). In the Islamic world, the art of ceramic tilework reached its peak in the 16th and 17th centuries in Iran and Turkey. Employed as a veneer over a brick core, tiles could sheathe entire buildings (FIG. 5-2), including domes and minarets.

One of the masterworks of Iranian tilework is the 14th-century mihrab (FIG. 5-11) from the Madrasa Imami in Isfahan. (A *madrasa* is an Islamic theological college that often incorporates a mosque.) It is also a splendid example of Arabic *calligraphy*, or ornamental writing. The Islamic world held the art of calligraphy in high esteem, and the

walls of buildings often displayed the sacred words of the Koran. Quotations from the Koran appear, for example, in a mosaic band above the outer ring of columns inside the Dome of the Rock (FIG. 5-3). The Isfahan mihrab exemplifies the perfect aesthetic union between the calligrapher's art and abstract ornamentation. The pointed arch that immediately enframes the mihrab niche bears an inscription from the Koran in an early stately rectilinear script called *Kufic*, after the city of Kufa, one of the renowned centers of Arabic calligraphy. A cursive style, *Muhaqqaq*, fills the mihrab's outer rectangular frame. The tile ornament on the curving surface of the niche and the area above the pointed arch are composed of tighter and looser networks of geometric and abstract floral motifs. The technique used here is the most difficult of all the varieties Islamic artisans practiced: *mosaic tilework*. Every piece had to be chiseled and cut to fit its specific place in the mihrab, even the inscriptions. The mosaicist smoothly integrated the framed inscription in the center of the niche—proclaiming that the mosque is the domicile of the pious believer—with the subtly varied patterns. The mihrab's outermost inscription—detailing the five pillars of Islamic faith—serves as a fringelike extension, as well as a border, for the entire design. The calligraphic and geometric elements are so completely unified that only the practiced eye can distinguish them.

LUXURY ARTS

In the smaller-scale, and often private, realm of the luxury arts, Muslim artists also excelled. Indeed, in the Islamic world, the term "minor arts" is especially inappropriate. Although of modest size, the books, textiles, ceramics, and metalwork Muslim artists produced in great quantities are among the finest works of any age. From the vast array of Islamic luxury arts, a few masterpieces may serve to suggest both the range and quality of small-scale Islamic art.

The Koran Although the chief Islamic book, the sacred Koran, was codified in the mid-seventh century, the earliest preserved Korans date to the ninth century. Koran pages were either bound into books or stored as loose sheets in boxes. The writing in most of the early examples is the angular Kufic script used in the central panel of the mihrab in FIG. 5-11. Arabic is written from right to left, with certain characters connected by a baseline. In Kufic script, the uprights almost form right angles with the baseline. As with Hebrew and other Semitic languages, the usual practice was to write in consonants only. But to facilitate recitation of the Koran, scribes often indicated vowels by red or yellow symbols above or below the line.

On a 9th- or early 10th-century Koran page (FIG. 5-12), five text lines in black ink with red vowels appear below a decorative band incorporating the chapter title in gold and ending in a palm-tree *finial* (a crowning ornament). This approach to page design has parallels at the extreme northwestern corner of the then-known world—in the early medieval manuscripts of the British Isles, where artists similarly

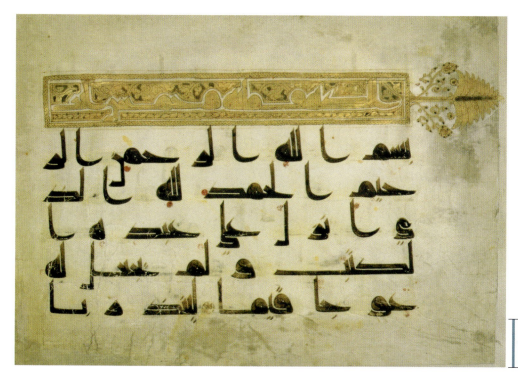

5-12 Koran page, 9th or early 10th century. Ink and gold on vellum, $7\frac{1}{4}$″ × $10\frac{1}{4}$″. Chester Beatty Library and Oriental Art Gallery, Dublin.

Muslim scribes used the stately rectilinear Kufic script for the text of the oldest known Korans. This page has five text lines and a palm-tree finial. Islamic tradition shuns the representation of fauna in sacred books.

united text and ornament (FIG. 6-4). But the stylized human and animal forms that populate those Christian books never appear in Korans. Islamic tradition shuns the representation of fauna of any kind in sacred contexts. This also explains the total absence of figural ornamentation in mosques, setting the Islamic world sharply apart from both the classical world and Christian Europe and Byzantium.

Mosque Lamps Well-endowed mosques possessed luxurious furnishings, including highly decorated glass lamps. Islamic artists perfected this art form and fortunately, despite their exceptionally fragile nature, many examples survive, in large part because the lamps were revered by those who handled them. One of the finest is the mosque lamp (FIG. 5-13) made for Sayf al-Din Tuquztimur (d. 1345), an official in the court of the Mamluk sultan al-Nasir Muhammad. (The Mamluk capital was at Cairo, Egypt, which was the largest Muslim city of the late Middle Ages.) The glass lamps hung on chains from the mosque's ceilings. The shape of Tuquztimur's lamp is typical of the period, consisting of a conical neck, wide body with six vertical handles, and a tall foot. Inside, a small glass container held the oil and wick. *Enamel* adornment enlivens the surfaces. The decoration includes Tuquztimur's emblem—an eagle over a cup (Tuquztimur served as the sultan's cup-bearer)—and cursive Arabic calligraphy giving the official's name and titles as well as a quotation of the Koranic verse (24:35) comparing God's light to the light in a lamp. When the lamp was lit, the verse (and Tuquztimur's name) would have been dramatically illuminated.

Timurid *Bustan* In the late 14th century, a new Islamic empire arose in Central Asia under the leadership of Timur (r. 1370–1405), known in the Western world as Tamerlane. Timur, a successor of the Mongol Genghis Khan (see Chap-

ter 16), quickly extended his dominions to include Iran and parts of Anatolia. The Timurids ruled until 1501 and were great patrons of art and architecture in cities such as Herat, Bukhara, and Samarqand. Herat in particular became

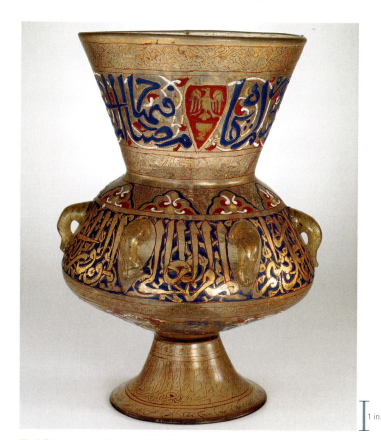

5-13 Mosque lamp of Sayf al-Din Tuquztimur, from Egypt, 1340. Glass with enamel decoration, 1′ 1″ high. British Museum, London.

The enamel decoration of this glass mosque lamp includes a quotation from the Koran comparing God's light to the light in a lamp. The burning wick dramatically illuminated the sacred verse.

a leading center for the production of luxurious books under the patronage of the Timurid sultan Husayn Mayqara (r. 1470–1506). These books often contained full-page narrative paintings with human and animal figures. In secular artworks, Islamic artists freely depicted figures.

The most famous Persian painter active around 1500 was BIHZAD, who worked at the Herat court and illustrated the sultan's copy of Sadi's *Bustan (Orchard)*. One page (FIG. 5-1) represents a story in both the Bible and the Koran—the seduction of Yusuf (Joseph) by Potiphar's wife Zulaykha. Sadi's text is dispersed throughout the page in elegant Arabic script in a series of beige panels. According to the tale as told by Jami (1414–1492), an influential mystic theologian and poet whose Persian text appears in blue in the white pointed arch at the lower center of the composition, Zulaykha lured Yusuf into her palace and led him through seven rooms, locking each door behind him. In the last room she threw herself at Yusuf, but he resisted and was able to flee when the seven doors opened miraculously. Bihzad's painting of the story features vivid color, intricate decorative detailing suggesting luxurious textiles and tiled walls, and a brilliant balance between two-dimensional patterning and perspectival depictions of balconies and staircases.

Ardabil Carpet Wood is scarce in most of the Islamic world, and the typical furniture used in the West—beds, tables, chairs—is rarely found in Muslim structures. Architectural spaces, therefore, are not defined by the type of furniture placed in them. A room's function (eating or sleeping, for example) can change simply by rearranging the carpets and cushions. Textiles are among the glories of Islamic art. Unfortunately, because of their fragile nature and the heavy wear carpets endure, early Islamic textiles are rare today and often fragmentary. One of the best—and largest—later examples comes from Ardabil in Iran. The carpet (FIG. 5-14), one of a pair, adorned the funerary mosque of Shaykh Safi al-Din (1252–1334), but it dates to 1540, two centuries after the erection of the mosque, during the reign of Shah Tahmasp (r. 1524–1576). Tahmasp elevated carpet weaving to a national industry and set up royal factories at Isfahan, Kashan, Kirman, and Tabriz. The name MAQSUD OF KASHAN is woven into the fabric. He must be the designer who supplied the master pattern to two teams of royal weavers (one for each of the two carpets). The carpet, almost 35 by 18 feet, consists of roughly 25 million knots (some 340 to the square inch; its twin has even more knots).

The design consists of a central sunburst medallion, representing the inside of a dome, surrounded by 16 pendants. Mosque lamps (appropriate motifs for the Ardabil funerary mosque) are suspended from two pendants on the long axis of the carpet. The lamps are of different sizes, and some scholars have suggested that this is an optical device to make the two appear equal in size when viewed from the end of the carpet at the room's threshold (the bottom end of FIG. 5-14). The rich blue background is covered with leaves and flowers attached to a framework of delicate stems that

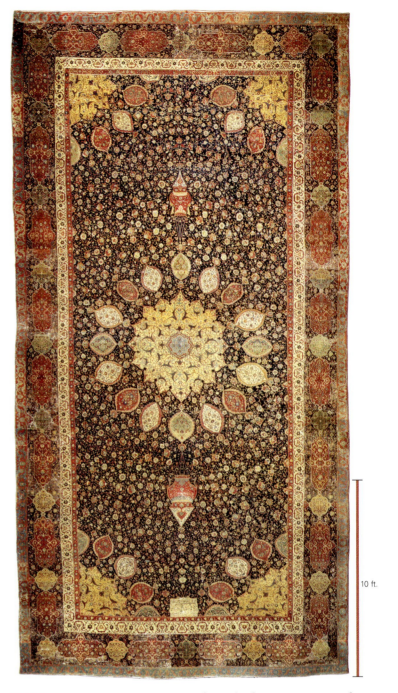

10 ft.

5-14 MAQSUD OF KASHAN, carpet from the funerary mosque of Shaykh Safi al-Din, Ardabil, Iran, 1540. Knotted pile of wool and silk, 34′ 6″ × 17′ 7″. Victoria & Albert Museum, London.

This carpet consists of roughly 25 million knots. The decoration presents the illusion of a heavenly dome with lamps reflected in a pool of water with floating lotus blossoms.

spread over the whole field. The entire composition presents the illusion of a heavenly dome with lamps reflected in a pool of water full of floating lotus blossoms.

Islam in Asia Islamic artists and architects also brought their distinctive style to South Asia, where a Muslim sultanate was established at Delhi in India in the early 13th century. These important Islamic works are an integral part of the history of Asian art and are treated in Chapter 15.

The Islamic World

ARCHITECTURE

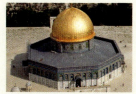

Dome of the Rock, Jerusalem, 687–692

- The Umayyads (r. 661–750) were the first Islamic dynasty. They ruled from their capital at Damascus in Syria until they were overthrown by the Abbasids (r. 750–1258), who established their capital at Baghdad in Iraq.

- The first great Islamic building is the Dome of the Rock. The domed octagon commemorated the triumph of Islam in Jerusalem, which the Muslims captured from the Byzantines in 638. Umayyad and Abbasid mosques were of the hypostyle hall type and incorporated arcaded courtyards and minarets.

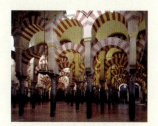

Great Mosque, Córdoba, 8th to 10th centuries

- The Umayyad capital in Spain was Córdoba, where the caliphs (r. 756–1031) erected and expanded the Great Mosque between the 8th and 10th centuries. The mosque features horseshoe and multilobed arches and mosaic-clad domes. The last Spanish Muslim dynasty was the Nasrid (r. 1230–1492), whose capital was Granada. The Alhambra is the best surviving example of Islamic palace architecture. It is famous for its stuccoed walls and arches and its muqarnas vaults and domes.

- The Timurid (r. 1370–1501) and Safavid (r. 1501–1732) dynasties ruled Iran and Central Asia for almost four centuries and were great patrons of art and architecture. The art of tilework reached its peak under the patronage of the Safavid dynasty, when builders frequently used mosaic tiles to cover the walls and vaults of mosques and madrasas.

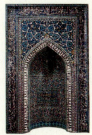

Mihrab, Madrasa Imami, Isfahan, ca. 1354

LUXURY ARTS

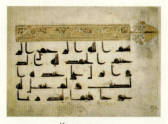

Koran page, 9th or early 10th century

- The earliest preserved Korans date to the 9th century and feature Kufic calligraphy and decorative motifs but no figural illustrations. Islamic tradition shuns the representation of fauna of any kind in sacred contexts.

- The Timurid court at Herat, Afghanistan, employed the most famous painters of the day, who specialized in illustrating secular books with narrative scenes incorporating people and animals. The most famous Persian painter active around 1500 was Bihzad.

- Muslim artists also excelled in the art of enamel-decorated glass lamps, which illuminated mosque interiors. They hung on chains from the mosque's ceilings.

- Textiles are among the glories of Islamic art. Some carpets, for example, the pair designed by Maqsud of Kashan for a 16th-century Iranian funerary mosque at Ardabil, were woven with millions of knots.

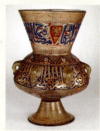

Mosque lamp of Sayf al-Din Tuquztimur, 1340

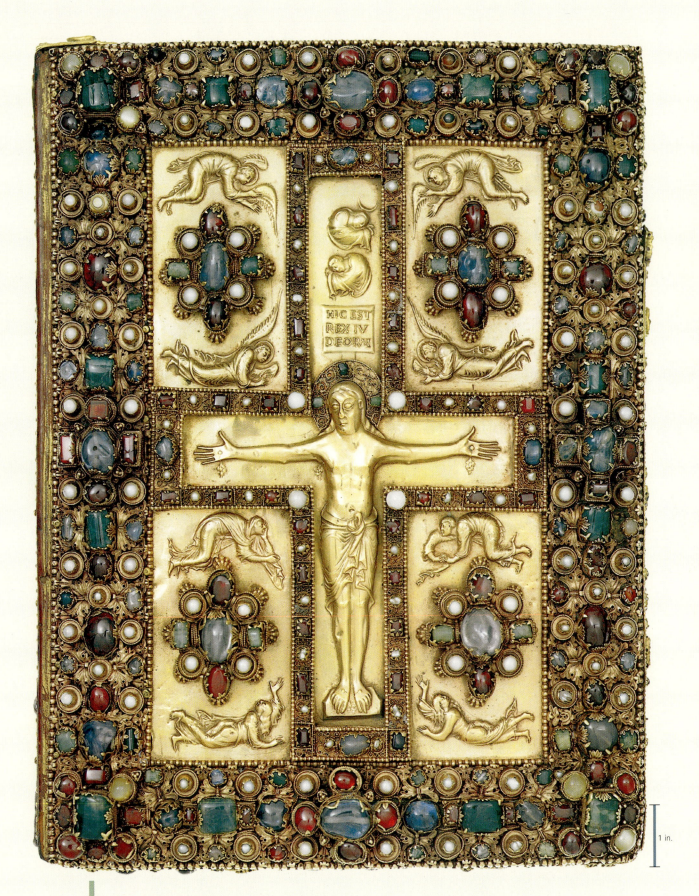

6-1 Crucifixion, front cover of the *Lindau Gospels*, from Saint Gall, Switzerland, ca. 870. Gold, precious stones, and pearls, $1' 1\frac{3}{8}'' \times 10\frac{3}{8}''$. Pierpont Morgan Library, New York.

Sacred books with covers of gold and jewels were among the most costly and revered art objects produced in medieval Europe. This Carolingian cover revives the Early Christian imagery of the youthful Christ.

1 in.

Early Medieval and Romanesque Europe

Historians once referred to the thousand years (roughly 400 to 1400) between the dying Roman Empire's official adoption of Christianity and the rebirth (Renaissance) of interest in classical art as the Dark Ages. They viewed this period as a blank between classical antiquity and the beginning of modern Europe. This negative assessment, a legacy of the humanist scholars of Renaissance Italy, persists today in the retention of the noun "Middle Ages" and the adjective "medieval" to describe this "era in between" and its art. Modern scholars, however, long ago ceased to see the art of medieval Europe as unsophisticated or inferior. On the contrary, medieval artists produced some of the most innovative and beautiful artworks in world history.

EARLY MEDIEVAL ART

Early medieval (ca. 500–1000) art in western Europe (MAP **6-1**) was a unique fusion of the classical heritage of Rome's former northwestern provinces, the cultures of the non-Roman peoples north of the Alps, and Christianity. Over the centuries, the various population groups merged, and a new order gradually replaced what had been the Roman Empire, resulting eventually in the foundation of today's European nations.

Art of the Warrior Lords

Art historians do not know the full range of art and architecture the early medieval transalpine peoples produced. What has survived is not truly representative and consists almost exclusively of small "status symbols"—weapons and items of personal adornment such as bracelets, pendants, and belt buckles discovered in lavish burials. Earlier scholars, who viewed medieval art through a Renaissance lens, ignored these "minor arts" because of their small scale, seemingly utilitarian nature, and abstract decoration, and because their creators rejected the classical idea that the representation of organic nature should be the focus of artistic endeavor. In their own time, however, people regarded these objects as treasures. They enhanced the prestige of their owners and testified to the stature of those buried with them. In the great Anglo-Saxon epic *Beowulf*, the hero's comrades cremate him and place his ashes in a huge *tumulus* (burial mound) overlooking the sea. As an everlasting tribute, they "buried rings and brooches in the barrow, all those adornments that brave men had brought out from the hoard after

Beowulf died. They bequeathed the gleaming gold, treasure of men, to the earth."[1]

Sutton Hoo Ship Burial The *Beowulf* saga also recounts the funeral of the warrior lord Scyld, who was laid to rest in a ship set adrift in the North Sea overflowing with arms and armor and costly adornments. In 1939 archaeologists uncovered a treasure-laden ship in a burial mound at Sutton Hoo, England. Although unique, it epitomizes the early medieval tradition of burying great lords with rich furnishings. Among the many precious finds were a gold belt buckle, 10 silver bowls, 40 gold coins, and 2 silver spoons inscribed "Saulos" and "Paulos" (Saint Paul's names in Greek before and after his baptism). The spoons may allude to a conversion to Christianity. Some historians have associated the burial with the East Anglian king Raedwald (r. 599?–625), who was baptized a Christian before his death in 625.

The most extraordinary Sutton Hoo find was a purse cover (FIG. **6-2**) decorated with *cloisonné* plaques. Early medieval metalworkers produced cloisonné jewelry by soldering small metal strips, or *cloisons* (French, "partitions"), edge up, to a metal background, and then filling the compartments with semiprecious stones, pieces of colored glass, or glass paste fired to resemble sparkling jewels. On the Sutton Hoo purse cover, four symmetrically arranged groups of cloisonné figures make up the lower row. The end groups consist of a front-facing man standing between two profile beasts. The trio is a pictorial parallel to the epic sagas of the era in which heroes like Beowulf battle and conquer horrific monsters. The two center groups represent eagles attacking ducks. The convex beaks of the eagles fit against the concave beaks of the ducks. The two figures fit together so snugly that they

seem at first to be a single dense abstract design. This is true also of the man-animals motif.

Above these figures are three geometric designs. The outer ones are purely linear. The central design is an interlace pattern, in which the lines turn into writhing animal figures. Elaborate intertwining patterns are characteristic of many times and places, but the combination of interlace with animal figures was uncommon outside the realm of the early medieval warlords. In fact, metalcraft with a vocabulary of interlace patterns and other motifs beautifully integrated with animal forms was the premier art of the early Middle Ages in western Europe.

MAP 6-1 Western Europe around 1100.

6-2 Purse cover, from the Sutton Hoo ship burial in Suffolk, England, ca. 625. Gold, glass, and enamel cloisonné with garnets and emeralds, $7\frac{1}{2}$" long. British Museum, London.

One of many treasures found in a ship beneath a royal burial mound, this purse cover combines abstract interlace ornamentation with animal figures— a hallmark of early medieval art in western Europe.

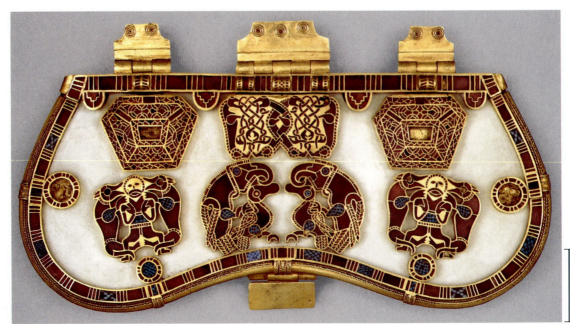

Hiberno-Saxon Art

The Christianization of the British Isles began in the fifth century. The new converts quickly founded monasteries throughout Ireland and in Britain and Scotland. In 563, for example, Saint Columba established an important monastery on the Scottish island of Iona, where he successfully converted the native Picts to Christianity. Iona monks built a monastery at Lindisfarne off the northern coast of Britain in 635. These and other later foundations became great centers of learning. Art historians call the art that flourished within the monasteries of the British Isles *Hiberno-Saxon* (Irish-English).

The most important extant Hiberno-Saxon artworks are the illuminated manuscripts of the Christian Church. Liturgical books were the primary vehicles in the effort to Christianize the British Isles. They literally brought the Word of God to a predominantly illiterate populace who regarded the monks' sumptuous volumes with awe. Books were scarce and jealously guarded treasures of the libraries, *scriptoria* (writing studios), and churches of early medieval monasteries.

One of the most characteristic features of Hiberno-Saxon book illumination is the inclusion of full pages devoted neither to text nor to illustration but to pure embellishment. Interspersed between the text pages are so-called *carpet pages*, resembling textiles, made up of decorative panels of abstract and zoomorphic forms. Many books also contain pages on which the painter enormously enlarged the initial letters of an important passage of sacred text and transformed them into elaborate decorative patterns. This type of manuscript decoration merged the abstraction of early medieval personal adornment with the pictorial tradition of Early Christian art.

Lindisfarne Gospels The marriage between Christian imagery and the animal-interlace style of the northern warlords is on display in the *Lindisfarne Gospels*. The *Gospels* ("good news"), the opening four books of the New Testament, tell the story of the life of Christ, but the painter of the *Lindisfarne Gospels* had little interest in narrative. A cross-inscribed carpet page (FIG. **6-3**) is typical of this lavish book. Fantastic serpentine animals devour each other, curling over and returning on their intertwined writhing, elastic shapes. The rhythm of expanding and contracting forms produces a vivid effect of motion and change, but the painter held it in check by the regularity of the design and by

the dominating motif of the inscribed cross. The cross—the all-important symbol of the imported religion—stabilizes the rhythms of the serpentines and, perhaps by contrast with its heavy immobility, seems to heighten the effect of motion. The illuminator placed the motifs in detailed symmetries, with inversions, reversals, and repetitions that must be studied closely to appreciate not so much their variety as their mazelike complexity. The zoomorphic forms intermingle with clusters and knots of line, and the whole design vibrates with energy. The color is rich yet cool. The painter adroitly adjusted shape and color to achieve a smooth and perfectly even surface.

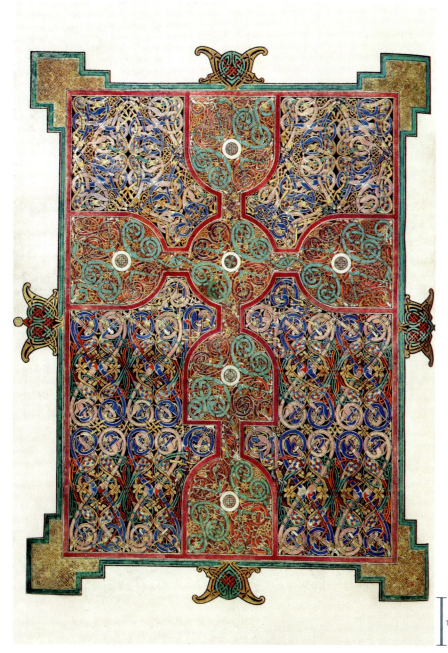

1 in.

6-3 Cross and carpet page, folio 26 verso of the *Lindisfarne Gospels*, from Northumbria, England, ca. 698–721. Tempera on vellum, 1' 1½" × 9¼". British Library, London.

The marriage between Christian imagery and the animal-interlace style of the early medieval warrior lords can be seen in this full-page painting in one of the oldest known Hiberno-Saxon Gospel books.

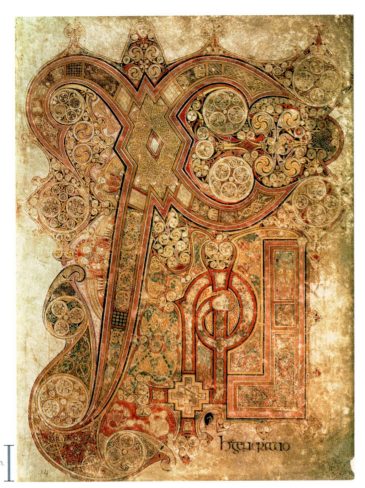

6-4 Chi-rho-iota page, folio 34 recto of the *Book of Kells*, from Iona, Scotland, late eighth or early ninth century. Tempera on vellum, 1′ 1″ × 9½″. Trinity College Library, Dublin.

In this opening page to the Gospel of Saint Matthew, the illuminator transformed the biblical text into abstract pattern, literally making God's words beautiful. The design recalls early medieval metalwork.

Book of Kells The greatest achievement of Hiberno-Saxon art is the *Book of Kells*, which boasts an unprecedented number of full-page illuminations, including carpet pages, New Testament figures and narrative scenes, and monumentalized and embellished words from the Bible. One medieval commentator described the book in the *Annals of Ulster* for the year 1003 as "the chief relic of the western world." From an early date it was housed in an elaborate metalwork box on a church altar, befitting a greatly revered "relic." The page reproduced here (FIG. **6-4**) opens the account of the nativity of Jesus in the Gospel of Saint Matthew. The initial letters of Christ in Greek (XPI, *chi-rho-iota*) occupy nearly the entire page, although two words—*autem* (abbreviated simply as *h*) and *generatio*—appear at the lower right. Together they read, "Now this is how the birth of Christ came about." The page corresponds to the opening of Matthew's Gospel, the passage read in church on Christmas Day. The illuminator transformed the holy words into abstract pattern, literally making God's words beautiful. The intricate design recalls early medieval metalwork, but the cloisonné-like interlace is not pure abstraction. The letter *rho*, for example, ends in a male head, and animals are at its base to the left of *h generatio*. Half-

figures of winged angels appear to the left of *chi*, accompanying the monogram as if accompanying Christ himself. Close observation reveals many other figures, human and animal.

Carolingian Art

On Christmas Day of the year 800 in Saint Peter's (FIG. **4-4**), Pope Leo III (r. 795–816) crowned Charles the Great (Charlemagne), king of the Franks since 768, as emperor of Rome (r. 800–814). In time, Charlemagne became known as the first Holy (that is, Christian) Roman Emperor, a title his successors in the West did not formally adopt until the 12th century. Born in 742, when northern Europe was still in chaos, Charlemagne consolidated the Frankish kingdom his father and grandfather bequeathed him and defeated the Lombards in Italy. He thus united Europe and laid claim to reviving the glory of the ancient Roman Empire. His official seal bore the words *renovatio imperii Romani* (renewal of the Roman Empire). Charlemagne gave his name (Carolus Magnus in Latin) to an entire era, the *Carolingian* period.

Charlemagne was a sincere admirer of learning, the arts, and classical culture. He invited to his court the best minds of his age, among them Alcuin, master of the *cathedral* (bishop's church) school at York, the center of Northumbrian learning. One of Charlemagne's dearest projects was the recovery of the true text of the Bible, which, through centuries of errors in copying, had become quite corrupt. Alcuin of York's revision of the Bible became the most widely used. Charlemagne himself could read and speak Latin fluently, in addition to Frankish, his native tongue. He also could understand Greek, and held books, both sacred and secular, in especially high esteem, importing many and sponsoring the production of far more.

Coronation Gospels The most famous of Charlemagne's books is the *Coronation Gospels*. The text is in handsome gold letters on purple vellum. The major full-page illuminations show the four Gospel authors at work—Saints Matthew, Mark, Luke, and John, the four *evangelists* (from the Greek word for "one who announces good news"). The page (FIG. **6-5**) depicting Saint Matthew follows the venerable tradition of author portraits, which were familiar features of Greek and Latin books. Similar representations of seated philosophers or poets writing or reading abound in ancient art. The Matthew of the *Coronation Gospels* also reveals the legacy of classical art. Deft, illusionistic brushwork defines the massive drapery folds wrapped around the body beneath. The Carolingian painter used color and modulation of light and shade to create the illusion of three-dimensional form. The cross-legged chair, the lectern, and the saint's toga are familiar Roman accessories, and the placement of the book and lectern top at an angle suggests a Mediterranean model employing classical perspective. The landscape background is also a classical feature, and the frame consists of the kind of acanthus leaves commonly found in Roman art. Almost nothing is known in the Hiberno-Saxon British Isles or Frankish Europe that could have prepared the way

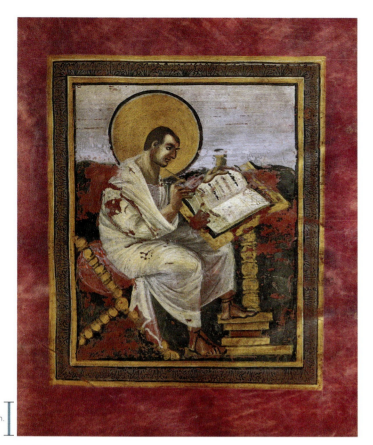

6-5 Saint Matthew, folio 15 recto of the *Coronation Gospels (Gospel Book of Charlemagne)*, from Aachen, Germany, ca. 800–810. Ink and tempera on vellum, $1' \frac{3}{4}'' \times 10''$. Schatz-kammer, Kunsthistorisches Museum, Vienna.

The painted manuscripts produced for Charlemagne's court reveal the legacy of classical art. The Carolingian painter used light, shade, and perspective to create the illusion of three-dimensional form.

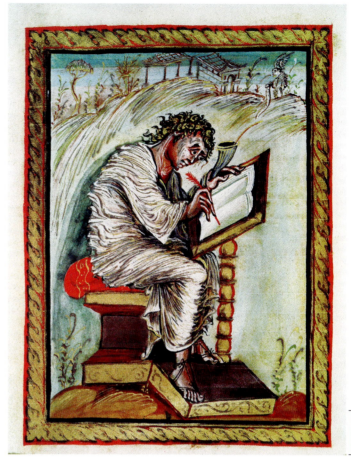

6-6 Saint Matthew, folio 18 verso of the *Ebbo Gospels (Gospel Book of Archbishop Ebbo of Reims)*, from Hautvillers (near Reims), France, ca. 816–835. Ink and tempera on vellum, $10\frac{1}{4}'' \times 8\frac{3}{4}''$. Bibliothèque Municipale, Épernay.

Saint Matthew writes in frantic haste, and the folds of his drapery writhe and vibrate. This Carolingian painter merged classical illusionism with the northern linear tradition.

for this portrayal of Saint Matthew. If a Frank, rather than an Italian or a Byzantine, painted the Saint Matthew and the other evangelist portraits of the *Coronation Gospels*, the Carolingian artist had fully absorbed the classical manner. Classical painting style was one of the many components of Charlemagne's program to establish himself as the head of a renewed Christian Roman Empire.

Ebbo Gospels Another Saint Matthew (FIG. **6-6**), in a gospel book made for Archbishop Ebbo of Reims, France, may be an interpretation of an author portrait very similar to the one the *Coronation Gospels* master used as a model. It resembles it in pose and in brushwork technique, but there the resemblance stops. The *Ebbo Gospels* illuminator replaced the classical calm and solidity of the *Coronation Gospels* evangelist with an energy that amounts to frenzy. Matthew writes in frantic haste. His hair stands on end, his eyes open wide, the folds of his drapery writhe and vibrate, the landscape behind him rears up alive. The painter even set the page's leaf border in motion. This evangelist portrait contrasts strongly with the *Coronation Gospels* Matthew. The *Ebbo Gospels* painter translated a classical prototype into a new Carolingian style, merging classical illusionism and the northern linear tradition.

Lindau Gospels The taste for luxurious portable objects, shown previously in the art of the early medieval warrior lords, persisted under Charlemagne and his successors. They commissioned numerous works employing costly materials, including book covers made of gold and jewels and sometimes also ivory or pearls. Gold and gems not only glorified the Word of God but also evoked the heavenly Jerusalem. One of the most sumptuous Carolingian book covers (FIG. **6-1**) is the one later added to the *Lindau Gospels*. The gold cover, fashioned in one of the royal workshops of Charles the Bald (r. 840–875), Charlemagne's grandson, presents a youthful Christ in the Early Christian tradition, nailed to the cross but oblivious to pain. Surrounding Christ are pearls and jewels (raised on golden claw feet so that they can catch and reflect the light even more brilliantly and protect the delicate metal relief from denting). The statuesque open-eyed figure, rendered in hammered relief, is classical both in conception and in execution. In contrast, the four angels and the personifications of the moon and the sun above and the crouching figures of the Virgin Mary and Saint John (and two other figures of uncertain identity) in the quadrants below display the vivacity and nervous energy

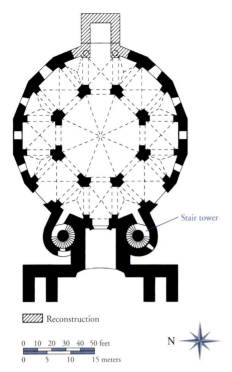

6-7 Restored plan of the Palatine Chapel of Charlemagne, Aachen, Germany, 792–805.

Charlemagne often visited Ravenna and sought to emulate Byzantine splendor in the North. The plan of his German palace chapel is based on that of San Vitale (FIG. 4-16), but the Carolingian plan is simpler.

of the *Ebbo Gospels* Matthew (FIG. **6-6**). This eclectic work highlights the stylistic diversity of early medieval art in Europe. Here, however, the translated figural style of the Mediterranean prevails, in keeping with the classical tastes and imperial aspirations of the Frankish "emperors of Rome."

Aachen In his eagerness to reestablish the imperial past, Charlemagne looked to Rome and Ravenna for models for his buildings. One was the former heart of the Roman Empire, which he wanted to "renew." The other was the western outpost of Byzantine might and splendor (see Chapter 4), which he wanted to emulate in his own capital at Aachen, Germany. Charlemagne often visited Ravenna, and once brought from there porphyry columns to adorn his Palatine (palace) Chapel. The plan (FIG. **6-7**) of the Aachen chapel resembles that of Ravenna's San Vitale (FIG. 4-16), and a direct relationship very likely exists between the two.

A comparison between the Carolingian chapel, the first vaulted structure of the Middle Ages north of the Alps, and its southern counterpart is instructive. The Aachen plan is simpler. Omitted were San Vitale's apselike extensions reaching from the central octagon into the ambulatory. At Aachen, the two main units stand in greater independence of each other. This solution may lack the subtle sophistication of the Byzantine building, but the Palatine Chapel gains geometric clarity. A view of its interior (FIG. **6-8**) shows that the architect converted the "floating" quality of San Vitale (FIG. 4-17) into massive geometric form.

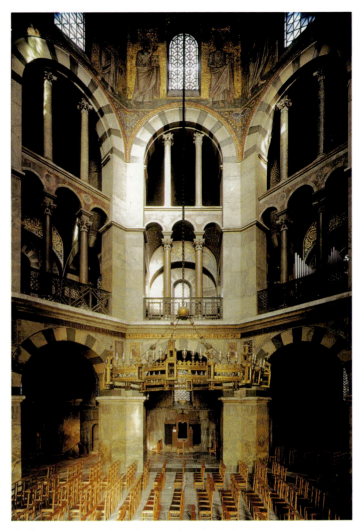

6-8 Interior of the Palatine Chapel of Charlemagne, Aachen, Germany, 792–805.

Charlemagne's chapel is the first vaulted structure of the Middle Ages north of the Alps. The architect transformed the complex interior of San Vitale (FIG. 4-17) into a simple and massive geometric form.

On the exterior, two cylindrical towers with spiral staircases flank the entrance portal. This was a first step toward the great dual-tower facades of western European churches from the 10th century to the present. Above the portal, Charlemagne could appear in a large framing arch and be seen by those gathered in the atrium in front of the chapel. (The plan includes only part of the atrium.) Directly behind that second-story arch was Charlemagne's marble throne. From there he could peer down at the altar in the apse. Charlemagne's imperial gallery followed the model of the western imperial gallery at Hagia Sophia (FIGS. 4-12 and 4-13) in Constantinople, even if the design of the facade broke sharply from Byzantine tradition.

Saint Gall The construction and expansion of many monasteries also characterized the Carolingian period. About 819, Haito, the abbot of Reichenau and bishop of Basel, commissioned a schematic plan (FIG. **6-9**) for a Benedictine monastic community (see "Medieval Monaster-

Medieval Monasteries and Benedictine Rule

Monastic foundations appeared in western Europe beginning in Early Christian times. The monks who established monasteries also made the rules that governed them. The most significant of these monks was Benedict of Nursia (Saint Benedict), who founded the Benedictine order in 529. By the ninth century, the "Rule" Benedict wrote *(Regula Sancti Benedicti)* had become standard for all European monastic establishments, in part because Charlemagne encouraged its adoption throughout the Frankish territories.

Saint Benedict believed the corruption of the clergy accompanying the increasing worldliness of the Christian Church had its roots in the lack of firm organization and regulation. As he saw it, idleness and selfishness had led to neglect of the commandments of God and of the Church. The cure for this was communal association in an *abbey* under the absolute rule of an *abbot* the monks elected (or an *abbess* the nuns chose), who would see to it that the monks spent each hour of the day in useful work or sacred reading. The emphasis on work and study and not on meditation and austerity is of great historical significance. Since antiquity, manual labor had been considered disgraceful, the business of the lowborn or of slaves. Benedict raised it to the dignity of religion. By thus exalting the virtue of manual labor, Benedict not only rescued it from its age-old association with slavery but also recognized it as the path to self-sufficiency for the entire religious community.

Whereas some of Saint Benedict's followers emphasized spiritual "work" over manual labor, others, most notably the Cistercians, put his teachings about the value of physical work into practice. These monks reached into their surroundings and helped reduce the vast areas of daunting wilderness of early medieval Europe. They cleared dense forest teeming with wolves, bear, and wild boar; drained swamps; cultivated wastelands; and built roads, bridges, and dams, as well as monastic churches and their associated living and service quarters. An ideal monastery (FIG. 6-9) provided all the facilities necessary for the conduct of daily life—a mill, bakery, infirmary, vegetable garden, and even a brewery—so that the monks felt no need to wander outside its protective walls.

These religious communities were critically important to the revival of learning. The clergy, who were also often scribes and scholars, had a monopoly on the skills of reading and writing in an age of almost universal illiteracy. The monastic libraries and scriptoria, where the monks read, copied, illuminated, and bound books with ornamented covers, became centers of study. Monasteries were almost the sole repositories of what remained of the literary culture of the Greco-Roman world and early Christianity. Saint Benedict's requirements of manual labor and sacred reading came to include writing and copying books, studying music for chanting the day's offices, and—of great significance—teaching. The monasteries were also the schools of the early Middle Ages.

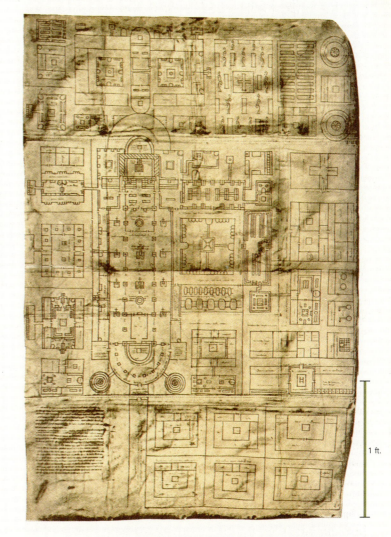

1 ft.

6-9 Schematic plan for a monastery at Saint Gall, Switzerland, ca. 819. Red ink on parchment, $3' 8\frac{1}{8}'' \times 2' 4''$. Stiftsbibliothek, Saint Gall.

The purpose of this plan for an ideal, self-sufficient monastery was to separate the monks from the laity. Near the center is the church with its cloister, an earthly paradise reserved for the monks.

ies and Benedictine Rule," above) and sent it to the abbot of Saint Gall in Switzerland to use as a guide in rebuilding the monastery there. It constitutes a treasure trove of information about Carolingian monastic life. The design's fundamental purpose was to separate the monks from the laity (nonclergy) who also inhabited the community. Later monasteries all across western Europe are variations of the Saint Gall scheme.

Near the center, dominating everything, was the church with its *cloister*, a colonnaded courtyard (compare FIG. **6-17**, *top*) not unlike the Early Christian atrium (FIG. **4-4**) but situated to the side of the church rather than in front of its main portal. Reserved for the monks alone, the cloister, a kind of earthly paradise removed from the world at large, provided the peace and quiet necessary for contemplation. Clustered around the cloister were the most essential buildings:

dormitory, refectory, kitchen, and storage rooms. Other structures, including an infirmary, school, guest house, bakery, brewery, and workshops, were grouped around this central core of church and cloister.

Haito invited the abbot of Saint Gall to adapt the plan as he saw fit, and the Saint Gall builders did not, in fact, follow the Reichenau model exactly. Nonetheless, if the abbot had wished, Haito's plan could have served as a practical guide for the Saint Gall masons because it was laid out on a *module* (standard unit) of two and a half feet. Parts or multiples of this module appear consistently throughout the plan. For example, the nave's width, indicated on the plan as 40 feet, equals 16 modules; the length of each monk's bed, two and a half modules.

The models that carried the greatest authority for Charlemagne and his builders were those from the Christian phase of the Roman Empire. The widespread adoption of the Early Christian basilica, at Saint Gall and elsewhere, rather than the domed central plan of Byzantine churches, was crucial to the subsequent development of western European church architecture. Unfortunately, no Carolingian basilica has survived in anything approaching its original form. Nevertheless, it is possible to reconstruct the appearance of some of them with fair accuracy. The monastery church at Saint Gall, for example, was essentially a traditional basilica, but it had features not found in any Early Christian church. Most obvious is the addition of a second apse on the west end of the building.

Not quite as evident but much more important to the subsequent development of church architecture north of the Alps was the presence of a transept at Saint Gall, a rare feature but one that characterized the two greatest Early Christian basilicas in Rome, Saint Peter's (FIG. 4-4) and Saint Paul's. The Saint Gall transept is as wide as the nave on the plan and was probably the same height. Early Christian builders had not been concerned with proportional relationships. They assembled the various portions of their buildings only in accordance with the dictates of liturgical needs. On the Saint Gall plan, however, the various parts of the building relate to one another by a geometric scheme that ties them together into a tight, cohesive unit. Equalizing the widths of nave and transept automatically makes the area where they cross (the *crossing*) a square. Most Carolingian churches shared this feature. But Haito's planner also used the *crossing square* as the unit of measurement for the remainder of the church plan. The transept arms are equal to one crossing square, the distance between transept and apse is one crossing square, and the nave is four and a half crossing squares long. The fact that the two aisles are half as wide as the nave integrates all parts of the church in a rational, orderly plan.

The Saint Gall plan also reveals another important feature of many Carolingian basilicas: towers framing the end(s) of the church. Haito's plan shows only two towers, both cylindrical and on the west side of the church, as at the Pala-tine Chapel (FIG. 6-7) at Aachen, but they stand apart from the church facade. If a tower existed above the crossing, the silhouette of Saint Gall would have shown three towers altering the horizontal profile of the traditional basilica and identifying the church even from afar. Other Carolingian basilicas had towers incorporated in the fabric of the west end of the building, as in Charlemagne's Palatine Chapel, thereby creating a unified monumental facade that greeted all those who entered the church. Architectural historians call this feature of Carolingian and some later churches the *westwork* (German *Westwerck*, "western entrance structure").

Ottonian Art

Charlemagne was buried in the Palatine Chapel at Aachen. His empire survived him by fewer than 30 years. When his son Louis the Pious (r. 814–840) died, Louis's sons—Charles the Bald, Lothair, and Louis the German—divided the Carolingian Empire among themselves. In 843, after bloody conflicts, the brothers signed a treaty partitioning the Frankish lands into western, central, and eastern areas, very roughly foreshadowing the later nations of France and Germany and a third realm corresponding to a long strip of land stretching from the Netherlands and Belgium to Rome. In the mid-10th century, the eastern part of the former empire consolidated under the rule of a new Saxon line of German emperors called, after the names of the three most illustrious family members, the *Ottonians*. The pope crowned the first Otto (r. 936–973) in Rome in 962. The three Ottos not only preserved but enriched the culture and tradition of the Carolingian period.

Hildesheim One of the great patrons of Ottonian art and architecture was Bishop Bernward of Hildesheim, Germany. He was the tutor of Otto III (r. 983–1002) and builder of the abbey church of Saint Michael (FIGS. **6-10** and **6-11**) at Hildesheim. Bernward, who made Hildesheim a center of learning, was an expert craftsman and bronze caster as well as a scholar. In 1001 he traveled to Rome as the guest of Otto III. During this stay, Bernward studied at first hand the ancient monuments the Carolingian and Ottonian emperors revered.

Constructed between 1001 and 1031 (and rebuilt after being bombed during World War II), Bernward's Saint Michael's is an elaborate version of a Carolingian basilica. It has two apses, two transepts, and multiple towers. The transepts create eastern and western centers of gravity. The nave seems to be merely a hall that connects them. Lateral entrances leading into the aisles from the north and south (FIG. **6-11**) additionally make for an almost complete loss of the traditional basilican orientation toward the east. Some ancient Roman basilicas, such as the Basilica Ulpia in Trajan's Forum (FIG. **3-34**, no. 4), also had two apses and entrances on the side, and Bernward probably was familiar with this variant basilican plan.

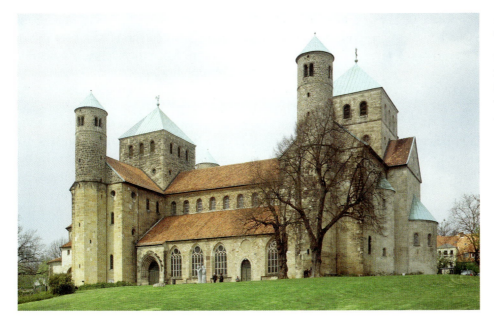

6-10 Saint Michael's, Hildesheim, Germany, 1001–1031.

Built by Bishop Bernward, a great art patron, Saint Michael's is a masterpiece of Ottonian basilica design. The church's two apses, two transepts, and multiple towers give it a distinctive profile.

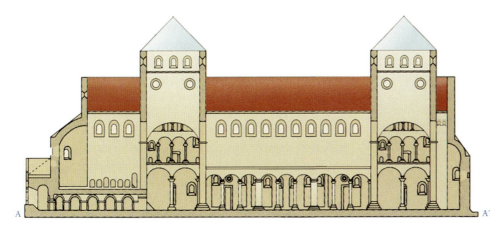

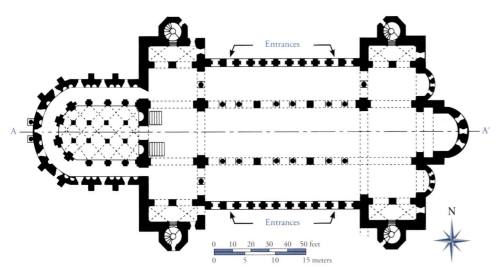

6-11 Longitudinal section (*top*) and plan (*bottom*) of the abbey church of Saint Michael's, Hildesheim, Germany, 1001–1031.

Saint Michael's entrances are on the sides. Alternating piers and columns divide the space in the nave into vertical units. These features transformed the tunnel-like horizontality of Early Christian basilicas.

At Hildesheim, as in the plan of the monastery at Saint Gall (FIG. 6-9), the builders adopted a modular approach. The crossing squares, for example, are the basis for the nave's dimensions—three crossing squares long and one square wide. The placement of heavy piers at the corners of each square gives visual emphasis to the three units. These piers alternate with pairs of columns to form what architectural historians call the *alternate-support system*. The alternating piers and columns divide the nave into vertical units, mitigating the tunnel-like horizontality of the Early Christian basilica.

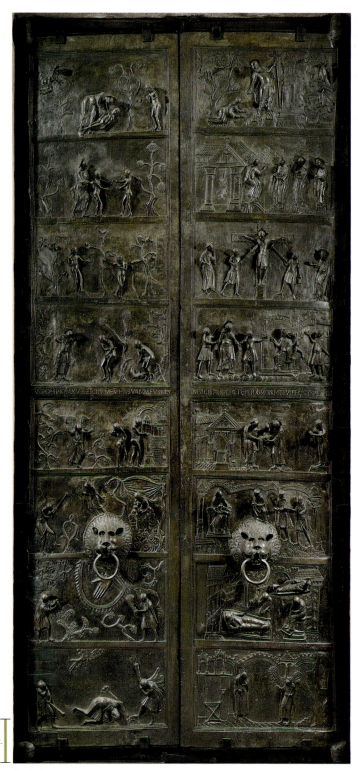

1 ft.

6-12 Doors with relief panels (Genesis, left door; life of Christ, right door), commissioned by Bishop Bernward for Saint Michael's, Hildesheim, Germany, 1015. Bronze, 16′ 6″ high. Dom-Museum, Hildesheim.

Bernward's doors vividly tell the story of Original Sin and Redemption, and draw parallels between the Old and New Testaments, pairing the expulsion from Paradise and the infancy and suffering of Christ.

Bernward's Doors In 1001, when Bishop Bernward was in Rome, he resided in Otto III's palace on the Aventine hill in the neighborhood of Santa Sabina, an Early Christian church renowned for its carved wooden doors. Those doors, decorated with episodes from both the Old and New Testa-

ments, may have inspired the remarkable bronze doors the bishop had cast for Saint Michael's. The Hildesheim doors (FIG. **6-12**) are more than 16 feet tall. Each was cast in a single piece with the figural sculpture, a technological marvel. Carolingian sculpture, like most sculpture since the fall of Rome, consisted primarily of small-scale art executed in ivory and precious metals, often for book covers (FIG. **6-1**). The Hildesheim doors are huge in comparison, but the 16 individual panels stem from that tradition.

The panels of the left door illustrate highlights from the book of Genesis, beginning with the Creation of Adam (at the top) and ending with the murder of Adam and Eve's son Abel by his brother Cain (at the bottom). The right door recounts the life of Christ (reading from the bottom up), starting with the Annunciation and terminating with the appearance to Mary Magdalene of Christ after the Resurrection. Together, the doors tell the story of Original Sin and ultimate Redemption, showing the expulsion from the Garden of Eden and the path back to Paradise through the Church. As in Early Christian times, theologians interpreted the Old Testament as prefiguring the New Testament. The panel depicting the Fall of Adam and Eve, for example, is juxtaposed with the Crucifixion on the other door. Eve nursing the infant Cain is opposite Mary with the Christ Child in her lap. The figures show a vivid animation that recalls the Saint Matthew of the *Ebbo Gospels*, but the narrative compositions also reveal the Hildesheim artist's genius for anecdotal detail. For example, in the fourth panel from the top on the left door, God, portrayed as a man, accuses Adam and Eve after their fall from grace. He jabs his finger at them with the force of his whole body. The frightened pair crouch, both to hide their shame and to escape the lightning bolt of divine wrath. Each passes the blame—Adam pointing backward to Eve, and Eve pointing downward to the deceitful serpent. Both figures struggle to point with one arm while attempting to shield their bodies from sight with the other. With an instinct for expressive pose and gesture, the artist brilliantly communicated Adam and Eve's newfound embarrassment at their nakedness and their unconvincing denials of wrongdoing.

Gero Crucifix Nowhere is the Ottonian revival of interest in monumental sculpture more evident than in the crucifix (FIG. **6-13**) Archbishop Gero commissioned and presented to Cologne Cathedral in 970. Carved in oak and then painted and gilded, the six-foot-tall image of Christ nailed to the cross presents a dramatically different conception of the Savior than that seen on the *Lindau Gospels* cover (FIG. **6-1**), with its Early Christian imagery of the youthful Christ triumphant over death. The bearded Christ of the Cologne crucifix is more akin to Byzantine representations (FIG. **4-22**) of the suffering Jesus, but the emotional power of the Ottonian work is greater still. The sculptor depicted Christ as an all-too-human martyr. Streaks of blood trickle down his forehead from the (missing) crown of thorns. His eyelids are closed, and his face is contorted in pain. Christ's body sags under its own weight. The muscles stretch to their limit—those of his right shoulder and chest seem almost to

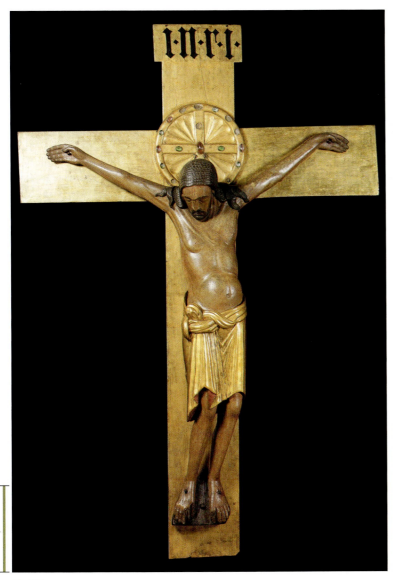

1 ft.

6-13 Crucifix commissioned by Archbishop Gero for Cologne Cathedral, Germany, ca. 970. Painted wood, height of figure, 6′ 2″. Cathedral, Cologne.

In this early example of the revival of monumental sculpture in the Middle Ages, an Ottonian sculptor depicted with unprecedented emotional power the intense agony of Christ's ordeal on the cross.

architectural elements of this period, principally barrel and groin vaults based on the round arch, resembled those of ancient Roman architecture. Thus, the word distinguished most Romanesque buildings from earlier medieval timber-roofed structures, as well as from later Gothic churches with vaults resting on pointed arches. Scholars in other fields quickly borrowed the term. Today "Romanesque" broadly designates the history and culture of western Europe between about 1050 and 1200 (MAP 6-1).

During the 11th and 12th centuries, thousands of ecclesiastical buildings were remodeled or newly constructed. This immense building enterprise reflected in part the rise of independent and increasingly prosperous towns during the Romanesque period. But it also was an expression of the widely felt relief and thanksgiving that the conclusion of the first Christian millennium in the year 1000 had not brought an end to the world, as many had feared. In the Romanesque age, the construction of churches became almost an obsession. As the monk Raoul Glaber observed in 1003, "it was as if the whole earth . . . were clothing itself everywhere in the white robe of the church."[2]

The enormous investment in ecclesiastical buildings and furnishings also reflected a significant increase in pilgrimage traffic in Romanesque Europe (see "Pilgrimages and the Cult of Relics," page 170). Pilgrims were important sources of funding for monasteries that possessed the *relics* of venerated saints. The clergy of the various monasteries vied with one another to provide magnificent settings for the display of their relics. Justification for such heavy investment to attract donations could be found in the Bible itself, for example in Psalm 26:8: "Lord, I have loved the beauty of your house, and the place where your glory dwells." Traveling pilgrims fostered the growth of towns as well as monasteries. Pilgrimages were, in fact, a major economic and conceptual catalyst for the art and architecture of the Romanesque period.

Although art historians use the term "Romanesque" to describe 11th- and 12th-century art and architecture throughout Europe, pronounced regional differences existed. To a certain extent, Romanesque art and architecture parallel European Romance languages, which vary regionally but have a common core in Latin, the language of the Romans.

rip apart. The halo behind Christ's head may foretell his subsequent Resurrection, but the worshiper can sense only his pain. Gero's crucifix is the most powerful characterization of intense agony of the early Middle Ages.

ROMANESQUE ART

The Romanesque era is the first since Archaic and Classical Greece to take its name from an artistic style rather than from politics or geography. Unlike Carolingian and Ottonian art, named for emperors, or Hiberno-Saxon art, a regional term, *Romanesque* is a title art historians invented to describe medieval art and architecture that appeared "Roman-like." Architectural historians first employed the adjective in the early 19th century to describe European architecture of the 11th and 12th centuries. Scholars noted that certain

France

Some of the most innovative developments in Romanesque architecture and architectural sculpture occurred in France.

Saint-Sernin, Toulouse Around 1070, construction of a great new church began in honor of Toulouse's first bishop, Saint Saturninus (Saint Sernin in French). Large congregations were common at the southwestern French shrines along the pilgrimage routes to Santiago de Compostela in Spain, and the unknown architect designed Saint-Sernin to

Pilgrimages and the Cult of Relics

The cult of *relics* was not new to the Romanesque era. For centuries, Christians had traveled to sacred shrines housing the body parts of, or objects associated with, the holy family or the saints. The faithful had long believed that bones, clothing, instruments of martyrdom, and the like had the power to heal body and soul. The veneration of relics reached a high point in the 11th and 12th centuries.

In Romanesque times, pilgrimage was the most conspicuous feature of public devotion, proclaiming the pilgrim's faith in the power of saints and hope for their special favor. The major shrines—Saint Peter's and Saint Paul's in Rome and the Church of the Holy Sepulchre in Jerusalem—drew pilgrims from all over Europe. To achieve salvation, Christians braved bad roads and hostile wildernesses infested with robbers who preyed on innocent travelers. The journeys could take more than a year to complete—when they were successful. People often undertook pilgrimage as an act of repentance or as a last resort in their search for a cure for some physical disability. Hardship and austerity were means of increasing pilgrims' chances for the remission of sin or of disease. The distance and peril of the pilgrimage were measures of pilgrims' sincerity of repentance or of the reward they sought.

For those with insufficient time or money to make a pilgrimage to Rome or Jerusalem, holy destinations could be found closer to home. In France, for example, the church at Vézelay housed the bones of Mary Magdalene. Pilgrims could also view Saint Lazarus's remains at Autun (FIG. 6-20) and Saint Saturninus's at Toulouse (FIG. 6-14). Each of these great shrines was also an important way station en route to the most venerated Christian shrine in western Europe, the tomb of Saint James at Santiago de Compostela in northwestern Spain (MAP 6-1).

Large crowds of pilgrims paying homage to saints placed a great burden on the churches that stored their relics, but they also provided significant revenues, making possible the erection of ever grander and more luxuriously appointed structures. The popularity of pilgrimages led to changes in church design, necessitating longer and wider naves and aisles, transepts and ambulatories with additional chapels (FIG. 6-15), and second-story galleries (FIG. 6-16).

6-14 Aerial view (looking northwest) of Saint-Sernin, Toulouse, France, ca. 1070–1120.

Pilgrimages were a primary economic catalyst for the art and architecture of the Romanesque period. The clergy vied with one another to provide magnificent settings for the display of holy relics.

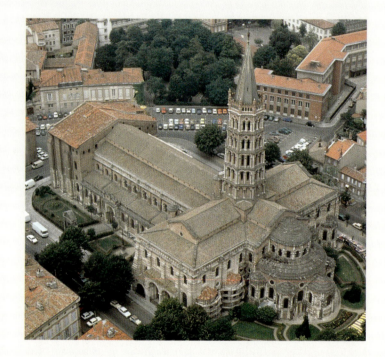

6-15 Plan of Saint-Sernin, Toulouse, France, ca. 1070–1120 (after Kenneth John Conant).

Increased traffic led to changes in church design. "Pilgrimage churches" such as Saint-Sernin have longer and wider naves and aisles, as well as transepts and ambulatories with radiating chapels for viewing relics.

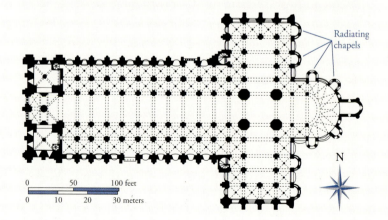

Radiating chapels

0   50   100 feet
0 10 20 30 meters

N

accommodate them. The grand scale of the building is apparent in the aerial view (FIG. **6-14**), which for relative size shows automobiles, trucks, and nearly invisible pedestrians. The church's 12th-century exterior is still largely intact, although the two towers of the western facade (at the left in FIG. 6-14) were never completed, and the prominent *crossing tower* is largely Gothic and later.

Saint-Sernin's plan (FIG. **6-15**) is extremely regular and geometrically precise. The crossing square, flanked by massive piers and marked off by heavy arches, served as the module for the entire church. Each nave *bay*, for example, measures exactly one-half of the crossing square, and each aisle bay measures exactly one-quarter. The Toulouse design is a highly refined realization of the planning scheme first seen at Saint Gall (FIG. **6-9**). But the Toulouse plan differs in significant ways from the designs of earlier monastic churches. It exemplifies what has come to be called the "pilgrimage church" type, one intended to provide additional space for curious pilgrims, worshipers, and liturgical processions. To achieve this expansion, builders increased the length of the nave, doubled the side aisles, and added a transept and am-

bulatory with *radiating chapels* housing the church's relics so that the faithful could view them without having to enter the choir where the main altar stood.

Saint-Sernin also has upper galleries, or *tribunes*, over the inner aisle and opening onto the nave (FIG. **6-16**), which housed overflow crowds on special occasions. The tribunes played an important role in buttressing the continuous semicircular cut-stone *barrel vault* that covers Saint-Sernin's nave. *Groin vaults* (indicated by Xs on the plan, FIG. **6-15**) in the tribune galleries as well as in the ground-floor aisles absorbed the pressure *(thrust)* exerted by the barrel vault along the entire length of the nave and transferred the main thrust to the thick outer walls.

The builders of Saint-Sernin were not content with just buttressing the massive nave vault. They also carefully coordinated the vault's design with that of the nave arcade below and with the modular plan of the building as a whole. The geometric floor plan (FIG. **6-15**) is fully reflected in the nave walls (FIG. **6-16**), where *engaged columns* embellish the piers marking the corners of the bays. Architectural historians refer to piers with columns or pilasters attached to their rectangular cores as *compound piers*. At Saint-Sernin, the engaged columns rise from the bottom of the compound piers to the vault's *springing* (the lowest stone of an arch) and continue across the nave as *transverse arches*. As a result, the Saint-Sernin nave seems to be composed of numerous identical vertical volumes of space placed one behind the other, marching down the building's length in orderly procession. Saint-Sernin's spatial organization corresponds to and renders visually the plan's geometric organization. This rationally integrated scheme, with repeated units decorated and separated by moldings, had a long future in later church architecture.

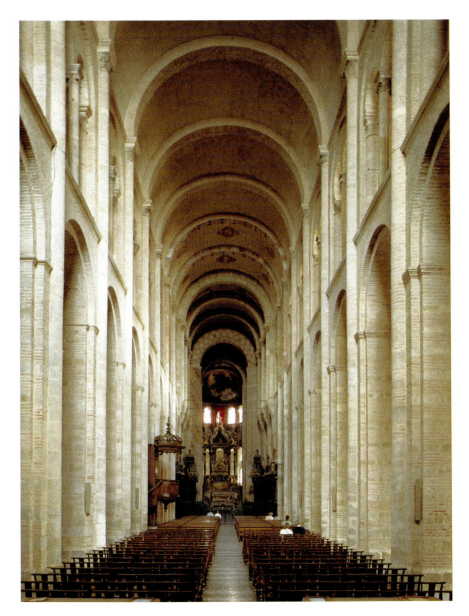

Saint-Sernin's stone vaults provided protection from the devastating conflagrations that regularly destroyed traditional timber-roofed basilicas. But although fireproofing was no doubt one of the attractions of vaulted naves and aisles in an age when candles provided interior illumination, other factors probably played a greater role in the decision to make the enormous investment that stone masonry required. A desire to provide a suitably majestic setting for the display of relics—and the competition for pilgrimage traffic and the donations pilgrims brought

6-16 Interior of Saint-Sernin, Toulouse, France, ca. 1070–1120.

Saint-Sernin's groin-vaulted tribune galleries housed overflow crowds and buttressed the stone barrel vault over the nave. The transverse arches continue the lines of the compound piers.

6-17 General view of the cloister (*top*) and detail of the pier with the relief of Abbot Durandus (*bottom*), Saint-Pierre, Moissac, France, ca. 1100–1115. Relief: limestone, 6' high.

The revived tradition of stone-carving probably began with artists decorating capitals with reliefs. The most extensive preserved ensemble of sculptured early Romanesque capitals is in the Moissac cloister. The pier reliefs are early examples of large-scale sculpture.

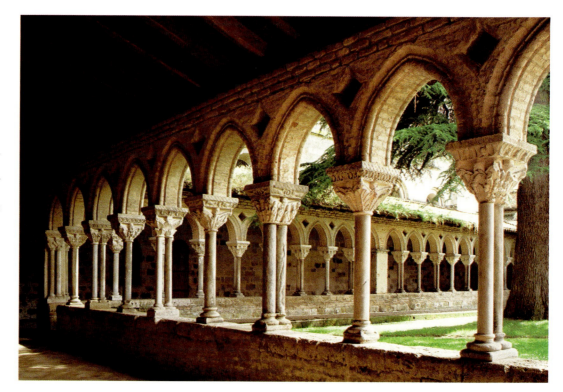

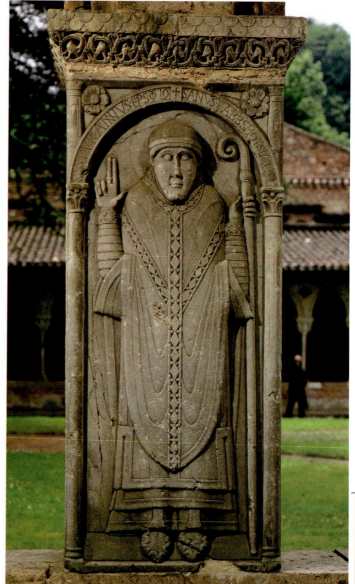

1 ft.

with them—as well as enhanced acoustics for the Christian liturgy and the music that accompanied it, probably better explain the rapid spread of stone vaulting throughout Romanesque Europe. Some texts of the time, in fact, comment on the "wondrous" visual impact of costly stone vaults.

Saint-Pierre, Moissac Saint-Sernin also features a group of seven marble slabs representing angels, apostles, and Christ. Dated to the year 1096, they are among the earliest known examples of large-scale Romanesque sculpture. Stone sculpture had almost disappeared from the art of western Europe during the early Middle Ages. The revival of stonecarving is a hallmark of the Romanesque age—and one reason the period is aptly named. The revived tradition of stone carving probably began with builders adding decorative reliefs on column and pier capitals. The most extensive preserved ensemble of sculptured early Romanesque capitals is in the cloister (FIG. **6-17**) of Saint-Pierre at Moissac in southwestern France. The monks of the Moissac abbey joined the Cluniac order in 1047, and Moissac quickly became an important stop along the pilgrimage route to Santiago de Compostela. The monks, enriched by the gifts of pilgrims and noble benefactors, adorned their church with an elaborate series of relief sculptures.

At Moissac, as elsewhere, the cloister and its garden provided the monks (and nuns) with a foretaste of Paradise. In the cloister, they could read their devotions, pray, and meditate in an atmosphere of calm serenity, each monk withdrawn into the private world where the soul communes only with God. Moissac's cloister sculpture program consists of large figural reliefs on the piers as well as *historiated* (ornamented with figures) capitals on the columns. The pier reliefs (FIG. **6-17**, *bottom*) portray the 12 apostles and the first Cluniac abbot of Moissac, Durandus (1047–1072), who was bur-

The Romanesque Church Portal

Although sculpture in a variety of materials adorned different areas of Romanesque churches, it was most often found in the grand stone portals through which the faithful had to pass. Sculpture had been employed in church doorways before. For example, Ottonian bronze doors (FIG. 6-12) decorated with Old and New Testament scenes marked one entrance to Saint Michael's at Hildesheim. In the Romanesque era (and during the Gothic period that followed), sculpture usually appeared in the area around the doors rather than on them. Romanesque sculptors regularly decorated several parts of church portals (FIG. 6-18) with figural reliefs:

■ *Tympanum* (FIGS. 6-19 to 6-21), the prominent semicircular *lunette* above the doorway proper, comparable in importance to the triangular pediment of a Greco-Roman temple

■ *Voussoirs* (FIG. 6-21), the wedge-shaped blocks that together form the *archivolts* of the arch framing the tympanum

■ *Lintel* (FIGS. 6-20 and 6-21), the horizontal beam above the doorway

■ *Trumeau* (FIG. 6-19), the center post supporting the lintel in the middle of the doorway

■ *Jambs* (FIG. 6-19), the side posts of the doorway

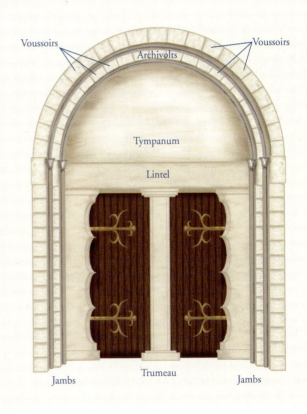

6-18 The Romanesque church portal.

The clergy considered the church doorway the beginning of the path to salvation through Christ. Many Romanesque churches feature didactic sculptural reliefs above and beside the entrance portals.

---

ied in the cloister. The 76 capitals alternately crown single and paired column shafts (FIG. 6-17, *top*). They are variously decorated, some with abstract patterns, many with biblical scenes or the lives of saints, others with fantastic monsters of all sorts. *Bestiaries*—collections of illustrations of real and imaginary animals—became very popular in the Romanesque age. The monstrous forms were reminders of the chaos and deformity of a world without God's order. Medieval artists delighted in inventing composite beasts with multiple heads and other fantastic creations.

Bernard of Clairvaux Historiated capitals were common in Cluniac monasteries. Many medieval monks, especially those of the Cluniac order, equated piety with the construction of beautiful churches having elegant carvings. But one of the founding principles of monasticism was the rejection of worldly pleasures in favor of a life of contemplation. Some monks were appalled by the costly churches being erected all around them. One group of Benedictine monks founded a new order at Cîteaux in eastern France in 1098. The Cistercians (so called from the Latin name for Cîteaux) were Benedictine monks who split from the Cluniac order to return to the strict observance of the Rule of Saint Benedict. The Cistercian movement expanded with astonishing rapidity. Within a half century, more than 500 Cistercian monasteries had been established. The Cister-

cians rejected figural sculptures as distractions from their devotions. The most outspoken Cisterican critic of the new Romanesque sculptures was Abbot Bernard of Clairvaux (1090–1153). In a letter Bernard wrote in 1127 to William, abbot of Saint-Thierry, he complained about the sculptural adornment of non-Cistercian churches: "In the cloisters . . . so plentiful and astonishing a variety of [monstrous] forms is seen that one would rather read in the marble than in books, and spend the whole day wondering at every single one of them than in meditating on the law of God."[3]

During the Romanesque period, stone sculpture also spread to other areas of the church, both inside and out. The proliferation of sculpture reflects the changing role of many churches in western Europe. In the early Middle Ages, most churches served small monastic communities, and the worshipers were primarily or exclusively clergy. With the rise of towns in the Romanesque period, churches, especially those on the major pilgrimage routes, increasingly served the lay public. To reach this new, largely illiterate audience and to draw a wider population into their places of worship, church officials decided to display Christian symbols and stories throughout their churches, especially in the portals (see "The Romanesque Church Portal," above, and FIG. 6-18) opening onto the town squares. Stone, rather than painting or mosaic, was the most suitable durable medium for exterior decorative programs.

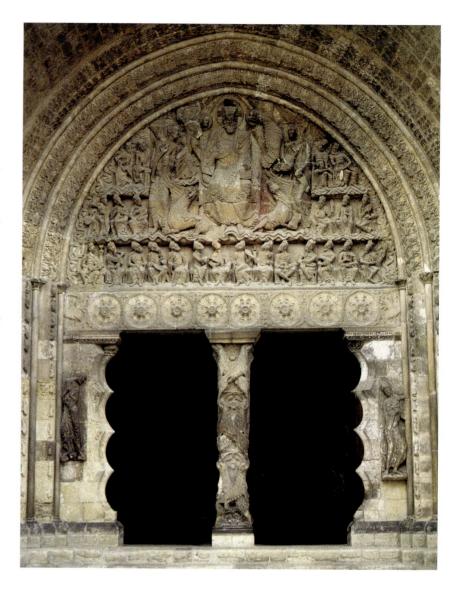

6-19 South portal of Saint-Pierre, Moissac, France, ca. 1115–1135.

Romanesque churches served a largely illiterate lay public. To attract worshipers, the clergy commissioned sculptors to carve Christian symbols and stories on the portals opening onto the town squares.

South Portal, Moissac The tympanum of the south portal (FIG. **6-19**) of Saint-Pierre at Moissac, facing the town square, depicts the Second Coming of Christ as King and Judge of the world in its last days. The pictorial programs of Romanesque church facades reflect the idea that Christ is the door to salvation ("I am the door; who enters through me will be saved"—John 10:9). As befits his majesty, the enthroned Christ is at the center of the Moissac tympanum. The signs of the four evangelists—Matthew's winged man, Mark's lion, John's eagle, and Luke's ox—flank him. To one side of each pair of signs is an attendant angel holding scrolls to record human deeds for judgment. The figures of crowned musicians, which complete the design, are the 24 elders who accompany Christ as the kings of this world and make music in his praise. Two courses of wavy lines symbolizing the clouds of Heaven divide the elders into three tiers.

Many variations exist within the general style of Romanesque sculpture, as within Romanesque architecture. The extremely elongated bodies of the recording angels, the cross-legged dancing pose of Saint Matthew's angel, the jerky movement of the elders' heads, the zigzag and dovetail lines of the draperies, the bandlike folds of the torsos, and the bending back of the hands against the body are all characteristic of the anonymous Moissac sculptor's distinctive style. The animation of the individual figures, however, contrasts with the stately monumentality of the composition as a whole, producing a dynamic tension in the tympanum.

Below the tympanum are a richly decorated trumeau and elaborate door jambs with scalloped contours, the latter a borrowing from Islamic Spain (FIG. 5-7). On the trumeau's right face is a prophet displaying the scroll where his prophetic vision is written. Six roaring interlaced lions fill the trumeau's outer face. Lions were the church's ideal protectors. In the Middle Ages, people believed lions slept with their eyes open.

Saint-Lazare, Autun In 1132 the Cluniac bishop Étienne de Bage consecrated the Burgundian cathedral of Saint-Lazare (Saint Lazarus) at Autun. For its tympanum (FIG. **6-20**), he commissioned the sculptor GISLEBERTUS to carve a dramatic vision of the Last Judgment, which four trumpet-blowing angels announce. In the tympanum's center, far larger than any other figure, is Christ, enthroned in a *mandorla*. He dispassionately presides over the separation of the blessed from the damned. At the left, an obliging angel boosts one of the blessed into the heavenly city. Below, the souls of the dead line up to await their fate. Two of the men at the left end of the lintel carry bags emblazoned with a cross and a shell. These are the symbols of pilgrims to Jerusalem and Santiago de Compostela. Those who had made the difficult journey would be judged favorably. To their right, three small figures beg an angel to intercede on their behalf. The angel responds by pointing to the Judge above. On the right side are those who will be condemned to Hell. Giant hands pluck one poor soul from the earth. Directly above, in the tympanum, is an unforgettable vision of the weighing of souls. Angels and devils contest at the scales, each trying to manipulate the balance for or against a soul. Hideous demons guffaw and roar. Their gaunt, lined bodies, with legs ending in sharp claws, writhe and bend like long, loathsome insects. A devil, leaning from the dragon mouth of Hell, drags souls in, while above him a howling demon crams souls headfirst into a furnace.

The Autun tympanum must have inspired terror in the believers who passed beneath it as they entered the cathedral. Even those who could not read could, in the words of Bernard of Clairvaux, "read in the marble." For the literate,

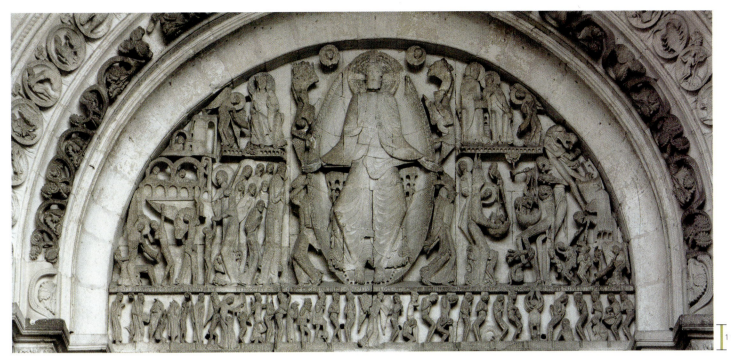

6-20 GISLEBERTUS, *Last Judgment*, west tympanum of Saint-Lazare, Autun, France, ca. 1120–1135. Marble, 21' wide at base.

Christ, enthroned in a mandorla, presides over the separation of the blessed from the damned in this dramatic vision of the Last Judgment, designed to terrify those guilty of sin and beckon them into the church.

the Autun clergy composed explicit written warnings to reinforce the pictorial message and had the words engraved in Latin on the tympanum. For example, beneath the weighing of souls, the inscription reads, "May this terror terrify those whom earthly error binds, for the horror of these images here in this manner truly depicts what will be."[4]

La Madeleine, Vézelay Another large tympanum (FIG. **6-21**)—at the Church of La Madeleine (Mary Magdalene) at Vézelay, not far from Autun—depicts the Pentecost and the Mission of the Apostles. As related in Acts 1:4–9, Christ foretold that the 12 apostles would receive the power of the Holy Spirit and become the witnesses of the truth of

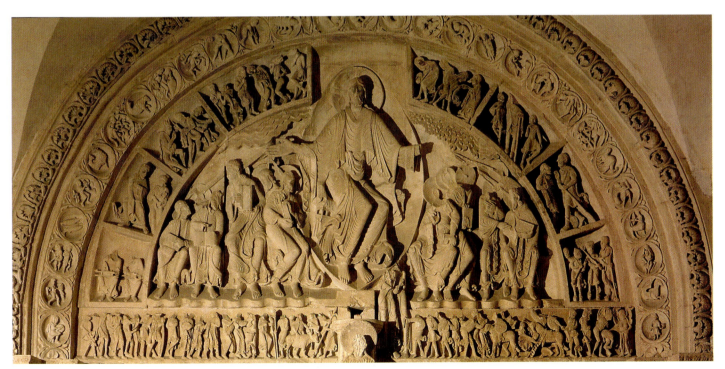

6-21 Pentecost and Mission of the Apostles, tympanum of the center portal of the narthex of La Madeleine, Vézelay, France, 1120–1132.

The light rays emanating from Christ's hands represent the instilling of the Holy Spirit in the apostles. On the lintel and in eight compartments around the tympanum, the heathen wait to be converted.

Romanesque Art | 175

the Gospels throughout the world. The light rays emanating from Christ's hands represent the instilling of the Holy Spirit in the apostles (Acts 2:1–42) at the Pentecost (the seventh Sunday after Easter). The apostles, holding the Gospel books, receive their spiritual assignment, to preach the Gospel to all nations. The Christ figure is a splendid essay in calligraphic theme and variation. The drapery lines shoot out in rays, break into quick zigzag rhythms, and spin into whorls, wonderfully conveying the spiritual light and energy that flow from Christ over and into the equally animated apostles. The overall composition, as well as the detailed treatment of the figures, contrasts with the much more sedate representation of the Second Coming (FIG. 6-19) at Moissac, where a grid of horizontal and vertical lines contains almost all the figures. The sharp differences between the two tympana highlight the regional diversity of Romanesque art.

The world's heathen peoples, the objects of the apostles' mission, appear on the lintel below and in eight compartments around the tympanum. The portrayals of the yet-to-be-converted constitute a medieval anthropological encyclopedia. Present are the legendary giant-eared Panotii of India, Pygmies (who require ladders to mount horses), and a host of other races, some characterized by a dog's head, others by a pig's snout, and still others by flaming hair. The assembly of agitated figures also includes hunchbacks, mutes, blind men, and lame men. Humanity, still suffering, awaits the salvation to come. As at Moissac and Autun, as worshipers entered the building, the tympanum established God's omnipotence and presented the Church as the road to salvation.

Crusades The Mission of the Apostles theme was an ideal choice for the Vézelay tympanum. Vézelay is more closely associated with the Crusades than any other church in Europe. The *Crusades* ("taking of the Cross") were mass armed pilgrimages, whose stated purpose was to wrest the Christian shrines of the Holy Land from Muslim control. Similar vows bound Crusaders and pilgrims. They hoped not only to atone for sins and win salvation but also to glorify God and extend the power of the Christian Church. Pope Urban II had intended to preach the launching of the First Crusade at Vézelay in 1095. In 1147, Bernard of Clairvaux called for the Second Crusade at Vézelay, and King Louis VII of France took up the cross there. In 1190, King Richard the Lionhearted of England and King Philip

Augustus of France set out from Vézelay on the Third Crusade. The spirit of the Crusades determined in part the iconography of the Vézelay tympanum. The Crusades were a kind of "second mission of the apostles" to convert the infidel.

Moralia in Job Unlike monumental stone sculpture, the art of painting did not need to be "revived" in the Romanesque period. Early medieval monasteries produced large numbers of illuminated manuscripts (FIGS. 6-3 to 6-6). One of the major Romanesque scriptoria was at the abbey of Cîteaux, mother church of the Cistercian order. Just before Bernard of Clairveaux joined the monastery in 1112, the monks completed work on an illuminated copy of Saint Gregory's (Pope Gregory the Great, r. 590–604) *Moralia in Job*. It is an example of Cistercian illumination before Bernard's passionate opposition to figural art in monasteries led

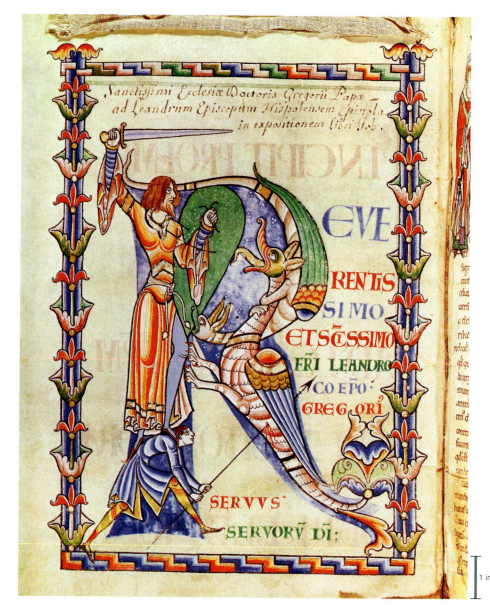

6-22 Initial *R* with knight fighting a dragon, folio 4 verso of the *Moralia in Job*, from Cîteaux, France, ca. 1115–1125. Ink and tempera on vellum, 1′ 1¾″ × 9¼″. Bibliothèque Municipale, Dijon.

Ornamented initials date to the Hiberno-Saxon era (FIG. 6-4), but this artist translated the theme into Romanesque terms. The duel between knight and dragons may symbolize monks' spiritual struggle.

in 1134 to a Cistercian ban on elaborate paintings in manuscripts. After 1134 the Cistercian order prohibited full-page illustrations, and even initial letters had to be nonfigurative and of a single color. The historiated initial reproduced here (FIG. 6-22) clearly would have been in violation of Bernard's ban had it not been painted before his prohibitions took effect. A knight, his squire, and two roaring dragons form an intricate letter *R*, the initial letter of the salutation *Reverentissimo*. This page is the opening of Gregory's letter to "the very reverent" Leander (ca. 534–600), bishop of Seville. The knight is a slender, regal figure who raises his shield and sword against the dragons while the squire, crouching beneath him, runs a lance through one of the monsters. Ornamented initials date to the Hiberno-Saxon period (FIG. 6-4), but in the *Moralia in Job* the artist translated the theme into Romanesque terms. The page may be a reliable picture of a medieval baron's costume. The typically French Romanesque banding of the torso and partitioning of the folds are evident, but the master painter deftly avoided stiffness and angularity. The partitioning actually accentuates the knight's verticality and elegance and the thrusting action of his squire. The flowing sleeves add a spirited flourish to the swordsman's gesture. The knight, handsomely garbed, cavalierly wears no armor and calmly aims a single stroke, unmoved by the ferocious dragons lunging at him. The duel between knight and dragons may be an allegory of the spiritual struggle of monks.

Holy Roman Empire and Italy

The Romanesque successors of the Ottonians were the Salians (r. 1027–1125), a dynasty of Franks of the Salian tribe. They ruled an empire that corresponds roughly to present-day Germany and the Lombard region of northern Italy (MAP 6-1). Like their predecessors, the Salian emperors were important patrons of art and architecture, although, as elsewhere in Romanesque Europe, the monasteries remained great centers of artistic production.

Hildegard of Bingen The most prominent nun of the 12th century and one of the greatest religious figures of the Middle Ages, Hildegard of Bingen (1098–1179), was born into an aristocratic family that owned large estates in the German Rhineland. At a very early age she began to have visions, and her parents had her study to become a nun. In 1141, God instructed Hildegard to disclose her visions to the world. Bernard of Clairvaux certified in 1147 that those visions were authentic. Archbishop Heinrich of Mainz joined him in endorsing Hildegard. In 1148 the Cistercian pope Eugenius III (r. 1145–1153) formally authorized Hildegard "in the name of Christ and Saint Peter to publish all that she had learned from the Holy Spirit." At this time Hildegard became the abbess of a new convent built for her near Bingen. As reports of Hildegard's visions spread, kings, popes, barons, and prelates sought her counsel.

One of the most interesting Romanesque books is Hildegard's *Scivias (Know the Ways [Scite vias] of God)*. On the opening page (FIG. 6-23), Hildegard sits within a monastery experiencing her divine vision. Five long tongues of fire emanating from above enter her brain, just as she describes the experience in the accompanying text. She immediately sets down what has been revealed to her on a wax tablet resting on her left knee. Nearby, the monk Volmar, Hildegard's confessor, copies into a book all she has written. Here, in a singularly dramatic context, is a picture of the essential nature of ancient and medieval book manufacture—individual scribes copying and recopying texts by hand.

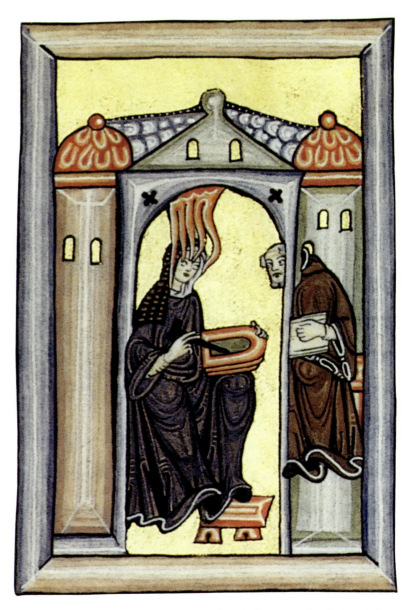

6-23 Hildegard receives her visions, detail of a facsimile of a lost folio in the Rupertsberger *Scivias* by Hildegard of Bingen, from Trier or Bingen, Germany, ca. 1180. Abbey of St. Hildegard, Rüdesheim/Eibingen.

Hildegard of Bingen was one of the great religious figures of the Middle Ages. Here, she experiences a divine vision, shown as five tongues of fire emanating from above and entering her brain.

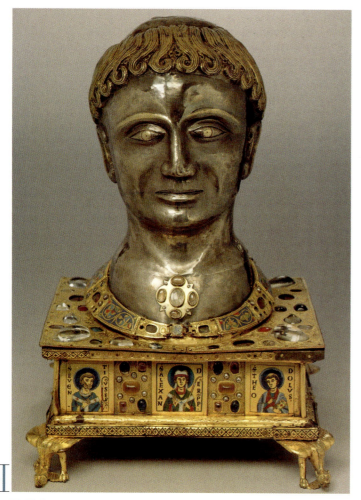

Reliquary of Saint Alexander As noted, Romanesque church officials competed with one another in the display of relics and often expended large sums on elaborate containers to house them. The *reliquary* of Saint Alexander (FIG. **6-24**), made in 1145 for Abbot Wibald of Stavelot in Belgium to house the relics of Pope Alexander II (r. 1061–1073), is one of the finest examples. The almost life-size idealized head, fashioned in beaten (*repoussé*) silver with bronze gilding for the hair, resembles portraits of youthful Roman emperors such as Augustus (FIG. **3-1**) and Constantine (FIG. **3-48**). The saint wears a collar of jewels and *enamel* plaques around his neck. Enamels and gems also adorn the box on which the head is mounted. The three plaques on the front depict Saints Eventius, Alexander, and Theodolus. The nine plaques on the other three sides represent female allegorical figures—Wisdom, Piety, and Humility among them. Although a local artist produced these enamels in the Meuse River region, the models were surely Byzantine. Saint Alexander's reliquary underscores the multiple sources of Romanesque art as well as its stylistic diversity. Not since antiquity had people journeyed as extensively as they did in the Romanesque period, and artists regularly saw works of wide geographic origin. Abbot Wibald himself epitomized the well-traveled 12th-century clergyman. He was abbot of Montecassino in southern Italy and participated in the Second Crusade. Frederick Barbarossa (Holy Roman Emperor, r. 1152–1190) sent Wibald to Constantinople to arrange Frederick's wedding to the niece of the Byzantine emperor Manuel Comnenus.

6-24 Head reliquary of Saint Alexander, from Stavelot Abbey, Belgium, 1145. Silver repoussé (partly gilt), gilt bronze, gems, pearls, and enamel, 1′ 5½″ high. Musées Royaux d'Art et d'Histoire, Brussels.

This reliquary is typical in the use of costly materials. The combination of an idealized classical head with Byzantine-style enamels underscores the stylistic diversity of Romanesque art.

Sant'Ambrogio, Milan Nowhere is the regional diversity of Romanesque art and architecture more readily apparent than in Italy, where developments in Lombardy parallel those elsewhere in the Holy Roman Empire, but in central Italy the Early Christian tradition remained very strong. The Lombard church of Sant'Ambrogio (FIG. **6-25**),

6-25 Interior of Sant'Ambrogio, Milan, Italy, late 11th to early 12th century.

The architect of this Milanese church was one of the first to use groin vaults in the nave as well as the aisles. Each nave bay corresponds to two aisle bays. The alternate-support system complements this modular plan.

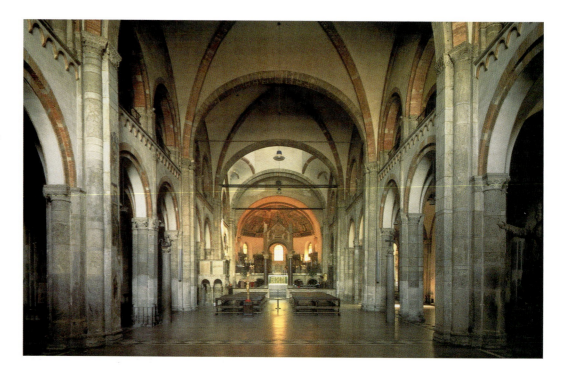

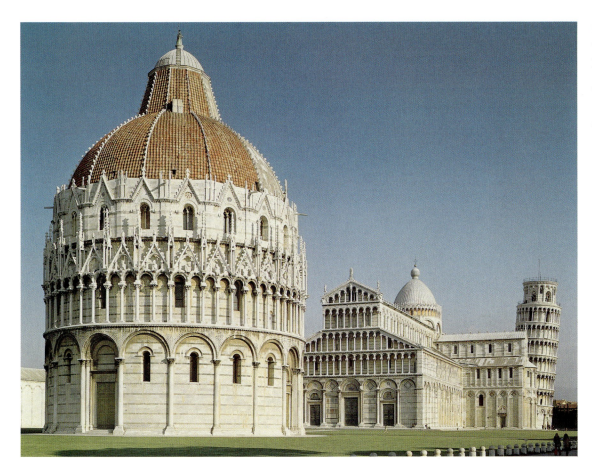

6-26 Cathedral complex, Pisa, Italy; cathedral begun 1063; baptistery begun 1153; campanile begun 1174.

Pisa's cathedral continues the tradition of the Early Christian basilica and is structurally less experimental than contemporaneous northern buildings, highlighting the regional diversity of Romanesque architecture.

erected in the late 11th or early 12th century in honor of Saint Ambrose, Milan's first bishop (d. 397), is an example of the experimentation with different kinds of vaulting that characterizes Romanesque architecture north of the Alps. Sant'Ambrogio has a nave and two aisles but no transept. Above each inner aisle is a tribune gallery. Each nave bay consists of a full square flanked by two small squares in each aisle, all covered with groin vaults. The technical problems of building groin vaults of cut stone (as opposed to concrete, knowledge of which did not survive the fall of Rome) at first limited their use to the covering of small areas, such as the individual bays of the aisles of Saint-Sernin (FIG. 6-15) at Toulouse. In Sant'Ambrogio the nave vaults are slightly domical, rising higher than the transverse arches. An octagonal dome covers the last bay, its windows providing the major light source (the building lacks a clerestory) for the otherwise rather dark interior. The emphatic alternate-support system perfectly reflects the plan's geometric regularity. The lightest pier moldings are interrupted at the gallery level, and the heavier ones rise to support the nave vaults. The compound piers even continue into the ponderous vaults, which have supporting arches, or *ribs*, along their groins. This is an early instance of rib vaulting, a salient characteristic of mature Romanesque and of later Gothic architecture (see "The Gothic Rib Vault," Chapter 7, page 189).

Pisa Although the widespread use of stone vaults in 11th- and 12th-century churches inspired the term "Romanesque," Italian Romanesque churches outside Lombardy usually retained the wooden roofs of their Early Christian predecessors. The cathedral complex (FIG. **6-26**) at Pisa dramatically testifies to the regional diversity of Romanesque architecture. The cathedral, its freestanding *campanile* (bell tower), and the *baptistery*, where infants and converts were initiated into the Christian community, present a rare opportunity to study a coherent group of three Romanesque buildings. Save for the upper portion of the baptistery, with its remodeled Gothic exterior, the three structures are stylistically homogeneous.

Construction of Pisa Cathedral began first—in 1063, the same year work began on Saint Mark's (FIG. 4-1) in Venice, another prosperous maritime city. The spoils of a naval victory over the Muslims off Palermo in Sicily in 1062 funded the Pisan project. Pisa Cathedral is large, with a nave and four aisles, and is one of the most impressive and majestic of all Romanesque churches. At first glance, the cathedral resembles an Early Christian basilica, but its broadly projecting transept, its crossing dome, and the facade's multiple arcade galleries distinguish the church as Romanesque. So too does the rich marble *incrustation* (wall decoration consisting of bright panels of different colors, as in the Pantheon's interior; FIG. 3-39). The cathedral's campanile is Pisa's famous Leaning Tower (FIG. 6-26, *right*). The tilted vertical axis of the bell tower is the result of a settling foundation. It began to "lean" even while under construction and now inclines some 15 perilous feet out of plumb at the top. Graceful arcaded galleries mark the tower's stages and repeat the cathedral's facade motif, effectively relating the round campanile to its mother building.

Normandy and England

After their conversion to Christianity in the early 10th century, the Vikings settled the northern French coast. Their territory came to be called Normandy—home of the Norsemen, or Normans. The Normans quickly developed a distinctive Romanesque architectural style that became the major source of French Gothic architecture.

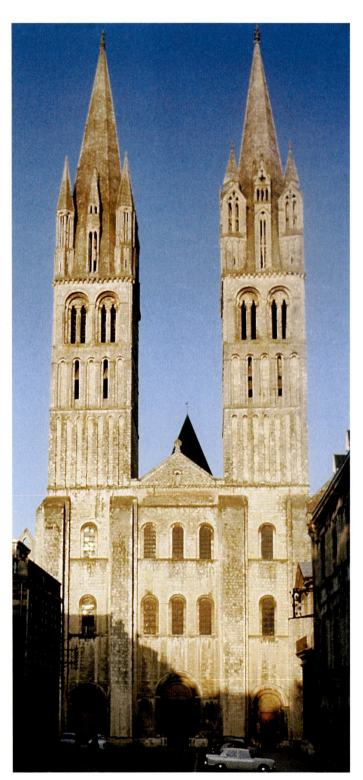

6-27 West facade of Saint-Étienne, Caen, France, begun 1067.

The division of Saint-Étienne's facade into three parts corresponding to the nave and aisles reflects the methodical planning of the entire church. The towers also have a tripartite design.

Saint-Étienne, Caen The abbey church of Saint-Étienne at Caen is the outstanding example of Norman Romanesque architecture. Begun by William of Normandy (William the Conqueror; see page 182) in 1067, work must have advanced rapidly, because he was buried there in 1087. Saint-Étienne's west facade (FIG. **6-27**) is a striking design rooted in the tradition of Carolingian and Ottonian westworks, but it reveals a new unified design. Four large buttresses divide the facade into three bays that correspond to the nave and aisles. Above the buttresses, the towers also display a triple division and a progressively greater piercing of their walls from lower to upper stages. (The culminating spires are a Gothic addition.) The tripartite division extends throughout the facade, both vertically and horizontally, organizing it into a close-knit, well-integrated design that reflects the careful and methodical planning of the entire structure.

The original design of Saint-Étienne called for a wooden roof, but the Caen nave (FIG. **6-28**) had compound piers

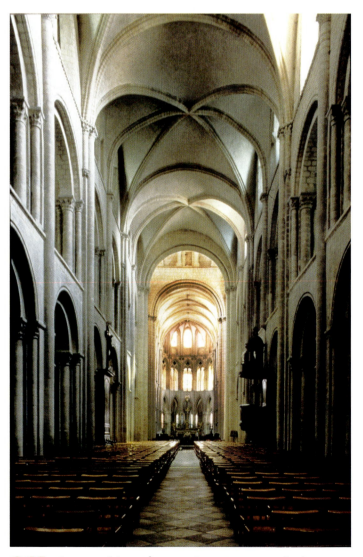

6-28 Interior of Saint-Étienne, Caen, France, vaulted ca. 1115–1120.

The six-part groin vaults of Saint-Étienne made possible an efficient clerestory. The three-story elevation with its large arched openings provides ample light and makes the nave appear taller than it is.

with simple engaged half-columns alternating with piers with half-columns attached to pilasters. When the builders decided to install groin vaults around 1115, the alternating nave piers proved a good match. Those piers soar all the way to the vaults' springing. Their branching ribs divide the large square-vault compartments into six sections, making a *sexpartite vault*. The vaults rise high enough to provide room for an efficient clerestory. The resulting three-story elevation, with its large arched openings, admits ample light to the interior. It also makes the nave appear even taller than it is. As in Sant'Ambrogio (FIG. 6-25), the Norman building has rib vaults. The diagonal and transverse ribs compose a structural skeleton that partially supports the still fairly massive paneling between them. Despite the heavy masonry, the large windows and reduced interior wall surface give Saint-Étienne's nave a light and airy quality.

Durham Cathedral William of Normandy's conquest of Anglo-Saxon England in 1066 began a new epoch in English history. In architecture, it signaled the importation of French Romanesque building and design methods. Construction of Durham Cathedral (FIG. **6-29**), on the Scottish frontier of northern England, began around 1093, in the generation following the Norman conquest. It predates the remodeled Caen church but was a vaulted structure from the very beginning. Consequently, the pattern of the ribs of the nave's groin vaults corresponds perfectly to the design of the arcade below. Each seven-part nave vault covers two bays. Large, simple pillars ornamented with abstract designs (diamond, chevron, and cable patterns, all originally painted) alternate with compound piers that carry the transverse arches of the vaults. The pier-vault relationship

scarcely could be more visible or the building's structural rationale better expressed.

The bold surface patterning of the Durham nave is a reminder that construction of imposing stone edifices such as the Romanesque churches of England and Normandy required more than just the talents of master designers. A corps of expert masons had to transform rough stone blocks into the precise shapes necessary for their specific place in the church's fabric. Although thousands of simple quadrangular blocks make up the great walls of these structures, the builders needed large numbers of blocks in much more complex shapes. To cover the nave and aisles, the stonecutters had to carve blocks with concave faces to conform to the curve of the vault. Also required were blocks with projecting moldings for the ribs, blocks with convex surfaces for the pillars or with multiple profiles for the compound piers, and so forth. It was an immense undertaking, and it is no wonder that medieval building campaigns often lasted for decades.

Durham Cathedral is the earliest example known of a ribbed groin vault placed over a three-story nave. And in the nave's western parts, completed before 1130, the rib vaults have slightly *pointed arches*, bringing together for the first time two of the key elements that determined the structural evolution of Gothic architecture. Also of great significance is the way the English builders buttressed the nave vaults. The lateral section (FIG. **6-29**, *right*) reveals that simple *quadrant arches* (arches whose curve extends for one-fourth of a circle's circumference) take the place of groin vaults. The structural descendants of these quadrant arches are the flying buttresses that epitomize the mature Gothic solution to church construction (see "The Gothic Cathedral," Chapter 7, page 193).

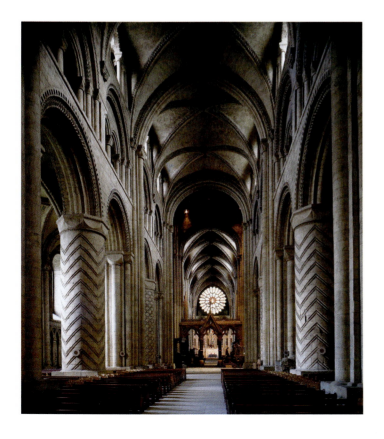

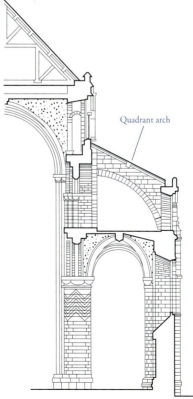

Quadrant arch

6-29 Interior (*left*) and lateral section (*right*) of Durham Cathedral, England, begun ca. 1093.

Durham Cathedral is the first example of a ribbed groin vault placed over a three-story nave. The architect used quadrant arches in place of groin vaults in the tribune to buttress the nave vaults.

Bayeux Tapestry Many of the finest illustrated manuscripts of the Romanesque age were the work of monks in English scriptoria, following in the tradition of Hiberno-Saxon book production. But the most famous work of English Romanesque art is neither a book nor Christian in subject. The so-called *Bayeux Tapestry* (FIG. 6-30) is unique in medieval art. It is not a woven *tapestry* but rather an *embroidery* made of wool sewn on linen. Closely related to Romanesque manuscript illumination, its borders contain the kinds of real and imaginary animals found in contemporaneous books, and an explanatory Latin text sewn in thread accompanies many of the pictures.

Some 20 inches high and about 230 feet long, the *Bayeux Tapestry* is a continuous, friezelike, pictorial narrative of a crucial moment in England's history and of the events that led up to it. The Norman defeat of the Anglo-Saxons at Hastings in 1066 brought England under the control of the Normans, uniting all of England and much of France under one rule. The dukes of Normandy became the kings of England. Commissioned by Bishop Odo, the half brother of the conquering Duke William, the embroidery may have been sewn by women at the Norman court. Many art historians, however, believe it was the work of English stitchers in Kent, where Odo was earl after the Norman conquest. Odo donated the work to Bayeux Cathedral (hence its nickname), but it is uncertain whether it was originally intended for display in the church's nave, where the theme would have been a curious choice.

The circumstances leading to the Norman invasion of England are well documented. In 1066, Edward the Confessor, the Anglo-Saxon king of England, died. The Normans believed Edward had recognized William of Normandy as his rightful heir. But the crown went to Harold, earl of Wessex, the king's Anglo-Saxon brother-in-law, who had sworn an oath of allegiance to William. The betrayed Normans, descendants of the seafaring Vikings, boarded their

6-30 Funeral procession to Westminster Abbey (*top*) and Battle of Hastings (*bottom*), details of the *Bayeux Tapestry*, from Bayeux Cathedral, Bayeux, France, ca. 1070–1080. Embroidered wool on linen, 1' 8" high (entire embroidery 229' 8" long). Centre Guillaume le Conquérant, Bayeux.

The *Bayeux Tapestry* is unique in Romanesque art. Like the historical narratives of ancient Roman art, it depicts a contemporaneous event in full detail, as in the scroll-like frieze of Trajan's Column (FIG. 3-35).

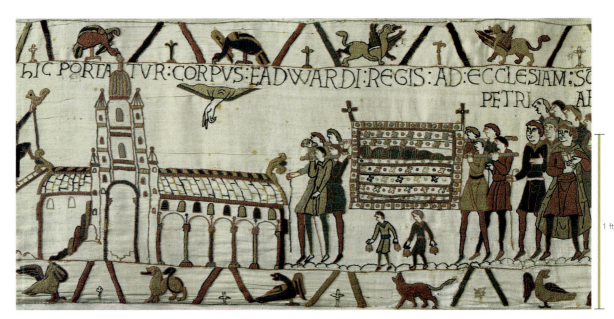

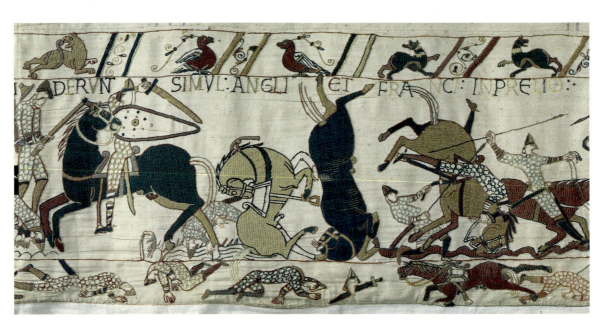

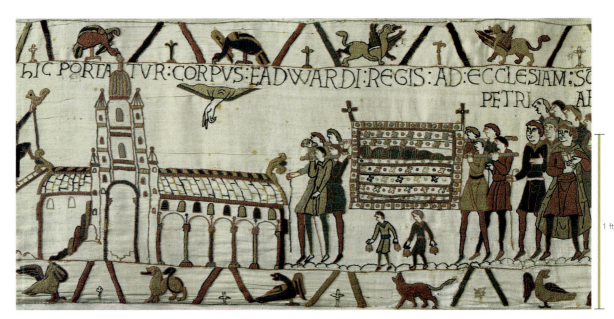1 ft.

ships, crossed the English Channel, and crushed Harold's forces.

Illustrated here are two episodes of the epic tale as represented in the *Bayeux Tapestry*. The first detail (FIG. **6-30**, *top*) depicts King Edward's funeral procession. The hand of God points the way to the church where he was buried—Westminster Abbey, consecrated on December 28, 1065, just a few days before Edward's death. The church was one of the first Romanesque buildings erected in England, and the embroiderers took pains to record its main features, including the imposing crossing tower and the long nave with tribunes. Here William was crowned king of England on Christmas Day, 1066. The second detail (FIG. **6-30**, *bottom*) shows the Battle of Hastings in progress. The Norman cavalry cuts down the English defenders. The lower border is filled with the dead and wounded, although the upper register continues the animal motifs of the rest of the embroidery. The Romanesque artist co-opted some of the characteristic motifs of Greco-Roman battle scenes, for example, the horses with twisted necks and contorted bodies (compare FIG. **2-50**). But the artists rendered the figures in the Romanesque manner. Linear patterning and flat color replaced classical three-dimensional volume and modeling in light and dark hues.

The *Bayeux Tapestry* stands apart from all other Romanesque artworks in that it depicts an event in full detail at a time shortly after it occurred, recalling the historical narratives of ancient Roman art. Art historians have often likened the Norman embroidery to the scroll-like frieze of the Column of Trajan (FIG. **3-35**). Like the Roman account, the story told on the *Bayeux Tapestry* is the conqueror's version of history, a proclamation of national pride, and is not confined to battlefield successes. It is a complete chronicle of events. Included are the preparations for war, with scenes depicting the felling and splitting of trees for ship construction, the loading of equipment onto the vessels, the cooking and serving of meals, and so forth. In this respect, the *Bayeux Tapestry* is the most *Roman*-esque work of Romanesque art.

Bury Bible Produced at the Bury Saint Edmunds abbey in England around 1135, the *Bury Bible* exemplifies the lavish illustration common to the large Bibles used in wealthy Romanesque abbeys not subject to the Cistercian ban on luxurious books. The frontispiece (FIG. **6-31**) to the book of Deuteronomy shows two scenes framed by symmetrical leaf motifs in softly glowing harmonized colors. The upper register depicts Moses and Aaron proclaiming the law to the Israelites. Moses has horns, consistent with Saint Jerome's translation of the Hebrew word that also means "rays." The lower panel portrays Moses pointing out the clean and un-

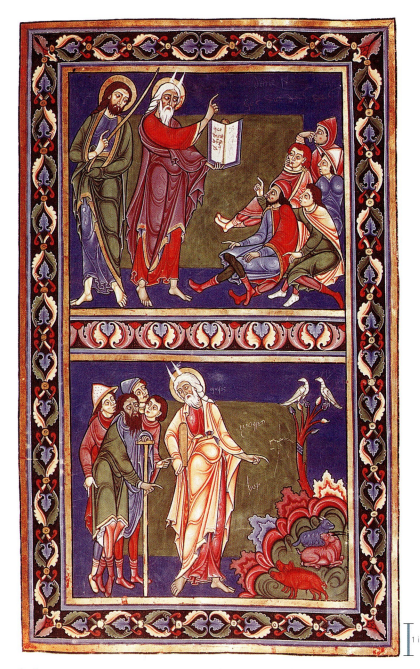

6-31 MASTER HUGO, *Moses expounding the Law*, folio 94 recto of the *Bury Bible*, from Bury Saint Edmunds, England, ca. 1135. Ink and tempera on vellum, 1′ 8″ × 1′ 2″. Corpus Christi College, Cambridge.

Master Hugo apparently was a rare Romanesque lay artist, one of the emerging class of professional artists and artisans who depended for their livelihood on commissions from well-endowed monasteries.

clean beasts. The gestures are slow and gentle and have quiet dignity. The figures of Moses and Aaron seem to glide. This presentation is quite different from the abrupt emphasis and spastic movement of contemporaneous Romanesque relief sculptures. Yet the patterning remains in the multiple divisions of the draped limbs, the lightly shaded volumes connected with sinuous lines and ladderlike folds.

The artist responsible for the *Bury Bible* is known: MASTER HUGO, who was also a sculptor and metalworker. With Gislebertus (FIG. **6-20**), Hugo is one of the small but growing number of Romanesque artists who signed their works or whose names were recorded. In the 12th century, artists—illuminators as well as sculptors—increasingly began to identify themselves. Although most medieval artists remained anonymous, the contrast of the Romanesque period with the early Middle Ages is striking. Hugo apparently was a secular artist, one of the emerging class of professional artists and artisans who depended for their livelihood on commissions from well-endowed monasteries. These artists resided in towns rather than within secluded abbey walls, and they traveled frequently to find work. They were the exception, however, and the typical Romanesque scribes and illuminators continued to be monks and nuns working anonymously in the service of God.

Eadwine Psalter Named for the English monk EADWINE THE SCRIBE, the *Eadwine Psalter* (*psalters* are separate books containing the 150 psalms of King David) contains 166 illustrations. The last page (FIG. 6-32), however, presents a rare picture of a Romanesque artist at work. The style of the Eadwine portrait is related to that of the *Bury Bible*, but, although the patterning is still firm (notably in the cowl and the thigh), the drapery falls more softly and follows the movements of the body beneath it. Here, the arbitrariness of many Romanesque painted and sculpted garments yielded slightly, but clearly, to the requirements of more naturalistic representation. The Romanesque artist's instinct for decorating the surface remained, as is apparent in the gown's whorls and spirals. But, significantly, the artist painted those interior lines very lightly to avoid conflict with the functional lines that contain them.

The "portrait" of Eadwine—it is probably a generic type and not a specific likeness—is in the long tradition of author portraits in ancient and medieval manuscripts, although the true author of the *Eadwine Psalter* is King David. Eadwine exaggerated his importance by likening his image to that of an evangelist writing his gospel (FIGS. 6-5 and 6-6) and by including an inscription within the inner frame that identifies him and proclaims him a "prince among scribes." He declares that due to the excellence of his work, his fame will endure forever and that he can offer his book as an acceptable gift to God. Eadwine, like

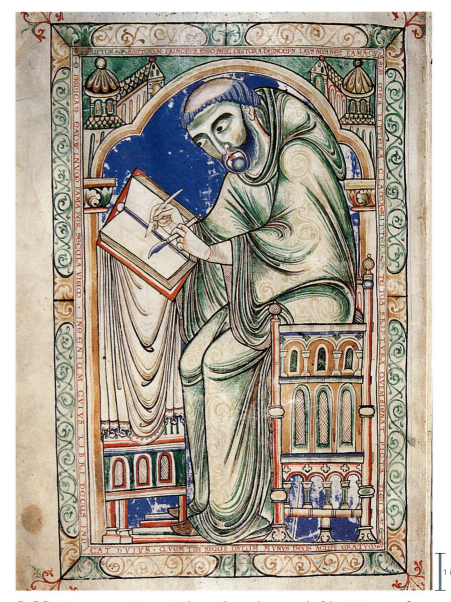

1 in.

6-32 EADWINE THE SCRIBE, Eadwine the scribe at work, folio 283 verso of the *Eadwine Psalter*, ca. 1160–1170. Ink and tempera on vellum. Trinity College, Cambridge.

Although he humbly offered his book as a gift to God, the English monk Eadwine added an inscription to his portrait declaring himself a "prince among scribes" whose fame would endure forever.

other Romanesque sculptors and painters who signed their works, may have been concerned for his fame, but these artists, whether monks or laity, were not yet aware of the concepts of fine art and fine artist. To them, their work existed not for its own sake but for God's. Nonetheless, works such as this one are an early sign of a new attitude toward the role of the artist in society that presages the emergence of the notion of individual artistic genius in the Renaissance.

Early Medieval and Romanesque Europe

EARLY MEDIEVAL ART

▌ The surviving art of the period following the fall of Rome in 410 consists almost exclusively of small-scale status symbols, especially portable items of personal adornment featuring cloisonné ornamentation. The decoration of these objects displays a variety of abstract and zoomorphic motifs. Especially characteristic are intertwined animal and interlace patterns.

▌ The Christian art of the early medieval British Isles is called Hiberno-Saxon. The most important extant artworks are the illuminated manuscripts produced in the monastic scriptoria of Ireland and Northumbria. The most distinctive features of these books are the full pages devoted neither to text nor to illustration but to pure embellishment. Some text pages feature enlarged initial letters of important passages transformed into elaborate decorative patterns.

▌ In 800, Pope Leo III crowned Charlemagne, king of the Franks since 768, emperor of Rome (r. 800–814). Charlemagne reunited much of western Europe and initiated a conscious revival of the art and culture of Early Christian Rome during the Carolingian period (768–877). Carolingian illuminators merged the illusionism of classical painting with the northern linear tradition. Carolingian sculptors revived the Early Christian tradition of depicting Christ as a statuesque youth. Carolingian architects looked to Ravenna and Early Christian Rome for models but transformed their sources, introducing, for example, the twin-tower western facade for basilicas and employing strict modular plans in their buildings.

▌ In the 10th century, a new line of emperors, the Ottonians (r. 919–1024), consolidated the eastern part of Charlemagne's former empire and sought to preserve and enrich the culture and tradition of the Carolingian period. Ottonian architects built basilican churches with the towering spires and imposing westworks of their Carolingian models but introduced the alternate-support system into the interior elevation of the nave. Ottonian sculptors also began to revive the art of monumental sculpture in works such as the Gero crucifix and the colossal bronze doors of Saint Michael's at Hildesheim.

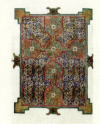

Lindisfarne Gospels, ca. 698–721

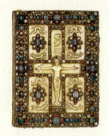

Lindau Gospels, ca. 870

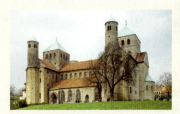

Saint Michael's, Hildesheim, 1001–1031

ROMANESQUE ART

▌ *Romanesque* takes its name from the Roman-like barrel and groin vaults based on round arches employed in many European churches built between 1050 and 1200. Romanesque vaults, however, were made of stone, not concrete. Numerous churches sprang up along the French pilgrimage roads leading to the shrine of Saint James at Santiago de Compostela in Spain. These churches were large enough to accommodate crowds of pilgrims who came to view the relics displayed in radiating chapels off the ambulatory and transept. Elsewhere, especially in the Holy Roman Empire and in Normandy and England, innovative architects began to use groin vaults in naves and introduced the three-story elevation of nave arcade, tribune, and clerestory.

▌ The Romanesque period also brought the revival of monumental stone relief sculpture, especially on church facades, where scenes of Christ as Last Judge often greeted the faithful as they entered the doorway to salvation. The sculptor Gislebertus was one of a growing number of Romanesque artists who signed their works.

▌ The names of some Romanesque manuscript painters are also known, including Master Hugo, a rare instance of a professional lay artist during the early Middle Ages.

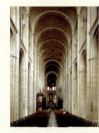

Saint-Sernin, Toulouse, ca. 1070–1120

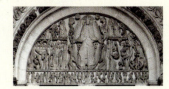

Gislebertus, Last Judgment, Autun, ca. 1120–1135

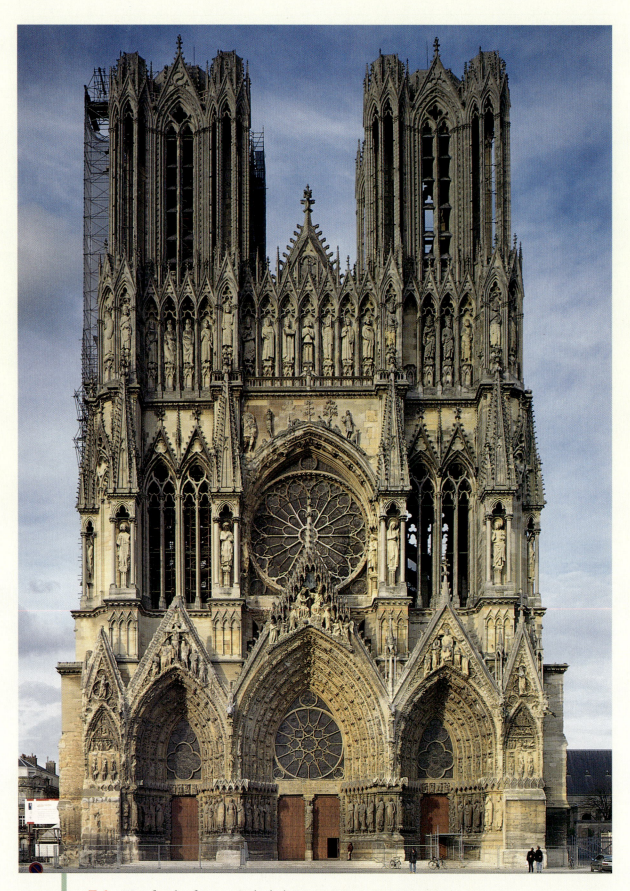

7-1 West facade of Reims Cathedral, Reims, France, ca. 1225–1290.

The facade of Reims Cathedral exemplifies French High Gothic architects' desire to reduce sheer mass and replace it with intricately framed voids. Stained-glass windows, not stone sculpture, fill the tympana.

Gothic Europe

The 12th through 14th centuries were a time of profound change in European society. The focus of both intellectual and religious life shifted definitively from pilgrimage churches and monasteries in the countryside to rapidly expanding secular cities with enormous cathedrals reaching to the sky. In these new urban centers, prosperous merchants made their homes, and *guilds* (professional associations) of scholars founded the first universities. Modern Europe's independent secular nations began to take shape (MAP **7-1**).

To describe the art and architecture of this pivotal period, Giorgio Vasari (1511–1574), the Italian artist and biographer known as "the father of art history," used the term *Gothic*. Vasari chose the term to ridicule what he considered the "monstrous and barbarous" art of the uncouth Goths whom he believed were responsible for both Rome's downfall and the destruction of the classical style in art and architecture.[1] Italian Renaissance artists and scholars regarded Gothic art with contempt and considered it ugly and crude. In the 13th and 14th centuries, however, when the Gothic style was the rage in most of Europe, especially north of the Alps, contemporaries referred to Gothic architecture as *opus modernum* (Latin, "modern work") or *opus francigenum* ("French work"). They recognized that Gothic buildings displayed an exciting new style—and that the style originated in France. For them, Gothic cathedrals were not distortions of the classical style but images of the City of God, the Heavenly Jerusalem.

Although the Gothic style achieved international acclaim, it was a regional phenomenon. To the east and south of Europe, the Islamic and Byzantine styles still prevailed. And many regional variants existed within European Gothic, just as distinct regional styles characterized the Romanesque period. Gothic began and ended at different dates in different places, but it first appeared in northern France in the mid-12th century.

FRANCE

About 1130, King Louis VI (r. 1108–1137) moved his official residence to Paris, spurring much commercial activity and a great building boom. Paris soon became the leading city of France, indeed of northern Europe. Although Rome remained the religious center of western Christendom, Paris became its intellectual capital. The University of Paris attracted the best minds from all over Europe. Virtually every thinker of note in the Gothic world at some point studied or taught at the Parisian university. Even in the Romanesque period, Paris was a learning center. Its Cathedral School professors, known as Schoolmen, developed the philosophy

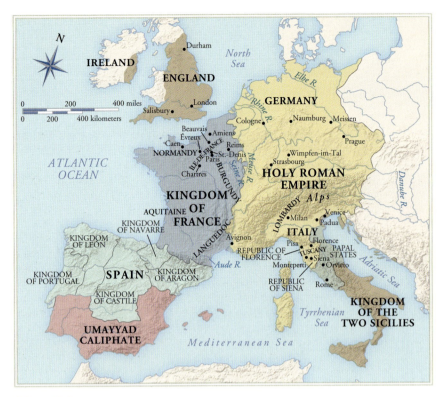

MAP 7-1 Europe around 1200.

called *Scholasticism*. Until the 12th century, both clergy and lay individuals considered truth the exclusive property of divine revelation as given in the Holy Scriptures. But the Schoolmen sought to demonstrate that reason alone could lead to certain truths. Their goal was to prove the central

articles of Christian faith by argument *(disputatio)*. By the 13th century, the Schoolmen of Paris already had organized as a professional guild of master scholars, separate from the numerous Church schools the bishop of Paris oversaw. The structure of the Parisian guild served as the model for many other European universities.

Architecture and Architectural Decoration

The earliest manifestations of the Gothic spirit in art and architecture appeared concurrently with the first stages of Scholastic philosophy. Both originated in Paris and its environs. Many art historians have noted the parallels between them—how the logical thrust and counterthrust of Gothic construction, the geometric relationships of building parts, and the systematic organization of the iconographical programs of Gothic church portals coincide with Scholastic principles and methods. No documents exist, however, linking the scholars, builders, and sculptors.

Suger and Saint-Denis On June 11, 1144, King Louis VII of France (r. 1137–1180), Queen Eleanor of Aquitaine, and an entourage of court members, together with five French archbishops and other distinguished clergy, converged on the Benedictine abbey church of Saint-Denis for the dedication of its new east end (FIGS. 7-2 and 7-3). The

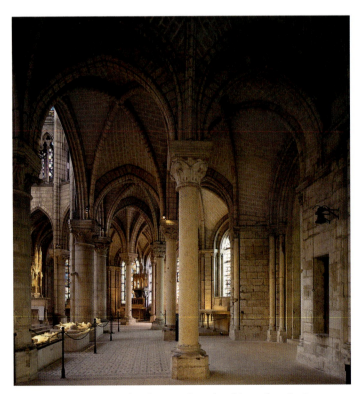

7-2 Ambulatory and radiating chapels, abbey church, Saint-Denis, France, 1140–1144.

The remodeling of the east end of Saint-Denis marked the beginning of Gothic architecture. Rib vaults with pointed arches spring from slender columns. The radiating chapels have stained-glass windows.

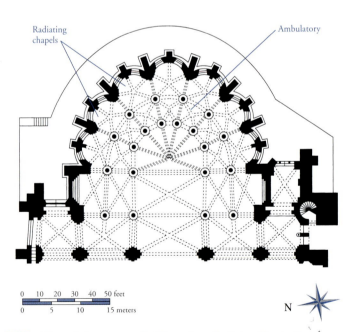

7-3 Plan of the east end, abbey church, Saint-Denis, France, 1140–1144 (after Sumner Crosby).

The innovative plan of the east end of Saint-Denis dates to Abbot Suger's lifetime. By using lightweight rib vaults, the builders were able to eliminate the walls between the radiating chapels.

The Gothic Rib Vault

The ancestors of the Gothic *rib vault* are the Romanesque vaults found at Caen (FIG. 6-28), Durham (FIG. 6-29), and elsewhere. The rib vault's distinguishing feature is the crossed, or diagonal, *ribs* (arches) under its groins, as seen in the Saint-Denis ambulatory and chapels (FIG. 7-2). The ribs form the *armature*, or skeletal framework, for constructing the vault. Gothic vaults generally have more thinly vaulted *webs* (the masonry between the ribs) than found in Romanesque vaults. But the chief difference between the two styles of rib vaults is the *pointed arch*, an integral part of the Gothic skeletal armature. French Romanesque architects (FIG. 6-19) borrowed the form from Muslim Spain and passed it to their Gothic successors. Pointed arches allowed Gothic builders to make the crowns of all the vault's arches approximately the same level, regardless of the space to be vaulted. The Romanesque architects could not achieve this with their semicircular arches.

The drawings in FIG. 7-4 illustrate this key difference. In FIG. 7-4a, the rectangle *ABCD* is an oblong nave bay to be vaulted. *AC* and *BD* are the diagonal ribs; *AB* and *CD*, the transverse arches; and *AD* and *BC*, the nave arcade's arches. If the architect uses semicircular arches (*AFB, BJC,* and *DHC*), their radii and, therefore, their heights (*EF, IJ,* and *GH*) will be different, because the width of a semicircular arch determines its height. The result will be a vault (FIG. 7-4b) with higher transverse arches (*DHC*) than the arcade's arches (*CJB*). The vault's crown (*F*) will be still higher. If the builder uses pointed arches, the transverse (*DLC*) and arcade (*BKC*) arches can have the same heights (*GL* and *IK* in FIG. 7-4a). The result will be a Gothic rib vault (FIG. 7-4c), where the points of the arches (*L* and *K*) are at the same level as the vault's crown (*F*).

A major advantage of the Gothic vault is its flexibility, which permits the vaulting of compartments of varying shapes, as at Saint-Denis (FIG. 7-3). Pointed arches also channel the weight of the vaults more directly downward than do semicircular arches. The vaults therefore require less buttressing to hold them in place, in turn permitting builders to open up the walls and insert large windows beneath the arches. Because pointed arches also lead the eye upward, they make the vaults appear taller than they are. In FIG. 7-4, the crown (*F*) of both the Romanesque (b) and Gothic (c) vaults is the same height from the pavement, but the Gothic vault seems taller. Both the physical and visual properties of rib vaults with pointed arches aided Gothic builders in their quest for soaring height in church interiors.

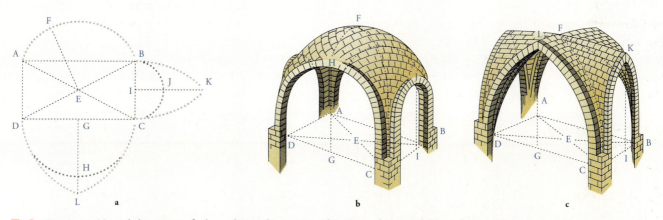

7-4 Diagram (a) and drawings of rib vaults with semicircular (b) and pointed (c) arches.

Pointed arches channel the weight of the rib vaults more directly downward than do semicircular arches, requiring less buttressing. Pointed arches also make the vaults appear taller than they are.

church, a few miles north of Paris, had been erected centuries before in honor of Saint Dionysius, the apostle who brought Christianity to Gaul. It housed the saint's tomb and those of almost all the French kings. The basilica was France's royal church, the very symbol of the monarchy. By the early 12th century, however, the Carolingian building was in disrepair and had become too small to accommodate the growing number of pilgrims. Its abbot, Suger, also believed it was of insufficient grandeur to serve as the official church of the French kings. He began to rebuild Saint-Denis in 1135 by erecting a new west facade with sculptured portals. In 1140 work began on the east end. Suger died before he could remodel the nave, but he attended the 1144 dedication of the new choir, ambulatory, and radiating chapels.

The mid-12th-century portion of Saint-Denis represented a sharp break from past practice. Innovative rib vaults resting on pointed, or *ogival*, arches (see "The Gothic Rib Vault," above, and FIG. 7-4c) cover the ambulatory and chapels (FIG. 7-2). These pioneering, exceptionally lightweight vaults spring from slender columns in the ambulatory and from the thin masonry walls framing the chapels. The lightness of the vaults enabled the builders to eliminate the walls between the chapels and open up the outer walls and fill them with stained-glass windows (see "Stained-Glass Windows," page 195). Suger and his contemporaries marveled at the "wonderful and uninterrupted light" that poured in through these "most sacred windows."[2] The abbot called the colored light *lux nova*, "new light." The polychrome rays

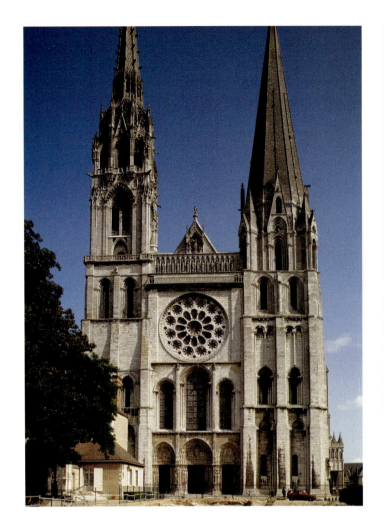

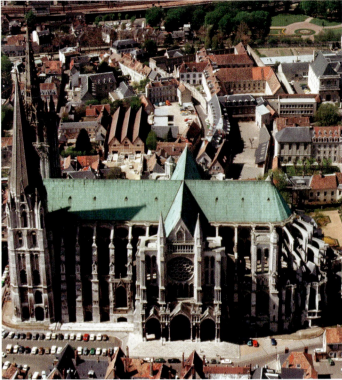

7-5 West facade (*left*) and aerial view looking north (*right*) of Chartres Cathedral, Chartres, France, begun 1134; rebuilt after 1194.

The Early Gothic west facade was all that remained of Chartres Cathedral after the fire of 1194. Architectural historians consider the rebuilt church the first great monument of High Gothic architecture.

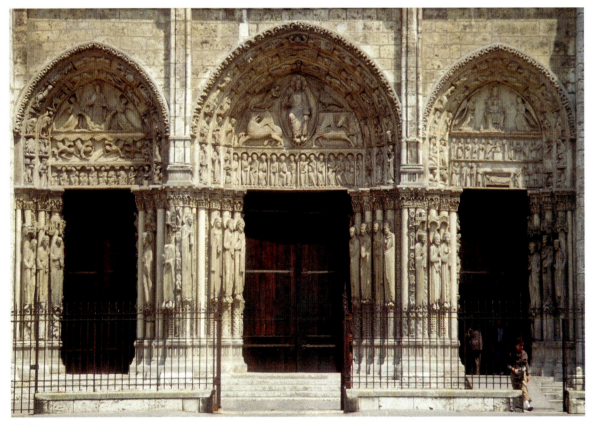

7-6 Royal Portal, west facade, Chartres Cathedral, Chartres, France, ca. 1145–1155.

The sculptures of the Royal Portal proclaim the majesty and power of Christ. The tympana depict, from left to right, Christ's Ascension, the Second Coming, and Jesus in the lap of the Virgin Mary.

coming through the windows shone on the walls and columns, almost dissolving them. The light-filled space made Suger feel as if he were "dwelling . . . in some strange region of the universe which neither exists entirely in the slime of the earth nor entirely in the purity of Heaven." In Suger's eyes, his splendid new church was a way station on the road to Paradise, which "transported [him] from this inferior to that higher world."[3]

Royal Portal, Chartres Suger's stained-glass windows and the new type of vaulting employed at Saint-Denis quickly became hallmarks of French Gothic architecture. Saint-Denis is also the key monument of Early Gothic sculpture. Little of the sculpture that Suger commissioned for the west facade of the abbey church survived the French Revolution of the late 18th century, but in the mid-12th century, statues of Old Testament kings, queens, and prophets attached to columns screened the jambs of all three doorways. This innovative design appeared immediately afterward at Chartres Cathedral (FIG. **7-5**)—Notre-Dame (the shrine of "Our Lady," that is, the Virgin Mary)—also in the Île-de-France, the region centered on Paris. Work on the west facade began around 1145. Called the "Royal Portal" because of the statue-columns of kings and queens flanking its three doorways (FIGS. **7-5**, *left*, and **7-6**), the west entrance and its towers are almost all that remain of the church begun in 1134 and destroyed by fire in 1194 before it had been completed.

The sculptures of the Royal Portal proclaim the majesty and power of Christ. Christ's Ascension into Heaven appears in the tympanum of the left doorway. The Second Coming is the subject of the center tympanum. The theme—in essence, the Last Judgment—was still of central importance, as it was in Romanesque portals. But at Early Gothic Chartres, the Second Coming promised salvation rather than damnation to those entering the church. In the tympanum of the right portal, Christ appears in the lap of the Virgin Mary. Mary's prominence on the Chartres facade has no parallel in the decoration of Romanesque church portals. At Chartres the designers gave her a central role in the sculptural program, a position she maintained throughout the Gothic period. As the Mother of Christ, Mary stood compassionately between the Last Judge and the horrors of Hell, interceding for all her faithful. Worshipers in the later 12th and 13th centuries sang hymns to Notre Dame, put her image everywhere, and dedicated great cathedrals to her. Soldiers carried the Virgin's image into battle on banners, and her name joined Saint Denis's as part of the French king's battle cry. She became the spiritual lady of chivalry, and the Christian knight dedicated his life to her. The severity of Romanesque themes stressing the Last Judgment yielded to the gentleness of Gothic art, in which Mary is the kindly Queen of Heaven.

Statues of Old Testament kings and queens decorate the jambs flanking each doorway of the Royal Portal (FIGS. **7-6** and **7-7**). They are the royal ancestors of Christ and, both figuratively and literally, support the New Testament figures above the doorways. They wear 12th-century clothes, and

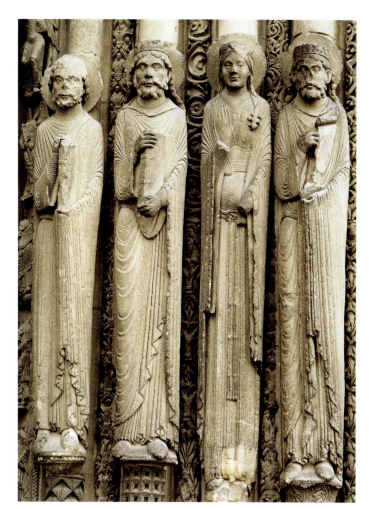

7-7 Old Testament kings and queen, jamb statues, central doorway of Royal Portal, Chartres Cathedral, Chartres, France, ca. 1145–1155.

The biblical kings and queens of the Royal Portal are the royal ancestors of Christ. These Early Gothic statue-columns display the first signs of a new naturalism in European sculpture.

medieval observers also regarded them as images of the kings and queens of France. (This was the motivation for vandalizing the comparable figures at Saint-Denis during the French Revolution.) The figures stand rigidly upright with their elbows held close against their hips. The linear folds of their garments—inherited from the Romanesque style, along with the elongated proportions—generally echo the vertical lines of the columns behind them. (In this respect, Gothic jamb statues differ significantly from classical caryatids; FIGS. **2-42**. The Gothic figures are *attached* to columns. The classical statues *replaced* columns.) And yet, within and despite this architectural straitjacket, the statues display the first signs of a new naturalism. The sculptors conceived and treated the statues as three-dimensional volumes, not reliefs, and they stand out from the plane of the wall. The new naturalism—enhanced by painting, as was the norm for medieval stone sculpture—is noticeable particularly in the statues' heads, where kindly human faces replace the masklike features of most Romanesque figures. The sculptors of the Royal Portal statues initiated an era of artistic concern with personality and individuality.

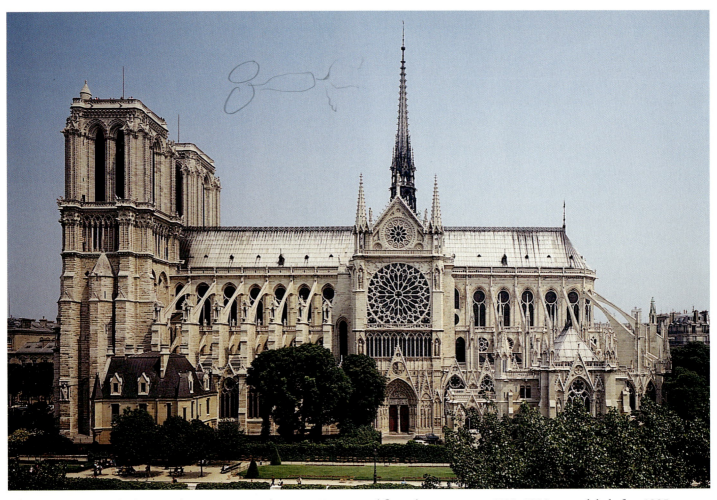

7-8 Notre-Dame (looking north), Paris, France, begun 1163; nave and flying buttresses, ca. 1180–1200; remodeled after 1225.

Architects first used flying buttresses on a grand scale at the Cathedral of Notre-Dame in Paris. The buttresses countered the outward thrust of the nave vaults and held up the towering nave walls.

Notre-Dame, Paris The rapid urbanization of Paris under Louis VI and his successors and the accompanying increase in population made a new cathedral a necessity. Notre-Dame (FIG. **7-8**) occupies a picturesque site on an island in the Seine River called the Île-de-la-Cité. The Gothic church replaced an earlier basilica and has a complicated building history. The choir and transept were completed by 1182, the nave by around 1225, and the facade not until about 1250–1260. The original nave elevation had four stories, with stained-glass *oculi* (singular *oculus*, a small round window) inserted between the vaulted tribune and clerestory typical of Norman Romanesque churches like Saint-Étienne (FIG. **6-28**) at Caen. As a result, windows fill two of the four stories, significantly reducing the masonry area. (This four-story nave elevation can be seen in only one bay in FIG. **7-8**, immediately to the right of the south transept and partially hidden by it.)

To hold the much thinner—and taller—walls of Notre-Dame in place, the unknown architect introduced *flying buttresses*, exterior arches that spring from the lower roofs over the aisles and ambulatory (FIG. **7-8**) and counter the outward thrust of the nave vaults. Gothic builders employed flying buttresses as early as 1150 in a few smaller churches, but at Notre-Dame in Paris they circle a great urban cathedral. The internal quadrant arches (FIG. **6-29**, *right*) beneath the aisle roofs at Durham Cathedral perform a similar function and are forerunners of exposed Gothic flying buttresses. The combination of precisely positioned flying buttresses and rib vaults with pointed arches was the ideal solution to the problem of constructing towering naves with huge windows. The flying buttresses, like slender extended fingers holding up the walls, are key components of the distinctive "look" of Gothic cathedrals (see "The Gothic Cathedral," page 193, and FIG. **7-9**).

Chartres after 1194 Churches burned frequently in the Middle Ages, and church officials often had to raise money suddenly for new building campaigns. In contrast to monastic churches, which usually were small and completed rather quickly, the building histories of urban cathedrals often extended over decades and sometimes over centuries. The rebuilding of Chartres Cathedral after the devastating fire of 1194 took a relatively short 27 years. Most architectural historians consider the post-1194 Chartres Cathedral

The Gothic Cathedral

Most of the architectural components of Gothic cathedrals appeared in earlier structures, but the way Gothic architects combined these elements made these later buildings unique expressions of medieval faith. The key ingredients of the Gothic "recipe" were rib vaults with pointed arches, flying buttresses, and huge windows of colored glass (see "Stained-Glass Windows," page 195). The cutaway view (FIG. 7-9) of a typical Gothic cathedral illustrates how these and other important architectural devices worked together.

- *Pinnacle:* A sharply pointed ornament capping the piers or flying buttresses; also used on cathedral facades.

- *Flying buttresses:* Masonry struts that transfer the thrust of the nave vaults across the roofs of the side aisles and ambulatory to a tall pier rising above the church's exterior wall. (Compare FIG. I-13, *right.*)

- *Vaulting web:* The masonry blocks that fill the area between the ribs of a groin vault.

- *Diagonal rib:* In plan, one of the ribs that form the X of a groin vault. In FIG. 7-4, the diagonal ribs are the lines *AC* and *BD*.

- *Transverse rib:* A rib that crosses the nave or aisle at a 90-degree angle (lines *AB* and *CD* in FIG. 7-4).

- *Springing:* The lowest stone of an arch; in Gothic vaulting, the lowest stone of a diagonal or transverse rib.

- *Clerestory:* The windows below the vaults that form the nave elevation's uppermost level. By using flying buttresses and rib vaults on pointed arches, Gothic architects could build huge clerestory windows and fill them with *stained glass* held in place by ornamental stonework called *tracery.*

- *Oculus:* A small round window.

- *Lancet:* A tall, narrow window crowned by a pointed arch.

- *Triforium:* The story in the nave elevation consisting of arcades, usually *blind* (FIG. 7-10) but occasionally filled with stained glass (FIGS. I-2 and 7-23).

- *Nave arcade:* The series of arches supported by piers separating the nave from the side aisles.

- *Compound pier with shafts (responds):* Also called the *cluster pier,* a pier with a group, or cluster, of attached shafts, or *responds,* extending to the springing of the vaults.

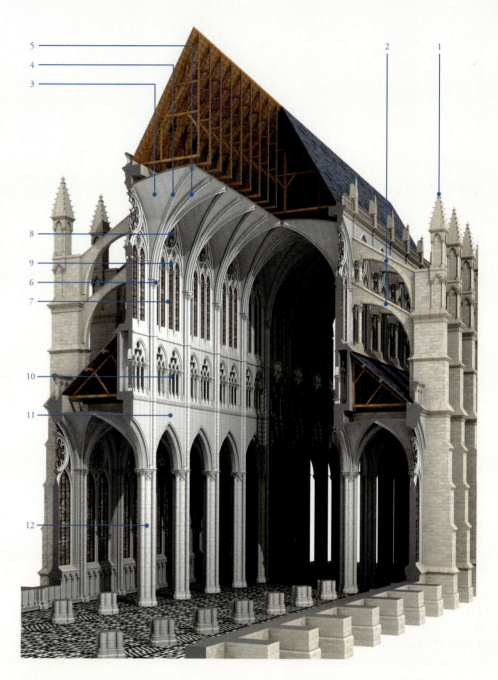

7-9 Cutaway view of a typical French Gothic cathedral (John Burge). (1) pinnacle, (2) flying buttress, (3) vaulting web, (4) diagonal rib, (5) transverse rib, (6) springing, (7) clerestory, (8) oculus, (9) lancet, (10) triforium, (11) nave arcade, (12) compound pier with responds.

Rib vaults with pointed arches, flying buttresses, and stained-glass windows are the major ingredients in the Gothic cathedral "recipe," but other elements also contributed to the distinctive look of these churches.

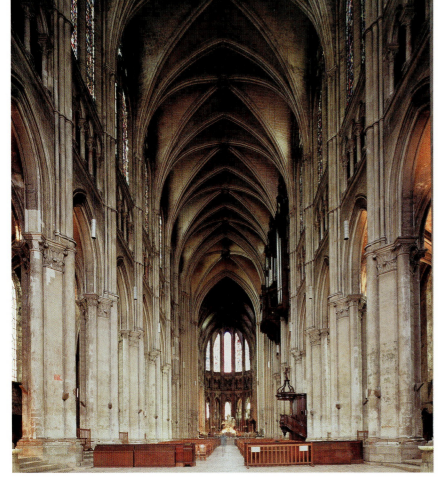

7-10 Interior of Chartres Cathedral (looking east), Chartres, France, begun 1194.

The post-1194 Chartres Cathedral was the first church planned from the beginning with flying buttresses, which made possible the substitution of the triforium for the tribune gallery in the nave.

the first High Gothic building. At Chartres (FIG. 7-10), rectangular nave bays with four-part vaults replaced the square bays with six-part vaults and the alternate-support system seen at Saint-Étienne (FIG. 6-28) at Caen and in Early Gothic churches. The new system, in which a rectangular unit in the nave, defined by its own vault, was flanked by a single square in each aisle rather than two, as before, became the High Gothic norm. The High Gothic vault covered a smaller area and therefore could be braced more easily than its Early Gothic predecessor, making taller naves more practical to build.

The 1194 Chartres Cathedral was also the first church planned from the beginning with flying buttresses, another key High Gothic feature. The flying buttresses made it possible to eliminate the tribune gallery above the aisle, which had partially braced Romanesque and Early Gothic naves. Taking its place was the *triforium*, the band of arcades between the clerestory and the nave arcade. The triforium occupies the space corresponding to the exterior strip of wall covered by the sloping timber roof above the galleries. The new High Gothic tripartite nave elevation consisted of arcade, triforium, and clerestory with greatly enlarged

windows. The Chartres windows are almost as high as the main arcade and consist of double lancets crowned by a single oculus. The strategic placement of flying buttresses permitted the construction of nave walls with so many voids that heavy masonry played a minor role.

Chartres Stained Glass Despite the vastly increased size of the clerestory windows, the Chartres nave (FIG. 7-10) is relatively dark because the colored glass that fills the windows suppresses light. The purpose of these windows was not to illuminate the interior with bright sunlight but to transform natural light into Suger's mystical lux nova (see "Stained-Glass Windows," page 195). Chartres retains almost the full complement of its original stained glass, which, although it has a dimming effect, transforms the character of the interior in dramatic fashion. The immense (approximately 43 feet in diameter) *rose window* (circular stained-glass window) and tall lancets of Chartres Cathedral's north transept (FIG. 7-11) were the gift of the Queen of France, Blanche of Castile, around 1220. The royal motifs of yellow castles on a red ground and yellow *fleurs-de-lis* (three-petaled iris flowers) on a blue ground fill the eight narrow windows in the rose's lower spandrels. The iconography is also fitting for a queen. The enthroned Virgin and Child appear in the roundel at the center of the rose, which resembles a gem-studded book cover. Around her are four doves of the Holy Spirit and eight angels. Twelve square panels contain images of Old Testament kings, including David and Solomon (at the 12 and 1 o'clock positions respectively). These are the royal ancestors of Christ. Isaiah (11:1–3) had prophesied that the Messiah would come from the family of the patriarch Jesse, father of David. The genealogical "tree of Jesse" is a familiar motif in medieval art. Below, in the lancets, are Saint Anne and the baby Virgin flanked by four of Christ's Old Testament ancestors, Melchizedek, David, Solomon, and Aaron, echoing the royal genealogy of the rose but at a larger scale.

The rose and lancets change in hue and intensity with the hours, turning solid architecture into a floating vision of the celestial heavens. Almost the entire mass of wall opens up into stained glass, which is held in place by an intricate stone armature of *bar tracery*. Here, the Gothic passion for light led to a daring and successful attempt to subtract all superfluous material bulk just short of destabilizing the structure in order to transform hard substance into insubstantial, luminous color. That this vast, complex fabric of stone-set glass has maintained its structural integrity for almost 800 years attests to the Gothic builders' engineering genius.

Stained-Glass Windows

Stained-glass windows are almost synonymous with Gothic architecture. They differ from the mural paintings and mosaics that adorned earlier churches in one all-important respect: They do not conceal walls—they replace them. Also, they transmit rather than reflect light, filtering and transforming the natural sunlight. Abbot Suger called this colored light *lux nova*. According to Suger's contemporary, Hugh of Saint-Victor (1096–1142), a prominent Parisian theologian, "stained-glass windows are the Holy Scriptures . . . and since their brilliance lets the splendor of the True Light pass into the church, they enlighten those inside."* William Durandus, Bishop of Mende, expressed a similar sentiment at the end of the 13th century: "The glass windows in a church are Holy Scriptures, which expel the wind and the rain, that is, all things hurtful, but transmit the light of the True sun, that is, God, into the hearts of the faithful."†

The manufacture of stained-glass windows was labor-intensive and costly. A Benedictine monk named Theophilus recorded the full process around 1100. First, the master designer drew the exact composition of the planned window on a wooden panel, indicating all the linear details and noting the colors for each section. Glassblowers provided flat sheets of glass of different colors to *glaziers* (glassworkers), who cut the windowpanes to the required size and shape with special iron shears. Glaziers produced an even greater range of colors by *flashing* (fusing one layer of colored glass to another). Next, painters added details such as faces, hands, hair, and clothing in enamel by tracing the master design on the wood panel through the colored glass. Then they heated the painted glass to fuse the enamel to the surface. At that point, the glaziers "leaded" the various fragments of glass—that is, they joined them by strips of lead called *cames*. The *leading* not only held the (usually quite small) pieces together but also separated the colors to heighten the design's effect as a whole. The distinctive character of Gothic stained-glass windows is largely the result of this combination of fine linear details with broad flat expanses of color framed by black lead. Finally, the glassworkers strengthened the completed window with an armature of iron bands (FIG. 7-11).

The form of the stone frames for the stained-glass windows also evolved. Early rose windows have stained glass held in place by *plate tracery* (FIG. 7-5, *left*). The glass fills only the "punched holes" in the heavy ornamental stonework. *Bar tracery* (FIGS. 7-5, *right*, and 7-11), a later development, is much more slender. The stained-glass windows fill almost the entire opening, and the stonework is unobtrusive, appearing more as if it were delicate leading than masonry wall.

*Attributed to Hugh of Saint-Victor, *Speculum de mysteriis ecclesiae,* Sermon 2.
†William Durandus, *Rationale divinorum officiorum,* 1.1.24. Translated by John Mason Neale and Benjamin Webb, *The Symbolism of Churches and Church Ornaments* (Leeds: Green, 1843), 28.

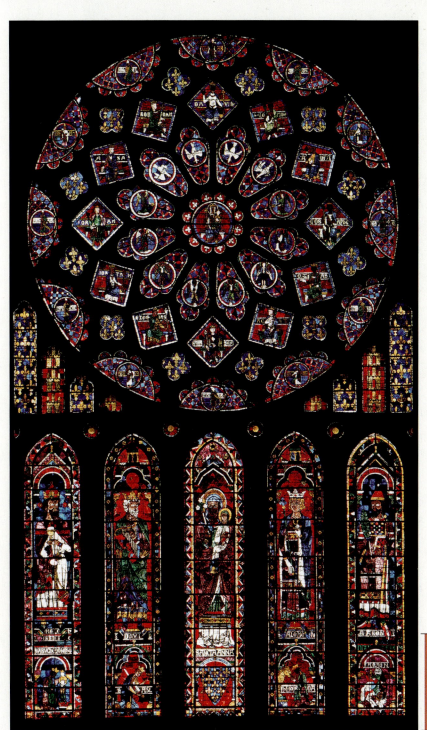

10 ft.

7-11 Rose window and lancets, north transept, Chartres Cathedral, Chartres, France, ca. 1220. Stained glass, rose window 43′ in diameter.

Stained-glass windows transformed natural light into Suger's lux nova. This immense rose window and the tall lancets were the gift of Blanche of Castile, Queen of France, to Chartres Cathedral.

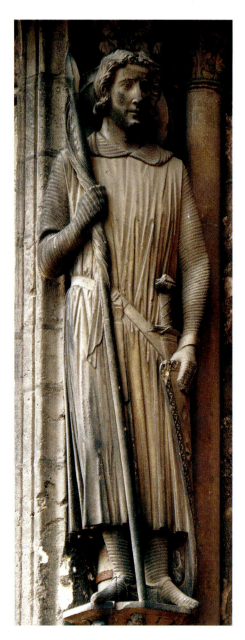

7-12 Saint Theodore, jamb statue, Porch of the Martyrs (left doorway), south transept, Chartres Cathedral, Chartres, France, ca. 1230.

Although this statue of Theodore is still attached to a column, the setting no longer determines its pose. The High Gothic sculptor portrayed the saint swinging out one hip, as in Greek statuary (FIG. 2-34).

Chartres South Transept The sculptures adorning the portals of the two new Chartres transepts erected after the 1194 fire are also prime examples of the new High Gothic spirit. The Chartres transept portals (FIG. 7-5, *right*) project more forcefully from the church than do the Early Gothic portals of its west facade (FIGS. 7-5, *left*, and 7-6). Similarly, the statues of saints on the portal jambs are more independent of the architectural framework. Saint Theodore (FIG. **7-12**) from the Porch of the Martyrs in the south transept reveals the great changes Gothic sculpture had undergone since the Royal Portal statues (FIG. 7-7) of the mid-12th century. These changes recall in many ways the revolutionary developments in ancient Greek sculpture during the transition from the Archaic to the Classical style (see Chapter 2). The High Gothic sculptor portrayed Theodore as the ideal Christian knight and clothed him in the cloak and chain-mail armor of Gothic Crusaders. The handsome, long-haired youth holds his spear firmly in his right hand and rests his left hand on his shield. Although the statue is

still attached to a column, the architectural setting no longer determines its pose. The saint turns his head to the left and swings out his hip to the right, breaking the rigid vertical line that, on the Royal Portal, fixes the figures immovably. The body's resulting torsion and pronounced sway call to mind Classical Greek statuary, especially the contrapposto stance of Polykleitos's *Spear Bearer* (FIG. 2-34). It is not inappropriate to speak of the changes that occurred in 13th-century Gothic sculpture as a "second Classical revolution."

Amiens Cathedral Chartres Cathedral set a pattern that many other Gothic architects followed, even if they refined the details. Construction of Amiens Cathedral began in 1220, while work was still in progress at Chartres. The architects were ROBERT DE LUZARCHES, THOMAS DE CORMONT, and RENAUD DE CORMONT. The builders finished the nave (FIG. **7-13**) by 1236 and the radiating chapels by 1247, but work on the choir continued until almost 1270. The Amiens elevation derived from the High Gothic formula established at

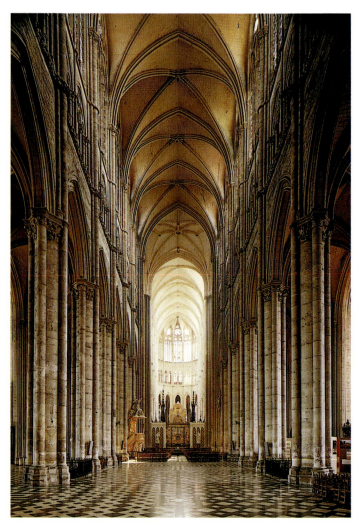

7-13 ROBERT DE LUZARCHES, THOMAS DE CORMONT, and RENAUD DE CORMONT, interior of Amiens Cathedral (looking east), Amiens, France, begun 1220.

The concept of a self-sustaining skeletal architecture reached full maturity at Amiens Cathedral. The four-part High Gothic vaults on pointed arches rise an astounding 144 feet above the nave floor.

Chartres (FIG. 7-10). But Amiens Cathedral's proportions are even more elegant, and the number and complexity of the lancet windows in both its clerestory and triforium are even greater. The whole design reflects the builders' confident use of the complete High Gothic structural vocabulary: the rectangular-bay system, the four-part rib vault, and a buttressing system that permitted almost complete dissolution of heavy masses and thick weight-bearing walls. At Amiens, the concept of a self-sustaining skeletal architecture reached full maturity.

The nave vaults of Chartres Cathedral rise to a height of 118 feet. Those at Amiens are 144 feet above the floor, reflecting the French Gothic obsession with constructing ever-taller cathedrals. The tense, strong lines of the Amiens vault ribs converge to the colonnettes and speed down the walls to the compound piers. Almost every part of the superstructure has its corresponding element below. The overall effect is of effortless strength, of a buoyant lightness not normally associated with stone architecture. The light flooding in from the clerestory—and, in the choir, also from the triforium—makes the vaults seem even more insubstantial. The effect recalls another great building, one utterly different from Amiens but where light also plays a defining role: Hagia Sophia (FIG. 4-13) in Constantinople. Once again, the designers reduced the building's physical mass by structural ingenuity and daring, and light further dematerializes what remains. If Hagia Sophia is the perfect expression of Byzantine spirituality in architecture, Amiens, with its soaring vaults and giant windows admitting divine colored light, is its Gothic counterpart.

Reims Cathedral Construction of Reims Cathedral (FIG. 7-1) began only a few years after work commenced at Amiens. Its west facade displays the Gothic desire to reduce sheer mass and replace it with intricately framed voids. The builders punctured almost the entire stone skin of the building. The deep piercing of walls and towers left few continuous surfaces for decoration, and the stonemasons covered the ones that remained with colonnettes, arches, pinnacles, rosettes, and other decorative stonework that visually screen and nearly dissolve the structure's solid core. Sculpture also extends to the areas above the portals, especially the band of statues (the so-called kings gallery) running the full width of the facade directly above the rose window. Below, sculpture-lined funnel-like portals project boldly from the rest of the facade. The treatment of the tympana over the doorways is telling. There, stained-glass windows replaced the stone relief sculpture of earlier facades. The contrast with Romanesque heavy masonry construction (FIG. 6-27) is extreme. But the rapid transformation of the Gothic facade since Saint-Denis and Chartres (FIG. 7-5, left) is no less noteworthy.

The Reims jamb statues are also prime examples of the High Gothic style. Four of the most prominent statues (FIG. 7-14) represent the *Annunciation* and *Visitation* and are further testimony to the Virgin's central role in Gothic iconography. The sculpted figures appear almost completely detached from their architectural background, with the sup-

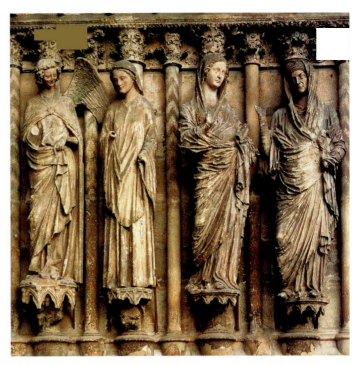

7-14 *Annunciation* and *Visitation*, jamb statues of central doorway, west facade, Reims Cathedral, Reims, France, ca. 1230–1255.

Different sculptors working in diverse styles carved the Reims jamb statues, but all detached their figures from the columns and set the bodies and arms in motion. The figures converse through gestures.

porting columns reduced so significantly as to in no way restrict the free and easy movements of the full-bodied figures. (Compare the Reims statue-columns with those of the Royal Portal of Chartres, FIG. 7-7, where the background columns occupy a volume equal to that of the figures.)

The Reims statues also vividly illustrate that the sculptured ornamentation of Gothic cathedrals took decades to complete and required many sculptors often working in diverse styles. Art historians believe that three different sculptors carved these four statues at different times during the quarter century from 1230 to 1255. The *Visitation* group (FIG. 7-14, *right*) is the work of an artist who probably studied classical statuary. Although art historians have been unable to pinpoint specific models in the Reims region, the heads of both women resemble ancient Roman portraits. Whatever the sculptor's source, the statues are astonishing approximations of the classical naturalistic style. The Reims master even incorporated the Greek contrapposto posture, far exceeding the stance of the Chartres Saint Theodore (FIG. 7-12). The swaying of the hips is much more pronounced. (It is even more exaggerated in the elegant elongated body of the angel Gabriel in the *Annunciation* group, FIG. 7-14, *left*.) The right legs of the *Visitation* figures bend, and the knees press through the rippling folds of the garments. The sculptor also set the figures' arms in motion. Mary and Elizabeth not only turn their faces toward each other but also converse through gestures. In the Reims *Visitation* group, the formerly isolated Gothic jamb statues have become actors in a biblical narrative.

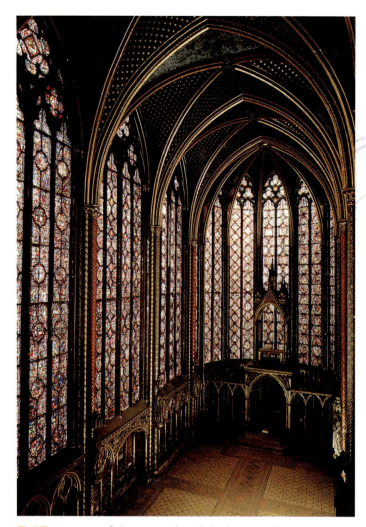

7-15 Interior of the upper chapel (looking northeast), Sainte-Chapelle, Paris, France, 1243–1248.

At Louis IX's Sainte-Chapelle, the architect succeeded in dissolving the walls to the point that 6,450 square feet of stained glass make up more than three-quarters of the Rayonnant Gothic structure.

Sainte-Chapelle, Paris If the stained-glass windows inserted into the portal tympana of Reims Cathedral exemplify the wall-dissolving High Gothic architectural style, Sainte-Chapelle (FIG. 7-15) in Paris demonstrates this principle applied to a whole building. Louis IX (Saint Louis, r. 1226–1270) built Sainte-Chapelle, joined to the royal palace, as a repository for the crown of thorns and other relics of Christ's Passion he had purchased in 1239. The chapel is a masterpiece of the so-called *Rayonnant* (radiant) style of the High Gothic age, which was the preferred style of the royal Parisian court of Saint Louis. Sainte-Chapelle's architect reduced walls and the bulk of supports to such an extent that 6,450 square feet of stained glass constitute more than three-quarters of the structure. The supporting elements are hardly more than large *mullions*, or vertical stone bars. The emphasis is on the extreme slenderness of the architectural forms and on linearity in general. Sainte-Chapelle's enormous stained-glass windows filter the light and fill the interior with an unearthly rose-violet atmosphere. Approximately 49 feet high and 15 feet wide, these windows were the largest designed up to their time.

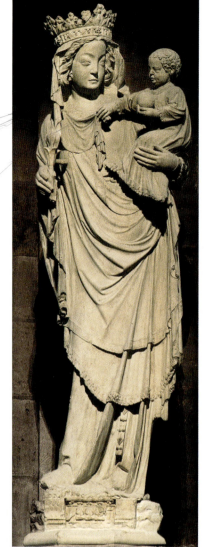

7-16 Virgin and Child (*Virgin of Paris*), Notre-Dame, Paris, France, early 14th century.

Late Gothic sculpture is elegant and mannered. Here, the solemnity of Early and High Gothic religious figures gave way to a tender and anecdotal portrayal of Mary and Jesus as royal mother and son.

Virgin of Paris The "court style" of Sainte-Chapelle has its pictorial parallel in the mannered elegance of the Reims Gabriel statue (FIG. 7-14, *left*), but the style long outlived Saint Louis. The best French Late Gothic example of this sculptural style is the statue nicknamed the *Virgin of Paris* (FIG. 7-16) because of its location in the Parisian Cathedral of Notre-Dame. The sculptor portrayed Mary in an exaggerated S-curve posture. She is a worldly queen, decked out in royal garments and wearing a heavy gem-encrusted crown. The Christ Child is equally richly attired and is very much the infant prince in the arms of his young mother. The tender, anecdotal characterization of mother and son represents a further humanization of the portrayal of religious figures in Gothic sculpture. Late Gothic statuary is very different in tone from the solemnity of most High Gothic figures, just as Late Classical Greek statues of the Olympian gods (FIG. 2-48) differ from High Classical depictions.

Book Illumination and Luxury Arts

Paris's claim as the intellectual center of Gothic Europe did not rest solely on the stature of its university faculty and on the reputation of its architects, masons, sculptors, and stained-glass makers. The city was also a renowned center for the production of fine books. The Florentine poet Dante Alighieri (1265–1321), in fact, referred to Paris in his *Divine Comedy* (ca. 1310–1320) as the city famed for the art of illumination.[4] Indeed, the Gothic period is when book manufacture shifted from scriptoria in isolated monasteries to urban workshops. Owned and staffed by laypersons who sold their products to the royal family, scholars, and prosperous merchants, these for-profit secular businesses, concentrated in Paris, were the forerunners of modern publishing houses.

God as Architect One of the finest examples of French Gothic book illustration is the frontispiece (FIG. **7-17**) of a *moralized Bible* produced in Paris during the 1220s. Moralized Bibles are lavish books in which each page pairs Old and New Testament episodes with illustrations explaining their moral significance. (The page reproduced here does not conform to this formula because it is the introduction to all that follows.) Above the illustration, the scribe wrote (in French rather than Latin): "Here God creates heaven and earth, the sun and moon, and all the elements." God appears as the architect of the world, shaping the universe with the aid of a compass. Within the perfect circle already created are the spherical sun and moon and the unformed matter that will become the earth once God applies the same geometric principles to it. In contrast to the biblical account of Creation, where God created the sun, moon, and stars after

the earth had been formed, and made the world by sheer force of will and a simple "Let there be . . ." command, on this page the Gothic artist portrayed God as an industrious architect, creating the universe with some of the same tools mortal builders use.

Blanche of Castile Not surprisingly, most of the finest Gothic books known today belonged to the French monarchy. One of these is a moralized Bible now in the Pierpont Morgan Library. Saint Louis inherited the throne when he was only 12 years old, so until he reached adulthood, his mother, Blanche of Castile, served as France's regent. Blanche ordered this Bible for her teenage son during her regency (1226–1234). The dedication page (FIG. **7-18**) has a costly gold background and depicts Blanche and Louis enthroned beneath triple-lobed arches and miniature cityscapes. Below, in similar architectural frames, are a monk and a scribe. The older clergyman dictates a sacred text to his young apprentice. The scribe already has divided his page into two columns of four roundels each, a format often used for the

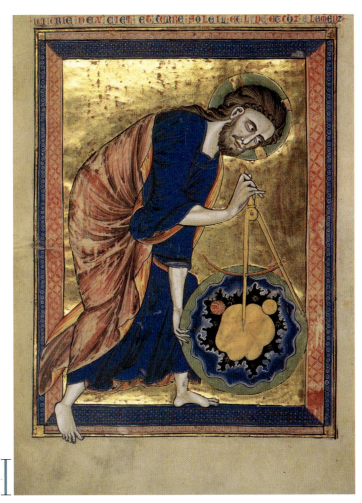

7-17 God as architect of the world, folio 1 verso of a moralized Bible, from Paris, ca. 1220–1230. Ink, tempera, and gold leaf on vellum, 1′ 1½″ × 8¼″. Österreichische Nationalbibliothek, Vienna.

Paris was the intellectual capital of Europe and the center of production for fine books. This artist portrayed God as an industrious architect creating the universe using the same tools as Gothic builders.

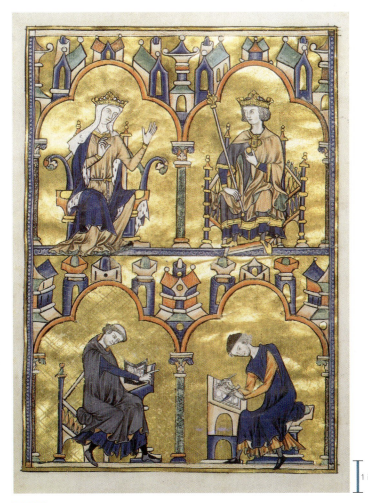

7-18 Blanche of Castile, Louis IX, and two monks, dedication page (folio 8 recto) of a moralized Bible, from Paris, France, 1226–1234. Ink, tempera, and gold leaf on vellum, 1′ 3″ × 10½″. Pierpont Morgan Library, New York.

The costly gold dedication page of this royal book depicts Saint Louis, his mother, and two monks. The younger monk is at work on the paired illustrations of a moralized Bible.

France | 199

paired illustrations of moralized Bibles. The inspirations for these designs were probably the roundels of Gothic stained-glass windows (compare the windows of Louis's own, later Sainte-Chapelle, FIG. 7-15).

The picture of Gothic book production on the dedication page of this moralized Bible is greatly abbreviated. The manufacturing process used in the workshops of 13th-century Paris involved many steps and numerous specialized artists, scribes, and assistants of varying skill levels. The Benedictine abbot Johannes Trithemius (1462–1516) described the way books were still made in his day in his treatise *In Praise of Scribes:*

> If you do not know how to write, you still can assist the scribes in various ways. One of you can correct what another has written. Another can add the rubrics [headings] to the corrected text. A third can add initials and signs of division. Still another can arrange the leaves and attach the binding. Another of you can prepare the covers, the leather, the buckles and clasps. All sorts of assistance can be offered the scribe to help him pursue his work without interruption. He needs many things which can be prepared by others: parchment cut, flattened and ruled for script, ready ink and pens. You will always find something with which to help the scribe.[5]

The preparation of the illuminated pages also involved several hands. Some artists, for example, specialized in painting borders or initials. Only the workshop head or one of the most advanced assistants would paint the main figural scenes. Given this division of labor and the assembly-line nature of Gothic book production, it is astonishing how uniform the style is on a single page, as well as from page to page, in most illuminated manuscripts. Inscriptions in some Gothic illuminated books state the production costs—the prices paid for materials, especially gold, and for the execution of initials, figures, flowery script, and other embellishments. By this time, illuminators were professional guild members, and their personal reputation, like modern "brand names," guaranteed the quality of their work. Though the cost of materials was still the major factor determining a book's price, individual skill and reputation increasingly decided the value of the illuminator's services. The centuries-old monopoly of the Church in book production had ended.

Virgin of Jeanne d'Evreux The royal family also patronized goldsmiths, silversmiths, and other artists specializing in the production of luxury works in metal and enamel for churches, palaces, and private homes. Especially popular were statuettes of sacred figures, which the wealthy purchased either for private devotion or as gifts to the churches they frequented. The Virgin Mary was a favored subject. Perhaps the finest of these costly statuettes is the large silver-gilt figurine known as the *Virgin of Jeanne d'Evreux* (FIG. 7-19). The queen, wife of Charles IV (r. 1322–1328), donated the image of the Virgin and Child to the royal abbey church of Saint-Denis in 1339. Mary stands on a rectangular base decorated with enamel scenes of Christ's Passion. But no hint of grief appears in the beautiful young Mary's face. The Christ Child, also without a care in the world, playfully

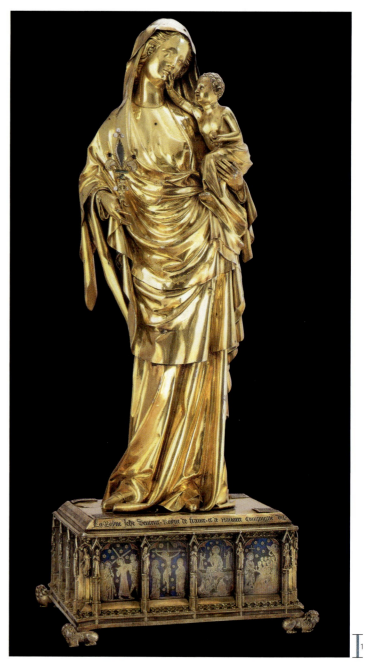

7-19 *Virgin of Jeanne d'Evreux,* from the abbey church of Saint-Denis, France, 1339. Silver gilt and enamel, 2′ 3½″ high. Louvre, Paris.

Queen Jeanne d'Evreux donated this luxurious reliquary-statuette to the royal abbey church of Saint-Denis. The intimate human characterization of the holy figures recalls that of the *Virgin of Paris* (FIG. 7-16).

reaches for his mother. The elegant proportions of the two figures, Mary's swaying posture, the heavy drapery folds, and the intimate human characterization of the holy figures are also features of the roughly contemporary *Virgin of Paris* (FIG. 7-16). In the *Virgin of Jeanne d'Evreux,* as in the *Virgin of Paris,* Mary appears not only as the Mother of Christ but as the Queen of Heaven. The Saint-Denis Mary also originally wore a crown, and the scepter she holds is in the form of the fleur-de-lis, the French monarchy's floral emblem. The statuette also served as a reliquary. The Virgin's scepter contained hairs believed to come from Mary's head.

ENGLAND

In 1269 the prior (deputy abbot) of the Church of Saint Peter at Wimpfen-im-Tal in the German Rhineland hired "a very experienced architect who had recently come from the city of Paris" to rebuild his monastery church.[6] The architect reconstructed the church *opere francigeno* ("in the French manner")—that is, in the Gothic style of the Île-de-France. The Parisian Gothic style had begun to spread even earlier, but in the second half of the 13th century the new style became dominant throughout western Europe. European architecture did not, however, turn Gothic all at once or uniformly. Almost everywhere, patrons and builders modified the Rayonnant court style of the Île-de-France according to local preferences.

Salisbury Cathedral Salisbury Cathedral (FIG. **7-20**) embodies the essential characteristics of English Gothic architecture. Begun in 1220, construction required about 40 years, which makes Salisbury almost exactly contemporaneous with Amiens and Reims cathedrals. Thus, the differences between the French and English buildings are very instructive. Although Salisbury's facade has lancet windows and blind arcades with pointed arches and statuary, it presents a striking contrast to the Reims design (FIG. **7-1**). The English facade is a squat screen in front of the nave, wider than the building behind it. The soaring height of the French facade is absent. The Salisbury facade also does not correspond to the three-part division of the interior (nave and two aisles). Different, too, is the emphasis on the great crossing tower (added about 1320–1330), which dominates the silhouette. Salisbury's height is modest compared with that of Amiens and Reims. And because height is not a decisive factor in the English building, the architect used the flying buttress sparingly and as a rigid prop, rather than as an integral part of the vaulting system within the church. In short, the English builders adopted some of the superficial motifs of French Gothic architecture but did not embrace its structural logic or emphasis on height.

Salisbury's interior (FIG. **7-21**), although Gothic in its three-story elevation, pointed arches, four-part rib vaults, compound piers, and the tracery of the triforium, conspicuously departs from the French Gothic style seen at Amiens (FIG. **7-13**). The pier colonnettes stop at the springing of the nave arches and do not connect with the vault ribs. Instead, the vault ribs rise from corbels in the triforium, producing a strong horizontal emphasis. Underscoring this horizontality is the rich color contrast between the light stone of the walls and vaults and the dark Purbeck marble used for the triforium moldings and corbels, compound pier responds, and other details.

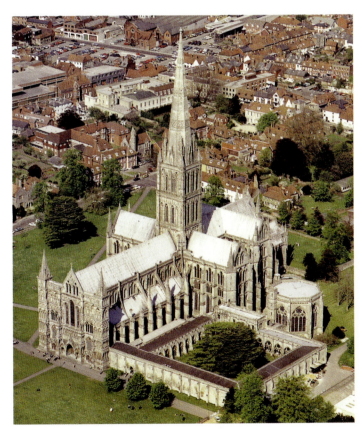

7-20 Aerial view of Salisbury Cathedral (looking northeast), Salisbury, England, 1220–1258; west facade completed 1265; spire ca. 1320–1330.

Exhibiting the distinctive regional features of English Gothic architecture, Salisbury Cathedral has a squat facade that is wider than the building behind it. The architects used flying buttresses sparingly.

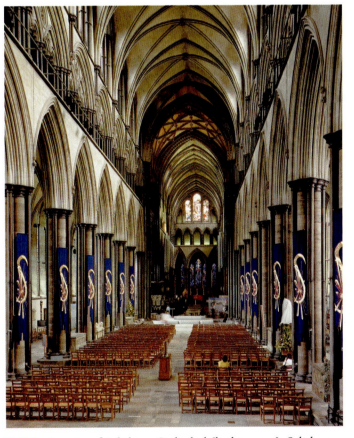

7-21 Interior of Salisbury Cathedral (looking east), Salisbury, England, 1220–1258.

Salisbury Cathedral's interior differs from contemporaneous French Gothic designs in the strong horizontal emphasis of its three-story elevation and the use of dark Purbeck marble for moldings.

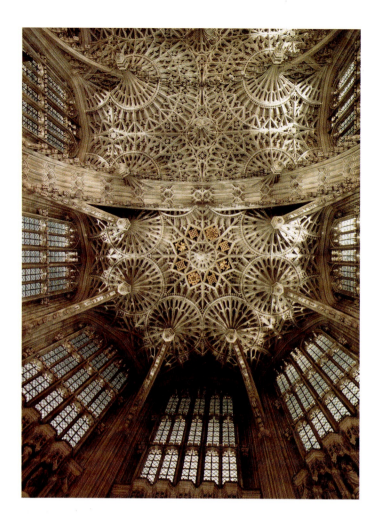

7-22 ROBERT and WILLIAM VERTUE, fan vaults of the chapel of Henry VII, Westminster Abbey, London, England, 1503–1519.

Two hallmarks of the Perpendicular style of English Late Gothic architecture are the multiplication of ribs and the use of fan vaults with lacelike tracery and large hanging pendants resembling stalactites.

overwhelms the cones hanging from the ceiling. The chapel represents the dissolution of structural Gothic into decorative fancy. The designers released the French Gothic style's original lines from their function and multiplied them into the uninhibited architectural virtuosity and theatrics of the English Perpendicular style.

HOLY ROMAN EMPIRE

The architecture of the Holy Roman Empire remained conservatively Romanesque well into the 13th century. In many German churches, the only Gothic feature was the rib vault, buttressed solely by the heavy masonry of the walls. By mid-century, though, the French Gothic style began to have a profound impact.

Cologne Cathedral Begun in 1248 under the direction of GERHARD OF COLOGNE, Cologne Cathedral was not completed until more than 600 years later. It is the largest cathedral in northern Europe and boasts a giant (422-foot-long) nave with two aisles on each side. The 150-foot-high

Chapel of Henry VII English Gothic architecture found its native language in the elaboration of architectural pattern for its own sake. Structural logic, expressed in the building fabric, was secondary. The pier, wall, and vault elements, still relatively simple at Salisbury, became increasingly complex and decorative in the 14th century and later. In the early-16th-century chapel of Henry VII adjoining Westminster Abbey in London, the so-called *Perpendicular* style of Late English Gothic is on display. The style takes its name from the pronounced verticality of its decorative details, in contrast to the horizontal emphasis of Salisbury and Early English Gothic. In Henry's chapel, the architects ROBERT and WILLIAM VERTUE multiplied the vault ribs (FIG. **7-22**) and pulled them into uniquely English *fan vaults* with large hanging *pendants* resembling stalactites. Intricate tracery recalling lace

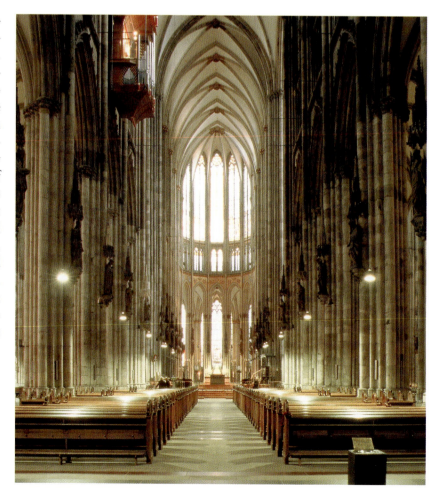

7-23 GERHARD OF COLOGNE, choir of Cologne Cathedral (looking east), Cologne, Germany, completed 1322.

Cologne Cathedral is the largest church in northern Europe. Its 150-foot-high choir, a variation of the Amiens Cathedral choir (FIG. 7-13), is a prime example of the Gothic quest for height.

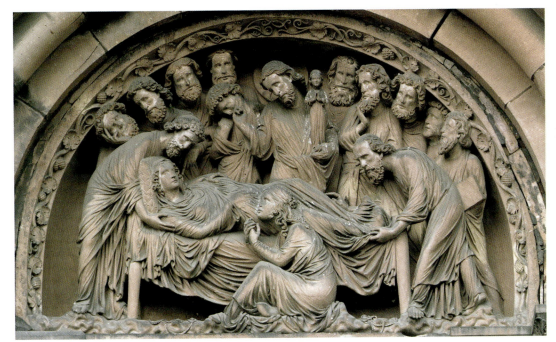

7-24 Death of the Virgin, tympanum of left doorway, south transept, Strasbourg Cathedral, Strasbourg, France, ca. 1230.

Stylistically akin to the *Visitation* group (FIG. 7-14, *right*) of Reims Cathedral, the figures in Strasbourg's south-transept tympanum express profound sorrow through dramatic poses and gestures.

14th-century choir (FIG. 7-23) is a skillful variation of the Amiens Cathedral choir (FIG. 7-13) design, with double lancets in the triforium and tall, slender single windows in the clerestory above and choir arcade below. The Cologne choir expresses the Gothic quest for height even more emphatically than many French Gothic buildings.

Strasbourg Cathedral Like French Gothic architects, French sculptors also often set the standard for their counterparts in other countries. In the German Rhineland, work began in 1176 on a new cathedral for Strasbourg, today a French city. The apse, choir, and transepts were in place by around 1240. Stylistically, these sections of the new church are Romanesque. But the reliefs of the two south-transept portals are fully Gothic and reveal the influence of contemporaneous French sculpture, especially that of Reims.

The subject of the left tympanum (FIG. 7-24) is the death of the Virgin Mary. A comparison of the Strasbourg Mary on her deathbed with the Mary of the Reims *Visitation* group (FIG. 7-14, *right*) suggests that the German master had studied the recently installed French jamb statues. The 12 apostles gather around the Virgin, forming an arc of mourners well suited to the semicircular frame. At the center, Christ receives his mother's soul (the doll-like figure he holds in his left hand). Mary Magdalene, wringing her hands in grief, crouches beside the deathbed. The sorrowing figures express emotion in varying degrees of intensity, from serene resignation to gesturing agitation. The sculptor organized the group by dramatic pose and gesture but also by the rippling flow of deeply incised drapery that passes among them like a rhythmic electric pulse. The sculptor's objective was to imbue the sacred figures with human emotions and to stir emotional responses in observers. In Gothic France, as already noted, art became increasingly humanized and natural. In Gothic Germany, artists carried this humanizing trend even further by emphasizing passionate drama.

Naumburg Cathedral The Strasbourg style, with its feverish emotionalism, was particularly appropriate for narrating dramatic events in relief. The sculptor entrusted with the decoration of the west choir of Naumburg Cathedral faced a very different challenge. The task was to carve statues of the 12 benefactors of the original 11th-century church. The vivid gestures and agitated faces of the Strasbourg portal contrast with the quiet solemnity of the Naumburg statues. Two of the figures (FIG. 7-25) stand out

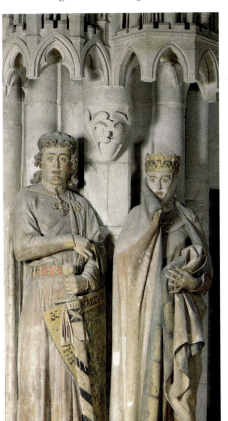

7-25 Ekkehard and Uta, statues in the west choir, Naumburg Cathedral, Naumburg, Germany, ca. 1249–1255. Painted limestone, Ekkehard 6′ 2″ high.

The period costumes and individualized features of these donor portraits give the impression that Ekkehard and Uta posed for their statues, but they lived long before the Naumburg sculptor's time.

1 ft.

from the group because of their exceptional quality. They represent the margrave (German military governor) Ekkehard II of Meissen and his wife Uta. The statues are attached to columns and stand beneath architectural canopies, a common framing device on French Gothic portal statuary. Their location indoors accounts for the preservation of much of the original paint. Ekkehard and Uta give an idea of how the facade and transept sculptures of Gothic cathedrals once looked.

The period costumes and the individualized features and personalities of the margrave and his wife give the impression that they sat for their own portraits, although the subjects lived well before the sculptor's time. Ekkehard, the intense knight, contrasts with the beautiful and aloof Uta. With a wonderfully graceful gesture, she draws the collar of her gown partly across her face while she gathers up a soft fold of drapery with a jeweled, delicate hand. The sculptor subtly revealed the shape of Uta's right arm beneath her cloak and rendered the fall of drapery folds with an accuracy that indicates the use of a model. The two statues are arresting images of real people, even if they bear the names of aristocrats the artist never met. By the mid-13th century, life-size images of secular personages had found their way into churches.

Röttgen Pietà The confident Naumburg donors stand in marked contrast to a haunting 14th-century German painted wooden statuette (FIG. **7-26**) of the Virgin Mary holding the dead Christ in her lap. The widespread troubles of the 14th century—war, plague, famine, social strife—brought on an ever more acute awareness of suffering. This sensibility found its way readily into religious art. A fevered and fearful piety sought comfort and reassurance in the reflection that Christ and the Virgin Mother shared humanity's woes. To represent this, artists emphasized the traits of human suffering in powerful, expressive exaggeration. In the illustrated group (called a *Pietà*, "pity" or "compassion" in Italian), the sculptor portrayed Christ as a stunted, distorted human wreck, stiffened in death and covered with streams of blood gushing from a huge wound. Mary, who cradles him like a child in her lap, is the very image of maternal anguish, her oversized face twisted in an expression of unbearable grief. This statue expresses nothing of the serenity of earlier Gothic depictions of the Virgin (FIG. **7-6**, right tympanum). Nor does the *Röttgen Pietà* (named after a collector) have anything in common with the aloof, iconic images of the Theotokos with the infant Jesus in her lap common in Byzantine art (FIG. **4-20**). Here the artist forcibly confronts the devout with an appalling icon of agony, death, and sorrow that humanizes—to the point of heresy—the sacred personages. The work calls out to the horrified believer, "What is your suffering compared to this?"

Throughout Europe, the humanizing of religious themes and religious images accelerated steadily after the 12th century. By the 14th century, art addressed the private person (often in a private place) in a direct appeal to the emotions. The expression of feeling accompanied the representation of the human body in motion. As the figures of the church portals began to twist on their columns, then move within their

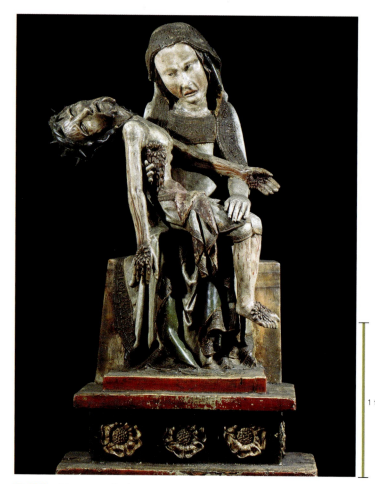

7-26 Virgin with the Dead Christ (*Röttgen Pietà*), from the Rhineland, Germany, ca. 1300–1325. Painted wood, 2′ 10½″ high. Rheinisches Landemuseum, Bonn.

This statuette of the Virgin grieving over the distorted dead body of Christ in her lap reflects the widespread troubles of the 14th century and the German interest in emotional imagery.

niches, and then stand independently, their details became more outwardly related to the human audience as expressions of recognizable human emotions.

ITALY

Nowhere is the regional diversity of Gothic art and architecture more evident than in Italy. In fact, art historians debate whether late-13th- and 14th-century Italian art should be considered Late Gothic, the last phase of medieval art, or Early *Renaissance*, the dawn of a new artistic age when artists broke away from medieval conventions and consciously revived the classical style. Both of these characterizations have merit.

The word *renaissance* in French and English (*rinascità* in Italian) refers to a "rebirth" of art and culture. A revived interest in classical cultures—indeed, the veneration of classical antiquity as a model—was central to this rebirth. The notion that the Renaissance represented the restoration of the glorious past of Greece and Rome is the root of the concept of the "Middle Ages," that is, the era in between antiquity and the Renaissance. It also gave rise to Vasari's disdainful labeling of medieval art as "Gothic."

A significant development in 14th-century Italy was the blossoming of a vernacular (commonly spoken) literature, which dramatically affected Italy's intellectual and cultural life. Latin remained the official language of church liturgy and state documents, but the creation of an Italian vernacular literature was one important sign that the religion-oriented view of the world that dominated medieval Europe was about to change dramatically. Although religion continued to occupy a primary position in the lives of Europeans, a growing concern with the natural world, the individual, and humanity's worldly existence characterized the Renaissance period—the 14th through the 16th centuries.

Fundamental to the development of the Italian Renaissance was *humanism*. Humanism was more a code of civil conduct, a theory of education, and a scholarly discipline than a philosophical system. As their name suggests, the Italian humanists celebrated human values and interests as distinct from—but not opposed to—religion's otherworldly values. Humanists held up classical cultures as particularly praiseworthy. This enthusiasm for antiquity involved study of Latin literature and a conscious emulation of what proponents thought were the Roman civic virtues. These included self-sacrificing service to the state, participation in government, defense of state institutions (especially the administration of justice), and stoic indifference to personal misfortune in the performance of duty. Classical cultures provided humanists with a model for living in this world, a model primarily of human focus that derived not from an authoritative and traditional religious dogma but from reason.

Sculpture and Painting

The Renaissance humanists quickly developed a keen interest in classical art as well as literature. Although the *Visitation* statues of Reims Cathedral (FIG. 7-14) show a familiarity with Roman statuary in 13th-century France, the emulation of Greco-Roman art was, not surprisingly, far more common in Italy, where the Holy Roman Emperor Frederick II (r. 1220–1250) had been king of Sicily since 1197. Frederick's nostalgia for Rome's past grandeur fostered a revival of Roman sculpture in Sicily and southern Italy not unlike the neoclassical *renovatio* that Charlemagne encouraged four centuries earlier in Germany (see Chapter 6).

Nicola Pisano The sculptor known as NICOLA PISANO (Nicola of Pisa, active ca. 1258–1278) received his early training in southern Italy. After Frederick's death in 1250, Nicola traveled northward and eventually settled in Pisa. The city, then at the height of its political and economic power, was a magnet for artists seeking lucrative commissions. Nicola Pisano's sculpture, unlike the French sculpture of the period, was not part of the extensive decoration of great portals. He carved marble reliefs and ornamentation for large *pulpits* (raised platforms from which priests lead church services), completing the first in 1260 for Pisa's baptistery (FIG. 6-26, *left*). Some elements of the pulpit's design carried on medieval traditions, but Nicola incorporated classical elements into this medieval type of structure. The large, bushy capitals are a Gothic variation of the Corinthian capital. The arches are round, as in Roman architecture, rather than pointed, as in Gothic buildings. And each of the large rectangular relief panels resembles the front of a Roman sarcophagus (FIG. 3-46).

One of these panels (FIG. 7-27) depicts scenes from the Infancy cycle of Christ (see "The Life of Jesus in Art," Chapter 4, pages 124–125), including the *Annunciation* (*top left*), the *Nativity* (*center* and *lower half*), and the *Adoration of the Shepherds* (*top right*). The Virgin reclines like a lid figure on an Etruscan (FIG. 3-4) or Roman sarcophagus, and the face types, beards, coiffures, and draperies, as well as the bulk and weight of the figures, reveal the influence of classical relief sculpture. Scholars have even been able to pinpoint the models for some of Nicola's figures on Roman sarcophagi in Pisa.

1 ft.

7-27 NICOLA PISANO, *Annunciation, Nativity, and Adoration of the Shepherds,* relief panel on the pulpit of the baptistery, Pisa, Italy, 1259–1260. Marble relief, 2′ 10″ × 3′ 9″.

Classical sculpture inspired the face types, beards, coiffures, and draperies as well as the bulk and weight of Nicola's figures. The Madonna of the *Nativity* resembles lid figures on Roman sarcophagi.

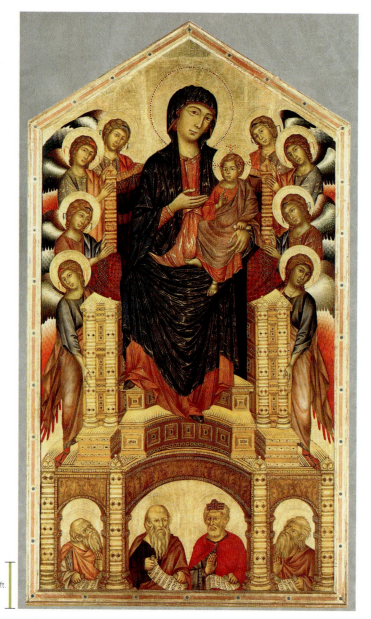

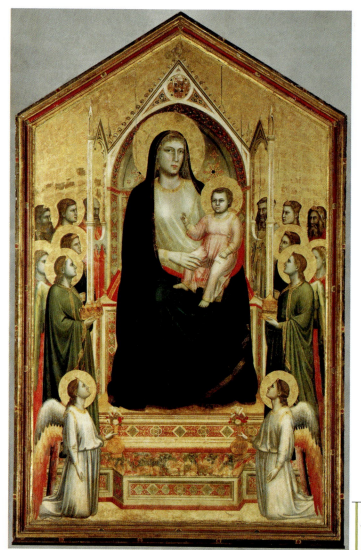

7-28 CIMABUE, *Madonna Enthroned with Angels and Prophets*, ca. 1280–1290. Tempera on wood, 12′ 7″ × 7′ 4″. Galleria degli Uffizi, Florence.

Cimabue was a master of the Italo-Byzantine style, which dominated Italian painting throughout the Middle Ages. Here, the heritage of Byzantine icon painting (FIGS. 4-20 and 4-25) is apparent.

7-29 GIOTTO DI BONDONE, *Madonna Enthroned*, ca. 1310. Tempera on wood, 10′ 8″ × 6′ 8″. Galleria degli Uffizi, Florence.

Giotto displaced the Byzantine style in Italian painting and revived the naturalism of classical art. His figures have substance, dimensionality, and bulk, and give the illusion that they could throw shadows.

Cimabue Late-13th-century Italian painting also differs sharply from the elegant court style popular north of the Alps. Byzantine style dominated Italian painting throughout the Middle Ages. The Italo-Byzantine style, or *maniera greca* ("Greek style"), still characterizes the art of Cenni di Pepo (ca. 1240–1302), better known by his nickname, CIMABUE (Bull's Head). In Cimabue's *Madonna Enthroned with Angels and Prophets* (FIG. 7-28), the heritage of Byzantine icon painting (FIGS. 4-20 and 4-25) is apparent in the careful structure and symmetry, the poses of the figures, the gold lines of Mary's garments, and the gold background. However, Cimabue constructed a deeper space for the Madonna and the surrounding figures to inhabit than is common in Byzantine painting, and he convincingly depicted the throne as receding into space.

Cimabue also enhanced the three-dimensionality of the drapery folds of the angels and prophets.

Giotto The Italian painter who made a much more radical break with the *maniera greca* was GIOTTO DI BONDONE (ca. 1266–1337), whom art historians from Vasari to the present day have regarded as the first Renaissance painter, a pioneer in pursuing *naturalism*—representation based on observation of the natural world. Scholars still debate the sources of Giotto's style, although one source must have been the work of the man Vasari identified as his teacher, Cimabue. Late medieval mural painting in Rome, French Gothic sculpture, and ancient Roman sculpture and painting must also have contributed to Giotto's artistic education. Yet no synthesis of these varied sources could have produced the significant shift in artistic approach that has led some scholars to describe Giotto as the father of Western pictorial art. Renowned in his own day, his reputation has never faltered. Regardless of the other influences on his artistic style, his true teacher was nature—the world of visible things.

Giotto's revolution in painting did not consist only of displacing the Byzantine style, establishing painting as a major art form for the next seven centuries, and restoring the naturalistic approach the ancients developed and medieval artists largely abandoned. He also inaugurated a method of pictorial expression based on observation and initiated an age that might be called "early scientific." By stressing the preeminence of sight for gaining knowledge of the world, Giotto and his successors contributed to the foundation of empirical science. They recognized that the visual world must be observed before it could be analyzed and understood. Praised in his own and later times for his fidelity to nature, Giotto was more than a mere imitator of it. He revealed nature while observing it and divining its visible order. In fact, he showed his generation a new way of seeing. With Giotto, Western artists turned resolutely toward the visible world as their source of knowledge of nature.

Madonna Enthroned On nearly the same great scale as Cimabue's enthroned Madonna (FIG. 7-28) is Giotto's panel (FIG. **7-29**) depicting the same subject. Giotto's Virgin rests within her Gothic throne with the unshakable stability of an ancient marble goddess. Giotto replaced Cimabue's slender Virgin, fragile beneath the thin gold ripplings of her drapery, with a sturdy, queenly mother. He even showed Mary's breasts pressing through the thin fabric of her white undergarment. Gold highlights have disappeared from her heavy robe. Giotto aimed, before all else, to construct a figure that has substance, dimensionality, and bulk. Works painted in the new style portray statuesque figures that project into the light and give the illusion that they could throw shadows. Giotto's *Madonna Enthroned* marks the end of medieval painting in Italy and the beginning of a new, naturalistic approach to art.

Arena Chapel To project onto a flat surface the illusion of solid bodies moving through space presents a double challenge. Constructing the illusion of a body also requires constructing the illusion of a space sufficiently ample to contain that body. In his *fresco* cycles (see "Fresco Painting," page 208), Giotto constantly strove to reconcile these two aspects of illusionistic painting. His frescoes in the Arena Chapel (Cappella Scrovegni; FIG. **7-30**) at Padua show his art at its finest. Enrico Scrovegni, a wealthy Paduan merchant, built the chapel, which takes its name from an ancient Roman amphitheater nearby, on a site adjacent to his now-razed palace. Some scholars have suggested that Giotto himself may have been the chapel's architect because its design so perfectly suits its interior decoration.

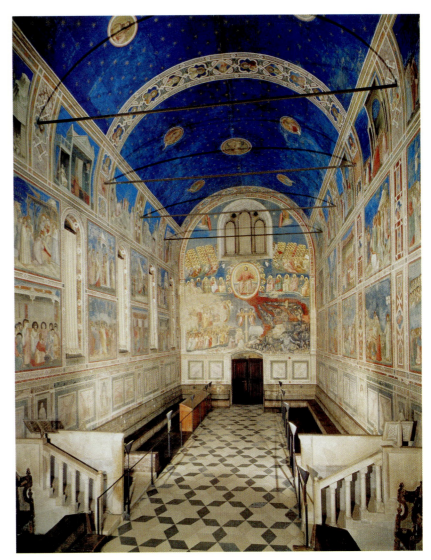

7-30 GIOTTO DI BONDONE, Arena Chapel (Cappella Scrovegni; interior looking west), Padua, Italy, 1305–1306.

The frescoes Giotto painted for the Arena Chapel show his art at its finest. In 38 framed panels, he presented the complete cycle of the life of Christ, culminating in the Last Judgment covering the entrance wall.

The rectangular barrel-vaulted hall has six narrow windows only in its south wall (FIG. 7-30, *left*), which leaves the entire north wall an unbroken and well-illuminated surface for painting. The whole building seems to have been designed to provide Giotto with as much flat surface as possible for presenting one of the most impressive and complete Christian pictorial cycles ever rendered. With 38 framed pictures, arranged on three levels, the artist related the most poignant incidents from the lives of the Virgin and her parents Joachim and Anna (top level), the life and mission of Christ (middle level), and his Passion, Crucifixion, and Resurrection (bottom level). These three pictorial levels rest on a coloristically neutral base. Imitation marble veneer, reminiscent of ancient Roman wall decoration (FIG. 3-39), alternates with the Virtues and Vices painted in *grisaille* (monochrome grays, often used for modeling in paintings) to resemble sculpture. The climactic event of the cycle of human salvation, the Last Judgment, covers most of the west wall above the chapel's entrance.

Fresco Painting

Fresco painting has a long history, particularly in the Mediterranean region, where the Minoans (FIGS. 2-5 and 2-6) used it as early as 1650 BCE. *Fresco* (Italian for "fresh") is a mural-painting technique that involves applying permanent lime-proof pigments, diluted in water, on freshly laid lime plaster. Because the surface of the wall absorbs the pigments as the plaster dries, fresco is one of the most permanent painting techniques. The stable condition of frescoes such as those in the Arena Chapel (FIGS. 7-30 and 7-31) in Padua and the Sistine Chapel (FIGS. 9-1 and 9-10 to 9-12) in Rome, now hundreds of years old, attest to the longevity of this painting method. The colors have remained vivid because of the chemically inert pigments the artists used. In addition to this *buon fresco* ("true" fresco) technique, artists used *fresco secco* (dry fresco). Fresco secco involves painting on dried lime plaster. Although the finished product visually approximates buon fresco, the plaster wall does not absorb the pigments, which simply adhere to the surface. Thus fresco secco does not have buon fresco's longevity.

The buon fresco process is time-consuming and demanding and requires several layers of plaster. Although buon fresco methods vary, generally the artist prepares the wall with a rough layer of lime plaster called the *arriccio* (brown coat). The artist then transfers the composition to the wall, usually by drawing directly on the arriccio with a burnt-orange pigment called *sinopia* (most popular during the 14th century) or by transferring a *cartoon* (a full-size preparatory drawing). Cartoons increased in usage in the 15th and 16th centuries, largely replacing sinopia underdrawings. Finally, the painter lays the *intonaco* (painting coat) smoothly over the drawing in sections (called *giornate,* Italian for "days") only as large as the artist expects to complete in that session. The buon fresco painter must apply the colors fairly quickly, because once the plaster is dry, it will no longer absorb the pigment. Any areas of the intonaco that remain unpainted after a session must be cut away so that fresh plaster can be applied for the next giornata.

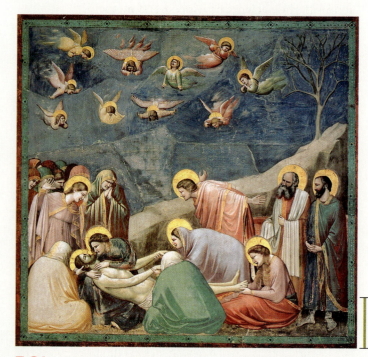

7-31 GIOTTO DI BONDONE, *Lamentation,* Arena Chapel (Cappella Scrovegni), Padua, Italy, ca. 1305. Fresco, 6′ 6¾″ × 6′ ¾″.

In this dramatic fresco, Giotto arranged his sculpturesque figures on a shallow stage and used the rocky landscape to direct the viewer's attention toward the head of the dead Christ.

Subtly scaled to the chapel's space (only about half life-size), Giotto's stately and slow-moving actors present their dramas convincingly and with great restraint. *Lamentation* (FIG. 7-31) reveals the essentials of his style. In the presence of angels darting about in hysterical grief, a congregation mourns over the dead body of the Savior just before its entombment. Mary cradles her son's body, while Mary Magdalene looks solemnly at the wounds in Christ's feet and Saint John the Evangelist throws his arms back dramatically. Giotto arranged a shallow stage for the figures, bounded by a thick diagonal rock incline that defines a horizontal ledge in the foreground. Though rather narrow, the ledge provides firm visual support for the figures, and the steep slope indicates the picture's dramatic focal point at the lower left. The figures are sculpturesque, simple, and weighty, but this mass did not preclude motion and emotion. Postures and gestures that might have been only rhetorical and mechanical convey, in *Lamentation,* a broad spectrum of grief. They range from Mary's almost fierce despair to the passionate outburst of Saint John to the philosophical resignation of the two disciples at the right and the mute sorrow of the two hooded mourners in the foreground.

Giotto constructed a "stage" that served as a model for artists who depicted human dramas in many subsequent paintings. His style broke sharply from the isolated episodes and figures seen in art until the late 13th century. In *Lamentation,* a single event provokes an intense response. Painters before Giotto rarely attempted, let alone achieved, this combination of compositional complexity and emotional resonance.

The formal design of the *Lamentation* fresco—the way Giotto grouped the figures within the constructed space—is worth close study. Each group has its own definition, and each contributes to the rhythmic order of the composition. The strong diagonal of the rocky ledge, with its single dead tree (the tree of knowledge of good and evil, which withered at the Fall of Adam), concentrates the viewer's attention on the group around the head of Christ, whose positioning is dynamically off center. The massive bulk of the seated mourner in the painting's left corner arrests and contains all movement beyond this group. The seated mourner to the right establishes a relation with the central figures, who, by gazes and gestures, draw the viewer's attention back to Christ's head. Figures seen from the back, which are frequent in Giotto's compositions, represent an innovation in the development away from the formal Italo-Byzantine style. These figures emphasize the foreground, aiding the visual placement of the intermediate figures farther back in space. This device, the very contradiction of the old frontality, in effect puts the viewer behind the "observer" figures, who, facing the action as spectators, reinforce the sense of stagecraft as a model for painting.

Giotto's new devices for depicting spatial depth and body mass could not, of course, have been possible without his management of light and shade. He shaded his figures to indicate both the direction of the light that illuminates them and the shadows (the diminished light), giving the figures volume. In *Lamentation*, light falls upon the upper surfaces of the figures (especially the two central bending figures) and passes down to dark in their draperies, separating the volumes one from the other and pushing one to the fore, the other to the rear. The graded continuum of light and shade, directed by an even, neutral light from a single steady source—not shown in the picture—was the first step toward the development of *chiaroscuro* (the use of contrasts of dark and light to produce modeling).

Giotto's stagelike settings are pictorial counterparts to contemporaneous *mystery plays*, in which the drama of the Mass was extended into one- and two-act narratives at church portals and in city squares. The great increase in popular sermons to huge city audiences prompted a public taste for narrative, recited as dramatically as possible. The arts of illusionistic painting, of drama, and of sermon rhetoric with all their theatrical flourishes developed simultaneously and were mutually influential. Giotto's art masterfully synthesized dramatic narrative, holy lesson, and truth to human experience in a visual idiom of his own invention, accessible to all.

Duccio The Republics of Siena and Florence were two of the leading city-states of 14th-century Italy. The Sienese were particularly proud of their victory over the Florentines at the battle of Monteperti in 1260 and believed the Virgin Mary had sponsored their triumph. This belief reinforced Sienese devotion to the Virgin, which was paramount in the religious life of the city. Sienese citizens could boast of Siena's dedication to the Queen of Heaven as more ancient and venerable than that of all others. To honor the Virgin, in 1308 the Sienese commissioned DUCCIO DI BUONINSEGNA (active ca. 1278–1318) to paint an immense *altarpiece*, the *Maestà* (Virgin Enthroned in Majesty), for Siena Cathedral. He and his assistants completed the ambitious work in 1311. As originally executed, the altarpiece consisted of a 7-foot-high center panel (FIG. **7-32**), surmounted by 7 pinnacles above, and a *predella*, or raised shelf, of panels at the base, altogether some 13 feet high.

The main panel of the front side represents the Virgin as the enthroned Queen of Heaven amid choruses of angels and saints. Duccio derived the composition's formality and symmetry, along with the figures and facial types of the principal angels and saints, from Byzantine tradition. But the artist relaxed the strict frontality and rigidity of the Byzantine compositions. Duccio's figures turn to each other in quiet conversation. Further, he individualized the faces of the four saints kneeling in the foreground, who perform their ceremonial

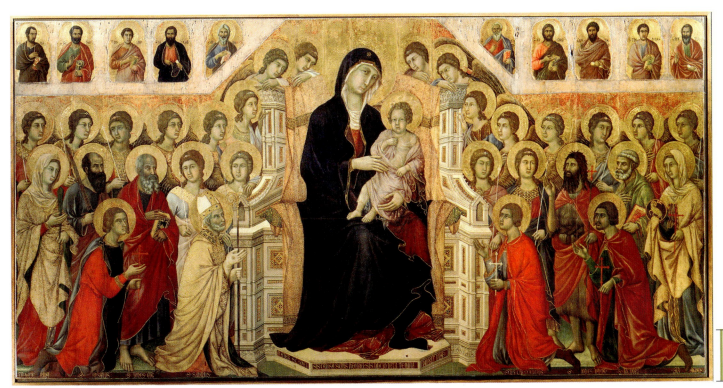

7-32 DUCCIO DI BUONINSEGNA, *Virgin and Child Enthroned with Saints*, principal panel of the *Maestà* altarpiece, from Siena Cathedral, Siena, Italy, 1308–1311. Tempera on wood, panel 7′ × 13′. Museo dell'Opera del Duomo, Siena.

Duccio derived the formality and symmetry of his composition from Byzantine tradition, but relaxed the rigidity and frontality of the figures, softened the drapery, and individualized the faces.

gestures without stiffness. Similarly, Duccio softened the usual Byzantine hard body outlines and drapery patterning. The drapery, particularly that of the female saints at both ends of the panel, falls and curves loosely. This feature is familiar in French Gothic works (FIG. 7-19) and is a mark of the artistic dialogue that occurred between Italy and the North in the 14th century.

Despite these changes that reveal Duccio's interest in the new naturalism, he respected the age-old requirement that as an altarpiece, the *Maestà* would be the focus of worship in Siena's largest and most important church. As such, Duccio knew the *Maestà* should be an object holy in itself—a work of splendor to the eyes, precious in its message and its materials. Duccio thus recognized that the function of this work naturally limited experimentation with depicting narrative action and producing illusionistic effects (such as Giotto's) by modeling forms and adjusting their placement in pictorial space. Instead, the Queen of Heaven panel is a miracle of color composition and texture manipulation, unfortunately not apparent in a photograph. Close inspection of the original reveals what the Sienese artist learned from other sources. In the 13th and 14th centuries, Italy was the distribution center for the great silk trade from China and the Middle East. After processing the silk in city-states such as Lucca and Florence, the Italians exported the fabric widely to satisfy the immense European market for sumptuous dress. People throughout Europe prized fabrics from China, Byzantium, and the Islamic realms. In the *Maestà* panel, Duccio created the glistening and shimmering effects of textiles, adapting the motifs and design patterns of exotic materials.

Simone Martini Duccio's successors in Siena included his pupil SIMONE MARTINI (ca. 1285–1344), who may have assisted in painting the *Maestà*. Martini was a close friend of the poet and scholar Francesco Petrarch (1304–1374), who praised the Sienese painter highly for his portrait of "Laura" (the woman to whom Petrarch dedicated his sonnets). Martini worked for the French kings in Naples and Sicily and, in his last years, produced paintings for the papal court, which in the 14th century was at Avignon, France, where he came in contact with Northern painters. By adapting the insubstantial but luxuriant patterns of the French Gothic manner to Sienese art and, in turn, by acquainting Northern painters with the Sienese style, Martini was instrumental in creating the so-called *International Style*. This new style swept Europe during the late 14th and early 15th centuries because it appealed to the aristocratic taste for brilliant colors, lavish costumes, intricate ornamentation, and themes involving splendid processions.

Martini's *Annunciation* altarpiece (FIG. 7-33) features elegant shapes and radiant color, flowing, fluttering line, and weightless figures in a spaceless setting—all hallmarks of the artist's style. The complex etiquette of the European chivalric courts dictated the presentation. Gabriel has just alighted, the breeze of his passage lifting his mantle, his iridescent wings still beating. The gold of his sumptuous gown is representative of the celestial realm from which he has descended. The Virgin, putting down her book of devotions, shrinks demurely from the angel's reverent genuflection, an appropriate gesture in the presence of royalty. She draws about her the deep blue, golden-hemmed mantle, the heral-

7-33 SIMONE MARTINI and LIPPO MEMMI (?), *Annunciation*, 1333 (frame reconstructed in the 19th century). Tempera and gold leaf on wood; center panel, 10′ 1″ × 8′ 8¾″. Galleria degli Uffizi, Florence.

A pupil of Duccio, Martini was instrumental in the creation of the International Style. Its hallmarks are elegant shapes, radiant color, flowing line, and weightless figures in golden, spaceless settings.

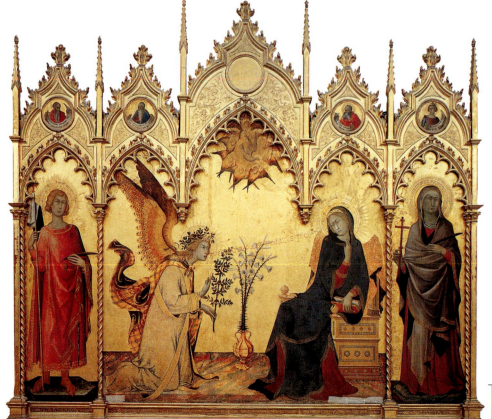

1 ft.

dic colors she wears as Queen of Heaven. Despite the Virgin's modesty and the tremendous import of the angel's message, the scene subordinates drama to court ritual, and structural experimentation to surface splendor. The intricate tracery of the richly tooled French Gothic–inspired frame and the elaborate *punchwork* halos enhance the tactile magnificence of the *Annunciation*.

Simone Martini and his student and assistant, Lippo Memmi (active ca. 1317–1350), signed the altarpiece and dated it (1333). The latter's contribution to the *Annunciation* is still a matter of debate, but art historians generally agree he painted the two lateral saints. These figures, which are reminiscent of the jamb statues of Gothic church portals, have greater solidity and lack the linear elegance of Martini's central pair. Given medieval and Renaissance workshop practices, it is often next to impossible to distinguish the master's hand from that of an assistant, especially if the master corrected or redid part of the assistant's work.

Ambrogio Lorenzetti

Another of Duccio's students was Ambrogio Lorenzetti (active 1319–1348), who contributed significantly to the general experiments in pictorial realism that characterized 14th-century Italian painting. In a vast fresco program he executed in Siena's Palazzo Pubblico (city hall), Lorenzetti both elaborated in spectacular fashion the advances in illusionistic representation made by other Italian painters and gave visual form to Sienese civic concerns.

Ambrogio produced three frescoes for the Palazzo Pubblico: *Allegory of Good Government*, *Bad Government and the Effects of Bad Government in the City*, and *Effects of Good Government in the City and in the Country*. The turbulent politics of the Italian cities—the violent party struggles, the overthrow and reinstatement of governments—certainly would have called for solemn reminders of fair and just administration. And the city hall was just the place for paintings such as Ambrogio Lorenzetti's. Indeed, the leaders of the Sienese government who commissioned this fresco series had undertaken the "ordering and reformation of the whole city and countryside of Siena."

In *Peaceful City* (FIG. **7-34**), a detail of *Effects of Good Government in the City and in the Country*, the artist depicted the urban effects of good government. The fresco is a panoramic view of Siena, with its palaces, markets, towers, churches, streets, and walls. The city's traffic moves peacefully, guild members ply their trades and crafts, and several radiant maidens, hand in hand, perform a graceful circling dance. Dancers were regular features of festive springtime rituals. Here, their presence also serves as a metaphor for a peaceful commonwealth. The artist fondly observed the life of his city, and its architecture gave him an opportunity to apply Sienese artists' rapidly growing knowledge of perspective.

In the *Peaceful Country* section of the fresco (not illustrated), Lorenzetti presented a bird's-eye view of the undulating Tuscan countryside, with its villas, castles, plowed farmlands, and peasants going about their seasonal occupations. An allegorical figure of Security hovers above the landscape, unfurling a scroll that promises safety to all who live under the rule of law. Lorenzetti's "portrait" of the Sienese countryside represents one of the first appearances of landscape in Western art since antiquity.

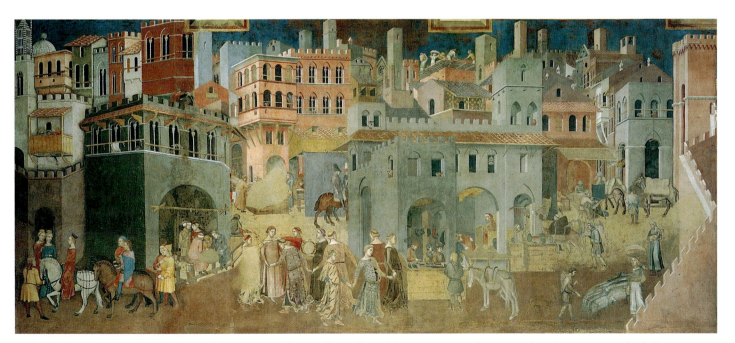

7-34 Ambrogio Lorenzetti, *Peaceful City*, detail from *Effects of Good Government in the City and in the Country*, Sala della Pace, Palazzo Pubblico, Siena, Italy, 1338–1339. Fresco.

Also a student of Duccio, Lorenzetti explored illusionistic representation in this panorama of the bustling city of Siena. The fresco, in the city's Palazzo Pubblico, served as an allegory of good government.

Architecture

The picture of Siena in Ambrogio Lorenzetti's *Peaceful City* (FIG. 7-34) could not be confused with a view of a French, German, or English city of the 14th century. Italian architects stood apart from developments north of the Alps, and, as noted, some architectural historians even have questioned whether the term "Gothic" should be applied to late medieval Italian buildings.

Orvieto Cathedral The west facade of Orvieto Cathedral (FIG. 7-35) is typical of "Gothic" architecture in Italy. Designed in the early 14th century by the Sienese architect LORENZO MAITANI, the Orvieto facade imitates some elements of the French Gothic architectural repertoire, especially the pointed gables over the three doorways, the rose window

and statues in niches in the upper zone, and the four large pinnacles that divide the facade into three bays. The outer pinnacles serve as miniature substitutes for the tall Northern European towers. Maitani's facade, however, is merely a Gothic overlay masking a marble-revetted structure in the Tuscan Romanesque tradition, as the three-quarter view of the cathedral reveals. The Orvieto facade resembles a great altar screen, its single plane covered with carefully placed carved and painted decoration. In principle, Orvieto belongs with Pisa Cathedral (FIG. 6-26) and other Italian buildings, rather than with Reims Cathedral (FIG. 7-1). Inside, Orvieto Cathedral has a timber-roofed nave with a two-story elevation (columnar arcade and clerestory). Both the chancel arch framing the apse and the nave arcade's arches are round as opposed to pointed.

7-35 LORENZO MAITANI, west facade of Orvieto Cathedral (looking northeast), Orvieto, Italy, begun 1310.

The pointed gables over the doorways, the rose window, and the large pinnacles derive from French architecture, but the facade of Orvieto Cathedral is merely a Gothic overlay masking a timber-roofed basilica.

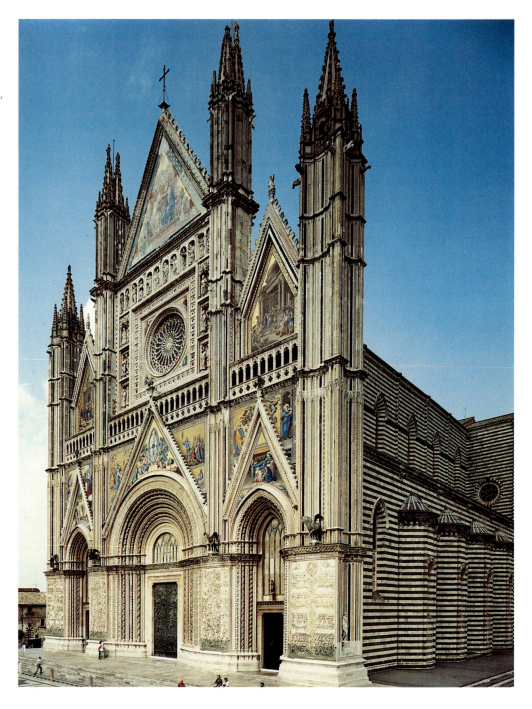

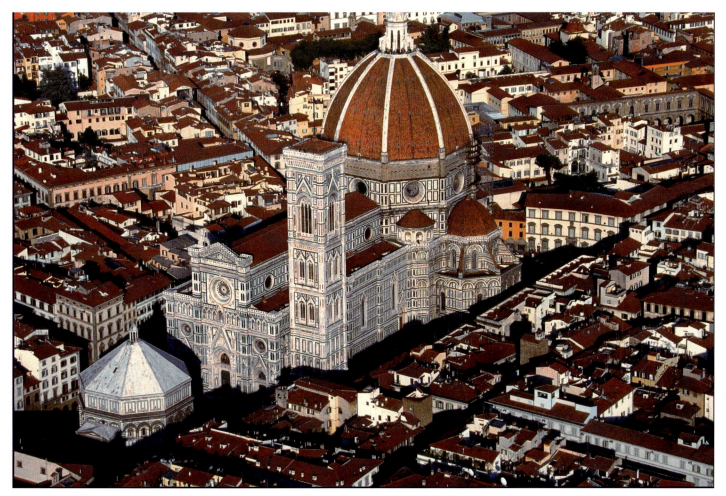

7-36 ARNOLFO DI CAMBIO and others, aerial view of Florence Cathedral (looking northeast), Florence, Italy, begun 1296.

This longitudinal basilican church with its Tuscan-style marble-encrusted walls forms a striking contrast to Reims Cathedral (FIG. 7-1) and underscores the regional diversity of Gothic architecture.

Florence Cathedral Like Siena, the Republic of Florence was a dominant city-state during the 14th century. The historian Giovanni Villani (ca. 1270–1348) described Florence as "the daughter and the creature of Rome," suggesting a preeminence inherited from the Roman Empire. Florentines took great pride in what they perceived as their economic and cultural superiority. Florence controlled the textile industry in Italy, and the republic's gold *florin* was the standard coin of exchange everywhere in Europe.

The city's citizens translated their pride in their predominance into landmark buildings, such as Florence Cathedral (FIG. **7-36**). ARNOLFO DI CAMBIO (ca. 1245–1302) began work on the cathedral in 1296. Intended as the "most beautiful and honorable church in Tuscany," this structure reveals the competitiveness Florentines felt with such cities as Siena and Pisa. Cathedral authorities planned for the church to hold the city's entire population, and although it holds only about 30,000 (Florence's population at the time was slightly less than 100,000), it seemed so large that the architect Leon Battista Alberti (see Chapter 8) commented that it seemed to cover "all of Tuscany with its shade." The vast gulf that separates this low, longitudinal basilican church with its Tuscan-style marble-encrusted walls from its towering transalpine counterparts is strikingly evident in a comparison between the Italian church and Reims Cathedral (FIG. 7-1), completed several years before work began in Florence.

Giotto di Bondone designed Florence Cathedral's campanile in 1334. In keeping with the Italian tradition (FIG. 6-26), the bell tower stands apart from the cathedral. In fact, it is essentially self-sufficient and could stand anywhere else in Florence without looking out of place. The same hardly can be said of Northern Gothic towers. They are integral elements of the building behind them, and it would be unthinkable to detach one of them and place it somewhere else. In contrast, not only could Giotto's tower be removed from the building without adverse effects, but also each of the parts—cleanly separated from each other by continuous moldings—seems capable of existing independently as an object of considerable aesthetic appeal. This compartmentalization is reminiscent of the Romanesque style, but it also forecasts the ideals of Renaissance architecture. Artists hoped to express structure in the clear, logical relationships of the component parts and to produce self-sufficient works that could exist in complete independence.

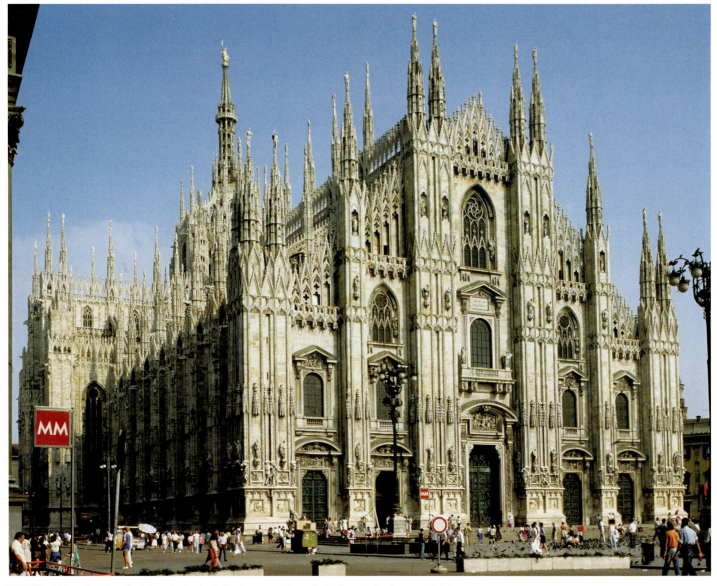

7-37 West facade of Milan Cathedral (looking southeast), Milan, Italy, begun 1386.

Milan Cathedral's elaborate facade is a confused mixture of Late Gothic pinnacles and tracery and Renaissance pediment-capped rectilinear portals. It marks the waning of the Gothic style.

Milan Cathedral Not all of Italy was as fiercely resistant to the French Gothic manner as was Tuscany. Since Romanesque times, Northern European influences had been felt strongly in Lombardy. When Milan's citizens decided to build their own cathedral (FIG. **7-37**) in 1386, they invited experts from France, Germany, and England, as well as Italy. These masters argued among themselves and with the city council, and no single architect ever played a dominant role. The result of this attempt at "architecture by committee" was, not surprisingly, a compromise. The building's proportions, particularly the nave's, became Italian (that is, wide in relation to height), but the surface decorations and details remained Gothic. Clearly derived from France are the cathedral's multitude of pinnacles and the elaborate tracery on the facade, flank, and transept. Long before completion of the building, however, the new classical style of the Italian Renaissance had been well launched (see Chapter 8), and the Gothic design had become outdated. Thus, Milan Cathedral's elaborate facade represents a confused mixture of Late Gothic and Renaissance elements. With its classical pediment-capped rectilinear portals amid Gothic pinnacles, the cathedral stands as a symbol of the waning of the Gothic style.

Gothic Europe

FRANCE

▪ The birthplace of Gothic art and architecture was Saint-Denis, where Abbot Suger used rib vaults with pointed arches and stained-glass windows to rebuild the Carolingian royal church. The Early Gothic (1140–1194) west facade of Suger's church also introduced statue-columns on the portal jambs, which appeared shortly later on the Royal Portal of Chartres Cathedral.

▪ After a fire in 1194, Chartres Cathedral was rebuilt with flying buttresses, four-part nave vaults, and a three-story elevation of nave arcade, triforium, and clerestory, setting the pattern for High Gothic (1194–1300) cathedrals, including Amiens with its 144-foot-high vaults.

▪ Flying buttresses made possible huge stained-glass windows. The divine colored light *(lux nova)* they admitted transformed the character of church interiors.

▪ High Gothic statue-columns broke out of the architectural straitjacket of their Early Gothic predecessors. At Chartres, Reims, and elsewhere, the sculpted figures move freely and sometimes converse with their neighbors.

▪ In the 13th century, Paris was the center of production of costly illuminated manuscripts in urban workshops of professional artists, which usurped the role of monastic scriptoria.

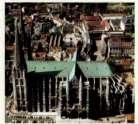

Chartres Cathedral, begun 1134; rebuilt after 1194

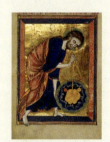

God as architect of the world, ca. 1220–1230

ENGLAND AND THE HOLY ROMAN EMPIRE

▪ English Gothic churches like Salisbury Cathedral differ from their French counterparts in their wider and shorter facades and sparing use of flying buttresses. Especially characteristic of English Gothic architecture is the elaboration of architectural patterns, as seen in the Perpendicular-style fan vaults of the chapel of Henry VII.

▪ German architects eagerly embraced the French Gothic architectural style at Cologne Cathedral and elsewhere. German originality manifested itself most clearly in sculptures depicting emotionally charged figures in dramatic poses. The statues of secular historical figures in Naumburg Cathedral signal a revival of interest in portraiture.

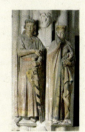

Ekkehard and Uta, Naumburg Cathedral, ca. 1249–1255

ITALY

▪ Nicola Pisano carved pulpits incorporating marble panels that, both stylistically and in individual motifs, depend on ancient Roman sarcophagi.

▪ The leading Italian painter of the late 13th century was Cimabue, who worked in the Italo-Byzantine style, or *maniera greca*.

▪ Giotto di Bondone forged a new path in the early 14th century. Giotto was a pioneer in pursuing a naturalistic approach to representation based on observation, which was at the core of the classical tradition in art. He is widely considered the first Renaissance painter.

▪ The greatest master of the Sienese school of painting was Duccio di Buoninsegna, whose *Maestà* still incorporates many Byzantine elements, but he relaxed the frontality and rigidity of his figures.

▪ Secular themes also came to the fore in 14th-century Italy, most notably in Ambrogio Lorenzetti's frescoes for Siena's Palazzo Pubblico. His depictions of the city and its surrounding countryside are among the first landscapes in Western art since antiquity.

▪ Italian 14th-century architecture underscores the regional character of late medieval art. Orvieto Cathedral's facade imitates some elements of the French Gothic repertoire, but it is merely an overlay masking a traditional timber-roofed structure with round arches in the nave arcade.

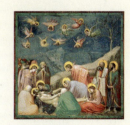

Giotto, Arena Chapel, Padua, ca. 1305

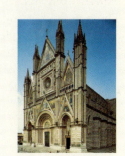

Maitani, Orvieto Cathedral, begun 1310

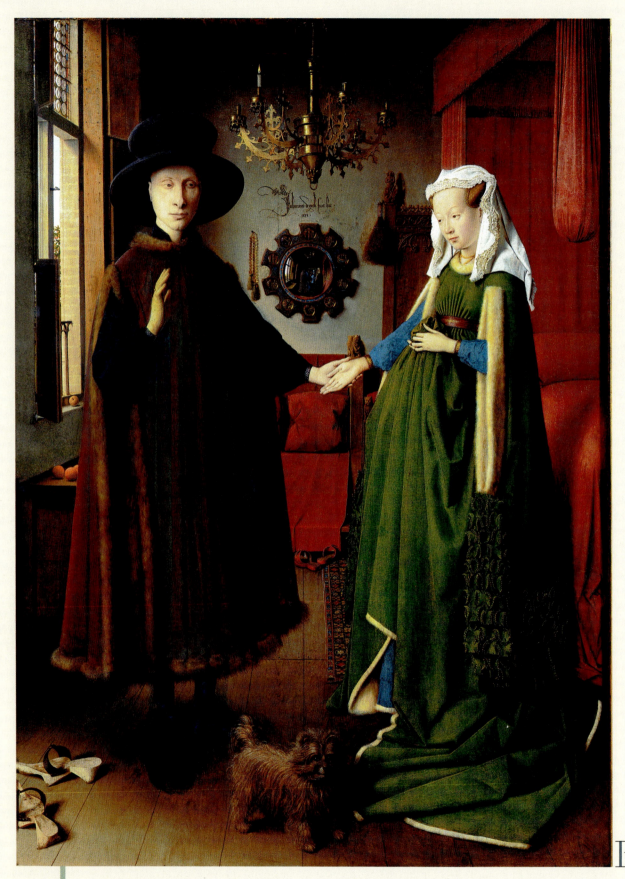

8-1 JAN VAN EYCK, *Giovanni Arnolfini and His Bride*, 1434. Oil on wood, 2′ 9″ × 1′ 10½″. National Gallery, London.

Van Eyck played a major role in popularizing oil painting and in establishing portraiture as an important art form. In this portrait of an Italian financier and his wife, the artist also portrayed himself in the mirror.

1 in.

Europe, 1400 to 1500

In the 14th and 15th centuries, Europe experienced the calamities of plague, war, and social upheaval. The Black Death that ravaged Italy in 1348, killing 50 to 60 percent of the population in the largest cities, also spread to much of the rest of Europe. The Hundred Years' War (1337–1453) further contributed to instability across the Continent. Primarily a protracted series of conflicts between France and England, the war also involved Flanders, a region corresponding to parts of what are today northern France, Belgium, Holland, and Luxembourg (MAP **8-1**). Crisis in the religious realm exacerbated the period's political instability. In 1305 the College of Cardinals elected a French pope, Clement V. He and the French popes who succeeded him chose to reside in Avignon. Understandably, this did not sit well with Italians, who saw Rome as the rightful capital of the universal church. The conflict between the French and Italians resulted in the election in 1378 of two popes—Clement VII, who remained in Avignon, and Urban VI, who resided in Rome. Thus began what became known as the Great Schism, which lasted until the election in 1417 of Martin V, a Roman pope acceptable to all.

Despite the troubles of the age, a new economic system evolved—the early stage of European capitalism. Responding to the financial requirements of trade, new credit and exchange systems created an economic network of enterprising European cities. The trade in money accompanied the trade in commodities, and the former financed industry. Both were in the hands of trading companies with central offices and international branches. In Italy, the most prominent financiers were the Medici of Florence. North of the Alps, the Flemish established the first international commercial stock exchange at Antwerp in 1460. It became pivotal for Europe's integrated economic activity. The thriving commerce, industry, and finance contributed to the evolution of cities, as did the migration of a significant portion of the rural population to urban centers. With successful merchants and bankers joining kings, dukes, and popes as major patrons of painting, sculpture, and architecture, the arts also flourished.

BURGUNDY AND FLANDERS

In the early 15th century, Philip the Good (r. 1419–1467) ruled a region known as the duchy of Burgundy (MAP 8-1), the fertile east-central region of France still known for its wines. In 1369 one of Philip the Good's predecessors, Philip the Bold (r. 1364–1404), married the daughter of the count of Flanders and acquired territory in the Netherlands. Thereafter, the major source of Burgundian wealth and power was Bruges, the city that made Burgundy a dangerous rival of royal France. Bruges initially derived its wealth from the wool trade and soon expanded into banking, becoming the financial clearinghouse for all of Northern Europe.

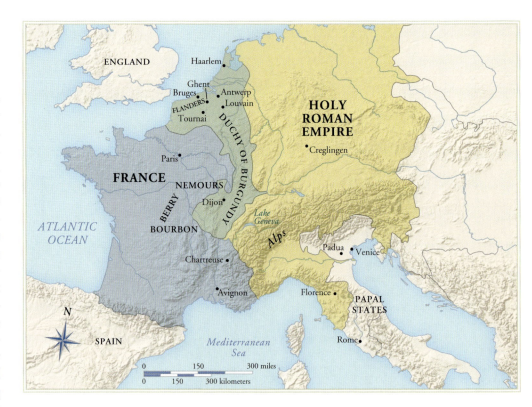

Indeed, Bruges so dominated Flanders that the duke of Burgundy eventually designated the city his capital and moved his court there from Dijon in the early 15th century. Due to the expanded territory and the prosperity of the duchy of Burgundy, Philip the Bold and his successors were probably the most powerful rulers in Northern Europe during the first three-quarters of the 15th century. Although cousins of the French kings, they usually supported England (on which they relied for the raw materials used in their wool industry) during the Hundred Years' War and, at times, controlled much of northern France, including Paris, the seat of the French monarchy. At the height of Burgundian power, the reigning duke's lands stretched from the Rhône River to the North Sea.

Chartreuse de Champmol Philip the Bold was among the greatest art patrons in Northern Europe. His largest artistic enterprise was the building of the Chartreuse de Champmol, near Dijon. Founded in the late 11th century by Saint Bruno, the Carthusian order consisted of monks who devoted their lives to solitary living and prayer. Saint Bruno established the order at Chartreuse in southeastern France; hence, the term *chartreuse* ("charter house" in English) refers to a Carthusian monastery. Inspired by Saint-Denis, the burial site of the kings of France (see Chapter 7), Philip intended the Dijon chartreuse to become a ducal mausoleum and serve both as a means of securing salvation in perpetuity for the Burgundian dukes and as a dynastic symbol of Burgundian power.

For the Champmol cloister, Philip the Bold's head sculptor, CLAUS SLUTER (active ca. 1380–1406) of Haarlem, designed a large fountain located in a well that provided water for the monastery. It seems improbable, however, that the fountain spouted water, because the Carthusian commitment to silence and prayer would have precluded anything that produced sound. Although Sluter died before completing the entire fountain, he did finish *Well of Moses* (FIG. 8-2) in 1406. Moses and five other Old Testament prophets (David, Daniel, Isaiah, Jeremiah, and Zachariah) ring a base that once supported a Crucifixion group. The Carthusians called it a *fons vitae*, a fountain of life. The blood of the crucified Christ symbolically flowed down over the prophets, spilling into the well below, washing over Christ's prophetic predecessors and redeeming anyone who would drink water from the well.

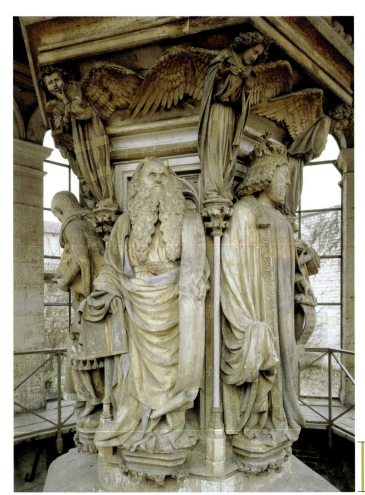

1 ft.

8-2 CLAUS SLUTER, *Well of Moses*, Chartreuse de Champmol, Dijon, France, 1395–1406. Limestone with traces of paint, figures 6' high.

Well of Moses, a symbolic fountain of life made for the duke of Burgundy, supported a Crucifixion group. Sluter's figures recall the jamb statues of French Gothic portals but are far more realistic.

Tempera and Oil Painting

The generic words "paint" and "pigment" encompass a wide range of substances artists have used over the years. Fresco aside (see "Fresco Painting," Chapter 7, page 208), during the 14th century, egg *tempera* was the material of choice for most painters, both in Italy and Northern Europe. Tempera consists of egg combined with a wet paste of ground pigment. In his influential treatise *Il libro dell'arte (The Craftsman's Handbook)*, Cennino Cennini (ca. 1370–1440), an Italian painter, mentioned that artists mixed only the egg yolk with the ground pigment, but analysis of paintings from this period has revealed that some artists used the whole egg. Images painted with tempera have a velvety sheen. Artists usually applied tempera to the painting surface with a light touch because thick application of the pigment mixture results in premature cracking and flaking.

Artists used oil paints as far back as the 8th century, but not until the early 15th century did oil painting become widespread. Flemish artists were among the first to employ oils extensively (often mixing them with tempera), and Italian painters quickly followed suit. The discovery of better drying components in the early 15th century enhanced the setting capabilities of oils. Rather than apply these oils in the light, flecked brushstrokes that tempera encouraged, artists laid the oils down in transparent glazes over opaque or semiopaque underlayers. In this manner, painters could build up deep tones through repeated glazing. Unlike tempera, whose surface dries quickly due to water evaporation, oils dry more uniformly and slowly, providing the artist time to rework areas. This flexibility must have been particularly appealing to artists who worked very deliberately, such as the Flemish masters Robert Campin (FIG. 8-3) and Jan van Eyck (FIGS. 8-1, 8-4, and 8-5) and the Italian Leonardo da Vinci (see Chapter 9). Leonardo also preferred oil paint because its gradual drying process and consistency permitted him to blend the pigments, thereby creating the impressive *sfumato* (smoky effect) that contributed to his fame.

Both tempera and oils can be applied to various surfaces. Through the early 16th century, wooden panels served as the foundation for most paintings. Italians painted on poplar. Northern European artists used oak, lime, beech, chestnut, cherry, pine, and silver fir. Availability of these timbers determined the choice of wood. Linen canvas became increasingly popular in the late 16th century. Although evidence suggests that artists did not intend permanency for their early images on canvas, the material proved particularly useful in areas such as Venice where high humidity warped wood panels and made fresco unfeasible. Further, until artists began to use wooden bars to stretch the canvas to form a taut surface, canvas paintings were more portable than wood panels.

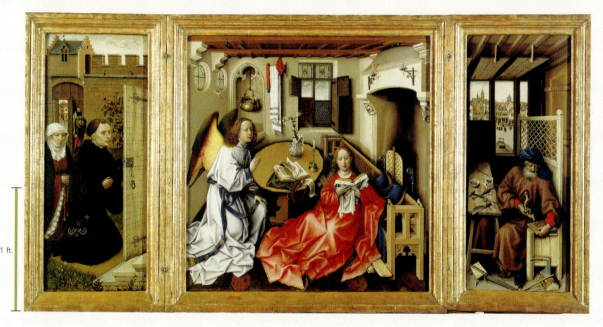

8-3 ROBERT CAMPIN (MASTER OF FLÉMALLE), *Mérode Altarpiece* (open), ca. 1425–1428. Oil on wood, center panel 2' 1⅜" × 2' ⅞", each wing 2' 1⅜" × 10⅞". Metropolitan Museum of Art, New York (The Cloisters Collection, 1956).

Campin set the *Annunciation* in a Flemish merchant's home in which the everyday objects represented have symbolic significance. Oil paints permitted Campin to depict all the details with loving fidelity.

Although the six prophets recall the jamb statues (FIG. 7-14) of Gothic portals, they are much more realistically rendered. Sluter's intense observation of natural appearance enabled him to sculpt the figures with portraitlike features and to differentiate textures ranging from coarse drapery to smooth flesh and silky hair. Originally, paint, much of which has flaked off, further augmented the naturalism of the figures. (The painter was Jean Malouel [ca. 1365–1415], another Netherlandish master.) This fascination with the specific and tangible in the visible world became one of the chief characteristics of 15th-century Flemish painting.

Robert Campin One of the earliest Flemish masters—and one of the first to use the new medium of *oil painting* (see "Tempera and Oil Painting," above)—was the "Master of Flémalle," who scholars generally agree was ROBERT CAMPIN (ca. 1378–1444) of Tournai (FIG. 8-3). Although traditional scholarship credited Jan van Eyck (discussed next) with the invention of oil painting, recent evidence has revealed that oil paints had been known for some time and that another Flemish painter, Melchior Broederlam (active ca. 1387–1409), was using oils in the 1390s. Flemish painters built up their pictures by superimposing translucent paint layers, called *glazes*, on a layer of underpainting, which in turn had been built up from a carefully planned drawing made on a panel prepared with a white ground. With the oil medium, Flemish painters were able to create richer colors than previously had been possible, giving their paintings an intense tonality, the illusion of glowing light, and enamel-like surfaces. These traits differed significantly from the high-keyed color, sharp light, and rather *matte* (dull) surfaces of *tempera*. The brilliant and versatile oil medium suited perfectly the formal intentions of 15th-century Flemish painters, who aimed for sharply focused clarity of detail in their representation of thousands of objects ranging in scale from large to almost invisible.

Campin's most famous work is the *Mérode Altarpiece* (FIG. 8-3), a private commission for household prayer. It was not unusual in that respect. Based on an accounting of extant Flemish religious paintings, lay patrons outnumbered clerical patrons by a ratio of two to one. At the time, various reform movements advocated personal devotion, and in the years leading up to the Protestant Reformation in the early 16th century, private devotional exercises and prayer grew in popularity. One of the more prominent features of these private images is the integration of religious and secular concerns. Artists often presented biblical scenes as taking place in a Flemish house. Although this might seem inappropriate or even sacrilegious today, religion was such an integral part of Flemish life that separating the sacred from the secular became virtually impossible. Moreover, the presentation in religious art of familiar settings and objects no doubt strengthened the direct bond the patron or viewer felt with biblical figures.

The *Mérode Altarpiece* is a small *triptych* (three-paneled painting) in which the center panel represents the popular *Annunciation* theme (as prophesied in Isaiah 7:14). The archangel Gabriel approaches Mary, who sits reading. The artist depicted a well-kept, middle-class Flemish home as the site of the event. The carefully rendered architectural scene in the background of the right wing confirms this identification of the locale. The depicted accessories, furniture, and utensils also help identify the setting as Flemish. However, the objects represented are not merely decorative. They also function as religious symbols. The book, extinguished candle, and lilies on the table, the copper basin in the corner niche, the towels, fire screen, and bench all symbolize, in different ways, the Virgin's purity and her divine mission. In the right panel, Joseph has made a mousetrap, symbolic of the theological tradition that Christ is bait set in the trap of the world to catch the Devil. The ax, saw, and rod in the foreground not only are tools of the carpenter's trade but also are mentioned in Isaiah 10:15.

In the left panel, the closed garden is symbolic of Mary's purity, and the flowers depicted all relate to Mary's virtues, especially humility. The altarpiece's donor, Peter Inghelbrecht, a wealthy merchant, and his wife kneel in the garden and witness the momentous event through an open door. *Donor portraits*—portraits of the individual(s) who commissioned (or "donated") the work—became very popular in the

15th century. In this instance, in addition to asking to be represented in their altarpiece, the Inghelbrechts probably specified the subject. Inghelbrecht means "angel bringer," a reference to the *Annunciation* theme of the central panel. The wife's name, Scrynmakers, means "cabinet- or shrine-makers," referring to the workshop scene in the right panel.

Jan van Eyck The first Netherlandish painter to achieve international fame was JAN VAN EYCK (ca. 1390–1441), who in 1425 became Philip the Good's court painter. The artist moved his studio to Bruges, where the duke maintained his official residence, in 1432, the year he completed the *Ghent Altarpiece* (FIGS. 8-4 and 8-5) for the church in Ghent originally dedicated to Saint John the Baptist (since 1540 Saint Bavo Cathedral). One of the most characteristic art forms in 15th-century Flanders was the monumental freestanding altarpiece, and the *Ghent Altarpiece* is one of the largest. Placed behind the altar, these imposing works served as backdrops for the Mass. Given their function, it is not surprising that many altarpieces depict scenes directly related to Christ's sacrifice. Flemish altarpieces most often took the form of *polyptychs* (hinged multipaneled paintings or relief panels). The hinges allowed the clergy to close the polyptych's side wings over the center panel(s). Artists decorated both the exterior and interior of the altarpieces. This multiple-image format allowed artists to construct narratives through a sequence of images, somewhat as in manuscript illustration. Although scholars do not have concrete information about when the clergy opened and closed these altarpieces, evidence suggests they remained closed on regular days and were opened on Sundays and feast days. This schedule would have allowed viewers to see both the interior and exterior—diverse imagery at various times according to the liturgical calendar.

Jodocus Vyd and his wife Isabel Borluut commissioned the *Ghent Altarpiece*. Vyd's largesse contributed to his appointment as burgomeister (chief magistrate) of Ghent shortly after the unveiling of the work. Two of the exterior panels (FIG. 8-4) depict the donors. The husband and wife, painted in illusionistically rendered niches, kneel with their hands clasped in prayer. They gaze piously at illusionistic stone sculptures of Ghent's patron saints, Saint John the Baptist and Saint John the Evangelist. The *Annunciation* appears on the upper register, with a careful representation of a Flemish town outside the painted window of the center panel. In the uppermost arched panels, van Eyck depicted the Old Testament prophets Zachariah and Micah, along with *sibyls*, classical mythological prophetesses whose writings the Church interpreted as prophecies of Christ.

When opened (FIG. 8-5), the altarpiece reveals a sumptuous, superbly colored painting of the medieval conception of humanity's *Redemption*. In the upper register, God the Father—wearing the pope's triple tiara, with a worldly crown at his feet, and resplendent in a deep-scarlet mantle—presides in majesty. To God's right is the Virgin, represented as the Queen of Heaven, with a crown of 12 stars upon her head. Saint John the Baptist sits to God's left. To either side is a choir of angels, with an angel playing an organ on the

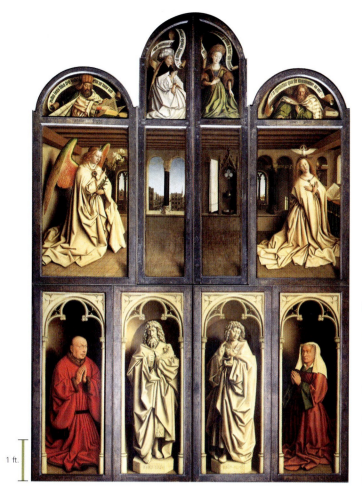

8-4 JAN VAN EYCK, *Ghent Altarpiece* (closed), Saint Bavo Cathedral, Ghent, Belgium, completed 1432. Oil on wood, 11′ 5″ × 7′ 6″.

Monumental painted altarpieces were popular in 15th-century Flemish churches. Artists decorated both the interiors and exteriors of these hinged polyptychs, which often, as here, included donor portraits.

1 ft.

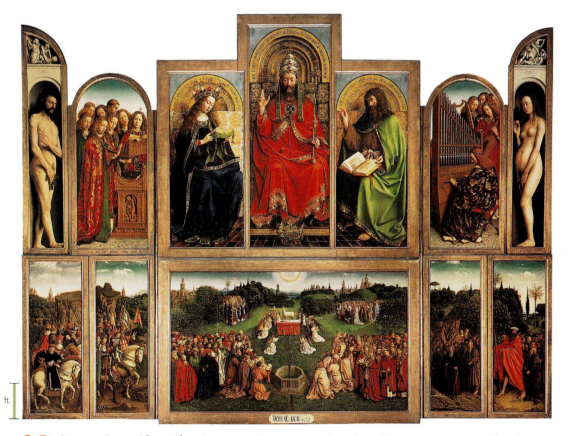

1 ft.

8-5 JAN VAN EYCK, *Ghent Altarpiece* (open), Saint Bavo Cathedral, Ghent, Belgium, completed 1432. Oil on wood, 11′ 5″ × 15′ 1″.

In this sumptuous painting of salvation from the Original Sin of Adam and Eve, God the Father presides in majesty. Van Eyck rendered every figure, garment, and object with meticulous fidelity to appearance.

right. Adam and Eve appear in the far panels. The inscriptions in the arches above Mary and Saint John extol the Virgin's virtue and purity and Saint John's greatness as the forerunner of Christ. The inscription above the Lord's head translates as "This is God, all-powerful in his divine majesty; of all the best, by the gentleness of his goodness; the most liberal giver, because of his infinite generosity." The step behind the crown at the Lord's feet bears the inscription, "On his head, life without death. On his brow, youth without age. On his right, joy without sadness. On his left, security without fear." The entire altarpiece amplifies the central theme of salvation. Even though humans, symbolized by Adam and Eve, are sinful, they will be saved because God, in his infinite love, will sacrifice his own son for this purpose.

The panels of the lower register extend the symbolism of the upper. In the center panel, the community of saints comes from the four corners of the earth through an opulent, flower-spangled landscape. They proceed toward the altar of the Lamb and toward the octagonal fountain of life. The Lamb symbolizes the sacrificed Son of God, whose heart bleeds into a chalice, while into the fountain spills the "pure river of water of life, clear as crystal, proceeding out of the throne of God and of the Lamb" (Rev. 22:1). On the right, the 12 apostles and a group of martyrs in red robes advance. On the left appear prophets. In the right background come the Virgin martyrs, and in the left background the holy confessors approach. On the lower wings, hermits, pilgrims, knights, and judges approach from left and right. They symbolize the four cardinal virtues: Temperance, Prudence, Fortitude, and Justice, respectively. The altarpiece celebrates the full Christian cycle from the Fall to the Redemption, presenting the Church triumphant in heavenly Jerusalem.

Van Eyck, like Campin, used oil paints to render the entire altarpiece in a shimmering splendor of color that defies reproduction. No small detail escaped the artist's eye. With pristine specificity, he revealed the beauty of the most insignificant object as if it were a work of piety as much as a work of art. He captured the soft texture of hair, the glitter of gold in the heavy brocades, the luster of pearls, and the flashing of gems, all with loving fidelity to appearance.

Giovanni Arnolfini Both the *Mérode Altarpiece* and the *Ghent Altarpiece* include painted portraits of their donors. These paintings marked a significant revival of portraiture, a genre that had languished since antiquity. A purely secular portrait, but one with religious overtones, is Jan van Eyck's oil painting *Giovanni Arnolfini and His Bride* (FIG. **8-1**). Van Eyck depicted the Lucca financier (who had established himself in Bruges as an agent of the Medici family) and his betrothed in a Flemish bedchamber that is simultaneously mundane and charged with the spiritual. As in the *Mérode Altarpiece*, almost every object portrayed conveys the sanctity of the event, specifically, the holiness of matrimony. Arnolfini and his bride, Giovanna Cenami, hand in hand, take the marriage vows. The cast-aside clogs indicate that this event is taking place on holy ground. The small dog symbolizes fidelity. Behind the pair, the curtains of the marriage bed have been opened. The bedpost's *finial* (crowning ornament) is a tiny statue of Saint Margaret, patron saint of childbirth. From the finial hangs a whisk broom, symbolic of

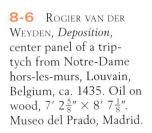

8-6 ROGIER VAN DER WEYDEN, *Deposition*, center panel of a triptych from Notre-Dame hors-les-murs, Louvain, Belgium, ca. 1435. Oil on wood, 7' 2⅝" × 8' 7⅛". Museo del Prado, Madrid.

Rogier's *Deposition* resembles a relief carving in which the biblical figures act out a drama of passionate sorrow as if on a shallow theatrical stage. The emotional impact of the painting is unforgettable.

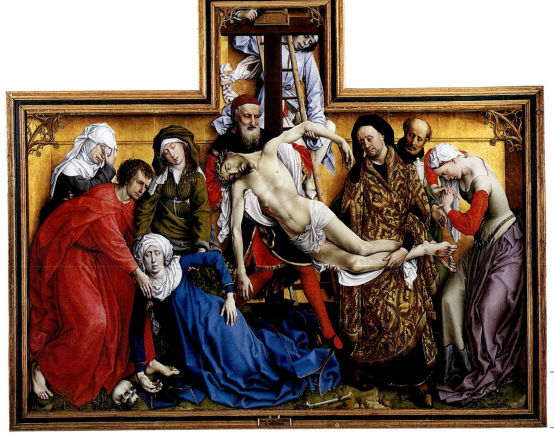

1 ft.

domestic care. The oranges on the chest below the window may refer to fertility. The single candle burning in the left rear holder of the ornate chandelier and the mirror, in which the viewer sees the entire room reflected, symbolize the all-seeing eye of God. The small medallions set into the mirror frame show tiny scenes from the Passion of Christ and represent God's promise of salvation for the figures reflected on the mirror's convex surface. Flemish viewers would have been familiar with many of the objects included in the painting because of traditional Flemish customs. Husbands presented brides with clogs, and the solitary lit candle in the chandelier was also part of Flemish marriage practices. Van Eyck's placement of the two figures suggests conventional gender roles—the woman stands near the bed and well into the room, whereas the man stands near the open window, symbolic of the outside world.

Van Eyck enhanced the documentary nature of this scene by exquisitely painting each object. He carefully distinguished textures and depicted the light from the window on the left reflecting off various surfaces. He augmented the scene's credibility by including the convex mirror, because the viewer can see not only the principals, Arnolfini and his wife, but also two persons who look into the room through the door. One of these must be the artist himself, as the florid inscription above the mirror, "Johannes de Eyck fuit hic" (Jan van Eyck was here) announces he was present. The picture's purpose, then, seems to have been to record and sanctify this marriage. However, some scholars recently have taken issue with this reading, suggesting that Arnolfini is conferring legal privileges on his wife to conduct business in his absence. In either case, the artist functions as a witness. The self-portrait of van Eyck in the mirror also underscores the painter's self-consciousness as a professional artist whose role deserves to be recorded and remembered.

Van Eyck and his contemporaries established portraiture as a major art form. Great patrons embraced the opportunity to have their likenesses painted. They wanted to memorialize themselves in their dynastic lines and to establish their identities, ranks, and stations with images far more concrete than heraldic coats of arms. Portraits also served to represent state officials at events they could not attend. Sometimes, royalty, nobility, and the very rich would send artists to paint the likeness of a prospective bride or groom. When young King Charles VI (r. 1380–1422) of France sought a bride, a painter journeyed to three different royal courts to make portraits of the candidates for queen.

Rogier van der Weyden A painter whose fame rivaled that of Jan van Eyck was ROGIER VAN DER WEYDEN (ca. 1400–1464), who was an assistant in the workshop of Robert Campin when van Eyck received the commission for the *Ghent Altarpiece*. Rogier, as scholars refer to him, soon became renowned for his dynamic compositions stressing human action and drama. He concentrated on Christian themes such as the Crucifixion and the Pietà, moving observers emotionally by relating the sufferings of Christ. *Deposition* (FIG. **8-6**) is the center panel of a triptych the

Archers Guild of Louvain commissioned. Rogier acknowledged the patrons of this altarpiece by incorporating the crossbow (the guild's symbol) into the decorative tracery in the corners. Instead of creating a deep landscape setting, as Jan van Eyck might have, Rogier compressed the figures and action onto a shallow stage to concentrate the viewer's attention. The painting, with the artist's crisp drawing and precise modeling of forms, resembles a stratified relief carving. A series of lateral undulating movements gives the group a compositional unity, a formal cohesion that Rogier strengthened by imbuing the figures with desolating anguish. The similar poses of Christ and the Virgin Mary further unify the composition. Few painters have equaled Rogier in the rendering of passionate sorrow as it vibrates through a figure or distorts a tear-stained face. His depiction of the agony of loss is among the most authentic in religious art. The emotional impact on the viewer is immediate and unforgettable.

Saint Luke Slightly later in date is Rogier's *Saint Luke Drawing the Virgin* (FIG. **8-7**), probably painted for the Guild of Saint Luke, the artists guild in Brussels. The panel depicts the patron saint of painters making a *silverpoint* drawing (see "Renaissance Drawings," Chapter 9, page 259) of the Virgin

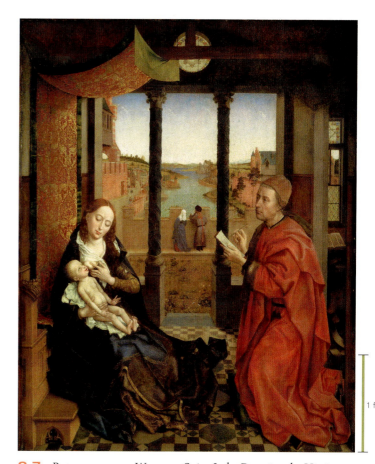

1 ft.

8-7 ROGIER VAN DER WEYDEN, *Saint Luke Drawing the Virgin*, ca. 1435–1440. Oil and tempera on wood, 4' 6$\frac{1}{8}$" × 3' 7$\frac{5}{8}$". Museum of Fine Arts, Boston (gift of Mr. and Mrs. Henry Lee Higginson).

Probably commissioned by the artists guild in Brussels, this painting honors the first Christian artist and the profession of painting. Saint Luke may be a self-portrait of the artist.

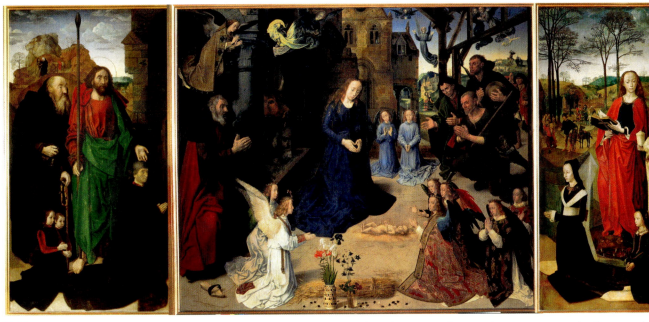

8-8 HUGO VAN DER GOES, *Portinari Altarpiece* (open), from Sant'Egidio, Florence, Italy, ca. 1476. Tempera and oil on wood, center panel 8' 3½" × 10', each wing 8' 3½" × 4' 7½". Galleria degli Uffizi, Florence.

This altarpiece is a rare instance of the awarding of a major commission in Florence to a Flemish painter. The Italians admired the incredibly realistic details and Hugo's brilliant portrayal of human character.

Mary. The theme paid tribute to the profession of painting in Flanders by drawing attention to the venerable history of the painter's craft. Many scholars believe Rogier's Saint Luke is a self-portrait, identifying the Flemish painter with the first Christian artist and underscoring the holy nature of painting as well as the growing self-awareness of Renaissance artists. Rogier shared with van Eyck the aim of recording every detail of the scene with loving fidelity to optical appearance, from the rich fabrics to the floor pattern to the landscape seen through the window. And, like Campin and van Eyck, Rogier imbued much of the representation with symbolic significance. At the right, the ox identifies the figure recording the Virgin's features as Saint Luke. The carved armrest of the Virgin's bench depicts Adam, Eve, and the serpent, reminding the viewer that Mary is the new Eve and Christ the new Adam who will redeem humanity from the Original Sin.

Hugo van der Goes By the mid-15th century, Flemish art had achieved renown throughout Europe. The *Portinari Altarpiece* (FIG. **8-8**) is a large-scale Flemish triptych in a family chapel in Florence, Italy. The artist who received the commission was HUGO VAN DER GOES (ca. 1440–1482) of Ghent. Hugo painted the altarpiece for Tommaso Portinari, an Italian shipowner and agent for the Medici family. Portinari appears on the wings of the triptych with his family and their patron saints. The central panel depicts the *Adoration of the Shepherds*. The Virgin, Joseph, and the angels seem to brood on the suffering to come rather than to meditate on the Nativity miracle. Mary kneels, somber and monumental, on a tilted ground that has the expressive function of center-

ing the main actors. The composition may also reflect the tilted stage floors of contemporary mystery plays. From the right rear enter three shepherds, represented with powerful realism in attitudes of wonder, piety, and gaping curiosity. Their lined faces, work-worn hands, and uncouth dress and manner seem immediately familiar.

After Portinari placed his altarpiece in the family chapel in the Florentine church of Sant'Egidio, it created a considerable stir among Italian artists. Although the painting as a whole may have seemed unstructured to them and the varying scale of the figures according to their importance perpetuated medieval conventions, Hugo's masterful technique and incredible realism in representing drapery, flowers, animals, and, above all, human character and emotion made a deep impression on the Italians.

FRANCE

In France, the anarchy of the Hundred Years' War and the weakness of the French kings gave rise to a group of powerful duchies. The dukes of Burgundy, patrons of the Chartreuse de Champmol (FIG. 8-2), were the strongest of these. Their counterparts—the dukes of Berry, Bourbon, and Nemours—and members of the French court were also significant art patrons.

Limbourg Brothers During the 15th century, French artists built on the achievements of Gothic manuscript painters (see Chapter 7). Among the most significant developments was a new conception and presentation of space. The

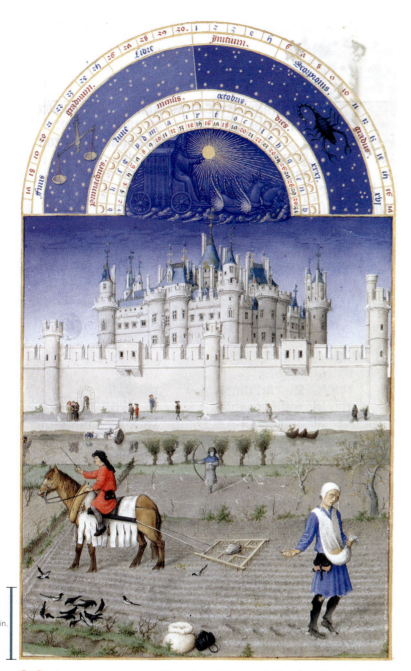

8-9 LIMBOURG BROTHERS (POL, JEAN, HERMAN), *October*, from *Les Très Riches Heures du Duc de Berry*, 1413–1416. Ink on vellum, $8\frac{7}{8}'' \times 5\frac{3}{8}''$. Musée Condé, Chantilly.

The sumptuous pictures in *Les Très Riches Heures* depict characteristic activities of each month and give unusual prominence to genre subjects, reflecting the increasing integration of religious and secular art.

LIMBOURG BROTHERS—POL, JEAN, and HERMAN—three nephews of Jean Malouel, painter of the *Well of Moses* (FIG. 8-2), were pioneers in expanding the illusionistic capabilities of manuscript illumination. The Limbourgs produced a gorgeously illustrated Book of Hours for Jean, the duke of Berry (r. 1360–1416) and brother of King Charles V (r. 1364–1380) of France and Philip the Bold of Burgundy. The duke was an avid art patron and focused much of his collecting energy on jewels, rare artifacts, and more than 300 manuscripts. The three brothers worked on *Les Très Riches Heures du Duc de Berry (The Very Sumptuous Hours of the Duke of Berry)* until

their deaths in 1416. A *Book of Hours*, like a *breviary*, was a collection of prayers. As prayer books, they replaced the traditional *psalters* (books of Psalms), which had been the only liturgical books in private hands until the mid-13th century. A Book of Hours contained liturgical passages to be read privately at set times during the day, as well as penitential psalms, devotional prayers, litanies to the saints, other prayers, and an illustrated calendar containing local religious feast days. Books of Hours became favorite possessions of the Northern European aristocracy during the 14th and 15th centuries. They eventually became available to affluent merchants and contributed to the decentralization of religious practice that was one factor in the Protestant Reformation in the early 16th century (see Chapter 9).

The calendar pictures of *Les Très Riches Heures* represent the 12 months in terms of the associated seasonal tasks, alternating scenes of nobility and peasantry. Above each picture is a lunette depicting the chariot of the sun as it makes its yearly cycle through the 12 months and zodiac signs. Beyond its function as a religious book, *Les Très Riches Heures* also visually captures the power of the duke and his relationship to the peasants. The illustration for *October* (FIG. 8-9) focuses on the peasantry. The Limbourgs depicted a sower, a harrower on horseback, and washerwomen, along with city dwellers, who promenade in front of the Louvre (the French king's residence at the time). The peasants do not appear particularly disgruntled as they go about their tasks. Surely this imagery flattered the duke's sense of himself as a compassionate master. The growing artistic interest in naturalism is evident in the careful architectural detail with which the brothers rendered the Louvre and in the convincing shadows of the people, animals, and objects (such as the archer scarecrow and the horse) in the scene.

As a whole, *Les Très Riches Heures* reinforced the image of the duke of Berry as a devout man, cultured bibliophile, sophisticated art patron, and powerful and magnanimous leader. Further, the expanded range of subject matter, especially the prominence of genre subjects in a religious book, reflected the increasing integration of religious and secular concerns in both art and life at the time. Although all three Limbourg brothers worked on *Les Très Riches Heures*, art historians have never been able to ascertain which brother painted which images. Given the common practice then of collaboration on artistic projects, this determination of specific authorship is of minor importance.

Jean Fouquet Images for private devotional use were popular in France, as in Flanders. Among the French artists whose paintings were in demand was JEAN FOUQUET (ca. 1420–1481), who worked for Charles VII and for the duke of Nemours. Fouquet painted a *diptych* (two-paneled

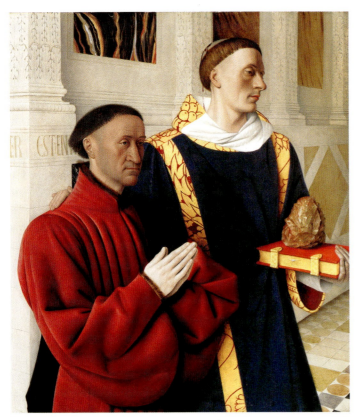
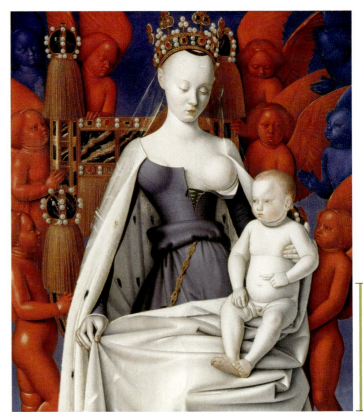

8-10 JEAN FOUQUET, *Melun Diptych. Étienne Chevalier and Saint Stephen* (left wing), ca. 1450. Oil on wood, 3′ ½″ × 2′ 9½″. Gemälde-galerie, Staatliche Museen, Berlin. *Virgin and Child* (right wing), ca. 1451. Oil on wood, 3′ 1¼″ × 2′ 9½″. Koninklijk Museum voor Schone Kunsten, Antwerp.

Fouquet's meticulous representation of a pious kneeling donor with a standing patron saint recalls Flemish painting (FIG. 8-4), as do the three-quarter stances and the sharp focus of the portraits.

painting; FIG. **8-10**) for Étienne Chevalier, the royal trea-surer of France. In the left panel, Chevalier appears with his patron saint, Saint Stephen (Étienne in French). Appropri-ately, Fouquet depicted Chevalier as devout—kneeling, with hands clasped in prayer. The representation of the pious do-nor with his standing saint recalls Flemish art (FIG. 8-4), as do the three-quarter stances, the sharp, clear focus of the portraits, and the painting medium (oil on wood). The artist depicted Stephen holding the stone of his martyrdom (death by stoning) atop a volume of the Scriptures, thereby ensur-ing that the viewer could properly identify the saint. Fouquet rendered the entire image in meticulous detail and included a highly ornamented architectural setting.

In its original diptych form (the two panels are now in different museums), the viewer would follow the gaze of Che-valier and Saint Stephen over to the right panel, which depicts the Virgin Mary and Christ Child. The juxtaposition of these two images allowed the patron to bear witness to the sacred. However, the integration of sacred and secular (especially the political or personal) common in other Northern European artworks complicates the reading of this diptych. Agnès Sorel, the mistress of Charles VII, was the model for Fouquet's de-piction of the Virgin Mary. Sorel was a pious individual, and, according to an inscription, Chevalier commissioned this

painting to fulfill a vow he made after Sorel's death in 1450. Thus, in addition to the religious interpretation of this dip-tych, there is surely a personal narrative here as well.

HOLY ROMAN EMPIRE

Because the Holy Roman Empire (whose core was Germany) did not participate in the long, drawn-out saga of the Hun-dred Years' War, its economy was stable and prosperous. Without a dominant court culture, wealthy merchants and clergy became the leading German art patrons during the 15th century.

Tilman Riemenschneider Carved wooden *retables* (altarpieces) were popular commissions for German churches. One prominent sculptor who specialized in producing re-tables was TILMAN RIEMENSCHNEIDER (ca. 1460–1531), who created the *Creglingen Altarpiece* for a parish church in Creg-lingen, incorporating intricate Gothic forms, especially in the elaborate canopy. The center panel (FIG. **8-11**) depicts the *Assumption of the Virgin*. By employing a restless line that runs through the garments of the figures, Riemenschneider succeeded in setting the whole design into fluid motion, and no individual element functions without the rest. The drap-

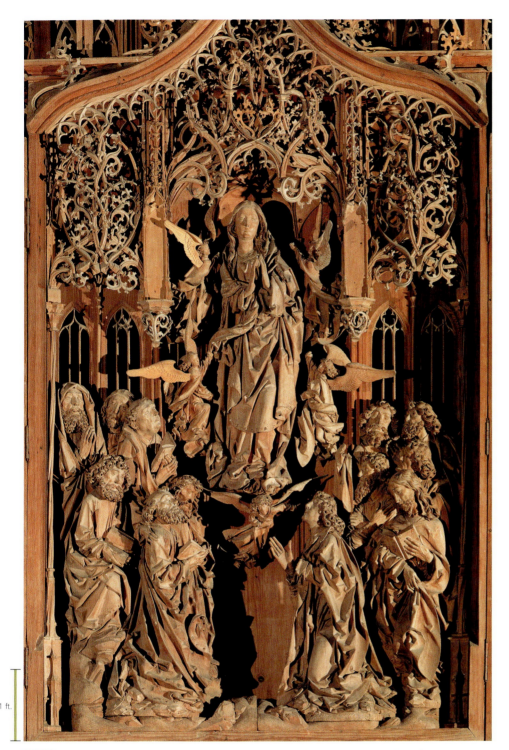

1 ft.

8-11 TILMAN RIEMENSCHNEIDER, *Assumption of the Virgin*, center panel of the *Creglingen Altarpiece*, parish church, Creglingen, Germany, ca. 1495–1499. Lindenwood, 6′ 1″ wide.

Tilman Riemenschneider specialized in carving large wooden retables. His works feature intricate Gothic tracery and religious figures whose bodies are almost lost within their swirling garments.

Martin Schongauer A new age blossomed with the invention by Johannes Gutenberg (ca. 1398–1468) of movable type around 1450 and the development of the printing press. Printing had been known in China centuries before but had never fostered, as it did in 15th-century Europe, a revolution in written communication and in the generation and management of information. Printing provided new and challenging media for artists, and the earliest form was the *woodcut* (see "Woodcuts, Engravings, and Etchings," page 228). Artists produced woodblock prints well before the development of movable-type printing. But when a rise in literacy and the improved economy necessitated production of illustrated books on a grand scale, artists met the challenge of bringing the woodcut picture onto the same page as the letterpress. The woodcut medium hardly had matured when the technique of *engraving*, begun in the 1430s and well developed by 1450, proved much more flexible. Predictably, in the second half of the century, engraving began to replace the woodcut process for making both book illustrations and widely popular single prints.

MARTIN SCHONGAUER (ca. 1430–1491) was the most skilled and subtle early master of metal engraving in Northern Europe. His *Saint Anthony Tormented by Demons* (FIG. **8-12**) shows both the versatility of the medium and the artist's mastery of it. The stoic saint is caught in a revolving thornbush of spiky demons, who claw and tear at him furiously. With unsurpassed skill and subtlety, Schongauer created marvelous distinctions of tonal values and textures—from smooth skin to rough cloth, from the furry and feathery to the hairy and scaly. The use of *cross-hatching* to describe forms, which Schongauer probably developed, became standard among German graphic artists. The Italians preferred *parallel hatching* (FIG. **8-28**) and rarely adopted the other method, which, in keeping with the general Northern European approach to art, tends to describe the surfaces of things rather than their underlying structures.

eries float and flow around bodies lost within them, serving not as descriptions but as design elements that tie the figures to one another and to the framework. A look of psychic strain, a facial expression common in Riemenschneider's work, heightens the spirituality of the figures, immaterial and weightless as they appear.

Woodcuts, Engravings, and Etchings

With the invention of movable type in the 15th century and the new widespread availability of paper from commercial mills, the art of printmaking developed rapidly in Europe. A *print* is an artwork on paper, usually produced in multiple impressions. The set of prints an artist creates from a single print surface is called an *edition*. The printmaking process involves the transfer of ink from a printing surface to paper. This can be accomplished in several ways. During the 15th and 16th centuries, artists most commonly used the relief and *intaglio* methods of printmaking.

Artists produce relief prints, the oldest printing method, by carving into a surface, usually wood. Relief printing requires artists to conceptualize their images negatively—that is, they remove the surface areas around the images. Thus, when the printmaker inks the surface, the carved-out areas remain clean, and a positive image results when the artist presses the printing block against paper. Because artists produce *woodcuts* through a subtractive process (removing parts of the material), it is difficult to create very thin, fluid, and closely spaced lines. As a result, woodcut prints tend to exhibit stark contrasts and sharp edges (for example, FIG. I-5).

In contrast to the production of relief prints, the intaglio method involves a positive process. The artist *incises* (scratches) an image on a metal plate, often copper. The image can be created on the plate manually (*engraving* or *drypoint*) using a tool (*burin* or *stylus*; for example, FIGS. 8-12 and 8-28) or chemically (*etching*; for example FIG. 10-24). In the latter process, an acid bath eats into the exposed parts of the plate where the artist has drawn through an acid-resistant coating. When the artist inks the surface of the intaglio plate and wipes it clean, the ink is forced into the incisions. Then the printmaker runs the plate and paper through a roller press, and the paper absorbs the remaining ink, creating the print. Because the engraver "draws" the image onto the plate, intaglio prints differ in character from relief prints. Engravings, drypoints, and etchings generally present a wider variety of linear effects. They also often reveal to a greater extent evidence of the artist's touch, the result of the hand's changing pressure and shifting directions.

The paper and ink artists use also affect the finished look of the printed image. During the 15th and 16th centuries, European printmakers used papers produced from cotton and linen rags that papermakers mashed with water into a pulp. The papermakers then applied a thin layer of this pulp to a wire screen and allowed it to dry to create the paper. As contact with Asia increased, printmakers made greater use of what was called Japan paper (of mulberry fibers) and China paper. Artists, then as now, could select from a wide variety of inks. The type and proportion of the ink ingredients affect the consistency, color, and oiliness of inks, which various papers absorb differently.

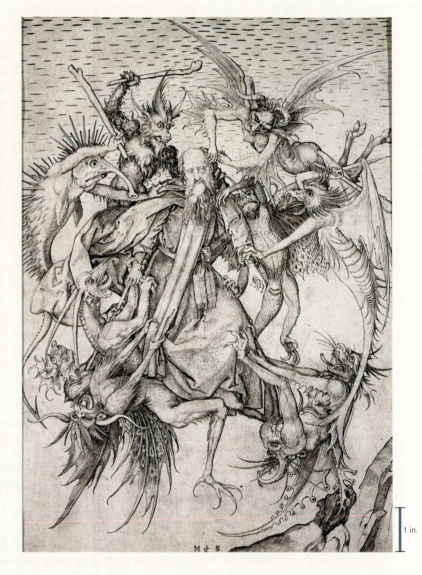

8-12 MARTIN SCHONGAUER, *Saint Anthony Tormented by Demons*, ca. 1480–1490. Engraving, $1' \frac{1}{4}'' \times 9''$. Fondazione Magnani Rocca, Corte di Mamiano.

Martin Schongauer was the most skilled of the early masters of metal engraving. By using a burin to incise lines in a copper plate, he was able to create a marvelous variety of tonal values and textures.

ITALY

During the 15th century, Italy witnessed constant fluctuations in its political and economic spheres, including shifting power relations among the numerous city-states and republics and the rise of princely courts (MAP **8-2**). *Condottieri* (military leaders) with large numbers of mercenary troops at their disposal played a major role in the ongoing struggle for power. Papal Rome and the courts of Urbino, Mantua, and other cities emerged as cultural and artistic centers alongside the great art centers of the 14th century, especially the Republic of Florence. The association of humanism with educa-

MAP 8-2 Italy around 1400.

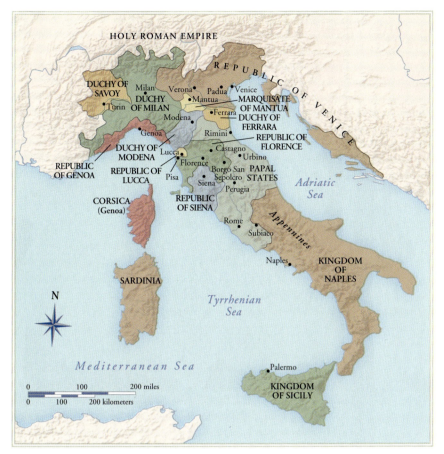

since antiquity. His grandson Lorenzo (1449–1492), called "the Magnificent," was a talented poet himself and gathered about him a galaxy of artists and gifted men in all fields, extending the library Cosimo had begun and revitalizing his academy for instructing artists. He also participated in what some scholars have called the Platonic Academy of Philosophy (most likely an informal reading group) and lavished funds (often the city's rather than his own) on splendid buildings, festivals, and pageants.

Baptistery Competition The history of 15th-century Florentine art, however, does not begin with the Medici but with a competition in 1401 sponsored by the Arte di Calimala (wool merchants guild). The guild invited artists to submit designs for the new east doors of Florence's baptistery. The commission was prestigious because the doors faced the entrance to Florence Cathedral (FIG. 7-36). The judges required each entrant to submit a relief panel depicting the sacrifice of Isaac, an important Old Testament subject (see Chapter 4). Historical developments of the time, however, may have been an important factor in the selection of this theme. In the late 1390s, the duke of Milan, Giangaleazzo Visconti, began a military campaign to take over the Italian peninsula. By 1401, Visconti's troops had surrounded Florence, and the republic's independence was in serious jeopardy. Despite dwindling water and food supplies, Florentine officials exhorted the public to defend the city's freedom. For example, the humanist chancellor Coluccio Salutati urged his fellow citizens to adopt the republican ideal of civil and political liberty associated with ancient Rome and to identify with its spirit. To be Florentine was to be Roman. Freedom was the distinguishing virtue of both. The story of Abraham and Isaac, with its theme of sacrifice, paralleled the message city officials had conveyed to inhabitants. The Florentines' reward for their faith and sacrifice came in 1402 when Visconti died suddenly, ending the invasion threat.

Only the panels of the two finalists, FILIPPO BRUNELLESCHI (1377–1446) and LORENZO GHIBERTI (1378–1455), have survived. As the jury instructed, both artists used the same French Gothic *quatrefoil* frames employed earlier for the panels on the baptistery's south doors, and depicted the same moment of the narrative—the angel's halting of Abraham's

tion and culture appealed to accomplished individuals of high status, and humanism had its greatest impact among the elite and powerful, whether in the republics or the princely courts. These individuals were in the best position to commission art. As a result, humanist ideas permeate Italian Renaissance art. The intersection of art with humanist doctrines during the Renaissance is evident in the popularity of subjects selected from classical history or mythology; increased concern with developing perspectival systems and depicting anatomy accurately; revival of portraiture and other self-aggrandizing forms of patronage; and citizens' extensive participation in civic and religious art commissions.

Florence

Because high-level patronage required significant accumulated wealth, those individuals and families that most prospered economically came to the fore in artistic circles. The best-known Italian Renaissance art patrons were the Medici of Florence, who acquired their vast fortune through banking. Although they were not a court family, the Medici used their tremendous wealth to wield great power and to commission art and architecture on a scale rarely seen. Scarcely a major architect, painter, sculptor, philosopher, or humanist scholar escaped the family's notice. The Medici were Renaissance humanists in the broadest sense of the term. Cosimo de' Medici (1389–1464), in fact, expended a fortune on manuscripts and books and opened the first public library

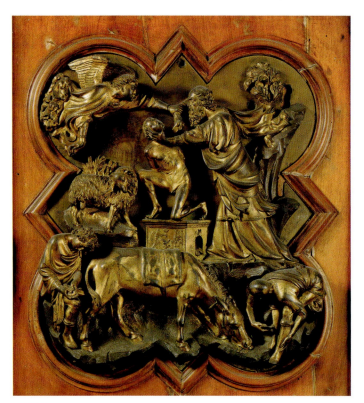

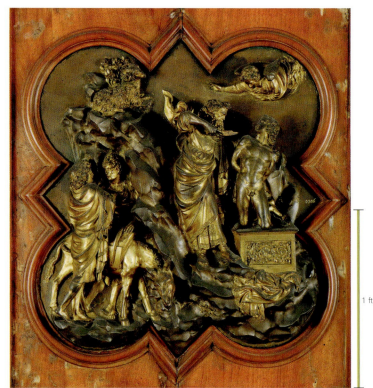

8-13 FILIPPO BRUNELLESCHI, *Sacrifice of Isaac*, competition panel for the east doors of the baptistery, Florence, Italy, 1401–1402. Gilded bronze, 1′ 9″ × 1′ 5½″. Museo Nazionale del Bargello, Florence.

Brunelleschi's entry in the competition to create new bronze doors for the Florentine baptistery shows a frantic angel about to halt an emotional, lunging Abraham clothed in swirling Gothic robes.

8-14 LORENZO GHIBERTI, *Sacrifice of Isaac*, competition panel for the east doors of the baptistery, Florence, Italy, 1401–1402. Gilded bronze, 1′ 9″ × 1′ 5½″. Museo Nazionale del Bargello, Florence.

In contrast to Brunelleschi's panel (FIG. 8-13), Ghiberti's entry in the baptistery competition features gracefully posed figures that recall classical statuary. Even Isaac's altar has a Roman acanthus frieze.

sacrifice. Brunelleschi's panel (FIG. **8-13**) shows a sturdy and vigorous interpretation of the theme, with something of the emotional agitation characteristic of Italian Gothic sculpture. Abraham seems suddenly to have summoned the dreadful courage needed to kill his son at God's command. He lunges forward, robes flying, exposing Isaac's throat to the knife. Matching Abraham's energy, the saving angel darts in from the left, grabbing Abraham's arm to prevent the killing. Brunelleschi's figures demonstrate his ability to observe carefully and represent faithfully all the elements in the biblical narrative.

Whereas Brunelleschi imbued his image with dramatic emotion, Ghiberti, the youngest artist in the competition, emphasized grace and smoothness. In his panel (FIG. **8-14**), Abraham appears in a typically Gothic S-curve pose with outthrust hip (FIG. 7-19) and seems to contemplate the act he is to perform, even as he draws his arm back to strike. The figure of Isaac, beautifully posed and rendered, recalls Greco-Roman statuary. Unlike his medieval predecessors, Ghiberti revealed a genuine appreciation of the nude male form and a deep interest in how the muscular system and skeletal structure move the human body. Even the altar on which Isaac kneels displays Ghiberti's emulation of antique models. Decorating it are acanthus scrolls of a type that commonly adorned Roman buildings. These classical references reflect the increasing influence of humanism. Ghiberti's *Sacrifice of*

Isaac is also noteworthy for the artist's interest in spatial illusion. The rocky landscape seems to emerge from the blank panel toward the viewer, as does the strongly foreshortened angel. Brunelleschi's image, in contrast, emphasizes the planar orientation of the surface.

Ghiberti's training included both painting and metalwork. His careful treatment of the gilded bronze surfaces, with their sharply and accurately incised detail, proves his skill as a goldsmith. That Ghiberti cast his panel in only two pieces (thereby reducing the amount of bronze needed) no doubt impressed the selection committee. (Brunelleschi's panel consists of several cast pieces.) Thus, not only would Ghiberti's doors, as proposed, be lighter and more impervious to the elements, but they also represented a significant cost savings. The younger artist's submission clearly had much to recommend it, both stylistically and technically, and the judges awarded the commission to him.

Gates of Paradise Ghiberti completed the baptistery's east doors in 1424, but church officials moved them to the north side of the building so that he could execute another pair of doors for the eastern entrance. This second project (1425–1452) produced the famous east doors (FIG. **8-15**) that Michelangelo later declared were "so beautiful that they would do well for the gates of Paradise."[1] In the *Gates of Paradise*, Ghiberti abandoned the quatrefoil frames

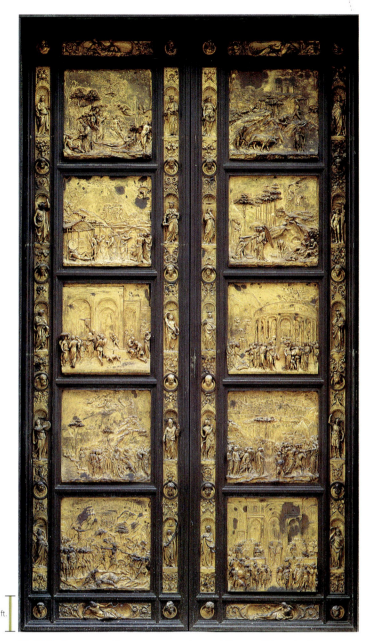

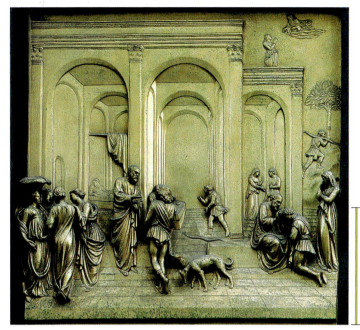

8-16 LORENZO GHIBERTI, *Isaac and His Sons* (detail of FIG. 8-15), east doors (*Gates of Paradise*), baptistery, Florence, Italy, 1425–1452. Gilded bronze, 2′ 7½″ × 2′ 7½″. Museo dell'Opera del Duomo, Florence.

In this relief, Ghiberti employed linear perspective to create the illusion of distance, but he also used sculptural atmospheric perspective, with forms appearing less distinct the deeper they are in space.

means. He represented buildings using *linear perspective* (see "Renaissance Perspectival Systems," page 232, and FIG. **8-17**), but the figures (in the bottom section of the relief, which actually projects slightly toward the viewer) appear almost fully in the round, some of their heads standing completely free. As the eye progresses upward, the relief increasingly flattens, concluding with the architecture in the background, which Ghiberti depicted in barely raised lines. In this manner, the artist created a sort of sculptor's *aerial perspective*, with forms appearing less distinct the deeper they are in space.

In these panels, Ghiberti achieved a greater sense of depth than had previously seemed possible in a relief, but his principal figures do not occupy the architectural space he created for them. Rather, the artist arranged them along a parallel plane in front of the grandiose architecture. (According to Alberti in *On the Art of Building*, the grandeur of the architecture reflects the dignity of the events shown in the foreground.) Ghiberti's figure style mixes a Gothic patterning of rhythmic line, classical poses and motifs, and a new realism in characterization, movement, and surface detail. Ghiberti retained the medieval narrative method of presenting several episodes within a single frame. In *Isaac and His Sons*, the women in the left foreground attend the birth of Esau and Jacob in the left background. In the central foreground, Isaac sends Esau and his dogs to hunt game. In the right foreground, Isaac blesses the kneeling Jacob as Rebecca looks on. Yet viewers experience little confusion because of Ghiberti's careful and subtle placement of each scene. The figures, in varying degrees of projection, grace-

8-15 LORENZO GHIBERTI, east doors (*Gates of Paradise*), baptistery, Florence, Italy, 1425–1452. Gilded bronze, 17′ high. Modern copy, ca. 1980. Original panels in Museo dell'Opera del Duomo, Florence.

In Ghiberti's later doors for the Florentine baptistery, the sculptor abandoned the Gothic quatrefoil frames for the biblical scenes (compare FIG. 8-14) and employed painterly illusionistic devices.

and reduced the number of panels from 28 to 10. Each panel contains a relief set in plain moldings and depicts a scene from the Old Testament. The complete gilding of the reliefs creates an effect of great splendor and elegance.

The individual panels, such as *Isaac and His Sons* (FIG. **8-16**), clearly recall painting techniques in their depiction of space as well as in their treatment of the narrative. Some exemplify more fully than painting many of the principles the architect and theorist Leon Battista Alberti (FIGS. 8-33, 8-36, and 8-37) formulated in his 1435 treatise, *On Painting*. In his relief, Ghiberti created the illusion of space partly through the use of pictorial perspective and partly by sculptural

Renaissance Perspectival Systems

Scholars long have noted the Renaissance fascination with perspective. In essence, portraying perspective involves constructing a convincing illusion of space in two-dimensional imagery while unifying all objects within a single spatial system. Renaissance artists were not the first to focus on depicting illusionistic space. Both the Greeks and the Romans were well versed in perspectival rendering (FIG. 3-19, *right*). However, the Renaissance rediscovery of and interest in perspective contrasted sharply with the portrayal of space during the Middle Ages, when spiritual concerns superseded the desire to depict objects illusionistically.

Renaissance perspectival systems included both linear perspective and atmospheric perspective. Developed by Filippo Brunelleschi, *linear perspective* allows artists to determine mathematically the relative size of rendered objects to correlate them with the visual recession into space. Linear perspective can be either one-point or two-point.

■ In one-point linear perspective (FIG. 8-17*a*) the artist first must identify a horizontal line that marks, in the image, the horizon in the distance (hence the term *horizon line*). The artist then selects a *vanishing point* on that horizon line (often located at the exact center of the line). By drawing *orthogonals* (diagonal lines) from the edges of the picture to the vanishing point, the artist creates a structural grid that organizes the image and determines the size of objects within the image's illusionistic space. Among the works that provide clear examples of one-point linear perspective are Masaccio's *Holy Trinity* (FIG. 8-23), Piero della Francesca's *Flagellation* (FIG. 8-35), Leonardo da Vinci's *Last Supper* (FIG. 9-3), and Raphael's *School of Athens* (FIG. 9-7). All of these are representations of figures in architectural settings, but linear perspective can also be applied to single figures. An especially dramatic example of the use of one-point perspective to depict a body receding into the background is Andrea Mantegna's *Foreshortened Christ* (FIG. 8-40).

■ Two-point linear perspective (FIG. 8-17*b*) also involves the establishment of a horizon line. Rather than choosing a single vanishing point along this horizon line, the artist identifies two points. The orthogonals that result from drawing lines from an object to each of the vanishing points creates, as in one-point perspective, a grid that indicates the relative size of objects receding into space.

■ Unlike linear perspective, which relies on a structured mathematical system, *atmospheric* (or *aerial*) *perspective* involves optical phenomena. Artists using atmospheric perspective exploit the principle that the farther back the object is in space, the blurrier, less detailed, and bluer it appears. Leonardo da Vinci used atmospheric perspective to great effect, as seen in works such as *Madonna of the Rocks* (FIG. 9-2) and *Mona Lisa* (FIG. 9-4).

Earlier Italian artists, such as Duccio (FIG. 7-32) and Lorenzetti (FIG. 7-34), had used several devices to indicate distance, but with the development of linear perspective, Renaissance artists acquired a way to make the illusion of distance certain and consistent. In effect, they conceived the picture plane as a transparent window through which the observer looks to see the constructed pictorial world. This discovery was enormously important, for it made possible what has been called the "rationalization of sight." It brought all random and infinitely various visual sensations under a simple rule that could be expressed mathematically. Indeed, Renaissance artists' interest in perspective reflects the emergence of science itself. Of course, the 15th-century artists were not primarily scientists. They simply found perspective an effective way to order and clarify their compositions. Nonetheless, perspective, with its new mathematical certitude, conferred a kind of aesthetic legitimacy on painting and relief sculpture by making the picture measurable and exact. According to Plato, measure is the basis of beauty, and Classical Greek art reflects this belief (see Chapter 2). In the Renaissance, when humanists rediscovered Plato and eagerly read his works, artists once again exalted the principle of measure as the foundation of the beautiful in the fine arts. The projection of measurable objects on flat surfaces influenced the character of Renaissance paintings and made possible scale drawings, maps, charts, graphs, and diagrams—means of exact representation that laid the foundation for modern science and technology. Mathematical truth and formal beauty conjoined in the minds of Renaissance artists.

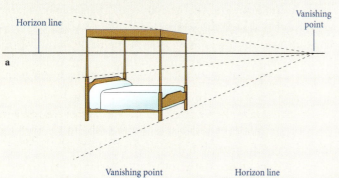

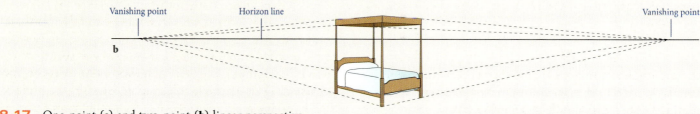

8-17 One-point (**a**) and two-point (**b**) linear perspective.

Linear perspective reflected the emergence of modern science itself. With its mathematical certitude, perspective also elevated the stature of painting by making pictures rational and measurable.

fully twist and turn, appearing to occupy and move through a convincing stage space, which Ghiberti deepened by showing some figures from behind. The classicism derives from the artist's close study of ancient art. Ghiberti admired and collected classical sculpture, bronzes, and coins. Their influence appears throughout the panel, particularly in the figure of Rebecca, which Ghiberti based on a popular Greco-Roman statuary type. The emerging practice of collecting

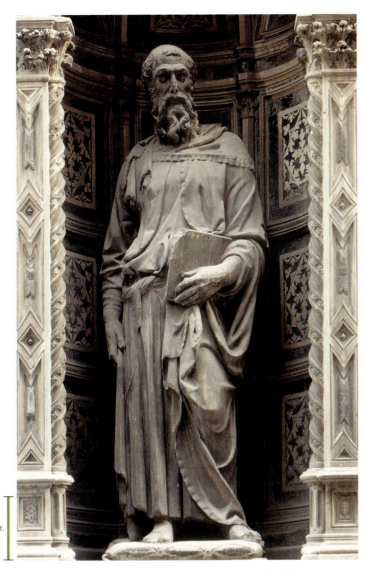

1 ft.

8-18 DONATELLO, *Saint Mark*, Or San Michele, Florence, Italy, ca. 1411–1413. Marble, 7′ 9″ high. Modern copy in exterior niche. Original sculpture in museum on second floor of Or San Michele, Florence.

In this statue carved for the guild of linen drapers, Donatello introduced the classical principle of contrapposto into Early Renaissance sculpture. The drapery falls naturally and moves with the body.

classical art in the 15th century had much to do with the incorporation of classical motifs and the emulation of classical style in Renaissance art.

Donatello A younger contemporary of Ghiberti was Donato di Niccolo Bardi, or DONATELLO (ca. 1386–1466). He participated along with other esteemed sculptors, including Ghiberti, in another major Florentine art program of the early 1400s, the decoration of Or San Michele. The building housed a church, a granary, and the headquarters of Florence's guilds. City officials assigned each of the niches on the building's exterior to a specific guild for decoration with a statue of its patron saint. Donatello completed *Saint Mark* (FIG. **8-18**) for the guild of linen drapers in 1413. In this sculpture, Donatello introduced the classical principle of weight shift, or *contrapposto* (see Chapter 2), into Early Renaissance sculpture. As the saint's body moves, the drap-

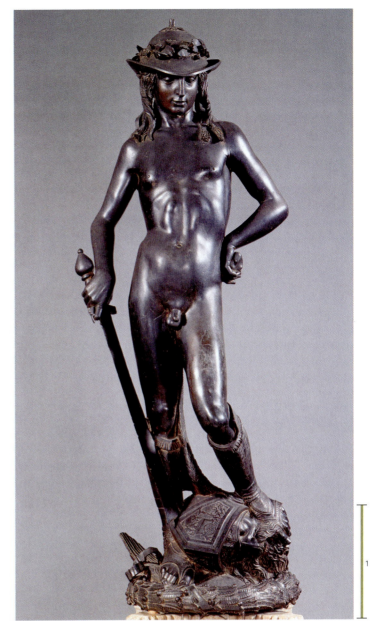

1 ft.

8-19 DONATELLO, *David*, ca. 1440–1460. Bronze, 5′ 2¼″ high. Museo Nazionale del Bargello, Florence.

Donatello's *David* possesses both the relaxed nude contrapposto and the sensuous beauty of nude Greek gods (FIG. 2-48). The revival of classical statuary style appealed to the sculptor's patrons, the Medici.

ery moves with it, hanging and folding naturally from and around different body parts so that the viewer senses the figure as a draped nude human, not a stone statue with arbitrarily incised drapery. Donatello's *Saint Mark* is the first Renaissance statue whose voluminous drapery (the pride of the Florentine guild that paid for the statue) does not conceal but accentuates the movement of the arms, legs, shoulders, and hips. This development further contributed to the sculpted figure's independence from its architectural setting. Saint Mark's stirring limbs, shifting weight, and mobile drapery suggest impending movement out of the niche.

David Donatello also enjoyed the patronage of the Medici. He cast the bronze statue *David* (FIG. **8-19**) sometime between 1440 and 1460 for the Palazzo Medici courtyard

(FIG. 8-32). The Medici were aware of Donatello's earlier *David*, a sculpture located in the Palazzo della Signoria, the center of political activity in Florence. The artist had produced it during the threat of invasion by King Ladislaus (r. 1399–1414) of Naples, and it had become a symbol of Florentine strength and independence. That the Medici selected the same subject for their private residence suggests that they identified themselves with Florence or, at the very least, saw themselves as responsible for the city's prosperity and freedom. Donatello's *David* was the first nude statue since ancient times. During the Middle Ages, the clergy regarded nude statues as both indecent and idolatrous, and nudity in general appeared only rarely in art—and then only in biblical or moralizing contexts, such as the story of Adam and Eve or depictions of sinners in Hell. With *David*, Donatello reinvented the classical nude. His subject, however, was not a pagan god, hero, or athlete but the youthful biblical slayer of Goliath who had become the symbol of the independent Florentine republic. *David* possesses both the relaxed classical contrapposto stance and the proportions and sensuous beauty of Greek gods (FIG. 2-48), qualities absent from medieval figures. The invoking of classical poses and formats appealed to the humanist Medici.

Gattamelata Given the increased emphasis on individual achievement and recognition that humanism fostered, it is not surprising that portraiture enjoyed a revival in 15th-century Italy. The grandest portrait of the era was an 11-foot-tall bronze equestrian statue (FIG. 8-20) that Donatello produced for the Republic of Venice. His assignment was to create a commemorative monument in honor of the recently deceased Venetian *condottiere* (mercenary general) Erasmo da Narni, nicknamed Gattamelata, or "honeyed cat"—a word play on his mother's name, Melania Gattelli. Equestrian statues occasionally had been set up in Italy in the late Middle Ages, but Donatello's *Gattamelata* was the first to rival the grandeur of the mounted portraits of antiquity, such as that of Marcus Aurelius (FIG. 3-40), which the artist must have seen in Rome. Donatello's contemporaries, one of whom described Gattamelata as sitting "there with great magnificence like a triumphant Caesar,"[2] recognized this reference to antiquity. The figure stands high on a lofty elliptical base in the square in front of the church of Sant'Antonio in Padua, the condottiere's birthplace. Massive and majestic, the great horse bears the armored general easily, for, unlike the sculptor of Marcus Aurelius, Donatello did not represent the Venetian commander as superhuman and more than life-size. The condottiere dominates his mighty steed by force of character rather than sheer size. His face set in a mask of dauntless resolution and unshakable will, Gattamelata is the very portrait of the male Renaissance individualist. Such a man—intelligent, courageous, ambitious, and frequently of humble origin—could, by his own resourcefulness and on his own merits, rise to a commanding position in the world. Together, man and horse convey an overwhelming image of irresistible strength

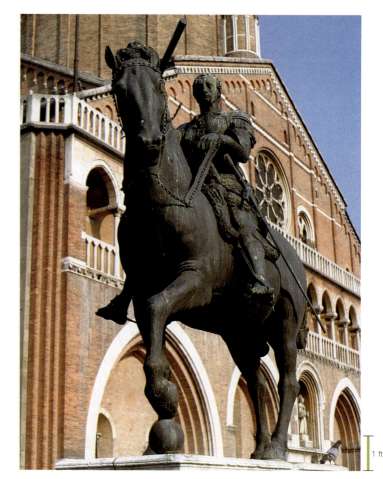

1 ft.

8-20 DONATELLO, *Gattamelata* (equestrian statue of Erasmo da Narni), Piazza del Santo, Padua, Italy, ca. 1445–1453. Bronze, 12′ 2″ high.

Donatello based his giant portrait of a Venetian general on equestrian statues of ancient Roman emperors (FIG. 3-40). Together, man and horse convey an overwhelming image of irresistible strength.

and unlimited power—an impression Donatello reinforced visually by placing the left forehoof of the horse on an orb, reviving a venerable ancient symbol for hegemony over the earth—a remarkable conceit because Erasmo da Narni was not a head of state.

Gentile da Fabriano In 15th-century Italy, humanism and the celebration of classical artistic values also characterized panel and mural painting. The new Renaissance style did not, however, immediately displace all vestiges of the Late Gothic style. In particular, the International Style, the dominant painting style around 1400 (see Chapter 7), persisted well into the century. The leading Florentine master of the International Style was GENTILE DA FABRIANO (ca. 1370–1427), who in 1423 painted *Adoration of the Magi* (FIG. 8-21) as the altarpiece for the family chapel of Palla Strozzi in the church of Santa Trinità in Florence. At the beginning of the 15th century, the Strozzi family was the wealthiest in Florence. The altarpiece, with its elaborate gilded Gothic frame, is testimony to the patron's lavish

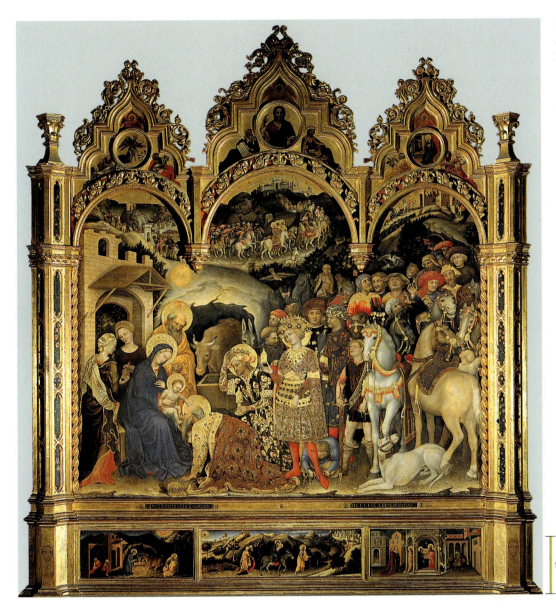

8-21 GENTILE DA FABRIANO, *Adoration of the Magi*, altarpiece from the Strozzi Chapel, Santa Trinità, Florence, Italy, 1423. Tempera on wood, 9' 11" × 9' 3". Galleria degli Uffizi, Florence.

Gentile was the leading Florentine painter working in the International Style, but he successfully blended naturalistic details with Late Gothic splendor in color, costume, and framing ornament.

1 ft.

tastes. So too is the painting itself, with its gorgeous surface and sumptuously costumed kings, courtiers, captains, and retainers accompanied by a menagerie of exotic animals. Gentile portrayed all these elements in a rainbow of color with extensive use of gold. The painting presents all the pomp and ceremony of chivalric etiquette in a scene that sanctifies the aristocracy in the presence of the Madonna and Child. Although the style is fundamentally Late Gothic, Gentile inserted striking naturalistic details. For example, the artist depicted animals from a variety of angles and foreshortened the forms convincingly, most notably the horse at the far right seen in a three-quarter rear view. Gentile did the same with human figures, such as the kneeling man removing the spurs from the standing *magus* (wise man) in the center foreground. In the left panel of the predella, Gentile painted what may have been the very first nighttime Nativity with the central light source—the radiant Christ Child—introduced into the picture itself. Although predominantly conservative, Gentile demonstrated that he was not oblivi-

ous to experimental trends and that he could blend naturalistic and inventive elements skillfully and subtly into a traditional composition without sacrificing Late Gothic splendor in color, costume, and framing ornament.

Masaccio The artist who epitomizes the innovative spirit of early-15th-century Florentine painting was Tommaso di ser Giovanni di Mone Cassai, known as **MASACCIO** (1401–1428). Although his presumed teacher, Masolino da Panicale, had worked in the International Style, Masaccio moved suddenly, within the short span of six years, into unexplored territory. Most art historians recognize no other painter in history to have contributed so much to the development of a new style in so short a time as Masaccio, whose untimely death at age 27 cut short his brilliant career. Masaccio was the artistic descendant of Giotto (FIGS. 7-29 to 7-31), whose calm monumental style he revolutionized with a whole new repertoire of representational devices that generations of Renaissance painters later studied and developed.

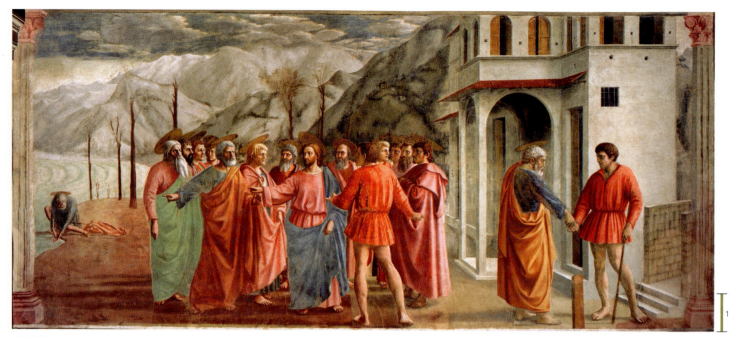

8-22 MASACCIO, *Tribute Money*, Brancacci Chapel, Santa Maria del Carmine, Florence, Italy, ca. 1424–1427. Fresco, 8′ 4⅛″ × 19′ 7⅛″.

Masaccio's figures recall Giotto's in their simple grandeur, but they convey a greater psychological and physical credibility. He modeled his figures with the light coming from outside the picture.

Tribute Money (FIG. 8-22), in the Brancacci Chapel of Santa Maria del Carmine in Florence, displays Masaccio's innovations. The fresco depicts an episode from the Gospel of Matthew (17:24–27). As the tax collector confronts Christ at the entrance to the Roman town of Capernaum, Christ directs Saint Peter to the shore of Lake Galilee. There, as Christ foresaw, Peter finds the tribute coin in the mouth of a fish and returns to pay the tax. Masaccio divided this narrative into three episodes within the fresco. In the center, Christ, surrounded by his disciples, tells Saint Peter to retrieve the coin from the fish, while the tax collector stands in the foreground, his back to spectators and hand extended, awaiting payment. At the left, in the middle distance, Peter extracts the coin from the fish's mouth, and, at the right, he thrusts the coin into the tax collector's hand. Masaccio's figures recall Giotto's in their simple grandeur, but they convey a greater psychological and physical credibility. Masaccio created the bulk of the figures by modeling not with a flat, neutral light lacking an identifiable source but with a light coming from a specific source outside the picture. The light comes from the right and strikes the figures at an angle, illuminating the parts of the solids that obstruct its path and leaving the rest in deep shadow, producing the illusion of deep sculptural relief. Between the extremes of light and dark, the light appears as a constantly active but fluctuating force highlighting the scene in varying degrees, almost a tangible substance independent of the figures. In his frescoes, Giotto used light only to model the masses. In Masaccio's work, light has its own nature, and the masses are visible only because of its direction and intensity. The viewer can imagine the light as playing over forms—reveal-ing some and concealing others, as the artist directs it. The individual figures in *Tribute Money* are solemn and weighty, but they also move freely and reveal body structure, as do Donatello's statues. Masaccio's representations adeptly suggest bones, muscles, and the pressures and tensions of joints. Each figure conveys a maximum of contained energy. *Tribute Money* helps the viewer understand Giorgio Vasari's comment: "The works made before his [Masaccio's] day can be said to be painted, while his are living, real, and natural."[3]

Masaccio's arrangement of the figures was equally inventive. They do not appear as a stiff screen in the foreground. Instead, the artist grouped them in circular depth around Christ, and he placed the whole group in a spacious landscape, rather than in the confined stage space of earlier frescoes. The group itself generates the foreground space that the architecture on the right amplifies. Masaccio depicted the building in one-point perspective, locating the vanishing point, where all the orthogonals converge, at Christ's head. Atmospheric perspective (see "Renaissance Perspectival Systems," page 232) unites the foreground with the background. Although ancient Roman painters used atmospheric perspective (FIG. 3-20), medieval artists had abandoned it. Thus it virtually disappeared from art until Masaccio and his contemporaries rediscovered it. They came to realize that light and air interposed between viewers and what they see are parts of the visual experience called "distance."

Holy Trinity Masaccio's *Holy Trinity* fresco (FIG. 8-23) in Santa Maria Novella is another of the young artist's masterworks and the premier early-15th-century example of the application of mathematics to convey perspective in picto-

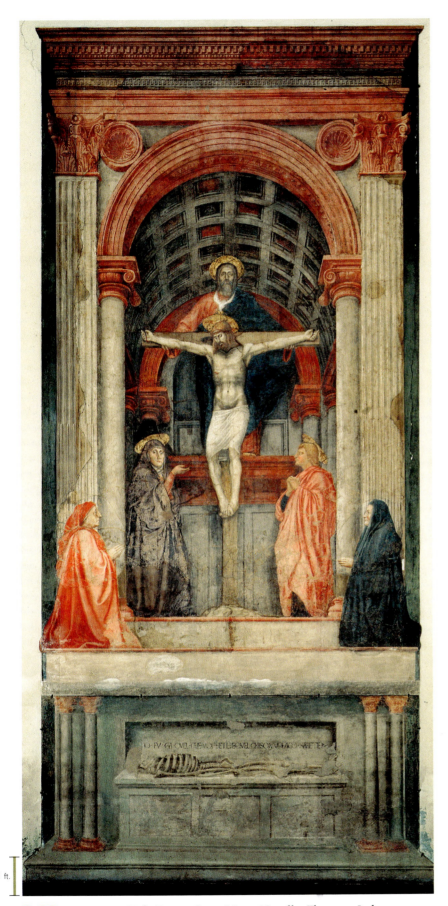

1 ft.

8-23 MASACCIO, *Holy Trinity*, Santa Maria Novella, Florence, Italy, ca. 1424–1427. Fresco, 21′ 10⅝″ × 10′ 4¾″.

Masaccio's *Holy Trinity* is the premier early-15th-century example of the application of mathematics to pictorial organization in Brunelleschi's new science of perspective. The illusionism is breathtaking.

rial organization. Masaccio painted the composition on two levels of unequal height. Above, in a coffered barrel-vaulted chapel reminiscent of a Roman triumphal arch (FIG. **3-31**), the Virgin Mary and Saint John appear on either side of the crucified Christ. God the Father emerges from behind Christ, supporting the arms of the cross and presenting his Son to the worshiper as a devotional object. The dove of the Holy Spirit hovers between God's head and Christ's head. Masaccio also included portraits of the donors of the painting, Lorenzo Lenzi and his wife, who kneel just in front of the pilasters that frame the chapel. Below, the artist painted a tomb containing a skeleton. An inscription in Italian painted above the skeleton reminds spectators that "I was once what you are, and what I am you will become."

The illusionism of *Holy Trinity* is breathtaking. In this fresco, Masaccio brilliantly demonstrated the principles and potential of Brunelleschi's new science of perspective. Indeed, this work so thoroughly incorporates those principles that some historians have suggested Brunelleschi may have collaborated with Masaccio. The vanishing point of the composition is at the foot of the cross. With this point at eye level, spectators look up at the Trinity and down at the tomb. About five feet above the floor level, the vanishing point pulls the two views together, creating the illusion of a stone structure that transects the wall's vertical plane. Whereas the tomb appears to project forward into the church, the chapel recedes visually behind the wall and appears as an extension of the spectators' space. This adjustment of the pictured space to the viewer's position was an important innovation in illusionistic painting, which other artists of the Renaissance and the later Baroque period would advance. Masaccio was so exact in his metrical proportions that it is possible to calculate the dimensions of the chapel (for example, the span of the painted vault is seven feet and the depth of the chapel is nine feet). Thus, he achieved not only a successful illusion but also a rational measured coherence that is responsible for the unity and harmony of this monumental composition. *Holy Trinity* is, however, much more than a demonstration of Brunelleschi's perspective or of the painter's ability to represent fully modeled figures bathed in light. In this painting, Masaccio also powerfully conveyed one of the central tenets of Christian faith. The ascending pyramid of figures leads viewers from the despair of death to the hope of resurrection and eternal life through Christ's crucifixion.

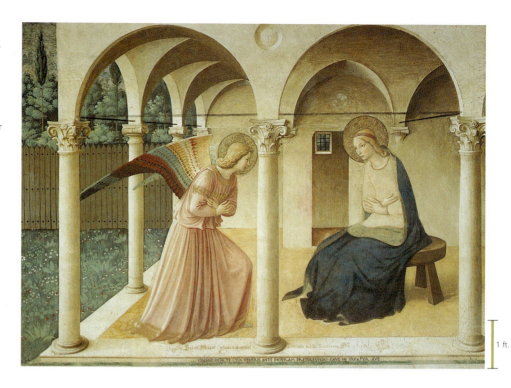

8-24 FRA ANGELICO, *Annunciation*, San Marco, Florence, Italy, ca. 1438–1447. Fresco, 7' 1" × 10' 6".

Painted for the Dominican monks of San Marco, Fra Angelico's fresco is characteristically simple and direct. Its figures and architecture have a pristine clarity that befits their function as devotional images.

1 ft.

Fra Angelico As Masaccio's *Holy Trinity* clearly demonstrates, humanism and religion were not mutually exclusive in 15th-century Florence. Nevertheless, for many 15th-century Italian artists, humanist concerns were not a primary consideration. FRA ANGELICO (ca. 1400–1455) was a leading painter whose art focused on serving the Roman Catholic Church. In the late 1430s, the abbot of the Dominican monastery of San Marco (Saint Mark) in Florence asked Fra Angelico to produce a series of frescoes for the monastery. The Dominicans had dedicated themselves to lives of prayer and work, and their Florentine religious compound was mostly spare and austere to encourage the monks to immerse themselves in their devotional lives. Fra Angelico's frescoes illustrated a 13th-century text, *The Way of Prayer*, which describes Saint Dominic's nine styles of prayer. *Annunciation* (FIG. **8-24**) appears at the top of the stairs leading to the friars' cells.

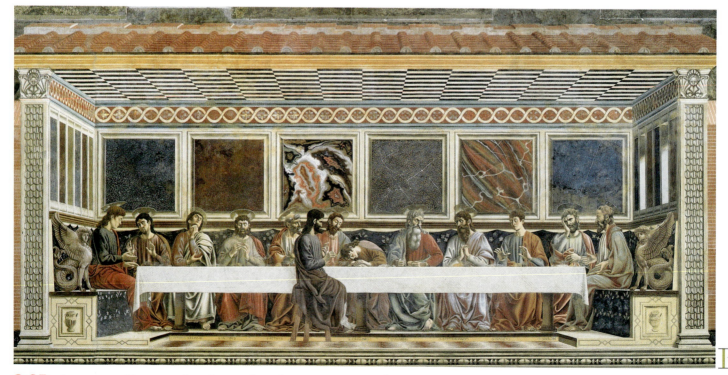

1 ft.

8-25 ANDREA DEL CASTAGNO, *Last Supper*, the refectory, monastery of Sant'Apollonia, Florence, Italy, 1447. Fresco, 15' 5" × 32'.

Judas sits isolated in this *Last Supper* fresco based on the Gospel of Saint John. The figures are small compared with the setting, reflecting Castagno's preoccupation with perspective painting.

Appropriately, the artist presented the scene of the Virgin Mary and the Archangel Gabriel with simplicity and serenity. The two figures appear in a plain *loggia*, and Fra Angelico painted all the fresco elements with a pristine clarity. As an admonition to heed the devotional function of the images, he included a small inscription at the base of the image: "As you venerate, while passing before it, this figure of the intact Virgin, beware lest you omit to say a Hail Mary." Like most of Fra Angelico's paintings, *Annunciation*'s simplicity and directness still have an almost universal appeal and fully reflect the artist's simple and humble character.

Andrea del Castagno Another painter who accepted a commission to produce a series of frescoes for a religious establishment was ANDREA DEL CASTAGNO (ca. 1421–1457). His *Last Supper* (FIG. **8-25**), painted in the *refectory* (dining hall) of Sant'Apollonia in Florence, a convent for Benedictine nuns, manifests both a commitment to the biblical narrative and an interest in perspective. The lavishly painted room that Christ and his 12 disciples occupy suggests Castagno's absorption with creating the illusion of three-dimensional space. However, closer scrutiny reveals inconsistencies, such as the fact that Renaissance perspectival systems make it impossible to see both the ceiling from inside and the roof from outside, as Castagno depicted. Further, the two side walls do not appear parallel. The artist chose a conventional compositional format, with the figures seated at a horizontally placed table. Castagno derived the apparent self-absorption of most of the disciples and the malevolent features of Judas (who sits alone on the outside of the table) from the Gospel of Saint John, rather than the more familiar version of the Last Supper recounted in the Gospel of Saint Luke. Castagno's dramatic and spatially convincing depiction of the event no doubt was a powerful presence for the nuns during their daily meals.

Fra Filippo Lippi A younger contemporary of Fra Angelico, FRA FILIPPO LIPPI (ca. 1406–1469), was also a friar—but there all resemblance ends. Fra Filippo was unsuited for monastic life. He indulged in misdemeanors ranging from forgery and embezzlement to the abduction of a pretty nun, Lucretia, who became his mistress and the mother of his son, the painter Filippino Lippi (1457–1504). Only the intervention of the Medici on his behalf at the papal court preserved Fra Filippo from severe punishment and total disgrace. An orphan, Fra Filippo spent his youth in a monastery adjacent to the Church of Santa Maria del Carmine and must have met Masaccio there and witnessed the decoration of the Brancacci Chapel. Fra Filippo's early work survives only in fragments, but these show that he tried to work with Masaccio's massive forms. Later, probably under the influence of Ghiberti's and Donatello's relief sculptures, he developed a linear style that emphasized the contours of his figures and permitted him to suggest movement through flying and swirling draperies.

A painting from Fra Filippo's later years, *Madonna and Child with Angels* (FIG. **8-26**), shows his skill in employing

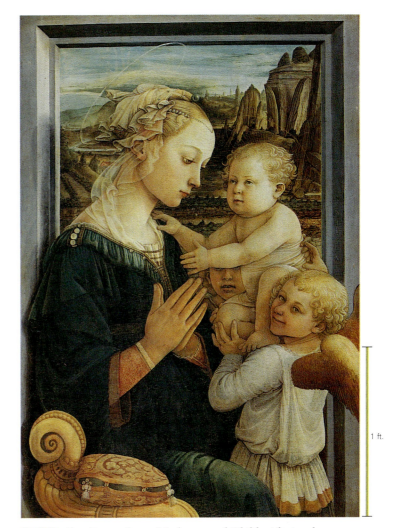

8-26 FRA FILIPPO LIPPI, *Madonna and Child with Angels*, ca. 1455. Tempera on wood, 2′ 11½″ × 2′ 1″. Galleria degli Uffizi, Florence.

Fra Filippo, a monk guilty of many misdemeanors, represented the Virgin and Christ Child in a distinctly worldly manner, carrying the humanization of the holy family further than ever before.

a wonderfully fluid line, which unifies the composition and contributes to the precise and smooth delineation of forms. Fra Filippo interpreted his subject here in a surprisingly worldly manner. The Madonna, a beautiful young mother, is not at all spiritual or fragile, and neither is the Christ Child, whom two angels hold up. One of the angels turns with the mischievous, puckish grin of a boy refusing to behave for the pious occasion. Significantly, all figures reflect the use of live models (perhaps even Lucretia for the Madonna). Fra Filippo plainly relished the charm of youth and beauty as he found it in this world. He preferred the real in landscape also. The background, seen through the window, incorporates recognizable features of the Arno River valley. Compared with the earlier Madonnas by Giotto (FIG. **7-29**) and Duccio (FIG. **7-32**), this work shows how far artists had carried the humanization of the religious theme. Whatever the ideals of spiritual perfection may have meant to artists in past centuries, Renaissance artists realized those ideals in terms of the sensuous beauty of this world.

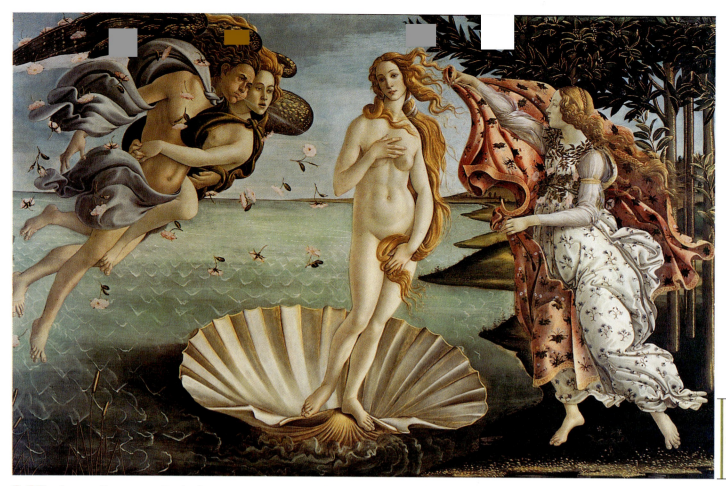

8-27 Sandro Botticelli, *Birth of Venus*, ca. 1484–1486. Tempera on canvas, 5′ 9″ × 9′ 2″. Galleria degli Uffizi, Florence.

Inspired by an Angelo Poliziano poem and classical statues of Aphrodite (FIG. 2-47), Botticelli revived the theme of the female nude in this elegant and romantic representation of Venus born of the sea foam.

Sandro Botticelli Fra Filippo's most famous pupil was Sandro Botticelli (1444–1510), whom the Medici frequently employed and whom art historians universally recognize as one of the great masters of line. One of the works Botticelli painted in tempera on canvas for the Medici is *Birth of Venus* (FIG. 8-27). The theme was the subject of a poem by Angelo Poliziano (1454–1494), a leading humanist of the day. In Botticelli's lyrical painting of the poet's retelling of the Greek myth, Zephyrus (the west wind), carrying Chloris, blows Venus, born of the sea foam and carried on a cockle shell, to her sacred island, Cyprus. There, the nymph Pomona runs to meet her with a brocaded mantle. The lightness and bodilessness of the winds propel all the figures without effort. Draperies undulate easily in the gentle gusts, perfumed by rose petals that fall on the whitecaps. The nudity of Botticelli's Venus was in itself an innovation. As noted earlier, the nude, especially the female nude, was exceedingly rare during the Middle Ages. The artist's use (especially on such a large scale) of an ancient Venus statue—a Hellenistic variant of Praxiteles' famous *Aphrodite of Knidos* (FIG. 2-47)—as a model could have drawn the charge of paganism and infidelity. But in the more accommodating Renaissance culture and under the protection of the powerful Medici, the depiction went unchallenged.

Botticelli's style is clearly distinct from the earnest search many other artists pursued to comprehend humanity and the natural world through a rational, empirical order. Indeed, Botticelli's elegant and beautiful style seems to have ignored all of the scientific knowledge 15th-century artists had gained in the understanding of perspective and anatomy. For example, the seascape in *Birth of Venus* is a flat backdrop devoid of atmospheric perspective. Botticelli's style paralleled the allegorical pageants that acting troupes staged in Florence as chivalric tournaments but structured around allusions to classical mythology. The same trend is evident in the poetry of the 1470s and 1480s. Artists and poets at this time did not directly imitate classical antiquity but used the myths, with delicate perception of their charm, in a way still tinged with medieval romance. Ultimately, Botticelli created a lyrical and courtly style of visual poetry parallel to the love poetry of Lorenzo de' Medici.

The wide range of Medici commissions illustrated in this chapter makes clear that the Florentine banking family did not restrict its collecting to any specific style or artist. Medici acquisitions ranged from mythological to biblical to historical subject matter and included both paintings and sculptures. Collectively, the art of the Medici reveals their wide and eclectic tastes and sincere love of art and learning, and

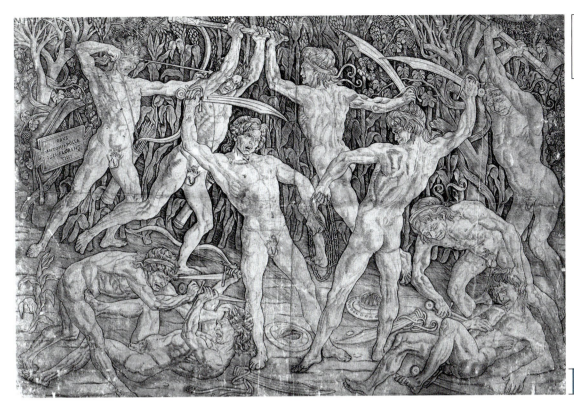

8-28 ANTONIO DEL POLLAIUOLO, *Battle of the Ten Nudes*, ca. 1465. Engraving, 1′ 3⅛″ × 1′ 11¼″. Metropolitan Museum of Art, New York (bequest of Joseph Pulitzer, 1917).

How muscles and sinews activate the human skeleton fascinated Pollaiuolo. The Florentine artist delighted in showing nude figures in violent action and from numerous foreshortened viewpoints.

1 in.

it makes a statement about the patrons themselves as well. Careful businessmen that they were, the Medici were not sentimental about their endowment of art and scholarship. Cosimo acknowledged that his good works were not only for the honor of God but also to construct his own legacy. Like the motivation for other great patrons throughout the ages, the desire of the Medici to promote their own fame led to the creation of many of the most cherished masterpieces in the history of Western art.

Antonio Pollaiuolo Another of the many artists who produced sculptures and paintings for the Medici was ANTONIO POLLAIUOLO (ca. 1431–1498), who took delight in showing human figures in violent action. Masaccio and his contemporaries had dealt effectively with the problem of rendering human anatomy, but their figures were usually at rest or in restrained motion. Pollaiuolo favored subjects dealing with combat. He conceived the body as a powerful machine and liked to display its mechanisms, such as knotted muscles and taut sinews that activate the skeleton as ropes pull levers. To show this to best effect, Pollaiuolo developed a figure so lean and muscular that it appears *écorché* (as if without skin), with strongly accentuated delineations at the wrists, elbows, shoulders, and knees. His engraving *Battle of the Ten Nudes* (FIG. 8-28), an early Italian example of the new medium that Northern European artists (FIG. 8-12) had pioneered, shows this figure type in a variety of poses and from numerous viewpoints, allowing Pollaiuolo to demonstrate his prowess in rendering the nude male figure. In this, he was a kindred spirit of late-sixth-century BCE Greek vase painters, such as Euthymides (FIG. 2-26), who had ex-

perimented with foreshortening for the first time in history. Even though Pollaiuolo's figures hack and slash at each other without mercy, they nevertheless seem somewhat stiff and frozen, because the artist showed *all* the muscle groups at maximum tension. Not until several decades later did an even greater anatomist, Leonardo da Vinci, observe that only part of the body's muscle groups are involved in any one action, while the others remain relaxed.

Florence Cathedral Filippo Brunelleschi's ability to codify a system of linear perspective derived in part from his skill as an architect. Although in a biography of him written around 1480, Giannozzo Manetti (1423–1497) reported that Brunelleschi turned to architecture out of disappointment over the loss of the commission for Florence's baptistery doors, he continued to work as a sculptor for several years and received commissions for sculpture as late as 1416. It is true, however, that as the 15th century progressed, Brunelleschi's interest turned increasingly toward architecture. Several trips to Rome (the first in 1402, probably with his friend Donatello), where the ruins of ancient Rome captivated him, heightened his fascination with architecture. His close study of Roman monuments and his effort to make an accurate record of what he saw may have been the catalyst that led Brunelleschi to develop his revolutionary system of linear perspective.

Brunelleschi's broad knowledge of Roman construction principles, combined with an analytical and inventive mind, permitted him to solve an engineering problem that no other 15th-century architect could tackle. The challenge was the design and construction of a dome

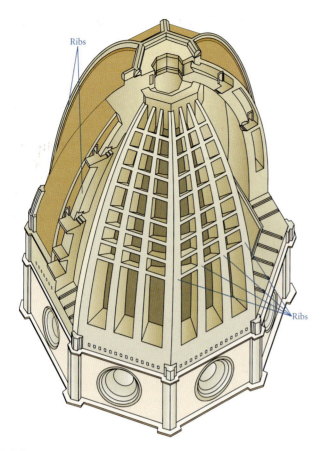

8-29 FILIPPO BRUNELLESCHI, cutaway view of the dome of Florence Cathedral, Florence, Italy, 1420–1436 (after Piero Sanpaolesi).

Brunelleschi solved the problem of placing a dome over the 140-foot crossing of Florence Cathedral by designing a thin double shell that was ogival in section. A heavy lantern anchors the dome at the top.

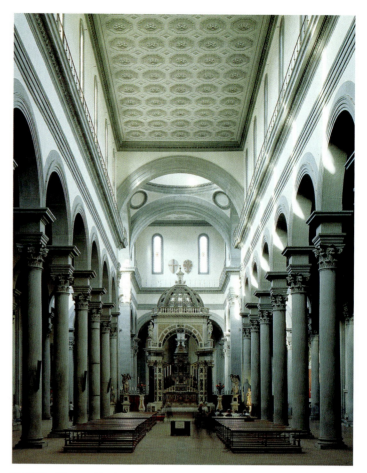

8-30 FILIPPO BRUNELLESCHI, interior of Santo Spirito (looking northeast), Florence, Italy, begun ca. 1436.

Santo Spirito displays the classical rationality of Brunelleschi's mature architectural style in its all-encompassing modular scheme based on the dimensions of the dome-covered crossing square.

(FIG. **8-29**) for the huge crossing of the unfinished Florence Cathedral (FIG. **7-36**). The problem was staggering. The space to be spanned (140 feet) was much too wide to permit construction with the aid of traditional wooden centering. Nor was it possible (because of the crossing plan) to support the dome with buttressed walls. With exceptional ingenuity, Brunelleschi not only discarded traditional building methods and devised new ones but also invented much of the machinery necessary for the job. Although he might have preferred the hemispheric shape of Roman domes, Brunelleschi raised the center of his dome and designed it around an ogival section, which is inherently more stable because it reduces the outward thrust around the dome's base. To minimize the structure's weight, he designed a relatively thin double shell (the first in history) around a skeleton of 24 ribs. The eight most important are visible on the exterior. Finally, in almost paradoxical fashion, Brunelleschi anchored the structure at the top with a heavy lantern. Despite Brunelleschi's knowledge of and admiration for Roman building techniques, and even though the Florence Cathedral dome was his most outstanding engineering achievement, he arrived at the solution to this critical structural problem through what were essentially Gothic building principles. Thus, the dome, which also had to harmonize in formal terms with the century-old building, does not really express Brunelleschi's architectural style.

Santo Spirito Santo Spirito (FIG. **8-30**), begun around 1436, showcases the clarity and classically inspired rationality that characterize Brunelleschi's mature designs. Brunelleschi established the dimensions of every part of this cruciform basilica as either multiples or segments of the dome-covered crossing square, creating a rhythmic harmony throughout the interior. For example, the nave is twice as high as it is wide, and the arcade and clerestory are of equal height, which means that the height of the arcade equals the nave's width. The austerity of the decor enhances the tranquil atmosphere. The calculated logic of the design—in essence, a series of mathematical equations—echoes that of classical buildings. The rationality of Santo Spirito contrasts sharply with the soaring drama and spirituality of the vaults and nave arcades of Gothic churches (FIGS. **7-10** and **7-13**). Santo Spirito fully expresses the new Renaissance spirit that placed its faith in reason rather than in the emotions.

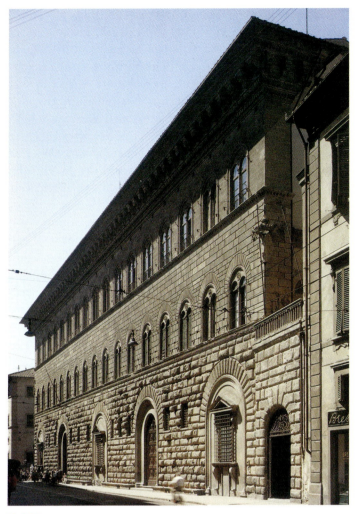

Palazzo Medici The Medici family's consolidation of power in a city that prided itself on its republicanism did not go unchallenged. In the early 1430s, a power struggle with other wealthy families led to the expulsion of the Medici from Florence. In 1434 the family returned, but Cosimo, aware of the importance of public perception, attempted to maintain a lower profile and to wield his power from behind the scenes. He rejected an ostentatious design that Brunelleschi had proposed for a new Medici residence not far from the cathedral and awarded the commission instead to MICHELOZZO DI BARTOLOMMEO (1396–1472), a young architect who had collaborated with Donatello in several sculptural enterprises. Although Cosimo passed over Brunelleschi, his architectural style in fact deeply influenced Michelozzo. To a limited extent, the Palazzo Medici (FIGS. **8-31** and **8-32**) reflects Brunelleschian principles.

Later bought by the Riccardi family (hence the name Palazzo Medici-Riccardi), who almost doubled the facade's length in the 18th century, the palace, both in its original and extended form, is a simple, massive structure. Heavy *rustication* (rough, unfinished masonry) on the ground floor accentuates its strength. Michelozzo divided the building block into stories of decreasing height by using long, unbroken *stringcourses* (horizontal bands), which give it coherence. *Dressed masonry* (smooth, finished stone blocks) on the upper levels produces a smoother surface with each successive story and modifies the severity of the ground floor. The building thus appears progressively lighter as the eye moves upward. The extremely heavy *cornice*, which Michelozzo related not to the top story but to the building as a whole, dramatically reverses this effect. Like the ancient Roman cornices that served as Michelozzo's models, the Palazzo Medici-Riccardi cornice is a very effective lid for the structure, clearly and emphatically defining its proportions. Michelozzo also may

8-31 MICHELOZZO DI BARTOLOMMEO, facade of the Palazzo Medici-Riccardi, Florence, Italy, begun 1445.

The Medici palace, with its combination of dressed and rusticated masonry and classical moldings, draws heavily on ancient Roman architecture, but Michelozzo creatively reinterpreted his models.

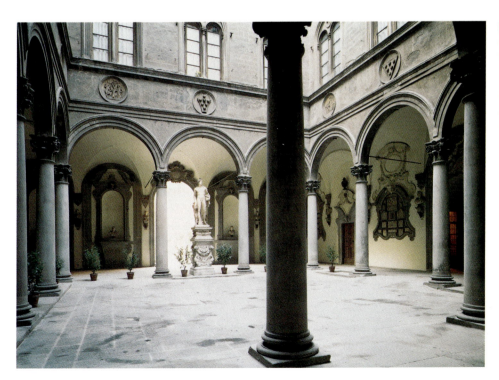

8-32 MICHELOZZO DI BARTOLOMMEO, interior court of the Palazzo Medici-Riccardi, Florence, Italy, begun 1445.

The Medici palace's interior court surrounded by a round-arched colonnade was the first of its kind, but the austere design clearly reveals Michelozzo's debt to Brunelleschi (FIG. 8-30).

have been inspired by the many extant examples of Roman rusticated masonry. However, nothing in the ancient world precisely compares with Michelozzo's design. The Palazzo Medici-Riccardi is an excellent example of the simultaneous respect for and independence from the antique that characterize the Early Renaissance in Italy.

The heart of the palace is an open colonnaded court (FIG. 8-32) that clearly shows Michelozzo's debt to Brunelleschi. The round-arched colonnade, although more massive in its proportions, closely resembles the nave of Santo Spirito (FIG. 8-30). This interior court surrounded by an arcade was the first of its kind, however, and it influenced a long line of descendants in Renaissance domestic architecture.

Leon Battista Alberti Although he entered the profession of architecture rather late in life, LEON BATTISTA ALBERTI (1404–1472) made a remarkable contribution to architectural design. He was the first to study seriously the ancient Roman architectural treatise of Vitruvius (see Chapter 3), and his knowledge of it, combined with his own archaeological investigations, made him the first Renaissance architect to understand Roman architecture in depth. Alberti's most influential theoretical work, *On the Art of Building* (written about 1450, published 1486), although inspired by Vitruvius, contains much original material. Alberti advocated a system of ideal proportions and considered the central plan to be the ideal form for a Christian church. He also regarded the combination of column and arch, which had persisted since Roman times and throughout the Middle Ages, as incongruous. He argued that the arch is a wall opening that should be supported only by a section of wall (a pier), not by an independent sculptural element (a column), as in Brunelleschi's and Michelozzo's buildings (FIGS. 8-30 and 8-32).

Alberti's own architectural style represents a scholarly application of classical elements to contemporary buildings. For the new facade (FIG. 8-33) he designed for the 13th-century Gothic church of Santa Maria Novella in Florence, Alberti chose a small, pseudoclassical, pediment-capped temple front supported by a broad base of pilaster-framed arcades. Throughout the facade, Alberti defined areas and related them

to one another in terms of proportions that can be expressed in simple numerical ratios (1:1, 1:2, 1:3, 2:3, and so on). For example, the upper structure can be encased in a square one-fourth the size of the main square. The cornice separating the two levels divides the major square in half so that the lower portion of the building is a rectangle twice as wide as it is high. In his treatise, Alberti wrote at length about the necessity of employing harmonic proportions to achieve beautiful buildings. Alberti shared this conviction with Brunelleschi, and this fundamental dependence on classically derived mathematics distinguished their architectural work from that of their medieval predecessors. They believed in the eternal and universal validity of numerical ratios as the source of beauty. In this respect, Alberti and Brunelleschi revived the true spirit of the High Classical age of ancient Greece, as epitomized by the sculptor Polykleitos and the architect Iktinos, who produced canons of proportions for the perfect statue and the perfect temple (see Chapter 2). But it was not only a desire to emulate Vitruvius and the Greek masters that motivated Alberti to turn to mathematics in his quest for beauty. His contemporary, the Florentine humanist Giannozzo Manetti (1396–1459), had argued that Christianity itself possessed the order and logic of mathematics. In his 1452 treatise, *On the Dignity and Excellence of Man*, Manetti stated that Christian religious truths were as self-evident as mathematical axioms.

The Santa Maria Novella facade was an ingenious solution to a difficult design problem. Alberti succeeded in subjecting preexisting and quintessentially medieval features, such as the large round window on the second level, to a rigid geometrical order that instilled a quality of classical calm and reason. This facade also introduced a feature of great historical consequence—the scrolls that simultaneously

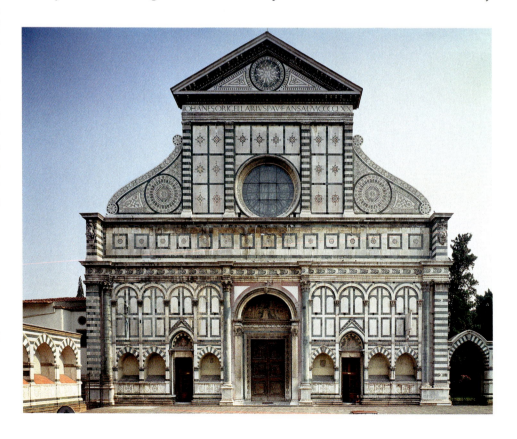

8-33 LEON BATTISTA ALBERTI, west facade of Santa Maria Novella, Florence, Italy, 1456–1470.

Alberti's design for the facade of this Gothic church features a pediment-capped temple front and pilaster-framed arcades. Numerical ratios are the basis of the proportions of all parts of the facade.

unite the broad lower and narrow upper level and screen the sloping roofs over the aisles. With variations, similar spirals appeared in literally hundreds of church facades throughout the Renaissance and Baroque periods.

Girolamo Savonarola In the 1490s, Florence underwent a political, cultural, and religious upheaval. Florentine artists and their fellow citizens responded then not only to humanist ideas but also to the incursion of French armies and especially to the preaching of the Dominican monk Girolamo Savonarola (1452–1498), the reforming priest-dictator who denounced the paganism of the Medici and their artists, philosophers, and poets. Savonarola exhorted the people of Florence to repent their sins, and, when Lorenzo de' Medici died in 1492 and the Medici fled, he prophesied the downfall of the city and of Italy and assumed absolute control of the state. Together with a large number of citizens, Savonarola believed that the Medici's political, social, and religious power had corrupted Florence and had invited the scourge of foreign invasion. The monk denounced humanism and encouraged citizens to burn their classical texts, scientific treatises, and philosophical publications. Modern scholars still debate the significance of Savonarola's brief span of power. Apologists for the undoubtedly sincere monk deny that his actions played a role in the decline of Floren-

tine culture at the end of the 15th century. But the puritanical spirit that moved Savonarola must have dampened considerably the neopagan enthusiasm of the Florentine Early Renaissance. Certainly, his condemnation of humanism as heretical nonsense and his expulsion of the Medici and other wealthy families from Florence deprived local artists of some of their major patrons. There were, however, abundant commissions for artists elsewhere in Italy.

The Princely Courts

Although Florentine artists led the way in creating the Renaissance in art and architecture, art production flourished throughout Italy in the 15th century. The papacy in Rome and the princely courts in Urbino, Mantua, and elsewhere also deserve credit for nurturing Renaissance art.

Perugino Between 1481 and 1483, Pope Sixtus IV (r. 1414–1484) summoned to Rome a group of artists, including Sandro Botticelli and Pietro Vannucci of Perugia, known as PERUGINO (ca. 1450–1523), to decorate with frescoes the walls of the newly completed Sistine Chapel. Perugino's contribution to the fresco cycle was *Christ Delivering the Keys of the Kingdom to Saint Peter* (FIG. **8-34**). The papacy had, from the beginning, based its claim to infallible and total

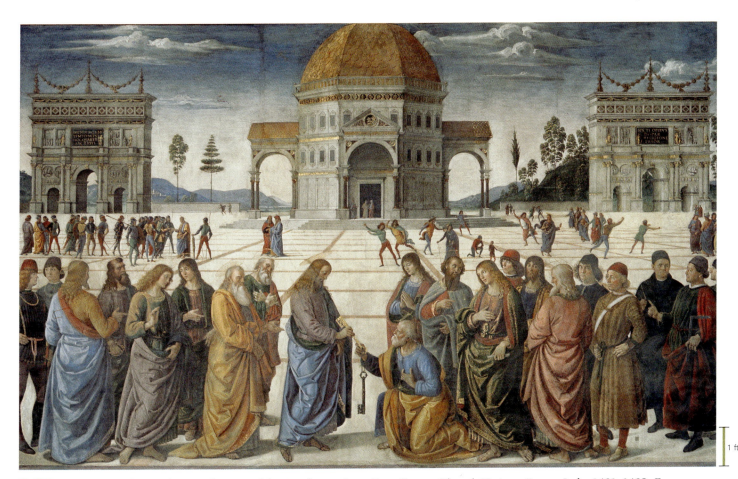

1 ft.

8-34 PERUGINO, *Christ Delivering the Keys of the Kingdom to Saint Peter*, Sistine Chapel, Vatican, Rome, Italy, 1481–1483. Fresco, 11' 5½" × 18' 8½".

Painted for the Vatican, this fresco depicts the event on which the papacy bases its authority. The converging lines of the pavement connect the action in the foreground with the background.

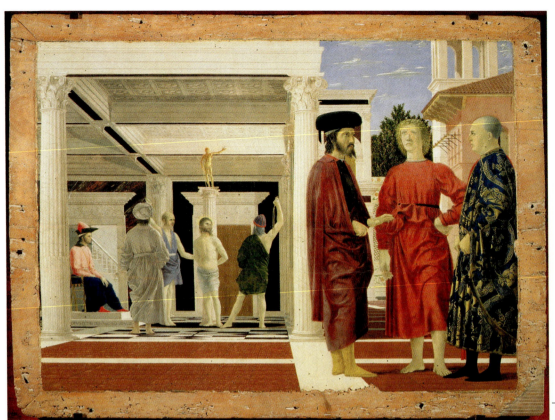

8-35 Piero della Francesca, *Flagellation of Christ*, ca. 1455–1465. Oil and tempera on wood, 1′ 11⅛″ × 2′ 8¼″. Galleria Nazionale delle Marche, Urbino.

The identification of the foreground figures continues to elude scholars. They appear to discuss the biblical tragedy that takes place in Pilate's palace, which Piero rendered in perfect linear perspective.

1 in.

authority over the Roman Catholic Church on this biblical event. In Perugino's version, Christ hands the keys to Saint Peter, who stands amid an imaginary gathering of the 12 apostles and Renaissance contemporaries. These figures occupy the apron of a great stage space that extends into the distance to a point of convergence in the doorway of a central-plan temple. (Perugino used parallel and converging lines in the pavement to mark off the intervening space.) Figures in the middle distance complement the near group, emphasizing its density and order by their scattered arrangement. At the corners of the great *piazza*, duplicate triumphal arches serve as the base angles of a distant compositional triangle whose apex is in the central building. Perugino modeled the arches very closely on the Arch of Constantine (FIG. 3-50) in Rome. Although an anachronism in a painting depicting a scene from Christ's life, the arches served to underscore the close ties between Constantine and Saint Peter and of the great basilica (FIG. 4-4) the first Christian emperor built over Saint Peter's tomb in Rome. Christ and Peter flank the triangle's central axis, which runs through the temple's doorway, the perspective's vanishing point. Thus, the composition interlocks both two-dimensional and three-dimensional space, and the placement of central actors emphasizes the axial center. This spatial science allowed the artist to organize the action systematically. Perugino, in this single picture, incorporated the learning of generations.

Urbino Under the patronage of Federico da Montefeltro (1422–1482), Urbino, southeast of Florence across the Appenines (MAP 8-2), became an important center of Renaissance art and culture. In fact, the humanist writer Paolo Cortese (1465–1540) described Federico as one of the two greatest artistic patrons of the 15th century (the other was Cosimo de' Medici). Federico was a condottiere so renowned for his military expertise that he was in demand by popes and kings, and soldiers came from across Europe to study under his direction.

Piero della Francesca One artist who received several commissions from Federico was PIERO DELLA FRANCESCA (ca. 1420–1492) of San Sepolcro in Tuscany, who had earlier painted for the Medici, among others. One of Piero's best, but most enigmatic, paintings is *Flagellation of Christ* (FIG. 8-35). The setting for the New Testament drama is the portico of Pontius Pilate's palace in Jerusalem. Curiously, the focus of the composition is not Christ but the group of three large figures in the foreground, whose identity scholars still debate. Some have identified the bearded figure as a Turk and interpreted the painting as a commentary on the capture in 1453 of Christian Constantinople by the Muslims (see Chapter 5). Other scholars, however, identify the three men as biblical figures, including the Old Testament's King David, one of whose psalms theologians believed predicted the conspiracy against Christ. In any case, the three men appear to discuss the event in the background. As Pilate, the seated judge, watches, Christ, bound to a column topped by a classical statue, is about to be whipped. Piero's perspective is so meticulous that the floor pattern can be reconstructed perfectly as a central porphyry (purple marble) circle with surrounding squares composed of various geo-

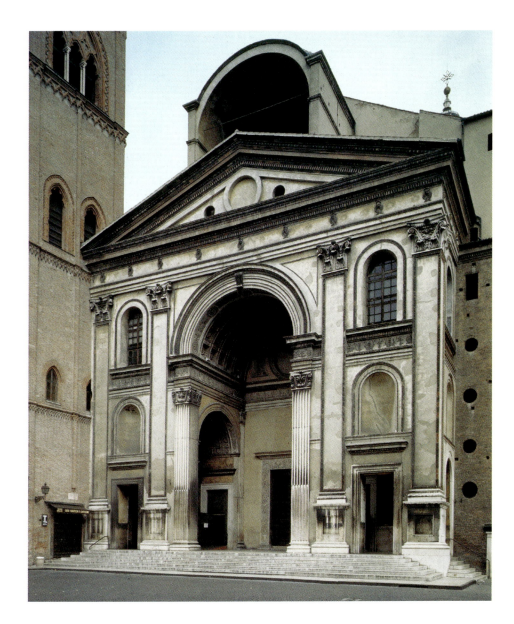

8-36 Leon Battista Alberti, west facade of Sant'Andrea, Mantua, Italy, designed 1470, begun 1472.

Alberti's design for Sant'Andrea reflects his study of ancient Roman architecture. Employing a colossal order, the architect locked together a triumphal arch and a Roman temple front with pediment.

metric shapes. Whatever the solution is to the iconographical puzzle of Piero's *Flagellation*, the panel reveals a mind cultivated by mathematics. The careful delineation of detail suggests an architect's vision. Piero believed the highest beauty resides in forms that have the clarity and purity of geometric figures. Toward the end of his long career he wrote the first theoretical treatise on systematic perspective, after having practiced the art with supreme mastery for almost a lifetime. His association with the architect Alberti at Ferrara and at Rimini around 1450–1451 probably turned his attention fully to perspective (a science in which Alberti was an influential pioneer) and helped determine his later, characteristically architectonic compositions. This approach appealed to Federico, a patron fascinated by architectural space and its depiction.

Sant'Andrea, Mantua Marquis Ludovico Gonzaga (1412–1478) ruled one of the wealthiest princely courts of the 15th century, the marquisate of Mantua in northeastern Italy (MAP 8-2). A famed condottiere like Federico de Monte-feltro, Gonzaga established his reputation as a fierce military leader while general of the Milanese armies. The visit to Mantua by Pope Pius II (r. 1458–1464) in 1459 stimulated the marquis's determination to transform Mantua into a spectacular city that all Italy would envy.

One of the major projects Gonzaga instituted was the redesigning of the church of Sant'Andrea to replace an 11th-century church. Gonzaga turned to Alberti for this important commission. The facade (FIG. **8-36**) Alberti designed locked together two complete ancient Roman architectural motifs—the temple front and the triumphal arch. The combination was already a feature of Roman buildings still standing in Italy. For example, many Roman triumphal arches incorporated a pediment over the arcuated passageway and engaged columns, but there is no close parallel in antiquity for Alberti's eclectic and ingenious design. The Renaissance architect's concern for proportion led him to equalize the vertical and horizontal dimensions of the facade, which left it considerably shorter than the church behind it. Because of the primary importance of visual appeal, many Renaissance

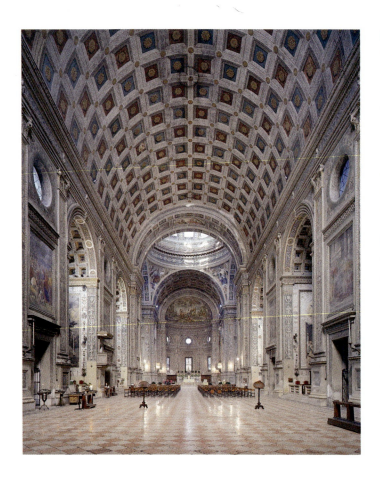

Alberti abandoned the medieval columnar arcade for the nave of Sant'Andrea. The tremendous vaults suggest that he may have been inspired by Constantine's Basilica Nova (FIG. 3-49) in Rome.

architects made this concession not only to the demands of a purely visual proportionality in the facade but also to the facade's relation to the small square in front of it, even at the expense of continuity with the body of the building. Yet structural correspondences to the building do exist in Sant'Andrea's facade. The pilasters are the same height as those on the nave's interior walls, and the central barrel vault over the main exterior entrance, with smaller barrel vaults branching off at right angles, introduces on a smaller scale the arrangement of the nave and aisles. The facade pilasters, as part of the wall, run uninterrupted through three stories in an early application of the *colossal (giant) order* that became a favorite motif of Michelangelo (see Chapter 9).

Inside (FIG. **8-37**), Alberti abandoned the medieval columned arcade Brunelleschi used in Santo Spirito (FIG. 8-30). Thick walls alternating with vaulted chapels and interrupted by a massive dome over the crossing support the huge barrel vault. The vaulted interior calls to mind the vast spaces and

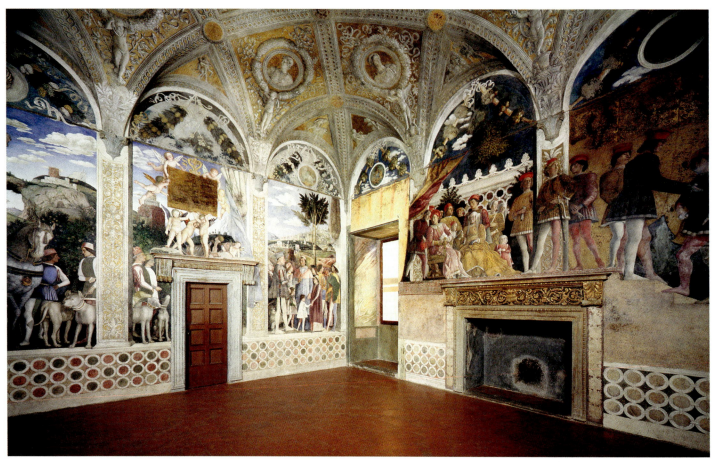

8-38 ANDREA MANTEGNA, interior of the Camera Picta (Painted Chamber), Palazzo Ducale, Mantua, Italy, 1465–1474. Fresco.

Working for Ludovico Gonzaga, who established Mantua as a great art city, Mantegna produced for the duke's palace the first completely consistent illusionistic fresco decoration of an entire room.

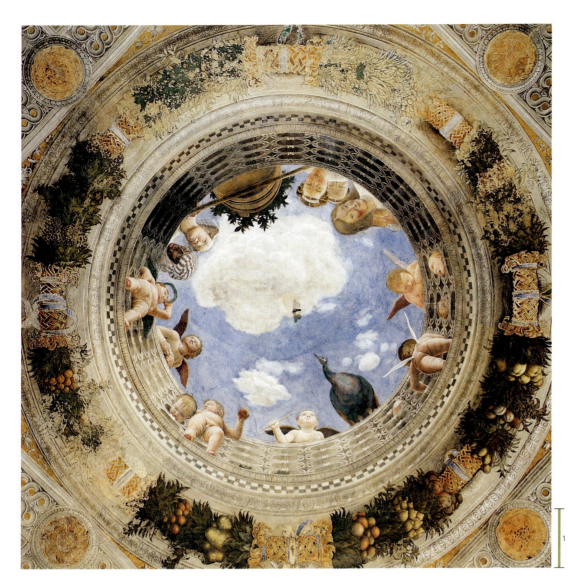

8-39 ANDREA MANTEGNA, ceiling of the Camera Picta (Painted Chamber), Palazzo Ducale, Mantua, Italy, 1465–1474. Fresco, 8′ 9″ diameter.

Inside the Camera Picta, the viewer becomes the viewed as figures look down into the room from a painted oculus opening onto a blue sky. This is the first perspectival view of a ceiling from below.

1 ft.

dense enclosing masses of Roman architecture. In his architectural treatise, Alberti criticized the traditional basilican plan (with continuous aisles flanking the central nave) as impractical because the colonnades conceal the ceremonies from the faithful in the aisles. For this reason, he designed a single huge hall with independent chapels branching off at right angles. This break with a Christian building tradition that had endured for a thousand years was extremely influential in later Renaissance and Baroque church planning.

Andrea Mantegna Like other princes, Ludovico Gonzaga believed that an impressive palace was an important visual expression of his authority. One of the most spectacular rooms in the Palazzo Ducale (Duke's Palace) in Mantua was the so-called Camera degli Sposi (Room of the Newlyweds; FIG. 8-38), originally the Camera Picta (Painted Room), decorated by ANDREA MANTEGNA (ca. 1431–1506) of Padua. Taking almost nine years to complete the extensive fresco program, Mantegna produced a series of images that aggrandize Ludovico Gonzaga and his family and reveal the activities and rhythm of courtly life. The scenes depict vignettes that include Ludovico, his wife, his

children, courtiers, and attendants, among others. Standing in the Camera degli Sposi, surrounded by the spectacle and majesty of these scenes, the viewer cannot help but be thoroughly impressed by both the commanding presence and elevated status of the patron and the dazzling artistic skills of Mantegna.

In the Camera degli Sposi, Mantegna performed a triumphant feat of pictorial illusionism, producing the first completely consistent illusionistic decoration of an entire room. Mantegna painted away the room's walls in a manner that foretold later Baroque decoration (see Chapter 10). It recalls the efforts of Italian painters more than 15 centuries earlier at Pompeii and elsewhere to integrate mural painting and architecture in frescoes of the so-called Second Style (FIGS. 3-18 and 3-19) of Roman painting. Mantegna's *trompe l'oeil* (French, "deceives the eye") design, however, far surpassed anything preserved from ancient Italy. The Renaissance painter's daring experimentalism led him to complete the room's decoration with the first perspective of a ceiling (FIG. 8-39) seen from below (called, in Italian, *di sotto in sù*, "from below upward"). Baroque ceiling decorators later broadly developed this technique. Inside the Camera Picta,

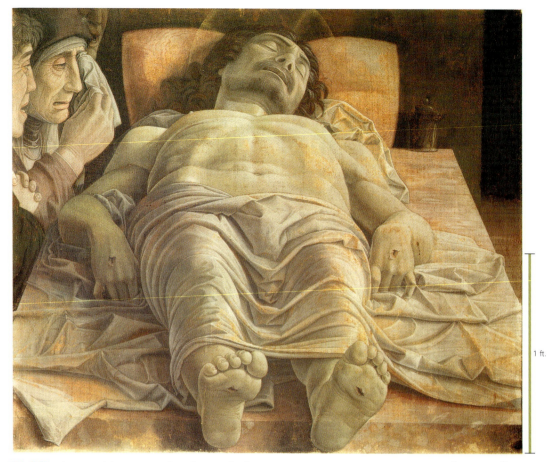

1 ft.

8-40 Andrea Mantegna, *Foreshortened Christ*, ca. 1500. Tempera on canvas, 2′ 2¾″ × 2′ 7⅞″. Pinacoteca di Brera, Milan.

In this work of overwhelming emotional power, Mantegna presented both a harrowing study of a strongly foreshortened cadaver and an intensely poignant depiction of a biblical tragedy.

the viewer becomes the viewed as figures look down into the room from the painted *oculus* ("eye"). Seen against the convincing illusion of a cloud-filled blue sky, several *putti* (cupids), strongly foreshortened, set the amorous mood of the Room of the Newlyweds, as the painted spectators (who are not identified) smile down on the scene. The prominent peacock is an attribute of Juno, Jupiter's bride, who oversees lawful marriages. This brilliant feat of illusionism climaxes almost a century of experimentation with perspective.

Foreshortened Christ One of Mantegna's later paintings, *Foreshortened Christ* (FIG. **8-40**), is a work of overwhelm-

ing power. At first glance, this painting seems to be a strikingly realistic study in foreshortening. Careful scrutiny, however, reveals that the artist reduced the size of the figure's feet, which, as he must have known, would cover much of the body if done in proper perspective. Thus, tempering naturalism with artistic license, Mantegna presented both a harrowing study of a strongly foreshortened cadaver and an intensely poignant depiction of a biblical tragedy. The painter's harsh, sharp line seems to cut the surface as if it were metal and conveys, by its grinding edge, the theme's corrosive emotion. Remarkably, all the science of the 15th century here serves the purpose of religious devotion.

Europe, 1400 to 1500

BURGUNDY AND FLANDERS

▌ The most powerful rulers north of the Alps during the first three-quarters of the 15th century were the dukes of Burgundy, who controlled Flanders.

▌ Flemish painters popularized the use of oil paints on wooden panels. By superimposing translucent glazes, they created richer colors than possible using tempera or fresco. Robert Campin's *Mérode Altarpiece* is an early example. Typical of Northern Renaissance painting, the everyday objects depicted often have symbolic significance.

▌ Jan van Eyck, Rogier van der Weyden, and others established portraiture as an important art form.

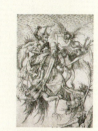

Campin, *Mérode Altarpiece,*
ca. 1425–1428

FRANCE AND THE HOLY ROMAN EMPIRE

▌ During the 15th century, the Hundred Years' War crippled the French economy, but art commissions continued. The Limbourg brothers expanded the illusionistic capabilities of manuscript illumination with calendar pictures depicting naturalistic settings.

▌ The major German innovation of the 15th century was the development of the printing press, which printers soon used to produce books with woodcut illustrations. Woodcuts are relief prints in which the artist carves out the areas around the printed lines. German artists were also the earliest masters of engraving. This intaglio technique allows for a wider variety of linear effects because the artist incises the image directly onto a metal plate.

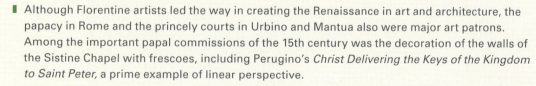

Schongauer, *Saint Anthony
Tormented by Demons,*
ca. 1480–1490

ITALY

▌ The fortunate congruence of artistic genius, the spread of humanism, and economic prosperity nourished the flowering of the new artistic culture that historians call the Renaissance—the rebirth of classical values in art and life. The greatest center of Renaissance art in the 15th century was Florence, home of the powerful Medici family, who were among the most ambitious art patrons in history.

▌ Some of the earliest examples of the new Renaissance style in sculpture are Donatello's *Saint Mark,* which reintroduced the classical concept of contrapposto into Renaissance statuary, and his later *David,* the first nude male statue since antiquity.

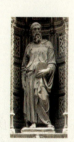

Donatello, *Saint Mark,* 1411–1413

▌ Although some painters continued to work in the Late Gothic International Style, others broke fresh ground by exploring new modes of representation. Masaccio's figures recall Giotto's but have a greater psychological and physical credibility, and the light shining on Masaccio's figures comes from a source outside the picture. His *Holy Trinity* epitomizes Early Renaissance painting in its convincing illusionism, achieved through Filippo Brunelleschi's new science of linear perspective, yet it remains effective as a devotional painting in a church setting.

▌ Italian architects also revived the classical style. Brunelleschi's Santo Spirito basilica showcases the clarity and Roman-inspired rationality of 15th-century Florentine architecture.

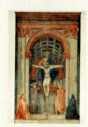

Masaccio, *Holy Trinity,*
ca. 1424–1427

▌ Although Florentine artists led the way in creating the Renaissance in art and architecture, the papacy in Rome and the princely courts in Urbino and Mantua also were major art patrons. Among the important papal commissions of the 15th century was the decoration of the walls of the Sistine Chapel with frescoes, including Perugino's *Christ Delivering the Keys of the Kingdom to Saint Peter,* a prime example of linear perspective.

▌ Mantua became an important art center under Marquis Ludovico Gonzaga, who brought in Leon Battista Alberti to rebuild the church of Sant'Andrea. Alberti applied the principles he developed in his influential 1450 treatise *On the Art of Building* to the project and freely adapted forms from Roman religious, triumphal, and civic architecture.

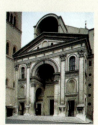

Alberti, Sant'Andrea, Mantua, 1470

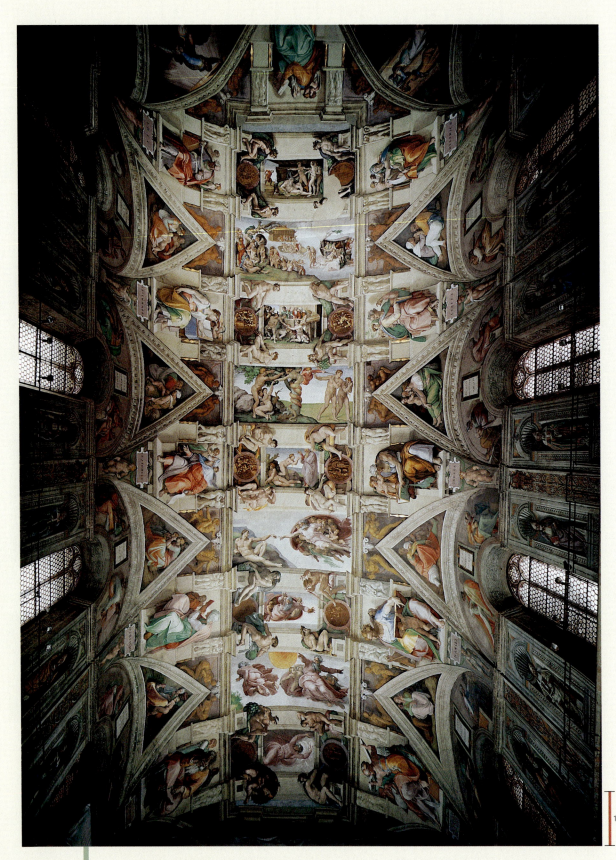

10 ft.

9-1 Michelangelo Buonarroti, ceiling of the Sistine Chapel, Vatican City, Rome, Italy, 1508–1512. Fresco, 128' × 45'.

Michelangelo, the Renaissance genius who was a painter, sculptor, and architect, labored almost four years in the Sistine Chapel (FIG. 9-10) painting more than 300 biblical figures on the ceiling illustrating the Creation and Fall of humankind.

Europe, 1500 to 1600

The 16th century brought major upheaval and change in Europe (MAP **9-1**), particularly in the realm of religion. Widespread dissatisfaction with the leadership and policies of the Roman Catholic Church instigated the Protestant Reformation. Led by theologians such as Martin Luther (1483–1546) and John Calvin (1509–1564) in the Holy Roman Empire, early-16th-century reformers directly challenged papal authority. Disgruntled Catholics voiced concerns about the sale of *indulgences* (pardons for sins, reducing the time a soul spent in Purgatory—equated with buying one's way into Heaven) and about nepotism (the appointment of relatives to important positions). Particularly damaging was the perception that the Roman popes concerned themselves more with temporal power and the accumulation of worldly goods than with the salvation of Church members. The fact that many 15th-century popes and cardinals came from wealthy families, such as the Medici, intensified this perception.

Protestantism The Northern European reform movement resulted in the establishment of Protestantism, with sects such as Lutheranism and Calvinism. Central to Protestantism was a belief in personal faith rather than adherence to decreed Church practices and doctrines. Because the Protestants believed the only true religious relationship was the personal one between individuals and God, they were, in essence, eliminating the need for Church intercession, which is central to Catholicism.

In 1517, in Wittenberg, Luther posted for discussion his *Ninety-five Theses*, which enumerated his objections to Church practices. Luther's goal was significant reform and clarification of major spiritual issues, but his ideas ultimately led to the splitting of Christendom. According to Luther, the Catholic Church's extensive ecclesiastical structure needed to be eliminated, for it had no basis in scripture. The Bible—nothing else—could serve as the foundation for Christianity. Luther declared the pope the Antichrist (for which the pope excommunicated him), called the Church the "whore of Babylon," and denounced ordained priests. Save for baptism and the Eucharist, Luther also rejected most of Catholicism's sacraments, decrying them as pagan obstacles to salvation. He believed that for Christianity to be restored to its original purity, the Church needed cleansing of all the impurities of doctrine that had collected through the ages.

A central concern of the Protestant reformers was the question of how Christians achieve salvation. Luther did not perceive salvation as something for which weak and sinful humans must constantly strive through good deeds performed under a punitive God's watchful eye. Instead, he argued, faithful individuals

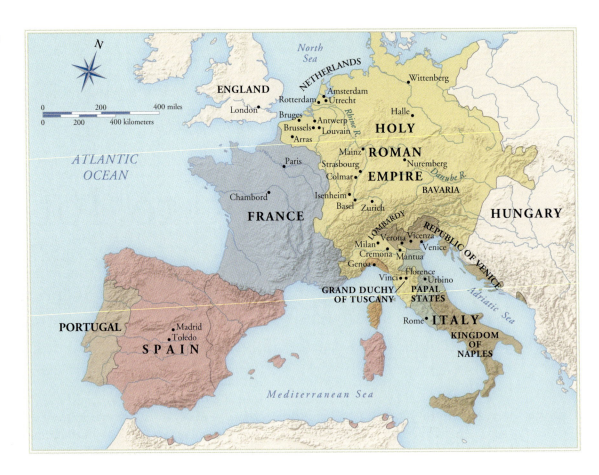

Map 9-1 Europe in the early 16th century.

attained redemption solely by God's bestowal of grace. Therefore, people cannot earn salvation. Further, no ecclesiastical machinery with all its miraculous rites and indulgences could save sinners from God's judgment. Only absolute faith in Christ could ensure salvation. Justification by faith alone, with the guidance of scripture, was the fundamental doctrine of Protestantism. Luther advocated the Bible as the source of all religious truth. The Bible—the sole scriptural authority—was the word of God, and the Church's councils, laws, and rituals carried no weight. Luther facilitated the lay public's access to biblical truths by producing the first translation of the Bible in a vernacular language (German).

In addition to doctrinal differences, Catholics and Protestants took divergent stances on the role of visual imagery in religion. Protestants believed religious imagery could lead to idolatry and distract viewers from focusing on the real reason for their presence in church—to communicate directly with God. Because of this belief, Protestant churches were relatively austere and unadorned. The Protestant concern over the role of religious imagery at times progressed to outright *iconoclasm*—the destruction of religious artworks. Particularly violent waves of iconoclastic fervor swept Basel, Zurich, Strasbourg, and Wittenberg in the 1520s. In an episode known as the Great Iconoclasm, bands of Calvinists visited Catholic churches in the Netherlands in 1566, shattering stained-glass windows, smashing statues, and destroying paintings and other artworks they perceived as idolatrous. These strong reactions to art not only reflected the religious fervor of the time but also served as dramatic demonstrations of the power of art—and how much art mattered.

Counter-Reformation In striking contrast, Catholics embraced church decoration as an aid to communicating with God. Under Pope Paul III (r. 1534–1549), the Catholic Church mounted a full-fledged campaign to counteract the defection of its members to Protestantism. This response, the Counter-Reformation, consisted of numerous initiatives. The Council of Trent, which met intermittently from 1545 through 1563, was a major element of this effort. Composed of cardinals, archbishops, bishops, abbots, and theologians, the Council of Trent dealt with issues of Church doctrine, including many the Protestants contested. Papal art commissions during this period were an integral part of this Counter-Reformation effort. Popes long had been aware of the power of visual imagery to construct and reinforce ideological claims, and the 16th-century popes exploited this capability (see "Religious Art in Counter-Reformation Italy," page 255). In fact, papal commissions constituted a high percentage of the most important artistic projects in High and Late Renaissance Italy.

ITALY

The 15th-century artistic developments in Italy (for example, interest in perspective systems, anatomical depictions, and classical cultures) matured during the early 16th

Religious Art in Counter-Reformation Italy

Both Catholics and Protestants took seriously the role of devotional imagery in religious life. However, their views differed dramatically. Whereas Catholics deemed art as valuable for cultivating piety, Protestants believed religious imagery could lead the faithful astray in their effort to seek a personal relationship with God. As part of the Counter-Reformation effort, Pope Paul III convened the Council of Trent in 1545 to review controversial Church doctrines. At its conclusion in 1563, the council issued an edict on the veneration of saints' relics and the role of sacred images:

[T]he images of Christ, of the Virgin Mother of God, and of the other saints are to be placed and retained especially in the churches, and . . . due honor and veneration is to be given them; . . . because the honor which is shown them is referred to the prototypes which they represent, so that by means of the images which we kiss and before which we uncover the head and prostrate ourselves, we adore Christ and venerate the saints whose likeness they bear. . . . Moreover, let the bishops diligently teach that by means of the stories of the mysteries of our redemption portrayed in paintings and other representations the people are instructed and confirmed in the articles of faith, which ought to be borne in mind and constantly reflected upon; also that great profit is derived from all holy images, not only because the people are thereby reminded of the benefits and gifts bestowed on them by Christ, but also because through the saints the miracles of God and salutary examples are set before the eyes of the faithful, so that they may give God thanks for those things, may fashion their own life and conduct in imitation of the saints and be moved to adore and love God and cultivate piety.*

*Canons and Decrees of the Council of Trent, December 3–4, 1563, in Robert Klein and Henri Zerner, Italian Art 1500–1600: Sources and Documents (Evanston, Ill.: Northwestern University Press, 1966), 120–121.

century in the brief era that art historians call the High Renaissance—the period between 1495 and the deaths of Leonardo da Vinci in 1519 and Raphael in 1520. The Renaissance style, however, dominated the remainder of the 16th century (the Late Renaissance), although a new style, called Mannerism, challenged it almost as soon as Raphael had been laid to rest (in the ancient Roman Pantheon, FIG. 3-39).

Thus, no single artistic style characterizes 16th-century Italy, but Italian art of this period uniformly exhibits an astounding mastery, both technical and aesthetic. The extraordinary quality of the artworks produced during this period by numerous masters elevated the prestige of all artists. Renaissance painters and sculptors raised visual art to a status formerly held only by poetry. The artists of 16th-century Italy in essence created a new profession—the fine arts—with its own rights of expression and its own venerable character.

Three of those most responsible for establishing the modern notion of the artist-genius worked primarily in Florence and Rome—Leonardo da Vinci, Raphael, and Michelangelo.

Leonardo da Vinci

Born in the small town of Vinci, near Florence, LEONARDO DA VINCI (1452–1519) was the quintessential "Renaissance man." Art was but one of his innumerable interests. Exploring Leonardo's art in conjunction with his other endeavors considerably enhances an understanding of his artistic production. Leonardo revealed his unquenchable curiosity in his voluminous notes, liberally interspersed with sketches dealing with botany, geology, geography, cartography, zoology, military engineering, animal lore, anatomy, and aspects of physical science, including hydraulics and mechanics. These

studies informed his art. For example, Leonardo's in-depth exploration of optics gave him an understanding of perspective, light, and color that he used in his painting. His scientific drawings (FIG. 9-5) are themselves artworks.

Leonardo's great ambition in his painting, as well as in his scientific endeavors, was to discover the laws underlying the processes and flux of nature. With this end in mind, he also studied the human body and contributed immeasurably to knowledge of physiology and psychology. Leonardo believed that reality in an absolute sense was inaccessible and that humans could know it only through its changing images. He considered the eyes the most vital organs and sight the most essential function, as, using the eyes, individuals could grasp the images of reality most directly and profoundly. In his notes, he stated repeatedly that all his scientific investigations made him a better painter.

Around 1481, Leonardo left Florence, offering his services to Ludovico Sforza (1451–1508), the son and heir apparent of the ruler of Milan. The political situation in Florence was uncertain, and Leonardo perhaps believed his particular skills would be in greater demand in Milan, providing him with the opportunity for increased financial security. He devoted most of a letter to Ludovico to advertising his competence and his qualifications as a military engineer, mentioning only at the end his abilities as a painter and sculptor:

And in short, according to the variety of cases, I can contrive various and endless means of offence and defence. . . . In time of peace I believe I can give perfect satisfaction and to the equal of any other in architecture and the composition of buildings, public and private; and in guiding water from one place to another. . . . I can carry out sculpture in marble, bronze, or clay, and also I can do in painting whatever may be done, as well as any other, be he whom he may."[1]

Leonardo da Vinci on Painting

In his *Madonna of the Rocks* (FIG. 9-2), begun in 1483, Leonardo da Vinci achieved a groundbreaking feat—the unified representation of objects in an atmospheric setting. This innovation was a manifestation of the artist's scientific curiosity about the invisible substance surrounding things. The Madonna, Christ Child, infant John the Baptist, and angel emerge through nuances of light and shade from the half-light of the cavernous visionary landscape. Light simultaneously veils and reveals the forms, immersing them in a layer of atmosphere between them and the observer. Leonardo's effective use of atmospheric perspective was the result in large part of his mastery of the relatively new medium of oil painting, which had previously been used primarily by Northern European painters (see "Tempera and Oil Painting," Chapter 8, page 219).

Leonardo wrote about the importance of atmospheric perspective in his so-called *Treatise on Painting,* where he set forth the reasons he believed painting was a greater art than sculpture:

> The painter will show you things at different distances with variation of color due to the air lying between the objects and the eye; he shows you mists through which visual images penetrate with difficulty; he shows you rain which discloses within it clouds with mountains and valleys; he shows the dust which discloses within it and beyond it the combatants who stirred it up; he shows streams of greater or lesser density; he shows fish playing between the surface of the water and its bottom; he shows the polished pebbles of various colors lying on the washed sand at the bottom of rivers, surrounded by green plants; he shows the stars at various heights above us, and thus he achieves innumerable effects which sculpture cannot attain.*

*Leonardo da Vinci, *Treatise on Painting,* 51, in Robert Klein and Henri Zerner, *Italian Art 1500–1600: Sources and Documents* (Evanston, Ill.: Northwestern University Press, 1966), 7–8.

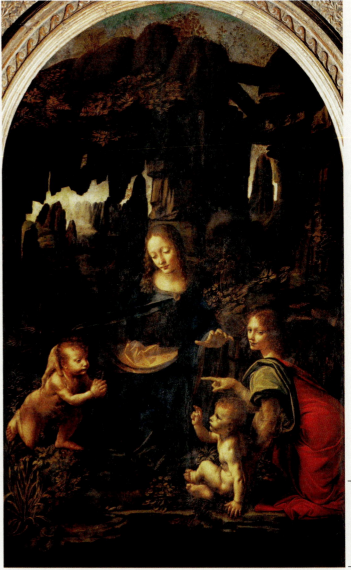

9-2 LEONARDO DA VINCI, *Madonna of the Rocks,* from San Francesco Grande, Milan, Italy, begun 1483. Oil on wood (transferred to canvas), 6′ 6½″ × 4′. Louvre, Paris.

In this groundbreaking work, Leonardo used gestures and a pyramidal composition to unite the Virgin, John the Baptist, the Christ Child, and an angel. The figures share the same light-infused environment.

1 ft.

Madonna of the Rocks Ludovico accepted Leonardo's offer. Shortly after settling in Milan, the Florentine artist painted *Madonna of the Rocks* (FIG. 9-2) as the center panel of an altarpiece in San Francesco Grande. The painting builds on Masaccio's understanding and use of chiaroscuro, the subtle play of light and dark. Modeling with light and shadow and expressing emotional states were, for Leonardo, the heart of painting: "A good painter has two chief objects to paint—man and the intention of his soul. The former is easy, the latter hard, for it must be expressed by gestures and the movement of the limbs. . . . A painting will only be wonderful for the beholder by making that which is not so appear raised and detached from the wall."[2]

Leonardo presented the figures in *Madonna of the Rocks* in a pyramidal grouping. They pray, point, and bless, and these acts and gestures, although their meanings are uncertain, visually unite the individuals portrayed. The angel points to the infant John and, through his outward glance, draws the viewer into the tableau. John prays to the Christ Child, who blesses him in return. The Virgin herself completes the series of interlocking gestures, her left hand reaching toward the Christ Child and her right hand resting protectively on John's shoulder. A melting mood of tenderness suffuses the entire composition. What the eye sees is fugitive, as are the states of the soul, or, in Leonardo's term, its "intentions." Nonetheless, the most remarkable aspect of

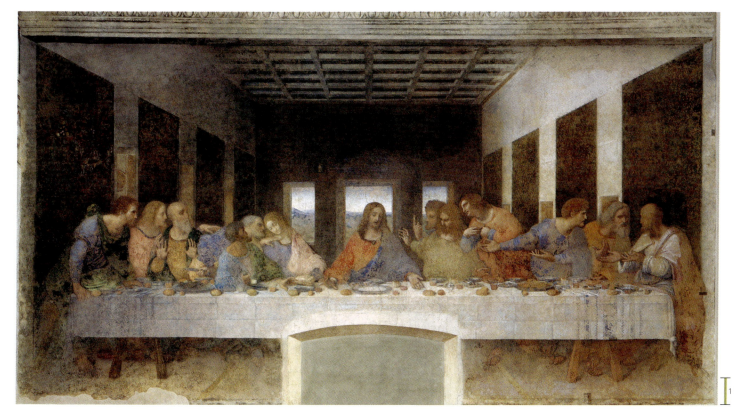

9-3 Leonardo da Vinci, *Last Supper*, ca. 1495–1498. Oil and tempera on plaster, 13′ 9″ × 29′ 10″. Refectory, Santa Maria delle Grazie, Milan.

Christ has just announced that one of his disciples will betray him, and each one reacts. Christ is both the psychological focus of the fresco and the focal point of all the converging perspective lines.

Madonna of the Rocks is that the holy figures share the same light-infused environment (see "Leonardo da Vinci on Painting," page 256).

Last Supper For the refectory of the Church of Santa Maria delle Grazie in Milan, Leonardo painted *Last Supper* (FIG. **9-3**). Cleaned and restored in 1999, the mural is still in a poor state, in part because of the painter's experiment in mixing oil and tempera and applying the colors *a secco* (to dried, rather than wet, plaster). Thus, the wall did not absorb the pigment as in the *buon fresco* technique (see "Fresco Painting," Chapter 7, page 208), and the paint quickly began to flake. The humidity of Milan further accelerated the deterioration. Nonetheless, the painting is both formally and emotionally Leonardo's most impressive work. Christ and his 12 disciples sit at a long table placed parallel to the picture plane in a simple, spacious room. The austere setting amplifies the painting's highly dramatic action. Christ, with outstretched hands, has just said, "One of you is about to betray me" (Matt. 26:21). A wave of intense excitement passes through the group as each disciple asks himself and, in some cases, his neighbor, "Is it I?" (Matt. 26:22). Leonardo linked Christ's dramatic statement about betrayal with the initiation of the ancient liturgical ceremony of the Eucharist, when, blessing bread and wine, Christ said, "This is my body, which is given for you. Do this for a commemoration of me. . . . This is the chalice, the new testament in my blood, which shall be shed for you" (Luke 22:19–20).

In the center, Christ appears isolated from the disciples and in perfect repose, the calm eye of the emotion swirling around him. The central window at the back, whose curved pediment arches above his head, frames his figure. The pediment is the only curve in the architectural framework, and it serves here, along with the diffused light, as a halo. Christ's head, which is at the center of the two-dimensional surface, is the focal point of all converging perspective lines in the composition. Thus, Leonardo made Christ the perspectival focus as well as the psychological focus and cause of the action. The two-dimensional, the three-dimensional, and the psychodimensional focuses are the same.

Leonardo presented the agitated disciples in four groups of three, united among and within themselves by the figures' gestures and postures. The artist sacrificed traditional iconography (FIG. **8-25**) to pictorial and dramatic consistency by placing Judas on the same side of the table as Jesus and the other disciples. The light source in the painting corresponds to the windows in the refectory. Judas's face is in shadow, and he clutches a money bag in his right hand as he reaches his left forward to fulfill the Master's declaration: "But yet behold, the hand of him that betrayeth me is with me on the table" (Luke 22:21). The two disciples at the table ends are quieter than the others, as if to bracket the energy of the composition, which is more intense closer to Christ, whose serenity both halts and intensifies it. The disciples register a broad range of emotional responses, including fear, doubt, protestation, rage, and love. Leonardo's numerous preparatory studies suggest he

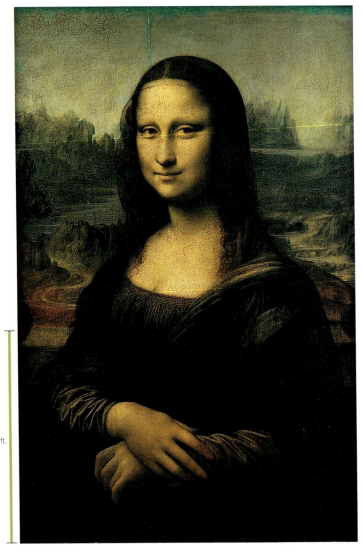

9-4 LEONARDO DA VINCI, *Mona Lisa*, ca. 1503–1505. Oil on wood, 2′ 6¼″ × 1′ 9″. Louvre, Paris.

Leonardo's skill with chiaroscuro and atmospheric perspective is on display in this new kind of portrait depicting the sitter as an individual personality who engages the viewer psychologically.

thought of each figure as carrying a particular charge and type of emotion. Like a stage director, he read the Gospel story carefully, and scrupulously cast his actors as the New Testament described their roles. In this work, as in his other religious paintings, Leonardo revealed his extraordinary ability to apply his voluminous knowledge about the observable world to the pictorial representation of a religious scene, resulting in a psychologically complex and compelling painting.

Mona Lisa Leonardo's *Mona Lisa* (FIG. **9-4**) is probably the world's most famous portrait. The sitter's identity is still the subject of scholarly debate, but in his biography of Leonardo, Giorgio Vasari asserted that she was Lisa di Antonio Maria Gherardini, the wife of Francesco del Giocondo, a wealthy Florentine—hence, "Mona (an Italian contraction of *ma donna*, 'my lady') Lisa." Despite the uncertainty of this identification, Leonardo's portrait is a convincing representation of an individual. Unlike earlier portraits, it does not serve solely as an icon of status. Indeed, Mona Lisa neither

wears jewelry nor holds any attribute associated with wealth. She sits quietly, her hands folded, her mouth forming a gentle smile, and her gaze directed at the viewer. Renaissance etiquette dictated that a woman should not look directly into a man's eyes. Leonardo's portrayal of this self-assured young woman without the trappings of power but engaging the audience psychologically is thus quite remarkable. The painting is darker today than 500 years ago, and the colors are less vivid, but *Mona Lisa* still reveals the artist's fascination and skill with chiaroscuro and atmospheric perspective. The portrait is a prime example of Leonardo's famous smoky *sfumato* (misty haziness)—his subtle adjustment of light and blurring of precise planes.

The lingering appeal of *Mona Lisa* derives in large part from Leonardo's decision to set his subject against the backdrop of a mysterious uninhabited landscape. This vista, with roads and bridges that seem to lead nowhere, recalls his *Madonna of the Rocks* (FIG. **9-2**). The composition also resembles Fra Filippo Lippi's *Madonna and Child with Angels* (FIG. **8-26**) with figures seated in front of a window through which the viewer looks out onto a distant landscape. Originally, the artist represented Mona Lisa in a *loggia* (columnar gallery). When the painting was trimmed (not by Leonardo), these columns were eliminated, but the remains of the column bases may still be seen to the left and right of Mona Lisa's shoulders.

Anatomical Studies Leonardo completed very few paintings. His perfectionism, relentless experimentation, and far-ranging curiosity diffused his efforts. However, the drawings in his notebooks preserve an extensive record of his ideas. His interests focused increasingly on science in his later years, and he embraced knowledge of all facets of the natural world. His investigations in anatomy yielded drawings of great precision and beauty of execution (see "Renaissance Drawings," page 259). *The Fetus and Lining of the Uterus* (FIG. **9-5**), although it does not meet 21st-century standards for accuracy (for example, Leonardo regularized the uterus's shape to a sphere, and his characterization of the lining is incorrect), was an astounding achievement in its day. Analytical anatomical studies such as this one epitomize the scientific spirit of the Renaissance, establishing that era as a prelude to the modern world and setting it in sharp contrast to the preceding Middle Ages. Although Leonardo may not have been the first scientist of the modern world (at least not in the modern sense of the term), he certainly originated a method of scientific illustration, especially *cutaway* views. Scholars have long recognized the importance of these drawings for the development of anatomy as a science, especially in an age predating photographic methods such as X-rays.

Leonardo also won renown in his time as an architect and sculptor, although no surviving buildings or sculptures can be definitively attributed to him. From his many drawings of central-plan buildings, it appears he shared the interest of other Renaissance architects in this building type. As for sculpture, Leonardo left numerous drawings of monumental equestrian statues, and one resulted in a full-scale model for a monument

Renaissance Drawings

In the 16th century, drawing (or *disegno*) assumed a position of greater prominence than ever before in artistic production. Until the late 15th century, the expense and relative scarcity of drawing surfaces limited the production of preparatory sketches. Most artists drew on *parchment* (prepared from the skins of calves, sheep, and goats) or on *vellum* (made from the skins of young animals). Because of the high cost of these materials, especially vellum, drawings in the 14th and 15th centuries tended to be extremely detailed and meticulously executed. Artists often drew using *silverpoint* (a *stylus* made of silver; compare FIG. 8-7) because of the fine line it produced and the sharp point it maintained. The introduction in the late 15th century of less expensive paper made of fibrous pulp, from the developing printing industry (see "Woodcuts," Chapter 8, page 228), allowed artists to experiment more and to draw with greater freedom. As a result, sketches abounded. Artists executed these drawings in pen and ink, chalk, charcoal, brush, and graphite or lead. Leonardo da Vinci was especially prolific. His drawings are not only small-scale artworks of the highest quality but also invaluable records of his wide range of interests, both artistic and scientific (FIG. 9-5).

The importance of drawing transcended the mechanical or technical possibilities that it afforded artists, however. The term *disegno* referred also to design, an integral component of good art. Design was the foundation of art, and drawing was the fundamental element of design. Federico Zuccaro (1542–1609) summed up this philosophy when he stated that drawing was the external physical manifestation *(disegno esterno)* of an internal intellectual idea or design *(disegno interno)*.

The design dimension of art production became increasingly important as artists cultivated their personal styles. The early stages of an apprentice's training largely focused on the study and copying of exemplary artworks. But to achieve widespread recognition, artists had to forgo this dependence on prestigious models and develop their own styles. Although the artistic community and public at large acknowledged technical skill, the conceptualization of the artwork—its theoretical and formal development—was paramount. Disegno—design in this case—represented an artist's conceptualization and intention. In Renaissance texts, the terms writers and critics often invoked to praise esteemed artists included *invenzione* (invention), *ingegno* (innate talent), *fantasia* (imagination), and *capriccio* (originality).

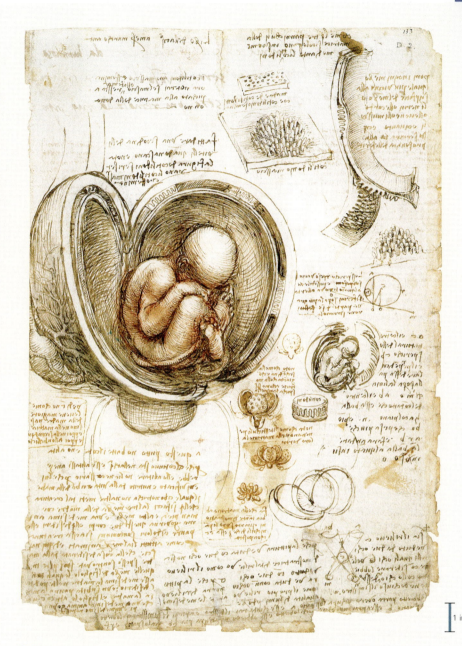

1 in.

9-5 LEONARDO DA VINCI, *The Fetus and Lining of the Uterus*, ca. 1510. Pen and ink with wash, over red chalk and traces of black chalk on paper, 1′ 8$\frac{5}{8}$″. Royal Library, Windsor Castle.

Leonardo's drawings document his wide range of interests. His analytical anatomical studies epitomize the scientific spirit of the Renaissance, establishing that era as a prelude to the modern world.

to Francesco Sforza (Ludovico's father). The French used it as a target and shot it to pieces when they occupied Milan in 1499. Due to the French presence, Leonardo left Milan and served for a while as a military engineer for Cesare Borgia, who, with the support of his father, Pope Alexander VI

(r. 1492–1503), tried to conquer the cities of the Romagna region in north-central Italy and create a Borgia duchy. Leonardo eventually returned to Milan in the service of the French. At the invitation of King Francis I, he then went to France, where he died at the château of Cloux in 1519.

Raphael

Raffaello Santi (or Sanzio), known as RAPHAEL (1483–1520) in English, was born in a small town in Umbria near Urbino. He probably learned the rudiments of his art from his father, Giovanni Santi, a painter connected with the ducal court of Federico da Montefeltro. Raphael spent the four years from 1504 to 1508 in Florence, where he studied the works of Leonardo and Michelangelo and developed his craft further. Raphael's powerful and original mature style epitomizes the ideals of High Renaissance art.

Madonna in the Meadow In 1505–1506, Raphael painted *Madonna in the Meadow* (FIG. **9-6**), using the pyramidal composition of Leonardo's *Madonna of the Rocks* (FIG. **9-2**) and modeling the faces and figures with the older master's subtle chiaroscuro. But Raphael retained the lighter tonalities of Umbrian painting, preferring clarity to obscurity. Dusky modeling and mystery did not fascinate Raphael, as they did Leonardo. Raphael's great series of Madonnas, of which this is an early example, unifies Christian devotion and pagan beauty. No artist ever has rivaled Raphael in his definitive rendering of this sublime theme of grace and dignity, of sweetness and lofty idealism.

School of Athens In 1508, Pope Julius II (r. 1503–1513) called Raphael to Rome. Beyond his responsibility as the spiritual leader of Christendom, Julius II extended his quest for authority to the temporal realm, as other medieval and Renaissance popes had done. An immensely ambitious man, Julius II indulged his enthusiasm for engaging in battle, which earned him the designation "warrior-pope." His selection of the name Julius, after Julius Caesar, reinforced the perception that the Roman Empire served as his governmental model. Julius II's papacy, however, was most notable for his contributions to the arts. He was an avid art patron and understood well the propagandistic value of visual imagery. After his election, he immediately commissioned artworks that would present an authoritative image of his rule and reinforce the primacy of the Catholic Church. Among the many projects Julius commissioned were a new design for Saint Peter's basilica (FIG. **9-14**), the painting of the Sistine Chapel ceiling (FIG. **9-1**), and the decoration of the papal apartments (FIG. **9-7**). These large-scale projects clearly required considerable financial resources. Many Church members perceived the increasing sale of indulgences as a revenue-generating mechanism to fund papal art, architecture, and lavish lifestyles. This perception, accurate or not, prompted disgruntlement among the faithful. Thus, Julius's patronage, despite its exceptional artistic legacy, also contributed to the rise of the Reformation.

Although the commissions for Saint Peter's and the Sistine Chapel went to others, Julius entrusted Raphael with the responsibility of decorating the papal apartments. Of the suite's several rooms *(stanze)*, Raphael painted two himself, including the Stanza della Segnatura (Room of the Signature—the

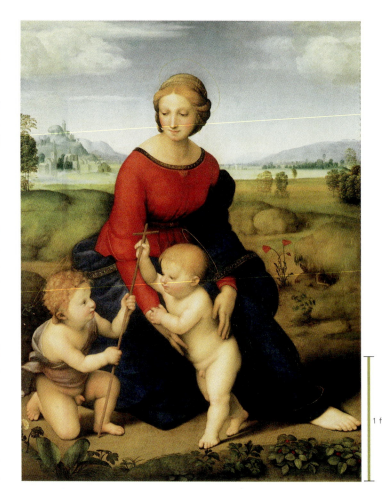

9-6 RAPHAEL, *Madonna in the Meadow*, 1505–1506. Oil on wood, 3′ 8½″ × 2′ 10¼″. Kunsthistorisches Museum, Vienna.

Emulating Leonardo's pyramidal composition (FIG. **9-2**) but rejecting his dusky modeling and mystery, Raphael set his Madonna in a well-lit landscape and imbued her with grace, dignity, and beauty.

papal library, where the pope signed official documents). Raphael's pupils completed the others, following his sketches. On the four walls of the library, under the headings *Theology, Law, Poetry,* and *Philosophy,* Raphael presented images that symbolized and summed up Western learning as Renaissance society understood it. The frescoes refer to the four branches of human knowledge and wisdom while pointing out the virtues and the learning appropriate to a pope. Given Julius II's desire for recognition as both a spiritual and temporal leader, it is appropriate that the *Theology* and *Philosophy* frescoes face each other. The two images present a balanced picture of the pope—as a cultured, knowledgeable individual and as a wise, divinely ordained religious authority.

In Raphael's *Philosophy* mural (popularly known as *School of Athens*, FIG. **9-7**), the setting is not a "school" but a congregation of the great philosophers and scientists of the ancient world. Raphael depicted these luminaries, revered by Renaissance humanists, conversing and explaining their various theories and ideas. The figures gather in a vast hall covered by massive vaults that recall Roman architecture—and approximate the appearance of the new Saint Peter's (FIG. **10-4**) in 1509, when Raphael began the fresco. Colossal

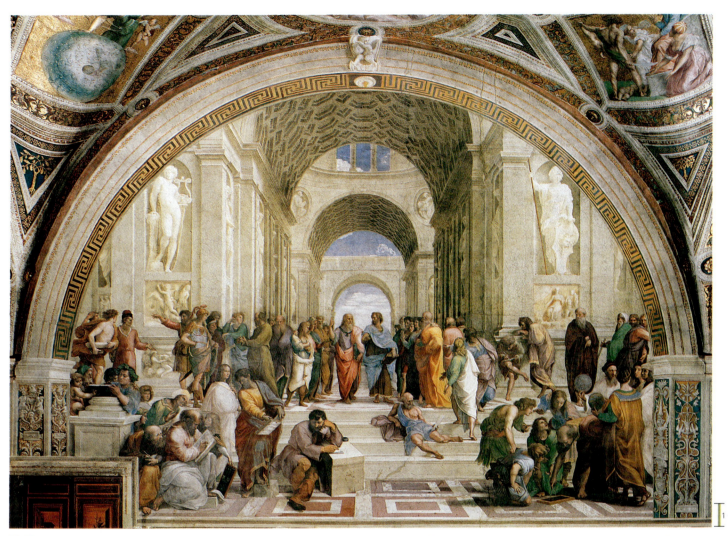

9-7 Raphael, *Philosophy (School of Athens)*, Stanza della Segnatura, Vatican Palace, Rome, Italy, 1509–1511. Fresco, 19′ × 27′.

Raphael included himself in this gathering of great philosophers and scientists whose self-assurance conveys calm reason. The setting resembles the interior of the new Saint Peter's (FIG. 10-4).

statues of Apollo and Athena, patron deities of the arts and of wisdom, oversee the interactions. Plato and Aristotle serve as the central figures around whom Raphael carefully arranged the others. Plato holds his book *Timaeus* and points to Heaven, the source of his inspiration, while Aristotle carries his book *Nicomachean Ethics* and gestures toward the earth, from which his observations of reality sprang. Appropriately, ancient philosophers, men concerned with the ultimate mysteries that transcend this world, stand on Plato's side. On Aristotle's side are the philosophers and scientists who studied nature and human affairs. At the lower left, Pythagoras writes as a servant holds up the harmonic scale. In the foreground, Heraclitus (probably a portrait of Michelangelo) broods alone. Diogenes sprawls on the steps. At the right, students surround Euclid, who demonstrates a theorem. Euclid may be a portrait of the architect Bramante (discussed later). At the extreme right, just to the right of the astronomers Zoroaster and Ptolemy, both holding globes, Raphael portrayed himself as a young man wearing a dark cap.

The groups appear to move easily and clearly, with eloquent poses and gestures that symbolize their doctrines and present an engaging variety of figural positions. Their self-assurance and natural dignity convey the very nature of calm reason, that balance and measure the great Renaissance minds so admired as the heart of philosophy. Significantly, in this work Raphael placed himself among the mathematicians and scientists rather than the humanists. Certainly the evolution of pictorial science came to its perfection in *School of Athens*. Raphael's convincing depiction of a vast perspectival space on a two-dimensional surface was the consequence of the union of mathematics with pictorial science, here mastered completely.

The artist's psychological insight matured along with his mastery of the problems of physical representation. All the characters in *School of Athens*, like those in Leonardo's *Last Supper* (FIG. 9-3), communicate moods that reflect their beliefs, and the artist's placement of each figure tied these moods together. Raphael carefully considered his design devices for relating individuals and groups to one another and to the whole. These compositional elements demand close study. From the center, where Plato and Aristotle stand, Raphael arranged the groups of figures in an ellipse with a wide opening in the foreground. Moving along the floor's perspectival pattern, the viewer's eye penetrates the assembly of philosophers and continues, by way of the reclining Diogenes, up to the here-reconciled leaders of the two great opposing camps of Renaissance philosophy. The perspectival vanishing point falls on Plato's left hand, drawing attention to *Timaeus*. In the Stanza della Segnatura, Raphael reconciled and harmonized not only the Platonists and Aristotelians but also paganism and Christianity, surely a major factor in his appeal to Julius II.

Michelangelo

The artist who received the most coveted commissions from Julius II was MICHELANGELO BUONARROTI (1475–1564). Although Michelangelo was an architect, sculptor, painter, poet, and engineer, he thought of himself first as a sculptor, regarding that calling as superior to that of a painter because the sculptor shares in something like the divine power to "make man." Drawing a conceptual parallel to Plato's ideas, Michelangelo believed the image produced by the artist's hand must come from the idea in the artist's mind. The idea, then, is the reality the artist's genius has to bring forth. But artists are not the creators of the ideas they conceive. Rather, they find their ideas in the natural world, reflecting the absolute idea, which, for the artist, is beauty. One of Michelangelo's best-known observations about sculpture is that the artist must proceed by finding the idea—the image locked in the stone. By removing the excess stone, the sculptor extricates the idea (FIG. I-12). The artist, Michelangelo felt, works many years at this unceasing process of revelation and "arrives late at novel and lofty things."[3]

Michelangelo did indeed arrive at "novel and lofty things," for he broke sharply from the lessons of his predecessors and contemporaries in one important respect. He mistrusted the application of mathematical methods as guarantees of beauty in proportion. Measure and proportion, he believed, should be "kept in the eyes." Vasari quoted Michelangelo as declaring that "it was necessary to have the compasses in the eyes and not in the hand, because the hands work and the eye judges."[4] Thus, Michelangelo set aside the ancient Roman architect Vitruvius, as well as Alberti, Leonardo, and others who tirelessly sought the perfect measure, and

asserted that the artist's inspired judgment could identify other pleasing proportions. In addition, Michelangelo argued that the artist must not be bound, except by the demands made by realizing the idea. This insistence on the artist's own authority was typical of Michelangelo and anticipated the modern concept of the right to a self-expression of talent limited only by the artist's own judgment. The artistic license to aspire far beyond the "rules" was, in part, a manifestation of the pursuit of fame and success that humanism fostered. In this context, Michelangelo created works in architecture, sculpture, and painting that departed from High Renaissance regularity. He put in its stead a style of vast, expressive strength conveyed through complex, eccentric, and often titanic forms that loom before the viewer in tragic grandeur. Michelangelo's self-imposed isolation, creative furies, proud independence, and daring innovations led Italians to speak of the dominating quality of the man and his works in one word—*terribilità*, the sublime shadowed by the awesome and the fearful.

Pietà Michelangelo began his career in Florence, but when the Medici fell in 1494 (see Chapter 8), he fled to Bologna and then moved to Rome. There, around 1498, still in his early 20s, he produced his first masterpiece—a *Pietà* (FIG. 9-8)—for the French cardinal Jean de Bilhères Lagraulas. The cardinal commissioned the statue to adorn the chapel in Old Saint Peter's (FIG. 4-4) in which he was to be

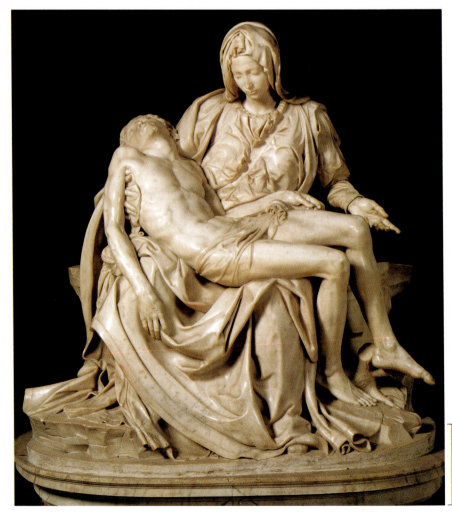

9-8 MICHELANGELO BUONARROTI, *Pietà*, ca. 1498–1500. Marble, 5′ 8½″ high. Saint Peter's, Vatican City, Rome.

Michelangelo's representation of Mary cradling Christ's corpse brilliantly captures the sadness and beauty of the young Virgin but was controversial because the Madonna seems younger than her son.

1 ft.

buried. The work is now on view in the new church (FIG. 10-3) that replaced the fourth-century basilica. The theme—Mary cradling the dead body of Christ in her lap—was a staple in the repertoire of French and German (FIG. 7-26) artists, and Michelangelo's French patron doubtless chose the subject. The Italian, however, rendered the Northern theme in an unforgettable manner. Michelangelo transformed marble into flesh, hair, and fabric with a sensitivity for texture that is almost without parallel. The polish and luminosity of the exquisite marble surface cannot be captured fully in photographs and can be appreciated only by viewing the original. Breathtaking, too, is the tender sadness of the beautiful and youthful Mary as she mourns over the death of her son. In fact, her age—seemingly less than that of Christ—was a subject of controversy from the moment of the unveiling of the statue. Michelangelo explained Mary's ageless beauty as an integral part of her purity and virginity. Beautiful, too, is the son she holds. Christ seems less to have died than to have drifted off into peaceful sleep in Mary's maternal arms. His wounds are barely visible.

David Michelangelo returned to Florence in 1501, when the Florence Cathedral building committee asked him to fashion a statue of *David* (FIG. 9-9) from a great block of marble left over from an earlier aborted commission. In 1495 the Florentine republic had ordered the transfer of Donatello's *David* (FIG. 8-19) from the Medici palace to the Palazzo della Signoria, the seat of government. Michelangelo's *David* stood outside the west door of the city hall and, like Donatello's statue, served as a symbol of Florentine liberty. The statue—which Florentines referred to as "the Giant"—immediately established Michelangelo's reputation as an extraordinary talent. Only 40 years after completion of *David*, Vasari extolled the work and claimed that "without any doubt the figure has put in the shade every other statue, ancient or modern, Greek or Roman."[5]

Despite the traditional association of David with heroism, Michelangelo chose to represent the young biblical warrior not after the victory, with Goliath's head at his feet, but turning his head to his left, sternly watchful of the approaching foe. Every aspect of his muscular body, including his face, is tense with gathering power. *David* exhibits the characteristic representation of energy in reserve that imbues Michelangelo's later figures with the tension of a coiled spring. The anatomy of David's body plays an important part in this prelude to action. His rugged torso, sturdy limbs, and large hands and feet alert viewers to the strength to come. The swelling veins and tightening sinews amplify the psychological energy of the pose.

Michelangelo doubtless had the classical nude in mind. Like many of his colleagues, he greatly admired Greco-Roman statues, in particular the skillful and precise rendering of heroic physique. Without strictly imitating the antique style, the Renaissance sculptor captured the tension of Lysippan athletes (FIG. 2-49) and the psychological insight and emotionalism of Hellenistic statuary (FIG. 2-54). His *David* differs from Donatello's (FIG. 8-19) in much the

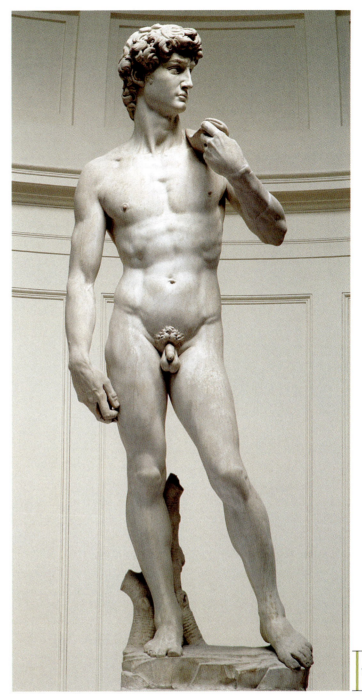

9-9 MICHELANGELO BUONARROTI, *David*, from Piazza della Signoria, Florence, Italy, 1501–1504. Marble, 17′ high. Galleria dell'Accademia, Florence.

In this colossal statue, Michelangelo represented David in heroic classical nudity, capturing the tension of Lysippan athletes (FIG. 2-49) and the emotionalism of Hellenistic statuary (FIG. 2-54).

same way later Hellenistic statues departed from their Classical predecessors (see Chapter 2). Michelangelo abandoned the self-contained composition of the 15th-century statue by abruptly turning the hero's head toward his gigantic adversary. His *David* is compositionally and emotionally connected to an unseen presence beyond the statue, a feature also of Hellenistic sculpture. As early as 1501, then, Michelangelo invested his efforts in presenting towering, pent-up emotion rather than calm, ideal beauty.

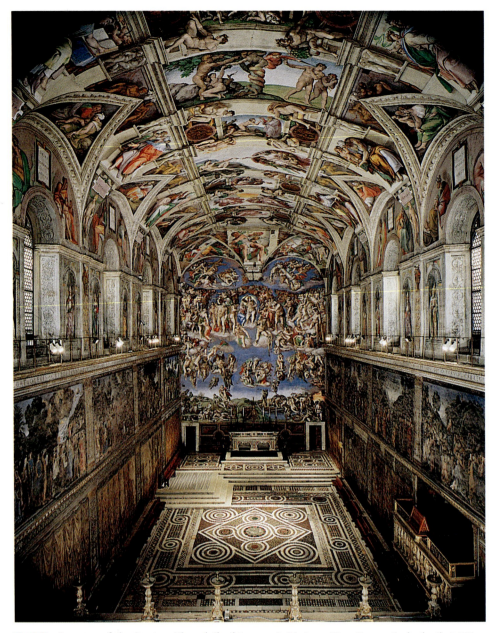

9-10 Interior of the Sistine Chapel (looking east), Vatican City, Rome, Italy, built 1473.

Michelangelo reluctantly agreed to paint the ceiling (FIG. 9-1) of the Sistine Chapel for Pope Julius II. He had to overcome the complicated perspective problems that the height and curve of the vault presented.

his patron's agenda, Church doctrine, and the artist's interests. Depicting the most august and solemn themes of all, the Creation, Fall, and Redemption of humanity, Michelangelo spread a colossal decorative scheme across the vast surface. He succeeded in weaving together more than 300 figures in a grand drama of the human race.

A long sequence of narrative panels describing the Creation, as recorded in Genesis, runs along the crown of the vault, from God's *Separation of Light and Darkness* (above the altar) to *Drunkenness of Noah* (nearest the entrance to the chapel). Thus, as viewers enter the chapel, look up, and walk toward the altar, they review, in reverse order, the history of the Fall of humankind. The Hebrew prophets and pagan sibyls who foretold the coming of Christ appear seated in large thrones on both sides of the central row of scenes from Genesis, where the vault curves down. In the four corner *pendentives*, Michelangelo placed four Old Testament scenes with David, Judith, Haman, and Moses and the Brazen Serpent. Scores of lesser figures also appear. The ancestors of Christ fill the triangular compartments above the windows, nude youths punctuate the corners of the central panels, and small pairs of putti in *grisaille* (monochrome painting using shades of gray to imitate sculpture) support the painted cornice surrounding the entire central corridor. The overall conceptualization of the ceiling's design and narrative structure not only presents a sweeping chronology of Christianity but also is in keeping with Renaissance ideas about Christian history. These ideas included interest in the conflict between good and evil and between the energy of youth and the wisdom of age. The conception of the entire ceiling was astounding in itself, and the articulation of it in its thousand details was a superhuman achievement.

Unlike Andrea Mantegna's decoration of the Camera Picta (FIGS. 8-38 and 8-39) in Mantua, the strongly marked unifying architectural framework in the Sistine Chapel does not produce "picture windows." Rather, the viewer focuses on figure after figure, each sharply outlined against the neutral tone of the architectural setting or the plain background of

Sistine Chapel In 1508, the same year Julius II asked Raphael to decorate the papal *stanze*, the pope convinced a reluctant Michelangelo to paint the ceiling of the Sistine Chapel (FIGS. 9-1 and 9-10). Michelangelo insisted that painting was not his profession (a protest that rings hollow after the fact, although his major works until then had been in sculpture), but he accepted the commission. Michelangelo faced enormous difficulties in painting the Sistine ceiling. He had to address its dimensions (some 5,800 square feet), its height above the pavement (almost 70 feet), and the complicated perspective problems the vault's height and curve presented, as well as his inexperience as a fresco painter. Yet, in less than four years, Michelangelo produced a monumental fresco incorporating

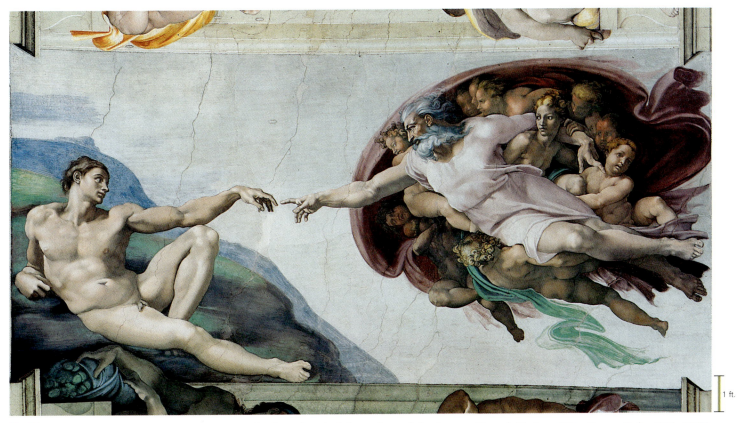

9-11 MICHELANGELO BUONARROTI, *Creation of Adam*, detail of the ceiling of the Sistine Chapel, Vatican City, Rome, Italy, 1511–1512. Fresco, 9′ 2″ × 18′ 8″.

Life leaps to Adam like a spark from the extended hand of God in this fresco, which recalls the communication between gods and heroes in the classical myths so admired by Renaissance humanists.

the panels. Here, as in his sculpture, Michelangelo relentlessly concentrated his expressive purpose on the human figure. To him, the body was beautiful not only in its natural form but also in its spiritual and philosophical significance. The body was the manifestation of the soul or of a state of mind and character. Michelangelo represented the body in its most simple, elemental aspect—in the nude or simply draped, with no background and no ornamental embellishment. He always painted with a sculptor's eye for how light and shadow communicate volume and surface. It is no coincidence that many of the figures seem to be tinted reliefs or freestanding statues.

Creation of Adam One of the ceiling's central panels is *Creation of Adam* (FIG. **9-11**). Michelangelo did not paint the traditional representation but instead produced a bold, humanistic interpretation of the momentous event. God and Adam confront each other in a primordial unformed landscape of which Adam is still a material part, heavy as earth. The Lord transcends the earth, wrapped in a billowing cloud of drapery and borne up by his powers. Life leaps to Adam like a spark flashed from the extended, mighty hand of God. The communication between gods and heroes, so familiar in classical myth, is here concrete. This blunt depiction of the Lord as ruler of Heaven in the Olympian pagan sense indicates how easily High Renaissance thought joined classical

and Christian traditions. Yet the classical trappings do not obscure the essential Christian message.

Beneath the Lord's sheltering left arm is a female figure, apprehensively curious but as yet uncreated. Scholars traditionally believed her to represent Eve, but many now think she is the Virgin Mary (with the Christ Child at her knee). If the second identification is correct, it suggests that Michelangelo incorporated into his fresco one of the essential tenets of Christian faith—the belief that Adam's Original Sin eventually led to the sacrifice of Christ, which in turn made possible the Redemption of all humankind. As God reaches out to Adam, the viewer's eye follows the motion from right to left, but Adam's extended left arm leads the eye back to the right, along the Lord's right arm, shoulders, and left arm to his left forefinger, which points to the Christ Child's face. The focal point of this right-to-left-to-right movement—the fingertips of Adam and the Lord—is dramatically off-center. Michelangelo replaced the straight architectural axes found in Leonardo's compositions with curves and diagonals. For example, the bodies of the two great figures are complementary—the concave body of Adam fitting the convex body and billowing "cloak" of God. Thus, motion directs not only the figures but also the whole composition. The reclining positions of the figures, the heavy musculature, and the twisting poses are all intrinsic parts of Michelangelo's style.

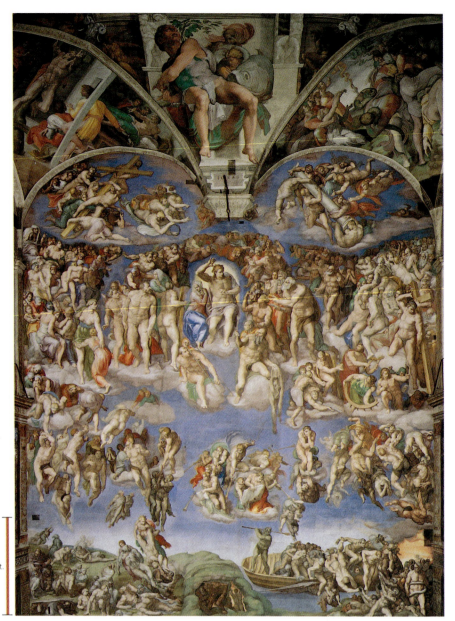

9-12 MICHELANGELO BUONARROTI, *Last Judgment*, altar wall of the Sistine Chapel, Vatican City, Rome, Italy, 1534–1541. Fresco, 48′ × 44′.

Michelangelo completed his fresco cycle in the Sistine Chapel with this terrifying vision of the fate awaiting sinners. Near the center, he placed his own portrait on the flayed skin Saint Bartholomew holds.

10 ft.

Last Judgment After the death of Julius II, Leo X (r. 1513–1521), Clement VII (r. 1523–1534), and Paul III (r. 1534–1549) also employed Michelangelo. Among Paul III's first papal commissions was *Last Judgment* (FIG. **9-12**), a large fresco for the Sistine Chapel's altar wall (FIG. **9-10**). Here, Michelangelo depicted Christ as the stern judge of the world—a giant who raises his mighty right arm in a gesture of damnation so broad and universal as to suggest he will destroy all creation. The choirs of Heaven surrounding him pulse with anxiety and awe. Crowded into the spaces below are trumpeting angels, the ascending figures of the just, and the downward-hurtling figures of the damned. On the left, the dead awake and assume flesh. On the right, demons,

whose gargoyle masks and burning eyes revive the demons of Romanesque tympana (FIG. **6-20**), torment the damned.

Michelangelo's terrifying vision of the fate that awaits sinners goes far beyond any previous rendition. Martyrs who suffered especially agonizing deaths crouch below the judge. One of them, Saint Bartholomew, who was skinned alive, holds the flaying knife and the skin, its face a grotesque self-portrait of Michelangelo. The figures are huge and violently twisted, with small heads and contorted features. Although this immense fresco impresses on viewers Christ's wrath on Judgment Day, it also holds out hope. A group of saved souls—the elect—crowd around Christ, and on the far right appears a figure with a cross, most likely the Good Thief (crucified with Christ) or a saint martyred by crucifixion, such as Saint Andrew.

Architecture

During the High Renaissance, architects and patrons alike turned to classical antiquity to find a suitable architectural vocabulary for conveying the new humanist worldview. In the buildings of ancient Rome, they discovered the perfect prototypes for the domed architecture that became the hallmark of the 16th century.

Bramante The leading architect of this classical-revival style at the opening of the century was DONATO D'ANGELO BRAMANTE (1444–1514). Born in Urbino and trained as a painter (perhaps by Piero della Francesca, FIG. **8-35**), Bramante went to Milan in 1481 and, like Leonardo, stayed there until the French arrived in 1499. In Milan he abandoned painting for architecture. Under the influence of Brunelleschi, Alberti, and perhaps Leonardo, all of whom strongly favored the art and architecture of classical antiquity, Bramante developed the High Renaissance form of the central-plan church.

Bramante's approach to design is on display in the architectural gem known as the Tempietto (FIG. **9-13**), so named because, to contemporaries, the building had the look of a small ancient temple. In fact, the round temples of Roman Italy provided the direct models for the lower story of Bramante's "Little Temple." The architect relied on the composition of volumes and masses and on a sculptural handling of solids and voids to set apart this building, all but devoid of ornament, from structures built in the preceding century.

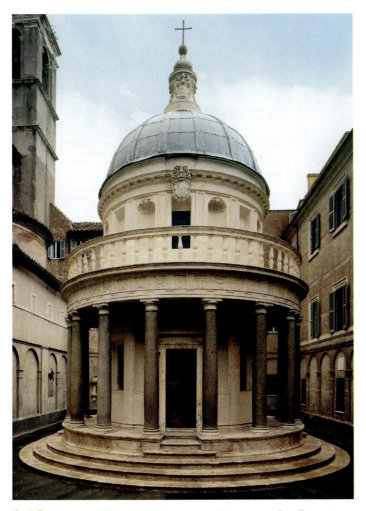

9-13 DONATO D'ANGELO BRAMANTE, Tempietto, San Pietro in Montorio, Rome, Italy, 1502(?).

Contemporaries celebrated Bramante as the first to revive the classical style in architecture. Roman round temples inspired this "little temple," but Bramante combined the classical parts in new ways.

Standing inside the cloister of the Church of San Pietro in Montorio, Rome, the Tempietto marked the conjectural location of Saint Peter's crucifixion. It resembles a sculptured reliquary and would have looked even more so standing inside the circular colonnaded courtyard Bramante planned for it but never executed.

The structure is severely rational with its sober circular *stylobate* (stepped temple platform) and the cool *Tuscan* style of the colonnade, neither feature giving any indication of the placement of an interior altar or of the entrance. However, Bramante achieved a truly wonderful balance and harmony in the relationship of the parts (dome, drum, and base) to one another and to the whole. Conceived as a tall, domed cylinder projecting from the lower, wider cylinder of its colonnade, this small building incorporates all the qualities of a sculptured monument. Light and shadow play around the columns and balustrade and across the deep-set rectangular windows, which alternate with shallow shell-capped niches in the walls and drum. Although the Tempietto, superficially at least, may resemble a Greco-Roman *tholos* (a circular shrine), and although antique models inspired all its details, the combination of parts and details was new and original. (Classical tholoi, for instance, had neither drum nor balustrade.)

One of the main differences between the Early and High Renaissance styles of architecture is the former's emphasis on detailing flat wall surfaces versus the latter's sculptural handling of architectural masses. Bramante's Tempietto initiated the High Renaissance era. Andrea Palladio, an influential theorist as well as a major architect (FIG. 9-16), included the Tempietto in his survey of ancient temples because Bramante was "the first to bring back to light the good and beautiful architecture that from antiquity to that time had been hidden."[6] Round in plan and elevated on a base that isolates it from its surroundings, the Tempietto conforms to Alberti's and Palladio's strictest demands for an ideal church.

New Saint Peter's Perhaps the most important artistic project Pope Julius II initiated was the replacement of the Constantinian basilica, Old Saint Peter's (FIG. 4-4), with a new structure. The earlier building had fallen into considerable disrepair and, in any event, did not suit this ambitious pope's taste for the colossal. Julius wanted to gain control over the whole of Italy and to make the Rome of the popes reminiscent of (if not more splendid than) the Rome of the caesars. As the symbolic seat of the papacy, Saint Peter's represented the history of the Church. The choice of an architect for the new church was therefore of the highest importance. Julius chose Bramante.

Bramante originally designed the new Saint Peter's to consist of a cross with arms of equal length, each terminating in an apse. The pope intended the new building to serve as a *martyrium* to mark Saint Peter's grave and also hoped to have his own tomb in it. A large dome would have covered the crossing, and smaller domes over subsidiary chapels would have covered the diagonal axes of the roughly square plan. Thus, Bramante's ambitious design called for a boldly sculptural treatment of the walls and piers under the dome. His organization of the interior space was complex in the extreme, with the intricate symmetries of a crystal. It is possible to detect in the plan some nine interlocking crosses, five of them supporting domes. The scale was titanic. According to sources, Bramante boasted he would place the dome of the Pantheon (FIG. 3-39) over the Basilica of Constantine (FIG. 3-49).

During Bramante's lifetime, construction of the new Saint Peter's basilica advanced only to the building of the crossing piers and the lower choir walls. After his death, the work passed from one architect to another and, in 1546, to Michelangelo, whose work on Saint Peter's became a long-term show of dedication, thankless and without pay. When Michelangelo died in 1564 at age 89, he was still hard at work on the project. Among Michelangelo's difficulties was his struggle to preserve Bramante's central-plan design, which he praised. Michelangelo carried his obsession with human form over to architecture and reasoned that buildings should follow the form of the human body. This meant organizing their units symmetrically around a central and unique axis, as the arms relate to the body or the eyes to the nose. "For it is an established fact," he once wrote, "that the members of architecture resemble the members of man. Whoever neither has been nor is a master at figures, and especially at anatomy, cannot really understand architecture."[7]

In his modification of Bramante's plan, Michelangelo reduced the central component from a number of interlocking crosses to a compact domed Greek cross inscribed in a square and fronted with a double-columned portico (FIG. **9-14**). Without destroying the centralizing features of Bramante's plan, Michelangelo, with a few strokes of the pen, converted its snowflake complexity into massive, cohesive unity. His treatment of the building's exterior further reveals his interest in creating a unified and cohesive design. Because of later changes to the front of the church, the west (apse) end (FIG. **9-15**) offers the best view of his style and intention. Michelangelo employed the device of the colossal order, which Alberti (FIG. **8-36**) had introduced in the 15th century, to great effect. The giant pilasters seem to march around the undulating wall surfaces, confining the movement without interrupting it. The architectural sculpturing here extends up from the ground through the attic stories and into the drum and the dome, unifying the whole building from base to summit.

The domed west end—as majestic as it is today and as influential architecturally as it has been throughout the centuries—is not quite as Michelangelo intended it. Originally, he had planned a dome with an ogival section, like that of

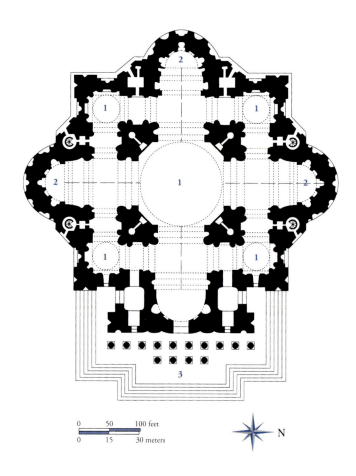

9-14 MICHELANGELO BUONARROTI, plan for Saint Peter's, Vatican City, Rome, Italy, 1546. (1) dome, (2) apse, (3) portico.

Michelangelo's plan for the new Saint Peter's was radically different from that of the original basilica (FIG. **4-4**). His central plan called for a domed Greek cross inscribed in a square and fronted by columns.

9-15
MICHELANGELO BUONARROTI, Saint Peter's (looking northeast), Vatican City, Rome, Italy, 1546–1564. Dome completed by GIACOMO DELLA PORTA, 1590.

The west end of Saint Peter's offers the best view of Michelangelo's intentions. The giant pilasters of his colossal order march around the undulating wall surfaces of the central-plan building.

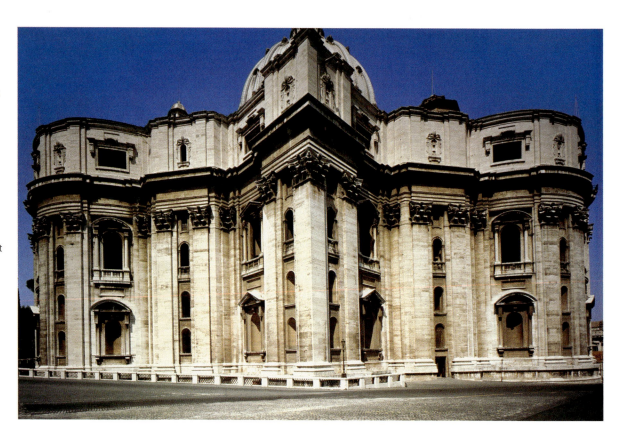

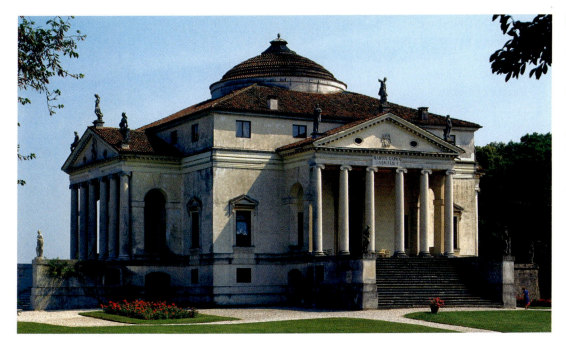

9-16 Andrea Palladio, Villa Rotonda, near Vicenza, Italy, ca. 1550–1570.

Palladio's Villa Rotonda has four identical facades, each one resembling a Roman temple with a columnar porch. In the center is a great dome-covered rotunda modeled on the Pantheon (FIG. **3-37**).

Florence Cathedral (FIG. **8-29**). But in his final version, he decided on a hemispherical dome to temper the verticality of the design of the lower stories and to establish a balance between dynamic and static elements. However, when GIACOMO DELLA PORTA (ca. 1533–1602) executed the dome after Michelangelo's death, he restored the earlier high design, ignoring Michelangelo's later version (FIG. **10-3**). Giacomo's reasons were probably the same ones that had impelled Brunelleschi to use an ogival section for his Florentine dome—greater stability and ease of construction. The result is that the dome seems to rise from its base, rather than rest firmly on it—an effect Michelangelo might not have approved. Nevertheless, Saint Peter's dome is probably the most impressive in the world.

Andrea Palladio The classical-revival style of High Renaissance architecture in Rome spread far and wide. One of its most accomplished practitioners was ANDREA PALLADIO (1508–1580), the chief architect of the Venetian republic. In order to study the ancient buildings firsthand, Palladio made several trips to Rome. In 1556 he illustrated Daniel Barbaro's edition of Vitruvius's *De architectura* and later wrote his own treatise on architecture, *I quattro libri dell'architettura (The Four Books of Architecture)*. Originally published in 1570, Palladio's treatise had wide-ranging influence on succeeding generations of architects throughout and beyond Europe. Palladio's influence outside Italy, most significantly in England and in colonial America, was stronger and more lasting than that of any other architect.

Palladio's significant reputation stemmed from his many designs for villas, built on the Venetian mainland. The same spirit that prompted the ancient Romans to build villas in the countryside motivated a similar villa-building boom in 16th-century Venice, which, with its very limited space, must have been highly congested. But a longing for the countryside was not the only motive. Declining fortunes prompted the Venetians to develop their mainland possessions with new land investment and reclamation projects. Citizens who could afford it set themselves up as aristocratic farmers and developed swamps into productive agricultural land. Wealthy families could regard their villas as providential investments. The villas were thus aristocratic farms (like the much later American plantations, which emulated Palladio's architectural style). Palladio generally arranged the outbuildings in long, low wings branching out from the main building and enclosing a large rectangular court area.

His most famous villa, Villa Rotonda (FIG. **9-16**), near Vicenza, is exceptional because the architect did not build it for an aspiring gentleman farmer but for a retired monsignor who wanted a villa for hosting social events. Palladio planned and designed Villa Rotonda, located on a hilltop, as a kind of *belvedere* (literally, "beautiful view"; in architecture, a residence on a hill), without the usual wings of secondary buildings. It has a central plan, with four identical facades and projecting porches, which served as platforms for enjoying different views of the surrounding landscape. Each facade of the villa resembles a Roman Ionic temple. In placing a traditional temple porch in front of a dome-covered interior, Palladio doubtless had the Pantheon (FIG. **3-37**) in mind as a model.

Venetian Painting

In addition to Palladio, 16th-century Venice boasted some of the most renowned painters of the Renaissance era. Artists in the maritime republic showed a special interest in recording the effect of Venice's soft-colored light on figures and landscapes, and Venetian paintings are easy to distinguish from contemporaneous works created in Florence and Rome.

Giovanni Bellini One artist who contributed significantly to creating the High Renaissance painting style in Venice was GIOVANNI BELLINI (ca. 1430–1516), who favored the new medium of oil paint developed in 15th-century Flanders (see "Tempera and Oil Painting," Chapter 8, page 219). This more flexible medium has a wider color range than either tempera or fresco. Venetian oil painting became the great complement of the painting schools of Florence and Rome.

Bellini earned great recognition for his many Madonnas, especially his monumental altarpieces of the *sacra conversazione* (holy conversation) type. In the sacra conversazione, which gained wide popularity as a theme for religious paintings from the middle of the 15th century on, saints from different epochs occupy the same space and seem to converse either with each other or with the audience. (Raphael employed much the same conceit in his *School of Athens*, FIG. 9-7, in which he assembled Greek philosophers of different eras.) Bellini carried on the tradition in one of his earliest major commissions, the *San Zaccaria Altarpiece* (FIG. 9-17). The Virgin Mary sits enthroned, holding the Christ Child, with four saints flanking her: Saint Peter with his key and book, Saint Catherine with the palm of martyrdom and the broken wheel, Saint Lucy with a tray that holds her plucked-out eyes, and Saint Jerome with a book (representing his translation of the Bible into Latin). At the foot of the throne sits an angel playing a viol.

The painting radiates a feeling of serenity and spiritual calm. Viewers derive this sense less from the figures (no interaction occurs among them) than from Bellini's harmonious and balanced presentation of color and light. Outlines dissolve in light and shadow. Glowing oil color produces a soft radiance that envelops the forms with an atmospheric haze and enhances their majestic serenity. Bellini's approach

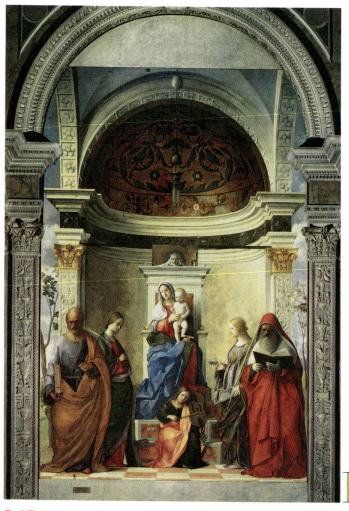

9-17 GIOVANNI BELLINI, *San Zaccaria Altarpiece*, 1505. Oil on wood transferred to canvas, 16' 5½" × 7' 9". San Zaccaria, Venice.

In this *sacra conversazione* uniting saints from different eras, Bellini created a feeling of serenity and spiritual calm through the harmonious and balanced presentation of color and light.

9-18 GIORGIONE DA CASTELFRANCO (and/or TITIAN?), *Pastoral Symphony*, ca. 1508–1510. Oil on canvas, 3' 7¼" × 4' 6¼". Louvre, Paris.

Venetian art is often described as poetic. In this painting, Giorgione so eloquently evoked the pastoral mood that the uncertainty about the picture's meaning is not distressing. The mood and rich color are enough.

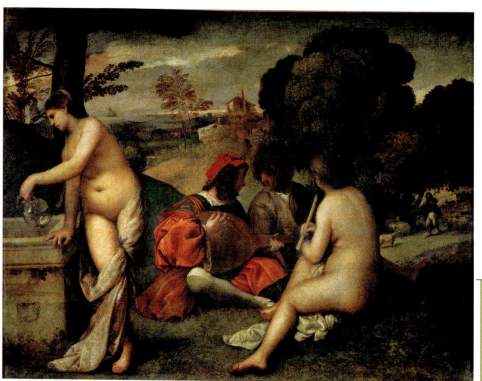

to painting differed sharply from that of his Central Italian contemporaries. Color was the primary instrument of Bellini and his Venetian successors, whereas the Florentines and Romans focused on sculpturesque form. Scholars often distill the contrast between these two approaches down to *colorito* (colored or painted) versus *disegno* (drawing and design). Venetian artists also preferred to paint the poetry of the senses and delighted in nature's beauty and the pleasures of humanity. Artists in Florence and Rome gravitated toward more intellectual themes—the epic of humanity, the masculine virtues, the grandeur of the ideal, and the lofty conceptions of religion involving the heroic and sublime. Much of the history of later Western art involves a dialogue between these two traditions.

Giorgione Describing Venetian art as "poetic" is particularly appropriate, given the development of *poesia*, or painting meant to operate in a manner similar to poetry. Both classical and Renaissance poetry inspired Venetian artists, and their paintings focused on the lyrical and sensual. Thus, in many Venetian artworks, discerning concrete narratives or subjects (in the traditional sense) is virtually impossible. The Venetian artist who deserves much of the credit for developing poesia-style painting was GIORGIONE DA CASTELFRANCO (ca. 1477–1510). Vasari reported that Giorgione was an accomplished lutenist and singer, and adjectives from poetry and music seem best suited for describing the pastoral air and muted chords of his works.

Giorgione's so-called *Pastoral Symphony* (FIG. 9-18; some believe it an early work by his student Titian) exemplifies poesia. Out of dense shadow emerge the soft forms of figures and landscape. Giorgione cast a mood of tranquil reverie and dreaminess over the entire scene, evoking the landscape of a lost but never forgotten paradise. The theme is as enigmatic as the lighting. Two nude women, accompanied by two clothed young men, occupy the rich, abundant landscape through which a shepherd passes. In the distance, a villa crowns a hill. The artist so eloquently evoked the pastoral mood that the viewer does not find the uncertainty about the picture's precise meaning distressing. The mood is enough. The shepherd symbolizes the poet. The pipes and the lute symbolize his poetry. The two women accompanying the young men may be thought of as their invisible inspiration, their muses. One turns to lift water from the sacred well of poetic inspiration. The voluptuous bodies of the women, softly modulated by the smoky shadow, became the standard in Venetian art. The fullness of their figures contributes to their effect as poetic personifications of nature's abundance.

Titian Giorgione's pastoralism passed to Tiziano Vecelli, called TITIAN (ca. 1490–1576) in English. Titian was a supreme colorist and the most extraordinary and prolific of the great Venetian painters. His remarkable coloristic sense and ability to convey light through color emerge in a major altarpiece, *Assumption of the Virgin* (FIG. 9-19), painted in oil (see "Palma il Giovane on Titian," page 272) for the main altar of Santa Maria Gloriosa dei Frari in Venice. The monumental

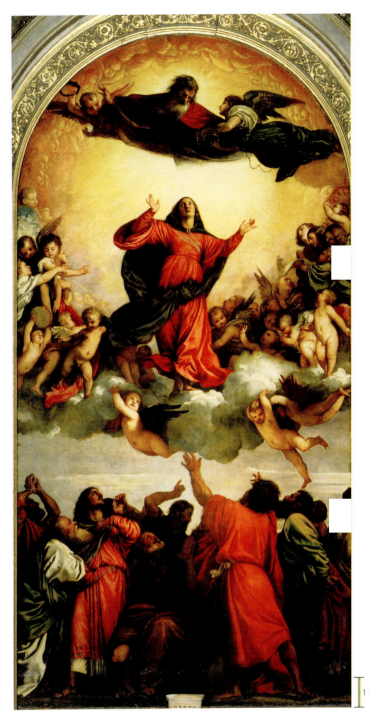

1 ft.

9-19 TITIAN, *Assumption of the Virgin*, 1516–1518. Oil on wood, 22' 7½" × 11' 10". Santa Maria Gloriosa dei Frari, Venice.

Titian won renown for his ability to convey light through color. In this dramatic depiction of the Virgin Mary's ascent to Heaven, the golden clouds seem to glow and radiate light into the church.

altarpiece (nearly 23 feet high) depicts the glorious ascent of the Virgin's body to Heaven on a great cloud borne aloft by putti. Above, golden clouds, so luminous they seem to glow and radiate light into the church interior, envelop the Virgin. God the Father appears above, awaiting Mary with open arms. Below, apostles gesticulate wildly as they witness this momentous event. Through vibrant color, Titian infused the image with a drama and intensity that assured his lofty reputation, then and now.

Palma il Giovane on Titian

An important change in art occurring in Titian's time was the almost universal adoption of canvas, with its rough-textured surface, in place of wood panels for paintings. Titian's works established oil color on canvas as the typical medium of the Western pictorial tradition thereafter. One of Titian's students and collaborators was Jacopo Negretti, known as Palma il Giovane (ca. 1548–1628), or "Palma the Younger." He wrote a valuable account of his teacher's working methods and described how he used the new medium to great advantage:

> Titian [employed] a great mass of colors, which served . . . as a base for the compositions. . . . I too have seen some of these, formed with bold strokes made with brushes laden with colors, sometimes of a pure red earth, which he used, so to speak, for a middle tone, and at other times of white lead; and with the same brush tinted with red, black and yellow he formed a highlight; and observing these principles he made the promise of an exceptional figure appear in four brushstrokes. . . . Having constructed these precious foundations he used to turn his pictures to the wall and leave them there without looking at them, sometimes for

several months. When he wanted to apply his brush again he would examine them with the utmost rigor . . . to see if he could find any faults. . . . In this way, working on the figures and revising them, he brought them to the most perfect symmetry that the beauty of art and nature can reveal. . . . [T]hus he gradually covered those quintessential forms with living flesh, bringing them by many stages to a state in which they lacked only the breath of life. He never painted a figure all at once and . . . in the last stages he painted more with his fingers than his brushes.*

*Quoted in Francesco Valcanover, "An Introduction to Titian," in *Titian: Prince of Painters* (Venice: Marsilio, 1990), 23–24.

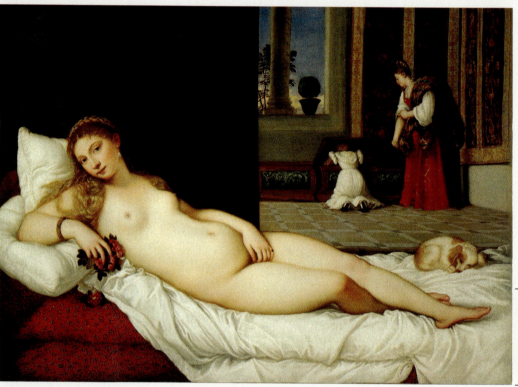

9-20 TITIAN, *Venus of Urbino*, 1538. Oil on canvas, 3′ 11″ × 5′ 5″. Galleria degli Uffizi, Florence.

Titian established oil-based pigments on canvas as the preferred painting medium in Western art. Here, he also set the standard for representations of the reclining female nude, whether divine or mortal.

1 ft.

Venus of Urbino In 1538, at the height of his powers, Titian painted the so-called *Venus of Urbino* (FIG. **9-20**) for Guidobaldo II, who became the duke of Urbino the following year. The title (given to the painting later) elevates to the status of classical mythology what is actually a representation of an Italian woman in her bedchamber. Indeed, no evidence suggests that Guidobaldo intended the commission as anything more than a female nude for his private enjoyment. Whether the subject is divine or mortal, Titian based his version on an earlier (and pioneering) painting of Venus (not illustrated) by Giorgione. Here, Titian established the compositional elements and the standard for paintings of the reclining female nude, regardless of the many variations

that ensued. This "Venus" reclines on the gentle slope of her luxurious pillowed couch, the linear play of the draperies contrasting with her body's sleek, continuous volume. At her feet is a slumbering lapdog. Behind her, a simple drape both places her figure emphatically in the foreground and frames a vista into the background at the right half of the picture. Two servants bend over a chest, apparently searching for garments to clothe "Venus." Beyond them, a smaller vista opens into a landscape. Titian masterfully constructed the view back into space and the division of the space into progressively smaller units.

As in other Venetian paintings, color plays a prominent role in *Venus of Urbino*. The red tones of the matron's skirt and the muted reds of the tapestries against the neutral whites of the matron's sleeves and of the kneeling girl's gown echo the deep Venetian reds set off against the pale neutral whites of the linen and the warm ivory gold of the flesh. The viewer must study the picture carefully to realize the subtlety of color planning. For instance, the two deep reds (in the foreground cushions and in the background skirt) play a critical role in the composition as a gauge of distance and as indicators of an implied diagonal opposed to the real one of the reclining figure. Here, Titian used color not simply to record surface appearance but also to organize his placement of forms.

Mannerism

Mannerism emerged in the 1520s in Italy as a distinctive artistic style in reaction to the High Renaissance style of Florence, Rome, and Venice. The term derives from the Italian word *maniera* ("style" or "manner"). Art historians usually define "style" as a characteristic or representative mode, especially of an artist or period (see Introduction), but the term can also refer to an absolute quality of fashion (someone has "style"). Mannerism's style (or representative mode) is characterized by style (being stylish, cultured, elegant).

Among the features most closely associated with Mannerism is artifice. Of course, all art involves artifice, in the sense that art is not "natural"—it is a representation of a scene or idea. But many artists, including High Renaissance painters such as Leonardo and Raphael, chose to conceal that artifice by using devices such as perspective and shading to make their art look natural. In contrast, Mannerist artists consciously revealed the constructed nature of their art. In other words, Renaissance artists generally strove to create art that appeared natural, whereas Mannerist artists were less inclined to disguise the contrived nature of art production. This is why artifice is a central feature of discussions about Mannerism, and why Mannerist works can seem, appropriately, "mannered." The conscious display of artifice in Mannerism often reveals itself in imbalanced compositions and unusual complexities, both visual and conceptual. Ambiguous spaces, departures from expected conventions, and unique presentations of traditional themes also surface frequently in Mannerist art.

Pontormo *Entombment of Christ* (FIG. **9-21**) by JACOPO DA PONTORMO (1494–1557) exhibits almost all the stylistic features characteristic of Mannerism's early phase. Painters had frequently depicted this subject, and Pontormo exploited viewers' familiarity with it by playing off of their expectations. For example, he omitted from the painting both the cross and Christ's tomb, and instead of presenting the action as occurring across the perpendicular picture plan, as artists such as Rogier van der Weyden (FIG. **8-6**) had done in their paintings of this scene, Pontormo rotated the conventional figural groups along a vertical axis. As a result, the Virgin Mary falls back (away from the viewer) as she releases her dead son's hand. Unlike High Renaissance artists, who had concentrated their masses in the center of the

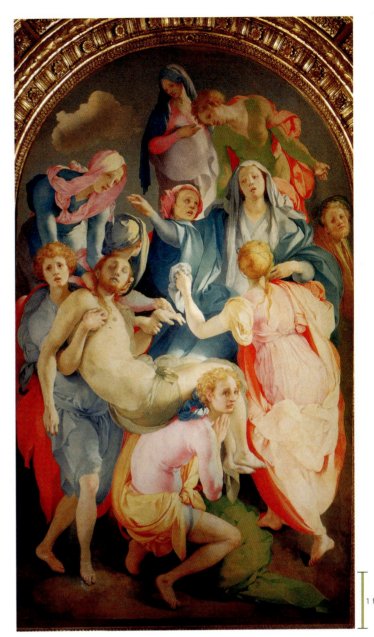

9-21 JACOPO DA PONTORMO, *Entombment of Christ*, Capponi Chapel, Santa Felicità, Florence, Italy, 1525–1528. Oil on wood, 10′ 3″ × 6′ 4″.

Mannerist paintings such as this one represent a departure from the compositions of the earlier Renaissance. Instead of concentrating masses in the center of the painting, Pontormo left a void.

painting, Pontormo left a void. This emptiness accentuates the grouping of hands that fill that hole, calling attention to the void—symbolic of loss and grief. In another departure from the norm, the Mannerist artist depicted the figures with curiously anxious glances cast in all directions. (The bearded young man at the upper right is probably a self-portrait.) Athletic bending and distorted twisting also characterize many of the figures, which have elastically elongated limbs and uniformly small and oval heads. The contrasting colors, primarily light blues and pinks, add to the dynamism and complexity of the work. The painting breaks sharply from the balanced, harmoniously structured compositions of the earlier Renaissance.

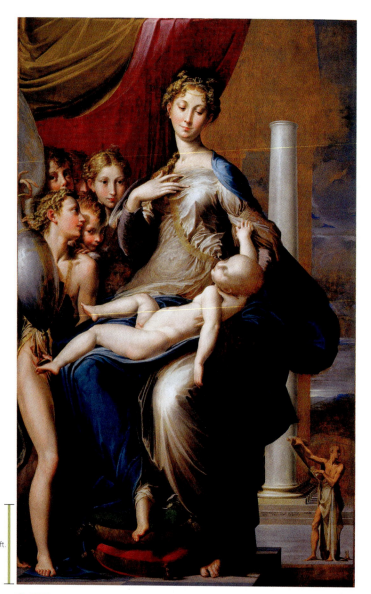

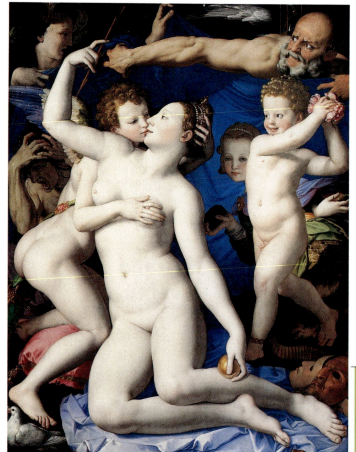

9-23 Bronzino, *Venus, Cupid, Folly, and Time*, ca. 1546. Oil on wood, 5' 1" × 4' 8¼". National Gallery, London.

In this painting of Cupid fondling his mother Venus, Bronzino demonstrated an appreciation for learned allegories with lascivious undertones. As in many Mannerist paintings, the meaning is ambiguous.

9-22 Parmigianino, *Madonna with the Long Neck*, from the Baiardi Chapel, Santa Maria dei Servi, Parma, Italy, 1534–1540. Oil on wood, 7' 1" × 4' 4". Galleria degli Uffizi, Florence.

Parmigianino's Madonna displays the stylish elegance that was a principal aim of Mannerism. Mary has a small oval head, a long, slender neck, attenuated hands, and a sinuous body.

Parmigianino Girolamo Francesco Maria Mazzola, known as **Parmigianino** (1503–1540), achieved in his best-known work, *Madonna with the Long Neck* (fig. **9-22**), the stylish elegance that was a principal aim of Mannerism. Parmigianino's rendition of this traditionally sedate subject is a picture of exquisite grace and precious sweetness. The Madonna's small oval head, her long and slender neck, the attenuation and delicacy of her hand, and the sinuous, swaying elongation of her frame—all are marks of the aristocratic, sumptuously courtly taste of a later phase of Mannerism. Parmigianino amplified this elegance by expanding the Madonna's form as viewed from head to toe. On the left stands a bevy of angelic creatures, melting with emotions as soft and smooth as their limbs. On the right, the artist included a line of columns without capitals and an enigmatic

figure with a scroll, whose distance from the foreground is immeasurable and ambiguous—the antithesis of rational Renaissance perspective. Although the elegance and sophisticated beauty of the painting are due in large part to the Madonna's attenuated limbs, that exaggeration is not solely decorative in purpose. *Madonna with the Long Neck* takes its subject from a metaphor in medieval hymns that compared the Virgin's neck to a great ivory tower or column. Thus, the work contains religious meaning in addition to the power derived from its beauty alone.

Bronzino Pontormo's pupil, Agnolo di Cosimo, called **Bronzino** (1503–1572), painted *Venus, Cupid, Folly, and Time* (fig. **9-23**) for Cosimo I de' Medici, the first grand duke of Tuscany, as a gift for King Francis I of France. In this painting, Bronzino demonstrated the Mannerists' fondness for learned allegories that often had lascivious undertones, a shift from the simple and monumental statements and forms of the High Renaissance. Bronzino depicted Cupid fondling his mother Venus, while Folly prepares to shower them with rose petals. Time, who appears in the upper right corner, draws back the curtain to reveal the playful incest

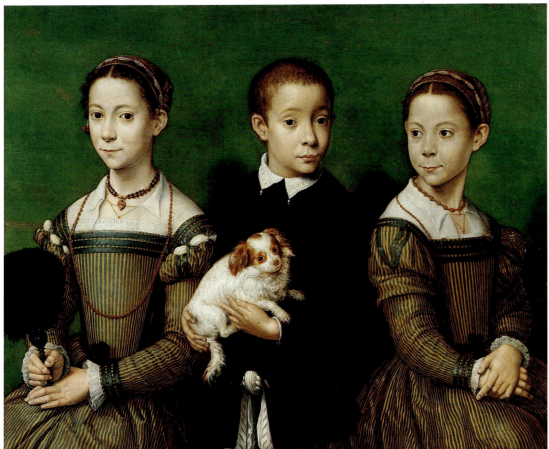

9-24 Sofonisba Anguissola, *Portrait of the Artist's Sisters and Brother*, ca. 1555. Oil on wood, 2′ 5$\frac{1}{4}$″ × 3′ 1$\frac{1}{2}$″. Methuen Collection, Corsham Court, Wiltshire.

Anguissola was the leading female artist of her time. Her contemporaries greatly admired her use of relaxed poses and expressions in intimate and informal group portraits like this one of her own family.

1 ft.

in progress. Other figures in the painting represent other human qualities and emotions, including Envy. The masks, a favorite device of the Mannerists, symbolize deceit. The picture seems to suggest that love—accompanied by envy and plagued by inconstancy—is foolish and that lovers will discover its folly in time. But, as in many Mannerist paintings, the meaning is ambiguous, and interpretations of the painting vary. Compositionally, Bronzino placed the figures around the front plane, and they almost entirely block the space. The contours are strong and sculptural, the surfaces of enamel smoothness. The heads, hands, and feet are especially elegant. The Mannerists considered the extremities the carriers of grace, and Bronzino's polished depiction of them was evidence of his skill.

Sofonisba Anguissola Men far outnumbered women as artists during the Renaissance, as they had since ancient times. In the 16th century, the rarity of female artists reflects the obstacles they faced. In particular, training practices mandating residence at a master's house precluded women from acquiring the necessary experience. In addition, social proscriptions, such as those preventing women from drawing from nude models, further hampered an aspiring female artist's advancement through the accepted avenues of artistic training. Still, there were determined women who surmounted these barriers and managed to develop not only considerable bodies of work but enviable reputations as well.

Chief among them was Sofonisba Anguissola (1527–1625) of Cremona, the first Italian woman to become an international art celebrity. She introduced a new kind of group portrait of irresistible charm, characterized by an informal intimacy and subjects that are often moving, conversing, or engaged in activities—in contrast to the stiff hypercorrectness of most earlier portraits. In *Portrait of the Artist's Sisters and Brother* (FIG. **9-24**), Anguissola placed her siblings against a neutral ground in an affectionate pose meant not for official display but for private showing. The sisters, wearing matching striped gowns, flank their brother, who caresses a lapdog. The older sister (at the left) summons the dignity required for the occasion, while the boy looks quizzically at the portraitist with an expression of naive curiosity, and the other girl diverts her attention toward something or someone to the painter's left. Anguissola's use of relaxed poses and expressions, her sympathetic personal presentation, and her graceful treatment of the forms won wide admiration, and she became the court painter of Philip II of Spain.

Tintoretto Jacopo Robusti, known as Tintoretto (1518–1594), claimed to be a student of Titian and aspired to combine Titian's color with Michelangelo's drawing, but he also adopted many Mannerist pictorial devices, which he employed to produce works imbued with dramatic power, depth of spiritual vision, and glowing Venetian color schemes. Toward the end of Tintoretto's life, his art became

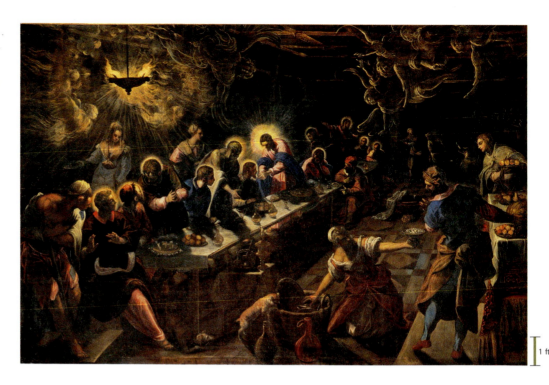

9-25 TINTORETTO, *Last Supper*, 1594. Oil on canvas, 12' × 18' 8". San Giorgio Maggiore, Venice.

Tintoretto adopted many Mannerist pictorial devices to produce oil paintings imbued with emotional power, depth of spiritual vision, glowing Venetian color schemes, and dramatic lighting.

1 ft

spiritual, even visionary, as solid forms melted away into swirling clouds of dark shot through with fitful light.

In *Last Supper* (FIG. 9-25), the figures appear in a dark interior illuminated by a single light in the upper left of the image. The shimmering halos establish the biblical nature of the dramatic scene, which immediately engages viewers. Tintoretto incorporated many Mannerist elements in his rendition of this traditional subject, including visual complexity and an imbalanced composition. In terms of design, the contrast with Leonardo's *Last Supper* (FIG. 9-3) is both extreme and instructive. Leonardo's composition, balanced and symmetrical, parallels the picture plane in a geometrically organized and closed space. The figure of Christ is the tranquil center of the drama and the perspectival focus. In Tintoretto's painting, Christ is above and beyond the converging perspective lines that race diagonally away from the picture surface, creating disturbing effects of limitless depth and motion. The viewer locates Tintoretto's Christ via the light flaring, beaconlike, out of darkness. The contrast of the two works reflects the direction Renaissance painting took in the 16th century, as it moved away from architectonic clarity of space and neutral lighting toward

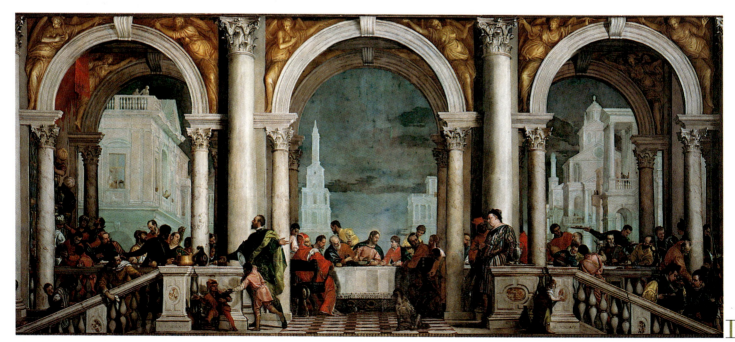

1 ft

9-26 PAOLO VERONESE, *Christ in the House of Levi*, from the refectory of Santi Giovanni e Paolo, Venice, Italy, 1573. Oil on canvas, 18' 3" × 42'. Galleria dell'Accademia, Venice.

Veronese's paintings feature superb color and majestic classical settings. The Catholic Church accused him of impiety for including dogs and dwarfs near Christ in this work originally titled *Last Supper*.

the dynamic perspectives and dramatic chiaroscuro of the coming Baroque.

Veronese Among the great Venetian masters was Paolo Cagliari of Verona, called PAOLO VERONESE (1528–1588). Whereas Tintoretto gloried in monumental drama and deep perspectives, Veronese specialized in splendid pageantry painted in superb color and set within majestic classical architecture. Like Tintoretto, Veronese painted on a huge scale, with canvases often as large as 20 by 30 feet or more. As Andrea Palladio looked to the example of classically inspired High Renaissance architecture, so Veronese returned to High Renaissance composition, its symmetrical balance, and its ordered architectonics. His shimmering colors span the spectrum, although he avoided solid colors for half shades (light blues, sea greens, lemon yellows, roses, and violets), creating veritable flowerbeds of tone.

Veronese's usual subjects, painted for the refectories of wealthy monasteries, afforded him an opportunity to display magnificent companies at table. *Christ in the House*

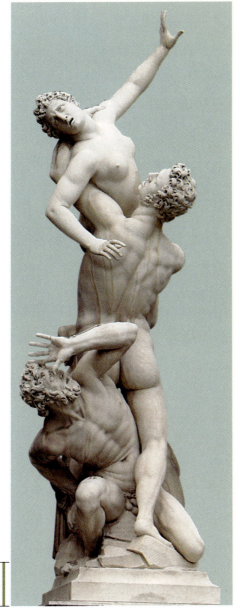

9-27 GIOVANNI DA BOLOGNA, *Abduction of the Sabine Women*, Loggia dei Lanzi, Piazza della Signoria, Florence, Italy, 1579–1583. Marble, 13′ 5½″ high.

This sculpture was the first large-scale group since classical antiquity designed to be seen from multiple viewpoints. The three bodies interlock to create a vertical spiral movement.

1 ft.

of Levi (FIG. **9-26**), originally called *Last Supper*, is an example. In a great open loggia framed by three monumental arches, Christ sits at the center of the splendidly garbed elite of Venice. In the foreground, with a courtly gesture, the very image of gracious grandeur, the chief steward welcomes guests. Robed lords, their colorful retainers, clowns, dogs, and dwarfs crowd into the spacious loggia. Painted during the Counter-Reformation, this depiction prompted criticism from the Catholic Church. The Holy Office of the Inquisition accused Veronese of impiety for painting such creatures so close to the Lord, and it ordered him to make changes at his own expense. Reluctant to do so, he simply changed the painting's title, converting the subject to a less solemn one.

Giovanni da Bologna The lure of Italy drew a brilliant young Flemish sculptor, Jean de Boulogne, to Florence, where he practiced his art under the equivalent Italian name of GIOVANNI DA BOLOGNA (1529–1608). Giovanni's *Abduction of the Sabine Women* (FIG. **9-27**) exemplifies Mannerist principles of figure composition in sculpture. Drawn from the legendary history of Rome, the group received its present title—relating how the early Romans abducted wives for themselves from the neighboring Sabines—only after its exhibition. Giovanni did not depict any particular subject. His goal was to achieve a dynamic spiral figural composition involving an old man, a young man, and a woman, all nude in the tradition of ancient statues portraying mythological figures. *Abduction of the Sabine Women* includes references to *Laocoön* (FIG. **2-58**)—once in the crouching old man and again in the woman's up-flung arm. The three bodies interlock on a vertical axis, creating an ascending spiral movement.

To appreciate the sculpture fully, the viewer must walk around it, because the work changes radically according to the vantage point. One factor contributing to the shifting imagery is the prominence of open spaces that pass through the masses (for example, the space between an arm and a body), giving the spaces an effect equal to that of the solids. Giovanni's figures, however, do not break out of the spiral vortex of the composition but remain as if contained within a cylinder. Nonetheless, this sculpture was the first large-scale group since classical antiquity designed to be seen from multiple viewpoints.

HOLY ROMAN EMPIRE

The dissolution of the Burgundian Netherlands in 1477 led to a realignment in the European geopolitical landscape in the early 16th century (MAP **9-1**). France and the Holy Roman Empire absorbed the former Burgundian territories and increased their power. Overshadowing these political developments, however, was the crisis in the religious realm that gave rise to the Protestant movement in Germany. Because of Martin Luther's presence, the Reformation initially was strongest there. But at the opening of the 16th century, Luther had not yet posted his *Ninety-five Theses*, and the Catholic Church was still an important art patron in the Holy Roman Empire.

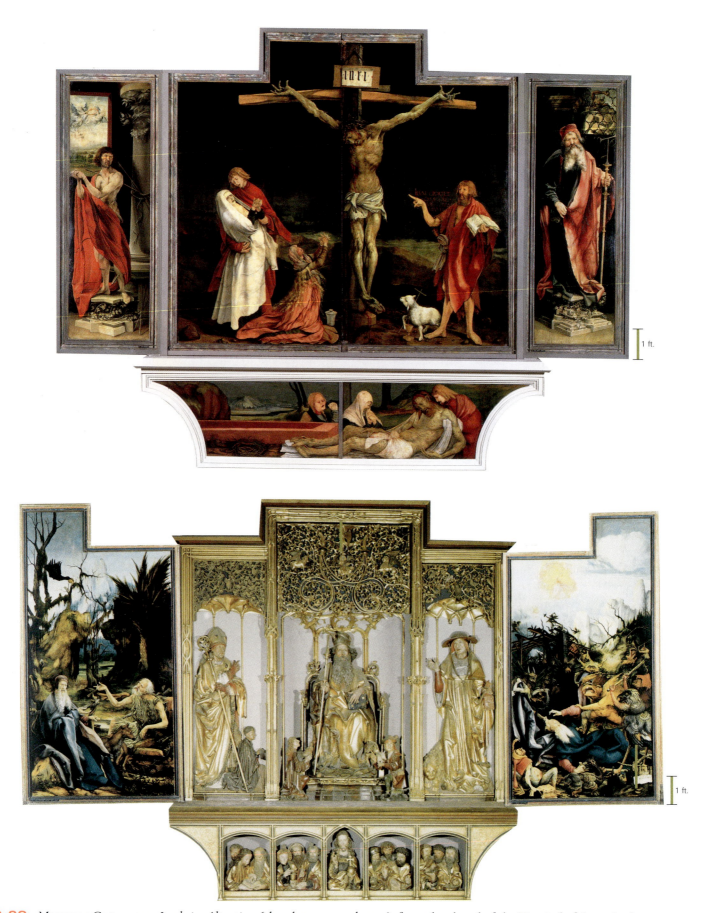

9-28 MATTHIAS GRÜNEWALD, *Isenheim Altarpiece* (closed, *top*; open, *bottom*), from the chapel of the Hospital of Saint Anthony, Isenheim, Germany, ca. 1510–1515. Oil on wood, 9′ 9½″ × 10′ 9″ (center panel); 8′ 2½″ × 3′ ½″ (each wing); 2′ 5½″ × 11′ 2″ (predella). Shrine carved by NIKOLAUS HAGENAUER in 1490. Painted and gilt limewood, 9′ 9½″ × 10′ 9″. Musée d'Unterlinden, Colmar.

Befitting its setting in a monastic hospital, Matthias Grünewald's *Isenheim Altarpiece* includes painted panels depicting suffering and disease but also miraculous healing, hope, and salvation.

Matthias Grünewald Around 1510, Matthias Neithardt, known conventionally as MATTHIAS GRÜNEWALD (ca. 1480–1528), who worked for the archbishops of Mainz from 1511 on, began work on the *Isenheim Altarpiece* (FIG. 9-28). The piece is a complex and fascinating monument that reflects Catholic beliefs and incorporates several references to Catholic doctrines, such as the lamb (symbol of the Son of God), whose wound spurts blood into a chalice in the exterior *Crucifixion* scene. Created for the monastic hospital order Saint Anthony of Isenheim, the work consists of a wooden shrine (carved by NIKOLAUS HAGENAUER in 1490) that includes gilded and polychromed statues of Saints Anthony Abbot, Augustine, and Jerome (FIG. 9-28, *bottom*) in addition to Grünewald's two pairs of movable wings that open at the center. Hinged together at the sides, one pair stands directly behind the other. Painted between 1510 and 1515, the exterior panels of the first pair (visible when the altarpiece is closed; FIG. 9-28, *top*) present four subjects—*Crucifixion* in the center, *Saint Sebastian* on the left, *Saint Anthony* on the right, and *Lamentation* in the predella. When these exterior wings are open, four additional scenes (not illustrated) appear—*Annunciation, Angelic Concert, Madonna and Child,* and *Resurrection*. Opening this second pair of wings exposes Hagenauer's interior shrine, flanked by Grünewald's *Meeting of Saints Anthony and Paul* and *Temptation of Saint Anthony* (FIG. 9-28, *bottom*).

The placement of this altarpiece in the choir of a church adjacent to the monastery hospital dictated much of the imagery. Saints associated with the plague and other diseases and with miraculous cures, such as Saints Anthony and Sebastian, appear prominently in the iconographical program. Grünewald's panels specifically address the themes of dire illness and miraculous healing and emphasize the suffering of the order's patron saint, Anthony. The painted images served as warnings, encouraging increased devotion from monks and hospital patients. They also functioned therapeutically by offering some hope to the afflicted. Indeed, Saint Anthony's legend encompassed his role as both vengeful dispenser of justice (by inflicting disease) and benevolent healer. Grünewald brilliantly used color to enhance the potency of the altarpiece. He intensified the contrast of horror and hope by playing subtle tones and soft harmonies against shocking dissonance of color.

One of the most memorable scenes is *Temptation of Saint Anthony* (FIG. 9-28, *bottom*). It is a terrifying image of the five temptations, depicted as an assortment of ghoulish and bestial creatures in a dark landscape, attacking the saint. In the foreground, Grünewald painted a grotesque image of a man, whose oozing boils, withered arm, and distended stomach all suggest a horrible disease. Medical experts have connected these symptoms with ergotism (a disease caused by ergot, a fungus that grows especially on rye). Although doctors did not discover the cause of ergotism until about 1600, people lived in fear of its recognizable symptoms (convulsions and gangrene). The public referred to this illness as "Saint Anthony's fire," and it was one of the major diseases treated at the Isenheim hospital. The gangrene often compelled amputation, and scholars have noted that the two movable halves of the altarpiece's predella (FIG. 9-28, *top*), if slid apart, make it appear as if Christ's legs have been amputated. The same observation can be made with regard to the two main exterior panels. Due to the off-center placement of the cross, opening the left panel "severs" one arm from the crucified figure.

Thus, Grünewald carefully selected and presented his altarpiece's iconography to be particularly meaningful for viewers at the hospital. In the interior shrine, the artist balanced the horrors of the disease and the punishments awaiting those who did not repent with scenes such as the *Meeting of Saints Anthony and Paul*, depicting the two saints, healthy and aged, conversing peacefully. Even the exterior panels (the closed altarpiece; FIG. 9-28, *top*) convey these same concerns. *Crucifixion* emphasizes Christ's pain and suffering, but the knowledge that this act redeemed humanity tempers the misery. In addition, Saint Anthony appears in the right wing as a devout follower of Christ who, like Christ and for Christ, endured intense suffering for his faith. Saint Anthony's presence on the exterior thus reinforces the themes Grünewald intertwined throughout this entire altarpiece—themes of pain, illness, and death juxtaposed with those of hope, comfort, and salvation.

Albrecht Dürer The dominant artist of the early 16th century in the Holy Roman Empire was ALBRECHT DÜRER (1471–1528) of Nuremberg. Like Leonardo da Vinci, he wrote theoretical treatises on a variety of subjects, such as perspective, fortification, and the ideal in human proportions. He traveled extensively, visiting and studying in Colmar, Basel, Strasbourg, Antwerp, Brussels, and Venice among other locales, and became personally acquainted with many of the leading humanists and artists of his time. A man of exceptional talents and tremendous energy, Dürer was the first artist outside Italy to become an international celebrity, and he has enjoyed a lofty reputation ever since—primarily as a printmaker. Indeed, few artists have ever rivaled the body of graphic work in woodcut and engraving that he produced. Dürer employed an agent to help sell his prints. His wife, who served as his manager, and his mother also sold his work at markets. The lawsuit Dürer brought in 1506 against an Italian artist for copying his prints reveals his business acumen. Scholars generally regard this lawsuit as the first in history over artistic copyright.

Fascinated with classical ideas as passed along by Italian Renaissance artists, Dürer was among the first Northern European artists to travel to Italy expressly to study Italian art and its underlying theories at their source. After his first journey in 1494–1495 (the second was in 1505–1506), he incorporated many Italian Renaissance developments into his art. Art historians have acclaimed Dürer as the first Northern European artist to understand fully the basic aims of the Renaissance in Italy.

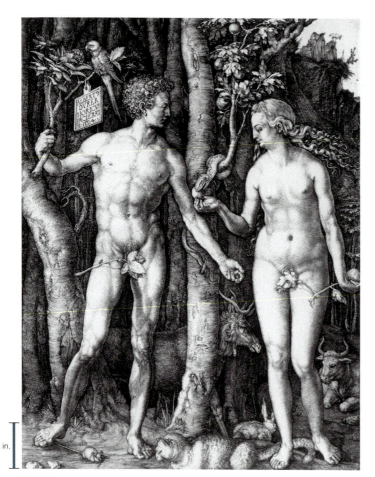

9-29 ALBRECHT DÜRER, *Fall of Man (Adam and Eve)*, 1504. Engraving, $9\frac{7}{8}'' \times 7\frac{5}{8}''$. Museum of Fine Arts, Boston (centennial gift of Landon T. Clay).

Dürer was the first Northern European artist to become an international celebrity. *Fall of Man,* with two figures based on ancient statues, reflects his studies of the Vitruvian theory of human proportions.

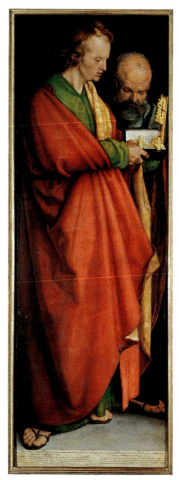
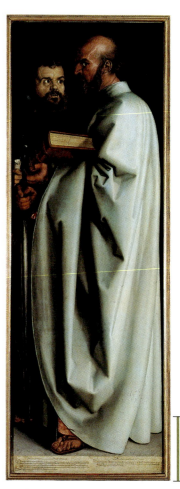

9-30 ALBRECHT DÜRER, *Four Apostles*, 1526. Oil on wood, each panel 7′ 1″ × 2′ 6″. Alte Pinakothek, Munich.

Dürer's support for Lutheranism surfaces in these portraitlike depictions of four saints on two panels. Peter, representative of the pope in Rome, plays a secondary role behind John the Evangelist.

An engraving, *Fall of Man* (*Adam and Eve;* FIG. **9-29**), represents the first distillation of Dürer's studies of the Vitruvian theory of human proportions, a theory based on arithmetic ratios. Clearly outlined against the dark background of a Northern European forest, the two idealized figures of Adam and Eve stand in poses reminiscent of specific classical statues probably known to the German artist through graphic representations. Preceded by numerous geometric drawings in which he attempted to systematize sets of ideal human proportions in balanced contrapposto poses, the final print presents Dürer's concept of the "perfect" male and female figures. Yet he tempered this idealization with naturalism. The gnarled bark of the trees and the feathery leaves authenticate the scene, as do the various creatures skulking underfoot. The animals populating the print are also symbolic. The choleric cat, the melancholic elk, the sanguine rabbit, and the phlegmatic ox represent humanity's temperaments based on the "four humors," fluids that were the basis of theories of the body's function developed by the ancient Greek physician Hippocrates and practiced in medieval physiology. The tension between cat and mouse in the foreground symbolizes the relation between Adam and Eve at the crucial moment in *Fall of Man*.

Four Apostles Dürer's impressive technical facility with different media extended also to painting. *Four Apostles* (FIG. **9-30**) is a two-panel oil painting he produced without commission and presented to the city fathers of Nuremberg in 1526 to be hung in the city hall. Saints John and Peter appear on the left panel, Mark and Paul on the right. In addition to showcasing Dürer's mastery of the oil technique, his brilliant use of color and light and shade, and his ability to imbue the four saints with individual personalities and portraitlike features, *Four Apostles* documents the artist's support for Martin Luther by his positioning of the figures. Dürer relegated Saint Peter (as representative of the pope in Rome) to a secondary role by placing him behind John the Evangelist. John assumed particular prominence for Luther because of the evangelist's focus on Christ's person in his Gospel. In addition, Peter and John both read from the Bible, the single authoritative source of religious truth, according to Luther. Dürer emphasized the Bible's centrality by depicting it open to the passage "In the beginning was the Word, and the Word was with God, and the Word was God" (John 1:1). At the bottom of the panels, Dürer included quotations from each of the apostles' books, using Luther's German translation of the New Testament. The excerpts warn

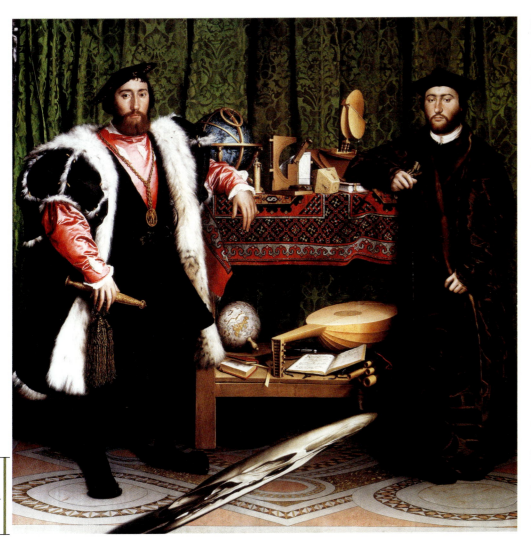

9-31 HANS HOLBEIN THE
YOUNGER, *The French Ambassadors*,
1533. Oil and tempera on wood,
6' 8" × 6' 9½". National Gallery,
London.

In this double portrait, Holbein
depicted two humanists with a
collection of objects reflective of
their worldliness and learning, but
he also included an anamorphic
skull, a reminder of death.

1 ft.

against the coming of perilous times and the preaching of
false prophets who will distort God's word.

Hans Holbein

The leading artist of the Holy Roman
Empire in the generation after Dürer was HANS HOLBEIN THE
YOUNGER (ca. 1497–1543). Holbein produced portraits that reflected the Northern European tradition of close realism that
had emerged in 15th-century Flemish art (see Chapter 8). Yet
he also incorporated Italian ideas about monumental composition and sculpturesque form. The surfaces of his paintings
are as lustrous as enamel, his detail is exact and exquisitely
drawn, and his contrasts of light and dark are never heavy.

Holbein began his artistic career in Basel, but due to the
immediate threat of a religious civil war, he left for England,
where he became painter to the court of King Henry VIII.
While there, Holbein produced a superb double portrait
of the French ambassadors to England, Jean de Dinteville
and Georges de Selve. *The French Ambassadors* (FIG. **9-31**)
exhibits Holbein's considerable talents—his strong sense of
composition, his subtle linear patterning, his gift for portraiture, his marvelous sensitivity to color, and his faultlessly
firm technique. The two men, both ardent humanists, stand
at opposite ends of a side table covered with an oriental rug
and a collection of objects reflective of their worldliness and
their interest in learning and the arts. These include math-

ematical and astronomical models and implements, a lute with a
broken string, compasses, a sun-
dial, flutes, globes, and an open
hymnbook with Luther's translation of *Veni, Creator Spiritus* and
of the Ten Commandments.

Of particular interest is the
long gray shape that slashes di-
agonally across the picture plane and interrupts the stable,
balanced, and serene composition. This form is an *anamorphic image*, a distorted image recognizable only when viewed
with a special device, such as a cylindrical mirror, or by
looking at the painting at an acute angle. In this case, if the
viewer stands off to the right, the gray slash becomes a skull.
Although scholars do not agree on the skull's meaning, at
the very least it refers to death. Artists commonly incorporated skulls into paintings as reminders of mortality. Indeed,
Holbein depicted a skull on the metal medallion on Jean
de Dinteville's hat. Holbein may have intended the skulls,
in conjunction with the crucifix that appears half hidden
behind the curtain in the upper left corner, to encourage
viewers to ponder death and resurrection. This painting may
also allude to the growing tension between secular and religious authorities. Jean de Dinteville was a titled landowner,
Georges de Selve a bishop. The inclusion of Luther's trans-
lations next to the lute with the broken string (a symbol of
discord) may also subtly refer to the religious strife. Despite
the uncertainty about the precise meaning of *The French
Ambassadors*, it is a painting of supreme artistic achievement. Holbein rendered the still-life objects with the same
meticulous care as the men themselves, the woven design of
the deep emerald curtain behind them, and the floor tiles,
constructed in faultless perspective.

FRANCE

As *The French Ambassadors* illustrates, France in the early 16th century continued its efforts to secure widespread recognition as a political power and cultural force. Under Francis I (r. 1515–1547), the French established a firm foothold in Milan and its environs. Francis waged a campaign (known as the Habsburg-Valois Wars) against Charles V (the Spanish king and Holy Roman Emperor; r. 1516–1558), which occupied him from 1521 to 1544. These wars involved disputed territories—southern France, the Netherlands, the Rhinelands, northern Spain, and Italy—and reflected France's central role in the shifting geopolitical landscape. Despite these military preoccupations, Francis I also endeavored to elevate his country's cultural profile. To that end, he invited several esteemed Italian artists, including Leonardo da Vinci, to his court. Francis's attempt to glorify the state and himself meant that the religious art dominating the Middle Ages no longer prevailed, for the king and not the Church held the power.

Château de Chambord Francis I indulged his passion for building by commissioning several large-scale *châteaux*, among them the Château de Chambord (FIG. **9-32**). These châteaux, developed from medieval fortified castles, served as country houses for royalty, who usually built them near forests for use as hunting lodges. Construction on Chambord began in 1519, but Francis I never saw its completion. Chambord's plan includes a central square block with four corridors, in the shape of a cross, and a broad, central staircase that gives access to groups of rooms—ancestors of the modern suite of rooms or apartments. At each of the four corners, a round tower punctuates the square plan, and a moat surrounds the whole. From the exterior, Chambord presents a carefully contrived horizontal accent on three levels, with continuous moldings separating its floors. Windows align precisely, one exactly over another. The Italian Renaissance palazzo (FIG. **8-31**) served as the model for this matching of horizontal and vertical features, but above the third level the structure's lines break chaotically into a jumble of high dormers, chimneys, and lanterns that recall soaring ragged Gothic silhouettes on the skyline.

THE NETHERLANDS

With the demise of the duchy of Burgundy in 1477 and the division of that territory between France and the Holy Roman Empire, the Netherlands at the beginning of the 16th century consisted of 17 provinces (corresponding to modern Holland, Belgium, and Luxembourg). The Netherlands was among the most commercially advanced and prosperous European countries. Its extensive network of rivers and easy access to the Atlantic Ocean provided a setting conducive to overseas trade, and shipbuilding was one of the most profitable businesses. The region's commercial center shifted toward the end of the 15th century, partly because of buildup of silt in the Bruges estuary. Traffic relocated to Antwerp, which became the hub of economic activity in the Netherlands after 1510. As many as 500 ships a day passed through Antwerp's harbor, and large trading colonies from England, the Holy Roman Empire, Italy, Portugal, and Spain established themselves in the city.

During the 16th century, the Netherlands was under the political control of Philip II (r. 1556–1598) of Spain, who had inherited the region from his father, Charles V (r. 1519–1556). The economic prosperity of the Netherlands served as a potent incentive for Philip to strengthen his control over the territory. However, his heavy-handed tactics and repressive measures led in 1579 to revolt, resulting in the formation of two federations. The Union of Arras, a Catholic association of southern Netherlandish provinces, remained under Spanish dominion, and the Union of Utrecht, a Protestant group of northern provinces, became the Dutch Republic. The increasing number of Netherlandish citizens converting to Protestantism affected the arts, as evidenced by a cor-

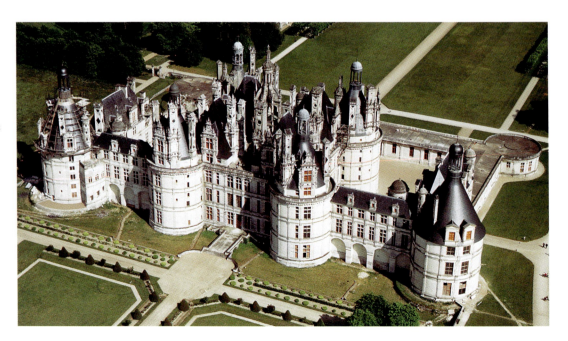

9-32 Château de Chambord, Chambord, France, begun 1519.

French Renaissance châteaux, which developed from medieval castles, served as country houses for royalty. King Francis I's Château de Chambord reflects Italian palazzo design, but it has a Gothic roof.

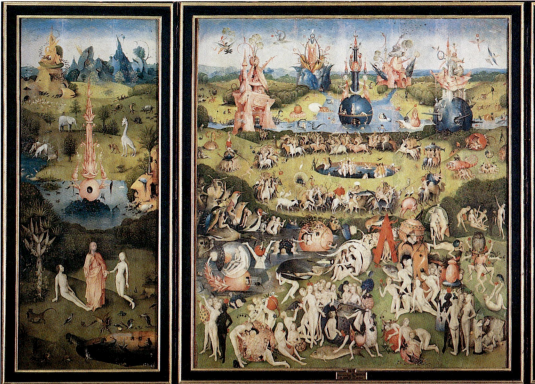
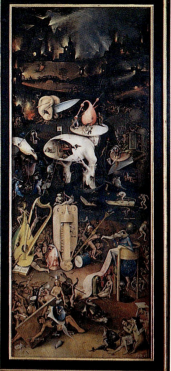

1 ft.

9-33 HIERONYMUS BOSCH, *Garden of Earthly Delights*, 1505–1510. Oil on wood, center panel, 7′ 2⅝″ × 6′ 4¾″, each wing 7′ 2⅝″ × 3′ 2¼″. Museo del Prado, Madrid.

Bosch was the most imaginative and enigmatic painter of his era. In this triptych, which may commemorate a wedding, he created a fantasy world filled with nude men and women and bizarre creatures and objects.

responding decrease in large-scale altarpieces and religious works (although such works continued to be commissioned for Catholic churches). Much of Netherlandish art of this period provides a wonderful glimpse into the lives of various strata of society, from nobility to peasantry, capturing their activities, environment, and values.

Hieronymus Bosch The most famous Netherlandish painter at the turn of the 16th century was HIERONYMUS BOSCH (ca. 1450–1516), one of the most fascinating and puzzling artists in history. Interpretations of Bosch differ widely. Scholars debate whether he was a satirist, an irreligious mocker, or a pornographer, a heretic or an orthodox fanatic like Girolamo Savonarola, his Italian contemporary (page 245).

Bosch's most famous work, the so-called *Garden of Earthly Delights* (FIG. **9-33**), is also his most enigmatic, and no interpretation of it has ever won universal acceptance. This large-scale work takes the familiar form of a triptych. The format suggests a religious function for Bosch's painting, but *Garden of Earthly Delights* resided in the palace of Henry III of Nassau, regent of the Netherlands, seven years after its completion. This location suggests a secular commission for private use. Scholars have proposed that, given the work's central themes of marriage, sex, and procreation, the painting probably commemorates a wedding, a subject seen earlier in Jan van Eyck's *Giovanni Arnolfini and His Bride* (FIG. 8-1). Any similarities between the two paintings

end there, however. Whereas van Eyck grounded his depiction of a betrothed couple in 15th-century life and custom, Bosch portrayed a visionary world of fantasy and intrigue.

In the left panel, God presents Eve to Adam in a landscape, presumably the Garden of Eden. Bosch placed the event in a wildly imaginative setting that includes an odd pink fountainlike structure in a body of water and an array of fanciful and unusual animals. These details may hint at an interpretation involving *alchemy*—the medieval study of seemingly magical changes, especially chemical changes. The right panel, in contrast, bombards viewers with the horrors of Hell. Beastly creatures devour people, while others are impaled or strung on musical instruments, as if on a medieval rack. A gambler is nailed to his own table. A spidery monster embraces a girl while toads bite her. A sea of inky darkness envelops all of these horrific scenes. Observers must search through the hideous enclosure of Bosch's Hell to take in its fascinating though repulsive details.

Sandwiched between Paradise and Hell is the huge center panel, in which nude people blithely cavort in a landscape dotted with bizarre creatures and unidentifiable objects. The numerous fruits and birds (fertility symbols) in the scene suggest procreation, and, indeed, many of the figures are paired off as couples. The orgiastic overtones of this panel, in conjunction with the terrifying image of Hell, have led some scholars to interpret this triptych—as they have other Last Judgment images—as a warning of the fate awaiting the sinful, decadent, and immoral.

Quinten Massys Antwerp's growth and prosperity, along with its wealthy merchants' propensity for collecting and purchasing art, attracted artists to the city. Among them was QUINTEN MASSYS (ca. 1466–1530), who became Antwerp's leading painter after 1510. Son of a Louvain blacksmith, Massys demonstrated a willingness to explore the styles and modes of a variety of models, from Jan van Eyck to Hieronymus Bosch and from Rogier van der Weyden to Albrecht Dürer and Leonardo da Vinci. Yet his eclecticism was subtle and discriminating, enriched by an inventiveness that gave a personal stamp to his paintings.

In *Money-Changer and His Wife* (FIG. **9-34**), Massys presented a professional man transacting business. He holds scales, checking the weight of coins on the table. The artist's detailed rendering of the figures, setting, and objects suggests a fidelity to observable fact. But the painting is also a commentary on Netherlandish values and mores. In it, Massys highlighted the financial transactions that were an increasingly prominent part of 16th-century secular life in the Netherlands and that distracted Christians from their religious duties. The man's wife, for example, shows more interest in watching her husband weigh money than in reading her prayer book. Massys incorporated into his painting numerous references to the importance of a moral, righteous, and spiritual life, including a carafe with water and a candlestick, traditional religious symbols. The couple ignores them, focusing solely on money. On the right, through a window, an old man talks with another man, suggesting idleness and gossip. The reflected image in the convex mirror on the counter offsets this image of sloth and foolish chatter. There, a man reads what is most likely a Bible or prayer book. Behind him is a church steeple. An inscription on the original frame (now lost) read, "Let the balance be just and the weights equal" (Lev. 19:36), a caution that applies both to the money-changer's professional conduct and the eventual Last Judgment. The couple in this painting, however, has tipped the balance in favor of the pursuit of wealth.

Pieter Aertsen This tendency to inject reminders about spiritual well-being also emerges in *Butcher's Stall* (FIG. **9-35**) by PIETER AERTSEN (ca. 1507–1575), who worked in Antwerp for more than three decades. At first glance, this painting

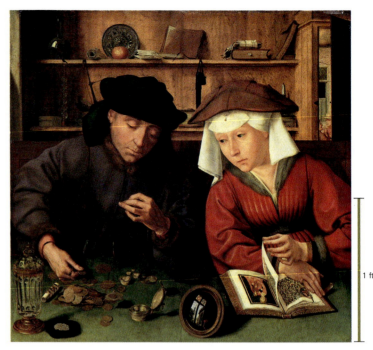

9-34 QUINTEN MASSYS, *Money-Changer and His Wife*, 1514. Oil on wood, 2′ 3¾″ × 2′ 2⅜″. Louvre, Paris.

Massys's painting depicting a secular financial transaction is also a commentary on 16th-century Netherlandish values. The banker's wife shows more interest in the money-weighing than in her prayer book.

appears to be a descriptive *genre* scene (one from everyday life). On display is an array of meat products—a side of a hog, chickens, sausages, a stuffed intestine, pig's feet, meat pies, a cow's head, a hog's head, and hanging entrails. Also visible are fish, pretzels, cheese, and butter. Like Massys, Aertsen embedded strategically placed religious images in his painting. In the background, Joseph leads a donkey carrying Mary and the Christ Child. The Holy Family stops to offer alms to a beggar and his son, while the people behind

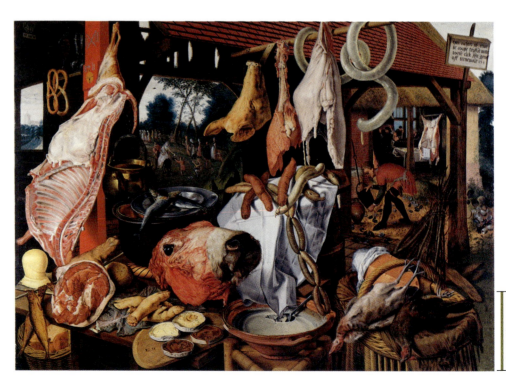

9-35 PIETER AERTSEN, *Butcher's Stall*, 1551. Oil on wood, 4′ ⅜″ × 6′ 5¾″. Uppsala University Art Collection, Uppsala.

At first glance *Butcher's Stall* appears to be a genre painting, but in the background Joseph leads a donkey carrying Mary and the Christ Child. Aertsen balanced images of gluttony with allusions to salvation.

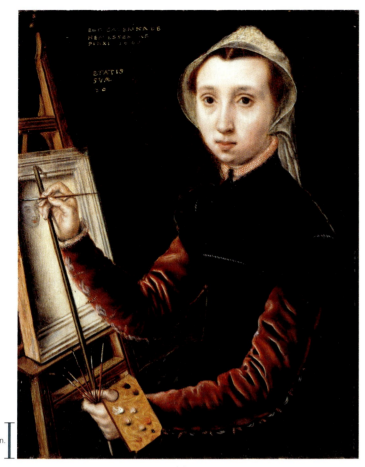

9-36 CATERINA VAN HEMESSEN, *Self-Portrait*, 1548. Oil on wood, 1′ $\frac{3}{4}$″ × 9 $\frac{7}{8}$″. Kunstmuseum, Öffentliche Kunstsammlung Basel, Basel.

In this first known Northern European self-portrait by a woman, Caterina van Hemessen represented herself as a confident artist momentarily interrupting her work to look out at the viewer.

the sacred figures wend their way toward a church. Furthermore, the crossed fishes on the platter and the pretzels and wine in the rafters on the upper left all refer to "spiritual food" (pretzels often served as bread during Lent). Aertsen accentuated these allusions to salvation through Christ by contrasting them to their opposite—a life of gluttony, lust, and sloth. He represented this degeneracy with the oyster and mussel shells (which Netherlanders believed possessed aphrodisiacal properties) scattered on the ground on the painting's right side, along with the people seen eating and carousing nearby under the roof.

Caterina van Hemessen With the accumulation of wealth in the Netherlands, portraits increased in popularity. CATERINA VAN HEMESSEN (1528–1587) painted the first known Northern European self-portrait (FIG. **9-36**) by a woman. She had learned her craft from her father, Jan Sanders van Hemessen, a well-known painter. Here, the daughter confidently presented herself as an artist who interrupts her painting to look toward the viewer. She holds brushes, a palette, and a *maulstick* (a stick used to steady the hand while painting) in her left hand, and delicately applies pigment to the canvas with her right hand. Caterina ensured proper identification (and credit) through the inscription in the painting: "Caterina van Hemessen painted me / 1548 / her age 20."

Pieter Bruegel the Elder The greatest Netherlandish painter of the mid-16th century was PIETER BRUEGEL THE ELDER (ca. 1528–1569). Like many of his contemporaries, Bruegel traveled to Italy, where he apparently spent almost two years, venturing as far south as Sicily. Unlike other artists, however, Bruegel chose not to incorporate classical elements into his paintings. Instead, his works reveal an interest in the interrelationship of human beings and nature. But in Bruegel's paintings, no matter how huge a slice of the world the artist shows, human activities remain the dominant theme.

Bruegel's *Netherlandish Proverbs* (FIG. **9-37**) depicts a Netherlandish village populated by a wide range of people (nobility, peasants, and

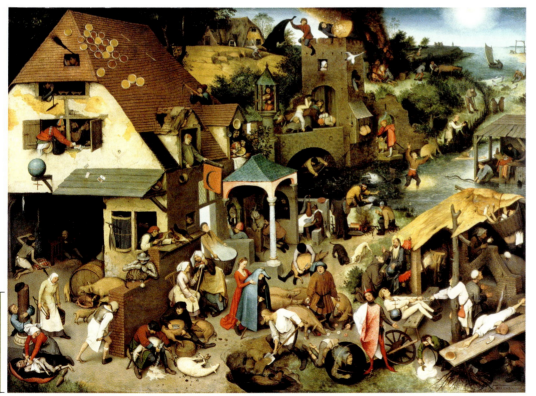

9-37 PIETER BRUEGEL THE ELDER, *Netherlandish Proverbs*, 1559. Oil on wood, 3′ 10″ × 5′ 4 $\frac{1}{8}$″. Gemäldegalerie, Staatliche Museen, Berlin.

In this painting of a crowded Netherlandish village, Bruegel indulged his audience's obsession with proverbs and passion for clever imagery, and demonstrated his deep understanding of human nature.

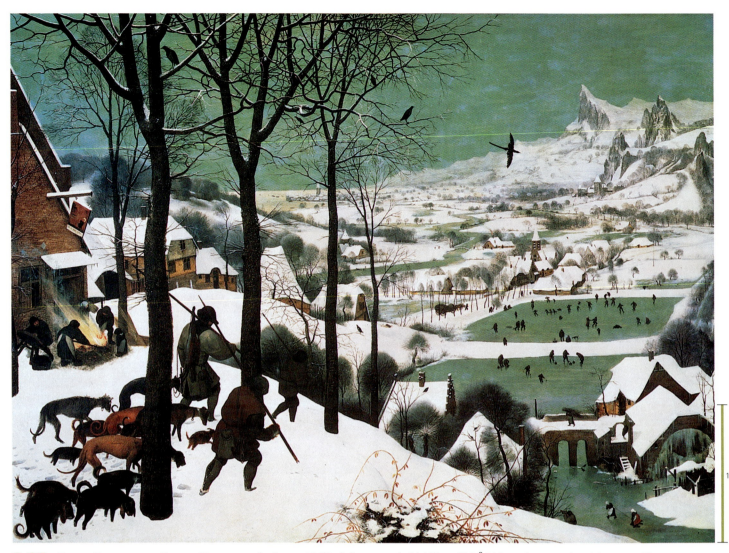

9-38 PIETER BRUEGEL THE ELDER, *Hunters in the Snow*, 1565. Oil on wood, 3′ 10″ × 5′ 3¾″. Kunsthistorisches Museum, Vienna.

In *Hunters in the Snow,* one of a series of six paintings illustrating annual seasonal changes, Bruegel draws the viewer diagonally into its depth by his mastery of line, shape, and composition.

1 ft.

clerics). From a bird's-eye view, the spectator encounters a mesmerizing array of activities reminiscent of the topsy-turvy scenes of Bosch (FIG. 9-33), but the purpose and meaning of Bruegel's anecdotal details are clear. By illustrating more than a hundred proverbs in this single painting, the artist indulged his Netherlandish audience's obsession with proverbs and passion for detailed and clever imagery. As the viewer scrutinizes the myriad vignettes within the painting, Bruegel's close observation and deep understanding of human nature become apparent. The proverbs depicted include, on the far left, a man in blue gnawing on a pillar ("He bites the column"—an image of hypocrisy). To his right, a man "beats his head against a wall" (an ambitious idiot). On the roof a man "shoots one arrow after the other, but hits nothing" (a shortsighted fool). In the far distance, the "blind lead the blind."

Hunters in the Snow (FIG. **9-38**) is very different in character and illustrates the dynamic variety of Bruegel's work. One of a series of six paintings illustrating seasonal changes in the year, *Hunters* refers back to older Netherlandish traditions of depicting seasons and peasants in Books of Hours (FIG. 8-9). Bruegel's painting shows human figures and

landscape locked in winter cold. The weary hunters return with their hounds, women build fires, skaters skim the frozen pond, the town and its church huddle in their mantle of snow. The artist rendered the landscape in an optically accurate manner. It develops smoothly from foreground to background and draws the viewer diagonally into its depths. Bruegel's consummate skill in using line and shape and his subtlety in tonal harmony make this one of the great landscape paintings in the history of European art.

SPAIN

Spain emerged as the dominant European power at the end of the 16th century. Under Charles V of Habsburg (r. 1516–1556) and his son, Philip II (r. 1556–1598), the Spanish Empire dominated a territory greater in extent than any ever known—a large part of Europe, the western Mediterranean, a strip of North Africa, and vast expanses in the New World. Spain acquired many of its New World colonies through aggressive overseas exploration. Among the most notable conquistadors sailing under the Span-

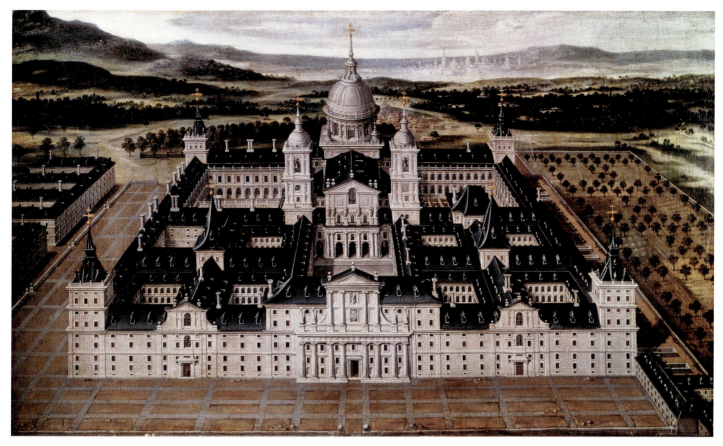

9-39 Juan de Herrera and Juan Bautista de Toledo, El Escorial, near Madrid, Spain, 1563–1584 (detail of an anonymous 18th-century painting).

Conceived by Charles V and built by Philip II, El Escorial is a combined royal mausoleum, church, monastery, and palace. The complex is classical in style with severely plain walls and massive towers.

ish flag were Christopher Columbus (1451–1506), Vasco Nuñez de Balboa (ca. 1475–1517), Ferdinand Magellan (1480–1521), Hernán Cortés (1485–1547), and Francisco Pizarro (ca. 1470–1541). The Habsburg Empire, enriched by New World plunder, supported the most powerful military force in Europe. Spain defended and then promoted the interests of the Catholic Church in its battle against the inroads of the Protestant Reformation. In fact, Philip II earned the title "Most Catholic King." Spain's crusading spirit, nourished by centuries of war with Islam, engaged body and soul in forming the most Catholic civilization of Europe and the Americas. In the 16th century, for good or for ill, Spain left the mark of Spanish power, religion, language, and culture on two hemispheres.

El Escorial In architecture, Philip II favored an Italian-derived classicism, which is on display in the expansive complex called El Escorial (FIG. **9-39**), built by Juan Bautista de Toledo (d. 1567) and Juan de Herrera (ca. 1530–1597), principally the latter. In his will, Charles V stipulated that a "dynastic pantheon" be constructed to house the remains of past and future monarchs of Spain. Philip II, obedient to his father's wishes, chose a site some 30 miles northwest of Madrid in rugged terrain with barren mountains. There he built El Escorial, not only a royal mausoleum but also a church,

a monastery, and a palace. Legend has it that the gridlike plan for the enormous complex, 625 feet wide and 520 feet deep, symbolized the gridiron on which Saint Lawrence, El Escorial's patron saint, suffered his martyrdom.

The vast structure is in keeping with Philip's austere and conscientious character, his passionate Catholic religiosity, his proud reverence for his dynasty, and his stern determination to impose his will worldwide. He insisted that in designing El Escorial, the architects focus on simplicity of form, severity in the whole, nobility without arrogance, and majesty without ostentation. Only the three entrances, with the dominant central portal framed by superimposed orders and topped by a pediment in the Italian fashion, break the long sweep of the structure's severely plain walls. Massive square towers punctuate the four corners. The stress on the central axis, with its subdued echoes in the two flanking portals, anticipates the three-part organization of later Baroque facades (see Chapter 10). The construction material for the entire complex (including the church)—granite, a difficult stone to work—conveys a feeling of starkness and gravity. The church's massive facade and the austere geometry of the interior complex, with its blocky walls and ponderous arches, produce an effect of overwhelming strength and weight. El Escorial stands as the overpowering architectural expression of Spain's spirit in its heroic epoch.

9-40 EL GRECO, *Burial of Count Orgaz,*
Santo Tomé, Toledo, Spain, 1586. Oil on canvas,
16′ × 12′.

El Greco's art is a blend of Byzantine and Italian
Mannerist elements. His intense emotional content
captured the fervor of Spanish Catholicism, and his
dramatic use of light foreshadowed the Baroque
style.

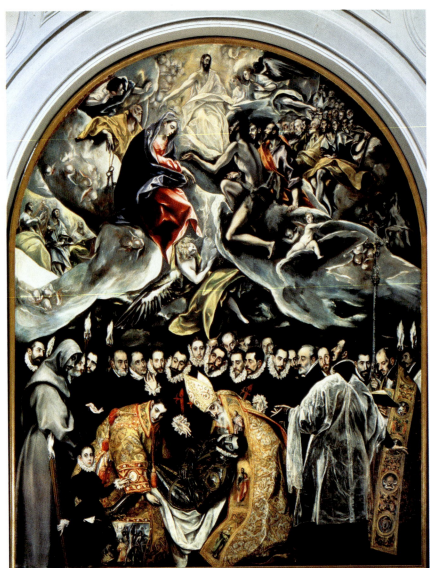

1 ft.

El Greco The most renowned painter in
16th-century Spain was, ironically, not a Spaniard. Doménikos Theotokópoulos, called EL
GRECO (ca. 1547–1614), was born on Crete but
emigrated to Italy as a young man. In his youth,
he absorbed the traditions of Late Byzantine
frescoes and mosaics. While still young, El
Greco ("the Greek") went to Venice, where he
worked in Titian's studio, although Tintoretto's
painting apparently made a stronger impression
on him. A brief trip to Rome explains the influences of Roman and Florentine Mannerism
on his work. By 1577 he had left for Spain to
spend the rest of his life in Toledo. El Greco's
art is a strong personal blending of Byzantine
and Mannerist elements. The intense emotionalism of his paintings, which naturally appealed
to Spanish piety, and a great reliance on color
bound him to 16th-century Venetian art and
to Mannerism. El Greco's art was not strictly
Spanish (although it appealed to certain sectors
of that society), for it had no Spanish antecedents and little effect on later Spanish painters.
Nevertheless, El Greco's hybrid style captured
the fervor of Spanish Catholicism.

This passion is vividly expressed in the artist's masterpiece, *The Burial of Count Orgaz* (FIG. **9-40**), painted in
1586 for the Church of Santo Tomé in Toledo. El Greco
based the artwork on the legend that the count of Orgaz,
who had died some three centuries before and who had been
a great benefactor of Santo Tomé, was buried in the church
by Saints Stephen and Augustine, who miraculously descended from Heaven to lower the count's body into its sepulchre. The brilliant Heaven that opens above irradiates the
earthly scene. The painter represented the terrestrial with a
firm realism, whereas he depicted the celestial, in his quite
personal manner, with elongated undulating figures, fluttering draperies, and a visionary swirling cloud. Below, the two
saints lovingly lower the count's armor-clad body, the armor
and heavy draperies painted with all the rich sensuousness of
the Venetian school. A solemn chorus of black-clad Spanish
personages fills the background. In the carefully individualized features of these figures, El Greco demonstrated that
he was also a great portraitist. These men call to mind both
the conquistadors of the 16th century and the Spanish naval
officers who, two years after the completion of this painting,
led the Great Armada against both Protestant England and
the Netherlands.

The upward glances of some of the figures below and
the flight of an angel above link the painting's lower and upper spheres. The action of the angel, who carries the count's
soul in his arms as Saint John and the Virgin intercede for
it before the throne of Christ, reinforces this connection. El
Greco's deliberate change in style to distinguish between
the two levels of reality gives the viewer an opportunity to
see the artist's early and late manners in the same work, one
below the other. His sumptuous and realistic presentation
of the earthly sphere is still strongly rooted in Venetian art,
but the abstractions and distortions El Greco used to show
the immaterial nature of the heavenly realm characterize
his later style. His elongated figures existing in undefined
spaces, bathed in a cool light of uncertain origin, explain El
Greco's usual classification as a Mannerist, but it is difficult
to apply that label to him without reservations. Although he
used Mannerist formal devices, El Greco's primary concerns
were to depict emotion and convey his religious passion or
arouse that of observers. The forcefulness of his paintings
is the result of his unique, highly developed expressive
style. His strong sense of movement and use of light prefigured the Baroque style of the 17th century, examined next
in Chapter 10.

Europe, 1500 to 1600

ITALY

- During the High (1500–1520) and Late (1520–1600) Renaissance, the major Italian artistic centers were Florence, Rome, and Venice. Whereas most Florentine and Roman artists emphasized careful design preparation based on preliminary drawing *(disegno),* Venetian artists focused on color and the process of paint application *(colorito).*

- Leonardo da Vinci was a master of chiaroscuro and atmospheric perspective. He was famous for his *sfumato* (misty haziness) and for his psychological insight in depicting biblical narrative.

- Raphael favored lighter tonalities than Leonardo and clarity over obscurity. His sculpturesque figures appear in landscapes under blue skies or in grandiose architectural settings rendered in perfect perspective.

- Michelangelo's carved and painted figures have heroic physiques and great emotional impact. He preferred pent-up energy to Raphael's calm, ideal beauty.

- The leading architect of the early 16th century was Bramante, who championed the classical style of the ancients but combined classical elements in original ways. He favored the central plan for ecclesiastical buildings.

- The two greatest masters of the Venetian painting school were Giorgione, who developed the concept of *poesia,* poetical painting, and Titian, who won renown for his rich surface textures and dazzling display of color in all its nuances. Titian established oil paint on canvas as the typical medium of the Western pictorial tradition.

- Mannerism (1520–1600) was a reaction to the High Renaissance style. A prime feature of Mannerist art is artifice. Renaissance artists generally strove to create art that appeared natural, whereas Mannerist artists such as Pontormo and Parmigianino were less inclined to disguise the contrived nature of art production. Ambiguous space, departures from expected conventions, and unique presentations of traditional themes are common features of Mannerist art.

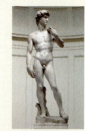

Michelangelo, *David,* 1501–1504

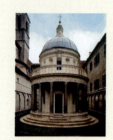

Bramante, Tempietto, Rome, 1502(?)

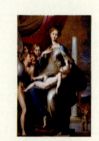

Parmigianino, *Madonna with the Long Neck,* 1534–1540

NORTHERN EUROPE AND SPAIN

- Dissatisfaction with the Church in Rome led to the Protestant Reformation. Protestants objected to the sale of indulgences, rejected most Catholic sacraments, and condemned ostentatious church decoration as a form of idolatry. Still, art, especially prints, played a role in Protestantism. Albrecht Dürer, the first artist outside Italy to become an international celebrity, was a master printmaker. *Fall of Man* reflects his studies of classical statues and the Vitruvian theory of human proportions.

- The Netherlands was one of the most prosperous countries in 16th-century Europe. Netherlandish art provides a picture of contemporary life and values. Pieter Aertsen's *Butcher's Stall* seems to be a straightforward genre scene but includes the Holy Family offering alms to a beggar, providing a stark contrast between gluttony and religious piety.

- Landscapes were the specialty of Pieter Bruegel. His *Hunters in the Snow* is one of a series of paintings depicting the seasonal changes of the year and the activities associated with them.

- The leading painter of 16th-century Spain was the Greek-born El Greco, whose art combined Byzantine style, Italian Mannerism, and the religious fervor of Catholic Spain.

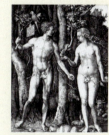

Albrecht Dürer, *Fall of Man,* 1504

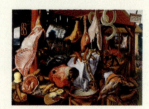

Pieter Aertsen, *Butcher's Stall,* 1551

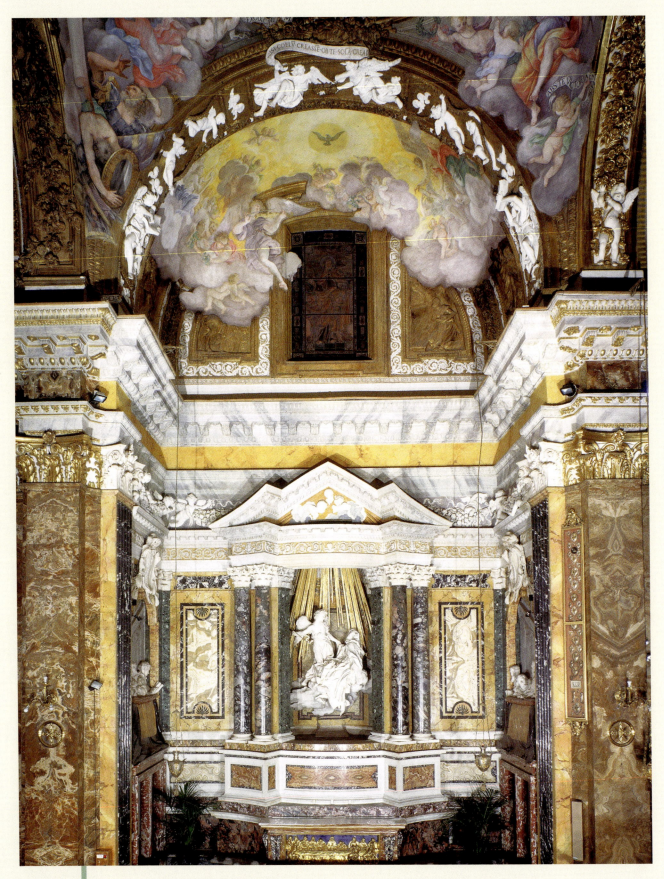

10-1 GIANLORENZO BERNINI, interior of the Cornaro Chapel, Santa Maria della Vittoria, Rome, Italy, 1645–1652.

Bernini was the quintessential Baroque artist. For the Cornaro Chapel, he drew on the full capabilities of architecture, sculpture, and painting to create an intensely emotional experience for worshipers.

Europe, 1600 to 1700

During the 17th century, numerous geopolitical shifts occurred in Europe as the fortunes of the individual countries waxed and waned. Pronounced political and religious friction resulted in widespread unrest and warfare. Indeed, between 1562 and 1721, all of Europe was at peace for a mere four years. The major conflict of this period was the Thirty Years' War (1618–1648), which ensnared Spain, France, Sweden, Denmark, the Netherlands, Germany, Austria, Poland, the Holy Roman Empire, and the Ottoman Empire. Although the outbreak of this war had its roots in the religious conflict between militant Catholics and militant Protestants, the driving force quickly shifted to secular, dynastic, and nationalistic concerns. Among the major political entities vying for expanded power and authority in Europe were the Bourbon dynasty of France and the Habsburg dynasties of Spain and the Holy Roman Empire. The war, which concluded with the Treaty of Westphalia in 1648, was largely responsible for the political restructuring of Europe (MAP 10-1). As a result, the United Provinces of the Netherlands (the Dutch Republic), Sweden, and France expanded their authority. Spanish and Danish power diminished. In addition to reconfiguring territorial boundaries, the Treaty of Westphalia in essence granted freedom of religious choice throughout Europe. This treaty thus marked the abandonment of the idea of a united Christian Europe, and recognized the practical realities of secular political systems. The building of today's nation-states was emphatically under way.

The 17th century also brought heightened economic competition to Europe. Much of the foundation for worldwide mercantilism—extensive geographic exploration, improved maps, advances in shipbuilding—had been laid in the previous century. In the 17th century, however, changes in financial systems, lifestyles, and trading patterns, along with expanding colonialism, fueled the creation of a worldwide marketplace. The Dutch founded the Bank of Amsterdam in 1609, which eventually became the center of European transfer banking. By establishing a system in which merchant firms held money on account, the bank relieved traders of having to transport precious metals as payment. Trading practices became more complex. Rather than reciprocal trade, triangular trade (trade among three parties) allowed for a larger pool of desirable goods. Exposure to a wider array of goods affected European diets and lifestyles. Coffee (from island colonies) and tea (from China) became popular beverages during the early 17th century. Equally explosive was the growth of sugar use. Sugar, tobacco, and rice were slave crops, and the slave trade expanded to meet the demand for these goods. The resulting worldwide mercantile system permanently changed the face of Europe. The prosperity international trade generated affected social and political

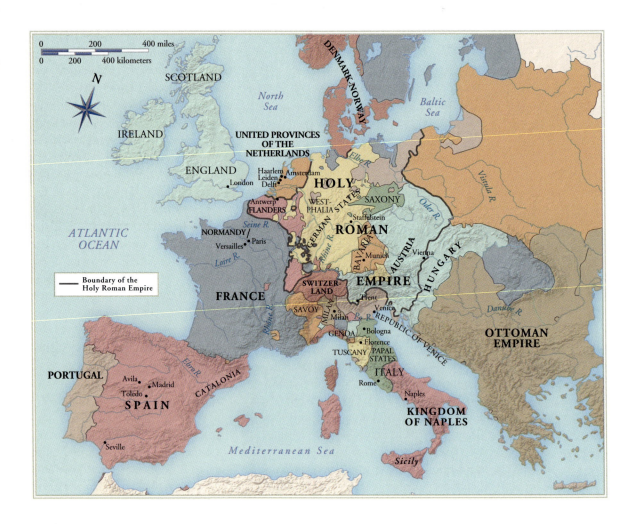

MAP 10-1
Europe in 1648 after the Treaty of Westphalia.

relationships, necessitating new rules of etiquette and careful diplomacy. With increased disposable income, more of the newly wealthy spent money on art, expanding the number of possible sources of patronage.

Art historians traditionally describe 17th-century European art as *Baroque*, but the term is problematic because the period encompasses a broad range of styles and genres. Although its origin is unclear, "Baroque" may have come from the Portuguese word *barroco*, meaning an irregularly shaped pearl. Use of the term emerged in the late 18th and early 19th centuries, when critics disparaged the Baroque period's artistic production, in large part because of perceived deficiencies in comparison with the art of the Italian Renaissance. Over time, this negative connotation faded, but the term is still useful to describe the distinctive new style that emerged during the 17th century—a style of complexity and drama seen especially in Italian art. Whereas Renaissance artists reveled in the precise, orderly rationality of classical models, Italian Baroque artists embraced dynamism, theatricality, and elaborate ornamentation, all used to spectacular effect, often on a grandiose scale.

ITALY

Although in the 16th century the Catholic Church launched the Counter-Reformation as a response to—and a challenge to—the Protestant Reformation (see Chapter 9), the consid-

erable appeal of Protestantism continued to preoccupy the popes in Rome throughout the 17th century. Protestantism changed the nature of artistic patronage in many European countries, but in Italy, the Catholic Church remained the leading source of artistic commissions. The aim of much of Italian Baroque art was to restore Catholicism's predominance and centrality.

Architecture and Sculpture

Italian 17th-century art and architecture, especially in Rome, reflected the renewed energy of the Counter-Reformation. At the end of the 16th century, Sixtus V (r. 1585–1590) had augmented the papal treasury and intended to rebuild Rome as an even more magnificent showcase of the Catholic Church's power. Between 1606 and 1667, several strong and ambitious popes—Paul V, Urban VIII, Innocent X, and Alexander VII—brought many of Sixtus V's dreams to fruition. Rome still bears the marks of their patronage everywhere.

Carlo Maderno In 1606, Pope Paul V (r. 1605–1621) commissioned CARLO MADERNO (1556–1629) to complete Saint Peter's in Rome. As the symbolic seat of the papacy, Saint Peter's radiated enormous metaphorical presence. In light of Counter-Reformation concerns, the Baroque popes wanted to conclude the already century-long rebuilding

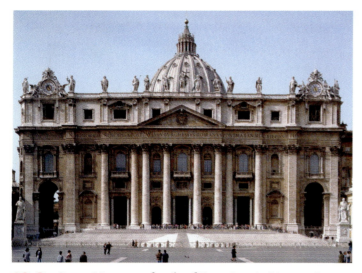

10-2 CARLO MADERNO, facade of Saint Peter's, Vatican City, Rome, Italy, 1606-1612.

Maderno's facade embodies the design principles of early Baroque architecture. Vigorously projecting columns mount dramatically toward the emphatically stressed pediment-capped central section.

project and reestablish the majesty embodied in the mammoth structure. Because of the preexisting core of an incomplete building, Maderno lacked the luxury of formulating a totally new concept for Saint Peter's. But Maderno's new facade (FIG. 10-2) does incorporate the design principles of early Italian Baroque architecture. Vigorously projecting columns and pilasters mount dramatically toward the pediment-capped central section. Strong shadows cast by the columns heighten the sculptural effect. The two outside bell-tower bays were not part of Maderno's original plan, however. Had the facade been constructed according to the architect's initial design, it would have exhibited greater verticality and visual coherence.

In plan, Maderno's expanded Saint Peter's also departed from the 16th-century central plans of Bramante and Michelangelo (FIGS. 9-14 and 9-15). Paul V asked Maderno to add three nave bays to the earlier nucleus because he decided the Renaissance architects' central plan was too closely associated with pagan buildings, such as the Pantheon (FIG. 3-37). Moreover, the traditional longitudinal plan reinforced the symbolic distinction between clergy and laity and provided a space for the processions of ever-growing assemblies. Lengthening the nave, unfortunately, pushed the dome farther back from the facade and all but destroyed the effect Michelangelo had planned—a structure pulled together and dominated by its dome. When viewed at close range, the dome barely emerges above the facade's soaring frontal plane. Seen from farther back (FIG. 10-2), it appears to have no drum. Visitors must move back quite a distance from the front to see the dome and drum together (FIG. 10-3).

Gianlorenzo Bernini Old Saint Peter's had a large forecourt, or *atrium* (FIG. 4-4, no. 6), in front of the church proper, and in the mid-17th century GIANLORENZO BERNINI (1598–1680) received the prestigious commission to construct a monumental colonnade-framed *piazza* ("plaza"; FIG. 10-3) in front of Maderno's facade. Architect, painter, and sculptor, Bernini was one of the most important and imaginative artists of the Italian Baroque era and its most characteristic spirit. Bernini's design had to accommodate two preexisting structures on the site—a fountain Maderno designed and an ancient obelisk the Romans brought from Egypt, which Pope Sixtus V had moved to its present location in 1585 as part of his vision of Christian triumph in Rome. Bernini co-opted these features to define the long axis of a vast oval embraced by two colonnades joined to Maderno's facade. Four rows of huge Tuscan columns make up the two colonnades, which terminate in classical temple fronts. The colonnades extend a dramatic gesture of embrace to all who enter the piazza, symbolizing the welcome the Roman Catholic Church offered its members during the Counter-Reformation. Bernini himself referred to his colonnades as the welcoming arms

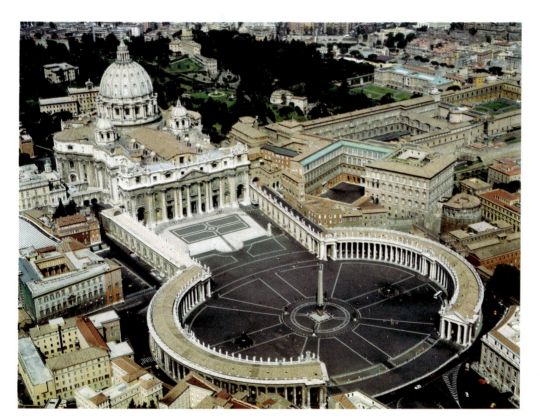

10-3 Aerial view (looking northwest) of Saint Peter's, Vatican City, Rome, Italy, 1506–1666.

The dramatic gesture of embrace the colonnades make as worshipers enter Saint Peter's piazza symbolizes the welcome the Roman Catholic Church extended its members during the Counter-Reformation.

of the church. Beyond their symbolic resonance, the colonnades visually counteracted the natural perspective and brought the facade closer to the viewer. By emphasizing the facade's height in this manner, Bernini subtly and effectively compensated for its extensive width. Thus, a Baroque transformation expanded the compact central designs of Bramante and Michelangelo into a dynamic complex of axially ordered elements that reach out and enclose spaces of vast dimension. By its sheer scale and theatricality, the complete Saint Peter's fulfilled the desire of the Counter-Reformation Church to present an awe-inspiring and authoritative vision of itself.

Baldacchino Long before being invited to design the piazza, Bernini had been at work decorating the interior of Saint Peter's. His first commission, completed between 1624 and 1633, called for the design and erection of a gigantic bronze *baldacchino* (FIG. **10-4**) under the great dome. The canopy-like structure (*baldacco* is Italian for "silk from Baghdad," such as for a cloth canopy) is as tall as an eight-story building. The baldacchino serves both functional and symbolic purposes. It marks the high altar and the tomb of Saint Peter, and it visually bridges human scale to the lofty vaults and dome above. Further, for worshipers entering the nave of the huge church, it provides a dramatic, compelling presence at the crossing. Its columns also create a visual frame for the elaborate sculpture representing the throne of Saint Peter (the Cathedra Petri) at the far end of Saint Peter's (FIG. **10-4**, *rear*). On a symbolic level, the structure's decorative elements speak to the power of the Catholic Church and of Pope Urban VIII (r. 1623–1644). Partially fluted and wreathed with vines, the baldacchino's four spiral columns recall those of the ancient baldacchino over the same spot in Old Saint Peter's, thereby invoking the past to reinforce the primacy of the Roman Catholic Church in the 17th century. At the top of the columns, four colossal angels stand guard at the upper corners of the canopy. Forming the canopy's apex are four serpentine brackets that elevate the orb and the cross. Since the time of the emperor Constantine, builder of the original Saint Peter's basilica, the orb and the cross had served as symbols of the Church's triumph. The baldacchino also features numerous bees, symbols of Urban VIII's family, the Barberini. The structure effectively gives visual form to the triumph of Christianity and the papal claim to doctrinal supremacy.

David Although Bernini was a great and influential architect, his fame rests primarily on his sculpture. The biographer Filippo Baldinucci (1625–1696) said about Bernini: "[No sculptor] manipulated marble with more facility and boldness. He gave his works a marvelous softness . . . making the marble, so to say, flexible."[1] In keeping with the Italian Baroque spirit, Bernini's sculpture is expansive and theatrical, and the element of time usually plays an important role in it. His *David* (FIG. **10-5**) fundamentally differs from the earlier portrayals of the same subject by Donatello (FIG. 8-19)

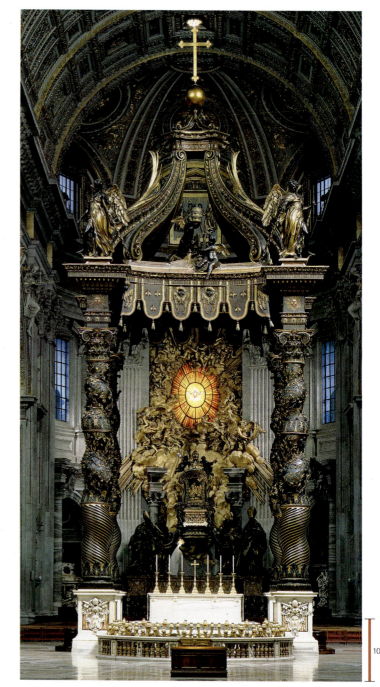

10-4 GIANLORENZO BERNINI, baldacchino, Saint Peter's, Vatican City, Rome, Italy, 1624–1633. Gilded bronze, 100' high.

Bernini's baldacchino serves both functional and symbolic purposes. It marks Saint Peter's tomb and the high altar of the church, and it visually bridges human scale to the lofty vaults and dome above.

and Michelangelo (FIG. 9-9). Donatello depicted David after his triumph over Goliath. Michelangelo portrayed David before his encounter with the giant. Bernini chose to represent the combat itself. Unlike his Renaissance predecessors, the Baroque sculptor aimed to catch the split-second of maximum action. Bernini's *David*, his muscular legs widely and firmly planted, begins the violent, pivoting motion that will launch the stone from his sling. Unlike Myron, the fifth-century BCE Greek sculptor who froze his *Diskobolos* (FIG. 2-1) at a fleeting moment of inaction, Bernini selected the most dramatic of

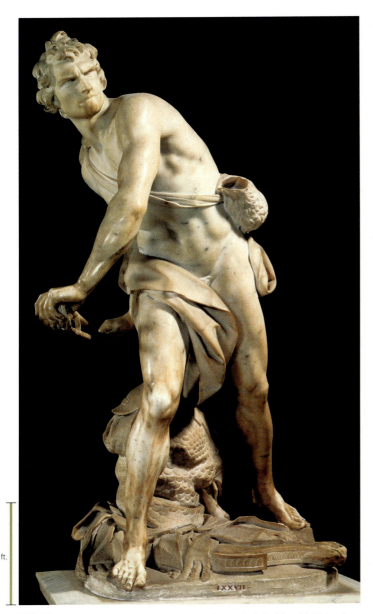

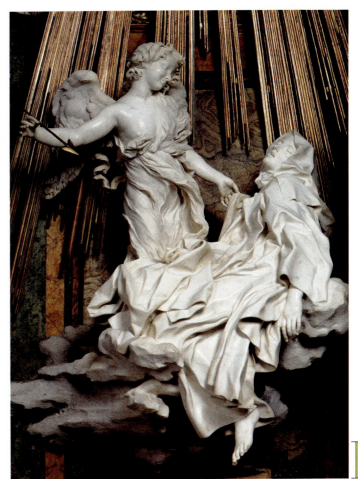

10-6 GIANLORENZO BERNINI, *Ecstasy of Saint Teresa*, Cornaro Chapel, Santa Maria della Vittoria, Rome, Italy, 1645–1652. Marble, 11′ 6″ high.

The passionate drama of Bernini's depiction of Saint Teresa correlated with the ideas of Ignatius Loyola, who argued that the re-creation of spiritual experience would do much to increase devotion and piety.

10-5 GIANLORENZO BERNINI, *David*, 1623. Marble, 5′ 7″ high. Galleria Borghese, Rome.

Bernini's sculptures are expansive and theatrical, and the element of time plays an important role in them. His emotion-packed *David* seems to be moving through both time and space.

an implied sequence of poses, so that the viewer has to think simultaneously of the continuum and of this tiny fraction of it. The suggested continuum imparts a dynamic quality to the statue that conveys a bursting forth of energy. Bernini's statue seems to be moving through time and through space. This kind of sculpture cannot be inscribed in a cylinder or confined in a niche. Its dynamic action demands space around it. Nor is the statue self-sufficient in the Renaissance sense, as its pose and attitude direct attention beyond it to the unseen Goliath. Bernini's sculpted figure moves out into the space that surrounds it. Further, the expression of intense concentration on David's face contrasts vividly with the classically placid visages of Renaissance Davids. The tension in the young hero's face augments the dramatic impact of Bernini's sculpture.

Cornaro Chapel Another work that displays the motion and emotion of Italian Baroque art and exemplifies Bernini's refusal to limit his statues to firmly defined spatial settings is *Ecstasy of Saint Teresa* in the Cornaro Chapel (FIG. **10-1**) of the Roman church of Santa Maria della Vittoria. For this chapel, Bernini marshaled the full capabilities of architecture, sculpture, and painting to charge the entire area with palpable tension. He accomplished this by drawing on the considerable knowledge of the theater he absorbed from writing plays and producing stage designs. The marble sculpture (FIG. **10-6**) that serves as the chapel's focus depicts Saint Teresa, one of the great mystical saints of the Spanish Counter-Reformation. Her conversion occurred after the death of her father, when she fell into a series of trances, saw visions, and heard voices. Feeling a persistent pain, she attributed it to the fire-tipped arrow of divine love that an angel had thrust repeatedly into her heart. In her writings, Saint Teresa described this experience as making her swoon in delightful anguish. In Bernini's hands, the entire Cornaro Chapel became a theater for the production of this mystical drama. The niche in which it takes place appears as a shallow *proscenium* (the part of the stage in front of the curtain) crowned with a broken Baroque pediment and ornamented with polychrome marble. On either side of the chapel, sculpted relief portraits of the family of Cardinal Federico Cornaro watch the heavenly drama unfold from choice balcony seats. Bernini depicted the saint in ecstasy, unmistakably a mingling of spiritual and physical passion, swooning back on a cloud, while the smiling angel aims his arrow. The sculptor's supreme technical virtuosity is evident in the visual differentiation in texture among the clouds, rough monk's cloth, gauzy material, smooth flesh, and feathery wings—all carved from the same white marble. Light from a hidden window of yellow glass pours down on golden rays that suggest the radiance of Heaven, whose painted representation covers the vault.

The passionate drama of Bernini's *Ecstasy of Saint Teresa* correlated with the ideas disseminated earlier by Ignatius Loyola (1491–1556), who founded the Jesuit order in 1534 and whom the Church canonized as Saint Ignatius in 1622. In his book *Spiritual Exercises*, Ignatius argued that the re-creation of spiritual experiences in artworks would do much to increase devotion and piety. Thus, theatricality and sensory impact were useful vehicles for achieving Counter-Reformation goals. Bernini was a devout Catholic, which undoubtedly contributed to his understanding of those goals. His inventiveness, technical skill, sensitivity to his patrons' needs, and energy account for his position as the quintessential Italian Baroque artist.

Francesco Borromini As gifted as Bernini was, FRANCESCO BORROMINI (1599–1667) took Italian Baroque architecture to even greater dramatic heights. In the small church of San Carlo alle Quattro Fontane (Saint Charles at the Four Fountains; FIG. **10-7**), Borromini surpassed any of his predecessors or contemporaries in emphasizing a building's sculptural qualities. Maderno incorporated sculptural elements in Saint Peter's facade (FIG. **10-2**), but Borromini set his facade in undulating motion, creating a dynamic counterpoint of concave and convex elements on two levels

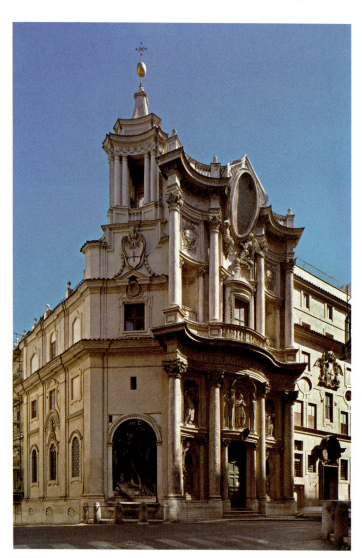

10-7 FRANCESCO BORROMINI, facade of San Carlo alle Quattro Fontane, Rome, Italy, 1665–1676.

Borromini rejected the traditional notion that a building's facade should be a flat frontispiece. He set San Carlo's facade in undulating motion, making a counterpoint of concave and convex elements.

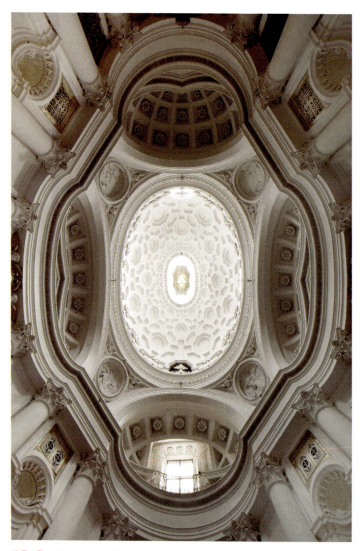

10-8 FRANCESCO BORROMINI, dome of San Carlo alle Quattro Fontane, Rome, Italy, 1638–1641.

In place of a traditional round dome, Borromini capped the interior of San Carlo with a deeply coffered oval dome that seems to float on the light entering through windows hidden in its base.

(for example, the sway of the cornices). He emphasized the three-dimensional effect with deeply recessed niches. This facade is not the traditional flat frontispiece that defines a building's outer limits. It is a pulsating, engaging component inserted between interior and exterior space, designed not to separate but to provide a fluid transition between the two. Underscoring this functional interrelation of the building and its environment is the curious fact that it has not one but two facades. The second, a narrow bay crowned with its own small tower, turns away from the main facade and, tracking the curve of the street, faces an intersection. (The upper facade dates seven years after Borromini's death, and it is uncertain to what degree the present design reflects his original intention.)

San Carlo's interior (FIG. **10-8**) is a hybrid of a Greek cross and an oval, with a long axis between entrance and apse. The side walls move in an undulating flow that reverses the facade's motion. Vigorously projecting columns define the space into which they protrude just as much as they accent the walls attached to them. Capping this molded interior space

is a deeply coffered oval dome that seems to float on the light entering through windows hidden in its base. Rich variations on the basic theme of the oval, dynamic relative to the static circle, create an interior that appears to flow from entrance to altar, unimpeded by the segmentation so characteristic of Renaissance buildings.

Painting

Although architecture and sculpture provided the most obvious vehicles for manipulating space and creating theatrical effects, painting continued to be an important art form in the Baroque era, as it was in previous centuries.

Annibale Carracci One of the most renowned 17th-century Italian painters was ANNIBALE CARRACCI (1560–1609) of Bologna, who received much of his training at the academy of art founded cooperatively by his family members, among them his cousin Ludovico Carracci (1555–1619) and brother Agostino Carracci (1557–1602). The Bolognese academy was the first significant institution of its kind in the history of Western art. The Carracci founded it on the premises that art can be taught—the basis of any academic philosophy of art—and that its instruction must include the classical and Renaissance traditions in addition to the study of anatomy and life drawing.

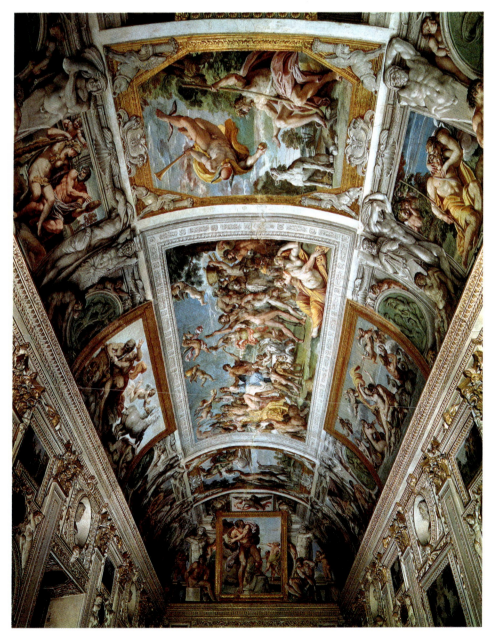

Annibale Carracci's most notable work is his decoration of the Palazzo Farnese gallery (FIG. **10-9**) in Rome. Cardinal Odoardo Farnese, a wealthy descendant of Pope Paul III, commissioned this ceiling fresco to celebrate the wedding of the cardinal's brother. Appropriately, the title of its iconographic program is *Loves of the Gods*—interpretations of the varieties of earthly and divine love in classical mythology. Carracci arranged the scenes in a format resembling framed easel paintings on a wall, but he painted them on the surfaces of a shallow curved vault. This type of simulated easel painting for ceiling design is called *quadro riportato*

10-9 ANNIBALE CARRACCI, *Loves of the Gods*, ceiling frescoes in the gallery, Palazzo Farnese, Rome, Italy, 1597–1601.

On the shallow curved vault of this large gallery in the Palazzo Farnese, Carracci arranged the mythological scenes in a quadro riportato format—a fresco resembling easel paintings on a wall.

Giovanni Pietro Bellori on Caravaggio

The written sources to which art historians turn as aids in understanding the art of the past are invaluable, but they reflect the personal preferences and prejudices of the writers. Giovanni Pietro Bellori (1613–1696), the leading biographer of Baroque artists, was an outspoken admirer of Renaissance classicism, especially the art of Raphael, and an ardent critic of Mannerism and of Caravaggio. In his *Vita* of Annibale Carracci, for example, Bellori praised "the divine Raphael . . . [whose art] raised its beauty to the summit, restoring it to the ancient majesty of . . . the Greeks and the Romans" and lamented that, soon after, "artists, abandoning the study of nature, corrupted art with the *maniera,* that is to say, with the fantastic idea based on practice and not on imitation."*

Bellori characterized Caravaggio (FIGS. 10-10 and 10-11) as talented and widely imitated but condemned him for his rejection of classicism in favor of realism. Two excerpts from Bellori's *Vita* of Caravaggio record some of the painter's own memorable remarks.

> [Caravaggio] began to paint according to his own inclinations; not only ignoring but even despising the superb statuary of antiquity and the famous paintings of Raphael, he considered nature to be the only subject fit for his brush. As a result, when he was shown the most famous statues of [the ancient Greek masters] Phidias and Glykon in order that he might use them as models, his only answer was to point toward a crowd of people, saying that nature had given him an abundance of masters. . . . [W]hen he came upon someone in town who pleased him he made no attempt to improve on the creations of nature.†

> [Caravaggio] claimed that he imitated his models so closely that he never made a single brushstroke that he called his own, but said rather that it was nature's. Repudiating all other rules, he considered the highest achievement not to be bound to art. For this innovation he was greatly acclaimed, and many talented and educated artists seemed compelled to follow him. . . . Nevertheless he lacked *invenzione,* decorum, *disegno,* or any knowledge of the science of painting. The moment the model was taken from him, his hand and his mind became empty . . . [With Caravaggio] began the imitation of common and vulgar things, seeking out filth and deformity.‡

* Giovanni Pietro Bellori, *Le vite de' pittori, scultori e architetti moderni* (Rome, 1672). Translated by Catherine Enggass, *The Lives of Annibale and Agostino Carracci by Giovanni Pietro Bellori* (University Park: Pennsylvania University Press, 1968), 5–6.
† Translated by Howard Hibbard, *Caravaggio* (New York: Harper & Row, 1983), 362.
‡ Ibid., 371–372.

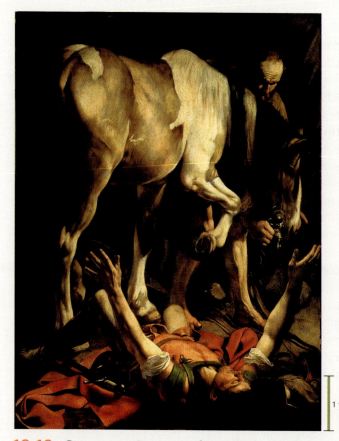

1 ft.

10-10 CARAVAGGIO, *Conversion of Saint Paul,* ca. 1601. Oil on canvas, 7′ 6″ × 5′ 9″. Cerasi Chapel, Santa Maria del Popolo, Rome.

Caravaggio used perspective, chiaroscuro, and dramatic lighting to bring viewers into this painting's space and action, almost as if they were participants in Saint Paul's conversion to Christianity.

(transferred framed painting), and Carracci's great influence made it fashionable for more than a century. Flanking the framed pictures are polychrome seated nude youths, who turn their heads to gaze at the scenes around them, and standing Atlas figures painted to resemble marble statues. Carracci derived these motifs from Michelangelo's Sistine Chapel ceiling (FIG. 9-1) but did not copy the figures. Notably, Caracci's chiaroscuro in the Farnese ceiling differs for the pictures and the figures surrounding them. The painter modeled the figures inside each quadro in an even light. In contrast, light from beneath seems to illuminate the outside figures, as if they were tangible three-dimensional beings or statues illuminated by torches in the gallery below. In the crown of the vault, a long panel, *Triumph of Bacchus,* is an ingenious mixture of Raphael's drawing style and lighting and Titian's more sensuous and animated figures. It reflects Carracci's adroitness in adjusting their authoritative styles to make something of his own.

Caravaggio Michelangelo Merisi, known as CARAVAGGIO (1573–1610) after the northern Italian town from which he came, developed a unique Baroque painting style that had tremendous influence throughout Europe. His outspoken disdain for the classical masters (probably more vocal than real) drew bitter criticism from many painters, one of whom denounced him as the "anti-Christ of painting." For Giovanni Pietro Bellori, the most authoritative critic of the age and an admirer of Annibale Carracci, Caravaggio's refusal to emulate the models of his distinguished predecessors threatened the entire classical tradition of Italian painting that had reached its zenith in Raphael's work (see "Giovanni Pietro Bellori on Caravaggio," above). Yet despite this criticism and the problems in Caravaggio's troubled life (reconstructed from documents such as police records), Caravaggio received many commissions, both public and private. Numerous artists paid him the supreme compliment of borrowing from his innovations. His influence on later artists, as much outside Italy as within, was immense. In his art, Caravaggio injected naturalism into both religion and the classics, reducing them to human dramas played out in the harsh and dingy settings of his time and place by unidealized figures selected from the fields and the streets.

Conversion of Saint Paul Around 1601, Caravaggio painted *Conversion of Saint Paul* (FIG. **10-10**) for the Cerasi Chapel in the Roman church of Santa Maria del Popolo. The painting depicts the conversion of the Pharisee Saul to Christianity, when he became the disciple Paul. Caravaggio represented the saint-to-be flat on his back with his arms thrown up. In the background, an old hostler seems preoccupied with caring for the horse. At first inspection, little here suggests the momentous significance of the spiritual event in progress. The audience could interpret the scene as a mere stable accident, not a man overcome by a great miracle.

Although criticized for departing from the traditional representations of this and other religious scenes, Caravaggio imbued his paintings with eloquence and humanity. To compel interest and involvement in Paul's conversion, the painter used perspective and chiaroscuro to bring viewers as close as possible to the scene's space and action, becoming almost participants in the event. The low horizon line augments this sense of inclusion. Caravaggio designed *Conversion of Saint Paul* for its location in the church, positioned at the line of sight of a person standing at the chapel entrance.

The sharply lit figures emerge from the dark of the background as if lit by the light from the chapel's windows. The lighting resembles that of a stage production analogous to the rays in Bernini's *Ecstasy of Saint Teresa* (FIG. **10-6**). The stark contrast of light and dark was a feature of Caravaggio's style that first shocked and then fascinated his contemporaries. Art historians call Caravaggio's use of dark settings enveloping their occupants *tenebrism*, from the Italian word *tenebroso*, or "shadowy" manner. In Caravaggio's work, tenebrism contributed mightily to the essential meaning of his pictures. In *Conversion of Saint Paul*, the dramatic spotlight shining down upon the fallen Pharisee is the light of divine revelation converting Saul to Christianity.

Calling of Saint Matthew A piercing ray of light illuminating a world of darkness and bearing a spiritual message is also a central feature of Caravaggio's *Calling of Saint Matthew* (FIG. **10-11**). It is one of two large canvases honoring Saint Matthew the artist painted for the side walls of the Contarelli Chapel in San Luigi dei Francesi in Rome. The commonplace setting—a tavern with unadorned walls—is typical of Caravaggio. Into this mundane environment, cloaked in mysterious shadow and almost unseen, Christ, identifiable initially only by his indistinct halo, enters from the right. With a commanding gesture that recalls the Lord's hand in Michelangelo's *Creation of Adam* (FIG. 9-11), he summons Levi, the Roman tax collector, to a higher calling. The astonished Levi—his face highlighted for the viewer by the beam of light emanating from an unspecified source above Christ's head and outside the picture—points to himself in disbelief. Although Christ's extended arm is reminiscent of the Lord's in *Creation of Adam*, the position of Christ's hand and wrist is similar to that of Adam's. This reference was highly appropriate, because the Church considered Christ to be the second Adam. Whereas Adam was responsible for the Fall, Christ is responsible for Redemption. The conversion of Levi (who became Matthew) brought his salvation.

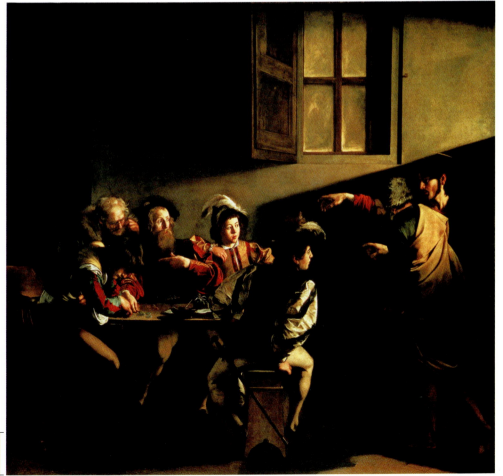

1 ft.

10-11 CARAVAGGIO, *Calling of Saint Matthew*, ca. 1597–1601. Oil on canvas, 11′ 1″ × 11′ 5″. Contarelli Chapel, San Luigi dei Francesi, Rome.

The stark contrast of light and dark was a key feature of Caravaggio's style. Here, Christ, cloaked in mysterious shadow and almost unseen, summons Levi the tax collector (Saint Matthew) to a higher calling.

The Letters of Artemisia Gentileschi

Artemisia Gentileschi (FIG. 10-12) was the most renowned woman painter in Europe during the first half of the 17th century and the first woman ever admitted to membership in Florence's Accademia del Disegno. In addition to scores of paintings created for wealthy patrons that included the king of England and the grand duke of Tuscany, Gentileschi left behind 28 letters, some of which reveal that she believed patrons treated her differently because of her gender.

Two 1649 letters written in Naples to Don Antonio Ruffo in Messina make her feelings explicit.

> I fear that before you saw the painting you must have thought me arrogant and presumptuous. . . . [I]f it were not for Your Most Illustrious Lordship . . . I would not have been induced to give it for one hundred and sixty, because everywhere else I have been I was paid one hundred *scudi* per figure. . . . You think me pitiful, because a woman's name raises doubts until her work is seen.*

> As for my doing a drawing and sending it, [tell the gentleman who wishes to know the price for a painting that] I have made a solemn vow never to send my drawings because people have cheated me. In particular, just today I found myself [in the situation] that, having done a drawing of souls in Purgatory for the Bishop of St. Gata, he, in order to spend less, commissioned another painter to do the painting using my work. If I were a man, I can't imagine it would have turned out this way, because when the concept has been realized and defined with lights and darks, and established by means of planes, the rest is a trifle.†

* Letter dated January 30, 1649. Translated by Mary D. Garrard, *Artemisia Gentileschi: The Image of the Female Hero in Italian Baroque Art* (Princeton, N.J.: Princeton University Press, 1989), 390.
† Letter dated November 13, 1649. Ibid., 397–398.

Narratives involving heroic women were a favorite theme for Gentileschi. In *Judith Slaying Holofernes,* the controlled highlights on the action in the foreground recall Caravaggio's paintings and heighten the drama.

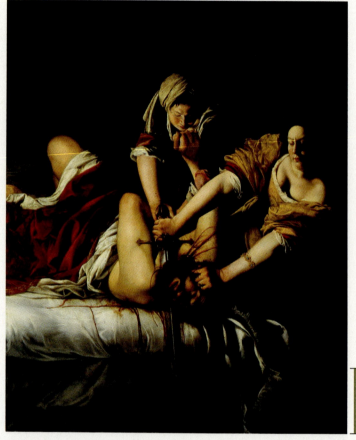

1 f

10-12 Artemisia Gentileschi, *Judith Slaying Holofernes,* ca. 1614–1620. Oil on canvas, 6′ 6⅓″ × 5′ 4″. Galleria degli Uffizi, Florence.

Artemisia Gentileschi Caravaggio's combination of naturalism and drama appealed both to patrons and artists, and he had many followers. One of the most accomplished was Artemisia Gentileschi (ca. 1593–1653), whose father Orazio (1563–1639), her teacher, was himself strongly influenced by Caravaggio. The daughter's successful career, pursued in Florence, Venice, Naples, and Rome (see "The Letters of Artemisia Gentileschi," above), helped to disseminate Caravaggio's manner throughout Italy. In *Judith Slaying Holofernes* (FIG. 10-12), Gentileschi used the tenebrism and even the "dark" subject matter Caravaggio favored. Significantly, she chose a narrative involving a heroic female, a favorite theme of hers. The story, from the Old Testament book of Judith, relates the delivery of Israel from its enemy, Holofernes. Having succumbed to Judith's charms, the Assyrian general Holofernes invited her to his tent for the night. When he fell asleep, Judith cut off his head. In this version of the scene (Gentileschi produced more than one painting of the subject), Judith and her maidservant behead Holofernes. Blood spurts everywhere as the two women summon all their strength to wield the heavy sword. The tension and strain are palpable. The controlled highlights on the action in the foreground recall Caravaggio's work and heighten the drama here as well.

Fra Andrea Pozzo Inspired by the Sistine Chapel (FIG. 9-1) and the Farnese gallery (FIG. 10-9), many Italian painters created ceiling decorations for churches and palaces. A leading practitioner of this genre was Fra Andrea Pozzo (1642–1709), a lay brother of the Jesuit order and a master of perspective, on which he wrote an influential treatise. Pozzo designed and executed the vast ceiling fresco *Glorification of Saint Ignatius* (FIG. 10-13) for Sant'Ignazio in Rome. The church was prominent in Counter-Reformation Rome because of its dedication to Saint Ignatius, the founder of the Jesuit order. The Jesuits played a major role in Counter-

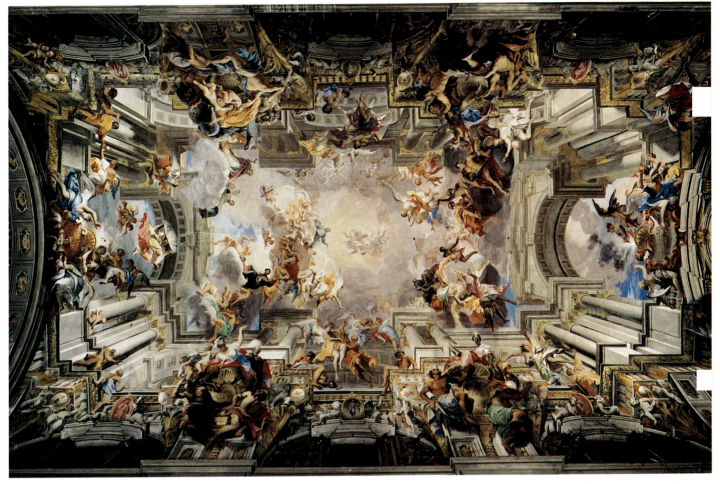

10-13 FRA ANDREA POZZO, *Glorification of Saint Ignatius*, ceiling fresco in the nave of Sant'Ignazio, Rome, Italy, 1691–1694.

Pozzo created the illusion that Heaven is opening up above the viewer's head by continuing the church's architecture into the painted vault. The fresco gives the appearance that the roof has been lifted off.

Reformation education and sent legions of missionaries to the New World and Asia. In *Glorification of Saint Ignatius*, Pozzo created the illusion that Heaven is opening up above the congregation. To accomplish this, the artist illusionistically continued the church's architecture into the vault so that the roof seems to be lifted off. As Heaven and Earth commingle, Christ receives Saint Ignatius in the presence of figures personifying the four corners of the world. A disk in the nave floor marks the ideal standpoint for the whole perspectival illusion. For worshipers looking upward from this spot, the vision is complete. They find themselves in the presence of the heavenly and spiritual.

The effectiveness of Italian Baroque religious art depended on the drama and theatricality of individual images, as well as on the interaction and fusion of architecture, sculpture, and painting. Sound enhanced this experience. Architects designed churches with acoustical effect in mind, and in an Italian Baroque church filled with music, the power of both image and sound must have been immensely moving. Through simultaneous stimulation of both the visual and auditory senses, the faithful might well have been transported into a trancelike state that would, indeed, as the great English poet John Milton (1608–1674) eloquently stated in *Il Penseroso* (1631), "bring all Heav'n before [their] eyes."[2]

SPAIN

During the 16th century, Spain had established itself as an international power. The Habsburg kings had built a dynastic state that encompassed Portugal, part of Italy, the Netherlands, and extensive areas of the New World. By the beginning of the 17th century, however, the Habsburg Empire was struggling, and although Spain mounted an aggressive effort during the Thirty Years' War, by 1660 the imperial age of the Spanish Habsburgs was over. In part, the demise of their empire was due to economic woes. The military campaigns of Philip III (r. 1598–1621) and his son Philip IV (r. 1621–1665) waged during the Thirty Years' War were costly and led to higher taxes on Spanish subjects. This burden in turn incited revolts and civil war in Catalonia and Portugal in the 1640s, further straining an already fragile economy. Thus, the dawn of the Baroque period in Spain found the country's leaders struggling to maintain control of their dwindling empire. But realizing the value of visual imagery in communicating to a wide audience, both Philip III and Philip IV continued to spend lavishly on art.

In a country passionately committed to Catholic orthodoxy, Spanish Baroque artists, like their Italian contemporaries, sought ways to move viewers and to encourage greater devotion and piety. Particularly appealing in this regard

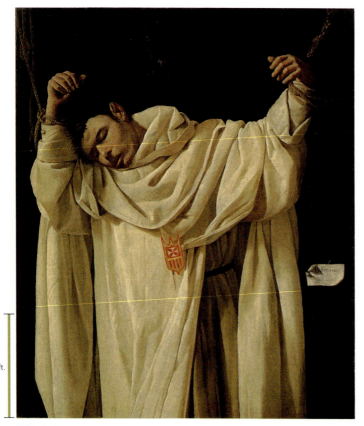

10-14 Francisco de Zurbarán, *Saint Serapion*, 1628. Oil on canvas, 3′ 11½″ × 3′ 4¾″. Wadsworth Atheneum, Hartford (Ella Gallup Sumner and Mary Catlin Sumner Collection Fund).

The light shining on Serapion calls attention to his tragic death and increases the painting's dramatic impact. The monk's coarse features label him as common, evoking empathy from a wide audience.

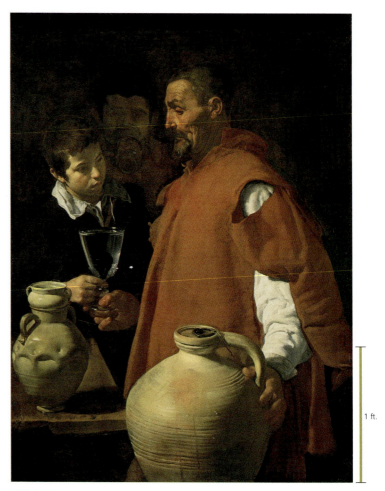

10-15 Diego Velázquez, *Water Carrier of Seville*, ca. 1619. Oil on canvas, 3′ 5½″ × 2′ 7½″. Victoria & Albert Museum, London.

In this early work—a genre scene that seems to convey a deeper significance—the contrast of darks and lights and the plebeian nature of the figures reveal Velázquez's indebtedness to Caravaggio.

were scenes of death and martyrdom, which provided artists with opportunities both to depict extreme feelings and to instill those feelings in viewers. Spain prided itself on its saints—Saint Teresa of Avila (FIG. 10-6) and Saint Ignatius Loyola (FIG. 10-13) were both Spanish-born—and martyrdom scenes surfaced frequently in Spanish Baroque art.

Francisco de Zurbarán A leading 17th-century Spanish painter was FRANCISCO DE ZURBARÁN (1598–1664), whose primary patrons were rich monastic orders. Many of his paintings are quiet and contemplative, appropriate for prayer. Zurbarán painted *Saint Serapion* (FIG. 10-14) as a devotional image for the funerary chapel of the Order of Mercy in Seville. The saint, who participated in the Third Crusade, suffered martyrdom while preaching the Gospel to Muslims. According to one account, the monk's captors tied him to a tree, then tortured and decapitated him. The Order of Mercy dedicated itself to self-sacrifice, and Serapion's membership in this order amplified the resonance of Zurbarán's painting. In *Saint Serapion* the monk emerges from a dark background and fills the foreground. The bright light shining on him calls attention to the saint's tragic death and increases the dramatic impact of the image. In the background are two barely visible tree branches. A small note next to the saint identifies him. The coarse features of the

Spanish monk label him as common, no doubt evoking empathy from a wide audience.

Diego Velázquez The greatest Spanish painter of the Baroque age was DIEGO VELÁZQUEZ (1599–1660). Like many other Spanish artists, he produced religious pictures as well as genre scenes, but his renown in his day rested primarily on the works he painted for his major patron, King Philip IV. Trained in Seville, Velázquez was quite young when he came to the attention of the king, who, struck by the artist's immense talent, appointed him court painter. With the exception of two extended trips to Italy and a few excursions, Velázquez remained in Madrid for the rest of his life. His close relationship with Philip IV and his high office as chamberlain of the palace gave him prestige and a rare opportunity to fulfill the promise of his genius.

An early work, *Water Carrier of Seville* (FIG. 10-15), painted when Velázquez was only about 20, already reveals his impressive command of his craft. Velázquez rendered the figures with clarity and dignity, and his careful depiction of the water jugs in the foreground, complete with droplets

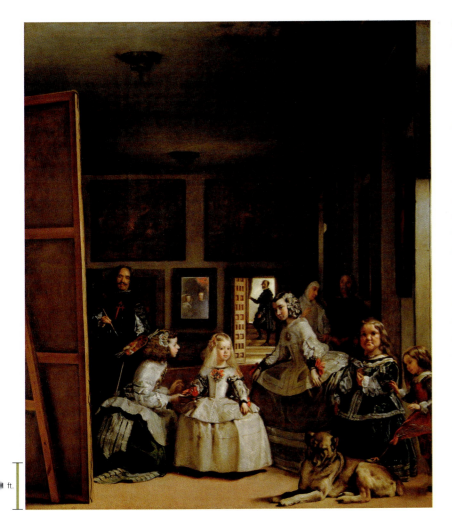

10-16 Diego Velázquez, *Las Meninas (The Maids of Honor)*, 1656. Oil on canvas, 10′ 5″ × 9′. Museo del Prado, Madrid.

Velázquez intended this huge and complex work, with its cunning contrasts of true spaces, mirrored spaces, and picture spaces, to elevate both himself and the profession of painting.

may be painting this very picture—an informal image of the infanta and her entourage. Alternately, Velázquez may be painting a portrait of King Philip IV and Queen Mariana, whose reflections appear in the mirror on the far wall. If so, that would suggest the presence of the king and queen in the viewer's space, outside the confines of the picture. Other scholars have proposed that the mirror image reflects not the physical appearance of the royal couple in Velázquez's studio but the image that he is in the process of painting on the canvas before him. This question has never been definitively resolved.

More generally, *Las Meninas* is Velázquez's attempt to elevate both himself and his profession. As first painter to the king and as chamberlain of the palace, Velázquez was conscious not only of the importance of his court office but also of the honor and dignity belonging to his profession as a painter. Throughout his career, Velázquez hoped to be ennobled by royal appointment to membership in the ancient and illustrious Order of Santiago. Because he lacked a sufficiently noble background, he gained entrance only with difficulty at the very end of his life, and then only through the pope's dispensation. In the painting, he wears the order's red cross on his doublet, painted there, legend says, by the king himself. In all likelihood, the artist painted it. In Velázquez's mind, *Las Meninas* might have embodied the idea of the great king visiting his studio, as Alexander the Great visited the studio of the painter Apelles in ancient Greece. The figures in the painting all appear to acknowledge the royal presence. Placed among them in equal dignity is Velázquez, face-to-face with his sovereign. The location of the completed painting reinforced this act of looking—of seeing and being seen. *Las Meninas* hung in the personal office of Philip IV in another part of the palace. Thus, although occasional visitors admitted to the king's private quarters may have seen this painting, Philip IV was the primary audience. Each time he stood before the canvas, he again participated in the work as the probable subject of the painting within the painting and as the object of the figures' gazes. In *Las Meninas*, Velázquez elevated the art of painting, in the person of the painter, to the highest status. The king's presence enhanced this status—either in person as the viewer of *Las Meninas* or as a reflected image in the painting itself. The paintings that appear in *Las Meninas* further reinforced this celebration of the painter's craft. On the wall above the doorway and

of water, adds to the credibility of the genre scene, which seems to convey a deeper significance. As in Zurbarán's *Saint Serapion* (FIG. **10-14**), the contrast of darks and lights and the plebeian nature of the figures reveal the influence of Caravaggio, whose work Velázquez had studied.

Las Meninas After an extended visit to Rome from 1648 to 1651, Velázquez returned to Spain and painted his greatest masterpiece, *Las Meninas* (*The Maids of Honor;* FIG. **10-16**). The painter represented himself in his studio standing before a large canvas. The young Infanta (Princess) Margarita appears in the foreground with her two maids-in-waiting, her favorite dwarfs, and a large dog. In the middle ground are a woman in widow's attire and a male escort. In the background, a chamberlain stands in a brightly lit open doorway. Scholars have been able to identify everyone in the room, including the two meninas and the dwarfs. The room was the artist's studio in the palace of the Alcázar in Madrid. After the death of Prince Baltasar Carlos in 1646, Philip IV ordered part of the prince's chambers converted into a studio for Velázquez.

Las Meninas is noteworthy for its visual and narrative complexity. Indeed, art historians have yet to agree on any particular reading or interpretation. A central issue has been what, exactly, is taking place in *Las Meninas*. What is Velázquez depicting on the huge canvas in front of him? He mirror, two faintly recognizable pictures have been identified as copies of paintings by Peter Paul Rubens (discussed next). The paintings depict the immortal gods as the source of art. Ultimately, Velázquez sought ennoblement not for himself alone but for his art.

Las Meninas is extraordinarily complex visually. Velázquez's optical report of the event, authentic in every detail, pictorially summarizes the various kinds of images in their different levels and degrees of reality. He portrayed the realities of image on canvas, of mirror image, of optical image, and of the two painted images. This work—with its cunning contrasts of mirrored spaces, "real" spaces, picture spaces, and pictures within pictures—itself appears to have been taken from a large mirror reflecting the whole scene. This would mean that the artist did not paint the princess and her suite as the main subjects of *Las Meninas* but himself in the process of painting them. *Las Meninas* is a pictorial summary and a commentary on the essential mystery of the visual world, as well as on the ambiguity that results when different states or levels interact or are juxtaposed.

Velázquez achieved these results in several ways. The extension of the composition's pictorial depth in both directions is noteworthy. The open doorway and its ascending staircase lead the eye beyond the artist's studio, and the mirror device and the outward glances of several of the figures incorporate the viewer's space into the picture as well. (Compare how the mirror in Jan van Eyck's *Giovanni Arnolfini and His Bride*, FIG. 8-1, similarly incorporates the area in front of the canvas into the picture, although less obviously and without a comparable extension of space beyond the rear wall of the room.) Velázquez also masterfully observed and represented form and shadow. Instead of putting lights abruptly beside darks,

following Caravaggio, Velázquez allowed a great number of intermediate values of gray to come between the two extremes. His matching of tonal gradations approached effects that were only later discovered in the age of photography.

FLANDERS

In the 16th century, the Netherlands had come under the crown of Habsburg Spain when the emperor Charles V retired, leaving the Spanish kingdoms, their Italian and American possessions, and the Netherlandish provinces to his only legitimate son, Philip II (r. 1556–1598). (Charles gave the imperial title and the German lands to his brother.) Philip's repressive measures against the Protestants led the northern provinces to break from Spain and to set up the Dutch Republic. The southern provinces remained under Spanish control, and they retained Catholicism as their official religion. The political distinction between modern Holland and Belgium more or less reflects this original separation, which in the 17th century signaled not only religious but also artistic differences. The Baroque art of Flanders (the Spanish Netherlands) retained close connections to the Baroque art of Catholic Europe, whereas the Dutch schools of painting developed their own subjects and styles.

Peter Paul Rubens   The renowned Flemish master PETER PAUL RUBENS (1577–1640) drew together the main contributions of the Italian Renaissance and Baroque masters to formulate the first truly pan-European painting style. Rubens's art is an original and powerful synthesis of the manners of many painters, especially Michelangelo, Titian, Carracci, and Caravaggio. Rubens's style had wide appeal,

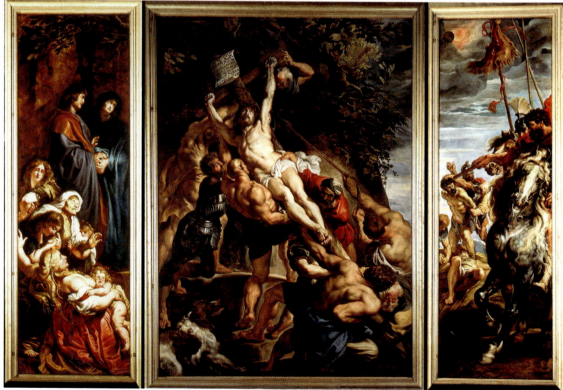

10-17 PETER PAUL RUBENS, *Elevation of the Cross*, from Saint Walburga, Antwerp, 1610. Oil on wood, 15′ 1⅞″ × 11′ 1½″ (center panel), 15′ 1⅞″ × 4′ 11″ (each wing). Antwerp Cathedral, Antwerp.

In this triptych, Rubens explored foreshortened anatomy and violent action. The composition seethes with a power that comes from heroic exertion. The tension is emotional as well as physical.

and his influence was international. Among the most learned individuals of his time, Rubens possessed an aristocratic education and a courtier's manner, diplomacy, and tact, which, with his facility for language, made him the associate of princes and scholars. He became court painter to the dukes of Mantua, friend of King Philip IV of Spain and his adviser on art collecting, painter to Charles I (r. 1625–1649) of England and Marie de' Medici (1573–1642) of France, and permanent court painter to the Spanish governors of Flanders. Rubens also won the confidence of his royal patrons in matters of state, and they often entrusted him with diplomatic missions of the highest importance. In the practice of his art, scores of associates and apprentices assisted Rubens, turning out numerous paintings for an international clientele. In addition, he functioned as an art dealer, buying and selling contemporary artworks and classical antiquities. His many enterprises made him a rich man, with a magnificent town house and a castle in the countryside.

Elevation of the Cross Rubens became a master in 1598 and departed for Italy two years later, where he remained until 1608. During these years, he formulated the foundations of his style. Shortly after returning home, he painted *Elevation of the Cross* (FIG. 10-17) for the church of Saint Walburga in Antwerp. The triptych reveals his careful study of the works of Michelangelo and Caravaggio as well as ancient statuary. In his Latin treatise *De imitatione statuarum (On the Imitation of Statues)*, Rubens stated: "I am convinced that in order to achieve the highest perfection one needs a full understanding of the [ancient] statues, indeed a complete absorption in them; but one must make judicious use of them and before all avoid the effect of stone."[3] The scene brings together tremendous straining forces and counterforces as heavily muscled men labor to lift the cross. Here, as in his *Lion Hunt* (FIG. I-9), Rubens used the subject as an opportunity to show foreshortened anatomy and the contortions of violent action reminiscent of the twisted figures of Michelangelo (FIG. I-12). Rubens placed the body of Christ on the cross as a diagonal that cuts dynamically across the picture while receding into it. The whole composition seethes with a power that comes from genuine exertion, from elastic human sinew taut with effort. The tension is emotional as well as physical, as reflected not only in Christ's face but also in the features of his followers. Strong modeling in dark and light, which heightens the drama, marks Rubens's work at this stage of his career. He later developed a much subtler coloristic style.

Marie de' Medici Rubens's interaction with royalty and aristocrats provided him with an understanding of the ostentation and spectacle of Baroque (particularly Italian) art that appealed to the wealthy and privileged. Rubens, the born courtier, reveled in the pomp and majesty of royalty. Likewise, those in power embraced the lavish spectacle that served the Catholic Church so well in Italy. The magnificence and splendor of Baroque imagery reinforced the authority and right to rule of the highborn. Among Rubens's royal patrons was Marie de' Medici, a member of the famous Floren-

tine house and widow of Henry IV (r. 1589–1610), the first Bourbon king of France. She commissioned Rubens to paint a series memorializing and glorifying her career. Between 1622 and 1626, Rubens, working with amazing creative energy, produced 21 huge historical-allegorical pictures designed to hang in the queen's new palace, the Luxembourg, in Paris.

In *Arrival of Marie de' Medici at Marseilles* (FIG. 10-18), Marie disembarks after her sea voyage from Italy. An allegorical personification of France, draped in a cloak decorated with the royal *fleur-de-lis* (compare FIG. 10-31), welcomes her. The sea and sky rejoice at her safe arrival. Neptune and the Nereids (daughters of the sea god Nereus) salute her, and winged, trumpeting Fame swoops overhead. Conspicuous in the galley's opulently carved stern-castle, under the Medici coat of arms, stands the imperious commander of the vessel, the only immobile figure in the composition. In black and silver, this figure makes a sharp accent amid the swirling tonality of ivory, gold, and red. Rubens enriched the surfaces with a decorative splendor that pulls the whole composition together. The audacious vigor that customarily enlivens the artist's figures, beginning with the monumental, twisting sea creatures, vibrates through the entire design.

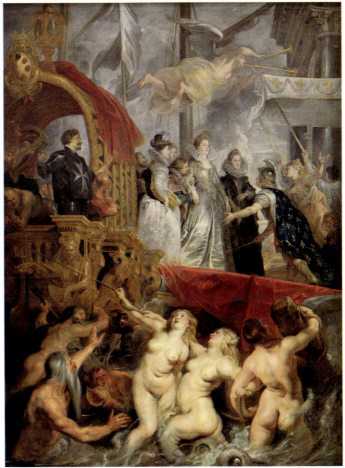

1 ft.

10-18 PETER PAUL RUBENS, *Arrival of Marie de' Medici at Marseilles*, 1622–1625. Oil on canvas, 12' 11½" × 9' 7". Louvre, Paris.

Marie de' Medici asked Rubens to paint 21 large canvases glorifying her career. In this historical-allegorical picture of robust figures in an opulent setting, the sea and sky rejoice at the queen's arrival in France.

Anthony Van Dyck Most of Rubens's successors in Flanders were at one time his assistants. The most famous was ANTHONY VAN DYCK (1599–1641). Early on, the younger man, unwilling to be overshadowed by the master's undisputed stature, left his native Antwerp for Genoa and then London, where he became court portraitist to Charles I. Although Van Dyck created dramatic compositions of high quality, his specialty became the portrait. He developed a courtly manner of great elegance that was influential internationally. In one of his finest works, *Charles I Dismounted* (FIG. 10-19), the ill-fated Stuart king stands in a landscape with the Thames River in the background. An equerry and a page attend him. The portrait is a stylish image of relaxed authority, as if the king is out for a casual ride in his park, but no one can mistake the regal poise and the air of absolute authority that his Parliament resented and was soon to rise against. Here, King Charles turns his back on his attendants as he surveys his domain. The king's placement is exceedingly artful. He stands off-center but balances the picture with a single keen glance at the viewer. Van Dyck even managed to portray the monarch, a man of short stature, in a position to look down on the observer. Van Dyck's elegant style resounded in English portrait painting well into the 19th century.

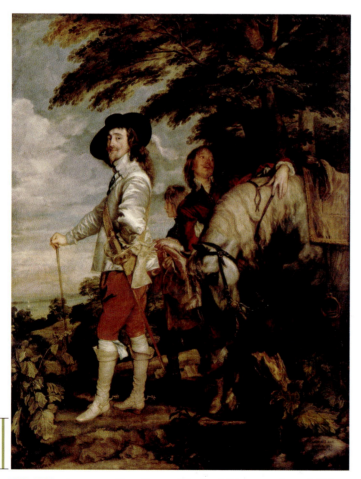

10-19 ANTHONY VAN DYCK, *Charles I Dismounted*, ca. 1635. Oil on canvas, 8' 11" × 6' 11½". Louvre, Paris.

Van Dyck specialized in court portraiture. In this painting, he depicted the absolutist monarch Charles I at a sharp angle so that the king, a short man, appears to be looking down at the viewer.

1 ft.

DUTCH REPUBLIC

The Dutch succeeded in securing their independence from the Spanish in the late 16th century. Not until 1648, however, after years of continual border skirmishes with the Spanish, did the northern Netherlands achieve official recognition as the United Provinces of the Netherlands (the Dutch Republic; MAP 10-1). The country owed its ascendance during the 17th century largely to its economic prosperity. With the founding of the Bank of Amsterdam in 1609, Amsterdam emerged as the financial center of the Continent. The Dutch economy also benefited enormously from the country's expertise on the open seas, which facilitated establishing far-flung colonies. By 1650, Dutch trade routes extended to North and South America, the west coast of Africa, China, Japan, Southeast Asia, and much of the Pacific.

Due to this prosperity and in the absence of an absolute ruler, political power increasingly passed into the hands of an urban class of merchants and manufacturers, especially in cities such as Amsterdam, Haarlem, and Delft. They in turn became the most important sources of art commissions. This shift in patronage and the Calvinist rejection of most religious art produced works emphasizing different pictorial content. Dutch Baroque art centered on genre scenes, landscapes, portraits, and still lifes, often of small scale, in sharp contrast with the Italian Baroque penchant for ostentatious ceiling frescoes depicting religious or mythological themes.

Frans Hals The leading painter in Haarlem was FRANS HALS (ca. 1581–1666), who made portraits his specialty. Portrait artists traditionally had relied heavily on convention—for example, specific poses, settings, and attire—to convey a sense of the sitter. Because the subject was usually someone of status or note, such as a pope, king, duchess, or wealthy banker, the artist's goal was to produce an image appropriate to the subject's station in life. With the increasing numbers of Dutch middle-class patrons, the tasks for Dutch portraitists became more challenging. Not only were the traditional conventions inappropriate and thus unusable, but also the Calvinists shunned ostentation, instead wearing subdued and dark clothing with little variation or decoration. Despite these difficulties, or perhaps because of them, Hals produced lively portraits that seem far more relaxed than traditional formulaic portraiture. He injected an engaging spontaneity into his images and conveyed the individuality of his sitters as well. His manner of execution intensified the casualness, immediacy, and intimacy in his paintings. Because the touch of Hals's brush was as light and fleeting as the momentary pose he captured, so the figure, the highlights on clothing, and the facial expression all seem instantaneously created.

Hals also excelled at group portraits, which multiplied the challenges of depicting a single sitter. *Archers of Saint Hadrian* (FIG. 10-20) depicts the members of one of the many Dutch civic militia groups that claimed credit for liberating the Dutch Republic from Spain. Like other companies,

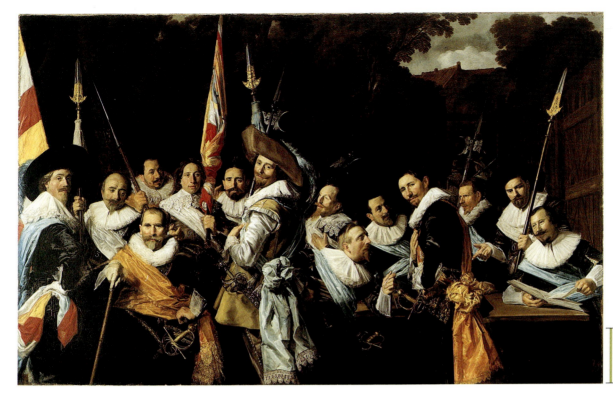

10-20 FRANS HALS, *Archers of Saint Hadrian*, ca. 1633. Oil on canvas, 6′ 9″ × 11′. Frans Halsmuseum, Haarlem.

In this brilliant composition, Hals solved the difficult problem of adequately representing each individual in a group portrait while retaining action and variety in the painting as a whole.

the Archers met on their saint's feast day in dress uniform for a grand banquet. These events often involved a group portrait, giving Hals the opportunity to attack the problem of how to represent each group member adequately yet retain action and variety in the composition. Whereas earlier group portraits in the Netherlands were rather ordered and regimented images, Hals sought to enliven his depictions. In *Archers of Saint Hadrian*, each man is both a troop member and an individual with a distinct physiognomy. The sitters' movements and moods also vary enormously. Some engage the viewer directly. Others look away or at a companion. Whereas one is stern, another is animated. Each man is equally visible and clearly recognizable. The uniformity of attire—black military dress, white ruffs, and sashes—did not deter Hals from injecting spontaneity into the work. Indeed, he used those elements to create a lively rhythm that extends throughout the composition and energizes the portrait. The impromptu effect—the preservation of every detail and fleeting facial expression—is, of course, due to careful planning. Yet Hals's vivacious brush appears to have moved instinctively, directed by a plan in his mind but not traceable in any preparatory scheme on the canvas.

Judith Leyster Some of Hals's students developed thriving careers of their own as portraitists. One was JUDITH LEYSTER (1609–1660), whose *Self-Portrait* (FIG. **10-21**) suggests the strong training she received. The picture is detailed, precise, and accurate but also imbued with a spontaneity found in Hals's works. In this self-portrait, Leyster succeeded at communicating a great deal about herself. She depicted herself as an artist, seated in front of a painting resting on an easel. The palette in her left hand and brush in her right announce that the painting is her creation. She thus allows the viewer to evaluate her skill, which both the

fiddler on the canvas and the image of herself demonstrate as considerable. Although she produced a wide range of paintings, including still lifes and floral pieces, Leyster's specialty

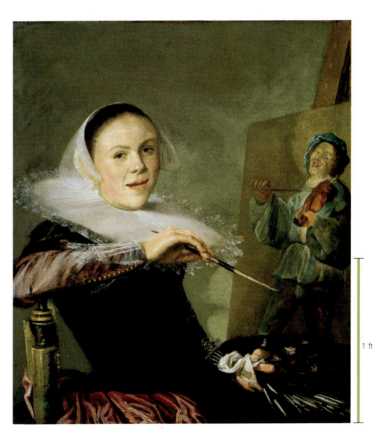

10-21 JUDITH LEYSTER, *Self-Portrait*, ca. 1630. Oil on canvas, 2′ 5 3/8″ × 2′ 1 5/8″. National Gallery of Art, Washington, D.C. (gift of Mr. and Mrs. Robert Woods Bliss).

Although presenting herself as an artist specializing in genre scenes, Leyster wears elegant attire instead of a painter's smock, placing her socially as a member of a well-to-do family.

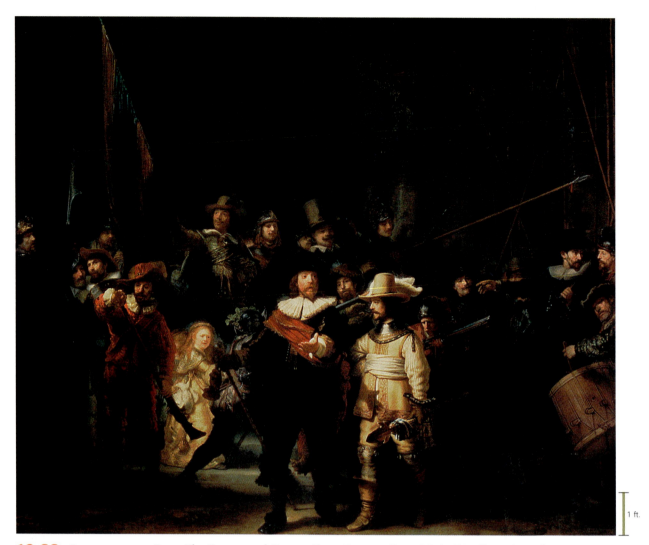

10-22 REMBRANDT VAN RIJN, *The Company of Captain Frans Banning Cocq (Night Watch)*, 1642. Oil on canvas, 11′ 11″ × 14′ 4″ (cropped from original size). Rijksmuseum, Amsterdam.

Rembrandt's dramatic use of light contributes to the animation of this militia group portrait in which the artist showed the members scurrying about as they organize themselves for a parade.

was genre scenes such as the comic image seen on the easel. Her quick smile and relaxed pose reflect her self-assurance as she stops her work to meet the viewer's gaze. Although presenting herself as an artist, Leyster did not depict herself wearing the traditional artist's smock (compare FIG. 10-23). Her elegant attire distinguishes her socially as a member of a well-to-do family, another important aspect of her identity.

Rembrandt van Rijn The premier Dutch artist of the 17th century was REMBRANDT VAN RIJN (1606–1669), who moved from his native Leiden to Amsterdam around 1631 because the larger city promised to provide him with a more extensive clientele. He quickly gained renown for his portraits, which delve deeply into the psyche and personality of his sitters. Like Hals, Rembrandt also produced memorable group portraits. The most famous is *The Company of Captain Frans Banning Cocq* (FIG. 10-22), better known as *Night Watch*. This more commonly used title is a misnomer, however. The nocturnal look of the scene is due more to the varnish the artist used, which darkened considerably

over time, than to the subject depicted. From the limited information available about the commission, it appears that Captain Frans Banning Cocq and his lieutenant Willem van Ruytenburch, along with 16 members of their militia, each contributed to Rembrandt's fee. *Night Watch* was one of six paintings by different artists that various civic groups commissioned around 1640 for the assembly and banquet hall of Amsterdam's new Musketeers Hall. Unfortunately, in 1715, when city officials moved Rembrandt's painting to the town hall, they cropped it on all sides. But even in its truncated form, *Night Watch* succeeds in capturing the excitement and frenetic activity of the men preparing for the parade. A comparison with Hals's *Archers of Saint Hadrian* (FIG. 10-20) reveals Rembrandt's inventiveness in enlivening what was, by then, becoming a conventional portrait format. Rather than present assembled men posed in orderly fashion, the younger artist chose to portray the company scurrying about in the act of organizing themselves, thereby animating the image considerably. At the same time, Rembrandt managed to record the three most important stages of using a musket—

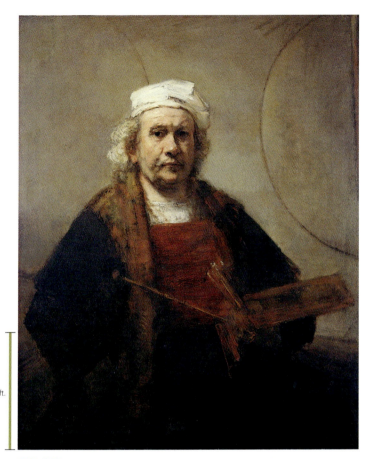

1 ft.

10-23 REMBRANDT VAN RIJN, *Self-Portrait*, ca. 1659–1660. Oil on canvas, 3′ 8¾″ × 3′ 1″. Kenwood House, London (Iveagh Bequest).

In this self-portrait, Rembrandt's interest in revealing the human soul is evident in the attention given to his expressive face. The controlled use of light and the nonspecific setting contribute to this focus.

loading, firing, and readying the weapon for reloading—details that must have pleased his patrons.

Rembrandt's use of light is among the hallmarks of his style. His pictorial method involved refining light and shade into finer and finer nuances until they blended with one another. Earlier painters' use of abrupt lights and darks gave way to gradation in the work of artists such as Rembrandt and Velázquez. Although these later artists may have sacrificed some of the dramatic effects of sharp chiaroscuro, a greater fidelity to true appearances offset those sacrifices. This technique is closer to reality because the eyes perceive light and dark not as static but as always subtly changing. In general, Renaissance artists represented forms and faces in a flat, neutral modeling light (even Leonardo's shading is of a standard kind). They represented the *idea* of light, rather than the real look of it. Artists such as Rembrandt discovered degrees of light and dark, degrees of differences in pose, in the movements of facial features, and in psychic states. They arrived at these differences optically, not conceptually or in terms of some ideal. Rembrandt found that by manipulating the direction, intensity, distance, and surface texture of light and shadow, he could render the most subtle nuances of character and mood, both in persons and

entire scenes. He discovered for the modern world that variation of light and shade, subtly modulated, could be read as emotional differences. In the visible world, light, dark, and the wide spectrum of values between the two are charged with meanings and feelings that sometimes are independent of the shapes and figures they modify. The theater and the photographic arts have used these discoveries to great dramatic effect.

Self-Portrait In his portraits, Rembrandt employed what could be called the "psychology of light." Light and dark are not in conflict. They are reconciled, merging softly and subtly to produce the visual equivalent of quietness. Their prevailing mood is that of tranquil meditation, of philosophical resignation, of musing recollection—indeed, a whole cluster of emotional tones heard only in silence. In a self-portrait (FIG. **10-23**) produced late in Rembrandt's life, the light that shines from the upper left of the painting bathes the artist's face in soft highlights, leaving the lower part of his body in shadow. Rembrandt depicted himself here as possessing dignity and strength, and the portrait serves as a summary of the many stylistic and professional concerns that occupied him throughout his career. Rembrandt's distinctive use of light is evident, as is the assertive brushwork that suggests a quiet confidence and self-assurance. He presented himself as a working artist holding his brushes, palette, and maulstick and wearing his studio garb—a smock and painter's turban. The circles on the wall behind him may allude to a legendary sign of artistic virtuosity—the ability to draw a perfect circle freehand. Ultimately, Rembrandt's abiding interest in revealing the human soul emerged here in his careful focus of the viewer's attention on his expressive visage. His controlled use of light and the nonspecific setting contribute to this focus. Further, X-rays of the painting have revealed that Rembrandt originally depicted himself in the act of painting. His final resolution, with the viewer's attention drawn to his face, produced a portrait not just of the artist but of the man as well.

Hundred-Guilder Print Many artists rapidly took up etching (see "Woodcuts, Engravings, and Etchings," Chapter 8, page 228) early in the 17th century, because etching permitted greater freedom in drawing the design. For etching, the printmaker covers a copper plate with a layer of wax or varnish. The artist incises the design into this surface with a pointed tool, exposing the metal below but not cutting into its surface. The printer then immerses the plate in acid, which etches, or eats away, the exposed parts of the metal, acting the same as the burin in engraving. The medium's softness gives etchers greater carving freedom than woodcutters and engravers have working directly in their more resistant media of wood and metal.

If Rembrandt had never painted, he still would be renowned, as he principally was in his lifetime, for his prints. Prints were a major source of income for him. *Christ with the*

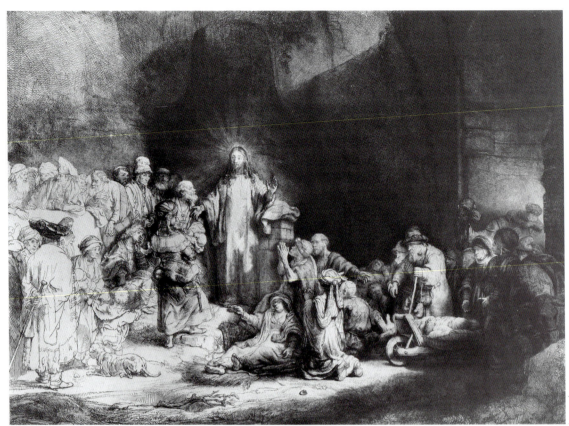

Rembrandt's mastery of the new printmaking medium of etching is evident in his expert use of light and dark to draw attention to Christ as he preaches compassionately to the blind and lame.

Sick around Him, Receiving the Children (FIG. **10-24**) is one of Rembrandt's most celebrated etchings. Indeed, the title by which the print has been known since the early 18th century, *Hundred-Guilder Print*, refers to the high price it brought during Rembrandt's lifetime. The artist suffused this print with a deep and abiding piety, presenting the viewer not the celestial triumph of the Catholic Church but the humanity and humility of Jesus. Christ appears in the center preaching compassionately to, and simultaneously blessing, the blind, the lame, and the young whom Rembrandt spread throughout the composition in a dazzling array of standing, kneeling, and lying positions. Also present is a young man in elegant garments with his head in his hand, lamenting Christ's insistence that the wealthy must give their possessions to the poor in order to gain entrance to Heaven. The tonal range of the print is remarkable. At the right, the figures near the city gate are in deep shadow. At the left, the figures, some rendered almost exclusively in outline, are in bright light—not the light of day but the illumination radiating from Christ himself. A second, unseen source of light comes from the right and casts the shadow of the praying man's arms and head onto Christ's tunic. Technically and in terms of its humanity, the *Hundred-Guilder Print* is Rembrandt's supreme achievement as a printmaker.

Jacob van Ruisdael In addition to portraiture, the Dutch avidly collected landscapes, interior scenes, and still lifes. Each of these painting genres dealt directly with the daily lives of the urban mercantile public, accounting for their appeal. Landscape scenes abound in 17th-century Dutch art. Due to topography and politics, the Dutch had a unique relationship to the terrain, one that differed from those of other European countries. After gaining independence from Spain, the Dutch undertook an extensive land reclamation project that lasted almost a century. Dikes and drainage systems cropped up across the countryside. Because of the effort expended on these endeavors, the Dutch developed a very direct relationship to the land. Most Dutch families owned and worked their own farms.

Jacob van Ruisdael (ca. 1628–1682) became famous for his precise and sensitive depictions of the Dutch landscape. In *View of Haarlem from the Dunes at Overveen* (FIG. **10-25**), van Ruisdael provided an overarching view of this major Dutch city. The specifics of the artist's image—the Saint Bavo church in the background, the numerous windmills that recall the land reclamation efforts, and the figures in the foreground stretching linen to be bleached (a major industry in Haarlem)—reflect the pride Dutch painters took in recording their homeland and the activities of their fellow citizens. Nonetheless, in this painting the inhabitants and dwellings are so minuscule that they blend into the land itself. Further, the horizon line is low, so the sky fills almost three-quarters of the picture space, and the sun illuminates the landscape only in patches, where it has broken through the clouds above. In *View of Haarlem*, van Ruisdael not only captured the appearance of a specific locale but also succeeded in imbuing the work with a quiet serenity that approaches the spiritual.

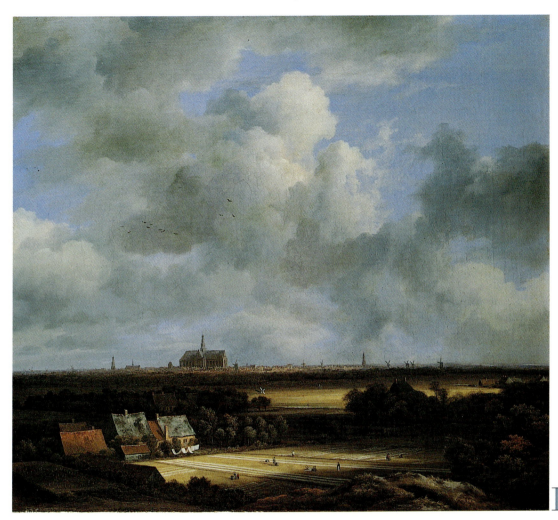

10-25 JACOB VAN RUISDAEL, *View of Haarlem from the Dunes at Overveen*, ca. 1670. Oil on canvas, 1′ 10″ × 2′ 1″. Mauritshuis, The Hague.

In this painting, van Ruisdael succeeded in capturing a specific view of Haarlem, its windmills, and Saint Bavo church, but he also imbued the landscape with a quiet serenity that approaches the spiritual.

1 in.

Jan Vermeer The sense of peace, familiarity, and comfort that Dutch landscape paintings exude also emerges in interior scenes, another popular subject among middle-class patrons. These paintings offer glimpses into the lives of prosperous, responsible, and cultured citizens. The foremost Dutch painter of interior scenes was JAN VERMEER (1632–1675) of Delft. Vermeer earned most of his income as an innkeeper and art dealer, and he produced no more than 35 paintings definitively attributable to him. Earlier Flemish artists, such as Robert Campin (FIG. 8-3), had painted domestic interiors, but sacred personages often occupied those scenes. In contrast, Vermeer and his contemporaries composed neat, quietly opulent interiors of Dutch middle-class dwellings with men, women, and children engaging in household tasks or some small recreation. Women are the primary occupants of Vermeer's homes, and his paintings are highly idealized depictions of the social values of Dutch burghers.

Vermeer was a master of pictorial light and used it with immense virtuosity. He could render space so convincingly through his depiction of light that in his works, the picture surface functions as an invisible glass pane through which the viewer looks into the constructed illusion. Historians are confident that Vermeer used as tools both mirrors and the *camera obscura* (literally, "dark room"), an ancestor of the modern camera based on passing light through a tiny pinhole or lens to project an image on a screen or the wall of a room. (In later versions, artists projected the image on a ground-glass wall of a box whose opposite wall contained the pinhole or lens.) This does not mean that Vermeer merely copied the image. Instead, these aids helped him obtain results he reworked compositionally, placing his figures and the furniture of a room in a beautiful stability of quadrilateral shapes. His designs have a matchless classical serenity. Enhancing this quality are colors so true to the optical facts and so subtly modulated that they suggest Vermeer was far ahead of his time in color science. Close examination of his paintings shows that Vermeer realized shadows are not colorless and dark, that adjoining colors affect each other, and that light is composed of colors. Thus, he painted reflections off of surfaces in colors modified by others nearby. Some experts have suggested Vermeer also perceived the phenomenon modern photographers call "circles of confusion," which appear on out-of-focus negatives. Vermeer could have seen them in images projected by the camera obscura's primitive lenses. He approximated these effects with light dabs that, in close view, give the impression of an image slightly "out of focus." When the observer draws back a step, however, as if adjusting the lens, the color spots cohere, giving an astonishingly accurate illusion of a third dimension.

The Art of Painting Vermeer's stylistic precision and commitment to his profession are evident in *Allegory of the Art of Painting* (FIG. **10-26**). The artist himself appears in the painting, sitting with his back to the viewer and dressed in "historical" clothing (reminiscent of Burgundian attire). He is hard at work on a painting of the model standing before him wearing a laurel wreath and holding a trumpet and book, traditional attributes of Clio, the muse of history. The map of the provinces (an increasingly common wall adornment in Dutch homes) on the back wall serves as yet another reference to history. As in other Vermeer paintings, the viewer is outside the space of the action, looking through the drawn curtain that separates the artist in his studio from the rest of the house—and from the viewer. Some art historians have suggested that the light radiating from an unseen window on the left that illuminates both the model and the canvas being painted alludes to the light of artistic inspiration. Accordingly, many scholars have interpreted this painting as an allegory—a reference to painting inspired by history. Vermeer's mother-in-law confirmed this allegorical reading in 1677 when she sought to retain the painting after the artist's death, when 26 of his works were scheduled to be sold to pay his widow's debts. She listed the painting in her written claim as "the piece . . . wherein the Art of Painting is portrayed."[4]

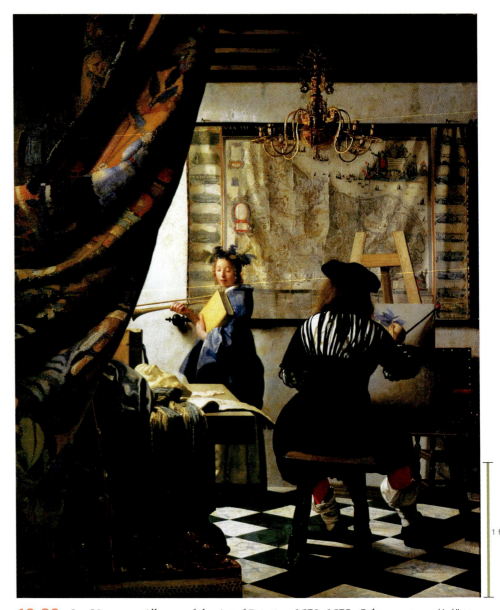

10-26 JAN VERMEER, *Allegory of the Art of Painting*, 1670–1675. Oil on canvas, 4′ 4″ × 3′ 8″. Kunsthistorisches Museum, Vienna.

Vermeer used both mirrors and the camera obscura to depict opulent 17th-century Dutch domestic interiors so convincingly. He was also far ahead of his time in understanding the science of color.

Pieter Claesz The prosperous Dutch were justifiably proud of their accomplishments, and the popularity of still-life paintings—particularly images of accumulated material goods—reflected this pride. These still lifes, like Vermeer's interior scenes, are beautifully crafted images that are both scientific in their optical accuracy and poetic in their beauty and lyricism. Paintings such as *Vanitas Still Life* (FIG. **10-27**) by PIETER CLAESZ (1597–1660) celebrate material possessions, here presented as if strewn across a tabletop or dresser. The ever-present morality and humility central to the Calvinist faith tempered Dutch pride in worldly goods, however. Thus, while Claesz fostered the appreciation and enjoyment of the beauty and value of the objects depicted, he also reminded the viewer of life's transience by incorporating references to death. Paintings with these features are

called *vanitas* (vanity) paintings. Each feature is referred to as a *memento mori*. In *Vanitas Still Life*, references to mortality include the skull, timepiece, tipped glass, and cracked walnut. All suggest the passage of time or a presence that has disappeared. Something or someone was here, and now is gone. Claesz emphasized this element of time (and demonstrated his technical virtuosity) by including a self-portrait, reflected in the glass ball on the left side of the table. He appears to be painting this still life. But in an apparent challenge to the message of inevitable mortality that vanitas paintings convey, the portrait serves to immortalize the subject—in this case, the artist himself.

Rachel Ruysch As living objects that soon die, flowers, particularly cut blossoms, appeared frequently in vanitas

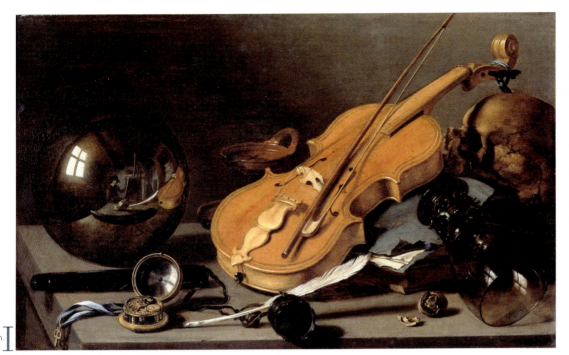

10-27 PIETER CLAESZ, *Vanitas Still Life*, 1630s. Oil on panel, 1′ 2″ × 1′ 11½″. Germanisches Nationalmuseum, Nuremberg.

Vanitas still lifes reflect the pride Dutch citizens had in their material possessions, but Calvinist morality and humility tempered that pride. The skull and timepiece remind the viewer of life's transience.

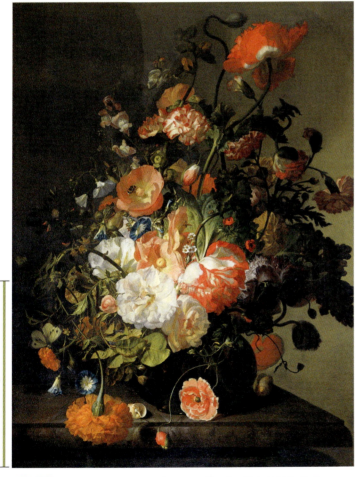

10-28 RACHEL RUYSCH, *Flower Still Life*, after 1700. Oil on canvas, 2′ 5¾″ × 1′ 11⅞″. Toledo Museum of Art, Toledo (purchased with funds from the Libbey Endowment, gift of Edward Drummond Libbey).

Flower paintings were very popular in the Dutch Republic. Ruysch achieved international renown for her lush paintings of floral arrangements, noted also for their careful compositions.

paintings. However, floral painting as a distinct genre also flourished in the Dutch Republic. Among the leading practitioners of this art was RACHEL RUYSCH (1663–1750). Ruysch's father was a professor of botany and anatomy, which may account for her interest in and knowledge of plants and insects. She acquired an international reputation for lush paintings such as *Flower Still Life* (FIG. **10-28**). In this image, the lavish floral arrangement is so full that many of the blossoms seem to be spilling out of the vase. Ruysch carefully constructed her paintings. Here, for example, she positioned the flowers to create a diagonal that runs from the lower left of the painting to the upper right corner and that offsets the opposing diagonal of the table edge.

FRANCE

In France, monarchical authority had been increasing for centuries, culminating in the reign of Louis XIV (r. 1661–1715), who sought to determine the direction of French society and culture. Although its economy was not as expansive as that of the Dutch Republic, France became Europe's largest and most powerful country in the 17th century. Against this backdrop, the arts flourished.

Nicolas Poussin Rome's ancient and Renaissance monuments enticed many French artists to study there. For example, Normandy-born NICOLAS POUSSIN (1594–1665) spent most of his life in Rome, where he produced grandly severe paintings modeled on those of Titian and Raphael. He also carefully worked out a theoretical explanation of his method and was ultimately responsible for establishing classical painting as an important ingredient of 17th-century French art (see "Poussin's Notes for a Treatise on Painting," on page 314). Poussin's classical style presents a striking contrast to the contemporaneous Baroque style of his Italian

Poussin's Notes for a Treatise on Painting

As the leading exponent of classical painting in 17th-century Rome, Nicolas Poussin (FIG. 10-29) outlined the principles of classicism in notes for an intended treatise on painting, left incomplete at his death. In those notes, Poussin described the essential ingredients necessary to produce a beautiful painting in "the grand manner":

> The grand manner consists of four things: subject-matter or theme, thought, structure, and style. The first thing that, as the foundation of all others, is required, is that the subject-matter shall be grand, as are battles, heroic actions, and divine things. But assuming that the subject on which the painter is laboring is grand, his next consideration is to keep away from minutiae . . . [and paint only] things magnificent and grand . . . . Those who elect mean subjects take refuge in them because of the weakness of their talents.*

The idea of beauty does not descend into matter unless this is prepared as carefully as possible. This preparation consists of three things: arrangement, measure, and aspect or form. Arrangement means the relative position of the parts; measure refers to their size; and form consists of lines and colors. Arrangement and relative position of the parts and making every limb of the body hold its natural place are not sufficient unless measure is added, which gives to each limb its correct size, proportionate to that of the whole body [compare Polykleitos's *Canon,* page 67], and unless form joins in, so that the lines will be drawn with grace and with a harmonious juxtaposition of light and shadow.†

* Translated by Robert Goldwater and Marco Treves, eds., *Artists on Art,* 3d ed. (New York: Pantheon Books, 1958), 155.
† Ibid., 156.

10-29 NICOLAS POUSSIN, *Et in Arcadia Ego,* ca. 1655. Oil on canvas, 2′ 10″ × 4′. Louvre, Paris.

Poussin was the leading proponent of classicism in Baroque Rome. His works incorporate the rational order and stability of Raphael's compositions as well as figures inspired by ancient statuary.

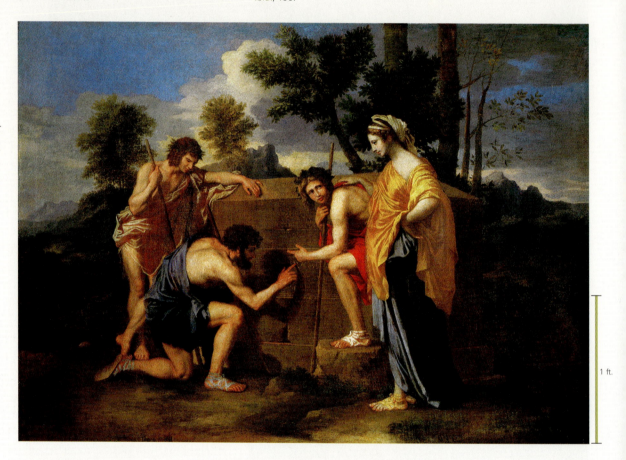

1 ft.

counterparts in Rome, underscoring the multifaceted character of the art of 17th-century Europe.

Poussin's *Et in Arcadia Ego (Even in Arcadia, I [am present];* FIG. 10-29) draws on the rational order and stability of Raphael's paintings and on antique statuary. Landscape, of which Poussin became increasingly fond, provides the setting for the picture. Dominating the foreground, however, are three shepherds, living in the idyllic land of Arcadia, who study an inscription on a tomb as a statuesque female figure quietly places her hand on the shoulder of one of them. She may be the spirit of death, reminding these mortals, as does the inscription, that death is found even in Arcadia, supposedly a spot of paradisiacal bliss. The countless draped female statues surviving in Italy from Roman times supplied the models for this figure, and the posture of the youth with one foot resting on a boulder derives from Greco-Roman statues of Neptune, the sea god, leaning on his trident. The classically compact, balanced grouping of the figures, the even light, and the thoughtful and reserved mood complement Poussin's classical figure types.

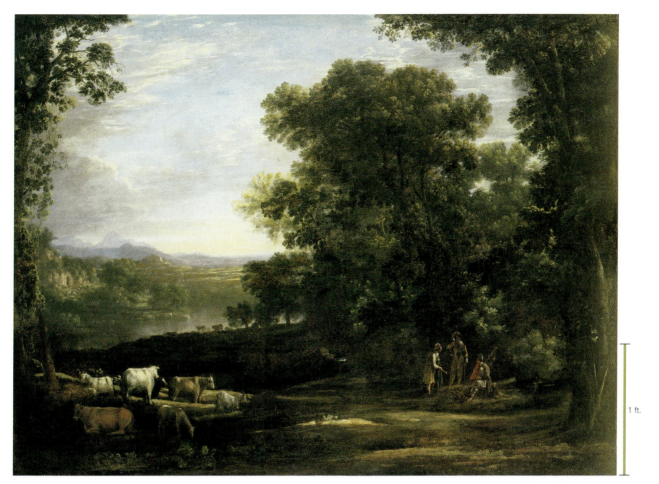

10-30 CLAUDE LORRAIN, *Landscape with Cattle and Peasants*, 1629. Oil on canvas, 3′ 6″ × 4′ 10½″. Philadelphia Museum of Art, Philadelphia (George W. Elkins Collection).

Claude used atmospheric and linear perspective to transform the rustic Roman countryside filled with peasants and animals into an ideal classical landscape bathed in sunlight in infinite space.

Claude Lorrain Claude Gellée, called CLAUDE LORRAIN (1600–1682) after his birthplace in the duchy of Lorraine, rivaled Poussin in fame. Claude modulated in a softer style the disciplined rational art of Poussin. Unlike the figures in Poussin's pictures, those in Claude's landscapes tell no dramatic story, point out no moral, and praise no hero. Indeed, his figures often appear to be added as mere excuses for the radiant landscape itself. For Claude, painting involved essentially one theme—the beauty of a broad sky suffused with the golden light of dawn or sunset glowing through a hazy atmosphere and reflecting brilliantly off the rippling water.

In *Landscape with Cattle and Peasants* (FIG. **10-30**), the figures in the right foreground chat in animated fashion. In the left foreground, cattle relax contentedly. In the middle ground, cattle amble slowly away. The well-defined foreground, distinct middle ground, and dim background recede in serene orderliness, until all form dissolves in a luminous mist. Atmospheric and linear perspective reinforce each other to turn a vista into a typical Claudian vision, an ideal classical world bathed in sunlight in infinite space. Claude's formalizing of nature with balanced groups of architectural masses, screens of trees, and sheets of water followed the

great tradition of classical landscape. It began with the backgrounds of Venetian painting (FIG. 9-18) and continued in the art of Poussin (FIG. 10-29). Yet Claude, like the Dutch painters, studied the light and the atmospheric nuances of nature, making a unique contribution. He recorded carefully in hundreds of sketches the look of the Roman countryside, its gentle terrain accented by stone-pines, cypresses, and poplars and by ever-present ruins of ancient aqueducts, tombs, and towers. He made these the fundamental elements of his compositions.

The artist achieved his marvelous effects of light by painstakingly placing tiny value gradations, which imitated, though on a very small scale, the true range of values of outdoor light and shade. Avoiding the problem of high-noon sunlight overhead, Claude preferred, and convincingly represented, the sun's rays as they gradually illuminated the morning sky or, with their dying glow, set the pensive mood of evening. Thus, he matched the moods of nature with those of human subjects. Claude's infusion of nature with human feeling and his recomposition of nature in a calm equilibrium greatly appealed to the landscape painters of the 18th and early 19th centuries.

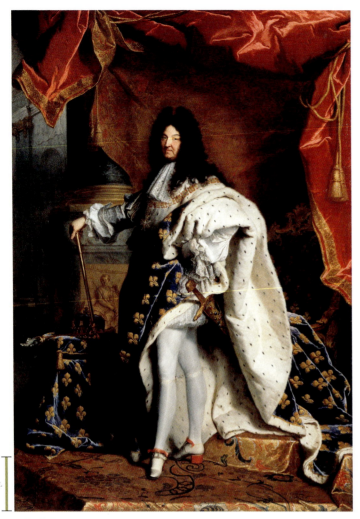

10-31 HYACINTHE RIGAUD, *Louis XIV*, 1701. Oil on canvas, 9′ 2″ × 6′ 3″. Louvre, Paris.

In this portrait set against a stately backdrop, Rigaud portrayed the 5′ 4″ Sun King wearing red high-heeled shoes and with his ermine-lined coronation robes thrown over his left shoulder.

Louis XIV The preeminent French art patron of the 17th century was King Louis XIV. Determined to consolidate and expand his power, Louis was a master of political strategy and propaganda. He established a carefully crafted and nuanced relationship with the nobility, granting them sufficient benefits to keep them pacified but simultaneously maintaining rigorous control to forestall insurrection or rebellion. He also ensured subservience by anchoring his rule in divine right (belief in a king's absolute power as being God's will). So convinced was Louis of his importance and centrality to the French kingdom that he eagerly adopted the title "the Sun King." Like the sun, Louis was the center of the universe, and his desire for control extended to all realms of French life, including art. The king and his principal adviser, Jean-Baptiste Colbert (1619–1683), strove to organize art and architecture in the service of the state. They understood well the power of art as propaganda and the value of visual imagery for cultivating a public persona, and they spared no pains to raise great symbols and monuments to the king's absolute power. Louis and Colbert sought to regularize taste and establish the classical style as the preferred French manner. The founding of the Royal Academy of Painting and Sculpture in 1648 served to advance this goal.

The portrait of Louis XIV (FIG. **10-31**) by HYACINTHE RIGAUD (1659–1743) successfully conveys the image of an absolute monarch. The king, age 63 when Rigaud painted this work, looks out at the viewer with directness. He stands with his left hand on his hip and with his elegant ermine-lined, fleur-de-lis coronation robes (compare FIG. **10-18**) thrown over his shoulder, suggesting an air of haughtiness. Louis also draws back his garment to expose his legs. (The king was a ballet dancer in his youth and was proud of his well-toned legs.) The portrait's majesty derives in large part from the composition. The Sun King is the unmistakable focal point of the image, and Rigaud placed him so that he seems to look down on the viewer. Given that Louis XIV was only 5′ 4″ tall—a fact that drove him to invent the high-heeled shoes he wears in the portrait—the artist apparently catered to his patron's wishes. The carefully detailed environment in which the king stands also contributes to the painting's stateliness and grandiosity. Indeed, when the king was not present, Rigaud's portrait, which hung over the throne, served in his place, and courtiers were not permitted to turn their backs on the painting.

Versailles Louis XIV was also a builder on a grand scale. One of his projects was to convert a royal hunting lodge at Versailles, a few miles outside Paris, into a great palace. He assembled a veritable army of architects, decorators, sculptors, painters, and landscape architects under the general management of CHARLES LE BRUN (1619–1690). In their hands, the conversion of a simple lodge into the palace of Versailles (FIG. **10-32**) became the greatest architectural project of the age—a defining statement of French Baroque style and an undeniable symbol of Louis XIV's power and ambition. Planned on a gigantic scale, the project called not only for a large palace flanking a vast park but also for the construction of a satellite city to house court and government officials, military and guard detachments, courtiers, and servants (undoubtedly to keep them all under the king's close supervision). Le Brun laid out this town to the east of the palace along three radial avenues that converge on the palace structure. Their axes, in a symbolic assertion of the ruler's absolute power over his domains, intersected in the king's spacious bedroom, which also served as an official audience chamber. The palace itself, more than a quarter mile long, is perpendicular to the dominant east-west axis that runs through the associated city and park.

Every detail of the extremely rich decoration of the palace's interior received careful attention. The architects and decorators designed everything from wall paintings to doorknobs in order to reinforce the splendor of Versailles and to exhibit the very finest sense of artisanship. Of the literally hundreds of rooms within the palace, the most famous is the Galerie des Glaces, or Hall of Mirrors (FIG. **10-33**), designed by JULES HARDOUIN-MANSART (1646–1708) and

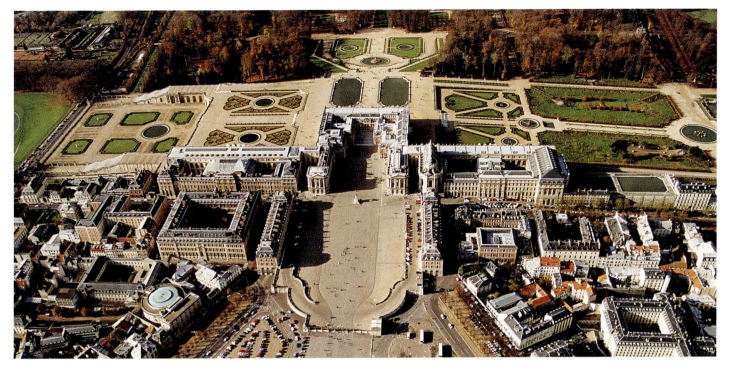

10-32 JULES HARDOUIN-MANSART, CHARLES LE BRUN, and ANDRÉ LE NÔTRE, aerial view (looking west) of the palace and gardens, Versailles, France, begun 1669.

Louis XIV ordered his architects to convert a royal hunting lodge at Versailles into a gigantic palace and park with a satellite city whose three radial avenues intersect in the king's bedroom.

Le Brun. This hall overlooks the park from the second floor and extends along most of the width of the central block. Although deprived of its original sumptuous furniture, which included gold and silver chairs and bejeweled trees, the Galerie des Glaces retains much of its splendor today. Hundreds of mirrors, set into the wall opposite the windows, alleviate the hall's tunnel-like quality and illusionistically extend the width of the room. The mirror, that ultimate source of illusion, was a favorite element of Baroque interior design. Here, it also enhanced the dazzling extravagance of the great festivals Louis XIV was so fond of hosting.

The enormous palace might appear unbearably ostentatious were it not for its extraordinary setting in the vast park that makes it almost an adjunct. From the Galerie des Glaces, the king and his guests could gaze out on a sweeping vista down the park's tree-lined central axis and across terraces,

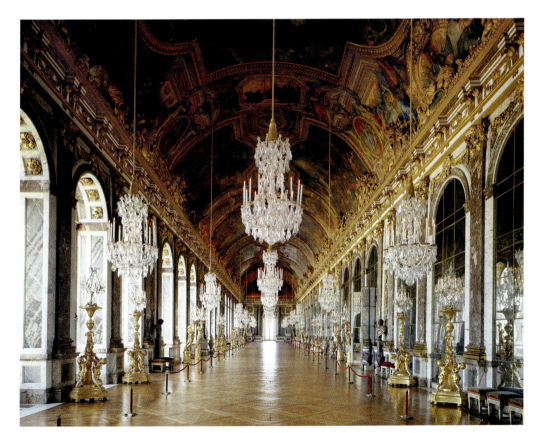

10-33 JULES HARDOUIN-MANSART and CHARLES LE BRUN, Galerie des Glaces (Hall of Mirrors), palace of Versailles, Versailles, France, ca. 1680.

This hall overlooks the Versailles park from the second floor of Louis XIV's palace. Hundreds of mirrors illusionistically extend the room's width and once reflected gilded and jeweled furnishings.

lawns, pools, and lakes toward the horizon. The park of Versailles, designed by ANDRÉ LE NÔTRE (1613–1700), must rank among the world's greatest artworks in both size and concept. Here, the French architect transformed an entire forest into a park. Although the geometric plan may appear stiff and formal, the park in fact offers an almost unlimited assortment of vistas, as Le Nôtre used not only the multiplicity of natural forms but also the terrain's slightly rolling contours with stunning effectiveness.

The formal gardens near the palace provide a rational transition from the frozen architectural forms to the natural living ones. Here, the elegant forms of trimmed shrubs and hedges define the tightly designed geometric units. Each unit is different from its neighbor and has a focal point in the form of a sculptured group, a pavilion, a reflecting pool, or a fountain. Farther away from the palace, the design loosens as trees, in shadowy masses, screen or frame views of open countryside. Le Nôtre carefully composed all vistas for maximum effect. Light and shadow, formal and informal, dense growth and open meadows—all play against one another in unending combinations and variations. No photograph or series of photographs can reveal the design's full richness. The park unfolds itself only to people who actually walk through it.

ENGLAND

In England, in sharp distinction to France, the common law and the Parliament kept royal power in check. England also differed from France (and Europe in general) in other significant ways. Although an important part of English life, religion was not the contentious issue it was on the Continent. The religious affiliations of the English included Catholicism, Anglicanism, Protestantism, and Puritanism (the English version of Calvinism). In the economic realm, England was the one country (other than the Dutch Republic) to take advantage of the opportunities offered by overseas trade. England, like the Dutch Republic, possessed a large and powerful navy as well as excellent maritime capabilities. In the realm of art, the most important English contributions were in the field of architecture, much of it, as in France, incorporating classical elements.

Christopher Wren London's majestic Saint Paul's Cathedral (FIG. **10-34**) is the work of England's most renowned architect, CHRISTOPHER WREN (1632–1723). A mathematical genius and skilled engineer whose work won Isaac Newton's praise, Wren became professor of astronomy in London at age 25. Mathematics led to architecture, and Charles II (r. 1660–1685) asked Wren to prepare a plan for restoring the old Gothic church of Saint Paul. Wren proposed to remodel the building based on Roman structures. Within a few months, the Great Fire of London, which destroyed the old structure and many churches in the city in 1666, gave Wren his opportunity. Wren had traveled through France, where the splendid palaces and state buildings being created in and around Paris must have impressed him. He also closely studied prints illustrating Baroque architecture in

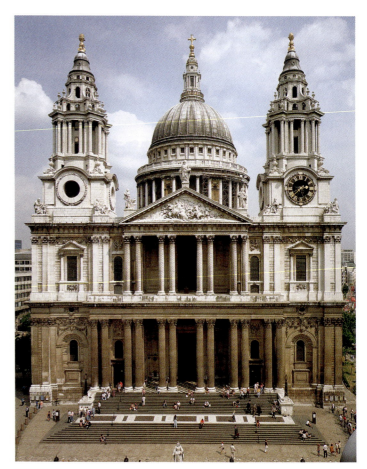

10-34 SIR CHRISTOPHER WREN, new Saint Paul's Cathedral, London, England, 1675–1710.

Wren's cathedral replaced an old Gothic church. The facade design owes much to the Italian architects Palladio and Borromini. The dome recalls that of Saint Peter's in Rome (FIGS. **10-2** and **10-3**).

Italy. In Saint Paul's, he harmonized Palladian, French, and Italian Baroque features.

For its size, the cathedral was built with remarkable speed—in little more than 30 years—and Wren lived to see it completed. The building's form underwent constant refinement during construction, and Wren did not determine the final appearance of the towers until after 1700. In the striking skyline composition, two foreground towers act effectively as foils to the great dome. Wren must have known similar schemes that Italian architects devised for Saint Peter's (FIGS. **10-2** and **10-3**) in Rome to solve the problem of the relationship between the facade and dome. Certainly the influence of Borromini (FIG. **10-7**) appears in the upper levels and lanterns of the towers and that of Palladio in the lower levels. Further, the superposed paired columnar porticos have parallels in contemporaneous French architecture. Wren's skillful eclecticism integrated all these foreign features into a monumental unity.

Wren designed many other London churches after the Great Fire. Even today, his towers and domes punctuate the skyline of that great city, with Saint Paul's dome the tallest of all. Wren's legacy was significant and long-lasting, in both England and colonial America (see Chapter 11).

Europe, 1600 to 1700

ITALY AND SPAIN

- In contrast to the precision and orderly rationality of Renaissance classicism, Italian Baroque art is dynamic, theatrical, and ornate. In architecture, Francesco Borromini emphasized the sculptural qualities of buildings. The facades of his churches are not flat frontispieces but undulating surfaces that provide a fluid transition from exterior to interior space. The interiors of his buildings pulsate with energy and feature complex domes that grow organically from curving walls.

- The greatest Italian Baroque sculptor was Gianlorenzo Bernini, who was also an important architect. In *Ecstasy of Saint Teresa,* he marshaled the full capabilities of architecture, sculpture, and painting to create an intensely emotional experience for worshipers, consistent with the Counter-Reformation principle of using artworks to inspire devotion and piety.

- In painting, Caravaggio broke new ground by employing stark and dramatic contrasts of light and dark (tenebrism) and by setting religious scenes in everyday locales filled with rough-looking common people.

- The greatest Spanish Baroque painter was Diego Velázquez, court painter to Philip IV (r. 1621–1665). His masterwork, *Las Meninas,* is a celebration of the art of painting. It mixes true spaces, mirrored spaces, picture spaces, and pictures within pictures.

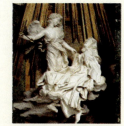

Bernini, *Ecstasy of Saint Teresa,* 1645–1652

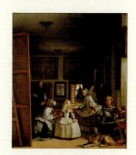

Velázquez, *Las Meninas,* 1656

FLANDERS AND THE DUTCH REPUBLIC

- In the 17th century, Flanders remained Catholic and under Spanish control. Flemish Baroque art is closely tied to the Baroque art of Italy. The leading Flemish painter of this era was Peter Paul Rubens. His paintings of the career of Marie de' Medici exhibit Baroque splendor in color and ornament, and feature Rubens's characteristic robust and foreshortened figures in swirling motion.

- The Dutch Republic received official recognition of its independence from Spain in the Treaty of Westphalia of 1648. Worldwide trade and banking brought prosperity to its predominantly Protestant citizenry, which largely rejected church art in favor of private commissions of portraits, genre scenes, landscapes, and still lifes.

- Rembrandt van Rijn, the greatest Dutch artist of the age, treated a broad range of subjects, including religious themes and portraits. His oil paintings are notable for their dramatic impact and subtle gradations of light and shade as well as the artist's ability to convey human emotions. Rembrandt was also a master printmaker renowned for his etchings.

- Frans Hals produced innovative portraits of middle-class patrons in which a lively informality replaced the formulaic patterns of traditional portraiture. Jacob van Ruisdael specialized in landscapes depicting specific places, not idealized Renaissance settings. Peter Claesz painted vanitas still lifes featuring meticulous depictions of worldly goods and reminders of death. Jan Vermeer specialized in painting Dutch families in serenely opulent homes. Vermeer's convincing representation of interior spaces depended in part on his use of the camera obscura.

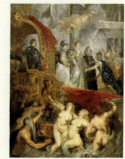

Rubens, *Arrival of Marie de' Medici,* 1622–1625

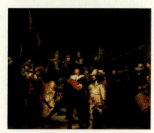

Rembrandt, *Night Watch,* 1642

FRANCE AND ENGLAND

- The major art patron in 17th-century France was the "Sun King," Louis XIV, who built a gigantic palace-and-garden complex at Versailles featuring sumptuous furnishings and sweeping vistas. Among the architects Louis employed were Charles Le Brun and Jules Hardouin-Mansart, who succeeded in marrying Italian Baroque and French classical styles. The leading French proponent of classical painting was Nicolas Poussin, who spent most of his life in Rome and championed the "grand manner" of painting, which called for heroic or divine subjects and classical compositions with figures often modeled on ancient statues.

- In England, architecture was the most important art form. Christopher Wren harmonized the architectural principles of Palladio with the Italian Baroque and French classical styles.

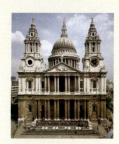

Wren, new Saint Paul's, London, 1675–1710

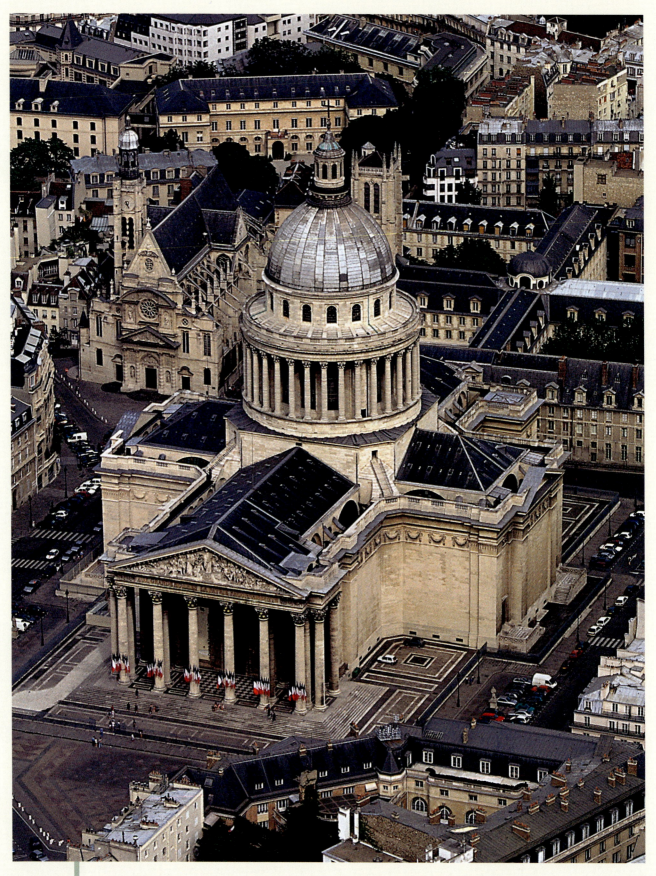

11-1 JACQUES-GERMAIN SOUFFLOT, Panthéon (Sainte-Geneviève), Paris, France, 1755–1792.

The Enlightenment revived interest in the art and culture of ancient Greece and Rome. Soufflot's Panthéon combines a portico based on an ancient Roman temple with a colonnaded dome and a Greek-cross plan.

Europe and America, 1700 to 1800

In 1700, Louis XIV still ruled as the Sun King of France, presiding over his realm and French culture from his palatial residence at Versailles (FIG. 10-32). By 1800 revolutions had overthrown the monarchy in France and achieved independence for the British colonies in America. The 18th century also gave birth to a revolution of a different kind—the Industrial Revolution, which began in England and soon transformed the economies of continental Europe and North America. Against this backdrop of revolutionary change came major transformations in the arts.

ROCOCO

The death of Louis XIV in 1715 had important repercussions in French high society. The grandiose palace-based culture of Baroque France gave way to a much more intimate and decentralized culture based in the elegant town houses of Paris. These private homes became the centers of a new style called *Rococo*, which was primarily a style of interior design. The term derived from the French word *rocaille* (literally, "pebble"), but it referred especially to the small stones and shells used to decorate grotto interiors. Shells or shell forms were the principal motifs in Rococo ornament.

In the early 18th century, Paris was the social capital of Europe, and the Rococo salon was the center of Parisian society. Wealthy, ambitious, and clever society hostesses competed to attract the most famous and the most accomplished people to their salons. The medium of social intercourse was conversation spiced with wit, repartee as quick and deft as a fencing match. Artifice reigned supreme, and participants considered enthusiasm or sincerity in bad taste. French Rococo salons were complete works of art with guests surrounded by elegant furniture, enchanting small sculptures, ornamented mirror frames, delightful ceramics and silver, and decorative tapestry complementing the architecture, relief sculptures, and wall paintings.

Amalienburg One of the finest examples of French Rococo interior design is, ironically, not in Paris but in Germany. The Amalienburg is a small lodge the French architect FRANÇOIS DE CUVILLIÉS (1695–1768) built in the park of the Nymphenburg Palace in Munich. The most spectacular room in the lodge is the circular Hall of Mirrors (FIG. 11-2), a silver-and-blue ensemble of architecture, stucco relief, silvered bronze mirrors, and crystal. The hall dazzles the eye with myriad scintillating motifs, forms, and figurations and represents the Rococo style

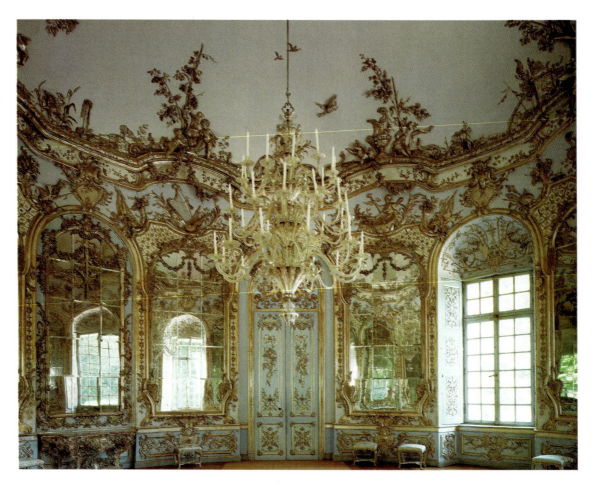

11-2

Françs de Cuvilliés, Hall of Mirrors, the Amalienburg, Nymphenburg Palace park, Munich, Germany, early 18th century.

Designed by a French architect, this circular hall in a German lodge displays the Rococo architectural style at its zenith, dazzling the eye with the organic interplay of mirrors, crystal, and stucco relief.

at its zenith. Silvery light, reflected and multiplied by windows and mirrors, bathes the room and creates shapes and contours that weave rhythmically around the upper walls and the ceiling coves. Everything seems organic, growing, and in motion, an ultimate refinement of illusion that the architect, artists, and artisans, all magically in command of their varied media, created with virtuoso flourishes.

Antoine Watteau The painter most closely associated with French Rococo is ANTOINE WATTEAU (1684–1721). He was largely responsible for creating a specific type of Rococo painting, called a *fête galante* (French, "amorous festival") painting. These works depicted the outdoor amusements of French high society. Watteau's masterpiece, *Pilgrimage to Cythera* (FIG. **11-3**), is probably the most famous fête galante picture. It was the artist's entry for admission to the French Royal Academy of Painting and Sculpture. In 1717 the fête galante was not an acceptable category for submission, but rather than reject Watteau's candidacy, the academy created a new category to accommodate his entry.

At the turn of the century, two competing doctrines sharply divided the membership of the French academy. Many members followed Nicolas Poussin (FIG. **10-29**) in teaching that form was the essential element in painting, whereas colors served only a decorative purpose: "Colors in painting are as allurements for persuading the eyes," Poussin argued.[1] The other group took Peter Paul Rubens (FIGS. **10-17** and **10-18**) as its model and proclaimed the supremacy of color. Depend-

ing on which doctrine they supported, academy members were either *Poussinistes* or *Rubénistes*. Watteau was Flemish, and Rubens's coloristic style heavily influenced his work. With Watteau in their ranks, the Rubénistes carried the day, establishing Rococo as the preferred style of the early 18th century.

Pilgrimage to Cythera portrays luxuriously costumed lovers who have made a "pilgrimage" to Cythera, the island of eternal youth and love, sacred to Aphrodite. The elegant figures move gracefully from the protective shade of a woodland park filled with amorous cupids and voluptuous statuary. Watteau's figural poses blend sophistication and sweetness. He composed his generally quite small paintings from albums of superb drawings in which he sought to capture slow movement from difficult and unusual angles, searching for the smoothest, most poised, and most refined attitudes. Watteau also strove for the most exquisite shades of color, defining in a single stroke the shimmer of silk at a bent knee or the iridescence that touches a glossy surface as it emerges from shadow. The haze of color, the subtly modeled shapes, the gliding motion, and the air of suave gentility appealed greatly to the Rococo artist's wealthy patrons.

Jean-Honoré Fragonard Watteau died when he was only 37 years old, but JEAN-HONORÉ FRAGONARD (1732–1806) and others carried on the Rococo painting manner Watteau pioneered. In *The Swing* (FIG. **11-4**), a young gentleman has managed an arrangement whereby an unsuspecting old

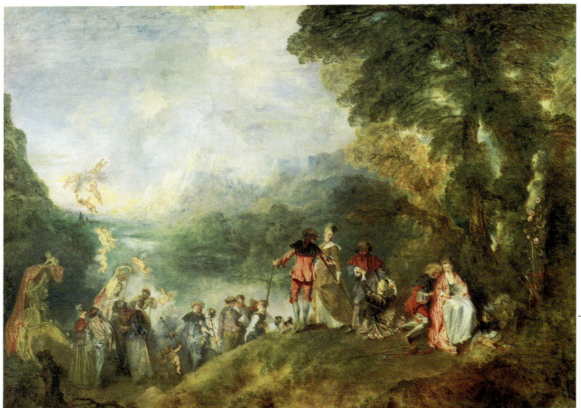

11-3 ANTOINE WATTEAU, *Pilgrimage to Cythera*, 1717. Oil on canvas, 4′ 3″ × 6′ 4½″. Louvre, Paris.

Watteau's fête galante paintings depict the outdoor amusements of French high society. The haze of color, subtly modeled shapes, gliding motion, and air of suave gentility match Rococo taste.

1 ft.

bishop swings the young man's pretty sweetheart higher and higher, while her lover (and the work's patron), in the lower left-hand corner, stretches out to admire her ardently from a strategic position on the ground. The young lady flirtatiously and boldly kicks off her shoe toward the little statue of Cupid. The infant love god holds his finger to his lips. The landscape setting is out of Watteau—a luxuriant perfumed bower in a park that very much resembles a stage scene for comic opera. The glowing pastel colors and soft light convey, almost by themselves, the theme's sensuality.

Clodion *The Swing* is a small painting. Indeed, Rococo was a style best suited for small-scale works that projected a mood of sensual intimacy in elegant salons. Many 18th-century artists, including Claude Michel, called CLODION (1738–1814), specialized in small sculptures representing sensuous Rococo fantasies. *Satyr Crowning*

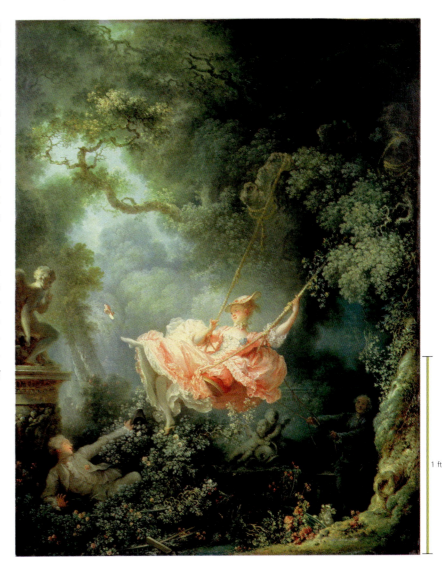

11-4 JEAN-HONORÉ FRAGONARD, *The Swing*, 1766. Oil on canvas, 2′ 8⅝″ × 2′ 2″. Wallace Collection, London.

In this painting epitomizing Rococo style, pastel colors and soft light complement a sensuous scene in which a young lady flirtatiously kicks off her shoe at a statue of Cupid while her lover watches.

1 ft.

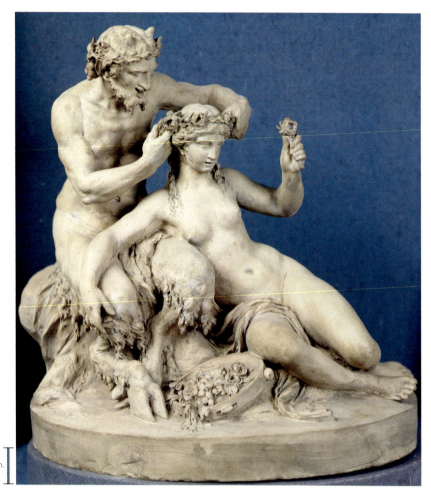

11-5 CLODION, *Satyr Crowning a Bacchante*, 1770. Terracotta, 1′ $\frac{5}{8}$″ high. Louvre, Paris.

The erotic playfulness of Fragonard's paintings is evident in Clodion's tabletop terracotta sculptures representing sensuous fantasies often involving satyrs and bacchantes, the followers of Bacchus.

a Bacchante (FIG. **11-5**) is a characteristic example of Clodion's work. It depicts two mythological followers of Bacchus, the Roman god of wine. The erotic playfulness of the sculptor's semihuman satyr and languorous bacchante typifies the Rococo spirit. In this group, Clodion captured the sensual exhilaration of the Rococo style in diminutive scale and inexpensive terracotta. As is true of so many Rococo artifacts, the artist designed this group for a tabletop.

THE ENLIGHTENMENT

A major factor in the political, social, and economic changes that led to revolution at the end of the 18th century was the *Enlightenment*. The Enlightenment was a new way of thinking critically about the world and about humankind, independently of religion, myth, or tradition. The basis of Enlightenment thought was empirical evidence. Enlightenment thinkers promoted the scientific questioning of all assertions and rejected unfounded beliefs about the nature of humankind and of the world.

This new approach to the acquisition of knowledge had its roots in the 17th century with the mathematical and scientific achievements of René Descartes (1596–1650), Blaise Pascal (1623–1662), Isaac Newton (1642–1727), and Gottfried Wilhelm von Leibnitz (1646–1716). England and France were the principal centers of the Enlightenment, though its dictums influenced the thinking of intellectuals throughout Europe and in the American colonies. Benjamin Franklin (1706–1790), Thomas Jefferson (1743–1826), and other American notables embraced its principles.

Newton and Locke Of particular importance for Enlightenment thought was the work of Great Britain's Isaac Newton (1642–1727) and John Locke (1632–1704). In his scientific studies, Newton insisted on empirical proof of his theories and encouraged others to avoid metaphysics and the supernatural—realms that extended beyond the natural physical world. This emphasis on both tangible data and concrete experience became a cornerstone of Enlightenment thought. John Locke, whose works acquired the status of Enlightenment gospel, developed these ideas further. According to Locke's "doctrine of empiricism," knowledge comes to people through their sense perception of the material world. From these perceptions alone people form ideas. Locke asserted that human beings are born good, not cursed by Original Sin. The laws of Nature grant them the natural rights of life, liberty, and property as well as the right to freedom of conscience. Government is by contract, and its purpose is to protect these rights. If and when government abuses these rights, the citizenry has the further natural right of revolution.

Philosophes The work of Newton and Locke also inspired many French intellectuals, or *philosophes*. These thinkers conceived of individuals and societies at large as parts of physical nature. They shared the conviction that the ills of humanity could be remedied by applying reason and common sense to human problems. They criticized the powers of church and state as irrational limits placed on political and intellectual freedom. They believed that by the accumulation and propagation of knowledge, humanity could advance by degrees to a happier state than it had ever known. This conviction matured into the "doctrine of progress" and its corollary doctrine of the "perfectibility of humankind."

Animated by their belief in human progress and perfectibility, the philosophes took on the task of gathering knowledge and making it accessible to all who could read. Their program was, in effect, the democratization of knowledge. Denis Diderot (1713–1784) became editor of the groundbreaking 35-volume *Encyclopédie*, a compilation of illustrated

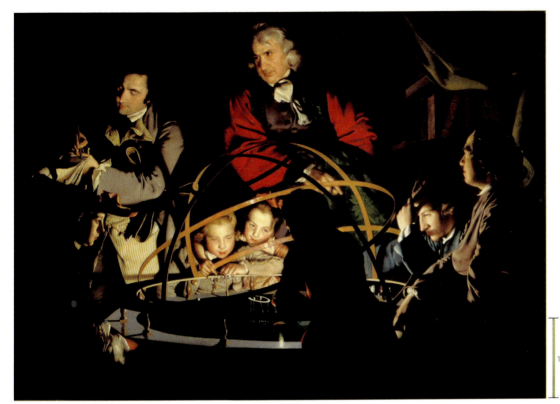

11-6 JOSEPH WRIGHT OF DERBY, *A Philosopher Giving a Lecture at the Orrery (in which a lamp is put in place of the sun)*, ca. 1763–1765. Oil on canvas, 4′ 10″ × 6′ 8″. Derby Museums and Art Gallery, Derby.

Wright's commemoration of recent inventions was in tune with the Enlightenment doctrine of progress. In this dramatically lit scene, the wonders of scientific knowledge mesmerize everyone.

1 ft.

articles written by more than a hundred contributors, including all the leading philosophes. The *Encyclopédie* was truly comprehensive (its formal title was *Systematic Dictionary of the Sciences, Arts, and Crafts*) and included all available knowledge—historical, scientific, and technical, as well as religious and moral—and political theory.

François Marie Arouet, better known as Voltaire (1694–1778), became, and still is, the most representative figure—almost the personification—of the Enlightenment spirit. Voltaire was instrumental in introducing Newton and Locke to the French intelligentsia. Voltaire hated, and attacked through his writings, the arbitrary despotic rule of kings, the selfish privileges of the nobility and the church, religious intolerance, and, above all, the injustice of the *ancien régime* (the "old order"). He converted a whole generation to the conviction that fundamental changes were necessary. This conviction paved the way for the French Revolution as well as the American Revolution.

Joseph Wright The Enlightenment's emphasis on scientific investigation and technological invention opened up new possibilities for human understanding of the world and for control of its material forces. Research into the phenomena of electricity and combustion, along with the discovery of oxygen and the power of steam, had enormous consequences. Steam power as an adjunct to, or replacement for, human labor marked a new era in world history, beginning with the Industrial Revolution. Most scholars mark the start of the Industrial Revolution with the invention of steam engines in England for industrial production and, later, their use for transportation in the 1740s.

The fascination technological progress held for ordinary people as well as for the learned is the subject of *A Philosopher Giving a Lecture at the Orrery* (FIG. **11-6**) by the English painter JOSEPH WRIGHT OF DERBY (1734–1797). Wright specialized in painting dramatic candlelit and moonlit scenes. He favored subjects such as the orrery demonstration, which could be illuminated by a single light from within the picture. In the painting, a scholar demonstrates a mechanical model of the solar system called an *orrery*, in which each planet (represented by a metal orb) revolves around the sun (a lamp) at the correct relative velocity. Light from the lamp pours forth from in front of the boy silhouetted in the foreground to create dramatic light and shadows that heighten the drama of the scene. Awed children crowd close to the tiny orbs that represent the planets within the arcing bands that symbolize their orbits. An earnest listener makes notes, while the lone woman seated at the left and the two gentlemen at the right look on with rapt attention. The wonders of scientific knowledge mesmerize everyone in the painting. Wright elevated the theories and inventions of the Industrial Revolution to the plane of history painting.

Rousseau The second key figure of the French Enlightenment, who was also instrumental in preparing the way ideologically for the French Revolution, was Jean-Jacques Rousseau (1712–1778). Voltaire believed the salvation of humanity was in the advancement of science and in the rational improvement of society. In contrast, Rousseau declared that the arts, sciences, society, and civilization in general had corrupted "natural man." According to Rousseau, "Man by nature is good . . . he is depraved and perverted by society."

The Enlightenment | **325**

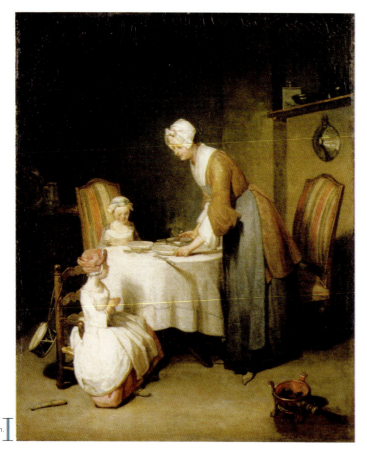

1 in.

11-7 Jean-Baptiste-Siméon Chardin, *Saying Grace*, 1740. Oil on canvas, 1′ 7″ × 1′ 3″. Louvre, Paris.

Consistent with the ideas of Rousseau, Chardin celebrated the simple goodness of ordinary people, especially mothers and children, who lived in a world far from the frivolous Rococo salons of Paris.

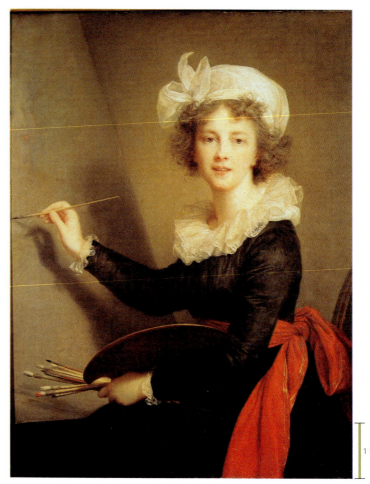

1 ft.

11-8 Élisabeth Louise Vigée-Lebrun, *Self-Portrait*, 1790. Oil on canvas, 8′ 4″ × 6′ 9″. Galleria degli Uffizi, Florence.

Vigée-Lebrun was one of the few women admitted to France's Royal Academy of Painting and Sculpture. In this self-portrait, she depicted herself confidently painting the likeness of Queen Marie Antoinette.

He rejected the idea of progress, insisting that "Our minds have been corrupted in proportion as the arts and sciences have improved."[2] Rousseau's elevation of feelings above reason as the most "natural" human expression led him to exalt as the ideal the peasant's simple life, with its honest and unsullied emotions.

Chardin Rousseau's influential views caused both artists and the public to turn away from the Rococo sensibility in art in favor of the "natural," as opposed to the artificial and frivolous. Jean-Baptiste-Siméon Chardin (1699–1779) painted quiet scenes of domestic life, which offered the opportunity to praise the simple goodness of ordinary people, especially mothers and young children, who in spirit, occupation, and environment lived far from corrupt society. In *Saying Grace* (FIG. **11-7**), Chardin ushers the viewer into a modest room where a mother and her small daughters are about to dine. The mood of quiet attention is at one with the hushed lighting and mellow color and with the closely studied still-life accessories whose worn surfaces tell their own humble domestic history. The viewer witnesses a moment of social instruction, when mother and older sister supervise the younger sister in the simple, pious ritual of giving thanks to God before a meal. The simplicity of the composition

reinforces the subdued charm of this scene, with the three figures highlighted against the dark background. Chardin was the poet of the commonplace and the master of its nuances. A gentle sentiment prevails in all his pictures, an emotion not contrived and artificial but born of the painter's honesty, insight, and sympathy. Chardin's paintings had wide appeal, even in unexpected places. Louis XV, the royal personification of the Rococo in his life and tastes, once owned *Saying Grace.*

Vigée-Lebrun *Self-Portrait* (FIG. **11-8**) by Élisabeth Louise Vigée-Lebrun (1755–1842) is another variation of the "naturalistic" impulse in 18th-century French art. The artist pauses in her work to look directly at viewers and return their gaze. Although her mood is lighthearted and her costume's details echo the serpentine curve Rococo artists and wealthy patrons loved, nothing about Vigée-Lebrun's pose or her mood speaks of Rococo frivolity. Hers is the self-confident stance of a woman whose art has won her an independent role in society. She portrayed herself in a close-up, intimate view at work on one of the portraits that won her

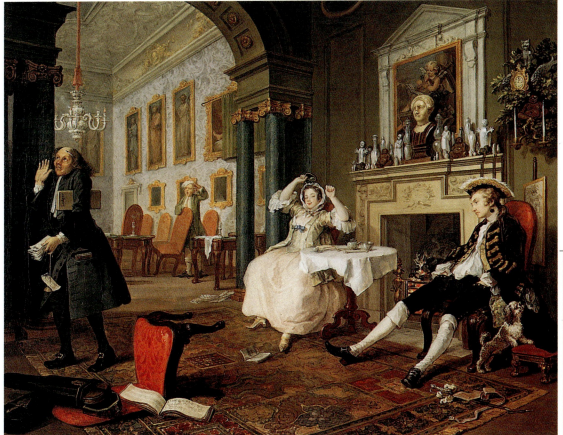

11-9 WILLIAM HOGARTH, *Breakfast Scene*, from *Marriage à la Mode*, ca. 1745. Oil on canvas, 2' 4" × 3'. National Gallery, London.

Hogarth won fame for his paintings and prints satirizing 18th-century English life with comic zest. This is one of a series of six paintings in which he chronicled the marital immoralities of the moneyed class.

renown, that of Queen Marie-Antoinette (1755–1793). Like many of her contemporaries, Vigée-Lebrun lived a life of extraordinary personal and economic independence, working for the nobility throughout Europe. She was famous for the force and grace of her portraits, especially those of highborn ladies and royalty. She was successful during the age of the late monarchy in France and was one of the few women admitted to the Royal Academy of Painting and Sculpture. After the French Revolution, however, the academy rescinded her membership, because women were no longer welcome, but she enjoyed continued success owing to her talent, wit, and ability to forge connections with those in power in the postrevolutionary period.

William Hogarth Across the Channel, a truly English style of painting emerged with WILLIAM HOGARTH (1697–1764), who satirized the lifestyle of the newly prosperous middle class with comic zest. Traditionally, the British imported painters from the Continent—Holbein, Rubens, and Van Dyck among them. Hogarth waged a lively campaign throughout his career against the English feeling of dependence on, and inferiority to, these artists. Although Hogarth would have been the last to admit it, his painting owed much to the work of his contemporaries in France, the Rococo artists. Yet his subject matter, frequently moral in tone, was distinctively English. It was the great age of English satirical writing, and Hogarth saw himself as translating satire into the visual arts.

Hogarth's favorite device was to make a series of narrative paintings and prints, in a sequence like chapters in a book or scenes in a play, following a character or group of characters in their encounters with some social evil. *Breakfast Scene* (FIG. 11-9), from *Marriage à la Mode*, is one in a sequence of six paintings satirizing the marital immoralities of the moneyed classes in England. In it, a marriage is just beginning to founder. The husband and wife are tired after a long night spent in separate pursuits. While the wife stayed at home for an evening of cards and music-making, her young husband had been away from the house for a night of suspicious business. He thrusts his hands deep into the empty money-pockets of his breeches, while his wife's small dog sniffs inquiringly at a woman's lacy cap protruding from his coat pocket. A steward, his hands full of unpaid bills, raises his eyes to Heaven in despair at the actions of his noble master and mistress.

The house is palatial, but Hogarth filled it with witty clues to the dubious taste of its occupants. For example, the row of pious religious paintings on the upper wall of the distant room concludes with a curtain-shielded work that undoubtedly depicts an erotic subject. According to the custom of the day, ladies could not view this discreetly hidden painting, but at the pull of a cord, the master and his male guests could gaze at the cavorting figures. In *Breakfast Scene*, as in all his work, Hogarth proceeded as a novelist might, elaborating on his subject with carefully chosen detail, whose discovery heightens the comic aspects of the story.

Thomas Gainsborough A contrasting blend of "naturalistic" representation and Rococo setting is found in *Mrs. Richard Brinsley Sheridan* (FIG. **11-10**) by the British painter THOMAS GAINSBOROUGH (1727–1788). This portrait shows a lovely woman, dressed informally, seated in a rustic landscape faintly reminiscent of Watteau (FIG. 11-3) in its soft-hued light and feathery brushwork. Gainsborough intended to match the natural, unspoiled beauty of the landscape with that of his sitter. Mrs. Sheridan's dark brown hair blows freely in the slight wind, and her clear "English" complexion and air of ingenuous sweetness contrast sharply with the pert sophistication Continental Rococo artists portrayed. Gainsborough originally had planned to give the picture a more pastoral air by adding several sheep, but he did not live long enough to paint them in. Even without this element, the painting clearly expresses the artist's deep interest in the landscape setting. Although he won greater fame in his time for his portraits, he began as a landscape painter and always preferred painting scenes of nature to the depiction of human likenesses.

The portrait of Mrs. Sheridan is representative of what became known as *Grand Manner portraiture*, and Gainsborough was one of the leading practitioners of this genre. Although clearly depicting individualized people, Grand Manner portraiture also elevated the sitter by conveying refinement and elegance. Painters communicated a person's grace and class through certain standardized conventions, such as the large scale of the figures relative to the canvas, the controlled poses, the landscape setting, and the low horizon line. Thus, despite the naturalism central to Gainsborough's portraits, he tempered it with a degree of artifice. This combination of aristocratic Rococo sophistication with rustic naturalism is an example of the hybrid nature of much 18th-century art.

Benjamin West Some American artists also became well known in England. BENJAMIN WEST (1738–1820), born in Pennsylvania on what was then the colonial frontier, traveled to Europe early in life to study art and then went to England, where he met with almost immediate success. A cofounder of the Royal Academy of Arts, West became official painter to King George III (r. 1760–1801) and retained that position during the strained period of the American Revolution. In *Death of General Wolfe* (FIG. **11-11**), West depicted the mortally wounded young English commander just after his defeat of the French in the decisive battle of Quebec in 1759, which gave Canada to Great Britain. In portraying a recent historical subject, he put his characters in contemporary costume (although the military uniforms are not completely accurate in all details). However, West blended this realism of detail with the grand tradition of history painting by arranging his figures in a complex, theatrically ordered composition. His modern hero dies among grieving officers on the field of victorious battle in a way that suggests the death of a great saint. West wanted to present this hero's death in the service of the state as a martyrdom charged with religious emotions. His innovative combination of the conventions of traditional heroic painting with

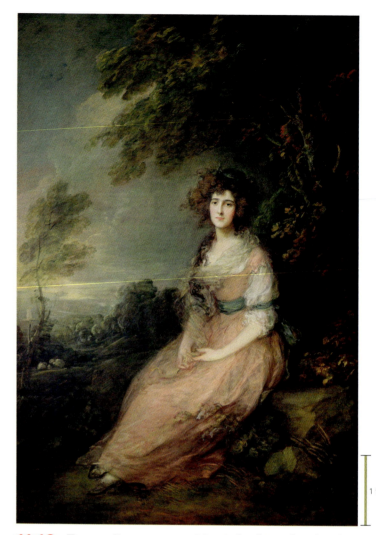

11-10 THOMAS GAINSBOROUGH, *Mrs. Richard Brinsley Sheridan*, 1787. Oil on canvas, 7' 2$\frac{5}{8}$" × 5' $\frac{5}{8}$". National Gallery of Art, Washington, D.C. (Andrew W. Mellon Collection).

In this life-size portrait, Gainsborough sought to match the natural beauty of Mrs. Sheridan with that of the landscape. The rustic setting, soft-hued light, and feathery brushwork recall Rococo painting

a look of modern realism was so effective that it won viewers' hearts in his own day and continued to influence history painting well into the 19th century.

John Singleton Copley American artist JOHN SINGLETON COPLEY (1738–1815) matured as a painter in the Massachusetts Bay Colony. Like West, Copley later emigrated to England, where he absorbed the fashionable English portrait style. But unlike Grand Manner portraiture, Copley's *Portrait of Paul Revere* (FIG. **11-12**), painted before Copley left Boston, conveys a sense of directness and faithfulness to visual fact that marked the taste for honesty and plainness many visitors to America noticed during the 18th and 19th centuries. When Copley painted his portrait, Revere was not yet the familiar hero of the American Revolution. In the picture, he is working at his everyday profession of silversmithing. The setting is plain, the lighting clear and revealing. Revere sits in his shirtsleeves, bent over a teapot in progress. He pauses and turns his head to look the observer

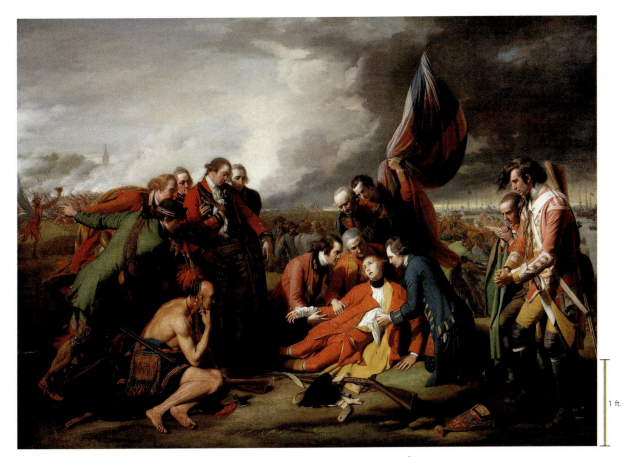

11-11 Benjamin West, *Death of General Wolfe*, 1771. Oil on canvas, 4′ 11½″ × 7′. National Gallery of Canada, Ottawa (gift of the Duke of Westminster, 1918).

West's great innovation was to blend contemporaneous subject matter and costumes with the grand tradition of history painting. Here, West likened General Wolfe's death to that of a martyred saint.

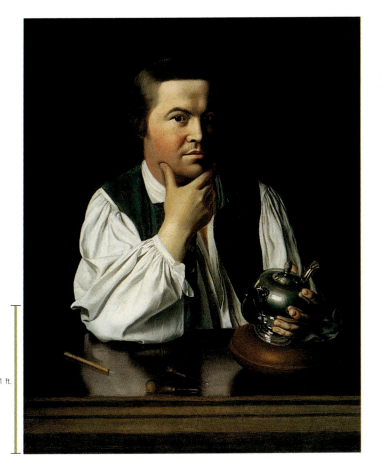

straight in the eye. Copley treated the reflections in the polished wood of the tabletop with as much care as Revere's figure, his tools, and the teapot resting on its leather graver's pillow. The painter gave special prominence to Revere's eyes by reflecting intense reddish light onto the darkened side of the face and hands. The informality and the sense of the moment link this painting to contemporaneous English and French portraits. But the spare style and the emphasis on the sitter's down-to-earth character differentiate this American work from its European counterparts.

The Grand Tour The 18th-century public also sought "naturalness" in artists' depictions of landscapes. Documentation of particular places became popular, in part due to growing travel opportunities and expanding colonialism. These depictions of geographic settings also served the needs of the many scientific expeditions mounted during the century and satisfied the desires of genteel tourists for mementos of

11-12 John Singleton Copley, *Portrait of Paul Revere*, ca. 1768–1770. Oil on canvas, 2′ 11⅛″ × 2′ 4″. Museum of Fine Arts, Boston (gift of Joseph W., William B., and Edward H.R. Revere).

In contrast to Grand Manner portraiture, Copley's *Paul Revere* emphasizes his subject's down-to-earth character, differentiating this American work from its British and Continental counterparts.

The Enlightenment | 329

The Grand Tour and Veduta Painting

Although travel throughout Europe was commonplace in the 18th century, Italy became a particularly popular destination. This "pilgrimage" of the wealthy from France, England, Germany, the United States, and elsewhere came to be known as the Grand Tour. The Grand Tour was not simply leisure travel. The education available in Italy to the inquisitive mind made the trip an indispensable experience for anyone who wished to make a mark in society. The Enlightenment had made knowledge of ancient Rome and Greece imperative, and a steady stream of visitors traveled to Italy in the late 18th and early 19th centuries. These tourists aimed to increase their knowledge of literature, the visual arts, architecture, theater, music, history, customs, and folklore. Given this extensive agenda, it is not surprising that a Grand Tour could take a number of years to complete, and most travelers followed an established itinerary.

The British were the most avid travelers, and they conceived the initial "tour code," including important destinations and required itineraries. Although they designated Rome early on as the primary destination, visitors traveled as far north as Venice and as far south as Naples and even Sicily. Many of those who completed a Grand Tour returned home with a painting by Antonio Canaletto, the leading painter of scenic views *(vedute)* of Venice. It must

have been very cheering on a gray winter afternoon in England to look up and see a sunny, panoramic view such as that in Canaletto's *Riva degli Schiavoni, Venice* (FIG. 11-13), with its cloud-studded sky, picturesque water traffic, and well-known Venetian landmarks painted in scrupulous perspective and minute detail.

Canaletto usually made drawings "on location" to take back to his studio and use as sources for paintings. To help make the on-site drawings true to life, he often used a camera obscura, as Vermeer (FIG. 10-26) did before him, a device that enabled Canaletto to create visually convincing paintings that included variable focus of objects at different distances. Canaletto's *vedute* give the impression of capturing every detail, with no omissions. In fact, he presented each site within Renaissance perspectival rules and exercised great selectivity about which details to include and which to omit to make a coherent and engagingly attractive painting.

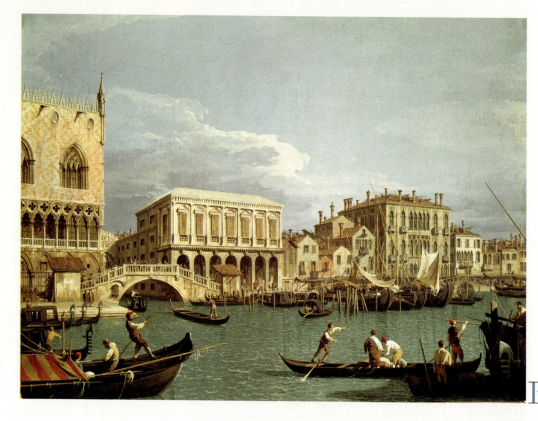

11-13 ANTONIO CANALETTO, *Riva degli Schiavoni, Venice*, ca. 1735–1740. Oil on canvas, 1′ 6½″ × 2′ ⅞″. Toledo Museum of Art, Toledo.

Canaletto was the leading painter of Venetian vedute, which were treasured souvenirs for 18th-century travelers visiting Italy on a Grand Tour. He used a camera obscura for his on-site drawings.

their journeys. By this time, a "Grand Tour" of the major sites of Europe was an essential part of every well-bred person's education (see "The Grand Tour," above). Naturally, those on tour wished to return with items that would help them remember their experiences and impress those at home with the wonders they had seen. The English were especially eager collectors of pictorial souvenirs. Many artists in Venice specialized in painting the most characteristic scenes, or *vedute* (views), of that city to sell to British visitors. Chief among the Venetian painters was ANTONIO CANALETTO (1697–1768), whose works, for example *Riva degli Schiavoni, Venice* (FIG.

11-13), English tourists avidly acquired as evidence of their visit to the city of the Grand Canal.

NEOCLASSICISM

One of the defining characteristics of the late 18th century was a renewed interest in classical antiquity, which the Grand Tour was instrumental in fueling. Admiration for Greek and Roman art and culture gave rise to the artistic movement known as *Neoclassicism*. The geometric harmony and rationality of classical art and architecture seemed to

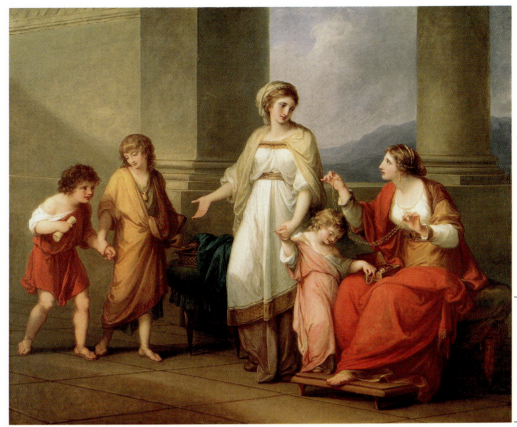

11-14 Angelica Kauffmann, *Cornelia Presenting Her Children as Her Treasures,* or *Mother of the Gracchi,* ca. 1785. Oil on canvas, 3′ 4″ × 4′ 2″. Virginia Museum of Fine Arts, Richmond (Adolph D. and Wilkins C. Williams Fund).

Kauffmann's painting of a virtuous Roman mother who presented her children to a visitor as her jewels exemplifies the Enlightenment fascination with classical antiquity and classical art.

1 ft.

embody Enlightenment ideals. In addition, classical cultures represented the height of civilized society, and Greece and Rome served as models of enlightened political organization. These cultures, with their traditions of liberty, civic virtue, morality, and sacrifice, were ideal models during a period of great political upheaval. Given these traditional associations, it is not coincidental that Neoclassicism was particularly appealing during the French and American Revolutions.

Winckelmann In the late 18th century, the ancient world also increasingly became the focus of scholarly attention. In 1755, Johann Joachim Winckelmann (1717–1768), the first modern art historian, published *Reflections on the Imitation of Greek Art in Painting and Sculpture,* uncompromisingly designating Greek art as the most perfect to come from human hands—and far preferable to "natural" art: "[An enlightened person] will find beauties hitherto seldom revealed when he compares the total structure of Greek figures with most modern ones, especially those modelled more on nature than on Greek taste."[3]

In his *History of Ancient Art* (1764), Winckelmann described each monument and positioned it within a huge inventory of works organized by subject matter, style, and period. Before Winckelmann, art historians had focused on biography, as did Giorgio Vasari and Giovanni Pietro Bellori in the 16th and 17th centuries. Winckelmann thus initiated one modern art historical method thoroughly in accord with Enlightenment ideas of ordering knowledge—a system of description and classification that provided a pioneering model for the understanding of stylistic evolution. Winckelmann's writings also laid a theoretical foundation for Neoclassical art.

Angelica Kauffmann One of the pioneers of Neoclassical painting was Angelica Kauffmann (1741–1807). Born in Switzerland and trained in Italy, Kauffmann spent many of her productive years in England. With West and others, she was a founding member of the British Royal Academy of Arts and enjoyed an enviable reputation. Her *Cornelia Presenting Her Children as Her Treasures* (FIG. **11-14**) is an *exemplum virtutis* (example or model of virtue) drawn from Greek and Roman history and literature. The moralizing pictures of Hogarth (FIG. 11-9) already had marked a change in taste, but Kauffmann replaced the modern setting and characters of his works. She clothed her actors in ancient Roman garb and posed them in statuesque attitudes within Roman interiors. The theme in this painting is the virtue of Cornelia, mother of the future political leaders Tiberius and Gaius Gracchus, who, in the second century BCE, attempted to reform the Roman Republic. Cornelia reveals her character in this scene, which takes place after the seated visitor showed off her fine jewelry and then insisted that Cornelia show hers. Instead of rushing to get her own precious adornments, Cornelia brought her sons forward, presenting them as her jewels. The architectural setting is severely Roman, with no Rococo motif in evidence, and the composition and drawing have the simplicity and firmness of low-relief carving.

Jacques-Louis David Although his early paintings were in the Rococo manner, a period of study in Rome converted Jacques-Louis David (1748–1825) to Neoclassicism. David's preferred models were the works of the ancient and Renaissance masters. He condemned the Rococo style as an "artificial taste" and exalted the "perfect form" of Greek

David on Greek Style and Public Art

Jacques-Louis David was the leading Neoclassical painter in France at the end of the 18th century. He championed a return to Greek style and the painting of inspiring heroic and patriotic subjects. In 1796 he made the following statement to his pupils:

> I want to work in a pure Greek style. I feed my eyes on antique statues, I even have the intention of imitating some of them. The Greeks had no scruples about copying a composition, a gesture, a type that had already been accepted and used. They put all their attention and all their art on perfecting an idea that had been already conceived. They thought, and they were right, that in the arts the way in which an idea is rendered, and the manner in which it is expressed, is much more important than the idea itself. To give a body and a perfect form to one's thought, this—and only this—is to be an artist.*

David also strongly believed that paintings depicting noble events in ancient history, such as *Oath of the Horatii* (FIG. 11-15), would instill patriotism and civic virtue in the public at large in postrevolutionary France. In November 1793 he wrote:

> [The arts] should help to spread the progress of the human spirit, and to propagate and transmit to posterity

the striking examples of the efforts of a tremendous people who, guided by reason and philosophy, are bringing back to earth the reign of liberty, equality, and law. The arts must therefore contribute forcefully to the education of the public. . . . The arts are the imitation of nature in her most beautiful and perfect form. . . . [T]hose marks of heroism and civic virtue offered the eyes of the people [will] electrify the soul, and plant the seeds of glory and devotion to the fatherland.†

* Translated by Robert Goldwater and Marco Treves, eds., *Artists on Art*, 3d ed. (New York: Pantheon Books, 1958), 206.
† Ibid., 205.

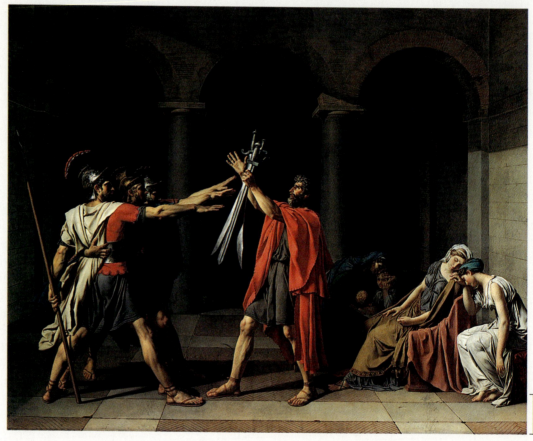

11-15 JACQUES-LOUIS DAVID, *Oath of the Horatii*, 1784. Oil on canvas, 10′ 10″ × 13′ 11″. Louvre, Paris.

David was the Neoclassical painter-ideologist of the French Revolution. This huge canvas celebrating ancient Roman patriotism and sacrifice features statuesque figures and classical architecture.

1 ft.

art (see "David on Greek Style and Public Art," above). David, who became the Neoclassical painter-ideologist of the French Revolution, concurred with the Enlightenment belief that subject matter should have a moral and should be presented so that noble deeds in the past could inspire virtue in the present.

A milestone painting in David's career, *Oath of the Horatii* (FIG. 11-15) depicts a story from pre-Republican Rome, the heroic phase of Roman history. The topic was not too arcane for David's audience. Pierre Corneille (1606–1684) had retold this story of conflict between love and patriotism, first recounted by the ancient Roman historian

Livy, in a play performed in Paris several years earlier. The leaders of the warring cities of Rome and Alba decided to resolve their conflicts in a series of encounters waged by three representatives from each side. The Romans chose as their champions the three Horatius brothers, who had to face the three sons of the Curatius family from Alba. A sister of the Horatii, Camilla, was the bride-to-be of one of the Curatius sons, and the wife of the youngest Horatius was the sister of the Curatii. David's painting shows the Horatii as they swear on their swords, held high by their father, to win or die for Rome, oblivious to the anguish and sorrow of their female relatives. In its form, *Oath of the Horatii* is a paragon of the

Neoclassical style. Not only was the subject a narrative of patriotism and sacrifice excerpted from Roman history, but the painter presented it with force and clarity. David depicted the scene in a shallow space much like a stage setting, defined by a severely simple architectural framework. He deployed his statuesque and carefully modeled figures across the space, close to the foreground, in a manner reminiscent of ancient relief sculpture. The rigid, angular, and virile forms of the men on the left effectively contrast with the soft curvilinear shapes of the distraught women on the right. This pattern visually pits virtues the Enlightenment leaders ascribed to men (such as courage, patriotism, and unwavering loyalty to a cause) against the emotions of love, sorrow, and despair that the women in the painting express. The French viewing audience perceived such emotionalism as characteristic of the female nature. The message was clear and of a type readily identifiable to the prerevolutionary French public. The picture created a sensation at its first exhibition in Paris in 1785, and although David painted it under royal patronage and did not intend the painting as a revolutionary statement, the Neoclassical style of *Oath of the Horatii* soon became the semiofficial voice of the revolution.

Death of Marat When the French Revolution broke out in 1789, David threw in his lot with the Jacobins, the radical and militant faction. He accepted the role of de facto minister of propaganda, organizing political pageants and ceremonies that included floats, costumes, and sculptural props. David believed that art could play an important role in educating the public and that dramatic paintings emphasizing patriotism and civic virtue would prove effective as rallying calls. However, rather than continue to create artworks focused on scenes from antiquity, David began to portray events from the French Revolution itself. He intended *Death of Marat* (FIG. 11-16) not only to serve as a record of an important episode in the struggle to overthrow the monarchy but also to provide inspiration and encouragement to the revolutionary forces. Jean-Paul Marat (1743–1793), a writer and David's friend, was tragically assassinated in 1793. David depicted the martyred revolutionary after Charlotte Corday (1768–1793), a member of a rival political faction, stabbed him to death in his medicinal bath. (Marat suffered from a painful skin disease.) The cold neutral space above Marat's figure slumped in the tub produces a chilling oppressiveness. David vividly placed narrative details—the knife, the wound, the blood, the letter with which the young woman gained entrance—to sharpen the sense of pain and outrage and to confront viewers with the scene itself. *Death of Marat* is convincingly real, yet David masterfully composed the painting to present Marat as a tragic martyr who died in the service of the revolution. David based the figure of Marat on Christ in Michelangelo's *Pietà* (FIG. 9-8). The reference to Christ's martyrdom made the painting a kind of "altarpiece" for the new civic "religion," inspiring the French people with the saintly dedication of their slain leader.

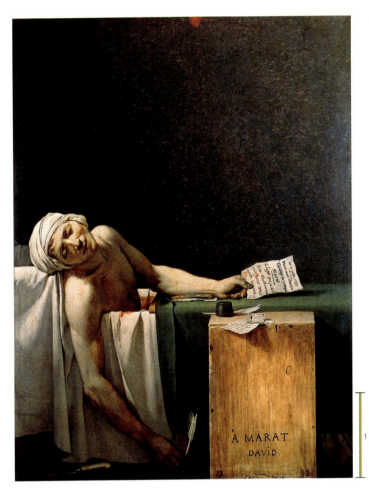

11-16 JACQUES-LOUIS DAVID, *Death of Marat*, 1793. Oil on canvas, 5′ 5″ × 4′ 2½″. Musées Royaux des Beaux-Arts de Belgique, Brussels.

David depicted the revolutionary Marat as a tragic martyr, stabbed to death in his bath. Although the painting displays severe Neoclassical spareness, its convincing realism conveys pain and outrage.

Panthéon, Paris Architecture in the Enlightenment era also exhibits a dependence on classical models. Early in the 18th century, architects began to turn away from the theatricality and ostentation of Baroque and Rococo design and embraced a more streamlined, antique look. The portico of the Parisian church of Sainte-Geneviève, now the Panthéon (FIG. 11-1), by JACQUES-GERMAIN SOUFFLOT (1713–1780), stands as testament to the revived interest in Greek and Roman cultures. The columns, based on those of a Roman temple in Lebanon (reproduced with studied archaeological precision), stand out from walls that are severely blank, except for a repeated garland motif near the top. The colonnaded dome, a Neoclassical version of the domes of Saint Peter's (FIG. 10-3) in Rome and Saint Paul's (FIG. 10-34) in London, rises above a Greek-cross plan. Both the dome and the vaults rest on an interior grid of splendid freestanding Corinthian columns, as if the portico's colonnade continued within. Although the overall effect, inside and out, is Roman, the structural principles employed are essentially Gothic. Soufflot was one of the first 18th-century builders to suggest that the logical engineering of Gothic cathedrals (see "The Gothic Cathedral," Chapter 7, page 193) could be applied to modern buildings.

Jefferson led the
movement to adopt
Neoclassicism as the
architectural style of the
United States. Although
built of local materials,
his Virginia home recalls
Palladio's Villa Rotonda
(fig. 9-16).

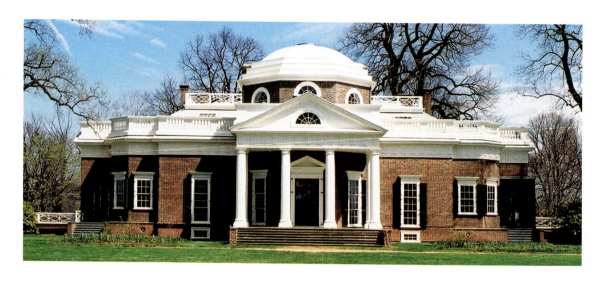

Thomas Jefferson Part of the appeal of Neoclassicism was due to its associative values—morality, idealism, patriotism, and civic virtue. Thus, it is not surprising that in the new American republic, THOMAS JEFFERSON (1743–1826)—scholar, economist, educational theorist, statesman, and gifted amateur architect—spearheaded a movement to adopt Neoclassicism as the national architectural style. Jefferson admired Andrea Palladio immensely and read carefully the Italian architect's *Four Books of Architecture*. After serving as minister to France, Jefferson returned to America and completely remodeled his own home, Monticello (FIG. 11-17), near Charlottesville, Virginia, emulating Palladio's manner. The final version of Monticello is somewhat reminiscent of the Villa Rotonda (FIG. 9-16), but its materials are the local wood and brick used in Virginia.

Jean-Antoine Houdon Neoclassicism also became the preferred style for public sculptural commissions in the newly independent United States. When the Virginia legislature wanted to erect a life-size marble statue of Virginia-born George Washington, the commission turned to the leading French Neoclassical sculptor of the late 18th century, JEAN-ANTOINE HOUDON (1741–1828). Houdon had already carved a bust portrait of Benjamin Franklin when he was U.S. ambassador to France. Although in Houdon's portrait of Washington (FIG. 11-18), the first American president wears the fashion of the times, the artist made an overt reference in this statue to the Roman Republic. The "column" on which Washington leans is a bundle of rods with an ax attached—the ancient Roman *fasces*, an emblem of authority. The 13 rods symbolize the 13 original states. The plow behind Washington and the fasces allude to Cincinnatus, a patrician of the early Roman Republic who was elected dictator during a time of war and resigned his position as soon as victory had been achieved in order to return to his farm. Washington wears the badge of the Society of the Cincinnati (visible beneath the bottom of his waistcoat), an association founded in 1783 for army officers who had resumed their peacetime roles after America won independence from England. Tellingly, Washington no longer holds his sword in Houdon's statue.

The Neoclassical style, so closely associated with revolution and democracy in the late 18th century, ironically also became the ideal vehicle for promoting the empire of Napoleon Bonaparte in the opening decade of the 19th century. Napoleonic art and the revolutionary new styles that eventually displaced Neoclassicism are the subject of Chapter 12.

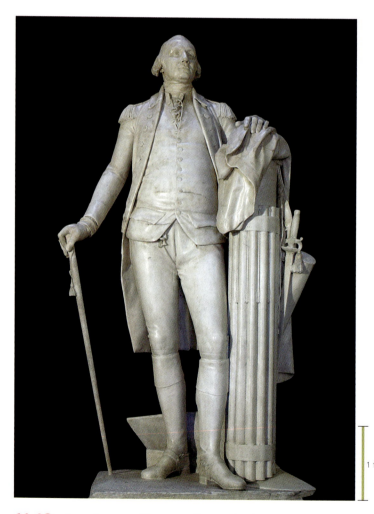

1 ft.

11-18 JEAN-ANTOINE HOUDON, *George Washington*, 1788–1792. Marble, 6′ 2″ high. State Capitol, Richmond.

Houdon portrayed Washington in contemporary garb, but he incorporated the Roman fasces and Cincinnatus's plow in the statue because Washington had returned to his farm after his war service.

Europe and America, 1700 to 1800

ROCOCO

▌ In the early 18th century, the centralized and grandiose palace-based culture of Baroque France gave way to the much more intimate Rococo culture of Parisian town houses. There, aristocrats and intellectuals gathered for witty conversation in salons featuring delicate colors, sinuous lines, gilded mirrors, elegant furniture, and small paintings and sculptures.

▌ The leading Rococo painter was Antoine Watteau, whose usually small canvases feature light colors and elegant figures in ornate costumes moving gracefully through lush landscapes. His fête galante paintings depict the outdoor amusements of French high society.

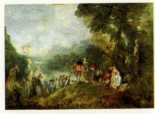

Watteau, *Pilgrimage to Cythera*, 1717

THE ENLIGHTENMENT

▌ By the end of the 18th century, revolutions had overthrown the monarchy in France and achieved independence for the British colonies in America. A major factor was the Enlightenment, a new way of thinking critically about the world independently of religion and tradition that also helped foster the Industrial Revolution, which began in England in the 1740s. The Enlightenment promoted scientific questioning of all assertions and embraced the doctrine of progress. The first modern encyclopedias appeared during the 18th century, making accumulated knowledge widely available.

▌ The Enlightenment also made knowledge of ancient Rome imperative for the cultured elite, and Europeans and Americans in large numbers undertook a Grand Tour of Italy. Among the most popular souvenirs of the Grand Tour were Antonio Canaletto's vedute of Venice rendered in precise Renaissance perspective with the aid of a camera obscura.

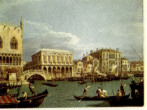

Canaletto, *Riva degli Schiavoni, Venice*, ca. 1735–1740

▌ Rejecting the idea of progress, Jean-Jacques Rousseau, one of the leading French philosophes, argued for a return to natural values and exalted the simple, honest life of peasants. His ideas had a profound impact on artists such as Jean-Baptiste-Siméon Chardin, who painted sentimental narratives about rural families.

▌ The taste for the natural also led to the popularity of portrait paintings set against landscape backgrounds, a specialty of Thomas Gainsborough, among others, and to a reawakening of an interest in realism. Benjamin West represented the protagonists in his history paintings attired in contemporary dress.

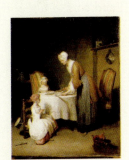

Chardin, *Saying Grace*, 1740

NEOCLASSICISM

▌ The Enlightenment revival of interest in Greece and Rome also gave rise in the late 18th century to the artistic movement known as Neoclassicism, which incorporated the subjects and styles of ancient art. Classical art also became a subject for scholarly inquiry. Johann Joachim Winckelmann, the first modern art historian, extolled Greek art as the most perfect ever to come from human hands.

▌ One of the pioneers of the new style was Angelica Kauffmann, who often chose subjects drawn from Roman history for her paintings. Jacques-Louis David, who exalted classical art as the imitation of nature in its most beautiful and perfect form, also favored ancient Roman themes. Painted on the eve of the French Revolution, *Oath of the Horatii,* set in a severe classical hall, extolled patriotism and sacrifice.

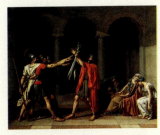

David, *Oath of the Horatii*, 1784

▌ Neoclassicism also became the dominant style in 18th-century European architecture. Ancient Roman temples and Italian Renaissance churches inspired Jacques-Germain Soufflot's Panthéon in Paris.

▌ In the United States, Thomas Jefferson adopted the Neoclassical style in his design for his Virginia home, Monticello. He championed Neoclassicism as the official architectural style of the new American republic because it represented for him idealism, patriotism, and civic virtue.

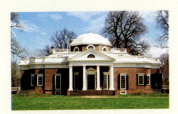

Jefferson, Monticello, Charlottesville, 1770–1806

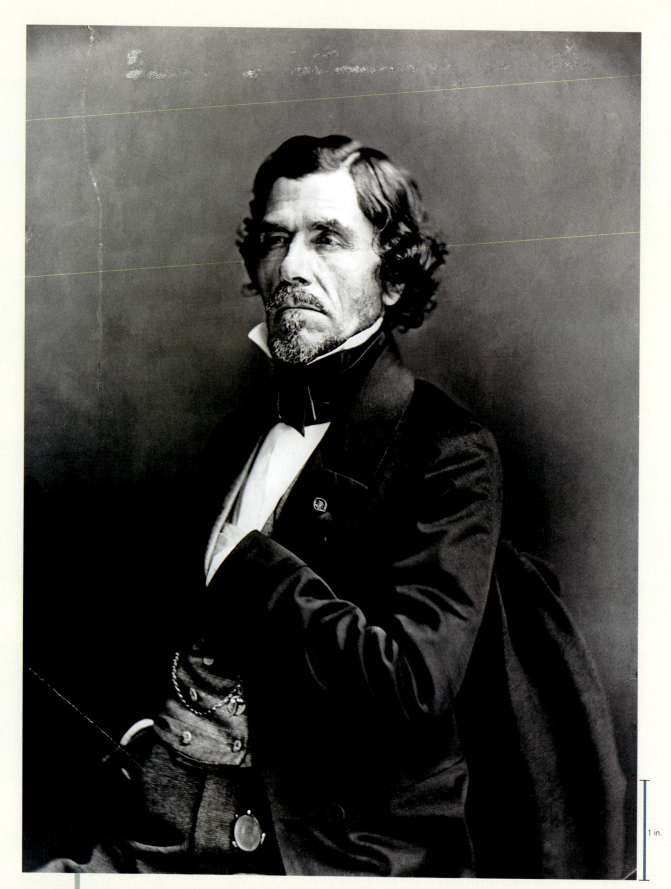

1 in.

12-1 NADAR, *Eugène Delacroix*, ca. 1855. Modern print, $8\frac{1}{2}'' \times 6\frac{2}{3}''$, from the original negative. Bibliothèque Nationale, Paris.

Eugène Delacroix, the great Romantic painter, was one of many 19th-century artists intrigued by how photography presented reality. Here, he sat for Nadar, one of the earliest portrait photographers.

Europe and America, 1800 to 1870

The revolution of 1789 initiated a new era in France, but the overthrow of the monarchy also opened the door for Corsican-born Napoleon Bonaparte (1769–1821) to exploit the resulting disarray and establish a different kind of monarchy with himself at its head. In 1799, after serving in various French army commands, Napoleon became first consul of the French Republic, a title with clear and intentional links to the ancient Roman Republic (see Chapter 3). During the next 15 years, the ambitious general gained control of almost all of continental Europe in name or through alliances, and in 1804 the pope journeyed to Paris for Napoleon's coronation as Emperor of the French. But in 1812, Napoleon launched a disastrous invasion of Russia that ended in retreat, and in 1815 he suffered a devastating loss at the hands of the British at Waterloo in present-day Belgium. Forced to abdicate the imperial throne, Napoleon went into exile on the island of Saint Helena in the South Atlantic, dying there six years later.

Following Napoleon's death, the political geography of Europe changed dramatically (MAP **12-1**), but in many ways the more significant changes during the first half of the 19th century were technological and economic. The Industrial Revolution caused a population boom in European cities, and railroads spread to many parts of the Continent, facilitating the transportation of both goods and people. During this period, the arts also underwent important changes. The century opened with Neoclassicism still supreme, but by 1870 Romanticism and Realism in turn had captured the imagination of artists and public alike. New construction techniques had a major impact on architectural design, and the invention of photography revolutionized picture making of all kinds.

ART UNDER NAPOLEON

Napoleon embraced all links with the classical past as sources of symbolic authority for his short-lived imperial state. Not surprisingly, the artistic style that most appealed to him was Neoclassicism. He offered Jacques-Louis David (FIGS. **11-15** and **11-16**) the position of First Painter of the Empire and commissioned various architects to design buildings and monuments based on ancient Roman models.

Antonio Canova Napoleon's favorite sculptor was ANTONIO CANOVA (1757–1822), who somewhat reluctantly left a successful career in Italy to settle in Paris and serve the emperor. Once in France, Canova became Napoleon's admirer and made numerous portraits, all in the Neoclassical style, of the emperor and his family. Perhaps the best known of these works is the marble portrait

Map 12-1

Europe around 1850.

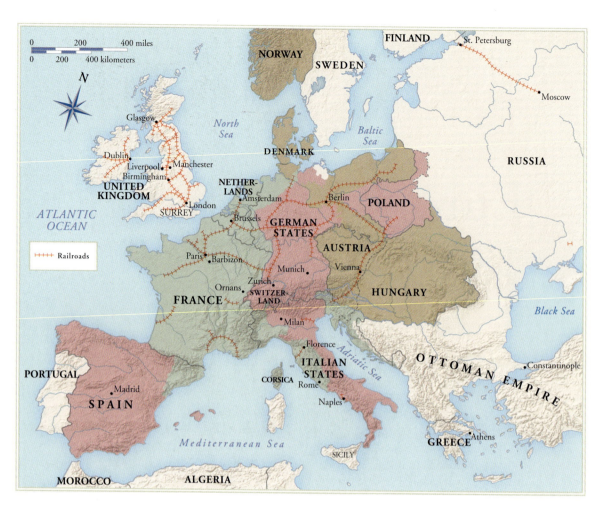

of Napoleon's sister, Pauline Borghese, as Venus (FIG. **12-2**). Initially, Canova had suggested depicting Borghese as Diana, goddess of the hunt. Pauline, however, demanded to be shown as Venus, the goddess of love. Thus she appears reclining on a divan and gracefully holding the golden apple, the symbol of the goddess's triumph in the judgment of Paris. Canova clearly based his work on Greek statuary—the semi-nude body and sensuous pose recall Hellenistic statues such as *Venus de Milo* (FIG. **2-56**). The French public was never able to admire Canova's portrait, however. Napoleon had arranged the marriage of his sister to an heir of the noble Roman Borghese family. Once Pauline was in Rome, her behavior was less than dignified, and the public gossiped extensively about her affairs. Her insistence on

being portrayed as the goddess of love reflected her self-perception. Due to his wife's questionable reputation, Prince Camillo Borghese (1775–1832), the work's official patron, kept the sculpture sequestered in the Villa Borghese. The prince allowed relatively few people to see it (and then only by torchlight).

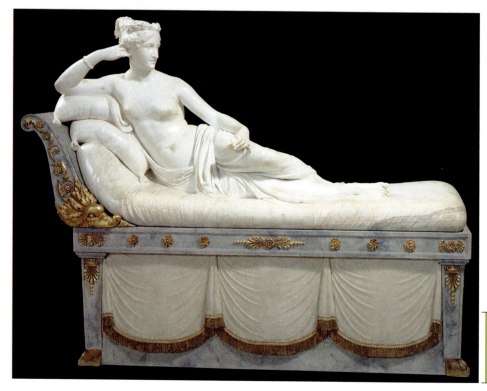

12-2 ANTONIO CANOVA, *Pauline Borghese as Venus*, 1808. Marble, 6' 7" long. Galleria Borghese, Rome.

Canova was Napoleon Bonaparte's favorite sculptor. In this marble statue inspired by classical models, the artist depicted the emperor's sister—at her request—as the nude Roman goddess of love.

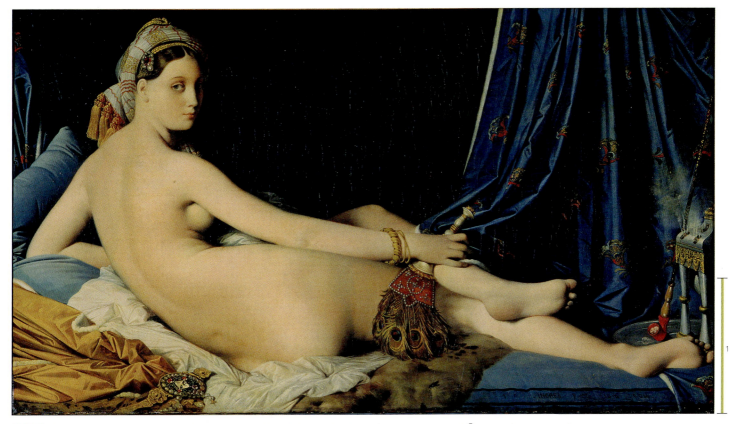

12-3 Jean-Auguste-Dominique Ingres, *Grande Odalisque*, 1814. Oil on canvas, 2′ 11$\frac{7}{8}$″ × 5′ 4″. Louvre, Paris.

The reclining female nude was a Greco-Roman subject, but Ingres converted his Neoclassical figure into an odalisque in a Turkish harem, consistent with the new Romantic taste for the exotic.

1 ft.

Ingres In the late 1790s, Jean-Auguste-Dominique Ingres (1780–1867) arrived at David's studio, but his study there was to be brief, and he soon broke with the Neoclassical master on matters of style. This difference of opinion involved Ingres's adoption of what he believed to be a truer and purer Greek style than David's. The younger artist adopted flat and linear forms approximating those found in Greek vase painting (see Chapter 2). In many of his works, Ingres placed the figure in the foreground, much like a piece of low-relief sculpture. In *Grande Odalisque* (FIG. **12-3**), Ingres's subject, the reclining nude figure, followed the tradition of Giorgione and Titian (FIG. **9-20**) and classical antiquity. The work also shows Ingres's admiration for Raphael in his borrowing of that master's type of female head. However, by converting the figure to an *odalisque* (a woman in a Turkish harem), the artist made a strong concession to the contemporary Romantic taste for the exotic (discussed next).

When Ingres first exhibited *Grande Odalisque* in 1814, the painting drew acid criticism. Critics initially saw Ingres as a rebel in terms of both the form and content of his works. They did not cease their attacks until the mid-1820s, when Eugène Delacroix appeared on the scene. Ingres soon led the academic forces in their battle against the "barbarism" of Delacroix, Théodore Géricault, and the Romantic movement.

ROMANTICISM

Whereas Neoclassicism's rationality reinforced Enlightenment thought (see Chapter 11), particularly Voltaire's views, Rousseau's ideas contributed to the rise of *Romanticism*. Rousseau's exclamation "Man is born free, but is everywhere in chains!"—the opening line of his *Social Contract* (1762)—summarizes a fundamental Romantic premise. Romanticism emerged from a desire for freedom—not only political freedom but also freedom of thought, of feeling, of action, of worship, of speech, and of taste. Romantics asserted that freedom was the right and property of all. They believed the path to freedom was through imagination rather than reason. Romanticism as a phenomenon began around 1750 and ended about 1850, but most art historians use the term more narrowly to denote an artistic movement that was in vogue from about 1800 to 1840, between Neoclassicism and Realism.

The transition from Neoclassicism to Romanticism constituted a shift in emphasis from reason to feeling, from calculation to intuition, and from objective nature to subjective emotion. Among Romanticism's manifestations were the interests in the medieval period and in the sublime. For people living in the 18th century, the Middle Ages were the "dark ages," a time of barbarism, superstition, dark mystery, and miracle. The Romantic imagination stretched its

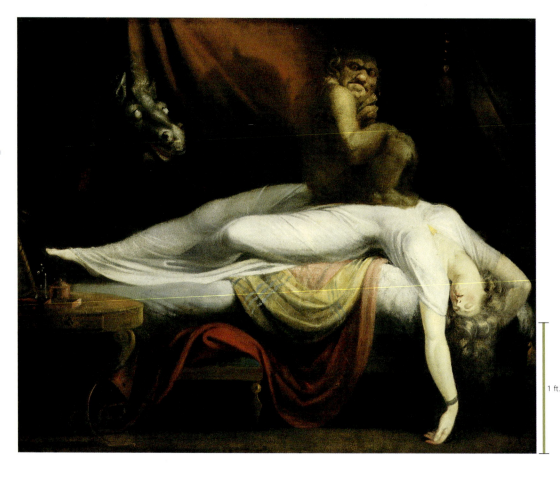

12-4 HENRY FUSELI, *The Nightmare*, 1781. Oil on canvas, 3′ 3¾″ × 4′ 1½″. Detroit Institute of the Arts, Detroit (Founders Society purchase with funds from Mr. and Mrs. Bert L. Smokler and Mr. and Mrs. Lawrence A. Fleishman).

The transition from Neoclassicism to Romanticism marked a shift in emphasis from reason to feeling. Fuseli was among the first painters to depict the dark terrain of the human subconscious.

1 ft.

perception of the Middle Ages into all the worlds of fantasy open to it, including the ghoulish, the infernal, the terrible, the nightmarish, the grotesque, the sadistic, and all the imagery that emerges from the chamber of horrors when reason sleeps. Related to the imaginative sensibility was the period's notion of the sublime. Among the individuals most involved in studying the sublime was the British politician and philosopher Edmund Burke (1729–1797). In *A Philosophical Enquiry into the Origins of Our Ideas of the Sublime and Beautiful* (1757), Burke articulated his definition of the sublime—feelings of awe mixed with terror. Burke observed that pain or fear evoked the most intense human emotions and that these emotions could also be thrilling. Thus, raging rivers and great storms at sea can be sublime to their viewers. Accompanying this taste for the sublime was the taste for the fantastic, the occult, and the macabre—for the adventures of the soul voyaging into the dangerous reaches of consciousness.

Henry Fuseli The concept of the nightmare is the subject of a 1781 painting (FIG. **12-4**) by HENRY FUSELI (1741–1825). Swiss by birth, Fuseli settled in England and eventually became a member of the Royal Academy. Largely self-taught, he contrived a distinctive manner to express the fantasies of his vivid imagination. Fuseli specialized in night moods of horror and in dark fantasies—in the demonic, in the macabre, and often in the sadistic. In *The Nightmare*, a beautiful young woman lies asleep, draped across the bed with her

limp arm dangling over the side. An *incubus*, a demon believed in medieval times to prey, often sexually, on sleeping women, squats ominously on her body. In the background, a ghostly horse with flaming eyes bursts into the scene from beyond the curtain. Fuseli was among the first to attempt to depict the dark terrain of the human subconscious that became fertile ground for later artists to harvest.

Spain and France

From its roots in the work of Fuseli and other late-18th-century artists, Romanticism gradually displaced Neoclassicism as the dominant painting style of the first half of the 19th century. The leading Romantic painters were Francisco Goya in Spain and Théodore Géricault and Eugène Delacroix in France.

Francisco Goya Although FRANCISCO JOSE DE GOYA LUCIENTES (1746–1828) was David's contemporary, their work has little in common. Both, however, rose to prominence as official court artists. When he was 40, Goya became Pintor del Rey (Painter to the King), and in 1799 Charles IV (r. 1788–1808) promoted him to First Court Painter. Goya did not arrive at his general dismissal of Neoclassicism without considerable thought about the Enlightenment and the Neoclassical penchant for rationality and order. In *The Sleep of Reason Produces Monsters* (FIG. **12-5**), a print from a series titled *Los Caprichos (The Caprices)*, Goya depicted himself

The Romantic Spirit in Music and Literature

The appeal of Romanticism, with its emphasis on freedom and emotions unrestrained by rational thought (FIG. 12-5), extended well beyond the realm of the visual arts. In European music, literature, and poetry, the Romantic spirit was a dominant presence during the late 18th and early 19th centuries. These artistic endeavors rejected classicism's structured order in favor of the emotive and expressive. In music, the compositions of Franz Schubert (1797–1828), Franz Liszt (1811–1886), Frédéric Chopin (1810–1849), and Johannes Brahms (1833–1897) all emphasized the melodic or lyrical. These composers believed music had the power to express the unspeakable and to communicate the subtlest and most powerful human emotions.

In literature, Romantic poets such as John Keats (1795–1821), William Wordsworth (1770–1850), and Samuel Taylor Coleridge (1772–1834) published volumes of poetry that manifested the Romantic interest in lyrical drama. *Ozymandias,* by Percy Bysshe Shelley (1792–1822), speaks of faraway, exotic locales. The setting of *Sardanapalus* (1821) by Lord Byron (1788–1824) is the ancient Assyrian Empire (see Chapter 1). Byron's poem conjures images of eroticism and fury unleashed—images of the kind that appear in Delacroix's painting *Death of Sardanapalus* (FIG. 12-8). One of the best examples of the Romantic spirit is the engrossing novel *Frankenstein,* written in 1818 by Shelley's wife, Mary Wollstonecraft Shelley (1797–1851). This fantastic tale of a monstrous creature run amok not only embraced the emotional but also rejected the rationalism that underlay Enlightenment thought. Dr. Frankenstein's monster was a product of science, and the novel is an indictment of the tenacious belief in science that thinkers such as Voltaire promoted. *Frankenstein* served as a cautionary tale of the havoc that could result from unrestrained scientific experimentation and from the arrogance of scientists like Dr. Frankenstein.

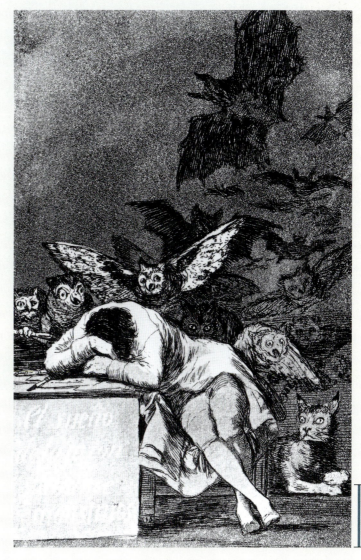

12-5 Francisco Goya, *The Sleep of Reason Produces Monsters,* from *Los Caprichos,* ca. 1798. Etching and aquatint, $8\frac{7}{16}'' \times 5\frac{7}{8}''$. Metropolitan Museum of Art, New York (gift of M. Knoedler & Co., 1918).

In this print, Goya depicted himself asleep while threatening creatures converge on him, revealing his commitment to the Romantic spirit—the unleashing of imagination, emotions, and nightmares.

1 in.

asleep, slumped onto a table or writing stand, while threatening creatures converge on him. Seemingly poised to attack the artist are owls (symbols of folly) and bats (symbols of ignorance). The viewer might read this as a portrayal of what emerges when reason is suppressed and, therefore, as an espousal of Enlightenment ideals. However, it also can be interpreted as Goya's commitment to the creative process and the Romantic spirit—the unleashing of imagination, emotions, and even nightmares (see "The Romantic Spirit in Music and Literature," above).

Third of May, 1808 As dissatisfaction with the rule of Charles IV increased, the political situation grew more tenuous. The Spanish people eventually threw their support behind Ferdinand VII, son of Charles IV and Queen Maria Luisa, in the hope that he would initiate reform. To overthrow his father and mother, Ferdinand enlisted the aid of Napoleon Bonaparte, who had designs on the Spanish throne and thus willingly sent French troops to Spain. Not surprisingly, as soon as he ousted Charles IV, Napoleon revealed his plan to rule Spain himself by installing his brother Joseph Bonaparte (r. 1808–1813) on the Spanish throne. The Spanish people, finally recognizing the French as invaders, sought a way to expel the foreign troops. On May 2, 1808, in frustration, the Spanish attacked Napoleon's soldiers in a chaotic and violent clash. In retaliation and as a show of force, the French responded the next day by executing numerous Spanish citizens.

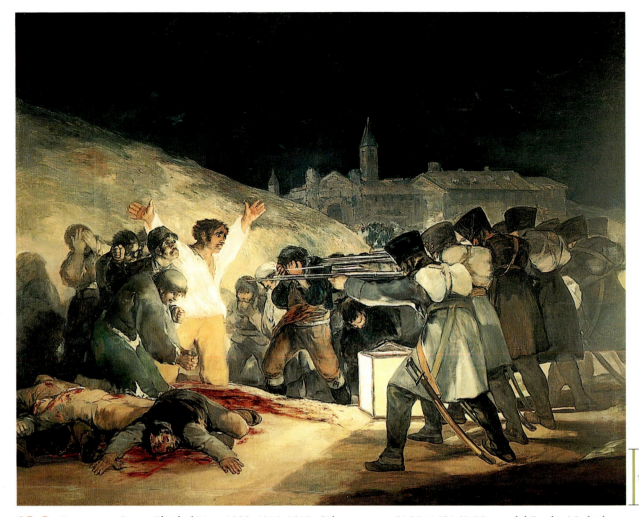

12-6 Francisco Goya, *Third of May, 1808*, 1814–1815. Oil on canvas, 8′ 9″ × 13′ 4″. Museo del Prado, Madrid.

Goya encouraged viewer empathy for the massacred Spanish peasants by portraying horrified expressions and anguish on their faces, endowing them with a humanity lacking in the French firing squad.

1 ft.

This tragic event is the subject of Goya's most famous painting, *Third of May, 1808* (FIG. **12-6**). In emotional fashion, Goya depicted the anonymous murderous wall of French soldiers ruthlessly executing the unarmed and terrified Spanish peasants. The artist encouraged empathy for the Spaniards by portraying horrified expressions and anguish on their faces, endowing them with a humanity lacking in the firing squad. Moreover, the peasant about to be shot throws his arms out in a cruciform gesture reminiscent of Christ's position on the cross. Goya enhanced the emotional drama of this tragic event through his stark use of darks and lights and by extending the time frame. Although Goya captured the specific moment when one man is about to be executed, he also depicted the bloody bodies of others already lying dead on the ground. Still others have been herded together to be shot in a few moments.

Théodore Géricault In France, one of the two greatest Romantic painters was THÉODORE GÉRICAULT (1791–1824). Although Géricault retained an interest in the heroic and the epic and was well trained in classical drawing, he chafed at the rigidity of the Neoclassical style, instead producing works that captivate the viewer with their drama, visual complexity, and emotional force.

Géricault's most ambitious project was *Raft of the Medusa* (FIG. **12-7**). In this gigantic (16 by 23 feet) depiction of a historical event, the artist abandoned the idealism of Neoclassicism and invoked the theatricality of Romanticism. The painting's subject is an 1816 shipwreck off the African coast. The French frigate *Medusa* ran aground on a reef due to the incompetence of the captain, a political appointee. In an attempt to survive, 150 passengers built a makeshift raft from pieces of the disintegrating ship. The raft drifted for 12 days, and the number of survivors dwindled to 15. Finally, a ship spotted the raft and rescued the emaciated survivors. This horrendous event was political dynamite once it became public knowledge.

In *Raft of the Medusa*, which Géricault took eight months to complete, the artist sought to capture the horror, chaos, and emotion of the tragedy yet invoke the grandeur and impact of large-scale history painting. The few despairing survivors summon what little strength they have left to flag down the passing ship far on the horizon. Géricault departed from the straightforward organization of Neoclassical compositions and

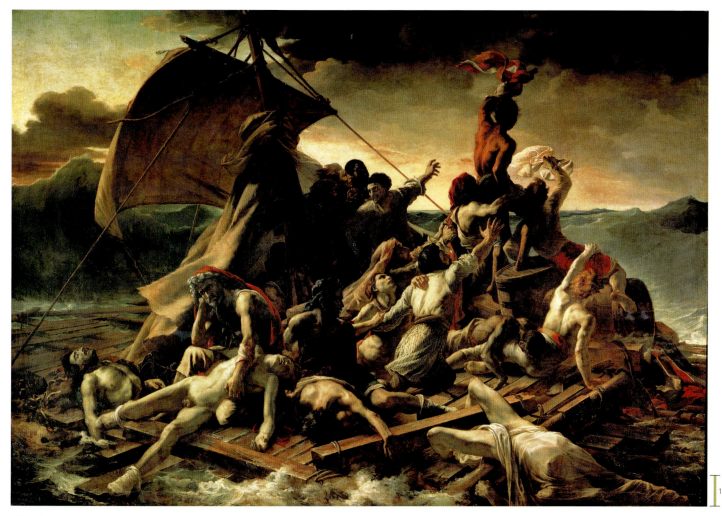

12-7 THÉODORE GÉRICAULT, *Raft of the Medusa*, 1818–1819. Oil on canvas, 16′ 1″ × 23′ 6″. Louvre, Paris.

In this huge history painting, Géricault rejected Neoclassical compositional principles and, consistent with the Romantic spirit, presented a jumble of writhing bodies in every attitude of suffering, despair, and death.

instead presented a jumble of writhing bodies. He arranged the survivors and several corpses in a powerful X-shaped composition, and piled one body on another in every attitude of suffering, despair, and death. One light-filled diagonal axis stretches from bodies at the lower left up to the black man raised on his comrades' shoulders and waving a piece of cloth toward the horizon. The cross axis descends from the storm clouds and the dark, billowing sail at the upper left to the shadowed upper torso of the body trailing in the open sea. Géricault's decision to place the raft at a diagonal so that a corner juts outward further compels the viewer to participate in this scene. Indeed, it seems as though some of the corpses are sliding off the raft into the viewing space. The subdued palette and prominent shadows lend an ominous pall to the scene.

Despite the theatricality and dramatic action that imbue this work with a Romantic spirit, Géricault went to great lengths to ensure the accuracy of his representation. He visited hospitals and morgues to examine corpses, interviewed the survivors, and had a model of the raft constructed in his studio. Géricault also took this opportunity to insert a comment on the practice of slavery. The artist was a member of an abolitionist group that sought ways to end the slave trade

in the colonies. Given Géricault's antipathy to slavery, it is appropriate that he placed Jean Charles, a black soldier and one of the few survivors, at the top of the pyramidal heap of bodies.

Eugène Delacroix Art historians often present the history of painting during the first half of the 19th century as a contest between two major artists—Ingres, the Neoclassical draftsman, and EUGÈNE DELACROIX (1798–1863), the Romantic colorist. Their dialogue recalls the quarrel at the end of the 17th century and into the 18th (see Chapter 11) between the Poussinistes, the conservative defenders of academism who regarded drawing as superior to color, and the Rubénistes, who championed the importance of color over line. No other painter of the time explored the domain of Romantic subject and mood as thoroughly and definitively as Delacroix. His technique was impetuous, improvisational, and instinctive, rather than the deliberate, studious, and cold application of pigment of the Neoclassicists (see "Delacroix on Neoclassicism," page 344). His work epitomized Romantic colorist painting, catching the impression quickly and developing it in the execution process. His contemporaries commented on

Romanticism | 343

Delacroix on Neoclassicism

Eugène Delacroix, the leading French Romantic painter of the 19th century, expressed his contempt for the Neoclassical style of Jacques-Louis David (FIGS. 11-15 and 11-16) and others in a series of letters he wrote in 1832 from Morocco. Romantic artists often depicted exotic faraway places they had never seen, but Delacroix actually made the journey to northern Africa in search of fresh inspiration for his paintings. He discovered in the sundrenched Moroccan landscape and in the hardy and colorful men dressed in robes reminiscent of the Roman toga a culture more classical than anything European Neoclassicism could conceive. In a letter to his friend Fréderic Villot dated February 29, 1832, he wrote:

> This place is made for painters. . . . [B]eauty abounds here; not the overpraised beauty of fashionable paintings. The heroes of David and Co. with their rose-pink limbs would cut a sorry figure beside these children of the sun, who moreover wear the dress of classical antiquity with a nobler air, I dare assert.*

In a second letter, written June 4, 1832, he reported to Auguste Jal:

> I have Romans and Greeks on my doorstep: it makes me laugh heartily at David's Greeks, . . . I know now what they were really like; . . . If painting schools persist in [depicting classical subjects], I am convinced, and you will agree with me, that they would gain far more from being shipped off as cabin boys on the first boat bound for the Barbary coast than from spending any more time wearing out the classical soil of Rome. Rome is no longer to be found in Rome.†

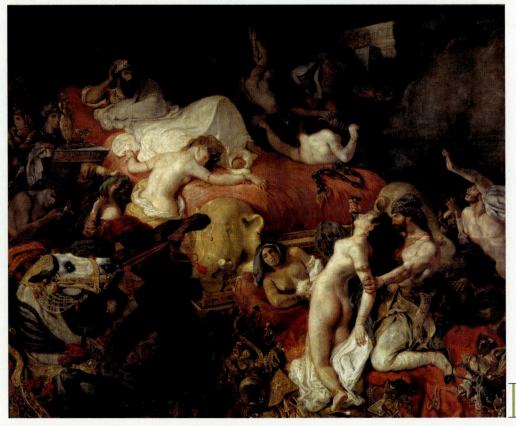

12-8 EUGÈNE DELACROIX, *Death of Sardanapalus*, 1827. Oil on canvas, 12′ 1½″ × 16′ 2⅞″. Louvre, Paris.

Inspired by Lord Byron's 1821 poem, Delacroix painted the Romantic spectacle of an Assyrian king on his funeral pyre. The richly colored and emotionally charged canvas is filled with exotic figures.

1 ft.

* Translated by Jean Stewart, in Charles Harrison, Paul Wood, and Jason Gaiger, eds., *Art in Theory 1815–1900: An Anthology of Changing Ideas* (Oxford: Blackwell, 1998), 87.
† Ibid., 88.

how furiously Delacroix worked once he had an idea, keeping the whole painting progressing at once. The fury of his attack matched the fury of his imagination and his subjects.

Death of Sardanapalus

Delacroix's richly colored and emotionally charged *Death of Sardanapalus* (FIG. 12-8) is a grand Romantic pictorial drama. Although inspired by Lord Byron's poem *Sardanapalus* (see "The Romantic Spirit," page 341), the painting does not illustrate that text. Instead, Delacroix depicted the last hour of the Assyrian king (who had just received news of his armies' defeat and the enemies' entry into his city) in a much more tempestuous and crowded setting than Byron described. Here, orgiastic destruction replaces the sacrificial suicide found in the poem.

In the painting, the king reclines on his funeral pyre, soon to be set alight, and gloomily watches the destruction of all of his most precious possessions—his women, slaves, horses, and treasure. Sardanapalus's favorite concubine throws herself on the bed, determined to perish in the flames with her master. The king presides like a genius of evil over the tragic scene. Most conspicuous are the tortured and dying bodies of the harem women. In the foreground, a muscular slave plunges his knife into the neck of one woman. Delacroix filled this awful spectacle of suffering and death with the most daringly difficult and tortuous poses, and chose the richest intensities of hue. With its exotic and erotic overtones, *Death of Sardanapalus* tapped into the fantasies of Romantic-era viewers.

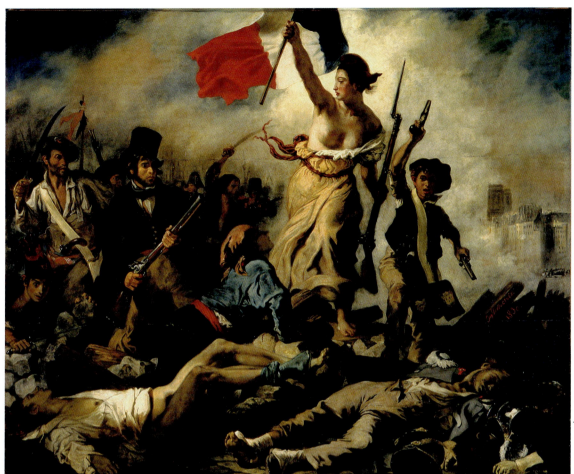

12-9 Eugène Delacroix, *Liberty Leading the People*, 1830. Oil on canvas, 8′ 6″ × 10′ 8″. Louvre, Paris.

Balancing contemporaneous historical fact with poetic allegory, Delacroix captured the passion and energy of the 1830 revolution in this painting of Liberty leading the Parisian uprising against Charles X.

1 ft.

Liberty Leading the People Although *Death of Sardanapalus* is a seventh-century BCE drama, Delacroix, like Géricault, also turned to current events, particularly tragic or sensational ones, for his subject matter. For example, he produced several images based on the Greek war for independence (1821–1829). Certainly, the French perception of the Greeks locked in a brutal struggle for freedom from the cruel and exotic Ottoman Turks generated great interest in Romantic circles. Closer to home, Delacroix captured the passion and energy of the 1830 revolution in France in his painting *Liberty Leading the People* (FIG. **12-9**). Based on the Parisian uprising against Charles X (r. 1824–1830) at the end of July 1830, it depicts the allegorical personification of Liberty, defiantly thrusting forth the French Republic's tricolor banner as she urges the masses to fight on. She wears a scarlet Phrygian cap (the symbol of a freed slave in antiquity), which reinforces the urgency of this struggle. Arrayed around Liberty are bold Parisian types—the street boy brandishing his pistols, the menacing worker with a cutlass, and the intellectual dandy in top hat with sawed-off musket. As in Géricault's *Raft of the Medusa* (FIG. **12-7**), dead bodies lie all around. In the background, the Gothic towers of Notre-Dame (FIG. **7-8**) rise through the smoke and haze. The painter's inclusion of this recognizable Parisian landmark specifies the locale and event, balancing contemporary historical fact with poetic allegory.

Landscape Painting

Landscape painting came into its own in the 19th century as a fully independent and respected genre. Briefly eclipsed at the century's beginning by the taste for ideal form, which favored figural composition and history, landscape painting expressed the Romantic view, first extolled by Rousseau, of nature as a "being" that included the totality of existence in organic unity and harmony. In nature—"the living garment of God," as German poet and dramatist Johann Wolfgang von Goethe (1749–1832) called it—artists found an ideal subject to express the Romantic theme of the soul unified with the natural world. As all nature was mysteriously permeated by "being," landscape artists had the task of interpreting the signs, symbols, and emblems of universal spirit disguised within visible material things. Artists no longer merely beheld a landscape, but rather participated in its spirit, becoming translators of nature's transcendent meanings.

Caspar David Friedrich Among the first artists to depict the Romantic transcendental landscape was CASPAR DAVID FRIEDRICH (1774–1840). For Friedrich, landscapes were temples and his paintings were altarpieces. The reverential mood of his works demands from the viewer the silence appropriate to sacred places filled with a divine presence. *Abbey*

12-10 CASPAR DAVID FRIEDRICH, *Abbey in the Oak Forest*, 1810. Oil on canvas, 4′ × 5′ 8½″. Nationalgalerie, Staatliche Museen zu Berlin, Berlin.

Friedrich was a master of the Romantic transcendental landscape. The reverential mood of this winter scene with the ruins of a Gothic church and cemetery demands the silence appropriate to sacred places.

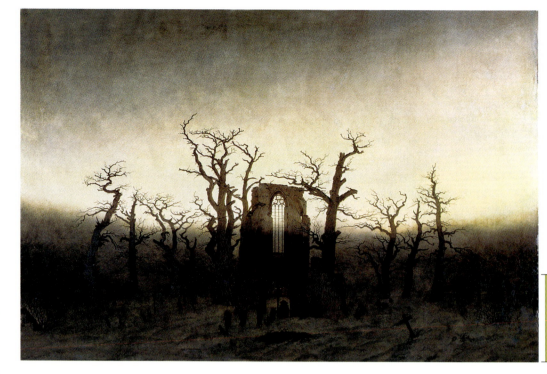

1 ft.

in the Oak Forest (FIG. **12-10**) serves as a solemn requiem. Under a winter sky, through the leafless oaks of a snow-covered cemetery, a funeral procession bears a coffin into the ruins of a Gothic church. The emblems of death are everywhere—the season's desolation, the leaning crosses and tombstones, the black of mourning that the grieving wear, the skeletal trees, and the destruction time wrought on the church. The painting is a meditation on human mortality. As Friedrich himself remarked: "Why . . . do I so frequently choose death, transience, and the grave as subjects for my paintings? One must submit oneself many times to death in order some day to attain life everlasting."[1] The artist's sharp-focused rendering of details demonstrates his keen perception of everything in the physical environment relevant to his message. Friedrich's work balances inner and outer experience. "The artist," he wrote, "should not only paint what he sees before him, but also what he sees within him."[2] Although Friedrich's works may not have the theatrical energy of the paintings of Géricault or Delacroix, a resonant and deep emotion pervades them.

John Constable One of the most momentous developments in Western history—the Industrial Revolution—greatly influenced the evolution of Romantic landscape painting in England. Although discussion of the Industrial Revolution invariably focuses on technological advances,

12-11 JOHN CONSTABLE, *The Haywain*, 1821. Oil on canvas, 4′ 3¼″ × 6′ 1″. National Gallery, London.

The Haywain is a nostalgic view of the disappearing English countryside during the Industrial Revolution. Constable had a special gift for capturing the texture that climate and weather give to landscape.

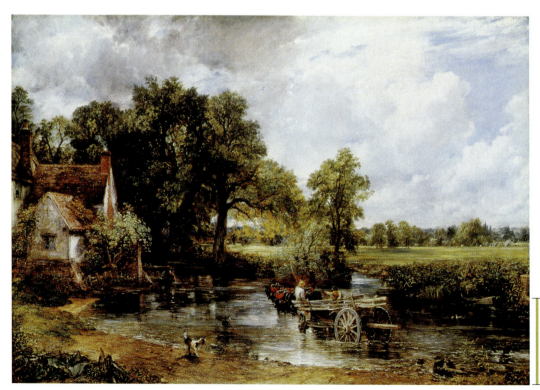

1 ft.

factory development, and growth of urban centers, its effect on the countryside and the land itself was no less severe. The decline in prices for agrarian products caused by industrialization produced significant unrest in the English countryside. In particular, increasing numbers of displaced farmers could no longer afford to farm their small land plots. JOHN CONSTABLE (1776–1837) addressed the agrarian situation in his landscape paintings. *The Haywain* (FIG. **12-11**) is a placid, picturesque scene of the countryside. A small cottage is on the left, and in the center foreground a man leads a horse and wagon across the stream. Billowy clouds float lazily across the sky. The muted greens and golds and the delicacy of Constable's brush strokes augment the scene's tranquility. The artist portrayed the oneness with nature that the Romantic poets sought. The relaxed figures are not observers but participants in the landscape's being. Constable made countless sketches from nature for each of his canvases, studying nature as a meteorologist (which he was by avocation). His special gift was for capturing textures the climate and the weather gave to landscape. Constable's use of tiny dabs of local color, stippled with white, created a sparkling shimmer of light and hue across the canvas surface—the vibration itself suggestive of movement and process.

The Haywain is also significant for precisely what it does not show—the civil unrest of the agrarian working class and the outbreaks of violence and arson that resulted. The people that populate Constable's landscapes blend into the scenes and are one with nature. Rarely does the viewer see workers engaged in tedious labor. Indeed, this painting has a nostalgic, wistful air to it—a lament to a disappearing rural pastoralism. (Constable came from a rural landowning family of considerable wealth.) This nostalgia, presented in such naturalistic terms, renders Constable's works Romantic in tone. That Constable felt a kindred spirit with the Romantic artists is revealed by his comment "painting is but another word for feeling."[3]

J.M.W. Turner Constable's contemporary in the English school of landscape painting, JOSEPH MALLORD WILLIAM TURNER (1775–1851), produced work that also responded to encroaching industrialization. However, whereas Constable's paintings are serene and precisely painted, Turner's feature turbulent swirls of frothy pigment. The passion and energy of Turner's works reveal the Romantic sensibility that was the foundation for his art and also clearly illustrate Edmund Burke's concept of the sublime—awe mixed with terror.

Among Turner's most notable works is *The Slave Ship* (FIG. **12-12**). Its subject is a 1783 incident reported in a widely read book by Thomas Clarkson, *The History of the Abolition of the Slave Trade.* Because the book had just been reprinted in 1839, Clarkson's account probably prompted Turner's choice of subject for this 1840 painting. The incident involved the captain of a slave ship who, on realizing that his insurance company would reimburse him only for slaves lost at sea but not for those who died en route, ordered the sick and dying slaves thrown overboard. Turner's frenzied emotional depiction of this act matches its barbaric nature. The artist transformed the sun into an incandescent comet amid flying scarlet clouds. The slave ship moves into the distance, leaving in its wake a turbulent sea choked with the bodies of slaves sinking to their deaths. The scale of the minuscule human forms compared with the vast sea and overarching sky reinforces the sense of the sublime, especially the immense power of nature over humans. Almost lost in the boiling colors are the event's particulars, but on close inspection, the viewer can discern the iron shackles and manacles around the wrists and ankles of the drowning slaves, denying them any chance of saving themselves.

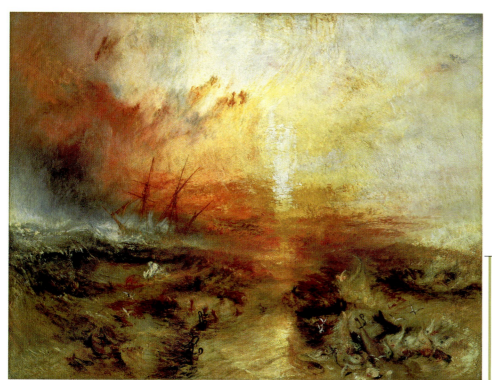

12-12 JOSEPH MALLORD WILLIAM TURNER, *The Slave Ship (Slavers Throwing Overboard the Dead and Dying, Typhoon Coming On)*, 1840. Oil on canvas, 2′ 11¼″ × 4′. Museum of Fine Arts, Boston (Henry Lillie Pierce Fund).

The essence of Turner's innovative style is the emotive power of color. He released color from any defining outlines to express both the forces of nature and the painter's emotional response to them.

1 ft.

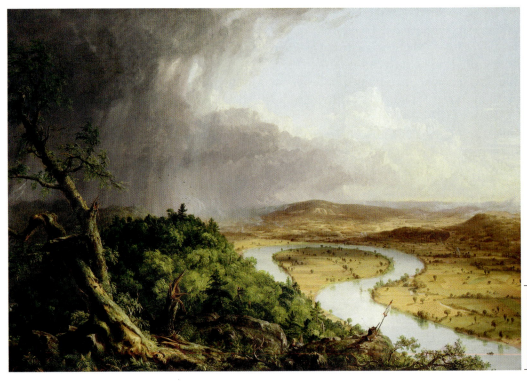

12-13 THOMAS COLE, *The Oxbow (View from Mount Holyoke, Northampton, Massachusetts, after a Thunderstorm)*, 1836. Oil on canvas, 4′ 3½″ × 6′ 4″. Metropolitan Museum of Art, New York (gift of Mrs. Russell Sage, 1908).

Cole divided his canvas into dark, stormy wilderness on the left and sunlit civilization on the right. The minuscule painter at the bottom center seems to be asking for advice about America's future course.

1 ft.

A key ingredient in Turner's highly personal style is the emotive power of pure color. The haziness of the picture's forms and the indistinctness of his compositions intensify the colors and energetic brush strokes. Turner's great innovation was to release color from any defining outlines so as to express both the forces of nature and the painter's emotional response to them. In his paintings, the reality of color is at one with the reality of feeling. Turner's methods had an incalculable effect on the later development of painting. His discovery of the aesthetic and emotive power of pure color and his pushing of the medium's fluidity to a point where the paint itself is almost the subject were important steps toward 20th-century abstract art, which dispensed with shape and form altogether (see Chapter 15).

Thomas Cole In America, landscape painting was the specialty of a group of artists known as the Hudson River School, so named because its members drew their subjects primarily from the uncultivated regions of New York State's Hudson River valley, although many of these painters depicted scenes from across the country. Like the early-19th-century landscape painters in Germany and England, the artists of the Hudson River School not only presented Romantic panoramic landscape views but also participated in the ongoing exploration of the individual's and the country's relationship to the land. American landscape painters frequently focused on identifying qualities that made America unique. An American painter of English birth, THOMAS COLE (1801–1848), often considered the leader of the Hudson River School, articulated this idea:

> Whether he [an American] beholds the Hudson mingling waters with the Atlantic—explores the central wilds of this vast continent, or stands on the margin of the distant Oregon, he is still in the midst of American scenery—it is his own land;

its beauty, its magnificence, its sublimity—all are his; and how undeserving of such a birthright, if he can turn towards it an unobserving eye, an unaffected heart![4]

Another issue that surfaced frequently in Hudson River School paintings was the moral question of America's direction as a civilization. Cole presented the viewer with this issue in *The Oxbow* (FIG. **12-13**). A splendid scene opens before the viewer, dominated by the lazy oxbow-shaped curve of the Connecticut River near Mount Holyoke, Massachusetts. Cole divided the composition in two, with the dark, stormy wilderness on the left and sunlit civilization on the right. The minuscule artist in the bottom center of the painting (wearing a top hat), dwarfed by the landscape's scale, turns to the viewer as if to ask for input in deciding the country's future course. Cole's depiction of expansive wilderness incorporated reflections and moods romantically appealing to the public.

REALISM

Realism was a movement that developed in France around midcentury against the backdrop of an increasing emphasis on science. Advances in industrial technology during the early 19th century reinforced the Enlightenment's foundation of rationalism. Both intellectuals and the general public increasingly embraced *empiricism* (the search for knowledge based on observation and direct experience). Indicative of the widespread faith in science was the influence of *positivism*, a Western philosophical model developed by the French philosopher Auguste Comte (1798–1857). Positivists promoted science as the mind's highest achievement and advocated a purely empirical approach to nature and society. Comte believed that scientific laws governed the environment and human activity and could be revealed through careful recording and analysis of observable data. Like the empiricists and positivists, Realist

Courbet on Realism

The Parisian academic jury selecting work for the 1855 Salon (part of the Exposition Universelle in that year) rejected two of Courbet's paintings on the grounds that his subjects and figures were too coarse and too large. In response, Courbet withdrew all of his works and set up his own exhibition outside the grounds, calling it the Pavilion of Realism. Courbet was the first artist ever to stage a private exhibition of his own work. His pavilion and the statement he issued to explain the paintings shown there amounted to the new movement's manifestos.

The title of "realist" has been imposed upon me . . . . Titles have never given a just idea of things; were it otherwise, the work would be superfluous. . . . I have studied the art of the moderns, avoiding any preconceived system and without prejudice. I have no more wanted to imitate the former than to copy the latter; nor have I thought of achieving the idle aim of "art for art's sake." No! I have simply wanted to draw from a thorough knowledge of tradition the reasoned and free sense of my own individuality. . . . To be able to translate the customs, ideas, and appearances of my time as I see them—in a word, to create a living art—this has been my aim.*

On Christmas Day, 1861, six years after distributing that statement at his Pavilion of Realism, Courbet wrote an open letter, published a few days later in the Courier *du dimanche,* addressed to prospective students.

[An artist must apply] his personal faculties to the ideas and the events of the times in which he lives. . . . [A]rt in painting should consist only of the representation of things that are visible and tangible to the artist. Every age should be represented only by its own artists, that is to say, by the artists who have lived in it. I also maintain that painting is an essentially concrete art form and can consist only of the representation of both real and existing things. . . . An abstract object, not visible, nonexistent, is not within the domain of painting.[†]

Courbet's most famous statement, however, is his blunt dismissal of academic painting, in which he concisely summed up the core principle of Realist painting: "I have never seen an angel. Show me an angel, and I'll paint one."[‡]

12-14 GUSTAVE COURBET, *The Stone Breakers*, 1849. Oil on canvas, 5′ 3″ × 8′ 6″. Formerly at Gemäldegalerie, Dresden (destroyed in 1945).

Courbet was the leading figure in the Realist movement. In this large work, he used a palette of dirty browns and grays to convey the dreary and dismal nature of menial labor in mid-19th-century France.

1 ft.

* Translated by Robert Goldwater and Marco Treves, eds., *Artists on Art from the XIV to the XX Century,* 3d ed. (New York: Pantheon, 1958), 295.
† Translated by Petra ten-Doesschate Chu, *Letters of Gustave Courbet* (Chicago: University of Chicago Press, 1992), 203–204.
‡ Quoted by Vincent van Gogh in a July 1885 letter to his brother Theo. Ronald de Leeuw, *The Letters of Vincent van Gogh* (New York: Penguin, 1996), 302.

artists argued that only the things of one's own time—what people could see for themselves—were "real." Accordingly, Realists focused their attention on the experiences and sights of everyday contemporary life and disapproved of historical and fictional subjects on the grounds that they were neither real and visible nor of the present.

France

Gustave Courbet The leading figure of the Realist movement in 19th-century art was GUSTAVE COURBET (1819–1877). In fact, Courbet used the term *Realism* when exhibiting his works, even though he shunned labels (see "Courbet on Realism," above). The Realists' sincerity about scrutinizing their environment led them to portray objects and im-

ages that in recent centuries artists had deemed unworthy of depiction—the mundane and trivial, working-class laborers and peasants, and so forth. Moreover, the Realists depicted these scenes on a scale and with an earnestness and seriousness previously reserved for grand history painting

Stone Breakers In *The Stone Breakers* (FIG. **12-14**), Courbet captured on canvas in a straightforward manner two men—one about 70, the other quite young—in the act of breaking stones, traditionally the lot of the lowest in French society. By juxtaposing youth and age, Courbet suggested that those born to poverty remain poor their entire lives. The artist neither romanticized nor idealized the men's menial labor but depicted their thankless toil with directness and accuracy. Courbet's palette of dirty browns and grays conveys the dreary and dismal nature of the task, while the angular positioning of the older stone breaker's limbs suggests a mechanical monotony. The heroic, the sublime, and the dramatic are not found here. Theatricality was at the heart of Romanticism. Realism captured the ordinary rhythms of daily life.

Courbet's choice of the working poor as subject matter had special meaning for the mid-19th-century French audience. In 1848 workers rebelled against the bourgeois leaders of the newly formed Second Republic and against the rest of the nation, demanding better working conditions and a redistribution of property. The army quelled the revolution in three days, but not without long-lasting trauma and significant loss of life. That uprising thus raised the issue of labor as a national concern and placed workers on center stage, both literally and symbolically. Courbet's depiction of stone breakers in 1849 was both timely and populist.

Of great importance for the later history of art, Realism also involved a reconsideration of the painter's primary goals and departed from the established priority on illusionism. Accordingly, Realists called attention to painting as a pictorial construction by the way they applied pigment or manipulated composition. Courbet's intentionally simple and direct methods of expression in composition and technique seemed unbearably crude to many of his more traditional contemporaries, who called him a primitive. Although his bold, somber palette was essentially traditional, Courbet often used the *palette knife* for placing and unifying large daubs of paint, producing a roughly wrought surface. His example

inspired later Impressionists, such as Claude Monet and Auguste Renoir (see Chapter 13), but the public accused him of carelessness, and critics wrote of his "brutalities."

Jean-François Millet Like Courbet, JEAN-FRANÇOIS MILLET (1814–1878) found his subjects in the people and occupations of the everyday world. Millet was one of a group of French painters of country life who, to be close to their rural subjects, settled near the village of Barbizon. This Barbizon School specialized in detailed pictures of forest and countryside. In *The Gleaners* (FIG. **12-15**), Millet depicted three peasant women performing the back-breaking task of gleaning the last wheat scraps. These impoverished women were members of the lowest level of peasant society. Landowning nobles traditionally permitted them to glean—to pick up the remainders left in the field after the harvest. Millet characteristically placed his monumental figures in the foreground, against a broad sky. Although the field stretches back to a rim of haystacks, cottages, trees, and distant workers and a flat horizon, the gleaners quietly going about their tedious and time-consuming work dominate the canvas.

Although Millet's works have a sentimentality absent from those of Courbet, the French public still reacted to his paintings with disdain and suspicion. In the aftermath of the 1848 revolution, for Millet to invest the poor with solemn grandeur did not meet with the approval of the prosperous classes. Further, the middle class linked the poor with the dangerous, newly defined working class, which was finding outspoken champions in social theorists such as Karl

12-15 JEAN-FRANÇOIS MILLET, *The Gleaners*, 1857. Oil on canvas, 2′ 9″ × 3′ 8″. Musée d'Orsay, Paris.

Millet and the Barbizon School painters specialized in depictions of French country life. Here, Millet portrayed three impoverished women gathering the remainders left in the field after a harvest.

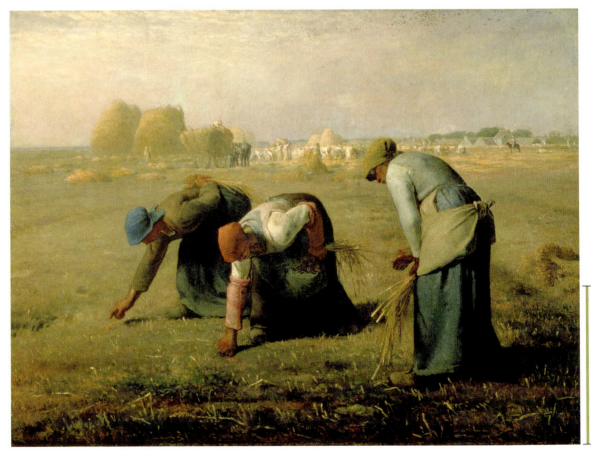

1 ft.

Lithography

Lithography (Greek, "stone writing") was the invention of the German printmaker Alois Senefelder (1771–1834), who in 1798 created the first prints using stone instead of metal plates or wooden blocks. In contrast to earlier printing techniques (see "Woodcuts, Engravings, and Etchings," Chapter 8, page 228) in which the artist applied ink either to a raised or incised surface, in lithography the printing and nonprinting areas of the plate are on the same plane.

The chemical phenomenon fundamental to lithography is the repellence of oil and water. The lithographer uses a greasy, oil-based crayon to draw directly on a stone plate and then wipes water onto the stone, which clings only to the areas the drawing does not cover. Next, the artist rolls oil-based ink onto the stone, which adheres to the drawing but is repelled by the water. When the artist presses the stone against paper, only the inked areas—the drawing—transfer to the paper.

Color lithography requires multiple plates, one for each color, and the printmaker must take special care to make sure each impression lines up perfectly with the previous one so that each color prints in its proper place.

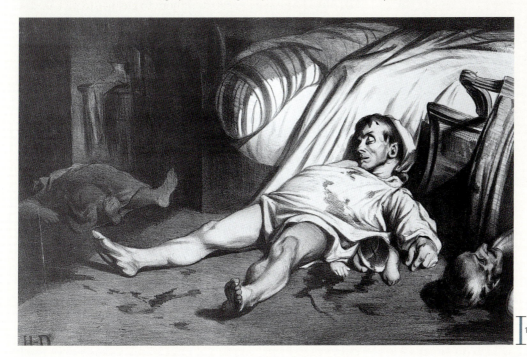

12-16 Honoré Daumier, *Rue Transnonain*, 1834. Lithograph, $1' \times 1' 5\frac{1}{2}''$. Philadelphia Museum of Art, Philadelphia (bequest of Fiske and Marie Kimball).

Daumier used the recent invention of lithography to reach a wide audience for his social criticism and political protest. This print records the horrific 1834 massacre in a workers' housing block in Paris.

1 in.

Marx (1818–1883) and Friedrich Engels (1820–1895), and the novelists Émile Zola (1840–1902) and Charles Dickens (1812–1870). Socialism was a growing movement, and its views on property and its call for social justice, even economic equality, frightened the bourgeoisie. In Millet's sympathetic portrayal of the poor, many saw a political manifesto.

Honoré Daumier Because people widely recognized the power of art to serve political means, the political and social agitation accompanying the violent revolutions in France and the rest of Europe in the later 18th and early 19th centuries prompted the French people to suspect artists of subversive intention. Honoré Daumier (1808–1879) was a defender of the urban working classes, and through his Realist art, he boldly confronted authority with social criticism and political protest. In response, the authorities imprisoned Daumier. A painter, sculptor, and one of the world's great printmakers, Daumier produced *lithographs* (see "Lithography," above) that allowed him to create an unprecedented number of prints,

thereby reaching a broader audience. Daumier also contributed satirical lithographs to the widely read, liberal French Republican journal *Caricature*. In these prints, he mercilessly lampooned the foibles and misbehavior of politicians, lawyers, doctors, and the rich bourgeoisie in general.

Daumier's lithograph *Rue Transnonain* (FIG. 12-16) depicts an atrocity with the same shocking impact as Goya's *Third of May, 1808* (FIG. 12-6). The lithograph's title refers to a street in Paris where an unknown sniper killed a civil guard, part of a government force trying to repress a worker demonstration. Because the fatal shot had come from a workers' housing block, the remaining guards immediately stormed the building and massacred all of its inhabitants. With Goya's power, Daumier created a view of the slaughter from a sharp, realistic angle of vision. He depicted not the dramatic moment of execution but the terrible, quiet aftermath. The broken, scattered forms lie amid violent disorder. Daumier's pictorial manner is rough and spontaneous. How it carries expressive exaggeration is part of its remarkable force.

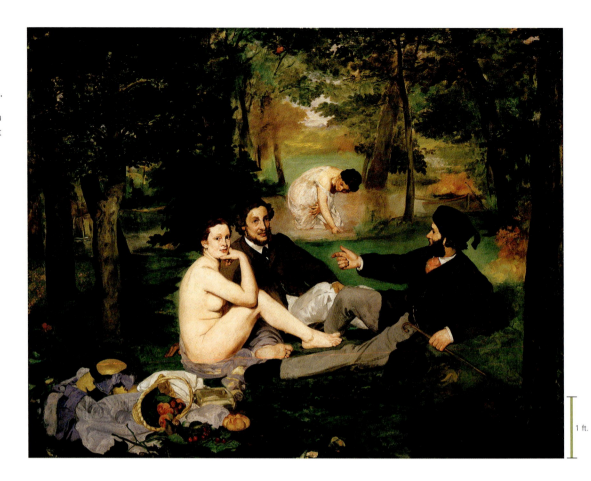

12-17 ÉDOUARD MANET, *Le Déjeuner sur l'Herbe (Luncheon on the Grass),* 1863. Oil on canvas, 7′ × 8′ 8″. Musée d'Orsay, Paris.

Manet drew intense criticism both for his shocking subject matter and his manner of painting. Moving away from illusionism, he used colors to flatten form and to draw attention to the painting surface.

1 ft.

Édouard Manet Like Gustave Courbet, ÉDOUARD MANET (1832–1883) was a pivotal artist during the 19th century. Not only was his work critical for the articulation of Realist principles, but his art also played an important role in the development of Impressionism in the 1870s (see Chapter 13). Manet's masterpiece, *Le Déjeuner sur l'Herbe (Luncheon on the Grass;* FIG. **12-17**), depicts two women, one nude, and two clothed men enjoying a picnic of sorts. Consistent with Realist principles, Manet based all of the foreground figures on living people. The seated woman is Manet's favorite model at the time, and the gentlemen are his brother (with cane) and the sculptor Ferdinand Leenhof. The two men wear fashionable Parisian attire of the 1860s. In contrast, the nude woman is an unidealized figure type. She also seems disturbingly unabashed and at ease, gazing directly at the viewer without shame or flirtatiousness.

This audacious painting outraged the public. Rather than depicting a traditional pastoral scene, *Le Déjeuner* represented ordinary men and promiscuous women in a Parisian park. Manet surely anticipated criticism of his painting, but shocking the public was not his primary aim. His goal was more complex and involved a reassessment of the entire range of art. *Le Déjeuner* contains sophisticated references and allusions to many painting genres—history painting, portraiture, pastoral scenes, nudes, and even religious scenes. It is, in fact, a synthesis and critique of the history of painting.

The negative response to *Le Déjeuner* by public and critics alike extended beyond Manet's subject matter to his manner of painting. He rendered in soft focus and broadly painted the landscape, including the pool in which the second woman bathes. This loose manner of painting contrasts with the clear forms of the harshly lit foreground trio and the pile of discarded female attire and picnic foods at the lower left. The lighting creates strong contrasts between darks and highlighted areas. In the main figures, many values are summed up in one or two lights or darks. The effect is both to flatten the forms and to give them a hard, snapping presence. Form, rather than being a matter of line, is only a function of paint and light. Manet himself declared that the chief actor in the painting is the light. Manet used art to call attention to art. In other words, he was moving away from illusion and toward open acknowledgment of painting's properties, such as the flatness of the painting surface, which would become a core principle of many later 19th- and 20th-century painters.

Olympia Even more scandalous to the French viewing public was Manet's *Olympia* (FIG. **12-18**). This work depicts a young white prostitute (Olympia was at the time a common "professional" name for prostitutes) reclining on a bed. Entirely nude except for a thin black ribbon tied around her neck, a bracelet on her arm, an orchid in her hair, and fashionable slippers on her feet, Olympia meets the viewer's eyes with a look of cool indifference. Behind her appears a black maid, who presents her a bouquet of flowers from a client.

Olympia horrified public and critics alike. Although images of prostitutes were not unheard of during this period, the shamelessness of Olympia and her look that verges on defiance shocked viewers. The depiction of a black woman was also not new to painting, but the public perceived Manet's inclusion of both a black maid and a nude prostitute as evoking

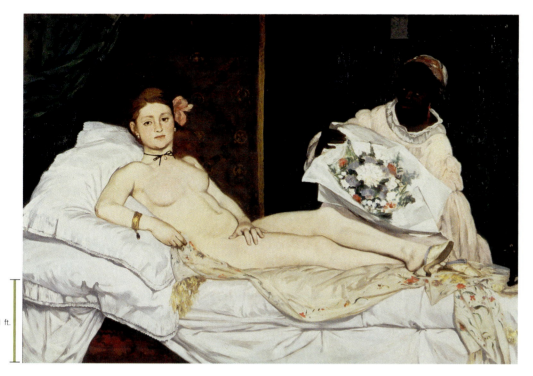

12-18 ÉDOUARD MANET, *Olympia*, 1863. Oil on canvas, 4′ 3″ × 6′ 2¼″. Musée d'Orsay, Paris.

Manet scandalized the public with this painting of a nude prostitute and her black maid carrying a bouquet from a client. Critics also faulted him for using rough brush strokes and abruptly shifting tonality.

moral depravity, inferiority, and animalistic sexuality. The contrast of the black servant with the fair-skinned courtesan also made reference to racial divisions. One critic described Olympia as "a courtesan with dirty hands and wrinkled feet . . . her body has the livid tint of a cadaver displayed in the morgue; her outlines are drawn in charcoal and her greenish, bloodshot eyes appear to be provoking the public, protected all the while by a hideous Negress."[5] From this statement, it is clear that the critic was responding to Manet's artistic style as well as his subject matter. Manet's brush strokes are rougher and the shifts in tonality more abrupt than those found in traditional academic painting. This departure from accepted practice exacerbated the audacity of the subject matter.

United States

Although French artists took the lead in promoting Realism and the notion that artists should depict the realities of modern life, this movement was not exclusively French. The Realist foundation in empiricism and positivism appealed to artists in many European countries and in the United States.

Winslow Homer One of the leading American Realist painters was WINSLOW HOMER (1836–1910) of Boston. During the Civil War, Homer joined the Union campaign as an artist-reporter for *Harper's Weekly*. At the end of the war, he painted *Veteran in a New Field* (FIG. 12-19). Although it is fairly simple and direct, this painting provides significant

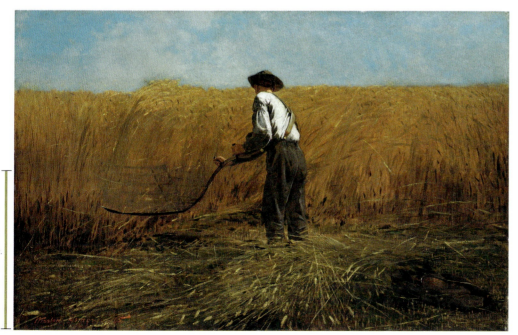

12-19 WINSLOW HOMER, *Veteran in a New Field*, 1865. Oil on canvas, 2′ ⅛″ × 3′ 2⅛″. Metropolitan Museum of Art, New York (bequest of Miss Adelaide Milton de Groot, 1967).

This veteran's productive work implies a smooth transition to peace after the American Civil War, but Homer placed a single-bladed scythe in his hands, a symbol of the deaths of soldiers and of Abraham Lincoln.

commentary on the effects and aftermath of America's catastrophic national conflict. The painting depicts a man with his back to the viewer, harvesting wheat. Homer identified him as a veteran by the uniform and canteen carelessly thrown on the ground. The veteran's involvement in meaningful and productive work implies a smooth transition from war to peace. This was seen as evidence of America's strength. "The peaceful and harmonious disbanding of the armies in the summer of 1865," poet Walt Whitman (1819–1892) wrote, was one of the "immortal proofs of democracy, unequall'd in all the history of the past."[6]

Veteran in a New Field also comments symbolically about death. By the 1860s, farmers used cradled scythes to harvest wheat. In this instance, however, Homer rejected realism in favor of symbolism. He painted a single-bladed scythe, thereby transforming the veteran into a symbol of Death—the Grim Reaper himself—and the painting into an elegy to the thousands of soldiers who died in the Civil War and into a lamentation on the death of recently assassinated President Abraham Lincoln.

Thomas Eakins Even more resolutely a Realist than Homer was Philadelphia-born THOMAS EAKINS (1844–1916). The too-brutal realism of Eakins's early masterpiece, *The Gross Clinic* (FIG. **12-20**), prompted the art jury to reject

it for the Philadelphia exhibition that celebrated the American independence centennial in 1876. The work presents the surgeon Dr. Samuel Gross in the operating amphitheater of the Jefferson Medical College in Philadelphia. Gross, with bloody fingers and scalpel, lectures about his surgery on a young man's leg. Watching the surgeon are several colleagues, all of whom historians have identified, and the patient's mother, who covers her face. The painting is an unsparing description of an unfolding event, with a good deal more reality than many viewers could endure. "It is a picture," one critic said, "that even strong men find difficult to look at long, if they can look at it at all."[7]

Edmonia Lewis Realism also appealed to some American sculptors. EDMONIA LEWIS (ca. 1845–after 1909) produced work that was stylistically indebted to Neoclassicism but depicted contemporary Realist themes. *Forever Free* (FIG. **12-21**) is a marble sculpture Lewis carved while living in

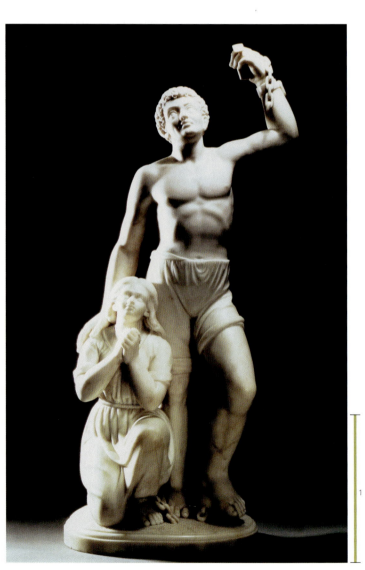

12-21 EDMONIA LEWIS, *Forever Free*, 1867. Marble, 3′ 5¼″ high. James A. Porter Gallery of Afro-American Art, Howard University, Washington, D.C.

Edmonia Lewis's *Forever Free,* carved in Rome four years after Abraham Lincoln's Emancipation Proclamation, owes a stylistic debt to Neoclassicism but depicts a Realist subject—two freed slaves.

12-20 THOMAS EAKINS, *The Gross Clinic*, 1875. Oil on canvas, 8′ × 6′ 6″. Philadelphia Museum of Art, Philadelphia.

The too-brutal realism of Eakins's depiction of the Jefferson Medical College operating amphitheater caused rejection of this painting from the Philadelphia exhibition celebrating America's centennial.

Rome, surrounded by examples of both classical and Renaissance art. It represents two freed African American slaves. The man stands heroically in a contrapposto stance reminiscent of classical statues. His right hand rests on the shoulder of the kneeling woman, and his left hand holds aloft a broken manacle and chain as literal and symbolic references to his former servitude. Produced four years after Lincoln's issuance of the Emancipation Proclamation, *Forever Free* was widely perceived as an abolitionist statement. However, because Lewis was female, African American, and Native American (she was the daughter of a Chippewa mother and African American father), scholars have debated the degree to which the sculptor attempted to inject a statement about African American gender relationships into this statue. For example, does the kneeling position of the woman represent Lewis's acceptance of female subordination?

Lewis's accomplishments as a sculptor speak to the increasing access to training that was available to women in the 19th century. Educated at Oberlin College (the first American college to grant degrees to women), Lewis financed her trip to Rome with the sale of medallions and marble busts. Her success in a field dominated by white male artists is a testament to both her skill and her determination.

England

Realism did not appeal to all artists, however. In England, a group of painters called the Pre-Raphaelite Brotherhood refused to be limited to the contemporary scenes strict Realists portrayed. These artists chose instead to represent fictional and historical subjects with a significant degree of convincing illusion. The Pre-Raphaelites wished to create fresh and sincere art, free from what they considered the tired, artificial manner propagated in the academies by the successors of Raphael.

Influenced by the critic, artist, and writer John Ruskin (1819–1900), the Brotherhood, organized in 1848, agreed with his distaste for the materialism and ugliness of the contemporary industrializing world. The Pre-Raphaelites also appreciated the spirituality and idealism (as well as the art and artisanship) of past times, especially the Middle Ages and the Early Renaissance.

John Everett Millais One of the Pre-Raphaelite Brotherhood's founders was JOHN EVERETT MILLAIS (1829–1896). Millais's painstaking observation of nature is apparent in *Ophelia* (FIG. **12-22**), which he exhibited in the 1855 Universal Exposition in Paris, where Courbet set up his Pavilion of Realism. The subject, from Shakespeare's *Hamlet*, is the drowning of Ophelia. To make the pathos of the scene visible, Millais became a faithful and feeling witness of its every detail, reconstructing it with a lyricism worthy of the original poetry. Although the scene is fictitious, Millais worked diligently to present it with unswerving fidelity to visual fact. He painted the background at a spot along the Hogsmill River in Surrey. For the figure of Ophelia, Millais had a friend lie in a heated bathtub full of water for hours at a stretch.

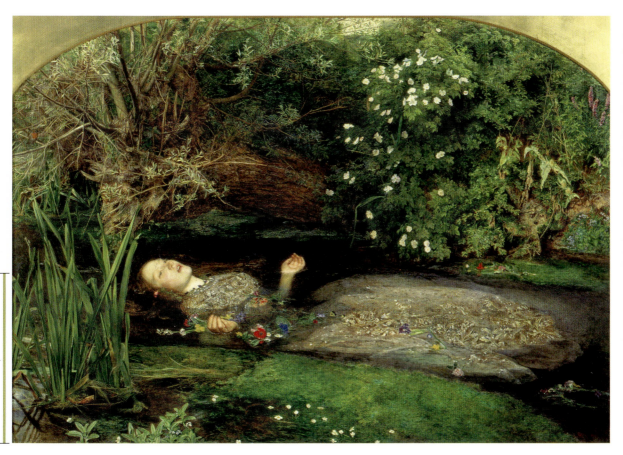

1 ft.

12-22 JOHN EVERETT MILLAIS, *Ophelia*, 1852. Oil on canvas, 2′ 6″ × 3′ 8″. Tate Gallery, London.

Millais was a founder of the Pre-Raphaelite Brotherhood, whose members refused to be limited to the contemporary scenes strict Realists portrayed. The drowning of Ophelia is a Shakespearean subject.

ARCHITECTURE

In architecture, the 19th century brought not only the revival of many earlier styles, including the Gothic, the Classical, and the Baroque, but also the introduction of new building materials that would have an important future in design and construction.

Houses of Parliament England celebrated its medieval heritage with *Neo-Gothic* buildings. In London, after the old Houses of Parliament burned in 1834, CHARLES BARRY (1795–1860), with the assistance of A.W.N. PUGIN (1812–1852), submitted the winning design (FIG. 12-23) for the new building. By this time, style had become a matter of selection from the historical past. Barry had traveled widely in Europe, Greece, Turkey, Egypt, and Palestine, studying the architecture of each place. He preferred the classical Renaissance styles, but he had designed some earlier Neo-Gothic buildings, and Pugin successfully influenced him in the direction of English Late Gothic. Pugin was one of a group of English artists and critics who saw moral purity and spiritual authenticity in the religious architecture of the Middle Ages. They also glorified the careful medieval artisans who built the great cathedrals. The Industrial Revolution was flooding the market with cheaply made and ill-designed commodities, and machine work was replacing handicraft. Pugin believed in the necessity of restoring the old artisanship, which had honesty and quality. The design of the Houses of Parliament, however, is not genuinely Gothic, despite its picturesque tower groupings (the Clock Tower, containing Big Ben, at one end, and the Victoria Tower at the other). The building has a formal axial plan and a kind of Palladian regularity beneath its Neo-Gothic detail.

Paris Opéra In contrast, for the Paris Opéra (FIG. 12-24), CHARLES GARNIER (1825–1898) designed a festive and spectacularly theatrical Neo-Baroque facade with two wings resembling domed central-plan churches. Inside, intricate arrangements of corridors, vestibules, stairways, balconies, alcoves, entrances, and exits facilitate easy passage throughout the building and provide space for entertainment and socializing at intermissions. The Baroque grandeur of the layout and of the opera house's decorative appointments are characteristic of an architectural style called *Beaux-Arts*, which flourished in the late 19th and early 20th centuries in France. Based on ideas taught at the dominant École des Beaux-Arts (School of Fine Arts) in Paris, the Beaux-Arts style incorporated classical principles (such as symmetry in design, including interior spaces that extended radially from a central core or axis) and featured extensive exterior ornamentation. As an example of a Beaux-Arts building, Garnier's Opéra proclaims, through its majesty and opulence, its function as a gathering place for glittering audiences in an age of conspicuous wealth.

Crystal Palace Work on Garnier's opera house began in 1861, but by then many architects had already abandoned sentimental and Romantic designs from the past. They turned instead to honest expressions of a building's purpose. Since the 18th century, bridges had been built of cast iron, and most other utilitarian architecture—factories, warehouses, dockyard structures, mills, and the like—long had been built simply and without historical ornamentation. Iron, along with other industrial materials, permitted engineering advancements in the construction of larger, stronger, and more fire-resistant structures than before. The tensile

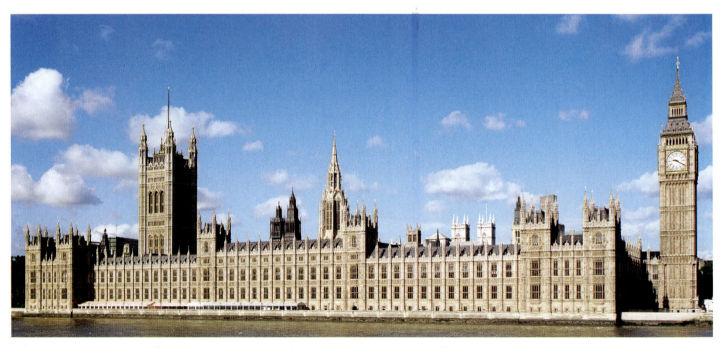

12-23 CHARLES BARRY and A.W.N. PUGIN, Houses of Parliament, London, England, designed 1835.

The 19th century brought the revival of many architectural styles, often reflecting nationalistic pride. The Houses of Parliament have an exterior veneer and towers that recall late English Gothic style.

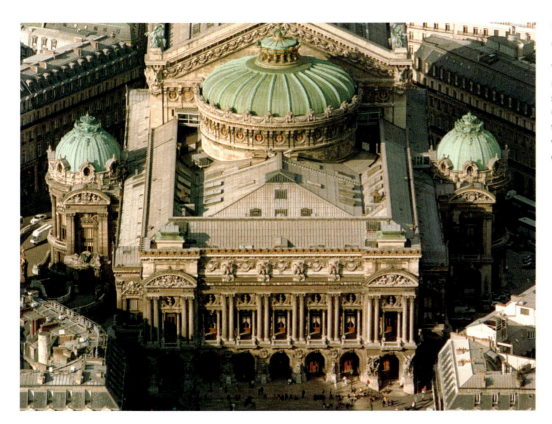

strength of iron (and especially of steel, available after 1860) permitted architects to create new designs involving vast enclosed spaces, as in the great train sheds of railroad stations and in exposition halls.

JOSEPH PAXTON (1801–1865) had built several conservatories (greenhouses) on the country estate of the duke of Devonshire. In the largest—300 feet long—he used an experimental system of glass-and-metal roof construction. En-

couraged by the success of this building technique, Paxton submitted the winning glass-and-iron design in the competition for the hall to house the Great Exhibition of 1851 in London. Paxton's hall, called the Crystal Palace (FIG. **12-25**), was the centerpiece of this exhibition organized to gather together "works of industry of all nations." Constructed using prefabricated parts, the vast structure was erected in the then-unheard-of time of six months and dismantled at the

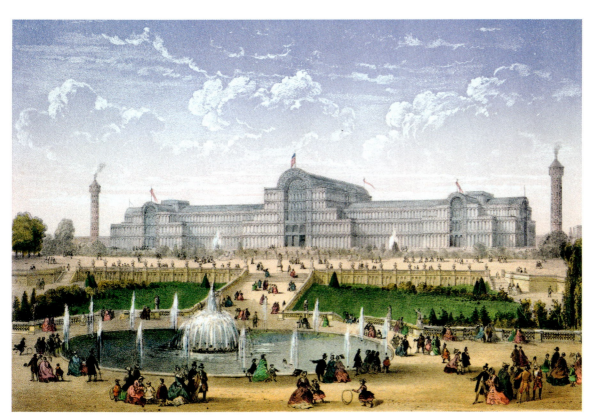

exhibition's closing to avoid permanent obstruction of the park. The plan borrowed much from ancient Roman and Christian basilicas, with a central flat-roofed "nave" and a barrel-vaulted crossing "transept." The design provided ample interior space to contain displays of huge machines as well as to accommodate decorative touches in the form of large working fountains and giant trees. The public admired the building so much that the workers who dismantled it erected an enlarged version of the Crystal Palace at a new location on the outskirts of London, where it remained until fire destroyed it in 1936.

PHOTOGRAPHY

Ever since Frenchman LOUIS-JACQUES-MANDÉ DAGUERRE (1789–1851) and Briton William Henry Fox Talbot (1800–1877) announced the first practical photographic processes in 1839, people have celebrated photography as a revelation of visible things. The relative ease of the process, even in its earliest and most primitive form, seemed a dream come true for 19th-century scientists and artists, who for centuries had grappled with less satisfying methods for capturing accurate images of their subjects. Photography also perfectly suited an age that saw artistic patronage continue to shift away from the elite few toward a broader base of support. The growing and increasingly powerful middle class embraced both the comprehensible images of the new medium and its lower cost.

For the traditional artist, photography suggested new answers to the great debate about what is real and how to represent the real in art. It also challenged the place of traditional modes of pictorial representation originating in the Renaissance. Artists as diverse as Delacroix, Ingres, Courbet, and the Impressionist Edgar Degas (see Chapter 13) welcomed photography as a helpful auxiliary to painting. They marveled at the ability of photography to translate three-dimensional objects onto a two-dimensional surface. Other artists, however, saw photography as a mechanism capable of displacing the painstaking work of skilled painters dedicated to representing the optical truth of chosen subjects. Photography's challenge to painting, both historically and technologically, seemed to some artists an expropriation of the realistic image, until then the exclusive property of painting.

Artists themselves were instrumental in the development of this new technology. The camera obscura was familiar to 18th-century artists. In 1807 the invention of the *camera lucida* (lighted room) replaced the enclosed chamber of the camera obscura. Now the photographer aimed a small prism lens, hung on a stand, downward at an object. The lens projected the image of the object onto a sheet of paper. Artists using either of these devices found this process long and arduous, no matter how accurate the resulting work. All yearned for a more direct way to capture a subject's image. Two very different scientific inventions that accomplished this—the *daguerreotype* and the *calotype* (see "Daguerreotype, Calotype, and Wet-Plate Photography," page 359)—were announced almost simultaneously in France and England in 1839.

Daguerreotypes The French government presented the new daguerreotype process at the Academy of Science in Paris on January 7, 1839, with the understanding that its details would be made available to all interested parties without charge (although the inventor received a large annuity in appreciation). Soon, people worldwide were taking pictures with the daguerreotype "camera" in a process almost immediately christened *photography*, from the Greek *photos* (light) and *graphos* (writing). Each daguerreotype is a unique work with amazing detail and finely graduated tones from black to white. *Still Life in Studio* (FIG. **12-26**) is one of the first successful plates Daguerre produced after perfecting his method. The process captured every detail—the subtle forms, the varied textures, the diverse tones of light and shadow—in Daguerre's carefully constructed tableau. The three-dimensional forms of the sculptures, the basket, and the bits of cloth spring into high relief and are convincingly represented. The inspiration for the composition came from 17th-century Dutch still lifes, such as those by Pieter Claesz (FIG. **10-27**). Like Claesz, Daguerre arranged his objects to reveal their textures and shapes clearly. Unlike a painter, Daguerre could not alter anything within his arrangement to effect a stronger image. However, he could suggest a symbolic meaning through his choice of objects. Like the skull and timepiece in Claesz's painting, Daguerre's sculptural and architectural fragments and the framed print of an embrace suggest that even art is vanitas and will not endure forever.

Nadar Making portraits was an important economic opportunity for most photographers, and portraiture quickly became one of the most popular early photographic genres. The greatest of the early portrait photographers was Gaspar-Félix Tournachon, known simply as NADAR (1828–1910), a French novelist, journalist, and caricaturist. Photographic studies for his caricatures led Nadar to open a portrait studio. So talented was he at capturing the essence of his subjects that the most important people in France, including Delacroix, Daumier, Courbet, and Manet, flocked to his studio to have their portraits made. Nadar said he sought in his work "that instant of understanding that puts you in touch with the model—helps you sum him up, guides you to his habits, his ideas, and character and enables you to produce . . . a really convincing and sympathetic likeness, an intimate portrait."[8] Nadar's *Eugène Delacroix* (FIG. **12-1**) shows the painter at the height of his career. In this photograph, the artist imparts remarkable presence. Even in half-length, his gesture and expression create a mood that reveals much about him. Perhaps Delacroix responded to Nadar's famous gift for putting his clients at ease by assuming the pose that best expressed his personality. The new calotype photographic process made possible the rich range of tones in Nadar's images.

Daguerreotype, Calotype, and Wet-Plate Photography

The earliest photographic processes were the *daguerreotype* (FIG. 12-26), named after L.-J.-M. Daguerre, and the *calotype*. Daguerre was an architect and theatrical set painter and designer who created a popular entertainment called the Diorama. Audiences witnessed performances of "living paintings" created by changing the lighting effects on a "sandwich" composed of a painted backdrop and several layers of painted translucent front curtains. Daguerre used a camera obscura for the Diorama, but he sought a more efficient and effective procedure. Through a mutual acquaintance, he met Joseph Nicéphore Niépce (1765–1833), who in 1826 had successfully made a permanent picture of the cityscape outside his upper-story window by exposing, in a camera obscura, a metal plate covered with a light-sensitive coating. Niépce's process, however, had the significant drawback that it required an eight-hour exposure time. After Niépce died in 1833, Daguerre continued his work, making two important discoveries. Latent development—that is, bringing out the image through treatment in chemical solutions—considerably shortened the length of time needed for exposure. Daguerre also discovered a better way to "fix" the image by chemically stopping the action of light on the photographic plate, which otherwise would continue to darken until the image turned solid black.

The daguerreotype reigned supreme in photography until the 1850s, but the second major photographic invention, the ancestor of the modern negative-print system, eventually replaced it. On January 31, 1839, less than three weeks after Daguerre unveiled his method in Paris, W.H.F. Talbot presented a paper on his "photogenic drawings" to the Royal Institution in London. As early as 1835, Talbot made "negative" images by plac-

ing objects on sensitized paper and exposing the arrangement to light. This created a design of light-colored silhouettes recording the places where opaque or translucent objects had blocked light from darkening the paper's emulsion. In his experiments, Talbot next exposed sensitized papers inside simple cameras and, with a second sheet, created "positive" images. He further improved the process with more light-sensitive chemicals and a chemical development of the negative image. This technique allowed multiple prints. However, in Talbot's process, which he named the calotype (from the Greek *kalos*, "beautiful"), the photographic images incorporated the texture of the paper. This produced a slightly blurred, grainy effect very different from the crisp detail and wide tonal range available with the daguerreotype. Also discouraging widespread adoption of the calotype were the stiff licensing and equipment fees charged for many years after Talbot patented his new process in 1841.

An early master of an improved kind of calotype photography was the multitalented Frenchman Nadar (FIG. 12-1). He used glass negatives and albumen printing paper (prepared with egg white), which could record finer detail and a wider range of light and shadow than Talbot's calotype process. The new *wet-plate* technology (so named because the photographic plate was exposed, developed, and fixed while wet) almost at once became the universal way of making negatives until 1880. However, wet-plate photography (FIG. 12-27) had drawbacks. The plates had to be prepared and processed on the spot. Working outdoors meant taking along a portable darkroom of some sort—a wagon, tent, or box with light-tight sleeves for the photographer's arms.

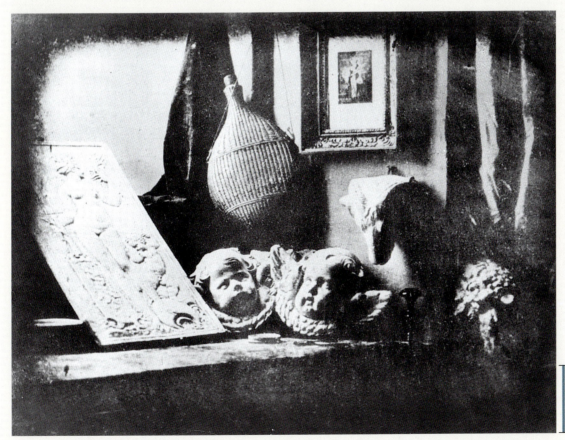

12-26 LOUIS-JACQUES-MANDÉ DAGUERRE, *Still Life in Studio*, 1837. Daguerreotype, $6\frac{1}{4}$" × $8\frac{1}{4}$". Collection Société Française de Photographie, Paris.

One of the first plates Daguerre produced after perfecting his new photographic process was this still life, in which he was able to capture amazing detail and finely graduated tones from black to white.

1 in.

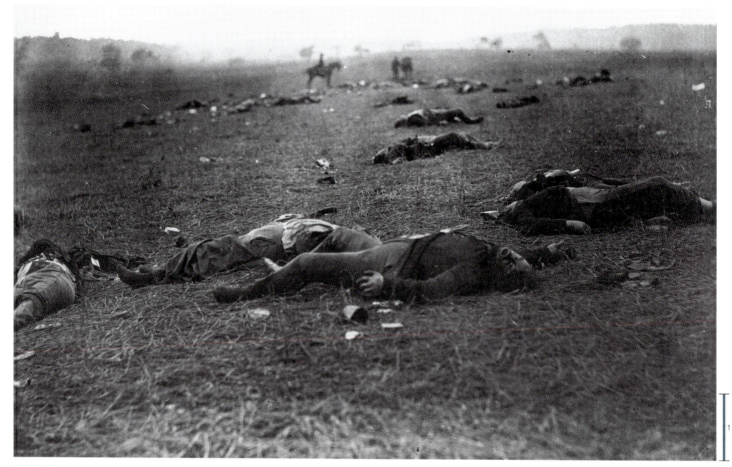

1 in.

12-27 TIMOTHY O'SULLIVAN, *A Harvest of Death, Gettysburg, Pennsylvania, July 1863*. Negative by Timothy O'Sullivan. Original print by ALEXANDER GARDNER, 6¾" × 8¾". New York Public Library (Astor, Lenox and Tilden Foundations, Rare Books and Manuscript Division), New York.

Wet-plate technology enabled photographers to record historical events on the spot—and to comment on the high price of war, as in this photograph of dead Union soldiers at Gettysburg in 1863.

Timothy O'Sullivan Photographers were quick to realize the documentary power of their new medium. Thus began the story of photography's influence on modern life and of the immense changes it brought to communication and information management. Historical events could be recorded in permanent form on the spot for the first time. The photographs taken of the Crimean War (1856) and of the American Civil War remain unsurpassed as incisive accounts of military life, unsparing in their truthful detail and poignant as expressions of human experience.

Of the Civil War photographs, the most moving are the inhumanly objective records of combat deaths. Perhaps the most reproduced is *A Harvest of Death, Gettysburg, July 1863* (FIG. **12-27**) by TIMOTHY O'SULLIVAN (1840–1882).

Although viewers could regard this image as simple news reportage, it also functions to impress on people the high price of the Civil War. Corpses litter the battlefield as far as the eye can see. As the photograph modulates from the precise clarity of the bodies of Union soldiers in the foreground, boots stolen and pockets picked, to the almost indistinguishable corpses in the distance, the suggestion of innumerable other dead soldiers is unavoidable. This "harvest" is far more sobering and depressing than that in Winslow Homer's Civil War painting *Veteran in a New Field* (FIG. **12-19**). Though it was years before photolithography could reproduce photographs like this in newspapers, photographers exhibited them publicly. These images made an impression that newsprint engravings never could.

Europe and America, 1800 to 1870

NAPOLEONIC ART AND ROMANTICISM

▪ As Emperor of France from 1804 to 1815, Napoleon embraced the Neoclassical style in order to associate his regime with the empire of ancient Rome. Napoleon chose Jacques-Louis David as First Painter of the Empire. Napoleon's favorite sculptor was Antonio Canova, who carved marble Neoclassical portraits of the imperial family, including a reclining image of Napoleon's sister, Pauline Borghese, in the guise of Venus.

▪ The roots of Romanticism are in the 18th century, but usually the term more narrowly denotes the artistic movement that flourished from 1800 to 1840, between Neoclassicism and Realism. Romantic painters gave precedence to feeling and imagination over Enlightenment reason, and explored the exotic, erotic, and fantastic in their art.

▪ The leading Romantic painter in Spain was Francisco Goya, whose works include the *Caprichos* series celebrating the unleashing of imagination, emotions, and even nightmares. In France, Eugène Delacroix led the way in depicting Romantic narratives set in faraway places and distant times. He set his colorful *Death of Sardanapalus* in ancient Assyria.

▪ Romantic painters often chose landscapes as an ideal subject to express the Romantic theme of the soul unified with the natural world. Masters of the transcendental landscape include Friedrich in Germany, Constable and Turner in England, and Cole in the United States.

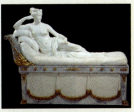

Canova, *Pauline Borghese as Venus*, 1808

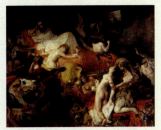

Delacroix, *Death of Sardanapalus*, 1827

REALISM

▪ Realism developed as an artistic movement in mid-19th-century France. Its leading proponent was Gustave Courbet, whose paintings of menial labor and ordinary people exemplify his belief that painters should depict only their own time and place. Honoré Daumier boldly confronted authority with his satirical lithographs commenting on the plight of the urban working classes. Édouard Manet shocked the public with his paintings featuring promiscuous women and rendered in rough brush strokes, which emphasized the flatness of the painting surface, paving the way for modern abstract art.

▪ American Realists include Winslow Homer and Thomas Eakins. Eakins's *The Gross Clinic,* a painting of surgery in progress, was too brutally realistic for the Philadelphia art jury that rejected it.

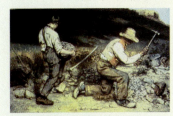

Courbet, *The Stone Breakers,* 1849

ARCHITECTURE

▪ Territorial expansion, the Romantic interest in exotic locales and earlier eras, and nationalistic pride led to the revival in the 19th century of older architectural styles, especially the Gothic. By the middle of the century, many architects had already abandoned sentimental and Romantic designs from the past in favor of exploring the possibilities of cast-iron construction, as in Joseph Paxton's Crystal Palace in London.

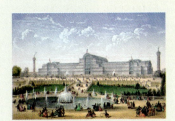

Paxton, Crystal Palace, London, 1850–1851

PHOTOGRAPHY

▪ In 1839, L.-J.-M. Daguerre in Paris and W.H.F. Talbot in London invented the first practical photographic processes. Many of the earliest photographers specialized in portrait photography, but others, including Timothy O'Sullivan in the United States, quickly realized the documentary power of the new medium.

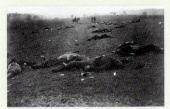

O'Sullivan, *A Harvest of Death,* 1863

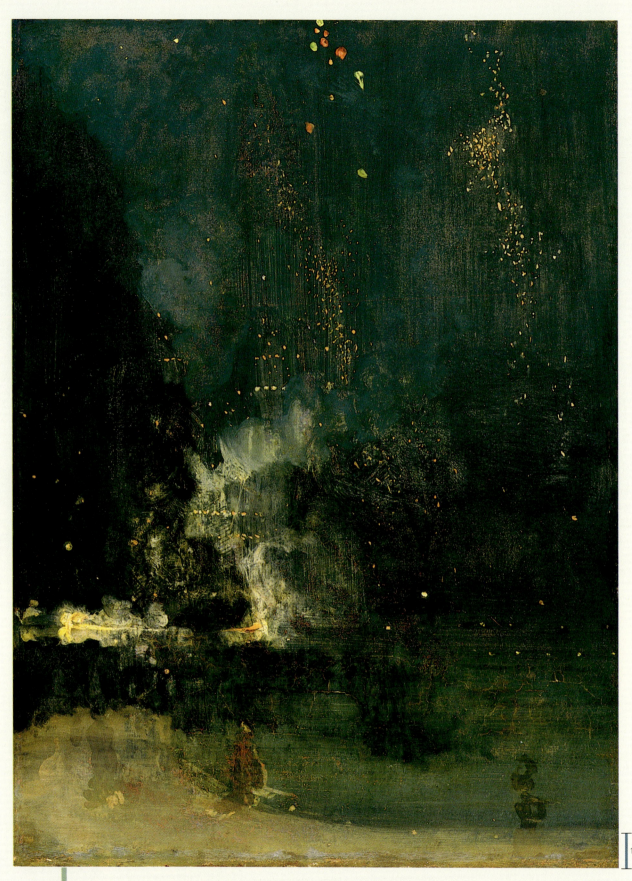

1 in.

13-1 JAMES ABBOTT MCNEILL WHISTLER, *Nocturne in Black and Gold (The Falling Rocket)*, ca. 1875. Oil on panel, 1' 11$\frac{5}{8}$" × 1' 6$\frac{1}{3}$". Detroit Institute of the Arts, Detroit (gift of Dexter M. Ferry Jr.).

Whistler shared the Impressionists' interest in conveying atmospheric effects in oil painting, but he also emphasized the abstract arrangement of shapes and colors, foreshadowing 20th-century art.

Europe and America, 1870 to 1900

During the latter half of the 19th century, the Industrial Revolution in England spread to France (MAP **13-1**) and throughout Europe and to the United States. Because of this dramatic expansion, historians often refer to the third quarter of the 19th century as the second Industrial Revolution. Whereas the first Industrial Revolution centered on textiles, steam, and iron, the second focused on steel, electricity, chemicals, and oil. Discoveries in these fields provided the foundation for developments in plastics, machinery, building construction, and automobile manufacturing and paved the way for the invention of the radio, electric light, telephone, and electric streetcar.

Among the significant consequences of industrialization was urbanization. The number and size of Western cities grew dramatically during the latter part of the 19th century, largely due to migration from rural regions. Rural dwellers relocated to urban centers because expanded agricultural enterprises squeezed smaller property owners from the land. The widely available work opportunities in the cities, especially in factories, were also a major factor in this migration. In addition, improving health and living conditions in the cities contributed to their explosive growth.

The rise of the urban working class was fundamental to the ideas of the German political and social theorist Karl Marx (1818–1883), whose *Communist Manifesto* (1848), written with Friedrich Engels (1820–1895), called for workers to overthrow the capitalist system. Like other 19th-century empiricists, Marx believed that scientific, rational laws governed nature and, indeed, all human history. For Marx, economic forces based on class struggle induced historical change. Throughout history, insisted Marx, those who controlled the means of production conflicted with those whose labor they exploited for their own enrichment. Marxism's ultimate goal was to create a socialist state in which the working class seized power. Marxism attracted a wide following and was instrumental in the rise of trade unions.

Equally influential was the English naturalist Charles Darwin (1809–1882), whose theory of natural selection did much to increase interest in science. Darwin's concept of evolution based on a competitive system in which only the fittest survived, as presented in *On the Origin of Species by Means of Natural Selection* (1859), sharply contrasted with the biblical narrative of creation. By challenging traditional Christian beliefs, Darwinism contributed to a growing secular attitude. Other theorists and social thinkers, notably British philosopher Herbert Spencer (1820–1903), applied Darwin's principles to the rapidly changing socioeconomic realm. As in the biological world, they asserted, intense competition led to the survival of the most economically fit companies, enterprises, and countries. These "social Darwinists" provided Western leaders with justification for the colonization of peoples and cultures they deemed less advanced. By 1900 the major Western economic and political powers had divided up much of the world (MAP 14-1).

Modernism The combination of extensive technological changes and increased exposure to other cultures, coupled with the rapidity of these changes, led to an acute sense in Western cultures of the world's impermanence. These societal changes in turn fostered a new and multifaceted artistic approach that historians call *modernism*. Modernist artists seek to capture the images and sensibilities of their age, but modernism transcends the simple present to involve the artist's critical examination of or reflection on the premises of art itself. Modernism thus implies certain concerns about art and aesthetics that are internal to art production, regardless of whether the artist is producing scenes from contemporary social life.

Clement Greenberg (1909–1994), an influential American art critic, explained modernism this way:

> [T]he essence of Modernism lies . . . in the use of the characteristic methods of a discipline to criticize the discipline itself. . . . Realistic, illusionist art had dissembled the medium, using art to conceal art. Modernism used art to call attention to art. The limitations that constitute the medium of painting—the flat surface, the shape of the support, the properties of pigment—were treated by the Old Masters as negative factors that could be acknowledged only implicitly or indirectly. Modernist painting has come to regard these same limitations as positive factors that are to be acknowledged openly.[1]

The work of Gustave Courbet and the Realists (see Chapter 12) already expressed this modernist viewpoint, but modernism emerged even more forcefully in the late-19th-century movements that art historians call Impressionism and Post-Impressionism.

IMPRESSIONISM

Impressionism, both in content and in style, was an art of industrialized, urbanized Paris, a reaction to the sometimes brutal and chaotic transformation of French life that occurred during the latter half of the 19th century. The rapidity of these changes made the world seem unstable and insubstantial. As the poet and critic Charles Baudelaire (1821–1867) observed in 1860 in his essay "The Painter of Modern Life": "[M]odernity is the transitory, the fugitive, the contingent."[2] Accordingly, Impressionist works represent an attempt to capture a fleeting moment—not in the absolutely fixed,

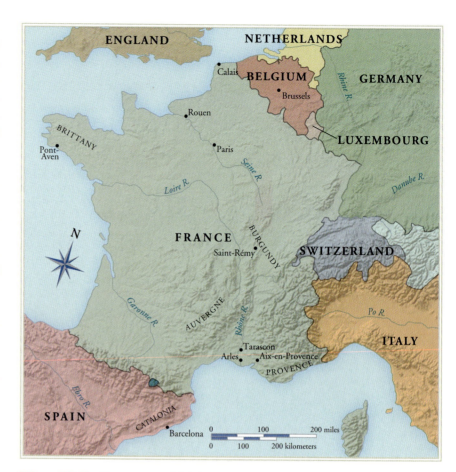

MAP 13-1 France around 1870.

precise sense of a Realist painting but by conveying the elusiveness and impermanence of images and conditions.

Claude Monet A hostile critic applied the label "Impressionism" in response to the painting *Impression: Sunrise* (FIG. 13-2) by CLAUDE MONET (1840–1926) exhibited in the first Impressionist show in 1874 (see "Academic Salons and Independent Art Exhibitions," page 365). Although the critic intended the label to be derogatory, by the third Impressionist show in 1878, the artists had embraced it and were calling themselves Impressionists. Artists and critics had used the term before, but only in relation to sketches. Impressionist paintings do incorporate the qualities of sketches—abbreviation, speed, and spontaneity. This is apparent in *Impression: Sunrise*, in which Monet made no attempt to disguise the brush strokes or blend the pigment to create smooth tonal gradations and an optically accurate scene. Although this painting is not technically a sketch, it has a sketchy quality. Monet's concern with acknowledging the paint and the canvas surface continued the modernist exploration the Realists began. Impressionism operated at the intersection of what the artists saw and what they felt. In other words, the "impressions" these artists recorded in their paintings were neither purely objective descriptions of the exterior world nor solely subjective responses but the interaction between the two. They were sensations—the artists' subjective and personal responses to nature.

Academic Salons and Independent Art Exhibitions

For both artists and art historians, modernist art stands in marked contrast—indeed, in forceful opposition—to academic art, that is to the art promoted by established art schools such as the Royal Academy of Painting and Sculpture in France (founded 1648) and the Royal Academy of Arts in Britain (founded 1768). These government-subsidized academies, which supported a limited range of artistic expression focusing on traditional subjects and highly polished technique, held annual exhibitions, called "Salons" in France. Because of the challenges modernist art presented to established artistic conventions, the juries for the Salons and other official exhibitions often rejected the works more adventurous artists wished to display. As noted, Gustave Courbet's reaction to the rejection of some of his paintings in 1855 was to set up his own Pavilion of Realism (see "Courbet on Realism," Chapter 12, page 349).

Growing dissatisfaction with the decisions of the French Academy's jurors prompted Napoleon III (r. 1852–1870) in 1863 to establish the Salon des Refusés (Salon of the Rejected) to show all of the works not accepted for exhibition in the regular Salon. Manet's *Le Déjeuner sur l'Herbe* (FIG. **12-17**) was among them. The public greeted it and the entire exhibition with derision. In 1867, after further rejections, Manet, following Courbet, mounted a private exhibition of 50 of his paintings outside the Paris World's Fair. Six years later, Claude Monet (FIGS. **13-2** and **13-3**) and other Impressionists formed their own society and began mounting shows of their works in Paris. This decision gave the Impressionists much more freedom, for they did not have to contend with the Academy's authoritative and confining viewpoint, and thereafter they held exhibitions at one- or two-year intervals from 1874 until 1886. Another group of artists unhappy with the Salon's conservative nature adopted the same renegade approach. In 1884 these artists formed the Société des Artistes Indépendants (Society of Independent Artists) and held annual Salons des Indépendants. Georges Seurat's *A Sunday on La Grande Jatte* (FIG. **13-8**) was one of the paintings in the Independents' 1886 Salon.

As the art market expanded, venues for the exhibition of art increased. Art circles and societies sponsored private shows in which both amateurs and professionals participated. Dealers became more aggressive in promoting the artists they represented by mounting exhibitions in a variety of spaces, some fairly intimate and small, others large and grandiose. All of these proliferating opportunities for exhibition gave artists alternatives to the traditional constraints of the Salon and provided fertile breeding ground for the development of radically new art forms and styles.

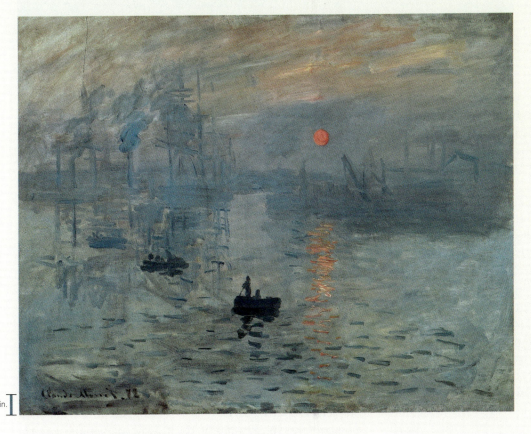

1 in.

13-2 CLAUDE MONET, *Impression: Sunrise*, 1872. Oil on canvas, 1' 7½" × 2' 1½". Musée Marmottan, Paris.

A hostile critic disparagingly labeled Monet's style "Impressionism" because of this painting's sketchy quality and prominent brush strokes. Monet and his circle, however, embraced the label for their movement.

In sharp contrast to traditional artists, Monet painted outdoors, which sharpened his focus on the roles light and color play in capturing an instantaneous representation of atmosphere and climate. Scientific studies of light and the invention of chemically synthesized pigments increased artists' sensitivity to the multiplicity of colors in nature and gave them new colors for their work. After scrutinizing the effects of light and color on forms, the Impressionists concluded that *local color*—an object's true color in white light—becomes modified by the quality of the light shining on it, by reflec-tions from other objects, and by the effects juxtaposed colors produce. Shadows do not appear gray or black, as many earlier painters thought, but are composed of colors modified by reflections or other conditions. Using various colors and short, choppy brush strokes, Monet was able to catch accurately the vibrating quality of light. The fact that Impressionist canvas surfaces look incomprehensible at close range and their forms and objects appear only when the eye fuses the strokes at a certain distance accounts for much of the early adverse criticism leveled at Monet and his fellow Impressionists.

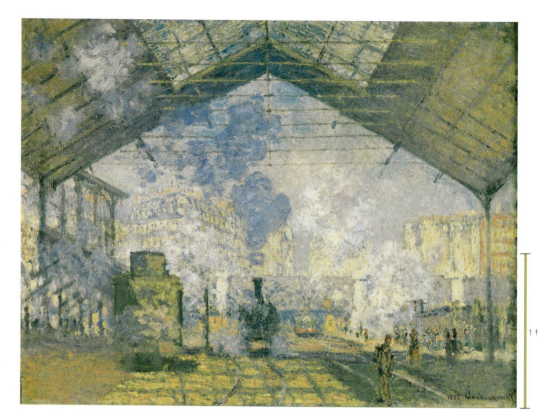

13-3 CLAUDE MONET, *Saint-Lazare Train Station*, 1877. Oil on canvas, 2' 5¾" × 3' 5". Musée d'Orsay, Paris.

Impressionist canvas surfaces look indecipherable at close range, but the eye fuses the brush strokes at a distance. Monet's agitated application of paint contributes to the sense of energy and vitality in this urban scene.

Saint-Lazare Most of the Impressionists depicted scenes in and around Paris, the heart of modern life in France. Monet's *Saint-Lazare Train Station* (FIG. **13-3**) shows a dominant aspect of the contemporary urban scene. The expanding railway network had made travel more convenient, bringing throngs of people into Paris. In this painting, Monet captured the energy and vitality of Paris's modern transportation hub. The train, emerging from the steam and smoke it emits, rumbles into the station. In the background haze are the tall buildings that were becoming a major component of the Parisian landscape. Monet's agitated paint application contributes to the sense of energy and conveys the atmosphere of urban life.

Pierre-Auguste Renoir Another facet of Paris that drew the Impressionists' attention was the leisure activities of its inhabitants. Scenes of dining, dancing, the café-concerts, the opera, and the ballet were mainstays of Impressionism. Although seemingly unrelated, industrialization facilitated these pursuits. With the advent of set working hours, people's schedules became more regimented, allowing them to plan their favorite pastimes. *Le Moulin de la Galette* (FIG. **13-4**) by PIERRE-AUGUSTE RENOIR (1841–1919) depicts a popular Parisian dance hall. Some people crowd the tables and chatter, while others dance energetically. So lively is the atmosphere that the viewer can virtually hear the sounds of music, laughter, and tinkling glasses. The painter dappled the whole scene with sunlight and shade, artfully blurred into the figures to produce just the effect of floating and fleeting light the Impressionists cultivated. Renoir's casual placement of the figures and the suggested continuity of space, spreading in all directions and only accidentally limited by the frame, position the viewer as a participant rather than as an outsider. Whereas classical artists sought to express universal and timeless qualities, the Impressionists attempted to depict just the opposite—the incidental and the momentary.

Edgar Degas Impressionists also depicted more formal leisure activities. The fascination EDGAR DEGAS (1834–1917) had with patterns of motion brought him to the Paris Opéra (FIG. **12-24**) and its ballet school. There, his great observational power took in the formalized movements of classical ballet, one of his favorite subjects. In *The Rehearsal* (FIG. **13-5**), Degas used several devices to bring the observer into the pictorial space. The frame cuts off the spiral stair, the windows in the background, and the group of figures in the right foreground. The figures are not at the center of a classically balanced composition. Instead, Degas arranged them in a seemingly random manner. The prominent diagonals of the wall bases and floorboards carry the viewer into and along the directional lines of the dancers. Finally, as is customary in Degas's ballet pictures, a large, off-center, empty space creates the illusion of a continuous floor that connects the observer with the pictured figures.

The often arbitrarily cut-off figures, the patterns of light splotches, and the blurriness of the images in this and other Degas works indicate the artist's interest in reproducing single moments. Further, they reveal his fascination with photography. Degas not only studied the photographs of others but also used the camera to make preliminary studies for his works, particularly photographing figures in interiors. Japanese art was another inspirational source for Degas's paintings. The cunning spatial projections in works such as *The Rehearsal* probably derived in part from Japanese prints (see "Japanese Woodblock Prints," Chapter 18, page 506). Japanese artists used diverging lines not only to organize the flat shapes of figures but also to direct attention into the picture space (FIG. **18-16**). The Impressionists, acquainted with these prints as early as the 1860s, greatly admired their spatial organization, familiar and intimate themes, and flat, unmodeled color areas.

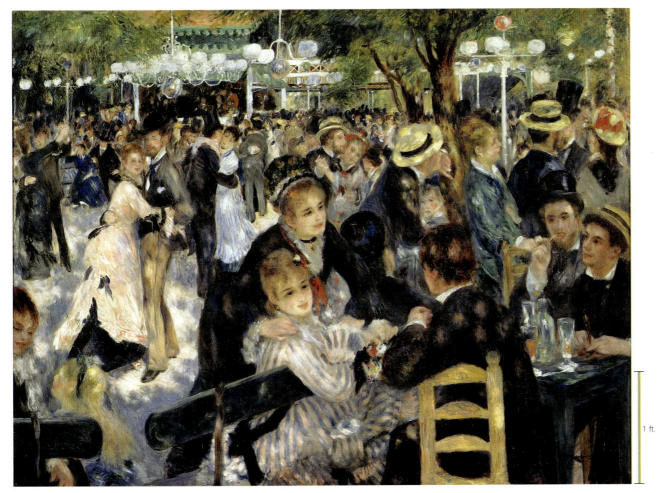

13-4 PIERRE-AUGUSTE RENOIR, *Le Moulin de la Galette*, 1876. Oil on canvas, 4′ 3″ × 5′ 8″. Musée d'Orsay, Paris.

Renoir's painting of this popular Parisian dance hall is dappled by sunlight and shade, artfully blurred into the figures to produce just the effect of floating and fleeting light the Impressionists cultivated.

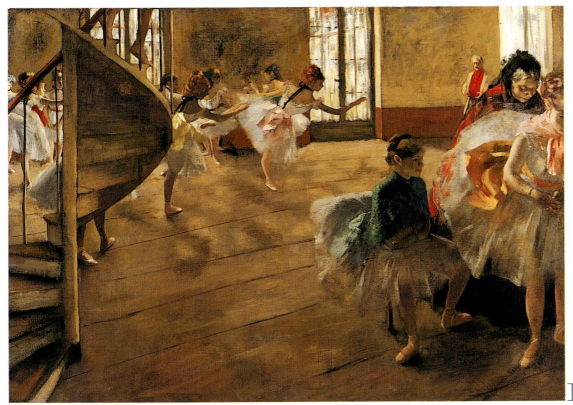

1 in.

13-5 EDGAR DEGAS, *The Rehearsal*, 1874. Oil on canvas, 1′ 11″ × 2′ 9″. Glasgow Art Galleries and Museum, Glasgow (Burrell Collection).

The arbitrarily cut-off figures, the patterns of light splotches, and the blurriness of the images in this work reveal Degas's interest in reproducing single moments, as well as his fascination with photography.

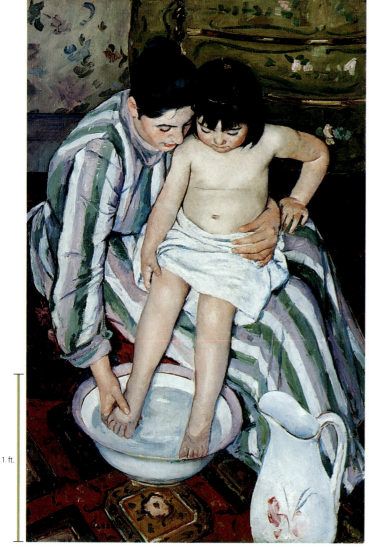

13-6 MARY CASSATT, *The Bath*, ca. 1892. Oil on canvas, 3' 3" × 2' 2". Art Institute of Chicago, Chicago (Robert A. Walker Fund).

Cassatt owed much to the compositions of Degas and Japanese print-makers, but her subjects differ from those of most Impressionists, in part because, as a woman, she could not frequent Parisian cafés.

Mary Cassatt In the Salon of 1874, Degas admired a painting by a young Philadelphia artist, MARY CASSATT (1844–1926), who had moved to Europe to study master-works in France and Italy. Degas befriended Cassatt, who exhibited regularly with the Impressionists, but as a woman, she could not easily frequent the cafés with her male artist friends. She was also responsible for the care of her aging parents, who had joined her in Paris. Because of these restrictions, Cassatt's subjects were principally women and children, whom she presented with a combination of objectivity and genuine sentiment. Works such as *The Bath* (FIG. **13-6**) show the tender relationship between a mother and child. The visual solidity of the mother and child contrasts with the flattened patterning of the wallpaper and rug. Cassatt's style in this work owed much to the compositional devices of Degas and of Japanese printmakers, but the painting's design has an originality and strength all its own.

James Whistler Another American expatriate artist in Europe was JAMES ABBOTT MCNEILL WHISTLER (1834–1903), who spent time in Paris before settling finally in London. He met many of the French Impressionists, and his art is a unique combination of some of their concerns and his own. Whistler shared the Impressionists' interest in the subjects of contemporary life and the sensations color produces on the eye. To these influences he added his own desire to create harmonies paralleling those achieved in music. To underscore his artistic intentions, Whistler began calling his paintings "arrangements" or "nocturnes." *Nocturne in Black and Gold*, or *The Falling Rocket* (FIG. **13-1**) is a daring painting with gold flecks and splatters that represent the exploded fireworks punctuating the darkness of the night sky. More interested in conveying the atmospheric effects than in providing details of the scene, Whistler emphasized creating a harmonious arrangement of shapes and colors on the rectangle of his canvas, an approach that appealed to many 20th-century artists. His works angered many 19th-century viewers, however. The British critic John Ruskin (1819–1900) responded to this painting with a scathing review accusing Whistler of "flinging a pot of paint in the public's face."[3] In reply, Whistler sued Ruskin for libel. Although Whistler won the case, his victory had sadly ironic consequences for him. The judge, showing where his—and the public's—sympathies lay, awarded the artist only one farthing (less than a penny) in damages and required him to pay all of the court costs, which ruined Whistler financially.

POST-IMPRESSIONISM

By 1886 most critics and a large segment of the public accepted the Impressionists as serious artists. Just when their images of contemporary life no longer seemed crude and unfinished, however, a group of younger artists came to feel that the Impressionists were neglecting too many of the traditional elements of picture making in their attempts to capture momentary sensations of light and color on canvas. These artists were much more interested in systematically examining the properties and expressive qualities of line, pattern, form, and color. Because their art had its roots in Impressionism, but is not stylistically homogeneous, these artists have become known as the *Post-Impressionists*.

Henri de Toulouse-Lautrec Closest to the Impressionists in many ways was the French artist HENRI DE TOULOUSE-LAUTREC (1864–1901), who deeply admired Degas and shared his interest in capturing the sensibility of modern life. Toulouse-Lautrec's work, however, has an added satirical edge to it and often borders on caricature. Genetic defects that stunted his growth and in part crippled him led to the artist's self-exile from the high society his ancient aristocratic name entitled him to enter. He became a denizen of the night world of Paris, consorting with a tawdry population of entertainers, prostitutes, and other social outcasts. He reveled in the energy of cheap music halls, cafés,

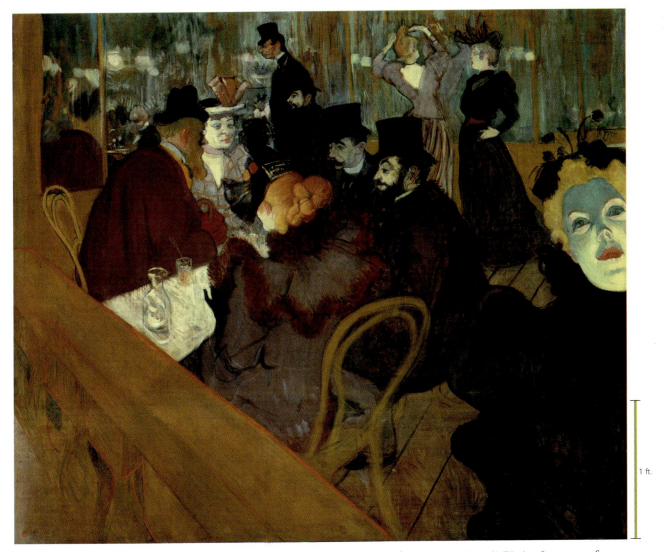

13-7 HENRI DE TOULOUSE-LAUTREC, *At the Moulin Rouge*, 1892–1895. Oil on canvas, 4' × 4' 7". Art Institute of Chicago, Chicago (Helen Birch Bartlett Memorial Collection).

The influences of Degas, Japanese prints, and photography show in this painting's oblique composition, but the glaring lighting, masklike faces, and dissonant colors are Toulouse-Lautrec's own idiom.

and bordellos. *At the Moulin Rouge* (FIG. **13-7**) reveals the influences of Degas, of Japanese prints, and of photography in the oblique and asymmetrical composition, the spatial diagonals, and the strong line patterns with added dissonant colors. But Toulouse-Lautrec so emphasized or exaggerated each element that the tone is new. Compare, for example, this painting's mood with the relaxed and casual atmosphere of Renoir's *Le Moulin de la Galette* (FIG. **13-4**). Toulouse-Lautrec's scene is nightlife, with its glaring artificial light, brassy music, and assortment of corrupt, cruel, and masklike faces. (He included himself in the background—the tiny man with the derby accompanying the very tall man, his cousin.) Such distortions by simplification of the figures and faces anticipated Expressionism (see Chapter 14), when artists' use of formal elements—for example, brighter colors and bolder lines than ever before—increased the impact their images had on observers.

Georges Seurat The themes GEORGES SEURAT (1859–1891) addressed in his paintings were also Impressionist subjects, but he depicted them in a resolutely intellectual way. Seurat devised a disciplined and painstaking system of painting that focused on color analysis. He was less concerned with recording immediate color sensations than with organizing colors carefully and systematically into a new kind of pictorial order. Seurat harnessed the free and fluent play of color that characterized Impressionism into a calculated arrangement based on scientific color theory (see "19th-Century Color Theory," page 370). His system, known as *pointillism* or *divisionism*, involves carefully observing color and separating it into its component parts. The artist then applies these pure component colors to the canvas in tiny dots (points) or daubs. Thus, the shapes, figures, and spaces in the image become totally comprehensible only from a distance when the viewer's eye blends the many pigment dots.

Post-Impressionism   369

19th-Century Color Theory

In the 19th century, advances in the sciences contributed to changing theories about color and how people perceive it. Many physicists and chemists studied optical reception and the behavior of the human eye in response to light of differing wavelengths. They also investigated the psychological dimension of color. Their discoveries provided a framework within which artists such as Georges Seurat (FIG. 13-8), the inventor of pointillism, worked.

Discussions of color often focus on *hue* (for example, red, yellow, and blue), but it is important to consider the other facets of color—*saturation* (the hue's brightness or dullness) and *value* (the hue's lightness or darkness). Most artists during the 19th century understood the concepts of *primary, secondary,* and *complementary colors* (see Introduction, page 8). Chemist Michel-Eugène Chevreul (1786–1889) extended artists' understanding of color dynamics by formulating the law of *simultaneous contrasts* of colors. Chevreul asserted that juxtaposed colors affect the eye's reception of each, making the two colors as dissimilar as possible, both in hue and value. For example, placing light green next to dark green has the effect of making the light green look even lighter and the dark green darker. Chevreul further provided an explanation of *successive contrasts*—the phenomenon of colored afterimages. When a person looks intently at a color (green, for example) and then shifts to a white area, the eye momentarily perceives the complementary color (red).

Charles Blanc (1813–1882), who coined the term *optical mixture* to describe the visual effect of juxtaposed complementary colors, asserted that the smaller the areas of adjoining complementary colors, the greater the tendency for the eye to "mix" the colors, so that the viewer perceives a grayish or neutral tint. Seurat used this principle frequently in his paintings.

Also influential for Seurat was the work of physicist Ogden Rood (1831–1902), who constructed an accurate and understandable diagram of contrasting colors. Further (and particularly significant to Seurat), Rood suggested that artists could achieve color gradation by placing small dots or lines of color side by side that would blend in the eye.

The color experiments of Seurat and other late-19th-century artists were also part of a larger discourse about human vision and how people see and understand the world. The theories of physicist Ernst Mach (1838–1916) focused on the psychological experience of sensation. He believed humans perceive their environments in isolated units of sensation that the brain then recomposes into a comprehensible world. Another scientist, Charles Henry (1859–1926), also pursued research into the psychological dimension of color—how colors affect people, and under what conditions. He went even further to explore the physiological effects of perception.

13-8 GEORGES SEURAT, *A Sunday on La Grande Jatte,* 1884–1886. Oil on canvas, 6′ 9″ × 10′. Art Institute of Chicago, Chicago (Helen Birch Bartlett Memorial Collection).

Seurat's color system—pointillism—involved dividing colors into their component parts and applying those colors to the canvas in tiny dots. The forms become comprehensible only from a distance.

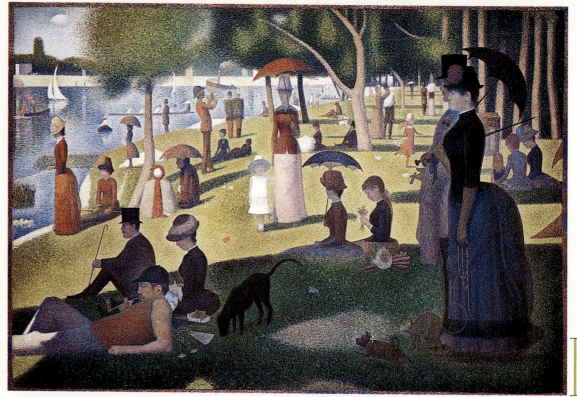

1 ft.

Pointillism was on view at the eighth and last Impressionist exhibition in 1886, when Seurat showed his *A Sunday on La Grande Jatte* (FIG. 13-8). The subject of the painting is consistent with Impressionist recreational themes, but Seurat's rendition is strangely rigid and remote, unlike the spontaneous representations of most Impressionists. By using meticulously calculated values, Seurat carved out a deep rectangular space. He played on repeated motifs both to create flat patterns and to suggest spatial depth. Reiterating the profile of the female form, the parasol, and the cylindrical forms

The Letters of Vincent van Gogh

Throughout his life, Vincent van Gogh wrote letters to his brother Theo van Gogh (1857–1891), a Parisian art dealer, on matters both mundane and philosophical. The letters are precious documents of the vicissitudes of the painter's life and reveal his emotional anguish. In many of the letters, van Gogh also forcefully stated his views about art. In one letter, he told Theo: "In both my life and in my painting, I can very well do without God but I cannot, ill as I am, do without something which is greater than I, . . . the power to create."* For van Gogh, the power to create involved the expressive use of color. "Instead of trying to reproduce exactly what I

have before my eyes, I use color more arbitrarily so as to express myself forcibly."† Color in painting, he argued, is "not locally true from the point of view of the delusive realist, but color suggesting some emotion of an ardent temperament."‡

Some of van Gogh's letters contain vivid descriptions of his paintings. For example, about *Night Café* (FIG. 13-9), he wrote:

I have tried to express the terrible passions of humanity by means of red and green. The room is blood red and dark yellow with a green billiard table in the middle; there are four citron-yellow lamps with a glow of orange and green. Everywhere there is a clash and contrast of the most disparate reds and greens in the figures of little sleeping hooligans, in the empty, dreary room, in violet and blue. The blood-red and the yellow-green of the billiard table, for instance, contrast with the soft, tender Louis XV green of the counter, on which there is a pink nosegay. The white coat of the landlord, awake in a corner of that furnace, turns citron-yellow, or pale luminous green.§

* Vincent van Gogh to Theo van Gogh, September 3, 1888, in W. H. Auden, ed., *Van Gogh: A Self-Portrait. Letters Revealing His Life as a Painter* (New York: Dutton, 1963), 319.
† August 11, 1888. Ibid., 313.
‡ September 8, 1888. Ibid., 321.
§ September 8, 1888. Ibid., 320.

13-9 VINCENT VAN GOGH, *Night Café*, 1888. Oil on canvas, 2' 4½" × 3'. Yale University Art Gallery, New Haven (bequest of Stephen Carlton Clark).

In *Night Café,* van Gogh explored the capabilities of colors and distorted forms to express emotions. The thickness, shape, and direction of his brush strokes create a tactile counterpart to the intense colors.

1 ft.

---

of the figures, Seurat placed each in space to set up a rhythmic movement in depth as well as from side to side. Sunshine fills the picture, but the painter did not break the light into transient patches of color. Light, air, people, and landscape are fixed in an abstract design in which line, color, value, and shape cohere in a precise and tightly controlled organization.

Vincent van Gogh In marked contrast to Seurat, VINCENT VAN GOGH (1853–1890) explored the capabilities of colors and distorted forms to express his emotions. The son of a Dutch Protestant pastor, van Gogh believed he had a religious calling and did missionary work in the coal-mining area of Belgium. Repeated professional and personal failures brought him close to despair. Only after he turned to painting did he find a way to communicate his experiences. When van Gogh died of a self-inflicted gunshot wound at age 37,

he considered himself a failure as an artist. He sold only one painting during his lifetime. Since his death, however, his reputation and the appreciation of his art have grown dramatically. Subsequent painters, especially the Fauves and German Expressionists (see Chapter 14), built on the use of color and the expressiveness of van Gogh's art. It is no exaggeration to state that today van Gogh is one of the most revered artists in history.

After relocating to Arles in southern France in 1888, van Gogh painted *Night Café* (FIG. 13-9). Although the subject is apparently benign, van Gogh invested it with a charged energy. As he stated in a letter to his brother Theo (see "The Letters of Vincent van Gogh," above), he wanted the painting to convey an oppressive atmosphere—"a place where one can ruin oneself, go mad, or commit a crime."[4] The proprietor rises like a specter from the edge of the billiard table, which the painter depicted in such a steeply tilted perspective that it threatens to slide out of the painting into the viewer's space. Van Gogh communicated the "madness" of the place by selecting vivid hues whose juxtaposition augmented their intensity. His insistence on the expressive values of color led him to develop a corresponding expressiveness in his paint application. The thickness, shape, and direction of his brush strokes created a tactile counterpart to his intense color schemes. He often moved the brush vehemently back and forth or at right angles, giving a textilelike effect, even squeezing dots or streaks directly onto his canvas from his paint tube. This bold, almost slapdash attack enhanced the intensity of his colors.

Starry Night Similarly illustrative of van Gogh's "expressionist" method is *Starry Night* (FIG. **13-10**), which the artist painted in 1889, the year before his death. At this time, van Gogh was living in an asylum in Saint-Rémy, where he had committed himself. In *Starry Night*, the artist did not represent the sky's appearance. Rather, he communicated his feelings about the electrifying vastness of the universe, filled with whirling and exploding stars and galaxies of stars, the earth and humanity huddling beneath it. Given van Gogh's determination to "use color . . . to express himself forcibly," the dark, deep blue that pervades the entire painting cannot be overlooked. Together with the turbulent brush strokes, the color suggests a quiet but pervasive depression. Van Gogh expressed his feelings about death and the stars in a letter to his brother: "[L]ooking at the stars always makes me dream, . . . Why, I ask myself, shouldn't the shining dots of the sky be as accessible as the black dots on the map of France? Just as we take the train to get to Tarascon or Rouen, we take death to reach a star."[5]

Paul Gauguin Like van Gogh, the French painter PAUL GAUGUIN (1848–1903) rejected objective representation in favor of subjective expression. He also broke with the Impressionists' studies of minutely contrasted hues because he believed color above all must be expressive and the artist's power to determine the colors in a painting was a central element of creativity. However, whereas van Gogh's heavy, thick brush strokes were an important component of his expressive style, Gauguin's color areas appear flatter, often visually dissolving into abstract patches or patterns.

In 1883, Gauguin gave up his prosperous career in the brokerage business to devote his time entirely to painting. Three years later, attracted by Brittany's unspoiled culture, Gauguin moved from Paris to Pont-Aven. Although in the 1870s and 1880s Brittany had been transformed into a profitable market economy, Gauguin still viewed the Bretons as "natural" men and women at ease in their environment. At Pont-Aven, he painted *Vision after the Sermon*, or *Jacob Wrestling with the Angel* (FIG. **13-11**), a work that decisively rejects both Realism and Impressionism. The painting shows Breton women, wearing their starched white Sunday caps and black dresses, visualizing the sermon they have just heard at church on Jacob's encounter with the Holy Spirit (Gen. 32:24–30). The women pray devoutly before the apparition. Gauguin departed from optical realism and composed the picture elements to focus the viewer's attention on the idea and intensify its message. The images are not what the Impressionist eye would have seen and replicated but what memory would have recalled and imagination would have modified. Thus the artist twisted the perspective and allotted the space to emphasize the innocent faith of the unquestioning women, and he shrank Jacob and the

13-10 VINCENT VAN GOGH, *Starry Night*, 1889. Oil on canvas, 2′ 5″ × 3′ ¼″. Museum of Modern Art, New York (acquired through the Lillie P. Bliss Bequest).

In this late work, van Gogh painted the vast night sky filled with whirling and exploding stars, the earth huddled beneath it. The painting is an almost abstract pattern of expressive line, shape, and color.

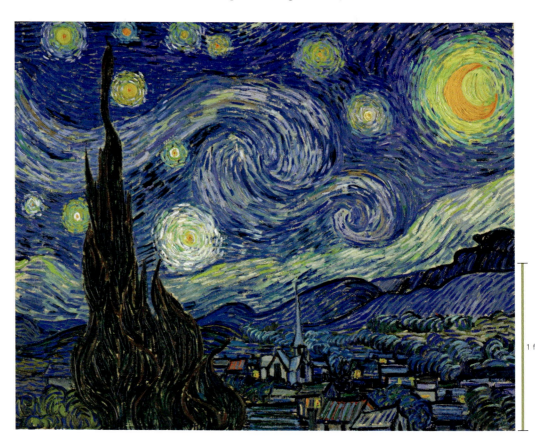

1 ft.

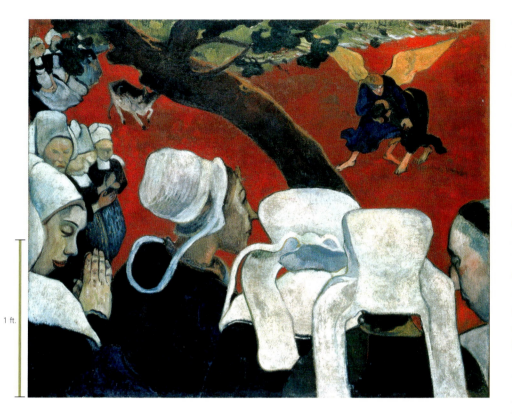

1 ft.

13-11 PAUL GAUGUIN, *Vision after the Sermon*, or *Jacob Wrestling with the Angel*, 1888. Oil on canvas, 2′ 4¾″ × 3′ ½″. National Gallery of Scotland, Edinburgh.

Gauguin admired Japanese prints, stained glass, and cloisonné enamels. Their influences are evident in this painting of Breton women, in which firm outlines enclose large areas of unmodulated color.

ritual. Like many of his contemporaries, Gauguin admired Japanese prints as well as medieval stained glass (FIG. 7-11) and cloisonné metalwork (FIG. 6-2). These art forms contributed to his own daring experiment to transform traditional painting and Impressionism into abstract, expressive patterns of line, shape, and pure color.

Where Do We Come From?

After a brief period of association with van Gogh in Arles in 1888, Gauguin settled in Tahiti. Gauguin believed the South Pacific island would offer him a life far removed from materialistic Europe and an opportunity to reconnect with nature. Upon his arrival, he was disappointed to find that Tahiti, under French control since 1842, had been extensively colonized. Gauguin tried to maintain his vision of an untamed paradise by moving to the Tahitian countryside, where he expressed his fascination with primitive life and brilliant color in a series of striking decorative canvases. Gauguin often based the design, although indirectly, on native motifs, and the color owed its peculiar harmonies of lilac, pink, and lemon to the tropical flora of the islands.

angel, wrestling in a ring enclosed by a Breton stone fence, to the size of fighting cocks. Wrestling matches were regular features at the entertainment held after high mass, so Gauguin's women are spectators at a contest that was, for them, a familiar part of their culture.

Gauguin did not unify the picture with a horizon perspective, light and shade, or a naturalistic use of color. Instead, he abstracted the scene into a pattern. Pure unmodulated color fills flat planes and shapes bounded by firm lines: white caps, black dresses, and the red field of combat. The shapes are angular, even harsh. The caps, the sharp fingers and profiles, and the hard contours suggest the austerity of peasant life and

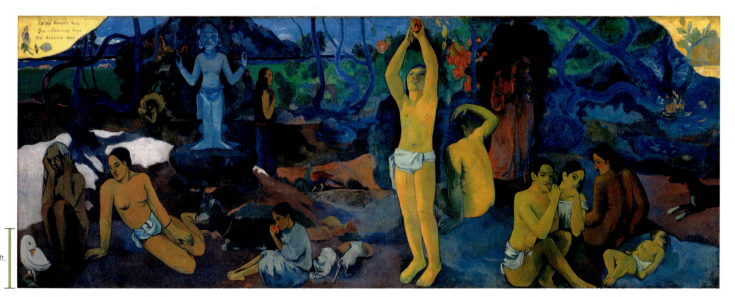

1 ft.

13-12 PAUL GAUGUIN, *Where Do We Come From? What Are We? Where Are We Going?* 1897. Oil on canvas, 4′ 6¹³⁄₁₆″ × 12′ 3″. Museum of Fine Arts, Boston (Tompkins Collection).

In search of a place far removed from European materialism, Gauguin moved to Tahiti, where he used native women and tropical colors to present a pessimistic view of the inevitability of the life cycle.

Post-Impressionism   373

In 1897, worn down by failing health and the hostile reception of his work, Gauguin tried unsuccessfully to take his own life, but not before painting *Where Do We Come From? What Are We? Where Are We Going?* (FIG. **13-12**). This monumental work can be read as a summary of Gauguin's art and his views on life. The scene is a tropical landscape, populated with native women and children. He described it in a letter to a friend:

> Where are we going? Near to death an old woman. . . . What are we? Day to day existence. . . . Where do we come from? Source. Child. Life begins. . . . Behind a tree two sinister figures, cloaked in garments of sombre colour, introduce, near the tree of knowledge, their note of anguish caused by that very knowledge in contrast to some simple beings in a virgin nature, which might be paradise as conceived by humanity, who give themselves up to the happiness of living.[6]

Where Do We Come From? is, therefore, a sobering, pessimistic image of the life cycle's inevitability. Gauguin died a few years later in the Marquesas Islands, his artistic genius still unrecognized.

Paul Cézanne Like Seurat, the French artist PAUL CÉZANNE (1839–1906) turned from Impressionism to develop a more analytical style. Although at first he accepted the Impressionists' color theories and their faith in subjects chosen from everyday life, his own studies of Renaissance and Baroque paintings in the Louvre persuaded him that Impressionism lacked form and structure. Cézanne declared he wanted to "make of Impressionism something solid and durable like the art of the museums."[7]

The basis of Cézanne's art was his unique way of studying nature, as seen in works such as *Mont Sainte-Victoire* (FIG. **13-13**), one of many views Cézanne painted of this mountain near his home in Aix-en-Provence. Cézanne's aim was not truth in appearance, especially not photographic truth, nor was it the "truth" of Impressionism. Rather, he sought a lasting structure behind the formless and fleeting visual information the eye absorbs. Instead of employing the Impressionists' random approach when he was face-to-face with nature, Cézanne attempted to order the lines, planes, and colors that comprised nature. He constantly and painstakingly checked his painting against the part of the real scene—he called it the "motif"—he was studying at the moment. When Cézanne wrote that his goal was "[to do] Poussin [FIG. 10-29] over entirely from nature . . . in the open air, with color and light, instead of . . . in a studio,"[8] he meant that he sought to achieve Poussin's effects of distance, depth, structure, and solidity not by using traditional perspective and chiaroscuro but by recording the color patterns an optical analysis of nature provides.

With special care, Cézanne explored the properties of line, plane, and color and their interrelationships. He studied the effect of every kind of linear direction, the capacity of planes to create the sensation of depth, the intrinsic qualities of color, and the power of colors to modify the direction and depth of lines and planes. To create the illusion of three-

13-13 PAUL CÉZANNE, *Mont Sainte-Victoire,* 1902–1904. Oil on canvas, 2' 3½" × 2' 11¼". Philadelphia Museum of Art, Philadelphia (George W. Elkins Collection).

In his landscapes, Cézanne replaced the transitory visual effects of shifting atmospheric conditions, a focus for the Impressionists, with careful analysis of the lines, planes, and colors of nature.

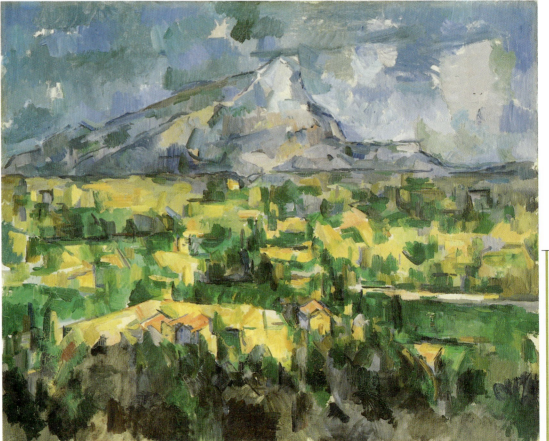

1 ft.

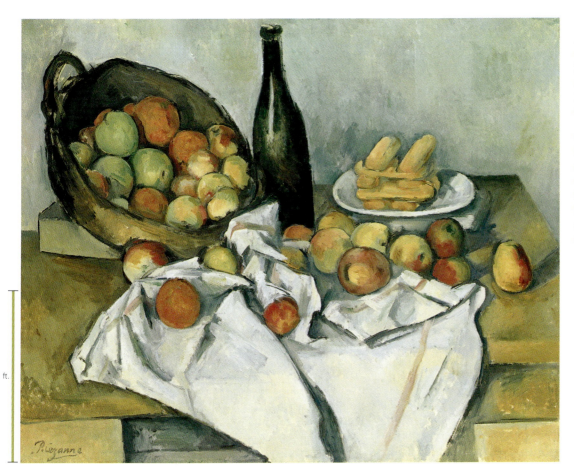

13-14 PAUL CÉZANNE, *Basket of Apples*, ca. 1895. Oil on canvas, 2′ $\frac{3}{8}$″ × 2′ 7″. Art Institute of Chicago, Chicago (Helen Birch Bartlett Memorial Collection, 1926).

Cézanne's still lifes reveal his analytical approach to painting. He captured the solidity of bottles and fruit by juxtaposing color patches, but the resulting abstract shapes are not optically realistic.

1 ft.

dimensional form and space, Cézanne focused on carefully selecting colors. He understood that the visual properties—hue, saturation, and value—of different colors vary (see "Color Theory," page 370). Cool colors tend to recede, warm ones advance. By applying to the canvas small patches of juxtaposed colors, some advancing and some receding, Cézanne created volume and spatial depth in his works. On occasion, the artist depicted objects chiefly in one hue and achieved convincing solidity by modulating the intensity (or saturation). At other times, he juxtaposed contrasting colors of like saturation to compose specific objects, such as fruit or bowls.

In *Mont Sainte-Victoire*, he replaced the transitory visual effects of changing atmospheric conditions—effects that occupied Monet—with a more concentrated, lengthier analysis of the colors in large lighted spaces. The main space stretches out behind and beyond the canvas plane and includes numerous small elements, such as roads, fields, houses, and the viaduct at the far right, each seen from a slightly different viewpoint. Above this shifting, receding perspective rises the largest mass of all, the mountain, with an effect—achieved by equally stressing background and foreground contours—of being simultaneously near and far away. This portrayal approximates the real experience a person has when viewing a landscape's forms piecemeal. The relative proportions of objects vary rather than being fixed by a strict one- or two-point perspective, such as that normally found in a photograph. Cézanne immobilized the shifting colors of Impressionism into an array of clearly defined planes that compose the objects and spaces in his scene.

Basket of Apples Still-life painting was another good vehicle for Cézanne's experiments, as he could arrange a limited number of selected objects to provide a well-ordered point of departure. So analytical was Cézanne in preparing, observing, and painting still lifes (in contrast to the Impressionist emphasis on the idea of the spontaneous) that he had to abandon using real fruit and flowers because they tended to rot. In *Basket of Apples* (FIG. 13-14), the objects have lost something of their individual character as bottles and fruit and almost become cylinders and spheres. Cézanne captured the solidity of each object by juxtaposing color patches. His interest in the study of volume and solidity is evident from the disjunctures in the painting—the table edges are discontinuous, and various objects seem to be depicted from different vantage points. In his zeal to understand three-dimensionality and to convey the placement of forms relative to the space around them, Cézanne explored his still-life arrangements from different viewpoints. This resulted in paintings that, although conceptually coherent, do not appear optically realistic. In keeping with the modernist concern with the integrity of the painting surface, Cézanne's methods never permit the viewer to disregard the two-dimensionality of the picture plane. In this manner, Cézanne achieved a remarkable feat—presenting the viewer with two-dimensional and three-dimensional images simultaneously.

SYMBOLIST AND FIN-DE-SIÈCLE PAINTING

The Impressionists and Post-Impressionists believed their emotions and sensations were important elements for interpreting nature, but the depiction of objects, people, and nature remained the primary focus of their efforts. By the end of the 19th century, the representation of nature became completely subjective. Artists rejected the optical world as observed in favor of a fantasy world, of forms they conjured in their free imagination, with or without reference to things conventionally seen. Color, line, and shape, divorced from conformity to the optical image, became symbols of personal emotions in response to the world. Many artists following this path adopted an approach to subject and form that associated them with a general European movement called *Symbolism*. Symbolists, whether painters or writers, disdained Realism as trivial. The task of Symbolist visual and verbal artists was not to see things but to see through them to a significance and reality far deeper than what superficial appearance gave. Symbolists cultivated all the resources of imagination, and their subjects became increasingly esoteric and exotic, mysterious, visionary, dreamlike, and fantastic. Perhaps not coincidentally, at about this time Sigmund Freud (1856–1939), the founder of psychoanalysis, published his classic work *Interpretations of Dreams* (1900), an introduction to the concept and the world of unconscious experience.

Henri Rousseau Paul Gauguin had journeyed to the South Seas in search of primitive innocence. French artist HENRI ROUSSEAU (1844–1910) was a "primitive" without leaving Paris—an untrained amateur painter. Rousseau produced an art of dream and fantasy in a style that had its own

sophistication and made its own departure from the artistic currency of the time. He compensated for his apparent visual, conceptual, and technical naïveté with a natural talent for design and an imagination teeming with exotic images of mysterious tropical landscapes. In *Sleeping Gypsy* (FIG. 13-15), the recumbent figure occupies a desert world, silent and secret, and dreams beneath a pale, perfectly round moon. In the foreground, a lion that resembles a stuffed, but somehow menacing, animal doll sniffs at the gypsy. A critical encounter impends—an encounter of the type that recalls the uneasiness of a person's vulnerable subconscious self during sleep.

Edvard Munch Linked in spirit to the Symbolists was the Norwegian painter and graphic artist EDVARD MUNCH (1863–1944), who felt deeply the pain of human life. His belief that humans were powerless before the great natural forces of death and love and the emotions associated with them—jealousy, loneliness, fear, desire, despair—became the theme of most of his art. Because Munch's goal was to describe the conditions of "modern psychic life," as he put it, Realist and Impressionist techniques were inappropriate, focusing as they did on the tangible world. In the spirit of Symbolism, Munch developed a style of putting color, line, and figural distortion to expressive ends.

Munch's *The Scream* (FIG. 13-16) exemplifies his style. The image—a man standing on a bridge or jetty in a landscape—comes from the real world, but Munch's treatment of the image departs significantly from visual reality. *The Scream* evokes a visceral, emotional response from the viewer because of the painter's dramatic presentation. The man in the foreground, simplified to almost skeletal form, emits a primal scream. The landscape's sweeping curvilinear lines reiterate the curvilinear shape of the mouth and head,

13-15 HENRI ROUSSEAU, *Sleeping Gypsy*, 1897. Oil on canvas, 4′ 3″ × 6′ 7″. Museum of Modern Art, New York (gift of Mrs. Simon Guggenheim).

In *Sleeping Gypsy*, Henri Rousseau depicted a doll-like but menacing lion sniffing at a recumbent dreaming figure in a mysterious landscape. The painting conjures the vulnerable subconscious during sleep.

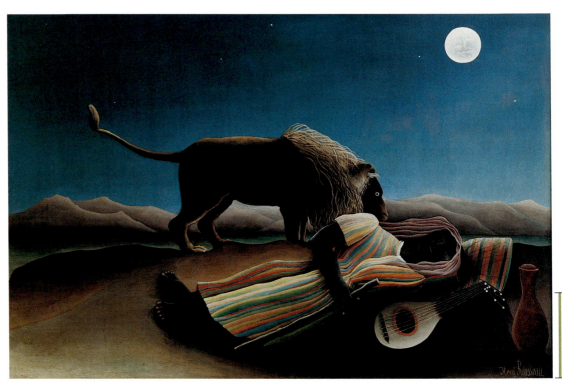

1 ft.

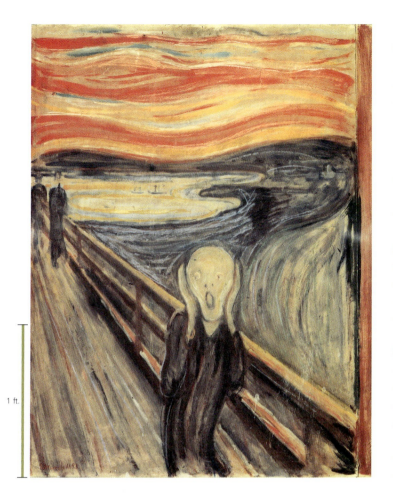

13-16 EDVARD MUNCH, *The Scream*, 1893. Tempera and pastels on cardboard, 2′ 11¾″ × 2′ 5″. National Gallery, Oslo.

Although grounded in the real world, *The Scream* departs significantly from visual reality. Munch used color, line, and figural distortion to evoke a strong emotional response from the viewer.

almost like an echo, as the cry reverberates through the setting. The fiery red and yellow stripes that give the sky an eerie glow also contribute to this work's resonance. Munch wrote a revealing epigraph to accompany the painting: "I stopped and leaned against the balustrade, almost dead with fatigue. Above the blue-black fjord hung the clouds, red as blood and tongues of fire. My friends had left me, and alone, trembling with anguish, I became aware of the vast, infinite cry of nature."[9] Appropriately, the original title of this work was *Despair*.

Fin-de-Siècle Historians have adopted the term *fin-de-siècle* (French, "end of the century") to describe the culture of the late 1800s. This designation is not merely chronological but also refers to a certain sensibility. The increasingly large and prosperous middle classes dominated European society and aspired to the advantages the aristocracy traditionally enjoyed. They too strove to live "the good life," which evolved into a culture of decadence and indulgence. Characteristic of the fin-de-siècle period was an intense preoccupation with sexual drives, powers, and perversions. People at the end of the century also immersed themselves in an exploration of the unconscious. This culture was unrestrained and freewheeling, but the determination to enjoy life masked an anxiety prompted by significant political upheaval and an uncertain future. The country most closely associated with fin-de-siècle culture was Austria.

Gustav Klimt The Viennese artist GUSTAV KLIMT (1863–1918) captured this period's flamboyance in his work but tempered it with unsettling undertones. In *The Kiss* (FIG. **13-17**), Klimt depicted a couple locked in an embrace. All that is visible of the couple,

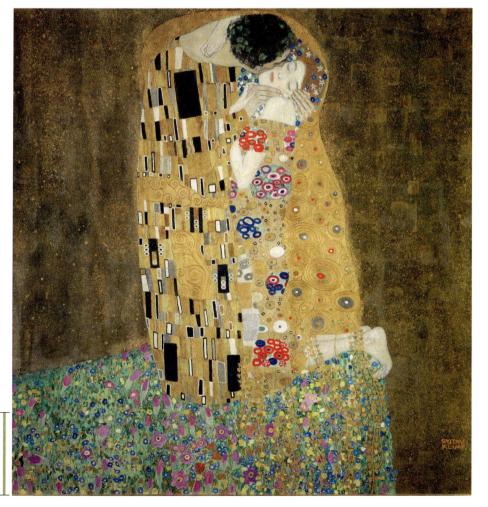

13-17 GUSTAV KLIMT, *The Kiss*, 1907–1908. Oil on canvas, 5′ 10¾″ × 5′ 10¾″. Österreichische Galerie Belvedere, Vienna.

In this opulent Viennese fin-de-siècle painting, Gustav Klimt revealed only a small segment of each lover's body. The rest of the painting dissolves into shimmering, extravagant flat patterning.

however, is a small segment of each person's body. The rest of the painting dissolves into shimmering, extravagant flat patterning, evoking the conflict between two- and three-dimensionality intrinsic to the work of many other modernists. Paintings such as *The Kiss* were visual manifestations of fin-de-siècle spirit because they captured a decadence conveyed by opulent and sensuous images.

SCULPTURE

The three-dimensional art of sculpture was not suited to capturing the optical sensations many late-19th-century painters favored. Sculpture's very nature—its tangibility and solidity—suggests permanence. Consequently, sculptors of this period pursued artistic goals markedly different from those of contemporaneous painters.

Auguste Rodin The leading French sculptor of the later 19th century was AUGUSTE RODIN (1840–1917). Rodin conceived and executed his sculptures with a Realist sensibility, but he was also well aware of the innovations of the Impressionists. Although color was not a significant factor in Rodin's work, Impressionist influence is evident in the artist's abiding concern for the effect of light on the three-dimensional surface. When focusing on the human form, he joined his profound knowledge of anatomy and movement with special attention to the body's exterior, saying, "The sculptor must learn to reproduce the surface, which means all that vibrates on the surface, soul, love, passion, life. . . . Sculpture is thus the art of hollows and mounds, not of smoothness, or even polished planes."[10] Primarily a modeler of pliable material rather than a carver of hard wood or stone, Rodin worked his sculptures with fingers sensitive to the subtlest variations of surface, catching the fugitive play of constantly shifting light on the body. In his studio, he often would have a model move around in front of him while he made sketches with coils of clay. Rodin was able to capture the quality of the transitory through his highly textured surfaces while revealing larger themes and deeper, lasting sensibilities.

Rodin's masterpiece is the cast-bronze life-size group *Burghers of Calais* (FIG. 13-18), which commemorates a heroic episode in the Hundred Years' War. During the English siege of Calais, France, in 1347, six of the city's leading citizens agreed to offer their lives in return for the English king's promise to lift the siege and spare the rest of the populace. Each of the bedraggled-looking figures is a convincing study of despair, resignation, or quiet defiance. Rodin enhanced the psychic effects through his choreographic placement of the group members. Rather than clustering in a tightly formal composition, the *burghers* (middle-class citizens) wander aimlessly. The roughly textured surfaces add to the pathos of the figures and compel the viewer's continued interest. Rodin designed the monument without the traditional high base in the hope that the citizens of Calais would be inspired by the sculptural representation of their ancestors standing eye-level in the city center and preparing eternally to

13-18 AUGUSTE RODIN, *Burghers of Calais*, 1884–1889, cast ca. 1953–1959. Bronze, 6′ 10½″ high, 7′ 11″ long, 6′ 6″ deep. Musée Rodin, Paris.

Rodin was able to capture the quality of the transitory through his highly textured surfaces while also revealing larger themes, as in this poignant group of six citizens who sacrificed their lives for their city.

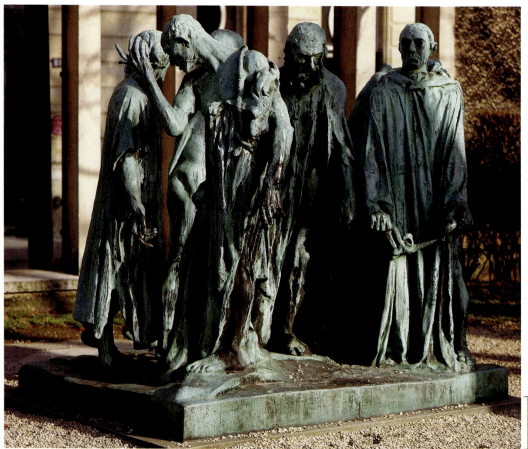

1 ft.

set off on their sacrificial journey. However, the city officials who commissioned the group found Rodin's vision so offensive that they banished the monument to a remote site and modified the work's effect by placing it high on an isolating pedestal.

ARCHITECTURE

In the late 19th century, new technologies and the changing needs of urbanized, industrialized society affected architecture throughout the Western world. Since the 18th century, bridges had been built of cast iron, which permitted engineering advancements in the construction of larger,

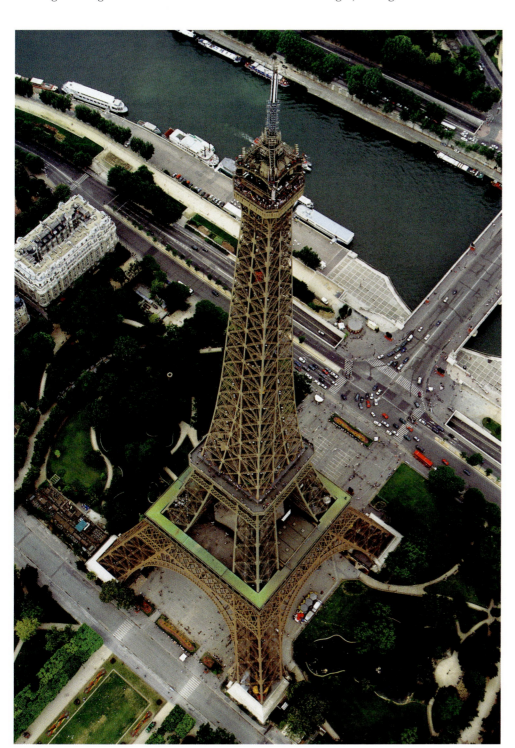

stronger, and more fire-resistant structures. Steel, available after 1860, allowed architects to enclose larger spaces, such as those found in railroad stations (FIG. 13-3). The Realist impulse also encouraged an architecture that honestly expressed a building's purpose rather than elaborately disguised a building's function.

Alexandre-Gustave Eiffel The elegant metal skeleton structures of the French engineer-architect ALEXANDRE-GUSTAVE EIFFEL (1832–1923) were responses to that idea. Eiffel created the interior armature for France's anniversary gift to the United States—the *Statue of Liberty*—but he designed his best-known work, the Eiffel Tower (FIG. **13-19**), for a great exhibition in Paris in 1889. Originally seen as a symbol of modern Paris, the metal tower thrusts its needle shaft 984 feet above the city, making it at the time of its construction the world's tallest structure. The tower rests on four giant supports connected by gracefully arching open-frame skirts that provide a pleasing mask for the heavy horizontal girders needed to strengthen the legs. The transparency of the structure blurs the distinction between interior and exterior to an extent never before achieved or even attempted. Eiffel jolted the architectural profession into a realization that newly available materials and processes could generate a radically innovative approach to architectural design.

13-19 ALEXANDRE-GUSTAVE EIFFEL, Eiffel Tower, Paris, France, 1889.

Eiffel's metal skeleton structures jolted the architectural profession into a realization that newly available materials and processes could effect a radically new approach to architectural design.

13-20 Louis Henry Sullivan, Guaranty (Prudential) Building, Buffalo, 1894–1896.

Sullivan used the latest technologies to create this light-filled, well-ventilated, early steel-and-glass skyscraper. He added ornate embellishments to both the exterior and interior to impart a sense of refinement and taste.

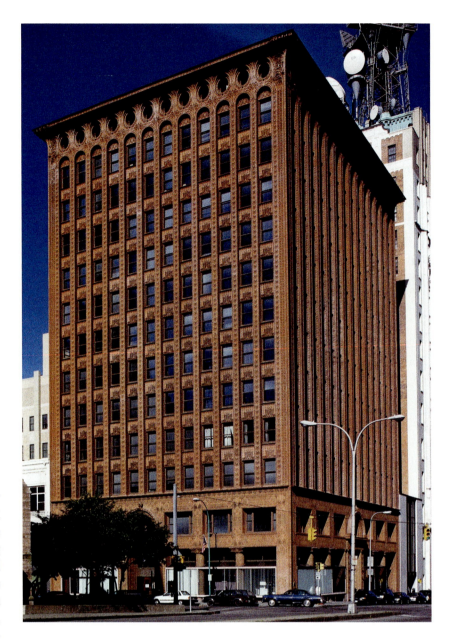

Louis Henry Sullivan The desire for greater speed and economy in building, as well as for a reduction in fire hazards, prompted the use of cast and wrought iron for many building programs. Architects enthusiastically developed cast-iron architecture until a series of disastrous fires in the early 1870s demonstrated that cast iron by itself was far from impervious to fire. This discovery led to encasing the metal in masonry, combining the first material's strength with the second's fire resistance. In cities, convenience required closely grouped buildings, and increased property values forced architects literally to raise the roof. The new construction materials, which could support structures of unprecedented height, gave birth to the American skyscraper. As skyscrapers proliferated, in large part because of the introduction of elevators beginning in 1868, architects refined the visual vocabulary of these buildings.

Louis Henry Sullivan (1856–1924), deemed by many architectural historians the first truly modern architect, arrived at a synthesis of industrial structure and ornamentation that perfectly expressed the spirit of late-19th-century commerce. To achieve this, he employed the latest technological developments to create light-filled, well-ventilated office buildings and adorned both exteriors and interiors with ornate embellishments. These characteristics are evident in the Guaranty (Prudential) Building (FIG. **13-20**) in Buffalo, New York, built between 1894 and 1896. The structure is steel, sheathed with terracotta. The imposing size of the building and the regularity of the window placements served as an expression of the large-scale, refined, and orderly office work that took place within. Sullivan tempered the severity of the structure with lively ornamentation, both on the piers and cornice on the exterior of the building and on the stairway balustrades, elevator cages, and ceiling in the interior. The Guaranty Building illustrates Sullivan's famous dictum that "form follows function," which became the slogan of many early-20th-century architects.

Thus, in architecture as well as in the pictorial arts, the late 19th century was a period during which artists challenged traditional modes of expression, often emphatically rejecting the past. Architects and painters as different as Sullivan, Monet, van Gogh, and Cézanne, each in his own way, contributed significantly to the entrenchment of modernism as the new cultural orthodoxy of the early 20th century (see Chapter 14).

Europe and America, 1870 to 1900

IMPRESSIONISM

▌ A hostile critic applied the term "Impressionism" to the paintings of Claude Monet because of their sketchy quality. The Impressionists—Monet, Pierre-Auguste Renoir, Edgar Degas, and others—strove to capture fleeting moments and transient effects of light and climate on canvas. The Impressionists also focused on recording contemporary urban life in Paris. They frequently painted scenes from bars, dance halls, the ballet, and railroad stations.

▌ Complementing the Impressionists' sketchy, seemingly spontaneous brush strokes are the compositions of their paintings. Reflecting the influence of Japanese prints and photography, Impressionist works often have arbitrarily cut-off figures and settings seen at sharply oblique angles.

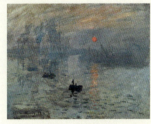

Monet, *Impression: Sunrise,* 1872

POST-IMPRESSIONISM

▌ Post-Impressionism is not a unified style. The term refers to the group of late-19th-century artists who followed the Impressionists and took painting in new directions.

▌ Georges Seurat refined the Impressionist approach to color and light into pointillism—the disciplined application of pure color in tiny daubs. Vincent van Gogh explored the capabilities of colors and distorted forms to express emotions, as in his dramatic depiction of the sky in *Starry Night.* Paul Gauguin, an admirer of Japanese prints, moved away from Impressionism in favor of large areas of flat color bounded by firm lines. Paul Cézanne replaced the transitory visual effects of the Impressionists with a rigorous analysis of the lines, planes, and colors that make up landscapes and still lifes.

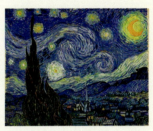

Van Gogh, *Starry Night,* 1889

SYMBOLIST AND FIN-DE-SIÈCLE PAINTING

▌ The Symbolists disdained Realism as trivial and sought to depict a reality beyond that of the everyday world. They rejected materialism and celebrated fantasy and imagination. Their subjects were often mysterious, exotic, and sensuous. Henri Rousseau's *Sleeping Gypsy,* which alludes to the world of the subconscious during sleep, is a characteristic example.

▌ Late-19th-century fin-de-siècle artists, such as Edvard Munch in Norway and Gustav Klimt in Austria, explored the opulent, decadent, sensuous, and unconscious in their paintings.

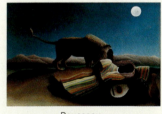

Rousseau, *Sleeping Gypsy,* 1897

SCULPTURE

▌ Sculpture is not suited to capturing transitory optical effects or exploring the properties of color and line, and late-19th-century sculptors thus pursued goals different from those of the Impressionists and Post-Impressionists.

▌ The leading sculptor of the era was Auguste Rodin, who explored Realist themes and the representation of movement, as in his moving portrayal of six leading citizens of Calais who sacrificed their lives for their countrymen.

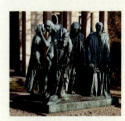

Rodin, *Burghers of Calais,* 1884–1889

ARCHITECTURE

▌ New technologies and the changing needs of urbanized, industrialized society transformed Western architecture at the close of the 19th century. The exposed iron skeleton of the Eiffel Tower, which blurs the distinction between interior and exterior, jolted architects into a realization that modern materials and processes could revolutionize architectural design.

▌ In the United States, Louis Sullivan was a pioneer in designing the first metal, stone, and glass skyscrapers.

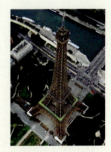

Eiffel, Eiffel Tower, Paris, 1889

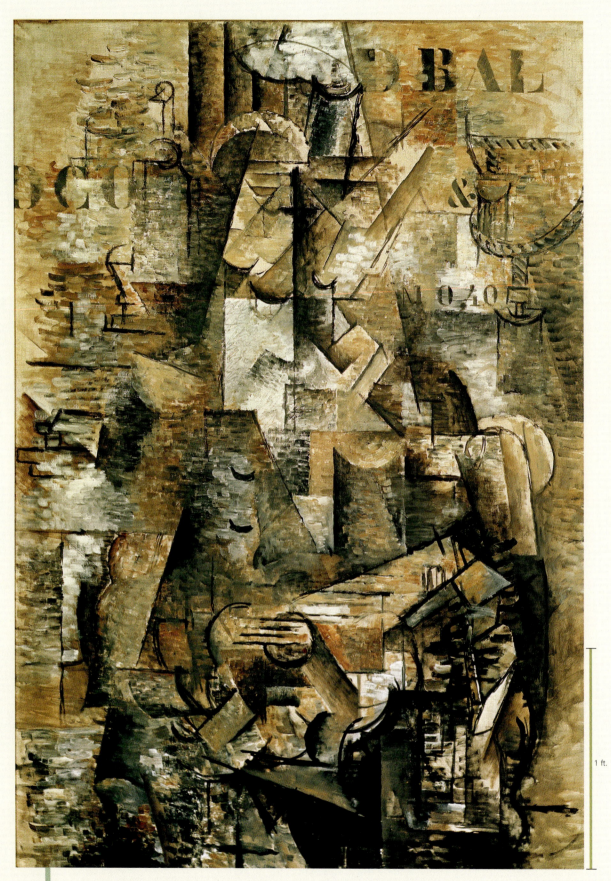

1 ft.

14-1 Georges Braque, *The Portuguese*, 1911. Oil on canvas, 3′ 10⅛″ × 2′ 8″. Kunstmuseum, Basel (gift of Raoul La Roche, 1952).

The Cubists were among the early-20th-century artists who rejected the pictorial illusionism of Western art after the Renaissance and challenged the most basic assumptions about the nature and purpose of art.

Europe and America, 1900 to 1945

The first half of the 20th century was a period of significant upheaval worldwide. Between 1900 and 1945, the major industrial powers expanded their colonial empires, fought two global wars, witnessed the rise of Communism, Fascism, and Nazism, and suffered the Great Depression. These decades were also a time of radical change in the arts when painters and sculptors challenged some of the most basic assumptions about the purpose of art and what form an artwork should take.

Early-20th-century imperialism was capitalist and expansionist, establishing colonies as raw-material sources, as manufacturing markets, and as territorial acquisitions. Colonialism also often had the missionary dimension of bringing the "light" of Christianity and civilization to "backward peoples" and educating "inferior races." Nationalism and rampant imperialism led to competition. Eventually, countries negotiated alliances to protect their individual interests. The conflicts between the two major blocs—the Triple Alliance (Germany, Austria-Hungary, and Italy) and the Triple Entente (Russia, France, and Great Britain)—led to World War I, which began in 1914. Although the United States tried to remain neutral, it finally felt compelled to enter the war in 1917. The slaughter and devastation of the Great War lasted until 1918. Not only were more than nine million soldiers killed in battle, but the introduction of poison gas in 1915 added to the horror of humankind's inhumanity to itself.

The Russian Revolution exacerbated the global chaos when it erupted in 1917. Dissatisfaction with the regime of Tsar Nicholas II (r. 1894–1917) led workers to stage a general strike, and the monarchy's rule ended with the tsar's abdication in March. In late 1917 the Bolsheviks, led by Vladimir Lenin (1870–1924), wrested control of the country, nationalized the land, and turned it over to the local rural soviets (councils of workers and soldiers deputies). After extensive civil war, the Communists, as they now called themselves, established the Union of Soviet Socialist Republics in 1923.

Economic upheaval followed on the heels of war and revolution. The Great Depression of the 1930s dealt a serious blow to the stability of Western countries. By 1932 unemployment in the British workforce stood at 25 percent, and 40 percent of German workers were without jobs. Production in the United States plummeted by 50 percent. This economic disaster, along with the failure of postwar treaties and the League of Nations to keep the peace, provided a fertile breeding ground for dangerous forces to emerge once again. Benito Mussolini (1883–1945) established the nationalistic Fascist regime in Italy, Joseph Stalin (1879–1953) gained control of the Communist Party in the Soviet Union, and Adolf Hitler

(1889–1945) consolidated his power in Germany by building the Nazi Party into a mass political movement.

These ruthless seizures of power led to the many conflicts that evolved into World War II, which erupted in 1939 when Germany invaded Poland, and Britain and France declared war on Germany. Eventually, this conflict earned its designation as a world war. While Germany and Italy fought most of Europe and the Soviet Union, Japan invaded China and occupied Indochina. After the Japanese bombing of Pearl Harbor in Hawaii in 1941, the United States declared war on Japan. Germany, in loose alliance with Japan, declared war on the United States. This catastrophic struggle drew to an end in 1945, when the Allied forces defeated Germany, and the United States dropped atomic bombs on Hiroshima and Nagasaki in Japan. The shock of the war's physical, economic, and psychological devastation tempered the elation people felt at the conclusion of global hostilities.

EUROPE, 1900 TO 1920

Like other members of society, artists deeply felt the effects of the political and economic disruptions of the early 20th century. As the old social orders collapsed and new ones, from communism to corporate capitalism, took their place, artists searched for new definitions of and uses for art in a radically changed world. Already in the 19th century, each successive modernist movement had challenged artistic conventions, giving rise to the *avant-garde* ("front guard"), a term derived from French military usage. Avant-garde artists were the vanguard, or trailblazers. They rejected the classical, academic, and traditional, and zealously explored the premises and formal qualities of painting and sculpture. In the early 1900s, avant-garde principles first emerged forcefully in the general movement that art historians call *Expressionism*. Although used in connection with a wide variety of art, at its essence the term refers to art that is the result of the artist's personal vision and that often has an emotional dimension. Expressionism contrasts strongly with most Western post-Renaissance art, which focused on visually describing the empirical world.

Fauvism

One of the first Expressionist movements of the 20th century was *Fauvism*. In 1905 a group of young painters exhibited canvases so simplified in design and so shockingly bright in color that a startled critic, Louis Vauxcelles (1870–1943), described the artists as *fauves* (wild beasts). Driving the Fauve movement was a desire to develop an art that had the directness of Impressionism but that also used intense color juxtapositions and their emotional capabilities, the legacy of artists such as van Gogh and Gauguin (see Chapter 13). Fauve artists went even further in liberating color from its descriptive function, using it for both expressive and structural ends.

Henri Matisse The dominant figure of the Fauve group was HENRI MATISSE (1869–1954), who believed color could play a primary role in conveying meaning and focused his efforts on developing this notion (see "Matisse on Color," page 385). Matisse explained his approach: "What characterized fauvism was that we rejected imitative colors, and that with pure colors we obtained stronger reactions."[1] In *Woman with the Hat* (FIG. 14-2), Matisse depicted his wife Amélie in a rather conventional manner compositionally, but he used seemingly arbitrary colors. The entire image—the woman's face, clothes, hat, and background—consists of patches and splotches of color juxtaposed in ways that sometimes produce jarring contrasts.

The maturation of Matisse's exploration of the expressive power of color is evident in *Red Room* (*Harmony in Red*; FIG. 14-3). The subject is the interior of a comfortable, prosperous household with a maid placing fruit and wine on the table, but Matisse's canvas is radically different from

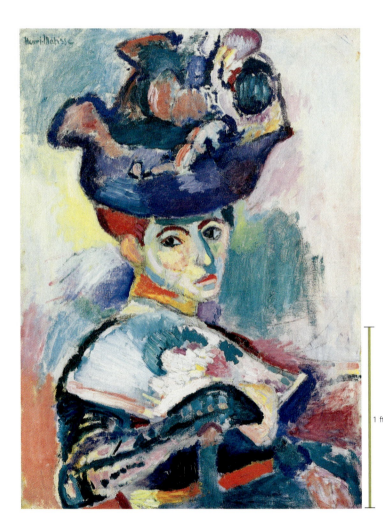

1 ft.

14-2 HENRI MATISSE, *Woman with the Hat*, 1905. Oil on canvas, 2′ 7¾″ × 1′ 11½″. San Francisco Museum of Modern Art, San Francisco (bequest of Elise S. Haas).

Matisse portrayed his wife Amélie using patches and splotches of seemingly arbitrary colors. He and the other Fauve painters used color not to imitate nature but to produce a reaction in the viewer.

Matisse on Color

In a 1908 essay entitled "Notes of a Painter," Henri Matisse set forth his principles and goals as a painter. The excerpts that follow help explain what Matisse was trying to achieve in paintings such as *Harmony in Red* (FIG. 14-3).

> What I am after, above all, is expression. . . . Expression, for me, does not reside in passions glowing in a human face or manifested by violent movement. The entire arrangement of my picture is expressive: the place occupied by the figures, the empty spaces around them, the proportions, everything has its share. Composition is the art of arranging in a decorative manner the diverse elements at the painter's command to express his feelings. . . . Both harmonies and dissonances of colour can produce agreeable effects. . . . Suppose I

have to paint an interior: I have before me a cupboard; it gives me a sensation of vivid red, and I put down a red which satisfies me. A relation is established between this red and the white of the canvas. Let me put a green near the red, and make the floor yellow; and again there will be relationships between the green or yellow and the white of the canvas which will satisfy me. . . . A new combination of colours will succeed the first. . . . From the relationship I have found in all the tones there must result a living harmony of colours, a harmony analogous to that of a musical composition. . . . My choice of colours does not rest on any scientific theory; it is based on observation, on sensitivity, on felt experiences. . . . I simply try to put down colours which render my sensation.*

* Translated by Jack D. Flam, *Matisse on Art* (London: Phaidon, 1973), 32–40.

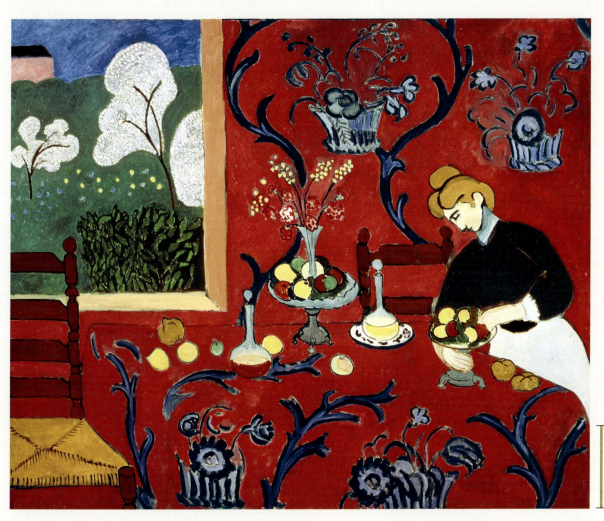

14-3

HENRI MATISSE, *Red Room (Harmony in Red)*, 1908–1909. Oil on canvas, 5′ 11″ × 8′ 1″. State Hermitage Museum, Saint Petersburg.

Matisse believed painters should choose compositions and colors that express their feelings. Here, the table and the wall seem to merge because they are the same color and have identical patterning.

1 ft.

traditional paintings of domestic interiors (FIG. 10-26). The Fauve painter depicted objects in simplified and schematized fashion and flattened the forms. For example, Matisse eliminated the front edge of the table, making the table, with its identical patterning, as flat as the wall behind it. The window at the upper left could also be a painting on the wall,

further flattening the space. Everywhere, the colors contrast richly and intensely. Initially, this work was predominantly green, and then Matisse repainted it blue. Neither seemed appropriate. Not until he repainted the canvas red did Matisse feel he had found the right color for the "harmony" he wished to compose.

German Expressionism

The immediacy and boldness of the Fauve images appealed to many artists, including the German Expressionists. However, although color plays a prominent role in contemporaneous German painting, the expressiveness of the German images is due as much to wrenching distortions of form, ragged outline, and agitated brush strokes. This approach resulted in savagely powerful, emotional canvases in the years leading to World War I.

Ernst Ludwig Kirchner The first group of German artists to explore Expressionist ideas gathered in Dresden in 1905 under the leadership of ERNST LUDWIG KIRCHNER (1880–1938). The group members thought of themselves as paving the way for a more perfect age by bridging the old age and the new. They derived their name, *Die Brücke* (The Bridge), from this concept. The Bridge artists protested the hypocrisy and materialism of those in power. Kirchner, in particular, focused much of his attention on the detrimental effects of industrialization, such as the alienation of individuals in cities, which he felt fostered a mechanized and impersonal society.

Kirchner's *Street, Dresden* (FIG. **14-4**) provides a glimpse into the frenzied activity of a German city before World War I. Rather than the distant, panoramic urban view the Impressionists favored, this street scene is jarring and dissonant. The women in the foreground loom large, approaching the viewer somewhat menacingly. The steep perspective of the street, which threatens to push the women into the viewer's space, increases their confrontational nature. Harshly rendered, the women's features make them appear ghoulish, and the garish, clashing colors—juxtapositions of bright orange, emerald green, acrid chartreuse, and pink—add to the expressive impact of the image. Kirchner's perspectival distortions, disquieting figures, and color choices reflect the influence of the work of Edvard Munch, who made similar expressive use of formal elements in *The Scream* (FIG. **13-16**).

Vassily Kandinsky A second major German Expressionist group, *Der Blaue Reiter* (The Blue Rider), formed in Munich in 1911. The two founding members, Vassily Kandinsky and Franz Marc, whimsically selected this name because of their mutual interest in the color blue and in horses. Like Die Brücke, this group produced paintings that captured the artists' feelings in visual form while also eliciting intense visceral responses from viewers.

Born in Russia, VASSILY KANDINSKY (1866–1944) moved to Munich in 1896 and soon developed a spontaneous and aggressively avant-garde expressive style. Indeed, Kandinsky was one of the first artists to explore complete abstraction, as in *Improvisation 28* (FIG. **14-5**). A true intellectual, Kandinsky was one of the few artists to read with some comprehension the new scientific theories of the era formulated by Max Planck (1858–1947), Ernest Rutherford (1871–1937), Albert Einstein (1879–1955), and Niels Bohr (1885–1962). Fundamental to Enlightenment thought was faith in science, but the work of these scientists shattered people's confidence in the objective reality of matter. Rutherford's exploration of atomic structure, for example, convinced Kandinsky that material objects had no real substance. The painter articulated his ideas in an influential 1912 treatise, *Concerning the Spiritual in Art*, which contributed to the growing interest in abstraction. Artists, Kandinsky believed, must express the spirit and their innermost feelings by orchestrating color, form, line, and space. He produced numerous works like *Improvisation 28*, conveying emotion through color juxtapositions, intersecting linear elements, and implied spatial relationships. Ultimately, Kandinsky saw these abstractions

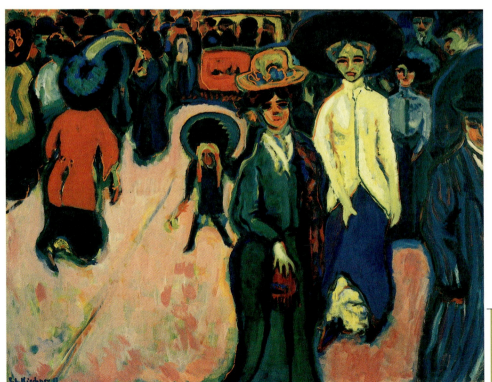

14-4 ERNST LUDWIG KIRCHNER, *Street, Dresden*, 1908 (dated 1907). Oil on canvas, 4′ 11¼″ × 6′ 6⅞″. Museum of Modern Art, New York.

Kirchner's perspectival distortions, disquieting figures, and color choices reflect the influence of the Fauves and of Edvard Munch (FIG. **13-16**), who made similar expressive use of formal elements.

1 ft.

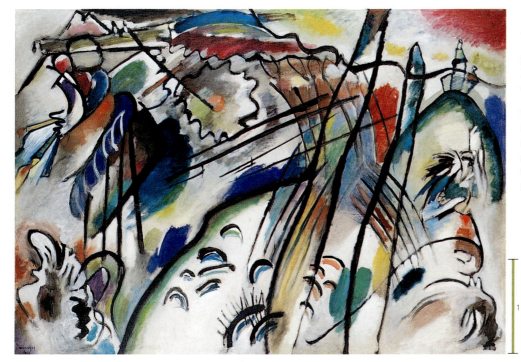

14-5 VASSILY KANDINSKY, *Improvisation 28* (second version), 1912. Oil on canvas, 3′ 7⅞″ × 5′ 3⅞″. Solomon R. Guggenheim Museum, New York (gift of Solomon R. Guggenheim, 1937).

Kandinsky believed that artists must express their innermost feelings by orchestrating color, form, line, and space. He was one of the first painters to explore complete abstraction in his canvases.

1 ft.

as evolving blueprints for a more enlightened and liberated society emphasizing spirituality.

Franz Marc Like many of the other German Expressionists, FRANZ MARC (1880–1916) grew increasingly pessimistic about the state of humanity, especially as World War I loomed on the horizon. His perception of human beings as deeply flawed led him to turn to the animal world for his subjects. Animals, he believed, were "more beautiful, more pure" than humanity and thus more appropriate as a vehicle to express an inner truth. In his quest to imbue his paintings with greater emotional intensity, Marc focused on color and

developed a system of correspondences between specific colors and feelings or ideas. According to Marc, "Blue is the *male* principle, severe and spiritual. Yellow is the *female* principle, gentle, happy and sensual. Red is *matter*, brutal and heavy."[2] Marc's attempts to create, in a sense, an iconography of color links him to other avant-garde artists struggling to redefine the practice of art.

Fate of the Animals (FIG. **14-6**) represents the culmination of Marc's color explorations. Painted in 1913, when the tension of impending cataclysm had pervaded society, the animals appear trapped in a forest, some apocalyptic event destroying both them and the trees. The painter distorted

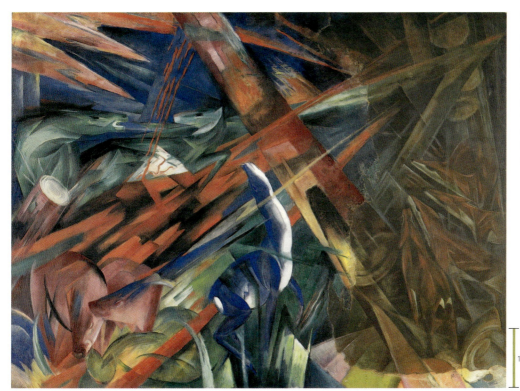

14-6 FRANZ MARC, *Fate of the Animals*, 1913. Oil on canvas, 6′ 4¼″ × 8′ 9½″. Kunstmuseum, Basel.

Marc developed a system of correspondences between specific colors and feelings or ideas. In this apocalyptic scene of animals trapped in a forest, the colors of severity and brutality dominate.

1 ft.

the entire scene and shattered it into fragments. Significantly, the lighter and brighter colors—the passive, gentle, and cheerful ones—are absent, and the colors of severity and brutality dominate the work. Marc discovered just how well his painting portended war's anguish and tragedy when the army sent him to the front the following year. His experiences in battle prompted him to write to his wife that *Fate of the Animals* "is like a premonition of this war—horrible and shattering. I can hardly conceive that I painted it."[3] His contempt for people's inhumanity and his attempt to express that through his art ended, with tragic irony, in his death in action in World War I in 1916.

Käthe Kollwitz The emotional power of postwar German Expressionism is evident in the graphic work of KÄTHE KOLLWITZ (1867–1945), although she had no formal association with any Expressionist group. Kollwitz explored a range of issues from the overtly political to the deeply personal. One image that she treated in a number of prints was that of a mother with her dead child. Kollwitz initially derived the theme from the Christian *Pietà* but transformed it into a universal statement of maternal loss and grief. In *Woman with Dead Child* (FIG. **14-7**), she disavowed the reverence and grace that pervaded most Christian depictions of Mary holding the dead Christ (FIG. **9-8**) and replaced those attributes with an animalistic passion, shown in the way the mother ferociously grips the body of her dead child. The primal nature of the image is in keeping with the aims of the Expressionists, and the scratchy lines the etching needle produced serve as evidence of Kollwitz's very personal touch. The emotional impact of this image is undeniably powerful. That

Kollwitz used her son Peter as the model for the dead child no doubt made the image all the more personal to her. The image stands as a poignant premonition. Peter died fighting in World War I at age 21.

Primitivism and Cubism

The Expressionist departure from any strict adherence to illusionism in art was a path other artists followed. Among those who most radically challenged prevailing artistic conventions and moved most aggressively into the realm of abstraction was Pablo Picasso.

Pablo Picasso A Spanish artist whose importance in the history of art is uncontested, PABLO PICASSO (1881–1973) made staggering contributions to new ways of representing the surrounding world. Perhaps the most prolific artist in history, he explored virtually every artistic medium during his lengthy career and experimented with a wide range of visual expression, first in Spain and then in Paris, where he settled in 1904. Picasso remained a traditional artist in making careful preparatory studies for each major work, but he epitomized modernism in his enduring quest for innovation, which resulted in sudden shifts from one style to another.

Les Demoiselles d'Avignon By 1906, Picasso was searching restlessly for new ways to depict form. He found clues in the late paintings of Cézanne and in ancient Iberian sculpture and the art of other "primitive" cultures (see "Primitivism and Colonialism," page 389). These diverse sources lie behind *Les Demoiselles d'Avignon* (*The Young Ladies of Avignon*; FIG. **14-8**), which opened the door to a radically new method of representing form in space. Picasso began the work as a symbolic picture to be titled *Philosophical Bordello*, portraying male clients intermingling with women in the reception room of a brothel on Avignon Street in Barcelona. By the time the artist finished, he had eliminated the male figures and simplified the room's details to a suggestion of drapery and a schematic foreground still life. Picasso had become wholly absorbed in the problem of finding a new way to represent the five female figures in their interior space. Instead of treating the figures as continuous volumes, he fractured their shapes and interwove them with the equally jagged planes that represent drapery and empty space. Indeed, the space, so entwined with the bodies, is virtually illegible. Here Picasso pushed Cézanne's treatment of form and space (FIGS. **13-13** and **13-14**) to a new level. The tension between Picasso's representation of three-dimensional space and his conviction that a painting is a two-dimensional design lying flat on the surface of a stretched canvas is a tension between representation and abstraction.

The artist extended the radical nature of *Les Demoiselles d'Avignon* even further by depicting the figures inconsistently. Ancient Iberian sculptures inspired the calm, ideal features of the three young women at the left. The energetic, violently striated features of the two heads to the right emerged late in Picasso's production of the work and grew directly from his

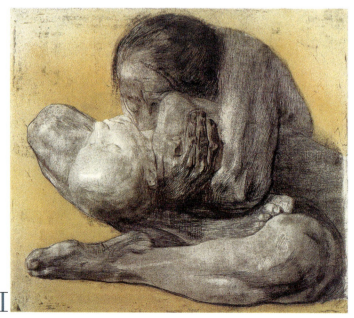

1 in.

14-7 KÄTHE KOLLWITZ, *Woman with Dead Child*, 1903. Etching overprinted lithographically with a gold tone plate, 1′ 4⅝″ × 1′ 7⅛″. British Museum, London.

The theme of the mother mourning over her dead child derives from images of the *Pietà in* Christian art, but Kollwitz transformed it into a powerful universal statement of maternal loss and grief.

Primitivism and Colonialism

Many early-20th-century artists incorporated in their work stylistic elements from the artifacts of Africa, Oceania, and the native peoples of the Americas—a phenomenon art historians call *primitivism*. Some of them, for example Henri Matisse and Pablo Picasso, were enthusiastic collectors of "primitive art," but all artists could view the numerous non-Western objects displayed in European and American anthropological and ethnographic museums, which began to proliferate during the late 19th century. The formation of these collections was a by-product of the rampant colonialism central to the geopolitical dynamics of the 19th century and much of the 20th century (MAP **14-1**). Most of the Western powers maintained colonies in Africa or the Pacific. Westerners often perceived these colonial cultures as "primitive" and referred to many of the non-Western artifacts displayed in museums as "artificial curiosities" or "fetish objects." These works, which often seemed to depict strange gods or creatures, reinforced the perception that these peoples were "barbarians" who needed to be "civilized" or "saved," thereby justifying colonialism worldwide.

Whether avant-garde artists were aware of the imperialistic implications of their appropriation of non-Western cultures is unclear. Certainly, however, many artists reveled in the energy and freshness of non-Western images and forms. These different cultural products provided European and American artists with new ways of looking at their own art. Picasso, for example, believed African masks "were magic things . . . mediators" between humans and the forces of evil, and he sought to capture their power as well as their forms in his paintings. "I understood why I was a painter. . . . All alone in that awful museum [the Trocadéro in Paris], with masks, dolls . . . *Les Demoiselles d'Avignon* [FIG. 14-8] must have come to me that day."*

* Jean-Louis Paudrat, "From Africa," in William Rubin, ed., *"Primitivism" in 20th Century Art: Affinity of the Tribal and the Modern* (New York: Museum of Modern Art, 1984), 1:141.

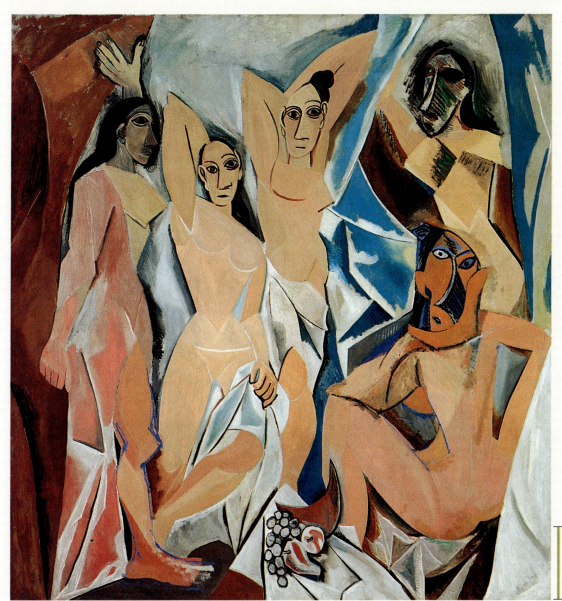

14-8 PABLO PICASSO, *Les Demoiselles d'Avignon*, 1907. Oil on canvas, 8' × 7' 8". Museum of Modern Art, New York (acquired through the Lillie P. Bliss Bequest).

African and ancient Iberian sculpture and the late paintings of Cézanne influenced this pivotal work, with which Picasso opened the door to a radically new method of representing forms in space.

1 ft.

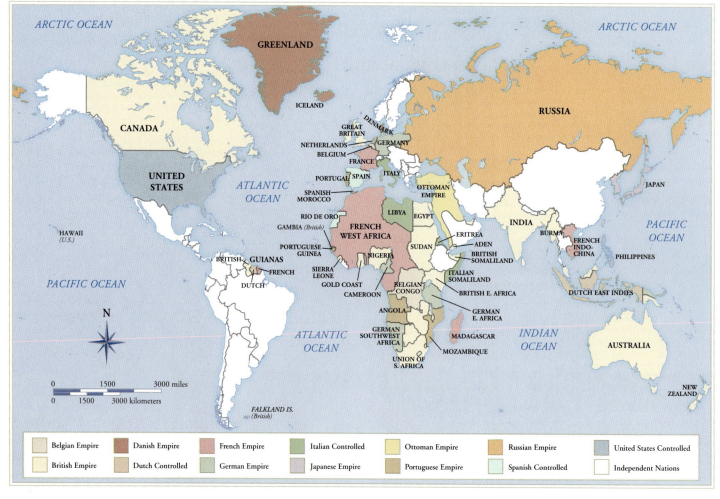

MAP 14-1 Colonial empires around 1900.

increasing fascination with the power of African sculpture, which he avidly collected. Perhaps responding to the energy of these two new heads, Picasso also revised their bodies. He broke them into more ambiguous planes suggesting a combination of views, as if the observer sees the figures from more than one point in space at once. The woman seated at the lower right shows these multiple angles most clearly, presenting the viewer simultaneously with a three-quarter back view from the left, another from the right, and a front view of the head that suggests seeing the figure frontally as well. Gone is the traditional concept of an orderly, constructed, and unified pictorial space that mirrors the world. In its place are the rudimentary beginnings of a new representation of the world as a dynamic interplay of time and space. Clearly, *Les Demoiselles d'Avignon* represents a dramatic departure from the careful presentation of a visual reality. Explained Picasso: "I paint forms as I think them, not as I see them."[4]

Georges Braque and Cubism For many years, Picasso showed *Les Demoiselles* only to other painters. One of the first to see it was GEORGES BRAQUE (1882–1963), a Fauve painter who found it so challenging that he began to rethink his own painting style. Using Picasso's revolutionary ideas as a point of departure, together Braque and Picasso formulated *Cubism* around 1908. Cubism represented

a radical turning point in the history of art, nothing less than a dismissal of the pictorial illusionism that had dominated Western art since the Renaissance. The Cubists rejected naturalistic depictions, preferring compositions of shapes and forms abstracted from the conventionally perceived world. These artists pursued the analysis of form central to Cézanne's artistic explorations, and they dissected life's continuous optical spread into its many constituent features, which they then recomposed, by a new logic of design, into a coherent aesthetic object. For the Cubists, the art of painting had to move far beyond the description of visual reality. This rejection of accepted artistic practice illustrates both the period's aggressive avant-garde critique of pictorial convention and the public's dwindling faith, in light of modern physics, in a safe, concrete Enlightenment world. The new style received its name after Matisse described some of Braque's work to the critic Louis Vauxcelles as having been painted "with little cubes." In his review, Vauxcelles described the new paintings as "cubic oddities."[5]

The French writer and theorist Guillaume Apollinaire summarized well the central concepts of Cubism in 1913:

Authentic cubism [is] the art of depicting new wholes with formal elements borrowed not from the reality of vision, but from that of conception. This tendency leads to a poetic kind of painting which stands outside the world of observation; for, even in a simple cubism, the geometrical surfaces of an object must be opened out in order to give a complete representation of it. . . . Everyone must agree that a chair, from whichever side it is viewed, never ceases to have four legs, a seat and back, and that if it is robbed of one of these elements, it is robbed of an important part.[6]

Art historians refer to the first phase of Cubism, developed jointly by Picasso and Braque, as *Analytic Cubism*. Because Cubists could not achieve Apollinaire's total view through the traditional method of drawing or painting models from one position, these artists began to dissect the forms of their subjects. They presented that dissection for the viewer to inspect across the canvas surface. In simplistic terms, Analytic Cubism involves analyzing the structure of forms.

The Portuguese Georges Braque's painting *The Portuguese* (FIG. **14-1**) exemplifies Analytic Cubism. The subject is a Portuguese musician the artist had seen years earlier in a bar in Marseilles. Braque concentrated his attention on dissecting the form and placing it in dynamic interaction with the space around it. Unlike the Fauves and German Expressionists, who used vibrant colors, the Cubists chose subdued hues—here solely brown tones—in order to focus attention on form. In *The Portuguese*, Braque carried his analysis so far that the viewer must work diligently to discover clues to the subject. The construction of large intersecting planes suggests the forms of a man and a guitar. Smaller shapes interpenetrate and hover in the large planes. The way Braque treated light and shadow reveals his departure from conventional artistic practice. Light and dark passages suggest both chiaroscuro modeling and transparent planes that allow the viewer to see through one level to another. As the observer looks, solid forms emerge only to be canceled almost immediately by a different reading of the subject.

The stenciled letters and numbers add to the painting's complexity. Letters and numbers are flat shapes, but as elements of a Cubist painting such as *The Portuguese*, they allow the artist to play with the viewer's perception of two- and three-dimensional space. The letters and numbers lie flat on the painted canvas surface, yet the image's shading and shapes flow behind and underneath them, pushing the letters and numbers forward into the viewing space. Occasionally, they seem attached to the surface of some object within the painting. Ultimately, the constantly shifting imagery makes it impossible to arrive at any definitive or final reading of the image. Analytical Cubist paintings radically disrupt expectations about the representation of space and time.

Synthetic Cubism In 1912, Cubism entered a new phase called *Synthetic Cubism*, in which artists constructed paintings and drawings from objects and shapes cut from paper or other materials to represent parts of a subject. The work marking the point of departure for this new style was Picasso's *Still Life with Chair-Caning* (FIG. **14-9**), a painting in which the artist imprinted a photolithographed pattern of a cane chair seat on the canvas and then pasted a piece of oilcloth on it. Framed with a piece of rope, this work

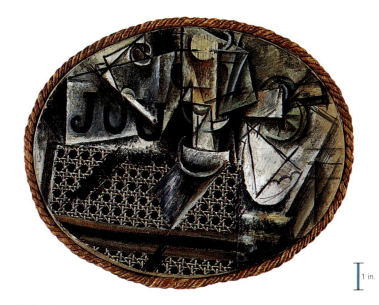

14-9 PABLO PICASSO, *Still Life with Chair-Caning*, 1912. Oil and oilcloth on canvas, $10\frac{5}{8}''$ × 1' $1\frac{3}{4}''$. Musée Picasso, Paris.

This painting includes a piece of oilcloth imprinted with the photo-lithographed pattern of a cane chair seat. Framed with a piece of rope, the still life challenges the viewer's understanding of reality.

challenges the viewer's understanding of reality. The photographically replicated chair-caning seems so "real" that one expects the holes to break any brush strokes laid upon it. But the chair-caning, although optically suggestive of the real, is only an illusion or representation of an object. In contrast, the painted abstract areas do not refer to tangible objects in the real world. Yet the fact that they do not imitate anything makes them more "real" than the chair-caning. No pretense exists. Picasso extended the visual play by making the letter *U* escape from the space of the accompanying *J* and *O* and partially covering it with a cylindrical shape that pushes across its left side. (The letters *JOU* appear in many Cubist paintings. These letters formed part of the masthead of the daily French newspapers [*journaux*] often found among the objects represented. Picasso and Braque especially delighted in the punning references to *jouer and jouir*—the French verbs meaning "to play" and "to enjoy.")

After *Still Life with Chair-Caning*, both Picasso and Braque continued to explore the medium of *collage*, introduced into the realm of high art in that work. From the French *coller* ("to stick"), a collage is a composition of bits of objects, such as newspaper or cloth, glued to a surface. Although most discussions of Cubism and collage focus on the innovations in artistic form they represented, it is important to note that the public also viewed the revolutionary and subversive nature of Cubism in sociopolitical terms. Indeed, the public saw Cubism's challenge to artistic convention and tradition as an attack on 20th-century society. Various artists and writers of the period allied themselves with different anarchist groups whose social critiques and utopian visions appealed to progressive thinkers. Many critics in the French press consistently equated Cubism with anarchism, revolution, and disdain for tradition.

Futurism

A contemporaneous modernist art movement, *Futurism*, did indeed have a well-defined sociopolitical agenda. Inaugurated and named by the charismatic Italian poet and playwright Filippo Tommaso Marinetti (1876–1944) in 1909, Futurism began as a literary movement but soon encompassed the visual arts, cinema, theater, music, and architecture. Indignant over the political and cultural decline of Italy, the Futurists published numerous manifestos in which they aggressively advocated revolution, both in society and in art. In their quest to launch Italian society toward a glorious future, the Futurists championed war as a means of washing away the stagnant past and agitated for the destruction of museums, libraries, and similar repositories of accumulated culture, which they described as mausoleums. They also called for radical innovation in the arts. Of particular interest to the Futurists were the speed and dynamism of modern technology. Marinetti insisted that a racing "automobile adorned with great pipes like serpents with explosive breath . . . is more beautiful than the *Victory of Samothrace*" (FIG. **2-55**, by then representative of classicism and the glories of past civilizations).[7] Appropriately, Futurist art often focuses on motion in time and space, incorporating the Cubist discoveries derived from the analysis of form.

Giacomo Balla The Futurists' interest in motion and in the Cubist dissection of form is evident in *Dynamism of a Dog on a Leash* (FIG. **14-10**) by GIACOMO BALLA (1871–1958). Here, observers focus their gaze on a passing dog and its owner, whose skirts the artist placed just within visual range. Balla achieved the effect of motion by repeating shapes, as in the dog's legs and tail and in the swinging line of the leash. Simultaneity of views was central to the Futurist program (see "Futurist Manifestos," page 393).

Umberto Boccioni One artist who cosigned the Futurist painting manifesto was UMBERTO BOCCIONI (1882–1916), who produced what is perhaps the definitive work of Futurist sculpture, *Unique Forms of Continuity in Space* (FIG. **14-11**). This piece highlights the formal and spatial effects of motion rather than their source, the striding human figure. The figure is so expanded, interrupted, and broken in plane and contour that it almost disappears behind the blur of its movement, much as the forms of roadside objects become blurred when seen through the window of an automobile traveling at great speed on a highway. Although Boccioni's figure bears a curious resemblance to the ancient *Nike of Samothrace* (FIG. **2-55**), a cursory comparison reveals how far the modern work departs from the ancient one.

This Futurist representation of motion in sculpture has its limitations. The eventual development of the motion picture, based on the rapid sequential projection of fixed images, produced more convincing illusions of movement. And several decades later in sculpture, Alexander Calder (FIG. **14-30**) pioneered the development of kinetic sculpture—sculpture with moving parts. However, in the early 20th century, Boccioni's sculpture was notable for its ability to capture the sensation of motion.

DADA

Although the Futurists celebrated World War I and the changes they hoped it would effect, the mass destruction and chaos that conflict unleashed horrified other artists. Humanity had never before witnessed such wholesale slaughter on so grand a scale over such an extended period. The new technology of armaments, bred of the age of steel, changed the nature of combat. In the face of massed artillery hurling millions of tons of high explosives and gas shells and in the sheets of fire from thousands of machine guns, attack was suicidal, and battle movement congealed into the stalemate of trench warfare. The mud, filth, and blood of the trenches, the pounding and shattering of incessant shell fire, and the terrible deaths and mutilations were a devastating psychological as well as physical experience for a generation brought up with the doctrine of progress and a belief in the fundamental values of civilization.

With the war as a backdrop, many artists contributed to an artistic and literary movement that became known as *Dada*. This movement emerged, in large part, in reaction to what many of these artists saw as nothing more than an insane spectacle of collective homicide. Although Dada began independently in New York and Zurich, it also emerged in Paris, Berlin, and Cologne, among other cities. Dada was

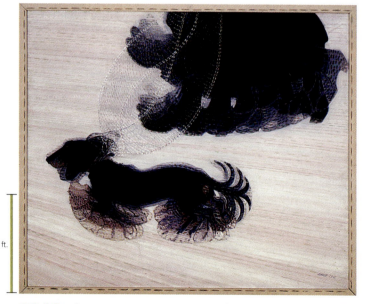

1 ft.

14-10 GIACOMO BALLA, *Dynamism of a Dog on a Leash*, 1912. Oil on canvas, 2′ 11⅜″ × 3′ 7¼″. Albright-Knox Art Gallery, Buffalo (bequest of A. Conger Goodyear, gift of George F. Goodyear, 1964).

The Futurists' interest in motion and in the Cubist dissection of form is evident in Balla's painting of a passing dog and its owner. Simultaneity of views was central to the Futurist program.

Futurist Manifestos

On April 11, 1910, a group of young Italian artists published *Futurist Painting: Technical Manifesto* in Milan in an attempt to apply the writer Filippo Tommaso Marinetti's views on literature to the visual arts. Signed jointly by Giacomo Balla (FIG. 14-10), Umberto Boccioni (FIG. 14-11), and three other artists, the manifesto states in part:

> On account of the persistency of an image on the retina, moving objects constantly multiply themselves [and] their form changes . . . . Thus a running horse has not four legs, but twenty.

> What was true for the painters of yesterday is but a falsehood today. . . . To paint a human figure you must not paint it; you must render the whole of its surrounding atmosphere.

> We declare . . . that all forms of imitation must be despised, all forms of originality glorified . . . that all subjects previously used must be swept aside in order to express our whirling life of steel, of pride, of fever and of speed . . . that movement and light destroy the materiality of bodies.*

Two years later, Boccioni published *Technical Manifesto of Futurist Sculpture,* in which he argued that traditional sculpture was "a monstrous anachronism" and that modern sculpture should be

> a translation, in plaster, bronze, glass, wood or any other material, of those atmospheric planes which bind and intersect things. . . . Let's . . . proclaim the absolute and complete abolition of finite lines and the contained statue. Let's split open our figures and place the environment inside them. We declare that the environment must form part of the plastic whole.†

Boccioni's own work (FIG. 14-11) is the perfect expression of these principles and goals.

* *Futurist Painting: Technical Manifesto* (*Poesia,* April 11, 1910). Translated by Filippo Tommaso Marinetti, in Umbro Apollonio, ed., *Futurist Manifestos* (Boston: Museum of Fine Arts, 1970), 27–31.
† Translated by Robert Brain, in ibid., 51–65.

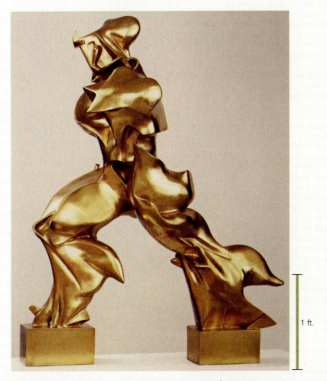

1 ft.

14-11 UMBERTO BOCCIONI, *Unique Forms of Continuity in Space*, 1913 (cast 1931). Bronze, $3' 7\frac{7}{8}'' \times 2' 10\frac{7}{8}'' \times 1' 3\frac{3}{4}''$. Museum of Modern Art, New York (acquired through the Lillie P. Bliss Bequest).

Boccioni's Futurist manifesto for sculpture advocated abolishing the enclosed statue. This running figure is so expanded and interrupted that it almost disappears behind the blur of its movement.

more a mind-set or attitude than a single identifiable style. The Dadaists believed reason and logic had been responsible for the unmitigated disaster of global warfare, and they concluded that the only route to salvation was through political anarchy, the irrational, and the intuitive. Thus, an element of absurdity is a cornerstone of Dada, even reflected in the movement's name. According to an often repeated anecdote, the Dadaists chose "Dada" at random from a French-German dictionary. The French word means a child's hobby horse. The term satisfied the Dadaists' desire for something irrational and nonsensical.

Art historians often describe Dada as a nihilistic enterprise because of its goal of undermining cherished notions about art. However, by attacking convention and logic, the Dada artists unlocked new avenues for creative invention, thereby fostering a more serious examination of the basic premises of art. But the Dadaists could also be lighthearted in their subversiveness. Although horror and disgust about the war initially prompted Dada, an undercurrent of humor and whimsy runs through much of the art. In its emphasis on the spontaneous and intuitive, Dada paralleled the views of Sigmund Freud (1856–1939) and Carl Jung (1875–1961). Freud was a Viennese doctor who formulated the fundamental principles of psychoanalysis. In *The Interpretation of Dreams* (1900), Freud argued that the unconscious controls human behavior. Jung, a Swiss psychiatrist who developed Freud's theories further, asserted that the unconscious has two facets, a personal and a collective unconscious. The latter comprises memories and associations all humans share. According to Jung, the collective unconscious accounts for the development of myths, religions, and philosophies. The Dadaists were particularly interested in exploring the unconscious. They believed art was a powerfully practical means of self-revelation and catharsis, and images arising out of the subconscious mind had a truth of their own, independent of conventional vision.

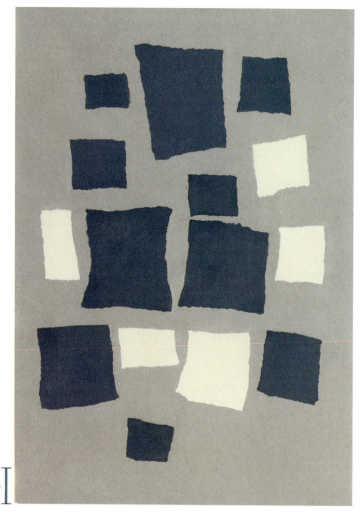

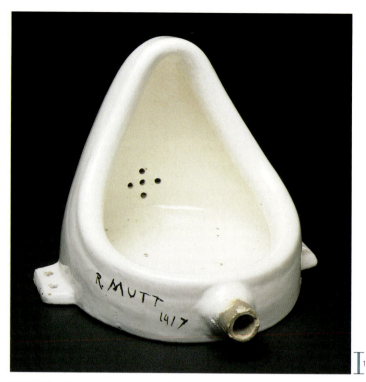

14-13 MARCEL DUCHAMP, *Fountain* (second version), 1950 (original version produced 1917). Readymade glazed sanitary china with black paint, 1' high. Philadelphia Museum of Art, Philadelphia.

Duchamp's "readymade" sculptures were mass-produced objects that the Dada artist modified. In *Fountain,* he conferred the status of art on a urinal and forced people to see the object in a new light.

14-12 JEAN (HANS) ARP, *Collage Arranged According to the Laws of Chance*, 1916–1917. Torn and pasted paper, 1' 1⅞" × 1' 1⅝". Museum of Modern Art, New York.

In this collage, Arp dropped torn paper squares onto a sheet of paper and then glued them into the resulting arrangement. His reliance on chance in composing images reinforced the anarchy inherent in Dada.

Jean Arp The Zurich-based Dada artist JEAN (HANS) ARP (1887–1966) pioneered the use of chance in composing his images. Tiring of the look of some Cubist-related collages he was making, he tore some sheets of paper into roughly shaped squares, haphazardly dropped them onto a sheet of paper on the floor, and glued them into the resulting arrangement. The rectilinearity of the shapes guaranteed a somewhat regular design, but chance introduced an imbalance that seemed to Arp to restore to his work a special mysterious vitality he wanted to preserve. *Collage Arranged According to the Laws of Chance* (FIG. **14-12**) is a work he created by this method. As the Dada filmmaker Hans Richter (1888–1976) stated, "For us chance was the 'unconscious mind' that Freud had discovered in 1900. . . . Adoption of chance had another purpose, a secret one. This was to restore to the work of art its primeval magic power and to find a way back to the immediacy it had lost through contact with . . . classicism."[8] Arp's renunciation of artistic control and reliance on chance in creating his compositions reinforced the anarchy and subversiveness inherent in Dada.

Marcel Duchamp Perhaps the most influential Dadaist was MARCEL DUCHAMP (1887–1968), a Frenchman who became the central artist of New York Dada. In 1913 he exhibited his first "readymade" sculptures, which were mass-produced common objects the artist selected and sometimes "rectified" by modifying their substance or combining them with another object. The creation of readymades, he insisted, was free from any consideration of either good or bad taste, qualities shaped by a society he and other Dada artists found aesthetically bankrupt. Perhaps his most outrageous readymade was *Fountain* (FIG. **14-13**), a porcelain urinal presented on its back, signed "R. Mutt," and dated. The "artist's signature" was, in fact, a witty pseudonym derived from the Mott plumbing company's name and that of the short half of the then-popular Mutt and Jeff comic-strip team. The "art" of this "artwork" lies in the artist's choice of object, which has the effect of conferring the status of art on it and forces the viewer to see the object in a new light.

Hannah Höch Dada spread throughout much of Western Europe, arriving as early as 1917 in Berlin, where it soon took on an activist political edge, partially in response to the economic, social, and political chaos in that city. The Berlin Dadaists developed Cubist collage to a new intensity, christening their version of the technique *photomontage*. Unlike Cubist collage (FIG. **14-9**), the parts of a Dada collage consisted almost entirely of "found" details, such as pieces of

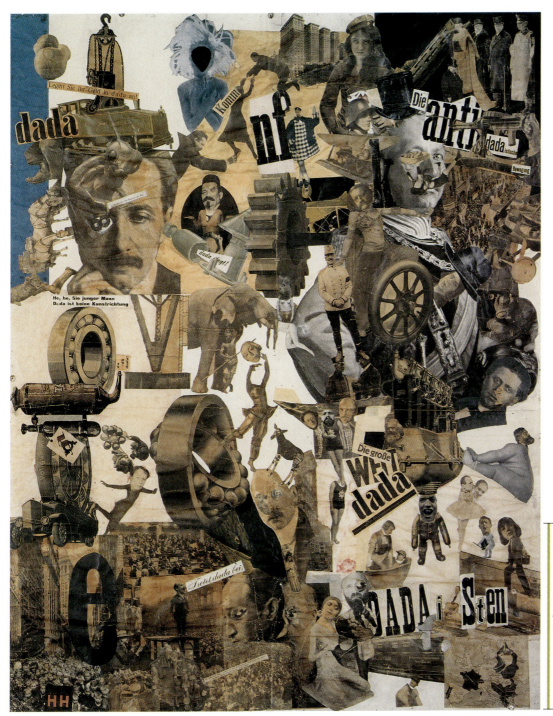

14-14 HANNAH HÖCH, *Cut with the Kitchen Knife Dada through the Last Weimar Beer Belly Cultural Epoch of Germany*, 1919–1920. Photomontage, 3′ 9″ × 2′ 11½″. Neue Nationalgalerie, Staatliche Museen zu Berlin, Berlin.

In Höch's photomontage, photographs of some of her fellow Dadaists appear among images of Marx and Lenin. The artist juxtaposed herself with a map of Europe showing the progress of women.

1 ft.

magazine photographs, usually combined into deliberately antilogical compositions. Collage lent itself well to the Dada desire to use chance when creating art and antiart.

One of the Berlin Dadaists who perfected the photomontage technique was HANNAH HÖCH (1889–1978). Höch's photomontages advanced the absurd illogic of Dada by presenting the viewer with chaotic, contradictory, and satiric compositions. They also provided scathing commentary on two of the most dramatic developments during the Weimar Republic (1918–1933) in Germany—the redefinition of women's social roles and the explosive growth of mass print media. She revealed these combined themes in *Cut with the Kitchen Knife Dada through the Last Weimar Beer Belly Cultural Epoch of Germany* (FIG. **14-14**). In this photomontage Höch arranged an eclectic mixture of cutout photos and letters, including, at the lower right, "Die grosse Welt dada" ("The great Dada world"). To align Dada with other revolutionary movements, Höch carefully placed photographs of some of her fellow Dadaists among images of Marx, Lenin, and other well-known figures. She also juxtaposed the heads of German military leaders with exotic dancers' bodies, which provided the wickedly humorous critique central to much of Dada. Finally, the artist positioned herself in this topsy-turvy world she created. A photograph of Höch's head appears on a walking woman's body in the lower right corner above a map of Europe, showing the progress of women's enfranchisement. Aware of the power that women and Dada had to destabilize society, Höch forcefully manifested that belief through her art.

Art "Matronage" in America

Until the 20th century, the dearth of women artists was often due to professional institutions that restricted women's access to artistic training. For example, the proscription against women participating in life-drawing classes, a staple of academic artistic training, in effect denied women the opportunity to become professional artists. By the early 20th century, many of the impediments to recognition of women as artists had been removed. Today, women are a major presence in the art world. One development in the early 20th century that laid the groundwork for this change was the prominent role women played as art patrons. These "art matrons" provided financial, moral, and political support to cultivate the advancement of the arts in America.*

Gertrude Vanderbilt Whitney (1875–1942) was a practicing sculptor and enthusiastic collector. To assist young American artists to exhibit their work, she opened the Whitney Studio in 1914. By 1929, dissatisfied with the recognition accorded young, progressive American artists, she offered her entire collection of 500 works to the Metropolitan Museum of Art. Her offer rejected, she founded her own museum, the Whitney Museum of American Art in New York City. She chose as the first director a visionary and energetic woman, Juliana Force (1876–1948), who inaugurated a pioneering series of monographs on living American artists and organized lecture series by influential art historians and critics. Through the efforts of these two women, the Whitney Museum became a major force in American art.

A trip to Paris in 1920 whetted the interest of Peggy Guggenheim (1898–1979) in avant-garde art. Like Whitney, she collected art. She eventually opened a gallery in England and continued her support for innovative artists after her return to the United States. Guggenheim's New York gallery, Art of This Century, was instrumental in advancing the careers of many artists. She eventually moved her art collection to a lavish Venetian palace, where the public can still see these important artworks.

Lillie P. Bliss (1864–1931), Mary Quinn Sullivan (1877–1939), and Abby Aldrich Rockefeller (1874–1948) were philanthropists, art collectors, and educators who saw the need for a museum to collect and exhibit modernist art. Together these visionary women established the Museum of Modern Art in New York City in 1929, which became (and continues to be) the most influential museum of modern art in the world.

Isabella Stewart Gardner (1840–1924) and Jane Stanford (1828–1905) also undertook the ambitious project of founding museums. The Isabella Stewart Gardner Museum in Boston, established in 1903, contains an impressive collection of art that is comprehensive in scope. The Stanford Museum, the first American museum west of the Mississippi, got its start in 1905 on the grounds of Stanford University, which Leland Stanford Sr. and Jane Stanford founded after the tragic death of their son. The Stanford Museum houses a wide range of objects, including archaeological and ethnographic artifacts. These two driven women committed much of their time, energy, and financial resources to ensure the success of these museums. Both were intimately involved in the day-to-day operations of their institutions.

The museums these women established flourish today, attesting to the extraordinary vision of these "art matrons" and the remarkable contributions they made to the advancement of art in the United States.

* Art historian Wanda Corn coined the term "art matronage" in the catalogue *Cultural Leadership in America: Art Matronage and Patronage* (Boston: Isabella Stewart Gardner Museum, 1997).

AMERICA, 1900 TO 1930

Avant-garde experiments in the arts were not limited to Europe. In the early 20th century, many American artists pursued modernist ideas—often with the support of visionary female patrons (see "Art 'Matronage' in America," above).

Armory Show A major vehicle for disseminating information about European artistic developments in the United States was the "Armory Show," held in early 1913 at the armory of the National Guard's 69th Regiment in New York City. The exhibition of more than 1,600 works by American and European artists included paintings by Matisse, Kandinsky, Picasso, Braque, and Duchamp. In addition to exposing American artists and the public to the latest in European artistic developments, this show also provided American artists with a prime showcase for their work. The provocative exhibition, which traveled to Chicago and Boston after New York, served as a lightning rod for commentary, immediately attracting heated controversy. Some critics even demanded the exhibition be closed as a menace to public morality. The work the press most maligned was Marcel Duchamp's *Nude Descending a Staircase, No. 2* (FIG. **14-15**). The painting, a single figure in motion down a staircase in a time continuum, suggests the effect of a sequence of overlaid film stills. Unlike Duchamp's Dadaist work (FIG. **14-13**), *Nude Descending a Staircase* has more in common with the work of the Cubists and the Futurists. The monochromatic palette is reminiscent of Analytic Cubism, as is Duchamp's faceted presentation of the human form. The artist's interest in depicting the figure in motion reveals an affinity to the Futurists' ideas. One critic described this work as "an explosion in a shingle factory,"[9] and newspaper cartoonists had a field day lampooning the painting.

Marsden Hartley One American painter who incorporated some of the latest European trends in his work was MARSDEN HARTLEY (1877–1943), who traveled to Europe in 1912, visiting Paris, where he became acquainted with the work of the Cubists, and Munich, where he gravitated to the Blaue Reiter circle. Kandinsky's work particularly im-

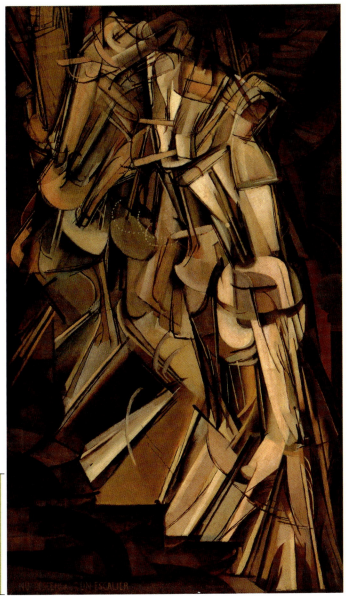

14-15 MARCEL DUCHAMP, *Nude Descending a Staircase, No. 2*, 1912. Oil on canvas, 4′ 10″ × 2′ 11″. Philadelphia Museum of Art, Philadelphia (Louise and Walter Arensberg Collection).

The Armory Show of 1913 introduced European avant-garde art to America. Duchamp's figure in motion down a staircase in a time continuum reveals the artist's indebtedness to Cubism and Futurism.

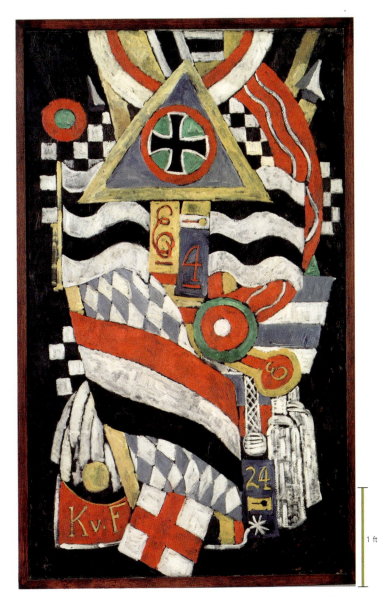

14-16 MARSDEN HARTLEY, *Portrait of a German Officer*, 1914. Oil on canvas, 5′ 8¼″ × 3′ 5⅜″. Metropolitan Museum of Art, New York (Alfred Stieglitz Collection).

In this elegy to a lover killed in battle, Hartley arranged military-related images against a somber black background. The flattened, planar presentation reveals the influence of Synthetic Cubism.

pressed Hartley, and he developed a style he called "Cosmic Cubism." He moved to Berlin in 1913. With the heightened militarism in Germany and the eventual outbreak of World War I, Hartley immersed himself in military imagery. Among his most famous paintings of this period is *Portrait of a German Officer* (FIG. **14-16**). It depicts an array of common military-related images: German imperial flags, regimental insignia, badges, and emblems such as the Iron Cross. But the painting also includes references to Hartley's lover, Lieutenant Karl von Freyberg, who lost his life in battle a few months before Hartley painted this work. Von Freyberg's initials appear in the lower left corner. His age when he died (24) is in the lower right corner, and von Freyberg's regiment number (4) appears in the center of the painting. Also incor-

porated is the letter *E* for von Freyberg's regiment, the Bavarian Eisenbahn. The influence of Synthetic Cubism is evident in the flattened, planar presentation of the elements, which appear almost as abstract patterns. The somber black background against which the artist placed the colorful stripes, patches, and shapes casts an elegiac pall over the painting.

Georgia O'Keeffe In 1918, Texas-born GEORGIA O'KEEFFE (1887–1986) moved from the tiny town of Canyon to New York City, where she met Alfred Stieglitz (FIG. **14-17**), who played a major role in promoting the avant-garde in the United States through "291," his gallery at 291 Fifth Avenue. Stieglitz had seen and exhibited some of O'Keeffe's earlier work, and he drew her into his circle of avant-garde painters and photographers. Stieglitz became one of O'Keeffe's staunchest supporters and, eventually, her husband. O'Keeffe is best known for her paintings of cow skulls and of flowers, for example, *Jack-in-the-Pulpit No. 4* (FIG. I-1), which reveals her interest in stripping subjects to their purest forms and colors in order to heighten their expressive power. In this work, O'Keeffe reduced the incredible details of a flower to a symphony of basic colors, shapes, textures, and vital rhythms, simplifying the flower's curved planes and contours almost to the point of complete abstraction. The fluid planes unfold like undulant petals from a subtly placed axis—the white jetlike streak—in a vision of the slow, controlled motion of growing life. O'Keeffe's painting, in its graceful, quiet poetry, reveals the organic reality of the object by strengthening its characteristic features.

Alfred Stieglitz As an artist, ALFRED STIEGLITZ (1864–1946) is best known for his photographs. He took his camera everywhere he went, photographing whatever he saw around him, from the bustling streets of New York City to cloudscapes in upstate New York to the faces of friends and relatives. He believed in making only "straight, unmanipulated"

photographs. Thus, he exposed and printed them using basic photographic processes, without resorting to techniques such as double-exposure or double-printing that would add information not present in the subject when he released the shutter. Stieglitz said he wanted the photographs he made with this direct technique "to hold a moment, to record something so completely that those who see it would relive an equivalent of what has been expressed."[10]

Stieglitz began a lifelong campaign to win a place for photography among the fine arts while a student of photochemistry in Germany. Returning to New York, he founded the Photo-Secession group, which mounted traveling exhibitions in the United States and sent loan collections abroad, and he also published an influential journal titled *Camera Work*. In his own works, Stieglitz specialized in photographs of his environment and saw these subjects in terms of arrangements of forms and of the "colors" of his black-and-white materials. He was attracted above all to arrangements of form that stirred his deepest emotions. His aesthetic approach crystallized in *The Steerage* (FIG. 14-17), taken during a voyage to Europe with his first wife and daughter in 1907. Traveling first class, Stieglitz rapidly grew bored with the company of prosperous passengers. From the first-class level of the ship, he could see over the rail to the lower deck reserved for steerage passengers the government sent back to Europe after refusing them entrance into the United States. Stieglitz described what he saw:

> The scene fascinated me: A round hat; the funnel leaning left, the stairway leaning right; the white drawbridge, its railing made of chain; white suspenders crossed on the back of a man below; circular iron machinery; a mast that cut into the sky, completing a triangle. I stood spellbound. I saw shapes related to one another—a picture of shapes, and underlying it, a new vision that held me: simple people; the feeling of ship, ocean, sky; a sense of release that I was away from the mob called rich. . . . I had only one plate holder with one unexposed plate. Could I catch what I saw and felt? I released the shutter. If I had captured what I wanted, the photograph would go far beyond any of my previous prints. It would be a picture based on related shapes and deepest human feeling—a step in my own evolution, a spontaneous discovery.[11]

This description reveals Stieglitz's abiding interest in the formal elements of the photograph—an insistently modernist focus. The finished print fulfilled Stieglitz's vision so well that it shaped his future photographic work, and its haunting mixture of found patterns and human activity continues to stir viewers' emotions to this day.

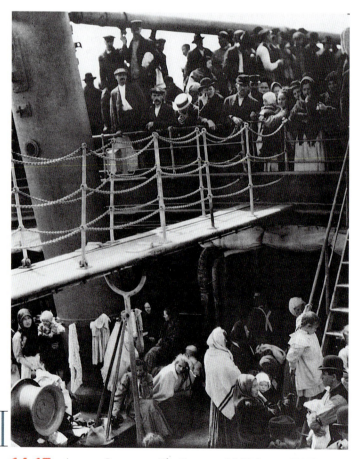

1 in.

14-17 ALFRED STIEGLITZ, *The Steerage*, 1907 (print 1915). Photogravure (on tissue), $1' \frac{3}{8}'' \times 10\frac{1}{8}''$. Amon Carter Museum, Fort Worth.

Stieglitz waged a lifelong campaign to win a place for photography among the fine arts. This 1907 image is a haunting mixture of found patterns of forms and human activity, stirring deep emotions.

Edward Weston Stieglitz's concern for positioning photography as an art form with the same fine-art status as painting and sculpture was also the aim of EDWARD WESTON (1886–1958). In addition to making "straight" photographs like those of Stieglitz, Weston experimented with photographs that moved toward greater abstraction, paralleling developments in other media. *Nude* (FIG. 14-18) is an example of the latter photographic style. The image's

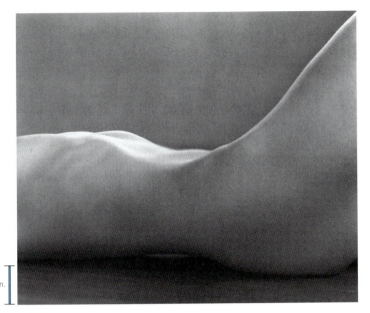

14-18 EDWARD WESTON, *Nude*, 1925. Platinum print, 7½″ × 9½″. Center for Creative Photography, University of Arizona, Tucson.

Weston experimented with photographs that moved toward abstraction. By selecting only a segment of a nude body as his subject, the artist converted the human form to a landscape.

simplicity and the selection of a small segment of the human body as the subject result in a lyrical photograph of dark and light areas that at first glance suggests a landscape. Further inspection reveals the fluid curves and underlying skeletal armature of the human form. This photograph, in its reductiveness, formally expresses a study of the body that verges on the abstract.

EUROPE, 1920 TO 1945

Because World War I was fought entirely on European soil, the Continent's artists experienced its devastating effects to a much greater degree than did their American counterparts. The war had a profound impact on Europe's geopolitical terrain, on individual and national psyches, and on the art of the 1920s and 1930s.

Guernica The previous discussion of Pablo Picasso focused on his immersion in aesthetic issues, but he was acutely aware of politics throughout his life. As Picasso watched his homeland descend into civil war in the late 1930s, his involvement in political issues grew even stronger. He declared: "[P]ainting is not made to decorate apartments. It is an instrument for offensive and defensive war against the enemy."[12] In January 1937, the Spanish Republican government-in-exile in Paris asked Picasso to produce a monumental work for the Spanish pavilion at the Paris International Exposition that summer. Picasso was well aware of the immense visibility and large international audience this opportunity afforded him, but he did not formally accept the invitation until he received word that Guernica, capital of the Basque region in southern France and northern Spain, had been almost totally destroyed in an air raid on April 26 by Nazi bombers acting on behalf of the rebel general Francisco Franco (1892–1975). Not only did the Germans attack the city itself, but because they dropped their bombs at the busiest hour of a market day, they killed or wounded many of Guernica's 7,000 citizens. The event jolted Picasso into action. By the end of June, he had completed *Guernica* (FIG. **14-19**), a mural-sized canvas of extraordinary power.

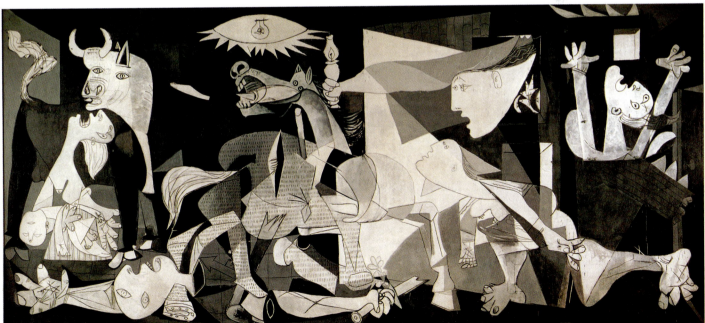

14-19 PABLO PICASSO, *Guernica*, 1937. Oil on canvas, 11′ 5½″ × 25′ 5¾″. Museo Nacional Centro de Arte Reina Sofía, Madrid.

Picasso used Cubist techniques, especially the fragmentation of objects and dislocation of anatomical features, to expressive effect in this condemnation of the Nazi bombing of the Basque capital.

Despite the painting's title, Picasso made no specific reference to the event in *Guernica*—no bombs, no German planes. Rather, the collected images in *Guernica* combine to create a visceral outcry of human grief. In the center, along the lower edge of the painting, lies a slain warrior clutching a broken and useless sword. A gored horse tramples him and rears back in fright as it dies. On the left, a shrieking, anguished woman cradles her dead child. On the far right, a woman on fire runs screaming from a burning building, while another woman flees mindlessly. In the upper right corner, a woman, represented only by a head, emerges from the burning building, thrusting forth a light to illuminate the horror. Overlooking the destruction is a bull, which, according to the artist, represents "brutality and darkness."[13]

Picasso used aspects of his Cubist discoveries to expressive effect in *Guernica*, particularly the fragmentation of objects and the dislocation of anatomical features. The dissections and contortions of the human form in *Guernica* parallel what happened to the figures in real life. To emphasize the scene's severity and starkness, Picasso reduced his palette to black, white, and shades of gray. Aware of the power of art to make political statements, Picasso refused to allow exhibition of *Guernica* in Spain while Generalissimo Franco was in power. At the artist's request, *Guernica* hung in the Museum of Modern Art in New York City after the 1937 World's Fair concluded. Not until after Franco's death in 1975 did Picasso allow the mural to be exhibited in his homeland.

Neue Sachlichkeit

In Germany, World War I gave rise to an artistic movement called *Neue Sachlichkeit* (New Objectivity). The artists associated with Neue Sachlichkeit served, at some point, in the German army, and their military experiences deeply influenced their worldviews and informed their art, which aimed to present an objective image of the war and its effects.

Max Beckmann Initially a supporter of the war, MAX BECKMANN (1884–1950) enlisted in the German army because he believed the chaos would lead to a better society, but over time the mass destruction increasingly disillusioned him. Soon his work began to emphasize the horrors of war and of a society he saw descending into madness. His disturbing view of society is evident in *Night* (FIG. **14-20**), which depicts a cramped room three intruders have forcibly invaded. A bound woman, apparently raped, is splayed across the foreground of the painting. At the left, one of the intruders hangs her husband, while another one twists his left arm out of its socket. An unidentified woman cowers in the background. On the far right, the third intruder prepares to flee with the child.

14-20

MAX BECKMANN, *Night*, 1918–1919. Oil on canvas, 4′ 4$\frac{3}{8}$″ × 5′ $\frac{1}{4}$″. Kunstsammlung Nordrhein-Westfalen, Düsseldorf.

Beckmann's treatment of forms and space in *Night* matched his view of the brutality of early-20th-century society. Objects are dislocated and contorted, and the space is buckled and illogical.

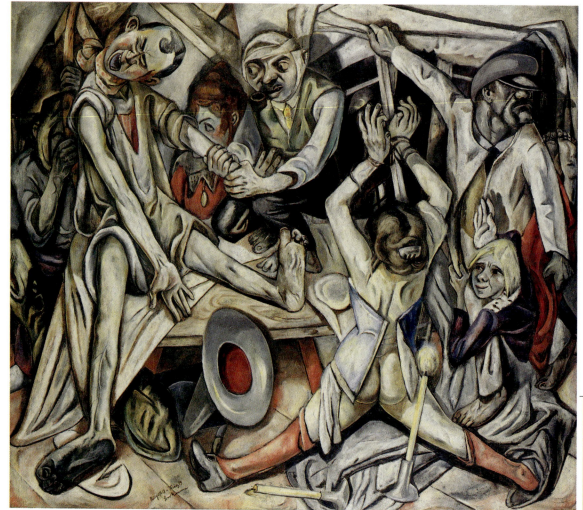

1 ft.

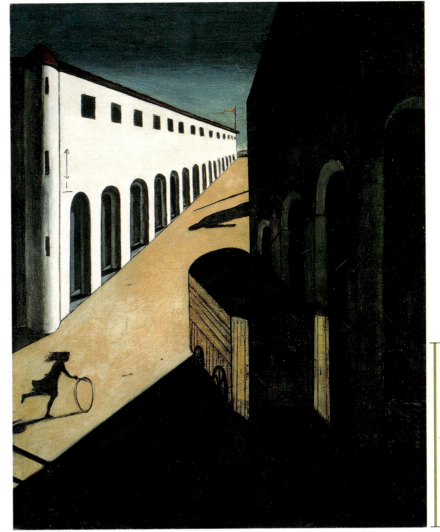

14-21 GIORGIO DE CHIRICO, *Melancholy and Mystery of a Street*, 1914. Oil on canvas, 2′ 10¼″ × 2′ 4½″. Private collection.

De Chirico's Metaphysical Painting movement was a precursor of Surrealism. In this street scene, filled with mysterious forms and shadows, the painter evoked a disquieting sense of foreboding.

1 ft.

Although this image does not depict a war scene, the wrenching, brutal violence pervading the home is a searing and horrifying comment on society's condition. Beckmann also injected a personal reference by using himself, his wife, and his son as the models for the three family members. The stilted angularity of the figures and the roughness of the paint surface contribute to the image's savageness. In addition, the artist's treatment of forms and space reflects the world's violence. Objects are dislocated and contorted, and the space is buckled and illogical. For example, the woman's hands are bound to the window that opens from the room's back wall, but her body appears to hang vertically, rather than lying across the plane of the intervening table.

Surrealism

In 1924 the *First Surrealist Manifesto* appeared in France, and most of the artists associated with Dada joined that new movement. Not surprisingly, *Surrealism* incorporated many Dada improvisational techniques. The Surrealists believed those methods important for engaging the elements of fantasy and activating the unconscious forces that lie deep within every human being. Inspired in part by the ideas of Freud and Jung, the Surrealists sought to explore the inner world of the psyche, the realm of fantasy and the unconscious, and were especially interested in the nature of dreams. According to André Breton (1896–1966), one of the movement's founders:

> Surrealism is based on the belief in the superior reality of certain forms of association heretofore neglected, in the omnipotence of dreams, in the undirected play of thought. . . . I believe in the future resolution of the states of dream and reality, in appearance so contradictory, in a sort of absolute reality, or surreality."[14]

Thus, the Surrealists' dominant motivation was to bring the aspects of outer and inner "reality" together into a single position, in much the same way life's seemingly unrelated fragments combine in the vivid world of dreams. Surrealism developed along two lines. In *Naturalistic Surrealism*, painters present recognizable scenes that seem to have metamorphosed into a dream or nightmare image. In *Biomorphic Surrealism*, artists create largely abstract compositions, although the imagery sometimes suggests organisms or natural forms.

Giorgio de Chirico The Italian painter GIORGIO DE CHIRICO (1888–1978) was an important precursor of the Surrealists. In his paintings of cityscapes and shop windows, he championed *Pittura Metafisica*, or Metaphysical Painting. Returning to Italy after study in Munich, de Chirico found hidden reality revealed through strange juxtapositions, such as those seen on late autumn afternoons in the city of Turin, when the long shadows of the setting sun transformed vast open squares and silent public monuments into what the painter called "metaphysical towns." De Chirico translated this vision into paint in works such as *Melancholy and Mystery of a Street* (FIG. **14-21**), in which the spaces and buildings evoke a disquieting sense of foreboding. The choice of the term "metaphysical" to describe de Chirico's paintings suggests that these images transcend their physical appearances. For all its clarity and simplicity, the painting takes on a rather sinister air. Only a few inexplicable and incongruous elements punctuate the scene's solitude—a small girl with her hoop in the foreground, the empty van, and the ominous shadow of a man emerging from behind the building. The sense of strangeness de Chirico could conjure with familiar objects and scenes recalls the observation of philosopher Friedrich Nietzsche (1844–1900) that "underneath this reality in which we live and have our being, another and altogether different reality lies concealed."[15]

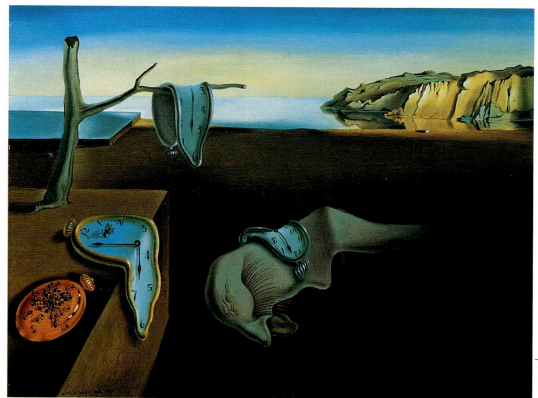

14-22 SALVADOR DALÍ, *The Persistence of Memory*, 1931. Oil on canvas, $9\frac{1}{2}$" × 1' 1". Museum of Modern Art, New York.

Dalí aimed to paint "images of concrete irrationality." In this realistically rendered landscape featuring three "decaying" watches, he created a haunting allegory of empty space where time has ended.

Salvador Dalí Spaniard SALVADOR DALÍ (1904–1989) was the most famous Naturalistic Surrealist painter. As he described it, in his painting he aimed "to materialize the images of concrete irrationality with the most imperialistic fury of precision . . . in order that the world of imagination and of concrete irrationality may be as objectively evident . . . as that of the exterior world of phenomenal reality."[16] All these aspects of Dalí's style appear in *The Persistence of Memory* (FIG. **14-22**), a haunting allegory of empty space where time has ended. An eerie, never-setting sun illuminates the barren landscape. An amorphous creature draped with a limp pocket watch sleeps in the foreground. Another watch hangs from the branch of a dead tree that springs unexpectedly from a blocky architectural form. A third watch hangs half over the edge of the rectangular form, beside a small timepiece resting face down on the block's surface. Ants swarm mysteriously over the small watch, while a fly walks along the face of its large neighbor, almost as if this assembly of watches were decaying organic life—soft and sticky. Dalí rendered every detail of this dreamscape with precise control, striving to make the world of his paintings as convincingly real as the most meticulously rendered landscape based on a real scene from nature.

René Magritte The Belgian painter RENÉ MAGRITTE (1898–1967) also expressed in exemplary fashion the Surrealist idea and method—the dreamlike dissociation of image and meaning. His works administer disruptive shocks because they subvert viewers' expectations based on logic and common sense. The danger of relying on rationality when viewing a Surrealist work is apparent in Magritte's *The Treachery (or Perfidy) of Images* (FIG. **14-23**). Magritte presented a meticulously rendered *trompe l'oeil* (French, "fools the eye") depiction of a briar pipe. The caption beneath the image, however, contradicts what seems obvious: "Ceci n'est pas une pipe" ("This is not a pipe"). The discrepancy between image and caption clearly challenges the assumptions underlying the reading of visual art. Like the other Surrealists' work, this painting wreaks havoc on the viewer's reliance on the conscious and the rational.

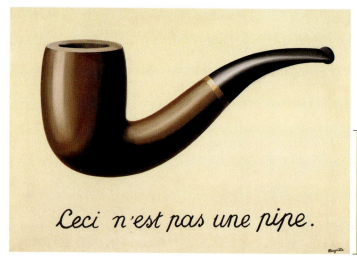

14-23 RENÉ MAGRITTE, *The Treachery (or Perfidy) of Images*, 1928–1929. Oil on canvas, 1' $11\frac{5}{8}$" × 3' 1". Los Angeles County Museum of Art, Los Angeles (purchased with funds provided by the Mr. and Mrs. William Preston Harrison Collection).

The discrepancy between Magritte's meticulously painted briar pipe and his caption, "This is not a pipe," challenges the viewer's reliance on the conscious and the rational in the reading of visual art.

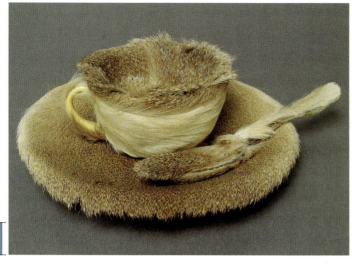

1 in.

14-24 MERET OPPENHEIM, *Object (Le Déjeuner en Fourrure)*, 1936. Fur-covered cup, $4\frac{3}{8}''$ in diameter; saucer, $9\frac{3}{8}''$ in diameter; spoon, 8″ long. Museum of Modern Art, New York.

The Surrealists loved the concrete tangibility of sculpture, which made their art even more disquieting. Oppenheim's functional fur-covered object captures the Surrealist flair for magical transformation.

Meret Oppenheim Sculpture especially appealed to the Naturalistic Surrealists, because its concrete tangibility made their art all the more disquieting. *Object* (FIG. **14-24**), also called *Le Déjeuner en Fourrure (Luncheon in Fur)*, by Swiss artist MERET OPPENHEIM (1913-1985) captures the incongruity, humor, visual appeal, and, often, eroticism characterizing Surrealism. The artist presented a fur-lined teacup inspired by a conversation she had with Picasso. After admiring a bracelet Oppenheim had made from a piece of brass covered with fur, Picasso noted that anything might be covered with fur. When her tea grew cold, Oppenheim responded to Picasso's comment by ordering "un peu plus de fourrure" (a little more fur), and the sculpture had its genesis. *Object* takes on an anthropomorphic quality, animated by the quirky combination of the fur with a functional object. Further, the sculpture captures the Surrealist flair for alchemical, seemingly magical or mystical, transformation. It incorporates a sensuality and eroticism (seen here in the seductively soft, tactile fur lining the concave form) that are also components of much of Surrealist art.

Joan Miró Like the Dadaists, the Surrealists used many methods to free the creative process from reliance on the kind of conscious control they believed society had shaped too much. The Spanish artist JOAN MIRÓ (1893–1983) used *automatism*—the creation of art without conscious control—and various types of planned "accidents" to provoke reactions closely related to subconscious experience. Although Miró resisted formal association with any movement or group, including the Surrealists, Breton identified him as "the most Surrealist of us all."[17] From the beginning, Miró's work contained an element of fantasy and hallucination. After Surrealist poets in Paris introduced him to the use of chance to create art, the young Spaniard devised a new painting method that allowed him to create works such as *Painting* (FIG. **14-25**). Miró began this piece by making a scattered collage composition with assembled fragments cut from a catalogue for machinery. The shapes in the collage became motifs the artist freely reshaped to create black silhouettes—solid or in outline, with dramatic accents of white and vermilion. They suggest, in the painting, a host of amoebic organisms or constellations in outer space floating in an immaterial background space filled with soft reds, blues, and greens.

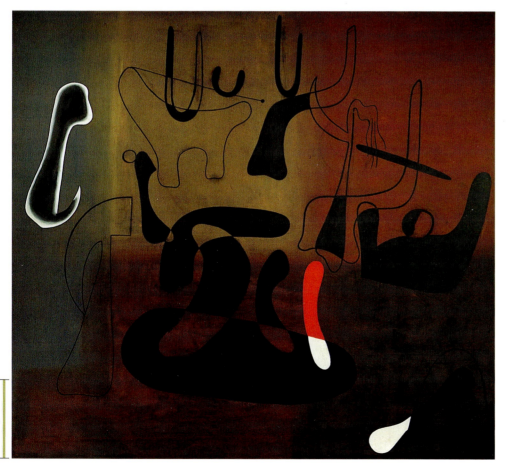

1 ft.

14-25 JOAN MIRÓ, *Painting*, 1933. 5′ 8″ × 6′ 5″. Museum of Modern Art, New York (Loula D. Lasker Bequest by exchange).

Miró promoted automatism, the creation of art without conscious control. He began this painting with a scattered collage and then added forms suggesting floating amoebic organisms.

Miró described his creative process as a switching back and forth between unconscious and conscious image-making: "Rather than setting out to paint something, I begin painting and as I paint the picture begins to assert itself, or suggest itself under my brush. The form becomes a sign for a woman or a bird as I work. . . . The first stage is free, unconscious. . . . The second stage is carefully calculated."[18] Even the artist could not always explain the meanings of pictures such as *Painting*. They are, in the truest sense, spontaneous and intuitive expressions of the little-understood, submerged unconscious part of life.

Suprematism and De Stijl

The pessimism and cynicism of movements such as Dada reflect the historical circumstances of the early 20th century. However, not all artists reacted to the profound turmoil of the times by retreating from society. Some avant-garde artists promoted utopian ideals, believing staunchly in art's ability to contribute to the improvement of society. These efforts often surfaced in the face of significant political upheaval, illustrating the link established early on between revolution in politics and revolution in art. Among the art movements espousing utopian notions were Suprematism in Russia and De Stijl in Holland.

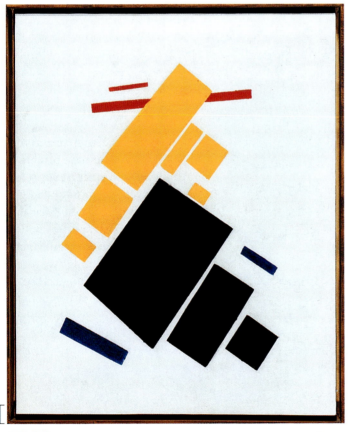

14-26 KAZIMIR MALEVICH, *Suprematist Composition: Airplane Flying*, 1915 (dated 1914). Oil on canvas, 1' $10\frac{7}{8}''$ × 1' 7". Museum of Modern Art, New York.

Malevich developed an abstract style he called Suprematism to convey that the supreme reality in the world is pure feeling. In this work, the brightly colored rectilinear shapes float against white space.

Kazimir Malevich Russian artist KAZIMIR MALEVICH (1878–1935) developed an abstract style to convey his belief that the supreme reality in the world is pure feeling, which attaches to no object. Thus, this belief called for new, nonobjective forms in art—shapes not related to objects in the visible world. Malevich christened his new artistic approach *Suprematism*, explaining: "Under Suprematism I understand the supremacy of pure feeling in creative art. To the Suprematist, the visual phenomena of the objective world are, in themselves, meaningless; the significant thing is feeling, as such, quite apart from the environment in which it is called forth."[19]

The basic form of Malevich's new Suprematist nonobjective art was the square. Combined with its relatives, the straight line and the rectangle, the square soon filled his paintings, such as *Suprematist Composition: Airplane Flying* (FIG. **14-26**). In this work, the brightly colored shapes float against and within a white space, and the artist placed them in dynamic relationship to one another. Malevich believed all people would easily understand his new art because of the universality of its symbols. It used the pure language of shape and color to which everyone could respond intuitively.

Piet Mondrian In 1917 a group of young Dutch artists including PIET MONDRIAN (1872–1944) formed a new movement and began publishing a magazine, calling both movement and magazine *De Stijl* (The Style). In addition to promoting utopian ideals, De Stijl artists believed in the birth of a new age in the wake of World War I. In their first manifesto, they declared: "There is an old and a new consciousness of the age. The old one is directed toward the individual. The new one is directed toward the universal."[20] The choice of the term "De Stijl" reflected confidence that this style—*the* style—revealed the underlying eternal structure of existence. Accordingly, De Stijl artists reduced their artistic vocabulary to simple geometric elements.

Time spent in Paris before World War I introduced Mondrian to Cubism. However, as his attraction to contemporary theological writings grew, Mondrian sought to purge his art of every overt reference to individual objects in the external world. He formulated a conception of nonobjective or pictorial design—"pure plastic art"—that he believed expressed universal reality:

> Art is higher than reality and has no direct relation to reality. . . . To approach the spiritual in art, one will make as little use as possible of reality, because reality is opposed to the spiritual. . . . [W]e find ourselves in the presence of an abstract art. Art should be above reality, otherwise it would have no value for man."[21]

Mondrian soon moved beyond Cubism because he felt "Cubism did not accept the logical consequences of its own discoveries; it was not developing towards its own goal, the expression of pure plastics."[22] To achieve "pure plastic art," or *Neoplasticism*, as Mondrian called it, he eventually limited his formal vocabulary to the three primary colors (red, blue, and yellow), the three primary values (black, white, and gray), and the two primary directions (horizontal and

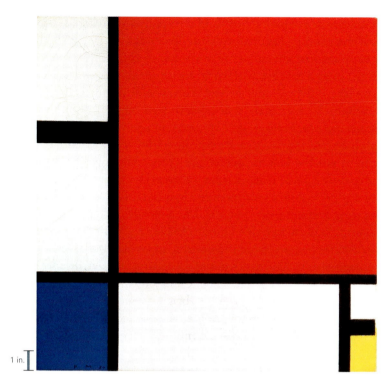

14-27 PIET MONDRIAN, *Composition with Red, Blue, and Yellow*, 1930. Oil on canvas, 1′ 6⅛″ × 1′ 6⅛″. Kunsthaus, Zurich. © Mondrian/Holtzman Trust c/o HCR International, VA, USA.

Mondrian created numerous "pure plastic" paintings in which he locked primary colors into a grid of intersecting vertical and horizontal lines. By altering the grid patterns, he created a dynamic tension.

vertical). He believed primary colors and values were the purest colors and therefore the perfect tools to help an artist construct a harmonious composition. Mondrian created numerous paintings locking color planes into a grid of intersecting vertical and horizontal lines, as in *Composition with Red, Blue, and Yellow* (FIG. **14-27**). In each of these paintings, he altered the grid patterns and the size and placement of the color planes to create an internal cohesion and harmony. This did not mean inertia. Rather, Mondrian worked to maintain a dynamic tension in his paintings through the size and position of lines, shapes, and colors.

Sculpture

During the second quarter of the 20th century, European sculptors also explored avant-garde ideas in their work, especially abstraction.

Constantin Brancusi In his sculptures, Romanian artist CONSTANTIN BRANCUSI (1876–1957) sought to move beyond surface appearances to capture the essence or spirit of the object depicted. He claimed: "What is real is not the external form but the essence of things. Starting from this truth it is impossible for anyone to express anything essentially real by imitating its exterior surface."[23] Brancusi's ability to design rhythmic, elegant sculptures conveying the essence of his subjects is evident in *Bird in Space* (FIG. **14-28**). Clearly not a literal depiction of a bird, the work is the final result of a long

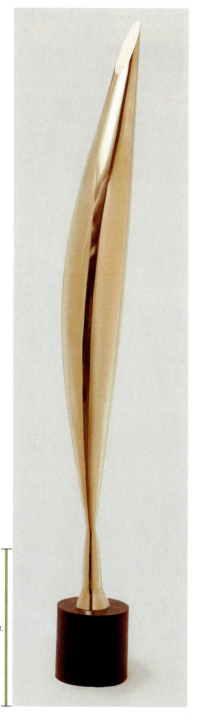

14-28 CONSTANTIN BRANCUSI, *Bird in Space*, 1924. Bronze, 4′ 2⁵⁄₁₆″ high. Philadelphia Museum of Art, Philadelphia (Louise and Walter Arensberg Collection, 1950).

Although not a literal depiction of a bird, Brancusi's softly curving, light-reflecting abstract sculpture in polished bronze suggests a bird about to soar in free flight through the heavens.

process. Brancusi started with the image of a bird at rest with its wings folded at its sides and ended with an abstract columnar form sharply tapered at each end. Despite the abstraction, the sculpture retains the suggestion of a bird about to soar in free flight through the heavens. The highly reflective surface of the polished bronze does not allow the eye to linger on the sculpture itself. Instead, the viewer's eye follows the gleaming reflection along the delicate curves right off the tip of the work, thereby inducing a feeling of flight.

The British sculptor Henry Moore (1898–1986) summed up Brancusi's contribution to the history of sculpture as follows: "Since the Gothic, European sculpture had become overgrown with moss, weeds—all sorts of surface excrescences which completely concealed shape. It has been Brancusi's special mission to get rid of this overgrowth, and to make us once more shape-conscious. To do this he has had to concentrate on very simple direct shapes . . . . Abstract qualities of design are essential to the value of a work."[24]

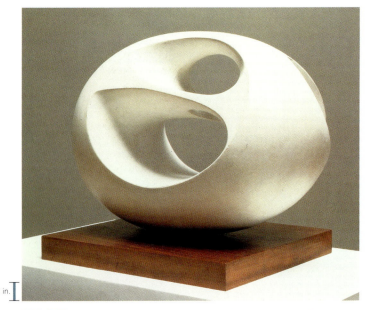

1 in.

14-29 Barbara Hepworth, *Oval Sculpture (No. 2)*, 1943. Plaster cast, $11\frac{1}{4}'' \times 1' \, 4\frac{1}{4}'' \times 10''$. Tate Gallery, London.

Hepworth's major contribution to the history of sculpture was the introduction of the hole, or negative space, as an abstract element that is as integral and important to the sculpture as its mass.

Barbara Hepworth Another leading British artist of this era was BARBARA HEPWORTH (1903–1975), who developed her personal kind of essential sculptural form, combining pristine shape with a sense of organic vitality. She sought a sculptural idiom that would express her sense both of nature and the landscape and of the person who is in and observes nature. By 1929, Hepworth arrived at a breakthrough that evolved into an enduring and commanding element in her work, an element that represents her major contribution to the history of sculpture: the use of the hole, or void. Of particular note is the fact that Hepworth introduced the hole, or negative space, in her sculpture as an abstract element—it does not represent anything specific—and one that is as integral and important to the sculpture as its mass. *Oval Sculpture (No. 2)* (FIG. **14-29**) is a plaster cast of an earlier wooden sculpture Hepworth carved in 1943. Pierced in four places, *Oval Sculpture* is as much defined by the smooth, curving holes as by the volume of white plaster. Like the forms in all of Hepworth's mature works, those in *Oval Sculpture* are basic and universal, expressing a sense of eternity's timelessness.

AMERICA, 1930 TO 1945

In the years leading up to and during World War II, many European artists emigrated to the United States. Their collective presence in the United States was critical for the development of American art in the decades following the 1913 Armory Show.

Alexander Calder One American artist who rose to international prominence at this time was ALEXANDER CALDER (1898–1976). Both the artist's father and grandfather were sculptors, but Calder initially studied mechanical engineering. Fascinated all his life by motion, he explored that phenomenon and its relationship to three-dimensional form in much of his sculpture. As a young artist in Paris in the late 1920s, Calder invented a circus full of wire-based miniature performers that he activated into realistic analogues of the motion of their real-life counterparts. After a visit to Mondrian's studio in the early 1930s, Calder set out to put the Dutch painter's brightly colored rectangular shapes (FIG. **14-27**) into motion. (Marcel Duchamp, intrigued by Calder's early motorized and hand-cranked examples of moving abstract pieces, named them *mobiles*.) Calder's engineering skills soon helped him to fashion a series of balanced structures hanging from rods, wires, and colored, organically shaped plates. This new kind of sculpture, which combined nonobjective organic forms and motion, succeeded in expressing the innate dynamism of the natural world.

An early Calder mobile is *Lobster Trap and Fish Tail* (FIG. **14-30**). The artist carefully planned each nonmechanized mobile so that any air current would set the parts moving to create a constantly shifting dance in space. Mondrian's work may have provided the initial inspiration for the mobiles, but their organic shapes resemble those in Joan Miró's Surrealist paintings (FIG. **14-25**). Indeed, a viewer can read Calder's forms as either geometric or organic. Geometrically, the lines suggest circuitry and rigging, and the shapes derive from circles and ovoid forms. Organically, the lines suggest nerve axons, and the shapes resemble cells, leaves, fins, wings, and other bioforms.

Great Depression The catastrophic U.S. stock market crash of October 1929 marked the onset of the Great Depression, which dramatically changed the nation. Artists were among the many economic victims. The already limited art market virtually disappeared, and museums curtailed both their purchases and exhibition schedules. Many artists sought financial support from the federal government, which established numerous programs to provide relief, assist recovery, and promote reform. Among the programs supporting artists were the Treasury Relief Art Project, founded in 1934 to commission art for federal buildings, and the Works Progress Administration (WPA), founded in 1935 to relieve widespread unemployment. Under the WPA, the federal art project paid artists, writers, and theater people a regular wage in exchange for work in their professions. Another important program was the Resettlement Administration (RA), later known as the Farm Securities Administration (FSA), which oversaw emergency aid programs for farm families.

Dorothea Lange The RA hired American photographer DOROTHEA LANGE (1895–1965) in 1936 and dispatched her to photograph the struggles of the rural poor. At the end of an assignment to document the lives of migratory pea pickers in California, Lange stopped at a camp in Nipomo and found the migrant workers there starving because the crops had frozen in the fields. Among the pictures Lange

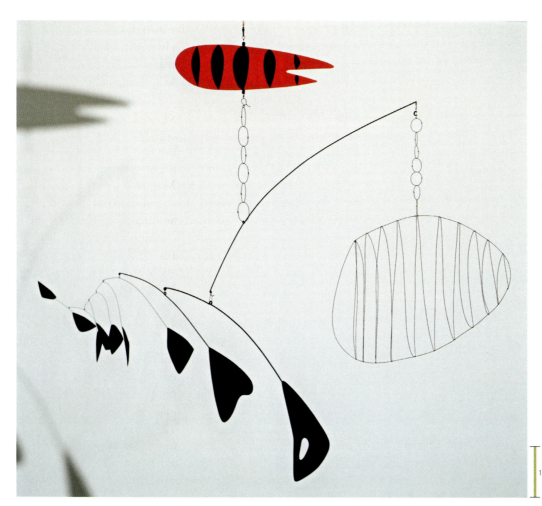

14-30 ALEXANDER CALDER, *Lobster Trap and Fish Tail*, 1939. Painted sheet aluminum and steel wire, 8′ 6″ × 9′ 6″. Museum of Modern Art, New York.

Using his thorough knowledge of engineering to combine non-objective organic forms and motion, Calder created a new kind of sculpture—the mobile—that expressed reality's innate dynamism.

1 ft.

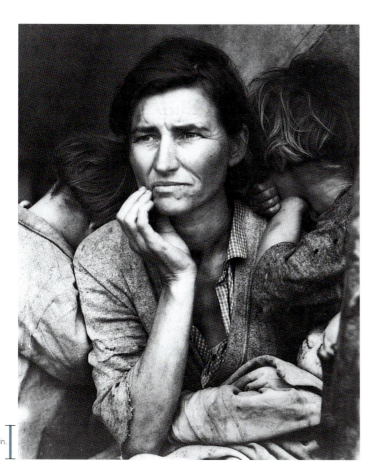

made on this occasion was *Migrant Mother, Nipomo Valley* (FIG. **14-31**), in which she captured the mixture of strength and worry in the raised hand and careworn face of a mother, who holds a baby on her lap. Two older children cling to her trustingly while shunning the camera. Within days after Lange's powerful photograph appeared in a San Francisco newspaper, people rushed food to Nipomo to feed the hungry workers.

Edward Hopper Trained as a commercial artist, EDWARD HOPPER (1882–1967) studied painting and printmaking in New York and then in Paris. When he returned to the United States, he concentrated on scenes of contemporary American city and country life. His paintings depict buildings, streets, and landscapes that are curiously muted, still, and filled with empty spaces, evoking the national mind-set during the Depression era. Hopper did not paint historically

14-31 DOROTHEA LANGE, *Migrant Mother, Nipomo Valley*, 1935. Gelatin silver print, 1′ 1″ × 9″. Oakland Museum of California, Oakland (gift of Paul S. Taylor).

While documenting the lives of migratory farm workers during the Depression, Lange made this unforgettable photograph of a mother in which she captured the woman's strength and worry.

1 in.

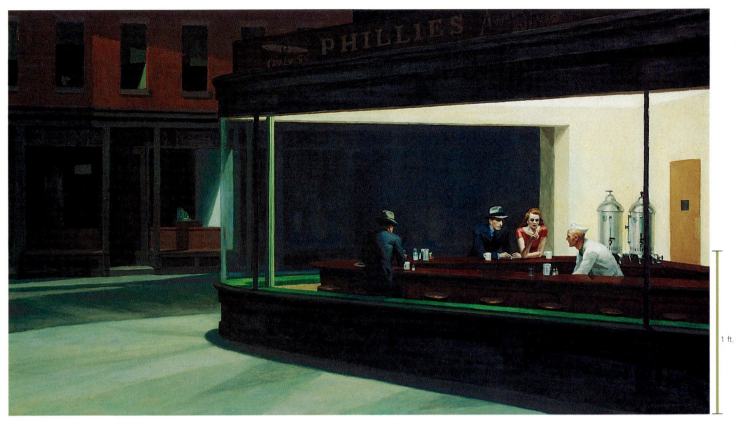

14-32 EDWARD HOPPER, *Nighthawks*, 1942. Oil on canvas, 2′ 6″ × 4′ 8$\frac{11}{16}$″. Art Institute of Chicago, Chicago (Friends of American Art Collection).

The seeming indifference of Hopper's characters to one another, and the echoing spaces that surround them, evoke the overwhelming loneliness and isolation of Depression-era life in the United States.

specific scenes. He took as his subject the more generalized theme of the overwhelming loneliness and echoing isolation of modern life in the United States. In his paintings, motion is stopped and time suspended, as if the artist recorded the major details of a poignant personal memory. From the darkened streets outside a restaurant in *Nighthawks* (FIG. **14-32**), the viewer glimpses the lighted interior through huge windows, which lend the inner space the paradoxical sense of being both a safe refuge and a vulnerable place for the three customers and the counterman. The seeming indifference of Hopper's characters to one another and the echoing spaces that surround them evoke the pervasive loneliness of modern humans. *Nighthawks* recalls the work of 19th-century Realist painters (see Chapter 12), but, consistent with more recent trends in painting, Hopper simplified the shapes in a move toward abstraction.

Jacob Lawrence In 1927, African American artist JACOB LAWRENCE (1917–2000) moved to Harlem, New York, and came under the spell of the African art and the African American history he found in lectures and exhibitions and in the special programs sponsored by the 135th Street New York Public Library. Inspired by the politically oriented art of Goya (FIG. 12-6), Daumier (FIG. 12-16), and others, Lawrence found his subjects in the everyday life of Harlem and in African American history. In 1941 he began a 60-painting series titled *The Migration of the Negro*, in which he defined

his own vision of the continuing African American struggle against discrimination. Unlike Lawrence's earlier historical paintings, this series called attention to a contemporaneous event—the ongoing exodus of black laborers from the southern United States. Disillusioned with their lives, hundreds of thousands of African Americans left the South in the years following World War I, seeking improved economic opportunities and more hospitable political and social conditions in the North. The "documentation" of the period, such as the RA program, ignored African Americans, and thus this major demographic shift remained largely invisible to most of the public. Lawrence and his family were part of that migration, and he knew the conditions African Americans encountered in the North were often as difficult and discriminatory as those they had left behind in the South.

Lawrence's series provides numerous vignettes capturing the experiences of these migrating people. Often, a sense of bleakness and of the degradation of African American life dominates the images. *No. 49* (FIG. **14-33**) in the series bears the caption "They also found discrimination in the North although it was much different from that which they had known in the South." The artist depicted a blatantly segregated dining room with a barrier running down the room's center separating the whites on the left from the African Americans on the right. To ensure a continuity and visual integrity among all 60 paintings, Lawrence interpreted his themes systematically in rhythmic arrangements of bold,

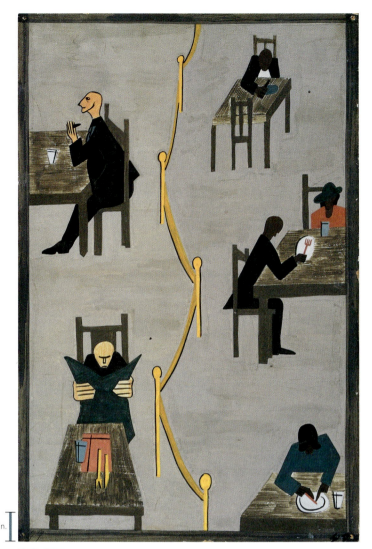

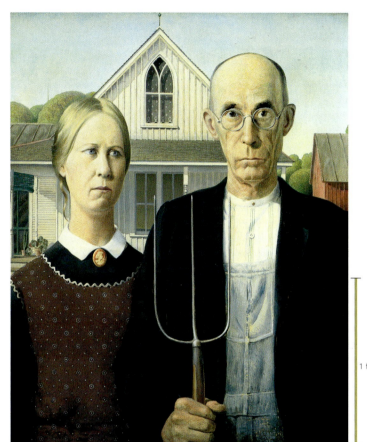

14-34 GRANT WOOD, *American Gothic*, 1930. Oil on beaverboard, 2′ 5⅞″ × 2′ ⅞″. Art Institute of Chicago, Chicago (Friends of American Art Collection). Licensed by VAGA, New York.

In reaction to modernist abstract painting, the Midwestern Regionalism movement focused on American subjects. Wood's painting of an Iowa farmer and his daughter is an American icon.

14-33 JACOB LAWRENCE, *No. 49*, from *The Migration of the Negro*, 1940–1941. Tempera on Masonite, 1′ 6″ × 1′. Phillips Collection, Washington, D.C.

The 49th in a series of 60 paintings documenting African American life in the North, Lawrence's depiction of a segregated dining room underscored that the migrants had not left discrimination behind.

flat, and strongly colored shapes. His style drew equally from his interest in the push-pull effects of Cubist space and his memories of the patterns made by the colored scatter rugs brightening the floors of his childhood homes. He unified the narrative with a consistent palette of bluish green, orange, yellow, and grayish brown throughout the entire series.

Grant Wood At a 1931 conference, GRANT WOOD (1891–1942) announced a new art movement developing in the Midwest, known as *Regionalism*, which he described as focused on American subjects and as standing in reaction to the modernist abstraction of Europe and New York. Wood and the Regionalists turned their attention instead to rural life as America's cultural backbone. Wood's paintings focus on rural Iowa, where he was born and raised. The work that catapulted Wood to national prominence was *American Gothic* (FIG. **14-34**), which became an American icon. The artist depicted a farmer and his spinster daughter standing

in front of a neat house with a small lancet window, typically found on Gothic cathedrals (see Chapter 7). The man and woman wear traditional attire. He appears in worn overalls, she in an apron trimmed with rickrack. Their dour expressions give the painting a severe quality, which Wood enhanced with his meticulous brushwork. The public immediately embraced *American Gothic* as embodying "strength, dignity, fortitude, resoluteness, integrity," qualities people felt represented the true spirit of America.[25]

Wood's Regionalist vision involved more than his subjects. It extended to a rejection of avant-garde styles in favor of a clearly readable, Realist style. Surely this approach appealed to many people alienated by the increasing presence of abstraction in art. But, despite the accolades this painting received, it also attracted criticism. Not everyone saw the painting as a sympathetic portrayal of Midwestern life. Indeed, some in Iowa considered the depiction insulting. In addition, notwithstanding the seemingly reportorial nature of *American Gothic*, some critics viewed it as a political statement—one of staunch nationalism. In light of Germany's problematic politics at the time, many observers found Wood's nationalistic attitude disturbing. Nonetheless, during the Great Depression, Regionalist paintings had a popular appeal because they often projected a reassuring image of America's heartland.

Rivera on Art for the People

Diego Rivera was an avid proponent of a social and political role for art in the lives of common people, and he wrote passionately about the proper goals for an artist—goals that he fully met in his own murals depicting Mexican history (FIG. 14-35). Rivera's views stand in sharp contrast to the growing interest in abstraction on the part of many early-20th-century painters and sculptors.

Art has always been employed by the different social classes who hold the balance of power as one instrument of domination—hence, as a political instrument. One can analyze epoch after epoch—from the stone age to our own day—and see that there is no form of art which does not also play an essential political role. . . . What is it then that we really need? . . . An art with revolu-

tion as its subject: because the principal interest in the worker's life has to be touched first. It is necessary that he find aesthetic satisfaction and the highest pleasure appareled in the essential interest of his life. . . . The subject is to the painter what the rails are to a locomotive. He cannot do without it. In fact, when he refuses to seek or accept a subject, his own plastic methods and his own aesthetic theories become his subject instead. . . . [H]e himself becomes the subject of his work. He becomes nothing but an illustrator of his own state of mind . . . . That is the deception practiced under the name of "Pure Art."*

* Quoted in Robert Goldwater and Marco Treves, eds., *Artists on Art from the XIV to the XX Century* (New York: Pantheon, 1945), 475–477.

14-35 DIEGO RIVERA, *Ancient Mexico*, from *History of Mexico*, Palacio Nacional, Mexico City, 1929–1935. Fresco.

A staunch Marxist, Rivera painted vast mural cycles in public buildings to dramatize the history of his native land. This fresco depicts the conflicts between indigenous Mexicans and the Spanish colonizers.

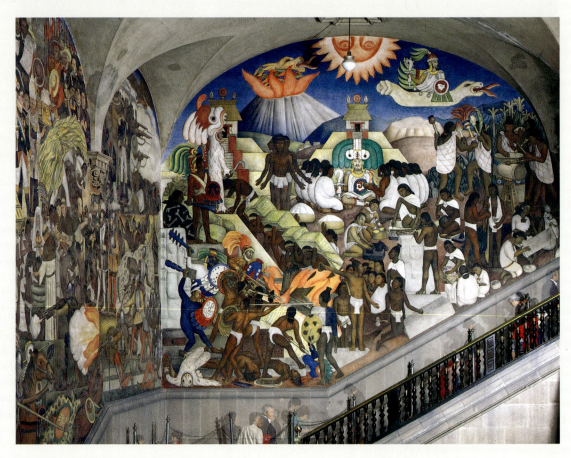

Diego Rivera During the period between the two world wars, several Mexican painters achieved international renown for their work. DIEGO RIVERA (1886–1957) was one of a group of Mexican artists determined to base their art on the culture of their homeland. The movement these artists formed was part of the idealistic rethinking of society that occurred in conjunction with the Mexican Revolution (1910–1920) and the lingering political turmoil of the 1920s. Among the projects these politically motivated artists undertook were vast *mural cycles* (series of frescoes with a common theme) placed in public buildings to dramatize and validate

the history of Mexico's native peoples. A staunch Marxist, Rivera strove to develop an art that served his people's needs (see "Rivera on Art for the People," above). Toward that end, he sought to create a national Mexican style incorporating a popular, generally accessible aesthetic in keeping with the socialist spirit of the Mexican Revolution.

Perhaps Rivera's finest mural cycle is the one lining the staircase of the National Palace in Mexico City. In these images, painted between 1929 and 1935, he depicted scenes from Mexico's history, of which *Ancient Mexico* (FIG. 14-35) is one. This section of the mural represents the conflicts between the indigenous people and the Spanish colonizers. Rivera included portraits of important figures in Mexican history and, in particular, in the struggle for Mexican independence. Although complex, the decorative, animated murals retain the legibility of folklore, and the figures consist of simple monumental shapes and areas of bold color.

Frida Kahlo Born to a Mexican mother and German father, the painter FRIDA KAHLO (1907–1954), who married Diego Rivera, used the details of her life as powerful symbols for the psychological pain of human existence. Art historians often consider Kahlo a Surrealist due to the psychic and autobiographical issues she dealt with in her art. Indeed, André Breton deemed her a Naturalistic Surrealist, although Kahlo herself rejected any association with Surrealism. Kahlo began painting seriously as a young student, during convalescence from an accident that tragically left her in constant pain. Her life became a heroic and tumultuous battle for survival against illness and stormy personal relationships. Typical of her long series of unflinching self-portraits is *The Two Fridas* (FIG. **14-36**), one of the few large-scale canvases Kahlo ever produced. The twin figures sit side by side on a low bench in a barren landscape under a stormy sky. The figures suggest different sides of the artist's personality, inextricably linked by the clasped hands and by the thin artery that stretches between them, joining their exposed hearts. The artery ends on one side in surgical forceps and on the other in a miniature portrait of her husband

as a child. Her deeply personal paintings touch sensual and psychological memories in her audience.

However, to read Kahlo's paintings solely as autobiographical overlooks the powerful political dimension of her art. Kahlo was deeply nationalistic and committed to her Mexican heritage. Politically active, she joined the Communist Party in 1920 and participated in public political protests. *The Two Fridas* incorporates Kahlo's commentary on the struggle facing Mexicans in the early 20th century in defining their national cultural identity. The Frida on the right (representing indigenous culture) appears in a Tehuana dress, the traditional costume of Zapotec women from the Isthmus of Tehuantepec, whereas the Frida on the left (representing imperialist forces) wears a European-style white lace dress. The heart, depicted here in such dramatic fashion, was an important symbol in the art of the Aztecs (see Chapter 19), whom Mexican nationalists idealized as the last independent rulers of an indigenous political unit. Thus *The Two Fridas* represents both Kahlo's personal struggles and the struggles of her homeland.

ARCHITECTURE

The first half of the 20th century was a time of great innovation in architecture too. As in painting, sculpture, and photography, new ideas came from both sides of the Atlantic.

Walter Gropius The De Stijl group not only developed an appealing simplified geometric style but also promoted the notion that art should be thoroughly incorporated into living environments. As Mondrian had insisted, "Art and life are one; art and life are both expressions of truth."[26] In Germany, WALTER GROPIUS (1883–1969) developed a particular vision of "total architecture." He made this concept the foundation of not only his own work but also the work of generations of pupils under his influence at a school called the *Bauhaus*. In 1919, Gropius became the director of the Weimar School of Arts and Crafts in Germany, founded in 1906. Under Gropius, the school assumed a new name—Das Staatliche Bauhaus (State School of Building). Gropius's goal was to train artists, architects, and designers to accept and anticipate 20th-century needs. He developed an extensive curriculum based on certain principles. First, Gropius staunchly advocated the importance of strong basic design and craftsmanship as fundamental to good art and architecture. Second, he promoted the unity of art, architecture, and design. Third, Gropius emphasized the need for thorough knowledge of machine-age technologies and materials. "Architects, painters, and sculptors," he insisted, "must recognize anew the composite character of a building as an entity."[27] To encourage the elimination of boundaries that traditionally separated art from architecture and art from craft, the Bauhaus offered courses in a wide range of artistic disciplines. These included weaving, pottery, bookbinding, carpentry, metalwork, stained glass, mural painting, stage design, advertising, and typography, in addition to painting, sculpture, and architecture. Ultimately, he hoped to achieve

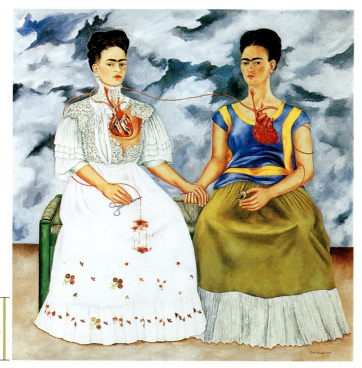

1 ft.

14-36 FRIDA KAHLO, *The Two Fridas*, 1939. Oil on canvas, 5′ 7″ × 5′ 7″. Museo de Arte Moderno, Mexico City.

Kahlo's deeply personal paintings touch sensual and psychological memories in her audience. Here, twin figures linked by clasped hands and a common artery suggest different sides of personality.

a marriage between art and industry—a synthesis of design and production. Like the De Stijl movement, the Bauhaus philosophy had its roots in utopian principles. Gropius declared: "Together let us conceive and create the new building of the future, which will embrace architecture and sculpture and painting in one unity and which will rise one day toward heaven from the hands of a million workers like a crystal symbol of a new faith."[28] The reference to a unity of workers also reveals the undercurrent of socialism in Germany at the time.

Bauhaus in Dessau

After encountering increasing hostility from a new government elected in 1924, the Bauhaus moved north to Dessau in early 1925. By this time, the Bauhaus program had matured. In a statement, Gropius listed the school's goals:

- A decidedly positive attitude to the living environment of vehicles and machines.
- The organic shaping of things in accordance with their own current laws, avoiding all romantic embellishment and whimsy.
- Restriction of basic forms and colours to what is typical and universally intelligible.
- Simplicity in complexity, economy in the use of space, materials, time, and money.[29]

The building Gropius designed for the Bauhaus at Dessau visibly expressed these goals. It is, in fact, the Bauhaus's architectural manifesto. The Dessau Bauhaus consisted of workshop and class areas, a dining room, a theater, a gymnasium, a wing with studio apartments, and an enclosed two-story bridge housing administrative offices. Of the major wings, the most dramatic was the Shop Block (FIG. **14-37**). Three stories tall, the Shop Block housed a printing shop and dye works facility, in addition to other work areas. The builders

constructed the skeleton of reinforced concrete but set these supports well back, sheathing the entire structure in glass to create a streamlined and light effect. This design's simplicity followed Gropius's dictum that architecture should avoid "all romantic embellishment and whimsy." Further, he realized his principle of "economy in the use of space" in his interior layout of the Shop Block, which consisted of large areas of free-flowing undivided space. Gropius believed that this spatial organization encouraged interaction and the sharing of ideas.

Ludwig Mies van der Rohe

In 1928, Gropius left the Bauhaus, and LUDWIG MIES VAN DER ROHE (1886–1969) eventually took over the directorship, moving the school to

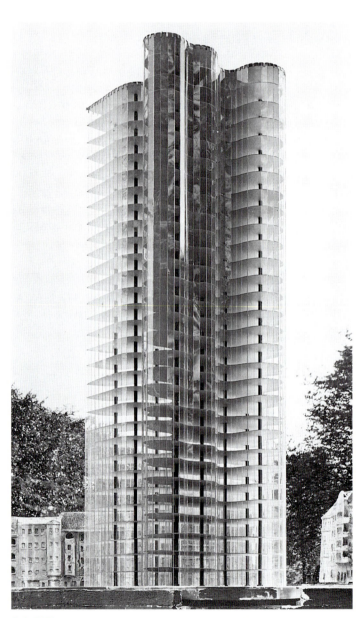

14-38 LUDWIG MIES VAN DER ROHE, model for a glass skyscraper, Berlin, Germany, 1922 (no longer extant).

In this technically and aesthetically adventurous design, the architect whose motto was "less is more" proposed a wholly transparent building that revealed its cantilevered floor planes and thin supports.

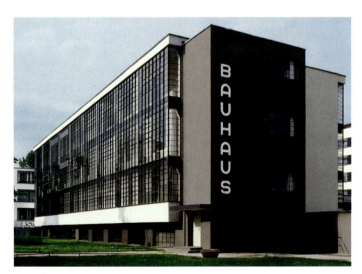

14-37 WALTER GROPIUS, Shop Block, the Bauhaus, Dessau, Germany, 1925–1926.

Gropius constructed this Bauhaus building by sheathing a reinforced concrete skeleton in glass. The design followed his dictum that architecture should avoid "all romantic embellishment and whimsy."

Berlin. Taking as his motto "less is more" and calling his architecture "skin and bones," the new Bauhaus director had already fully formed his aesthetic when in 1921 he conceived the model (FIG. 14-38) for a glass skyscraper building (unfortunately never constructed). Three irregularly shaped towers flow outward from a central court designed to hold a lobby, a porters room, and a community center. Two cylindrical entrance shafts rise at the ends of the court, each containing elevators, stairways, and toilets. Wholly transparent, the perimeter walls reveal the regular horizontal patterning of the cantilevered floor planes and their thin vertical supporting elements. The bold use of glass sheathing and inset supports was, at the time, technically and aesthetically adventurous. The weblike delicacy of the lines of the model as well as the illusion of movement created by reflection and by light changes seen through the glass prefigured the design of many of the glass skyscrapers found in major cities throughout the world today.

End of the Bauhaus One of Adolf Hitler's first acts after coming to power was to close the Bauhaus in 1933. During its 14-year existence, the school graduated fewer than 500 students, yet it achieved legendary status. Its phenomenal impact extended beyond painting, sculpture, and architecture to interior design, graphic design, and advertising. Moreover, art schools everywhere began to structure their curricula in line with the Bauhaus's pioneering program. The numerous Bauhaus instructors who fled Nazi Germany disseminated the school's philosophy and aesthetic widely. Many, including Gropius and Mies van der Rohe, settled in the United States.

Le Corbusier The simple geometric aesthetic Gropius and Mies van der Rohe developed became known as the *International Style* because of its widespread popularity. One of the purest adherents of this style was the Swiss architect Charles-Edouard Jeanneret, who took the name LE CORBUSIER (1887–1965). An influential theorist as well as practitioner, Le Corbusier sought to design a functional living space, which he described as a "machine for living."

Le Corbusier's Villa Savoye (FIG. 14-39) at Poissy-sur-Seine near Paris illustrates one of the major principles associated with the "purism" of the International Style—the elimination of the weight-bearing wall. New structural systems using materials such as steel and ferroconcrete (reinforced concrete) made such designs possible. A cube of lightly enclosed and deeply penetrated space, the Villa Savoye has only a partially confined ground floor (containing a three-car garage, bedrooms, a bathroom, and utility rooms). Much of the house's interior is open space, with the thin steel columns supporting the concrete main living floor and roof garden area. Le Corbusier inverted the traditional design practice of placing light elements above and heavy ones below by refusing to enclose the ground story of the Villa Savoye with masonry walls. This openness makes the "load" of the Villa Savoye's upper stories appear to hover lightly on the slender column supports. The major living rooms in the Villa Savoye are on the second floor, wrapping around an open central court. Strip windows that run along the membrane-like exterior walls provide illumination to the rooms. From the second-floor court, a ramp leads up to a flat roof-terrace and garden protected by a curving windbreak along one side. Several colors appear on the building's exterior—originally, a dark-green base, cream walls, and a rose-and-blue windscreen on top. The villa has no traditional facade. People must walk around and through the house to comprehend its layout. Spaces and masses interpenetrate so fluidly that inside and outside space intermingle.

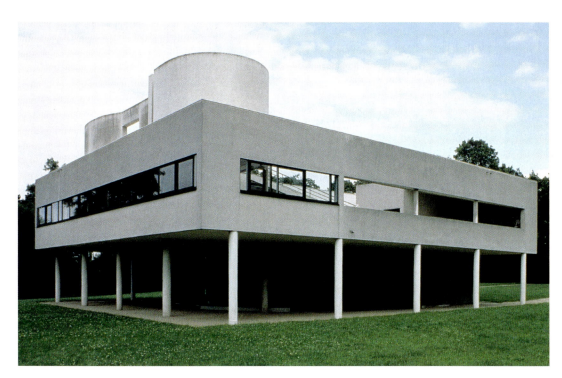

14-39 LE CORBUSIER, Villa Savoye, Poissy-sur-Seine, France, 1929.

Steel and ferroconcrete made it possible for Le Corbusier to invert the traditional practice of placing light architectural elements above heavy ones and to eliminate weight-bearing walls on the ground story.

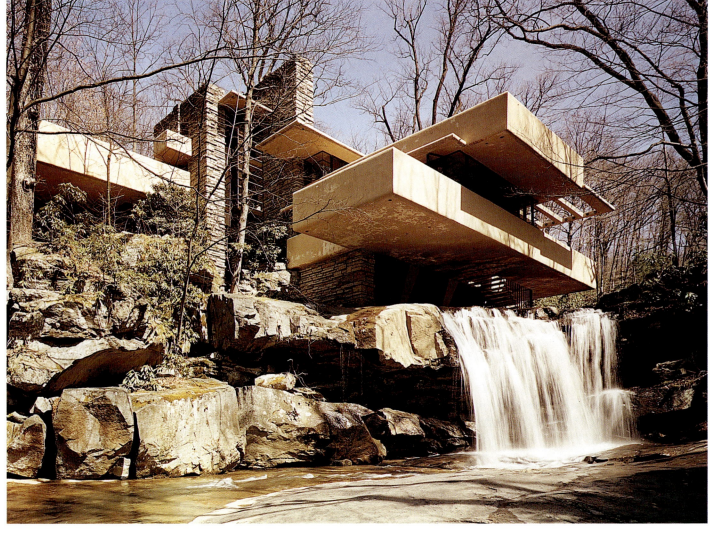

14-40 FRANK LLOYD WRIGHT, Kaufmann House (Fallingwater), Bear Run, Pennsylvania, 1936–1939.

Perched on a rocky hillside over a waterfall, Wright's Fallingwater has long sweeping lines, unconfined by abrupt wall limits, reaching out and capturing the expansiveness of the natural environment.

Frank Lloyd Wright A major figure in the development of early-20th-century architecture was FRANK LLOYD WRIGHT (1867–1959). Born in Wisconsin, Wright moved to Chicago, where he eventually joined the firm headed by Louis Sullivan (FIG. 13-20). Wright believed in "natural" or "organic" architecture serving free individuals who have the right to move within a "free" space, which he envisioned as a nonsymmetrical design interacting spatially with its natural surroundings. He sought to develop an organic unity of planning, structure, materials, and site.

The house nicknamed "Fallingwater" (FIG. **14-40**), which Wright designed as a weekend retreat at Bear Run, Pennsylvania, for the Pittsburgh department store magnate Edgar Kaufmann Sr., exemplifies his "naturalistic" approach to architecture. Perched on a rocky hillside over a small waterfall, Kaufmann's home has long sweeping lines, unconfined by abrupt wall limits, reaching out toward and capturing the expansiveness of the natural environment. Rather than build the house overlooking or next to the waterfall, Wright decided to build it over the waterfall, because he believed the inhabitants would become desensitized to the waterfall's presence and

power if they merely overlooked it. To take advantage of the location, Wright designed a series of terraces as independent cantilevers, or self-supporting shelves, that extend on three levels from a central core structure. Abandoning all symmetry, he eliminated a facade, extended the roofs far beyond the walls, and all but concealed the entrance. The contrasting textures of concrete, painted metal, and natural stones in the house's walls enliven its shapes, as does Wright's use of full-length strip windows to create a stunning interweaving of interior and exterior space. The implied message of Wright's new architecture was space, not mass—a space designed to fit the patron's life and enclosed and divided as required.

Wright achieved international fame. As early as 1940, Mies van der Rohe wrote that the "dynamic impulse from [Wright's] work invigorated a whole generation."[30] Wright's influence in Europe was rare for any American artist before World War II. But in the decades following that global conflict, American painters, sculptors, and architects often took the lead in establishing new styles that artists elsewhere quickly emulated. This new preeminence of America in the arts is the subject of Chapter 15.

Europe and America, 1900 to 1945

EUROPE, 1900 TO 1920

▌ During the early 20th century, avant-garde artists searched for new definitions of art in a changed world. Henri Matisse and the Fauves used bold colors as their primary means of conveying feeling. German Expressionist paintings feature clashing colors, disquieting figures, and perspectival distortions.

▌ Pablo Picasso and Georges Braque radically challenged prevailing artistic conventions with Cubism, in which artists dissect forms and place them in interaction with the space around them.

▌ The Futurists focused on motion in time and space in their effort to create paintings and sculptures that captured the dynamic quality of modern life. The Dadaists celebrated the spontaneous and intuitive, often incorporating found objects in their artworks.

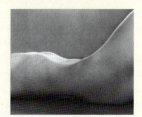

Picasso, *Les Demoiselles d'Avignon*, 1907

AMERICA, 1900 TO 1930

▌ The Armory Show of 1913 introduced European avant-garde art to American artists. The most notorious work in the exhibition was Marcel Duchamp's *Nude Descending a Staircase*.

▌ Photography emerged as an important American art form in the work of Alfred Stieglitz, who emphasized the careful arrangement of forms and patterns of light and dark. Edward Weston experimented with photographs of segments of the human body that verge on abstraction.

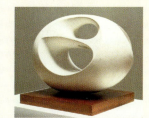

Weston, *Nude*, 1925

EUROPE, 1920 TO 1945

▌ World War I gave rise to the Neue Sachlichkeit movement in Germany. "New Objectivity" artists focused on depicting the horrors of war.

▌ The Surrealists investigated ways to express in art the world of dreams and the unconscious. Naturalistic Surrealists aimed for "concrete irrationality" in their naturalistic paintings of dreamlike scenes. Biomorphic Surrealists experimented with automatism and employed abstract imagery.

▌ Many European modernists pursued utopian ideals. The Suprematists developed an abstract style to express pure feeling. De Stijl artists employed simple geometric forms in their "pure plastic art." Constantin Brancusi, Barbara Hepworth, and other sculptors also increasingly turned to abstraction and emphasized voids as well as masses in their work.

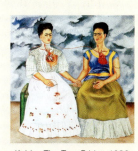

Hepworth, *Oval Sculpture (No. 2)*, 1943

AMERICA, 1930 TO 1945

▌ Although Alexander Calder created abstract works between the wars, other American artists favored figural art. Edward Hopper explored the loneliness of life in the Depression era. Jacob Lawrence recorded the struggle of African Americans. Grant Wood depicted life in rural Iowa.

▌ Mexican artists achieved international renown. Diego Rivera painted epic mural cycles of the history of Mexico. Frida Kahlo's powerful autobiographical paintings explored the human psyche.

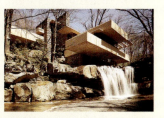

Kahlo, *The Two Fridas*, 1939

ARCHITECTURE

▌ Under Walter Gropius, the Bauhaus group in Germany promoted the vision of "total architecture," which called for the integration of all the arts in constructing modern living environments. In France, Le Corbusier used modern construction materials in his "machines for living"— simple houses with open plans and unadorned surfaces.

▌ The leading American architect of the first half of the 20th century was Frank Lloyd Wright. "Fallingwater" is a bold asymmetrical design integrating a private home with the natural environment.

Wright, Fallingwater, 1936–1939

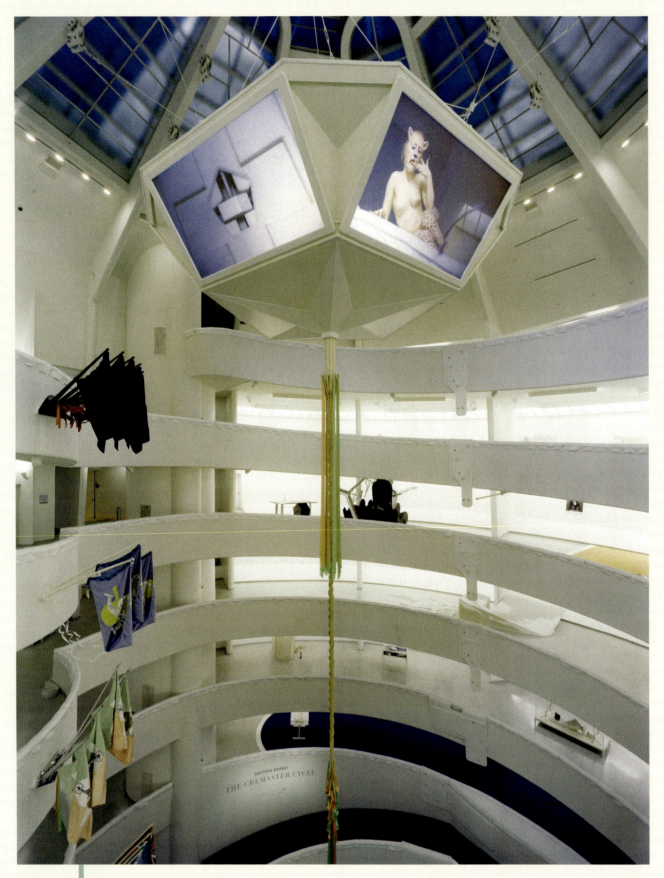

15-1 MATTHEW BARNEY, *Cremaster* cycle, installation at the Solomon R. Guggenheim Museum, New York, 2003.

Barney's vast multimedia installations of drawings, photographs, sculptures, and videos typify the relaxation of the traditional boundaries among artistic media at the opening of the 21st century.

Europe and America after 1945

World War II, with the global devastation it unleashed, set the stage for further conflict and upheaval during the second half of the 20th century. In 1947 the British left India, dividing the subcontinent into two hostile nations, India and Pakistan. After a catastrophic war, Communists came to power in China in 1949. North Korea invaded South Korea in 1950 and fought a grim three-year war with the United States and its allies. The Soviet Union brutally suppressed uprisings in East Germany, Poland, Hungary, and Czechoslovakia. The United States intervened in disputes in Central and South America. Almost as soon as many African nations—Kenya, Uganda, Nigeria, Angola, Mozambique, the Sudan, Rwanda, and the Congo—won their independence, civil wars broke out. In Indonesia, internal conflict left more than 100,000 dead. Algeria expelled France in 1962 after the French waged a prolonged war with Algeria's Muslim natives. After 15 years of bitter fighting in Southeast Asia, the United States suffered defeat in Vietnam. Arab nations fought wars with Israel in 1967, 1973, and the early 1980s. A revitalized Islam inspired a fundamentalist religious revolution in Iran and encouraged "holy war" with the West using terrorism as a weapon—most dramatically in the attacks on New York City and Washington, D.C., on September 11, 2001. In response, the United States and allied Western nations launched invasions of Afghanistan and Iraq.

Upheaval has also characterized the cultural sphere since the end of World War II. In the United States, for example, during the 1960s and 1970s the struggle for civil rights for African Americans, for free speech on university campuses, and for disengagement from the Vietnam War led to a rebellion of the young. A new system of values emerged—a "youth culture," expressed in radical rejection not only of national policies but often also of the society generating them. Young Americans derided their elders' lifestyles and adopted unconventional dress, manners, habits, and morals deliberately subversive of traditional social standards. The youth era brought the sexual revolution, the widespread use and abuse of drugs, and the development of rock music. Young people rejected mainstream society, embraced alternative belief systems, and dismissed university curricula as irrelevant.

The civil rights movement of the 1960s and the women's liberation movement of the 1970s reflected this spirit of rebellion, coupled with the rejection of racism and sexism. African Americans fought discrimination and sought equal rights. Women systematically began to challenge the male-dominated culture, which they perceived as having limited their opportunities for centuries. Gays and lesbians and various ethnic groups also mounted challenges to discriminatory policies and attitudes.

PAINTING AND SCULPTURE, 1945 TO 1970

The end of World War II in 1945 left devastated cities, ruptured economies, and governments in chaos throughout Europe. These factors, coupled with the massive loss of life and the indelible horror of the Holocaust and the dropping of atomic bombs on Hiroshima and Nagasaki, resulted in a pervasive sense of despair, disillusionment, and skepticism. Although many people (for example, the Futurists in Italy) had tried to find redemptive value in World War I, it was impossible to do the same with World War II, coming as it did so closely on the heels of the war that was supposed to "end all wars." Further, World War I was largely a European conflict in which roughly 10 million people died, whereas World War II was a truly global catastrophe, leaving 35 million dead in its wake.

Postwar Expressionism in Europe

The cynicism that emerged across Europe in the 1940s found voice in existentialism, a philosophy asserting the absurdity of human existence and the impossibility of achieving certainty. Many existentialists also promoted atheism. The writings of French author Jean-Paul Sartre (1905–1980) most clearly captured the existentialist spirit. According to Sartre, if God does not exist, then individuals must constantly struggle in isolation with the anguish of making decisions in a world without absolutes or traditional values. This spirit of pessimism and despair emerged frequently in European art of the immediate postwar period. A brutality or roughness characterized much of this art, appropriately expressing both the artist's state of mind and the larger cultural sensibility.

Alberto Giacometti The sculpture of Swiss artist **ALBERTO GIACOMETTI** (1901–1966) perhaps best expresses the spirit of existentialism. Although Giacometti never claimed he pursued existentialist ideas in his art, his works capture the essence of that philosophy. Indeed, Sartre, Giacometti's friend, saw the artist's figural sculptures as the epitome of existentialist humanity—alienated, solitary, and lost in the world's immensity. Giacometti's sculptures of the 1940s, such as *Man Pointing* (FIG. **15-2**), are thin, virtually featureless figures with rough, agitated surfaces. Rather than conveying the solidity and mass of conventional bronze sculpture, these severely attenuated figures seem swallowed up by the space surrounding them, imparting a sense of isolation and fragility. Giacometti's sculptures are evocative and moving, speaking to the pervasive despair in the aftermath of world war.

Francis Bacon Created in the year after World War II ended, *Painting* (FIG. **15-3**) by British artist **FRANCIS BACON** (1910–1992) is an indictment of humanity and a reflection of war's butchery. The painting is a compelling and revolting image of a powerful, stocky man with a gaping mouth and

a vivid red stain on his upper lip, as if he were a carnivore devouring the raw meat sitting on the railing surrounding him. Bacon may have based his depiction of this central figure on news photos of similarly dressed European and American leaders. The umbrella in particular recalls images of Neville Chamberlain (1869–1940), the wartime British prime minister who frequently appeared in photographs with an umbrella. Bacon added to the painting's visceral impact by depicting the flayed carcass hanging behind the central figure as if it were a crucified human form. Although the specific sources for the imagery in *Painting* may not be entirely clear, the work is, in Bacon's words, "an attempt to remake the violence of reality itself." Bacon often described his art as "the brutality of fact."[1]

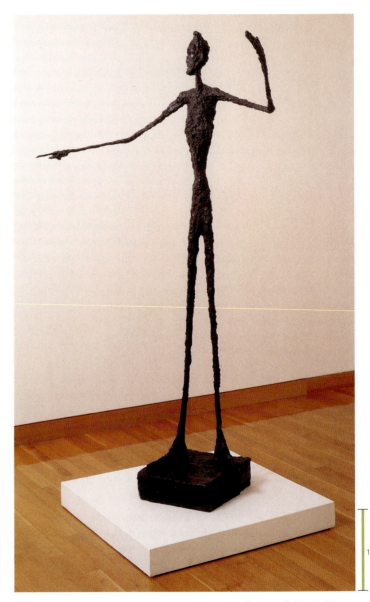

15-2 ALBERTO GIACOMETTI, *Man Pointing* (no. 5 of 6), 1947. Bronze, 5' 10" × 3' 1" × 1' 5$\frac{5}{8}$". Des Moines Art Center, Des Moines (Nathan Emory Coffin Collection).

The writer Jean-Paul Sartre considered Giacometti's thin and virtually featureless sculpted figures the epitome of existentialist humanity—alienated, solitary, and lost in the world's immensity.

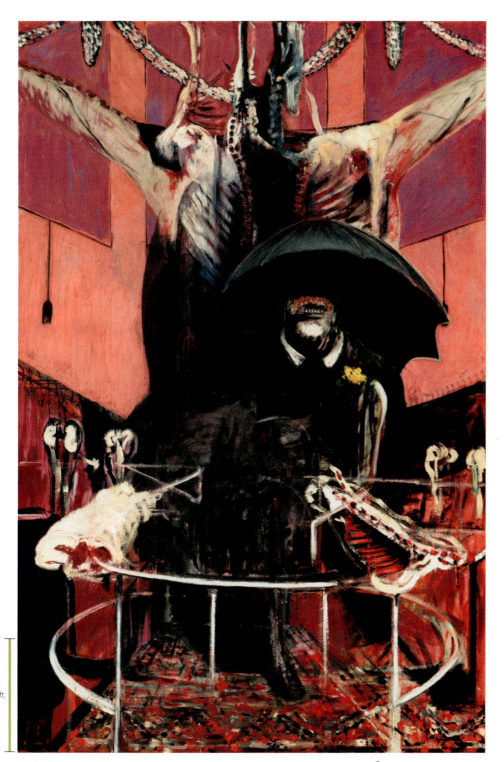

15-3 Francis Bacon, *Painting*, 1946. Oil and pastel on linen, 6′ 5$\frac{7}{8}$″ × 4′ 4″. Museum of Modern Art, New York.

Painted in the aftermath of World War II, this intentionally revolting image of a powerful figure presiding over a slaughter is Bacon's indictment of humanity and a reflection of war's butchery.

however, modernism increasingly became identified with a strict *formalism*—an emphasis on an artwork's visual elements rather than its subject. The most important champion of New York formalist painting was the American art critic Clement Greenberg (1909–1994), who wielded considerable influence from the 1940s through the 1970s. So dominant was Greenberg that scholars often refer to the general modernist tenets during this period as Greenbergian formalism. Greenberg promoted the idea of purity in art. He believed artists should strive for a more explicit focus on the properties exclusive to each medium—for example, two-dimensionality in painting and three-dimensionality in sculpture. To achieve this, artists had to eliminate illusion and embrace abstraction. Greenberg argued that

a modernist work of art must try, in principle, to avoid communication with any order of experience not inherent in the most literally and essentially construed nature of its medium. Among other things, this means renouncing illusion and explicit subject matter. The arts are to achieve concreteness, "purity," by dealing solely with their respective selves—that is, by becoming "abstract" or nonfigurative.[2]

Abstract Expressionism, the first major American avant-garde movement, emerged in New York in the 1940s. As the name suggests, the Abstract Expressionists produced paintings that are, for the most part, abstract but express the artist's state of mind with the goal also of striking emotional chords in the viewer. The movement developed along two lines—*gestural abstraction* and *chromatic abstraction*. The gestural abstractionists relied on the expressiveness of energetically applied pigment.

Abstract Expressionism

In the 1940s, the center of the Western art world shifted from Paris to New York because of the devastation World War II had inflicted across Europe and the resulting influx of émigré artists to the United States. American artists picked up the European avant-garde's energy, which movements such as Cubism and Dada had fostered. In the postwar years, In contrast, the chromatic abstractionists focused on color's emotional resonance.

Jackson Pollock The artist whose work best exemplifies gestural abstraction is Jackson Pollock (1912–1956), who developed his signature style in the mid-1940s. By 1950, Pollock had refined his technique and was producing large-scale abstract paintings such as *Number 1, 1950*

Jackson Pollock on Action Painting

The kind of physical interaction between the painter and the canvas that Jackson Pollock championed led the critic Harold Rosenberg (1896–1989) to label Pollock's work (FIG. **15-4**) *action painting*. In an influential 1952 article, Rosenberg described the attempts of Pollock and other Abstract Expressionists to get "in the painting":

> At a certain moment the canvas began to appear to one American painter after another as an arena in which to act—rather than as a space in which to reproduce, redesign, analyze or "express" an object, actual or imagined. What was to go on the canvas was not a picture but an event. The painter no longer approached his easel with an image in his mind; he went up to it with material in his hand to do something to that other piece of material in front of him. The image would be the result of this encounter.*

In an essay he published in 1947, Pollock explained the motivations for his action painting and described the manner in which he applied pigment to canvas.

My painting does not come from the easel. I hardly ever stretch my canvas before painting. I prefer to tack the unstretched canvas to the hard wall or the floor. I need the resistance of a hard surface. On the floor I am more at ease. I feel nearer, more a part of the painting, since this way I can walk around it, work from the four sides and literally be in the painting. . . . I continue to get further away from the usual painter's tools such as easel, palette, brushes, etc. I prefer sticks, trowels, knives and dripping fluid paint or a heavy impasto with sand, broken glass and other foreign matter added. When I am in my painting, I'm not aware of what I'm doing. . . . [T]he painting has a life of its own. I try to let it come through. . . . The source of my painting is the unconscious.†

* Harold Rosenberg, "The American Action Painters," reprinted in *The Tradition of the New* (New York: Horizon Press, 1959), 25.
† Quoted in Francis V. O'Connor, *Jackson Pollock* (New York: Museum of Modern Art, 1967), 39–40.

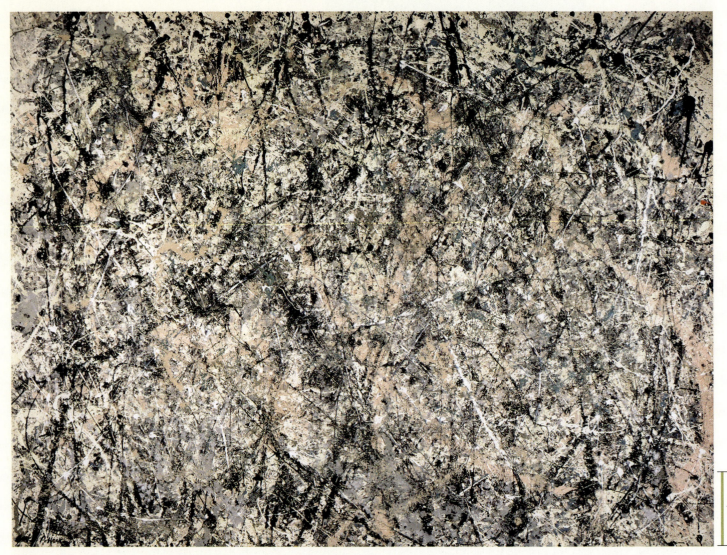

1 ft.

15-4 JACKSON POLLOCK, *Number 1, 1950 (Lavender Mist)*, 1950. Oil, enamel, and aluminum paint on canvas, 7′ 3″ × 9′ 10″. National Gallery of Art, Washington, D.C. (Ailsa Mellon Bruce Fund).

Pollock's "action paintings" emphasize the creative process. His mural-size canvases consist of rhythmic drips, splatters, and dribbles of paint that envelop viewers, drawing them into a lacy spider web.

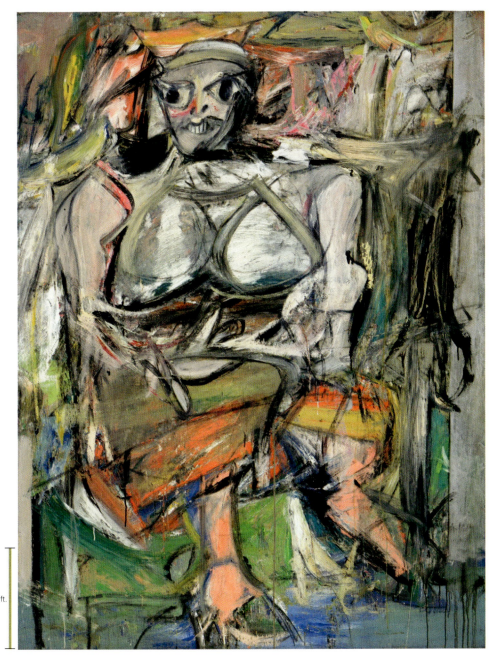

15-5 WILLEM DE KOONING, *Woman I*, 1950–1952. Oil on canvas, 6′ 3⅞″ × 4′ 10″. Museum of Modern Art, New York.

Although rooted in figuration, including pictures of female models on advertising billboards, de Kooning's *Woman I* displays the energetic application of pigment typical of gestural abstraction.

"Jackson Pollock on Action Painting," page 420). Art historians have linked his ideas about improvisation in the creative process to his interest in what psychiatrist Carl Jung called the collective unconscious. Pollock's reliance on improvisation and the subconscious has parallels in Surrealism and the work of Vassily Kandinsky (FIG. **14-5**), whom critics described as an abstract expressionist as early as 1919.

Willem de Kooning Despite the public's skepticism about Pollock's art, other artists enthusiastically pursued similar avenues of expression. Dutch-born WILLEM DE KOONING (1904–1997) also developed a gestural abstractionist style. Even images such as *Woman I* (FIG. **15-5**), although rooted in figuration, display the sweeping gestural brush strokes and energetic application of pigment typical of gestural abstraction. Out of the jumbled array of slashing lines and agitated patches of color appears a ferocious-looking woman with staring eyes and ponderous breasts. Her toothy smile, inspired by an ad for Camel cigarettes, becomes a grimace. Female models on advertising billboards partly inspired *Woman I*, one of a series of female images, but de Kooning's female forms also suggest fertility figures and a satiric inversion of the traditional image of Venus, goddess of love. Process was important to de Kooning, as it was for Pollock. Continually working on *Woman I* for almost two years, de Kooning painted an image and then scraped it away the next day and began anew. His wife Elaine, also a painter, estimated that he painted approximately 200 scraped-away images of women on this canvas before settling on the final one. Like Pollock, de Kooning was very much "in" his paintings.

Mark Rothko In contrast to the aggressively energetic images of the gestural abstractionists, the work of the chromatic abstractionists exudes a quieter aesthetic, exemplified by the work of Russian-born MARK ROTHKO (1903–1970). Rothko believed that references to anything specific in the physical world conflicted with the sublime idea of the universal, supernatural "spirit of myth," which he saw as the core of meaning in art. Rothko's mature paintings are compositionally simple, with color serving as the primary conveyor

(*Lavender Mist*; FIG. **15-4**). These works consist of rhythmic drips, splatters, and dribbles of paint. The mural-sized fields of energetic skeins of pigment envelop viewers, drawing them into a lacy spider web. Using sticks or brushes, Pollock flung, poured, and dripped paint (not only traditional oil paints but aluminum paints and household enamels as well) onto a section of canvas he simply unrolled across his studio floor. This working method earned the artist the derisive nickname "Jack the Dripper." Responding to the image as it developed, Pollock created art that was both spontaneous and choreographed. His painting technique highlights a particularly avant-garde aspect of gestural abstraction—its emphasis on the creative process. Indeed, Pollock literally immersed himself in the painting during its creation (see

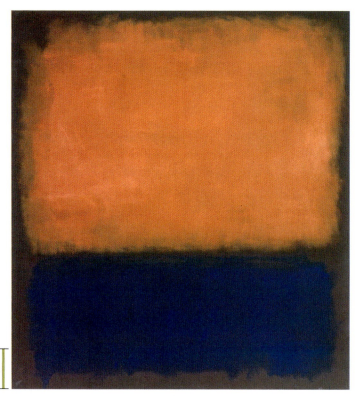

1 ft.

15-6 MARK ROTHKO, *No. 14*, 1960. Oil on canvas, 9′ 6″ × 8′ 9″. San Francisco Museum of Modern Art, San Francisco (Helen Crocker Russell Fund Purchase).

Rothko's chromatic abstractionist paintings—consisting of hazy rectangles of pure color hovering in front of a colored background— are compositionally simple but compelling visual experiences.

of meaning. In works such as *No. 14* (FIG. **15-6**), Rothko created compelling visual experiences consisting of two or three large rectangles of pure color with hazy, brushy edges

that seem to float on the canvas surface, hovering in front of a colored background. When properly lit, these paintings appear as shimmering veils of intensely luminous colors suspended in front of the canvases. Although the color juxtapositions are visually captivating, Rothko intended them as more than decorative. He saw color as a doorway to another reality, and insisted that color could express "basic human emotions—tragedy, ecstasy, doom. . . . The people who weep before my pictures are having the same religious experience I had when I painted them."[3] Like the other Abstract Expressionists, Rothko produced highly evocative, moving paintings that relied on formal elements rather than specific representational content to elicit emotions in the viewer.

Post-Painterly Abstraction

Post-Painterly Abstraction, another American art movement, developed out of Abstract Expressionism. Yet Post-Painterly Abstraction, a term Clement Greenberg coined, manifests a radically different sensibility from Abstract Expressionism. Whereas Abstract Expressionism conveys a feeling of passion and visceral intensity, a cool, detached rationality emphasizing tighter pictorial control characterizes Post-Painterly Abstraction. Greenberg saw this art as contrasting with "painterly" art, characterized by loose, visible pigment application. Evidence of the artist's hand, so prominent in gestural abstraction, is conspicuously absent in Post-Painterly Abstraction. Greenberg championed this art form because it embodied his idea of purity in art.

Frank Stella Attempting to arrive at pure painting, the Post-Painterly Abstractionists distilled painting down to its

15-7 FRANK STELLA, *Mas o Menos (More or Less)*, 1964. Metallic powder in acrylic emulsion on canvas, 9′ 10″ × 13′ 8½″. Musée National d'Art Moderne, Centre Georges Pompidou, Paris (purchase 1983 with participation of Scaler Foundation).

Stella tried to achieve purity in painting using evenly spaced pinstripes on colored grounds. His canvases have no central focus, no painterly or expressive elements, and no tactile quality.

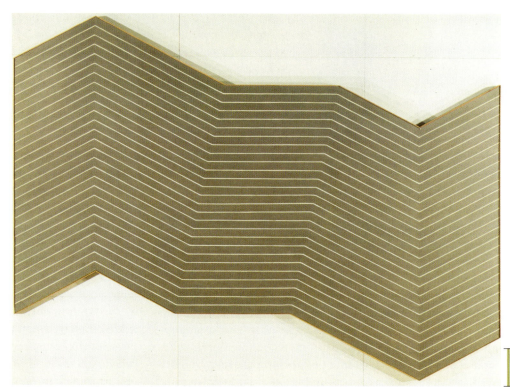

1 ft.

Helen Frankenthaler on Color-Field Painting

In 1965 the art critic Henry Geldzahler interviewed Helen Frankenthaler about her work as an abstract painter. In the following excerpt, Frankenthaler described her approach to placing color on canvas (FIG. 15-8) and compared her method with the way earlier modernist artists used color in their paintings.

> I will sometimes start a picture feeling "What will happen if I work with three blues and another color, and maybe more or less of the other color than the combined blues?" And very often midway through the picture I have to change the basis of the experience. . . .
>
> When you first saw a Cubist or Impressionist picture there was a whole way of instructing the eye or the subconscious. Dabs of color had to stand for real things; it was an abstraction of a guitar or a hillside. The opposite is going on now. If you have bands of blue, green, and pink, the mind doesn't think sky, grass, and flesh. These are colors and the question is what are they doing with themselves and with each other. Sentiment and nuance are being squeezed out.*

* Henry Geldzahler, "Interview with Helen Frankenthaler," *Artforum* 4, no. 2 (October 1965), 37–38.

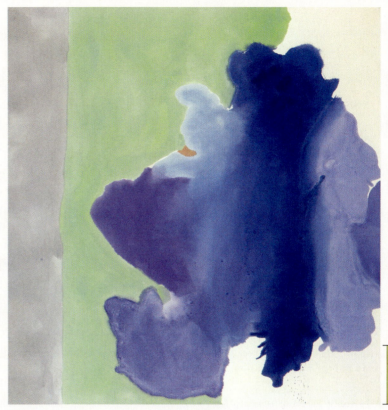

15-8 HELEN FRANKENTHALER, *The Bay*, 1963. Acrylic on canvas, 6′ 8⅞″ × 6′ 9⅞″. Detroit Institute of Arts, Detroit.

Color-field painters like Frankenthaler poured paint onto unprimed canvas, allowing the pigment to soak into the fabric. Her works underscore that a painting is simply pigment on a flat surface.

1 ft.

essential elements, producing spare, elemental, and resolutely two-dimensional images. An example of one variant of Post-Painterly Abstraction, *hard-edge painting*, is *Mas o Menos* (*More or Less;* FIG. **15-7**) by FRANK STELLA (b. 1936). Stella eliminated many of the variables associated with painting. His simplified images of thin, evenly spaced pinstripes on colored grounds have no central focus, no painterly or expressive elements, only limited surface modulation, and no tactile quality. Stella's systematic painting illustrates Greenberg's insistence on purity in art. The artist's famous comment on his work, "What you see is what you see," reinforces two notions: Painters interested in producing advanced art must reduce their work to its essential elements, and the viewer must acknowledge that a painting is simply pigment on a flat surface.

Helen Frankenthaler *Color-field painting*, another variant of Post-Painterly Abstraction, also emphasized painting's basic properties. However, rather than produce sharp, unmodulated shapes as the hard-edge artists did, the color-field painters poured diluted paint onto unprimed canvas, allowing the pigment to soak in. No other painting method

results in such literal flatness. The images created, such as *The Bay* (FIG. **15-8**) by HELEN FRANKENTHALER (b. 1928), appear spontaneous and almost accidental (see "Helen Frankenthaler on Color-Field Painting," above). These works differ from those of Rothko in the way Frankenthaler subordinated the emotional component, so integral to Abstract Expressionism, to resolving formal problems.

Sculpture

Painters were not the only artists interested in Greenberg's formalist ideas. American sculptors also aimed for purity in their medium. Whereas painters worked to emphasize flatness, sculptors, understandably, chose to focus on three-dimensionality as the unique characteristic and inherent limitation of the sculptural idiom.

David Smith American sculptor DAVID SMITH (1906–1965) produced metal sculptures that have affinities with the Abstract Expressionist movement in painting. Smith learned to weld in an automobile plant in 1925 and later applied to his art the technical expertise gained from handling metals.

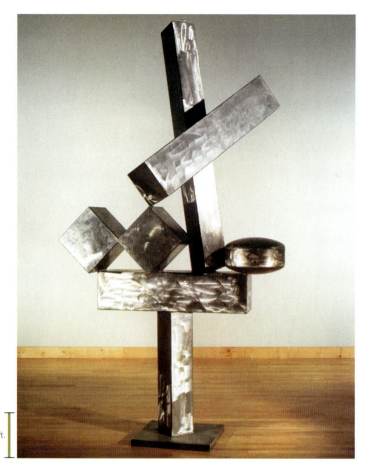

1 ft.

15-9 DAVID SMITH, *Cubi XIX*, 1964. Stainless steel, 9′ 4¾″ × 4′ 10¼″ × 3′ 4″. Tate Gallery, London.

David Smith's metal sculptures have affinities with Abstract Expressionism. They consist of simple geometric forms—cubes, cylinders, and rectangular bars—piled up and then welded together.

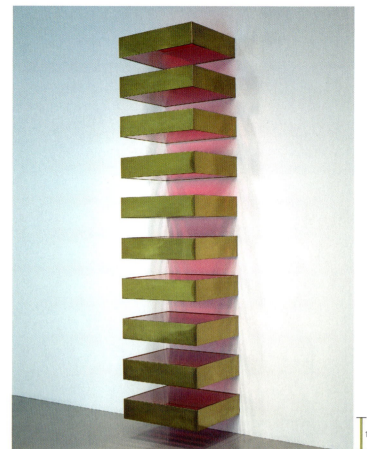

1 ft.

15-10 DONALD JUDD, *Untitled*, 1969. Brass and colored fluorescent Plexiglass on steel brackets, 10 units, 6⅛″ × 2′ × 2′ 3″ each, with 6″ intervals. Hirshhorn Museum and Sculpture Garden, Smithsonian Institution, Washington, D.C. (gift of Joseph H. Hirshhorn, 1972). © Donald Judd Estate/Licensed by VAGA, New York.

By rejecting illusionism and symbolism and reducing sculpture to basic geometric forms, Donald Judd and other Minimalist artists emphasized their works' "objecthood" and concrete tangibility.

After experimenting with a variety of sculptural styles and materials, Smith created his *Cubi* series in the early 1960s. These works, for example *Cubi XIX* (FIG. **15-9**), consist of simple geometric forms—cubes, cylinders, and rectangular bars. Made of stainless steel sections piled atop one another and then welded together, these large-scale sculptures make a striking visual statement. Smith added gestural elements reminiscent of Abstract Expressionism by burnishing the metal with steel wool, producing swirling random-looking patterns that draw attention to the two-dimensionality of the sculptural surface. This treatment, which captures the light hitting the sculpture, activates the surface and imparts a texture to his pieces.

Donald Judd A predominantly sculptural movement that emerged in the 1960s was *Minimalism*. Difficult to describe other than as three-dimensional objects, Minimalist artworks often lack identifiable subjects, colors, surface textures, and narrative elements. By rejecting illusionism and reducing sculpture to basic geometric forms, Minimalists emphasized their art's "objecthood" and concrete tangibility. In so doing, they reduced experience to its most fundamental level. One of the leading Minimalist sculptors was DONALD JUDD (1928–1994), who embraced a spare, universal

aesthetic corresponding to the core tenets of the movement. Judd's determination to arrive at a visual vocabulary that avoided deception or ambiguity propelled him away from representation and toward precise, simple sculpture. For Judd, a work's power derived from its character as a whole and from the specificity of its materials. *Untitled* (FIG. **15-10**) presents basic geometric boxes constructed of brass and red Plexiglass, undisguised by paint or other materials. The artist did not intend the work to be metaphorical or symbolic but a straightforward declaration of sculpture's objecthood. Judd used Plexiglass because its translucency permits the viewer to access the interior, thereby rendering the sculpture both open and enclosed. This aspect of the design reflects Judd's desire to banish ambiguity or falseness from his works.

Louise Nevelson Although Minimalism was a dominant sculptural trend in the 1960s, many sculptors pursued other styles. Russian-born LOUISE NEVELSON (1899–1988) created sculpture that combines a sense of the architectural fragment with the power of Dada and Surrealist found objects to express her personal sense of life's underlying significance.

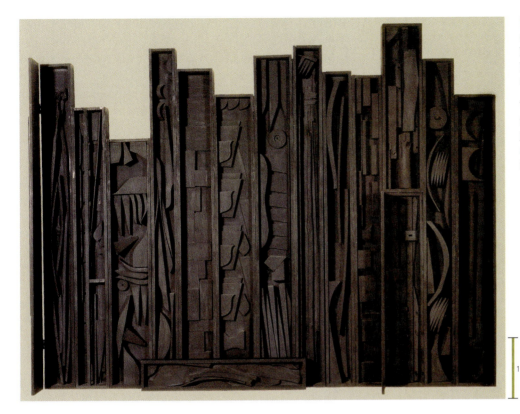

1 ft.

Beginning in the late 1950s, Nevelson assembled sculptures of found wooden objects and forms, enclosing small sculptural compositions in boxes of varied sizes, and joined the boxes to one another to form "walls," which she then painted in a single hue—usually black, white, or gold. This monochromatic color scheme unifies the diverse parts of pieces such as *Tropical Garden II* (FIG. **15-11**) and creates a mysterious field of shapes and shadows. The structures suggest magical environments resembling the treasured secret hideaways dimly remembered from childhood. Yet the boxy frames and the precision of the manufactured found objects create a rough geometric structure that the eye roams over freely, lingering on some details. The effect is rather like viewing the side of an apartment building from a moving elevated train.

Louise Bourgeois In contrast to the architectural nature of Nevelson's work, a sensuous organic quality recalling the evocative Biomorphic Surrealist forms of Joan Miró (FIG. 14-25) pervades the work of French-American artist LOUISE BOURGEOIS (b. 1911). *Cumul I* (FIG. **15-12**) is a collection of round-headed units huddled, with their heads protruding, within a collective cloak dotted with holes. The units differ in size, and their position within the group lends a distinctive personality to each. Although the shapes remain abstract, they refer strongly to human bodies. Bourgeois uses a wide variety of materials in her works, including wood, plaster, latex, and plastics, in addition to alabaster, marble, and bronze. She exploits each material's qualities to suit the expressiveness of the piece. In *Cumul I*, the alternating high gloss and matte finish of the marble increases the sensuous distinction between the group of swelling forms and the soft folds swaddling them. Bourgeois connects her sculpture with the body's multiple relationships to landscape: "[My pieces]

are anthropomorphic and they are landscape also, since our body could be considered from a topographical point of view, as a land with mounds and valleys and caves and holes." Sculptures like *Cumul I* are also often openly sexual: "There has always been sexual suggestiveness in my work. Sometimes I am totally concerned with female shapes—characters of breasts like clouds—but often I merge the activity—phallic breasts, male and female, active and passive."[4]

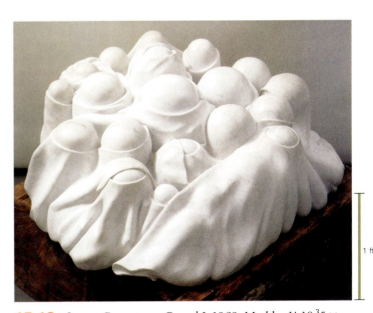

15-12 LOUISE BOURGEOIS, *Cumul I*, 1969. Marble, 1′ 10⅜″ × 4′ 2″ × 4′. Musée National d'Art Moderne, Centre Georges Pompidou, Paris. © Louise Bourgeois/Licensed by VAGA, New York.

1 ft.

Pop Art

Despite their differences, the Abstract Expressionists, Post-Painterly Abstractionists, and Minimalists all adopted an artistic vocabulary of resolute abstraction. The artists of the *Pop Art* movement, however, recognized that the insular and introspective attitude of the avant-garde had alienated the public, and they reintroduced in their work all the traditional artistic devices used to convey meaning, such as signs, symbols, and figural imagery. Pop artists not only embraced representation but also produced an art firmly grounded in consumer culture and the mass media, thereby making it much more accessible and understandable to the average person. Indeed, the name "Pop Art," short for "popular art," refers to the popular mass culture and familiar imagery of the modern urban environment.

Richard Hamilton   Art historians trace the roots of Pop Art to a group of young British artists, architects, and writers who formed the Independent Group at the Institute of Contemporary Art in London in the early 1950s. They sought to initiate fresh thinking in art, in part by sharing their fascination with the aesthetics and content of such facets of popular culture as advertising, comic books, and movies. In 1956 an Independent Group member, RICHARD HAMILTON (b. 1922), made a small collage, *Just What Is It That Makes Today's Homes So Different, So Appealing?* (FIG. **15-13**), that exemplifies British Pop Art of the period. Long intrigued by

Duchamp's ideas, Hamilton consistently combined elements of popular art and fine art in his work, seeing both as belonging to the whole world of visual communication. He created *Just What Is It?* for the poster and catalogue of one section of an exhibition titled *This Is Tomorrow*, which included images from Hollywood cinema, the mass media, and one reproduction of a van Gogh painting (to represent popular fine artworks).

The fantasy interior in Hamilton's collage reflects the values of modern consumer culture through figures and objects cut from glossy magazines. *Just What Is It?* includes references to the mass media (the television, the theater marquee outside the window, the newspaper), advertising (Hoover vacuums, Ford cars, Armour hams, Tootsie Pops), and popular culture (the cutout nude from a girlie magazine, bodybuilder Charles Atlas, romance comic books). Scholars have written much about the possible deep meaning of this piece, and few would deny the work's satirical effect, whether or not the artist intended to make a pointed comment. Artworks of this sort stimulated the viewer's wide-ranging speculation about society's values, and this kind of intellectual toying with mass-media meaning and imagery typified Pop Art in Europe.

Jasper Johns   Although Pop Art originated in England, the movement found its greatest articulation and success in the United States, in large part because the more fully matured American consumer culture provided a fertile environment for the movement. Indeed, Independent Group members claimed their inspiration came from Hollywood, Detroit, and New York's Madison Avenue, paying homage to America's predominance in the realms of mass media, mass production, and advertising. One artist pivotal to the early development of American Pop Art was JASPER JOHNS

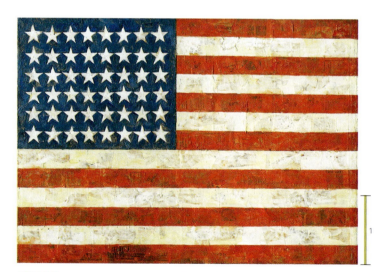

15-13   RICHARD HAMILTON, *Just What Is It That Makes Today's Homes So Different, So Appealing?* 1956. Collage, $10\frac{1}{4}$" × $9\frac{3}{4}$". Kunsthalle Tübingen, Tübingen.

The fantasy interior in Hamilton's collage reflects the values of the consumer culture through figures and objects cut from glossy magazines. Toying with mass-media imagery typifies British Pop Art.

15-14   JASPER JOHNS, *Flag*, 1954–1955, dated on reverse 1954. Encaustic, oil, and collage on fabric mounted on plywood, 3' $6\frac{1}{4}$" × 5' $\frac{5}{8}$". Museum of Modern Art, New York (gift of Philip Johnson in honor of Alfred H. Barr Jr.). © Jasper Johns/Licensed by VAGA, New York.

American Pop artist Jasper Johns wanted to draw attention to common objects that people view frequently but rarely scrutinize. He made several series of paintings of targets, flags, numbers, and letters.

(b. 1930), who sought to draw attention to common objects in the world—what he called things "seen but not looked at."[5] To this end, he created several series of paintings of targets, flags, numbers, and alphabets. For example, *Flag* (FIG. **15-14**) depicts an object people view frequently but rarely scrutinize. The highly textured surface of the work is the result of Johns's use of *encaustic*, an ancient method of painting with liquid wax and dissolved pigment (FIG. **3-41**). First, the artist embedded a collage of newspaper scraps or photographs in wax. He then painted over them with the encaustic. Because the wax hardened quickly, Johns worked rapidly, and the translucency of the wax allows the viewer to see the layered painting process.

Robert Rauschenberg Johns's friend ROBERT RAUSCHENBERG (1925–2008) began using mass-media images in his work in the 1950s. Rauschenberg set out to create works that would be open and indeterminate. He began making *combines*, combinations of paintings and sculptures. Some combines seem to be sculptures with painting incorporated into certain sections. Others are paintings with three-dimensional objects attached to the surface. In the early 1960s, Rauschenberg adopted the commercial medium of *silk-screen printing*, first in black and white and then in color, and began filling entire canvases with appropriated news images and anonymous photographs of city scenes.

Canyon (FIG. **15-15**) is typical of Rauschenberg's combines. Pieces of printed paper and photographs cover parts of the canvas. Much of the unevenly painted surface consists of pigment roughly applied in a manner reminiscent of de Kooning's work (FIG. **15-5**). A stuffed bald eagle attached to the lower part of the combine spreads its wings as if lifting off in flight toward the viewer. Completing the combine, a pillow dangles from a string attached to a wood stick below the eagle. The artist tilted or turned some of the images sideways, and each overlays part of another image. The compositional confusion may resemble that in a Dada collage, but the parts of Rauschenberg's combines maintain their individuality. The various recognizable images and objects seem unrelated and defy a consistent reading, although Rauschenberg chose all the elements of his combines with specific meanings in mind. For example, he based *Canyon* on a Rembrandt painting of Jupiter in the form of an eagle carrying the boy Ganymede heavenward. The photo in the combine is a reference to the Greek boy, and the hanging pillow is a visual pun on his buttocks.

Roy Lichtenstein As the Pop Art movement matured, the images became more concrete and tightly controlled. American artist ROY LICHTENSTEIN (1923–1997) turned his attention to the comic book as a mainstay of popular culture. In paintings such as *Hopeless* (FIG. **15-16**), Lichtenstein

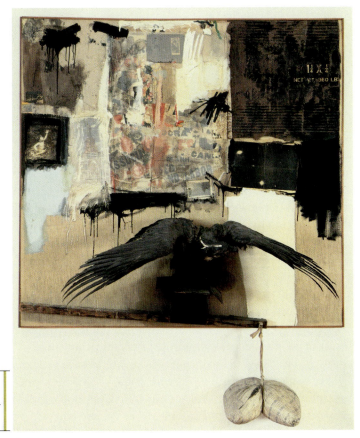

15-15 ROBERT RAUSCHENBERG, *Canyon*, 1959. Oil, pencil, paper, fabric, metal, cardboard box, printed paper, printed reproductions, photograph, wood, paint tube, and mirror on canvas, with oil on eagle, string, and pillow, 6′ 9¾″ × 5′ 10″ × 2′. Sonnabend Collection. © Robert Rauschenberg/Licensed by VAGA, New York.

Rauschenberg's "combines" intersperse painted passages with sculptural elements. *Canyon* incorporates pigment on canvas with pieces of printed paper, photographs, a pillow, and a stuffed eagle.

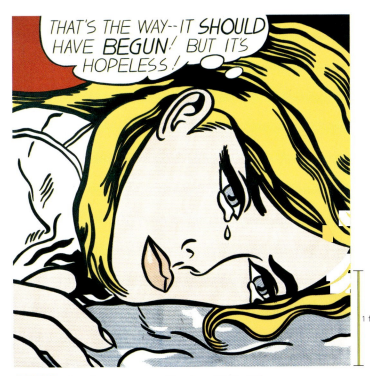

15-16 ROY LICHTENSTEIN, *Hopeless*, 1963. Oil on canvas, 3′ 8″ × 3′ 8″. Kunstmuseum, Basel. © Estate of Roy Lichtenstein.

Comic books appealed to Lichtenstein because they were a mainstay of American popular culture, meant to be read and discarded. The Pop artist, however, immortalized their images on large canvases.

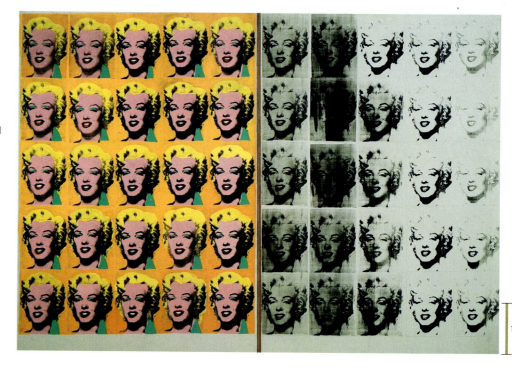

15-17 ANDY WARHOL, *Marilyn Diptych*, 1962. Oil, acrylic, and silk-screen enamel on canvas, each panel 6′ 8″ × 4′ 9″. Tate Gallery, London.

Warhol's repetition of Monroe's face reinforced her status as a consumer product, her glamorous, haunting visage confronting the viewer endlessly, as it did the American public in the aftermath of her death.

1 ft.

excerpted an image from a comic book, a form of entertainment meant to be read and discarded, and immortalized the image on a large canvas. Aside from that modification, Lichtenstein remained remarkably faithful to the original comic-strip image. His subject was one of the melodramatic scenes common to popular romance comic books of the time. Lichtenstein also used the visual vocabulary of the comic strip, with its dark black outlines and unmodulated color areas, and retained the familiar square dimensions. Moreover, his printing technique, *benday dots*, called attention to the mass-produced derivation of the image. Named after its inventor, the newspaper printer Benjamin Day (1810–1889), the benday-dot system involves the modulation of colors through the placement and size of colored dots.

Andy Warhol The quintessential American Pop artist was ANDY WARHOL (1928–1987). An early successful career as a commercial artist and illustrator grounded Warhol in the sensibility and visual rhetoric of advertising and the mass media, knowledge that proved useful for his Pop artworks. So immersed was Warhol in a culture of mass production that he not only produced numerous canvases of the same image but also named his studio "The Factory."

Warhol often produced images of Hollywood celebrities, such as Marilyn Monroe. Like his other paintings, these works emphasize the commodity status of the subjects depicted. Warhol created *Marilyn Diptych* (FIG. **15-17**) in the weeks following the movie star's tragic suicide in August 1962, capitalizing on the media frenzy her death prompted. Warhol selected a publicity photo that provides no insight into the woman herself. Rather, the viewer sees only a mask—the persona the Hollywood myth machine generated. The garish colors and the flat application of paint contribute to that image's masklike quality. The repetition of Monroe's face reinforces her status as a consumer product, her glamor-

ous, haunting visage seemingly confronting the viewer endlessly, as it did the American public in the aftermath of her death. The right half of this work, with its poor registration of pigment, suggests a sequence of film stills, a reference to the realm from which Monroe derived her fame.

Superrealism

Like the Pop artists, the artists associated with *Superrealism* sought a form of artistic communication that was more accessible to the public than the remote, unfamiliar visual language of the postwar abstractionists. The Superrealists expanded Pop Art's iconography in both painting and sculpture by making images in the late 1960s and 1970s involving scrupulous fidelity to optical fact. Because many Superrealists used photographs as sources for their imagery, art historians also refer to this movement as *Photorealism*.

Chuck Close American artist CHUCK CLOSE (b. 1940) is best known for his large-scale Photorealist portraits. For Close, however, realism, rather than an end in itself, was the result of an intellectually rigorous, systematic approach to painting. He based his paintings of the late 1960s and early 1970s, such as his *Big Self-Portrait* (FIG. **15-18**), on photographs, and his main goal was to translate photographic information into painted information. Because he aimed simply to record visual information about his subject's appearance, he deliberately avoided creative compositions, flattering lighting effects, and revealing facial expressions. Not interested in providing insight into the personalities of those portrayed, Close painted anonymous and generic people, mostly friends. By reducing the variables in his paintings (even their canvas size is a constant 9 by 7 feet), Close could focus on employing his methodical presentations of faces, thereby encouraging the viewer to deal with the formal

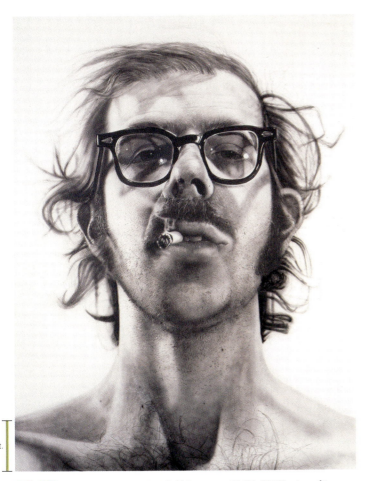

1 ft.

15-18 CHUCK CLOSE, *Big Self-Portrait*, 1967–1968. Acrylic on canvas, 8′ 11″ × 6′ 11″. Walker Art Center, Minneapolis (Art Center Acquisition Fund, 1969).

Close's goal was to translate photographic information into painted information. In his portraits, he deliberately avoided creative compositions, flattering lighting effects, and revealing facial expressions.

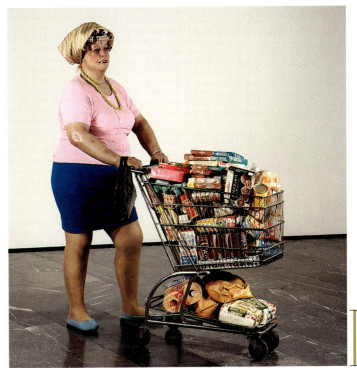

1 ft.

15-19 DUANE HANSON, *Supermarket Shopper*, 1970. Polyester resin and fiberglass polychromed in oil, with clothing, steel cart, and groceries, life-size. Nachfolgeinstitut, Neue Galerie, Sammlung Ludwig, Aachen. © Estate of Duane Hanson/Licensed by VAGA, New York.

Hanson used molds from live models to create his Superrealistic life-size painted plaster sculptures. His aim was to capture the emptiness and loneliness of average Americans in familiar settings.

aspects of his works. Indeed, because of the large scale of the artist's paintings, close scrutiny causes the images to dissolve into abstract patterns.

Duane Hanson Not surprisingly, many sculptors also were Superrealists, including DUANE HANSON (1925–1996), who perfected a casting technique that allowed him to create life-size sculptures that many viewers initially mistake for real people. Hanson first made plaster molds from live models and filled the molds with polyester resin. After the resin hardened, the artist removed the outer molds and cleaned, painted with an *airbrush* (a tool that uses compressed air to spray paint), and decorated the sculptures with wigs, clothes, and other accessories. These works, such as *Supermarket Shopper* (FIG. **15-19**), depict stereotypical average Americans, striking chords with the public precisely because of their familiarity. "The subject matter that I like best," said Hanson, "deals with the familiar lower and middle-class American types of today. To me, the resignation, emptiness and loneliness of their existence captures the true reality of life for these people. . . . I want to achieve a certain tough realism which speaks of the fascinating idiosyncrasies of our time."[6]

PAINTING AND SCULPTURE SINCE 1970

The Pop artists and Superrealists were not the only artists to challenge modernist formalist doctrine. By the 1970s, the range of art produced in both traditional and new media in reaction to Abstract Expressionism, Minimalism, and other formalist movements had become so diverse that only a broad general term can describe the phenomenon: *postmodernism*. There is no agreement about the definition of postmodern art. Some scholars assert that a major characteristic of postmodernism is the erosion of the boundaries between high culture and popular culture—a separation Clement Greenberg and the modernists had staunchly defended. With the appearance of Pop Art, that separation became more difficult to maintain. For many recent artists, postmodernism involves examining the process by which meaning is generated and the negotiation or dialogue that transpires between viewers and artworks. This kind of examination of the nature of art parallels the literary field of study known as critical theory. Critical theorists view art and architecture, as well as literature and the other humanities, as a culture's intellectual products, or "constructs." These constructs unconsciously suppress or conceal the true premises that inform the culture, primarily the values of those politically in control. Thus, cultural products function in an ideological capacity, obscuring, for example, racist or sexist attitudes. When revealed by analysis, the facts behind these constructs, according to critical theorists, contribute to a more substantial understanding of artworks, buildings, books, and the overall culture.

Many critical theorists use an analytical strategy called *deconstruction*, after a method developed in the 1960s and 1970s by French intellectuals, notably Michel Foucault (1926–1984) and Jacques Derrida (1930–2004). For those employing deconstruction, all cultural constructs are "texts." Acknowledging the lack of fixed or uniform meanings in these texts, critical theorists accept a variety of interpretations as valid. The enterprise of deconstruction is to reveal the contradictions and instabilities of these texts, whether written or visual. With primarily political and social aims, deconstructive analysis has the ultimate goal of effecting political and social change. Accordingly, critical theorists who employ this approach seek to uncover—to deconstruct—the facts of power, privilege, and prejudice underlying the practices and institutions of any given culture. Critical theorists do not agree upon any philosophy or analytical method, because in principle they oppose firm definitions. They do share a healthy suspicion of all traditional truth claims and value standards, all hierarchical authority and institutions. For them, deconstruction means destabilizing established meanings, definitions, and interpretations while encouraging subjectivity and individual differences.

Certainly, one thing all postmodern artists have in common is a self-consciousness about their place in the historical continuum of art. Consequently, many of them resurrect artistic traditions to comment on and reinterpret those styles or idioms. However defined, postmodern art comprises a dizzying array of artworks in different media. Only a representative sample can be presented here.

Neo-Expressionism

One of the first coherent movements to emerge during the postmodern era was *Neo-Expressionism*. This international movement's name reflects postmodern artists' interest in reexamining earlier art production and connects this art to the powerful, intense works of the German Expressionists (see Chapter 14) and the Abstract Expressionists.

Anselm Kiefer German artist ANSELM KIEFER (b. 1945) has produced some of the most lyrical and engaging Neo-Expressionist works. His paintings, such as *Nigredo* (FIG. 15-20), are monumental in scale, recall Abstract Expressionist canvases, and draw the viewer to their textured surfaces, made more complex by the addition of materials such as straw. It is not merely the impressive physicality of Kiefer's paintings that accounts for the impact of his work, however. His images function on a mythological or metaphorical level, as well as on a historically specific one. Kiefer's works of the 1970s and 1980s often involve a reexamination of German history, particularly the painful Nazi era of 1920–1945, and evoke the feeling of despair. Kiefer believes Germany's participation in World War II and the Holocaust left permanent scars on the souls of the German people and on the souls of all humanity. *Nigredo* ("blackening") pulls the viewer into an expansive landscape depicted using Renaissance perspectival principles. This landscape, however, is far from pastoral or carefully cultivated. Rather, it appears bleak and charred. Although it makes no specific reference to the Holocaust, this incinerated landscape indirectly alludes to the horrors of that tragedy. More generally, the blackness of the landscape may refer to the notion of alchemical change or transformation, a concept of great interest to Kiefer. Black is one of the four symbolic colors of the alchemist—a color that refers both to death and to the molten, chaotic state of substances

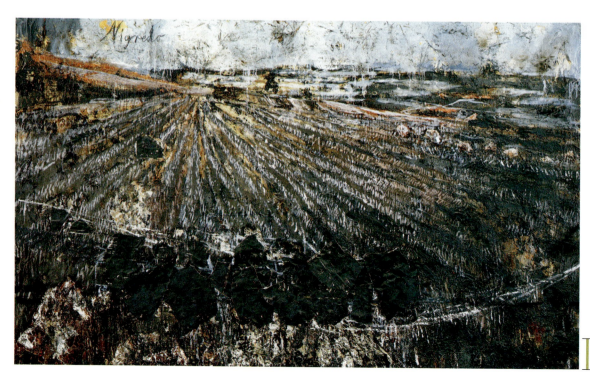

15-20 ANSELM KIEFER, *Nigredo*, 1984. Oil paint on photosensitized fabric, acrylic emulsion, straw, shellac, and relief paint on paper, 11′ × 18′. Philadelphia Museum of Art, Philadelphia (gift of Friends of the Philadelphia Museum of Art).

Kiefer's paintings have thickly encrusted surfaces incorporating materials such as straw. Here, the German artist used perspective to pull the viewer into an incinerated landscape alluding to the Holocaust.

1 ft.

Judy Chicago on *The Dinner Party*

One of the acknowledged masterpieces of feminist art is Judy Chicago's *The Dinner Party* (FIG. **15-21**), which required a team of nearly 400 to create and assemble. In 1979, Chicago published a book explaining the genesis and symbolism of the work.

> [By 1974] I had discarded [my original] idea of painting a hundred abstract portraits on plates, each paying tribute to a different historic female figure. . . . In my research I realized over and over again that women's achievements had been left out of history . . . . My new idea was to try to symbolize this. . . . [I thought] about putting the plates on a table with silver, glasses, napkins, and tablecloths, and over the next year and a half the concept of *The Dinner Party* slowly evolved. I began to think about the piece as a reinterpretation of the Last Supper from the point of view of women, who, throughout history, had prepared the meals and set the table. In my "Last Supper," however, the women would be the honored guests. Their representation in the form of plates set on the table would express the way women had been confined, and the piece would thus reflect both women's achievements and their oppression. . . . My goal with *The Dinner Party* was . . . to forge a new kind of art expressing women's experience. . . . [It] seemed appropriate to relate our history through art, particularly through techniques traditionally associated with women—china-painting and needlework.*

* Judy Chicago, "The Dinner Party": *A Symbol of Our Heritage* (Garden City, N.Y.: Anchor Press, 1979), 11–12.

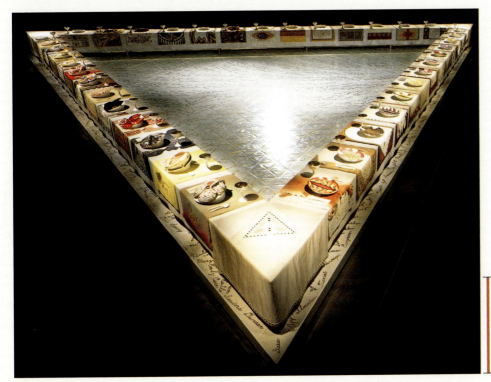

15-21 JUDY CHICAGO, *The Dinner Party*, 1979. Multimedia, including ceramics and stitchery, 48′ long on each side. Brooklyn Museum, Brooklyn.

Chicago's *Dinner Party* honors 39 women from antiquity to the 20th century. The triangular form and the materials she chose—painted china and fabric—are traditionally associated with women.

10 ft.

broken down by fire. The alchemist, however, focuses on the transformation of substances, and thus the emphasis on blackness is not absolute but can also be perceived as part of a process of renewal and redemption. Kiefer thus has imbued his work with a deep symbolic meaning that, when combined with the intriguing visual quality of his parched, congealed surfaces, results in paintings of enduring power.

Feminist Art

With the renewed interest in representation that Pop artists and Superrealists introduced in the 1960s and 1970s, painters and sculptors once again began to embrace the persuasive power of art to communicate with a wide audience. In recent decades, artists have investigated more insistently the dynamics of power and privilege, especially in relation to issues of gender, race, and ethnicity.

Judy Chicago In the 1970s, the feminist movement focused public attention on the history of women and their place in society. JUDY CHICAGO (Judy Cohen, b. 1939) cofounded the Feminist Art Program in California and sought to educate the public about women's role in history and the fine arts. She aimed to establish a respect for women and their art, to forge a new kind of art expressing women's experiences, and to find a way to make that art accessible to a large audience. Chicago developed a personal painting style that consciously included abstract organic vaginal images. In the early 1970s, she began planning an ambitious piece, *The Dinner Party* (FIG. **15-21**), using craft techniques (such as china painting and stitchery) traditionally practiced by women, to celebrate the achievements and contributions women made throughout history (see "Judy Chicago on *The Dinner Party*," page 431). She originally conceived the work as a feminist Last Supper for 13 "honored guests," as in the New Testament, but all women. There are also 13 women in a witches' coven, and Chicago's *Dinner Party* refers to witchcraft and the worship of the Mother Goddess. But because Chicago had uncovered so many worthy women in the course of her research, she expanded the number of guests threefold to 39 and placed them around a triangular table 48 feet long on each side. The triangular form refers to the ancient symbol for both woman and the Goddess. The notion of a dinner party also alludes to women's traditional role as homemakers.

The Dinner Party rests on a white tile floor inscribed with the names of 999 additional women of achievement to signify that the accomplishments of the 39 honored guests rest on a foundation other women laid. Among the "invited" women at the table are Georgia O'Keeffe (FIG. I-1), the Egyptian pharaoh Hatshepsut (FIG. 1-29), the British writer Virginia Woolf, the Native American guide Sacajawea, and the American suffragist Susan B. Anthony. Each woman's place has identical eating utensils and a goblet but a unique oversized porcelain plate and a long place mat or table runner covered with imagery that reflects significant facts about that woman's life and culture. The plates range from simple concave shapes with china-painted imagery to dishes whose sculptured three-dimensional designs almost seem to struggle to free themselves. The designs on each plate incorporate both butterfly and vulval motifs—the butterfly as the ancient symbol of liberation and the vulva as the symbol of female sexuality. Each table runner combines traditional needlework techniques, including needlepoint, embroidery, crochet, beading, patchwork, and appliqué.

Cindy Sherman Early attempts at dealing with feminist issues in art tended toward essentialism, emphasizing universal differences—either biological or experiential—between women and men. More recent discussions have gravitated toward the notion of gender as a socially constructed concept, and an extremely unstable one at that. Identity is multifaceted and changeable, making the discussion of feminist issues more challenging. Consideration of the many variables, however, results in a more complex understanding of gender roles. American artist CINDY SHERMAN (b. 1954) addresses in her work the way much of Western art presents female beauty for the enjoyment of the "male gaze," a primary focus of contemporary feminist theory. Since 1977, Sherman has produced a series of more than 80 black-and-white photographs titled *Untitled Film Stills*. She got the idea for the series after examining soft-core pornography magazines and noting the stereotypical ways they depicted women. She decided to produce her own series of photographs, designing, acting in, directing, and photographing the works. In so doing, Sherman took control of her own image and constructed her own identity, a primary feminist concern. In works from the series, such as *Untitled Film Still #35* (FIG.

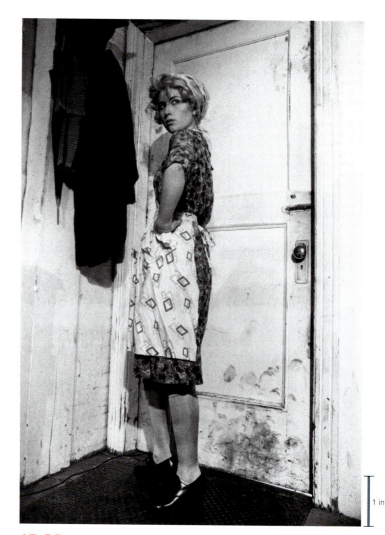

15-22 CINDY SHERMAN, *Untitled Film Still #35*, 1979. Gelatin silverprint, 10″ × 8″. Private collection.

Sherman assumed roles and posed for 80 photographs resembling film stills in which she addressed the way women have been presented in Western art for the enjoyment of the "male gaze."

15-22), Sherman appears, often in costume and wig, in a photograph that seems to be a film still. Most of the images in this series recall popular film genres but are sufficiently generic that the viewer cannot relate them to specific movies. Sherman often reveals the constructed nature of these images with the shutter release cable she holds in her hand to take the pictures. (The cord runs across the floor in #35.) Although the artist is still the object of the viewer's gaze in these images, the identity is one she alone chose to assume.

Barbara Kruger Another artist who has explored the male gaze and the culturally constructed notion of gender in her art is BARBARA KRUGER (b. 1945). Kruger's work draws on her early training as a graphic designer for *Mademoiselle* magazine. *Untitled* (*Your Gaze Hits the Side of My Face*; FIG. 15-23) incorporates layout techniques the mass media use to sell consumer goods. Although Kruger favored the reassuringly familiar format and look of advertising, her goal was to subvert the typical use of commercial imagery. Rather, she aimed to expose the deceptiveness of the media messages the viewer complacently absorbs. Kruger wanted to undermine

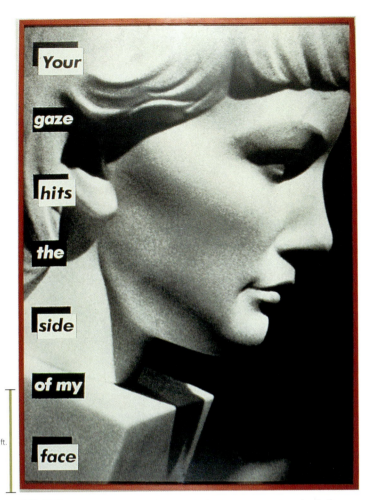

15-23 Barbara Kruger, *Untitled (Your Gaze Hits the Side of My Face)*, 1981. Photograph, red painted frame, 4′ 7″ × 3′ 5″. Courtesy Mary Boone Gallery, New York.

Kruger explored the male gaze in her art. Using the layout techniques of mass media, she constructed this huge word-and-photograph collage to challenge culturally constructed notions of gender.

THE ADVANTAGES OF BEING A WOMAN ARTIST:

Working without the pressure of success
Not having to be in shows with men
Having an escape from the art world in your 4 free-lance jobs
Knowing your career might pick up after you're eighty
Being reassured that whatever kind of art you make it will be labeled feminine
Not being stuck in a tenured teaching position
Seeing your ideas live on in the work of others
Having the opportunity to choose between career and motherhood
Not having to choke on those big cigars or paint in Italian suits
Having more time to work when your mate dumps you for someone younger
Being included in revised versions of art history
Not having to undergo the embarrassment of being called a genius
Getting your picture in the art magazines wearing a gorilla suit

A PUBLIC SERVICE MESSAGE FROM **GUERRILLA GIRLS** CONSCIENCE OF THE ART WORLD

1 in.

15-24 Guerrilla Girls, *The Advantages of Being a Woman Artist*, 1988. Offset print, 1′ 5″ × 1′ 10″. Collection of the artists.

The anonymous Guerrilla Girls wear gorilla masks in public performances and produce posters in which they call attention to injustice in the art world, especially what they perceive as sexism and racism.

the myths—particularly those about women—the media constantly reinforce. Her huge (often 4 by 6 feet) word-and-photograph collages challenge the cultural attitudes embedded in commercial advertising. Kruger overlaid a photograph of a classically beautiful sculpted head of a woman with a vertical row of text composed of eight words. The words cannot be taken in with a single glance, and reading them is a staccato exercise, with a cumulative quality that delays understanding and intensifies the meaning (rather like reading a series of roadside billboards from a speeding car). Kruger's use of text in her work is significant. Many cultural theorists have asserted that language is one of the most powerful vehicles for internalizing stereotypes and conditioned roles.

Guerrilla Girls The New York–based Guerrilla Girls, formed in 1984, bill themselves as the "conscience of the art world." This group sees its duty as calling attention to injustice in the art world, especially what it perceives as the sexist and racist orientation of the major art institutions. The women who are members of the Guerrilla Girls protect their identities by wearing gorilla masks in public. They employ guerrilla tactics by demonstrating in public, staging performances, and placing posters and flyers in public locations. One poster that reflects the group's agenda facetiously lists "the advantages of being a woman artist" (FIG. **15-24**). In fact, the list itemizes for readers the numerous obstacles women artists face in the contemporary art world. The Guerrilla Girls hope their publicizing of these obstacles will result in improvements in the situation for women artists.

Other Social and Political Art

Feminist issues are by no means the only social and political concerns that contemporary artists have addressed in their work. Race and ethnicity are among the other pressing issues that have given rise to important artworks during the past few decades.

Kiki Smith American sculptor Kiki Smith (b. 1954) has explored the question of who controls the human body, an interest that grew out of her training as an emergency medical service technician in New York City. Smith, however, also wants to reveal the socially constructed nature of the body, and she encourages the viewer to consider how external forces shape people's perceptions of their bodies. In *Untitled* (FIG. **15-25**), for example, Smith dramatically departed from conventional representations of the body, both in art and in the media. She suspended two life-size wax figures, one male and one female, both nude, from metal stands, and marked each of the sculptures with long white drips—body fluids running from the woman's breasts and down the man's leg. According to Smith:

Most of the functions of the body are hidden . . . from society. . . . [W]e separate our bodies from our lives. But, when

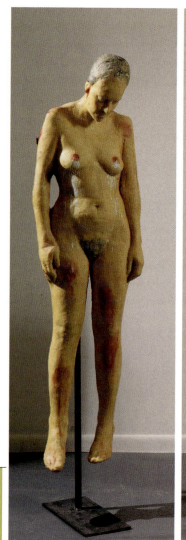
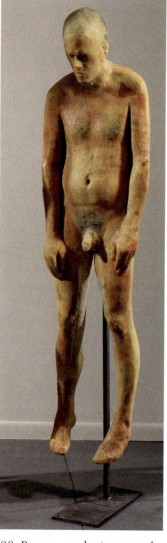

15-25 KIKI SMITH, *Untitled*, 1990. Beeswax and microcrystalline wax figures on metal stands, female figure installed height 6′ 1½″; male figure 6′ 4 15/16″. Whitney Museum of American Art, New York (purchased with funds from the Painting and Sculpture Committee).

Asking "who controls the body?" Kiki Smith sculpted two life-size wax figures of a nude man and woman with body fluids running from the woman's breasts and down the man's leg.

people are dying, they are losing control of their bodies. That loss of function can seem humiliating and frightening. But, on the other hand, you can look at it as a kind of liberation of the body. It seems like a nice metaphor—a way to think about the social—that people lose control despite the many agendas of different ideologies in society, which are trying to control the body(ies) . . . medicine, religion, law, etc. Just thinking about control—who has control of the body? . . . Does the mind have control of the body? Does the social?[7]

Faith Ringgold Other artists, reflecting their own identities and backgrounds, have used their art to address issues associated with African American women. Inspired by the civil rights movement, FAITH RINGGOLD (b. 1930) produced numerous works in the 1960s that provided incisive commentary on the realities of racial prejudice. She increasingly incorporated references to gender as well and, in the 1970s, turned to fabric as the predominant material in her art.

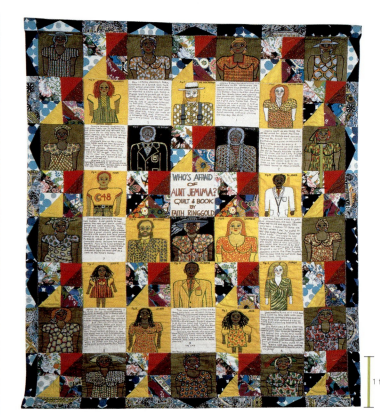

15-26 FAITH RINGGOLD, *Who's Afraid of Aunt Jemima?* 1983. Acrylic on canvas with fabric borders, quilted, 7′ 6″ × 6′ 8″. Private collection.

In this quilt, a medium associated with women, Ringgold presented a tribute to her mother that also addresses African American culture and the struggles of women to overcome oppression.

Using fabric allowed her to make more pointed reference to the domestic sphere, traditionally associated with women, and to collaborate with her mother, Willi Posey, a fashion designer. After her mother's death in 1981, Ringgold created *Who's Afraid of Aunt Jemima?* (FIG. **15-26**), a quilt composed of dyed, painted, and pieced fabric. A moving tribute to her mother, this work combines the personal and the political. The quilt includes a narrative—the witty story of the family of Aunt Jemima, most familiar as the stereotypical black "mammy" but here a successful African American business-woman. Ringgold conveyed this narrative using both text (written in black dialect) and embroidered portraits interspersed with traditional patterned squares. This work, while resonating with autobiographical references, also speaks to the larger issues of the history of African American culture and the struggles of women to overcome oppression.

Chris Ofili Another contemporary artist who has explored his ethnic and racial heritage in his art is CHRIS OFILI (b. 1968). One theme Ofili has treated is religion, interpreted through the eyes of a British-born Catholic of Nigerian descent. Ofili's *The Holy Virgin Mary* (FIG. **15-27**) depicts Mary in simplified form and floating in an indeterminate space. The artist employed brightly colored pigments, applied to the canvas in multiple layers of beadlike dots (inspired by images from ancient caves in Zimbabwe). Surrounding the

Public Funding of Controversial Art

Although art can be beautiful and uplifting, throughout history art has also challenged and offended. Since the early 1980s, a number of heated controversies about art have surfaced in the United States. There have been many calls to remove the "offensive" works from public view and, in reaction, accusations of censorship. The central questions in all cases have been whether there are limits to what art can appropriately be exhibited, and whether governmental authorities have the right to monitor and pass judgment on creative endeavors. A related question is whether the acceptability of a work should be a criterion in determining the public funding of art.

Two exhibits in 1989 placed the National Endowment for the Arts (NEA), a federal agency charged with distributing funds to support the arts, squarely in the middle of this debate. One of the exhibitions, devoted to recipients of the Awards for the Visual Arts (AVA), took place at the Southeastern Center for Contemporary Art in North Carolina. Among the award winners was Andres Serrano (b. 1950), whose *Piss Christ*, a photograph of a crucifix submerged in urine, sparked an uproar. Reverend Donald Wildmon, head of the American Family Association, expressed outrage that this work was in an exhibition funded by the NEA and the Equitable Life Assurance Society (a sponsor of the AVA). He demanded that *Piss Christ* be removed and launched a letter-writing campaign that led Equitable Life to cancel its sponsorship of the awards. To staunch conservatives, this exhibition, along with the show *Robert Mapplethorpe: The Perfect Moment,* served as evidence of cultural depravity and immorality, which they insisted should not receive public funding. Mapplethorpe (1946–1989) was a photographer well known for his elegant, spare photographs of flowers and vegetables as well as his erotic, homosexually oriented images. As a result of media furor over *The Perfect Moment,* the director of the Corcoran Museum of Art canceled the scheduled exhibition of this traveling show. But the director of the Contemporary Arts Center in Cincinnati decided to mount the show. The government indicted him on charges of obscenity, but a jury acquitted him six months later.

These controversies intensified public criticism of the NEA and its funding practices. The next year, the head of the NEA, John Frohnmayer, vetoed grants for four lesbian, gay, or feminist performance artists—Karen Finley, John Fleck, Holly Hughes, and Tim Miller—who became known as the "NEA Four." Infuriated by what they perceived as overt censorship, the artists filed suit, eventually settling the case and winning reinstatement of their grants. Congress responded by dramatically reducing the NEA's budget, and the agency no longer awards grants or fellowships to individual artists.

Controversies have also erupted on the municipal level. In 1999, Rudolph Giuliani, then mayor of New York, joined the protest over the inclusion of several artworks in the exhibition *Sensation: Young British Artists from the Saatchi Collection* at the Brooklyn Museum. Chris Ofili's *The Holy Virgin Mary* (FIG. 15-27) became the flashpoint for public furor. Denouncing the show as "sick stuff," the mayor threatened to cut off all city subsidies to the museum.

Art that seeks to unsettle and challenge is critical to the cultural, political, and psychological life of a society. The regularity with which provoca-

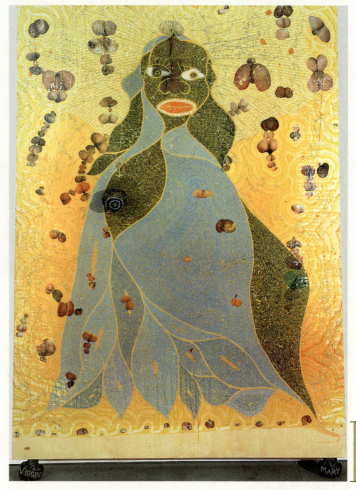

15-27 CHRIS OFILI, *The Holy Virgin Mary*, 1996. Paper collage, oil paint, glitter, polyester resin, map pins, elephant dung on linen, 7′ 11″ × 5′ 11$\frac{5}{16}$″. Saatchi Collection, London.

Ofili, a British-born Catholic of Nigerian descent, represented the Virgin Mary with African elephant dung on one breast and surrounded by genitalia and buttocks. The painting produced a public outcry.

tive art raises controversy suggests that it operates at the intersection of two competing principles: free speech and artistic expression on the one hand and a reluctance to impose images upon an audience that finds them repugnant or offensive on the other. These controversies demonstrate, beyond doubt, the enduring power of art.

Virgin are tiny images of genitalia and buttocks cut from pornographic magazines, which, to the artist, parallel the putti that often surround Mary in Renaissance paintings. Another reference to Ofili's African heritage surfaces in the clumps of elephant dung—one attached to the Virgin's breast, and two more on which the canvas rests, serving as supports. The

dung allowed Ofili to incorporate Africa into his work in a literal way. Still, he wants the viewer to move beyond the cultural associations of the materials and see those materials in new ways. Not surprisingly, *The Holy Virgin Mary* elicited strong reactions from the public and government officials (see "Public Funding of Controversial Art," above).

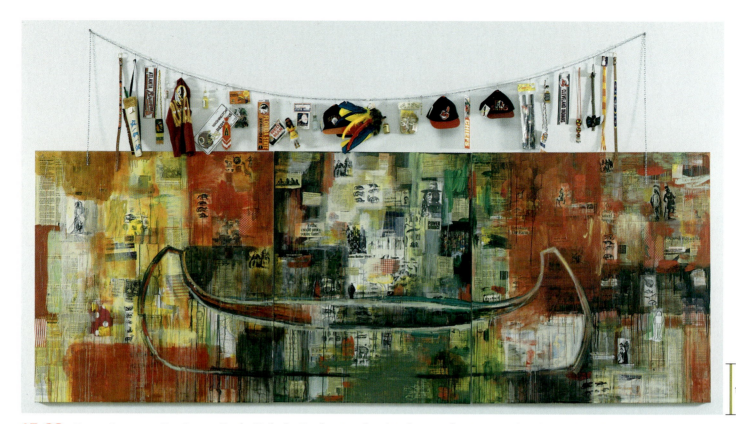

15-28 JAUNE QUICK-TO-SEE SMITH, *Trade (Gifts for Trading Land with White People)*, 1992. Oil and mixed media on canvas, 5′ × 14′ 2″. Chrysler Museum of Art, Norfolk.

Quick-to-See Smith's mixed-media canvases are full of references to her Native American identity. Some of the elements refer to the controversy surrounding sports teams that have American Indian names.

Jaune Quick-to-See Smith Another contemporary artist who has explored the politics of identity is JAUNE QUICK-TO-SEE SMITH (b. 1940), a Native American artist raised on the Flatrock Reservation in Montana. Quick-to-See Smith's heritage has always informed her art, and her concern about the invisibility of Native American artists has led her to organize exhibitions of their art. Yet she has acknowledged a wide range of influences, including "pictogram forms from Europe, the Amur [the river between Russia and China], the Americas; color from beadwork, parfleches [hide cases], the landscape; paint application from Cobra art, New York expressionism, primitive art; composition from Kandinsky, Klee or Byzantine art."[8]

Quick-to-See Smith's art challenges stereotypes and unacknowledged assumptions. *Trade (Gifts for Trading Land with White People;* FIG. **15-28**) is a large-scale painting with collage elements and attached objects, reminiscent of a Rauschenberg combine (FIG. 15-15). The painting's central image, a canoe, appears in an expansive field painted in loose Abstract Expressionist fashion and covered with clippings from Native American newspapers. Above the painting, as if hung from a clothesline, is an array of objects. These include Native American artifacts, such as beaded belts and feather headdresses, and contemporary sports memorabilia from teams with American Indian–derived names—the Cleveland Indians, Atlanta Braves, and Washington Redskins. The inclusion of these contemporary objects immediately recalls the vocal opposition to those names and to acts such as the Braves' "tomahawk chop." Quick-to-See Smith uses the past to comment on the present.

Magdalena Abakanowicz The stoic, everyday toughness of the human spirit has been the subject of the Polish fiber artist MAGDALENA ABAKANOWICZ (b. 1930). A leader in the recent exploration in sculpture of the expressive powers of weaving techniques, Abakanowicz gained fame with experimental freestanding pieces in both abstract and figural modes. For Abakanowicz, fiber materials are deeply symbolic:

> I see fiber as the basic element constructing the organic world on our planet, as the greatest mystery of our environment. It is from fiber that all living organisms are built—the tissues of plants and ourselves. . . . Fabric is our covering and our attire. Made with our hands, it is a record of our souls.[9]

To all of her work, Abakanowicz brought the experiences of her early life as a member of an aristocratic family disturbed by the dislocations of World War II and its aftermath. Best known for her works based on human forms, she multiplies each form for exhibition in groups as symbols for the individual in society, lost in the crowd yet retaining some distinctiveness. This impression is especially powerful in *80 Backs* (FIG. **15-29**). Abakanowicz made each piece by pressing layers of natural organic fibers into a plaster mold. Every

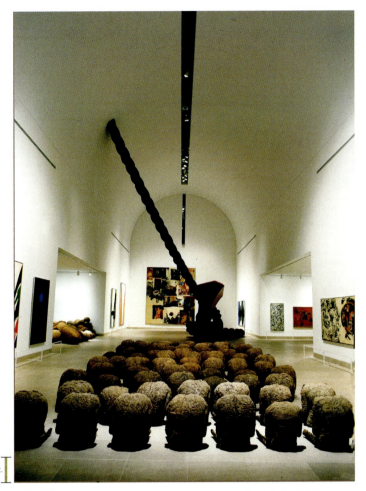

15-29 MAGDALENA ABAKANOWICZ, *80 Backs*, 1976–1980. Burlap and resin, each 2′ 3″ high. Museum of Modern Art, Dallas. © Magdalena Abakanowicz/Licensed by VAGA, New York.

Polish fiber artist Abakanowicz explored the stoic, everyday toughness of the human spirit in this group of nearly identical sculptures that serve as symbols of distinctive individuals lost in the crowd.

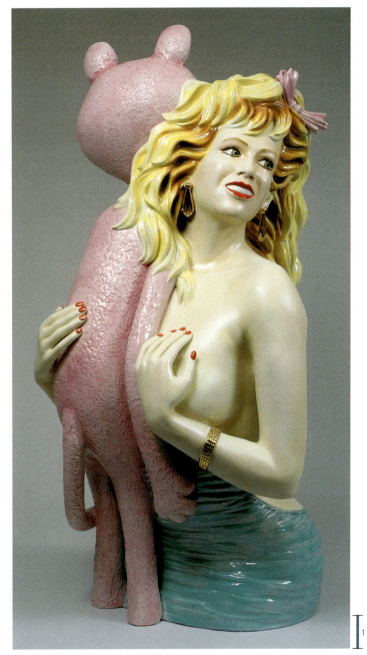

15-30 JEFF KOONS, *Pink Panther*, 1988. Porcelain, 3′ 5″ × 1′ 8½″ × 1′ 7″. Museum of Contemporary Art, Chicago (Gerald S. Elliot Collection).

In the 1980s, Koons created sculptures that highlight everything wrong with contemporary American consumer culture. In this work, he intertwined a centerfold nude and a cartoon character.

sculpture depicts the slumping shoulders, back, and arms of a figure of indeterminate sex and rests legless directly on the floor. The repeated pose of the figures in *80 Backs* suggests meditation, submission, and anticipation. Although made from a single mold, the figures achieve a touching sense of individuality because each assumed a slightly different posture as the material dried and because the artist imprinted a different pattern of fiber texture on each.

Jeff Koons While many contemporary artists have pursued personally meaningful agendas in their art, other have addressed society-wide concerns, for example postmodern commodity culture. American JEFF KOONS (b. 1955) first became prominent in the art world for a series of works in the early 1980s that involved exhibiting common purchased objects such as vacuum cleaners. Clearly following in the footsteps of artists such as Marcel Duchamp (FIG. 14-13), Koons made no attempt to manipulate or alter the objects. More recently, he has produced porcelain sculptures, such as *Pink Panther* (FIG. 15-30), in which he continued his immersion in contempo-

rary mass culture by intertwining a magazine centerfold nude with a famous cartoon character. Koons reinforced the trite and kitschy nature of this imagery by titling the exhibition of which this work was a part *The Banality Show*. Some art critics have argued that Koons and his work instruct viewers because both artist and work serve as the most visible symbols of everything wrong with contemporary American society. Whether or not this is true, Koons's prominence in the art world indicates that he, like Andy Warhol before him, has developed an acute understanding of the dynamics of consumer culture.

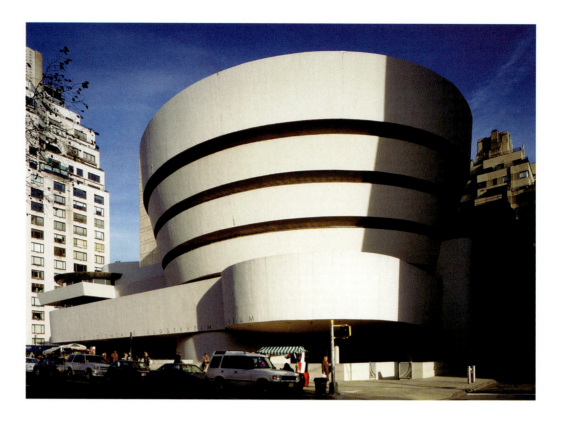

15-31 FRANK LLOYD WRIGHT, Solomon R. Guggenheim Museum (looking northeast), New York, 1943–1959.

Using reinforced concrete almost as a sculptor might use resilient clay, Wright designed a snail shell–shaped museum with a winding interior ramp for the display of artworks along its gently inclined path (FIG. 15-1).

ARCHITECTURE AND SITE-SPECIFIC ART

Some of the leading architects of the first half of the 20th century, most notably Frank Lloyd Wright (FIG. 14-40), Le Corbusier (FIG. 14-39), and Ludwig Mies van der Rohe (FIG. 14-38), concluded their long, productive careers in the postwar period. At the same time, younger architects rose to international prominence, some working in the modernist idiom but others taking architectural design in new directions, including postmodernism and Deconstructivism. Still, one common denominator exists in the diversity of contemporary architectural design: the breaking down of national boundaries, with major architects pursuing projects on several continents, often simultaneously.

Modernism

In parallel with the progressive movement toward formal abstraction in postwar painting and sculpture, modernist architects explored formalist simplicity and designed buildings that adhered to a rigid geometry as well as buildings that featured organic sculptural qualities.

Frank Lloyd Wright The last great building Frank Lloyd Wright designed was the Solomon R. Guggenheim Museum (FIG. 15-31) in New York City. Using reinforced concrete almost as a sculptor might use resilient clay, Wright designed a structure inspired by the spiral of a snail's shell. The shape of the shell expands toward the top, and a winding interior ramp (FIG. 15-1) spirals to connect the gallery

bays. A skylight strip embedded in the museum's outer wall provides illumination to the ramp, which visitors can stroll up or down, viewing the artworks displayed along the gently sloping pathway. Thick walls and the solid organic shape give the building, outside and inside, the sense of turning in on itself, and the long interior viewing area opening onto a 90-foot central well of space creates a sheltered environment, secure from the bustling city outside.

Le Corbusier Completed in 1955 at Ronchamp, France, Le Corbusier's Notre-Dame-du-Haut (FIG. 15-32) is an organic fusion of architecture and sculpture, and a testament to the boundless creativity of this great architect. The monumental impression of this small pilgrimage chapel seen from afar is deceptive. Although one massive exterior wall contains a pulpit facing a spacious outdoor area for large-scale open-air services on holy days, the interior holds at most 200 people. The intimate scale, stark and heavy walls, and mysterious illumination (jewel tones cast from the deeply recessed stained-glass windows) give this space an aura reminiscent of a sacred cave or a medieval monastery.

Notre-Dame-du-Haut's structure may look free-form to the untrained eye, but Le Corbusier based it, like a medieval cathedral, on an underlying mathematical system. The builders formed the fabric from a frame of steel and metal mesh, which they sprayed with concrete and painted white, except for two interior private chapel niches with colored walls and the roof, which Le Corbusier wished to have darken naturally with the passage of time. The preliminary sketches for the building indicate Le Corbusier linked the design with the shape of praying hands, with the wings of a dove (representing

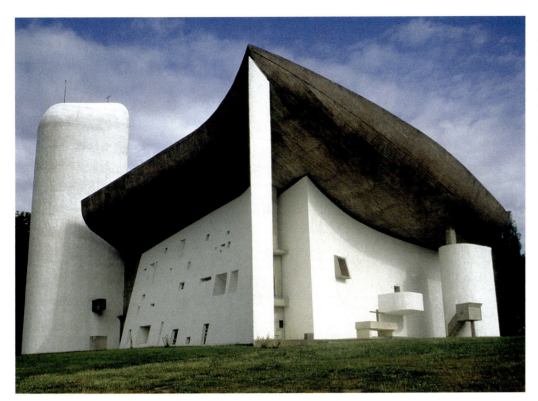

The organic forms of Le Corbusier's mountaintop chapel present a fusion of architecture and sculpture. The architect based the shapes on praying hands, a dove's wings, and a ship's prow.

both peace and the Holy Spirit), and with the prow of a ship (a reminder that the Latin word for the main gathering place in Christian churches is *nave*, meaning "ship"). The artist envisioned that in these powerful sculptural solids and voids, human beings could find new values—new interpretations of their sacred beliefs and of their natural environments.

Mies van der Rohe In contrast to the sculpturesque idiom of Wright and Le Corbusier, other modernist architects created massive, sleek, and geometrically rigid buildings, following Mies van der Rohe's contention that "less is more." Many of these more "Minimalist" designs are heroic presences in the urban landscape that effectively symbolize the giant corporations that often inhabit them. The "purest" example of these corporate skyscrapers is the rectilinear glass-and-bronze Seagram Building (FIG. **15-33**) in Manhattan, designed by Mies van der Rohe and American architect PHILIP JOHNSON (1906–2005). By the mid-1950s, the steel-and-glass towers pioneered by Louis Sullivan (FIG. **13-20**) and carried further by Mies van der Rohe (FIG. **14-38**) had become a familiar sight in cities all over the world. Appealing in its structural logic and clarity, the style, easily imitated, quickly became the norm for postwar commercial high-rise buildings. The architects of the Seagram Building deliberately designed it as a thin shaft, leaving the front quarter of its midtown site as an open pedestrian plaza. The tower appears to rise from the pavement on stilts. Glass walls even surround the recessed lobby. The building's recessed structural elements make it appear to have a glass skin, interrupted only by the thin strips of bronze anchoring the windows. The bronze strips and the amber glass windows give the tower a richness found in few of its neighbors.

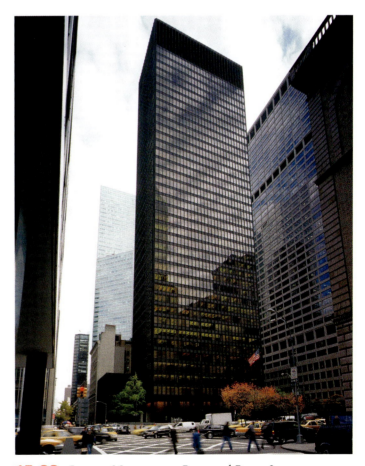

15-33 LUDWIG MIES VAN DER ROHE and PHILIP JOHNSON, Seagram Building, New York, 1956–1958.

Massive, sleek, and geometrically rigid, this modernist skyscraper has a bronze and glass skin that masks its concrete and steel frame. The giant corporate tower appears to rise from the pavement on stilts.

Maya Lin's Vietnam Veterans Memorial

The history of Maya Lin's Vietnam Veterans Memorial (FIG. 15-34) provides dramatic testimony to this monument's power. In 1981 a jury of architects, sculptors, and landscape architects selected Lin's design in a blind competition. Conceivably, the jurors not only found her proposal compelling but also thought her design's serene simplicity would be the least likely to provoke controversy. Nevertheless, the choice incited heated responses. Even the wall's color came under attack. One veteran charged that black is "the universal color of shame, sorrow and degradation in all races, all societies worldwide."* The sharpest protests, however, concerned the form and siting of the monument. Because of the stark contrast between the massive white memorials (the Washington Monument and the Lincoln Memorial) bracketing Lin's sunken wall, some people saw her Minimalist design as minimizing the Vietnam War and, by extension, the efforts of those who fought in the conflict. Lin herself, however, described the wall as follows:

> The Vietnam Veterans Memorial is not an object inserted into the earth but a work formed from the act of cutting open the earth and polishing the earth's surface—dematerializing the stone to pare surface, creating an interface between the world of the light and the quieter world beyond the names.[†]

Due to the vocal opposition, a compromise was necessary to ensure the memorial's completion. The Commission of Fine Arts, the federal group overseeing the project, commissioned an additional memorial in 1983: a larger-than-life-size realistic bronze sculpture by Frederick Hart (1943–1999) of three soldiers, armed and in uniform, which now stands approximately 120 feet from Lin's wall. Several years later, a group of nurses won approval for a sculpture honoring women's service in the Vietnam War. The seven-foot-tall bronze statue by Glenna Goodacre (b. 1939) depicts three female figures, one cradling a wounded soldier in her arms. Since 1993 the work has occupied a site about 300 feet south of the Lin memorial.

Whether celebrated or condemned, the Vietnam Veterans Memorial generates dramatic responses. Commonly, visitors react very emotionally, even those who know none of the soldiers named on the monument. The polished granite surface prompts individual soul-searching—viewers see themselves reflected among the names. Many visitors leave mementos at the foot of the wall in memory of loved ones they lost in the Vietnam War or make rubbings from the incised names. Arguably, much of this memorial's power derives from its Minimalist simplicity. It does not dictate response and therefore successfully encourages personal exploration.

* Elizabeth Hess, "A Tale of Two Memorials," *Art in America* 71, no. 4 (April 1983), 122.
[†] Excerpt from an unpublished 1995 lecture, quoted in Kristine Stiles and Peter Selz, *Theories and Documents of Contemporary Art: A Sourcebook of Artists' Writings* (Berkeley and Los Angeles: University of California Press, 1996), 525.

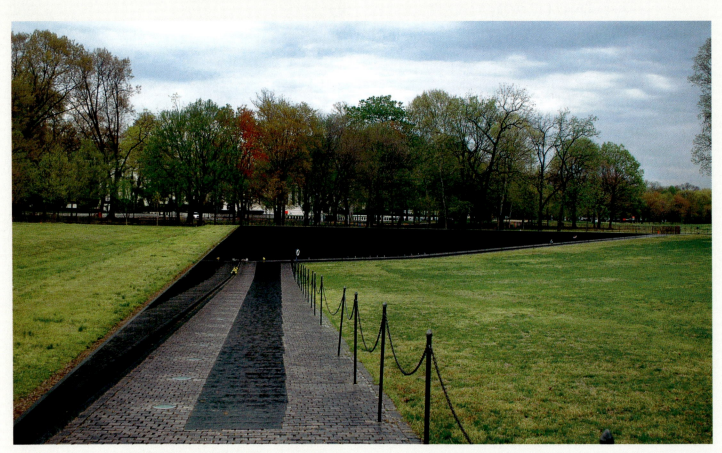

15-34 MAYA YING LIN, Vietnam Veterans Memorial (looking southwest), Washington, D.C., 1981–1983.

Like Minimalist sculpture, Lin's memorial to the veterans of the Vietnam War is a simple geometric form. Its inscribed polished walls actively engage the viewer in a psychological dialogue about the war.

Maya Ying Lin Often classified as a work of Minimalist sculpture rather than architecture, the Vietnam Veterans Memorial (FIG. **15-34**) in Washington, D.C., was designed in 1981 by MAYA YING LIN (b. 1960) when she was only 21. The austere, simple memorial, a V-shaped wall constructed of polished black granite panels, begins at ground level at each end and gradually ascends to a height of 10 feet at the center of the V. Each wing is 246 feet long. Lin set the wall into the landscape, enhancing visitors' awareness of descent as they walk along the wall toward the center. The names of the Vietnam War's 57,939 casualties (and those still missing) incised on the memorial's walls, in the order of their deaths, contribute to the monument's dramatic effect.

When Lin designed this pristinely simple monument, she gave a great deal of thought to the purpose of war memorials. She concluded that a memorial

> should be honest about the reality of war and be for the people who gave their lives. . . . [I] didn't want a static object that people would just look at, but something they could relate to as on a journey, or passage, that would bring each to his own conclusions. . . . I wanted to work with the land and not dominate it. I had an impulse to cut open the earth . . . an initial violence that in time would heal. The grass would grow back, but the cut would remain.[10]

In light of the tragedy of the war, this unpretentious memorial's allusion to a wound and long-lasting scar contributes to its communicative ability (see "Maya Lin's Vietnam Veterans Memorial," page 440).

Postmodernism

The impersonality and sterility of many modernist structures led to a rejection of modernism's authority in architecture, ushering in postmodernism, which, as in contemporary painting and sculpture, is not a unified style. In contrast to the simplicity of modernist architecture, postmodern architecture is complex, pluralistic, and eclectic. Whereas the modernist program was reductive, the postmodern vocabulary of the 1970s and 1980s was expansive and inclusive. Among the first to explore this new direction in architecture were Jane Jacobs (1916–2006) and Robert Venturi. In their influential books *The Death and Life of Great American Cities* (Jacobs, 1961) and *Complexity and Contradiction in Architecture* (Venturi, 1966), they argued that the uniformity and anonymity of modernist architecture (in particular, the corporate skyscrapers dominating many urban skylines) were unsuited to human social interaction and that diversity is the great advantage of urban life. Postmodern architects accepted, indeed embraced, the messy and chaotic nature of urban life. When designing these varied buildings, many postmodern architects consciously selected past architectural elements or references and juxtaposed them with contemporary elements or fashioned them of high-tech materials, thereby creating a dialogue between past and present. Postmodern architecture incorporates not only traditional architectural references but references to mass culture and popular imagery as well.

Michael Graves The Portland Building (FIG. **15-35**) by American architect MICHAEL GRAVES (b. 1934) reasserts the wall's horizontality against the verticality of modernist skyscrapers. Graves favored the square's solidity and stability, making it the main body of his composition (echoed in the windows), which rests on a wider base and carries a setback penthouse crown. Two paired facades support capital-like large hoods on one pair of opposite facades and a frieze of stylized Baroque roundels tied by bands on the other pair. A huge painted keystone motif joins five upper levels on one facade pair, and painted surfaces further define the building's base, body, and penthouse levels. The modernist purist surely would not welcome the ornamental wall, color painting, or symbolic reference. These features, taken together, raised a storm of criticism. Various critics denounced Graves's Portland Building as "an enlarged jukebox" and an "oversized Christmas package," but others approvingly noted its classical references as constituting a "symbolic temple" and praised the building as a courageous architectural adventure. Whatever will be history's verdict, the Portland Building is an early marker of postmodernist innovation.

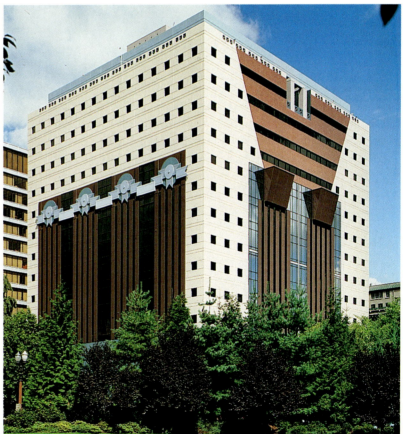

15-35 MICHAEL GRAVES, Portland Building, Portland, Oregon, 1980.

In this early example of postmodernist architecture, Graves reasserted the horizontality and solidity of the wall. He drew attention to the mural surfaces through polychromy and ornamental motifs.

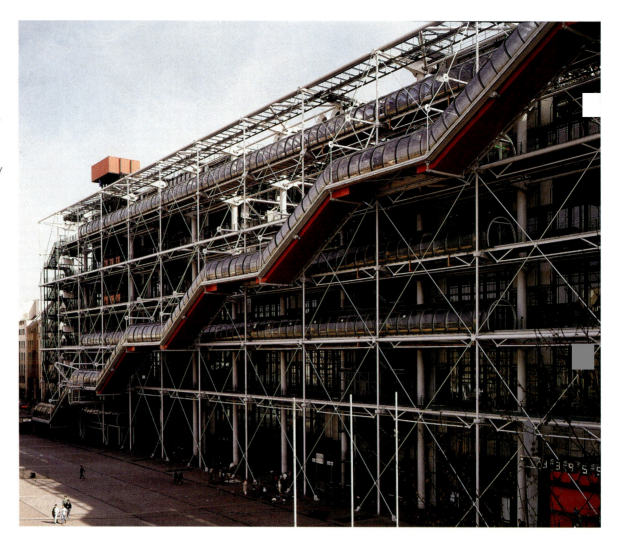

15-36 Richard Rogers and Renzo Piano, Georges Pompidou National Center of Art and Culture (the "Beaubourg"), Paris, France, 1977.

The architects fully exposed the anatomy of this six-level building, as in the century-earlier Crystal Palace (FIG. 12-24), and color-coded the internal parts according to function, as in a factory.

Rogers and Piano During their short-lived partnership, British architect RICHARD ROGERS (b. 1933) and Italian architect RENZO PIANO (b. 1937) used motifs and techniques from ordinary industrial buildings in their design for the Georges Pompidou National Center of Art and Culture (FIG. **15-36**) in Paris, known popularly as the "Beaubourg" after its location in the Place Beaubourg. The architects fully exposed the anatomy of this six-level building, which is a kind of updated version of the Crystal Palace (FIG. **12-24**), and made its "metabolism" visible. They color-coded pipes, ducts, tubes, and corridors according to function (red for the movement of people, green for water, blue for air-conditioning, and yellow for electricity), much as in a sophisticated factory. Critics who deplore the Beaubourg's vernacular qualities disparagingly refer to the complex as a "cultural supermarket" and point out that its exposed entrails require excessive maintenance to protect them from the elements. Nevertheless, the building has been popular with visitors since it opened in 1977. The flexible interior spaces and the colorful structural body provide a festive environment for the crowds flowing through the building enjoying its art galleries, industrial design center, library, science and music centers, conference rooms, research and archival facilities, movie theaters, rest areas, and restaurant.

Deconstructivism

In architecture, as in painting and sculpture, deconstruction as an analytical and design strategy emerged in the 1970s. Architectural *Deconstructivism* seeks to disorient the observer. To this end, Deconstructivist architects attempt to disrupt the conventional categories of architecture and to rupture the viewer's expectations based on them. Destabilization plays a major role in Deconstructivist architecture. Disorder, dissonance, imbalance, asymmetry, unconformity, and irregularity replace their opposites—order, consistency, balance, symmetry, regularity, and clarity, as well as harmony, continuity, and completeness. The haphazardly presented volumes, masses, planes, borders, lighting, locations, directions, spatial relations, as well as the disguised structural facts, challenge the viewer's assumptions about architectural form as it relates to function. According to Deconstructivist principles, the very absence of the stability of traditional categories of architecture in a structure announces a "deconstructed" building.

Frank Gehry The architect most closely identified with Deconstructivist architecture is the Canadian-born FRANK GEHRY (b. 1929). Trained in sculpture, Gehry works up his designs by constructing models and then cutting them up

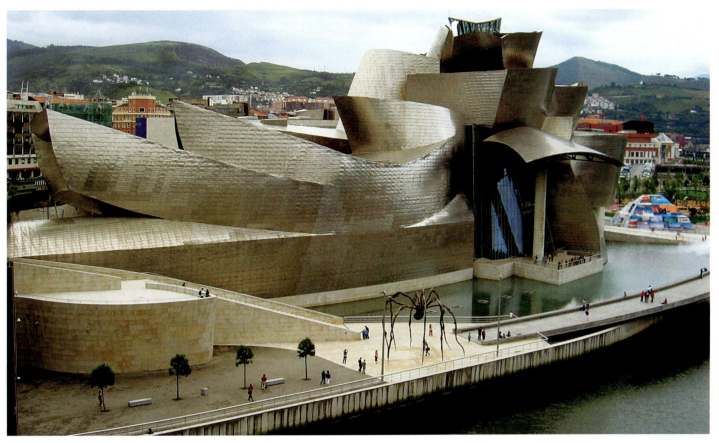

15-37 FRANK GEHRY, Guggenheim Bilbao Museo, Bilbao, Spain, 1997.

Gehry's limestone-and-titanium Bilbao museum is an immensely dramatic building. Its disorder and seeming randomness of design epitomize Deconstructivist architectural principles.

and arranging them until he has a satisfying composition. His Guggenheim Museum (FIG. **15-37**) in Bilbao, Spain, is an immensely dramatic building, a mass of asymmetrical and imbalanced forms that appear as a collapsed or collapsing aggregate of units whose irregular profiles change dramatically with every shift of a visitor's position. The scaled limestone and titanium exterior lends a space-age character to the building and highlights further the unique cluster effect of the many forms. A group of organic forms that Gehry refers to as a "metallic flower" tops the museum. Inside, an enormous glass-walled central atrium soars upward 165 feet, serving as the focal point for the three levels of galleries radiating from it. The seemingly weightless screens, vaults, and volumes of the interior float and flow into one another, guided only by light and dark cues. Overall, the Guggenheim in Bilbao is a profoundly compelling structure. Its disorder, its seeming randomness of design, and the disequilibrium it prompts in viewers epitomize Deconstructivist principles.

Environmental and Site-Specific Art

Like Maya Lin's Vietnam Veterans Memorial (FIG. **15-34**), works of *Environmental Art*, sometimes called *earthworks*, exist at the intersection of architecture and sculpture. The

Environmental Art movement emerged in the 1960s and included a wide range of artworks, most of them *site-specific* (created for only one location). Many artists associated with these sculptural projects also used natural or organic materials, including the land itself. It is no coincidence that this art form developed during a period of increased concern for the environment. The ecology movement of the 1960s and 1970s in America aimed to publicize and combat escalating pollution, depletion of natural resources, and the dangers of toxic waste. The problems of public aesthetics (for example, litter, urban sprawl, and compromised scenic areas) were also at issue. Widespread concern about the environment led to the passage of the U.S. National Environmental Policy Act in 1969 and the creation of the federal Environmental Protection Agency. Environmental artists used their art to call attention to the landscape and, in so doing, were part of this national dialogue.

As an innovative art form that challenged traditional assumptions about art making and artistic models, Environmental Art clearly had an avant-garde, progressive dimension. But like Pop artists, Environmental artists insisted on moving art out of the rarefied atmosphere of museums and galleries and into the public sphere. Most encouraged spectator interaction with their works. Ironically, the remote locations of many earthworks have limited public access.

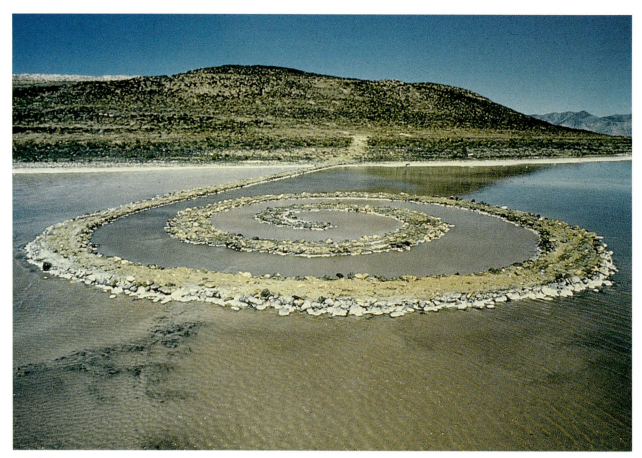

15-38 ROBERT SMITHSON, *Spiral Jetty*, Great Salt Lake, Utah, 1970. © Estate of Robert Smithson/Licensed by VAGA, New York.

Smithson used industrial equipment to create Environmental artworks by manipulating earth and rock. *Spiral Jetty* is a mammoth spiral of black basalt, limestone, and earth extending into Great Salt Lake.

Robert Smithson A leading American Environmental artist was ROBERT SMITHSON (1938–1973), who used industrial construction equipment to manipulate vast quantities of earth and rock on isolated sites. Smithson's best-known piece is *Spiral Jetty* (FIG. **15-38**), a mammoth coil of black basalt, limestone rocks, and earth that extends out into Great Salt Lake in Utah. Driving by the lake one day, Smithson came across some abandoned mining equipment, left there by a company that had tried and failed to extract oil from the site. Smithson saw this as a testament to the enduring power of nature and to humankind's inability to conquer it. He decided to create an artwork in the lake that ultimately became a monumental spiral curving out from the shoreline and running 1,500 linear feet into the water. Smithson insisted on designing his work in response to the location itself. He wanted to avoid the arrogance of an artist merely imposing an unrelated concept on the site. The spiral idea grew from Smithson's first impression of the location. Then, while researching Great Salt Lake, Smithson discovered that the molecular structure of the salt crystals coating the rocks at the water's edge was spiral in form.

As I looked at the site, it reverberated out to the horizons only to suggest an immobile cyclone while flickering light made the entire landscape appear to quake. A dormant earthquake spread into the fluttering stillness, into a spinning sensation without movement. The site was a rotary that enclosed itself in an immense roundness. From that gyrating space emerged the possibility of the Spiral Jetty.[11]

Christo and Jeanne-Claude Like Smithson, CHRISTO and JEANNE-CLAUDE (both b. 1935) seek to intensify the viewer's awareness of the space and features of rural and urban sites. However, rather than physically alter the land itself, as Smithson often did, Christo and Jeanne-Claude prompt this awareness by temporarily modifying the landscape with cloth. Christo studied art in his native Bulgaria and in Vienna. After a move to Paris, he began to encase objects in clumsy wrappings, thereby appropriating bits of the real world into the mysterious world of the unopened package whose contents can be dimly seen in silhouette under the wrap. Starting in 1961, Christo and Jeanne-Claude, husband and wife, began to collaborate on large-scale projects that normally deal with the environment itself. Their artworks require years of preparation and research and scores of meetings with local authorities and citizens groups. *Surrounded Islands 1980–83* (FIG. **15-39**), created in Biscayne Bay in Miami, Florida, for two weeks in May 1983, typifies Christo

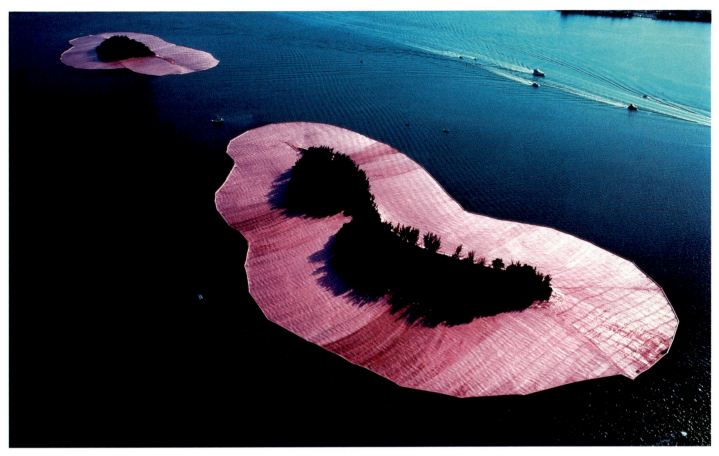

15-39 CHRISTO and JEANNE-CLAUDE, *Surrounded Islands 1980–83*, Biscayne Bay, Miami, Florida, 1980–1983.

Christo and Jeanne-Claude created this Environmental artwork by surrounding 11 small islands with 6.5 million square feet of pink fabric. Characteristically, the work existed for only two weeks.

and Jeanne-Claude's work. For this project, they surrounded 11 small human-made islands (from a dredging project) in the bay with 6.5 million square feet of pink polypropylene floating fabric. The project required three years of preparation to obtain the necessary permits, assemble the labor force, and raise the $3.2 million needed to execute the project. Huge crowds watched as crews removed accumulated trash from the 11 islands (to assure maximum contrast between their dark colors, the pink of the cloth, and the blue of the bay) and then unfurled the fabric "cocoons" to form magical floating "skirts" around each tiny bit of land.

PERFORMANCE ART, CONCEPTUAL ART, AND NEW MEDIA

Among the most significant developments in the art world after World War II has been the expansion of the range of works considered "art." Some of the new types of artworks are the result of the invention of new media, such as computers and video cameras. But the new art forms also reflect avant-garde artists' continued questioning of the status quo. For example, in keeping with the modernist critique of artistic principles, some artists, in a spirit reminiscent of Dada and Surrealism (see Chapter 14), developed the fourth dimension—time—as

an integral element of their artwork. The term art historians use to describe these temporal works is *Performance Art*.

Performance Art

Performance artists replace traditional stationary artworks with movements, gestures, and sounds carried out before an audience, whose members may or may not participate in the performance. Initially, these artists, anticipating the rebellion and youthful exuberance of the 1960s, staged informal and spontaneous events that pushed art outside the confines of mainstream art institutions (museums and galleries). Performance Art also served as an antidote to the affectation of most traditional art objects and challenged art's function as a commodity. In the later 1960s, however, museums commissioned performances with increasing frequency, thereby neutralizing much of the subversiveness that characterized this new art form.

Joseph Beuys German artist JOSEPH BEUYS (1921–1986) created actions aimed at illuminating the condition of modern humanity. He wanted to stimulate thought about art and life based in part on his experience as a pilot during World War II. After the enemy shot down his plane over the Crimea, nomadic Tatars nursed him back to health by swaddling his body in fat and felt to warm him. To Beuys,

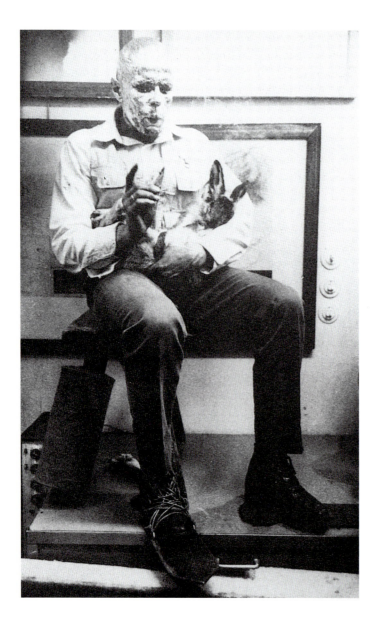

In this one-person event, Performance artist Beuys coated his head with honey and gold leaf. Assuming the role of a shaman, he used stylized actions to evoke a sense of mystery and sacred ritual.

fat and felt thus symbolized healing and regeneration, and he incorporated these materials into many of his performances, such as *How to Explain Pictures to a Dead Hare* (FIG. **15-40**). This one-person event consisted of stylized actions evoking a sense of mystery and sacred ritual. Beuys appeared in a room hung with his drawings, cradling a dead hare to which he spoke softly. Beuys coated his head with honey covered with gold leaf, creating a shimmering mask. In this manner, he took on the role of the shaman, an individual with special spiritual powers. Beuys believed he was acting to help revolutionize human thought so that each human being could become a truly free and creative person.

Conceptual Art

The relentless challenges to artistic convention fundamental to the historical avant-garde reached a logical conclusion with *Conceptual Art* in the late 1960s. Conceptual artists asserted that the "artfulness" of art lay in the artist's idea, rather than in its final expression. These artists regarded the idea, or concept, as the defining component of the artwork. Indeed, some Conceptual artists eliminated the object altogether.

Joseph Kosuth American artist JOSEPH KOSUTH (b. 1945) was a major proponent of Conceptual Art. His work operates at the intersection of language and vision, dealing with the relationship between the abstract and the concrete.

15-41 JOSEPH KOSUTH, *One and Three Chairs*, 1965. Wooden folding chair, photographic copy of a chair, and photographic enlargement of a dictionary definition of chair; chair, 2' 8$\frac{3}{8}$" × 1' 2$\frac{7}{8}$" × 1' 8$\frac{7}{8}$"; photo panel, 3' × 2' $\frac{1}{8}$"; text panel, 2' × 2' $\frac{1}{8}$". Museum of Modern Art, New York (Larry Aldrich Foundation Fund).

Conceptual artists regard the "concept" as an artwork's defining component. To portray "chairness," Kosuth juxtaposed a chair, a photograph of the chair, and a dictionary definition of "chair."

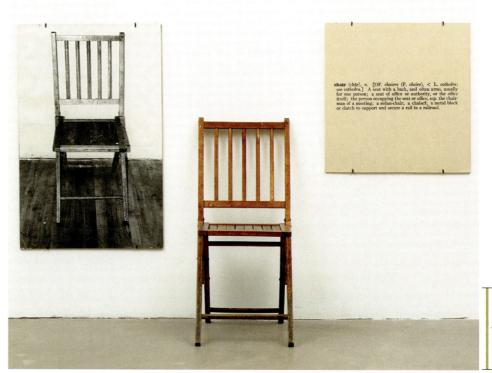

For example, in *One and Three Chairs* (FIG. **15-41**) Kosuth juxtaposed a real chair, a full-scale photograph of the chair, and an enlarged reproduction of a dictionary definition of the word "chair." By so doing, the Conceptual artist asked the viewer to ponder the notion of what constitutes "chairness." He explained:

> Like everyone else I inherited the idea of art as a set of *formal* problems. . . . [T]he radical shift was in changing the idea of art itself. . . . It meant you could have an art work which was that *idea* of an art work, and its formal components weren't important. I felt I had found a way to make art without formal components being confused for an expressionist composition. The expression was in the idea, not the form—the forms were only a device in the service of the idea.[12]

Conceptual artists like Kosuth challenge the very premises of artistic production, pushing art's boundaries to a point where no concrete definition of "art" is possible.

New Media

During the past half century, many avant-garde artists have eagerly embraced new technologies in their attempt to find fresh avenues of artistic expression. Among the most popular new media are video recording and computer graphics. Initially, only commercial television studios possessed video equipment, but in the 1960s, with the development of relatively inexpensive portable video recorders and of electronic devices allowing manipulation of recorded video material, artists began to explore in earnest the expressive possibilities of this new technology. In its basic form, video recording involves a special motion-picture camera that captures visible images and translates them into electronic data that can be displayed on a video monitor or television screen. Video pictures resemble photographs in the amount of detail they contain, but a video image consists of a series of points of light on a grid. Viewers looking at television or video art are not aware of the monitor's surface. Instead, fulfilling the Renaissance ideal, they concentrate on the image and look through the glass surface, as through a window, into the "space" beyond. Video images combine the optical realism of photography with the sense that the subjects move in real time in a deep space "inside" the monitor.

Nam June Paik When video introduced the possibility of manipulating subjects in real time, artists such as Korean-born NAM JUNE PAIK (1932–2006) were eager to work with the medium. After studying music performance, art history, and Eastern philosophy in Korea and Japan, Paik worked with electronic music in Germany in the late 1950s. In 1965, after relocating to New York City, Paik acquired the first inexpensive video recorder sold in Manhattan (the Sony Porta-Pak) and immediately recorded everything he saw out the window of his taxi on the return trip to his studio downtown. Experience acquired as artist-in-residence at television stations WGBH in Boston and WNET in New York allowed him to experiment with the most advanced broadcast video technology.

A grant permitted Paik to collaborate with the gifted Japanese engineer-inventor Shuya Abe in developing a video synthesizer. This instrument enables artists to manipulate and change the electronic video information in various ways, causing images or parts of images to stretch, shrink, change color, or break up. With the synthesizer, artists also can layer images, inset one image into another, or merge images from various cameras with those from video recorders to make a single visual kaleidoscopic "time-collage." This kind of compositional freedom permitted Paik to combine his interests in painting, music, Eastern philosophy, global politics for survival, humanized technology, and cybernetics. Paik called his video works "physical music" and said his musical background enabled him to understand time better than could video artists trained only in painting or sculpture.

Paik's best-known video work, *Global Groove* (FIG. **15-42**), combines in quick succession fragmented sequences of female tap dancers, poet Allen Ginsberg (1926–1997) reading his work, a performance by cellist Charlotte Moorman (1933–1991) using a man's back as her instrument, Pepsi commercials from Japanese television, Korean drummers, and a shot of the Living Theatre group performing a controversial piece called *Paradise Now*. Commissioned originally for broadcast over the United Nations satellite, the cascade of imagery in *Global Groove* gives viewers a glimpse of the rich worldwide television menu Paik had predicted would be available in the future.

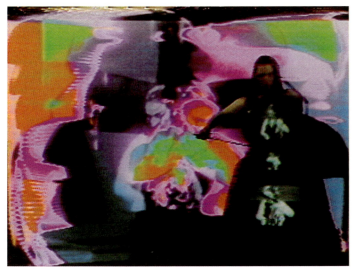

15-42 NAM JUNE PAIK, video still from *Global Groove*, 1973. Color videotape, sound, 30 minutes. Collection of the artist.

Korean-born video artist Paik's best-known work is a cascade of fragmented sequences of performances and commercials intended as a sample of the rich worldwide television menu of the future.

Bill Viola For much of his artistic career, BILL VIOLA (b. 1951) has explored the capabilities of digitized imagery, producing many video *installations* (artworks creating an artistic environment in a room or gallery). Often focused on sensory perception, the pieces not only heighten viewer

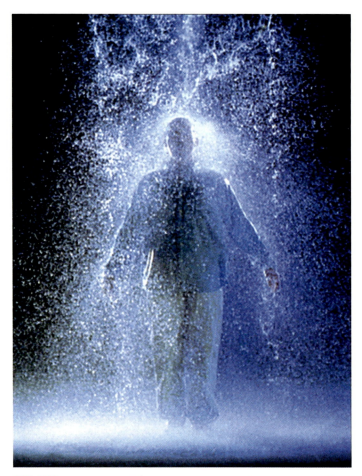

15-43 BILL VIOLA, *The Crossing*, 1996. Video/sound installation with two channels of color video projection onto screens 16′ high.

Viola's video projects use extreme slow motion, contrasts in scale, shifts in focus, mirrored reflections, and staccato editing to create dramatic sensory experiences rooted in tangible reality.

awareness of the senses but also suggest an exploration into the spiritual realm.

Viola, an American, spent years studying Buddhist, Christian, Sufi, and Zen mysticism. Because he fervently believes in art's transformative power and in a spiritual view of human nature, Viola designs works encouraging spectator introspection. His recent video projects involve techniques such as extreme slow motion, contrasts in scale, shifts in focus, mirrored reflections, staccato editing, and multiple or layered screens to achieve dramatic effects.

The power of Viola's work is evident in *The Crossing* (FIG. **15-43**), an installation piece involving video projection on two 16-foot-high screens. The artist either shows the two color videos on the front and back of the same screen or on two separate screens in the same installation. In these two companion videos, shown simultaneously on the two screens, a man surrounded in darkness appears, moving closer until he fills the screen. On one screen, drops of water fall from above onto the man's head, while on the other screen, a small

fire breaks out at the man's feet. Over the next few minutes, the water and fire increase in intensity until the man disappears in a torrent of water on one screen (shown in FIG. **15-43**), and flames consume the man on the other screen. The deafening roar of a raging fire and a torrential downpour accompanies these visual images. Eventually, everything subsides and fades into darkness. This installation's elemental nature and its presentation in a dark space immerse viewers in a pure sensory experience very much rooted in tangible reality.

Matthew Barney One of the major trends in the art world of the first decade of the 21st century is the relaxation of the traditional boundaries between and among artistic media. In fact, many artists today are creating vast and complex multimedia installations combining new and traditional media.

One of these artists is MATTHEW BARNEY (b. 1967). The 2003 installation (FIG. **15-1**) of his epic *Cremaster* cycle at the Solomon R. Guggenheim Museum in New York City typifies the expansive scale of many contemporary works. A multimedia extravaganza involving drawings, photographs, sculptures, video performances, and films, the *Cremaster* cycle is a lengthy narrative that takes place in a self-enclosed universe Barney created.

The title of the work refers to the cremaster muscle, which controls testicular contractions in response to external stimuli. Barney uses the development of this muscle in the embryonic process of sexual differentiation as the conceptual springboard for the entire *Cremaster* project, in which he explores the notion of creation in expansive and complicated ways. The cycle's narrative, revealed in the five feature-length films and the artworks, makes reference to, among other things, a musical revue in Boise, Idaho (Barney's hometown), the life cycle of bees, the execution of convicted murderer Gary Gilmore, Celtic mythology, Masonic rituals, a motorcycle race, and a lyric opera set in late-19th-century Budapest. In the installation, Barney tied the artworks together conceptually by a five-channel video piece projected on screens hanging in the Guggenheim's rotunda. Immersion in Barney's constructed world is disorienting and overwhelming and has a force that competes with the immense scale and often frenzied pace of contemporary life.

No one knows what the next years and decades will bring, but given the expansive scope of postmodernism, it is likely that no single approach to or style of art will dominate. New technologies certainly will continue to redefine what constitutes a "work of art." Thus, the universally expanding presence of computers, digital technology, and the Internet may well erode what few conceptual and geographical boundaries remain and make art and information about art available to virtually everyone, thereby creating a truly global artistic community.

Europe and America after 1945

PAINTING AND SCULPTURE

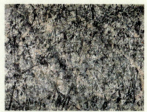

Pollock, *Lavender Mist*, 1950

▪ The art of the second half of the 20th century reflects cultural upheaval: the rejection of traditional values, and the emergence of the civil rights and feminist movements, and of the new consumer society.

▪ The first major postwar avant-garde art movement was Abstract Expressionism, which championed an artwork's formal elements rather than its subject. Gestural abstractionists, such as Pollock and de Kooning, sought expressiveness through energetically applied pigment. Chromatic abstractionists, such as Rothko, struck emotional chords through large areas of pure color.

▪ Post-Painterly Abstraction promoted a cool rationality in contrast to Abstract Expressionism's passion. Both hard-edge painters, such as Stella, and color-field painters, such as Frankenthaler, pursued purity in art by emphasizing the flatness of pigment on canvas.

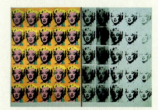

Warhol, *Marilyn Diptych*, 1962

▪ Pop artists, such as Johns, Lichtenstein, and Warhol, turned away from abstraction to the representation of subjects grounded in popular culture—flags, comic strips, Hollywood stars.

▪ Superrealists, such as Close and Hanson—kindred spirits to Pop artists in many ways—created paintings and sculptures featuring scrupulous fidelity to optical fact.

▪ The leading postwar sculptural movement was Minimalism. Judd created artworks consisting of simple unadorned geometric shapes to underscore sculpture's "objecthood."

▪ Much of the art since 1970 addresses pressing social issues, especially gender, race, and ethnicity. Leading feminist artists include Chicago, whose *Dinner Party* honors important women throughout history and features crafts traditionally associated with women, and Sherman and Kruger, who have explored the "male gaze" in their art. Ringgold and Simpson have addressed issues important to African American women, and Quick-to-See-Smith has examined Native American heritage.

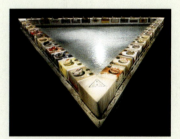

Chicago, *Dinner Party*, 1979

ARCHITECTURE AND SITE-SPECIFIC ART

▪ Some of the leading early-20th-century modernist architects were also active after 1945. Wright built the snail-shell Guggenheim Museum, Le Corbusier the sculpturesque Notre-Dame-du-Haut, and Mies van der Rohe the Minimalist Seagram skyscraper.

▪ In contrast to modernist architecture, postmodernist architecture is complex and eclectic and often incorporates references to historical styles, as in Graves's Portland Building. Deconstructivist architects seek to disorient the viewer with asymmetrical and irregular shapes, as Gehry did in his Guggenheim Museum in Bilbao.

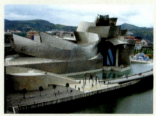

Gehry, Guggenheim Museum, Bilbao, 1997

▪ Site-specific art exists at the intersection of architecture and sculpture and is sometimes temporary in nature, as was Christo and Jeanne-Claude's *Surrounded Islands*.

PERFORMANCE AND CONCEPTUAL ART AND NEW MEDIA

▪ Among the most significant developments in the art world after World War II has been the expansion of the range of works considered "art." Performance artists replace traditional stationary artworks with movements and sounds carried out before an audience. Their Performance Art often addresses the same social and political issues painters and sculptors explore.

▪ Conceptual artists believe the "artfulness" of art is in the idea, not in the work resulting from the idea. Kosuth's chairs, for example, is an artwork at the intersection of language and vision.

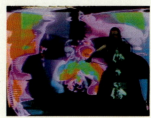

Paik, *Global Groove*, 1973

▪ Paik, Viola, and others have embraced video recording technology to produce artworks that combine images and sounds, sometimes viewed on small monitors, other times on huge screens. Other contemporary artists, including Barney, have explored computer graphics and other new media, often in vast and complex museum installations.

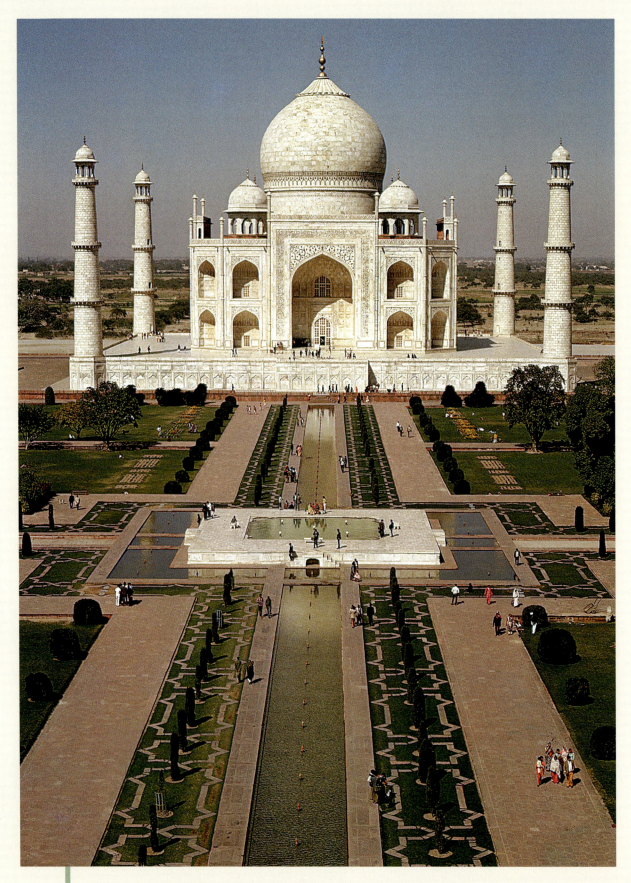

16-1 Taj Mahal, Agra, India, 1632–1647.

South Asia is home to the monuments of three great religions—Buddhism, Hinduism, and Islam. This famous Muslim mausoleum seems to float magically over reflecting pools in a vast garden symbolizing Paradise.

South and Southeast Asia

South and Southeast Asia is a vast geographic area comprising, among many others, the nations of India, Pakistan, Cambodia, Myanmar, Thailand, and Vietnam (MAP **16-1**). Not surprisingly, the region's inhabitants display tremendous cultural and religious diversity. The people of India alone speak more than 20 different major languages. The art of South and Southeast Asia is equally diverse—and very ancient. When Alexander the Great and his army reached India in 326 BCE, the civilization they encountered was already more than two millennia old.

INDIA AND PAKISTAN

In the mid-third millennium BCE, when the Sumerians were burying their dead in the Royal Cemetery at Ur and the Egyptians were erecting the Great Pyramids at Gizeh (see Chapter 1), a great civilization arose along the Indus River in present-day Pakistan and extended into India as far south as Gujarat and east beyond Delhi. Archaeologists have dubbed this early South Asian culture the Indus Civilization.

Indus Civilization

The Indus Civilization flourished from about 2600 to 1500 BCE, and evidence indicates there was active trade during this period between the Indus Valley and Mesopotamia. The most important excavated Indus sites are Harappa and Mohenjo-daro. These early, fully developed cities featured streets oriented to compass points and multistoried houses built of carefully formed and precisely laid kiln-baked bricks. The Indus cities also boasted one of the world's first sophisticated systems of water supply and sewage. In Mohenjo-daro, hundreds of wells throughout the city provided fresh water to homes boasting some of the oldest recorded private bathing areas and toilet facilities with drainage into public sewers. But in sharp contrast to the contemporaneous civilizations of Mesopotamia and Egypt, archaeologists have not yet identified any Indus building as a temple or palace.

Indus Seals Excavators have discovered surprisingly little art from the long-lived Indus Civilization, and all of the objects found are small. The most common are steatite seals with incised designs. They are similar in many ways to the seals found at contemporaneous sites in Mesopotamia. Most of the Indus examples have an animal or tiny narrative carved on the face, along with a still-untranslated script. On the back, a *boss* (circular knob) with a hole permitted insertion of a string so that the seal could be worn or hung on a wall. As in the ancient Near East, the Indus peoples sometimes used the seals to make impressions on clay,

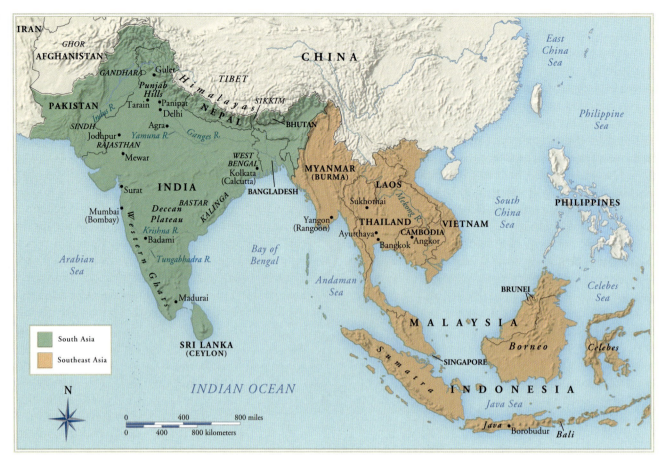

MAP 16-1   South and Southeast Asia.

apparently for securing trade goods wrapped in textiles. The animals most frequently represented include the humped bull, elephant, rhinoceros, and tiger—always in strict profile. Some of the narrative seals appear to show that the Indus peoples considered trees sacred, as both Buddhists and Hindus later did. Many historians have suggested religious and ritual continuities between the Indus Civilization and later Indian culture.

One of the most elaborate seals (FIG. 16-2) depicts a male figure with a horned headdress and, perhaps, three faces, seated (with erect penis) among the profile animals that regularly appear alone on other seals. The figure's folded legs with heels pressed together and arms resting on the knees suggest a *yogic* posture. *Yoga* is a method for controlling the body and relaxing the mind used in later Indian religions to yoke, or unite, the practitioner to the divine. Although most scholars reject the identification of this figure as a prototype of the multiheaded Hindu god Shiva (FIG. 16-10) as Lord of Beasts, the yogic posture argues that this important Indian meditative practice began as early as the Indus Civilization.

Vedic and Upanishadic Periods

By 1700 BCE, the urban phase of the Indus Civilization had ended in most areas. Very little art survives from the next thousand years, but the religious foundations laid during this period helped define most later South Asian art.

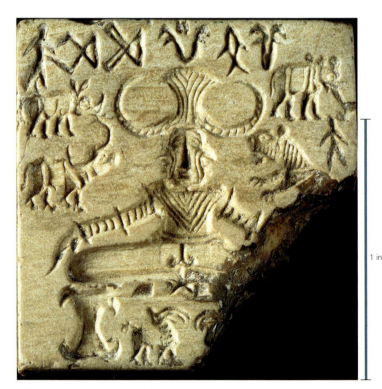

16-2   Seal with seated figure in yogic posture, from Mohenjo-daro, Pakistan, ca. 2300–1750 BCE. Steatite coated with alkali and baked, $1\frac{3}{8}'' \times 1\frac{3}{8}''$. National Museum, New Delhi.

This seal depicting a figure wearing a horned headdress and seated in a yogic posture is evidence that this important Indian meditative practice began as early as the Indus Civilization.

Vedas and Upanishads The basis for the new religious ideas were the oral hymns the Aryans brought to India from central Asia. The Aryans ("Noble Ones"), who spoke Sanskrit, the earliest language yet identified in South Asia, were a mobile herding people who occupied northwestern India in the second millennium BCE. Around 1500 BCE, the Aryans composed the first of four *Vedas*. These Sanskrit compilations of religious learning (Veda means "knowledge") included hymns intended for priests (called Brahmins) to chant or sing. The Aryan religion centered on sacrifice, the ritual enactment of often highly intricate and lengthy ceremonies in which the priests placed materials, such as milk and soma (an intoxicating drink), into a fire that took the sacrifices to the gods in the heavens. If the Brahmins performed these rituals accurately, the gods would fulfill the prayers of those who sponsored the sacrifices. These gods, primarily male, included Indra, Varuna, Surya, and Agni, gods associated, respectively, with the rains, the ocean, the sun, and fire. The Aryans did not make images of these deities.

The next phase of South Asian urban civilization developed east of the Indus heartland, in the Ganges River valley. Here, from 800 to 500 BCE, religious thinkers composed a variety of texts called the *Upanishads*. Among the innovative ideas of the Upanishads were *samsara*, *karma*, and *moksha* (or *nirvana*). *Samsara* is the belief that individuals are born again after death in an almost endless round of rebirths. The type of rebirth can vary. One can be reborn as a human being, an animal, or even a god. An individual's past actions *(karma)*, either good or bad, determine the nature of future rebirths. The ultimate goal of a person's religious life is to escape from the cycle of birth and death by merging the individual self into the vital force of the universe. This escape is called either *moksha* (liberation, for Hindus) or *nirvana* (cessation, for Buddhists).

Hinduism and Buddhism The two major modern religions originating in Asia, Hinduism and Buddhism, developed in the late centuries BCE and the early centuries CE. Hinduism, the dominant religion in India today, discussed in more detail later, has its origins in Aryan religion. The founder of Buddhism was the Buddha, a historical figure who advocated the path of *asceticism*, or self-discipline and self-denial, as the means to free oneself from attachments to people and possessions, thus ending rebirth (see "Buddhism and Buddhist Iconography," page 454). Unlike their predecessors in South Asia, both Hindus and Buddhists use images of gods and holy persons in religious rituals. Buddhism has the older artistic tradition. The earliest Buddhist monuments date to the Maurya period.

Maurya Dynasty

When Alexander the Great reached the Indus River in 326 BCE, his troops refused to go forward. Reluctantly, Alexander abandoned his dream of conquering India and headed home. After Alexander's death, his generals divided his empire among themselves. One of them, Seleucus Nicator, reinvaded India, but Chandragupta Maurya (r. 323–298 BCE), founder of the Maurya dynasty (r. 323–185 BCE), defeated him in 305 BCE and eventually consolidated almost all of present-day India under his domain.

Ashoka The greatest Maurya ruler was Ashoka (r. 272–231 BCE), who left his imprint on history by converting to Buddhism and spreading the Buddha's teaching throughout and beyond India. Ashoka formulated a legal code based on the Buddha's dharma and inscribed his laws on enormous monolithic stone columns erected throughout his kingdom. Ashoka's pillars reached 30 to 40 feet high and are the first known monumental stone artworks in India. The pillars penetrated deep into the ground, connecting earth and sky, forming an "axis of the universe," a pre-Buddhist concept that became an important motif in Buddhist architecture. The columns stood along pilgrimage routes to sites associated with the Buddha and on the roads leading to Pataliputra (modern Patna), the Maurya capital. Capping Ashoka's pillars were elaborate capitals, also carved from a single block of stone. The finest of these is the seven-foot lion capital (FIG. **16-3**) from Sarnath, where the Buddha gave his first sermon and set the Wheel of the Law into motion. Stylistically, Ashoka's capital owes much to the ancient Near East, but its iconography is Buddhist. Two

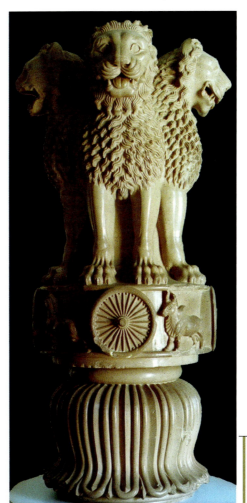

16-3 Lion capital from a column erected by Ashoka at Sarnath, India, ca. 250 BCE. Sandstone, 7' high. Archaeological Museum, Sarnath.

Ashoka formulated a legal code based on the Buddha's teachings and inscribed those laws on columns erected throughout his kingdom. The lions on this capital once supported the Buddha's Wheel of the Law.

1 ft.

Buddhism and Buddhist Iconography

The Buddha and Buddhism

The Buddha (Enlightened One) was born around 563 BCE as Prince Siddhartha Gautama, the eldest son of the king of the Shakya clan. A prophecy foretold that he would grow up to be either a world conqueror or a great religious leader. His father preferred the secular role for young Siddhartha and groomed him for kingship by shielding the boy from the hardships of the world. When he was 29, however, the prince rode out of the palace, abandoned his wife and family, and encountered firsthand the pain of old age, sickness, and death. Siddhartha responded to the suffering he witnessed by renouncing his opulent life and becoming a wandering ascetic searching for knowledge through meditation. Six years later, he achieved complete enlightenment, or buddhahood, while meditating beneath a pipal tree (the Bodhi tree) at Bodh Gaya ("place of enlightenment") in eastern India. Known from that day on as Shakyamuni (wise man of the Shakya clan), the Buddha preached his first sermon in the Deer Park at Sarnath. There he set in motion the Wheel (chakra) of the Law (dharma) and expounded the Four Noble Truths that are the core insights of Buddhism: (1) Life is suffering; (2) the cause of suffering is desire; (3) one can overcome and extinguish desire; (4) the way to conquer desire and end suffering is to follow the Buddha's Eightfold Path of right understanding, right thought, right speech, right action, right livelihood, right effort, right mindfulness, and right concentration. The Buddha's path leads to nirvana, the cessation of the endless cycle of painful life, death, and rebirth. The Buddha continued to preach until his death at 80 at Kushinagara. His disciples carried on his teaching and established monasteries where others could follow the Buddha's path to enlightenment and nirvana.

This earliest form of Buddhism is called Theravada (Path of the Elders) Buddhism. The new religion developed and changed over time as the Buddha's teachings spread from India throughout Asia. The second major school of Buddhist thought, Mahayana (Great Path) Buddhism, emerged around the beginning of the Common Era. Mahayana Buddhists refer to Theravada Buddhism as Hinayana (Lesser Path) Buddhism and believe in a larger goal than nirvana for an individual—namely, buddhahood for all. Mahayana Buddhists also revere bodhisattvas ("Buddhas-to-be"), exemplars of compassion who hold back at the threshold of nirvana to aid others in earning merit and achieving buddhahood.

A third important Buddhist sect venerates the Amitabha Buddha (Amida in Japanese), the Buddha of Infinite Light and Life. The devotees of this Buddha hope to be reborn in the Pure Land Paradise of the West, where the Amitabha resides and can grant them salvation. Pure Land teachings maintain that people have no possibility of attaining enlightenment on their own, but can achieve paradise and nirvana by faith alone.

Buddhist Iconography

The earliest (first century CE) depictions of the Buddha in human form show him as a robed monk. Artists distinguished the Enlightened One from monks and bodhisattvas by lakshanas, body attributes indicating the Buddha's suprahuman nature: an urna, or curl of hair between the eyebrows, shown as a dot; an ushnisha, a cranial bump shown as hair on the earliest images (FIG. 16-6) but later as an actual part of the head (FIG. 16-7); and elongated ears, the result of wearing heavy royal jewelry in his youth, but the enlightened Shakyamuni is rarely bejeweled, as are many bodhisattvas (FIG. 16-8). Sometimes the Buddha appears with a halo, or sun disk, behind his head (FIG. 16-7).

Representations of the Buddha also feature a repertory of mudras, or hand gestures, conveying fixed meanings. These include the dhyana (meditation) mudra, with the right hand over the left hand, palms upward; the bhumisparsha (earth-touching) mudra, right hand down reaching to the ground, calling the earth to witness the Buddha's enlightenment (FIG. 16-6b); the dharmachakra (Wheel of the Law, or teaching) mudra, a two-handed gesture with right thumb and index finger forming a circle (FIG. 16-7); and the abhaya (do not fear) mudra, right hand up, palm outward, a gesture of protection or blessing (FIG. 16-6c).

Episodes from the Buddha's life are among the most popular subjects in all Buddhist artistic traditions. No single text provides the complete or authoritative narrative of the Buddha's life and death. Thus, numerous versions and variations exist, allowing for a rich artistic repertory. Four of the most important events are his birth at Lumbini from the side of his mother, Queen Maya (FIG. 16-6a); his achievement of buddhahood while meditating beneath the Bodhi tree at Bodh Gaya (FIG. 16-6b); his first sermon at Sarnath (FIGS. 16-6c and 16-7); and his attainment of nirvana when he died (parinirvana) at Kushinagara (FIG. 16-6d).

pairs of back-to-back lions stand on a round abacus decorated with four wheels and four animals symbolizing the four quarters of the world. The lions once carried a large stone wheel on their backs. The wheel (chakra) referred to the Wheel of the Law but also indicated Ashoka's stature as a chakravartin ("holder of the wheel"), a universal king imbued with divine authority. The open mouths of the four lions that face the four quarters of the world may signify the worldwide announcement of the Buddha's message.

Kushan Dynasty

The Maurya dynasty came to an abrupt end when its last ruler was assassinated by one of his generals, who founded a new dynasty in his own name. The Shungas (r. 185–72 BCE),

however, ruled an empire confined to central India. Their successors were the Andhras (r. ca. 50–320 CE), who also controlled the Deccan plateau to the south. By the middle of the first century CE, an even greater empire, the Kushan (r. ca. 50–320 CE), rose in northern India. Its most celebrated king was Kanishka (r. 78–144 CE), whose capital was at Peshawar in Gandhara, a region largely in Pakistan today. The Kushans grew rich on trade between China and the west along one of the main caravan routes bringing the luxuries of the Orient to the Roman Empire.

Sanchi The unifying characteristic of this age of regional dynasties in South Asia was the patronage of Buddhism. One of the most important Buddhist monasteries, founded during Ashoka's reign and in use for more than a thousand years,

The Stupa

An essential element of Buddhist sanctuaries is the *stupa,* a grand circular mound modeled on earlier South Asian burial mounds of a type familiar in many other ancient cultures (for example, FIG. 2-11). The stupa was not, however, a tomb but a monument housing relics of the Buddha. When the Buddha died, his cremated remains were placed in eight reliquaries. Unlike their Western equivalents, which were put on display, the Buddha's relics were buried in solid earthen mounds (stupas) that could not be entered. In the mid-third century BCE, Ashoka opened the original eight stupas and spread the Buddha's relics among thousands of stupas in all corners of his realm. Buddhists venerated the Buddha's remains by *circumambulation,* walking around the stupa in a clockwise direction, following the path of the sun, bringing the devotee into harmony with the cosmos.

Stupas come in many sizes. The largest, such as the Great Stupa at Sanchi (FIG. 16-4), are three-dimensional *mandalas,* or sacred diagrams of the universe. The domed stupa itself represents the world mountain, with the cardinal points marked by *toranas,* or gateways. The *harmika,* positioned atop the stupa dome, is a stone fence that encloses a square area symbolizing the sacred domain of the gods. At the harmika's center, a *yasti,* or pole, corresponds to the axis of the universe, a motif already present in Ashoka's pillars. Three *chatras,* or stone disks, assigned various meanings, crown the yasti. The yasti rises from the mountain-dome and passes through the harmika, thus uniting this world with the heavenly paradise. A stone fence often encloses the entire structure, separating the sacred space containing the Buddha's relics from the profane world outside.

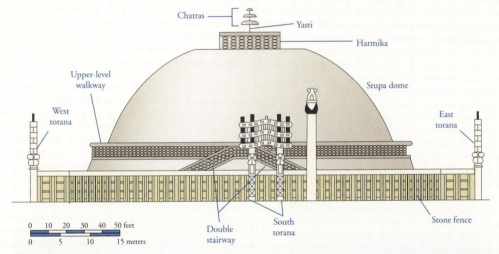

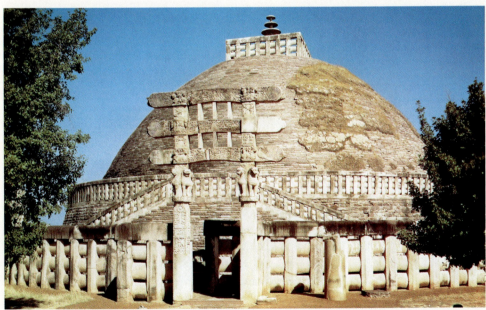

16-4 Diagram *(top)* and view looking north *(bottom)* of the Great Stupa, Sanchi, India, third century BCE to first century CE.

Stupas are earthen mounds containing relics of the Buddha. Buddhists walk around stupas in a clockwise direction, following the path of the sun, bringing the devotee into harmony with the cosmos.

is at Sanchi in central India. It consists of many buildings constructed over the centuries, including temples, *viharas* (celled structures where monks live), and large *stupas* (see "The Stupa," above). Sanchi's Great Stupa (FIG. 16-4) dates originally to Ashoka's reign, but its present form, with its tall stone fence and four gates, dates from around 50 BCE to 50 CE. The solid earth-and-rubble dome stands 50 feet high. Worshipers enter through one of the gateways, walk on the

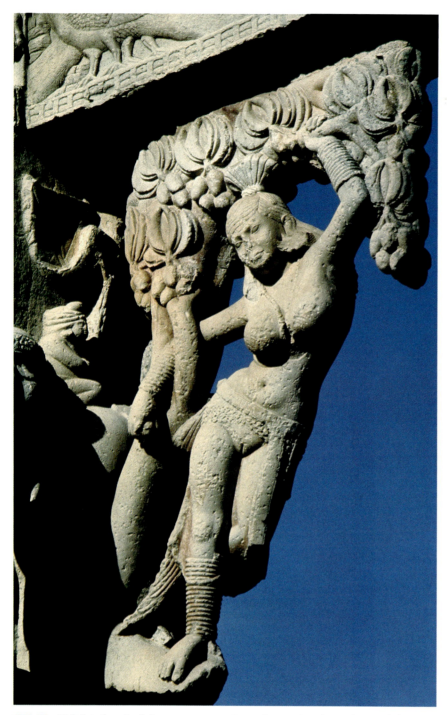

lives, as recorded in the jatakas, he accumulated sufficient merit to achieve enlightenment and become the Buddha. In the life stories recounted in the Great Stupa reliefs, however, the Buddha never appears in human form. Instead, the artists used symbols—for example, footprints, a parasol, or an empty seat—to indicate the Buddha's presence. Some scholars regard these symbols as markers of where the Buddha once was, enabling others to follow in his footsteps.

Also carved on the east torana is a scantily clad, sensuous woman called a *yakshi* (FIG. **16-5**), a goddess personifying fertility and vegetation. She reaches up to hold on to a mango tree branch while pressing her left foot against the trunk, an action that has brought the tree to flower. Buddhists later adopted this pose, with its rich associations of procreation and abundance, for representing the Buddha's mother, Maya, giving birth (FIG. **16-6***a*).

Gandhara The first anthropomorphic representations of the Buddha probably appeared in the first century CE. Scholars still debate what brought about this momentous shift in Buddhist iconography, but one factor may have been the changing perception of the Buddha himself. Originally revered as an enlightened mortal, the Buddha increasingly became regarded as a divinity. Consequently, the Buddha's followers desired images of him to worship. Many of the early portrayals of the Buddha in human form come from Gandhara in Pakistan. Gandharan art owes much to Greco-Roman art—the legacy of Alexander's incursions into the region.

One of the earliest pictorial narrative cycles in which the Buddha appears in human form is a Gandharan frieze (FIG. **16-6**) depicting, in chronological order from left to right, the Buddha's birth at Lumbini, his enlightenment at Bodh Gaya, his first sermon at Sarnath, and his death at Kushinagara. At the left, Queen Maya gives birth to Prince Siddhartha, who emerges from her right hip, already with his attributes of ushnisha, urna, and halo. Receiving him is the god Indra. Elegantly dressed ladies, one with a fan of peacock feathers, suggest the opulent court life the Buddha left behind. In the next scene, the Buddha sits beneath the Bodhi tree while the soldiers and demons of the evil Mara attempt to distract him from his quest for knowledge. They are unsuccessful, and the Buddha reaches down to touch the earth (bhumisparsha mudra) as witness to his enlightenment. Next, the Buddha preaches the Eightfold

16-5 Yakshi, detail of the east torana, Great Stupa, Sanchi, India, mid-first century BCE to early first century CE.

Yakshis personify fertility and vegetation. The Sanchi yakshis are scantily clad women who make mango trees flower. The yakshis' pose was later used to represent Queen Maya giving birth to the Buddha.

lower circumambulation path, and then climb the stairs on the south side to circumambulate at the second level. Veneration of the Buddha was open to all, not just the monks, and most of the dedications at Sanchi were by laypeople, who hoped to accrue merit for future rebirths with their gifts.

The reliefs on the four toranas at Sanchi depict not only the Buddha's life story but also the stories of his past lives (*jatakas*). In Buddhist belief, everyone has had innumerable past lives, including Siddhartha. During Siddhartha's former

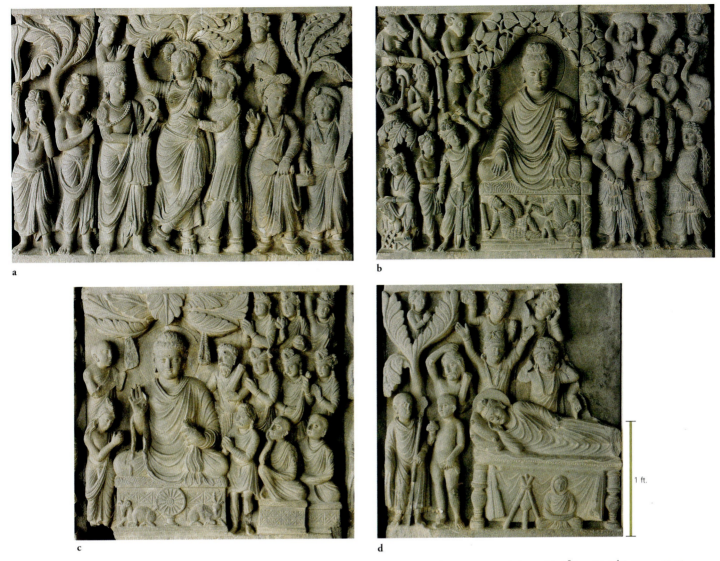

16-6 The life and death of the Buddha, frieze from Gandhara, Pakistan, second century CE. Schist, 2' 2$\frac{3}{8}$" × 9' 6$\frac{1}{8}$". Freer Gallery of Art, Washington, D.C. (a) birth at Lumbini, (b) enlightenment at Bodh Gaya, (c) first sermon at Sarnath, (d) death at Kushinagara.

This frieze is one of the earliest pictorial cycles in which the Buddha appears in human form. Although the iconography is Buddhist, Roman sculptures served as stylistic models for the Gandharan artist.

Path to nirvana in the Deer Park at Sarnath. The sculptor set the scene by placing two deer and the Wheel of the Law beneath the Buddha, who raises his right hand (abhaya mudra) to bless the monks and other devotees who have come to hear his first sermon. In the final section of the frieze, the parinirvana, the Buddha lies dying among his devotees, some of whom wail in grief, while one monk, who realizes that the Buddha has been permanently released from suffering, remains tranquil in meditation.

Although the iconography of the frieze is Buddhist, Roman sculptures must have served as stylistic models for the Gandharan artist. For example, the distribution of standing and equestrian figures over the relief ground, with those behind the first row seemingly suspended in the air, is familiar in Roman art of the second and third centuries CE (FIG. 3-46). The figure of the Buddha on his deathbed finds parallels in the reclining figures on the lids of Etruscan (FIG. 3-4) and Roman sarcophagi. The type of hierarchical com-

position in which a central large figure sits between balanced tiers of smaller onlookers is also common in Roman imperial art (FIG. 3-51).

The Gupta and Post-Gupta Periods

Around 320* a new empire arose in north-central India. The Gupta emperors (r. ca. 320–450) chose Pataliputra as their capital, deliberately associating themselves with the prestige of the former Maurya Empire. The heyday of this dynasty was under Chandragupta II (r. 375–415), whose very name recalled the first Maurya emperor.

---

*From this point on all dates in this chapter are CE unless otherwise stated.

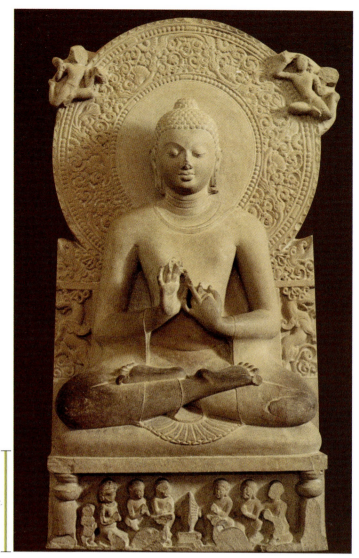

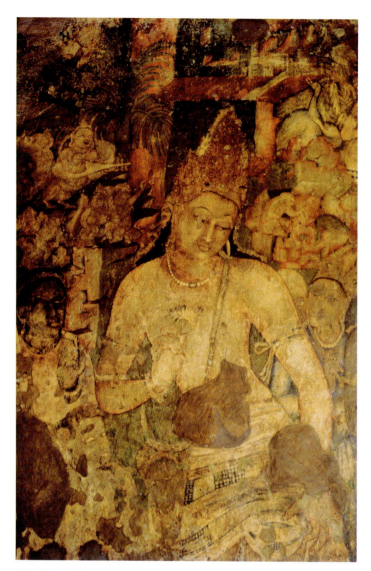

16-7 Seated Buddha preaching first sermon, from Sarnath, India, second half of fifth century. Tan sandstone, 5′ 3″ high. Archaeological Museum, Sarnath.

Under the Guptas, artists formulated the canonical image of the Buddha. This statue's smooth, unadorned surfaces conform to the Indian notion of perfect body form and emphasize the figure's spirituality.

16-8 Bodhisattva Padmapani, wall painting in cave 1, Ajanta, India, second half of fifth century.

The Ajanta caves are renowned for their mural paintings. This artist rendered the sensuous form of the richly attired bodhisattva with gentle gradations of color and delicate highlights and shadows.

Sarnath Under the Guptas, artists formulated what became the standard image of the Buddha. A fifth-century Buddha statue (FIG. **16-7**) from Sarnath is a characteristic example. The Buddha wears a clinging monastic robe covering both shoulders. His eyes are downcast in meditation, and he holds his hands in front of his body in the Wheel-turning gesture, preaching his first sermon. Below the Buddha is a scene with the Wheel of the Law at the center between two (now partially broken) deer symbolizing the Deer Park at Sarnath. The statue's smooth, unadorned surfaces conform to the Indian notion of perfect body form and emphasize the figure's spirituality. Buddha images such as this one became so popular that temples housing Buddha statues seem largely to have displaced the stupa as the norm in Buddhist sacred architecture.

Ajanta The new popularity of Buddha imagery may be seen at Ajanta, northeast of Bombay. Ajanta had been the site of a small Buddhist monastery for centuries, but royal patrons of

the local Vakataka dynasty, allied to the Guptas by marriage, added more than 20 new caves in the second half of the fifth century. Ajanta's fame today stems from the many caves that retain their painted wall and ceiling decoration. Illustrated here (FIG. **16-8**) is a detail of one of the restored painted walls in cave 1 depicting the bodhisattva Padmapani among a crowd of devotees, both princes and commoners. With long, dark hair hanging down below a jeweled crown, he stands holding his attribute, a blue lotus flower, in his right hand. The bodhisattva's face shows great compassion as he gazes downward at worshipers passing through the shrine entrance on their way to the rock-cut Buddha image housed in a cell at the back of the cave. The painter rendered the sensuous form of the richly attired bodhisattva with finesse, gently modeling the figure with gradations of color and delicate highlights and shadows, especially evident in the face and neck.

Buddhists and Hindus practiced their religions side by side in India, often at the same site. The Hindu Vakataka

Hinduism and Hindu Iconography

Unlike Buddhism (and Christianity, Islam, and other religions), Hinduism recognizes no founder or great prophet. Hinduism also has no simple definition but means "the religion of the Indians." Both "India" and "Hindu" have a common root in the name of the Indus River. The practices and beliefs of Hindus vary tremendously, but the literary origins of Hinduism can be traced to the Vedic period, and some aspects of Hindu practice seem already to have been present in the Indus Civilization of the third millennium BCE. Ritual sacrifice by Brahmin priests is central to Hinduism, as it was to the Aryans. The goal of sacrifice is to please a deity in order to achieve liberation (*moksha*) from the endless cycle of birth, death, and rebirth (*samsara*) and become one with the universal spirit.

Hinduism is a religion of many gods, who have various natures and take many forms. This multiplicity suggests the all-pervasive nature of the Hindu gods. The three most important deities are the gods Shiva and Vishnu and the goddess Devi.

Shiva (FIGS. 16-9 and 16-10) is the Destroyer, but, consistent with the multiplicity of Hindu belief, he is also a regenerative force, and, in the latter role, can be represented in the form of a *linga* (a phallus or cosmic pillar). When Shiva appears in human form in Hindu art, he frequently has multiple limbs and heads, signs of his suprahuman nature, and matted locks piled atop his head, crowned by a crescent moon. Sometimes he wears a serpent scarf and has a third eye on his forehead (the emblem of his all-seeing nature). Shiva rides the bull **Nandi** (FIG. 16-9) and often carries a trident, a three-pronged pitchfork.

Vishnu (FIG. 16-11) is the Preserver of the Universe. Artists frequently portray him with four arms holding various attributes. He sometimes reclines on a serpent floating on the waters of the cosmic sea. When the evil forces of the universe become too strong, he descends to earth to restore balance and assumes different forms (avatars, or incarnations), including a boar, fish, and tortoise, as well as **Krishna,** the divine lover (FIG. 16-17), and even the Buddha himself.

Devi is the Great Goddess who takes many forms and has many names. Hindus worship her alone or as a consort of male gods (**Parvati** or **Uma,** wife of Shiva; **Lakshmi,** wife of Vishnu), as well as **Radha,** lover of Krishna (FIG. 16-17). She has both benign and horrific forms, and she creates as well as destroys. In one manifestation, she is **Durga,** a multiarmed goddess who often rides a lion. Her son is the elephant-headed **Ganesha** (FIG. 16-9).

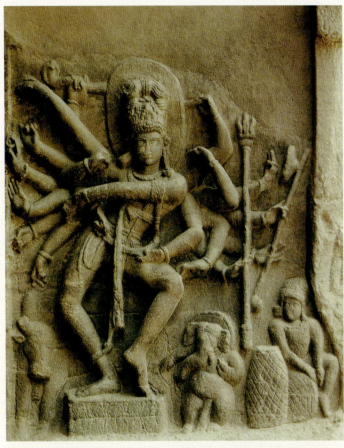

16-9 Dancing Shiva, rock-cut relief in cave temple, Badami, India, late sixth century.

Shiva dances the cosmic dance and has 18 arms, some holding objects, others forming mudras. Artists often portrayed Hindu gods with multiple limbs to indicate their suprahuman nature.

king Harishena (r. 462–481) and members of his court were the sponsors of the new caves at the Buddhist monastery at Ajanta. Buddhism and Hinduism are not monotheistic religions, such as Judaism, Christianity, and Islam. Instead, Buddhists and Hindus approach the spiritual through many gods and varying paths, which permits mutually tolerated differences. In fact, in Hinduism, the Buddha is one of the ten incarnations of Vishnu, one of the three principal Hindu deities (see "Hinduism and Hindu Iconography," above).

Badami More early Buddhist than Hindu art has survived in India because the Buddhists constructed large monastic institutions with durable materials such as stone and brick. But in the Gupta period, Hindu stone sculpture and architecture began to rival the great Buddhist monuments of South Asia. During the sixth century, the Huns brought down the Gupta Empire, and various regional dynasties rose to power. In the Deccan plateau of central India, the Chalukya kings ruled from their capital at Badami. There, Chalukya sculptors carved a series of reliefs in the walls of halls cut into the cliff above the city. One relief (FIG. 16-9) shows Shiva dancing the cosmic dance, his 18 arms swinging rhythmically in an arc. Some of the hands hold objects, and others form prescribed mudras. At the lower right, the elephant-headed Ganesha tentatively mimics Shiva. Nandi, Shiva's bull mount, stands at the left. Artists often represented Hindu deities as part human and part animal or, as in the Badami relief, as figures with multiple body parts. Composite and multilimbed forms indicate that the subjects are not human but suprahuman gods with supernatural powers.

Elephanta Another portrayal of Shiva as a suprahuman being is in a cave temple on Elephanta, an island in Bombay's harbor that in the sixth century was under the control of the Kalachuri dynasty. Deep within the temple is a nearly 18-foot-high rock-cut image (FIG. **16-10**) of Shiva as Mahadeva, the "Great God" or Lord of Lords. Mahadeva appears to emerge out of the depths of the cave as worshipers' eyes become accustomed to the darkness. This image of Shiva has three faces, each showing a different aspect of the deity. (A fourth, unseen at the back, is implied—the god has not emerged fully from the rock.) The central face expresses Shiva's quiet, balanced demeanor. The face's clean planes contrast with the richness of the piled hair encrusted with jewels. The two side faces differ significantly. That on the right is female, with framing hair curls. The left face is a grimacing male with a curling mustache who wears a cobra as an earring. The female (Uma) indicates the creative aspect of Shiva; the fierce male (Bhairava) represents Shiva's destructive side. Shiva holds these two opposing forces in check, and the central face expresses their balance. The cyclic destruction and creation of the universe, which the side faces also symbolize, are part of Indian notions of time, matched by the cyclic pattern of death and rebirth.

Deogarh The rock-cut Badami and Elephanta cave shrines are characteristic of early Hindu religious architecture, but temples constructed using quarried stone became more important as Hinduism evolved. The Vishnu Temple at Deogarh in north-central India, erected in the early sixth century, is among the first Hindu temples constructed with stone blocks. A simple square tower, it has an elaborately decorated doorway at the front and a relief in a niche on each of the other three sides. Sculpted guardians protect the doorway at Deogarh, because it is the transition point between the dangerous outside and the sacred interior.

The reliefs in the three niches of the Deogarh temple depict important episodes in the saga of Vishnu. On the south (FIG. **16-11**), Vishnu sleeps on the coils of the giant serpent Ananta, whose multiple heads form a kind of umbrella around the god's face. While Lakshmi massages her husband's legs (he has cramps as he gives birth), the four-armed Vishnu dreams the universe into reality. A lotus plant (said to have grown out of Vishnu's navel) supports the four-headed Hindu god of creation, Brahma. Flanking him are other important Hindu divinities, including Shiva on his bull. Below are six figures. The four at the right are personifications of Vishnu's various powers. They will defeat the two armed demons at the left. The sculptor carved all the figures in the classic Gupta style, with smooth bodies and clinging garments (compare FIG. 16-7).

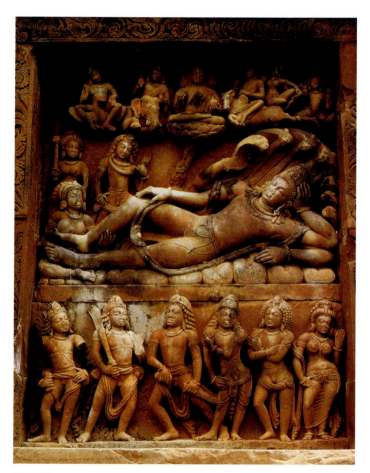

16-11 Vishnu asleep on the serpent Ananta, relief panel on the south facade of the Vishnu Temple, Deogarh, India, early sixth century.

The Deogarh temple is one of the first Hindu temples in the form of a stone tower. Its stone reliefs depict episodes from the saga of Vishnu, including this one in which the god dreams the universe into reality.

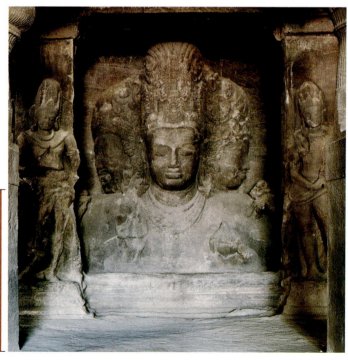

10 ft.

16-10 Shiva as Mahadeva, cave 1, Elephanta, India, ca. 550–575. Basalt, Shiva 17′ 10″ high.

This huge rock-cut image of Shiva as Mahadeva ("Great God") emerges out of the depths of the Elephanta cave as worshipers' eyes adjust to the darkness. Shiva has three faces, both male and female.

Hindu Temples

The Hindu temple is the home of the gods on earth and the place where they make themselves visible to humans. At the core of all Hindu temples is the *garbha griha,* the "womb chamber," which houses images or symbols of the deity, for example, Shiva's linga (see "Hinduism," page 459). Only the Brahmin priests can enter this inner sanctuary to make offerings to the gods. The worshipers can only stand at the threshold and behold the deity as manifest by its image. In the elaborate multiroomed temples of later Hindu architecture, the worshipers and priests progress through a series of ever more sacred spaces, usually on an east-west axis. Hindu priests and architects attached great importance to each temple's plan and sought to make it conform to the sacred geometric diagram (mandala) of the universe.

Architectural historians, following ancient Indian texts, divide Hindu temples into northern and southern typological groups:

The most important distinguishing feature of the **northern** style of temple (FIG. 16-13) is its beehivelike tower or *shikhara* ("mountain peak"), capped by an *amalaka,* a ribbed cushionlike form, derived from the shape of the amala fruit (believed to have medicinal powers). Amalakas appear on the corners of the lower levels of the shikhara too. Northern temples also have smaller towerlike roofs over the halls (*mandapas*) leading to the garbha griha.

Southern temples (FIG. 16-12) have flat roofs over their pillared mandapas, and shorter towered shrines, called *vimanas,* which lack the curved profile of their northern counterparts and resemble multilevel pyramids.

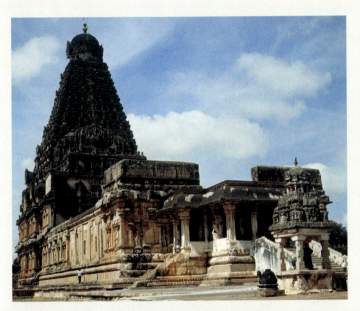

16-12 Rajarajeshvara Temple, Thanjavur, India, ca. 1010.

The Rajarajeshvara Temple at Thanjavur is an example of the southern type of Hindu temple. Two flat-roofed mandapas lead to the garbha griha in the base of its 210-foot-tall pyramidal vimana.

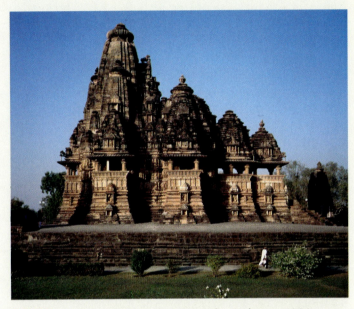

16-13 Vishvanatha Temple, Khajuraho, India, ca. 1000.

The Vishvanatha Temple at Khajuraho is of northern type and has four towers, each taller than the preceding one, symbolizing Shiva's mountain home. The largest tower is the beehive-shaped shikhara.

Early Medieval Period

During the seventh through the 12th centuries, regional dynasties ruled India. Elsewhere in Asia at this time, Buddhism spread rapidly, but in medieval India it gradually declined, and the various local kings vied with one another to erect glorious shrines to the Hindu gods.

Thanjavur Under the Chola dynasty, whose territories extended into part of Sri Lanka and even Java, architects constructed temples of unprecedented size and grandeur in the southern Indian tradition (see "Hindu Temples," above). The Rajarajeshvara Temple (FIG. **16-12**) at Thanjavur, dedicated in 1010 to Shiva as the Lord of Rajaraja, was the larg-

est and tallest temple (210 feet high) in India at its time. The temple stands inside a walled precinct. It consists of a stairway leading to two flat-roofed mandapas, the larger one having 36 pillars, and to the garbha griha in the base of the enormous pyramidal vimana that is as much an emblem of the Cholas' secular power as of their devotion to Shiva. On the exterior walls of the lower stories are numerous reliefs in niches depicting the god in his various forms.

Khajuraho At the same time the Cholas were building the Rajarajeshvara Temple at Thanjavur in the south, the Chandella dynasty was constructing temples—in northern style—at Khajuraho. The Vishvanatha Temple (FIG. **16-13**) is one of more than 20 large and elaborate temples at that site.

India and Pakistan | 461

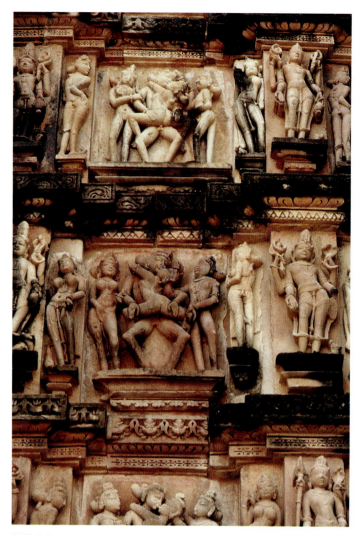

16-14 Mithuna reliefs, detail of the north side of the Vishvanatha Temple, Khajuraho, India, ca. 1000.

Northern Hindu temples often feature reliefs depicting deities and amorous couples (mithunas). The erotic sculptures suggest the propagation of life and serve as protectors of the sacred precinct.

Vishvanatha ("Lord of the World") is another of the many names for Shiva. Dedicated in 1002, the structure has three towers over the mandapas, each rising higher than the preceding one, leading to the tallest tower at the rear, in much the same way the foothills of the Himalayas, Shiva's home, rise to meet their highest peak. The mountain symbolism applies to the interior of the Vishvanatha Temple as well. Under the tallest tower, the shikhara, is the garbha griha, the small and dark inner sanctuary chamber, like a cave, which houses the image of the deity. Thus, temples such as the Vishvanatha symbolize constructed mountains with caves, comparable to the cave temples at other Indian sites. In all cases, the deity manifests himself or herself within the cave and takes various forms in sculptures. The temple mountains, however, are not intended to appear natural but rather are perfect mountains designed using ideal mathematical proportions.

The reliefs of Thanjavur's Rajarajeshvara Temple are typical of southern temple decoration, which is generally limited to images of deities. The exterior walls of Khajuraho's Vishvanatha Temple are equally typical of northern temples in the profusion of sculptures (FIG. 16-14) depicting mortals as well as gods, especially pairs of men and women (mithunas) embracing or engaged in sexual intercourse in an extraordinary range of positions. The use of seminude yakshis and amorous couples as motifs on religious buildings in India has a very long history, going back to the earliest architectural traditions, both Hindu and Buddhist (FIG. 16-5). As in earlier religious contexts, the erotic sculptures of Khajuraho suggest fertility and the propagation of life and serve as auspicious protectors of the sacred precinct.

Islam Arab armies first appeared in South Asia—at Sindh (Pakistan)—in 712. With them came Islam, the new religion that had already spread with astonishing speed from the Arabian peninsula to Syria, Iraq, Iran, Egypt, North Africa, and even southern Spain (see Chapter 5). At first, the Muslims established trading settlements but did not press deeper into the subcontinent. At the Battle of Tarain in 1192, however, Muhammad of Ghor (Afghanistan) defeated the armies of a confederation of Indian states. His general, Qutb al-Din Aybak, established the sultanate of Delhi (1206–1526) and, on his death in 1211, passed power on to his son. Iltutmish (r. 1211–1236) extended Ghorid rule across northern India. The Ghorids and other Islamic rulers gradually transformed Indian society, religion, and art.

Mughal Empire

In 1526 a Muslim prince named Babur defeated the last of the Ghorid sultans of northern India at the Battle of Panipat. Declaring himself the ruler of India, he established the Mughal Empire (1526–1857) at Delhi.

Akbar the Great The first great flowering of Mughal art and architecture occurred during the long reign of Babur's grandson, Akbar (r. 1556–1605), called the Great. Akbar enlarged the imperial painting workshop to about a hundred artists and kept them busy working on a series of ambitious projects. One of these was to illustrate the text of the biography he had commissioned Abul Fazl (1551–1602), a member of his court and a close friend, to write. The *Akbarnama (History of Akbar)* includes many full-page *miniatures*, so called because of their small size (about the size of a page in this book) compared with paintings on walls, wooden panels, or canvas. Indian miniatures were watercolor paintings on paper. They served either as illustrations in books or as loose-leaf pages in albums. Owners did not place the miniatures in frames and only rarely hung them on walls.

One extraordinary miniature (FIG. 16-15) in the emperor's personal copy of the *Akbarnama* was a collaborative effort between the painter BASAWAN, who designed and drew the composition, and CHATAR MUNI, who colored it. The painting depicts the episode of Akbar and Hawai, a wild elephant that the 19-year-old ruler mounted and pitted against another ferocious elephant. When the second animal fled in defeat, Hawai, still carrying Akbar, chased it to a pontoon bridge. The enormous weight of the elephants capsized the

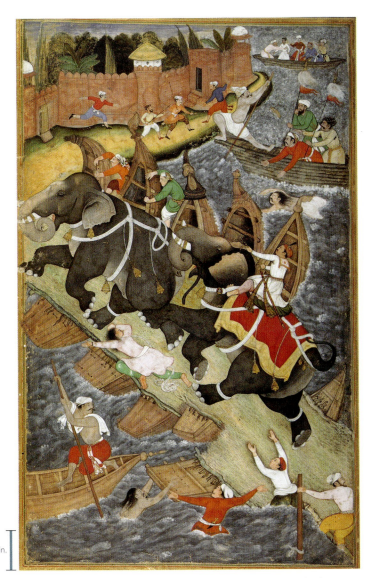

16-15 BASAWAN and CHATAR MUNI, *Akbar and the Elephant Hawai*, folio 22 from the *Akbarnama (History of Akbar)* by Abul Fazl, ca. 1590. Opaque watercolor on paper, 1′ 1⅞″ × 8¾″. Victoria & Albert Museum, London.

The Mughal rulers of India were great patrons of miniature painting. This example, showing the young emperor Akbar bringing an elephant under control, is also an allegory of his ability to rule.

sinks, and the oarsman just beyond the bridge who strains to steady his vessel while his three passengers stand up or lean overboard in reaction to the surrounding commotion.

Jahangir That the names Basawan and Chatar Muni are known is significant in itself. In contrast to the anonymity of pre-Mughal artists in India, many of those whom the Mughal emperors employed signed their artworks. Another of these was BICHITR, an artist in the imperial workshop of Akbar's son and successor, Jahangir (r. 1605–1627). The Mughals presided over a cosmopolitan court with refined tastes. British ambassadors and merchants were frequent visitors to the Mughal capital, and Jahangir, like his father, acquired many luxury goods from Europe, including globes, hourglasses, prints, and portraits.

The impact of European art on Mughal painting under Jahangir is evident in Bichitr's allegorical portrait (FIG. 16-16) of Jahangir seated on an hourglass throne, a

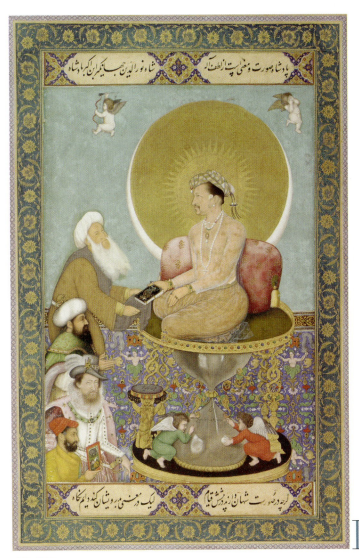

16-16 BICHITR, *Jahangir Preferring a Sufi Shaykh to Kings*, ca. 1615–1618. Opaque watercolor on paper, 1′ 6⅞″ × 1′ 1″. Freer Gallery of Art, Washington, D.C.

The influence of European art on Mughal painting is evident in this allegorical portrait of the haloed emperor Jahangir on an hourglass throne, seated above time, favoring spiritual over worldly power.

boats, but Akbar managed to bring Hawai under control and dismount safely. The young ruler viewed the episode as an allegory of his ability to govern—that is, to take charge of an unruly state.

For his pictorial record of that frightening day, Basawan chose the moment of maximum chaos and danger—when the elephants crossed the pontoon bridge, sending boatmen flying into the water. The composition is a bold one, with a very high horizon and two strong diagonal lines formed by the bridge and the shore. Together these devices tend to flatten out the vista, yet at the same time Basawan created a sense of depth by diminishing the size of the figures in the background. He was also a master of vivid gestures and anecdotal detail. Note especially the bare-chested figure in the foreground clinging to the end of a boat, the figure near the lower right corner with outstretched arms sliding into the water as the bridge

India and Pakistan | **463**

miniature from an album made for the emperor around 1615–1618. As the sands of time run out, two cupids (clothed, unlike their European models more closely copied at the top of the painting) inscribe the throne with the wish that Jahangir would live a thousand years. Bichitr portrayed his patron as an emperor above time and also placed behind Jahangir's head a radiant halo combining a golden sun and a white crescent moon, indicating that Jahangir is the center of the universe and its light source. One of the inscriptions on the painting gives the emperor's title as "Light of the Faith."

At the left are four figures. The lowest, both spatially and in the social hierarchy, is the Hindu painter Bichitr himself, wearing a red turban. He holds a miniature representing two horses and an elephant, costly gifts from Jahangir, and another self-portrait. In the miniature-within-the-miniature, Bichitr bows deeply before the emperor. In the larger painting, the artist signed his name across the top of the footstool Jahangir uses to step up to his hourglass throne. Thus, the ruler steps on Bichitr's name, further indicating the painter's inferior status.

Above Bichitr is a portrait in full European style of King James I of England (r. 1603–1625), copied from a painting by John de Critz (ca. 1552–1641) that the English ambassador to the Mughal court had given Jahangir as a gift. Above the king is a Turkish sultan, a convincing study of physiognomy but probably not a specific portrait. The highest member of the foursome is an elderly Muslim Sufi *shaykh* (mystic saint). Jahangir's father, Akbar, had gone to the mystic to pray for an heir. The current emperor, the answer to Akbar's prayers, presents the holy man with a sumptuous book as a gift. An inscription explains that "although to all appearances kings stand before him, Jahangir looks inwardly toward the dervishes [Islamic holy men]" for guidance. Bichitr's allegorical painting portrays his emperor in both words and pictures as favoring spiritual over worldly power.

Taj Mahal Monumental tombs were not part of either the Hindu or Buddhist traditions but had a long history in Islamic architecture. The Delhi sultans had erected tombs in India, but none could compare in grandeur to the fabled Taj Mahal (FIG. **16-1**) at Agra. Shah Jahan (r. 1628–1658), Jahangir's son, built the immense *mausoleum* as a memorial to his favorite wife, Mumtaz Mahal, although it eventually became the ruler's tomb as well. The dome-on-cube shape of the central block has antecedents in earlier Islamic mausoleums, but modifications and refinements in Agra created an almost weightless vision of glistening white marble. The Agra mausoleum seems to float magically above the tree-lined reflecting pools that punctuate the garden leading to it. Reinforcing the illusion that the marble tomb is suspended above the water is the absence of any visible means of ascent to the upper platform. A stairway does exist, but the architect intentionally hid it from the view of anyone who approaches the memorial.

The Taj Mahal follows the plan of Iranian garden pavilions, except that the building stands at one end rather than in the center of the formal garden. The tomb is octagonal in plan and has typically Iranian arcuated niches (FIGS. **5-10** and **5-11**) on each side. The interplay of shadowy voids with light-reflecting marble walls that seem paper-thin creates an impression of translucency. The pointed arches lead the eye in a sweeping upward movement toward the climactic dome, shaped like a crown *(taj)*. Carefully related minarets and corner pavilions enhance and stabilize this soaring central theme. The architect achieved this delicate balance between verticality and horizontality by strictly applying an all-encompassing system of proportions. The Taj Mahal (excluding the minarets) is exactly as wide as it is tall, and the height of its dome is equal to the height of the facade.

Abd al-Hamid Lahori (d. 1654), a court historian who witnessed the construction of the Taj Mahal, compared its minarets to ladders reaching toward Heaven and its surrounding gardens to Paradise. In fact, inscribed on the walls of the mausoleum and the gateway to the gardens are carefully selected excerpts from the Koran that confirm the historian's interpretation of the tomb's symbolism. The designer of the Taj Mahal may have conceived the mausoleum as the Throne of God perched above the gardens of Paradise on Judgment Day. The minarets hold up the canopy of that throne. In Islam, the most revered place of burial is beneath the Throne of God.

Later Hindu Kingdoms

The Mughal emperors ruled vast territories, but much of northwestern India (present-day Rajasthan) remained under the control of Hindu Rajput (literally, "sons of kings") dynasties. These small kingdoms had stubbornly resisted Mughal expansion, but even the strongest of them, Mewar, eventually submitted to the Mughal emperors. When Jahangir defeated the Mewar forces in 1615, the Mewar maharana (great king), like the other Rajput rulers, maintained a degree of independence but had to pay tribute to the Mughal treasury.

Rajput painting resembles Mughal painting in format and material, but it differs sharply in other respects. Most Rajput artists, for example, worked in anonymity, never inserting self-portraits into their paintings as the Mughal painter Bichitr did in his miniature (FIG. **16-16**) of Jahangir on an hourglass throne.

Krishna and Radha Some of the most frequent subjects for Rajput paintings were the amorous adventures of Krishna, the "Blue God," the most popular avatar of Vishnu. Krishna was a herdsman who spent an idyllic existence tending his cows, fluting, and sporting with beautiful herdswomen. His favorite lover was Radha. The 12th-century poet Jayadeva had related the story of Krishna and Radha in the *Gita Govinda (Song of the Cowherd)*. Their love was a model of the devotion, or *bhakti*, paid to Vishnu. Jayadeva's poem was the source for hundreds of later paintings, including *Krishna and Radha in a Pavilion* (FIG. **16-17**), a miniature painted in the Punjab Hills by a member of the "Pahari School," probably for Raja Govardhan Chand (r. 1741–1773)

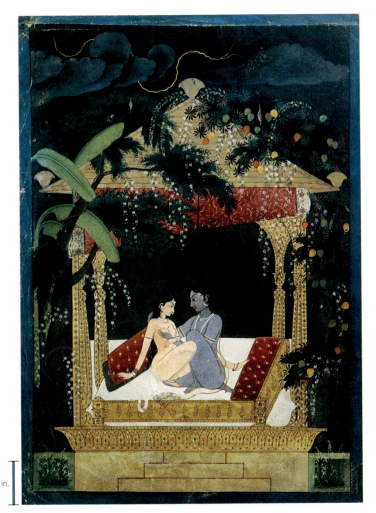

16-17 *Krishna and Radha in a Pavilion*, ca. 1760. Opaque watercolor on paper, $11\frac{1}{8}'' \times 7\frac{3}{4}''$. National Museum, New Delhi.

The love of Krishna (the "Blue God") for Radha is the subject of this colorful, lyrical, and sensual Pahari watercolor. Krishna's love was a model of the devotion paid to the Hindu god Vishnu.

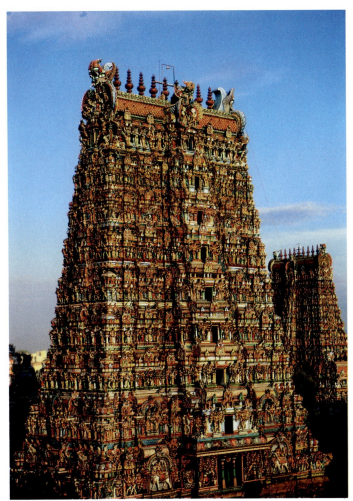

16-18 Outermost gopuras of the Great Temple, Madurai, India, completed 17th century.

The colossal gateway towers erected during the Nayak dynasty around the Great Temple at Madurai feature brightly painted stucco sculptures representing the vast pantheon of Hindu deities.

of Guler. Although Pahari painting owed much to Mughal drawing style, its coloration, lyricism, and sensuality are distinctive. In *Krishna and Radha in a Pavilion*, the lovers sit naked on a bed beneath a jeweled pavilion in a lush garden of ripe mangoes and flowering shrubs. Krishna gently touches Radha's breast while looking directly into her face. Radha shyly averts her gaze. It is night, the time of illicit trysts, and the dark monsoon sky momentarily lights up with a lightning flash indicating the moment's electric passion. Lightning is a standard element in Rajput and Pahari miniatures to symbolize sexual excitement.

Madurai Construction of some of the largest Hindu temple complexes in southern India occurred under the Nayak dynasty (r. 1529–1736). The most striking features of these huge complexes are their gateway towers called *gopuras*, decorated from top to bottom with painted sculptures. After erecting the gopuras, the builders constructed walls to connect them and then built more gopuras, always expanding outward from the center. Each set of gopuras was taller than those of the previous circuit. The outermost towers reached

colossal size, dwarfing the temples at the heart of the complexes. The largest gopuras (FIG. **16-18**) of the Great Temple at Madurai, dedicated to Shiva (under his local name, Sundareshvara, the Handsome One) and his consort Minakshi (the Fish-Eyed One), stand about 150 feet tall. Rising in a series of tiers of diminishing size, they culminate in a barrel-vaulted roof with *finials*. The ornamentation is extremely rich, consisting of row after row of brightly painted stucco sculptures representing the vast pantheon of Hindu deities and a host of attendant figures. Reconsecration of the temple occurs at 12-year intervals, at which time the gopura sculptures receive a new coat of paint, accounting for the vibrancy of their colors today.

The Mughal Empire came to an end in 1857, and for nearly a century thereafter, the British ruled India. Under the leadership of Mahatma Gandhi (1869–1948), India and Pakistan attained independence in 1947. Throughout the period of British sovereignty, local traditions mixed with imported European styles in both art and architecture. The rich and varied contemporary art of South Asia continues to draw upon these diverse traditions.

SOUTHEAST ASIA

Art historians once considered the art of Southeast Asia an extension of Indian civilization. Because of the Indian character of many Southeast Asian monuments, scholars hypothesized that Indian artists had constructed and decorated them and that Indians had colonized Southeast Asia. Today, researchers have concluded that the expansion of Indian culture to Southeast Asia during the first millennium CE was peaceful and nonimperialistic, a by-product of trade. Accompanying the trade goods from India were Sanskrit, Buddhism, and Hinduism—and Buddhist and Hindu art. But the Southeast Asian peoples soon modified Indian art to make it their own. Art historians now recognize Southeast Asian art and architecture as a distinctive and important tradition.

Java

On the island of Java, part of the modern nation of Indonesia, the period from the 8th to the 10th centuries witnessed the erection of both Hindu and Buddhist monuments.

Borobudur Borobudur (FIG. **16-19**), a Buddhist monument unique in both form and meaning, is colossal in size, measuring about 400 feet per side at the base and about 98 feet tall. Built over a small hill on nine terraces accessed by four stairways aligned with the cardinal points, the structure contains literally millions of blocks of volcanic stone. Visitors ascending the massive monument on their way to the summit encounter more than 500 life-size Buddha images, at least 1,000 relief panels, and some 1,500 stupas of various sizes.

Scholars debate the intended meaning of Borobudur. Most think the structure is a constructed cosmic mountain, a three-dimensional mandala where worshipers pass through various realms on their way to ultimate enlightenment. As they circumambulate Borobudur, pilgrims first see reliefs illustrating the karmic effects of various kinds of human behavior, then reliefs depicting jatakas of the Buddha's earlier lives, and, farther up, events from the life of Shakyamuni. On the circular terraces near the summit, each stupa is hollow and houses a statue of the seated Buddha, who has achieved spiritual enlightenment and preaches using the Wheel-turning mudra. At the very top is the largest, sealed stupa. It may once have contained another Buddha image, but some think it was left empty to symbolize the formlessness of true enlightenment. Although scholars have interpreted the iconographic program in different ways, all agree on two essential points: the dependence of Borobudur on Indian art, literature, and religion, and the fact that nothing comparable exists in India itself. Borobudur's sophistication, complexity, and originality underline how completely Southeast Asians had absorbed, rethought, and reformulated Indian religion and art by 800.

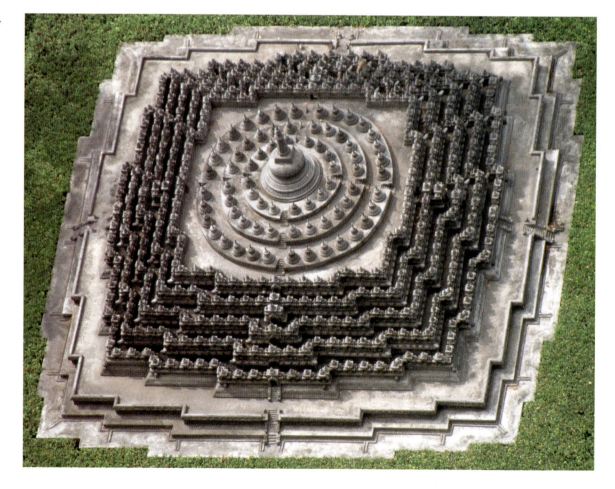

16-19 Aerial view of Borobudur, Java, Indonesia, ca. 800.

Borobudur is a colossal Buddhist monument of unique form. Built on nine terraces with more than 1,500 stupas and 1,500 statues and reliefs, it takes the form of a cosmic mountain, which worshipers circumambulate.

Cambodia

In 802, the Khmer king Jayavarman II (r. 802–850) founded the Angkor dynasty, which ruled Cambodia for the next 400 years and sponsored the construction of hundreds of monuments, including gigantic Buddhist monasteries *(wats)*.

Angkor Wat Founded by Indravarman (r. 877–889), Angkor is a vast complex of temples and palaces within a rectangular grid of canals and reservoirs fed by local rivers. For hundreds of years, each of the Khmer kings built a temple mountain at Angkor and installed his personal god—Shiva, Vishnu, or the Buddha—on top and gave the god part of his own royal name, implying that the king was a manifestation of the deity. When the king died, the Khmer believed the god reabsorbed him, because he had been the earthly portion of the deity during his lifetime, so they worshiped the king's image as the god. This concept of kingship approaches an actual deification of the ruler, familiar in many other societies, such as pharaonic Egypt (see Chapter 1).

Of all the monuments the Khmer kings erected, Angkor Wat (FIG. **16-20**) is the most spectacular. Built by Suryavarman II (r. 1113–1150), it is the largest of the many Khmer temple complexes. Angkor Wat rises from a huge rectangle of land delineated by a moat measuring about 5,000 by 4,000 feet. Like the other Khmer temples, its purpose was to associate the king with his personal god, in this case Vishnu. The centerpiece of the complex is a tall stepped tower surrounded by four smaller towers connected by covered galleries. The five towers symbolize the five peaks of Mount Meru, the sacred mountain at the center of the universe. Two more circuit walls with galleries, towers, and gates enclose the central block. Thus, as one progresses inward through the complex, the towers rise ever higher, in similar manner as the towers of Khajuraho's Vishvanatha Temple (FIG. 16-13) but in a more complex sequence and on a much grander scale. Throughout Angkor Wat, stone reliefs glorify both Vishnu in his various avatars and Suryavarman II.

Thailand

Southeast Asians practiced both Buddhism and Hinduism, but by the 13th century, in contrast to developments in India, Hinduism was in decline and Buddhism dominated much of the mainland. Historians date the beginning of the Sukhothai kingdom in Thailand to 1292, the year King Ramkhamhaeng (r. 1279–1299) erected a four-sided stele bearing the first inscription written in the Thai language.

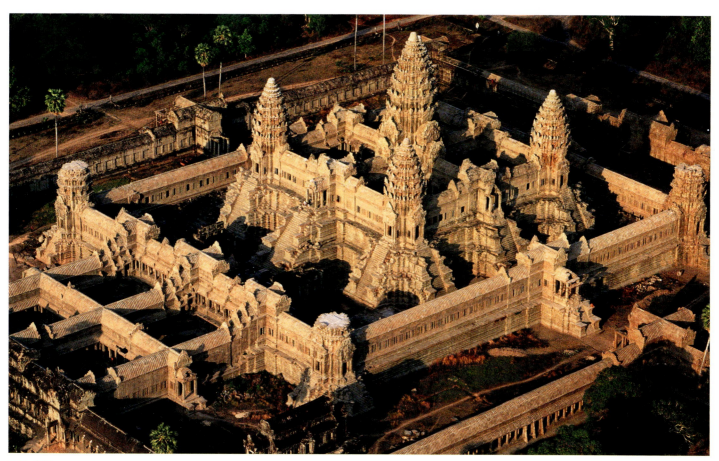

16-20 Aerial view (looking northeast) of Angkor Wat, Angkor, Cambodia, first half of 12th century.

Angkor Wat, built by Suryavarman II to associate the Khmer king with the god Vishnu, has five towers symbolizing the five peaks of Mount Meru, the sacred mountain at the center of the universe.

16-21 Walking Buddha, from Sukhothai, Thailand, 14th century. Bronze, 7′ 2½″ high. Wat Bechamabopit, Bangkok.

The walking-Buddha statuary type is unique to Thailand and displays a distinctive approach to body form. The Buddha's body is soft and elastic, and the right arm hangs loosely, like an elephant trunk.

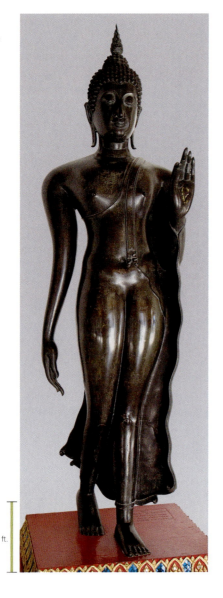

1 ft.

16-22 Schwedagon Pagoda, Rangoon (Yangon), Myanmar, 14th century or earlier (rebuilt several times).

The 344-foot-tall Schwedagon Pagoda houses two of the Buddha's hairs. Silver and jewels and 13,153 gold plates sheathe its exterior. The gold ball at the top is inlaid with 4,351 diamonds.

Walking Buddha Sukhothai's crowning artistic achievement was the development of a type of walking-Buddha statue (FIG. 16-21) displaying a distinctively Thai approach to body form. The bronze Buddha has broad shoulders and a narrow waist and wears a clinging monk's robe. He strides forward, his right heel off the ground and his left arm raised with the hand held in the do-not-fear mudra to encourage worshipers to come forward in reverence. A flame leaps from the top of the Buddha's head, and a sharp nose projects from his rounded face. The right arm hangs loosely, seemingly without muscles or joints, like an elephant's trunk. The Sukhothai artists intended the body type to suggest a supernatural being and to express the Buddha's beauty and perfection. Although images in stone exist, the Sukhothai artists handled bronze best, a material well suited to their conception of the Buddha's body as elastic. The Sukhothai walking-Buddha statuary type does not occur elsewhere in Buddhist art.

Myanmar

Myanmar, like Thailand, is overwhelmingly a Theravada Buddhist country today. Important Buddhist monasteries and monuments dot the countryside.

Schwedagon Pagoda In Rangoon, an enormous complex of buildings, including shrines filled with Buddha images, has as its centerpiece one of the largest stupas in the world, the Schwedagon Pagoda (FIG. 16-22). (*Pagoda* derives from the Portuguese version of a word for stupa.) The Rangoon pagoda houses two of the Buddha's hairs, traditionally said to have been brought to Myanmar by merchants who received them from the Buddha himself. Rebuilt several times, this highly revered stupa is famous for the gold, silver, and jewels encrusting its surface. The Schwedagon Pagoda stands 344 feet high. Covering its upper part are 13,153 plates of gold, each about a foot square. At the very top is a seven-tiered umbrella crowned with a gold ball inlaid with 4,351 diamonds, one of which weighs 76 carats. This great wealth was a gift to the Buddha from the laypeople of Myanmar to produce merit.

Buddhism and Buddhist art gradually spread from India not only to Southeast Asia but also to China, Korea, and Japan, where architects, sculptors, and painters created some of the most impressive surviving Buddhist monuments as well as a distinguished tradition of secular art (see Chapters 17 and 18).

South and Southeast Asia

INDUS CIVILIZATION AND MAURYA DYNASTY

▌ The Indus Civilization (ca. 2600–1500 BCE) was one of the world's earliest civilizations. Indus cities had streets oriented to the compass points and sophisticated water-supply and sewage systems, but little Indus art survives, most of it seals with incised designs and small-scale sculptures.

▌ The greatest ruler of the Maurya dynasty (323–185 BCE) was Ashoka (r. 272–231 BCE), who converted to Buddhism and spread the Buddha's teaching throughout South Asia. Ashoka's pillars are the first monumental stone artworks in India. Ashoka was also the builder of the original Great Stupa at Sanchi.

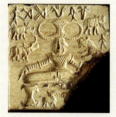

Seal, Mohenjo-daro, ca. 2300–1750 BCE

KUSHAN, GUPTA, POST-GUPTA PERIODS

▌ The first representations of the Buddha in human form date to the Kushan Empire (mid-first century to 320 CE). Gandharan Buddhist art owes a strong stylistic debt to Greco-Roman art. By the second century CE, the iconography of the life of the Buddha was well established.

▌ Gupta sculptors formulated the standard Buddha image in the fifth century, combining Gandharan iconography with a soft, full-bodied figure in clinging garments. The Gupta-period Buddhist caves of Ajanta are the best surviving examples of early mural painting in India.

▌ The oldest Hindu monumental stone temples and sculptures—at Badami, Elephanta, Deogarh, and elsewhere—date to the fifth and sixth centuries.

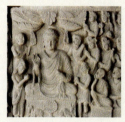

The Buddha's first sermon, Gandhara, second century CE

EARLY MEDIEVAL PERIOD

▌ The Chola, Chandella, and other regional dynasties ruled South Asia from the seventh to the 12th century, and distinctive regional styles emerged in Hindu religious architecture. Northern temples, such as the Vishvanatha Temple at Khajuraho, have a series of small towers leading to a tall beehive-shaped tower, or shikhara, over the garbha griha. Southern temples have flat-roofed pillared halls (mandapas) leading to a pyramidal tower (vimana).

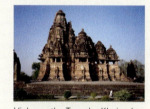

Vishvanatha Temple, Khajuraho, ca. 1000

MUGHAL EMPIRE

▌ The first great flowering of art and architecture in the Mughal Empire (1526–1857) occurred under Akbar the Great (r. 1556–1605), who oversaw an imperial workshop that specialized in painting miniatures. Shah Jahan (r. 1628–1658) built the Taj Mahal as a memorial to his favorite wife.

▌ During the Mughal Empire, Hindu Rajput kings ruled much of northwestern India. The coloration and sensuality of Rajput painting distinguish it from the contemporaneous Mughal style.

▌ Between 1529 and 1736, the Hindu Nayak dynasty controlled southern India and erected temple complexes with immense gateway towers (gopuras) decorated with painted stucco sculptures of Hindu deities.

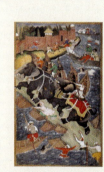

Basawan and Chatar Muni, *Akbar and the Elephant Hawai*, ca. 1590

SOUTHEAST ASIA

▌ Southeast Asian art and architecture reflect Indian prototypes, but many local styles developed. Borobudur in Indonesia depends on Indian prototypes but is unique in form. In Cambodia, the Khmer kings erected vast Buddhist temple complexes at Angkor. In Thailand, the Sukhothai walking-Buddha statuary type displays a unique approach to body form, for example, the Buddha's trunklike right arm. Myanmar's Schwedagon Pagoda in Rangoon is one of the largest stupas in the world and is encrusted with gold, silver, and jewels.

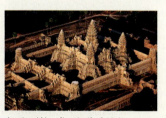

Angkor Wat, first half of 12th century

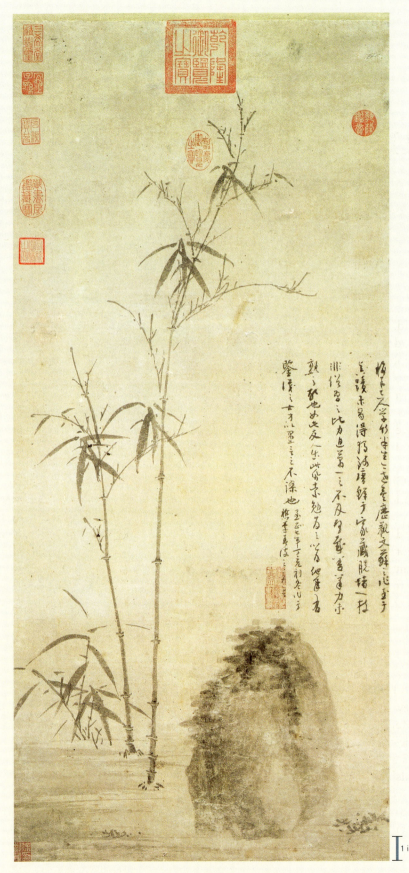

1 in.

17-1 Wu Zhen, *Stalks of Bamboo by a Rock*, Yuan dynasty, 1347. Hanging scroll, ink on paper, 2' 11½" × 1' 4⅝". National Palace Museum, Taibei.

Wu Zhen was one of the leading Yuan literati (scholar-artists). Chinese scroll painters favored bamboo as a subject because the plants' branches were perfect complements to the highly esteemed art of calligraphy.

China and Korea

CHINA

China (MAP **17-1**) is the only continuing civilization originating in the ancient world. Vast and varied both topographically and climatically, China's landscape includes sandy plains, mighty rivers, towering mountains, and fertile farmlands. Its political and cultural boundaries have varied over the millennia, and at times the country has grown to about twice the area of the United States. China boasts the world's largest population and is ethnically diverse. The spoken language varies so much that speakers of different dialects do not understand one another. However, the written language, which employs *characters* (signs that record meaning rather than sounds), has permitted different peoples living thousands of miles apart to share literary, philosophic, and religious traditions.

China traces its beginnings to long before the dawn of recorded history. Discoveries in recent years have provided evidence of settled village life as far back as the seventh or early sixth millennium BCE. Mastery of the art of pottery soon followed. The potters of the Yangshao Culture, which arose along the Yellow River in northeastern China, produced fine decorated ceramic bowls even before the invention of the potter's wheel in the fourth millennium BCE. Archaeologists have also found traces of China's earliest royal dynasty, the Xia (ca. 2000–1600 BCE), long thought to have been mythical.

Shang and Zhou Dynasties

The first great Chinese dynasty of the Bronze Age was the Shang (ca. 1600–1050 BCE), whose kings ruled from a series of royal capitals in the Yellow River valley. In 1928 excavations at Anyang (ancient Yin) brought to light the last Shang capital. There, archaeologists found a large number of objects inscribed in the earliest form of the Chinese language. These fragmentary records and the other finds at Anyang reveal a warlike, highly stratified society. The excavated tomb furnishings include weapons and a great wealth of objects in jade, ivory, *lacquer* (sap-coated wood), and bronze. Not only the Shang kings received lavish burials. The tomb of Fu Hao, the wife of Wu Ding (r. ca. 1215–1190 BCE), for example, contained more than a thousand bronze and jade objects and an ivory beaker inlaid with turquoise.

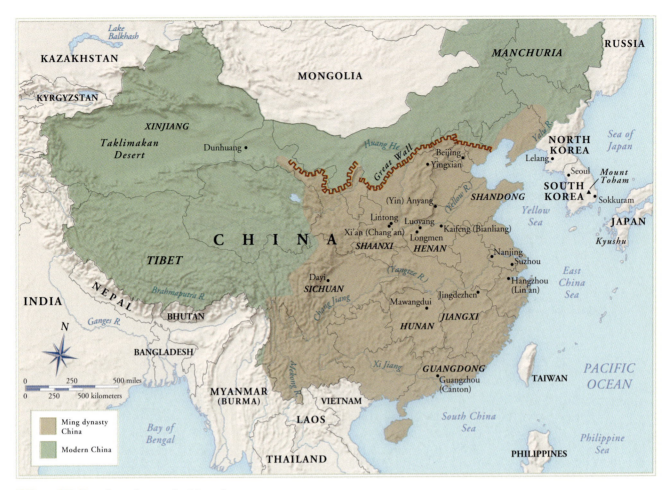

MAP 17-1 China during the Ming dynasty.

Shang Bronzes Shang artists perfected the casting of elaborate bronze vessels. Used in sacrifices to ancestors and in funerary ceremonies, Shang bronzes feature decorative motifs that range from mere suggestions of animal forms emerging out of linear patterns to identifiable representations of specific creatures. Often, distinct motifs stand out against a background of round or squared spirals ending in hooks. Sometimes the same motifs also cover the figures. Shang bronzes held wine, water, grain, or meat for sacrificial rites. Each vessel's shape matched its intended purpose.

One of the most dramatic Shang vessel forms is the *guang*, a libation vessel shaped like a covered gravy boat. In the illustrated example (FIG. **17-2**), the multiple designs and their fields of background spirals integrate so closely with the form of the vessel that they are not merely an external embellishment but an integral part of the sculptural whole. Some motifs on the guang's side may represent the eyes of a tiger and the horns of a ram. A horned animal forms the front of the lid, and at the rear is a horned head with a bird's beak.

Another horned head appears on the handle. Fish, birds, elephants, rabbits, and more abstract composite creatures swarm over the surface against a background of spirals. The

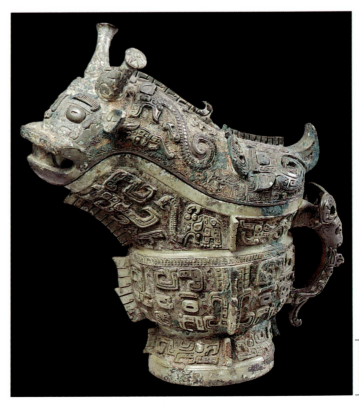

1 in.

17-2 Guang, probably from Anyang, China, Shang dynasty, 12th or 11th century BCE. Bronze, 6½" high. Asian Art Museum of San Francisco, San Francisco (Avery Brundage Collection).

Shang artists perfected the casting of elaborate bronze vessels decorated with animal motifs. The animal forms, real and imaginary, on this libation guang are probably connected with the world of spirits.

Daoism and Confucianism

Daoism and Confucianism are both philosophies and religions native to China. Both schools of thought attracted wide followings during the Warring States Period, when political turbulence led to social unrest.

Daoism emerged out of the metaphysical teachings attributed to Laozi (604?–531? BCE) and Zhuangzi (370?–301? BCE). It takes its name from Laozi's treatise *Daodejing (The Way and Its Power)*. Daoist philosophy stresses an intuitive awareness, nurtured by harmonious contact with nature, and eschews everything artificial. Daoists seek to follow the universal path, or principle, called the Dao, whose features cannot be described but only suggested through analogies. For example, the Dao is said to be like water, always yielding but eventually wearing away the hard stone that does not yield. For Daoists, strength comes from flexibility and inaction. Historically, Daoist principles encouraged retreat from society in favor of personal cultivation.

Confucius (551–479 BCE) was born in the state of Lu (roughly modern Shandong Province) to an aristocratic family that had fallen on hard times. From an early age, he showed a strong interest in the rites and ceremonies that helped unite people into an orderly society. As he grew older, he developed a deep concern for the suffering caused by the civil conflict of his day. Thus, he adopted a philosophy that he hoped would lead to order and stability. The *junzi* ("superior person" or "gentleman"), who possesses *ren* (human-heartedness), personifies the ideal social order Confucius sought. Although the term originally assumed noble birth, in Confucian thought anyone can become a junzi by cultivating the virtues

Confucius espoused, especially empathy for suffering, pursuit of morality and justice, respect for ancient ceremonies, and adherence to traditional social relationships, such as those between parent and child, elder and younger sibling, husband and wife, or ruler and subject.

Confucius's disciple Mencius (or Mengzi, 371?–289? BCE) developed the master's ideas further, stressing that the deference to age and rank that is at the heart of the Confucian social order brings a reciprocal responsibility. For example, a king's legitimacy depends on the goodwill of his people. A ruler should share his joys with his subjects and will know his laws are unjust if they bring suffering to the people.

Confucius spent much of his adult life trying to find rulers willing to apply his teachings, but he died in disappointment. However, he and Mencius had a profound impact on Chinese thought and social practice. Chinese traditions of venerating deceased ancestors and outstanding leaders encouraged the development of Confucianism as a religion as well as a philosophic tradition. Eventually, Emperor Wu (r. 140–87 BCE) of the Han dynasty established Confucianism as the state's official doctrine. Thereafter, it became the primary subject of the civil service exams required for admission into and advancement within government service.

"Confucian" and "Daoist" are broad, imprecise terms scholars often use to distinguish aspects of Chinese culture stressing social responsibility and order (Confucian) from those emphasizing cultivation of individuals, often in reclusion (Daoist). But both philosophies share the idea that anyone can cultivate wisdom or ability, regardless of birth.

---

fabulous animal forms, real and imaginary, are unlikely to have been purely decorative. They are probably connected with the world of spirits addressed in the rituals.

Zhou Dynasty Around 1050 BCE, the Zhou, former vassals of the Shang, captured Anyang and overthrew their Shang overlords. The Zhou dynasty (ca. 1050–256 BCE) proved to be the longest lasting in China's history. The closing centuries of Zhou rule include a long period of warfare among competing states, the so-called Warring States Period (ca. 475–221 BCE). This period of political and social turmoil was also a time of intellectual upheaval, when conflicting schools of philosophy, including Legalism, Daoism, and Confucianism, emerged (see "Daoism and Confucianism," above).

Qin Dynasty

The ruler of the state of Qin (from which the modern name "China" derives) brought the Warring States Period to an end by conquering all rival states, including the Zhou. Known to history by his title, Qin Shi Huangdi (First Emperor of Qin), between 221 and 210 BCE he controlled an area equal to about half of modern China. During his reign, Shi Huangdi ordered the linkage of active fortifications along the northern border of his realm to form the famous Great Wall

(MAP 17-1), which defended China against the fierce nomadic peoples of the north, especially the Huns. By sometimes brutal methods, the First Emperor consolidated rule through a centralized bureaucracy and adopted standardized written language, weights and measures, and coinage.

Shi Huangdi also repressed all schools of thought other than Legalism, which espoused absolute obedience to the state's authority and advocated strict laws and punishments. Chinese historians long have condemned the First Emperor, but the bureaucratic system he put in place had a long-lasting impact. Its success was due in large part to Shi Huangdi's decision to replace the hereditary feudal lords with talented salaried administrators and to reward merit rather than favor high birth.

Lintong In 1974, excavations started at the site of the immense burial mound of Shi Huangdi at Lintong. For its construction, the ruler conscripted more than 700,000 laborers and had the tomb filled with treasure. The mound itself remains largely unexcavated, but researchers believe it contains a vast underground funerary palace designed to match the fabulous palace the emperor occupied in life. The historian Sima Qian (136–85 BCE) described both palaces, but scholars did not take his account seriously until the discovery of pits around the tomb filled with more than 6,000 life-size painted terracotta figures of soldiers and horses, as well as

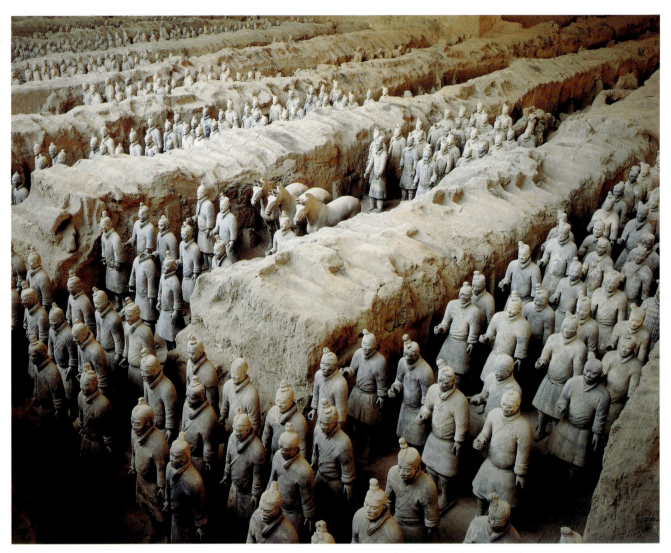

17-3 Army of the First Emperor of Qin in pits next to his burial mound, Lintong, China, Qin dynasty, ca. 210 BCE. Painted terracotta, average figure 5′ 10⅞″ high.

The First Emperor was buried beneath an immense mound guarded by more than 6,000 life-size terracotta soldiers. Although produced from common molds, every figure has an individualized appearance.

bronze horses and chariots (FIG. 17-3). The terracotta army served as the First Emperor's bodyguard deployed in perpetuity outside his tomb.

The Lintong army, comprising cavalry, chariots, archers, lancers, and hand-to-hand fighters, was one of the 20th century's greatest archaeological discoveries. The huge assemblage testifies to a very high degree of organization in the Qin imperial workshop. Manufacturing this army of statues required a veritable army of sculptors and painters as well as a large number of huge kilns. The First Emperor's artisans could have opted to use the same molds over and over again to produce thousands of identical soldiers standing in strict formation. In fact, they did employ the same molds repeatedly for different parts of the statues but assembled the parts in many different combinations. Consequently, the stances, arm positions, garment folds, equipment, coiffures, and facial features vary—sometimes slightly, sometimes markedly—from statue to statue. Additional hand modeling of the cast body parts before firing permitted the sculptors to differentiate the figures even more. The Qin painters undoubtedly

added further variations to the appearance of the terracotta army. The result of these efforts was a brilliant balance between uniformity and individuality.

Han Dynasty and Period of Disunity

Soon after the First Emperor's death, the people who had suffered under his reign revolted, assassinated his son, and founded the Han dynasty (206 BCE–220 CE). The Han ruled China for four centuries and extended its southern and western boundaries, penetrating far into Central Asia (modern Xinjiang) and even began to trade indirectly with distant Rome via the fabled Silk Road, a network of caravan tracts linking China and the Mediterranean world. Very few traders actually traveled the entire route. Along the way, goods usually passed through the hands of people from many lands, who often only dimly understood the origins and destinations of what they traded. The Roman passion for silk ultimately led to the modern name for the Central Asian routes, but gold,

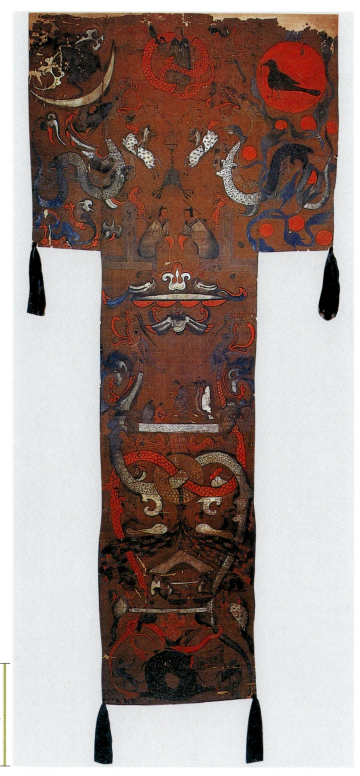

17-4 Funeral banner, from tomb 1 (tomb of the Marquise of Dai), Mawangdui, China, Han dynasty, ca. 168 BCE. Painted silk, 6' 8¾" × 3' ¼". Hunan Provincial Museum, Changsha.

This T-shaped silk banner was draped over the coffin of the Marquise of Dai, who is shown at the center awaiting her ascent to immortality in Heaven, the realm of the red sun and silvery moon.

1 ft.

tained a rich array of burial goods used during the funerary ceremonies and to accompany the deceased into the afterlife. Among the many finds are decorated lacquer utensils, various textiles, and an astonishingly well-preserved corpse in the innermost of four nested sarcophagi. Most remarkable of all, however, is the painted T-shaped silk banner (FIG. **17-4**) discovered draped over the marquise's coffin. Scholars generally agree that the area within the cross at the top of the T represents Heaven. Most of the vertical section below is the human realm, and at the very bottom is the Underworld. In the heavenly realm, dragons and immortal beings appear between and below two orbs—the red sun and its symbol, the raven, on the right, and the silvery moon and its symbol, the toad, on the left. Below, the standing figure on the first white platform near the center of the vertical section is probably the Marquise of Dai herself—one of the first portraits in Chinese art. The woman awaits her ascent to Heaven, where she will attain immortality. Nearer the bottom, the artist depicted her funeral. Between these two sections are two intertwining dragons. Their tails reach down to the Underworld and their heads point to Heaven, unifying the whole composition.

Disunity For three and a half centuries, from 220 to 589,* civil strife divided China into competing states. The history of this so-called Period of Disunity is extremely complex, but one development deserves special mention—the occupation of the north by peoples who were not ethnically Han Chinese and who spoke non-Chinese languages. It was in the northern states, connected to India by the desert caravan routes of the Silk Road, that Buddhism first took root in China during the Han dynasty. Certain practices shared with Daoism, such as withdrawal from ordinary society, helped Buddhism gain an initial foothold in the north. But Buddhism's promise of hope beyond the troubles of this world earned it an ever broader audience during the upheavals of the Period of Disunity. In addition, the fully developed Buddhist system of thought attracted intellectuals. Buddhism never fully displaced Confucianism and Daoism, but it did prosper throughout China for centuries and had a profound effect on the further development of the religious forms of those two native traditions.

Gu Kaizhi Secular arts also flourished in the Period of Disunity. Rulers sought calligraphers and painters to lend prestige to their courts. The most famous early Chinese painter with whom extant works can be associated was **GU KAIZHI** (ca. 344–406). Gu was a friend of important members of the Eastern Jin dynasty (317–420) and won renown as a calligrapher, a painter of court portraits, and a pioneer of landscape painting. A *handscroll* (see "Chinese Painting Materials and Formats," page 476) attributed to Gu Kaizhi in the 11th century is not actually by his hand, but it provides a good idea of the key elements of his art. Called *Admonitions of the Instructress to the Court Ladies*, the horizontal scroll contains painted scenes and accompanying explanatory text.

*From this point on, all dates in this chapter are CE unless otherwise stated.

ivory, gems, glass, lacquer, incense, furs, spices, cotton, linens, exotic animals, and other merchandise precious enough to warrant the risks also passed along the Silk Road.

Marquise of Dai In 1972 archaeologists excavated the tomb of the Marquise of Dai at Mawangdui. The tomb con-

Chinese Painting Materials and Formats

Mural paintings in caves (FIG. 17-7) were popular in China, as they were in South Asia (FIG. 16-8), but Chinese artists also employed several distinctive materials and formats for their paintings. The basic requirements for paintings not on walls were the same as for writing—a round tapered brush, soot-based ink, and either silk or paper. Chinese painters were masters of the brush. Sometimes they used modulated lines for contours and interior details that elastically thicken and thin to convey depth and mass. In other works, they used *iron-wire lines* (thin, unmodulated lines with a suggestion of tensile strength) to define the figures. Chinese painters also used richly colored minerals as pigments, finely ground and suspended in a gluey medium, and watery washes of mineral and vegetable dyes.

The formats of Chinese paintings on silk or paper tend to be personal and intimate, and they are usually best viewed by only one or two people at a time. The most common types are

Hanging scrolls (FIGS. 17-9 and 17-17). Chinese painters often mounted pictures on, or painted directly on, unrolled vertical scrolls for display on walls.

Handscrolls (FIGS. 17-5, 17-8, and 17-10). Paintings were also frequently attached to or painted on long, narrow scrolls that the viewer unrolled horizontally, section by section from right to left.

Album leaves (FIGS. 17-13 and 17-18). Many Chinese artists painted small panels on paper leaves, which collectors placed in albums.

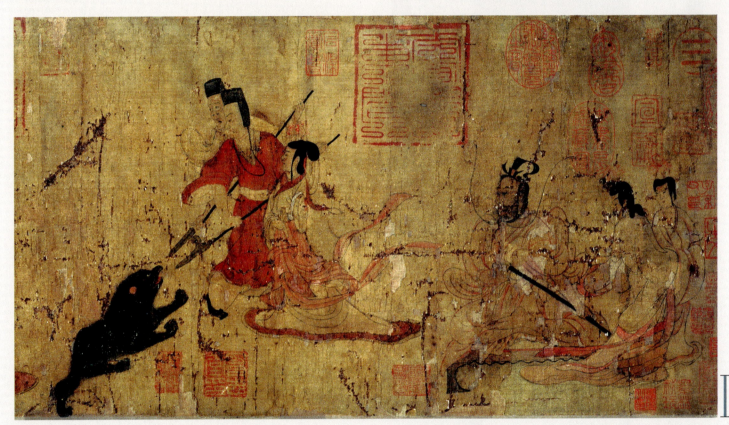

1 in.

17-5 Gu Kaizhi, *Lady Feng and the Bear*, detail of *Admonitions of the Instructress to the Court Ladies*, Period of Disunity, late fourth century. Handscroll, ink and colors on silk, entire scroll $9\frac{3}{4}$″ × 11′ $4\frac{1}{2}$″. British Museum, London.

Lady Feng's act of heroism to save the life of her emperor was a perfect model of Confucian behavior. In this early Chinese representation of the episode, the painter set the figures against a blank background.

Like all Chinese handscrolls, this one was unrolled and read from right to left, with only a small section exposed for viewing at one time. The section illustrated here (FIG. **17-5**) records a well-known act of heroism, the Lady Feng saving her emperor's life by placing herself between him and an attacking bear—a perfect model of Confucian behavior. As in many early Chinese paintings, the artist set the figures against a blank background with only a minimal setting for the scene, although in other works, Gu provided landscape settings for his narratives. The figures' poses and fluttering drapery ribbons, in concert with individualized facial expressions, convey a clear quality of animation.

Tang Dynasty

The emperors of the short-lived Sui dynasty (581–618) succeeded in reuniting China and prepared the way for the brilliant Tang dynasty (618–906). Under the Tang emperors,

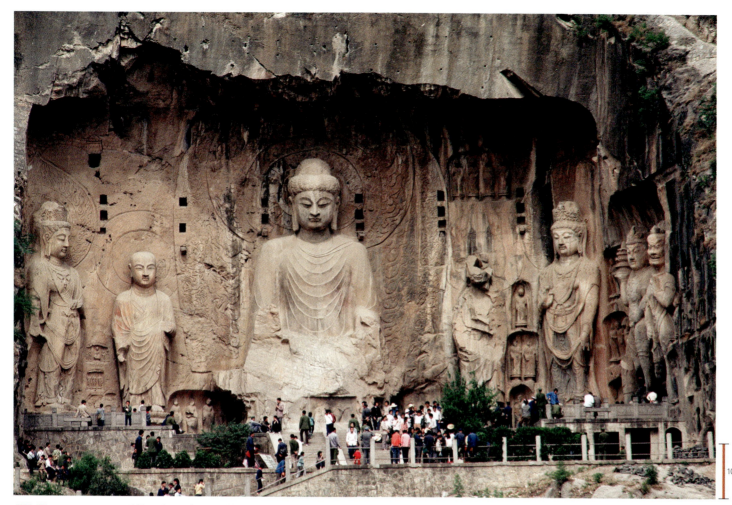

10 ft.

17-6 Vairocana Buddha, disciples, and bodhisattvas, Longmen Caves, Luoyang, China, Tang dynasty, completed 675. Buddha 44' high.

Empress Wu Zetian sponsored these colossal rock-cut sculptures. The Tang artists represented the Mahayana Cosmic Buddha in serene majesty, suppressing surface detail in favor of monumental simplicity.

China entered a period of unequaled magnificence. Chinese armies marched across Central Asia, prompting an influx of foreign peoples, wealth, and ideas into China. Traders, missionaries, and other travelers journeyed to the cosmopolitan Tang capital at Chang'an (modern Xi'an), and the Chinese, in turn, ventured westward. Chang'an occupied more than 30 square miles. Laid out on a grid scheme, it was the greatest city in the world during the seventh and eighth centuries.

Longmen Caves In its first century, the new dynasty sponsored great monuments for Buddhist worshipers. Cave complexes decorated with reliefs and paintings, modeled on those of India (see Chapter 16), were especially popular. One of the most spectacular Tang Buddhist sculptures is carved into the face of a cliff in the great Longmen Caves complex near Luoyang. Work at Longmen had begun almost two centuries earlier, during the Period of Disunity. The site's 2,435 shrines attest to its importance as a Buddhist center.

The colossal relief (FIG. **17-6**) that dominates the Longmen complex features a central figure of the Buddha that is 44 feet tall—seated. An inscription records that the project was completed in 676 when Gaozong (r. 649–683) was emperor and that in 672 the empress Wu Zetian underwrote a substantial portion of the considerable cost with her private

funds. Wu Zetian was an exceptional woman by any standard, and when Gaozong died in 683, she declared herself emperor and ruled until 705, when she was forced to abdicate at age 82.

Wu Zetian's Buddha is the Vairocana Buddha, or the Mahayana Cosmic Buddha, the Buddha of Boundless Space and Time (see "Buddhism," Chapter 16, page 454). Flanking him are two of his monks, attendant bodhisattvas, and guardian figures—all smaller than the Buddha but still of colossal size. (The tourists in FIG. 17-6 underscore the scale of the work.) The sculptors represented the Buddha in serene majesty. An almost geometric regularity of contour and smoothness of planes emphasize the volume of the massive figure. The folds of the Buddha's robes fall in a few concentric arcs. The artists suppressed surface detail in the interest of monumental simplicity and dignity.

Dunhuang Grottoes The westward expansion of the Tang Empire increased the importance of Dunhuang, the westernmost gateway to China on the Silk Road. Dunhuang long had been a wealthy, cosmopolitan trade center, a Buddhist pilgrimage destination, and home to thriving communities of Buddhist monks and nuns of varied ethnicity, as well as to adherents of other religions. In the course of several

17-7 *Paradise of Amitabha*, cave 172, Dunhuang, China, Tang dynasty, mid-eighth century. Wall painting, 10' high.

This richly detailed, brilliantly colored mural aided Tang worshipers at Dunhuang to visualize the wonders of the Pure Land Paradise promised to those who had faith in Amitabha, the Buddha of the West.

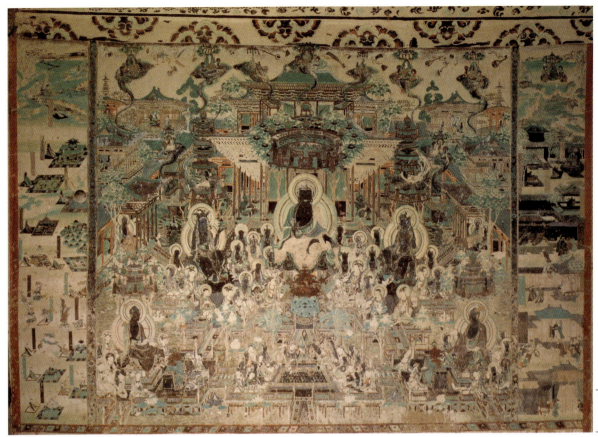

1 ft.

centuries, the Chinese cut hundreds of sanctuaries with painted murals into the soft rock of the cliffs near Dunhuang. Known today as the Mogao Grottoes and in antiquity as the Caves of a Thousand Buddhas, the Dunhuang caves are especially important because in 845, the emperor Wuzong instituted a major persecution, destroying 4,600 Buddhist temples and 40,000 shrines and forcing the return of 260,500 monks and nuns to lay life. Wuzong's policies did not affect Dunhuang, then under Tibetan rule, so the site preserves much of the type of art lost elsewhere.

Paradise of Amitabha (FIG. **17-7**), on the wall of one of the Dunhuang caves, shows how the splendor of the Tang era and religious teachings could come together in a powerful image. Buddhist Pure Land sects, especially those centered on Amitabha, Buddha of the West, had captured the popular imagination in the Period of Disunity and continued to flourish during the Tang dynasty. Pure Land teachings asserted that individuals had no hope of attaining enlightenment through their own power because of the waning of the Buddha's Law. Instead, they could obtain rebirth in a realm free from spiritual corruption simply through faith in Amitabha's promise of salvation. Richly detailed, brilliantly colored pictures steeped in the opulence of the Tang dynasty, such as this one, greatly aided worshipers in gaining faith by visualizing the wonders of the Pure Land Paradise. Amitabha sits in the center of a raised platform, his principal bodhisattvas and lesser divine attendants surrounding him. Before them a celestial dance takes place. Bodhisattvas had

strong appeal in East Asia as compassionate beings ready to achieve buddhahood but dedicated to humanity's salvation. Some received direct worship and became the main subjects of sculpture and painting.

Yan Liben The Tang emperors also fostered a brilliant tradition of scroll painting. Although few examples survive, many art historians regard the early Tang dynasty as the golden age of Chinese figure painting. *The Thirteen Emperors* (FIG. **17-8**), a masterpiece of line drawing and colored washes, has long been attributed to YAN LIBEN (d. 673). Born into an aristocratic family and the son of a famous artist, Yan Liben was prime minister under the Tang emperor Gaozong as well as a celebrated painter. This handscroll depicts 13 Chinese rulers from the Han to the Sui dynasties. Its purpose was to portray these historical figures as exemplars of moral and political virtue, in keeping with the Confucian ideal of learning from the past. Each emperor stands or sits in an undefined space. The emperor's great size relative to his attendants immediately establishes his superior stature. Simple shading in the faces and the robes gives the figures an added semblance of volume and presence. The detail in FIG. 17-8 represents Emperor Xuan of the Chen dynasty (557–589) seated among his attendants, two of whom carry the ceremonial fans that signify his rank. Xuan stands out easily from the others also because of his dark robes. His majestic serenity contrasts with his attendants' animated poses, which vary sharply from figure to figure, lending vitality to the composition.

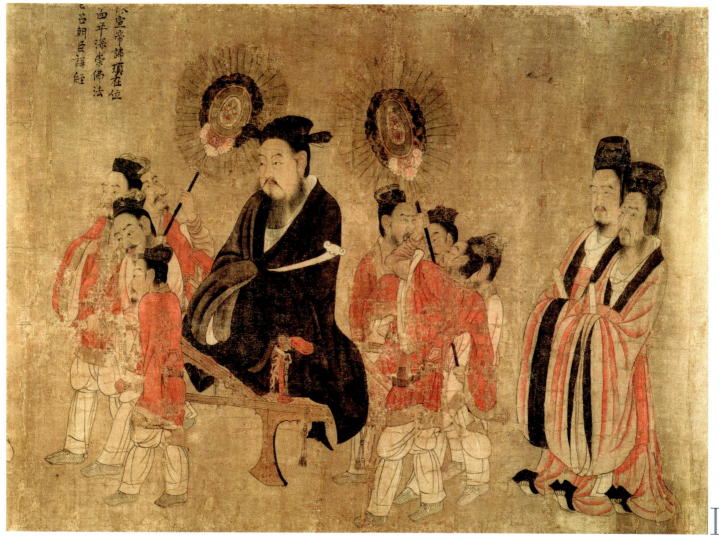

17-8 Attributed to YAN LIBEN, *Emperor Xuan and Attendants*, detail of *The Thirteen Emperors*, Tang dynasty, ca. 650. Handscroll, ink and colors on silk; detail, 1′ 8¼″ × 1′ 5½″; entire scroll, 17′ 5″ long. Museum of Fine Arts, Boston.

This handscroll portrays 13 Chinese rulers as Confucian exemplars of moral and political virtue. Yan Liben, a celebrated Tang painter, was a master of line drawing and colored washes.

Song Dynasty

The last century of Tang rule witnessed many popular uprisings and the empire's gradual disintegration. After an interim of internal strife known as the Five Dynasties period (907–960), General Zhao Kuangyin succeeded in consolidating the country once again. He established himself as the first emperor (r. 960–976) of the Song dynasty (960–1279), which ruled China from a capital in the north at Bianliang (modern Kaifeng) during the Northern Song period (960–1127). Under the Song emperors, many of the hereditary privileges of the elite class were curtailed. The emperors made political appointments on the basis of scores on civil service examinations, and education came to be a more important prerequisite for Song officials than high birth. The three centuries of Song rule, including the Southern Song period (1127–1279), when the capital was at Lin'an (modern Hangzhou) in southern China, were also a time of extraordinary technological innovation. Under the Song emperors, the Chinese invented the magnetic compass for sea navigation, printing with movable clay type, paper money, and gunpowder. Song China was the most technologically advanced society in the world in the early second millennium.

Fan Kuan For many art historians, the Song dynasty also marks the apogee of Chinese landscape painting, which first emerged as a major subject during the Period of Disunity. Although many of the great Northern Song masters worked for the imperial court, FAN KUAN (ca. 960–1030) was a Daoist recluse (see "Daoism and Confucianism," page 473) who shunned the cosmopolitan life of Bianliang. He believed nature was a better teacher than were other artists, and he spent long days in the mountains studying configurations of rocks and trees and the effect of sunlight and moonlight on natural forms. Song critics lauded Fan Kuan and other leading painters of his time as the first masters of the recording of light, shade, distance, and texture.

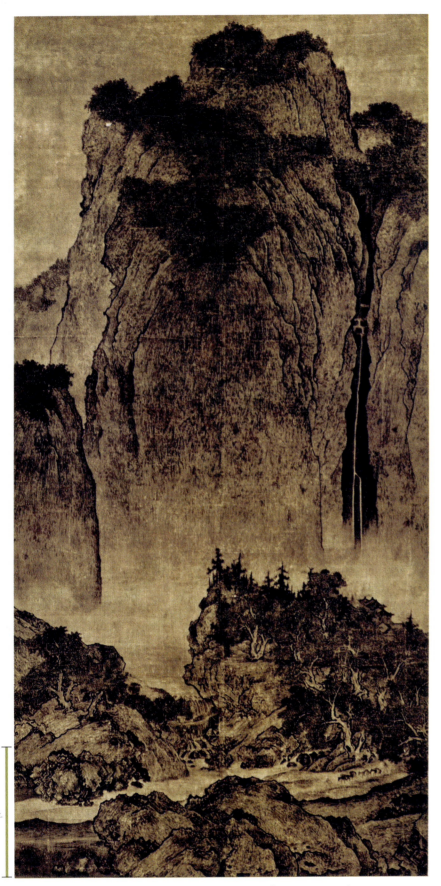

In *Travelers among Mountains and Streams* (FIG. **17-9**), Fan Kuan painted a vertical landscape of massive mountains rising from the distance. The overwhelming natural forms dwarf the few human and animal figures (for example, the mule train in the lower right corner), which the artist reduced to minute proportions. The nearly seven-foot-long silk hanging scroll cannot contain nature's grandeur. The landscape continues in all directions beyond its borders. The painter showed some elements from level ground (for example, the great boulder in the foreground), and others obliquely from the top (the shrubbery on the highest cliff). The shifting perspectives lead the viewer on a journey through the mountains. To appreciate the painted landscape fully, the viewer must focus not only on the larger composition but also on intricate details and on the character of each brush stroke. Numerous "texture strokes" help model massive forms and convey a sense of tactile surfaces. For the face of the mountain, for example, Fan Kuan employed small, pale brush marks, the kind of texture strokes the Chinese call "raindrop strokes."

Huizong A century after Fan Kuan painted in the mountains of Shanxi, HUIZONG (1082–1135; r. 1101–1126) assumed the Song throne at Bianliang. Less interested in governing than in the arts, he brought the country to near bankruptcy and lost much of China's territory to the armies of the Tartar Jin dynasty (1115–1234), who captured the Song capital in 1126 and took Huizong as a prisoner. He died in their hands nine years later. An accomplished poet, calligrapher, and painter, Huizong reorganized the imperial painting academy and required the study of poetry and calligraphy as part of the official training of court painters. *Calligraphy*, or the art of writing, was highly esteemed in China throughout its history, and prominent inscriptions are frequent elements of Chinese paintings (see "Calligraphy and Inscriptions on Chinese Paintings," page 481).

A short handscroll (FIG. **17-10**) usually attributed to Huizong is more likely the work of court painters under his direction, but it displays the emperor's style as both calligrapher and painter. Huizong's characters represent one of many styles of Chinese calligraphy. They are made up of thin strokes, and each character is meticulously aligned with its neighbors to form neat vertical rows. The painting depicts cranes flying over the roofs of

17-9 FAN KUAN, *Travelers among Mountains and Streams*, Northern Song period, early 11th century. Hanging scroll, ink and colors on silk, 6′ 7¼″ × 3′ 4¼″. National Palace Museum, Taibei.

Fan Kuan, a Daoist recluse, spent long days in the mountains studying the effects of light on rock formations and trees. He was one of the first masters of recording light, shade, distance, and texture.

1 ft.

Calligraphy and Inscriptions on Chinese Paintings

Many Chinese paintings (FIGS. 17-1, 17-10, 17-13, and 17-17) bear inscriptions, texts written on the same surface as the picture, or *colophons*, written texts on attached pieces of paper or silk.

Throughout Chinese history, calligraphy and painting have been closely connected and equally esteemed. Even the primary implements and materials for writing and drawing are the same—a brush, ink, and paper or silk (see "Chinese Painting Materials," page 476). Calligraphy depends for its effects on the controlled vitality of individual brush strokes and on the dynamic relationships of strokes within a character and among the characters themselves. Training in calligraphy was a fundamental part of the education and self-cultivation of Chinese scholars and officials, and inscriptions are especially common on *literati* paintings (see page 484).

Many stylistic variations exist in Chinese calligraphy. At the most formal extreme, each Chinese character consists of distinct straight and angular strokes and is separate from the next character. At the other extreme, the characters flow together as cursive abbreviations with many rounded forms.

A long tradition in China links pictures and texts. Famous poems frequently provided subjects for paintings, and poets composed poems inspired by paintings. Either practice might prompt inscriptions on artworks, some addressing painted subjects, some praising the painting's quality or the character of the painter. Some inscriptions explain the circumstances of the work. Later admirers and owners of paintings frequently inscribed their own appreciative words.

Painters, inscribers, and even owners usually also added *seal* impressions in red ink (FIGS. 17-1, 17-13, 17-17, and 17-18) to identify themselves. With all these textual additions, some paintings that have passed through many collections may seem cluttered to Western eyes. However, the historical importance given to these inscriptions and ownership history has been a critical aspect of painting appreciation in China.

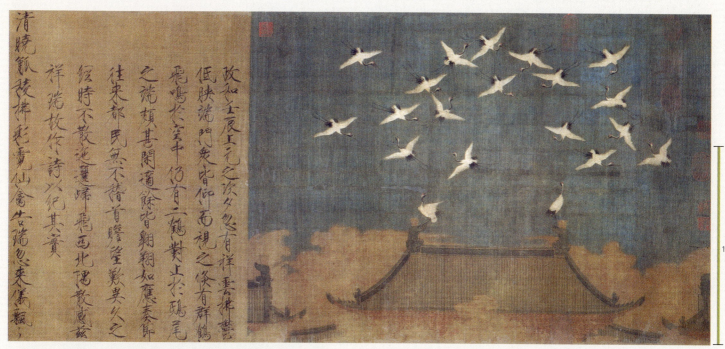

17-10 Attributed to HUIZONG, *Auspicious Cranes*, Northern Song period, 1112. Section of a handscroll, ink and colors on silk, 1' 8⅛" × 4' 6⅜". Liaoning Provincial Museum, Shenyang.

The Chinese regarded the 20 white cranes that appeared at Huizong's palace in 1112 as an auspicious sign. This painting of that event is a masterful combination of elegant composition, realistic observation, and beautiful calligraphy.

Bianliang. It is a masterful combination of elegant composition and realistic observation. The painter carefully recorded the black and red feathers of the white cranes and depicted the birds from a variety of viewpoints to suggest they were circling around the roof.

Huizong did not, however, choose this subject because of his interest in the anatomy and flight patterns of birds. The painting was a propaganda piece commemorating the appearance of 20 white cranes at the palace gates during a festival in 1112. The Chinese regarded the cranes as an auspicious sign, proof that Heaven had blessed Huizong's rule.

Foguang Si Pagoda For two centuries during the Northern Song period, the Liao dynasty (907–1125) ruled part of northern China. In 1056, at Yingxian, the Liao rulers built the tallest wooden building ever constructed (see "Chinese Wooden

China | 481

Architectural Basics

Chinese Wooden Construction

Although the basic unit of Chinese architecture, the rectangular hall with columns supporting a roof, was common in many ancient civilizations, Chinese buildings are distinguished by the curving silhouettes of their roofs and by their method of construction. The Chinese, like other ancient peoples, used wood to construct their earliest buildings. Although those structures do not survive, scholars believe that many of the features giving East Asian architecture its specific character may date to the Zhou dynasty.

The typical Chinese hall has a pitched roof with projecting eaves. Wooden columns, lintels, and brackets provide the support. The walls serve no weight-bearing function but act only as screens separating inside from outside and room from room. The colors of Chinese buildings, predominantly red, black, yellow, and white, are also distinctive. Chinese timber architecture is customarily multicolored throughout, save for certain parts left in natural color, such as railings made of white marble. The builders usually painted the walls and the columns red. Chinese designers often chose dazzling combinations of colors and elaborate patterns for the beams, brackets, eaves, rafters, and ceilings. Artisans painted or lacquered the surfaces to protect the timber from rot and wood parasites, as well as to produce an arresting aesthetic effect.

The basic construction method of Chinese architecture is illustrated in FIG. 17-11, with the major components of a Chinese building labeled. The builders laid *beams* between columns, decreasing the length of the beams as the structure rose. The beams supported vertical *struts,* which in turn supported higher beams and eventually the *purlins* running the length of the building and carrying the roof's sloping *rafters.* Unlike the rigid elements of the triangular trussed timber roof common in the West, which produce flat sloping rooflines, the varying lengths of the Chinese structure's cross beams and the variously placed purlins can create curved profiles, which eventually became the norm throughout East Asia. The interlocking clusters of brackets were capable of supporting roofs with broad overhanging *eaves,* another typical feature of Chinese architecture (FIG. 17-12). Multiplication of the *bays* (spaces between the columns) could extend the building's length to any dimension desired, although each bay could be no wider or longer than the length of a single tree trunk. The proportions of the structural elements could be fixed into modules, allowing for standardization of parts. This enabled rapid construction of a building. Remarkably, the highly skilled Chinese workers fit the parts together without using any adhesive substance, such as mortar or glue.

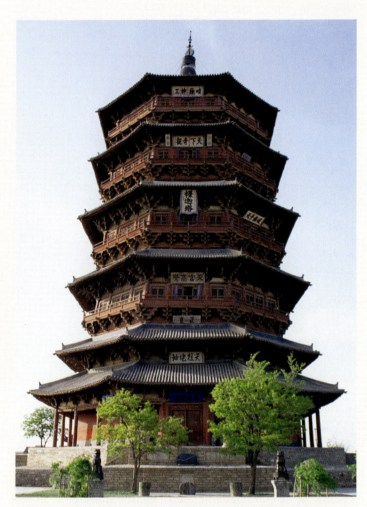

17-11 Chinese raised-beam construction (after L. Liu).

The walls of Chinese buildings serve no weight-bearing function. They act only as screens separating inside from outside and room from room. Curved rafters and eaves are also distinctive features.

17-12 Foguang Si Pagoda, Yingxian, China, Liao dynasty, 1056.

The tallest wooden building in the world is this pagoda in the Yingxian Buddhist temple complex. The nine-story tower shows the wooden beam-and-bracket construction system at its most ingenious.

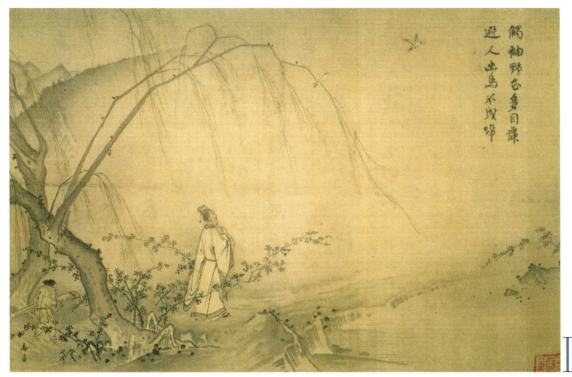

17-13 MA YUAN, *On a Mountain Path in Spring*, Southern Song period, early 13th century. Album leaf, ink and colors on silk, $10\frac{3}{4}''$ × 1′ 5″. National Palace Museum, Taibei.

Unlike Fan Kuan (FIG. 17-9), Ma Yuan reduced the landscape on this silk album leaf to a few elements and confined them to one part of the page. A tall solitary figure gazes out into the infinite distance.

1 in.

Construction," page 482, and FIG. 17-11)—the Foguang Si Pagoda (FIG. 17-12). The *pagoda*, or tower, the building type most often associated with Buddhism in China and other parts of East Asia, is the most eye-catching feature of a Buddhist temple complex. It somewhat resembles the tall towers of Indian temples and their distant ancestor, the Indian stupa (see "The Stupa," Chapter 16, page 455). Like stupas, many early pagodas housed relics and provided a focus for devotion to the Buddha. Later pagodas served other functions, such as housing sacred images and texts.

The octagonal pagoda at Yingxian is 216 feet tall. Sixty giant four-tiered bracket clusters carry the floor beams and projecting eaves of the five main stories. They rest on two concentric rings of columns at each level. Alternating main stories and windowless mezzanines with cantilevered balconies, set back farther on each story as the tower rises, form an elevation of nine stories altogether. Along with the open veranda on the ground level and the soaring pinnacle, the balconies visually lighten the building's mass.

Ma Yuan After Gaozong (r. 1127–1162), Huizong's sixth son, moved the Song capital to Lin'an, court sponsorship of the arts continued. During the reign of Ningzong (r. 1194–1224), members of the court, including Ningzong himself and the empress Yang, frequently added brief poems to the paintings created under their direction. Some of the painters belonged to families that had worked for the Song emperors for several generations. The most famous Song family of painters was the Ma family, which began working for the Song dynasty during the Northern Song period. MA YUAN (ca. 1160–1225) painted *On a Mountain Path in Spring*

(FIG. 17-13), a silk album leaf, for Ningzong in the early 13th century. In his composition, in striking contrast to Fan Kuan's much larger *Travelers among Mountains and Streams* (FIG. 17-9), the landscape is reduced to a few elements and confined to the foreground and left side of the page. A tall solitary figure gazes out into the infinite distance. Framing him are the carefully placed diagonals of willow branches. Near the upper right corner a bird flies toward the couplet that Ningzong added in ink:

> *Brushed by his sleeves, wild flowers dance in the wind;*
> *Fleeing from him, hidden birds cut short their songs.*

Some scholars have suggested that the author of the two-line poem is really Empress Yang, but the inscription is in Ningzong's hand. In any case, landscape paintings such as this one are perfect embodiments of the Chinese ideals of peace and unity with nature.

Yuan Dynasty

The 13th century was a time of profound political upheaval in Asia. During the opening decade, the Islamic armies of Muhammad of Ghor wrested power from India's Hindu kings and established a Muslim sultanate at Delhi (see Chapter 16). Then, in 1210, Genghis Khan (1167–1230) and the Mongols invaded northern China from Central Asia. By 1215 they had destroyed the Jin dynasty's capital at Beijing. In 1235 the Mongols attacked the Song dynasty in southern China, but it was not until 1279 that the last Song emperor fell at the hands of Genghis Khan's grandson, Kublai Khan (1215–1294). Kublai proclaimed himself the new emperor of China (r. 1279–1294) and founded the Yuan dynasty (1279–1368).

During the relatively brief tenure of the Yuan, trade between Europe and Asia increased dramatically. It was no coincidence that the most famous early European visitor to China, Marco Polo (1254–1324), arrived during the reign of Kublai Khan. Part fact and part fable, Marco Polo's chronicle of his travels to and within China was the only eyewitness description of East Asia available in Europe for several centuries. That account makes clear that the Venetian had a profound admiration for Yuan China. Marco Polo marveled not only at Kublai Khan's opulent lifestyle and palaces but also at the volume of commercial traffic on the Yangtze River; the splendors of Hangzhou; the use of paper currency, porcelain, and coal; the efficiency of the Chinese postal system; and the hygiene of the Chinese people. In the early second millennium, China was richer and technologically more advanced than late medieval Europe.

Wu Zhen The Mongols were great admirers of Chinese art and culture, but they were very selective in admitting former Southern Song subjects into their administration. In addition, many Chinese loyal to the former emperors refused to collaborate with their new foreign overlords, whom they considered barbarian usurpers. WU ZHEN (1280–1354), for example, chose to live as a hermit, far from the luxurious milieu of the Yuan emperors. He was among the *literati*, or scholar-artists, who emerged during the Song dynasty. The literati painted primarily for a small audience of their educational and social peers. Highly educated and steeped in traditional Chinese culture, these men and women came from prominent families. They cultivated poetry, calligraphy, painting, and other arts as a sign of social status and refined taste. Literati art is usually personal in nature and often shows nostalgia for the past.

Bamboo was a favorite subject of literati painters because the plant was a symbol of the ideal Chinese gentleman, who bends in adversity but does not break, and because depicting bamboo branches and leaves approximated the cherished art of calligraphy. In *Stalks of Bamboo by a Rock* (FIG. **17-1**), Wu Zhen clearly differentiated among the individual bamboo plants and reveled in the abstract patterns the stalks and leaves form. The bamboo plants are perfect complements to the calligraphic beauty of the Chinese black characters and red seals so prominently featured on this hanging scroll. Both the bamboo and the inscriptions gave Wu Zhen the opportunity to display his proficiency with the brush.

Jingdezhen Porcelain Chinese potters had produced stunning ceramic wares since the Neolithic period. By the Yuan period, Chinese potters had extended their mastery to fully developed porcelains, a very technically demanding medium. *Porcelain* is made from a fine white clay called kaolin mixed with ground petuntse (a type of feldspar). Firing takes place at an extremely high temperature (well over 2,000°F) in a kiln until the clay body fuses into a dense, hard substance resembling stone or glass. True porcelain is translucent and rings when struck. No other Chinese art

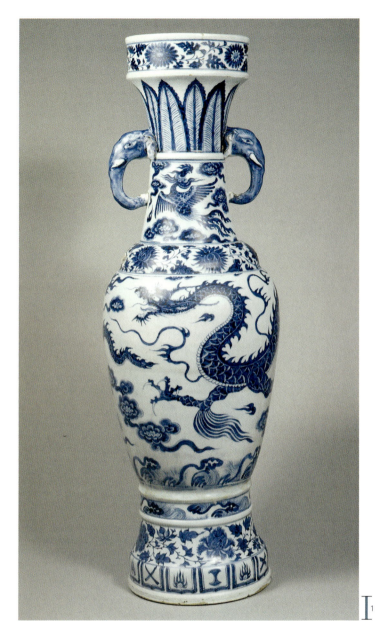

1 in.

17-14 Temple vase, Yuan dynasty, 1351. White porcelain with cobalt-blue underglaze, 2′ 1″ × 8$\frac{1}{8}$″. Percival David Foundation of Chinese Art, London.

This vase is an early example of porcelain with cobalt-blue underglaze decoration. Dragons and phoenixes, auspicious symbols of male and female energy, respectively, are the major painted motifs.

form has achieved such worldwide admiration, inspired such imitation, or penetrated so deeply into everyday life as porcelain. Long imported by neighboring countries as luxury goods, Chinese porcelains later captured great attention in the West, where potters did not succeed in mastering the production process until the early 18th century.

A tall porcelain vase (FIG. **17-14**) from the Jingdezhen kilns is one of a nearly identical pair dated by inscription to 1351. The inscription also says the vases, together with an incense burner, made up an altar set donated to a Buddhist temple as a prayer for peace, protection, and prosperity for the donor's family. The vase is one of the earliest dated examples of fine porcelain with cobalt-blue *underglaze* decoration.

The painter applied a cobalt compound to the clay surface before the main firing and then a clear *glaze* over the decoration. Underglaze decoration fully bonds to the piece in the kiln. The ornamentation on this example consists of bands of floral motifs between broader zones containing auspicious symbols, including phoenixes in the lower part of the neck and dragons on the main body of the vessel, both among clouds. These motifs may suggest the donor's high status or invoke prosperity blessings. Because of their vast power and associations with nobility and prosperity, the dragon and the phoenix also symbolize the emperor and empress, respectively. The dragon also may represent *yang*, the Chinese principle of active masculine energy, and the phoenix may represent *yin*, the principle of passive feminine energy.

Ming Dynasty

In 1368, Zhu Yuanzhong led a popular uprising that drove the last Mongol emperor from Beijing. After expelling the foreigners from China, he founded the native Chinese Ming dynasty (1368–1644), proclaiming himself its first emperor under the official name of Hongwu (r. 1368–1398). The new emperor built his capital at Nanjing, but the third Ming emperor, Yongle (r. 1403–1424), moved the capital back to Beijing (MAP 17-1). Although Beijing had been home to the Yuan dynasty, Ming architects designed much of the city as well as the imperial palace at its core.

Forbidden City The Ming builders laid out Beijing as three nested walled cities. The outer perimeter wall was 15 miles long and enclosed the walled Imperial City, with a perimeter of 6 miles, and the vast imperial palace compound, the moated Forbidden City (FIG. 17-15), so named because of the highly restricted access to it. There resided the Ming emperor, the Son of Heaven. The layout of the Forbidden City provided the perfect setting for the elaborate ritual of the imperial court. For example, the entrance gateway, the Noon Gate (in the foreground in the aerial view), has five portals. Only the emperor could walk through the central doorway. The two entrances to its left and right were reserved for the imperial family and high officials. Others had to use the outermost passageways. More gates and a series of courtyards and imposing buildings, all erected using the traditional Chinese bracketing system (see "Chinese Wooden Construction," page 482), led eventually to the Hall of Supreme Harmony, perched on an immense platform above marble staircases, the climax of a long north-south axis. Within the hall, the emperor sat on his throne on another high stepped platform.

Suzhou Gardens At the opposite architectural pole from the formality and rigid axiality of palace architecture is the Chinese pleasure garden. Several Ming gardens at Suzhou have been meticulously restored, including the huge (almost 54,000 square feet) Wangshi Yuan (Garden of the

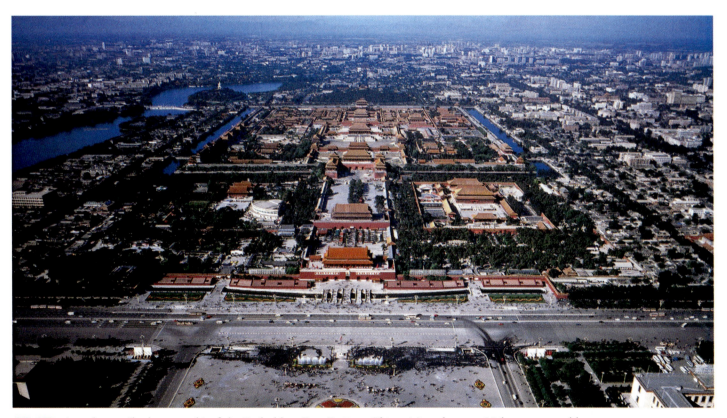

17-15 Aerial view (looking north) of the Forbidden City, Beijing, China, Ming dynasty, 15th century and later.

The layout of the Forbidden City provided the perfect setting for the elaborate ritual surrounding the Ming emperor, the Son of Heaven. Successive gates regulated access to the Hall of Supreme Harmony.

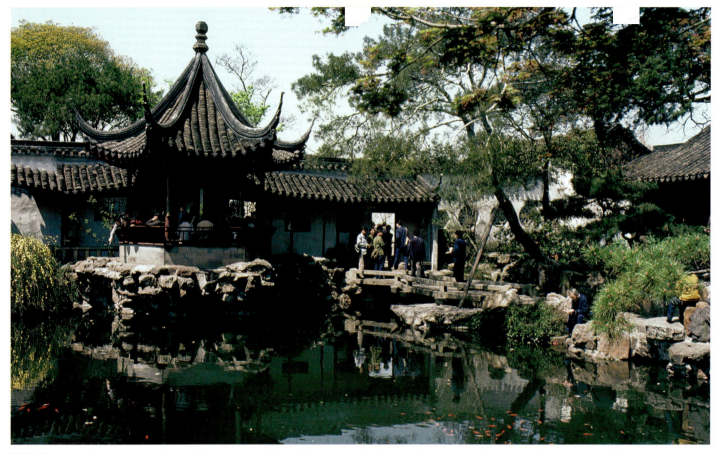

17-16 Wangshi Yuan (Garden of the Master of the Fishing Nets), Suzhou, China, Ming dynasty, 16th century and later.

Ming gardens are arrangements of natural and artificial elements intended to reproduce the irregularities of nature. This approach to design is the opposite of the formality and axiality of the Ming palace.

Master of the Fishing Nets; FIG. **17-16**). Designing a Ming garden was not a matter of cultivating plants in rows or of laying out terraces, flower beds, and avenues in geometric fashion, as was the case in many other cultures (compare, for example, the 17th-century French gardens at Versailles, FIG. **10-32**). Instead, the gardens are often scenic arrangements of natural and artificial elements intended to reproduce the irregularities of uncultivated nature. Verandas and pavilions rise on pillars above the water, and stone bridges, paths, and causeways encourage wandering through ever-changing vistas of trees, flowers, rocks, and their reflections in the ponds. The typical design is a sequence of carefully contrived visual surprises.

Dong Qichang The Ming emperors maintained an official workshop of painters in the Forbidden City itself, but the venerable tradition of literati painting also flourished. One of the most intriguing and influential literati of the late Ming dynasty was DONG QICHANG (1555–1636), a wealthy landowner and high official who was a poet, calligrapher, and painter. He also amassed a vast collection of Chinese art and achieved great fame as an art critic. In Dong Qichang's view, most Chinese landscape painters could be classified as belonging to either the Northern School of precise, academic painting or the Southern School of more subjective,

freer painting. "Northern" and "Southern" were therefore not geographic but stylistic labels. Dong Qichang chose these names for the two schools because he determined that their characteristic styles had parallels in the northern and southern schools of *Chan* Buddhism. Northern Chan Buddhists were "gradualists" and believed enlightenment could be achieved only after long training. The Southern Chan Buddhists believed enlightenment could come suddenly. The professional, highly trained court painters, whose role was to promote Ming ideology, belonged to the Northern School. The leading painters of the Southern School were the literati, whose freer and more expressive style Dong Qichang judged to be far superior.

Dong Qichang's own work—for example, *Dwelling in the Qingbian Mountains* (FIG. **17-17**), painted in 1617—belongs to the Southern School he so admired. Subject and style, as well as the incorporation of a long inscription at the top, immediately reveal his debt to earlier literati painters. But Dong Qichang was also an innovator, especially in his treatment of the towering mountains, where shaded masses of rocks alternate with flat, blank bands, flattening the composition and creating highly expressive and abstract patterns. Some critics have called Dong Qichang the first modernist painter, foreshadowing developments in 19th-century European landscape painting (FIG. **13-13**).

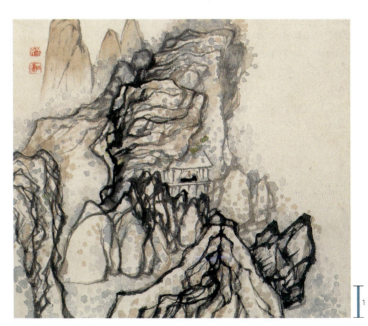

The Chinese calligraphy on the scroll (figure 17-17) reads top to bottom, right to left.

Qing Dynasty

The Ming bureaucracy's internal decay permitted another group of invaders, the Manchus of Manchuria, to overrun China in the 17th century. The Qing dynasty (1644–1911) the Manchus established quickly restored effective imperial rule, although southern China remained rebellious until the second Qing emperor, Kangxi (r. 1662–1722), succeeded in pacifying all of China. The Manchus adapted themselves to Chinese life and cultivated knowledge of China's arts.

Shitao Traditional literati painting continued to be fashionable among conservative Qing artists, but other painters experimented with extreme effects of massed ink or individualized brushwork patterns. Bold and freely manipulated compositions with a new, expressive force began to appear. A prominent painter in this mode was SHITAO (DAOJI, 1642–1707), a descendant of the Ming imperial family who became a Chan Buddhist monk at age 20. His theoretical writings, most notably his *Sayings on Painting from Monk Bitter Gourd* (his adopted name), called for use of the "single brush stroke" or "primordial line" as the root of all phenomena and representation. Although he carefully studied classical paintings, Shitao opposed mimicking earlier works and believed that he could not learn anything from them unless he changed them. In *Man in a House beneath a Cliff* (FIG. 17-18), Shitao surrounded the figure in a hut with vibrant, free-floating colored dots and multiple sinuous contour lines. Unlike traditional literati, Shitao did not so much depict the landscape's appearance as animate it, molding the forces running through it.

17-17 DONG QICHANG, *Dwelling in the Qingbian Mountains*, Ming dynasty, 1617. Hanging scroll, ink on paper, 7' 3½" × 2' 2½". Cleveland Museum of Art (Leonard C. Hanna Jr. bequest).

Dong Qichang, the "first modernist painter," conceived his landscapes as shaded masses of rocks alternating with blank bands, flattening the composition and creating expressive, abstract patterns.

17-18 SHITAO, *Man in a House beneath a Cliff*, Qing dynasty, late 17th century. Album leaf, ink and colors on paper, 9½" × 11". C. C. Wang Collection, New York.

Shitao experimented with extreme effects of massed ink and individualized brushwork patterns. In this album leaf, he surrounded a hut with vibrant, free-floating colored dots and sinuous contour lines.

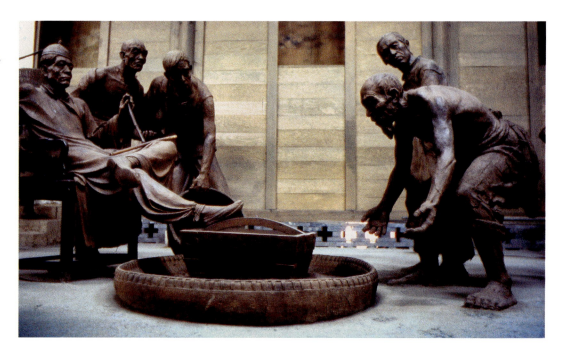

17-19 Ye Yushan and others, *Rent Collection Courtyard* (detail of larger tableau), Dayi, China, 1965. Clay, 100 yards long with life-size figures.

In this propagandistic tableau incorporating 114 figures, sculptors depicted the exploitation of peasants by their merciless landlords during the grim times before the Communists' takeover of China.

Modern China

The overthrow of the Qing dynasty and establishment of the Republic of China under the Nationalist Party in 1912 did not bring an end to the traditional themes and modes of Chinese art. But the Marxism that triumphed in 1949, when the Communists took control of China and founded the People's Republic, inspired a social realism that broke drastically with the past. The intended purpose of Communist art was to serve the people in the struggle to liberate and elevate the masses.

Ye Yushan In *Rent Collection Courtyard* (FIG. **17-19**), a 1965 tableau 100 yards long and incorporating 114 life-size figures, YE YUSHAN (b. 1935) and a team of sculptors grimly depicted the old times before the People's Republic. Peasants, worn and bent by toil, bring their taxes (in produce) to the courtyard of their merciless, plundering landlord. The message is clear—this kind of exploitation must not happen again. Initially, the authorities did not reveal the artists' names. The anonymity of those who depicted the event was significant in itself. The secondary message was that only collective action could effect the transformations the People's Republic sought.

KOREA

Korea is a peninsula that shares borders with China and Russia and faces the islands of Japan (MAP **17-1**). Korea's pivotal location is a key factor in understanding the relationship of its art to that of China and the influence of its art on that of Japan. About 100 BCE, during the Han dynasty, the Chinese established outposts in Korea. The most important was Lelang, which became a prosperous commercial center. By the middle of the century, however, three native kingdoms—Koguryo, Paekche, and Silla—controlled most of the Korean peninsula and reigned for more than seven centuries until

Silla completed its conquest of its neighbors in 668. During this era, known as the Three Kingdoms period (ca. 57 BCE–688 CE), Korea remained in continuous contact with both China and Japan. Buddhism was introduced into Korea from China in the fourth century CE. The Koreans in turn transmitted it from the peninsula to Japan in the sixth century.

Unified Silla Kingdom

Aided by China's emperor, the Silla kingdom conquered the Koguryo and Paekche kingdoms and unified Korea in 668. The era of the Unified Silla Kingdom (688–935) is roughly contemporary with the Tang dynasty's brilliant culture in China, and many consider it to be Korea's golden age. The Silla rulers embraced Buddhism both as a source of religious enlightenment and as a protective force. They considered the magnificent Buddhist temples they constructed in and around their capital of Kyongju to be supernatural defenses against external threats as well as places of worship.

Sokkuram Unfortunately, none of these temples survived Korea's turbulent history. However, at Sokkuram, near the summit of Mount Toham, northeast of the city, a splendid granite Buddhist monument is preserved. Surviving records suggest that Kim Tae-song, a member of the royal family who served as prime minister, supervised its construction. He initiated the project in 742 to honor his parents in his previous life. Certainly the intimate scale of Sokkuram and the quality of its reliefs and freestanding figures support the premise that the monument was a private chapel for royalty.

The main *rotunda* (circular area under a dome; FIG. **17-20**) measures about 21 feet in diameter. Despite its modest size, the Sokkuram project required substantial resources. Unlike the Chinese Buddhist caves at Longmen (FIG. **17-6**), the interior wall surfaces and sculpture were not cut

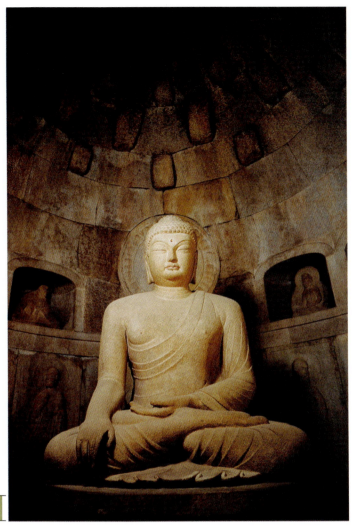

from the rock in the process of excavation. Instead, workers assembled hundreds of granite pieces of various shapes and sizes, attaching them with stone rivets instead of mortar. Sculpted images of bodhisattvas, arhats, and guardians line the lower zone of the wall. Above, 10 niches contain miniature statues of seated bodhisattvas and believers. All these figures face inward toward the 11-foot-tall statue of Shakyamuni, the historical Buddha, which dominates the chamber and faces the entrance. Carved from a single block of granite, the image represents the Buddha as he touched the earth to call it to witness the realization of his enlightenment at Bodh Gaya (FIG. 16-6b). Although remote in time and place from the Sarnath Buddha (FIG. 16-7) in India, this majestic image remains faithful to its iconographic prototypes in both South Asia and China. However, the figure has a distinctly broad-shouldered dignity combined with harmonious proportions that are without close precedents. Art historians consider it one of the finest images of the Buddha in East Asia.

17-20 Shakyamuni Buddha, in the rotunda of the cave temple, Sokkuram, Korea, Unified Silla Kingdom, 751–774. Granite, 11' high.

Unlike rock-cut Chinese Buddhist shrines, this Korean cave temple was constructed using granite blocks. Dominating the rotunda is a huge statue depicting the Buddha at the moment of his enlightenment.

1 ft.

Choson Dynasty

At the time the Yuan overthrew the Song dynasty in China, the Koryo dynasty (918–1392), which had ruled Korea since the downfall of China's Tang dynasty, was still in power. The Koryo kings outlasted the Yuan as well. Toward the end of the Koryo dynasty, however, the Ming emperors of China attempted to take control of northeastern Korea. General Yi Song-gye repelled them and founded the last Korean dynasty, the Choson in 1392. The long rule of the Choson kings ended only in 1910, when Japan annexed Korea.

Namdaemun, Seoul Public building projects helped give the new Korean state an image of dignity and power. One impressive early monument, built for the new Choson capital of Seoul, is the city's south gate, or Namdaemun (FIG. 17-21). It combines the imposing strength of its impressive

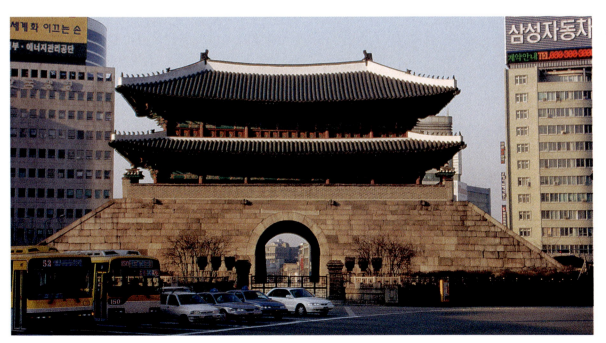

17-21
Namdaemun, Seoul, South Korea, Choson dynasty, first built in 1398.

The new Choson dynasty leaders constructed the south gate to their capital of Seoul as a symbol of their authority. Namdaemun combines stone foundations with Chinese-style bracketed wooden construction.

1 ft.

17-22 Song Su-nam, *Summer Trees*, 1983. Ink on paper, 2′ 1⅝″ high. British Museum, London.

Song Su-nam combined native and international traditions in *Summer Trees,* an ink painting that evokes Asian landscape painting but owes a great deal to American Post-Painterly Abstraction.

stone foundations with the sophistication of its intricately bracketed wooden superstructure. In East Asia, elaborate gateways, often in a processional series, are a standard element in city designs as well as royal and sacred compounds, all usually surrounded by walls, as at Beijing's Forbidden City (FIG. **17-15**). These gateways served as magnificent symbols of the ruler's authority, as did the triumphal arches of imperial Rome (see Chapter 3).

Modern Korea

After its annexation in 1910, Korea remained part of Japan until 1945, when the Western Allies and the Soviet Union took control of the peninsula nation at the end of World War II. Korea was divided into the Democratic People's Republic of Korea (North Korea) and the Republic of Korea (South Korea) in 1948. South Korea has emerged as a fully industrialized nation, and its artists have had a wide exposure to art styles from around the globe. While some Korean artists continue to work in a traditional East Asian manner, others have embraced developments in contemporary Europe and America.

Song Su-nam One painter who has very successfully combined native and international traditions is SONG SU-NAM (b. 1938), one of the founders of the Oriental Ink Movement of the 1980s. His *Summer Trees* (FIG. **17-22**) owes a great deal to the Post-Painterly Abstraction movement in the United States (see Chapter 15). But in place of acrylic resin on canvas, Song used ink on paper, the preferred medium of East Asian literati. He forsook, however, the traditional emphasis on brush strokes to explore the subtle tonal variations that broad stretches of ink wash made possible. Nonetheless, the painting's name recalls the landscapes of earlier Korean and Chinese masters. This simultaneous respect for tradition and innovation has been a hallmark of both Chinese and Korean art through their long histories.

China and Korea

SHANG TO QIN DYNASTIES

▍ The Shang dynasty (ca. 1600–1050 BCE) was the first great Chinese dynasty of the Bronze Age. The Shang kings ruled from a series of capitals in the Yellow River valley. Shang bronze-workers were among the best in the ancient world. The Zhou dynasty (ca. 1050–256 BCE) was the longest in China's history. During the last centuries of Zhou rule, Daoism and Confucianism gained wide followings. Shi Huangdi founded the Qin dynasty (221–206 BCE) after defeating the Zhou. A terracotta army of more than 6,000 soldiers guarded the First Emperor's burial mound at Lintong.

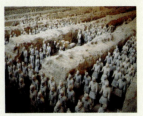

Army of the First Emperor of Qin, Lintong, ca. 210 BCE

HAN TO TANG DYNASTIES

▍ The Han dynasty (206 BCE–220 CE) extended China's boundaries, but civil strife divided China into competing states during the Period of Disunity (220–589 CE). Gu Kaizhi was a master scroll painter of the late fourth century CE. China enjoyed unequaled prosperity and power under the Tang emperors (618–906), whose capital at Chang'an became the most cosmopolitan city in the world. The Tang dynasty was the golden age of Chinese figure painting. Yan Liben's *The Thirteen Emperors* handscroll illustrates historical figures as exemplars of Confucian ideals. The Dunhuang mural paintings provide evidence of the magnificence of Tang Buddhist art.

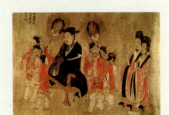

Yan Liben, *The Thirteen Emperors*, ca. 650

SONG AND YUAN DYNASTIES

▍ Song China (Northern Song, 960–1127, capital at Bianliang; Southern Song, 1127–1279, capital at Lin'an) was the most technologically advanced society in the world in the early second millennium. In art, the Song era marked the apogee of Chinese landscape painting. Fan Kuan, a Daoist recluse, was a pioneer in recording light, shade, distance, and texture in his hanging scrolls. The Mongols invaded northern China in 1210 and defeated the last Song emperor in 1279 to establish the Yuan dynasty (1279–1368). Yuan China was richer and technologically more advanced than Europe. The Jingdezhen kilns gained renown for porcelain pottery with cobalt-blue underglaze decoration.

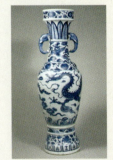

Temple vase, Yuan dynasty, 1351

MING DYNASTY TO THE PRESENT

▍ The Ming dynasty (1368–1644) constructed a vast new imperial palace compound, the Forbidden City, at its capital of Beijing. Surrounded by a moat and featuring an axial plan, it was the ideal setting for court ritual. At the opposite architectural pole are the gardens of Suzhou, which reproduce the irregularities of uncultivated nature.

▍ Under the Qing dynasty (1644–1911), traditional painting styles remained fashionable, but some Qing painters, such as Shitao, experimented with extreme effects of massed ink and free brushwork patterns. The overthrow of the Qing dynasty did not bring a dramatic change in Chinese art, but when the Communists gained control in 1949, state art focused on promoting Marxist ideals in vast propaganda pieces like *Rent Collection Courtyard*.

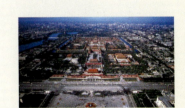

Forbidden City, Beijing, 15th century and later

KOREA

▍ The art of Korea is closely related to both Chinese and Japanese art. The first golden age of Korean art and architecture was under the Unified Silla Kingdom (688–935), when a magnificent Buddhist complex was constructed at Sokkuram. The last Korean dynasty was the Choson (1392–1910), which established its capital at Seoul and erected impressive public monuments like the Namdaemun gate to serve as symbols of imperial authority.

▍ Many modern Korean artists have successfully combined native and international traditions. Song Su-nam's landscapes owe a great deal to American Post-Painterly Abstraction.

Song Su-nam, *Summer Trees*, 1983

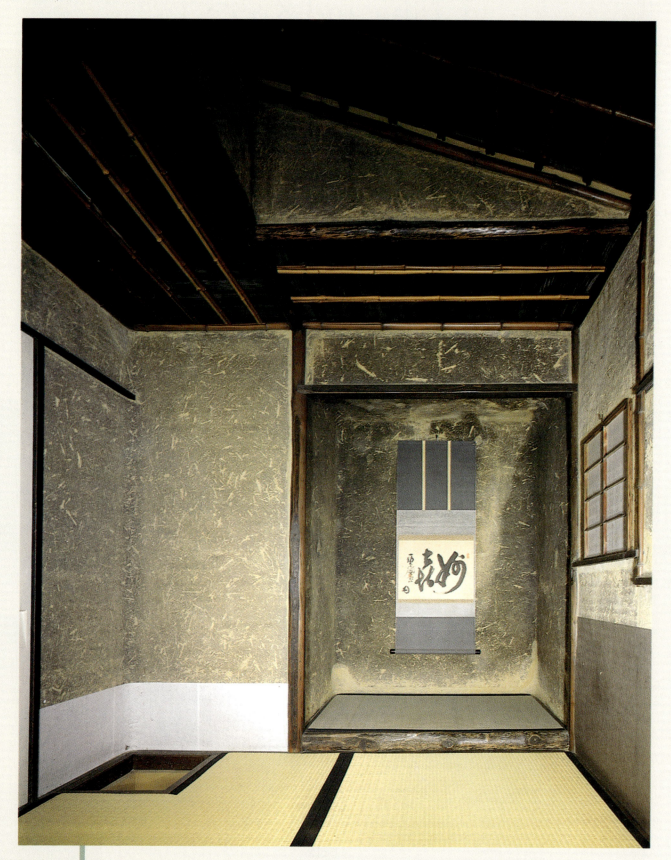

18-1 Sᴇɴ ɴᴏ Rɪᴋʏᴜ, Taian teahouse (interior view), Myokian Temple, Kyoto, Japan, Momoyama period, ca. 1582.

The Japanese developed the tea ceremony, which began in Zen Buddhist temples, into an important social ritual. To symbolize withdrawal from the world, guests must crawl through a small door to enter this teahouse.

Japan

The Japanese archipelago (MAP **18-1**) consists of four main islands—Hokkaido, Honshu, Shikoku, and Kyushu—and hundreds of smaller ones, a surprising number of them inhabited. Throughout history, the Japanese have demonstrated a remarkable ability to surmount challenges of geography, such as a mountainous island terrain that made travel and communication difficult. Japanese culture, however, does not reveal the isolation typical of some island civilizations but rather exhibits a responsiveness to imported ideas from continental eastern Asia, such as Buddhism and Chinese writing systems. Acknowledging these influences, however, does not suggest that Japan simply absorbed imported ideas and practices. On the contrary, Japan developed a truly distinct culture. Ultimately, Japan's close proximity to the Asian continent has promoted extensive exchange with mainland cultures, but the sea has helped protect it from outright invasions and allowed it to develop an individual and unique character.

JAPAN BEFORE BUDDHISM

Japan's earliest distinct culture is the Jomon (ca. 10,500–300 BCE). The term *jomon* ("cord markings") refers to the technique Japanese potters of this era used to decorate ceramic vessels. The Jomon people were hunter-gatherers, but unlike most hunter-gatherer societies, which were nomadic, the Jomon settled in villages, which permitted them to develop a distinctive ceramic technology, even before their development of agriculture. In fact, archaeologists have dated some pottery fragments found in Japan to before 10,000 BCE—older than the ceramics from any other area of the world.

Jomon culture gradually gave way to Yayoi (ca. 300 BCE–330 CE) in Kyushu, the southernmost of the main Japanese islands. Increased interaction with both China and Korea and immigration from Korea brought dramatic social and technological transformations. Japanese villages grew in size, and their inhabitants built fortifications around them, indicating a perceived need for defense. In the third century CE, Chinese visitors noted that Japan had walled towns, many small kingdoms, and a highly stratified social structure. Wet-rice agriculture provided the social and economic foundations for this development. During the Yayoi period, the Japanese also developed bronze casting and loom weaving.

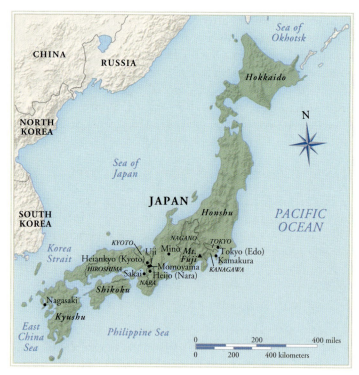

MAP 18-1 Japan.

Kofun Period

Historians named the succeeding Kofun period (ca. 300–552)* after the enormous earthen burial mounds, or *tumuli*, that had begun to appear in the third century. (*Ko* means "old"; *fun* means "tomb.") The tumuli recall the earlier Jomon practice of placing the dead on sacred mountains. The mounds grew dramatically in number and scale in the fourth century.

Tomb of Nintoku The largest tumulus (FIG. **18-2**) in Japan, at Sakai, is usually identified as the tomb of Emperor Nintoku, although many scholars think the tumulus postdates his death in 399. The central mound, which takes the standard Kofun "keyhole" form, is approximately 1,600 feet long and rises to a height of 90 feet. Surrounded by three moats, the entire site covers 458 acres. Kofun tumuli usually contained a coffin in a stone-walled burial chamber near the summit of the mound. The chamber also housed objects to assist in the deceased's transition to the next life. For exalted individuals like Emperor Nintoku, objects buried included important symbolic items and imperial regalia—mirrors, swords, and jewels. Bronze mirrors came from China, but the form of the tombs themselves and many of the burial goods suggest even closer connections with Korea.

Haniwa The Japanese also placed unglazed ceramic sculptures called *haniwa* on and around the Kofun tumuli. These sculptures, usually several feet in height, are distinctly Japanese. Compared with the Chinese terracotta soldiers and horses (FIG. 17-3) buried with the First Emperor of Qin, these statues appear deceptively whimsical as variations on a cylindrical theme. (*Hani* means "clay"; *wa* means "circle.") Yet haniwa sculptors skillfully adapted the basic clay cylinder into a host of forms, from abstract shapes to objects, animals, and human figures, such as warriors (FIG. **18-3**) and female shamans. These artists altered the shapes of the cylinders, emblazoned them with applied ornaments, excised or built up forms, and then painted the haniwa. The variety of figure types suggests that haniwa functioned not as military guards but as a spiritual barrier protecting both the living and the dead from contamination. The Japanese of the Kofun period set the statues both in curving rows around the tumulus and in groups around a haniwa house placed directly over the deceased's burial chamber. Presumably, the number

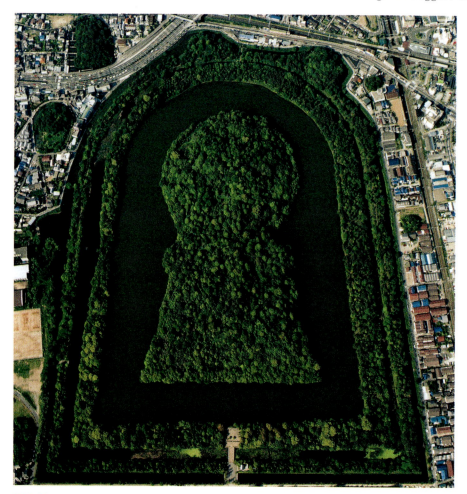

18-2 Tomb of Emperor Nintoku, Sakai, Osaka Prefecture, Japan, Kofun period, late fourth to early fifth century.

The largest Kofun tumulus, attributed to Emperor Nintoku, has a keyhole shape and three surrounding moats. About 20,000 clay haniwa (FIG. 18-3) were originally displayed on the giant earthen mound.

* From this point on, all dates in this chapter are CE unless otherwise stated.

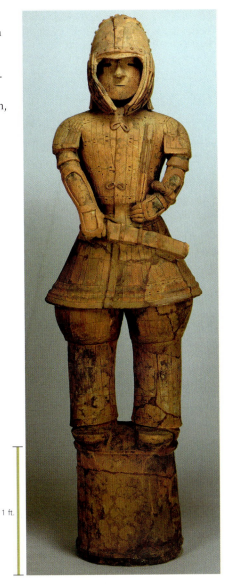

18-3 Haniwa warrior figure, from Gunma Prefecture, Japan, late Kofun period, fifth to mid-sixth century. Low-fired clay, 4′ 3¼″ high. Tokyo National Museum, Tokyo.

During the Kofun period, the Japanese set up cylindrical clay statues (haniwa) of humans and animals on burial tumuli. They served as a protective spiritual barrier between the living and the dead.

1 ft.

of sculptures reflected the stature of the dead person. Emperor Nintoku's tumulus had about 20,000 haniwa statues placed around the mound.

BUDDHIST JAPAN

In 552, according to traditional interpretation, the ruler of Paekche in Korea sent Japan's ruler a gilded bronze statue of the Buddha along with *sutras* (Buddhist scriptures) translated into Chinese, at the time the written language of eastern Asia. This event marked the beginning of the Asuka period (552–645), when Japan's ruling elite embraced major elements of continental culture that had been gradually filtering into Japan. These cultural components became firmly established in Japan and included Chinese writing, Confucianism, and Buddhism. The Japanese court, ruling from a series of capitals south of modern Kyoto, increasingly adopted the forms and rites of the Chinese court. In 710 the Japanese finally established what they intended as a permanent capital at Heijo (present-day Nara). City planners laid out the new capital on a symmetrical grid closely modeled on the plan of the Chinese capital of Chang'an.

For a half century after 552, Buddhism met with opposition, but by the seventh century, the new religion was established firmly in Japan. Older beliefs and practices (those that came to be known as Shinto) continued to have significance (and do to the present day), especially as agricultural rituals and imperial court rites. As time passed, Shinto deities even gained new identities as local manifestations of Buddhist deities.

Asuka and Nara Periods

In the arts associated with Buddhist practices, Japan followed Korean and Chinese prototypes very closely, especially during the Asuka and Nara (645–784) periods. In fact, early Buddhist architecture in Japan adhered so closely to mainland standards (although generally with a considerable time lag) that surviving Japanese temples have helped greatly in the reconstruction of what was almost completely lost on the continent.

Tori Busshi Among the earliest extant examples of Japanese Buddhist sculpture is a bronze *Buddha triad* (Buddha flanked by two bodhisattvas; FIG. **18-4**) dated 623. Empress Suiko commissioned the work as a votive offering when Prince

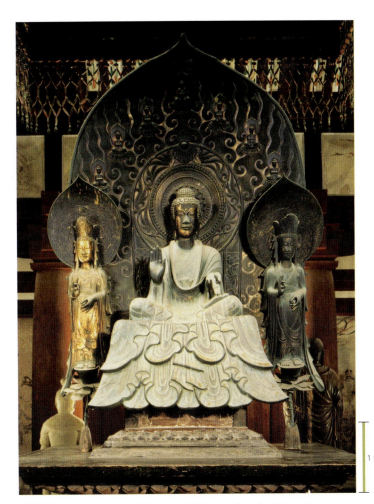

18-4 TORI BUSSHI, Shaka triad, Horyuji kondo, Nara, Japan, Asuka period, 623. Bronze, 5′ 9½″ high.

Nara's Shaka triad (the historical Buddha and two bodhisattvas) by Tori Busshi is among the earliest Japanese Buddhist sculptures. The bronze group reflects the sculptural style of sixth-century China.

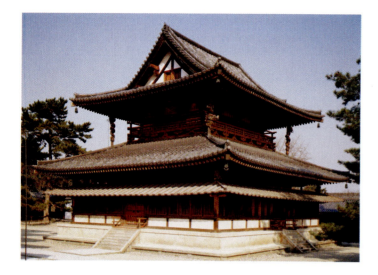

18-5 Kondo (*top*) and aerial view of the temple complex (*bottom*), Horyuji, Nara Prefecture, Japan, Nara period, ca. 680.

The kondo (Golden Hall) of a Buddhist temple complex housed statues of the Buddha and bodhisattvas. The Horyuji kondo follows Chinese models in its construction method and curved roofline.

Horyuji Kondo Tori Busshi created his Shaka triad for an Asuka Buddhist temple complex at Horyuji, seven miles south of modern Nara, but fire destroyed the temple. The statue was reinstalled around 680 in the *kondo* (Golden Hall; the main hall for worship that contained statues of the Buddha and the bodhisattvas to whom the temple was dedicated; FIG. **18-5,** *top*) of the successor Nara period complex (FIG. **18-5,** *bottom*). Although periodically repaired and somewhat altered, the structure retains its graceful but sturdy forms beneath the modifications. The main pillars (not visible in FIG. **18-5,** *top*, due to the addition of a porch in the eighth century) decrease in diameter from bottom to top. The tapering provides an effective transition between the more delicate brackets above and the columns' stout forms. Also somewhat masked by the later porch is the harmonious reduction in scale from the first to the second story. Following Chinese models, the builders used ceramic tiles as roofing material and adopted the distinctive curved roofline of Chinese architecture. Other buildings at the site include a five-story pagoda that serves as a reliquary. Until a disastrous fire in 1949, the interior walls of the Golden Hall at Horyuji preserved some of the finest early (ca. 710) examples of Buddhist wall painting in eastern Asia.

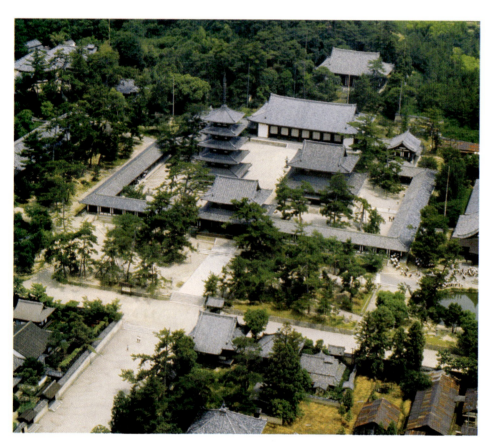

Shotuku fell ill in 621. When he died, the empress dedicated the triad to the prince's well-being in his next life and to his hoped-for rebirth in paradise. The central figure in the triad is Shaka (the Indian/Chinese Sakyamuni), the historical Buddha, seated with his right hand raised in the abhaya mudra (fear-not gesture; see "Buddhism and Buddhist Iconography," Chapter 16, page 454). Behind Shaka is a flaming *mandorla* (a lotus-petal-shaped *nimbus*) incorporating small figures of other Buddhas. The sculptor, TORI BUSSHI (*busshi* means "maker of Buddhist images"), was a descendant of a Chinese immigrant. Tori's Buddha triad reflects the style of the early to mid-sixth century in China and Korea and is characterized by elongated heads and elegantly stylized drapery folds that form gravity-defying swirls.

Heian Period

In 784, possibly to escape the power of the Buddhist priests in Nara, the imperial house moved its capital north, eventually relocating in 794 in what became its home until modern times. Originally called Heiankyo ("capital of peace and tranquility"), it is known today as Kyoto. The Heian period (794–1185) of Japanese art takes its name from the new capital. Early in the Heian period, Japan maintained fairly close ties with China, but from the middle of the ninth century on, relations between the two deteriorated so rapidly that court-sponsored contacts had ceased by the end of that century. Japanese culture became much more self-directed than it had been in the preceding few centuries.

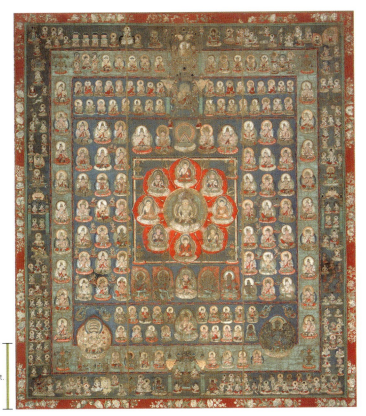

1 ft.

18-6 Taizokai (Womb World) of Ryokai Mandara, Kyoogo-kokuji (Toji), Kyoto, Japan, Early Heian period, second half of ninth century. Hanging scroll, color on silk, 6′ × 5′5⅝″.

The Womb World mandara is a diagram of the cosmic universe, composed of 12 zones, each representing one dimension of buddha nature. Mandaras played a central role in Esoteric Buddhist rituals and meditation.

Esoteric Buddhism
Among the major developments during the early Heian period was the introduction of Esoteric Buddhism to Japan from China. Esoteric Buddhism is so named because of the secret transmission of its teachings.

Two Esoteric sects made their appearance in Japan at the beginning of the Heian period: Tendai in 805 and Shingon in 806. The teachings of Tendai were based on the *Lotus Sutra*, one of the Buddhist scriptural narratives, and Shingon (True Word) teachings on two other sutras. Both Tendai and Shingon Buddhists believe all individuals possess buddha nature and can achieve enlightenment through meditation rituals and careful living. To aid focus during meditation, Shingon disciples use special hand gestures (mudras) and recite particular words or syllables. Shingon became the primary form of Buddhism in Japan through the mid-10th century.

Taizokai Mandara Because of the emphasis on ritual and meditation in Shingon, the arts flourished during the early Heian period. Both paintings and sculptures provided followers with visualizations of specific Buddhist deities and allowed them to contemplate the transcendental concepts central to the religion. Of particular importance in Shingon meditation was the *mandara* (mandala in Sanskrit), a diagram of the cosmic universe. Among the most famous Japanese mandaras is the Womb World (Taizokai), which usually hung on the wall of a Shingon kondo. The Womb World is composed of 12 zones, each representing one of the various dimensions of buddha nature (for example, universal knowledge, wisdom, achievement, and purity). The mandara illustrated here (FIG. **18-6**) is among the oldest and best preserved in Japan, and is located at Kyoogokokuji (Toji), the Shingon teaching center established at Kyoto in 823.

Phoenix Hall, Uji During the middle and later Heian period, belief in the vow of Amida, the Buddha of the Western Pure Land, to save believers through rebirth in his realm gained great prominence among the Japanese aristocracy. Eventually, the simple message of Pure Land Buddhism—universal salvation—facilitated the spread of Buddhism to all classes of Japanese society. The most important surviving monument in Japan related to Pure Land beliefs is the so-called Phoenix Hall (FIG. **18-7**) of Byodoin. Fujiwara Yorimichi, the powerful regent for three 11th-century

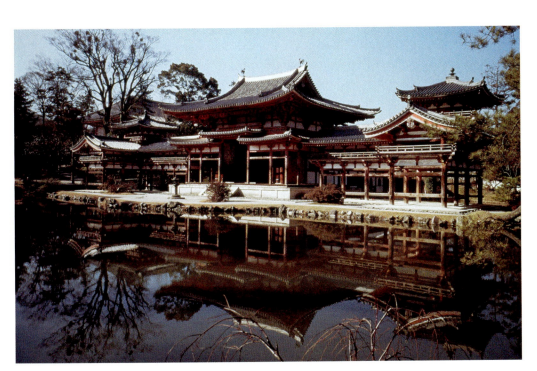

18-7 Phoenix Hall, Byodoin, Uji, Japan, Heian period, 1053.

The Phoenix Hall's elaborate winged form evokes images of Amida's palace in the Western Pure Land. Situated on a reflective pond, the temple suggests the floating weightlessness of celestial architecture.

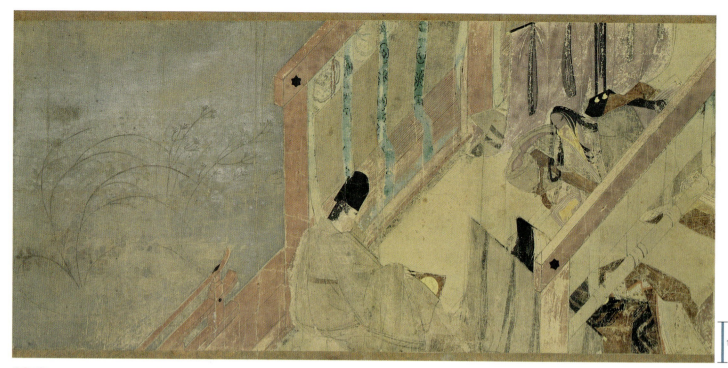

18-8 *Genji Visits Murasaki*, from the Minori chapter, *Tale of Genji*, Heian period, first half of 12th century. Handscroll, ink and color on paper, $8\frac{5}{8}$" high. Goto Art Museum, Tokyo.

In this Heian handscroll, the radically upturned ground plane and strong diagonal lines suggest three-dimensional space, but the flat fields of color emphasize the painting's two-dimensional character.

emperors, built the temple in memory of his father on the family's summer villa at Uji. Dedicated in 1053, the Phoenix Hall's elaborate winged form evokes images of the Buddha's palace in his Pure Land, as depicted in East Asian paintings (FIG. 17-7) in which the architecture reflects the design of Chinese palaces. By placing only light pillars on the exterior, elevating the wings, and situating the whole on a reflective pond, the Phoenix Hall builders suggested the floating weightlessness of celestial architecture. The building's name derives from its overall birdlike shape and from two bronze phoenixes decorating the ridgepole ends. In eastern Asia, these birds were believed to alight on lands properly ruled and were often associated with the empress. The authority of the Fujiwara family derived primarily from the marriage of daughters to the imperial line.

Tale of Genji Japan's most admired literary classic is *Tale of Genji*, written around 1000 by Murasaki Shikubu (usually referred to as Lady Murasaki), a lady-in-waiting at the court. Recounting the lives and loves of Prince Genji and his descendants, *Tale of Genji* provides readers with a view of Heian court culture.

The oldest extant examples of illustrated copies are fragments from a deluxe set of early-12th-century handscrolls produced by five teams consisting of a nobleman talented in calligraphy, a chief painter who drew the compositions in ink, and assistants who added the color. The script is pri-

marily *hiragana*, a sound-based writing system developed in Japan from Chinese characters. Hiragana originally served the needs of women (who were not taught Chinese) and became the primary script for Japanese court poetry. In these handscrolls, pictures alternate with text, as in Gu Kaizhi's *Admonitions* scrolls (FIG. 17-5). However, the Japanese work focuses on emotionally charged moments in personal relationships rather than on lessons in exemplary behavior.

In the scene illustrated here (FIG. **18-8**), Genji meets with his greatest love near the time of her death. The bush-clover in the garden identifies the season as autumn, a time associated with the fading of life and love. A radically upturned ground plane and strong diagonal lines suggest three-dimensional space. The painter omitted roofs and ceilings to provide a view of the interior spaces where the action takes place. Flat fields of color emphasize the painting's two-dimensional character. Rich patterns in the textiles and architectural ornamentation give a feeling of sumptuousness. The human figures appear constructed of stiff layers of contrasting fabrics, and the artist simplified and generalized the aristocratic faces, using a technique called "a line for the eye and a hook for the nose." This lack of individualization may reflect societal restrictions on looking directly at exalted persons. Several formal features of the *Genji* illustrations— native subjects, bright mineral pigments, lack of emphasis on strong brushwork, and general flatness—were later considered typical of *yamato-e*, or native-style painting. (The term *yamato* means "Japan.")

JAPAN UNDER THE SHOGUNS

In 1185 the Japanese emperor in Kyoto appointed the first *shogun* (military governor) at Kamakura in eastern Japan. Although the imperial family retained its right to reign and, in theory, the shogun managed the country on the emperor's behalf, in reality the emperor lost all governing authority. The Japanese *shogunate* was a political and economic arrangement in which *daimyo* (local lords), the leaders of powerful warrior bands composed of *samurai* (warriors), paid obeisance to the shogun. These local lords had considerable power over affairs within their domains. The Kamakura shogunate ruled Japan for more than a century.

Kamakura Period

During the Kamakura period (1185–1332), more frequent and positive contact with China brought with it an appreciation for more recent cultural developments there, ranging from new architectural styles to Chan (in Japan, *Zen*) Buddhism.

Shunjobo Chogen Rebuilding in Nara after the civil wars presented an early opportunity for architectural experimentation. A leading figure in planning and directing the reconstruction efforts was the priest Shunjobo Chogen (1121–1206), who reputedly made three trips to China between 1166 and 1176. After learning about contemporary Chinese architecture, he oversaw the rebuilding of Todaiji, among other projects. A portrait statue of him (FIG. **18-9**) is one of the most striking examples of the high level of naturalism prevalent in the early Kamakura period. Characterized by finely painted details, a powerful rendering of the signs of aging, and the inclusion of such personal attributes as prayer beads, the statue of Chogen exhibits the carving skill and style of the Kei School of sculptors. The Kei School traced its lineage to Jocho, a famous sculptor of the mid-11th century. Its works display expert craftsmanship combined with an increased concern for natural volume and detail. Enhancing the natural quality of Kei portrait statues is the use of inlaid rock crystal for the eyes, a technique found only in Japan.

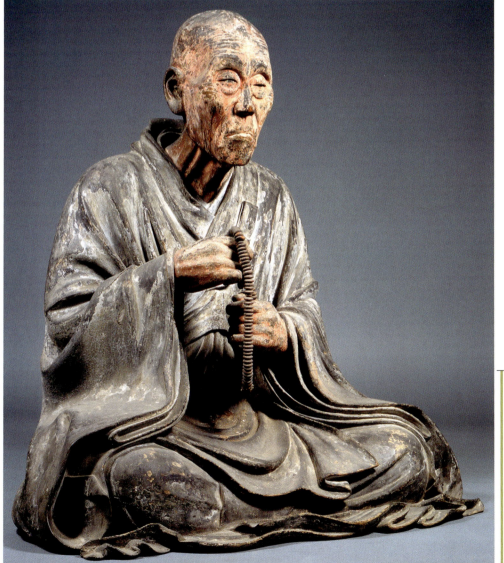

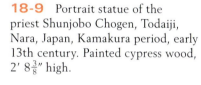

18-9 Portrait statue of the priest Shunjobo Chogen, Todaiji, Nara, Japan, Kamakura period, early 13th century. Painted cypress wood, 2' 8⅜" high.

The Kei School's interest in naturalism is seen in this moving portrait of a Kamakura priest. The statue is noteworthy for its finely painted details and powerful rendering of the signs of aging.

1 ft.

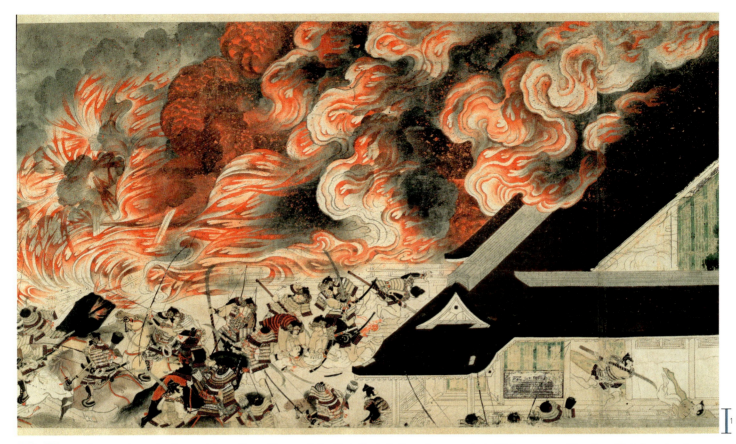

18-10 *Night Attack on the Sanjo Palace*, from *Events of the Heiji Period*, Kamakura period, 13th century. Handscroll, ink and colors on paper, 1′ 4¼″ high; complete scroll 22′ 10″ long. Museum of Fine Arts, Boston (Fenollosa-Weld Collection).

The *Heiji* scroll is an example of Japanese historical narrative painting. Staccato brushwork and vivid flashes of color capture the drama of the night attack and burning of Emperor Goshirakawa's palace.

The Kei School was typical of traditional Japanese artistic practice. Indeed, until recently, hierarchically organized male workshops produced most Japanese art. Membership in these workshops was often based on familial relationships. Dominating each workshop was a master, and many of his main assistants and apprentices were relatives. Outsiders of considerable skill sometimes joined workshops, often through marriage or adoption. The eldest son usually inherited the master's position, after rigorous training in the necessary skills from a very young age. Therefore, one meaning of the term "school of art" in Japan is a network of workshops tracing their origins back to the same master, a kind of artistic clan.

Attack on Sanjo Palace A striking example of Kamakura handscroll painting is *Events of the Heiji Period*, which dates to the 13th century and illustrates another facet of Japanese painting—historical narrative. The scroll depicts some of the battles in the civil wars at the end of the Heian period. The section reproduced here (FIG. **18-10**) represents the attack on the Sanjo palace in the middle of the night in which the retired emperor Goshirakawa was taken prisoner and his palace burned. Swirling flames and billowing

clouds of smoke dominate the composition. Below, soldiers on horseback and on foot do battle. As in other Heian and Kamakura scrolls, the painter depicted the buildings from above at a sharp angle. Noteworthy here are the staccato brushwork and the vivid flashes of color that beautifully capture the drama of the event.

Muromachi Period

In 1336, after years of upheaval and conflict, the shogun Ashikaga Takauji (1305–1358) managed to accrue sufficient power to establish the domination of his clan over all of Japan. This marked the beginning of the Muromachi period (1336–1573), named after the district of Kyoto in which the Ashikaga maintained their headquarters.

During the Muromachi period, Zen Buddhism (see "Zen Buddhism," page 502) gained many adherents. Unlike Pure Land Buddhism, which stressed reliance on the saving power of Amida, the Buddha of the West, Zen emphasized rigorous discipline and personal responsibility. For this reason, Zen held a special attraction for the upper echelons of samurai, whose behavioral codes placed high values on loyalty, courage, and self-control. Further, familiarity with Chinese

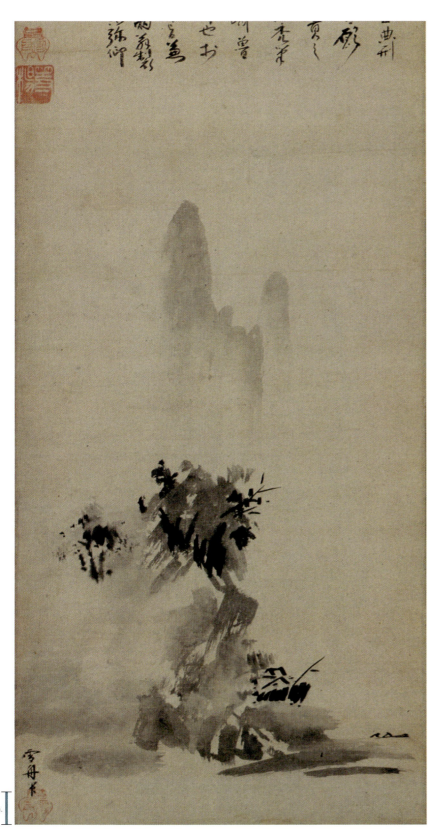

一典刑
夏え
香菜
也お
叩藏訊奶
弘義利前
弥御

1 in.

18-11 SESSHU TOYO, splashed-ink (haboku) land-scape, Muromachi period, 1495. Hanging scroll, ink on paper, full scroll 4' 10¼" × 1' ⅞", detail 2' 1" high. Tokyo National Museum, Tokyo.

In this splashed-ink landscape, the artist applied broad, rapid strokes, sometimes even dripping the ink on the paper. The result hovers at the edge of legibility, without dissolving into abstraction.

much greater attention to the problems of death and salvation. Zen temples stood out not only as religious institutions but also as centers of secular culture, where people could study Chinese art, literature, and learning, which the Japanese imported along with Zen Buddhism.

Sesshu Toyo As was common in earlier eras of Japanese history, Muromachi painters usually closely followed Chinese precedents (often arriving by way of Korea). Among the most celebrated Muromachi artists was the Zen priest SESSHU TOYO (1420–1506), one of the very few Japanese painters who traveled to China and studied contemporaneous Ming painting. His most dramatic works are in the *splashed-ink (haboku)* style, a technique with Chinese roots. The painter of a haboku picture paused to visualize the image, loaded the brush with ink, and then applied primarily broad, rapid strokes, sometimes even dripping the ink onto the paper. The result often hovers at the edge of legibility, without dissolving into pure abstraction. This balance between spontaneity and a thorough knowledge of the painting tradition gives the pictures their artistic strength. In the haboku landscape illustrated here (FIG. **18-11**), images of mountains, trees, and buildings emerge from the ink-washed surface. Two figures appear in a boat (to the lower right), and the two swift strokes nearby represent the pole and banner of a wine shop.

Kano Motonobu The opposite pole of Muromachi painting is represented by the Kano School, which by the 17th century had become a virtual national art academy. KANO MOTONOBU (1476–1559) was largely responsible for

Chan culture carried implications of superior knowledge and refinement, thereby legitimizing the elevated status of the warrior elite. Zen, however, was not simply the religion of Zen monks and highly placed warriors. Aristocrats, merchants, and others studied at and supported Zen temples. Zen Buddhists generally accepted other Buddhist teachings, especially ideas of the Pure Land sects. These sects gave

Japan under the Shoguns | 501

Zen Buddhism

Zen (Chan in Chinese), as a fully developed Buddhist tradition, began filtering into Japan in the 12th century and had its most pervasive impact on Japanese culture starting in the 14th century during the Muromachi period. As in other forms of Buddhism, Zen followers hoped to achieve enlightenment. Zen teachings assert that everyone has the potential for enlightenment, but worldly knowledge and mundane thought patterns suppress it. Thus, to achieve enlightenment, followers must break through the boundaries of everyday perception and logic. This is most often achieved through meditation. Indeed, the word *zen* means "meditation." Some Zen schools stress meditation as a long-term practice eventually leading to enlightenment, whereas others stress the benefits of sudden shocks to the worldly mind. One of these shocks is the subject of Kano Motonobu's *Zen Patriarch Xiangyen Zhixian Sweeping with a Broom* (FIG. 18-12), in which the shattering of a fallen roof tile opens the monk's mind.

The guidance of an enlightened Zen teacher is essential to arrive at enlightenment. Years of strict training involving manual labor under the tutelage of this master, coupled with meditation, provide the foundation for a receptive mind. According to Zen beliefs, by cultivating discipline and intense concentration, Buddhists can transcend their ego and release themselves from the shackles of the mundane world. Although Zen is not primarily devotional, followers do pray to specific deities. In general, Zen teachings view mental calm, lack of fear, and spontaneity as signs of a person's advancement on the path to enlightenment.

Zen training for monks in Japan took place at temples, some of which also served as centers of Chinese learning and handled funeral rites. Zen temples even embraced many traditional Buddhist observances, such as devotional rituals before images, which had little to do with meditation per se.

Zen ideals reverberated throughout Japanese culture as the teachings spread. Lay followers as well as Zen monks painted pictures and produced other artworks that appear to reach toward Zen ideals through their subjects and means of expression. Other cultural practices reflected the widespread appeal of Zen. For example, the tea ceremony offered a temporary respite from everyday concerns, a brief visit to a quiet retreat with a meditative atmosphere, such as the Taian teahouse (FIG. 18-1).

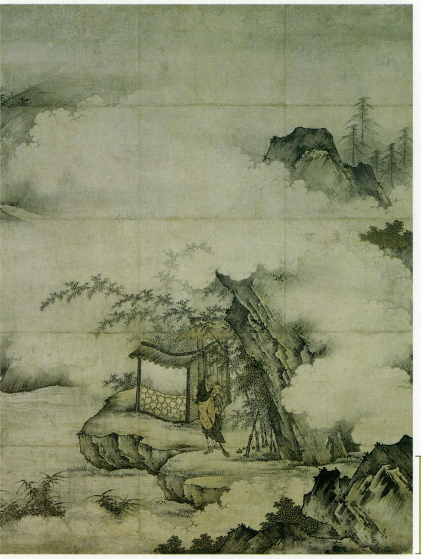

18-12 KANO MOTONOBU, *Zen Patriarch Xiangyen Zhixian Sweeping with a Broom*, from Daitokuji, Kyoto, Japan, Muromachi period, ca. 1513. Hanging scroll, ink and color on paper, 5′ 7 3/8″ × 2′ 10 3/4″. Tokyo National Museum, Tokyo.

The Kano School represents the opposite pole of Muromachi style from splashed-ink painting. In this scroll depicting a Zen patriarch experiencing enlightenment, the painter used bold outlines to define the forms.

establishing the Kano style. His *Zen Patriarch Xiangyen Zhixian Sweeping with a Broom* (FIG. 18-12) depicts the Zen patriarch at the moment he achieved enlightenment. As he sweeps the ground near his rustic retreat, a roof tile falls at his feet and shatters. The patriarch's Zen training is so deep that the resonant sound propels him into an awakening (see "Zen Buddhism," above). In contrast to Muromachi splashed-ink painting, Motonobu's work displays exacting precision in applying ink in bold outlines. Thick clouds obscure the mountainous setting and focus the viewer's attention on the sharp, angular rocks, bamboo branches, and modest hut that frame the patriarch. Lightly applied colors also draw attention to Xiangyen Zhixian, whom Motonobu portrayed as having let go of his broom with his right hand as he recoils in astonishment.

Momoyama Period

In 1573, Oda Nobunaga (1534–1582) overthrew the Ashigara shogunate in Kyoto but was later killed by one of his generals. Toyotomi Hideyoshi (1536–1598) then took control of the government until his death in 1598. In the ensuing power struggle, Tokugawa Ieyasu (1542–1616) emerged victorious and assumed the title of shogun in 1603. Ieyasu continued to face challenges, but by 1615 he had eliminated his last rival, initiating a new era in Japan's long history, the Edo period (see page 504). During the brief intervening Momoyama period (1573–1615), the successive warlords constructed huge castles with palatial residences—partly as symbols of their authority and partly as fortresses. The era's designation, Momoyama (Peach Blossom Hill), derives from the scenic foliage at one of those castles. Each warlord commissioned lavish decorations for the interior of his castle, including paintings, sliding doors, and folding screens *(byobu)* in ink, color, and gold leaf.

Hasegawa Tohaku A leading Momoyama screen painter was HASEGAWA TOHAKU (1539–1610), who studied the aesthetics and techniques of Chinese Chan and Japanese Zen painters such as Sesshu Toyo (FIG. 18-11). Tohaku painted in ink monochrome using loose brushwork with brilliant success in *Pine Forest* (FIG. 18-13). His wet brush strokes—long and slow, short and quick, dark and pale—present a grove of great pines shrouded in mist. His trees emerge from and recede into the heavy atmosphere, as if the landscape hovers at the edge of formlessness. In Zen terms, the picture suggests the illusory nature of mundane reality while evoking a calm, meditative mood.

Sen no Rikyu A favorite exercise of cultivation and refinement in the Momoyama period was the tea ceremony, which involved the ritual preparation, serving, and drinking of green tea. The host's responsibilities included serving the guests, selecting utensils, and determining the tearoom's decoration, which changed according to occasion and season. The tea ceremony eventually came to carry important political and ideological implications. It provided a means for those relatively new to political or economic power to assert authority in the cultural realm. For instance, upon returning from a major military campaign, Toyotomi Hideyoshi held an immense tea ceremony that lasted 10 days and was open to everyone in Kyoto. The tea ceremony's political implications became so serious that warlords granted or refused their vassals the right to practice it.

The most venerated tea master of the Momoyama period was SEN NO RIKYU (1522–1591), who was instrumental in establishing the rituals and aesthetics of the tea ceremony, for example, the manner of entry into a teahouse (crawling on one's hands and knees). Rikyu believed this behavior fostered humility and created the impression, however unrealistic, that there was no rank in a teahouse. Rikyu was the designer of the first Japanese teahouse built as an independent structure as opposed to being part of a house.

The Taian teahouse (FIG. 18-1) at the Myokian Temple in Kyoto, also attributed to Rikyu, is the oldest in Japan. The interior displays two standard features of late Muromachi

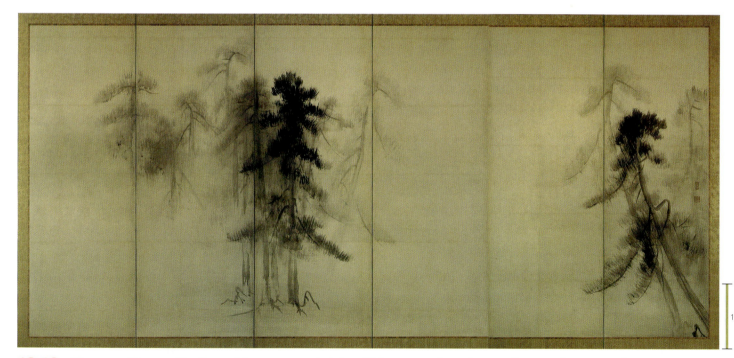

18-13 HASEGAWA TOHAKU, *Pine Forest*, Momoyama period, late 16th century. One of a pair of six-panel screens, ink on paper, 5' 1⅜" × 11' 4". Tokyo National Museum, Tokyo.

This Momoyama painter used wet brush strokes to depict a grove of great pines shrouded in mist. In Zen terms, the picture suggests the illusory nature of mundane reality while evoking a calm, meditative mood.

residential architecture—very thick, rigid straw mats called *tatami* (a Heian innovation) and an alcove called a *tokonoma*. The tatami accommodate the traditional Japanese customs of not wearing shoes indoors and of sitting on the floor. The tokonoma served as a place to hang scrolls of painting or calligraphy and to display other prized objects.

The Taian tearoom has unusually dark walls, with earthen plaster covering even some of the square corner posts. The room's dimness and tiny size (about six feet square) produce a cavelike feel and encourage intimacy among the tea host and guests. The guests enter from the garden outside through a small sliding door that forces them humbly to crawl inside. The means of entrance emphasizes a guest's passage into a ceremonial space set apart from the ordinary world.

Shino Ceramics

Sen no Rikyu was also influential in determining the aesthetics of tea ceremony utensils. He maintained that value and refinement lay in character and ability and not in bloodline or rank, and he therefore encouraged the use of tea items whose value was their inherent beauty rather than their monetary worth. Even before Rikyu, in the late 15th century, admiration of the technical brilliance of Chinese objects had begun to give way to greater appreciation of the virtues of rustic wares. This new aesthetic of refined rusticity, or *wabi*, was consistent with Zen concepts. Wabi suggests austerity and simplicity. Related to wabi and also important as a philosophical and aesthetic principle was *sabi*—the value found in the old and weathered, suggesting the tranquility reached in old age. Wabi and sabi aesthetics underlie the ceramic vessels produced for the tea ceremony, such as the Shino water jar named *kogan* (FIG. **18-14**). The name, which means "ancient stream bank," comes from the painted design on the jar's surface as well as from its coarse texture and rough form. The term *Shino* generally refers to ceramic wares produced during the late 16th and early 17th centuries in kilns in Mino. Shino wares typically have rough surfaces and feature heavy glazes containing feldspar. The kogan illustrated here has a prominent crack in one side and sagging contours (both intentional) to suggest the accidental and natural, qualities essential to the values of wabi and sabi.

Edo Period

When Tokugawa Ieyasu consolidated his power in 1615, he abandoned Kyoto, the official capital, and set up his headquarters in Edo (modern Tokyo), initiating the Edo period (1615–1868). The new regime instituted many policies designed to limit severely the pace of social and cultural change in Japan. Fearing the destabilization of the social order, the Tokugawa rulers banned Christianity and expelled all Westerners except the Dutch. The Tokugawa also transformed Confucian ideas of social stratification and civic responsibility into public policy, and they tried to control the social influence of urban merchants, some of whose wealth far outstripped that of most warrior leaders. However, the popula-

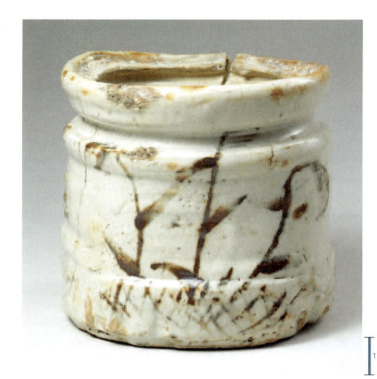

1 in.

18-14 Kogan, tea ceremony water jar, Momoyama period, late 16th century. Shino ware with underglaze design, 7″ high. Hatakeyama Memorial Museum, Tokyo.

Japanese tea ceremony vessels reflect the concepts of wabi, the aesthetic of refined rusticity, and sabi, the value found in weathered objects. These qualities suggest the tranquility achieved in old age.

tion's great expansion in urban centers, the spread of literacy in the cities and beyond, and a growing thirst for knowledge and diversion made for a very lively popular culture not easily subject to tight control.

Katsura Imperial Villa

In the Edo period, the imperial court's power remained as it had been for centuries, symbolic and ceremonial, but the court continued to wield influence in matters of taste and culture. For example, for a 50-year period in the 17th century, a princely family developed a modest country retreat into a villa that became the standard for domestic Japanese architecture. The Katsura Imperial Villa (FIG. **18-15**), built between 1620 and 1663 on the Katsura River southwest of Kyoto, has many features that derive from earlier teahouses, such as Rikyu's Taian (FIG. **18-1**), but the villa's designers incorporated elements of courtly gracefulness as well. Ornamentation that disguises structural forms has little place in this architecture's appeal, which relies instead on subtleties of proportion, color, and texture. A variety of textures (stone, wood, tile, and plaster) and subdued colors and tonal values enrich the villa's lines, planes, and volumes. Artisans painstakingly rubbed and burnished all surfaces to bring out the natural beauty of their grains and textures. The rooms are not large, but parting or removing the sliding doors between them can create broad rectangular spaces. Perhaps most important, the residents can open the doors to the outside to achieve a harmonious

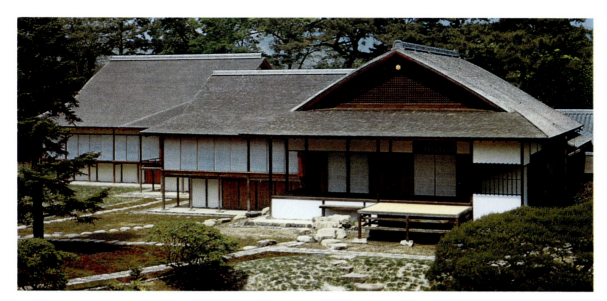

18-15 Eastern facade of the Katsura Imperial Villa, Kyoto, Japan, Edo period, 1620–1663.

This princely villa on the Katsura River has long been the standard for Japanese residential architecture. The design relies on subtleties of proportion, color, and texture instead of ornamentation for its aesthetic appeal.

integration of building and garden—one of the primary ideals of Japanese residential architecture.

Ogata Korin In painting, the Kano School enjoyed official governmental sponsorship during the Edo period, and its workshops provided paintings to the Tokugawa and their major vassals. By the mid-18th century, Kano masters also served as the primary painting teachers for nearly everyone aspiring to a career in the field. Even so, individualist painters and other schools emerged and flourished, working in quite distinct styles. The earliest major alternative school to emerge in the Edo period, Rinpa, was quite different in nature from the Kano School. It did not have a similar continuity of lineage and training through father and son, master and pupil. Instead, over time, Rinpa aesthetics and principles attracted a variety of individuals as practitioners and champions. Stylistically, Rinpa works feature vivid color and extensive use of gold and silver and often incorporate decorative patterns.

Rinpa takes its first syllable from the last syllable in the name of OGATA KORIN (1658–1716). One of Korin's masterpieces is a pair of two-panel folding screens (FIG. I-8) depicting red and white blossoming plum trees separated by a stream. Korin reduced the motifs to a minimum to offer a dramatic contrast of forms and visual textures. The landscape consists solely of delicate, slender branches, gnarled, aged tree trunks, and an undulating stream. Korin mixed viewpoints (he represented the stream as seen from above but the trees from the ground) to produce a striking two-dimensional pattern of dark forms on a gold ground. He even created a contrast between the dark motifs of stream and trees by varying painting techniques. The mottling of the trees comes from a signature Rinpa technique called *tarashikomi*, the dropping of ink and pigments onto surfaces still wet with previously applied ink and pigments. In sharp contrast, the pattern in the stream has the precision and elegant stylization of a textile design, produced by applying pigment through the forms cut in a paper stencil.

Ukiyo-e The growing urbanization in such cities as Osaka, Kyoto, and Edo led to an increase in the pursuit of sensual pleasure and entertainment in the brash popular theaters and the pleasure houses found in locales such as Edo's Yoshiwara brothel district. The Tokugawa tried to hold these activities in check, but their efforts were largely in vain. Those of lesser means could partake in the Yoshiwara pleasures and amusements vicariously. Rapid developments in the printing industry led to the availability of numerous books and printed images (see "Japanese Woodblock Prints," page 506), and these could convey the city's delights for a fraction of the cost of actual participation. Taking part in the emerging urban culture involved more than simple physical satisfactions and rowdy entertainments. Many participants were also admirers of literature, music, and art. The best-known products of this sophisticated counterculture were the *ukiyo-e*—"pictures of the floating world," a term that suggests the transience of human life and the ephemerality of the material world. The main subjects of these paintings and especially prints came from the realms of pleasure, but Edo printmakers also frequently depicted beautiful young women in domestic settings (FIG. 18-16) and landscapes (FIG. 18-17).

Suzuki Harunobu The urban appetite for ukiyo pleasures and for their depiction in ukiyo-e provided fertile ground for many print designers to flourish. Consequently, competition among publishing houses led to ever greater refinement and experimentation in printmaking. One of the most admired and emulated 18th-century designers, SUZUKI HARUNOBU (ca. 1725–1770), played a key role in developing multicolored prints. Called *nishiki-e* (brocade pictures) because of their sumptuous and brilliant color, these prints employed only the highest-quality paper and costly pigments. Harunobu gained a tremendous advantage over his fellow designers when he received commissions from members of a poetry club to design limited-edition nishiki-e prints. He transferred much of the knowledge he derived from nishiki-e

Japanese Woodblock Prints

During the Edo period, *ukiyo-e* woodblock prints became enormously popular. Sold in small shops and on the street, an ordinary print went for the price of a bowl of noodles. People of modest income could therefore collect prints in albums or paste them on walls. Ukiyo-e artists were generally painters who did not participate in the actual making of the prints that made them so famous. As the designers, they sold drawings to publishers, who in turn oversaw their printing. The publishers also played a role in creating ukiyo-e prints by commissioning specific designs or adapting them before printing. Certainly, the names of both designer and publisher appeared on the final prints. Unacknowledged in nearly all cases were the individuals who made the prints, the block carvers and printers. Using skills honed since childhood, they worked with both speed and precision for relatively low wages and thus made ukiyo-e prints affordable.

Stylistically, Japanese prints during the Edo period tend to have black outlines separating distinct color areas (FIG. 18-16). This format is a result of the printing process. A master carver pasted painted designs face down on a wooden block. Wetting and gently scraping the thin paper revealed the reversed image to guide the cutting of the block. After the carving, only the outlines of the forms and other elements that would be black in the final print remained raised in relief. The master printer then coated the block with black ink and printed several initial outline prints. These master prints became the guides for carving the other blocks, one for each color used. On each color block, the carver left in relief only the areas to be printed in that color. Even ordinary prints sometimes required up to 20 colors and thus 20 blocks. To print a color, a printer applied the appropriate pigment to a block's raised surface, laid a sheet of paper on it, and rubbed the back of the paper with a smooth flat object. Then another printer would print a different color on the same sheet of paper. Perfect alignment of the paper in each step was critical to prevent overlapping of colors, so the block carvers included printing guides—an L-shaped ridge in one corner and a straight ridge on one side—in their blocks. The printers could cover small alignment errors with a final printing of the black outlines from the last block.

The materials used in printing varied over time, but by the mid-18th century had reached a level of standardization. The blocks were planks of fine-grained hardwood, usually cherry. The best paper came from the white layer beneath the bark of mulberry trees, because its long fibers helped the paper stand up to repeated rubbing on the blocks. The printers used a few mineral pigments but favored inex-

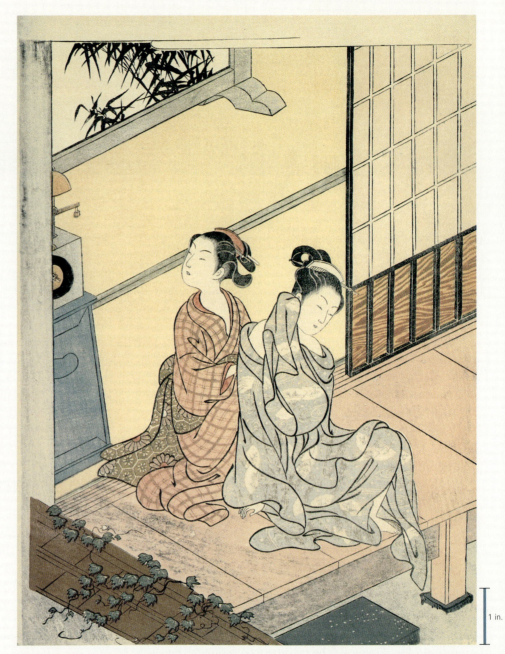

1 in.

18-16 Suzuki Harunobu, *Evening Bell at the Clock*, from *Eight Views of the Parlor*, Edo period, ca. 1765. Woodblock print, 11¼″ × 8½″. Art Institute of Chicago, Chicago (Clarence Buckingham Collection).

Harunobu's nishiki-e (brocade pictures) took their name from their costly pigments and paper. The rich color and flatness of the objects, women, and setting in this print are characteristic of the artist's style.

pensive dyes made from plants for most colors. As a result, the colors of ukiyo-e prints are highly susceptible to fading, especially when exposed to strong light. In the early 19th century, more permanent European synthetic dyes began to enter Japan. The first, Prussian blue, can be seen in Hokusai's *The Great Wave off Kanagawa* (FIG. 18-17).

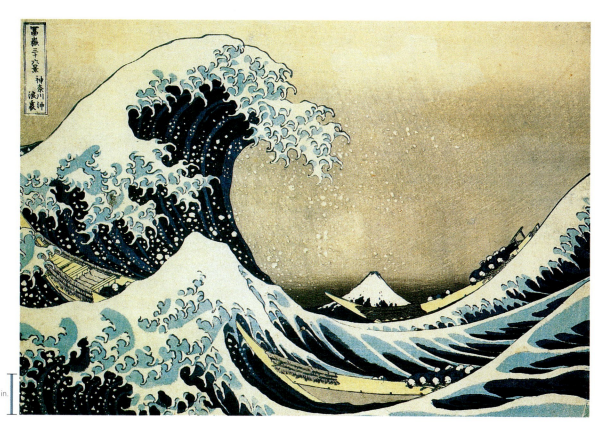

18-17 KATSUSHIKA HOKUSAI, *The Great Wave off Kanagawa*, from *Thirty-six Views of Mount Fuji*, Edo period, ca. 1826–1833. Woodblock print, ink and colors on paper, $9\frac{7}{8}''\times 1'\, 2\frac{3}{4}''$. Museum of Fine Arts, Boston (Bigelow Collection).

In this dramatic wood-block print, Hokusai used traditional Japanese flat and powerful graphic forms to depict a threatening wave seen against a low horizon line typical of Western painting.

1 in.

to his design of more commercial prints. Harunobu even issued some of the private designs later under his own name for popular consumption.

The sophistication of Harunobu's work is evident in *Evening Bell at the Clock* (FIG. **18-16**), from *Eight Views of the Parlor*. This series draws upon Chinese series, usually titled *Eight Views of the Xiao and Xiang Rivers*, in which each image focused on a particular time of day or year. In Harunobu's adaptation, beautiful young women and the activities that occupy their daily lives became the subject. In *Evening Bell at the Clock*, two young women seen from the typically Japanese elevated viewpoint (FIG. 18-8) sit on a veranda. One appears to be drying herself after a bath, while the other turns to face the chiming clock. Here, the artist has playfully transformed the great temple bell that rings over the waters in the Chinese series into a modern Japanese clock. This image incorporates the refined techniques characteristic of nishiki-e. Further, the flatness of the depicted objects and the rich color recall the traditions of court painting, a comparison many nishiki-e artists openly sought.

Katsushika Hokusai Woodblock prints afforded artists great opportunity for experimentation. For example, in producing landscapes, Japanese artists often incorporated Western perspective techniques. One of the foremost designers in this genre was KATSUSHIKA HOKUSAI (1760–1849). In *The Great Wave off Kanagawa* (FIG. **18-17**), part of a woodblock series called *Thirty-six Views of Mount Fuji*, the huge foreground wave dwarfs the artist's representation of a distant Fuji. This contrast and the whitecaps' ominous fingers magnify the wave's threatening aspect. The men in the trading boats bend low to dig their oars against the rough sea

and drive their long low vessels past the danger. Although Hokusai's print draws on Western techniques and incorporates the distinctive European color called Prussian blue, it also engages the Japanese pictorial tradition. Against a background with the low horizon typical of Western painting, Hokusai placed in the foreground the traditionally flat wave and its powerfully graphic forms.

MODERN JAPAN

The Edo period and the rule of the shoguns ended in 1868, when rebellious samurai from provinces far removed from Edo toppled the Tokugawa. Facilitating this revolution was the shogunate's inability to handle increasing pressure from Western nations for Japan to open itself to the outside world. Although the rebellion restored direct sovereignty to the imperial throne, real power rested with the emperor's cabinet. As a symbol of imperial authority, however, the official name of this new period was Meiji ("Enlightened Rule," 1868–1912), after the emperor's chosen reign name.

During the 20th century, Japan became increasingly prominent on the world stage in economics, politics, and culture. Among the events that propelled Japan into the spotlight was its participation in World War II during the Showa period (1926–1989). The most tragic consequences of that involvement were the widespread devastation and loss of life resulting from the atomic bombings of Hiroshima and Nagasaki in 1945. During the succeeding occupation period, the United States imposed new democratic institutions on Japan, with the emperor serving as only a ceremonial head of state. Japan's economy rebounded with remarkable speed, and during the ensuing half century Japan also assumed a

18-18 TANGE KENZO, national indoor Olympic stadiums, Tokyo, Japan, Showa period, 1961–1964.

Tange Kenzo was one of the most daring architects of post–World War II Japan. His Olympic stadiums employ a cable suspension system that allowed him to shape steel and concrete into remarkably graceful structures.

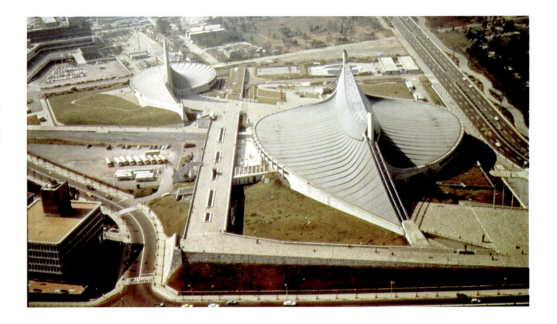

positive and productive place in the international art world. As they did in earlier times with the art and culture of China and Korea, Japanese artists internalized Western lessons and transformed them into a part of Japan's own vital culture.

Tange Kenzo In the postwar period, Japanese architecture, especially public and commercial building, underwent rapid transformation along Western lines. In fact, architecture may be the art form providing Japanese practitioners the most substantial presence on the world scene today. Japanese architects have made major contributions to both modern and postmodern developments. One of the most daringly experimental architects was TANGE KENZO (1913–2005). In the design of the stadiums (FIG. **18-18**) for the 1964 Olympics, he employed a cable suspension system that allowed him to shape steel and concrete into remarkably graceful structures. His attention to both the sculptural qualities of each building's raw concrete form and the fluidity of its spaces allied him with architects worldwide who carried on the legacy of the late style of Le Corbusier (FIG. **15-32**) in France.

Hamada Shoji No one style, medium, or subject dominates contemporary Japanese art, but much of it springs from ideas or beliefs that have long been integral to Japanese culture. One modern Japanese art form attracting great attention worldwide is ceramics. A formative figure in Japan's folk art movement, the philosopher Yanagi Soetsu (1889–1961), promoted an ideal of beauty inspired by the tea ceremony. He argued that true beauty could be achieved only in functional objects made of natural materials by anonymous craftspeople. Among the ceramists who produced this type of folk pottery, known as *mingei*, was HAMADA SHOJI (1894–1978). Although Hamada espoused Yanagi's selfless ideals, he still gained international fame and received official recognition in Japan as a Living National Treasure. Hamada's works (FIG. **18-19**) with casual slip designs are unsigned, but connoisseurs can easily recognize them as his. This kind of pottery is coarser, darker, and heavier than porcelain and lacks the latter's fine decoration. To those who appreciate simpler, earthier beauty, however, this dish holds great attraction. Hamada's artistic influence extended beyond the production of pots. He traveled to England in 1920 and, along with English potter Bernard Leach (1887–1978), established a community of ceramists committed to the mingei aesthetic. Together, Hamada and Leach expanded international knowledge of Japanese ceramics, and even now, the "Hamada-Leach aesthetic" is part of potters' education worldwide, underscoring the productive exchange of artistic ideas between Asia and the West today.

1 in.

18-19 HAMADA SHOJI, large bowl, Showa period, 1962. Black trails on translucent glaze, $5\frac{7}{8}$" × 1' $10\frac{1}{2}$" diameter. National Museum of Modern Art, Kyoto.

Hamada Shoji was a leading figure in the modern folk art movement in Japan who gained international fame. His unsigned ceramics feature casual slip designs and a coarser, darker texture than porcelain.

Japan

JAPAN BEFORE BUDDHISM

▌ The Jomon (ca. 10,500–300 BCE) is Japan's earliest distinct culture. It takes its name from the applied clay cordlike coil decoration of Jomon pottery.

▌ During the Kofun period (ca. 300–552 CE), the Japanese erected great earthen tumuli and placed clay cylindrical figures (haniwa) around and on top of them. Haniwa sculptures formed a protective spiritual barrier between the living and the dead.

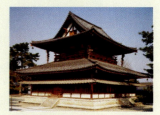

Haniwa warrior,
fifth to mid-sixth century

BUDDHIST JAPAN

▌ Buddhism was introduced to Japan in 552, and the first Japanese Buddhist artworks, such as Tori Busshi's Shaka triad, date to the Asuka period (552–645).

▌ During the Nara period (645–784), architecture, for example, the Horyuji kondo, followed Chinese models in construction technique and curved roofline.

▌ In 794 the imperial house moved its capital to Kyoto, initiating the Heian period (794–1185). A masterpiece of Heian Buddhist architecture is the Phoenix Hall at Uji, which evokes images of the celestial architecture of the Buddha's Pure Land of the West. Heian scroll paintings, for example, *Tale of Genji,* feature elevated viewpoints suggesting three-dimensional space and flat colors emphasizing the painting's two-dimensional character.

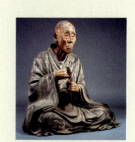

Kondo, Horyuji, ca. 680

JAPAN UNDER THE SHOGUNS

▌ In 1185 power shifted from the Japanese emperor to the Kamakura shogunate (1185–1332). Kamakura painting is diverse in both subject and style and includes historical narratives, such as *Events of the Heiji Period,* and Buddhist hanging scrolls. Kamakura wooden portraits, for example, that of Shunjobo Chogen, are noteworthy for their realism and the use of rock crystal for the eyes.

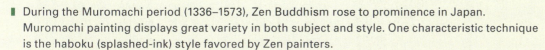

Shunjobo Chogen, early 13th century

▌ During the Muromachi period (1336–1573), Zen Buddhism rose to prominence in Japan. Muromachi painting displays great variety in both subject and style. One characteristic technique is the haboku (splashed-ink) style favored by Zen painters.

▌ The Momoyama period (1573–1615) was a brief interlude between two long-lasting shogunates, but it was then that the tea ceremony become an important social ritual. The tea master Sen no Rikyu designed the first teahouse built as an independent structure. The favored tea utensils were rustic Shino wares.

▌ The Edo period (1615–1868) began when Tokugawa Ieyasu moved his headquarters from Kyoto to Edo (modern Tokyo). Rinpa School paintings feature vivid colors and extensive use of gold. Ukiyo-e woodblock prints of Edo's "floating world" by Suzuki Harunobu and others depict scenes from brothels and the theater as well as beautiful women in domestic settings.

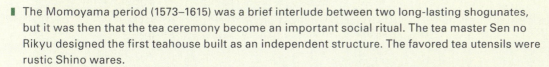

Harunobu, *Evening Bell at the Clock,* ca. 1765

MODERN JAPAN

▌ Rebellious samurai toppled the Tokugawa shogunate in 1868, opening the modern era of Japanese history.

▌ In the post–World War II period, Japanese architects achieved worldwide reputations. Tange Kenzo was a master of creating dramatic shapes using a cable suspension system for his concrete-and-steel buildings. Contemporary art in Japan is multifaceted, and the traditional and the modern flourish side by side.

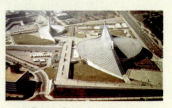

Tange, Olympic stadiums,
Tokyo, 1961–1964

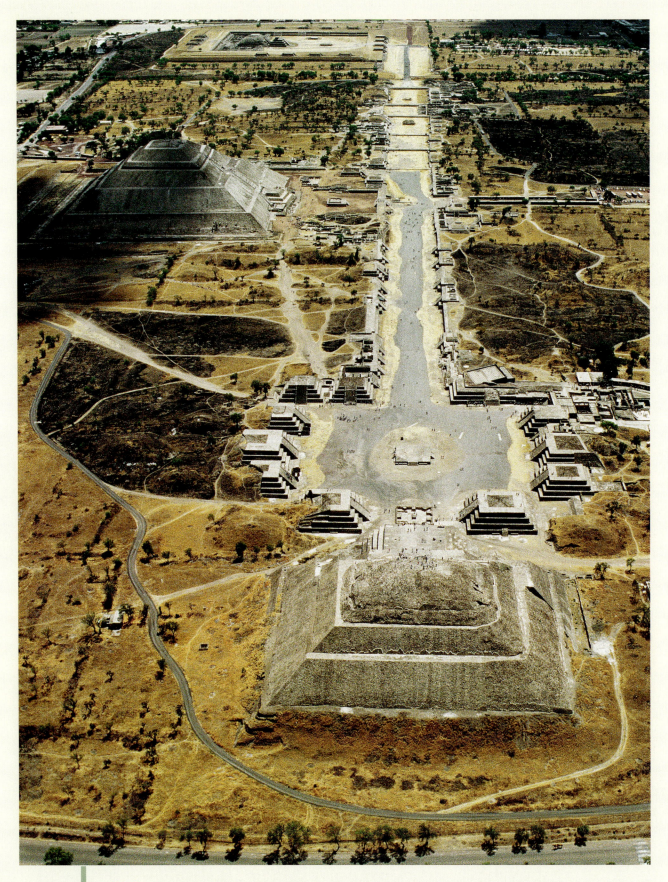

19-1 Aerial view of Teotihuacan (looking south), Mexico. Pyramid of the Moon (*foreground*), Pyramid of the Sun (*left*), and the Citadel (*top left*), all connected by the Avenue of the Dead; main structures ca. 50–200 CE.

At its peak around 600 CE, Teotihuacan was the sixth-largest city in the world. It had a rational grid plan and a two-mile-long main avenue. Its monumental pyramids echo the shapes of surrounding mountains.

The Americas

The origins of the indigenous peoples of the Americas are still uncertain. Sometime no later than 30,000 to 10,000 BCE, these first Americans probably crossed the now-submerged land bridge connecting the shores of the Bering Strait between Asia and North America. Some migrants may have reached the Western Hemisphere via boat. By 8000 to 2000 BCE, these Stone Age hunter-gatherer nomads had settled in villages and learned to fish and farm, and by the early centuries CE, several population groups had reached a high level of social complexity and technological achievement. Although most relied on stone tools, did not use the wheel (except for toys), and had no pack animals but the llama (in South America), ancient Americans excelled in the engineering arts associated with the planning and construction of cities, roads and bridges, and irrigation and drainage systems. They erected towering buildings, carved monumental stone statues and reliefs, painted extensive murals, and mastered the arts of weaving, pottery, and metalwork. This chapter examines in turn the artistic achievements of the native peoples of Mesoamerica, South America, and North America.

MESOAMERICA

The term *Mesoamerica* names the region that comprises part of present-day Mexico, Guatemala, Belize, Honduras, and the Pacific coast of El Salvador (MAP 19-1). Mesoamerica was the homeland of several of the great civilizations that flourished before the Spaniard Hernán Cortés (1485–1547) conquered the Aztec Empire in the 16th century. The Europeans destroyed most of the once-glorious American cities in their zeal to obliterate all traces of pagan beliefs. Other sites were abandoned to the forces of nature—erosion and the encroachment of tropical forests. But despite the ruined state of the pre-Hispanic cities, archaeologists and art historians have been able to reconstruct much of the history of the art and architecture of ancient Mesoamerica. Historians have established a widely accepted chronology divided into three epochs: Preclassic, from 2000 BCE to about 300 CE; Classic, from about 300 to 900; and Postclassic, from 900 to the Spanish conquest of 1521.

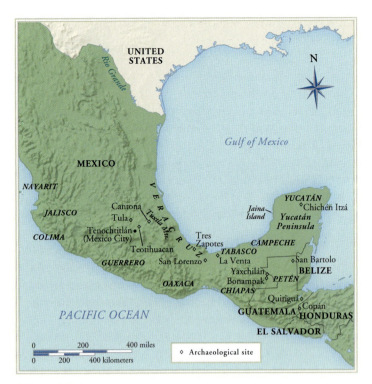

MAP 19-1 Mesoamerica.

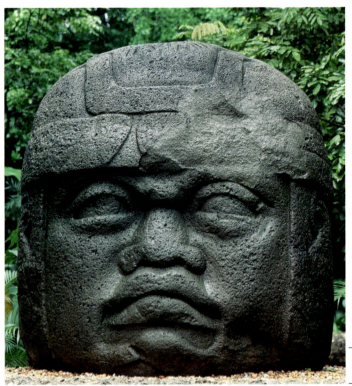

19-2 Colossal head, Olmec, La Venta, Mexico, 900–400 BCE. Basalt, 9′ 4″ high. Museo-Parque La Venta, Villahermosa.

The identities of the Olmec colossi are uncertain, but their individualized features and distinctive headgear, as well as later Maya practice, suggest that these heads portray rulers rather than deities.

1 ft.

Olmec

Scholars have often called the Preclassic Olmec culture of the present-day states of Veracruz and Tabasco the "mother culture" of Mesoamerica, because many distinctive Mesoamerican religious, social, and artistic traditions can be traced to it. Settling in the tropical lowlands of the Gulf of Mexico, the Olmec peoples cultivated a terrain of rain forest and alluvial lowland. Here, between approximately 1500 and 400 BCE, social organization assumed the form that later Mesoamerican cultures developed. The mass of the population—food-producing farmers scattered in hinterland villages—provided the sustenance and labor that maintained a hereditary caste of rulers, hierarchies of priests, functionaries, and artisans. At regular intervals, the whole community convened for ritual observances at religious-civic centers such as La Venta.

La Venta At La Venta, stone fences enclosed two great courtyards. At one end of the larger area was a pyramid almost 100 feet high, built of earth and adorned with colored clays. Its form may have mimicked a mountain, held sacred by Mesoamerican peoples as both a life-giving source of water and a feared destructive force. The La Venta layout is an early form of the temple-pyramid-plaza complex aligned on a north-south axis that characterized later Mesoamerican ceremonial center design.

Four colossal basalt heads (FIG. **19-2**), weighing about 10 tons each and standing between 6 and 10 feet high, face out from the plaza. Archaeologists have found more than a dozen similar heads at San Lorenzo and Tres Zapotes. Almost as much of an achievement as the carving of these huge heads with stone tools was their transportation across

the 60 miles of swampland from the nearest known basalt source, the Tuxtla Mountains. Although the identities of the colossi are uncertain, their individualized features and distinctive headgear and ear ornaments, as well as the later Maya practice of carving monumental ruler portraits, suggest that the Olmec heads portray rulers rather than deities. The sheer size of the heads and their intensity of expression evoke great power, whether mortal or divine.

Teotihuacan

The late Preclassic site of Teotihuacan (FIG. **19-1**), northeast of Mexico City, was a large, densely populated metropolis that fulfilled a central civic, economic, and religious role for the region and indeed for much of Mesoamerica. The city covers nine square miles, laid out in a grid pattern with the axes oriented by sophisticated surveying. Its major monuments date between 50 and 250 CE. At its peak, around 600 CE, Teotihuacan may have had as many as 125,000–200,000 residents, making it the sixth-largest city in the world at that time. Hundreds of years later, the Aztecs gave Teotihuacan its current name, which means "the place of the gods." Because the city's inhabitants left only a handful of undeciphered hieroglyphs, the names of many major features of the site are unknown. The Avenue of the Dead and the Pyramids of the Sun and Moon are Aztec designations that do not necessarily relate to the original names.

North-south and east-west axes, each four miles in length, divide the grid plan into quarters. The main north-south axis, the Avenue of the Dead (FIG. 19-1), is 130 feet wide and connects the Pyramid of the Moon complex with the Citadel and its Temple of Quetzalcoatl (FIG. 19-3). This two-mile stretch is not a continuously flat street but is broken by sets of stairs, giving pedestrians a constantly changing view of the surrounding buildings and landscape.

Pyramids The Pyramid of the Sun (FIG. 19-1, *left*), facing west on the east side of the Avenue of the Dead, dates to the first century CE. It is the city's centerpiece and its largest structure, rising to a height of more than 200 feet. The Pyramid of the Moon (FIG. 19-1, *foreground*) is a century or more later, about 150–250 CE. The shapes of the pyramids echo the surrounding mountains. Their imposing mass and scale surpass those of all other Mesoamerican sites. Rubble-filled and faced with the local volcanic stone, the pyramids consist of stacked square platforms diminishing in perimeter from the base to the top, like Djoser's much earlier Stepped Pyramid (FIG. 1-24) in Egypt. Ramped stairways led to crowning temples constructed of perishable materials such as wood and thatch, no longer preserved.

The Teotihuacanos built the Pyramid of the Sun over a cave that once may have contained a sacred spring. Excavators found children buried at the four corners of each of the pyramid's tiers. The later Aztec sacrificed children to bring rainfall, and Teotihuacan art abounds with references to water, so the Teotihuacanos may have shared the Aztec preoccupation with rain and agricultural fertility. The city's inhabitants rebuilt the Pyramid of the Moon at least five times in Teotihuacan's early history. The builders may have positioned it to mimic the shape of Cerro Gordo, the volcanic mountain behind it.

Quetzalcoatl At the south end of the Avenue of the Dead is the great quadrangle of the Citadel (FIG. 19-1, *top left*). It encloses a smaller pyramid datable to the third century CE, the Temple of Quetzalcoatl (FIG. **19-3**), the "feathered serpent," a major god in the Mesoamerican pantheon associated with wind, rain clouds, and life.

Beneath the temple, archaeologists found a tomb looted in antiquity, leading them to speculate that the Teotihuacanos, like the later Maya, buried their elite in or under pyramids. Surrounding the tomb both beneath and around the pyramid were the remains of at least a hundred sacrificial victims. Some wore necklaces made of strings of human jaws, both real and sculpted from shell. The presence of such a large number of victims may reflect Teotihuacan's militaristic expansion. Throughout Mesoamerica, the victors often sacrificed captured warriors.

The temple's sculptured panels, which feature projecting stone heads of Quetzalcoatl alternating with heads of a long-snouted scaly creature with rings on its forehead decorate each of the temple's six terraces. This is the first unambiguous representation of the feathered serpent in Mesoamerica. The scaly creature's identity is unclear. Linking these alternating heads are low-relief carvings of feathered-serpent bodies and seashells. The latter reflect Teotihuacan contact with the peoples of the Mexican coasts and also symbolize water, an essential ingredient for the sustenance of an agricultural economy. The Teotihuacanos established colonies as far away as the highlands of Guatemala, some 800 miles from the city.

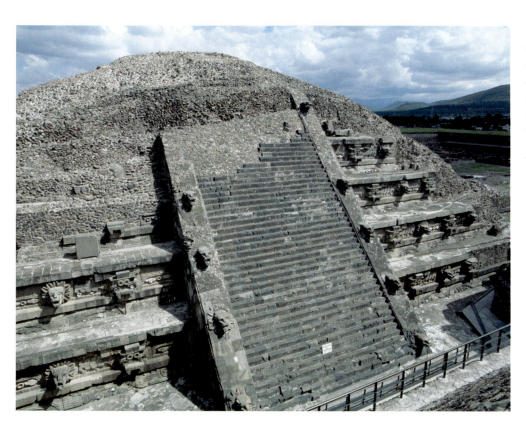

19-3 Partial view of the Temple of Quetzalcoatl, Teotihuacan, Mexico, third century CE.

The stone heads of Quetzalcoatl decorating this pyramid are the earliest representations of the feathered-serpent god. Beneath and around the pyramid, excavators found remains of sacrificial victims.

Maya

As was true of Teotihuacan, the foundations of Maya civilization can be traced to the Preclassic period, perhaps to 600 BCE or even earlier. At that time, the Maya, who occupied the moist lowland areas of Belize, southern Mexico, Guatemala, and Honduras, apparently abandoned their early, somewhat egalitarian pattern of village life and adopted a hierarchical autocratic society. This system evolved into the typical Classic Maya city-state governed by hereditary rulers and ranked nobility. How and why this happened are still uncertain.

Stupendous building projects signaled the change. Vast complexes of terraced temple-pyramids, palaces, plazas, and residences of the governing elite dotted the Maya area. Unlike at Teotihuacan, no single Maya site ever achieved complete dominance as the center of power. The new architecture, and the art embellishing it, advertised the power of the rulers, who appropriated cosmic symbolism and stressed their descent from gods to reinforce their claims to legitimate rulership. The unified institutions of religion and kingship were established so firmly, their hold on life and custom was so tenacious, and their meaning was so fixed in the symbolism and imagery of art that the rigidly conservative system of the Classic Maya lasted almost 600 years. Maya civilization began to decline in the eighth century CE. By 900 it had vanished, marking the beginning of the Postclassic era.

Although the causes of the beginning and end of Classic Maya civilization are obscure, researchers are gradually revealing its history, beliefs, ceremonies, conventions, and patterns of daily life through scientific excavation and progress made in decoding Mayan script. Two important breakthroughs in the 1950s radically altered the understanding of both Mayan writing and the Maya worldview. The first was the realization that the Maya depicted their rulers (rather than gods or anonymous priests) in their art and noted their rulers' achievements in their texts. The second was that Mayan writing is largely phonetic—that is, the hieroglyphs are composed of signs representing sounds in the Mayan language. Fortunately, the Spaniards recorded the various Mayan languages in colonial texts and dictionaries. Although perhaps only half of the ancient Mayan script can be translated accurately into today's spoken Mayan, experts can at least grasp the general meaning of many more hieroglyphs.

The Maya possessed a highly developed knowledge of mathematical calculation and the ability to observe and record the movements of the sun, the moon, and numerous planets. Their calendar, although radically different in form from the Western calendar used today, was just as precise and efficient. It allowed the Maya to establish the genealogical lines of their rulers and to create the only true written history in ancient America. Although other ancient Mesoamerican societies, even in the Preclassic period, also possessed calendars, only the Maya calendar can be translated directly into today's calendrical system.

Architecture and Ritual The Maya erected their most sacred and majestic buildings in enclosed, centrally located precincts within their cities. The religious-civic transactions that guaranteed the order of the state and the cosmos occurred in these settings. The Maya held dramatic rituals within a sculptured and painted environment, where huge symbols and images proclaimed the nature and necessity of that order. Maya builders designed spacious plazas for vast audiences who were exposed to overwhelming propaganda. In Maya paintings and sculptures, the Maya elite wear extravagant costumery of vividly colorful cotton textiles, feathers, jaguar skins, and jade, all emblematic of their rank and wealth. On the different levels of the painted and polished temple platforms, the ruling classes performed the offices of their rites in clouds of incense to the music of maracas, flutes, and drums. The Maya transformed the architectural complex at each city's center into a theater of religion and statecraft.

Copán Because Copán, on the western border of Honduras, has more hieroglyphic inscriptions and well-preserved carved monuments than any other site in the Americas, it was one of the first Maya sites excavated. It also has proved one of the richest in the trove of architecture, sculpture, and artifacts uncovered. In Copán's Great Plaza at the heart of the city, the Maya set up tall, sculpted stone stelae. Carved with the portraits of the rulers who erected them, these stelae also recorded their names, dates of reign, and notable achievements. Stele D (FIG. 19-4), erected in 736 CE, represents

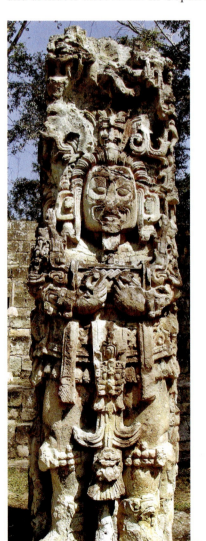

19-4 Stele D portraying Ruler 13 (Waxaklajuun-Ub'aah-K'awiil), Maya, Great Plaza, Copán, Honduras, 736 CE. Stone, 11′ 9″ high.

Ruler 13 reigned during the heyday of Copán. On this stele he wears an elaborate headdress and holds a double-headed serpent bar, symbol of the sky and of his absolute power.

The Mesoamerican Ball Game

After witnessing the native ball game of Mexico soon after their arrival, the 16th-century Spanish conquerors took Aztec ball players back to Europe to demonstrate the novel sport. Their chronicles remark on the athletes' great skill, the heavy wagering that accompanied the competition, and the ball itself, made of rubber, a substance the Europeans had never seen before.

The game was played throughout Mesoamerica and into the southwestern United States, beginning at least 3,400 years ago, the date of the earliest known ball court. The Olmec were apparently avid players. Their very name—a modern invention in Nahuatl, the Aztec language—means "rubber people," after the latex-growing region they inhabited. Not only do ball players appear in Olmec art, but archaeologists have found remnants of sunken earthen ball courts and even rubber balls at Olmec sites.

The Olmec earthen playing field evolved in other Mesoamerican cultures into a plastered masonry surface, I- or T-shaped in plan, flanked by two parallel sloping or straight walls. Sometimes the walls were wide enough to support small structures on top, as at Copán (FIG. 19-5). At other sites, temples stood at either end of the ball court. These structures were common features of Mesoamerican cities. At Cantona, for example, archaeologists have uncovered 22 ball courts even though only a small portion of the site has been excavated. Teotihuacan (FIG. 19-1) is an exception. Excavators have not yet found a ball court there, but mural paintings at the site illustrate people playing the game with portable markers and sticks. Most ball courts were adjacent to the important civic structures of Mesoamerican cities, such as palaces and temple-pyramids, as at Copán.

Surprisingly little is known about the rules of the ball game itself—how many players were on the field, how goals were scored and tallied, and how competitions were arranged. Unlike a modern soccer field with its standard dimensions, Mesoamerican ball courts vary widely in size.

The largest known—at Chichén Itzá—is nearly 500 feet long. Copán's is about 93 feet long. Some have stone rings set high up on their walls at right angles to the ground, which a player conceivably could knock a ball through, but many courts lack this feature. Alternatively, players may have bounced the ball against the walls and into the end zones. As in soccer, players could not touch the ball with their hands but used their heads, elbows, hips, and legs. They wore thick leather belts, and sometimes even helmets, and padded their knees and arms against the blows of the fast-moving solid rubber ball (FIG. 19-6).

Although widely enjoyed as a competitive spectator sport, the ball game did not serve solely for entertainment. The ball, for example, may have represented a celestial body such as the sun, its movements over the court imitating the sun's daily passage through the sky. Reliefs on the walls of ball courts at certain sites make clear that the game sometimes culminated in human sacrifice, probably of captives taken in battle and then forced to participate in a game they were predestined to lose.

Ball playing also had a role in Mesoamerican mythology. In the ancient Maya epic known as the *Popol Vuh (Council Book),* first written down in Spanish in the colonial period, the evil lords of the Underworld force a legendary pair of twins to play ball. The brothers lose and are sacrificed. The sons of one twin eventually travel to the Underworld and, after a series of trials including a ball game, outwit the lords and kill them. They revive their father, buried in the ball court after his earlier defeat at the hands of the Underworld gods. The younger twins rise to the heavens to become the sun and the moon, and the father becomes the god of maize (corn), principal sustenance of all Mesoamerican peoples. The ball game and its aftermath, then, were a metaphor for the cycle of life, death, and regeneration that permeated Mesoamerican religion.

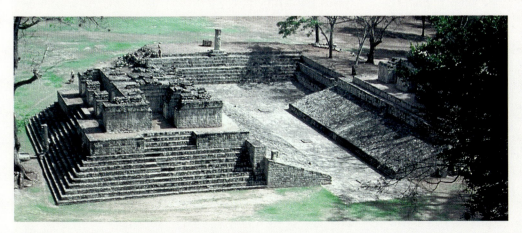

19-5 Ball court (looking north), Maya, Middle Plaza, Copán, Honduras, 738 CE.

Ball courts were common features of Mesoamerican cities. Copán's is 93 feet long. Little is known about the rules of the ball game, but games sometimes ended in human sacrifice, probably of captives taken in battle.

Waxaklajuun-Ub'aah-K'awiil (r. 695–738), the 13th in a dynastic sequence of 16 rulers. During his long reign, Copán may have reached its greatest physical extent and range of political influence. On Stele D, Ruler 13, as scholars call him, wears an elaborate headdress and ornamented kilt and sandals. He holds across his chest a double-headed serpent bar, symbol of the sky and of his absolute power. His features have the quality of a portrait likeness, although highly idealized. The Maya elite tended to have themselves portrayed in a conventionalized manner and as eternally youthful. The

dense, deeply carved ornamental details that frame the face and figure in florid profusion stand almost clear of the block and wrap around the sides of the stele. The high relief, originally painted, gives the impression of a freestanding statue, although a hieroglyphic text is carved on the flat back side of the stele. Ruler 13 erected many stelae and buildings at Copán, including one of Mesoamerica's best-preserved (and carefully restored) ball courts (FIG. 19-5; see "The Mesoamerican Ball Game," above), but the king of neighboring Quiriguá eventually captured and beheaded him.

Jaina The Maya produced small-scale sculptures as well, especially in clay. Remarkably lifelike, carefully descriptive, and even comic at times, they represent a wider range of human types and activities than those depicted on Maya stelae. Ball players (FIG. **19-6**), women weaving, older men, dwarfs, supernatural beings, and amorous couples, as well as elaborately attired rulers and warriors, make up the figurine repertory. Many of the hollow figurines are also whistles. The graves in the island cemetery of Jaina, off the western coast of Yucatán, yielded hundreds of these figures, including the ball player illustrated here. Traces of blue remain on the figure's belt—remnants of the vivid pigments that once covered many of these figurines. The Maya used "Maya blue," a combination of a particular kind of clay and indigo, a vegetable dye, to paint both ceramics and murals. This pigment has proved virtually indestructible, unlike the other colors that largely have disappeared over time. The Jaina figurines accompanied the dead on their inevitable voyage to the Underworld, but excavations have revealed nothing more that might clarify the meaning and function of the figures. Male figurines do not come exclusively from burials of male individuals, for example.

Bonampak Bonampak (Mayan, "painted walls") in southeastern Mexico is, as its name suggests, famous for its mural paintings. The example reproduced here (FIG. **19-7**) depicts the presentation of prisoners to Lord Chan Muwan. The figures have naturalistic proportions and overlap, twist, turn, and gesture. The artists used fluid lines to outline the forms, working with color to indicate both texture and volume. The Bonampak painters combined their pigments—

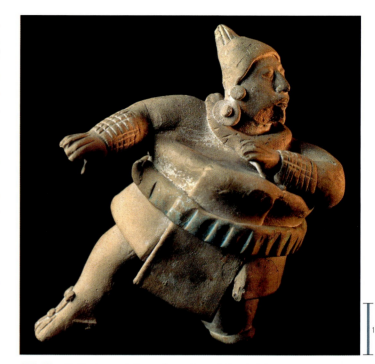

1 in.

19-6 Ball player, Maya, from Jaina Island, Mexico, 700–900 CE. Painted clay, $6\frac{1}{4}$" high. Museo Nacional de Antropología, Mexico City.

Maya ceramic figurines represent a wide range of human types and activities. This kneeling ball player wears a thick leather belt and arm- and kneepads to protect him from the hard rubber ball.

both mineral and organic—with a mixture of water, crushed limestone, and vegetable gums and applied them to their stucco walls in a technique best described as a cross between fresco and tempera.

19-7 Presentation of captives to Lord Chan Muwan, Maya, room 2 of structure 1, Bonampak, Mexico, ca. 790 CE. Mural, 17′ × 15′; watercolor copy by Antonio Tejeda. Peabody Museum of Archaeology and Ethnology, Harvard University, Cambridge.

The figures in this mural— a cross between fresco and tempera—may be standing on a pyramid's steps. At the top, the richly attired Chan Muwan reviews naked captives with mutilated hands awaiting their death.

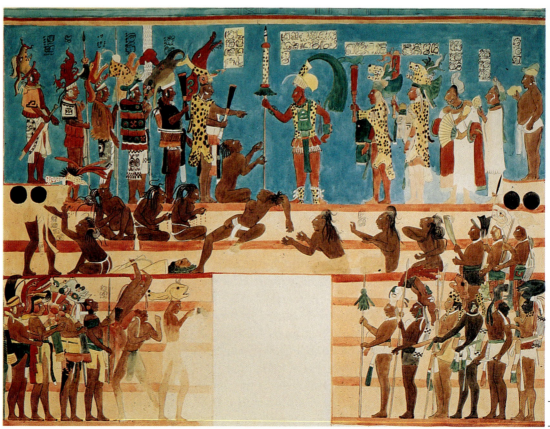

1 ft.

Circumstantial details fill Bonampak murals. The information given is comprehensive, explicit, and presented with the fidelity of an eyewitness report. The royal personages are identifiable by both their physical features and their costumes, and accompanying inscriptions provide the precise day, month, and year for the events recorded. All the scenes at Bonampak relate the events and ceremonies that welcome a new royal heir (shown as a toddler in some scenes). They include presentations, preparations for a royal fete, dancing, battle, and the taking and sacrificing of prisoners. On all occasions of state, public bloodletting was an integral part of Maya ritual. The ruler, his consort, and certain members of the nobility drew blood from their own bodies and sought union with the supernatural world. The slaughter of captives taken in war regularly accompanied this ceremony. Indeed, Mesoamerican cultures undertook warfare largely to provide victims for sacrifice. The torture and eventual execution of prisoners served both to nourish the gods and to strike fear into enemies and the general populace.

In the Chan Muwan mural (FIG. 19-7), the Bonampak painter arranged the figures in registers that may represent a pyramid's steps. On the uppermost step, against a blue background, is a file of gorgeously appareled nobles wearing animal headgear. Conspicuous among them on the right are retainers clad in jaguar pelts and jaguar headdresses. Also present is Chan Muwan's wife (third from right). The ruler himself, in jaguar jerkin and high-backed sandals, stands at the center, facing a crouching victim who appears to beg for mercy. Naked captives, anticipating death, crowd the middle level. One of them, already dead, sprawls at the ruler's feet. Others dumbly contemplate the blood dripping from their mutilated hands. The lower zone, cut through by a doorway, shows clusters of attendants who are doubtless of inferior rank to the lords of the upper zone. The stiff formality of the victors contrasts graphically with the supple imploring attitudes and gestures of the hapless victims. The Bonampak victory was short-lived. The murals were never finished, and soon after the dates written on the walls, the Maya abandoned the site.

The Bonampak murals are the most famous Maya wall paintings, but they are not unique. In 2001 at San Bartolo in northeastern Guatemala, American archaeologists discovered the earliest examples yet found. They date to about 100 BCE, almost a millennium before the Bonampak murals.

Yaxchilán Elite women played an important role in Maya society, and some surviving artworks, such as the painted lintels of temple 23 at Yaxchilán, document their high status. Lintel 24 (FIG. 19-8) depicts the ruler Itzamna Balam II (r. 681–742 CE), known as Shield Jaguar, and his principal wife, Lady Xoc. Lady Xoc is magnificently outfitted in an elaborate woven garment, headdress, and jewels. She pierces her tongue with a barbed cord in a bloodletting ceremony that, according to accompanying inscriptions, celebrated the birth of a son to one of the ruler's other wives as well as an alignment between the planets Saturn and Jupiter. The celebration must have been held in a dark chamber or at night

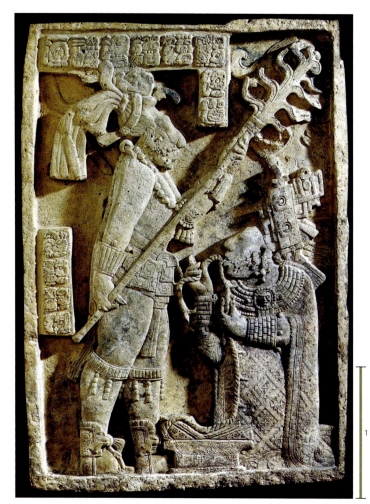

19-8 Shield Jaguar and Lady Xoc, Maya, lintel 24 of temple 23, Yaxchilán, Mexico, ca. 725 CE. Limestone, 3′ 7″ × 2′ 6½″. British Museum, London.

In this rare representation of a woman playing an important role in Maya ritual, Lady Xoc pierces her tongue in a bloodletting ceremony celebrating the birth of a new son to the ruler Shield Jaguar.

because Shield Jaguar provides illumination with a blazing torch. The purpose of these ceremonies was to produce hallucinations. (Lintel 25 depicts Lady Xoc and her vision of an ancestor emerging from the mouth of a serpent.)

Chichén Itzá Throughout Mesoamerica, the Classic period ended at different times with the disintegration of the great civilizations. Teotihuacan's political and cultural empire began to wane in the early sixth century. About 650, fire of unknown cause destroyed the city's center, and within a century Teotihuacan was deserted. Around 900, many of the major Maya sites were abandoned to the jungle, leaving a few northern Maya cities to flourish for another century or two during the Postclassic period before they, too, became depopulated. The war and confusion that followed the collapse of the Classic civilizations fractured the great states into small, local political entities isolated in fortified sites. In central Mexico the Toltec and the later Aztec peoples, both ambitious migrants from the north, forged empires by force of arms, while the militant city-state of Chichén Itzá dominated Yucatán, a flat, low, limestone peninsula covered

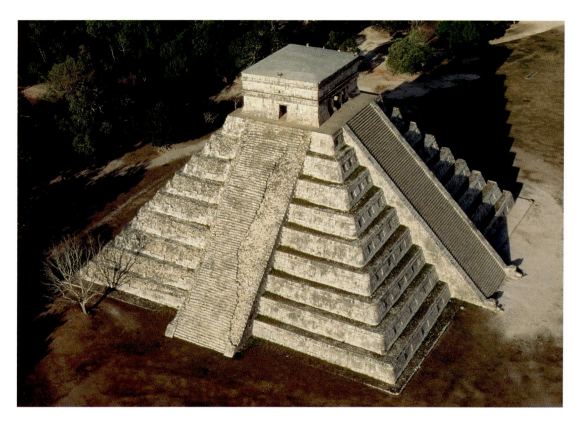

19-9 Aerial view of the Castillo (looking southwest), Maya, Chichén Itzá, Mexico, ca. 800–900 CE.

A temple to Kukulkan sits atop this pyramid with a total of 365 stairs on its four sides. At the winter and summer equinoxes, the sun casts a shadow in the shape of a serpent along the northern staircase.

with scrub vegetation. During the Classic period, Mayan-speaking peoples sparsely inhabited this northern region. For reasons scholars still debate, when the southern Classic Maya sites were abandoned after 900, the northern Maya continued to build many new temples in this area.

Dominating the main plaza of Chichén Itzá is the 98-foot-high pyramid (FIG. **19-9**) that the Spaniards nicknamed the Castillo (Castle). The pyramid has nine levels, probably a reference to the nine levels of the Underworld. The design of the Castillo is also tied to the solar year. The north side has 92 steps and the other three sides 91 steps each for a total of 365. At the winter and summer equinoxes, the sun casts a shadow along the northern staircase of the pyramid. Because of the pyramid's silhouette and the angle of the sun, the shadow takes the shape of a serpent that slithers along the pyramid's face as the sun moves across the sky. Atop the structure is a temple dedicated to Kukulkan, the Maya equivalent of Quetzalcoatl.

Excavations inside the Castillo in 1937 revealed an earlier nine-level pyramid within the later and larger structure. Inside was a royal burial chamber with a throne in the form of a red jaguar and a stone figure of a type called a *chacmool* depicting

19-10 Chacmool, Maya, from the Platform of the Eagles, Chichén Itzá, Mexico, ca. 800–900 CE. Stone, 4′ 10½″ high. Museo Nacional de Antropología, Mexico City.

Chacmools represent fallen warriors reclining on their backs with receptacles on their chests to receive sacrificial offerings. Excavators discovered one in the burial chamber inside the Castillo (FIG. 19-9).

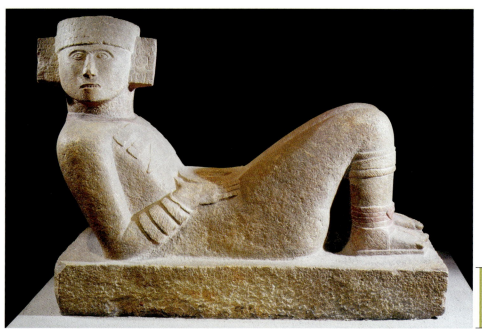

1 ft.

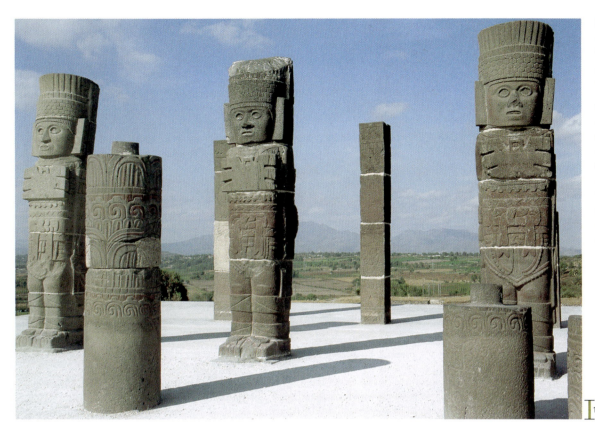

19-11 Colossal atlantids, pyramid B, Toltec, Tula, Mexico, ca. 900–1180 CE. Stone, each 16′ high.

The colossal statue-columns of Tula portraying warriors armed with darts and spear-throwers reflect the military regime of the Toltecs, whose arrival in central Mexico coincided with the decline of the Maya.

1 ft.

a fallen warrior. Chacmools (for example, FIG. **19-10**, found near the Castillo) recline on their backs and have receptacles on their chests to receive sacrificial offerings, probably of defeated enemies.

Toltec

The name Toltec, which signifies "makers of things," generally refers to a powerful tribe of invaders from the north, whose arrival in central Mexico coincided with the great disturbances that must have contributed to the fall of the Classic civilizations. The Toltecs were great political organizers and military strategists, dominating large parts of north and central Mexico. They were also master artisans and farmers. The later Aztecs admired the Toltecs and were proud to claim descent from them.

Tula The Toltec capital at Tula flourished from about 900 to 1200, the early part of the Postclassic period. Four colossal *atlantids* (male statue-columns; FIG. **19-11**) portraying armed warriors reflect the grim, warlike regime of the Toltecs. These images of brutal authority stand eternally at attention, warding off all hostile threats. Built up of four stone drums each, the sculptures stand atop pyramid B. They wear feathered headdresses and, as breastplates, stylized butterflies, heraldic symbols of the Toltec. In one hand they clutch a bundle of darts and in the other an *atlatl* (spear-thrower), typical weapons of highland Mexico. The figures originally supported a temple roof, now missing.

By 1180 the last Toltec ruler and most of his people abandoned Tula. Some years later, the city was catastrophically destroyed, its ceremonial buildings burned to their foundations, its walls demolished, and the straggling remainder of its population scattered. The exact reasons for the Toltecs' departure and for their city's destruction are unknown.

Aztec

The disintegration of the Toltec Empire brought a century of anarchy to the Valley of Mexico, the vast highland valley 7,000 feet above sea level that now contains sprawling Mexico City. Waves of northern invaders established warring city-states and wrought destruction in the valley. The last and greatest of these conquerors were the Aztecs, who called themselves Mexica. Following a legendary prophecy that they would build a city where they saw an eagle perched on a cactus with a serpent in its mouth, they settled on an island in Lake Texcoco (Lake of the Moon). Their settlement grew into the magnificent city of Tenochtitlán.

Recognized by those they subdued as fierce in war and cruel in peace, the Aztecs radically changed the social and political situation in Mexico. Subservient groups not only had to submit to Aztec military power but also had to provide victims to be sacrificed to Huitzilopochtli, the hummingbird god of war, and to other Aztec deities (see "Aztec Religion," page 521). The Aztecs practiced bloodletting and human sacrifice—which had a long history in Mesoamerica—to please the gods and sustain the great cycles of the universe. But the Mexica engaged in human sacrifice on a greater scale than any of their predecessors, even waging special battles, called the "flowery wars," expressly to obtain captives for future sacrifice.

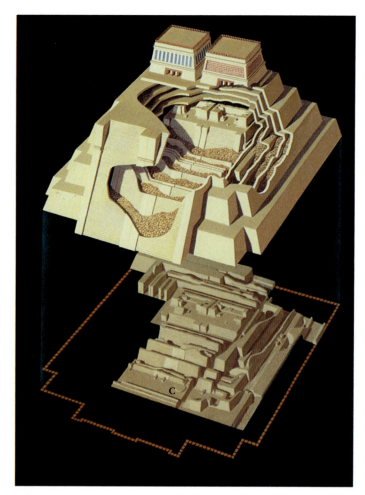

19-12 Reconstruction drawing with cutaway view of various rebuildings of the Great Temple, Aztec, Tenochtitlán, Mexico City, Mexico, ca. 1400–1500. C = Coyolxauhqui disk (FIG. 19-13).

The Great Temple in the Aztec capital encased successive earlier structures. The latest temple honored the gods Huitzilopochtli and Tlaloc, whose sanctuaries were at the top of a stepped pyramid.

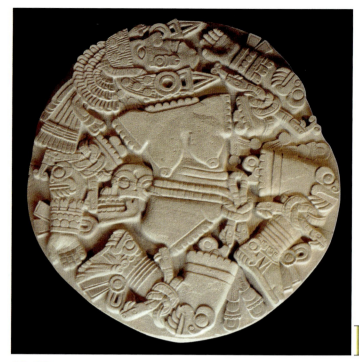

1 ft.

19-13 Coyolxauhqui (She of the Golden Bells), Aztec, from the Great Temple of Tenochtitlán, Mexico City, ca. 1469. Stone, diameter 10′ 10″. Museo del Templo Mayor, Mexico City.

The bodies of sacrificed foes that the Aztecs hurled down the Great Temple's stairs landed on this disk depicting the murdered, segmented body of the moon goddess Coyolxauhqui, Huitzilopochtli's sister.

Tenochtitlán The ruins of the Aztec capital, Tenochtitlán, lie directly beneath the center of Mexico City. In the late 1970s, Mexican archaeologists identified the exact location of many of the most important structures within the Aztec sacred precinct, and excavations continue. The principal building is the Great Temple (FIG. 19-12), a temple-pyramid honoring the Aztec god Huitzilopochtli and the local rain god, Tlaloc. Two great staircases originally swept upward from the plaza level to the double sanctuaries at the summit. The Great Temple is a remarkable example of *superimposition*, a common feature in Mesoamerican architecture, already noted in the Castillo (FIG. 19-9) at Chichén Itzá. The excavated structure, composed of seven shells, indicates how the earlier walls nested within the later ones. (Today, only two of the inner structures are visible. The Spaniards destroyed the later ones in the 16th century.) The sacred precinct also contained the temples of other deities, a ball court, a skull rack for the exhibition of the heads of victims killed in sacrificial rites, and a school for the children of the nobility.

The Aztecs laid out Tenochtitlán on a grid plan that divided the city into quarters and wards, reminiscent of Teotihuacan (FIG. 19-1), which, long abandoned, had become a pilgrimage site for the Aztecs. Tenochtitlán's island location required conducting communication and transport via canals and other waterways. Many of the Spaniards thought of Venice in Italy when they saw the city rising from the waters like a radiant vision. Crowded with buildings, plazas, and courtyards, the city also boasted a vast and ever-busy marketplace. In the words of Bernal Díaz del Castillo (1492–1581), a Spanish soldier who accompanied Cortés, "Some of the soldiers among us who had been in many parts of the world, in Constantinople, and all over Italy, and in Rome, said that so large a marketplace and so full of people, and so well regulated and arranged, they had never beheld before."[1] The city proper housed more than 100,000 people, but the Aztecs dominated an area with a population of approximately 11 million.

Coyolxauhqui The Temple of Huitzilopochtli at Tenochtitlán commemorated the god's victory over his sister and 400 brothers, who had plotted to kill their mother, Coatlicue (She of the Serpent Skirt). The myth signifies the birth of the sun at dawn, a role Huitzilopochtli sometimes assumed, and the sun's battle with the forces of darkness, the stars and moon. Huitzilopochtli chased away his brothers and dismembered the body of his sister, the moon goddess Coyolxauhqui (She of the Golden Bells, referring to the bells on her cheeks), at a hill near Tula (represented by the pyramid itself). A representation of the mythical event appears on a huge stone disk (FIG. 19-13) the Aztecs placed at the foot of the staircase

Aztec Religion

The Aztecs saw their world as a flat disk resting on the back of a monstrous earth deity. Tenochtitlán, their capital, was at its center, with the Great Temple (FIG. 19-12) representing a sacred mountain and forming the axis passing up to the heavens and down through the Underworld—a concept with parallels in other cultures (see, for example, "The Stupa," Chapter 16, page 455). Each of the four cardinal points had its own god, color, tree, and calendrical symbol. The sky consisted of 13 layers, whereas the Underworld had 9.

The Aztecs often adopted the gods of conquered peoples, and their pantheon was complex and varied. When the Aztecs arrived in the Valley of Mexico, their own patron, Huitzilopochtli, a war and sun deity, joined such well-established Mesoamerican gods as Tlaloc, the rain deity, and Quetzalcoatl, the feathered serpent, who was a benevolent god of life, wind, learning, and culture. Statues (FIG. 19-14) and reliefs (FIG. 19-13) depicting Aztec deities, often with political overtones, adorned their temple complexes.

The Aztec ritual cycle was very full, given that they celebrated events in two calendars—the sacred calendar (260 days) and the solar one (360 days plus 5 unlucky and nameless days). The two Mesoamerican calendars functioned simultaneously, requiring 52 years for the same date to recur in both. A ritual called the New Fire Ceremony commemorated this rare event. At midnight on a mountaintop, fire priests removed the heart of a sacrificial victim and with a fire drill lit a flame in the exposed cavity. They set ablaze bundles of sticks representing the 52 years that had just passed, ensuring that the sun would rise in the morning and that another cycle would begin. Rituals marked the completion of important religious structures as well. The dedication of the last major rebuilding of the Great Temple at Tenochtitlán in 1487, for example, reportedly involved the sacrifice of thousands of captives from recent wars in the Gulf Coast region.

Most Aztec ceremonies involved colorfully attired dancers and actors, and musicians playing conch-shell trumpets, drums, rattles, rasps, bells, and whistles. Almost every Aztec festival also included human sacrifice. To Tlaloc, the priests offered small children, because their tears brought the rains. Distinctive hairstyles, clothing, and black body paint identified the priests. Women served as priestesses, particularly in temples dedicated to various earth-mother cults. When Cortés and his men encountered a group of foul-smelling Aztecs with uncut fingernails, long hair matted with blood, and ears covered in cuts, they expressed shock, not realizing these people were priests performing rites in honor of the deities they served, including autosacrifice by piercing their skin with cactus spines to draw blood. These priests were the opposite of the "barbarians" the European conquerors considered them. They were, in fact, the most highly educated Aztecs. The religious practices that horrified their European conquerors, however, were not unique to the Aztecs but were deeply rooted in earlier Mesoamerican society.

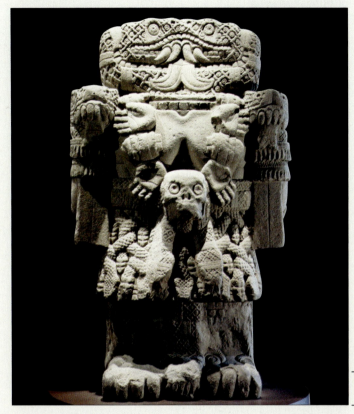

19-14 Coatlicue (She of the Serpent Skirt), Aztec, from Tenochtitlán, Mexico City, ca. 1487–1520. Andesite, 11′ 6″ high. Museo Nacional de Antropología, Mexico City.

This colossal statue stood near the Great Temple. The beheaded goddess wears a necklace of human hands and hearts. Entwined snakes form her skirt. Her attributes symbolize sacrificial death.

leading up to one of Huitzilopochtli's earlier temples on the site. (Cortés and his army never saw it because it lay within the outermost shell of the Great Temple.) Carved on the disk is an image of the murdered and segmented body of Coyolxauhqui. The mythological theme also carried a contemporary political message. The Aztecs sacrificed their conquered enemies at the top of the Great Temple and then hurled their bodies down the temple stairs to land on this stone. The victors thus forced their foes to reenact the horrible fate of the goddess that Huitzilopochtli dismembered. The unforgettable image of the fragmented goddess proclaimed the power of the Mexica over their enemies and the inevitable fate that must befall them when defeated. Marvelously composed, the relief has a kind of dreadful yet formal beauty. Within the circular space, the design's carefully balanced, richly detailed components have a slow turning rhythm reminiscent of a revolving galaxy. The carving is in low relief, a smoothly even, flat surface raised from a flat ground.

Coatlicue The Aztecs also produced freestanding statues. Perhaps the most impressive is the colossal image (FIG. 19-14) of Coatlicue discovered in 1790 near Mexico City's cathedral and probably once part of a group set up at the Great Temple. The main forms are in high relief, the details executed either in low relief or by incising. The overall impression is of an enormous blocky mass, its ponderous weight looming over awed viewers. From the beheaded goddess's neck writhe two serpents whose heads meet to form a tusked mask. Coatlicue wears a necklace of severed human hands and excised human hearts. The pendant of the necklace is a skull. Entwined snakes form her skirt. From between her legs emerges another serpent, symbolic perhaps of both menses and the male member. Like most Aztec deities, Coatlicue has both masculine and feminine traits. Her hands and feet have great claws, which she used to tear the human flesh she consumed. All of her attributes symbolize sacrificial death. Yet, in Aztec thought, this mother of the gods combined savagery and tenderness, for out of destruction arose new life.

Cortés and Moctezuma Unfortunately, most of the art the Aztecs produced did not survive the Spanish conquest and its aftermath. The conquerors took Aztec gold artifacts back to Spain and melted them down, and evangelical friars destroyed countless "idols" and illustrated books. The Europeans found it impossible to reconcile the beauty of the great city of Tenochtitlán with what they regarded as its hideous cults. They admired its splendid buildings ablaze with color, its luxuriant and spacious gardens, its sparkling waterways, its teeming markets, and its grandees resplendent in exotic bird feathers. But in 1519, when Emperor Moctezuma II (r. 1502–1521) brought Cortés and his entourage into Huitzilopochtli's temple, the Spaniards started back in horror and disgust from the huge statues clotted with dried blood. Denouncing Huitzilopochtli as a devil, Cortés proposed to put a high cross above the pyramid and a statue of the Virgin in the sanctuary to exorcise its evil. The ensuing clash of cultures led to a century of turmoil and an enormous population decline throughout the Spanish king's new domains, due in part to a host of new diseases for which the native Americans had no immunity.

SOUTH AMERICA

As in Mesoamerica, the indigenous civilizations of Andean South America (MAP 19-2) jarred against and stimulated one another, produced towering monuments and sophisticated paintings, sculptures, ceramics, and textiles, and were crushed in violent confrontations with the Spanish conquistadors. Although less well studied than the Mesoamerican cultures, those of South America are actually older, and in some ways they surpassed the accomplishments of their northern contemporaries. Andean peoples, for example, mastered metalworking much earlier, and their monumental architecture predates that of the Olmecs by more than a millennium.

The central Andean region of South America lies between Ecuador and northern Chile, with its western border the Pacific Ocean. Andean civilizations flourished both in the highlands and on the coast. The most important included the Paracas, Nasca, and Moche cultures and the Inka Empire.

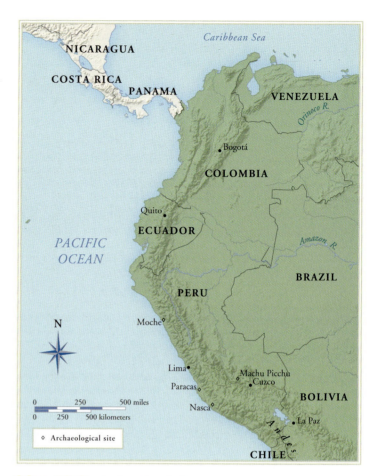

MAP 19-2 Andean South America.

Paracas, Nasca, and Moche

Three major coastal traditions developed during the millennium from ca. 400 BCE to 700 CE: the Paracas (ca. 400 BCE–200 CE), Nasca (ca. 200 BCE–600 CE), and Moche (ca. 1–700 CE). Together they exemplify the great variations within Peruvian art styles.

Paracas Outstanding among the Paracas arts are the mantles used to wrap the bodies of the dead in multiple layers. These textiles are among the enduring masterpieces of Andean art. Most are woven cotton with designs embroidered onto the fabric in alpaca or vicuña wool imported from the highlands. The weavers used more than 150 vivid colors, and sometimes sewed rare tropical bird feathers and small plaques of gold and silver onto cloth destined for the nobility. Feline, bird, and serpent motifs appear on many of the textiles, but the human figure, real or mythological, predominates. Humans dressed up as or transforming into animals are common motifs on the funerary mantles.

On one well-preserved example (FIG. 19-15), a figure with prominent eyes appears scores of times over the surface. The flowing hair and the slow kicking motion of the legs suggest airy, hovering movement. The flying or floating figure carries batons and fans or, according to some scholars, knives and hallucinogenic mushrooms. On other mantles the figures carry the skulls or severed heads of enemies. Art

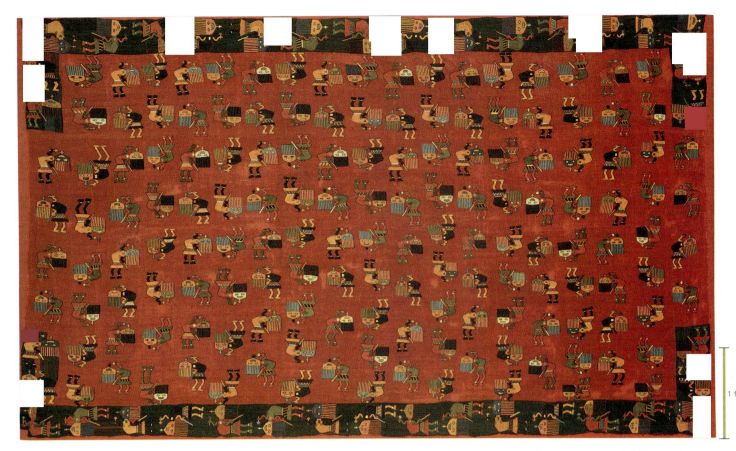

19-15 Embroidered funerary mantle, Paracas, from the southern coast of Peru, first century CE. Plain-weave camelid fiber with embroidery of camelid wool, 4' 7⅞" × 7' 10⅞". Museum of Fine Arts, Boston (William A. Paine Fund).

Outstanding among the Paracas arts are the woven mantles used to wrap the bodies of the dead. The flying or floating figure repeated endlessly on this mantle is probably either the deceased or a religious practitioner.

historians have interpreted the flying figures either as Paracas religious practitioners dancing or flying during an ecstatic trance or as images of the deceased. Despite endless repetitions of the motif, variations of detail occur throughout each textile, notably in the figures' positions and in subtle color changes.

Nasca The Nasca culture takes its name from the Nasca River valley south of Paracas. The Nasca are most famous for the figures they depicted on a gigantic scale. Some 800 miles of lines drawn in complex networks on the dry surface of the Nasca Plain have long attracted world attention because of their colossal size, which defies human perception from the ground. Preserved today are about three dozen images of plants, fish, and birds, including a hummingbird (FIG. **19-16**) several hundred feet long. The Nasca artists also drew geometric forms, such as trapezoids, spirals, and straight lines running for miles. Artists produced these Nasca

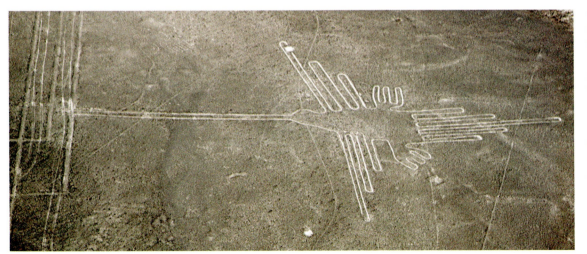

19-16
Hummingbird, Nasca Plain, Nasca, Peru, ca. 500 CE. Dark layer of pebbles scraped aside to reveal lighter clay and calcite beneath.

The earth drawings known as Nasca Lines represent birds, fish, plants, and geometric forms. They may have marked pilgrimage routes leading to religious shrines, but their function is uncertain.

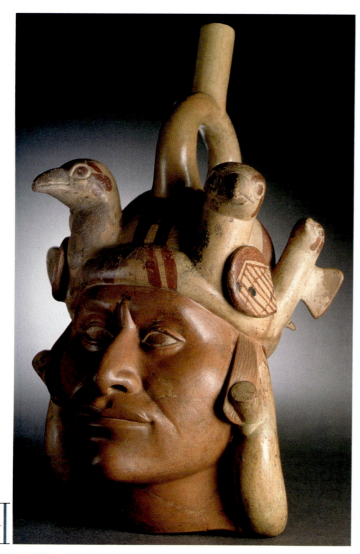

Moche The Moche occupied a series of river valleys on the north coast of Peru around the same time the Nasca flourished to the south. The Moche have left behind an extraordinary variety of painted vessels. Their pots illustrate architecture, metallurgy, weaving, the brewing of maize beer, human deformities and diseases, and even sexual acts. Moche vessels are predominantly flat-bottomed, stirrup-spouted jars, generally decorated with a two-color slip. Although the Moche made early vessels by hand without the aid of a potter's wheel, they fashioned later ones in two-piece molds. Thus, numerous near-duplicates survive. The portrait vessel illustrated here (FIG. **19-17**) is an elaborate example of a common Moche type. It may depict the face of a warrior, a ruler, or even a royal retainer whose image may have been buried with many other pots to accompany his dead master. The realistic rendering of the physiognomy is particularly striking.

Inka

The Inka were a small highland group who established themselves in the Cuzco Valley around 1000.* In the 15th century, however, they rapidly extended their power until their empire stretched from modern Quito, Ecuador, to central Chile, a distance of more than 3,000 miles. Perhaps 12 million subjects inhabited the area the Inka ruled. At the time of the Spanish conquest, the Inka Empire, although barely a century old, was the largest in the world. Expertise in mining and metalwork enabled the Inka to accumulate enormous wealth and to amass the fabled troves of gold and silver the Spaniards so coveted.

An empire as vast and rich as the Inka's required skillful organizational and administrative control, and the Inka had rare talent for both. They divided their Andean empire, which they called Tawantinsuyu ("Land of the Four Quarters"), into sections and subsections, provinces and communities, whose boundaries all converged on, or radiated from, the capital city of Cuzco.

The engineering prowess of the Inka matched their organizational talent. They mastered the difficult problems of Andean agriculture with terracing and irrigation, and knitted together the fabric of their empire with networks of roads and bridges. Shunning wheeled vehicles and horses, they used their highway system to move goods by llama and armies by foot throughout their territories. The Inka upgraded or built more than 14,000 miles of roads and established a swift, highly efficient communications system of relay runners who carried messages the length of the empire. Where the terrain was too steep for a paved flat surface, the Inka built stone steps, and their rope bridges crossed canyons high over impassable rivers. They established small settlements along the roads no more than a day apart where travelers could rest and obtain supplies for the journey.

19-17 Vessel in the shape of a portrait head, Moche, from north coast Peru, fifth to sixth century CE. Painted clay, 1′ ½″ high. Museo Arqueológico Rafael Larco Herrera, Lima.

The Moche produced an extraordinary variety of painted vessels. This one in the shape of a head may depict a warrior, ruler, or royal retainer. The realistic rendering of the face is particularly striking.

Lines, as the immense earth drawings are called, by selectively removing the dark top layer of stones to expose the light clay and calcite below. The Nasca created the lines quite easily from available materials and using rudimentary geometry. Small groups of workers have made modern reproductions of them with relative ease.

The lines seem to be paths laid out using simple stone-and-string methods. Some lead in traceable directions across the deserts of the Nasca River drainage. Others are punctuated by many shrinelike nodes, like the knots on a cord. Some lines converge at central places usually situated close to water sources and seem to be associated with water supply and irrigation. The lines may have marked routes for pilgrims journeying to local or regional shrines on foot. Altogether, the vast arrangement of the Nasca Lines is a system—not a meaningless maze but a map that plotted the whole terrain of Nasca material and spiritual concerns.

* From this point on all dates in this chapter are CE unless otherwise stated.

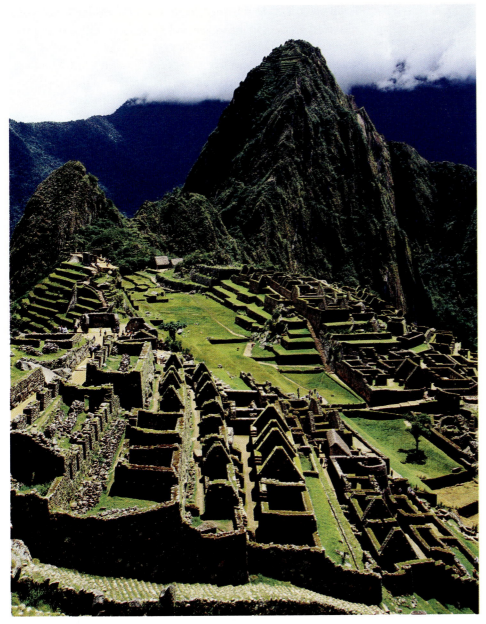

19-18 Machu Picchu (view from adjacent peak), Inka, Peru, 15th century.

Machu Picchu was the estate of an Inka ruler. The architects designed the buildings so that the windows and doors framed spectacular views of sacred peaks and facilitated astronomical observations.

Machu Picchu The imperial Inka were great architects, and their masons were masters at shaping and fitting stone. As a militant conquering people, they selected breathtaking, naturally fortified sites and further strengthened them by building various defensive structures. Inka city planning reveals an almost instinctive grasp of the proper relation of architecture to site.

One of the world's most awe-inspiring sights is the Inka city of Machu Picchu (FIG. **19-18**), which perches on a ridge between two jagged peaks 9,000 feet above sea level. Invisible from the Urubamba River valley some 1,600 feet below, the site remained unknown to the outside world until its rediscovery in 1911. In the very heart of the Andes, Machu Picchu is about 50 miles north of Cuzco and, like some of the region's other cities, was the private estate of a powerful mid-15th-century Inka ruler. Though relatively small and insignificant among its neighbors (with a resident population of little more than a thousand), the city is of great archaeological importance as a rare site left undisturbed since Inka times. The accommodation of its architecture to the landscape is so complete that Machu Picchu seems a natural part of the mountain ranges that surround it on all sides. The Inka even cut large stones to echo the shapes of the mountains beyond. Terraces spill down the mountainsides and extend even up to the very peak of Huayna Picchu, the great hill just beyond the city's main plaza. The Inka carefully sited buildings so that windows and doors framed spectacular views of sacred peaks and facilitated the recording of important astronomical events.

Pizarro and Atawalpa Smallpox spreading south from Spanish-occupied Mesoamerica killed the last Inka emperor and his heir before they ever laid eyes on a Spaniard. The Inka Empire quickly plunged into a civil war that only aided the Europeans in their conquest. In 1532, Francisco Pizarro (1471–1541) ambushed the would-be emperor Atawalpa on his way to be crowned at Cuzco after vanquishing his rival half-brother. Although Atawalpa paid a huge ransom of gold and silver, the Spaniards killed him and took control of his vast domain, only a decade after Cortés had defeated the

The Inka never developed a writing system, but they maintained strict control over their vast empire by developing a remarkably sophisticated recordkeeping device known as the *khipu*, with which they recorded calendrical and astronomical information, census and tribute totals, and inventories. For example, the Spaniards noted that Inka officials always knew exactly how much maize or cloth was in any storeroom in their empire. Not a book or a tablet, the khipu consisted of a main fiber cord and other knotted threads hanging perpendicularly off it. The color and position of each thread, as well as the kind of knot and its location, recorded numbers and categories of things, whether people, llamas, or crops. Studies of khipus have demonstrated that the Inka used the decimal system, were familiar with the zero concept, and could record numbers up to five digits.

Aztecs in Mexico. Following the murder of Atawalpa, the Spaniards erected the church of Santo Domingo, in an imported European style, on what remained of the Inka Temple of the Sun at Cuzco. A curved section of Inka wall serves to this day as the foundation for the church's apse. The two contrasting structures remain standing one atop the other. The juxtaposition is a symbol of the Spanish conquest of the Americas and serves as a composite monument to it.

NORTH AMERICA

In many parts of the United States and Canada, archaeologists have identified indigenous cultures dating back as far as 12,000 years ago. Most of the surviving art objects, however, come from the past 2,000 years. Scholars divide the vast and varied territory of North America (MAP 19-3) into cultural regions based on the relative homogeneity of language and social and artistic patterns. Lifestyles varied widely over the continent, ranging from small bands of migratory hunters to settled—at times even urban—agriculturalists, and Native American art and architecture are more varied in the United States and Canada than in Mesoamerica and Andean South America. Three major regions are of special interest: the Eastern Woodlands, the American Southwest, and the Northwest Coast (Washington and British Columbia).

Mississippian

The Mississippian culture, which emerged around 800 and eventually encompassed much of the eastern United States, surpassed all earlier Woodlands peoples in the size and complexity of their communities. One Mississippian mound site, Cahokia in southern Illinois, was the largest city in North America in the early second millennium, with a population of at least 20,000 and an area of more than six square miles. There were approximately 120 mounds at Cahokia. The grandest, 100 feet tall and built in stages between about 900 and 1200, was Monk's Mound. Aligned with the position of the sun at the equinoxes, it may have served as an astronomical observatory as well as the site of agricultural ceremonies. Each stage was topped by wooden structures that then were destroyed in preparation for the building of a new layer.

Serpent Mound The Mississippians also constructed *effigy mounds* (mounds built in the form of animals or birds). One of the best preserved is Serpent Mound, a twisting earthwork on a bluff overlooking a creek in Ohio. It measures nearly a quarter mile from its open jaw (FIG. **19-19**, *top right*), which seems to clasp an oval-shaped mound in its mouth, to its tightly coiled tail *(far left)*. Both its date and meaning are controversial. For a long time after the first excavations in the 1880s, archaeologists attributed the construction of Serpent Mound to the Adena culture, which flourished in the Ohio area during the last several centuries BCE. Radiocarbon dates taken from the mound, however, indicate that the Mississippians built it much later. Unlike most other ancient mounds, Serpent Mound contained no evidence of burials or temples. Serpents, however, were important in Mississippian iconography. These Native Americans strongly associated snakes with the earth and the fertility of crops.

Some researchers have proposed another possible meaning for the construction of Serpent Mound. The new date suggested for it is 1070, not long after the brightest appearance in recorded history of Halley's Comet in 1066. Could Serpent Mound have been built in response to this important astronomical event? Scholars have even suggested that the serpentine form of the mound replicates the comet itself streaking across the night sky. Whatever its meaning, such a large and elaborate earthwork could have been built only by a large labor force under the firm direction of powerful elites eager to leave their mark on the landscape forever.

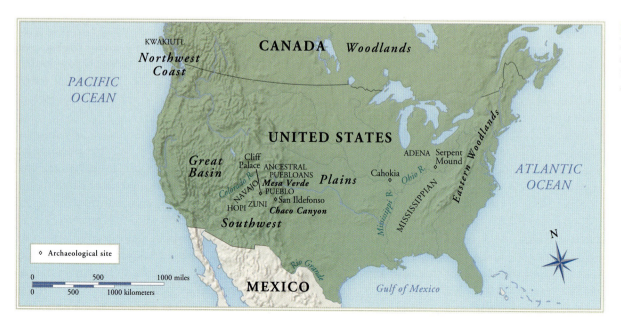

MAP 19-3 Native American sites in the United States and southern Canada.

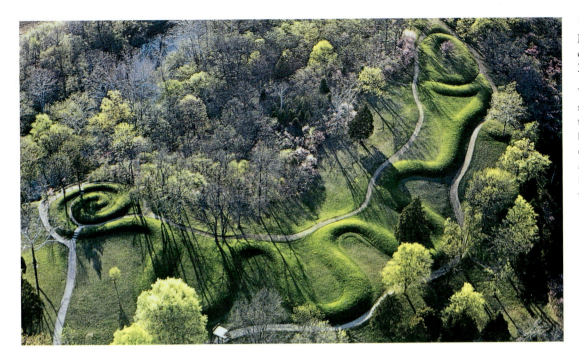

19-19 Serpent Mound, Mississippian, Ohio, ca. 1070. 1,200' long, 20' wide, 5' high.

The Mississippians constructed effigy mounds in the form of animals and birds. This well-preserved example seems to depict a serpent. Some scholars, however, think it replicates the path of Halley's Comet in 1066.

Southwest

The dominant culture of the American Southwest during the centuries preceding the arrival of Europeans was the Ancestral Puebloan, formerly known as the Anasazi (Navajo, "enemy ancestors"), which emerged around 200 but did not reach its peak until about 1000. The many ruined *pueblos* (Spanish, "urban settlements") scattered throughout the Southwest reveal the masterful building skills of the Ancestral Puebloans. In Chaco Canyon, New Mexico, they built a great semicircle of 800 rooms reaching to five stepped-back stories, the largest of several similar sites in and around the canyon. Chaco Canyon was the center of a wide trade network extending as far as Mexico.

Cliff Palace Sometime in the late 12th century, a drought occurred, and the Ancestral Puebloans largely abandoned their open canyon-floor dwelling sites to move farther north to the steep-sided canyons and lush environment of Mesa Verde in southwestern Colorado. Cliff Palace (FIG. **19-20**) is wedged into a sheltered ledge above a valley floor. It contains

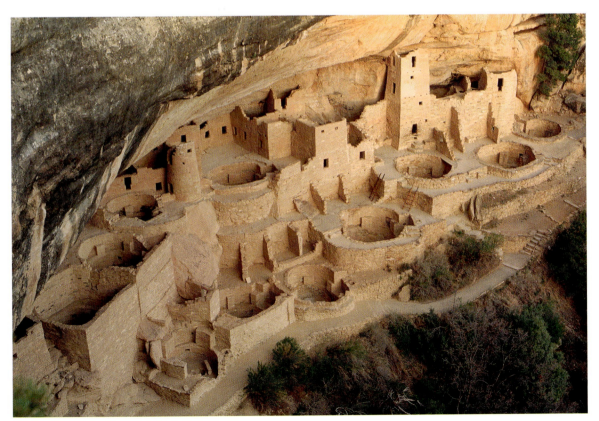

19-20 Cliff Palace, Ancestral Puebloan, Mesa Verde National Park, Colorado, ca. 1150–1300.

Cliff Palace is wedged into a sheltered ledge to heat the pueblo in winter and shade it during the hot summer months. It contains about 200 stone-and-timber rooms plastered inside and out with adobe.

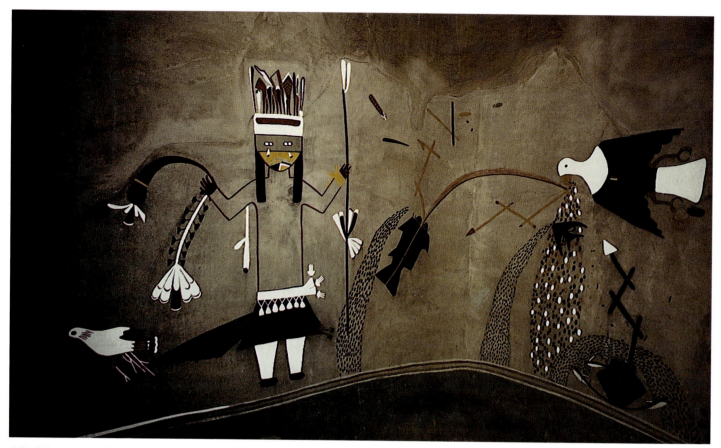

19-21 Detail of a kiva mural from Kuaua Pueblo (Coronado State Monument), Ancestral Puebloan, New Mexico, late 15th to early 16th century. Interior of the kiva, 18' × 18'. Museum of New Mexico, Santa Fe.

The kiva, or male council house, was the spiritual center of Puebloan life. Kivas were decorated with mural paintings associated with agricultural fertility. This painting depicts a lightning man, fish, birds, and seeds.

about 200 rectangular rooms (mostly communal dwellings) of carefully laid stone and timber, once plastered inside and out with *adobe* (sun-dried mud brick). The location for Cliff Palace was not accidental. The Ancestral Puebloans designed it to take advantage of the sun to heat the pueblo in winter and shade it during the hot summer months.

Kuaua Pueblo Scattered in the foreground of FIG. 19-20 are two dozen large circular semisubterranean structures, called *kivas*, which once were roofed over and entered with a ladder through a hole in the flat roof. These chambers were the spiritual centers of native Southwest life, male council houses where ritual regalia were stored and private rituals and preparations for public ceremonies took place—and still do.

Between 1300 and 1500, the Ancestral Puebloans decorated their kivas with elaborate mural paintings representing deities associated with agricultural fertility. According to their descendants, the present-day Hopi and Zuni, the detail of the Kuaua Pueblo mural shown here (FIG. 19-21) depicts a "lightning man" on the left side. Fish and eagle images (associated with rain) appear on the right side. Seeds, a lightning bolt, and a rainbow stream from the eagle's mouth. All these figures are associated with the fertility of the earth and

the life-giving properties of the seasonal rains, a constant preoccupation of Southwest farmers. The painter depicted the figures with great economy, using thick black lines, dots, and a restricted palette of black, brown, yellow, and white. The frontal figure of the lightning man seen against a neutral ground makes an immediate visual impact.

Hopi Katsinas Another art form from the Southwest is the *katsina* figurine. Katsinas are benevolent supernatural spirits personifying natural elements and living in mountains and water sources. Humans join their world after death. Among contemporary Pueblo groups, masked dancers ritually impersonate katsinas during yearly festivals dedicated to rain, fertility, and good hunting. To educate young girls in ritual lore, the Hopi traditionally give them miniature representations of the masked dancers. A Hopi katsina (FIG. 19-22) carved by OTTO PENTEWA (d. 1963) represents a rain-bringing deity who wears a mask painted in geometric patterns symbolic of water and agricultural fertility. Topping the mask is a stepped shape signifying thunderclouds and feathers to carry the Hopis' airborne prayers. The origins of the katsina figurines have been lost in time (they even may have developed from carved saints the Spaniards introduced during the colonial period). However, the cult is probably very ancient.

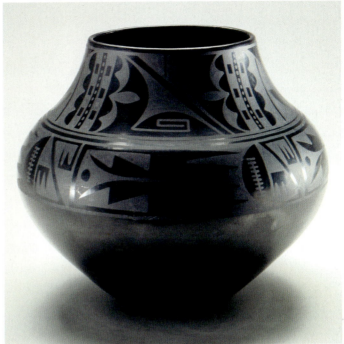

19-23 María Montoya Martínez, jar, San Ildefonso Pueblo, New Mexico, ca. 1939. Blackware, $11\frac{1}{8}$″ × 1′ 1″. National Museum of Women in the Arts, Washington, D.C. (gift of Wallace and Wilhelmina Hollachy).

María Montoya Martínez revived old techniques to produce 20th-century pottery of striking shapes, and textures. Her black-on-black pieces feature matte designs on highly polished surfaces.

Pueblo Pottery The Southwest has also provided the finest examples of North American pottery. Originally producing utilitarian forms, Southwest potters worked without the potter's wheel and instead formed shapes by hand that they then covered with slip, polished, and fired. Decorative motifs, often abstract and conventionalized, dealt largely with forces of nature—clouds, wind, and rain.

In the early decades of the 20th century, San Ildefonso Pueblo potter MARÍA MONTOYA MARTÍNEZ (1887–1980) revived old techniques to produce forms of striking shape, proportion, and texture. Her black-on-black pieces (FIG. **19-23**) feature matte designs on high-gloss surfaces achieved by extensive polishing and special firing in an oxygen-poor atmosphere. The elegant shapes, as well as the traditional but abstract designs, have made her pots popular with collectors.

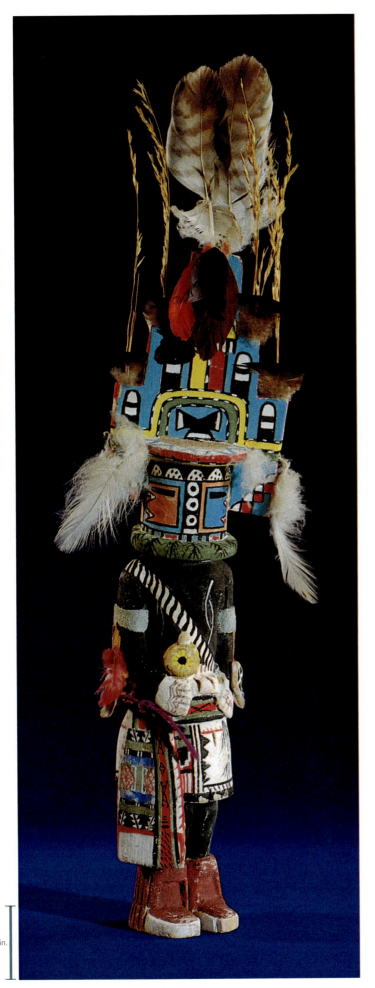

19-22 Otto Pentewa, katsina figurine, Hopi, New Oraibi, Arizona, carved before 1959. Cottonwood root, 1′ high. Arizona State Museum, University of Arizona, Tucson.

Katsinas are benevolent spirits living in mountains and water sources. This Hopi katsina represents a rain-bringing deity wearing a mask painted in geometric patterns symbolic of water and agricultural fertility.

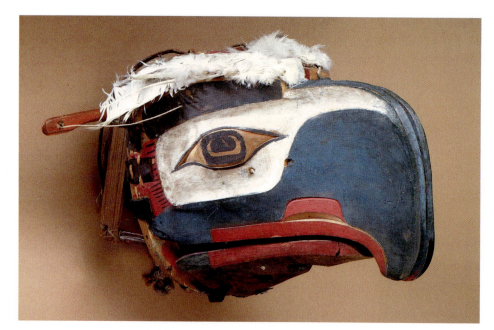

19-24 Eagle transformation mask, closed (*top*) and open (*bottom*) views, Kwakiutl, Alert Bay, Canada, late 19th century. Wood, feathers, and string, 1′ 10″ × 11″. American Museum of Natural History, New York.

The wearer of this Kwakiutl mask could open and close it rapidly by manipulating hidden strings, magically transforming himself from human to eagle and back again as he danced.

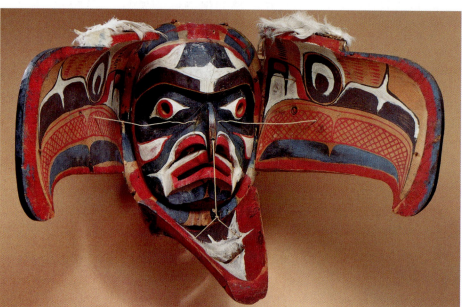

1 ft.

Northwest Coast

The Native Americans of the coasts and islands of northern Washington state, the province of British Columbia in Canada, and southern Alaska have long enjoyed a rich and reliable environment. They fished, hunted, gathered edible plants, and made their homes, utensils, and ritual objects from the region's great cedar forests.

Kwakiutl Among the numerous groups who settled the Northwest Coast are the Kwakiutl of southern British Columbia. Kwakiutl religious specialists used masks in their healing rituals. Men also wore masks in dramatic public performances during the winter ceremonial season. The animals and mythological creatures represented in masks and a host of other carvings derive from the Northwest Coast's rich oral tradition and celebrate the mythological origins and inherited privileges of high-ranking families. The artist who made the Kwakiutl mask illustrated here (FIG. **19-24**) meant it to be

seen in flickering firelight, and ingeniously constructed it to open and close rapidly when the wearer manipulated hidden strings. He could thus magically transform himself from human (FIG. 19-24, *bottom*) to eagle (FIG. 19-24, *top*) and back again as he danced. The transformation theme, in myriad forms, is a central aspect of the art and religion of the Americas. The Kwakiutl mask's human aspect also owes its dramatic character to the exaggeration and distortion of facial parts—such as the hooked beaklike nose and flat flaring nostrils—and to the deeply undercut curvilinear depressions, which form strong shadows. In contrast to the carved human face, but painted in the same colors, is the two-dimensional abstract image of the eagle painted on the inside of the outer mask.

Whether secular and decorative or spiritual and highly symbolic, the diverse styles and forms of Native American art in the United States and Canada reflect the indigenous peoples' reliance on and reverence toward the environment they considered it their privilege to inhabit.

The Americas

MESOAMERICA

▮ The Olmec (ca. 1200–400 BCE) is the "mother culture" of Mesoamerica. The Olmec built earthen pyramids and ball courts and carved colossal basalt portraits of their rulers during the Preclassic period.

▮ In contrast to Olmec sites, Teotihuacan, near modern Mexico City, was a huge metropolis laid out on a strict grid plan. Its major pyramids and plazas date to the late Preclassic period, ca. 50–250 CE.

▮ During the Classic period (ca. 300–900), the Maya built vast complexes of stone temple-pyramids, palaces, plazas, and ball courts and decorated them with monumental sculptures and mural paintings glorifying their rulers and gods.

▮ The Aztecs were the dominant power in Mesoamerica at the time of the Spanish conquest. Tenochtitlán, the capital, was a magnificent island city laid out on a grid plan. Statues and reliefs adorned the Great Temple complex.

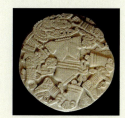

Castillo, Chichén Itzá, Maya, ca. 800–900

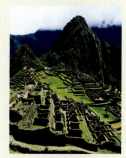

Coyolxauhqui, Great Temple, Tenochtitlán, ca. 1469

SOUTH AMERICA

▮ The ancient civilizations of South America are even older than those of Mesoamerica. The earliest Andean sites began to develop around 3000 BCE.

▮ The Paracas (ca. 400 BCE–200 CE) and Moche (ca. 1–700 CE) cultures of Peru produced extraordinary textiles and distinctive painted ceramics. The subjects range from composite human-animals to ruler portraits.

▮ The Nasca (ca. 200 BCE–600 CE) are famous for their colossal earth drawings known as Nasca Lines representing birds, fish, plants, and geometric forms.

▮ In the 15th century, the Inka ruled a vast empire with 14,000 miles of roads. The Inka were master architects who constructed Machu Picchu on a terraced site with spectacular views of sacred peaks.

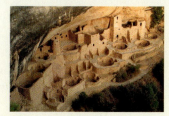

Machu Picchu, 15th century

NORTH AMERICA

▮ The indigenous cultures of the United States and Canada date as far back as 10,000 BCE, but most of the surviving art objects date from the past 2,000 years.

▮ The peoples of the Mississippian culture (ca. 800–1500) were great mound builders. Cahokia in Illinois with a population of at least 20,000 was the largest city in North America during the early second millennium.

▮ In the American Southwest, native peoples have been producing distinctive pottery for more than 2,000 years. María Montoya Martínez was the leading 20th-century ceramist.

▮ The Ancestral Puebloans constructed urban settlements (pueblos) and decorated their council houses (kivas) with mural paintings. Cliff Palace, Colorado, is noteworthy for its sophisticated design, wedged into a sheltered ledge above a valley floor to take advantage of the winter sun and the summer shade.

▮ On the Northwest Coast, masks played an important role in religious rituals. Some examples can open and close rapidly so that the wearer can magically transform himself from human to animal and back again.

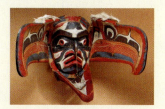

Cliff Palace, Colorado, ca. 1150–1300

Kwakiutl eagle transformation mask, late 19th century

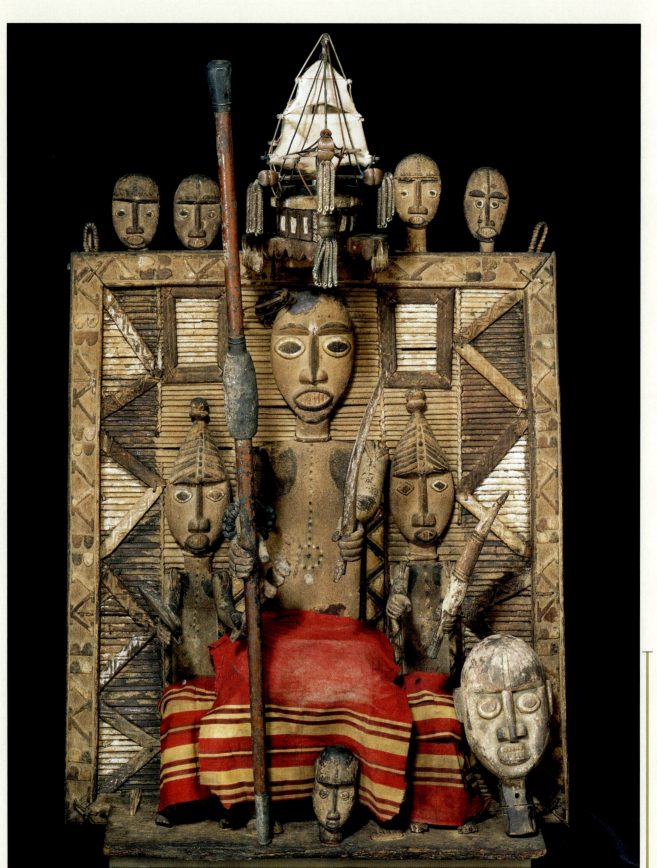

20-1 Ancestral screen (nduen fobara), Kalabari Ijaw, Nigeria, late 19th century. Wood, fiber, and cloth, 3′ 9½″ high. British Museum, London.

The hierarchical composition and the stylized human anatomy and facial features in this Kalabari ancestral screen are common in African art of all periods, but this shrine's complexity is exceptional.

1 ft.

Africa

Africa (MAP **20-1**) is a vast continent of 52 nations comprising more than one-fifth of the world's land mass and many distinct topographical and ecological zones. Parched deserts occupy northern and southern regions, high mountains rise in the east, and three great rivers—the Niger, the Congo, and the Nile—and their lush valleys support agriculture and large settled populations. More than 2,000 distinct ethnic, cultural, and linguistic groups, often but inaccurately called "tribes," long have inhabited this enormous continent. These population groups historically have ranged in size from a few hundred, in hunting and gathering bands, to 10 to 20 million or more. Councils of elders often governed smaller groups, whereas larger populations sometimes formed a centralized state under a king.

Despite this great variety, African peoples share many core beliefs and practices. These include honoring ancestors, worshiping nature deities, and elevating rulers to sacred status. Most peoples also consult diviners or fortune tellers. These beliefs have given rise to many richly expressive art traditions, including rock engraving and painting, body decoration, masquerades and other lavish festivals, figural sculpture, and sacred and secular architecture. Given the size of the African continent and the diversity of ethnic groups, it is not surprising that African art varies enormously in subject, materials, and function. Nomadic and seminomadic peoples excelled in the arts of personal adornment and also produced rock engravings and paintings depicting animals and rituals. Farmers, in contrast, often created figural sculpture in terracotta, wood, and metal for display in shrines to legendary ancestors or nature deities held responsible for the health of crops and the well-being of the people. The regalia, art, and architecture of kings and their courts, as elsewhere in the world, celebrated the wealth and power of the rulers themselves. Nearly all African peoples lavished artistic energy on the decoration of their own bodies to express their identity and status, and many communities mounted richly layered festivals, including masquerades, to celebrate harvests and the New Year, and to commemorate the deaths of leaders. In Africa, art helps define and create culture. Closely integrated within communal life and thought, African art was not created solely for display until the late 20th century.

PREHISTORY AND EARLY CULTURES

Thousands of rock engravings and paintings found at hundreds of sites across the continent constitute the earliest known African art. Some painted animals from the Apollo 11 Cave in Namibia date to perhaps as long ago as 23,000 BCE, earlier

MAP 20-1
Africa.

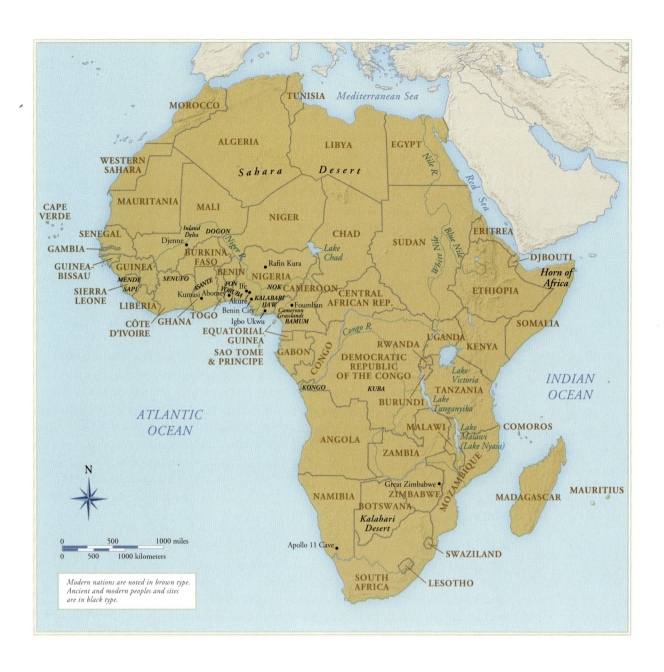

than all but the oldest Paleolithic art of Europe (see Chapter 1). As humankind apparently originated in Africa, the world's earliest art may yet be discovered there as well. The greatest concentrations of rock art are in the Sahara Desert to the north, the Horn of Africa in the east, and the Kalahari Desert to the south, as well as in caves and on rock outcroppings in southern Africa. Accurately naturalistic renderings as well as stylized images on rock surfaces show animals and humans in many different positions and activities, singly or in groups, stationary or in motion. Most of these works date to within the past 4,000 to 6,000 years, but some may have been created as early as 8000 BCE. They provide a rich record of the environment, human activities, and animal species in prehistoric times.

Although the precise dating and meaning of most African rock art remain uncertain, considerable literature exists that describes, analyzes, and interprets the varied human and animal activities shown, as well as the more symbolic and abstract patterns. The human and humanlike renderings depict people and a host of spirits and other supernatural beings and gods. The general significance and function of prehistoric art in Africa probably coincide with those of the later arts, which portray ideas and rituals about the origin, survival, health, and continuity of human populations.

Nok Outside Egypt and neighboring Nubia (see Chapter 1), the earliest African sculptures in the round have been found at several sites in central Nigeria that archaeologists collectively call the Nok culture. Scholars disagree on whether the Nok sites were unified politically or socially. Named after the site where these sculptures were first discovered in 1928, Nok art dates between 500 BCE and 200 CE. Hundreds of Nok-style figures and fragments, such as human and animal heads and body parts, have been found accidentally during tin-mining operations but not in their original context. A representative terracotta head (FIG. **20-2**), found at Rafin Kura, is a fragment of what was originally a full figure. Preserved fragments of other Nok statues indicate that sculptors

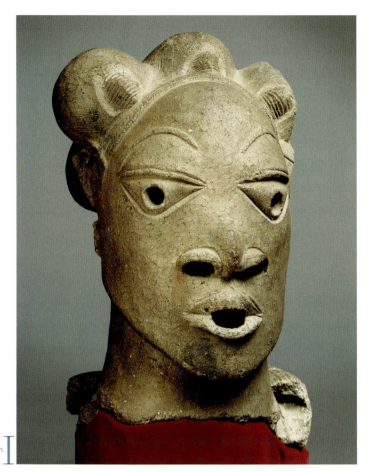

1 in.

20-2 Nok head, from Rafin Kura, Nigeria, ca. 500 BCE–200 CE. Terracotta, 1′ 2$\frac{3}{16}$″ high. National Museum, Lagos.

The earliest African sculptures in the round come from Nigeria. The Nok culture produced expressive terracotta heads with large eyes, mouths, and ears. Piercing equalized the heat during the firing process.

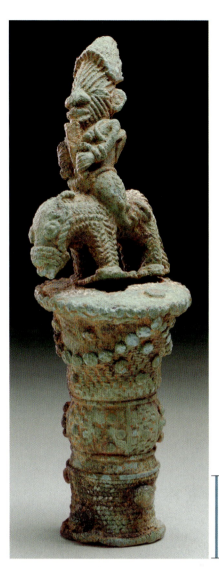

20-3 Equestrian figure on fly-whisk hilt, from Igbo Ukwu, Nigeria, 9th to 10th century CE. Copper-alloy bronze, figure 6$\frac{3}{16}$″ high. National Museum, Lagos.

The oldest known African lost-wax cast bronze is this fly-whisk hilt, which a leader used to extend his reach and magnify his gestures. The artist exaggerated the size of the ruler compared with his steed.

1 in.

fashioned standing, seated, and kneeling figures. The heads are disproportionately large compared with the bodies. The head shown here has an expressive face with large alert eyes, flaring nostrils, and parted lips. The pierced eyes, mouth, and ear holes are characteristic of Nok sculpture and probably helped to equalize the heating of the hollow clay head during the firing process. The coiffure with incised grooves, the raised eyebrows, the perforated triangular eyes, and the sharp jaw line suggest that the sculptor carved some details of the head while modeling the rest. Researchers are unclear about the function of the Nok terracottas, but the broken tube around the neck of the Rafin Kura figure may be a bead necklace, an indication that the person portrayed held an elevated position in Nok society. The gender of Nok artists is unknown. Because today the primary ceramists and clay sculptors across the continent are women, Nok sculptors may have been as well.

Igbo Ukwu By the 9th or 10th century CE, a West African bronze-casting tradition of great sophistication had developed in the Lower Niger area, just east of that great river. Dozens of refined, varied objects in an extremely intricate style have been unearthed at Igbo Ukwu. The ceramic, cop-per, bronze, and iron artifacts include basins, bowls, altar stands, staffs, swords, scabbards, knives, and pendants. One grave held numerous prestige objects—copper anklets, arm-lets, spiral ornaments, a fan handle, and more than 100,000 beads, which may have been used as a form of currency. The tomb also contained three elephant tusks, a crown, and a bronze leopard's skull. These items, doubtless the regalia of a leader (see "Art and Leadership in Africa," page 536), whether secular or religious, are the earliest cast-metal ob-jects known from regions south of the Sahara.

A lost-wax cast bronze (FIG. **20-3**), the earliest yet found in Africa, came from the same grave at Igbo Ukwu. It depicts an equestrian figure on a fly-whisk hilt. The Af-rican artist made the handle using a casting method similar to that documented much earlier in the Mediterranean and Near East (see "Hollow-Casting," Chapter 2, page 66). The hilt's upper section consists of a figure seated on a horselike animal, perhaps a donkey, and the lower part is an elabo-rately embellished handle with beaded and threadlike pat-terns. The rider's head is of exaggerated size, a common trait in the art of many early cultures. The prominent facial stripes probably represent marks of titled status, as can still be found among Igbo-speaking peoples today.

Art and Leadership in Africa

The relationships between leaders and art forms are strong, complex, and universal in Africa. Political, spiritual, and social leaders—kings, chiefs, titled people, and religious specialists—have the power and wealth to command the best artists and to require the finest materials to adorn themselves, furnish their homes, and make visible the cultural and religious organizations they lead. Leaders also possess the power to dispense art or the prerogative to use it.

Several formal or structural principles characterize the art of leaders and thus set it apart from the popular arts of ordinary Africans. Leaders' artworks—for example, the sumptuous and layered regalia of chiefs and kings (FIGS. 20-4 and 20-20)—tend to be durable and are often made of costly materials, such as ivory, beads, copper alloys, and other luxurious metals. Some of the objects made specifically for African leaders, such as thrones and footstools (FIG. 20-11), ornate clothing (FIG. 20-20), and special weaponry, draw attention to their superior status. Handheld objects—for example, staffs (FIG. 20-1), spears, knives (FIG. 20-1), scepters, pipes, and fly whisks (FIG. 20-3)—extend a leader's reach and magnify his or her gestures. Other objects associated with leaders, such as fans (FIG. I-11), shields, and umbrellas protect the leaders both physically and spiritually. Sometimes the regalia and implements of an important person are so heavy that they render the leader virtually immobile (FIG. 20-20), suggesting that the temporary holder of an office is less significant than the eternal office itself.

Although leaders' arts are easy to recognize in centralized, hierarchical societies, such as the Benin (FIGS. I-11, 20-7, 20-8, and 20-15) and Bamum (FIG. 20-11) kingdoms, leaders among less centralized peoples are no less conversant with the power of art to move people and effect change. For example, African leaders often establish and run masquerades and religious cults in which they may be less visible than the forms they commission and manipulate: shrines, altars, festivals, and rites of passage such as funerals, the last being especially elaborate and festive in many parts of Africa. The arts that leaders control thus help create pageantry, mystery, and spectacle, enriching and changing the lives of the people.

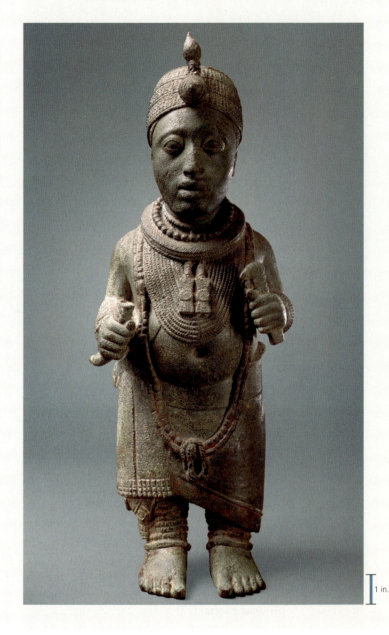

1 in.

20-4 King, from Ita Yemoo, Nigeria, 11th to 12th century. Zinc brass, 1′ 6½″ high. Museum of Ife Antiquities, Ife.

This royal figure with elaborate regalia has a naturalistically modeled torso and facial features that approach portraiture. The head, however, the locus of wisdom, is disproportionately large.

11TH TO 18TH CENTURIES*

Although kings ruled some African population groups from an early date, the best evidence for royal arts in Africa comes from the several centuries between about 1000 and the beginning of European colonization in the 19th century. This period also brought the construction of major houses of worship for the religions of Christianity and Islam, both of which originated in the Middle East but quickly gained adherents in Africa.

* From this point on all dates in this chapter are CE unless otherwise stated.

Ile-Ife Africans have long considered Ile-Ife, about 200 miles west of Igbo Ukwu in southwestern Nigeria, the cradle of Yoruba civilization, the place where the gods created the universe. Tradition also names the god Oduduwa the first *oni* (ruler) of Ile-Ife and the ancestor of all Yoruba kings. Ife artists often portrayed their sacred kings in sculpture. One of the most impressive examples is a statuette (FIG. 20-4), cast in a zinc-brass alloy, datable to the 11th or 12th century. This and many similar representations of Ife rulers are exceptional in Africa because of the naturalistic recording of facial features and fleshy anatomy, apart from blemishes or signs of age, which the artists intentionally omitted. Thus,

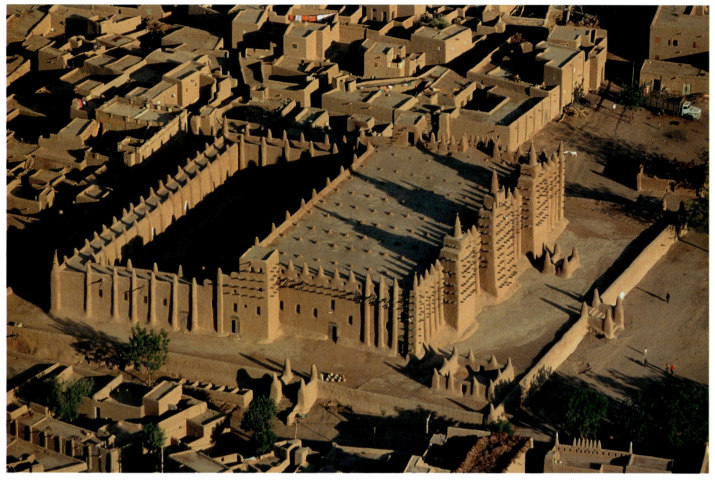

20-5 Aerial view (looking northwest) of the Great Mosque, Djenne, Mali, begun 13th century, rebuilt 1906–1907.

The Great Mosque at Djenne resembles Middle Eastern mosques in plan (large courtyard next to a roofed prayer hall), but the construction materials—adobe and wood—are distinctly African.

Ife style is lifelike but at the same time idealized. The sculptors portrayed most people as young adults in the prime of life and without any disfiguring warts or wrinkles. The naturalism does not extend to body proportions, however. The head of the statue, for example, is disproportionately large, as in Igbo Ukwu (FIG. 20-3) sculpture. For modern Yoruba, the head is the locus of wisdom, destiny, and the essence of being, and such ideas probably developed at least 800 years ago, accounting for the emphasis on the head in Ife statuary and African art in general. Indicating that the man portrayed was a sacred ruler was also a priority, and the sculptor of the statue illustrated here accurately recorded the precise details of the heavily beaded costume, crown, and jewelry.

Djenne The inland floodplain of the Niger River was for the African continent a kind of "fertile crescent," analogous to that of ancient Mesopotamia (see Chapter 2). Djenne in present-day Mali is the major city in this region. Djenne boasts one of the most ambitious examples of adobe architecture in the world, the city's Great Mosque (FIG. 20-5), first built in the 13th century and reconstructed in 1906–1907 after a fire destroyed the earlier building in 1830. The mosque has a large courtyard and a roofed prayer hall, emu-lating the plan of many of the oldest mosques known (see "The Mosque," Chapter 5, page 150). The facade, however, is unlike any in the Middle East and features soaring adobe towers and vertical buttresses resembling engaged columns that produce a majestic visual rhythm. The many rows of protruding wooden beams further enliven the walls but also serve a practical function as perches for workers undertaking the essential recoating of sacred clay on the exterior that occurs during an annual festival.

Great Zimbabwe The most famous southern African site of this period is a complex of stone ruins at the large southeastern political center called Great Zimbabwe. First occupied in the 11th century, the site features walled enclosures and towers that date from about the late 13th century to the middle of the 15th century. At that time, Great Zimbabwe had a wide trade network. Finds of beads and pottery from the Near East and China, along with copper and gold objects, underscore that Great Zimbabwe was a prosperous trade center well before Europeans began their coastal voyaging in the late 15th century.

Most scholars agree that Great Zimbabwe was a royal residence with special areas for the ruler (the royal hill complex),

20-6 Walls and tower, Great Enclosure, Great Zimbabwe, Zimbabwe, 14th century.

The Great Zimbabwe Empire in southern Africa had a trade network that extended to the Near East and China. The royal residence was surrounded by 30-foot-high stone walls and conical towers.

his wives, and nobles, including an open court for ceremonial gatherings. At the zenith of the empire's power, as many as 18,000 people may have lived in the surrounding area, with most of the commoners living outside the enclosed structures reserved for royalty. Although the actual habitations do not survive, the remaining enclosures are unusual for their size and the excellence of their stonework. Some perimeter walls reach heights of 30 feet. One of these, known as the Great Enclosure (FIG. **20-6**), houses one large and several small conical towerlike stone structures, which archaeologists have interpreted symbolically as masculine (large) and feminine (small) forms, but their precise significance is unknown. The form of the large tower suggests a granary. Grain bins were symbols of royal power and generosity, as the ruler received tribute in grain and dispensed it to the people in times of need.

Benin The Benin kingdom (not to be confused with the modern Republic of Benin; see MAP **20-1**) was established before 1400, most likely in the 13th century, just west of the lower reaches of the Niger River in what is today Nigeria. According to oral tradition, the first king of the new dynasty was the grandson of a Yoruba king of Ile-Ife. Benin reached its greatest power and geographical extent in the 16th century. The kingdom's vicissitudes and slow decline thereafter culminated in 1897, when the British burned and sacked the Benin palace and city. Benin City thrives today, however, and the palace, where the Benin king continues to live, has been partially rebuilt. Benin artists have produced many complex, finely cast copper-alloy sculptures as well as artworks in ivory, wood, ceramic, and wrought iron. The hereditary *oba*, or sacred king, and his court still use and dispense art objects as royal favors to title holders and other chiefs (see "Art and Leadership," page 536).

One of the masterworks of Benin ivory carving is a woman's head (FIG. **20-7**), displayed today in the Metropolitan Museum of Art. A Benin king almost certainly wore the head at his waist. A nearly identical pendant, fashioned from the same piece of ivory, is in the British Museum. Oba Esigie

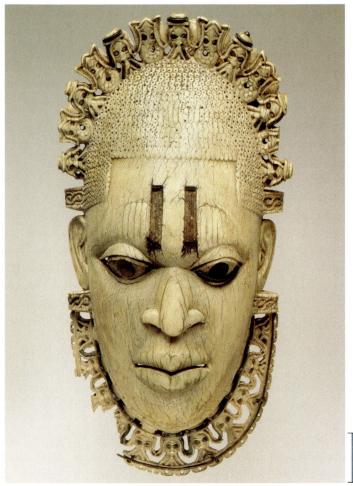

1 in.

20-7 Waist pendant of a Queen Mother, from Benin, Nigeria, ca. 1520. Ivory and iron, $9\frac{3}{8}$" high. Metropolitan Museum of Art, New York (Michael C. Rockefeller Memorial Collection, gift of Nelson A. Rockefeller, 1972).

This ivory head probably portrays Idia, mother of the Benin king Esigie. Above Idia's head are Portuguese heads and mudfish, symbols, respectively, of trade and of Olokun, the sea god.

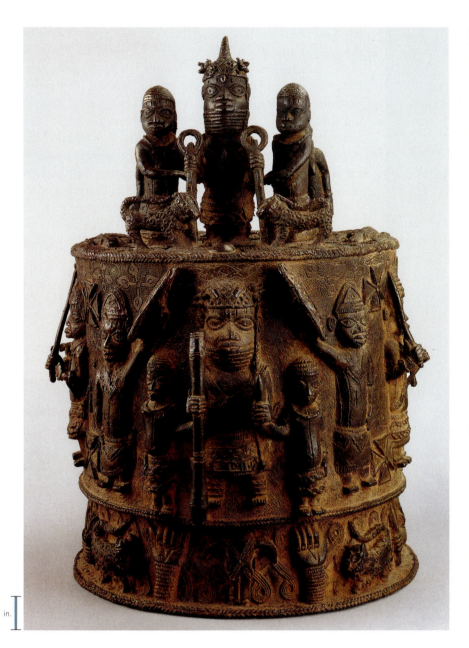

20-8 Altar to the Hand and Arm (ikegobo), from Benin, Nigeria, 17th to 18th century. Bronze, 1′ 5½″ high. British Museum, London.

One of the Benin king's praise names is "great head," and on this cast-bronze royal shrine, the artist represented him larger than all other figures and distorted his proportions to emphasize his head.

cal hierarchical compositions centered on the dominant king, probably Oba Eresonyen (r. 1735–1750). At the top, flanking and supporting the king, are smaller, lesser members of the court, usually identified as priests, and in front, a pair of leopards, animals the sacred king sacrificed and symbolic of his power over all creatures. Similar compositions are common in Benin arts, as exemplified by the royal plaque (FIG. I-11) discussed in the Introduction. Notably, too, the artist distorted the king's proportions to emphasize his head, the seat of his will and power. Benin men celebrate a festival of the head called Igue. One of the king's praise names is "great head." At these personal altars, the king and other high-ranking officials make sacrifices to their own power and accomplishments—symbolized by the hand and arm. The inclusion of leopards on the top and around the base, along with ram and elephant heads and crocodiles (not all visible in FIG. 20-8), reiterates royal power.

(r. ca. 1504–1550), under whom, with the help of the Portuguese, the Benin kingdom flourished and expanded, probably commissioned the pair. Esigie's mother, Idia, helped him in warfare, and in return he created for her the title of Queen Mother, Iy'oba, and built her a separate palace and court. The pendant, remarkable for its sensitive naturalism, most likely represents Idia. On its crown are alternating Portuguese heads and mudfish, symbolic allusions, respectively, to Benin's trade and diplomatic relationships with the Portuguese and to Olokun, god of the sea, wealth, and creativity. Another series of Portuguese heads also adorns the lower part of the carving. In the late 15th and 16th centuries, Benin people probably associated the Portuguese, with their large ships from across the sea, their powerful weapons, and their wealth in metals, cloth, and other goods, with Olokun, the deity they deemed responsible for abundance and prosperity.

The centrality of the sacred oba in Benin culture is well demonstrated by his depiction twice on a cast-brass royal shrine called an *ikegobo* (FIG. 20-8). It features symmetri-

Sapi Between 1490 and 1540, some peoples on the Atlantic coast of Africa in present-day Sierra Leone, whom the Portuguese collectively called the Sapi, created art not only for themselves but also for Portuguese explorers and traders, who took the objects back to Europe. The Portuguese commissions included delicate spoons, forks, and elaborate containers usually referred to as saltcellars, as well as boxes, hunting horns, and knife handles. Salt was a valuable commodity, used not only as a flavoring but also as a food preservative. Costly saltcellars were prestige items that graced the tables of the European elite. The Sapi export items were all meticulously carved from elephant tusk ivory with refined detail and careful finish. Ivory was plentiful in those early days and was one of the coveted exports in early West and Central African trade with Europe. The Sapi export ivories, the earliest examples of African "tourist art," are a fascinating hybrid art form.

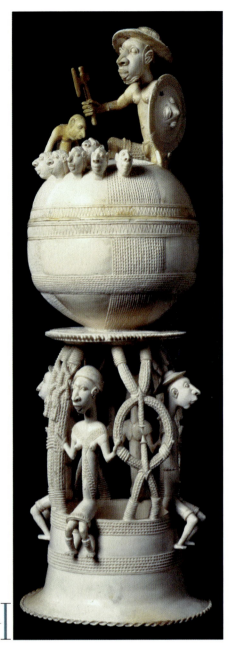

20-9 MASTER OF THE SYMBOLIC EXECUTION, saltcellar, Sapi-Portuguese, from Sierra Leone, ca. 1490–1540. Ivory, 1′ 4⅞″ high. Museo Nazionale Preistorico e Etnografico Luigi Pigorini, Rome.

The Sapi saltcellars made for export combine African and Portuguese traits. This one represents an execution scene with an African-featured man, who wears European pants, seated among severed heads.

1 in.

the base and the sphere, as well as certain elements of dress, such as the shirts and hats. Distinctly African are the style of the human heads and figures and their proportions, the latter skewed to emphasize the head. Identical large noses with flaring nostrils, as well as the conventions for rendering eyes and lips, characterize Sapi stone figures from the same region and period. Scholars cannot be sure whether the African carver or the European patron specified the subject matter and the configurations of various parts, but the Sapi works testify to a fruitful artistic interaction between Africans and Europeans during the early 16th century.

19TH CENTURY

Information gleaned from archaeology and field research in Africa (mainly interviews with local people) provides much more detail on the use, function, and meaning of African art objects produced during the past two centuries.

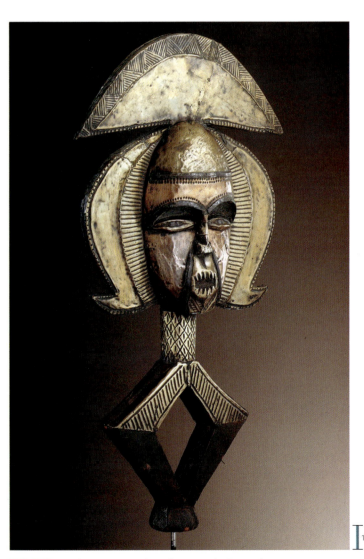

1 in.

20-10 Reliquary guardian figure (mbulu ngulu), Kota, Gabon, 19th or early 20th century. Wood, copper, iron, and brass, 1′ 9 1/16″ high. Musée Barbier-Mueller, Geneva.

Kota guardian figures have bodies in the form of an open lozenge and large heads. Polished copper and brass sheets cover the wood forms. The Kota believe that gleaming surfaces repel evil.

Art historians have attributed the saltcellar shown here (FIG. **20-9**), almost 17 inches high, to the MASTER OF THE SYMBOLIC EXECUTION, one of the three major Sapi ivory carvers during the period. It is his name piece and depicts an execution scene. A kneeling figure with a shield in one hand holds an ax (restored) in the other hand over another seated figure about to lose his head. On the ground before the executioner, severed heads grimly testify to the executioner's power. A double zigzag line separates the lid of the globular container from the rest of the vessel. This vessel rests in turn on a circular platform held up by slender rods adorned with crocodile images. Two male and two female figures sit between these rods, grasping them. The men wear European-style pants and have long, straight hair. The women wear skirts, and the elaborate raised patterns on their upper chests surely represent decorative scars. The European components of this saltcellar include the overall design of a spherical container on a pedestal and some of the geometric patterning on

Kota In modern times, as in earlier eras, Africans venerate ancestors for the continuing aid they believe they provide the living, including help in maintaining the productivity of the earth for bountiful crop production. Among the Kota of Gabon, ancestor veneration takes material form as collections of cranial and other bones *(relics)* gathered in special containers *(reliquaries)* crowned by guardian figures called *mbulu ngulu* (FIG. **20-10**). These figures have severely stylized bodies in the form of an open lozenge below a wooden head covered with strips and sheets of polished copper and brass. The Kota believe the gleaming surfaces repel evil. The simplified heads have hairstyles flattened out laterally above and beside the face. Geometric ridges, borders, and subdivisions add a textured elegance to the shiny forms. The copper alloy on most of these images was reworked sheet brass (or copper wire) taken from brass basins originating in Europe and traded into this area of equatorial Africa in the 18th and 19th centuries. The Kota inserted the lower portion of the image into the box of ancestral relics.

Kalabari Ijaw The Kalabari Ijaw of the eastern delta of the Niger River in present-day Nigeria have also lavished attention on shrines in honor of ancestors. The Kalabari shrines take a unique form and feature elaborate screens of wood, fiber, textiles, and other materials. An especially ornate example (FIG. **20-1**) is the almost four-foot-tall *nduen fobara* honoring a deceased chief of a trading corporation called a canoe house. Displayed in the house in which the chief lived, the screen represents the chief himself at the center holding a long silver-tipped staff in his right hand and a curved knife in his left hand. His chest is bare, and drapery covers the lower part of his body. His impressive headdress is in the form of a 19th-century European sailing ship, a reference to the chief's successful trading business. Flanking him are his attendants, smaller in size as appropriate for their lower rank. The heads of his slaves are at the top of the screen, and those of his conquered rivals are at the bottom. The hierarchical composition and the stylized rendition of human anatomy and facial features are common in African art, but the richness and complexity of this shrine are exceptional.

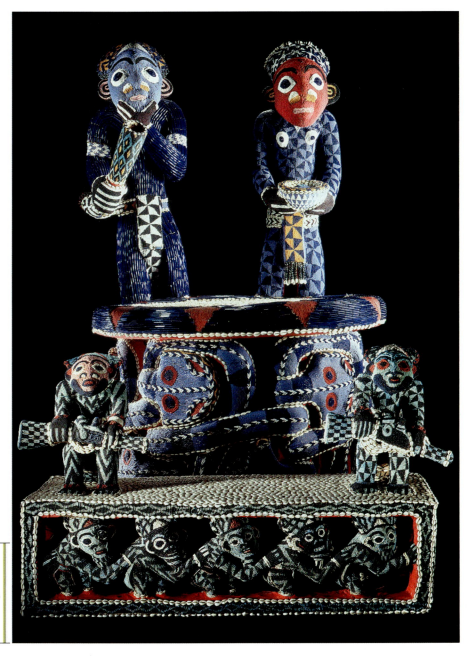

Bamum In the kingdom of Bamum in present-day Cameroon, the ruler lived in a palace compound at the capital city of Foumban until its destruction in 1910. The royal arts of Bamum make extensive use of richly colored textiles and luminous materials, such as glass beads and cowrie shells. The ultimate status symbol was the king's throne. The throne (FIG. **20-11**) that belonged to King Nsangu (r. 1865–1872 and 1885–1887) is a masterpiece of Bamum art. Intertwining blue and black serpents decorate the cylindrical seat. Above are the figures of two of the king's retainers, perpetually at his service. One, a man, holds the royal drinking horn. The other is a woman carrying a serving bowl in her hands. Below are two of the king's bodyguards wielding European rifles. Decorating the rectangular footstool are dancing figures. When the king sat on this throne, his rich garments complemented the bright colors of his seat, advertising his wealth and power to all who were admitted to his palace.

20-11 Throne and footstool of King Nsangu, Bamum, Cameroon, ca. 1870. Wood, textile, glass beads, and cowrie shells, 5′ 9″ high. Museum für Völkerkunde, Staatliche Museen zu Berlin, Berlin.

King Nsangu's throne features luminous beads and shells and richly colored textiles. The decoration includes intertwining serpents, male and female retainers, and bodyguards with European rifles.

1 ft.

Fon The foundation of the Fon kingdom in the present-day Republic of Benin dates to around 1600. Under King Guezo (r. 1818–1858), the Fon became a regional power with an economy based on trade in palm oil. After his first military victory, Guezo's son Glele (r. 1858–1889) commissioned a prisoner of war, Akati Akpele Kendo, to make a life-size iron statue (FIG. 20-12) of a warrior, probably the war god Gu, for a battle shrine in Glele's palace at Abomey. This *bocio*, or empowerment figure, was the centerpiece of a circle of iron swords and other weapons set vertically into the ground. The warrior strides forward with swords in both hands, ready to do battle. He wears a crown of miniature weapons and tools on his head. The form of the crown echoes the circle of swords around the statue. The Fon believed that the bocio protected their king, and they transported it to the battlefield whenever they set out to fight an enemy force. King Glele's iron warrior is remarkable for its size and for the fact that not only is the patron's name known but so too is the artist's name—a rare instance in Africa before the 20th century.

Kongo The Congo River formed the principal transportation route for the peoples of Central Africa during the 19th century. The large standing statue (FIG. 20-13) of a man bristling with nails and blades is a Kongo power figure *(nkisi n'kondi)* that a trained priest consecrated using precise ritual

formulas. These images embodied spirits believed to heal and give life or sometimes inflict harm, disease, or even death. Each figure had its specific role, just as it wore particular medicines—here protruding from the abdomen and featuring a large cowrie shell. The Kongo also activated every image differently. Owners appealed to a figure's forces every time they inserted a nail or blade, as if to prod the spirit to do its work. People invoked other spirits by repeating certain chants, by rubbing them, or by applying special powders. The roles of power figures varied enormously, from curing minor ailments to stimulating crop growth, from punishing thieves to weakening an enemy. Very large Kongo figures, such as this one, had exceptional ascribed powers and aided entire communities. Although benevolent for their owners, the figures stood at the boundary between life and death, and most villagers held them in awe. Compared with the sculptures of most other African peoples, this Kongo figure is relatively naturalistic, although the carver simplified the facial features and magnified the size of the head for emphasis.

Dogon The Dogon live in the inland delta region of the great Niger River in what is today Mali. One of the most common themes in Dogon art is the human couple. A characteristic Dogon linked-man-and-woman group (FIG. 20-14) of the early 19th century is probably a shrine or altar, although con-

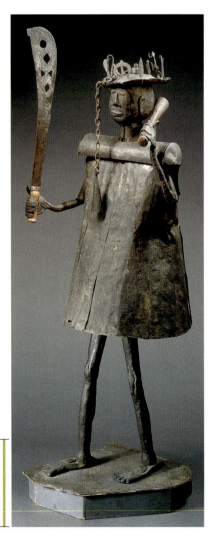

20-12 Akati Akpele Kendo, Warrior figure (Gu?), from the palace of King Glele, Abomey, Fon, Republic of Benin, 1858–1859. Iron, 5′ 5″ high. Musée du quai Branly, Paris.

This bocio, or empowerment figure, probably representing the war god Gu, was the centerpiece of a circle of iron swords. The Fon set it up on the battlefield, believing it protected their king.

1 ft.

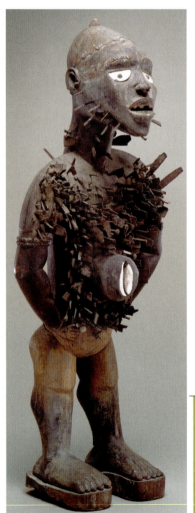

20-13 Nail figure (nkisi n'kondi), Kongo, from Shiloango River area, Democratic Republic of Congo, ca. 1875–1900. Wood, nails, blades, medicinal materials, and cowrie shell, 3′ 10¾″ high. Detroit Institute of Arts, Detroit.

Only priests using ritual formulas could consecrate Kongo power figures, which embody spirits that can heal or inflict harm. This statue has simplified anatomical forms and a very large head.

1 ft.

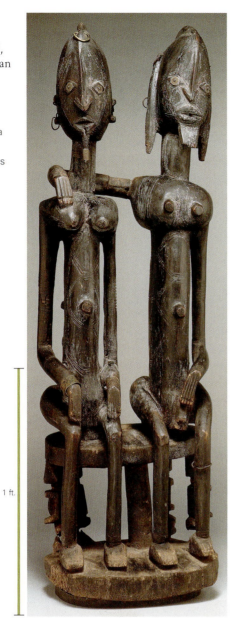

20-14 Seated couple, Dogon, Mali, ca. 1800–1850. Wood, 2′ 4″ high. Metropolitan Museum of Art, New York (gift of Lester Wunderman).

This Dogon carving of a linked man and woman documents gender roles in traditional African society. The protective man wears a quiver on his back. The nurturing woman carries a child on hers.

1 ft.

textual information is lacking. Interpretations vary, but the image vividly documents primary gender roles in traditional African society. The man wears a quiver on his back, and the woman carries a child on hers. Thus the man assumes a protective role as hunter or warrior, the woman a nurturing role. The slightly larger man reaches behind his mate's neck and touches her breast, as if to protect her. His left hand points to his genitalia. Four stylized figures support the stool upon which they sit. They are probably either spirits or ancestors, but the identity of the larger figures is uncertain.

The strong stylization of Dogon sculptures contrasts sharply with the organic, relatively realistic treatment of the human body in Kongo art (FIG. 20-13). The artist who carved the Dogon couple based the forms more on the idea or concept of the human body than on observation of individual heads, torsos, and limbs. The linked body parts are tubes and columns articulated inorganically. The carver reinforced the almost abstract geometry of the overall composition by incising rectilinear and diagonal patterns on the surfaces. The Dogon artist also understood the importance of space, and charged the voids, as well as the sculptural forms, with rhythm and tension.

20TH CENTURY

The art of Africa during the past 100 years ranges from traditional works depicting age-old African themes to modern works that are international in both content and style.

Benin In 1897, when the British sacked Benin City, there were still 17 shrines to ancestors in the Benin royal palace. Today only one 20th-century altar (FIG. 20-15) remains. According to oral history, it is similar to centuries-earlier versions. With a base of sacred riverbank clay, it is an assemblage of varied materials, objects, and symbols: a central copper-alloy altarpiece depicting a sacred king flanked by members

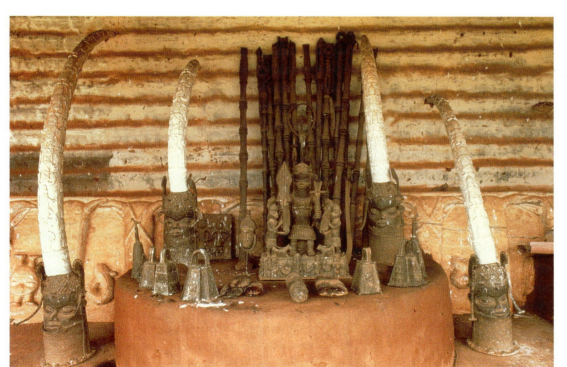

20-15 Royal ancestral altar of Benin King Eweka II, in the palace in Benin City, Nigeria, photographed in 1970. Clay, copper alloy, wood, and ivory.

This shrine to the heads of royal ancestors is an assemblage of varied materials, objects, and symbols. By sacrificing animals at this site, the Benin king annually invokes the collective strength of his ancestors.

of his entourage, plus copper-alloy heads, each fitted on top with an ivory tusk carved in relief. Behind are wood staffs and metal bells. The heads represent both the kings themselves and, through the durability of their material, the enduring nature of kingship. Their glistening surfaces, seen as red and signaling danger, repel evil forces that might adversely affect the shrine and thus the king and kingdom. Elephant-tusk relief carvings atop the heads commemorate important events and personages in Benin history. Their bleached white color signifies purity and goodness (probably of royal ancestors), and the tusks themselves represent male physical power. The carved wood rattle-staffs standing at the back refer to generations of dynastic ancestors by their bamboolike, segmented forms. The rattle-staffs and the pyramidal copper-alloy bells serve the important function of calling royal ancestral spirits to rituals performed at the altar.

The Benin king's head stands for wisdom, good judgment, and divine guidance for the kingdom. The several heads in the ancestral altar multiply these qualities. By means of animal sacrifices at this site, the living king annually purifies his own head (and being) by invoking the collective strength of his ancestors. Thus the varied objects, symbols, colors, and materials composing this shrine contribute both visually and ritually to the imaging of royal power, as well as to its history, renewal, and perpetuation.

Osei Bonsu Traditionally, Africans have tended not to exalt artistic individuality as much as Westerners have. Many people, in fact, consider African art as anonymous, but that is primarily because early researchers rarely asked for artists' names. Nonetheless, art historians can recognize many individual hands even when an artist's name has not been recorded. During the past century, art historians and anthropologists have been systematically noting the names and life histories of specific individual artists, many of whom have strong regional reputations. One of these was **Osei Bonsu** (1900–1976), a master carver based in the Asante capital, Kumasi, in present-day Ghana. A more naturalistic rendering of the face and crosshatched eyebrows are distinctive features of Bonsu's personal style.

The gold-covered wood sculpture (FIG. 20-16) depicting two men sitting at a table of food is a characteristic example of Bonsu's work. This object, commonly called a *linguist's staff* because its carrier often speaks for a king or chief, has

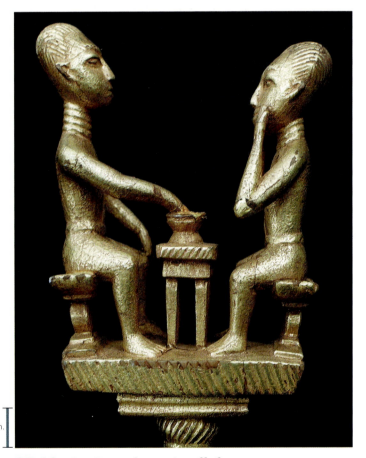

20-16 OSEI BONSU, linguist's staff of two men sitting at a table of food, Asante, Ghana, mid-20th century. Wood and gold leaf, section shown 10″ high. Collection of the Paramount Chief of Offinso, Asante.

Osei Bonsu carved this gold-covered wooden linguist's staff for someone who could speak for the Asante king. At the top are two men sitting at a table of food—a metaphor for the office of the king.

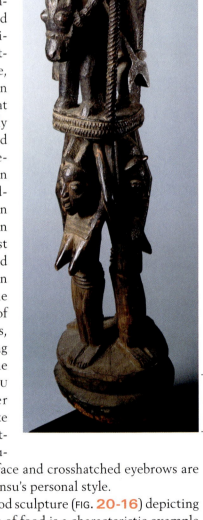

20-17 OLOWE OF ISE, veranda post, from Akure, Yoruba, Nigeria, 1920s. Wood and pigment, 14′ 6″ high. Denver Art Museum, Denver.

Olowe carved this post when Europeans were already familiar among the Yoruba. He recorded this colonialism by placing a European cap on one of the figures supporting the equestrian warrior.

a related proverb: "Food is for its rightful owner, not for the one who happens to be hungry." Food is a metaphor for the office the king or chief rightfully holds. The "hungry" man lusts for the office. The linguist, who is an important counselor and adviser to the king, might carry this staff to a meeting at which a rival is contesting the king's title to the stool (his throne, the office). Many hundreds of Asante sculptures have proverbs or other sayings associated with them, resulting in a rich verbal tradition related to Asante visual arts.

Olowe of Ise The leading Yoruba sculptor of the early 20th century was OLOWE OF ISE (ca. 1873–1938). Kings throughout Yorubaland (southern Nigeria and southern Benin) sought his services. The king of Ikere, for example, employed Olowe for four years starting in 1910. A tall veranda post (FIG. 20-17) that Olowe carved in the 1920s for the house of Chief Elefoshan of Akure is typical of his style. To achieve greater height, Olowe stacked his weapon-carrying equestrian warrior atop a platform supported on the heads and upraised arms of four attenuated figures, two men and two women, with long necks and enlarged heads. The latter trait is common among most Yoruba sculptors, but elongated bodies are an Olowe characteristic, along with finely textured detail, seen in the warrior's tunic. The post dates to a time when Europeans had already become a colonial presence among Yoruba peoples. Olowe subtly recorded this presence by placing a European-style billed cap on the head of one of the supporting figures. The overall design, more complex and with more open space than most posts by other carvers, signals Olowe's virtuosity.

Senufo The Senufo peoples of the western Sudan region in what is now northern Côte d'Ivoire have a population today of more than a million. Senufo men dance many masks (see "African Masquerades," page 546), mostly in the context of Poro, the primary men's association for socialization and initiation, a protracted process that takes nearly 20 years to complete. Maskers also perform at funerals and other public spectacles. Large Senufo masks (for example, FIG. 20-18) are composite creatures, combining characteristics of antelope, crocodile, warthog, hyena, and human: sweeping horns, a head, and an open-jawed snout with sharp teeth. These masks incarnate both ancestors and bush powers that combat witchcraft and sorcery, malevolent spirits, and the wandering dead. They are protectors who fight evil with their aggressively powerful forms and their medicines. At funerals, Senufo maskers attend the corpse and help expel the deceased from the village. This is the deceased individual's final transition, a rite of passage parallel to that undergone by all men during their years of Poro socialization. When an important person dies, the masquerades, music, dancing, costuming, and feasting together constitute a festive and complex work of art that transcends any one mask or character.

Mende The Mende are farmers who occupy the Atlantic coast of Africa in Sierra Leone. Although men own and perform most masks in Africa, in Mende society the women control and dance the masks. The Sande society of the Mende is the women's counterpart of the Senufo men's Poro society and controls the initiation, education, and acculturation of

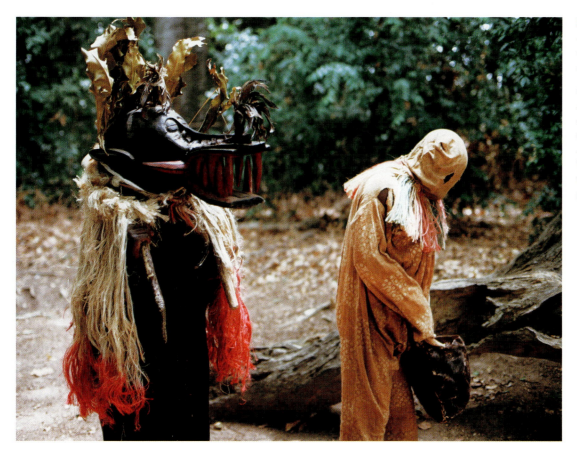

20-18 Gbon masquerader, Senufo, Côte d'Ivoire, photographed ca. 1980–1990.

Senufo masqueraders are always men. Their masks often represent composite creatures that incarnate both ancestors and bush powers. They fight malevolent spirits with their aggressively powerful forms.

African Masquerades

The art of masquerade has long been a quintessential African expressive form, replete with meaning and cultural importance. This is so today but was even more critically true in colonial times and earlier, when African masking societies boasted extensive regulatory and judicial powers. In stateless societies, such as those of the Senufo (FIG. 20-18) and Mende (FIG. 20-19), masks sometimes became so influential they had their own priests and served as power sources or as oracles. Societies empowered maskers to levy fines and to apprehend witches (usually defined as socially destructive people) and criminals, and to judge and punish them. Normally, however—especially today—masks are less threatening and more secular and educational, and they serve as diversions from the humdrum of daily life. Masked dancers usually embody either ancestors, seen as briefly returning to the human realm, or various nature spirits called upon for their special powers.

The mask, a costume ensemble's focal point, combines with held objects, music, and dance gestures to invoke a specific named character, almost always considered a spirit. A few masked spirits appear by themselves, but more often several characters come out together or in turn. Maskers enact a broad range of human, animal, and fantastic otherworldly behavior that is usually both stimulating and didactic. Masquerades, in fact, vary in function or effect along a continuum from weak spirit power and strong entertainment value to those rarely seen but possessing vast executive powers backed by powerful shrines. Most operate between these extremes, crystallizing varieties of human and animal behavior—caricatured, ordinary, comic, bizarre, serious, or threatening. These actions inform and affect audience members because of their dramatic staging. It is the purpose of most masquerades to move people, to affect them, to effect change.

Thus, masks and masquerades are mediators—between men and women, youths and elders, initiated and uninitiated, powers of nature and those of human agency, and even life and death. For many groups in West and Central Africa, masking plays (or once played) an active role in the socialization process, especially for men, who control most masks. Maskers carry boys (and, more rarely, girls) away from their mothers to bush initiation camps, put them through ordeals and schooling, and welcome them back to society as men months or even years later. A second major role is in aiding the transformation of important deceased persons into productive ancestors who, in their new roles, can bring benefits to the living community. Because most masking cultures are agricultural, it is not surprising that Africans often invoke masquerades to increase the productivity of the fields, to stimulate the growth of crops, and later to celebrate the harvest.

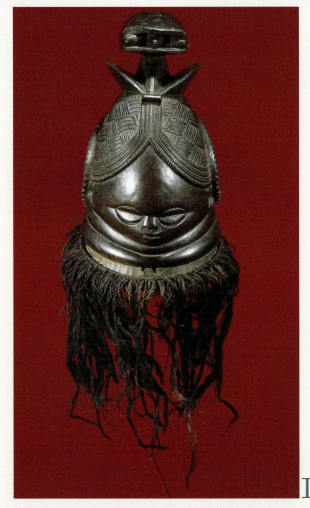

20-19 Female mask, Mende, Sierra Leone, 20th century. Wood and pigment, 1′ 2½″ high. Fowler Museum of Cultural History, University of California, Los Angeles (gift of the Wellcome Trust).

This Mende mask refers to ideals of female beauty, morality, and behavior. The large forehead signifies wisdom, the neck design beauty and health, and the plaited hair the order of ideal households.

Mende girls. The glistening black surface of Mende Sowie masks (FIG. 20-19) evokes female ancestral spirits newly emergent from their underwater homes (also symbolized by the turtle on top). The mask and its parts refer to ideals of female beauty, morality, and behavior. A high, broad forehead signifies wisdom and success. The neck ridges have multiple meanings. They are signs of beauty, good health, and prosperity and also refer to the ripples in the water from which the water spirits emerge. Intricately woven or plaited hair is the essence of harmony and order found in ideal households. A small closed mouth and downcast eyes indicate the silent, serious demeanor expected of recent initiates. Sande women wear these helmet masks on their heads as headdresses, with black raffia and cloth costumes to hide the wearers' identity during public performances. Elaborate coiffures, shiny black color, dainty triangular-shaped faces with slit eyes, rolls around the neck, and actual and carved versions of amulets and various emblems on the top commonly characterize Sowie masks. These symbolize the adult women's roles as wives, mothers, providers for the family, and keepers of medicines for use within the Sande association and the society at large.

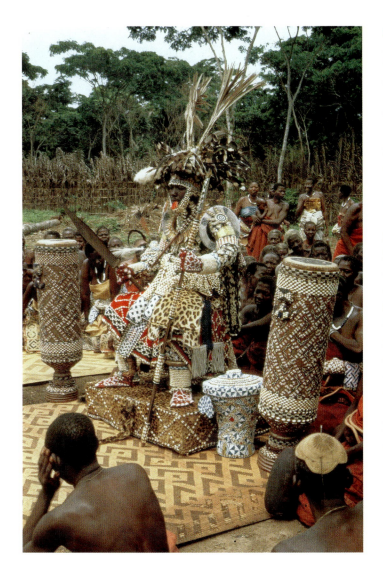

20-20 Kuba King Kot a-Mbweeky III during a display for photographer and filmmaker Eliot Elisofon in 1970, Mushenge, Democratic Republic of Congo.

Eagle feathers, leopard skin, cowrie shells, imported beads, raffia, and other materials combine to make the Kuba king larger than life. He is a collage of wealth, dignity, and military might.

Kuba Throughout history, African costumes have been laden with meaning and have projected messages that all members of the society could read. A photograph (FIG. **20-20**) taken in 1970 shows the Kuba (Democratic Republic of Congo) king Kot a-Mbweeky III (r. 1969–) seated in state before his court, bedecked in a dazzling multimedia costume with many symbolic elements. The king commissioned the costume he wears and now has become art himself. Eagle feathers, leopard skin, cowrie shells, imported beads, raffia, and other materials combine to overload and expand the image of the man, making him larger than life and most certainly a work of art. He is a human collage. He holds not one but two weapons, symbolic of his military might and underscoring his wealth, dignity, and grandeur. The man, with his regalia, embodies the office of sacred kingship. He is a superior being actually and figuratively, raised upon a dais, flanked by ornate drums, with a treasure basket of sacred relics by his left foot. The geometric patterns on the king's costume and nearby objects, and the abundance and redundancy of rich materials, epitomize the opulent style of Kuba court arts.

CONTEMPORARY ART

The art forms of contemporary Africa are immensely varied and defy easy classification. They range from the traditional, both in subject and technique, to Western-style oil-on-canvas paintings commenting on contemporary political and social issues.

Trigo Piula The Democratic Republic of Congo's TRIGO PIULA (b. ca. 1950) is a painter trained in Western artistic techniques and styles whose works fuse Western and Congolese images and objects in a pictorial blend that provides social commentary on present-day Congolese culture. *Ta Tele* (FIG. **20-21**) depicts a group of Congolese citizens staring transfixed at colorful pictures of life beyond Africa displayed on 14 television screens. The TV images include references to travel to exotic places (such as Paris with the Eiffel Tower, FIG. **13-19**), sports events, love, the earth

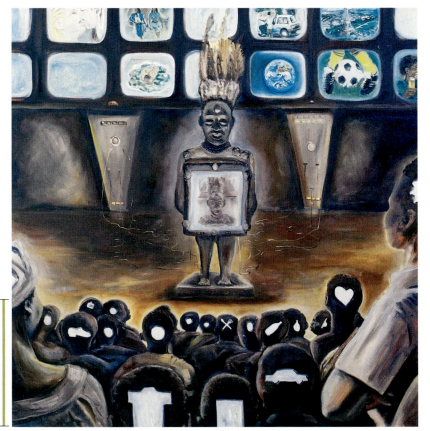

1 ft.

20-21 TRIGO PIULA, *Ta Tele*, Democratic Republic of Congo, 1988. Oil on canvas, 3′ 3$\frac{3}{8}$″ × 3′ 4$\frac{3}{8}$″. National Museum of African Art, Washington, D.C.

Ta Tele is a commentary on modern life showing Congolese citizens transfixed by television pictures of the world outside Africa. Even the traditional power figure at the center has a TV screen for a chest.

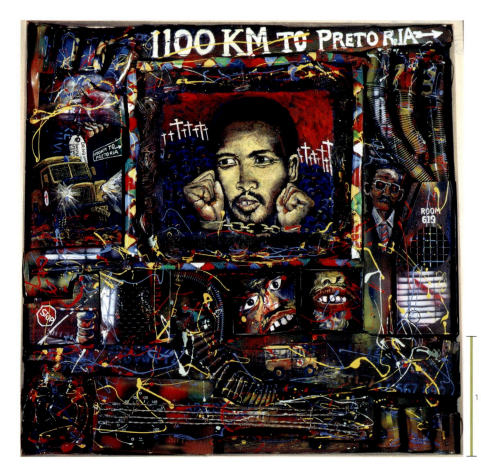

20-22 WILLIE BESTER, *Homage to Steve Biko*, South Africa, 1992. Mixed media, 3′ 7⅚″ × 3′ 7⅚″. Collection of the artist.

Homage to Steve Biko is a tribute to a leader of the Black Liberation Movement that protested apartheid in South Africa. References to the injustice of Biko's death fill this complex multimedia painting.

1 ft.

seen from a satellite, and Western worldly goods. A traditional Kongo power figure (compare FIG. 20-13) associated with warfare and divination stands at the composition's center as a visual mediator between the anonymous foreground viewers and the multiple TV images. In traditional Kongo contexts, this figure's feather headdress links it to supernatural and magical powers from the sky, such as lightning and storms. In Piula's rendition, the headdress perhaps refers to the power of airborne televised pictures. In the stomach area, where Kongo power figures often have glass in front of a medicine packet, Piula painted a television screen showing a second power figure, as if to double the figure's power. The artist shows most of the television viewers with a small white image of a foreign object—for example, a car, shoe, or bottle—on the backs of their heads. One meaning of this picture appears to be that television messages have deadened the minds of Congolese peoples to anything but modern thoughts or commodities. The power figure stands squarely on brown earth. Two speaker cabinets set against the back wall beneath the TV screens have wires leading to the figure, which in the past could inflict harm. In traditional Kongo thinking and color symbolism, the color white and earth tones are associated with spirits and the land of the dead. Perhaps Piula suggests that like earlier power figures, the contemporary world's new television-induced consumerism is poisoning the minds and souls of Congolese people as if by magic or sorcery.

Willie Bester Social and political issues also figure prominently in contemporary South African art. For example, artists first helped protest against South Africa's apartheid system (government-sponsored racial separation), then celebrated its demise and the subsequent democratically elected government under the first president, Nelson Mandela, in 1994. WILLIE BESTER (b. 1956) was among the critics of apartheid. His 1992 *Homage to Steve Biko* (FIG. 20-22) is a tribute to the gentle and heroic leader of the South African Black Liberation Movement whom the authorities killed while he was in detention. The exoneration of the two white doctors in charge of him sparked protests around the world. Bester packed his picture with references to death and injustice. Biko's portrait, at the center, is near another of the police minister, James Kruger, who had Biko transported 1,100 miles to Pretoria in the yellow Land Rover ambulance seen left of cen-

ter and again beneath Biko's portrait. Bester portrayed Biko with his chained fists raised in the recurrent protest gesture. This portrait memorializes both Biko and the many others killed during antiapartheid activities indicated by the white graveyard crosses above a blue sea of skulls beside Biko's head. The crosses stand out against a red background that recalls the inferno of burned townships. The stop sign (lower left) seems to mean "stop Kruger" or perhaps "stop apartheid." The tagged foot, as if in a morgue, above the ambulance (to the left) also refers to Biko's death. The red crosses on the ambulance door and on Kruger's reflective dark glasses echo, with sad irony, the graveyard crosses.

Blood red and ambulance yellow are in fact unifying colors dripped or painted on many parts of the work. Writing and numbers, found fragments and signs, both stenciled and painted—favorite Cubist motifs (FIGS. 14-1 and 14-9)—also appear throughout the composition. Numbers refer to dehumanized life under apartheid. Found objects—wire, sticks, cardboard, sheet metal, cans, and other discards—from which the poor construct fragile, impermanent township dwellings, remind viewers of the degraded lives of most South African people of color. The oil-can guitar (bottom center), another recurrent Bester symbol, refers both to the social harmony and joy provided by music and to the control imposed by apartheid policies. The whole composition is rich in texture and dense in its collage combinations of objects, photographs, signs, symbols, and painting. *Homage to Steve Biko* is a radical and powerful critique of an oppressive sociopolitical system, and it exemplifies the extent to which contemporary art can be invoked in the political process.

Africa

PREHISTORY AND EARLY CULTURES

▪ Humankind apparently originated in Africa, and some of the oldest known artworks are paintings dating ca. 23,000 BCE from the Apollo 11 Cave in Namibia.

▪ The Nok culture of central Nigeria produced the oldest African examples of sculpture in the round between 500 BCE and 200 CE. Bronze-casting using the lost-wax method is first documented in Africa in the 9th or 10th century CE at Igbo Ukwu (Nigeria).

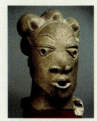

Nok terracotta head, ca. 500 BCE–200 CE

11TH TO 18TH CENTURIES

▪ The sculptors of Ile-Ife (Nigeria) fashioned images of their kings in an unusually naturalistic style during the 11th and 12th centuries, but the heads of the figures are disproportionately large, as in most African artworks.

▪ This period saw the construction of major shrines for Islamic and Christian worship that emulate foreign models but employ African building methods, for example, the adobe Great Mosque at Djenne (Mali).

▪ In southern Africa, the Great Zimbabwe Empire conducted prosperous trade with the Near East and China well before the first contact with Europeans. Impressive stone walls and towers enclosed the royal palace complex.

▪ The Benin kingdom in the Lower Niger region was probably founded in the 13th century but reached its zenith in the 16th century. Benin sculptors excelled in ivory carving and bronze-casting, producing artworks that glorified the royal family, for example, a waist pendant depicting the Queen Mother Idia.

▪ An early example of the interaction between African artists and European patrons is the series of Sapi ivory saltcellars from Sierra Leone datable between 1490 and 1540. They constitute the first African "tourist art."

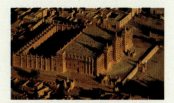

Great Mosque, Djenne, 13th century

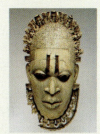

Benin ivory waist pendant, ca. 1520

19TH CENTURY

▪ Most of the traditional forms of African art continued into the 19th century. Among these are sculptures and shrines connected with the veneration of ancestors, such as the Kalabari Ijaw screen honoring a deceased chief. Although stylistically diverse, most African sculpture exhibits hierarchy of scale, both among figures and within the human body, where enlarged heads are common.

▪ Throughout history, African artists have been masters of woodcarving. Especially impressive examples are the Kongo power figures bristling with nails and blades and the Dogon sculptures of male and female couples.

▪ The royal arts also flourished in the 19th century. One of the earliest African artists whose name survives is Akati Akpele Kendo, who worked for the Fon king Glele around 1858, but most African art remains anonymous.

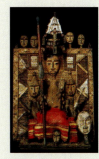

Kalabari Ijaw ancestral screen, late 19th century

20TH CENTURY

▪ The art forms of modern Africa range from the traditional to works of international character using Western techniques and motifs. The fashioning of masks for festive performances remains important in many parts of Africa today. Senufo masqueraders are almost always men, even when the masks they dance are female, but in Mende society, women are the maskers.

▪ The names of many more individual 20th-century artists are known. Two of the most famous are the Asante sculptor Osei Bonsu and the Yoruba sculptor Olowe of Ise. Among the most prominent contemporary artists are Trigo Piula of the Democratic Republic of Congo and Willie Bester of South Africa, whose work often incorporates social and political commentary.

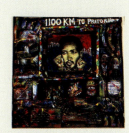

Bester, *Homage to Steve Biko*, 1992

Notes

INTRODUCTION

1. Quoted in George Heard Hamilton, *Painting and Sculpture in Europe, 1880–1940*, 6th ed. (New Haven, Conn.: Yale University Press, 1993), 345.

2. Quoted in *Josef Albers: Homage to the Square* (New York: Museum of Modern Art, 1964), n.p.

CHAPTER 1

1. Herodotus, *Histories*, 2.35.

2. The chronology adopted in this chapter is that of John Baines and Jaromír Malék, *Atlas of Ancient Egypt* (Oxford: Oxford University Press, 1980), 36–37. The division of kingdoms is that of, among others, Mark Lehner, *The Complete Pyramids* (New York: Thames & Hudson, 1997), 89, and David P. Silverman, ed., *Ancient Egypt* (New York: Oxford University Press, 1997), 20–39.

CHAPTER 2

1. Galen, *De placitis Hippocratis et Platonis*, 5. Translated by J. J. Pollitt, *The Art of Ancient Greece: Sources and Documents* (New York: Cambridge University Press, 1990), 76.

2. Pliny the Elder, *Natural History*, 34.55. Translated by Pollitt, 75.

3. Pliny, *Natural History*, 36.20.

4. Lucian, *Amores*, 13–14; *Imagines*, 6.

5. Pliny, *Natural History*, 35.110.

CHAPTER 3

1. Livy, *History of Rome*, 25.40.1–3.

2. Pliny the Elder, *Natural History*, 35.133.

CHAPTER 4

1. Augustine, *City of God*, 16.26.

2. Procopius, *De aedificiis*, 1.1.23ff. Translated by Cyril Mango, *The Art of the Byzantine Empire, 312–1453: Sources and Documents* (reprint of 1972 ed., Toronto: University of Toronto Press, 1986), 74.

3. Paulus Silentarius, *Descriptio Sanctae Sophiae*, 489, 668. Translated by Mango, 83, 86.

4. Procopius, 1.1.23ff. Translated by Mango, 75.

5. *Libri Carolini* 4.2. Translated by Herbert L. Kessler, *Spiritual Seeing: Picturing God's Invisibility in Medieval Art* (Philadelphia: University of Pennsylvania Press, 2000), 119.

CHAPTER 6

1. *Beowulf* 3162–3164. Translated by Kevin Crossley-Holland (New York: Farrar, Straus, Giroux, 1968), 119.

2. Translated by Charles P. Parkhurst Jr., in Elizabeth G. Holt, *A Documentary History of Art*, 2d ed. (Princeton, N.J.: Princeton University Press, 1981), 1: 18.

3. Bernard of Clairvaux, *Apologia* 12.28–29. Translated by Conrad Rudolph, *The "Things of Greater Importance": Bernard of Clairvaux's* Apologia *and the Medieval Attitude toward Art* (Philadelphia: University of Pennsylvania Press, 1990), 279, 283.

4. Translated by Calvin B. Kendall, *The Allegory of the Church: Romanesque Portals and Their Verse Inscriptions* (Toronto: University of Toronto Press, 1998), 207.

CHAPTER 7

1. Giorgio Vasari, *Introduzione alle tre arti del disegno* (1550), ch. 3; Paul Frankl, *The Gothic: Literary Sources and Interpretation through Eight Centuries* (Princeton, N.J.: Princeton University Press, 1960), 290–291, 859–860.

2. Translated by Erwin Panofsky, *Abbot Suger on the Abbey Church of Saint-Denis and Its Art Treasures*, 2d ed. (Princeton, N.J.: Princeton University Press, 1979), 101.

3. Ibid., 65.

4. Dante, *Divine Comedy*, Purgatory, 11.81.

5. Translated by Roland Behrendt, *Johannes Trithemius. In Praise of Scribes: De laude scriptorum* (Lawrence, Kans.: Coronado Press, 1974), 71.

6. Frankl, 55.

CHAPTER 8

1. Giorgio Vasari, *Lives of the Painters, Sculptors, and Architects*. Translated by Gaston du C. de Vere (New York: Knopf, 1996), 1: 304.

2. Quoted in H. W. Janson, *The Sculpture of Donatello* (Princeton, N.J.: Princeton University Press, 1965), 154.

3. Vasari, *Lives of the Painters, Sculptors, and Architects*, 1: 318.

CHAPTER 9

1. Leonardo da Vinci to Ludovico Sforza, ca. 1480–1481. Elizabeth Gilmore Holt, ed., *A Documentary History of Art*, 2d ed. (Princeton, N.J.: Princeton University Press, 1981), I: 274–275.

2. Quoted in Anthony Blunt, *Artistic Theory in Italy, 1450–1600* (London: Oxford University Press, 1964), 34.

3. Quoted in James M. Saslow, *The Poetry of Michelangelo: An Annotated Translation* (New Haven, Conn.: Yale University Press, 1991), 407.

4. Giorgio Vasari, *Lives of the Painters, Sculptors, and Architects*. Translated by Gaston du C. de Vere (New York: Knopf, 1996), 2: 736.

5. Quoted in A. Richard Turner, *Renaissance Florence: The Invention of a New Art* (New York: Abrams, 1997), 163.

6. Quoted in Bruce Boucher, *Andrea Palladio: The Architect in His Time* (New York: Abbeville, 1998), 229.

7. Quoted in Robert J. Clements, *Michelangelo's Theory of Art* (New York: New York University Press, 1961), 320.

CHAPTER 10

1. Filippo Baldinucci, *Vita del Cavaliere Giovanni Lorenzo Bernini* (1681). Translated by Robert Enggass, in Robert Enggass and Jonathan Brown, *Italian and Spanish Art, 1600–1750: Sources and Documents* (Evanston, Ill.: Northwestern University Press, 1992), 116.

2. John Milton, *Il Penseroso* (1631, published 1645), 166.

3. Translated by Kristin Lohse Belkin, *Rubens* (London: Phaidon, 1998), 47.

4. Albert Blankert, *Johannes Vermeer van Delft 1632–1675* (Utrecht: Spectrum, 1975), 133, no. 51. Translated by Bob Haak, *The Golden Age: Dutch Painters of the Seventeenth Century* (New York: Abrams, 1984), 450.

CHAPTER 11

1. Translated by Robert Goldwater and Marco Treves, eds., *Artists on Art, from the XIV to the XX Century*, 3d ed. (New York: Pantheon Books, 1958), 157.

2. Quoted in Thomas A. Bailey, *The American Pageant: A History of the Republic*, 2d ed. (Boston: Heath, 1961), 280.

3. Translated by Elfriede Heyer and Roger C. Norton, in Charles Harrison, Paul Wood, and Jason Gaiger, eds., *Art in Theory, 1648–1815: An Anthology of Changing Ideas* (Oxford: Blackwell, 2000), 453.

CHAPTER 12

1. Quoted in Helmut Borsch-Supan, *Caspar David Friedrich* (New York: Braziller, 1974), 7.

2. Translated by Jason Gaiger, in Charles Harrison, Paul Wood, and Jason Gaiger, eds., *Art in Theory, 1815–1900: An Anthology of Changing Ideas* (Oxford: Blackwell, 1998), 54.

3. Quoted by Brian Lukacher, in Stephen F. Eisenman, ed., *Nineteenth Century Art: A Critical History*, 2d ed. (New York: Thames & Hudson, 2002), 125.

4. Quoted in John W. McCoubrey, *American Art, 1700–1960: Sources and Documents* (Englewood Cliffs, N.J.: Prentice Hall, 1965), 98.

5. Quoted in Eisenman, 286.

6. Quoted in Nikolai Cikovsky Jr. and Franklin Kelly, *Winslow Homer* (Washington, D.C.: National Gallery of Art, 1995), 26.

7. Quoted in Lloyd Goodrich, *Thomas Eakins, His Life and Work* (New York: Whitney Museum of American Art, 1933), 51–52.

8. Quoted in Naomi Rosenblum, *A World History of Photography* (New York: Abbeville, 1984), 69.

CHAPTER 13

1. Clement Greenberg, "Modernist Painting," *Art and Literature*, no. 4 (Spring 1965): 193–194.

2. Quoted in Linda Nochlin, *Realism* (Harmondsworth: Penguin, 1971), 28.

3. Quoted in John McCoubrey, *American Art, 1700–1960: Sources and Documents* (Englewood Cliffs, N.J.: Prentice Hall, 1965), 184.

4. Vincent van Gogh to Theo van Gogh, September 1888, in J. van Gogh–Bonger and V. W. van Gogh, eds., *The Complete Letters of Vincent van Gogh* (Greenwich, Conn.: 1979), 3: 534.

5. Vincent van Gogh to Theo van Gogh, July 16, 1888, in W. H. Auden, ed., *Van Gogh: A Self-Portrait: Letters Revealing His Life as a Painter* (New York: Dutton, 1963), 299.

6. Quoted in Belinda Thompson, ed., *Gauguin by Himself* (Boston: Little, Brown, 1993), 270–271.

7. Cézanne to Émile Bernard, March 1904. Quoted in Sam Hunter, John Jacobus, and Daniel Wheeler, *Modern Art*, rev. 3d ed. (Upper Saddle River, N.J.: Prentice Hall, 2004), 28.

8. Cézanne to Émile Bernard, March 1904. Quoted in Robert Goldwater and Marco Treves, eds., *Artists on Art, from the XIV to the XX Century* (New York: Pantheon, 1945), 363.

9. Quoted in George Heard Hamilton, *Painting and Sculpture in Europe, 1880–1940*, 6th ed. (New Haven, Conn.: Yale University Press, 1993), 124.

10. Quoted in Victor Frisch and Joseph T. Shipley, *Auguste Rodin* (New York: Stokes, 1939), 203.

CHAPTER 14

1. Quoted in John Elderfield, *The "Wild Beasts": Fauvism and Its Affinities* (New York: Museum of Modern Art, 1976), 29.

2. Quoted in Frederick S. Levine, *The Apocalyptic Vision: The Art of Franz Marc as German Expressionism* (New York: Harper & Row, 1979), 57.

3. Quoted in Sam Hunter, John Jacobus, and Daniel Wheeler, *Modern Art*, rev. 3d ed. (Upper Saddle Hill, N.J.: Prentice Hall, 2004), 121.

4. Quoted in George Heard Hamilton, *Painting and Sculpture in Europe, 1880–1940*, 6th ed. (New Haven, Conn.: Yale University Press, 1993), 246.

5. Ibid., 238.

6. Quoted in Edward Fry, ed., *Cubism* (London: Thames & Hudson, 1966), 112–113.

7. Filippo Tommaso Marinetti, *The Foundation and Manifesto of Futurism* (*Le Figaro*, February 20, 1909). Translated by Joshua C. Taylor, in Herschel B. Chipp, *Theories of Modern Art: A Source Book by Artists and Critics* (Berkeley: University of California Press, 1968), 286.

8. Hans Richter, *Dada: Art and Anti-Art* (London: Thames & Hudson, 1961), 57.

9. Charles C. Eldredge, "The Arrival of European Modernism," *Art in America* 61 (July–August 1973): 35.

10. Dorothy Norman, *Alfred Stieglitz: An American Seer* (Millerton, N.Y.: Aperture, 1973), 9–10.

11. Ibid., 161.

12. Pablo Picasso, "Statement to Simone Téry," in Charles Harrison and Paul Wood, eds., *Art in Theory, 1900–2000: An Anthology of Changing Ideas* (Oxford: Blackwell, 2003), 649.

13. Quoted in Roland Penrose, *Picasso: His Life and Work*, rev. ed. (New York: Harper & Row, 1971), 311.

14. Quoted in William S. Rubin, *Dada, Surrealism, and Their Heritage* (New York: Museum of Modern Art, 1968), 64.

15. Quoted in Hamilton, *Painting and Sculpture*, 392.

16. Quoted in Rubin, *Dada, Surrealism*, 111.

17. Quoted in Hunter, Jacobus, and Wheeler, *Modern Art*, 179.

18. Quoted in William S. Rubin, *Miró in the Collection of the Museum of Modern Art* (New York: Museum of Modern Art, 1973), 32.

19. Translated by Howard Dearstyne, in Robert L. Herbert, *Modern Artists on Art*, 2d ed. (Mineola, N.Y.: Dover, 2000), 117.

20. Translated by Nicholas Bullock, quoted in Harrison and Wood, *Art in Theory, 1900–2000*, 281.

21. Quoted in Michel Seuphor, *Piet Mondrian: Life and Work* (New York: Abrams, 1956), 117.

22. Piet Mondrian, *Plastic Art and Pure Plastic Art* (1937), quoted in Hamilton, *Painting and Sculpture*, 319.

23. Quoted in Hamilton, *Painting and Sculpture*, 426.

24. Quoted in Herbert, *Modern Artists on Art*, 173–179.

25. Wanda M. Corn, *Grant Wood: The Regionalist Vision* (New Haven, Conn.: Yale University Press, 1983), 131.

26. Piet Mondrian, *Dialogue on the New Plastic* (1919). Translated by Harry Holzman and Martin S. James, in Harrison and Wood, *Art in Theory 1900–2000*, 285.

27. Walter Gropius, from *The Manifesto of the Bauhaus*, April 1919.

28. Ibid.

29. Quoted in John Willett, *Art and Politics in the Weimar Period: The New Sobriety, 1917–1933* (New York: Da Capo, 1978), 119.

30. Quoted in Philip Johnson, *Mies van der Rohe*, rev. ed. (New York: Museum of Modern Art, 1954), 200–201.

CHAPTER 15

1. Quoted in Dawn Ades and Andrew Forge, *Francis Bacon* (London: Thames & Hudson, 1985), 8; and David Sylvester, *The Brutality of Fact: Interviews with Francis Bacon*, 3d ed. (London: Thames & Hudson, 1987), 182.

2. Clement Greenberg, "Sculpture in Our Time," *Arts Magazine* 32, no. 9 (June 1956): 22.

3. Quoted in Selden Rodman, *Conversations with Artists* (New York: Devin-Adair, 1957), 93–94.

4. Quoted in Deborah Wye, *Louise Bourgeois* (New York: Museum of Modern Art, 1982), 25.

5. Quoted in Richard Francis, *Jasper Johns* (New York: Abbeville, 1984), 21.

6. Quoted in Christine Lindey, *Superrealist Painting and Sculpture* (London: Orbis, 1980), 130.

7. Quoted in Donald Hall, *Corporal Politics* (Cambridge: MIT List Visual Arts Center, 1993), 46.

8. Jaune Quick-to-See Smith and Harmony Hammond, *Women of Sweetgrass: Cedar and Sage* (New York: American Indian Center, 1984), 97.

9. Quoted in Mary Jane Jacob, *Magdalena Abakanowicz* (New York: Abbeville, 1982), 94.

10. Quoted in "Vietnam Memorial: America Remembers," *National Geographic* 167, no. 5 (May 1985): 557.

11. Quoted in Nancy Holt, ed., *The Writings of Robert Smithson* (New York: New York University Press, 1975), 111.

12. Quoted in "Joseph Kosuth: Art as Idea as Idea," in Jeanne Siegel, ed., *Artwords: Discourse on the 60s and 70s* (Ann Arbor, Mich.: UMI Research Press, 1985), 221, 225.

CHAPTER 19

1. Bernal Díaz del Castillo, *The Discovery and Conquest of Mexico.* Translated by A. P. Maudslay (New York: Farrar, Straus, Giroux, 1956), 218–219.

Glossary

A

à la grecque French, "in Greek style."

abacus The uppermost portion of the *capital* of a *column*, usually a thin slab.

abbess See *abbey*.

abbey A religious community under the direction of an abbot (for monks) or an abbess (for nuns).

abbot See *abbey*.

abhaya See *mudra*.

abrasion The rubbing or grinding of stone or another material to produce a smooth surface.

abstract Nonrepresentational; *forms* and *colors* arranged without reference to the depiction of an object.

Abstract Expressionism The first major American avant-garde movement, Abstract Expressionism emerged in New York City in the 1940s. The artists produced *abstract* paintings that expressed their state of mind and that they hoped would strike emotional chords in viewers. The movement developed along two lines: *gestural abstraction* and *chromatic abstraction*.

acropolis Greek, "high city." In ancient Greece, usually the site of the city's most important temple(s).

action painting Also called *gestural abstraction*. The kind of *Abstract Expressionism* practiced by Jackson Pollock, in which the emphasis is on the creative process, the artist's gesture in making art. Pollock poured liquid paint in linear webs on his canvases, which he laid out on the floor, thereby physically surrounding himself in the painting during its creation.

additive light Natural light, or sunlight, the sum of all the wavelengths of the visible *spectrum*. See also *subtractive light*.

additive sculpture A kind of sculpture technique in which materials (for example, clay) are built up or "added" to create form.

adobe The clay used to make a kind of sun-dried mud brick of the same name; also, a building made of adobe.

aerial perspective See *perspective*.

airbrush A tool that uses compressed air to spray paint onto a surface.

aisle The portion of a *basilica* flanking the *nave* and separated from it by a row of *columns* or *piers*.

ala (pl. alae) One pair of rectangular recesses at the back of the *atrium* of a Roman house.

album leaf A painting on a single sheet of paper for a collection stored in an album.

alchemy The medieval study of seemingly magical changes, especially chemical changes.

altarpiece A panel, or group of panels, painted or sculpted, situated above and behind an altar.

alternate-support system In church architecture, the use of alternating wall supports in the *nave*, usually *piers* and *columns* or *compound piers* of alternating form.

amalaka In Hindu temple design, the large flat disk with ribbed edges surmounting the beehive-shaped tower.

Amazonomachy In Greek mythology, the battle between the Greeks and Amazons.

ambulatory A covered walkway, outdoors (as in a church *cloister*) or indoors; especially the passageway around the *apse* and the *choir* of a church.

amphiprostyle A *classical* temple *plan* in which the *columns* are placed across both the front and back but not along the sides.

amphitheater Greek, "double theater." A Roman building type resembling two Greek theaters put together. The Roman amphitheater featured a continuous elliptical *cavea* around a central *arena*.

amphora An ancient Greek two-handled jar used for general storage purposes, usually to hold wine or oil.

amulet An object worn to ward off evil or to aid the wearer.

Analytic Cubism The first phase of *Cubism*, developed jointly by Pablo Picasso and Georges Braque, in which the artists analyzed form from every possible vantage point to combine the various views into one pictorial whole.

anamorphic image A distorted image that must be viewed by some special means (such as a mirror) to be recognized.

ancien régime French, "old order." The term used to describe the political, social, and religious order in France before the 1789 revolution.

antae The molded projecting ends of the walls forming the *pronaos* or *opisthodomos* of an ancient Greek temple.

apadana The great audience hall in ancient Persian palaces.

apostle Greek, "messenger." One of the 12 disciples of Jesus.

apse (adj. apsidal) A recess, usually semicircular, in the wall of a building, commonly found at the east end of a church.

arcade A series of *arches* supported by *piers* or *columns*.

arch A curved structural member that spans an opening and is generally composed of wedge-shaped blocks *(voussoirs)* that transmit the downward pressure laterally. See also *thrust*.

Archaic The artistic style of 600–480 BCE in Greece, characterized in part by the use of the *composite view* for painted and *relief* figures and of Egyptian stances for statues.

Archaic smile The smile that appears on all *Archaic* Greek statues from about 570 to 480 BCE. The smile is the Archaic sculptor's way of indicating that the person portrayed is alive.

architrave The *lintel* or lowest division of the *entablature*. In *classical* architecture, the epistyle.

archivolt The continuous molding framing an *arch*. In *Romanesque* and *Gothic* architecture, one of the series of concentric bands framing the *tympanum*.

arcuated *Arch*-shaped.

arena In a Roman *amphitheater*, the central area where bloody gladiatorial combats, wild animal hunts, and other boisterous events took place.

armature The crossed, or diagonal, *arches* that form the skeletal framework of a *Gothic rib vault*. In sculpture, the framework for a clay form.

arriccio In *fresco* painting, the first layer of rough lime plaster applied to the wall.

asceticism Self-discipline and self-denial.

ashlar masonry Carefully cut and regularly shaped blocks of stone used in construction, fitted together without mortar.

atlantid A male figure that functions as a supporting *column*. See also *caryatid*.

atlatl Spear-thrower, the typical weapon of the Toltecs of ancient Mexico.

atmospheric perspective See *perspective*.

atrium The central reception room of a Roman house that is partly open to the sky. Also, the open *colonnaded* court in front of and attached to a Christian *basilica*.

attic The uppermost story of a building, *triumphal arch*, or city gate.

attribute (n.) The distinctive identifying aspect of a person, for example, an object held, an associated animal, or a mark on the body. (v.) To make an *attribution*.

attribution Assignment of a work to a maker or makers.

automatism In painting, the process of yielding oneself to instinctive motions of the hands after establishing a set of conditions (such as size of paper or medium) within which a work is to be produced.

avant-garde French, "advance guard" (in a platoon). Late-19th- and 20th-century artists who emphasized innovation and challenged established convention in their work. Also used as an adjective.

avatar A manifestation of a deity incarnated in some visible form in which the deity performs a sacred function on earth.

axial plan See *plan*.

B

baldacchino A canopy on *columns*, frequently built over an altar. The term derives from *baldacco*.

baldacco Italian, "silk from Baghdad." See *baldacchino*.

baptism The Christian bathing ceremony in which an infant or a convert becomes a member of the Christian community.

baptistery In Christian architecture, the building used for *baptism*, usually situated next to a church.

Baroque The traditional blanket designation for European art from 1600 to 1750. The stylistic term *Baroque*, which describes art that features dramatic theatricality and elaborate ornamentation in contrast to the simplicity and orderly rationality of *Renaissance* art, is most appropriately applied to Italian art of this period. The term derives from *barroco*.

barrel vault See *vault*.

barroco Portuguese, "irregularly shaped pearl." See *Baroque*.

bar tracery See *tracery*.

base In ancient Greek architecture, the molded projecting lowest part of *Ionic* and *Corinthian* columns. (*Doric* columns do not have bases.)

basilica In Roman architecture, a civic building for legal and other civic proceedings, rectangular in plan with an entrance usually on a long side. In Christian architecture, a church somewhat resembling the Roman basilica, usually entered from one end and with an *apse* at the other.

bas-relief See *relief*.

Bauhaus A *school* of architecture in Germany in the 1920s under the direction of Walter Gropius, who emphasized the unity of art, architecture, and design.

bay The space between two columns in a building, or one unit in the *nave arcade* of a church; also, the passageway in an arcuated gate.

beam A horizontal structural member that carries the load of the superstructure of a building; a timber *lintel*.

Beaux-Arts An architectural *style* of the late 19th and early 20th centuries in France. Based on ideas taught at the École des Beaux-Arts in Paris, the Beaux-Arts style incorporated classical principles, such as symmetry in design, and featured extensive exterior ornamentation.

belvedere Italian, "beautiful view." A residence on a hill or any structure with a view of a *landscape* or seascape.

ben-ben A pyramidal stone; a fetish of the Egyptian god Re.

benday dots Named after the newspaper printer Benjamin Day, the benday-dot system involves the modulation of *colors* through the placement and size of colored dots.

bestiary A collection of illustrations of real and imaginary animals.

bhakti In Buddhist thought, the adoration of a personalized deity (*bodhisattva*) as a means of achieving unity with it; love felt by the devotee for the deity. In Hinduism, the devout, selfless direction of all tasks and activities of life to the service of one god.

bhumisparsha See *mudra*.

bilateral symmetry Having the same *forms* on either side of a central axis.

Biomorphic Surrealism See *Surrealism*.

black-figure painting In early Greek pottery, the silhouetting of dark figures against a light background of natural, reddish clay, with linear details *incised* through the silhouettes.

blind arcade An *arcade* having no actual openings, applied as decoration to a wall surface.

bocio A Fon (Republic of Benin) empowerment figure.

bodhisattva In Buddhist thought, one of the host of divinities provided to the Buddha to help him save humanity. A potential Buddha. See also *bhakti*.

Book of Hours A Christian religious book for private devotion containing prayers to be read at specified times of the day.

boss A circular knob.

breviary A Christian religious book of selected daily prayers and Psalms.

Buddha triad A three-figure group with a central Buddha flanked on each side by a *bodhisattva*.

buon fresco See *fresco*.

burgher A middle-class citizen.

burin A pointed tool used for *engraving* or *incising*.

buttress An exterior masonry structure that opposes the lateral *thrust* of an *arch* or a *vault*. A pier buttress is a solid mass of masonry. A flying buttress consists typically of an inclined member carried on an arch or a series of arches and a solid buttress to which it transmits lateral *thrust*.

byobu Japanese painted folding screens.

C

caduceus In ancient Greek mythology, a magical rod entwined with serpents, the attribute of Hermes (Roman, Mercury), the messenger of the gods.

caementa Latin, "small stones," one of the ingredients in Roman *concrete*.

caldarium The hot-bath section of a Roman bathing establishment.

caliph(s) Islamic rulers, regarded as successors of Muhammad.

calligrapher One who practices *calligraphy*.

calligraphy Greek, "beautiful writing." Handwriting or penmanship, especially elegant writing as a decorative art.

calotype A photographic process in which a positive image is made by shining light through a negative image onto a sheet of sensitized paper.

came A lead strip in a *stained-glass* window that joins separate pieces of colored glass.

camera lucida Latin, "lighted room." A device in which a small lens projects the image of an object downward onto a sheet of paper.

camera obscura Latin, "dark room." An ancestor of the modern camera in which a tiny pinhole, acting as a lens, projects an image on a screen, the wall of a room, or the ground-glass wall of a box; used by artists in the 17th, 18th, and early 19th centuries as an aid in drawing from nature.

campanile A bell tower of a church, usually, but not always, freestanding.

canon A rule, for example, of proportion. The ancient Greeks considered beauty to be a matter of "correct" proportion and sought a canon of proportion, both for the human figure and for buildings. The fifth-century BCE sculptor Polykleitos wrote the *Canon*, a treatise incorporating his formula for the perfectly proportioned statue.

capital The uppermost member of a *column*, serving as a transition from the *shaft* to the *lintel*. In *classical* architecture, the form of the capital varies with the *order*.

Capitolium An ancient Roman temple dedicated to the gods Jupiter, Juno, and Minerva.

capriccio Italian, "originality." One of several terms used in Italian *Renaissance* literature to praise the originality and talent of artists.

Carolingian (adj.) Pertaining to the empire of Charlemagne (Latin, Carolus Magnus) and his successors.

carpet page In early medieval manuscripts, a decorative page resembling a textile.

cartoon In painting, a full-size preliminary drawing from which a painting is made.

carving A *technique* of sculpture in which the artist cuts away material (for example, from a stone block) in order to create a *statue* or a *relief*.

caryatid A female figure that functions as a supporting *column*. See also *atlantid*.

casting A *technique* of sculpture in which the artist places a fluid substance, such as bronze or plaster, in a *mold*.

catacombs Subterranean networks of rock-cut galleries and chambers designed as cemeteries for the burial of the dead.

cathedral A bishop's church. The word derives from *cathedra*, referring to the bishop's seat.

cavea Latin, "hollow place or cavity." The seating area in ancient Greek and Roman theaters and *amphitheaters*.

cella The chamber at the center of an ancient temple; in a *classical* temple, the room (Greek, *naos*) in which the cult statue usually stood.

centaur In ancient Greek mythology, a creature with the front or top half of a human and the back or bottom half of a horse.

centauromachy In ancient Greek mythology, the battle between the Greeks and *centaurs*.

central plan See *plan*.

chacmool A Mesoamerican statuary type depicting a fallen warrior on his back with a receptacle on his chest for sacrificial offerings.

chakra The Buddha's wheel, set in motion at Sarnath.

chakravartin In South Asia, the ideal king, the Universal Lord who ruled through goodness.

Chan See *Zen*.

chaplet A metal pin used in hollow-casting to connect the *investment* with the clay core.

character In Chinese writing, a sign that records the meaning instead of the sound of spoken words.

chartreuse A Carthusian *monastery*.

château (pl. **châteaux**) French, "castle." A luxurious country residence for French royalty, developed from medieval castles.

chatra See *yasti*.

chiaroscuro In drawing or painting, the treatment and use of light and dark, especially the gradations of light that produce the effect of *modeling*.

chisel A tool with a straight blade at one end for cutting and shaping stone or wood.

chiton An ancient Greek linen tunic, the essential (and often only) garment of both men and women, the other being the *himation*.

choir The space reserved for the clergy and singers in the church, usually east of the *transept* but, in some instances, extending into the *nave*.

Christogram The three initial letters (chi-rho-iota) of Christ's name in Greek, which came to serve as a monogram for Christ.

chromatic abstraction A kind of *Abstract Expressionism* that focuses on the emotional resonance of color, as exemplified by the work of Mark Rothko.

chronology In art history, the dating of art objects and buildings.

chryselephantine Fashioned of gold and ivory.

circumambulation In Buddhist worship, walking around the *stupa* in a clockwise direction.

cire perdue See *lost-wax process*.

city-state An independent, self-governing city.

Classical The art and culture of ancient Greece between 480 and 323 BCE. Lower-case *classical* refers more generally to Greco-Roman art and culture.

clerestory The *fenestrated* part of a building that rises above the roofs of the other parts. The oldest known clerestories are Egyptian. In Roman *basilicas* and medieval churches, clerestories are the windows that form the *nave*'s uppermost level below the timber ceiling or the *vaults*.

cloison French, "partition." A cell made of metal wire or a narrow metal strip soldered edge-up to a metal base to hold *enamel*, semiprecious stones, pieces of colored glass, or glass paste fired to resemble sparkling jewels.

cloisonné A decorative metalwork technique employing *cloisons*; also, decorative brickwork in later Byzantine architecture.

cloister A *monastery* courtyard, usually with covered walks or *ambulatories* along its sides.

cluster pier See *compound pier*.

codex (pl. **codices**) Separate pages of *vellum* or *parchment* bound together at one side; the predecessor of the modern book. The codex superseded the *rotulus*.

coffer A sunken panel, often ornamental, in a *vault* or a ceiling.

collage A composition made by combining on a flat surface various materials, such as newspaper, wallpaper, printed text and illustrations, photographs, and cloth.

colonnade A series or row of *columns*, usually spanned by *lintels*.

colonnette A thin *column*.

colophon An inscription, usually on the last page, providing information regarding a book's manufacture. In Chinese painting, written texts on attached pieces of paper or silk.

color The value, or tonality, of a color is the degree of its lightness or darkness. The intensity, or saturation, of a color is its purity, its brightness or dullness. See also *primary*, *secondary*, and *complementary colors*.

color-field painting A variant of *Post-Painterly Abstraction* in which artists seek to reduce painting to its physical essence by pouring diluted paint onto unprimed canvas, allowing the pigment to soak into the fabric, as exemplified by the work of Helen Frankenthaler.

colorito Italian, "colored" or "painted." A term used to describe the application of paint. Characteristic of the work of 16th-century Venetian artists who emphasized the application of paint as an important element of the creative process. Central Italian artists, in contrast, largely emphasized *disegno*—the careful design preparation based on preliminary drawing.

colossal order An architectural design in which the *columns* or *pilasters* are two or more stories tall. Also called a giant order.

column A vertical, weight-carrying architectural member, circular in cross-*section* and consisting of a *base* (sometimes omitted), a *shaft*, and a *capital*.

combines The name American artist Robert Rauschenberg gave to his works combining painted passages and sculptural elements.

complementary colors Those pairs of *colors*, such as red and green, that together embrace the entire spectrum. The complement of one of the three *primary colors* is a mixture of the other two.

compose See *composition*.

composite view A convention of representation in which part of a figure is shown in profile and another part of the same figure is shown frontally; also called twisted perspective.

composition The way in which an artist organizes *forms* in an artwork, either by placing shapes on a flat surface or arranging forms in space.

compound pier A *pier* with a group, or cluster, of attached *shafts*, or *responds*, especially characteristic of *Gothic* architecture.

Conceptual Art An American *avant-garde* art movement of the 1960s holding that the "artfulness" of art lay in the artist's idea rather than its final expression.

conceptual representation The representation of the fundamental distinguishing properties of a person or object, not the way a figure or object appears in space at a specific moment. See *composite view*.

concrete A building material invented by the Romans and consisting of various proportions of lime mortar, volcanic sand, water, and small stones.

condottiere (pl. **condottieri**) An Italian mercenary general.

congregational mosque A city's main *mosque*, designed to accommodate the entire Muslim population for the Friday noon prayer. Also called the great mosque or Friday mosque.

connoisseur An expert in *attributing* artworks to one artist rather than another. More generally, an expert on artistic *style*.

contour line In art, a continuous line defining the outer shape of an object.

contrapposto The disposition of the human figure in which one part is turned in opposition to another part (usually hips and legs one way, shoulders and chest another), creating a counterpositioning of the body about its central axis. Sometimes called "weight shift" because the weight of the body tends to be thrown to one foot, creating tension on one side and relaxation on the other.

corbel A projecting wall member used as a support for some element in the superstructure. Also, *courses* of stone or brick in which each course projects beyond the one beneath it. Two such walls, meeting at the topmost course, create a corbeled arch or corbeled *vault*.

corbeled arch See *corbel*.

corbeled vault A *vault* formed by the piling of stone blocks in horizontal *courses*, cantilevered inward until the two walls meet in an *arch*.

Corinthian capital A more ornate form than *Doric* or *Ionic*; it consists of a double row of acanthus leaves from which tendrils and flowers grow, wrapped around a bell-shaped *echinus*. Although this *capital* form is often cited as the distinguishing feature of the Corinthian *order*, no such order exists, in strict terms, but only this type of capital used in the *Ionic* order.

cornice The projecting, crowning member of the *entablature* framing the *pediment*; also, any crowning projection.

course In masonry construction, a horizontal row of stone blocks.

cross-hatching See *hatching*.

crossing The space in a *cruciform* church formed by the intersection of the *nave* and the *transept*.

crossing square The area in a church formed by the intersection (*crossing*) of a *nave* and a *transept* of equal width, often used as a standard *module* of interior proportion.

crossing tower The tower over the *crossing* of a church.

cross vault See *vault*.

cruciform Cross-shaped.

Crusades In medieval Europe, armed pilgrimages aimed at recapturing the Holy Land from the Muslims.

cubiculum (pl. **cubicula**) A small cubicle or bedroom that opened onto the *atrium* of a Roman house. Also, a chamber in an Early Christian *catacomb* that served as a mortuary chapel.

Cubism An early-20th-century art movement that rejected *naturalistic* depictions, preferring *compositions* of shapes and forms abstracted from the conventionally perceived world. See also *Analytic Cubism* and *Synthetic Cubism*.

cult statue The statue of the deity that stood in the *cella* of an ancient temple.

cuneiform Latin, "wedge-shaped." A system of writing used in ancient Mesopotamia, in which wedge-shaped characters were produced by *incising* a soft clay tablet, which was then baked or otherwise allowed to harden.

cutaway An architectural drawing that combines an exterior view with an interior view of part of a building.

Cycladic Pertaining to the Cycladic islands of the Aegean Sea, except Crete; the prehistoric art of the Cyclades during the third millennium BCE.

Cyclopean masonry A method of stone construction, named after the mythical *Cyclopes*, using massive, irregular blocks without mortar, characteristic of the Bronze Age fortifications of Tiryns and other Mycenaean sites.

Cyclops (pl. **Cyclopes**) A mythical Greek one-eyed giant.

D

Dada An early-20th-century art movement prompted by a revulsion against the horror of World War I. Dada embraced political anarchy, the irrational, and the intuitive. A disdain for convention, often enlivened by humor or whimsy, is characteristic of the art the Dadaists produced.

Daedalic The Greek sculptural *style* of the seventh century BCE named after the legendary Daedalus.

daguerreotype A photograph made by an early method on a plate of chemically treated metal; developed by L.-J.-M. Daguerre.

daimyo Local lords who controlled small regions and owed obeisance to the *shogun* in the Japanese *shogunate* system.

damnatio memoriae The Roman decree condemning those who ran afoul of the Senate. Those who suffered damnatio memoriae had their memorials demolished and their names erased from public inscriptions.

deconstruction An analytical strategy developed in the late 20th century according to which all cultural "constructs" (art, architecture, literature) are "texts." People can read these texts in a variety of ways, but they cannot arrive at fixed or uniform meanings. Any interpretation can be valid, and readings differ from time to time, place to place, and person to person. For those employing this approach, deconstruction means destabilizing established meanings and interpretations while encouraging subjectivity and individual differences.

Deconstructivism An architectural *style* using *deconstruction* as an analytical strategy. Deconstructivist architects attempt to disorient the observer by disrupting the conventional categories of architecture. The haphazard presentation of volumes, masses, planes, lighting, and so forth challenges the viewer's assumptions about *form* as it relates to function.

demos Greek, "the people," from which the word *democracy* is derived.

Der Blaue Reiter German, "the blue rider." An early-20th-century German *Expressionist* art movement founded by Vassily Kandinsky and Franz Marc. The artists selected the whimsical name because of their mutual interest in the color blue and in horses.

De Stijl Dutch, "the style." An early-20th-century art movement (and magazine), founded by Piet Mondrian and Theo van Doesburg, whose members promoted utopian ideals and developed a simplified geometric style.

dharma In Buddhism, moral law based on the Buddha's teaching.

dharmachakra See *mudra*.

dhyana See *mudra*.

diagonal rib See *rib*.

Die Brücke German, "the bridge." An early-20th-century German *Expressionist* art movement under the leadership of Ernst Ludwig Kirchner. The group thought of itself as the bridge between the old age and the new.

diptych A two-paneled painting or *altarpiece*; also, an ancient Roman, Early Christian, or Byzantine hinged writing tablet, often of ivory and carved on the external sides.

disegno Italian, "drawing" and "design." *Renaissance* artists considered drawing to be the external physical manifestation *(disegno esterno)* of an internal intellectual idea of design *(disegno interno)*.

di sotto in sù Italian, "from below upward." A *perspectival* view seen from below.

disputatio Latin, "logical argument." The philosophical methodology used in *Scholasticism*.

divisionism See *pointillism*.

documentary evidence In art history, the examination of written sources in order to determine the date of an artwork, the circumstances of its creation, or the identity of the artist(s) who made it.

doge Duke; a ruler of the Republic of Venice, Italy.

dome A hemispherical *vault*; theoretically, an *arch* rotated on its vertical axis. In Mycenaean architecture, domes are beehive-shaped.

domus A Roman private house.

donor portrait A portrait of the individual(s) who commissioned (donated) a religious work, for example, an *altarpiece*, as evidence of devotion.

Doric One of the two systems (or *orders*) invented in ancient Greece for articulating the three units of the elevation of a *classical* building—the platform, the *colonnade*, and the superstructure *(entablature)*. The Doric order is characterized by, among other features, *capitals* with funnel-shaped *echinuses*, *columns* without *bases*, and a *frieze* of *triglyphs* and *metopes*. See also *Ionic*.

dressed masonry Stone blocks shaped to the exact dimensions required, with smooth faces for a perfect fit.

drum The cylindrical wall that supports a *dome*.

dry fresco See *fresco*.

drypoint An *engraving* in which the design, instead of being cut into the plate with a *burin*, is scratched into the surface with a hard steel "pencil." See also *engraving, etching, intaglio*.

E

earthworks See *Environmental Art*.

eaves The lower part of a roof that overhangs the wall.

echinus The convex element of a *capital* directly below the *abacus*.

écorché The representation of a nude body as if without skin.

edition A set of impressions taken from a single print surface.

effigy mounds Ceremonial mounds built in the shape of animals or birds by native North American peoples.

elevation In architecture, a head-on view of an external or internal wall, showing its features and often other elements that would be visible beyond or before the wall.

embroidery The technique of sewing threads onto a finished ground to form contrasting designs.

empiricism The search for knowledge based on observation and direct experience.

enamel A decorative coating, usually colored, fused onto the surface of metal, glass, or ceramics.

encaustic A painting *technique* in which pigment is mixed with wax, with the mixture applied to the surface while hot.

engaged column A half-round *column* attached to a wall. See also *pilaster*.

engraving The process of *incising* a design in hard material, often a metal plate (usually copper); also, the print or impression made from such a plate.

Enlightenment The Western philosophy based on empirical evidence that dominated the 18th century. The Enlightenment was a new way of thinking critically about the world and about humankind, independently of religion, myth, or tradition.

entablature The part of a building above the *columns* and below the roof. The entablature has three parts: *architrave, frieze,* and *pediment*.

entasis The convex profile (an apparent swelling) in the *shaft* of a *column*.

Environmental Art An American art form that emerged in the 1960s. Often using the land itself as their material, Environmental artists construct monuments of great scale and minimal form. Permanent or impermanent, these works transform some section of the environment, calling attention both to the land itself and to the hand of the artist. Sometimes referred to as earthworks.

epistyle See *architrave*.

etching A kind of *engraving* in which the design is *incised* in a layer of wax or varnish on a metal plate. The parts of the plate left exposed are then etched (slightly eaten away) by the acid in which the plate is immersed after incising. See also *drypoint, engraving, intaglio*.

Eucharist In Christianity, the partaking of the bread and wine, which believers hold to be either Christ himself or symbolic of him.

evangelist One of the four authors (Matthew, Mark, Luke, John) of the New Testament *Gospels*.

exedra Recessed area, usually semicircular.

exemplum virtutis Latin, "example or model of virtue."

Expressionism (adj. **Expressionist**) Twentieth-century art that is the result of the artist's unique inner or personal vision and that often has an emotional dimension. Expressionism contrasts with art focused on visually describing the empirical world.

F

facade Usually, the front of a building; also, the other sides when they are emphasized architecturally.

faience A low-fired opaque glasslike silicate.

fantasia Italian, "imagination." One of several terms used in Italian *Renaissance* literature to praise the originality and talent of artists.

fan vault See *vault*.

fasces A bundle of rods with an ax attached, an emblem of authority in ancient Rome.

fasciae In the *Ionic order*, the three horizontal bands that make up the *architrave*.

fauces Latin, "jaws." In a Roman house, the narrow foyer leading to the *atrium*.

Fauves French, "wild beasts." See *Fauvism*.

Fauvism An early-20th-century art movement led by Henri Matisse. For the *Fauves*, color became the formal element most responsible for pictorial coherence and the primary conveyor of meaning.

fenestrated Having windows.

fenestration The arrangement of the windows of a building.

fête galante French, "amorous festival." A type of *Rococo* painting depicting the outdoor amusements of upper-class French society.

fin-de-siècle French, "end of the century." A period in Western cultural history from the end of the 19th century until just before World War I, when decadence and indulgence masked anxiety about an uncertain future.

findspot Place where an artifact was found, or *provenance*.

finial A crowning ornament.

First Style mural The earliest style of Roman *mural* painting, in which the aim of the artist was to imitate, using painted stucco *relief*, the appearance of costly marble panels.

flashing In making *stained-glass* windows, fusing one layer of colored glass to another to produce a greater range of *colors*.

fleur-de-lis A three-petaled iris flower; the royal flower of France.

florin The denomination of gold coin of *Renaissance* Florence that became an international currency for trade.

flute or **fluting** Vertical channeling, roughly semicircular in cross-*section* and used principally on *columns* and *pilasters*.

flying buttress See *buttress*.

folio A page of a manuscript or book.

fons vitae Latin, "fountain of life." A symbolic fountain of everlasting life.

foreshortening The use of *perspective* to represent in art the apparent visual contraction of an object that extends back in space at an angle to the perpendicular plane of sight.

form In art, an object's shape and structure, either in two dimensions (for example, a figure painted on a surface) or in three dimensions (such as a *statue*).

formal analysis The visual analysis of artistic *form*.

formalism Strict adherence to, or dependence on, stylized shapes and methods of *composition*. An emphasis on an artwork's visual elements rather than its subject.

forum The public square of an ancient Roman city.

Fourth Style mural In Roman *mural* painting, the Fourth Style marks a return to architectural *illusionism*, but the architectural vistas of the Fourth Style are irrational fantasies.

freestanding sculpture A work of sculpture that the viewer can walk around.

fresco Painting on lime plaster, either dry (dry fresco, or fresco secco) or wet (true, or buon, fresco). In the latter method, the pigments are mixed with water and become chemically bound to the freshly laid lime plaster. Also, a painting executed in either method.

fresco secco See *fresco*.

Friday mosque See *congregational mosque*.

frieze The part of the *entablature* between the *architrave* and the *cornice*; also, any sculptured or painted band in a building. See *register*.

frigidarium The cold-bath section of a Roman bathing establishment.

Futurism An early-20th-century Italian art movement that championed war as a cleansing agent and that celebrated the speed and dynamism of modern technology.

G

garbha griha Hindi, "womb chamber." In Hindu temples, the *cella*, the holy inner sanctum, for the cult image or *symbol*.

genre A *style* or category of art; also, a kind of painting that realistically depicts scenes from everyday life.

Geometric The *style* of Greek art during the ninth and eighth centuries BCE, characterized by *abstract* geometric ornamentation and schematic figures.

gestural abstraction Also known as *action painting*. A kind of *abstract* painting in which the gesture, or act of painting, is seen as the subject of art. Its most renowned proponent was Jackson Pollock. See also *Abstract Expressionism*.

giant order See *colossal order*.

gigantomachy In ancient Greek mythology, the battle between gods and giants.

giornata (pl. **giornate**) Italian, "day." The section of plaster that a *fresco* painter expects to complete in one session.

gladiator (adj. **gladiatorial**) An ancient Roman professional fighter, usually a slave, who competed in an *amphitheater*.

glaze A vitreous coating applied to pottery to seal and decorate the surface. It may be colored, transparent, or opaque, and glossy or *matte*. In *oil painting*, a thin, transparent, or semitransparent layer applied over a *color* to alter it slightly.

glazed bricks Bricks painted and then kiln-fired to fuse the *color* with the baked clay.

glazier A glassworker.

gopuras The massive, ornamented entrance gateway towers of South Indian temple compounds.

gorgon In ancient Greek mythology, a hideous female demon with snake hair. Medusa, the most famous gorgon, was capable of turning anyone who gazed at her into stone.

Gospels The four New Testament books that relate the life and teachings of Jesus.

Gothic Originally a derogatory term named after the Goths, used to describe the history, culture, and art of western Europe in the 12th to 14th centuries.

Grand Manner portraiture A type of 18th-century portrait painting designed to communicate a person's grace and class through certain standardized conventions, such as the large scale of the figure relative to the canvas, the controlled pose, the landscape setting, and the low *horizon line*.

graver A sharp metal instrument for *incising* metal or stone or other materials.

great mosque See *congregational mosque*.

Greek cross A cross with four arms of equal length.

grisaille A monochrome painting done mainly in neutral grays to simulate sculpture.

groin The edge formed by the intersection of two *vaults*.

groin vault See *vault*.

ground line In paintings and *reliefs*, a painted or carved baseline on which figures appear to stand.

guang An ancient Chinese covered vessel, often in animal form, holding wine, water, grain, or meat for sacrificial rites.

guild An association of merchants, craftspersons, or scholars in medieval and *Renaissance* Europe.

H

haboku In Japanese art, a loose and rapidly executed painting *style* in which the ink seems to have been applied by flinging or splashing it onto the paper.

handscroll In Asian art, a horizontal painted scroll that is unrolled right to left, section by section, and often used to present illustrated religious texts or *landscapes*.

hanging scroll In Asian art, a vertical scroll hung on a wall with pictures mounted or painted directly on it.

haniwa Sculpted fired pottery cylinders, modeled in human, animal, or other forms and placed on Japanese *tumuli* of the Kofun period.

hard-edge painting A variant of *Post-Painterly Abstraction* that rigidly excludes all reference to gesture, and incorporates smooth knife-edge geometric forms to express the notion that painting should be reduced to its visual components.

harmika In Buddhist architecture, a stone fence or railing that encloses an area surmounting the dome of a *stupa* that represents one of the Buddhist heavens; from the center arises the *yasti*.

hatching A series of closely spaced drawn or *engraved* parallel lines. Cross-hatching employs sets of lines placed at right angles.

Hellenes (adj. **Hellenic**) The name the ancient Greeks called themselves as the people of Hellas.

Hellenistic The term given to the art and culture of the roughly three centuries between the death of Alexander the Great in 323 BCE and the death of Queen Cleopatra in 30 BCE, when Egypt became a Roman province.

henge An arrangement of *megalithic* stones in a circle, often surrounded by a ditch.

Hiberno-Saxon An art *style* that flourished in the *monasteries* of the British Isles in the early Middle Ages.

hierarchy of scale An artistic convention in which greater size indicates greater importance.

high relief See *relief*.

Hijra The flight of Muhammad from Mecca to Medina in 622, the year from which Islam dates its beginnings.

himation An ancient Greek woolen mantle worn by men and women over the *chiton* and draped in various ways.

hiragana A sound-based writing system developed in Japan from Chinese characters; it came to be the primary script for Japanese court poetry.

historiated Ornamented with representations, such as plants, animals, or human figures, that have a narrative—as distinct from a purely decorative—function.

horizon line See *perspective*.

hue The name of a *color*. See *primary colors, secondary colors,* and *complementary colors.*

humanism In the *Renaissance*, an emphasis on education and on expanding knowledge (especially of *classical* antiquity), the exploration of individual potential and a desire to excel, and a commitment to civic responsibility and moral duty.

hydria An ancient Greek three-handled water pitcher.

hypostyle hall A hall with a roof supported by *columns.*

I

icon A portrait or image; especially in Byzantine churches, a panel with a painting of sacred personages that are objects of veneration. In the visual arts, a painting, a piece of sculpture, or even a building regarded as an object of veneration.

iconoclasm The destruction of images. In Byzantium, the period from 726 to 843 when there was an imperial ban on images. The destroyers of images were known as iconoclasts. Those who opposed such a ban were known as iconophiles.

iconoclast See *iconoclasm.*

iconography Greek, the "writing of images." The term refers both to the content, or subject, of an artwork and to the study of content in art. It also includes the study of the symbolic, often religious, meaning of objects, persons, or events depicted in works of art.

iconophile See *iconoclasm.*

ikegobo A Benin royal shrine.

illuminated manuscript A luxurious handmade book with painted illustrations and decorations.

illusionism (adj. **illusionistic**) The representation of the three-dimensional world on a two-dimensional surface in a manner that creates the illusion that the person, object, or place represented is three-dimensional. See also *perspective.*

imagines (pl. n.) Latin, "images." In ancient Rome, wax portraits of ancestors.

imam In Islam, the leader of collective worship.

imperator Latin, "commander in chief," from which the word "emperor" is derived.

impluvium In a Roman house, the basin located in the *atrium* that collected rainwater.

Impressionism A late-19th-century art movement that sought to capture a fleeting moment, thereby conveying the elusiveness and impermanence of images and conditions.

in antis In ancient Greek architecture, between the *antae.*

incise To cut into a surface with a sharp instrument; also, a method of decoration, especially on metal and pottery.

incrustation Wall decoration consisting of bright panels of different *colors.*

incubus A demon believed in medieval times to prey, often sexually, on sleeping women.

indulgence A pardon for a sin committed.

ingegno Italian, "innate talent." One of several terms used in Italian *Renaissance* literature to praise the originality and talent of artists.

installation An artwork that creates an artistic environment in a room or gallery.

intaglio A graphic technique in which the design is *incised*, or scratched, on a metal plate, either manually *(engraving, drypoint)* or chemically *(etching)*. The incised lines of the design take the ink, making this the reverse of the *woodcut* technique.

internal evidence In art history, the examination of what an artwork represents (people, clothing, hairstyles, etc.) in order to determine its date. Also, the examination of the *style* of an artwork to identify the artist who created it.

International Style A *style* of 14th- and 15th-century painting begun by Simone Martini, who adapted the French *Gothic* manner to Sienese art fused with influences from the North. This style appealed to the aristocracy because of its brilliant *color,* lavish cos-tume, intricate ornamentation, and themes involving splendid processions of knights and ladies. Also, a style of 20th-century architecture associated with Le Corbusier, whose elegance of design came to influence the look of modern office buildings and skyscrapers.

intonaco In *fresco* painting, the last layer of smooth lime plaster applied to the wall; the painting layer.

invenzione Italian, "invention." One of several terms used in Italian *Renaissance* literature to praise the originality and talent of artists.

investment In hollow-casting, the final clay *mold* applied to the exterior of the wax model.

Ionic One of the two systems (or *orders*) invented in ancient Greece for articulating the three units of the elevation of a *classical* building: the platform, the *colonnade*, and the superstructure *(entablature)*. The Ionic order is characterized by, among other features, *volutes, capitals, columns* with *bases*, and an uninterrupted *frieze.*

iron-wire lines In ancient Chinese painting, thin brush lines suggesting tensile strength.

iwan In Islamic architecture, a *vaulted* rectangular recess opening onto a courtyard.

J

jambs In architecture, the side posts of a doorway.

jataka Tales of the past lives of the Buddha. See also *sutra.*

jomon Japanese, "cord markings." A type of Japanese ceramic technique characterized by ropelike markings.

K

ka In ancient Egypt, the immortal human life force.

Kaaba Arabic, "cube." A small cubical building in Mecca, the Islamic world's symbolic center.

kalos Greek, "beautiful."

karma In Vedic religions (see *Veda*), the ethical consequences of a person's life, which determine his or her fate.

katsina An art form of Native Americans of the Southwest, the katsina doll represents benevolent supernatural spirits (katsinas) living in mountains and water sources.

keystone See *voussoir.*

khipu Andean record-keeping device consisting of numerous knotted strings hanging from a main cord; the strings signified, by position and *color*, numbers and categories of items.

kiva A square or circular underground structure that is the spiritual and ceremonial center of Pueblo Indian life.

kogan A *Shino* water jar.

kondo Japanese, "golden hall." The main hall for worship in a Japanese Buddhist temple complex. The kondo contained *statues* of the Buddha and the *bodhisattvas* to whom the temple was dedicated.

Koran Islam's sacred book.

kore (pl. **korai**) Greek, "young woman." An *Archaic* Greek *statue* of a young woman.

kouros (pl. **kouroi**) Greek, "young man." An *Archaic* Greek *statue* of a young man.

krater An ancient Greek wide-mouthed bowl for mixing wine and water.

Kufic An early form of Arabic script, characterized by angularity, with the uprights forming almost right angles with the baseline.

L

lacquer A varnishlike substance made from the sap of the Asiatic sumac, used to decorate wood and other organic materials. Often colored with mineral pigments, lacquer cures to great hardness and has a lustrous surface.

lakshana One of the distinguishing marks of the Buddha. The lakshanas include the *urna* and *ushnisha.*

lamassu Assyrian guardian in the form of a man-headed winged bull.

lancet In *Gothic* architecture, a tall narrow window ending in a *pointed arch*.

landscape A picture showing natural scenery, without narrative content.

lateral section See *section*.

leading In the manufacture of *stained-glass* windows, the joining of colored glass pieces using lead *cames*.

lekythos (pl. **lekythoi**) A flask containing perfumed oil; lekythoi were often placed in Greek graves as offerings to the deceased.

line The extension of a point along a path, made concrete in art by drawing on or chiseling into a *plane*.

linear perspective See *perspective*.

linga In Hindu art, the depiction of Shiva as a phallus or cosmic *pillar*.

linguist's staff In Africa, a staff carried by a person authorized to speak for a king or chief.

lintel A horizontal *beam* used to span an opening.

literati In China, talented amateur painters and scholars from the landed gentry.

lithograph, lithography A print-making technique in which the artist uses an oil-based crayon to draw directly on a stone plate and then wipes water onto the stone. When ink is rolled onto the plate, it adheres only to the drawing.

liturgy (adj. **liturgical**) The official ritual of public worship.

local color An object's true *color* in white light.

loggia A gallery with an open *arcade* or a *colonnade* on one or both sides.

longitudinal plan See *plan*.

longitudinal section See *section*.

lost-wax (cire perdue) process A bronze-casting method in which a figure is modeled in wax and covered with clay; the whole is fired, melting away the wax (French, cire perdue) and hardening the clay, which then becomes a *mold* for molten metal.

low relief See *relief*.

lunette A semicircular area (with the flat side down) in a wall over a door, niche, or window; also, a painting or *relief* with a semicircular frame.

lux nova Latin, "new light." Abbot Suger's term for the light that enters a *Gothic* church through *stained-glass* windows.

M

madrasa An Islamic theological college adjoining and often incorporating a *mosque*.

magus (pl. **magi**) One of the three wise men from the East who presented gifts to the infant Jesus.

mandala Sacred diagram of the universe.

mandapa *Pillared* hall of a Hindu temple.

mandara See *mandala*.

mandorla An almond-shaped *nimbus* surrounding the figure of Christ or other sacred figure. In Buddhist Japan, a lotus-petal-shaped nimbus.

maniera Italian, "style" or "manner." See *Mannerism*.

maniera greca Italian, "Greek manner." The Italo-Byzantine painting *style* of the 13th century.

Mannerism A *style* of later *Renaissance* art that emphasized "artifice," often involving contrived imagery not derived directly from nature. Such artworks showed a self-conscious stylization involving complexity, caprice, fantasy, and polish. Mannerist architecture tended to flout the *classical* rules of order, stability, and symmetry, sometimes to the point of parody.

maqsura In some *mosques*, a screened area in front of the *mihrab* reserved for a ruler.

martyr A person who chooses to die rather than deny his or her religious belief. See *saint*.

martyrium A shrine to a Christian *martyr* or *saint*.

Mass The Catholic and Orthodox ritual in which believers understand that Christ's redeeming sacrifice on the cross is repeated when the priest consecrates the bread and wine in the *Eucharist*.

mastaba Arabic, "bench." An ancient Egyptian rectangular brick or stone structure with sloping sides erected over a subterranean tomb chamber connected with the outside by a shaft.

matte In painting, pottery, and photography, a dull finish.

maulstick A stick used to steady the hand while painting.

mausoleum A monumental tomb. The name derives from the mid-fourth-century BCE tomb of Mausolos at Halikarnassos, one of the Seven Wonders of the ancient world.

mbulu ngulu The wood-and-metal *reliquary* guardian figures of the Kota of Gabon.

meander An ornament, usually in bands but also covering broad surfaces, consisting of interlocking geometric motifs. An ornamental pattern of contiguous straight lines joined usually at right angles.

medium (pl. **media**) The material (for example, marble, bronze, clay, *fresco*) in which an artist works; also, in painting, the vehicle (usually liquid) that carries the pigment.

megalith (adj. **megalithic**) Greek, "great stone." A large, roughly hewn stone used in the construction of monumental prehistoric structures.

memento mori Latin, "reminder of death." In painting, a reminder of human mortality, usually represented by a skull.

Mesoamerica The region that comprises Mexico, Guatemala, Belize, Honduras, and the Pacific coast of El Salvador.

Mesolithic The "middle" Stone Age, between the *Paleolithic* and the *Neolithic* ages.

Messiah The savior of the Jews prophesied in the Old Testament. Christians believe that Jesus of Nazareth was the Messiah.

metope The panel between the *triglyphs* in a *Doric frieze*, often sculpted in *relief*.

mihrab A semicircular niche set into the *qibla* wall of a *mosque*.

minaret A distinctive feature of *mosque* architecture, a tower from which the faithful are called to worship.

minbar In a *mosque*, the pulpit on which the *imam* stands.

mingei A type of modern Japanese folk pottery.

miniatures Small individual Indian paintings intended to be held in the hand and viewed by one or two individuals at one time.

Minimalism A predominantly sculptural American trend of the 1960s characterized by works featuring a severe reduction of *form*, often to single, homogeneous units.

Minoan The second millennium BCE art of Crete, named after the legendary King Minos.

Minotaur The mythical beast, half man and half bull, that inhabited the *Minoan* palace at Knossos.

mithuna In South Asian art, a male-female couple embracing or engaged in sexual intercourse.

mobile A kind of sculpture, invented by Alexander Calder, combining nonobjective organic forms and motion in balanced structures hanging from rods, wires, and colored, organically shaped plates.

modeling The shaping or fashioning of three-dimensional *forms* in a soft material, such as clay; also, the gradations of light and shade reflected from the surfaces of matter in space, or the illusion of such gradations produced by alterations of value in a drawing, painting, or *print*.

modernism A movement in Western art that developed in the second half of the 19th century and sought to capture the images and sensibilities of the age. Modernist art goes beyond simply dealing with the present and involves the artist's critical examination of the premises of art itself.

module A basic unit of which the dimensions of the major parts of a work are multiples. The principle is used in sculpture and other art forms, but it is most often employed in architecture, where the module may be the dimensions of an important part of a building, such as the diameter of a *column*.

moksha See *nirvana*.

mold A hollow form for *casting*.

monastery A group of buildings in which monks live together, set apart from the secular community of a town.

monochromatic One color.

monolith (adj. **monolithic**) A *column shaft* that is all in one piece; a large, single block or piece of stone used in *megalithic* structures.

moralized Bible A heavily illustrated Bible, each page pairing paintings of Old and New Testament episodes with explanations of their moral significance.

mortuary temple In Egyptian architecture, a temple erected for the worship of a deceased pharaoh.

mosaic Patterns or pictures made by embedding small pieces *(tesserae)* of stone or glass in cement on surfaces such as walls and floors; also, the *technique* of making such works.

mosaicist A *mosaic* artist.

mosaic tilework An Islamic decorative *technique* in which large ceramic panels are fired, cut into smaller pieces, and set in plaster.

mosque The Islamic building for collective worship. From the Arabic word *masjid*, meaning a "place for bowing down."

mudra In Buddhist and Hindu iconography, a stylized and symbolic hand gesture. The dhyana (meditation) mudra consists of the right hand over the left, palms upward, in the lap. In the bhumisparsha (earth-touching) mudra, the right hand reaches down to the ground, calling the earth to witness the Buddha's enlightenment. The dharmachakra (Wheel of the Law, or teaching) mudra is a two-handed gesture with right thumb and index finger forming a circle. The abhaya (do not fear) mudra, with the right hand up, palm outward, is a gesture of protection or blessing.

Muhaqqaq A cursive style of Islamic *calligraphy*.

mullion A vertical member that divides a window or that separates one window from another.

mummification A *technique* used by ancient Egyptians to preserve human bodies so that they may serve as the eternal home of the immortal *ka*.

muqarnas Stucco decorations of Islamic buildings in which stalactite-like forms break a structure's solidity.

mural A wall painting.

mural cycle A series of *frescoes* with a common theme.

Mycenaean The prehistoric art of the Greek mainland, named after the city of Mycenae, although Mycenae was only one of the leading sites of the second millennium BCE.

mystery play A dramatic enactment of the holy mysteries of the Christian faith performed at church portals and in city squares.

N

naos See *cella*.

narthex A porch or vestibule of a church, generally *colonnaded* or *arcaded* and preceding the *nave*.

natatio The swimming pool in a Roman bathing establishment.

naturalism (adj. **naturalistic**) The style of painted or sculptured representation based on close observation of the natural world that was at the core of the *classical* tradition.

Naturalistic Surrealism See *Surrealism*.

nave The central area of an ancient Roman *basilica* or of a church, demarcated from *aisles* by *piers* or *columns*.

nduen fobara A Kalabari Ijaw (Nigeria) ancestral screen in honor of a deceased chief of a trading house.

necropolis Greek, "city of the dead." A large burial area or cemetery.

nemes In ancient Egypt, the linen headdress worn by the *pharaoh*, with the *uraeus* cobra of kingship on the front.

Neoclassicism A *style* of art and architecture that emerged in the later 18th century as part of a general revival of interest in *classi-*

cal cultures. Neoclassical artists adopted themes and styles from ancient Greece and Rome.

Neo-Expressionism An art movement that emerged in the 1970s reflecting artists' interest in the expressive capability of art, seen earlier in German *Expressionism* and *Abstract Expressionism*.

Neo-Gothic The revival of the *Gothic style* in architecture, especially in the 19th century.

Neolithic The "new" Stone Age.

Neoplasticism The Dutch artist Piet Mondrian's theory of "pure plastic art," an ideal balance between the universal and the individual using an *abstract* formal vocabulary.

Neue Sachlichkeit German, "new objectivity." An art movement that grew directly out of the World War I experiences of a group of German artists who sought to show the horrors of the war and its effects.

nimbus A halo or aureole appearing around the head of a holy figure to signify divinity.

nirvana In Buddhism and Hinduism, a blissful state brought about by absorption of the individual soul or consciousness into the supreme spirit. Also called moksha.

nishiki-e Japanese, "brocade pictures." Japanese polychrome *woodcut prints* valued for their sumptuous colors.

nkisi n'kondi A power figure carved by the Kongo people of the Democratic Republic of Congo. Such images embodied spirits believed to heal and give life or be capable of inflicting harm or death.

nymphs In *classical* mythology, female divinities of springs, caves, and woods.

O

oba An African sacred king.

oculus (pl. **oculi**) Latin, "eye." The round central opening of a *dome*. Also, a small round window in a *Gothic cathedral*.

odalisque A woman in a Turkish harem.

ogival Pointed, as in a *pointed arch*, a hallmark of *Gothic* architecture.

oil painting A painting *technique* using oil-based pigments that rose to prominence in Northern Europe in the 15th century and is now the standard medium for painting on canvas.

oni An African ruler.

opere francigeno See *opus francigenum*.

opisthodomos In ancient Greek architecture, a porch at the rear of a temple, set against the blank back wall of the *cella*.

optical mixture The visual effect of juxtaposed *complementary colors*.

opus francigenum Latin, "French work." Architecture in the *style* of *Gothic* France; *opere francigeno* (adj.), "in the French manner."

opus modernum Latin, "modern work." The late medieval term for *Gothic* art and architecture. Also called *opus francigenum*.

orant In Early Christian art, a figure with both arms raised in the ancient gesture of prayer.

oratory The church of a Christian *monastery*.

orchestra Greek, "dancing place." In ancient Greek theaters, the circular piece of earth with a hard and level surface on which the performance took place.

order In *classical* architecture, a *style* represented by a characteristic design of the *columns* and *entablature*.

orrery A mechanical model of the solar system demonstrating how the planets revolve around the sun.

orthogonal A line imagined to be behind and perpendicular to the picture plane; the orthogonals in a painting appear to recede toward a vanishing point on the horizon. See *perspective*.

Ottonian (adj.) Pertaining to the empire of Otto I and his successors.

P

pagoda An East Asian tower, usually associated with a Buddhist temple, having a multiplicity of winged *eaves*; thought to be derived from the Indian *stupa*.

palaestra An ancient Greek and Roman exercise area, usually framed by a *colonnade*. In Greece the palaestra was an independent building; in Rome palaestras were frequently incorporated into a bathing complex.

Paleolithic The "old" Stone Age, during which humankind produced the first sculptures and paintings.

palette A thin board with a thumb hole at one end on which an artist lays and mixes *colors*; any surface so used. Also, the colors or kinds of colors characteristically used by an artist. In ancient Egypt, a slate slab used for preparing makeup.

palette knife A flat tool used to scrape paint off the *palette*. Artists sometimes also used the palette knife in place of a brush to apply paint directly to the canvas.

Pantokrator Greek, "ruler of all." Christ as ruler and judge of heaven and earth.

papyrus A plant native to Egypt and adjacent lands used to make paperlike writing material; also, the material or any writing on it.

parallel hatching See *hatching*.

parapet A low, protective wall along the edge of a balcony, roof, or bastion.

parchment Lambskin prepared as a surface for painting or writing.

parinirvana Image of the reclining Buddha, often viewed as representing his death.

parthenos Greek, "virgin." The epithet of the goddess Athena.

paten A large shallow bowl or plate for the bread used in the *Eucharist*.

patriarch A Byzantine archbishop.

patrician A Roman freeborn landowner.

patron The person or entity that pays an artist to produce individual artworks or employs an artist on a continuing basis.

Pax Augusta Latin, "Augustan peace." The peace established in the Roman world by the emperor Augustus.

pebble mosaic A *mosaic* made of irregularly shaped stones of various *colors*.

pediment In *classical* architecture, the triangular space (gable) at the end of a building, formed by the ends of the sloping roof above the *colonnade*; also, an ornamental feature having this shape.

pendant The large hanging terminal element of a *Gothic* fan *vault*.

pendentive A concave, triangular section of a hemisphere, four of which provide the transition from a square area to the circular base of a covering *dome*. Although pendentives appear to be hanging (pendant) from the dome, they in fact support it.

peplos A simple, long woolen belted garment worn by ancient Greek women.

Performance Art An American *avant-garde* art trend of the 1960s that made time an integral element of art. In Performance works, movements, gestures, and sounds of persons communicating with an audience replace physical objects. Documentary photographs are generally the only evidence remaining after these events.

period style See *style*.

peripteral See *peristyle*.

peristyle In ancient Greek architecture, a *colonnade* all around the *cella* and its porch(es). A peripteral colonnade consists of a single row of *columns* on all sides; a dipteral colonnade has a double row all around. In Roman architecture, the colonnaded garden of a *domus*.

Perpendicular A Late English *Gothic style* of architecture distinguished by the pronounced verticality of its decorative details.

personal style See *style*.

personification An *abstract* idea represented in bodily form.

perspective (adj. **perspectival**) A method of presenting an illusion of the three-dimensional world on a two-dimensional surface. In linear perspective, the most common type, all parallel lines or surface edges converge on one, two, or three vanishing points located with reference to the eye level of the viewer (the horizon line of the picture), and associated objects are rendered smaller the farther from the viewer they are intended to seem. Atmospheric, or aerial, per-

spective creates the illusion of distance by the greater diminution of color intensity, the shift in color toward an almost neutral blue, and the blurring of *contour lines* as the intended distance between eye and object increases.

pharaoh (adj. **pharaonic**) An ancient Egyptian king.

philosophe French, "thinker, philosopher." The term applied to French intellectuals of the *Enlightenment*.

photomontage A *composition* made by pasting together pictures or parts of pictures, especially photographs. See also *collage*.

Photorealism See *Superrealism*.

physical evidence In art history, the examination of the materials used to produce an artwork in order to determine its date.

piazza Italian, "plaza." Also refers to the city square.

pier A vertical, freestanding masonry support.

Pietà A painted or sculpted representation of the Virgin Mary mourning over the body of the dead Christ.

pilaster A flat, rectangular, vertical member projecting from a wall of which it forms a part. It usually has a *base* and a *capital* and is often *fluted*. See also *engaged column*.

pillar Usually a weight-carrying member, such as a *pier* or a *column*; sometimes an isolated, freestanding structure used for commemorative purposes.

pinnacle In *Gothic* churches, a sharply pointed ornament capping the *piers* or flying *buttresses*; also used on church *facades*.

Pittura Metafisica Italian, "metaphysical painting." An early-20th-century Italian art movement led by Giorgio de Chirico, whose work conveys an eerie mood and visionary quality.

plan The horizontal arrangement of the parts of a building or of the buildings and streets of a city or town, or a drawing or diagram showing such an arrangement. In an axial plan, the parts of a building are organized longitudinally, or along a given axis; in a central plan, the parts of the structure are of equal or almost equal dimensions around the center.

plane A flat surface.

plate tracery See *tracery*.

poesia A term describing "poetic" art, notably Venetian *Renaissance* painting, which emphasizes the lyrical and sensual.

pointed arch A narrow *arch* of pointed profile, as opposed to a semicircular arch.

pointillism A system of painting devised by the 19th-century French painter Georges Seurat. The artist separates *color* into its component parts and then applies the component colors to the canvas in tiny dots (points). The image becomes comprehensible only from a distance when the viewer's eyes optically blend the pigment dots. Sometimes referred to as divisionism.

polyptych An *altarpiece* or a painting composed of more than three sections.

pontifex maximus Latin, "chief priest." The high priest of the Roman state religion, often the emperor himself.

Pop Art A term coined by British art critic Lawrence Alloway to refer to art, first appearing in the 1950s, that incorporates elements from consumer culture, the mass media, and popular culture, such as images from motion pictures and advertising.

porcelain An extremely hard white ceramic made from a fine white clay called kaolin mixed with ground petuntse, a type of feldspar. True porcelain is translucent and rings when struck.

portico A roofed *colonnade*; also, an entrance porch.

positivism A Western philosophical model that promoted science as the mind's highest achievement.

post-and-lintel system A system of construction in which two posts support a *lintel*.

Post-Impressionism The term used to describe the stylistically heterogeneous work of the group of late-19th-century painters in France, including van Gogh, Gauguin, Seurat, and Cézanne, who more systematically examined the properties and expressive qualities of *line*, pattern, *form*, and *color* than the Impressionists did.

postmodernism A reaction against *modernist formalism*, seen as elitist. Far more encompassing and accepting than the more rigid confines of modernist practice, postmodernism offers something for everyone by accommodating a wide range of styles, subjects, and formats, from traditional easel painting to *installation* and from *abstraction* to *illusionism*. Postmodern art often includes irony or reveals a self-conscious awareness on the part of the artist of art-making processes or the workings of the art world.

Post-Painterly Abstraction An American art movement that emerged in the 1960s, characterized by a cool, detached rationality emphasizing tighter pictorial control. See also *color-field painting* and *hard-edge painting*.

Poussiniste A member of the French Royal Academy of Painting and Sculpture during the early 18th century who followed Nicholas Poussin in insisting that *form* was the most important element of painting. See also *Rubéniste*.

predella The narrow ledge on which an *altarpiece* rests.

prefiguration In Early Christian art, the depiction of Old Testament persons and events as prophetic forerunners of Christ and New Testament events.

primary colors Red, yellow, and blue—the *colors* from which all other colors may be derived.

primitivism The incorporation in early-20th-century Western art of stylistic elements from the artifacts of Africa, Oceania, and the native peoples of the Americas.

princeps Latin, "first citizen." The official title of the ancient Roman emperors.

print An artwork on paper, usually produced in multiple impressions.

pronaos The space, or porch, in front of the *cella*, or *naos*, of an ancient Greek temple.

proportion The relationship in size of the parts of persons, buildings, or objects, often based on a *module*.

proscenium The part of a theatrical stage in front of the curtain.

prostyle A *classical* temple *plan* in which the *columns* are only in front of the *cella* and not on the sides or back.

provenance Origin or source; *findspot*.

psalter A book containing the Psalms.

pseudoperipteral In Roman architecture, a pseudoperipteral temple has a series of engaged *columns* all around the sides and back of the *cella* to give the appearance of a *peripteral colonnade*.

pueblo A communal multistoried dwelling made of stone or *adobe* brick by the Native Americans of the Southwest. Uppercase *Pueblo* (adj.) refers to various groups that occupied such dwellings.

pulpit A raised platform in a church or *mosque* on which a priest or *imam* stands while leading the religious service.

punchwork Tooled decorative work in gold foil.

purlins Horizontal *beams* in a roof structure, parallel to the *ridge-poles*, resting on the main *rafters* and giving support to the secondary rafters.

putto (pl. putti) A cherubic young boy.

pylon The wide entrance gateway of an Egyptian temple, characterized by its sloping walls.

pylon temple The type of Egyptian temple, characteristic of the New Kingdom, entered through a monumental *pylon*.

Q

qibla The direction (toward Mecca) Muslims face when praying.

quadrant arch An *arch* whose curve extends for one quarter of a circle's circumference.

quadro riportato A ceiling design in which painted scenes are arranged in panels that resemble framed pictures transferred to the surface of a shallow, curved *vault*.

quatrefoil A shape or plan in which the parts assume the form of a cloverleaf.

R

radiating chapels In medieval churches, chapels for the display of *relics* that opened directly onto the *ambulatory* and the *transept*.

rafters The sloping supporting timber planks that run from the *ridge-pole* of a roof to its edge.

raking cornice The *cornice* on the sloping sides of a *pediment*.

Rayonnant The "radiant" style of *Gothic* architecture, dominant in the second half of the 13th century and associated with the French royal court of Louis IX at Paris.

Realism A movement that emerged in mid-19th-century France. Realist artists represented the subject matter of everyday life (especially elements that until then had been considered inappropriate for depiction) in a relatively *naturalistic* mode.

red-figure painting In later Greek pottery, the silhouetting of red figures against a black background, with painted linear details; the reverse of *black-figure painting*.

refectory The dining hall of a Christian *monastery*.

Regionalism A 20th-century American art movement founded by Grant Wood that portrayed American rural life in a clearly readable, *Realist* style.

regional style See *style*.

register One of a series of superimposed bands or *friezes* in a pictorial narrative, or the particular levels on which motifs are placed.

relics The body parts, clothing, or objects associated with a holy figure, such as the Buddha, Christ, or a Christian *saint*, or, in Africa, an ancestor.

relief In sculpture, figures projecting from a background of which they are part. The degree of relief is designated high, low *(bas)*, or sunken. In the last, the artist cuts the design into the surface so that the highest projecting parts of the image are no higher than the surface itself. See also *repoussé*.

relieving triangle In Mycenaean architecture, the triangular opening above the *lintel* that serves to lighten the weight to be carried by the lintel itself.

reliquary A container for keeping *relics*.

Renaissance French, "rebirth." The term used to describe the history, culture, and art of 14th- through 16th-century western Europe during which artists consciously revived the *classical* style.

repoussé Formed in *relief* by beating a metal plate from the back, leaving the impression on the face. The metal is hammered into a hollow *mold* of wood or some other pliable material and finished with a *graver*. See also *relief*.

respond An engaged *column*, *pilaster*, or similar element that either projects from a *compound pier* or some other supporting device or is bonded to a wall and carries one end of an *arch*.

retable An architectural screen or wall above and behind an altar, usually containing painting, sculpture, carving, or other decoration. See also *altarpiece*.

revetment In architecture, a wall covering or facing.

rib A relatively slender, molded masonry *arch* that projects from a surface. In *Gothic* architecture, the ribs form the framework of the *vaulting*. A diagonal rib is one of the ribs that form the X of a *groin vault*. A transverse rib crosses the *nave* or *aisle* at a 90-degree angle.

rib vault A *vault* in which the diagonal and transverse *ribs* compose a structural skeleton that partially supports the masonry *web* between them.

ridgepole The *beam* running the length of a building below the peak of the gabled roof.

rocaille French, "pebble." See *Rococo*.

Rococo A style, primarily of interior design, that appeared in France around 1700. Rococo interiors featured lavish decoration, including small sculptures, ornamental mirrors, easel paintings, *tapestries*, *reliefs*, and wall paintings as well as elegant furniture. The term "Rococo" derived from the French word *rocaille* and referred to the small stones and shells used to decorate grotto interiors.

Romanesque "Romanlike." A term used to describe the history, culture, and art of medieval western Europe from ca. 1050 to ca. 1200.

Romanticism A Western cultural phenomenon, beginning around 1750 and ending about 1850, that gave precedence to feeling and imagination over reason and thought. More narrowly, the art movement that flourished from about 1800 to 1840.

rose window A circular *stained-glass* window.

rotulus The manuscript scroll used by Egyptians, Greeks, Etruscans, and Romans; predecessor of the *codex*.

rotunda The circular area under a *dome*; also, a domed round building.

Rubéniste A member of the French Royal Academy of Painting and Sculpture during the early 18th century who followed Peter Paul Rubens in insisting that color was the most important element of painting. See also *Poussiniste*.

rusticate (n. **rustication**) To give a rustic appearance by roughening the surfaces and beveling the edges of stone blocks to emphasize the joints between them. Rustication is a technique employed in ancient Roman architecture, and was also popular during the *Renaissance*, especially for stone *courses* at the ground-floor level.

S

sabi Japanese; the value found in the old and weathered, suggesting the tranquility reached in old age.

sacra conversazione Italian, "holy conversation." A style of *altarpiece* painting, popular after the middle of the 15th century, in which *saints* from different epochs are joined in a unified space and seem to be conversing either with each other or with the audience.

saint From the Latin *sanctus*, meaning "made holy by God." Persons who suffered and died for their Christian faith or who merited reverence for their Christian devotion while alive.

samsara In Hindu belief, the rebirth of the soul into a succession of lives.

samurai Medieval Japanese warriors.

sarcophagus (pl. **sarcophagi**) Latin, "consumer of flesh." A coffin, usually of stone.

saturation See *color*.

satyr A Greek mythological follower of Dionysos having a man's upper body, a goat's hindquarters and horns, and a horse's ears and tail.

Scholasticism The *Gothic* school of philosophy in which scholars applied Aristotle's system of rational inquiry to the interpretation of religious belief.

school A chronological and stylistic classification of works of art with a stipulation of place.

scriptorium (pl. **scriptoria**) The writing studio of a *monastery*.

sculpture in the round *Freestanding* figures, carved or modeled in three dimensions.

seal In Asian painting, a stamp affixed to a painting to identify the artist, the *calligrapher*, or the owner.

secondary colors Orange, green, and purple, obtained by mixing pairs of *primary colors* (red, yellow, blue).

Second Style mural The style of Roman *mural* painting in which the aim was to dissolve the confining walls of a room and replace them with the illusion of a three-dimensional world constructed in the artist's imagination.

section In architecture, a diagram or representation of a part of a structure or building along an imaginary plane that passes through it vertically. Drawings showing a theoretical slice across a structure's width are lateral sections. Those cutting through a building's length are longitudinal sections. See also *elevation* and *cutaway*.

senate Latin, "council of elders." The legislative body in Roman constitutional government.

serdab A small concealed chamber in an Egyptian *mastaba* for the statue of the deceased.

sexpartite vault See *vault*.

sfumato Italian, "smoky." A smokelike haziness that subtly softens outlines in painting; particularly applied to the painting of Leonardo da Vinci.

shaft The tall, cylindrical part of a *column* between the *capital* and the *base*.

shaykh An Islamic mystic saint.

shikhara The beehive-shaped tower of a northern-style Hindu temple.

Shino Japanese ceramic wares produced during the late 16th and early 17th centuries in kilns in Mino.

shogun In 12th- through 19th-century Japan, a military governor who managed the country on behalf of a figurehead emperor.

shogunate The Japanese military government of the 12th through 19th centuries.

sibyl A Greco-Roman mythological prophetess.

silk-screen printing An industrial printing technique that creates a sharp-edged image by pressing ink through a design on silk or a similar tightly woven porous fabric stretched tight on a frame.

silverpoint A *stylus* made of silver, used in drawing in the 14th and 15th centuries because of the fine line it produced and the sharp point it maintained.

simultaneous contrasts The phenomenon that juxtaposed *colors* affect the eye's reception of each, as when a painter places dark green next to light green, making the former appear even darker and the latter even lighter. See also *successive contrasts*.

sinopia A burnt-orange pigment used in *fresco* painting to transfer a *cartoon* to the *arriccio* before the artist paints the plaster.

site-specific art Art created for a specific location. See also *Environmental Art*.

skene Greek, "stage." The stage of a *classical* theater.

skenographia Greek, "scene painting." The Greek term for *perspective* painting.

slip A mixture of fine clay and water used in ceramic decoration.

space In art history, both the actual area an object occupies or a building encloses, and the *illusionistic* representation of space in painting and sculpture.

spandrel The roughly triangular space enclosed by the curves of adjacent *arches* and a horizontal member connecting their vertexes; also, the space enclosed by the curve of an *arch* and an enclosing right angle. The area between the arch proper and the framing *columns* and *entablature*.

spectrum The range or band of visible colors in natural light.

sphinx A mythical Egyptian beast with the body of a lion and the head of a human.

splashed-ink painting See *haboku*.

springing The lowest stone of an *arch*; in *Gothic* vaulting, the lowest stone of a diagonal or transverse *rib*.

stained glass In *Gothic* architecture, the colored glass used for windows.

stanza (pl. **stanze**) Italian, "room."

statue A three-dimensional sculpture.

stele (pl. **stelae**) A carved stone slab used to mark graves or to commemorate historical events.

still life A picture depicting an arrangement of inanimate objects.

strigil A tool ancient Greek athletes used to scrape oil from their bodies.

stringcourse A raised horizontal molding, or band, in masonry. Its principal use is ornamental but it usually reflects interior structure.

strut A timber plank or other structural member used as a support in a building. Also, a short section of marble used to support an arm or leg in a *statue*.

stupa A large, mound-shaped Buddhist shrine.

style A distinctive artistic manner. Period style is the characteristic style of a specific time. Regional style is the style of a particular geographical area. Personal style is an individual artist's unique manner.

stylistic evidence   In art history, the examination of the *style* of an artwork in order to determine its date or the identity of the artist.

stylobate   The uppermost course of the platform of a *classical* temple, which supports the *columns*.

stylus   A needlelike tool used in *engraving* and *incising*; also, an ancient writing instrument used to inscribe clay or wax tablets.

subtractive light   The painter's light in art; the light reflected from pigments and objects. See also *additive light*.

subtractive sculpture   A kind of sculpture *technique* in which materials are taken away from the original mass; carving.

successive contrasts   The phenomenon of colored afterimages. When a person looks intently at a *color* (green, for example) and then shifts to a white area, the fatigued eye momentarily perceives the *complementary color* (red). See also *simultaneous contrasts*.

sultan   A Muslim ruler.

Sunnah   The collection of the Prophet Muhammad's moral sayings and descriptions of his deeds.

superimposition   In *Mesoamerican* architecture, the erection of a new structure on top of, and incorporating, an earlier structure; the nesting of a series of buildings inside each other.

Superrealism   A *school* of painting and sculpture of the 1960s and 1970s that emphasized producing artworks based on scrupulous fidelity to optical fact. The Superrealist painters were also called Photorealists because many used photographs as sources for their imagery.

Suprematism   A type of art formulated by Kazimir Malevich to convey his belief that the supreme reality in the world is pure feeling, which attaches to no object and thus calls for new, nonobjective forms in art—shapes not related to objects in the visible world.

Surrealism   A successor to *Dada*, Surrealism incorporated the improvisational nature of its predecessor into its exploration of the ways to express in art the world of dreams and the unconscious. Biomorphic Surrealists, such as Joan Miró, produced largely *abstract compositions*. *Naturalistic* Surrealists, notably Salvador Dalí, presented recognizable scenes transformed into a dream or nightmare image.

sutra   In Buddhism, an account of a sermon by or a dialogue involving the Buddha. A scriptural account of the Buddha. See also *jataka*.

symbol   An image that stands for another image or encapsulates an idea.

Symbolism   A late-19th-century movement based on the idea that the artist was not an imitator of nature but a creator who transformed the facts of nature into a *symbol* of the inner experience of those facts.

symmetria   Greek, "commensurability of parts." Polykleitos's treatise on his *canon* of proportions for the human form incorporated the principle of symmetria.

Synthetic Cubism   A later phase of *Cubism*, in which paintings and drawings were constructed from objects and shapes cut from paper or other materials to represent parts of a subject, in order to engage the viewer with pictorial issues, such as figuration, realism, and abstraction.

T

taberna   In Roman architecture, a single-room shop usually covered by a barrel *vault*.

tablinum   The study or office in a Roman house.

taj   Arabic and Persian, "crown."

tapestry   A weaving *technique* in which the designs are woven directly into the fabric.

tarashikomi   In Japanese art, a painting *technique* involving the dropping of ink and pigments onto surfaces still wet with previously applied ink and pigments.

tatami   The traditional woven straw mat used for floor covering in Japanese architecture.

technique   The processes artists employ to create *form*, as well as the distinctive, personal ways in which they handle their materials and tools.

tempera   A *technique* of painting using pigment mixed with egg yolk, glue, or casein; also, the *medium* itself.

templon   The columnar screen separating the sanctuary from the main body of a Byzantine church.

tenebrism   Painting in the "shadowy manner," using violent contrasts of light and dark, as in the work of Caravaggio. The term derives from *tenebroso*.

tenebroso   Italian, "shadowy." See *tenebrism*.

tepidarium   The warm-bath section of a Roman bathing establishment.

terracotta   Hard-baked clay, used for sculpture and as a building material. It may be *glazed* or painted.

tessera (pl. tesserae)   Greek, "cube." A tiny stone or piece of glass cut to the desired shape and size for use in forming a *mosaic*.

tetrarch   One of four corulers.

tetrarchy   Greek, "rule by four." A type of Roman government established in the late third century CE by Diocletian in an attempt to establish order by sharing power with potential rivals.

texture   The quality of a surface, such as rough or shiny.

theatron   Greek, "place for seeing." In ancient Greek theaters, the slope overlooking the *orchestra* on which the spectators sat.

Theotokos   Greek, "she who bore God." The Virgin Mary, the mother of Jesus.

Third Style mural   In Roman *mural* painting, the style in which delicate linear fantasies were sketched on predominantly *monochromatic* backgrounds.

tholos (pl. tholoi)   A temple with a circular plan. Also, the burial chamber of a *tholos tomb*.

tholos tomb   In Mycenaean architecture, a beehive-shaped tomb with a circular plan.

thrust   The outward force exerted by an *arch* or a *vault* that must be counterbalanced by a *buttress*.

tokonoma   A shallow alcove in a Japanese room used to display a prized object, such as a painting or stylized flower arrangement.

tonality   See *color*.

torana   Gateway in the stone fence around a *stupa*, located at the cardinal points of the compass.

torque   A neckband worn by the ancient Gauls.

tracery   Ornamental stonework for holding *stained glass* in place, characteristic of *Gothic cathedrals*. In plate tracery the glass fills only the "punched holes" in the heavy ornamental stonework. In bar tracery the stained-glass windows fill almost the entire opening, and the stonework is unobtrusive.

transept   The part of a church with an axis that crosses the *nave* at a right angle.

transverse arch   An *arch* separating one vaulted *bay* from the next.

transverse rib   See *rib*.

tribune   In church architecture, a gallery over the inner *aisle* flanking the *nave*.

triclinium   The dining room of a Roman house.

trident   The three-pronged pitchfork associated with the ancient Greek sea god Poseidon (Roman, Neptune).

triforium   In a *Gothic cathedral*, the *blind arcaded* gallery below the *clerestory*; occasionally the *arcades* are filled with *stained glass*.

triglyph   A triple projecting, grooved member of a *Doric frieze* that alternates with *metopes*.

trilithon   A pair of *monoliths* topped with a *lintel*; found in *megalithic* structures.

triptych   A three-paneled painting or *altarpiece*.

triumphal arch In Roman architecture, a freestanding *arch* commemorating an important event, such as a military victory or the opening of a new road.

trompe l'oeil French, "deceives the eye." *Illusionistic* painting.

true fresco See *fresco*.

trumeau In church architecture, the *pillar* or center post supporting the *lintel* in the middle of the doorway.

tubicen Latin, "trumpeter."

tumulus (pl. **tumuli**) Burial mound; in Etruscan architecture, tumuli cover one or more subterranean multichambered tombs cut out of the local tufa (limestone). Also characteristic of Neolithic funerary architecture and of the Japanese Kofun period of the third and fourth centuries.

tunnel vault See *vault*.

Tuscan column The standard type of Etruscan *column*. It resembles ancient Greek *Doric* columns, but is made of wood, is unfluted, and has a *base*. Also, a popular motif in Renaissance and Baroque architecture.

twisted perspective See *composite view*.

tympanum (pl. **tympana**) The space enclosed by a *lintel* and an *arch* over a doorway.

U

ukiyo-e Japanese, "pictures of the floating world."

underglaze In *porcelain* decoration, the technique of applying mineral colors to the surface before the main firing, followed by an application of clear *glaze*.

Upanishads South Asian religious texts of ca. 800–500 BCE in which the concepts of *samsara*, *karma*, and *moksha* were introduced.

uraeus An Egyptian cobra; one of the emblems of pharaonic kingship.

urna A whorl of hair, represented as a dot, between the brows; one of the *lakshanas* of the Buddha.

ushabti In ancient Egypt, a figurine placed in a tomb to act as a servant to the deceased in the afterlife.

ushnisha A knot of hair on the top of the head; one of the *lakshanas* of the Buddha.

V

valley temple The temple closest to the Nile River associated with each of the Great Pyramids at Gizeh in ancient Egypt.

value See *color*.

vanishing point See *perspective*.

vanitas Latin, "vanity." A term describing paintings (particularly 17th-century Dutch *still lifes*) that celebrate material goods but also include reminders of death.

vault A masonry roof or ceiling constructed on the *arch* principle. A barrel (or tunnel) vault, semicylindrical in cross-*section*, is in effect a deep arch or an uninterrupted series of arches, one behind the other, over an oblong space. A quadrant vault is a half-barrel vault. A groin (or cross) vault is formed at the point at which two barrel vaults intersect at right angles. In a ribbed vault, there is a framework of *ribs* or arches under the intersections of the vaulting sections. A sexpartite vault is a vault whose ribs divide the vault into six compartments. A fan vault is a vault characteristic of English *Perpendicular Gothic*, in which radiating ribs form a fanlike pattern.

vaulting web In *Gothic* architecture, the masonry blocks that fill the area between the *ribs* of a *groin vault*.

Veda Sanskrit, "knowledge." One of four second-millennium BCE South Asian compilations of religious learning.

veduta (pl. **vedute**) Italian, "view." A painting of a characteristic scene of Venice and other locales, popular among British visitors taking the Grand Tour of Italy during the 18th century.

vellum Calfskin prepared as a surface for writing or painting.

veristic True to natural appearance; superrealistic.

vihara A Buddhist *monastery*, often cut into a hill.

vimana A pyramidal tower over the *garbha griha* of a southern-style Hindu temple.

vita Italian, "life." Also, the title of a biography.

volute A spiral, scroll-like form characteristic of the ancient Greek *Ionic capital*.

votive offering A gift of gratitude to a deity.

voussoir A wedge-shaped block used in the construction of a true *arch*. The central voussoir, which sets the arch, is the keystone.

W

wabi A 16th-century Japanese art style characterized by refined rusticity and an appreciation of simplicity and austerity.

wat A Buddhist *monastery* in Cambodia.

web See *vaulting web*.

westwork German, "western entrance structure." The *facade* and towers at the western end of a medieval church, principally in Germany. In contemporaneous documents, the westwork is called a castellum (Latin, "castle or fortress") or turris ("tower").

wet fresco See *fresco*.

wet-plate photography An early photographic process in which the photographic plate is exposed, developed, and fixed while wet.

white-ground painting An ancient Greek vase-painting *technique* in which the pot was first covered with a *slip* of very fine white clay, over which black *glaze* was used to outline figures, and diluted brown, purple, red, and white were used to color them.

woodcut A wooden block on the surface of which those parts not intended to print are cut away to a slight depth, leaving the design raised; also, the printed impression made with such a block.

Y

yaksha/yakshi Lesser local male and female Buddhist and Hindu divinities. Yakshis are goddesses associated with fertility and vegetation. Yakshas, the male equivalent of yakshis, are often represented as fleshy but powerful males.

yamato-e Also known as native-style painting, a purely Japanese style that often involved colorful, decorative representations of Japanese narratives or *landscapes*.

yang In Chinese cosmology, the principle of active masculine energy, which permeates the universe in varying proportions with yin, the principle of passive feminine energy.

yasti In Buddhist architecture, the mast or pole that arises from the dome of the *stupa* and its *harmika* and symbolizes the axis of the universe; it is adorned with a series of chatras (stone disks).

yin See *yang*.

yoga (adj. **yogic**) A method for controlling the body and relaxing the mind used in later Indian religions to yoke, or unite, the practitioner to the divine.

Z

Zen A Japanese Buddhist sect and its doctrine, emphasizing enlightenment through intuition and introspection rather than the study of scripture. In Chinese, Chan.

ziggurat In ancient Mesopotamian architecture, a monumental platform for a temple.

Bibliography

This list of books is very selective but comprehensive enough to satisfy the reading interests of the beginning art history student and general reader. The resources listed range from works that are valuable primarily for their reproductions to those that are scholarly surveys of schools and periods or monographs on individual artists. The emphasis is on recent in-print books and on books likely to be found in college and municipal libraries. No entries appear for periodical articles.

GENERAL STUDIES

Baxandall, Michael. *Patterns of Intention: On the Historical Explanation of Pictures*. New Haven: Yale University Press, 1985.

Boström, Antonia. *The Encyclopedia of Sculpture*. 3 vols. London: Routledge, 2003.

Broude, Norma, and Mary D. Garrard, eds. *The Expanding Discourse: Feminism and Art History*. New York: Harper Collins, 1992.

Bryson, Norman, Michael Ann Holly, and Keith Moxey. *Visual Theory: Painting and Interpretation*. New York: Cambridge University Press, 1991.

Chadwick, Whitney. *Women, Art, and Society*. 4th ed. New York: Thames & Hudson, 2007.

Cheetham, Mark A., Michael Ann Holly, and Keith Moxey, eds. *The Subjects of Art History: Historical Objects in Contemporary Perspective*. New York: Cambridge University Press, 1998.

Chilvers, Ian, and Harold Osborne, eds. *The Oxford Dictionary of Art*. 3d ed. New York: Oxford University Press, 2004.

Corbin, George A. *Native Arts of North America, Africa, and the South Pacific: An Introduction*. New York: Harper Collins, 1988.

Crouch, Dora P., and June G. Johnson. *Traditions in Architecture: Africa, America, Asia, and Oceania*. New York: Oxford University Press, 2000.

Curl, James Stevens. *Oxford Dictionary of Architecture and Landscape Architecture*. 2d ed. New York: Oxford University Press, 2006.

Encyclopedia of World Art. 17 vols. New York: McGraw-Hill, 1959–1987.

Fine, Sylvia Honig. *Women and Art: A History of Women Painters and Sculptors from the Renaissance to the 20th Century*. Montclair, N.J.: Alanheld & Schram, 1978.

Fleming, John, Hugh Honour, and Nikolaus Pevsner. *The Penguin Dictionary of Architecture and Landscape Architecture*. 5th ed. New York: Penguin, 2000.

Frazier, Nancy. *The Penguin Concise Dictionary of Art History*. New York: Penguin, 2000.

Freedberg, David. *The Power of Images: Studies in the History and Theory of Response*. Chicago: University of Chicago Press, 1989.

Gaze, Delia., ed. *Dictionary of Women Artists*. 2 vols. London: Routledge, 1997.

Hall, James. *Illustrated Dictionary of Subjects and Symbols in Eastern and Western Art*. New York: Icon Editions, 1994.

Harris, Anne Sutherland, and Linda Nochlin. *Women Artists, 1550–1950*. Los Angeles: Los Angeles County Museum of Art; New York: Knopf, 1977.

Hults, Linda C. *The Print in the Western World: An Introductory History*. Madison: University of Wisconsin Press, 1996.

Kemp, Martin. *The Science of Art: Optical Themes in Western Art from Brunelleschi to Seurat*. New Haven: Yale University Press, 1990.

Kleiner, Fred S. *Gardner's Art through the Ages: A Global History*. 13th ed. Belmont, Calif.: Wadsworth, 2008.

Kostof, Spiro, and Gregory Castillo. *A History of Architecture: Settings and Rituals*. 2d ed. Oxford: Oxford University Press, 1995.

Kultermann, Udo. *The History of Art History*. New York: Abaris, 1993.

Lucie-Smith, Edward. *The Thames & Hudson Dictionary of Art Terms*. 2d ed. New York: Thames & Hudson, 2004.

Moffett, Marian, Michael Fazio, and Lawrence Wadehouse. *A World History of Architecture*. Boston: McGraw-Hill, 2004.

Murray, Peter, and Linda Murray. *A Dictionary of Art and Artists*. 7th ed. New York: Penguin, 1998.

Nelson, Robert S., and Richard Shiff, eds. *Critical Terms for Art History*. Chicago: University of Chicago Press, 1996.

Penny, Nicholas. *The Materials of Sculpture*. New Haven: Yale University Press, 1993.

Pevsner, Nikolaus. *A History of Building Types*. London: Thames & Hudson, 1987. Reprint of 1979 ed.

———. *An Outline of European Architecture*. 8th ed. Baltimore: Penguin, 1974.

Pierce, James Smith. *From Abacus to Zeus: A Handbook of Art History*. 7th ed. Upper Saddle River, N.J.: Pearson Prentice Hall, 2003.

Placzek, Adolf K., ed. *Macmillan Encyclopedia of Architects*. 4 vols. New York: Macmillan, 1982.

Podro, Michael. *The Critical Historians of Art*. New Haven: Yale University Press, 1982.

Pollock, Griselda. *Vision and Difference: Femininity, Feminism and Histories of Art*. London: Routledge, 1988.

Preziosi, Donald, ed. *The Art of Art History: A Critical Anthology*. New York: Oxford University Press, 1998.

Read, Herbert. *The Thames & Hudson Dictionary of Art and Artists*. Rev. ed. New York: Thames & Hudson, 1994.

Reid, Jane D. *The Oxford Guide to Classical Mythology in the Arts, 1300–1990s*. 2 vols. New York: Oxford University Press, 1993.

Roth, Leland M. *Understanding Architecture: Its Elements, History, and Meaning*. 2d ed. Boulder, Colo.: Westview, 2006.

Slatkin, Wendy. *Women Artists in History: From Antiquity to the 20th Century*. 4th ed. Upper Saddle River, N.J.: Prentice Hall, 2000.

Steer, John, and Antony White. *Atlas of Western Art History: Artists, Sites and Monuments from Ancient Greece to the Modern Age*. New York: Facts on File, 1994.

Stratton, Arthur. *The Orders of Architecture: Greek, Roman and Renaissance*. London: Studio, 1986.

Sutton, Ian. *Western Architecture: From Ancient Greece to the Present*. New York: Thames & Hudson, 1999.

Trachtenberg, Marvin, and Isabelle Hyman. *Architecture, from Prehistory to Post-Modernism*. 2d ed. Upper Saddle River, N.J.: Prentice Hall, 2003.

Turner, Jane, ed. *The Dictionary of Art*. 34 vols. New York: Oxford University Press, 2003.

Wittkower, Rudolf. *Sculpture Processes and Principles*. New York: Harper & Row, 1977.

ANCIENT ART, GENERAL

Boardman, John. *The World of Ancient Art.* London: Thames & Hudson, 2006.

———, ed. *The Oxford History of Classical Art.* New York: Oxford University Press, 1997.

Gates, Charles. *Ancient Cities: The Archaeology of Urban Life in the Ancient Near East and Egypt, Greece, and Rome.* London: Routledge, 2003.

Renfrew, Colin, and Paul G. Bahn. *Archaeology: Theories, Methods, and Practices.* London: Thames & Hudson, 1991.

Trigger, Bruce. *Understanding Early Civilizations: A Comparative Study.* New York: Cambridge University Press, 2003.

CHAPTER 1 Prehistory and the First Civilizations

Prehistory

Bahn, Paul G. *The Cambridge Illustrated History of Prehistoric Art.* New York: Cambridge University Press, 1998.

Bahn, Paul G., and Jean Vertut. *Journey through the Ice Age.* Berkeley: University of California Press, 1997.

Cunliffe, Barry, ed. *The Oxford Illustrated Prehistory of Europe.* New York: Oxford University Press, 1994.

Hodder, Ian. *The Leopard's Tale: Revealing the Mysteries of Çatalhöyük.* London: Thames & Hudson, 2006.

Ruspoli, Mario. *The Cave of Lascaux: The Final Photographs.* New York: Abrams, 1987.

Scarre, Chris. *Exploring Prehistoric Europe.* New York: Oxford University Press, 1998.

Ancient Near East

Allen, Lindsay. *The Persian Empire.* Chicago: University of Chicago Press, 2005.

Amiet, Pierre. *Art of the Ancient Near East.* New York: Abrams, 1980.

Bahrani, Zainab. *The Graven Image: Representation in Babylonia and Assyria.* Philadelphia: University of Pennsylvania Press, 2003.

Collon, Dominique. *Ancient Near Eastern Art.* Berkeley: University of California Press, 1995.

Crawford, Harriet. *Sumer and the Sumerians.* New York: Cambridge University Press, 1991.

Curtis, John E., and Nigel Tallis. *Forgotten Empire: The World of Ancient Persia.* Berkeley: University of California Press, 2005.

Frankfort, Henri. *The Art and Architecture of the Ancient Orient.* 5th ed. New Haven: Yale University Press, 1996.

Meyers, Eric M., ed. *The Oxford Encyclopedia of Archaeology in the Near East.* 5 vols. New York: Oxford University Press, 1997.

Moortgat, Anton. *The Art of Ancient Mesopotamia.* New York: Phaidon, 1969.

Parrot, André. *The Arts of Assyria.* New York: Golden Press, 1961.

———. *Sumer: The Dawn of Art.* New York: Golden Press, 1961.

Reade, Julian E. *Assyrian Sculpture.* Cambridge, Mass.: Harvard University Press, 1999.

———. *Mesopotamia.* Cambridge, Mass.: Harvard University Press, 1991.

Roaf, Michael. *Cultural Atlas of Mesopotamia and the Ancient Near East.* New York: Facts on File, 1990.

Sasson, Jack M., ed. *Civilizations of the Ancient Near East.* 4 vols. New York: Scribner, 1995.

Snell, Daniel C. *Life in the Ancient Near East, 3100–332 B.C.* New Haven: Yale University Press, 1997.

Strommenger, Eva, and Max Hirmer. *5,000 Years of the Art of Mesopotamia.* New York: Abrams, 1964.

Egypt

Arnold, Dieter. *Building in Egypt: Pharaonic Stone Masonry.* New York: Oxford University Press, 1991.

Arnold, Dorothea, ed. *Egyptian Art in the Age of the Pyramids.* New York: Abrams, 1999.

Baines, John, and Jaromír Málek. *Atlas of Ancient Egypt.* New York: Facts on File, 1980.

Bard, Kathryn A. *An Introduction to the Archaeology of Ancient Egypt.* Oxford: Blackwell, 2007.

———, ed. *Encyclopedia of the Archaeology of Ancient Egypt.* London: Routledge, 1999.

Davis, Whitney. *The Canonical Tradition in Ancient Egyptian Art.* New York: Cambridge University Press, 1989.

Ikram, Salima, and Aidan Dodson. *The Mummy in Ancient Egypt: Equipping the Dead for Eternity.* New York: Thames & Hudson, 1998.

Kemp, Barry J. *Ancient Egypt: Anatomy of a Civilization.* 2d ed. New York: Routledge, 2006.

Lehner, Mark. *The Complete Pyramids: Solving the Ancient Mysteries.* New York: Thames & Hudson, 1997.

Málek, Jaromír. *Egyptian Art.* London: Phaidon, 1999.

Redford, Donald B., ed. *The Oxford Encyclopedia of Ancient Egypt.* 3 vols. New York: Oxford University Press, 2001.

Robins, Gay. *The Art of Ancient Egypt.* Cambridge, Mass.: Harvard University Press, 1997.

Schulz, Regina, and Matthias Seidel, eds. *Egypt: The World of the Pharaohs.* Cologne: Könemann, 1999.

Shafer, Byron E., ed. *Temples of Ancient Egypt.* Ithaca, N.Y.: Cornell University Press, 1997.

Shaw, Ian, and Paul Nicholson. *The Dictionary of Ancient Egypt.* London: British Museum, 1995.

Silverman, David P., ed. *Ancient Egypt.* New York: Oxford University Press, 1997.

Smith, William Stevenson, and William Kelly Simpson. *The Art and Architecture of Ancient Egypt.* Rev. ed. New Haven: Yale University Press, 1998.

Weeks, Kent R., ed. *Valley of the Kings.* Vercelli: White Star, 2001.

Wildung, Dietrich. *Egypt: From Prehistory to the Romans.* Cologne: Taschen, 1997.

CHAPTER 2 Greece

Prehistoric Aegean

Cullen, Tracey, ed. *Aegean Prehistory: A Review.* Boston: Archaeological Institute of America, 2001.

Dickinson, Oliver P.T.K. *The Aegean Bronze Age.* New York: Cambridge University Press, 1994.

Doumas, Christos. *The Wall-Paintings of Thera.* Athens: Thera Foundation, 1992.

Fitton, J. Lesley. *Cycladic Art.* Cambridge, Mass.: Harvard University Press, 1989.

———. *The Discovery of the Greek Bronze Age.* London: British Museum, 1995.

Forsyth, Phyllis Young. *Thera in the Bronze Age.* New York: Peter Lang, 1997.

Getz-Preziosi, Patricia. *Sculptors of the Cyclades: Individual and Tradition in the Third Millennium B.C.* Ann Arbor: University of Michigan Press, 1987.

Graham, James W. *The Palaces of Crete.* Princeton, N.J.: Princeton University Press, 1987.

Hood, Sinclair. *The Arts in Prehistoric Greece.* New Haven: Yale University Press, 1992.

Immerwahr, Sarah A. *Aegean Painting in the Bronze Age.* University Park: Pennsylvania State University Press, 1990.

Marinatos, Spyridon, and Max Hirmer. *Crete and Mycenae.* London: Thames & Hudson, 1960.

Preziosi, Donald, and Louise A. Hitchcock. *Aegean Art and Architecture.* New York: Oxford University Press, 1999.

Schofield, Louise. *The Mycenaeans.* Los Angeles: J. Paul Getty Museum, 2007.

Taylour, Lord William. *The Mycenaeans.* London: Thames & Hudson, 1990.

Warren, Peter. *The Aegean Civilisations from Ancient Crete to Mycenae.* 2d ed. Oxford: Elsevier-Phaidon, 1989.

Greece

Biers, William. *The Archaeology of Greece: An Introduction.* 2d ed. Ithaca, N.Y.: Cornell University Press, 1996.

Boardman, John. *Athenian Black Figure Vases.* Rev. ed. New York: Thames & Hudson, 1985.

———. *Athenian Red Figure Vases: The Archaic Period.* New York: Thames & Hudson, 1988.

———. *Athenian Red Figure Vases: The Classical Period.* New York: Thames & Hudson, 1989.

———. *Greek Sculpture: The Archaic Period.* Rev. ed. New York: Thames & Hudson, 1985.

———. *Greek Sculpture: The Classical Period.* New York: Thames & Hudson, 1987.

———. *Greek Sculpture: The Late Classical Period and Sculpture in Colonies and Overseas.* New York: Thames & Hudson, 1995.

Fullerton, Mark D. *Greek Art.* New York: Cambridge University Press, 2000.

Hurwit, Jeffrey M. *The Art and Culture of Early Greece, 1100–480 B.C.* Ithaca, N.Y.: Cornell University Press, 1985.

———. *The Athenian Acropolis: History, Mythology, and Archaeology from the Neolithic Era to the Present.* New York: Cambridge University Press, 1999.

Jenkins, Ian. *Greek Architecture and Its Sculpture.* Cambridge, Mass.: Harvard University Press, 2006.

Lawrence, Arnold W., and R. A. Tomlinson. *Greek Architecture.* Rev. ed. New Haven: Yale University Press, 1996.

Martin, Roland. *Greek Architecture: Architecture of Crete, Greece, and the Greek World.* New York: Electa/Rizzoli, 1988.

Mattusch, Carol C. *Classical Bronzes: The Art and Craft of Greek and Roman Statuary.* Ithaca, N.Y.: Cornell University Press, 1996.

Morris, Sarah P. *Daidalos and the Origins of Greek Art.* Princeton, N.J.: Princeton University Press, 1992.

Osborne, Robin. *Archaic and Classical Greek Art.* New York: Oxford University Press, 1998.

Palagia, Olga, ed. *Greek Sculpture: Functions, Materials, and Techniques in the Archaic and Classical Periods.* New York: Cambridge University Press, 2006.

Pedley, John Griffiths. *Greek Art and Archaeology.* 4th ed. Upper Saddle River, N.J.: Prentice Hall, 2007.

Pollitt, Jerome J. *Art in the Hellenistic Age.* New York: Cambridge University Press, 1986.

———. *The Art of Ancient Greece: Sources and Documents.* 2d ed. New York: Cambridge University Press, 1990.

Rhodes, Robin F. *Architecture and Meaning on the Athenian Acropolis.* New York: Cambridge University Press, 1995.

Ridgway, Brunilde S. *The Archaic Style in Greek Sculpture.* 2d ed. Chicago: Ares, 1993.

———. *Fifth Century Styles in Greek Sculpture.* Princeton, N.J.: Princeton University Press, 1981.

———. *Fourth-Century Styles in Greek Sculpture.* Madison: University of Wisconsin Press, 1997.

———. *Hellenistic Sculpture I: The Styles of ca. 331–200 B.C.* Madison: University of Wisconsin Press, 1990.

———. *Hellenistic Sculpture II: The Styles of ca. 200–100 B.C.* Madison: University of Wisconsin Press, 2000.

———. *Prayers in Stone: Greek Architectural Sculpture.* Berkeley: University of California Press, 1999.

Robertson, Martin. *A History of Greek Art.* Rev. ed. 2 vols. New York: Cambridge University Press, 1986.

Smith, R.R.R. *Hellenistic Sculpture.* New York: Thames & Hudson, 1991.

Spawforth, Tony. *The Complete Greek Temples.* London: Thames & Hudson, 2006.

Spivey, Nigel. *Greek Art.* London: Phaidon, 1997.

Stewart, Andrew. *Greek Sculpture: An Exploration.* 2 vols. New Haven: Yale University Press, 1990.

CHAPTER 3 The Roman Empire

Etruria

Bonfante, Larissa, ed. *Etruscan Life and Afterlife: A Handbook of Etruscan Studies.* Detroit, Mich.: Wayne State University Press, 1986.

Brendel, Otto J. *Etruscan Art.* 2d ed. New Haven: Yale University Press, 1995.

Haynes, Sybille. *Etruscan Civilization: A Cultural History.* Los Angeles: J. Paul Getty Museum, 2000.

Spivey, Nigel. *Etruscan Art.* New York: Thames & Hudson, 1997.

Sprenger, Maja, Gilda Bartoloni, and Max Hirmer. *The Etruscans: Their History, Art, and Architecture.* New York: Abrams, 1983.

Steingräber, Stephan. *Abundance of Life: Etruscan Wall Painting.* Los Angeles: J. Paul Getty Museum, 2006.

Torelli, Mario, ed. *The Etruscans.* New York: Rizzoli, 2001.

Rome

Andreae, Bernard. *The Art of Rome.* New York: Abrams, 1977.

Claridge, Amanda. *Rome: An Oxford Archaeological Guide.* New York: Oxford University Press, 1998.

Clarke, John R. *The Houses of Roman Italy, 100 B.C.–A.D. 250.* Berkeley: University of California Press, 1991.

Cornell, Tim, and John Matthews. *Atlas of the Roman World.* New York: Facts on File, 1982.

D'Ambra, Eve. *Roman Art.* New York: Cambridge University Press, 1998.

Dobbins, John J., and Pedar W. Foss. *The World of Pompeii.* London: Routledge, 2007.

Hannestad, Niels. *Roman Art and Imperial Policy.* Aarhus: Aarhus University Press, 1986.

Kleiner, Diana E. E. *Roman Sculpture.* New Haven: Yale University Press, 1992.

Kleiner, Fred S. *A History of Roman Art.* Belmont, Calif.: Wadsworth, 2007.

Kraus, Theodor. *Pompeii and Herculaneum: The Living Cities of the Dead.* New York: Abrams, 1975.

Lancaster, Lynne. *Concrete Vaulted Construction in Imperial Rome.* New York: Cambridge University Press, 2006.

Ling, Roger. *Roman Painting.* New York: Cambridge University Press, 1991.

MacDonald, William L. *The Architecture of the Roman Empire I: An Introductory Study.* Rev. ed. New Haven: Yale University Press, 1982.

Mazzoleni, Donatella. *Domus: Wall Painting in the Roman House.* Los Angeles: J. Paul Getty Museum, 2004.

Pollitt, Jerome J. *The Art of Rome, 753 B.C.–A.D. 337: Sources and Documents.* Rev. ed. New York: Cambridge University Press, 1983.

Richardson, Lawrence, Jr. *A New Topographical Dictionary of Ancient Rome.* Baltimore: Johns Hopkins University Press, 1992.

———. *Pompeii: An Architectural History.* Baltimore: Johns Hopkins University Press, 1988.

Taylor, Rabun. *Roman Builders.* New York: Cambridge University Press, 2003.

Toynbee, Jocelyn M. C. *Death and Burial in the Roman World.* London: Thames & Hudson, 1971.

Wallace-Hadrill, Andrew. *Houses and Society in Pompeii and Herculaneum.* Princeton, N.J.: Princeton University Press, 1994.

———. *Roman Imperial Architecture.* 2d ed. New Haven: Yale University Press, 1981.

Wilson-Jones, Mark. *Principles of Roman Architecture.* New Haven: Yale University Press, 2000.

Zanker, Paul. *The Power of Images in the Age of Augustus.* Ann Arbor: University of Michigan Press, 1988.

MEDIEVAL ART, GENERAL

Alexander, Jonathan J. G. *Medieval Illuminators and Their Methods of Work.* New Haven: Yale University Press, 1992.

Andrews, Francis B. *The Mediaeval Builders and Their Methods.* New York: Barnes & Noble, 1993.

Calkins, Robert G. *Medieval Architecture in Western Europe, from A.D. 300 to 1500.* New York: Oxford University Press, 1998.

Coldstream, Nicola. *Medieval Architecture.* New York: Oxford University Press, 2002.

Cross, Frank L., and Elizabeth A. Livingstone, eds. *The Oxford Dictionary of the Christian Church.* 3d ed. New York: Oxford University Press, 1997.

De Hamel, Christopher. *A History of Illuminated Manuscripts.* Oxford: Phaidon, 1986.

Kessler, Herbert L. *Seeing Medieval Art.* Toronto: Broadview, 2004.

Murray, Peter, and Linda Murray. *The Oxford Companion to Christian Art and Architecture.* New York: Oxford University Press, 1996.

Ross, Leslie. *Medieval Art: A Topical Dictionary.* Westport, Conn.: Greenwood, 1996.

Sekules, Veronica. *Medieval Art.* New York: Oxford University Press, 2001.

Snyder, James, Henry Luttikhuizen, and Dorothy Verkerk. *Art of the Middle Ages.* 2d ed. Upper Saddle River, N.J.: Prentice Hall, 2006.

Stokstad, Marilyn. *Medieval Art.* 2d ed. Boulder, Colo.: Westview, 2004.

CHAPTER 4 Early Christianity and Byzantium

Bowersock, G. W., Peter Brown, and Oleg Grabar, eds. *Late Antiquity: A Guide to the Postclassical World.* Cambridge, Mass.: Harvard University Press, 1998.

Cormack, Robin. *Byzantine Art.* New York: Oxford University Press, 2000.

Elsner, Jaś. *Art and the Roman Viewer: The Transformation of Art from the Pagan World to Christianity.* New York: Cambridge University Press, 1995.

———. *Imperial Rome and Christian Triumph.* New York: Oxford University Press, 1998.

Grabar, André. *The Beginnings of Christian Art, 200–395.* London: Thames & Hudson, 1967.

———. *Christian Iconography.* Princeton, N.J.: Princeton University Press, 1980.

———. *The Golden Age of Justinian: From the Death of Theodosius to the Rise of Islam.* New York: Odyssey, 1967.

Jensen, Robin Margaret. *Understanding Early Christian Art.* New York: Routledge, 2000.

Koch, Guntram. *Early Christian Art and Architecture.* London: SCM Press, 1996.

Krautheimer, Richard, and Slobodan Ćurčić. *Early Christian and Byzantine Architecture.* 4th ed. New Haven: Yale University Press, 1986.

Lowden, John. *Early Christian and Byzantine Art.* London: Phaidon, 1997.

Mango, Cyril. *Art of the Byzantine Empire, 312–1453: Sources and Documents.* Toronto: University of Toronto Press, 1986. Reprint of 1972 ed.

———. *Byzantine Architecture.* New York: Electa/Rizzoli, 1985.

Mathews, Thomas F. *Byzantium: From Antiquity to the Renaissance.* New York: Abrams, 1998.

———. *The Clash of Gods: A Reinterpretation of Early Christian Art.* Rev. ed. Princeton, N.J.: Princeton University Press, 1999.

Ousterhout, Robert. *Master Builders of Byzantium.* Princeton, N.J.: Princeton University Press, 2000.

Pelikan, Jaroslav. *Imago Dei: The Byzantine Apologia for Icons.* Princeton, N.J.: Princeton University Press, 1990.

Rodley, Lyn. *Byzantine Art and Architecture: An Introduction.* New York: Cambridge University Press, 1994.

Spier, Jeffrey, ed. *Picturing the Bible: The Earliest Christian Art.* New Haven: Yale University Press, 2007.

Webster, Leslie, and Michelle Brown, eds. *The Transformation of the Roman World,* A.D. *400–900.* Berkeley: University of California Press, 1997.

CHAPTER 5 The Islamic World

Blair, Sheila S., and Jonathan Bloom. *The Art and Architecture of Islam, 1250–1800.* New Haven: Yale University Press, 1994.

Bloom, Jonathan, and Sheila S. Blair. *Islamic Arts.* London: Phaidon, 1997.

Brend, Barbara. *Islamic Art.* Cambridge, Mass.: Harvard University Press, 1991.

Ettinghausen, Richard, Oleg Grabar, and Marilyn Jenkins-Madina. *The Art and Architecture of Islam, 650–1250.* Rev. ed. New Haven: Yale University Press, 2001.

Frishman, Martin, and Hasan-Uddin Khan. *The Mosque: History, Architectural Development and Regional Diversity.* New York: Thames & Hudson, 1994.

Grube, Ernst J. *Architecture of the Islamic World: Its History and Social Meaning.* 2d ed. New York: Thames & Hudson, 1984.

Hattstein, Markus, and Peter Delius, eds. *Islam: Art and Architecture.* Cologne: Könemann, 2000.

Hillenbrand, Robert. *Islamic Architecture: Form, Function, Meaning.* Edinburgh: Edinburgh University Press, 1994.

———. *Islamic Art and Architecture.* New York: Thames & Hudson, 1999.

Irwin, Robert. *Islamic Art in Context: Art, Architecture, and the Literary World.* New York: Abrams, 1997.

CHAPTER 6 Early Medieval and Romanesque Europe

Cahn, Walter. *Manuscripts: The Twelfth Century.* 2 vols. London: Miller, 1998.

Conant, Kenneth J. *Carolingian and Romanesque Architecture, 800–1200.* 4th ed. New Haven: Yale University Press, 1992.

Davis-Weyer, Caecilia. *Early Medieval Art, 300–1150: Sources and Documents.* Toronto: University of Toronto Press, 1986. Reprint of 1971 ed.

Diebold, William J. *Word and Image: An Introduction to Early Medieval Art.* Boulder, Colo.: Westview, 2000.

Dodwell, Charles R. *The Pictorial Arts of the West, 800–1200.* New Haven: Yale University Press, 1993.

Harbison, Peter. *The Golden Age of Irish Art: The Medieval Achievement, 600–1200.* New York: Thames & Hudson, 1999.

Hearn, Millard F. *Romanesque Sculpture: The Revival of Monumental Stone Sculpture in the Eleventh and Twelfth Centuries.* Ithaca, N.Y.: Cornell University Press, 1981.

Henderson, George. *From Durrow to Kells: The Insular Gospel-Books, 650–800.* London: Thames & Hudson, 1987.

Hubert, Jean, Jean Porcher, and Wolfgang Fritz Volbach. *The Carolingian Renaissance.* New York: Braziller, 1970.

McClendon, Charles. *The Origins of Medieval Architecture: Building in Europe,* A.D. *600–900.* New Haven: Yale University Press, 2005.

Minne-Sève, Viviane, and Hervé Kergall. *Romanesque and Gothic France: Architecture and Sculpture.* New York: Abrams, 2000.

Nees, Lawrence J. *Early Medieval Art.* New York: Oxford University Press, 2002.

Petzold, Andreas. *Romanesque Art.* New York: Abrams, 1995.

Stalley, Roger. *Early Medieval Architecture.* New York: Oxford University Press, 1999.

Toman, Rolf, ed. *Romanesque: Architecture, Sculpture, Painting.* Cologne: Könemann, 1997.

CHAPTER 7 Gothic Europe

Bony, Jean. *French Gothic Architecture of the Twelfth and Thirteenth Centuries.* Berkeley: University of California Press, 1983.

Branner, Robert. *Manuscript Painting in Paris during the Reign of St. Louis.* Berkeley: University of California Press, 1977.

———. *St. Louis and the Court Style in Gothic Architecture.* London: Zwemmer, 1965.

Camille, Michael. *Gothic Art: Glorious Visions.* New York: Abrams, 1996.

Courtenay, Lynn T., ed. *The Engineering of Medieval Cathedrals.* Aldershot: Scolar, 1997.

Erlande-Brandenburg, Alain. *The Cathedral: The Social and Architectural Dynamics of Construction.* New York: Cambridge University Press, 1994.

Frankl, Paul, and Paul Crossley. *Gothic Architecture.* New Haven: Yale University Press, 2000.

Frisch, Teresa G. *Gothic Art, 1140–c. 1450: Sources and Documents.* Toronto: University of Toronto Press, 1987. Reprint of 1971 ed.

Grodecki, Louis. *Gothic Architecture.* New York: Electa/Rizzoli, 1985.

Grodecki, Louis, and Catherine Brisac. *Gothic Stained Glass, 1200–1300.* Ithaca, N.Y.: Cornell University Press, 1985.

Maginnis, Hayden B. J. *Painting in the Age of Giotto: A Historical Reevaluation.* University Park: Pennsylvania State University Press, 1997.

———. *The World of the Early Sienese Painter.* University Park: Pennsylvania State University Press, 2001.

Minne-Sève, Viviane, and Hervé Kergall. *Romanesque and Gothic France: Architecture and Sculpture.* New York: Abrams, 2000.

Moskowitz, Anita Fiderer. *Italian Gothic Sculpture, c. 1250–c. 1400.* Cambridge: Cambridge University Press, 2001.

Norman, Diana, ed. *Siena, Florence, and Padua: Art, Society, and Religion, 1280–1400.* New Haven: Yale University Press, 1995.

Radding, Charles M., and William W. Clark. *Medieval Architecture, Medieval Learning.* New Haven: Yale University Press, 1992.

Rudolph, Conrad. *Artistic Change at St-Denis: Abbot Suger's Program and the Early Twelfth-Century Controversy over Art.* Princeton, N.J.: Princeton University Press, 1990.

Sauerländer, Willibald, and Max Hirmer. *Gothic Sculpture in France, 1140–1270.* New York: Abrams, 1973.

Toman, Rolf, ed. *The Art of Gothic: Architecture, Sculpture, Painting.* Cologne: Könemann, 1999.

White, John. *Art and Architecture in Italy, 1250–1400.* 3d ed. New Haven: Yale University Press, 1993.

Williamson, Paul. *Gothic Sculpture, 1140–1300*. New Haven: Yale University Press, 1995.

Wilson, Christopher. *The Gothic Cathedral: The Architecture of the Great Church, 1130–1530*. London: Thames & Hudson, 1990.

RENAISSANCE ART, GENERAL

Andrés, Glenn M., John M. Hunisak, and Richard Turner. *The Art of Florence*. 2 vols. New York: Abbeville, 1988.

Cole, Bruce. *Italian Art, 1250–1550: The Relation of Renaissance Art to Life and Society*. New York: Harper & Row, 1987.

———. *The Renaissance Artist at Work: From Pisano to Titian*. New York: Harper Collins, 1983.

Frommel, Christoph Luitpold. *The Architecture of the Italian Renaissance*. New York: Thames & Hudson, 2007.

Hartt, Frederick, and David G. Wilkins. *History of Italian Renaissance Art*. 6th ed. Upper Saddle River, N.J.: Prentice Hall, 2006.

Paoletti, John T., and Gary M. Radke. *Art, Power, and Patronage in Renaissance Italy*. Upper Saddle River, N.J.: Prentice Hall, 2005.

Richardson, Carol M., Kim W. Woods, and Michael W. Franklin. *Renaissance Art Reconsidered: An Anthology of Primary Sources*. Oxford: Blackwell, 2007.

Snyder, James, Larry Silver, and Henry Luttikhuizen. *Northern Renaissance Art: Painting, Sculpture, the Graphic Arts from 1350 to 1575*. Upper Saddle River, N.J.: Prentice Hall, 2005.

Thomson, David. *Renaissance Architecture: Critics, Patrons, and Luxury*. Manchester: Manchester University Press, 1993.

CHAPTER 8 Europe, 1400 to 1500

Baxandall, Michael. *Painting and Experience in Fifteenth Century Italy: A Primer in the Social History of Pictorial Style*. 2d ed. New York: Oxford University Press, 1988.

Campbell, Lorne. *The Fifteenth Century Netherlandish Schools*. London: National Gallery Publications, 1998.

Cole, Alison. *Virtue and Magnificence: Art of the Italian Renaissance Courts*. New York: Abrams, 1995.

Cole, Bruce. *Masaccio and the Art of Early Renaissance Florence*. Bloomington: Indiana University Press, 1980.

Edgerton, Samuel Y., Jr. *The Heritage of Giotto's Geometry: Art and Science on the Eve of the Scientific Revolution*. Ithaca, N.Y.: Cornell University Press, 1991.

Gilbert, Creighton, ed. *Italian Art, 1400–1500: Sources and Documents*. Evanston, Ill.: Northwestern University Press, 1992.

Hall, Marcia B. *Color and Meaning: Practice and Theory in Renaissance Painting*. Cambridge: Cambridge University Press, 1992.

Harbison, Craig. *The Mirror of the Artist: Northern Renaissance Art in Its Historical Context*. New York: Abrams, 1995.

Heydenreich, Ludwig H. *Architecture in Italy, 1400–1500*. 2d ed. New Haven: Yale University Press, 1996.

Hollingsworth, Mary. *Patronage in Renaissance Italy: From 1400 to the Early Sixteenth Century*. Baltimore: Johns Hopkins University Press, 1994.

Kemp, Martin. *Behind the Picture: Art and Evidence in the Italian Renaissance*. New Haven: Yale University Press, 1997.

Kempers, Bram. *Painting, Power, and Patronage: The Rise of the Professional Artist in the Italian Renaissance*. London: Penguin, 1992.

Lane, Barbara G. *The Altar and the Altarpiece: Sacramental Themes in Early Netherlandish Painting*. New York: Harper & Row, 1984.

Müller, Theodor. *Sculpture in the Netherlands, Germany, France and Spain, 1400–1500*. New Haven: Yale University Press, 1986.

Murray, Peter. *Renaissance Architecture*. New York: Electa/Rizzoli, 1985.

Olson, Roberta J. M. *Italian Renaissance Sculpture*. London: Thames & Hudson, 1992.

Parshall, Peter, and Rainer Schoch. *Origins of European Printmaking: Fifteenth-Century Woodcuts and Their Public*. New Haven: Yale University Press, 2005.

Seymour, Charles. *Sculpture in Italy, 1400–1500*. New Haven: Yale University Press, 1992.

Smith, Jeffrey Chipps. *The Northern Renaissance*. New York: Phaidon, 2004.

Turner, A. Richard. *Renaissance Florence: The Invention of a New Art*. New York: Abrams, 1997.

Welch, Evelyn. *Art and Society in Italy, 1350–1500*. Oxford: Oxford University Press, 1997.

White, John. *The Birth and Rebirth of Pictorial Space*. 3d ed. Boston: Faber & Faber, 1987.

Wolfthal, Diane. *The Beginnings of Netherlandish Canvas Painting, 1400–1530*. New York: Cambridge University Press, 1989.

CHAPTER 9 Europe, 1500 to 1600

Blunt, Anthony. *Art and Architecture in France, 1500–1700*. Rev. ed. New Haven: Yale University Press, 1999.

Brown, David Alan, and Sylvia Ferino-Pagden. *Bellini, Giorgione, Titian and the Renaissance of Venetian Painting*. New Haven: Yale University Press, 2006.

Brown, Patricia Fortini. *Art and Life in Renaissance Venice*. New York: Abrams, 1997.

Franklin, David. *Painting in Renaissance Florence, 1500–1550*. New Haven: Yale University Press, 2001.

Freedberg, Sydney J. *Painting in Italy, 1500–1600*. 3d ed. New Haven: Yale University Press, 1993.

Goffen, Rona. *Renaissance Rivals: Michelangelo, Leonardo, Raphael, Titian*. New Haven: Yale University Press, 2002.

Hall, Marcia B. *After Raphael: Painting in Central Italy in the Sixteenth Century*. Cambridge: Cambridge University Press, 1999.

Hall, Marcia B., ed. *Rome*. Artistic Centers of the Italian Renaissance series. New York: Cambridge University Press, 2005.

Holt, Elizabeth Gilmore, ed. *A Documentary History of Art*. Vol. 2, *Michelangelo and the Mannerists*. Rev. ed. Princeton, N.J.: Princeton University Press, 1982.

Humfry, Peter. *Painting in Renaissance Venice*. New Haven: Yale University Press, 1995.

Huse, Norbert, and Wolfgang Wolters. *The Art of Renaissance Venice: Architecture, Sculpture, and Painting*. Chicago: University of Chicago Press, 1990.

Koerner, Joseph Leo. *The Reformation of the Image*. Chicago: University of Chicago Press, 2004.

Landau, David, and Peter Parshall. *The Renaissance Print, 1470–1550*. New Haven: Yale University Press, 1994.

Lotz, Wolfgang. *Architecture in Italy, 1500–1600*. 2d ed. New Haven: Yale University Press, 1995.

Partridge, Loren. *The Art of Renaissance Rome*. New York: Abrams, 1996.

Shearman, John K. G. *Mannerism*. Baltimore: Penguin, 1978.

———. *Only Connect . . . Art and the Spectator in the Italian Renaissance*. Princeton, N.J.: Princeton University Press, 1990.

Smith, Jeffrey C. *German Sculpture of the Later Renaissance, c. 1520–1580: Art in an Age of Uncertainty*. Princeton, N.J.: Princeton University Press, 1993.

Stechow, Wolfgang. *Northern Renaissance Art, 1400–1600: Sources and Documents*. Upper Saddle River, N.J.: Prentice Hall, 1966.

Summers, David. *Michelangelo and the Language of Art*. Princeton, N.J.: Princeton University Press, 1981.

Zerner, Henri. *Renaissance Art in France: The Invention of Classicism*. Paris: Flammarion, 2003.

CHAPTER 10 Europe, 1600 to 1700

Alpers, Svetlana. *The Art of Describing: Dutch Art in the Seventeenth Century*. Chicago: University of Chicago Press, 1984.

Belkin, Kristin Lohse. *Rubens*. London: Phaidon, 1998.

Blunt, Anthony. *Art and Architecture in France, 1500–1700*. Rev. ed. New Haven: Yale University Press, 1999.

Brown, Jonathan. *The Golden Age of Painting in Spain*. New Haven: Yale University Press, 1991.

Enggass, Robert, and Jonathan Brown. *Italy and Spain, 1600–1750: Sources and Documents*. Upper Saddle River, N.J.: Prentice Hall, 1970.

Franits, Wayne. *Looking at Seventeenth-Century Dutch Art: Realism Reconsidered*. Cambridge: Cambridge University Press, 1997.

Haak, Bob. *The Golden Age: Dutch Painters of the Seventeenth Century*. New York: Abrams, 1984.

Harris, Ann Sutherland. *Seventeenth-Century Art & Architecture*. Upper Saddle River, N.J.: Prentice Hall, 2005.

Harrison, Charles, Paul Wood, and Jason Gaiger, eds. *Art in Theory, 1648–1815: An Anthology of Changing Ideas*. Oxford: Blackwell, 2000.

Held, Julius, and Donald Posner. *17th and 18th Century Art: Baroque Painting, Sculpture, Architecture*. New York: Abrams, 1971.

Lagerlöf, Margaretha R. *Ideal Landscape: Annibale Carracci, Nicolas Poussin and Claude Lorrain*. New Haven: Yale University Press, 1990.

Mérot, Alain. *French Painting in the Seventeenth Century*. New Haven: Yale University Press, 1995.

Montagu, Jennifer. *Roman Baroque Sculpture: The Industry of Art*. New Haven: Yale University Press, 1989.

Norberg-Schulz, Christian. *Baroque Architecture*. New York: Rizzoli, 1986.

North, Michael. *Art and Commerce in the Dutch Golden Age*. New Haven: Yale University Press, 1997.

Rosenberg, Jakob, Seymour Slive, and E. H. ter Kuile. *Dutch Art and Architecture, 1600–1800*. New Haven: Yale University Press, 1979.

Schama, Simon. *The Embarrassment of Riches: An Interpretation of Dutch Culture in the Golden Age*. Berkeley: University of California Press, 1988.

Toman, Rolf. *Baroque: Architecture, Sculpture, Painting*. Cologne: Könemann, 1998.

Varriano, John. *Italian Baroque and Rococo Architecture*. New York: Oxford University Press, 1986.

Vlieghe, Hans. *Flemish Art and Architecture, 1585–1700*. New Haven: Yale University Press, 1998.

Westermann, Mariët. *Rembrandt*. London: Phaidon, 2000.

———. *A Worldly Art: The Dutch Republic, 1585–1718*. New Haven: Yale University Press, 1996.

Wittkower, Rudolf. *Art and Architecture in Italy, 1600–1750*. 3 vols. 6th ed., revised by Joseph Connors and Jennifer Montagu. New Haven: Yale University Press, 1999.

CHAPTER 11 Europe and America, 1700 to 1800

Bermingham, Ann. *Landscape and Ideology: The English Rustic Tradition, 1740–1850*. Berkeley: University of California Press, 1986.

Boime, A. *Art in the Age of Revolution, 1750–1800*. Chicago: University of Chicago Press, 1987.

Crow, Thomas E. *Painters and Public Life in Eighteenth-Century Paris*. New Haven: Yale University Press, 1985.

Gaunt, W. *The Great Century of British Painting: Hogarth to Turner*. New York: Phaidon, 1971.

Herrmann, Luke. *British Landscape Painting of the Eighteenth Century*. New York: Oxford University Press, 1974.

Honour, Hugh. *Neo-Classicism*. Harmondsworth: Penguin, 1968.

Levey, Michael. *Rococo to Revolution: Major Trends in Eighteenth Century Painting*. London: Thames & Hudson, 1966.

Stillman, Damie. *English Neo-Classical Architecture*. 2 vols. London: Zwemmer, 1988.

Waterhouse, Ellis Kirkham. *Painting in Britain, 1530–1790*. 4th ed. New Haven: Yale University Press, 1979.

19TH AND 20TH CENTURIES, GENERAL

Arnason, H. H., and Peter Kalb. *History of Modern Art: Painting, Sculpture, Architecture, Photography*. 5th ed. Upper Saddle River, N.J.: Prentice Hall, 2004.

Ashton, Dore. *Twentieth-Century Artists on Art*. New York: Pantheon Books, 1985.

Chipp, Herschel B. *Theories of Modern Art*. Berkeley: University of California Press, 1968.

Chu, Petra ten-Doesschate. *Nineteenth-Century European Art*. 2d ed. Upper Saddle River, N.J.: Prentice Hall, 2006.

Coke, Van Deren. *The Painter and the Photograph from Delacroix to Warhol*. Rev. ed. Albuquerque: University of New Mexico Press, 1972.

Colquhoun, Alan. *Modern Architecture*. Oxford: Oxford University Press, 2002.

Craven, Wayne. *American Art: History and Culture*. Madison: Brown & Benchmark, 1994.

Doss, Erika. *Twentieth-Century American Art*. New York: Oxford University Press, 2002.

Eisenman, Stephen F., ed. *Nineteenth Century Art: A Critical History*. 3d ed. New York: Thames & Hudson, 2007.

Foster, Hal, Rosalind Krauss, Yve-Alain Bois, and Benjamin H. D. Buchloh. *Art since 1900: Modernism, Antimodernism, Postmodernism*. New York: Thames & Hudson, 2004.

Frampton, Kenneth. *A Critical History of Modern Architecture*. London: Thames & Hudson, 1985.

Goldwater, Robert, and Marco Treves, eds. *Artists on Art, from the XIV to the XX Century*. 3d ed. New York: Pantheon Books, 1958.

Hamilton, George H. *Painting and Sculpture in Europe, 1880–1940*. 6th ed. New Haven: Yale University Press, 1993.

Harrison, Charles, and Paul Wood. *Art in Theory, 1900–2000: An Anthology of Changing Ideas*. Oxford: Blackwell, 2003.

Herbert, Robert L., ed. *Modern Artists on Art*. Upper Saddle River, N.J.: Prentice Hall, 1971.

Hertz, Richard, and Norman M. Klein, eds. *Twentieth-Century Art Theory: Urbanism, Politics, and Mass Culture*. Englewood Cliffs, N.J.: Prentice Hall, 1990.

Heyer, Paul. *Architects on Architecture: New Directions in America*. New York: Van Nostrand Reinhold, 1993.

Hunter, Sam, John Jacobus, and Daniel Wheeler. *Modern Art: Painting, Sculpture, Architecture, Photography*. 3d ed. Upper Saddle River, N.J.: Prentice Hall, 2004.

Marien, Mary Warner. *Photography: A Cultural History*. 2d ed. Upper Saddle River, N.J.: Prentice Hall, 2006.

Pohl, Frances K. *Framing America: A Social History of American Art*. 2d ed. New York: Thames & Hudson, 2007.

Rosenblum, Robert, and Horst W. Janson. *19th-Century Art*. Rev. ed. Upper Saddle River, N.J.: Prentice Hall, 2005.

Upton, Dell. *Architecture in the United States*. Oxford: Oxford University Press, 1998.

Weaver, Mike. *The Art of Photography, 1839–1989*. New Haven: Yale University Press, 1989.

CHAPTER 12 Europe and America, 1800 to 1870

Bergdoll, Barry. *European Architecture, 1750–1890*. New York: Oxford University Press, 2000.

Boime, Albert. *The Academy and French Painting in the 19th Century*. London: Phaidon, 1971.

———. *Art in the Age of Bonapartism, 1800–1815*. Chicago: University of Chicago Press, 1990.

Brown, David Blayney. *Romanticism*. London: Phaidon, 2001.

Bryson, Norman. *Tradition and Desire: From David to Delacroix*. New York: Cambridge University Press, 1984.

Clark, T. J. *The Painting of Modern Life: Paris in the Art of Manet and His Followers*. Princeton, N.J.: Princeton University Press, 1984.

Eitner, Lorenz. *Neoclassicism and Romanticism, 1750–1850: An Anthology of Sources and Documents*. New York: Harper & Row, 1989.

Fried, Michael. *Manet's Modernism, or, The Face of Painting in the 1860s*. Chicago: University of Chicago Press, 1996.

Holt, Elizabeth Gilmore, ed. *From the Classicists to the Impressionists: A Documentary History of Art and Architecture in the Nineteenth Century*. Garden City, N.J.: Anchor Books/Doubleday, 1966.

Honour, Hugh. *Romanticism*. New York: Harper & Row, 1979.

Krell, Alain. *Manet and the Painters of Contemporary Life*. London: Thames & Hudson, 1996.

Kroeber, Karl. *British Romantic Art*. Berkeley: University of California Press, 1986.

Middleton, Robin. *Architecture of the Nineteenth Century*. London: Phaidon, 2003.

Middleton, Robin, and David Watkin. *Neoclassical and 19th-Century Architecture*. 2 vols. New York: Electa/Rizzoli, 1987.

Nochlin, Linda. *Realism and Tradition in Art, 1848–1900: Sources and Documents*. Upper Saddle River, N.J.: Prentice Hall, 1966.

Novotny, Fritz. *Painting and Sculpture in Europe, 1780–1880*. 3d ed. New Haven: Yale University Press, 1988.

Rubin, James Henry. *Courbet*. London: Phaidon, 1997.

Symmons, Sarah. *Goya*. London: Phaidon, 1998.

Vaughn, William. *German Romantic Painting*. New Haven: Yale University Press, 1980.

CHAPTER 13 Europe and America, 1870 to 1900

Broude, Norma. *Impressionism: A Feminist Reading*. New York: Rizzoli, 1991.

Escritt, Stephen. *Art Nouveau*. London: Phaidon, 2000.

Herbert, Robert L. *Impressionism: Art, Leisure, and Parisian Society.* New Haven: Yale University Press, 1988.

Lewis, Mary Tompkins. *Cézanne.* London: Phaidon, 2000.

Nochlin, Linda. *Impressionism and Post-Impressionism, 1874–1904: Sources and Documents.* Upper Saddle River, N.J.: Prentice Hall, 1966.

Rachman, Carla. *Monet.* London: Phaidon, 1997.

Rubin, James H. *Impressionism.* London: Phaidon, 1999.

Shiff, Richard. *Cézanne and the End of Impressionism: A Study of the Theory, Technique, and Critical Evaluation of Modern Art.* Chicago: University of Chicago Press, 1984.

Smith, Paul. *Impressionism: Beneath the Surface.* New York: Abrams, 1995.

Sund, Judy. *Van Gogh.* London: Phaidon, 2002.

CHAPTER 14 Europe and America, 1900 to 1945

Antliff, Mark. *Cultural Politics and the Parisian Avant-Garde.* Princeton, N.J.: Princeton University Press, 1993.

Antliff, Mark, and Patricia Leighten. *Cubism and Culture.* New York: Thames & Hudson, 2001.

Barron, Stephanie, ed. *Degenerate Art: The Fate of the Avant-Garde in Nazi Germany.* Los Angeles: Los Angeles County Museum of Art, 1991.

Bayer, Herbert, Walter Gropius, and Ise Gropius. *Bauhaus, 1919–1928.* New York: Museum of Modern Art, 1975.

Bearden, Romare, and Harry Henderson. *A History of African-American Artists from 1792 to the Present.* New York: Pantheon Books, 1993.

Breton, André. *Surrealism and Painting.* New York: Harper & Row, 1972.

Brown, Milton. *Story of the Armory Show: The 1913 Exhibition That Changed American Art.* 2d ed. New York: Abbeville, 1988.

Cox, Neil. *Cubism.* London: Phaidon, 2000.

Curtis, Penelope. *Sculpture, 1900–1945.* New York: Oxford University Press, 1999.

Curtis, William J. R. *Modern Architecture since 1900.* Upper Saddle River, N.J.: Prentice Hall, 1996.

Davidson, Abraham A. *Early American Modernist Painting, 1910–1935.* New York: Harper & Row, 1981.

Eberle, Matthias. *World War I and the Weimar Artists: Dix, Grosz, Beckmann, Schlemmer.* New Haven: Yale University Press, 1985.

Edwards, Steve, and Paul Wood, eds. *Art of the Avant-Gardes.* New Haven: Yale University Press, 2004.

Elderfield, John. *The "Wild Beasts": Fauvism and Its Affinities.* New York: Museum of Modern Art, 1976.

Gale, Matthew. *Dada and Surrealism.* London: Phaidon, 1997.

Gordon, Donald E. *Expressionism: Art and Idea.* New Haven: Yale University Press, 1987.

Harrison, Charles, Francis Frascina, and Gil Perry. *Primitivism, Cubism, Abstraction: The Early Twentieth Century.* New Haven: Yale University Press, 1993.

Hurlburt, Laurance P. *The Mexican Muralists in the United States.* Albuquerque: University of New Mexico Press, 1989.

Krauss, Rosalind. *The Originality of the Avant-Garde and Other Modernist Myths.* Cambridge, Mass.: MIT Press, 1986.

Lloyd, Jill. *German Expressionism: Primitivism and Modernity.* New Haven: Yale University Press, 1991.

Motherwell, Robert, ed. *The Dada Painters and Poets: An Anthology.* 2d ed. Boston: Hall, 1981.

Rhodes, Colin. *Primitivism and Modern Art.* New York: Thames & Hudson, 1994.

Richter, Hans. *Dada: Art and Anti-Art.* London: Thames & Hudson, 1961.

Rubin, William S. *Dada and Surrealist Art.* New York: Abrams, 1968.

———, ed. *Pablo Picasso: A Retrospective.* New York: Museum of Modern Art; Boston: New York Graphic Society, 1980.

———, ed. *"Primitivism" in 20th-Century Art: Affinity of the Tribal and the Modern.* 2 vols. New York: Museum of Modern Art, 1984.

Stott, William. *Documentary Expression and Thirties America.* New York: Oxford University Press, 1973.

Tisdall, Caroline, and Angelo Bozzolla. *Futurism.* New York: Oxford University Press, 1978.

Trachtenberg, Alan. *Reading American Photographs: Images as History—Mathew Brady to Walker Evans.* New York: Hill and Wang, 1989.

Vogt, Paul. *Expressionism: German Painting, 1905–1920.* New York: Abrams, 1980.

CHAPTER 15 Europe and America after 1945

Anfam, David. *Abstract Expressionism.* New York: Thames & Hudson, 1990.

Archer, Michael. *Art since 1960.* New ed. New York: Thames & Hudson, 2002.

Ashton, Dore. *American Art since 1945.* New York: Oxford University Press, 1983.

Battcock, Gregory, and Robert Nickas, eds. *The Art of Performance: A Critical Anthology.* New York: Dutton, 1984.

Beardsley, Richard. *Earthworks and Beyond: Contemporary Art in the Landscape.* New York: Abbeville, 1984.

Broude, Norma, and Mary D. Garrard. *The Power of Feminist Art: The American Movement of the 1970s, History and Impact.* New York: Abrams, 1994.

Causey, Andrew. *Sculpture since 1945.* New York: Oxford University Press, 1998.

Fineberg, Jonathan. *Art since 1940: Strategies of Being.* 2d ed. Upper Saddle River, N.J.: Prentice Hall, 2000.

Frascina, Francis, ed. *Pollock and After: The Critical Debate.* New York: Harper & Row, 1985.

Godfrey, Tony. *Conceptual Art.* London: Phaidon, 1998.

Goldberg, Rose Lee. *Performance Art: From Futurism to the Present.* Rev. ed. New York: Abrams, 1988.

Goldhagen, Sarah Williams, and Réjean Legault. *Anxious Modernisms: Experimentation in Postwar Architectural Culture.* Cambridge, Mass.: MIT Press, 2002.

Goodman, Cynthia. *Digital Visions: Computers and Art.* New York: Abrams, 1987.

Green, Jonathan. *American Photography: A Critical History since 1945 to the Present.* New York: Abrams, 1984.

Greenberg, Clement. *Clement Greenberg: The Collected Essays and Criticism.* Edited by J. O'Brien. 4 vols. Chicago: University of Chicago Press, 1986–1993.

Grundberg, Andy. *Photography and Art: Interactions since 1945.* New York: Abbeville, 1987.

Hertz, Richard, ed. *Theories of Contemporary Art.* 2d ed. Upper Saddle River, N.J.: Prentice Hall, 1993.

Hopkins, David. *After Modern Art, 1945–2000.* New York: Oxford University Press, 2000.

Jacobus, John. *Twentieth-Century Architecture: The Middle Years, 1940–1964.* New York: Praeger, 1966.

Jencks, Charles. *The Language of Post-Modern Architecture.* 6th ed. New York: Rizzoli, 1991.

———. *What Is Post-Modernism?* 3d ed. London: Academy Editions, 1989.

Joselit, David. *American Art since 1945.* New York: Thames & Hudson, 2003.

Kaprow, Allan. *Assemblage, Environments, and Happenings.* New York: Abrams, 1966.

Kirby, Michael. *Happenings.* New York: Dutton, 1966.

Leja, Michael. *Reframing Abstract Expressionism: Subjectivity and Painting in the 1940s.* New Haven: Yale University Press, 1993.

Lippard, Lucy R. *Mixed Blessings: New Art in a Multicultural America.* New York: Pantheon Books, 1990.

———. *Pop Art.* New York: Praeger, 1966.

Lovejoy, Margot. *Postmodern Currents: Art and Artists in the Age of the Electronic Media.* Ann Arbor, Mich.: UMI Research Press, 1989.

Lucie-Smith, Edward. *Movements in Art since 1945.* New ed. New York: Thames & Hudson, 2001.

Mamiya, Christin J. *Pop Art and Consumer Culture: American Super Market.* Austin: University of Texas Press, 1992.

Marder, Tod A. *The Critical Edge: Controversy in Recent American Architecture.* New Brunswick, N.J.: Rutgers University Press, 1980.

Norris, Christopher, and Andrew Benjamin. *What Is Deconstruction?* New York: St. Martin's, 1988.

Perry, Gill, and Paul Wood. *Themes in Contemporary Art.* New Haven: Yale University Press, 2004.

Risatti, Howard, ed. *Postmodern Perspectives: Issues in Contemporary Art.* Upper Saddle River, N.J.: Prentice Hall, 1990.

Rosen, Randy, and Catherine C. Brawer, eds. *Making Their Mark: Women Artists Move into the Mainstream, 1970–1985*. New York: Abbeville, 1989.

Rush, Michael. *New Media in Art*. 2d ed. New York: Thames & Hudson, 2005.

Sandford, Mariellen R., ed. *Happenings and Other Acts*. New York: Routledge, 1995.

Sandler, Irving. *Art of the Postmodern Era*. New York: Harper Collins, 1996.

Sayre, Henry M. *The Object of Performance: The American Avant-Garde since 1970*. Chicago: University of Chicago Press, 1989.

Schneider, Ira, and Beryl Korot. *Video Art: An Anthology*. New York: Harcourt Brace Jovanovich, 1976.

Shapiro, David, and Cecile Shapiro. *Abstract Expressionism: A Critical Record*. New York: Cambridge University Press, 1990.

Sonfist, Alan, ed. *Art in the Landscape: A Critical Anthology of Environmental Art*. New York: Dutton, 1983.

Stiles, Kristine, and Peter Selz. *Theories and Documents of Contemporary Art: A Sourcebook of Artists' Writings*. Berkeley and Los Angeles: University of California Press, 1996.

Taylor, Brendon. *Contemporary Art: Art since 1970*. Upper Saddle River, N.J.: Prentice Hall, 2005.

Venturi, Robert, Denise Scott-Brown, and Steven Isehour. *Learning from Las Vegas*. Cambridge, Mass.: MIT Press, 1972.

Waldman, Diane. *Collage, Assemblage, and the Found Object*. New York: Abrams, 1992.

Wheeler, Daniel. *Art since Mid-Century: 1945 to the Present*. Upper Saddle River, N.J.: Prentice Hall, 1991.

Wood, Paul. *Modernism in Dispute: Art since the Forties*. New Haven: Yale University Press, 1993.

CHAPTER 16 South and Southeast Asia

Asher, Catherine B. *Architecture of Mughal India*. New York: Cambridge University Press, 1992.

Beach, Milo Cleveland. *Mughal and Rajput Painting*. Cambridge: Cambridge University Press, 1992.

Blurton, T. Richard. *Hindu Art*. Cambridge, Mass.: Harvard University Press, 1993.

Chaturachinda, Gwyneth, Sunanda Krishnamurty, and Pauline W. Tabtiang. *Dictionary of South and Southeast Asian Art*. Chiang Mai, Thailand: Silkworm Books, 2000.

Craven, Roy C. *Indian Art: A Concise History*. Rev. ed. London: Thames & Hudson, 1997.

Dehejia, Vidya. *Indian Art*. London: Phaidon, 1997.

Fisher, Robert E. *Buddhist Art and Architecture*. New York: Thames & Hudson, 1993.

Harle, James C. *The Art and Architecture of the Indian Subcontinent*. 2d ed. New Haven: Yale University Press, 1994.

Huntington, Susan L., and John C. Huntington. *The Art of Ancient India: Buddhist, Hindu, Jain*. New York: Weatherhill, 1985.

McIntosh, Jane R. *A Peaceful Realm: The Rise and Fall of the Indus Civilization*. Boulder, Colo.: Westview, 2002.

Michell, George. *Hindu Art and Architecture*. New York: Thames & Hudson, 2000.

———. *The Hindu Temple: An Introduction to Its Meaning and Forms*. Chicago: University of Chicago Press, 1988.

Mitter, Partha. *Indian Art*. New York: Oxford University Press, 2001.

Srinivasan, Doris Meth. *Many Heads, Arms and Eyes: Origin, Meaning and Form of Multiplicity in Indian Art*. Leiden: E. J. Brill, 1997.

Stierlin, Henri. *Hindu India from Khajuraho to the Temple City of Madurai*. Cologne: Taschen, 1998.

Welch, Stuart Cary. *Imperial Mughal Painting*. New York: Braziller, 1978.

———. *India: Art and Culture, 1300–1900*. New York: Metropolitan Museum of Art, 1985.

CHAPTER 17 China and Korea

Cahill, James. *The Painter's Practice: How Artists Lived and Worked in Traditional China*. New York: Columbia University Press, 1994.

Clunas, Craig. *Art in China*. New York: Oxford University Press, 1997.

Fahr-Becker, Gabriele, ed. *The Art of East Asia*. Cologne: Könemann, 1999.

Fong, Wen C. *Beyond Representation: Chinese Painting and Calligraphy, 8th–14th Century*. New Haven: Yale University Press, 1992.

Fong, Wen C., and James C. Y. Watt. *Preserving the Past: Treasures from the National Palace Museum, Taipei*. New York: Metropolitan Museum of Art, 1996.

Howard, Angela Falco, Li Song, Wu Hong, and Yang Hong. *Chinese Sculpture*. New Haven: Yale University Press, 2006.

Nakata, Yujiro, ed. *Chinese Calligraphy*. New York: Weatherhill, 1983.

Rawson, Jessica. *Ancient China: Art and Archaeology*. New York: Harper & Row, 1980.

Sickman, Laurence, and Alexander C. Soper. *The Art and Architecture of China*. 3d ed. New Haven: Yale University Press, 1992.

Silbergeld, Jerome. *Chinese Painting Style: Media, Methods, and Principles of Form*. Seattle and London: University of Washington Press, 1982.

Steinhardt, Nancy S., ed. *Chinese Architecture*. New Haven: Yale University Press, 2002.

Sullivan, Michael. *Art and Artists of Twentieth-Century China*. Berkeley: University of California Press, 1996.

———. *The Arts of China*. 4th ed. Berkeley: University of California Press, 1999.

Thorp, Robert L., and Richard Ellis Vinograd. *Chinese Art and Culture*. New York: Abrams, 2001.

Vainker, S. J. *Chinese Pottery and Porcelain: From Prehistory to the Present*. New York: Braziller, 1991.

Watson, William. *The Arts of China to AD 900*. New Haven: Yale University Press, 1995.

———. *The Arts of China, 900–1620*. New Haven: Yale University Press, 2000.

Whitfield, Roger, and Anne Farrer. *Caves of the Thousand Buddhas: Chinese Art of the Silk Route*. New York: Braziller, 1990.

Wu, Hung. *Monumentality in Early Chinese Art*. Stanford, Calif.: Stanford University Press, 1996.

Xin, Yang, Nie Chongzheng, Lang Shaojun, Richard M. Barnhart, James Cahill, and Hung Wu. *Three Thousand Years of Chinese Painting*. New Haven: Yale University Press, 1997.

CHAPTER 18 Japan

Addiss, Stephen. *The Art of Zen*. New York: Abrams, 1989.

Brown, Kendall. *The Politics of Reclusion: Painting and Power in Muromachi Japan*. Honolulu: University of Hawaii Press, 1997.

Coaldrake, William H. *Architecture and Authority in Japan*. London: Routledge, 1996.

Elisseeff, Danielle, and Vadime Elisseeff. *Art of Japan*. Translated by I. Mark Paris. New York: Abrams, 1985.

Guth, Christine. *Art of Edo Japan: The Artist and the City, 1615–1868*. New York: Abrams, 1996.

Hickman, Money L., John T. Carpenter, Bruce A. Coats, Christine Guth, Andrew J. Pekarik, John M. Rosenfield, and Nicole C. Rousmaniere. *Japan's Golden Age: Momoyama*. New Haven: Yale University Press, 1996.

Mason, Penelope. *History of Japanese Art*. New York: Abrams, 1993.

Nishi, Kazuo, and Kazuo Hozumi. *What Is Japanese Architecture?* Translated by H. Mack Horton. New York: Kodansha International, 1985.

Nishikawa, Kyotaro, and Emily Sano. *The Great Age of Japanese Buddhist Sculpture*, A.D. 600–1300. Fort Worth, Tex.: Kimbell Art Museum, 1982.

Okudaira, Hideo. *Narrative Picture Scrolls*. Adapted by Elizabeth ten Grotenhuis. New York: Weatherhill, 1973.

Pearson, Richard J. *Ancient Japan*. New York: Braziller, 1992.

Rosenfield, John M. *Japanese Art of the Heian Period, 794–1185*. New York: Asia Society, 1967.

Sanford, James H., William R. LaFleur, and Masatoshi Nagatomi. *Flowing Traces: Buddhism in the Literary and Visual Arts of Japan*. Princeton, N.J.: Princeton University Press, 1992.

Shimizu, Yoshiaki, ed. *The Shaping of Daimyo Culture, 1185–1868*. Washington, D.C.: National Gallery of Art, 1988.

Singer, Robert T. *Edo. Art in Japan, 1615–1868*. Washington, D.C.: National Gallery of Art, 1998.

Stanley-Baker, Joan. *Japanese Art*. Rev. ed. New York: Thames & Hudson, 2000.

Stewart, David B. *The Making of a Modern Japanese Architecture, 1868 to the Present*. New York: Kodansha International, 1988.

CHAPTER 19 The Americas

Mesoamerica and South America

Bawden, Garth. *Moche*. Oxford: Blackwell, 1999.

Benson, Elizabeth P., and Beatriz de la Fuente, eds. *Olmec Art of Ancient Mexico*. Washington, D.C.: National Gallery of Art, 1996.

Berlo, Janet Catherine, ed. *Art, Ideology, and the City of Teotihuacan*. Washington, D.C.: Dumbarton Oaks, 1992.

Bruhns, Karen O. *Ancient South America*. New York: Cambridge University Press, 1994.

Carrasco, David. *The Oxford Encyclopedia of Mesoamerican Cultures: The Civilizations of Mexico and Central America*. New York: Oxford University Press, 2001.

Clark, John E., and Mary E. Pye, eds. *Olmec Art and Archaeology in Mesoamerica*. Washington, D.C.: National Gallery of Art, 2000.

Coe, Michael D. *The Maya*. 7th ed. New York: Thames & Hudson, 2005.

———. *Mexico: From the Olmecs to the Aztecs*. 5th ed. New York: Thames & Hudson, 2002.

D'Altroy, Terence N. *The Incas*. New ed. Oxford: Blackwell, 2003.

Fash, William. *Scribes, Warriors, and Kings: The City of Copan and the Ancient Maya*. New York: Thames & Hudson, 1991.

Grube, Nikolai, ed. *Maya: Divine Kings of the Rain Forest*. Cologne: Könemann, 2000.

Kubler, George. *The Art and Architecture of Ancient America: The Mexican, Maya, and Andean Peoples*. 3d ed. New Haven: Yale University Press, 1992.

McEwan, Gordon F. *The Incas: New Perspectives*. Santa Barbara, Calif.: ABC-CLIO, 2006.

Miller, Mary Ellen. *The Art of Mesoamerica, from Olmec to Aztec*. 4th ed. New York: Thames & Hudson, 2006.

———. *Maya Art and Architecture*. New York: Thames & Hudson, 1999.

Morris, Craig, and Adriana von Hagen. *The Inka Empire and Its Andean Origins*. New York: Abbeville, 1993.

Moseley, Michael E. *The Incas and Their Ancestors: The Archaeology of Peru*. Rev. ed. New York: Thames & Hudson, 2001.

Pasztory, Esther. *Aztec Art*. New York: Abrams, 1983.

———. *Pre-Columbian Art*. New York: Cambridge University Press, 1998.

Schele, Linda, and Mary E. Miller. *The Blood of Kings: Dynasty and Ritual in Maya Art*. Fort Worth, Tex.: Kimbell Art Museum, 1986.

Schmidt, Peter, Mercedes de la Garza, and Enrique Nalda, eds. *Maya*. New York: Rizzoli, 1998.

Silverman, Helaine. *The Nasca*. Oxford: Blackwell, 2002.

———, ed. *Andean Archaeology*. Oxford: Blackwell, 2004.

Smith, Michael Ernest. *The Aztecs*. 2d ed. Oxford: Blackwell, 2002.

Stone-Miller, Rebecca. *Art of the Andes from Chavin to Inca*. 2d ed. New York: Thames & Hudson, 2002.

Von Hagen, Adriana, and Craig Morris. *The Cities of the Ancient Andes*. New York: Thames & Hudson, 1998.

North America

Berlo, Janet Catherine, and Ruth B. Phillips. *Native North American Art*. New York: Oxford University Press, 1998.

Brose, David. *Ancient Art of the American Woodland Indians*. New York: Abrams, 1985.

Cordell, Linda S. *Ancient Pueblo Peoples*. Washington, D.C.: Smithsonian Institution Press, 1994.

Fagan, Brian. *Ancient North America: The Archaeology of a Continent*. 4th ed. New York: Thames & Hudson, 2005.

Feest, Christian F. *Native Arts of North America*. 2d ed. New York: Thames & Hudson, 1992.

Nabokov, Peter, and Robert Easton. *Native American Architecture*. New York: Oxford University Press, 1989.

Penney, David W. *North American Indian Art*. New York: Thames & Hudson, 2004.

CHAPTER 20 Africa

Bacquart, Jean-Baptiste. *The Tribal Arts of Africa*. New York: Thames & Hudson, 2002.

Bassani, Ezio. *Arts of Africa: 7,000 Years of African Art*. Milan: Skira, 2005.

Ben-Amos, Paula. *The Art of Benin*. New York: Thames & Hudson, 1980.

Blier, Suzanne P. *Royal Arts of Africa: The Majesty of Form*. New York: Abrams, 1998.

Cole, Herbert M., ed. *I Am Not Myself: The Art of African Masquerade*. Los Angeles: UCLA Fowler Museum of Cultural History, 1985.

Connah, Graham. *African Civilizations*. 2d ed. Cambridge: Cambridge University Press, 2001.

Drewal, Henry J., John Pemberton, and Rowland Abiodun. *Yoruba: Nine Centuries of African Art and Thought*. New York: Center for African Art, in association with Abrams, 1989.

Eyo, Ekpo, and Frank Willett. *Treasures of Ancient Nigeria*. New York: Knopf, 1980.

Fagg, Bernard. *Nok Terracottas*. Lagos: Ethnographica, 1977.

Fraser, Douglas F., and Herbert M. Cole, eds. *African Art and Leadership*. Madison: University of Wisconsin Press, 1972.

Garlake, Peter. *Early Art and Architecture of Africa*. Oxford: Oxford University Press, 2002.

Kasfir, Sidney L. *Contemporary African Art*. London: Thames & Hudson, 1999.

———. *West African Masks and Cultural Systems*. Tervuren: Musée Royal de l'Afrique Centrale, 1988.

Magnin, Andre, with Jacques Soulillou. *Contemporary Art of Africa*. New York: Abrams, 1996.

Phillips, Ruth B. *Representing Women: Sande Masquerades of the Mende of Sierra Leone*. Los Angeles: UCLA Fowler Museum of Cultural History, 1995.

Phillips, Tom, ed. *Africa, the Art of a Continent*. New York: Prestel, 1995.

Phillipson, D. W. *African Archaeology*. 2d ed. New York: Cambridge University Press, 1993.

Schädler, Karl-Ferdinand. *Earth and Ore: 2,500 Years of African Art in Terra-Cotta and Metal*. Munich: Panterra Verlag, 1997.

Sieber, Roy, and Roslyn A. Walker. *African Art in the Cycle of Life*. Washington, D.C.: Smithsonian Institution Press, 1987.

Visonà, Monica Blackmun, ed. *A History of Art in Africa*. 2d ed. Upper Saddle River, N.J.: Prentice Hall, 2007.

Vogel, Susan M. *Baule: African Art, Western Eyes*. New Haven: Yale University Press, 1997.

Walker, Roslyn A. *Olowe of Ise: A Yoruba Sculptor to Kings*. Washington, D.C.: National Museum of African Art, 1998.

Credits

Introduction—I-1: National Gallery of Art, Alfred Stieglitz Collection, Bequest of Georgia O'Keeffe. 1987.58.3. © 2008 The Georgia O'Keeffe Foundation/Artists Rights Society (ARS), New York; **I-2:** © English Heritage; **I-3:** akg-images/Rabatti—Domingie; **I-4:** Art © Estate of Ben Shahn/Licensed by VAGA, New York, NY. Whitney Museum of American Art, New York (gift of Edith and Milton Lowenthal in memory of Juliana Force); **I-5:** Metropolitan Museum of Art, Gift of Junius S. Morgan, 1919 (19.73.209) Image © The Metropolitan Museum of Art; **I-6:** Photo © Whitney Museum of American Art, © 2006 The Josef and Anni Albers Foundation/Artists Rights Society (ARS), New York; **I-7:** National Gallery, London. NG14. Bought, 1824; **I-8a,b:** MOA Art Museum, Shizuoka-ken, Japan; **I-9:** Bayerische Staatsgemäldesammlungen, Alte Pinakothek, Munich and Kunstdia-Archiv ARTOTHEK, Weilheim, Germany; **I-10:** Jürgen Liepe, Berlin; **I-11:** Metropolitan Museum of Art, Michael C. Rockefeller Memorial Collection, Gift of Nelson A. Rockefeller, 1965. (1987.412.309) Photograph © 1983 The Metropolitan Museum of Art; **I-12:** © Nimatallah/Art Resource, NY; **I-14a:** © National Library of Australia, Canberra, Australia/The Bridgeman Art Library; **I-14b:** From *The Childhood of Man* by Leo Frobenius (New York: J.B. Lippincott, 1909)

Chapter 1—1-1: © Yann Arthus-Bertrand/CORBIS; **1-2:** © Archivo Iconografico, S.A./CORBIS; **1-3:** Jean Vertut; **1-4:** Jean Vertut; **1-5:** Jean Vertut; **1-6:** Jean Vertut; **1-7:** © Gianni Dagli Orti/CORBIS; **1-8:** ANCIENT STATUES FROM JORDAN, These life size (human-form figures) made of plaster and bitumen date from 6500 BC and were recovered in 1985 from the statue pit at "Ain Ghazal" the Neolithic site located on the outskirts of 'Amman the capital of Jordan. Courtesy of the Hashemite Kingdom of Jordan, Dept. of Antiquities Statues from Ain Ghazal; **1-9:** © Adam Woolfitt/CORBIS; **1-10:** © Robert Harding Picture Library; **1-11:** Erwin Bohm; **1-12:** Erwin Bohm; **1-13:** © Erich Lessing/Art Resource, NY; **1-14a,b:** © British Museum, London, UK/The Bridgeman Art Library; **1-15:** © Joseph Scherschel/National Geographic Image Collection; **1-16:** © Réunion des Musées Nationaux/Art Resource, NY; **1-17:** © Réunion des Musées Nationaux/Art Resource, NY; **1-18:** Courtesy Saskia Ltd., © Dr. Ron Wiedenhoeft; **1-19:** © Copyright the Trustees of The British Museum; **1-20:** © Bildarchiv Preussischer Kulturbesitz/Art Resource, NY; **1-21:** The Art Archive/Dagli Orti (A); **1-22:** Hirmer Fotoarchiv, Munich; **1-24:** © Werner Forman/Art Resource, NY; **1-25:** © Robert Harding Picture Library; **1-26:** © Araldo de Luca; **1-27:** Museum of Fine Arts. Boston. Harvard University-Boston Museum of Fine Arts Expedition, 11.1738. Photograph © 2008 Museum of Fine Arts, Boston; **1-28:** Jean Vertut; **1-29:** Getty Research Library, Wim Swaan Photograph Collection, 96.P.21; **1-30:** © Carmen Redondo/CORBIS; **1-31:** Jean Claude Golvin; **1-32:** Metropolitan Museum of Art, Levi Hale Willard Bequest, 1890 (90.35.1), and the Frank H. McClung Museum, The University of Tennessee; **1-33:** © Araldo de Luca; **1-34:** © Bildarchiv Preussischer Kulturbesitz/Art Resource, NY; **1-35:** © Boltin Picture Library/Bridgeman Art Library; **1-36:** © Robert Harding Picture Library

Chapter 2—2-1: © Scala/Art Resource, NY; **2-2:** © Erich Lessing/Art Resource, NY; **2-3:** © Yann Arthus-Bertrand/CORBIS; **2-4:** © Roger Wood/CORBIS; **2-5:** The Art Archive/Heraklion Museum/Dagli Orti; **2-6:** © Nimatallah/Art Resource, NY; **2-7:** © Scala/Art Resource, NY; **2-8:** © Nimatallah/Art Resource, NY; **2-9:** Photo by Raymond V. Schoder, © 1987 by Bolchazy-Carducci Publishers, Inc.; **2-10:** Copyright © SIME s.a.s/eStock Photo—All rights reserved; **2-11:** © Vanni Archive/CORBIS; **2-12:** © Vanni Archive/CORBIS; **2-13:** © Archivo Iconografico, S.A./CORBIS ; **2-14:** The Metropolitan Museum of Art, Rogers Fund, 1914. (14.130.14) Photograph © 1996 The Metropolitan Museum of Art; **2-15:** © Réunion des Musées Nationaux/Art Resource, NY; **2-16:** The Metropolitan Museum of Art, Fletcher Fund, 1932. (32.11.1). Photograph © 1997 The Metropolitan Museum of Art; **2-17:** © Gianni Dagli Orti/CORBIS; **2-18:** © Nimatallah/Art Resource, NY; **2-21:** © Vanni/Art Resource, NY; **2-23:** © Vanni/Art Resource, NY; **2-24:** © Scala/Art Resource, NY; **2-25:** © Réunion des Musées Nationaux/Art Resource, NY; **2-26:** Courtesy Saskia Ltd., © Dr. Ron Wiedenhoeft; **2-27a:** Courtesy Saskia Ltd., © Dr. Ron Wiedenhoeft; **2-28:** © Gianni Dagli Orti/CORBIS; **2-29:** Courtesy Saskia Ltd., © Dr. Ron Wiedenhoeft; **2-30:** Courtesy Saskia Ltd., © Dr. Ron Wiedenhoeft; **2-31:** Studio Kontos; **2-32:** © Scala/Art Resource, NY; **2-34:** © Scala/Art Resource, NY; **2-36:** Studio Kontos; **2-38:** © British Museum, London, UK/Bridgeman Art Library; **2-39:** © Scala/Art Resource, NY; **2-40:** © Ancient Art and Architecture Collection Ltd.; **2-41b:** © Ancient Art and Architecture Collection Ltd.; **2-42:** © Scala/Art Resource, NY; **2-43:** Courtesy Saskia Ltd., © Dr. Ron Wiedenhoeft; **2-44:** © Nimatallah/Art Resource, NY; **2-45:** © Nimatallah/Art Resource, NY; **2-46:** © Scala/Art Resource, NY; **2-47:** © Scala/Art Resource, NY; **2-48:** © Archivo Iconografico, S.A./CORBIS; **2-49:** Canali Photobank, Italy; **2-50:** Canali Photobank, Italy; **2-51:** Photo by Raymond V. Schoder, © 1987 by Bolchazy-Carducci Publishers, Inc.; **2-52:** © Bildarchiv Preussischer Kulturbesitz/Art Resource, NY; **2-53:** © Bildarchiv Preussischer Kulturbesitz/Art Resource, NY; **2-54:** © Araldo de Luca/CORBIS; **2-55:** © Réunion des Musées Nationaux/Art Resource, NY; **2-56:** © Réunion des Musées Nationaux/Art Resource, NY; **2-57:** Courtesy Saskia Ltd., © Dr. Ron Wiedenhoeft; **2-58:** Image copyright © The Metropolitan Museum of Art/Art Resource, NY; **2-59:** © Araldo de Luca/CORBIS

Chapter 3—3-1: © Scala/Art Resource, NY; **3-2:** © David Lees/CORBIS; **3-3:** © Araldo de Luca/CORBIS; **3-4:** © Araldo de Luca/CORBIS; **3-5:** © Archivo Iconografico, S.A./CORBIS; **3-6:** © Ancient Art and Architecture Collection Ltd.; **3-7:** © Araldo de Luca/CORBIS; **3-8:** © Scala/Art Resource, NY; **3-9:** © Charles & Josette Lenars/CORBIS; **3-10:** James E. Packer; **3-11:** Photo © Valentino Renzoni, Osimo; **3-12:** © Alinari/Art Resource, NY; **3-13:** Pubbli Aer Foto; **3-15:** Photo, Henri Stierlin; **3-17:** Photo Archives Skira, Geneva, Switzerland; **3-18:** © Scala/Art Resource, NY; **3-19a, b:** Metropolitan Museum of Art, Rogers Fund, 1903. (03.14.13a-g). Photograph © 1986 The Metropolitan Museum of Art; **3-20:** © foto Luciano Romano; **3-21:** Metropolitan Museum of Art, Rogers Fund, 1920. (20.192.1). Photograph © 1987 The Metropolitan Museum of Art; **3-22:** Canali Photobank, Italy; **3-23:** Canali Photobank, Italy; **3-24:** Ny Carlsberg Glyptotek, Copenhagen; **3-25:** Courtesy Saskia Ltd., © Dr. Ron Wiedenhoeft; **3-26:** Courtesy Saskia Ltd., © Dr. Ron Wiedenhoeft; **3-27:** © Oliver Benn/Getty Images/Stone; **3-28:** © Robert Harding Picture Library; **3-29:** © Roy Rainford/Robert Harding Picture Library; **3-30:** © Araldo de Luca/CORBIS; **3-31:** Courtesy Saskia Ltd., © Dr. Ron Wiedenhoeft; **3-32:** © 2006 Fred S. Kleiner; **3-33:** © 2006 Fred S. Kleiner; **3-35:** Canali Photobank, Italy; **3-36:** © Scala/Art Resource, NY; **3-37:** © Scala/Art Resource, NY; **3-39:** Photo, Henri Stierlin; **3-40:** © 2006 Fred S. Kleiner; **3-41:** © The Trustees of The British Museum; **3-43:** © Scala/Art Resource, NY; **3-44:** The Metropolitan Museum of Art, New York, Samuel D. Lee Fund, 1940. (40.11.1a) Photograph © 1986 The Metropolitan Museum of Art; **3-45:** © Araldo de Luca; **3-46:** © Araldo de Luca/CORBIS; **3-47:** Canali Photobank, Italy; **3-48:** © 2006 Fred S. Kleiner; **3-50:** © Index/Artphoto; **3-51:** Instituto Centrale per il Catalogo e la Documentazione, (ICCD)

Chapter 4—4-1: © Alinari/Art Resource, NY; **4-2:** Pontificia Commissione per l'Archeologia Sacra; **4-3:** Foto Archivio di San Pietro in Vaticano; **4-5:** © Scala/Art Resource, NY; **4-6:** © Scala/Art Resource,

NY; **4-8:** © Scala/Art Resource, NY; **4-9:** © Scala/Art Resource, NY; **4-10:** Osterreichische Nationalbibliothek, Vienna, Bildarchiv. folio 7 recto of the Vienna Genesis; **4-11:** © Yann Arthus-Bertrand/CORBIS; **4-13:** Photo, Henri Stierlin; **4-15:** Archivio e Studio Folco Quilici, Roma; **4-17:** Canali Photobank, Italy; **4-18:** Canali Photobank, Italy; **4-19:** Canali Photobank, Italy; **4-20:** © Ronald Sheraton/Ancient Art and Architecture Collection Ltd.; **4-21:** The Art Archive/Dagli Orti; **4-22:** Studio Kontos; **4-23:** Josephine Powell; **4-24:** © Snark/Art Resource, NY; **4-25:** © Scala/Art Resource, NY

Chapter 5—5-1: © Erich Lessing/Art Resource, NY; **5-2:** © Moshe Shai/CORBIS; **5-3:** © Erich Lessing/Art Resource, NY; **5-4a:** © Yann Arthus-Bertrand/CORBIS; **5-5:** Photo, Henri Stierlin; **5-6:** www.bednorz-photo.de; **5-7:** © Adam Woolfit/Robert Harding Picture Library; **5-8:** The Art Archive/Dagli Orti; **5-9:** © Toyohiro Yamada/Getty Images/Taxi; **5-10:** photo Henri Stierlin; **5-11:** Metropolitan Museum of Art, Harris Brisbane Dick Fund, 1939 (39.20) Photograph © 1982 The Metropolitan Museum of Art; **5-12:** © The Trustees of the Chester Beatty Library, Dublin; **5-13:** © Copyright the Trustees of The British Museum; **5-14:** © Copyright the Trustees of The British Museum

Chapter 6—6-1: © The Pierpont Morgan Library/Art Resource, NY; **6-2:** © The Pierpont Morgan Library/Art Resource, NY; **6-3:** © British Library/HIP/Art Resource, NY; **6-4:** © The Board of Trinity College, Dublin, Ireland/The Bridgeman Art Library; **6-5:** Kunsthistorisches Museums, Wien; **6-6:** © Erich Lessing/Art Resource, NY; **6-8:** © Aachen Cathedral, Aachen, Germany, Bildarchiv Steffens/The Bridgeman Art Library; **6-9:** akg-images; **6-10:** www.bednorz-photo.de; **6-12:** Photo: Dom-Museum, Hildesheim (Frank Tomio); **6-13:** Rheinisches Bildarchiv; **6-14:** Jean Dieuzaide; **6-16:** akg-images/Stefan Drechsel; **6-17a, b:** © Michael Busselle/Robert Harding Picture Library; **6-19:** © Vanni/Art Resource, NY; **6-20:** akg-images/Paul M.R. Maeyaert; **6-21:** Hervé Champollion/akg-images; **6-22:** © Erich Lessing/Art Resource, NY; **6-23:** Abtei St. Hildegard; **6-24:** Photograph Speldoorn © Musées royaux d'Art et d'Histoire—Brussels; **6-25:** Canali Photobank, Italy; **6-27:** Universal Art Images; **6-28:** © Anthony Scibilia/Art Resource, NY **6-29a:** © Angelo Hornak/CORBIS; **6-30a, b:** By special permission of the City of Bayeux; **6-31:** The Master and Fellows of Corpus Christi College, Cambridge; **6-32:** Trinity College, Cambridge, England. MS R.17.1.f.283, Eadwine the Scribe

Chapter 7—7-1: www.bednorz-photo.de; **7-2:** www.bednorz-photo.de; **7-5a:** © Vanni/Art Resource, NY; **7-5b:** © Marc Garanger/CORBIS; **7-6:** © Vanni/Art Resource, NY; **7-7:** © SuperStock, Inc./SuperStock; **7-8:** Hirmer Fotoarchiv, Munich; **7-10:** © Chartres Cathedral, Chartres, France, Paul Maeyaert/The Bridgeman Art Library; **7-11:** © Angelo Hornak/CORBIS; **7-12:** © Anthony Scibilia/Art Resource, NY; **7-13:** Hirmer Fotoarchiv, Munich; **7-14:** © Scala/Art Resource, NY; **7-15:** © Giraudon/Art Resource, NY; **7-16:** www.bednorz-photo.de; **7-17:** Österreichische Nationalbibliothek, Vienna. Bildarchiv. folio 1 verso of a moralized Bible; **7-18:** © The Pierpont Morgan Library/Art Resource, NY; **7-19:** © Réunion des Musées Nationaux/Art Resource, NY; **7-20:** © English Heritage; **7-21:** © Archivo Iconografico, S.A./CORBIS; **7-22:** © Werner Forman/CORBIS; **7-23:** © Svenja-Foto/zefa/CORBIS ; **7-24:** www.bednorz-photo.de; **7-25:** www.bednorz-photo.de; **7-26:** © Erich Lessing/Art Resource, NY; **7-27:** © Scala/Art Resource, NY; **7-28:** © Scala/Art Resource, NY; **7-29:** © Summerfield Press/CORBIS ; **7-30:** © Scala/Art Resource, NY; **7-31:** © Scala/Art Resource, NY; **7-32:** © Scala/Art Resource, NY; **7-33:** Canali Photobank, Italy; **7-34:** © Scala/Art Resource, NY; **7-35:** Canali Photobank, Italy; **7-36:** © MUZZI FABIO/CORBIS SYGMA; **7-37:** © Scala/Art Resource, NY

Chapter 8—8-1: © Erich Lessing/Art Resource, NY; **8-2:** © Erich Lessing/Art Resource, NY; **8-3 left, right:** Image Copyright © The Metropolitan Museum of Art/Art Resource, NY; **8-4:** © Scala/Art Resource, NY; **8-5:** © Scala/Art Resource, NY; **8-6:** © Erich Lessing/Art Resource, NY; **8-7:** Museum of Fine Arts, Boston. Gift of Mr. and Mrs. Henry Lee Higginson. 93.153. Photograph © 2008 Museum of Fine Arts, Boston; **8-8a-c:** © Scala/Art Resource, NY; **8-9:** © Réunion des Musées Nationaux/Art Resource, NY; **8-10a:** © Bildarchiv Preussischer Kulturbesitz/Art Resource, NY; **8-10b:** © Scala/Art Resource, NY; **8-11:** © Erich Lessing/Art Resource, NY; **8-12:** © Scala/Art Resource, NY; **8-13:** © Erich Lessing/Art Resource, NY; **8-14:** © Erich Lessing/Art Resource, NY; **8-15:** © Scala/Art Resource, NY; **8-16:** © The Art Archive/Dagli Orti; **8-18:** © Scala/Art Resource, NY; **8-19:** © Scala/Art Resource, NY; **8-20:** © Elio Ciol/CORBIS; **8-21:** © Erich Lessing/Art Resource, NY; **8-22:** © Scala/Art Resource, NY; **8-23:** © Erich Lessing/Art Resource, NY; **8-24:** Canali Photobank, Italy; **8-25:** © Scala/Art Resource, NY; **8-26:** Canali Photo-

bank, Italy; **8-27:** © Summerfield Press Ltd.; **8-28:** Image Copyright © The Metropolitan Museum of Art/Art Resource, NY; **8-30:** © Alinari/Art Resource, NY; **8-31:** © Scala/Art Resource, NY; **8-32:** © Scala/Art Resource, NY; **8-33:** © The Bridgeman Art Library; **8-34:** © 1987 M. Sarri/Photo Vatican Museums; **8-35:** © Scala/Art Resource, NY; **8-36:** © Alinari/Art Resource, NY; **8-37:** Canali Photobank, Italy; **8-38:** © Scala/Art Resource, NY; **8-39:** © Scala/Art Resource, NY; **8-40:** © Erich Lessing/Art Resource, NY

Chapter 9—9-1: Photo Vatican Museums; **9-2:** © Erich Lessing/Art Resource, NY; **9-3:** © Alinari/Art Resource, NY; **9-4:** © Réunion des Musées Nationaux/Art Resource, NY; **9-5:** The Royal Collection © 2005, Her Majesty Queen Elizabeth II; **9-6:** © Erich Lessing/Art Resource, NY; **9-7:** © M. Sarri 1983/Photo Vatican Museums; **9-8:** © Araldo de Luca/CORBIS; **9-9:** © Arte & Immagini/CORBIS; **9-10:** Copyright © Nippon Television Network Corporation, Tokyo **9-11:** © Bracchietti-Zigrosi/Vatican Museums; **9-12:** Copyright © Nippon Television Network Corporation, Tokyo; **9-13:** © Scala/Art Resource, NY; **9-15:** © Scala/Art Resource, NY; **9-16:** © akg-images/Schütze/Rodemann; **9-17:** © Scala/Art Resource, NY; **9-18:** © Erich Lessing/Art Resource, NY; **9-19:** © Scala/Art Resource, NY; **9-20:** © Scala/Art Resource, NY; **9-21:** © Scala/Art Resource, NY; **9-22:** © Scala/Art Resource, NY; **9-23:** © National Gallery, London; **9-24** © The Bridgeman Art Library; **9-25:** © Scala/Art Resource, NY; **9-26:** © Scala/Art Resource, NY; **9-27:** © 2006 Fred S. Kleiner; **9-28a :**© Erich Lessing/Art Resource, NY; **9-28b:** © Musée d'Unterlinden Colmar, photo O. Zimmermann; **9-29:** Museum of Fine Arts, Boston (centennial gift of Landon T. Clay). 68.187. Photograph © 2008 Museum of Fine Arts, Boston; **9-30:** © Scala/Art Resource, NY; **9-31:** © National Gallery, London; **9-32:** © Charles E. Rotkin/CORBIS; **9-33:** © Institut Amatller D'art Hispànic; **9-34:** © Réunion des Musées Nationaux/Art Resource, NY; **9-35:** Uppsala University Art Collection; **9-36:** Oeffentliche Kunstsammlung Basel, photo Martin Bühler; **9-37:** © Bildarchiv Preussischer Kulturbesitz/Art Resource, NY; **9-38:** © Erich Lessing/Art Resource, NY; **9-39:** © Institut Amatller D'art Hispànic; **9-40:** © Scala/Art Resource, NY

Chapter 10—10-1: © akg-images/Pirozzi; **10-2:** © Andrea Jemolo/CORBIS; **10-3:** © Alinari/CORBIS; **10-4:** © akg-images/Joseph Martin; **10-5:** © Scala/Art Resource, NY; **10-6:** © Araldo de Luca; **10-7:** www.bednorz-photo.de; **10-8:** www.bednorz-photo.de; **10-9:** © Scala/Art Resource, NY; **10-10:** © Scala/Art Resource, NY; **10-11:** © Scala/Art Resource, NY; **10-12:** © Alinari/Art Resource, NY; **10-13:** © Summerfield Press Ltd.; **10-14:** Photograph © Wadsworth Atheneum Museum of Art; **10-15:** © Victoria & Albert Museum, London/Art Resource, NY; **10-16:** © Erich Lessing/Art Resource, NY; **10-17:** Copyright © IRPA-KIK, Brussels, www.kikirpa.be; **10-18:** © Erich Lessing/Art Resource, NY; **10-19:** © Réunion des Musées Nationaux/Art Resource, NY; **10-20:** © Frans Halsmuseum. Haarlem; **10-21:** Image © 2007 Board of Trustees, National Gallery of Art, Washington, D.C.; **10-22:** © The Bridgeman Art Library; **10-23:** English Heritage Photographic Library; **10-24:** © The Pierpont Morgan Library/Art Resource, NY; **10-25:** © Mauritshuis. The Hague; **10-26:** © Erich Lessing/Art Resource, NY; **10-27:** © Germanisches Nationalmuseum; Nuremberg; **10-28:** Photo Copyright © Toledo Museum of Art, Toledo, 1956.57; **10-29:** © Erich Lessing/Art Resource, NY; **10-30:** Photo copyright © Philadelphia Museum of Art, Philadelphia; **10-31:** © Réunion des Musées Nationaux/Art Resource, NY; **10-32:** © Yann Arthus-Bertrand/Altitude; **10-33:** © Massimo Listri/CORBIS; **10-34:** © Angelo Hornak/CORBIS

Chapter 11—11-1: © Yann Arthus-Bertrand/CORBIS; **11-2:** © Erich Lessing/Art Resource, NY; **11-3:** © Scala/Art Resource, NY; **11-4:** © The Bridgeman Art Library; **11-5:** © The Bridgeman Art Library; **11-6:** © Giraudon/Art Resource, NY; **11-7:** © Réunion des Musées Nationaux/Art Resource, NY; **11-8:** © The Bridgeman Art Library; **11-9:** National Gallery, London; **11-10:** © The Bridgeman Art Library; **11-11:** Photo © National Gallery of Canada; **11-12:** Museum of Fine Arts, Boston (gift of Joseph W., William B., and Edward H. R. Revere). 30.781. Photograph © 2008 Museum of Fine Arts, Boston; **11-13:** © Scala/Art Resource, NY; **11-14:** Photo: Katherine Wetzel © Virginia Museum of Fine Arts; **11-15:** © Réunion des Musées Nationaux/Art Resource, NY; **11-16:** © Scala/Art Resource, NY; **11-17:** © Monticello/Thomas Jefferson Foundation, Inc.; **11-18:** Photo © The Library of Virginia

Chapter 12—12-1: © Bettmann/CORBIS; **12-2:** © Scala/Art Resource, NY; **12-3:** © Réunion des Musées Nationaux/Art Resource, NY; **12-4:** Photograph © 1997 The Detroit Institute of Arts, 55.5.A; **12-5:** Image copyright © The Metropolitan Museum of Art/Art Resource, NY; **12-6:** © Erich Lessing/Art Resource, NY; **12-7:** © Erich Lessing/Art Resource,

NY; **12-8:** © Réunion des Musées Nationaux/Art Resource, NY; **12-9:** © Réunion des Musées Nationaux/Art Resource, NY; **12-10:** © Bildarchiv Preussischer Kulturbesitz/Art Resource, NY; **12-11:** © Art Resource, NY; **12-12:** Museum of Fine Arts, Boston (Henry Lillie Pierce Fund). 99.22. Photography © 2008 Museum of Fine Arts, Boston; **12-13:** Image copyright © The Metropolitan Museum of Art/Art Resource, NY; **12-14:** © The Bridgeman Art Library; **12-15:** © Réunion des Musées Nationaux/Art Resource, NY; **12-16:** Photo copyright © Philadelphia Museum of Art, 1995-86-42; **12-17:** © Erich Lessing/Art Resource, NY; **12-18:** © Réunion des Musées Nationaux/Art Resource, NY; **12-19:** Image copyright © The Metropolitan Museum of Art/Art Resource, NY; **12-20:** Gift of the Alumni Association to Jefferson Medical College in 1878 and purchased by the Pennsylvania Academy of the Fine Arts and the Philadelphia Museum of Art in 2007 with the generous support of more than 3,400 donors, photo copyright © Philadelphia Museum of Art; **12-21:** Photo © Howard University Gallery of Art, Washington, D.C.; **12-22:** © Tate Gallery, London/Art Resource, NY; **12-23:** © TravelPix/Robert Harding Picture Library; **12-24:** © Durand Patrick/CORBIS Sygma; **12-25:** © The Stapleton Collection/The Bridgeman Art Library; **12-26:** © Time & Life Pictures/Getty Images; **12-27:** © Hulton Archive/Getty Images

Chapter 13—13-1: Detroit Institute of Arts, Detroit (gift of Dexter M. Ferry Jr.) 46.309. Photograph © 1988 The Detroit Institute of Arts; **13-2:** © Erich Lessing/Art Resource, NY; **13-3:** © Erich Lessing/Art Resource, NY; **13-4:** © Réunion des Musées Nationaux/Art Resource, NY; **13-5:** Photo © Glasgow Art Galleries and Museum; **13-6:** Art Institute of Chicago, Chicago (Robert A. Walker Fund). 1910.2. Photography © The Art Institute of Chicago; **13-7:** Art Institute of Chicago, Chicago (Helen Birch Bartlett Memorial Collection). 1928.610. Photography © The Art Institute of Chicago; **13-8:** Art Institute of Chicago, Chicago (Helen Birch Bartlett Memorial Collection). 1926.224. Photography © The Art Institute of Chicago; **13-9:** © Yale University Art Gallery/Art Resource, NY; **13-10:** Digital Image © The Museum of Modern Art/Licensed by Scala/Art Resource, NY; **13-11:** Photo © National Gallery of Scotland, Edinburgh; **13-12:** Museum of Fine Arts, Boston (Tompkins Collection). 36.270. Photograph © 2008 Museum of Fine Arts, Boston; **13-13:** Philadelphia Museum of Art, Philadelphia (The George W. Elkins Collection). e1936-1-1 Photograph © Philadelphia Museum of Art; **13-14:** Art Institute of Chicago (Helen Birch Bartlett Memorial Collection, 1926). 1926.252 Photography © The Art Institute of Chicago; **13-15:** Digital Image © The Museum of Modern Art/Licensed by Scala/Art Resource, NY; **13-16:** Photo © Erich Lessing/Art Resource, NY; © 2008 Artists Rights Society (ARS), New York/The National Gallery, Oslo/BONO, Oslo; **13-17:** © Erich Lessing/Art Resource, NY; **13-18:** © akg-images; **13-19:** © Yann Arthus-Bertrand/CORBIS; **13-20:** © Thomas A. Heinz/CORBIS

Chapter 14—14-1: © Giraudon/Art Resource, NY, © 2008 Artists Rights Society (ARS), NY/ADAGP, Paris; **14-2:** Photo © San Francisco Museum of Modern Art, © 2008 Succession H. Matisse, Paris/Artists Rights Society (ARS), New York; **14-3:** © 2008 Succession H. Matisse, Paris/Artists Rights Society (ARS), New York; **14-4:** Digital Image © The Museum of Modern Art/Licensed by Scala/Art Resource, NY; **14-5:** Photo © David Heald © The Solomon R. Guggenheim Foundation, New York, © 2008 Artists Rights Society (ARS), New York/ADAGP, Paris; **14-6:** Oeffentliche Kunstsammlung, Basel, photo Martin Bühler; **14-7:** © Erich Lessing/Art Resource, NY; **14-8:** Digital Image © The Museum of Modern Art/Licensed by Scala/Art Resource, NY, 333.1939, © 2008 The Estate of Pablo Picasso/Artists Rights Society (ARS), NY; **14-9:** Photo: R, G. Ojeda © Réunion des Musées Nationaux/Art Resource, NY, © 2008 Estate of Pablo Picasso/Artists Rights Society (ARS), New York; **14-10:** © Albright-Knox Art Gallery, Buffalo/The Bridgeman Art Library; **14-11:** Digital Image © The Museum of Modern Art/Licensed by Scala/Art Resource, NY, 231.1948; **14-12:** Digital Image © The Museum of Modern Art/Licensed by Scala/Art Resource, NY, 457.1937, © 2008 Artists Rights Society (ARS), New York/VG Bild-Kunst, Bonn; **14-13:** Photo © Philadelphia Museum of Art, 1998-74-1, © 2008 Artists Rights Society (ARS), New York/ADAGP, Paris/Succession Marcel Duchamp; **14-14:** Photo © Bildarchiv Preussischer Kulturbesitz/Art Resource, NY, NG 57/61, © 2008 Artists Rights Society (ARS), New York/VG Bild-Kunst, Bonn; **14-15:** Photo © Philadelphia Museum of Art, 1950-134-59, © 2008 Artists Rights Society (ARS), New York/ADAGP, Paris/Succession Marcel Duchamp; **14-16:** Photo © Erich Lessing/Art Resource, NY, © 2008 Artists Rights Society (ARS), New York/ADAGP, Paris; **14-17:** Photo © Amon Carter Museum, Fort Worth, © 2008 Georgia O'Keeffe Museum/Artists Rights Society (ARS), New York; **14-18:** © 1981 Center for Creative Photography, Arizona Board of Regents; **14-19:** Photo © Erich Lessing/Art Resource, NY, © 2008 Estate of Pablo Picasso/Artists Rights Society (ARS), New York; **14-20:** Photo © Walter Klein, © 2008 Artists Rights Society (ARS), New York/VG Bild-Kunst, Bonn; **14-21:** Photo © The Bridgeman Art Library, © 2008 Artists Rights Society (ARS), New York/SIAE, Rome; **14-22:** Digital Image © The Museum of Modern Art/Licensed by Scala/Art Resource, NY, 162.1934, © 2008 Salvador Dali, Gala-Salvador Dali Foundation/Artists Rights Society (ARS), New York; **14-23:** Photo © Los Angeles County Museum of Art, 78.7, © 2008 C. Herscovici, Brussels/Artists Rights Society (ARS), New York; **14-24:** Digital Image © The Museum of Modern Art/Licensed by Scala/Art Resource, NY, 130.1946a-c, © 2008 Artists Rights Society (ARS), New York/ProLitteris, Zürich; **14-25:** Digital Image © The Museum of Modern Art/Licensed by Scala/Art Resource, NY, 229.1937, © 2008 Successi—Mir—Artists Rights Society (ARS), New York/ADAGP, Paris; **14-26:** Digital Image © The Museum of Modern Art/Licensed by Scala/Art Resource, NY, 248.1935; **14-27:** Digital Image © The Museum of Modern Art/Licensed by Scala/Art Resource, NY, 638.1967, © 2008 Mondrian-Holtzman Trust c/o HCR International, Warrenton, VA, USA; **14-28:** Photo © Philadelphia Museum of Art/CORBIS, 1950-134-14, 15, © 2008 Artists Rights Society (ARS), New York/ADAGP, Paris; **14-29:** Photo © Tate Gallery, London/Art Resource, NY, © Bowness, Hepworth Estate; **14-30:** Digital Image © The Museum of Modern Art/Licensed by Scala/Art Resource, NY, 590.1939.a-d, © 2008 Estate of Alexander Calder/Artists Rights Society (ARS), New York; **14-31:** Courtesy The Dorothea Lange Collection, The Oakland Museum of California; **14-32:** Photography The Art Institute of Chicago, 1942.51, Estate of Edward Hopper © The Whitney Museum of American Art; **14-33:** The Phillips Collection, Washington, D.C., © 2008 The Jacob and Gwendolyn Lawrence Foundation, Seattle/Artists Rights Society (ARS), New York; **14-34:** Photography © The Art Institute of Chicago, 1930.934, Art © Estate of Grant Wood/Licensed by VAGA, New York; **14-35:** Photo © 1986 The Detroit Institute of Arts/Dirk Bakker, © 2008 Banco de México Diego Rivera & Frida Kahlo Museums Trust. Av. Cinco de Mayo No. 2, Col. Centro, Del. Cuauhtémoc 06059, México, D.F; **14-36:** © Schalkwijk/Art Resource, NY; **14-37:** Photo © Vanni/Art Resource, NY, © 2008 Artists Rights Society (ARS), New York/VG Bild-Kunst, Bonn; **14-38:** Digital Image © The Museum of Modern Art/Licensed by Scala/Art Resource, NY, © 2008 Artists Rights Society (ARS), New York/VG Bild-Kunst, Bonn; **14-39:** Photo © Anthony Scibilia/Art Resource, NY, © 2008 Artists Rights Society (ARS), New York/ADAGP, Paris/FLC; **14-40:** Photo Ezra Stoller © Esto, All rights reserved, © 2008 Frank Lloyd Wright Foundation, Scottsdale, AZ/Artists Rights Society (ARS), New York

Chapter 15—15-1: Photograph by David Heald © The Solomon R. Guggenheim Foundation, New York; **15-2:** Photo © Des Moines Art Center, © 2008 Artists Rights Society (ARS), New York/ADAGP, Paris; **15-3:** Digital Image © The Museum of Modern Art/Licensed by Scala/Art Resource, NY, 229.1948, © 2008 The Estate of Francis Bacon/ARS, New York/DACS, London; **15-4:** National Gallery of Art, Washington DC, USA, © DACS/The Bridgeman Art Library. © 2008 The Pollock-Krasner Foundation/Artists Rights Society (ARS), New York; **15-5:** Digital Image © The Museum of Modern Art/Licensed by SCALA/Art Resource, NY. © 2008 The Willem de Kooning Foundation/Artists Rights Society (ARS), New York; **15-6** Photo © San Francisco Museum of Modern Art, © 1998 Kate Rothko Prizel & Christopher Rothko/Artists Rights Society (ARS), New York; **15-7:** Photo © CNAC/MNAM/Dist. © Réunion des Musées Nationaux/Art Resource, NY. © 2008 Frank Stella/Artists Rights Society (ARS), NY; **15-8:** Photo © The Detroit Institute of Arts, Founders Society Purchase, Dr. and Mrs. Hilbert H. DeLawter Fund/The Bridgeman Art Library, Art © Helen Frankenthaler; **15-9:** Photo © Tate Gallery, London/Art Resource, NY, Art © Estate of David Smith/Licensed by VAGA, New York; **15-10:** Photo © Hirshhorn Museum and Sculpture Garden, Smithsonian Institution, 72.154, Art © Judd Foundation/Licensed by VAGA, New York; **15-11:** Photo © CNAC/MNAM/Dist. © Réunion des Musées Nationaux/Art Resource, NY, © 2008 Estate of Louise Nevelson/Artists Rights Society (ARS), New York; **15-12:** Photo © CNAC/MNAM/Dist. © Réunion des Musées Nationaux/Art Resource, NY, Art © Louise Bourgeois/Licensed by VAGA, New York; **15-13:** Photo © The Bridgeman Art Library, © 2008 Artists Rights Society (ARS), New York/DACS, London; **15-14:** Digital Image © The Museum of Modern Art/Licensed by Scala/Art Resource, NY, 106.1973, Art © Jasper Johns/Licensed by VAGA, New York; **15-15:** Art © Robert Rauschenberg/Licensed by VAGA, New York; **15-16:** Oeffentliche Kunstsammlung Basel, Photo Martin Bühler, © Estate of Roy Lichtenstein; **15-17:** Photo © Tate Gallery, London/Art Resource, NY, © 2008 Andy Warhol Foundation for the Visual Arts/ARS, New York, Marilyn Monroe Estate/Curtis Management Agency;

15-18: Photo © Walker Art Center, Minneapolis, © Chuck Close; 15-19: Photo by Anne Gold, Art © Estate of Duane Hanson/Licensed by VAGA, New York; 15-20: Photo © Philadelphia Museum of Art, 1985-5-1, © Anselm Kiefer; 15-21: Photo © The Brooklyn Museum, © 2008 Judy Chicago/Artists Rights Society (ARS), New York; 15-22: © Cindy Sherman, courtesy the artist and Metro Pictures; 15-23: © Barbara Kruger, courtesy Mary Boone Gallery, New York; 15-24: Copyright © 1988 Guerrilla Girls, courtesy www.guerrillagirls.com; 15-25: Photo © Whitney Museum of American Art, © Kiki Smith; 15-26: © 1983 Faith Ringgold; 15-27: Courtesy and © Chris Ofili; 15-28: Chrysler Museum of Art, Norfolk, VA, Museum Purchase, 93.2, © Jaune Quick-to-See-Smith; 15-29: © Magdalena Abakanowicz, courtesy, Marlborough Gallery, New York; 15-30: Museum of Contemporary Art, Chicago, © Jeff Koons; 15-31: Photo © Angelo Hornak/CORBIS, © 2008 Frank Lloyd Wright Foundation, Scottsdale, AZ/Artists Rights Society (ARS), NY; 15-32: Photo akg-images/L. M. Peter, © 2008 Artists Rights Society (ARS), New York/ADAGP, Paris/FLC; 15-33: Photo © Angelo Hornak/CORBIS, © 2008 Artists Rights Society (ARS), New York/VG Bild-Kunst, Bonn; 15-34: © Kokyat Choong/The Image Works; 15-35: Peter Aaron © Esto; 15-36: © The Art Archive/Dagli Orti; 15-37: © Rolf Haid/dpa/CORBIS; 15-38: Art © Estate of Robert Smithson/Licensed by VAGA, New York, NY; 15-39: © 1983 Christo photo Wolfgang Volz. Christo and Jeanne-Claude; 15-40: Photo © Ute Klophaus, © 2008 Artists Rights Society (ARS), New York/VG Bild-Kunst, Bonn; 15-41: Digital Image © The Museum of Modern Art/Licensed by SCALA/Art Resource, NY. © 2008 Joseph Kosuth/Artists Rights Society (ARS), NY; 15-42: Courtesy Nam June Paik Studios, Inc.; 36.82: Adrian Piper Research Archives; 15-43: © Bill Viola, Photo: Kira Perov

Chapter 16—16-1: © Kevin R. Morris/CORBIS; 16-2: © National Museum of India, New Delhi/Bridgeman Art Library; 16-3: © Benoy K. Behl; 16-4b: © Scala/Art Resource, NY; 16-5: akg-images/Jean-Louis Nou; 16-6a-d: Freer Gallery of Art, Smithsonian Institution, Washington, DC. Purchase, F1949.9a-d; 16-7: © John C. Huntington; 16-8: © Benoy K. Behl; 16-9: akg-images/Jean-Louis Nou; 16-10: © Werner Forman/CORBIS; 16-11: akg-images/Jean-Louis Nou; 16-12: © JC Harle Collection; 16-13: © David Cumming; Eye Ubiquitous/CORBIS; 16-14: © Jack Fields/CORBIS; 16-15: © Victoria & Albert Museum, London/Art Resource, NY; 16-16: Freer Gallery of Art, Smithsonian Institution, Washington, D.C., Purchase, F1942.15; 16-17: National Museum, New Delhi; 16-18: © Christophe Boisvieux/CORBIS; 16-19: © Charles & Josette Lenars/CORBIS; 16-20: © Christophe Loviny/CORBIS; 16-21: © Stuart Westmorland; 16-22: © Ladislav Janicek/zefa/CORBIS

Chapter 17—17-1: Collection of the National Palace Museum, Taiwan, Republic of China; 17-2: © Asian Art Museum of San Francisco, The Avery Brundage Collection, B60B1032. Used by permission; 17-3: akg-images/Laurent Lecat; 17-4: © Hunan Provincial Museum, Changsa City; 17-5: © British Museum/HIP/Art Resource, NY; 17-6: © Lowell Georgia/CORBIS; 17-7: © Cultural Relics Publishing House, Beijing; 17-8: © Museum of Fine Arts, Boston, Massachusetts, USA, Denman Waldo Ross Collection/The Bridgeman Art Library; 17-9: The Art Archive/National Palace Museum, Taiwan; 17-10: © Cultural Relics Publishing House, Beijing; 17-12: © Liu Liqun/CORBIS; 17-13: © Collection of the National Palace Museum, Taiwan, Republic of China; 17-14: Percival David Foundation of Chinese Art, B614; 17-15: photos12.com, Panorama Stock; 17-16: © Carl and Ann Purcell/CORBIS; 17-17: Leonard C. Hanna Bequest, 1980, photo copyright © Cleveland Museum of Art, Cleveland; 17-18: John Taylor Photography, C. C. Wang Family Collection, NY; 17-19: © Audrey R. Topping; 17-20: © Archivo Iconografico, S.A./CORBIS; 17-21: © Ludovic Maisant/CORBIS; 17-22: Heritage Images, © The British Museum

Chapter 18—18-1: Photo Courtesy of the International Society for Educational Information, Inc. Tokyo; 18-2: © Georg Gerster/Photo Researchers, Inc.; 18-3: Toyko National Museum. Source: http://TnmArchives.jp; 18-4: Archivo Iconografico, S.A./CORBIS; 18-5a: © Archivo Iconografico, S.A./CORBIS; 18-5b: © DAJ/Getty Images; 18-6: Kyoogokokuji (Toji), Kyoto; 18-7: © Sakamoto Photo Research Laboratory/CORBIS; 18-8: © The Gotoh Art Museum, Tokyo; 18-9: Todaiji, Nara; 18-10: © Museum of Fine Arts, Boston, Massachusetts, USA, Fenollosa-Weld Collection/The Bridgeman Art Library; 18-11: TNM Image Archives, Source: http//TNMArchives.jp/; 18-12: TNM Image Archives, Source: http//TNMArchives.jp/; 18-13 left, right: TNM Image Archives, Source: http//TNMArchives.jp/; 18-14: © The Hatakeyama Memorial Museum of Fine Art, Tokyo; 18-16: Art Institute of Chicago, Chicago (Clarence Buckingham Collection).1925.2043, Photography © The Art Institute of Chicago; 18-17: Museum of Fine Arts, Boston (Bigelow Collection).11.17652, Photograph © 2008 Museum of Fine Arts, Boston; 18-18: National Yoyogi Stadium, photo courtesy Tokyo Convention and Visitors Bureau; 18-19: National Museum of Modern Art, Kyoto

Chapter 19—19-1: © Georg Gerster/Photo Researchers, Inc.; 19-2: © Danny Lehman/CORBIS; 19-3: © Gianni Dagli Orti/CORBIS; 19-4: © Sean Sprague/The Image Works; 19-5: © Philip Baird www.anthroarcheart.org; 19-6: akg-images/François Guénet; 19-7: © 2007 Peabody Museum of Archaeology and Ethnology, Harvard University, Cambridge. 48-63-20/17561 T1021.2 (detail); 19-8: © The British Museum/HIP/The Image Works; 19-9: © Yann Arthus-Bertrand/CORBIS; 19-10: © Scala/Art Resource, NY; 19-11: © Jonathan Blair/CORBIS; 19-12: adapted from an image by Ned Seidler/National Geographic Society; 19-13: © Gianni Dagli Orti/CORBIS; 19-14: © Gianni Dagli Orti/CORBIS; 19-15: Museum of Fine Arts, Boston William A. Paine Fund, 1931, 31.501. Photograph © 2008 Museum of Fine Arts, Boston; 19-16: © Charles & Josette Lenars/CORBIS; 19-17: © Nathan Benn/CORBIS; 19-18: Danny Lehman/CORBIS; 19-19: © Tony Linck/SuperStock; 19-20: © Kevin Fleming/CORBIS; 19-21: Photo © Museum of New Mexico, Santa Fe; 19-22: Arizona State Museum, University of Arizona, photo W. McLennan; 19-23: Photo © National Museum of Women in the Arts; 19-24: Photo © American Museum of Natural History, New York

Chapter 20—20-1: © The British Museum/HIP/Art Resource, NY; 20-2: Photograph © 1980 Dirk Bakker; 20-3: Photograph © 1980 Dirk Bakker; 20-4: Photograph © 1980 Dirk Bakker; 20-5: © Yann Arthus-Bertrand/CORBIS; 20-6: © I. Vanderharst/Getty Images/Robert Harding Picture Library; 20-7: Metropolitan Museum of Art. The Michael C. Rockefeller Memorial Collection, Gift of Nelson A. Rockefeller, 1972. (1978.412.323) Photograph © 1995 The Metropolitan Museum of Art; 20-8: © British Museum/HIP/Art Resource, NY; 20-9: © Museo Nazionale Preistorico e Etnografico Luigi Pigorini, Rome; 20-10: © abm-Archives Barbier Mueller, photographer Roger Asselberghs; 20-11: © Bildarchiv Preussischer Kulturbesitz/Art Resource, NY; 20-12: © 2006 Musée du quai Branly, photo Hugues Dubois/Scala, Florence; 20-13: © Detroit Institute of Arts. Founders Society Purchase, Eleanor Clay Ford Fund for African Art, 76.79; 20-14: Image copyright © The Metropolitan Museum of Art/Art Resource, NY; 20-15: National Museum of African Art, Smithsonian Institution/Eliot Eliosofon Photographic Archives; 20-16: Skip Cole; 20-17: Image © 2008 Denver Art Museum; 20-18: © Fulvio Roiter/CORBIS; 20-19: Photo © Fowler Museum of Cultural History, University of California, Los Angeles; 20-20: National Museum of African Art, Smithsonian Institution, Eliot Eliosofon Photographic Archives; 20-21: National Museum of African Art, Smithsonian Institution, Washington, D.C.; 20-22: © Willie Bester

Index